MW01040311

Extreme Exoticism

Extreme Exoticism

Japan in the American Musical Imagination

W. ANTHONY SHEPPARD

OXFORD

UNIVERSITY PRESS

OXFORD
UNIVERSITY PRESS

Oxford University Press is a department of the University of Oxford. It furthers
the University's objective of excellence in research, scholarship, and education
by publishing worldwide. Oxford is a registered trade mark of Oxford University
Press in the UK and certain other countries.

Published in the United States of America by Oxford University Press
198 Madison Avenue, New York, NY 10016, United States of America.

CIP data is on file at the Library of Congress
ISBN 978-0-19-007270-4

1 3 5 7 9 8 6 4 2

Printed by Sheridan Books, Inc., United States of America

To Lara, Ethan, and Maia

Contents

Illustrations

Boxes

Figures

Music Examples

Table

Glossary of Japanese Musical, Theatrical, and Aesthetic Terms

(Note: Japanese names will appear in the form of given name followed by family name throughout this text.)

benshi live narrator who performed at silent film screenings

biwa pear-shaped plucked fretted lute of four or five strings

bon-odori folk dance performed at *obon* festivals

bugaku ancient court dance genre accompanied by *gagaku* ensemble

bunraku puppet theater accompanied by solo vocalist (*gidayu*) and *shamisen*

butoh postwar avant-garde dance genre

charumera double-reed street instrument played by noodle sellers

enka mid-twentieth-century popular genre of sentimental lyrical ballads

fue/fuye bamboo flutes

gagaku court and Buddhist temple ensemble imported from China in seventh century

gidayu the narrative vocal and shamisen music in *bunraku*

gunka Western-influenced military songs from the Meiji period through World War II

hanamichi bridge/pathway extending through audience in *kabuki*, used for exits/entrances

hashigakari the covered walkway from backstage to the mainstage in *noh*

hayashi ensemble consisting of flute and drums in *noh* and *kabuki*

hichiriki oboe-like double reed melodic instrument in *gagaku*, piercing timbre

honkyoku classic genre of Zen Buddhist meditative *shakuhachi* music

hyoshigi wooden clappers used in *kabuki* and *bunraku*

in pentatonic scale with larger and smaller intervals, considered distinctly Japanese

issei first-generation/immigrant Japanese American

joruri narrative shamisen music as in *bunraku* puppet theater

kabuki all-male, popular theatrical genre since the seventeenth century

kakegoe the explosive vocal calls emitted by the drummers in *noh*

kakko hourglass-shaped drum played with sticks in *gagaku*

kawaisa/kawaii aesthetic of cuteness in fashion/entertainment since late twentieth century

keisu an inverted, bowl-shaped bell

kibigaku ritual ensemble music and dance derived from *gagaku* in late nineteenth century

kokoro aesthetic term meaning "heart" or "mind"

kokyu/kokiu bowed lute

koto plucked rectangular zither of thirteen strings

ko-tsuzumi smaller of two hourglass-shaped drums played in *noh*, held at the shoulder

kouta "little songs," central to geisha performance

kyogen comic theater typically performed as interludes in *noh*

ma aesthetic term signifying the powerful impact of space, silence, stillness

matsuri bayashi Shinto festival music

mei dramatic poses struck by actors at climactic moments in *kabuki*

mokugyo fish-head-shaped gong used in Buddhist ritual music

nagauta the vocal and *shamisen* music of *kabuki*, "long song"

nisei second-generation Japanese American

noh all-male, refined theatrical genre originating in the fourteenth century

obon/bon festival honoring ancestors

o-daiko large drum in *kabuki*

ondo folk songs and dances

onnagata female role performed by male actors in *kabuki*

otokoyaku male lead role performed by female actress in Takarazuka

o-tsuzumi larger of two hourglass-shaped drums played in *noh*, held at hip

rin small metal bowls played in Buddhist temple music

roppo dramatic exit by a male character on the *hanamichi* in *kabuki*

ryuteki transverse flute played in *gagaku*

sankyoku genre of chamber music, trio typically featuring *koto, shamisen*, and *shakuhachi*

sansei third-generation Japanese American

shakuhachi end-blown bamboo flute, employed both in Zen meditation and *sankyoku*

shamisen three stringed long-necked lute, central to geisha music, *kabuki, bunraku*

shinobue transverse bamboo flute

sho mouth reed organ, plays cluster chords in *gagaku* ensemble music

shomyo Buddhist chant

taiko barrel-shaped drum played with sticks, as in *noh* and *kabuki*

Takarazuka all-female form of popular theater originating in the early twentieth century

tayu the narrator/vocalist in *bunraku* puppet theater

tsugaru style of *shamisen* music characterized by rhythmic intensity

uchiwa-daiko fan drums used in Buddhist music

yo pentatonic scale consisting of roughly equal intervals (anhemitonic pentatonic)

Extreme Exoticism

Introductions and Acknowledgments

Over the course of the past century and a half, numerous composers, musicians, and audiences in the United States have imagined Japan through works created and experienced in every musical genre and medium. Some of these popular songs, film scores, and Broadway musicals reached large audiences over an extended period. The vast majority of these works proved more ephemeral, but nevertheless were culturally significant through their collective impact. This book investigates the reciprocal relationships among this diverse body of musical works, the ever protean political dynamic between the United States and Japan, and the evolving American social climate in which this music was created and experienced. To what extent was music employed to shape American perceptions of the Japanese, and to what extent was American music itself shaped in the process?

In the American imagination, Japan has represented the most exotic nation for well over 150 years. This perceived difference has inspired fantasies of both desire and repulsion. In addition, Japanese culture has had a profound impact on the arts and industry of the United States. The influence of Japan on American and European painting, architecture, design, theater, literature, and entertainment technology has been celebrated in numerous books and exhibitions. The impact of European and American music on Japan has also been studied by both Western and Japanese scholars. However, in the numerous studies of *japonisme* and Japan-US relations, the role of music has been virtually ignored.[1] Similarly, in musical studies of Orientalism and cross-cultural influence, rarely have scholars pursued in depth a longitudinal study of the musical interactions between two nations.[2] *Extreme Exoticism* offers a detailed and wide-ranging documentation and interpretation of the role of musical representation in shaping American perceptions of the Japanese, the reception of Japanese music encountered both in the United States and in Japan by American audiences, the influence of Japanese music and aesthetics on American composers, and the position of specific Japanese and Japanese American musicians in American musical life.

American interest in Japanese music and in representing Japan through music has directly paralleled Japanese and American actions on the global stage, resulting in specific periods of intense musical activity as well as periods of relative silence as Japan temporarily disappeared from the American culture radar. One can hear the development of Japan-US political relations in the silences and in the soundings of Japan-US musical encounters, from the 1853–1854 American "opening" of Japan, to Japan's victory in the 1904–1905 Russo-Japanese War and the US-led peace process, to the US Immigration Act of 1924 barring Japanese entry, to the 1941 bombing of Pearl Harbor, 1945 atomic bombing of Hiroshima and Nagasaki, and the subsequent US occupation of Japan, and on to the trade wars of the 1980s and the near ubiquity of Japanese computer games and cuisine in America by the end of the century. In the late nineteenth and early twentieth centuries, the passing of exotic "Old Japan" was lamented by many American aesthetes. Traditional Japanese culture was subsequently demonized leading up to and during World War II only to be met by American calls for its preservation in the postwar period. Similarly, the ultramodern "techno Japan" of the later twentieth century was simultaneously celebrated for bringing new forms of media technology and entertainment to American youth, and feared for its seeming inhuman technological dominance, unstoppable mass production, and mesmerizing entrapment. The appearance of specific Japanese cultural images, such as a *shamisen*-playing geisha in films from the early 1940s and then again in the late 1950s, has proven particularly polysemous.

Although American views of Japanese culture have vacillated dramatically, I have identified certain representational techniques and attitudes that have reappeared numerous times in different guises and in multiple musical genres. Composers, filmmakers, and theatrical producers have repeatedly sought to manufacture and manipulate "exotic authenticity" in their representations of Japan and in framing their audiences' encounters with Japanese music. The reception, representation, and influence of Japanese music have always been bound up with and impacted prevailing American artistic and social concerns. In the past 150 years Japanese music has served as material for modernist experimentation, as a sounding board allowing Americans to define their own music, as a tool for representing Japan either positively or negatively, and even therapeutically, as background relaxation music for massage. Specific features of Japanese traditional music were embraced as mid-twentieth-century composers sought to break with timbral, temporal, and harmonic norms of the European musical past. Japanese music has repeatedly played a significant role in shaping American perceptions of gender, as it helped to define Japanese women as embodying a feminine ideal to be emulated by white American women—many of whom themselves participated in creating works of *japonisme* as performers and composers. Music has also assisted in defining the Japanese and Japanese Americans racially over time and in counterpoint with other groups, particularly with African Americans, Native Americans, and Chinese Americans. *Japonisme* has inspired some of the most beautiful and engaging American works of architecture, literature, painting, dance, and music. It has also inspired some of the most trite and blatant expressions of racist Orientalism. From Tin Pan Alley songs during the Russo-Japanese War to Hollywood films of the 1980s trade wars, from the encounters with Japanese music of nineteenth-century Boston Brahmins to the *shakuhachi* recordings in today's day spas, from early cinematic versions of *Madame Butterfly* to Weezer's *Pinkerton* album, and from Perry's "opening" of Japan to the US Bicentennial opening of Sondheim's *Pacific Overtures* on Broadway, music has consistently reinscribed Japan as the land of extreme exoticism.

Two particularly illustrative contemporaneous works from a century ago will introduce many of the themes of this book—the first, a 1905 mass-marketed song in a comic vein that imagines a Japanese future for America; the second, a 1919 highbrow symphonic work that attempts through music to recover a lost, noble Old Japan. "When America Is Captured by the Japs," with lyrics by Paul West and music by John W. Bratton, was published in 1905 by the major New York company M. Witmark and Sons. Better known as the composer of "The Teddy Bears' Picnic," Bratton published multiple other Japanese-inspired songs and novelty piano pieces in the late nineteenth and early twentieth centuries, including "Japanese Lantern Dance" (1897), "My Little Belle of Japan: A Fan Tastic Episode" with words by Arthur L. Robb (1901), "In a Lotus Field" (1903), "Happy Jappy Soldier Man: Japanese War Song" with words by Paul West (1904), and (as lyricist) "In Cherry Blossom Time" (1914) with music by Eugene Salzer. "When America Is Captured by the Japs" stands out in this collection as it asks its audience and performers to imagine what would happen to American culture if the Japanese, fresh from their 1905 victory over Russia, were to push onward across the globe. The sheet music cover provides the answer, as may be seen in Figure 0.1. We see Uncle Sam dressed in a stars and stripes kimono, Japanese rice farmer's hat, and sandals, standing in front of a subtle silhouette of the Japanese flag's rising sun. Most strikingly, he plays a *shamisen* (with tuning pegs depicted upside down) and his lips are slightly parted as though in song. Such cultural cross-dressing had occurred in the reverse direction in late-nineteenth-century Meiji Era Japan as the Japanese attempted to modernize by copying many aspects of Western culture, including music. For example, to honor former president General Ulysses S. Grant during his 1879 visit to Japan, geishas clad in American-flag patterned kimonos danced and sang in praise of "the glory of America."[3] On this 1905 sheet music cover, however, the recent political and military ascendency of Japan has clearly turned this white American Japanese, both in his outer appearance and through his musical performance. Awkwardly placed below this male musician's spread legs is a photo of the Norwegian operatic soprano Inga Orner who, we are told, has sung this song "with Success," presumably in her recitals rather than in her Metropolitan Opera appearances. Orner's presence on this cover is but one of countless indications from this period that the boundary between high and low art was exceedingly porous. Her headshot is framed within an American shield and flanked by Japanese and American flag escutcheons. The placement of the photo suggests that her eyes are gazing upward to check on this culturally cross-dressed American male's masculinity.

In response to the new power and global prominence of Japan, the lyrics express both admiration and apprehension. The song predicts that America will be "captured," rather than "conquered," as Japanese culture will invade every aspect of American life. We learn that "when the yellow fellows own us," enthralled Americans will carry fans, wear kimonos, eat rice, and drink *sake* instead of whiskey and that the trains will run on time and political corruption will be a thing of the past. In typical Tin Pan Alley–era fashion, ethnic and racial representation becomes

Figure 0.1 "When America Is Captured by the Japs," sheet music cover (M. Witmark and Sons, 1905).

confused and interwoven in these verses and the term "Americans" refers solely to whites of Anglo-Saxon heritage. Besmirching African Americans as gamblers and referring to a Chinese card game, we are told that "coons will play fan tan in- stead of craps." In addition, the Japanese will displace Irish cooks and Americans will come to smoke opium—a stereotypical Chinese, rather than Japanese, vice in American popular culture of this period. As signaled on the cover by the *shamisen*- strumming Uncle Sam, American music, both high and low, will also be captured by the efficient exotic invaders, who will "write new comic operas, perhaps,/They'll import new prima donnas/To achieve our coin and honors,/And our tenors all will be wiped off the maps." Even "the show girls, goodness gracious, Will be driven out by geishas." Thus this song from 1905 predicted an anxiety expressed by many white American audiences and critics at the end of the century that "Western classical music" had been overtaken by East Asian musicians.[4] Bratton, however, clearly had not yet been "captured" by Japanese music. Instead, he efficiently signals a Japanese future musically by turning to a work of musical *japonisme* from the past, Gilbert and Sullivan's *The Mikado*, and quoting "Miya sama"—Sullivan's version of a Japanese *gunka* (military song) tune—in triple octaves and staccato articulation in the four opening bars. (The long-short-short rocking perfect fifth ostinato in the left hand accompaniment to the verses has more in common with representations of Native American drumming than with Japan.) Neither a fear of nor desire for musical miscegenation with Japanese music is evident in the score of this song, even though the cover art and lyrics suggest that Japanese exoticness could prove both dangerously contagious or temporarily and selectively assumed with pleasure.

Emerson Whithorne, a fairly conservative and successful composer of orchestral and piano music in the first decades of the twentieth century, did make an attempt to incorporate Japanese music more extensively in his 1919 orchestral suite *Adventures of a Samurai*.[5] Whithorne was known for his interest in East Asian music and professed to have studied Chinese music in particular. He composed numerous Japanese-inspired works including the 1911 set of songs *From Japan* and the 1916 piano pieces *Hototogisu: The Cuckoo* and *The Rain*, in addition to multiple Chinese-related works such as *Four Chinese Poems* (1912) and "Pell Street" from the suite *New York Days and Nights* (piano 1922; orchestral 1923). *Adventures of a Samurai* is a programmatic piece, subtitled "Just before the Battle" and in four movements titled "In the Temple," "Consecration of the Bells," "Serenade," and "Bushido." Like "When America Is Captured by the Japs," Whithorne's suite—the first version of which had been completed by 1914—was inspired by Japan's recent military prowess, though this work offers a far more reverential representation of the Japanese and is based on claims of exotic authenticity.[6] Announcements and reviews of Whithorne's piece emphasized that he had employed "a remarkable collection of genuine Japanese melodies," some of which had been offered to him by a friend who had spent time in Japan and others he had encountered through research at the British Museum, and that he had "allowed himself considerable freedom in their development."[7] Research and fieldwork appear to have been unnecessary as Whithorne employed the three most well-known and overused Japanese melodies in Western representations of Japan: "Miyasan"/"Tonyare-bushi" (Gilbert and Sullivan's "Miya sama"), "Sakura Sakura," and the anthem "Kimigayo." These melodies gradually emerge in fragmented form before receiving a more complete statement in Whithorne's score. For example, in the first movement the second half of the "Sakura Sakura" melody appears on page 4 of the score and the first half of the melody on page 20. In the fourth movement Whithorne expresses "Bushido," the samurai code of honor, through fragmented appearances of both "Kimigayo" and "Miya sama" before eventually superimposing the two melodies (p. 72) and climaxing with an orchestral apotheosis of "Kimigayo" (p. 85). *Adventures of a Samurai* also features the parallel fourths and fifths, staccato articulation, and general pentatonicism typical of Western musical representations of East Asia as well as some motives based on the *in* scale (a distinctively Japanese pentatonic scale featuring semitones). Though Whithorne attempted to capture this exotic music by drawing on Japanese melodies, his general musical style was clearly not "captured" by Japanese traditional music given that his score exhibits no traces of Japanese timbral or temporal sensibility. In short, he incorporated Japanese melodic material without altering his musical language very much to accommodate it. Exotic representation nearly always spurs some form of cross-cultural influence, however imaginatively and indirectly experienced it might be for the composer, and cross-cultural influence nearly always results in some degree of exotic representation, however dependent it might be on the audience's imagination.

In several chapters, I juxtapose examples separated by multiple decades and often created in strikingly different genres. In doing so, I reveal the profound continuities evident in exotic musical representation and influence throughout American music history and across the "high/low" cultural divide. A common assumption has been that "Romanticism," "modernism" and "postmodernism," "experimental" and "commercial," "cross-cultural influence" and "Orientalist representation" exist as files into which we can organize music of the past century and a half. In my historical research and analysis, I do not find evidence in support of this scholarly hardening of the categories and attempts at strict periodization. Rather than attempting to debunk such terms as "modernism" and "postmodernism" or "appropriation" and "influence"—indeed, I continue to rely on these terminological crutches—I argue that none of these categories has proven mutually exclusive in practice, and that these and other false binaries have warped the way we think about and hear twentieth- and twenty-first-century musics, even deafening us to otherwise audible similarities across time and across aesthetic and cultural boundaries. The terminological skepticism expressed here demands that we now turn to scrutinize the words employed in this book's title.

The title, *Extreme Exoticism: Japan in the American Musical Imagination*, contains terms and phrases denoting things that, strictly speaking, do not exist. After joining me in some titular deconstruction, I hope the reader will sense the presence of phantom scare quotes hovering around several of these words as they appear throughout this book. In addition, several of these terms should be understood as referring to a multiplicity and wide range of examples. For example, by "musical" I aim to signal all forms of music created in the United States, for I have not identified a single musical genre, style, medium, or format that has not at some point been harnessed to represent Japan or that lacks at least one example of a work shaped by Japanese cultural influences. I also intend to reveal the extensive imaginative work music has achieved throughout this history, how music has been harnessed to express individual composers', performers', and listeners' imagination of this exotic culture. Actually, this imaginative work is carried out socially, between individuals who assume multiple musical roles, both within and across cultures. As Arjun Appadurai explains: "The image, the imagined, the imaginary—these are all terms that direct us to something critical and new in global cultural processes: *the imagination as a social practice*. . . . the imagination has become an organized field of social practices, a form of work . . . and a form of negotiation between sites of agency (individuals) and globally defined fields of possibility."[8]

As a description of widespread and persistent American perceptions, "extreme" is the easiest word to justify historically in this title. Though Japanese culture is, obviously, not inherently any more exotic than American culture—and, indeed, has constituted part of American culture since the late nineteenth century—it has been consistently declared to be extremely foreign by a range of American figures of all racial and ethnic groups. Most of these cultural figures have been white. However, we will find that younger Japanese Americans of successive generations also tended to view the culture of their parents and grandparents as exotic, choosing either to embrace or distance themselves from Japanese culture at specific moments in a frequently precarious history. Furthermore, throughout the long and continuing civil rights struggle in the United States, some Asian American and African American musicians have aimed for an Afro-Asian cultural fusion, with Japanese culture serving as a particularly useful exotic wellspring located in stark opposition to mainstream Euro-American cultural norms.

Japan had been perceived as the *ne plus ultra* exotic land by Europeans for centuries—it is no coincidence that Tamino, the fairytale foreign prince in Mozart and Schikaneder's *The Magic Flute*, is identified as Japanese (though, as typical of exoticism, some sources indicate "Javanese"). It is clear that the sheer number and repetition of testimonials to Japan's alterity reinforced these perceptions over the centuries. Given the geographical distance and Japan's nearly 250 years of isolation prior to the arrival of Commodore Perry's gunboats in Edo Bay in 1853, it is also not surprising that Americans in all fields have consistently referred to the Japanese as culturally opposite and even uniquely unique. For example, Percival Lowell—the astronomer who theorized life on Mars, authored multiple books on East Asia, and traveled three times to Japan in the late nineteenth century—explained in 1888 that even though the Japanese do not actually stand on their heads on the other side of the world as a child might imagine, "they still appear quite as antipodal, mentally considered. Intellectually, at least, their attitude sets gravity at defiance. For to the mind's eye their world is one huge, comical antithesis of our own."[9] (Lowell did allow that "perhaps, could we once see ourselves as others see us, our surprise in the case of foreign peoples might be less pronounced.")[10] Writing as one of America's most well-known pundits on all things Asian, Pearl S. Buck declared in 1966: "For if there is one single truth about Asia, it is that while each country there is totally different from every other, Japan is the most different of all."[11] A similar view had been expressed with less charitable intent in congressional testimony leading up to the passage of the 1924 Immigration Act, when the Japanese were referred to as the "least assimilable" and "most dangerous" race.[12] A quarter century later, as the Cold

War was heating up, the eminent American Japanologist Edwin O. Reischauer took a broad view as he explained the particularity of the Japan-US relationship:

> In the meeting of Japan and the United States, the two extremities of the world, the problems, the hazards, and, possibly, the benefits of this head-on convergence of races and cultures in a shrinking world stand out in a clearer, starker light than they do in other parts of the world, where the meeting has come about more slowly and has been between less spectacularly contrasting cultures.[13]

Commentators both in the United States and elsewhere have continued to describe American and Japanese cultures as diametrically opposed. In a 1992 study of globalization, the British sociologist Roland Robertson referred to the United States and Japan as "polar sociocultural opposites in the contemporary global field."[14]

In quotations presented throughout this book it will become evident that, for many, Japanese music was a particularly clear indication of the ultimate otherness of the Japanese. During his tour of Japan, Albert Einstein confided in his travel diary on 3 November 1922: "It may be hard to understand them psychologically, I hesitate to try ever since the Japanese singing remained so entirely incomprehensible to me. Yesterday I heard another one singing away again to the point of making me dizzy."[15] When asked by me on 8 March 2006 at Williams College whether Japanese music and culture had impacted him and his film score for *Mishima: A Life in Four Chapters* (1985), Philip Glass professed that he found traveling to Japan "terrifying," akin to being sent "to Venus," and that he had "failed" at getting into the Japaneseness of Mishima in that score.

Coupled with the belief that Japanese music was extremely exotic, and the expressions of desire and loathing this inspired, was the recurring fear that this exoticism would be diminished through contact with the West. As early as 1903, Otto Abraham and Erich M. von Hornbostel concluded their study of Japanese music as follows:

> Unfortunately, with the expansion of European cultural influences, the charming originality of exotic art vanishes, and with it disappears material of exceedingly great value to the musicologist, ethnologist, and psychologist. Though we cannot preserve musical creations in our museums as we can other cultural products, we should attempt to collect durable phonographic recordings for our laboratories, so long as this is still possible. It is true that practical music, unlike the fine arts and crafts, cannot learn much from East Asia; but knowledge may well be indebted to her in times to come for a widening of musical horizons.[16]

For these German comparative musicologists, the Westernization of music in Japan would primarily constitute a loss to musical science. We will hear numerous Americans lamenting somewhat more passionately the loss of Old Japan and of Japanese musical exoticism, from the turn-of-the-century writings of Lafcadio

Hearn to the pronouncements of American scholars and composers at the 1961 East-West Music Encounter conference in Tokyo. We will also encounter numerous American composers who enthusiastically turned to elements of Japanese traditional music in an effort to widen their musical horizons, drawing on the ancient exotic even as it seemed to fade, in a modernist attempt to "make it new."

Repeated proclamations of Japan's utter difference led many Americans, somewhat paradoxically, to declare on first encounter that Japanese culture was somehow insufficiently exotic after all, that it had already been contaminated through contact with the West and had lost some of its authenticity. Of course, consuming Western artistic representations of and writings on exotic Old Japan back home had likely raised their expectations for encountering extreme exoticism to unsatisfiable levels. In 1891 Oscar Wilde identified the problem faced by those who would seek exotic authenticity in Japan, famously declaring that the Japan of the Japanese (and Western) painters did not actually exist, that "the whole of Japan is a pure invention," and that the Japanese people must actually be rather commonplace and not all that different from the English.[17] The French novelist Pierre Loti had wryly written of his own experiences in Japan along these lines in his 1887 semi-autobiographical novel *Madame Chrysanthème*, a seminal work for literary, theatrical, and musical *japonisme*. After arriving in Japan, Loti's protagonist explains how, *pace* Wilde, Japan proved just as artificial as its depictions in art: "At this moment, my impressions of Japan are charming enough; I feel myself fairly launched upon this tiny, artificial, fictitious world, which I felt I knew already from the paintings of lacquer and porcelains. It is so exact a representation!"[18] His preconceptions of Japanese women were likewise met at the moment he was presented with a potential temporary bride: "Heavens! why, I know her already! Long before setting foot in Japan, I had met with her, on every fan, on every tea-cup—with her silly air, her puffy little visage, her tiny eyes, mere gimlet-holes above those expanses of impossible pink and white which are her cheeks."[19] However, this exotic woman, along with numerous other aspects of Japanese culture, proves disappointing for this Frenchman, rather than exotically stimulating.

Repeatedly, European and American creative artists have claimed a desire to recreate an authentic representation of Japan in their works. With *Madama Butterfly*, Puccini stated that he hoped to create a "true Japan, not *Iris*,"[20] and many who have followed him have aspired to present a "true Japan, not *Madama Butterfly*." However, we will find that in works of exotic representation, Japanese and Japanese American performers have been repeatedly rejected as not being "Japanese" enough. Indeed, Western composers, film directors, and choreographers have rarely hesitated to teach these performers how to appear and sound more "Japanese." Conversely, actual Japanese music, dance, theatrical design, etc., was often rejected as being too foreign or incomprehensible when available for inclusion and, instead, was replaced by artistic translations and substitutions intended to make Japanese style and aesthetics more palatable for Western audiences. Aiming for exotic "authenticity" is an entirely quixotic project, in any case, given that cross-cultural presentation/

representation ultimately plays out diversely in the minds of individual audience members.

The exotic exists solely in the imaginations of composers, performers, and audiences. "Exotic" is most commonly employed as an adjective, describing something alien, either enticingly or repulsively different, that has traveled physically or conceptually across geographical distance or through time to the present experience of the observer. However, it is better understood in its predicate form. Labeling or describing peoples, places, and cultural practices as "exotic" requires the imaginative act of exoticizing—perceiving, representing, or classifying something as foreign or unusual from the perspective of the speaker.[21] Exotic representation has served a wide range of purposes throughout history and across the globe, defining one's culture in opposition to others and reinforcing perceptions of superiority, playing out domestic concerns in a foreign setting, didactically filling the vacuum of ignorance by instructing audiences how to perceive other peoples, and, most obviously, offering thrilling and "colorful" entertainment.[22] Exoticism has also proven useful in works of self-representation, as marginalized minority musicians, for example, played into mainstream expectations of exoticism aiming to secure a position in the musical marketplace or, conversely, to parody exoticism and thereby undermine the racist assumptions supporting this mode of representation.

Newly created music has frequently served the purposes of exotic representation. This has included representing the music of other cultures as being exotic, thereby exoticizing peoples and places associated with that music, and even displacing and substituting for those musical traditions in the minds of the intended audience. Musical exoticism has most often been achieved through the reuse of sonic stereotypes that work efficiently to signal otherness to the audience. Such musical signals of the exotic were frequently employed interchangeably and stylistic features from multiple exotic sources were commonly intermixed. Musical details such as parallel fourths or pentatonicism do not function in isolation in exoticism but instead are dependent on the immediate context and on previous representational usage. Whithorne's *Adventures of a Samurai* may serve here as a representative example of musical exoticism in multiple ways. First, Whithorne purported to represent an exotic culture through his newly composed music, as signaled in the work's programmatic titles. The score relied in part on several musical traits that had been repeatedly employed for representations of Asia more generally. Furthermore, particular passages based on Japanese melodies and scales in this suite stand out stylistically as exotic within the context of Whithorne's general orchestral style. Despite their orchestral setting, these melodies were likely received as actual "Japanese music," as though Whithorne's piece enabled the audience to listen directly to sounds from the exotic land. "Japanning" has referred for centuries to techniques of decoration in European and American furniture design in which an object was given a lacquered surface and, perhaps, other Japanese design elements. Whithorne had similarly Japanned his orchestral music in this piece without effecting a fundamental change in his musical language. Other American and European composers and musicians in the past century, however, stretched their musical style and techniques more extensively as they strove to represent the exotic through sound. Thus we will find that exoticism has repeatedly served as a major catalyst for musical experimentation.

Japan has inspired some particularly extreme forms of exoticism in American music history. We will encounter multiple bizarre representational situations and sudden reversals in representational intent throughout. We will also discover traces of Japanese musical and aesthetic influence in unexpected genres and in works by unlikely composers and musicians. As John Cage wrote in 1946, "Orientalisms occur in music where we least expect to find them."[23] Though the merging of traditional Japanese musical elements within European musical idioms and forms of exotic representation have appeared in works by Japanese composers over the past century and a half, our focus will remain on "Japan in" American music and culture, as signaled in this book's title, rather than on American music in Japan.[24] The impact of American music and musicians on Japanese musical life—from Luther Whiting Mason's pedagogical songs in the late nineteenth century, to jazz in Japan in the 1920s, and to John Cage and the Japanese avant-garde in the 1960s—has been studied, but a book titled "America in the Japanese Musical Imagination" remains to be written. Not only have Euro-American, Japanese American, Chinese American, and African American perceptions of Japan changed dramatically at different moments over the decades, what exactly constitutes the nation-state of "Japan" and "Japanese culture" has also evolved. Indeed, as noted above, the modernization and rapid transformations of Japan inspired a good deal of anxiety in the West and Japanese and Japanese American participation in "Western" music was frequently met with ridicule by white audiences in particular. Throughout this book we will encounter specific Japanese and Japanese American musicians, actors, choreographers, etc., who repeatedly served as token representatives of Japanese culture more broadly—including, for example, the modernist choreographer Michio Ito (whose range extended from W. B. Yeats to Hollywood) and the contemporary *sho* virtuoso Mayumi Miyata (who has collaborated with numerous figures including John Cage and Björk). We will discover that each of these Japanese and Japanese American figures had to determine the extent to which they wished to participate in and be identified with Japanese culture.

"The" is the most potentially misleading word in this book's title. Just as there was no one form of Japanese culture or one way of being Japanese or Japanese American in this period, there has never been a singular "American imagination" or "American music." As a cultural label, "American" must be understood both as an umbrella term—obscuring subcultural differences—and as signifying a superculture, the politically and financially dominant mainstream forces of cultural production that have broadly shaped public opinion and taste in the United States and, indeed, across the globe.[25] As Charles Hiroshi Garrett has argued, music played a particularly crucial role in defining "America" throughout the past century.[26] We will find throughout this study that musical representations of the Japanese frequently played out in a form of racial counterpoint, helping to define whiteness in opposition and often in triangulation with Chinese Americans and African Americans in particular.[27] Reflecting on the prediction that by 2055 the majority of Americans will be nonwhite, Hua Hsu concludes: "The question is whether whiteness, having arisen from a set of privileges accrued and institutionalized over centuries, can ever truly become a minority category, even if white people become a numerical minority. . . . we can now at least contemplate the possibility that white might become a color like all the rest. This is what it would mean to enter into history, rather than simply bending it to your will."[28] Extending Hsu's thought experiment, what would it take to represent "white" as exotic in the American musical imagination?

Throughout much of the history covered here, "American" and "white" were widely employed synonymously. In my archival work and in interviews with Japanese American musicians, particularly with *nisei* (children of Japanese immigrants), I was repeatedly struck by how casually they referred to themselves as "Japanese" and how frequently they used the term "American" in reference to whites, as though they had internalized mainstream racial discourse and the blunt racist messages of the 1924 Exclusion Act and of the internment of Japanese Americans during World War II. (The association of "American" with whiteness and the immigrant's experience of liminal status were both expressed in song as recently as 2016 in the Japanese American indie rock musician and songwriter Mitski's "Your Best American Girl," particularly in the rather devastating music video.) One of the more pernicious arguments for excluding "Japanese" from the definition of "American" was published in 1920 by Lothrop Stoddard, *The Rising Tide of Color against White World-Supremacy*.[29] Stoddard warned his intended (white) audience that "nothing is more *unstable* than the racial make-up of a people, while, conversely, nothing is more *unchanging* than the racial divisions of mankind."[30] He explained that given their "extraordinarily high birth-rate" in California, it was necessary to exclude Japanese from immigration to the United States and bluntly warned of the consequences of failing to do so: "What is absolutely certain is that any wholesale Oriental influx would inevitably doom the whites, first of the Pacific coast, and later of the whole United Sates, to social sterilization and ultimate racial extinction."[31]

Racial perceptions of the Japanese have proven quite unstable over time. Without having encountered any Japanese himself, Marco Polo referred to them as white and civilized and, as Rotem Kowner has revealed, this view appears to have persisted in Europe for several centuries until new Enlightenment formulations of racial hierarchy lowered their status and tinged the Japanese yellow.[32] Not only have perceptions of "the Japanese character" shifted dramatically in American popular culture (refined, sneaky, model minority, inscrutable, etc.), we will find that definitions of "the Japanese race" and even descriptions of Japanese skin color (tan, brown, yellow) have also proven unstable. Genomic studies over the past decades have revealed a far more complex and deep history of intermixing between human groups, undermining simplistic current or past racial categorizations. At the same time, psychological studies and neuroscience have shown that infants initially tend to respond negatively to individuals possessing physical features different from their own family members, but that these responses can be either changed or reinforced, and popular culture plays a major role in this educative process, in making race real in society. As Oscar Hammerstein put it, "you have to be carefully taught."

What is to be gained by learning about exotic representations of Japanese and Japanese Americans throughout American musical history? Arved Ashby has pointedly asked this very question, in a passage directly relevant to this study:

> In pointing out the latent—or less often, explicit—racism of earlier centuries without discussing its manifestations today, the historian would seem to imply that such no longer exists. Present-day discussions of minstrelsy or other such chauvinistic practices of the past seem born of a strange combination of penance and self-congratulation: the scholar does the convenient double-duty of recording the practice and rewriting the epitaph for something already dead. Along the way, he or she might become engrossed in the appalling question of how such practices might ever be instituted in musical terms. But are coon songs, anti-Chinese melodies, and wartime Japanese defamations worth discussing—as opposed simply to calling attention to them, the way a court of law records a felon's conviction—more than once, even as socio-cultural relics? Shouldn't the historical-scholarly impulse to "never forget" be weighed against the need to broach such new topics as the recent coercive practices of the RIAA [Recording Industry Association of America] and FCC [Federal Communications Commission]?[33]

The short answer is yes, it is worthwhile to investigate in detail past exotic musical representations of the Japanese, as I aim to demonstrate throughout this book. For now, it will prove useful to consider the implications of Ashby's questions in more detail. The election of President Obama in 2008 led to widespread claims that the United States had entered a post-racial period, that racism had been overcome, by and large. The presidential election of 2016, and numerous subsequent acts of hate speech and racially motivated crimes in the United States, have made it evident that this is not at all the case and that no "self-congratulation" is in order. I believe that studies offering a longitudinal history of racial representation and exoticism in music, leading right up to today, are as timely as ever and that it is worthwhile to call attention to parallels between such "new topics" as the Trump administration's actions and rhetoric concerning immigration and the anti-Japanese immigration movement leading to the 1924 Exclusion Act and the fear-driven decisions during wartime that led to the mass incarceration of US citizens of Japanese heritage. Though I hold no illusions that my scholarship will have a measurable positive impact on society at large, I feel it is rather premature to yield the field and to declare that penance and acknowledgment of the past are passé.

By investigating the position of American music in the US-Japan relationship, we will learn more broadly about the multiple roles played by music in racial representation, comparing across genres and media, and the dynamics of cross-cultural musical encounter and influence. This project necessarily engages with multiple fields and interdisciplinary topics, including Asian American studies, film studies, the analysis of propaganda and mass media, and the history of Orientalism in opera and film. I fully agree with Ashby's call to make connections to the present in such studies, and will do so by allowing incursions from the more recent past to appear throughout my otherwise chronological approach, turning more directly to recent decades in the concluding chapter. However, the implication that we should leave the past alone and move on to discussions of the present prompts me to wonder at what point, exactly, does the past end and the present begin? I would go further, paraphrasing William Faulkner and President Obama, to suggest that the past explored in *Extreme Exoticism* is no dead relic; it isn't even past.[34] We should not assume that there exists widespread knowledge of these "socio-cultural relics" and should keep in mind that the past cannot be forgotten if it was never actually known in the first place. I believe it is far too soon to ignore the past, or to allow it to remain silent.

A second question that must be addressed before proceeding with this book is one that I have been asked, either directly or indirectly, at multiple times over the past two decades. How did I come to write on these subjects, and from what personal perspective am I approaching these issues?[35] Searching back for the origin of things often proves a fool's errand, as I discovered at several points in this project, seeking to identify the earliest popular song referencing Japan or the first American composer to hear *gagaku*. Searching back for the personal origins of this book also proves problematic. I had first encountered Japanese performing arts in a classical Japanese literature course in college and began work on musical exoticism in graduate school. A major focus of my first book was the influence of Japanese *noh* theater on the works of specific European and American modernists. These academic pursuits point to an intellectual trajectory for this particular project, one I have been engrossed in—along with related investigations of exoticism in the works of Puccini, in postmodern operas, and in Chinese-language popular music—off and on for over two decades. However, I am able to pinpoint a specific moment when I decided to pursue this research project over other possibilities. Late one night in the spring of 1997, flipping through channels in search of a weather report, I chanced upon a scene in the 1957 movie *Sayonara*. I saw and heard a representation of a female *kabuki* character, followed by an approximation of a famous *kabuki* lion dance, interspersed with cuts to a smirking and wisecracking American Air Force officer played by Marlon Brando, who sat conspicuously costumed in uniform in this film's representation of a Japanese audience and theater and who served as a proxy for the film's actual intended audience. My initial attention was focused on Brando's character, on this white male's bemused reactions to exotic performance and, specifically, to the gender reversals of Japanese theater. I began to wonder to what extent such characters had shaped general American perceptions of Japanese culture since the mid-nineteenth century. However, what proved even more intriguing was the realization that the actor appearing as the female *kabuki* character and in the lion dance was the Mexican star Ricardo Montalbán performing in yellowface. Representations of Japanese culture and musical performance have led to many extreme forms of cultural cross-dressing.

As a white child, I performed in red, yellow, brown, and even blue face. As members of the YMCA Indian Guides program, my father and I belonged to the "Seminole tribe" and sat in a drum circle at our "long house" meetings. My Indian name, aptly enough, was Singing Brave and our "tribe" earned an award for most authentic costumes at a Florida state powwow. I later appeared as Pooh-Bah, the Lord High Everything Else, in a bathrobe and eye makeup in a performance of Gilbert and Sullivan's *The Mikado* at a downtown amphitheater in St. Petersburg, fortunately to a limited audience. Most extravagantly, I portrayed the High Linjafoon in a production of the 1974 "musical space trip" *Pardon Me, Is This Planet Taken* (music Gilbert M. Martin, book and lyrics John Jakes) in blue face and matching wig. Given the rhyming similarity between "Linja" and "ninja" and the fact that most English words mean the exact opposite for the Linjafoonians, these extremely alien characters seem inspired by representations of the exotic Japanese. In retrospect, the most significant of my culturally cross-dressed childhood performances occurred in a local high school production of Rodgers and Hammerstein's *South Pacific*. As a middle-school-aged actor, I was cast as Jerome, the mixed-race son of the white French planter Emile and his unnamed Polynesian wife. To pass as mixed race, I was made up with brown body paint on my arms, neck, and face. As I appeared on stage to sing "Dites-moi," the largely African American student audience erupted in riotous laughter and cat calls. Somehow I knew, I knew even then that the students were not reacting derisively to my singing voice or to my absurd French pronunciation, but that it was the brownface makeup that provoked their response. (The makeup permanently stained my shirt and I surreptitiously threw it away after the performance.) My later appearance in blackvoice was met with a more enthusiastic response when, running for junior class president in high school, I rapped my speech before the student body.[36] Seven years before presidential candidate Bill Clinton's 1992 saxophone performance on the Arsenio Hall show, my (literally) sophomoric rap in blackvoice and shades electrified the audience and I won in a landslide. I reused the same rap the following year to win the position of student government president—that time accompanied on beat box by two African American male friends from marching band. These rap performances were totally out of character for me and clearly seem, at this vantage point over three decades later, to have been acts of cross-cultural appropriation for the purposes of political advancement.

Throughout this book, my personal perspective will surely intrude now and again, but I have aimed not to presume to speak for Japanese or Japanese American musicians, avoiding a scholarly version of my childhood cultural cross-dressing. Nor do I claim to understand fully, despite my intensive historical research, the imaginative mindsets of the numerous white American composers whose work constitutes the bulk of the examples considered here. I also have attempted to avoid engaging in anachronistic condemnation from a presumed position of enlightenment, though I necessarily discuss in detail many works of exotic representation that I find deplorable. With each musical genre I have aimed to base my interpretations and descriptions on a large sample size. To achieve this, I carried out research across the country—from a garage in San Dimas, California, to a basement in Camden, New Jersey—and at numerous major libraries and archives in between. This work would not have been possible without the financial support of multiple granting agencies and the assistance and encouragement of many individuals whom I would like to acknowledge here.

*   *   *

My research and writing were funded through a National Endowment for the Humanities Summer Stipend (2002), Williams College Oakley Center Fellowships (2003–2004, Fall 2007, Fall 2015), a National Endowment for the Humanities Fellowship (2003–2004), an American Philosophical Society Sabbatical Fellowship (2007–2008), the Institute for Advanced Study, Princeton, New Jersey (2011–2012), and through Williams College faculty research and sabbatical funding, including several additional grants from the Dean of Faculty's Office. It is not possible to acknowledge the assistance of all the librarians and archivists at the institutions listed under "Archival Sources" in my bibliography, but I would like to thank several individuals who were particularly helpful: Robin Kibler and Alison O'Grady, Sawyer Library, Williams College; Ara Ghazarians, Armenian Cultural Foundation, Arlington, Massachusetts; Annette Fern, Harvard Theatre Collection; Leith Johnson, Cinema Archives, Wesleyan University; Rosemary Cullen, John Hay Library, Brown University; George Boziwick, Music Division, New York Public Library for the Performing Arts; Charles Silver and Ron Magliozzi, Celeste Bartos International Film Study Center, Museum of Modern Art; Paul Novosel, Archivist for the Dance Theatre of Harlem; Linda Wood, Free Library of Philadelphia; Gary Galván, Edwin A. Fleisher Collection of Orchestral Music, Free Library of Philadelphia; Maggie Kruesi, Annenberg Rare Book and Manuscript Library, University of Pennsylvania; Wayne Shirley, Music Division, Library of Congress; Aloha South, National Archives and Records Administration; James V. D'Arc and Norm Gillespie, Harold B. Lee Library Special Collections, Brigham Young University; Jean Cunningham, Paramount Theatre Music Library, Oakland, California; Ned Comstock, Cinema and Television Library, University of Southern California; Stuart Galbraith, Warner Bros. Archives, University of Southern California; Eldridge Walker, Music Department, Paramount Studios; and Marie Masumoto and Lisa Itagaki, Japanese American National Museum, Los Angeles.

I am also indebted to numerous scholars, collectors, and musicians who offered crucial information and guidance for my research work at various points over the past two decades. These individuals include William Blakefield, Christopher Yohmei Blasdel, Robert Bonfiglio, David H. Culbert, Linda C. Ehrlich, Philip Flavin, Victor Greene, Arthur Groos, Dolores M. Hsu, Paul Krzywicki, Robert C. Lancefield, William P. Malm, Sandra Marrone, Nancy Rayner, Ralph Samuelson, Takefusa Sasamori, Rose Rosengard Subotnik, John W. Waxman, and Shinichi Yuize. I have been fortunate in having multiple Williams College student research assistants who have contributed in several ways to the success of this project: Gregory Bloch, Augusta Caso, Melody Marchman, Maki Matsui, James O'Leary, Dan Perttu, Elizabeth Robie, and Emily Tiller.

Numerous colleagues, both near and far, have offered detailed comments, suggestions, and encouragement as this manuscript developed. In particular, I would like to thank Michael Beckerman, M. Jennifer Bloxam, Richard Crawford, Daniel Goldmark, Marjorie W. Hirsch, Ellie Hisama, Mary Hunter, Leta E. Miller, David Nicholls, Carol J. Oja, Jann Pasler, Christopher A. Reynolds, Lara Shore-Sheppard, Judy Tsou, and Deborah Wong. I also thank the anonymous readers of this manuscript in its various versions for providing critical guidance and necessary corrections. Finally, for their sustained support throughout my career, I am ever grateful to Carolyn Abbate, Philip V. Bohlman, the dearly missed Philip Brett, Suzannah Clark, Ralph Locke, and Richard Taruskin.

Some sections of this book have previously appeared in print and I remain indebted to the editorial teams who improved my prose for those publications. Much of chapter 5 appeared in the *Journal of the American Musicological Society* 54, no. 2 (2001), edited by Thomas S. Grey and copyedited by Catherine Gjerdingen. My discussion of the cinematic history of the "Madame Butterfly" narrative in chapter 4 appeared in the *Cambridge Opera Journal* 17, no. 1 (2005), under the editorship of Emanuele Senici and Mary Ann Smart. The sections of chapter 7 devoted to the career of Tak Shindo appeared in the online journal *ECHO* 6, no. 2 (2004), edited by Olivia Carter Mather. Finally, chapter 3's investigation of Japanese influence in the music of Henry Eichheim and Henry Cowell was previously published in the *Journal of the American Musicological Society* 61, no. 3 (2008), edited by Kate van Orden and copyedited by Louise Goldberg. (See the bibliography for detailed publication information.)

Seeing a book of this scope through to publication is a task requiring true expert assistance. I am profoundly grateful for the painstaking fact-checking and editorial work of Hannah Lewis, John Gabriel, and Elizabeth Elmi. Mika Hirai in the Office for Information Technology at Williams College provided crucial assistance in preparing many of the figures, and Andrew Maillet set the examples expertly and efficiently. Jeremy Toynbee of Newgen (UK) guided this manuscript throughout the production process and Timothy J. DeWerff proved an exceptionally skillful and knowledgeable copy editor. At Oxford University Press, I thank Victoria Dixon (Assistant Editor) for her work and Suzanne Ryan, Editor in Chief, Humanities, for her timely interventions, professionalism, and wit.

1

"Beyond Description"

Nineteenth-Century Americans Hearing Japan

In the official chronicle of Commodore Perry's 1853–1854 expedition to Japan—that display of American naval power ending Japan's 250 years of near isolation—Japanese music receives the following cursory recognition:

> The Japanese music, of which, by the way, the natives are passionately fond, has nothing in it to recommend it to the ears of Europeans or Americans. The principal instrument is the *samsic* [*sic*] or guitar, and every young female of the upper classes is taught to play upon it. It is the invariable accompaniment of ladies when they go to parties; and on these occasions the female guests sing and play by turns. They have, besides, various other instruments, but little can be said in commendation of their music.[1]

That is it—in some 600 pages, one paragraph is devoted to description of this exotic music. Such a summary dismissal of an entire nation's musical heritage is astonishing, particularly given the fact that the members of Perry's expedition could claim only the briefest encounter with this musical culture. This negative conclusion, however, echoes the virulent opinions of Japanese music expressed by those Europeans who had had more substantial opportunities to study it in the late sixteenth and early seventeenth centuries before the Japanese government's expulsion of foreigners in 1638.[2] The consistency and extremity of such responses reveals far more about Western listeners and their mechanisms for dealing with the exotic than it does about Japanese music.

Throughout the later nineteenth century numerous Americans recorded their reactions to encountering Japanese music and occasionally attempted to move beyond their initial culture shock to describe what they heard in detail. They frequently claimed to hear nothing musical in Japanese music and many complained of experiencing acute pain while listening to it. A select few grew to appreciate a variety of Japanese musical traditions and some even attempted to make this music their own. These first impressions, primarily formed by white affluent Americans, were shaped by the peculiar position of Japan in the American popular imagination as the cultural antipode to the United States. These initial exotic musical encounters need to be considered in the context of American *japonisme* (or "japanism")—the

late nineteenth-century craze for "all things Japanese"—and within the early political development of US-Japanese relations.

When and how did Americans first hear Japanese music and under what
circumstances? Why did Americans embrace Japanese art but reject Japanese
music? What can we learn from their reactions about cross-cultural encounters
more generally and about late nineteenth-century American musical values? In
tackling these questions, I have searched extensively through published and unpublished correspondence and diaries of Americans (from sailors to scholars to
Gilded Age socialites) who were either employed in Meiji Era Japan or who, as
globetrotters, just passed through. Bostonians—with their historical connection
to the China trade and whaling—constituted a disproportionate number of the
Americans who spent extended periods in Japan in the late nineteenth century.[3]
These included the *yatoi*, the several thousand American and European "foreign
helpers" who were invited by the Japanese in the 1870s and 1880s to teach a variety of subjects and thus serve the grand campaign of rapid Westernization. (By
the 1890s, Westerners in Japan experienced a backlash and were less welcome.)
Americans in Japan also included more casual travelers such as Charles Longfellow,
the famous poet's son, who journeyed to Japan on a whim in 1871 and ended up
encountering multiple forms of Japanese music and theater; accumulating a large
collection of Japanese decorative objects and photographs of *kabuki* actors, geishas,
and musicians; having his body tattooed in the Japanese style; building a Japanese
home; taking a Japanese lover; and staying for nearly two years. As Christine Guth
has put it, for Longfellow and numerous other Gilded Age American males, "travel
to Japan was a kind of ritual in which Euro-American travelers could use their political and economic power symbolically to reconcile their sense of themselves
as men."[4] This particular ritualistic role is one that Japan would periodically play
throughout the next century.

Pinpointing the first white American encounter with Japanese music is impossible, but the event most likely occurred not on Japanese soil but aboard a whaling
ship bound from Salem or New Bedford, Massachusetts. Or perhaps an American
citizen sailing for the Dutch in the late eighteenth century heard a Japanese musician on Deshima, the artificial island created by the Japanese for the limited trade
allowed during the period of isolation.[5] Such early American encounters with
Japanese music are documented in captains' diaries and by artifacts such as the
shamisen left aboard by Japanese castaways on an 1850 New Bedford whaler.[6] One
particularly determined individual actually beat the Perry expedition into Japan
by some five years. Ranald MacDonald, of Scottish-Chinook heritage, intuited
that Japanese and Native American peoples must have been related and therefore deliberately posed as a castaway in order to enter Japan in 1848. He managed
to stay for ten months, learning some Japanese and teaching English to Japanese
men who would later serve as interpreters during Perry's negotiations with the
Shogunate. Kept in captivity, MacDonald at one point was transported by boat and
he commented on the singing of the Ainu crew in his published narrative: "those in

forward, rowing, sang a great variety of songs—pretty much as we do—one singing a piece, then all joining in chorus. They all had fine, pleasant voices."[7] Arriving in Japan two decades after MacDonald, Samuel Pellman Boyer enjoyed a rather different musical experience, reporting in his published travel diary that "moosmie" women could be hired by the month and that at the geisha parties he attended "the girls commence singing a solemn air through their noses."[8] Boyer expressed his clear preference for the Japanese over the Chinese ("we all love Japan and almost hate China"),[9] despite finding everything about Japan to be utterly exotic: "Except that they do not walk on their heads instead of their feet, there are few things in which they [the Japanese] do not seem by some occult law to have been impelled in a perfectly opposite direction and a reversed order" (p. 33).

Of course, most American impressions of Japan and Japanese music were shaped not by experiences in Japan or at sea, but by reading numerous accounts by travelers in personal letters and newspaper reports and in the multiple travel guides and novels set in Japan published during the period. I have combed such sources for any and all reference to Japanese music and have tracked down some of the earliest songs, musicals, and plays representing Japan and Japanese music to the American public. In attempting to collect such historical traces the possibility of fully reconstructing these first exotic musical encounters assumes quixotic proportions rather early on. However, it is evident that nearly all of the major themes central to the history of American musical interaction with Japan over the past 150 years were initiated in this early period. The accumulative impact of the numerous late nineteenth-century published comments on Japanese music shaped American perceptions far into the future. To a large extent, America's first impressions of Japanese music proved lasting.

A Lexicon of Exotic Musical Invective

In encountering a foreign music for the first time, one may experience a range of possible reactions. At one extreme, the listener might be attracted to the novelties of the exotic musical system and sounds, even to the point of fetishizing such differences. At the other, the listener might be repulsed by the unfamiliar timbres, melodic shapes, and rhythmic patterns. Those American listeners attracted to exotic musical traditions historically have tended to be somewhat dissatisfied with Euro-American music, while those repulsed by the exotic have rarely failed to trumpet the superiority of their own musical culture. (Those who felt simultaneously attracted to and repulsed by the exotic were indulging in the full Orientalist experience.) In nearly all cases, nineteenth-century Americans appear to have been preconditioned to focus on difference rather than on similarity in their encounters with Japanese culture and, by and large, their reactions to Japanese music were hostile. The language employed by nineteenth-century Americans in describing Japanese music presents a veritable lexicon of musical invective. Numerous auditors confessed a fundamental inability to process Japanese music as music, labeling it: "beyond description," "unfathomable," "unintelligible," "incomprehensible," etc. For example, in his widely read 1876 book *The Mikado's Empire*, William Elliot Griffis, who lived in Japan for eight years, referred to sacred Shinto music as "the strangest and most weird system of sounds I ever heard."[10] (Griffis later claimed, rather oddly given the style of Japanese military band music, that when the international parade of allied troops entered triumphantly into the Forbidden City suppressing the Boxer Rebellion in China, the Russian band played the anthems of each nation, but "could not play the Japanese national air" when the "little brown men" marched by.)[11] Numerous other American reports on Japanese music employed far stronger terms such as "gruesome," "harsh," "strident," "hideous," "exasperating," "infernal," "ear-splitting," and "fiendish." Americans consistently referred to Japanese music as being like no other in the world, the *ne plus ultra* in revolting noise. Arthur Collins Maclay, an American teacher of English in Tokyo, wrote in 1886:

> For you must bear in mind that there is nothing like Japanese singing, either on the earth, or in the heavens above, or in the waters beneath. The operator first makes a prolonged hissing sound by drawing his breath between his lips. He then closes his eyes so tight that you fancy he never intends opening them again upon this cruel world. Then a series of groans and grunts begin to wallow up from the depths of his abdominal recesses, finally exploding from his mouth in a succession of fiendish hoots and yells. . . . I shall never forget the first time I heard one of these execrable productions of the infernal muse.[12]

Maclay appears to be describing *joruri*, the powerful vocal production of the *tayu* soloist accompanied by *shamisen* in the *bunraku* puppet theater—a style that in the late twentieth century would be celebrated and emulated by several American avant-garde composers and performers.

Particularly striking are the consistent references to pain in descriptions of Japanese musical performance—pain both experienced by the American auditors and observed in the physical deportment of the Japanese performers. Americans complained of this "piercing," "agonizing," and "deafening" music that gave rise to "acute neuralgia." In the earliest American account of Japanese music I have located, a sailor from Salem, Massachusetts (George Cleveland) described in 1801 the "distortions of countenence" in the Japanese musician which "made it apparent, that it was no small effort, to *make music*."[13] Others referred to the "unnatural" means of vocal production by Japanese singers and on their disfigurement while singing.[14] Several of these published descriptions reached a very wide audience in the United States. For instance, Isabella Bird, a highly successful travel writer, reported on her 1878 experience of Japanese music as follows:

> The power and penetrating qualities of the *sho* and flutes are tremendous; they leave not a single nerve untortured! The vocal performance was most excruciating.

It seemed to me to consist of a hyena-like howl, long and high . . . varied by frequent guttural, half-suppressed sounds, a bleat, or more respectfully "an impure
shake," very delicious to a musically-educated Japanese audience which is both
scientific and highly critical, but eminently distressing to European ears.[15]

Bird's reference to hyenas points to the entire bestiary of descriptive language
leveled at Japanese music by Americans who heard squeaking, howling, screeching,
and the noise of insects in this music. One officer on the Perry Expedition described
a cross-cultural musical exchange at an 1854 dinner reception for the Japanese
aboard his ship: "Lieutenant Brown sang a song, which they answered with a verse
or two of a Japanese song. I trust the difference of taste did not make our song sound
in their ears as their song did in ours, for it was more like the roaring of lions with
bad colds than anything else I can compare it to."[16] This quotation is striking in its
blunt assumption that the Japanese would naturally prefer Western music—an assumption that would mark American musical interactions with Japan for the next
150 years. Other writers simultaneously stated that Japanese music was unnatural
while also blaming the natural fauna of Japan for the defects of Japanese music.
Here I quote from Alice Mabel Bacon's 1891 *Japanese Girls and Women*:

It seems to me quite fortunate that the musical art is not more generally practiced,
as Japanese music, as a rule, is far from agreeable to the untrained ear of the outside barbarian. No one who has been in Japan can have failed to notice the peculiarly strident quality of the Japanese voice in singing, a quality that is gained by
professional singers through much labor and actual physical suffering. That this
is not a natural characteristic of the Japanese voice is shown by the fact that in
speaking, the voices, both of children and adults, are low and sweet. It seems to me
to be brought about by the pursuit of a wrong musical ideal, or at least, of a musical
ideal quite distinct from that of the Western world.[17]

Bacon then continues by suggesting that this defective musical ideal derives from
the fact that the Japanese keep caged noisy insects rather than singing birds: "These
insects delight the ears of the Japanese with their melody, and it seems to me that
the voices of singers throughout the empire are modeled after the shrill, rattling
chirp of the insect, rather than after the fuller notes of the bird's song."[18] Laura
Alexandrine Smith went even further in this direction in 1894: "Nature in Japan is a
silent teacher, singing-birds are rare, the most frequently heard being the unmusical
crow, the air and the water seem motionless, and the result of this wan and weirdly-
peaceful environment is a peculiarly calm and monotonous style of music."[19] The
notion that the natural environment shaped the evolution of Japanese music reflected contemporaneous evolutionary discourse.[20]

   Those writers who attempted to diagnose the ills of Japanese music in more musical detail consistently emphasized its specific deficiencies and defects. Japanese
music was faulted for lacking harmony, employing a "wrong scale," of having no

"real melody," of always being in the minor mode, of being both monotonous and prone to abrupt discontinuities, of featuring "paltry string and percussion instruments," and of not "striving to touch, by means of the divine art, the deepest sentiments in the human mind."[21] Francis Hall, an American who lived in Japan from 1859 to 1866 and whose numerous articles in the *New York Tribune* played a large role in shaping public perceptions of the Japanese, echoed the more wide-spread conviction that the Japanese had an innate disability when it came to music. In 1862, Hall described suffering through *matsuri* music as follows:

> Imagine a half-a-dozen wooden drums accompanied by several shrill fifes playing a tune with just three notes—and those discordant ones—from nine o'clock at night till three in the morning, accompanied with shouting and screeching, and all the hideous noises an unmusical people make when they are trying to be jolly . . . it would have been a better arrangement of things that a people who are so fond of celebrating holiday occasions with vocal efforts as the Japanese are should have been blessed with some ideas of melody.[22]

The evident American despair over the defects of Japanese music also found expression in works of fiction as in the following scene at a *matsuri* festival in the 1915 novel *The House of the Misty Star*:

> A group of priests were marching around it chanting some ritual. They were very solemn and their voices most weird. "What are they doing with their throats, Miss Jenkins?" asked Zura. "Singing." "Singing! Well, they know as much about singing as tit-willows do about grand opera."[23]

An encounter by American characters with the music of a Japanese female *kotoist* in Edward Greey's 1882 *Young Americans in Japan* fictionalized what numerous actual travelers claimed to have experienced in Japan itself:

> Sometimes the Jewetts imagined she was about to execute a tune, and listened to catch it, but in another moment she struck an inharmonious note, and to their disappointment ended the melody. After playing several times, she bowed, received their thanks and retired. "Your music is like your singing," said Mrs. Jewett. "Just as one thinks one can make out a connected tune, off goes the air at a tangent, and, oh dear! it is not what we call harmony."[24]

One fictional encounter with Japanese music by Americans in Japan calls for particular mention. The Canadian novelist Winnifred Eaton published multiple works set in Japan under the name Onoto Watanna in the first decade of the twentieth century, despite having an English father and Chinese mother. By assuming a Japanese-sounding name and occasionally appearing in kimono, Eaton positioned her novels within a frame of exotic authenticity. Eaton's 1901 *A Japanese Nightingale* was particularly successful and resulted in a staged play (1903) and silent film (1918).[25] At first glance, the description of Japanese music in this novel appears to accord with the general negative tone we have encountered in other writings from this period. Describing an arrival at a teahouse in the pleasure quarters, Eaton writes: "Suddenly they were in a blaze of swinging, dazzling lights, laughter and music, chatter, the clattering of dishes, the twang of the samisen, the ron-ton-ton of the biwa" (p. 3). Japanese music is introduced as simply one part of a noisy and exotic soundscape. However, the extended description of Western perceptions of Japanese musical performance that follows is quite intriguing, vacillating, as it does, between feelings of repulsion and attraction:

> Meanwhile the nerve-scraping dzin, dzin, dzin of a samisen was disturbing the air with teasing persistence. There is something provoking and still alluring in the music of the samisen. It startles the chills in the blood like the maddening scraping of a piece of metal against stone, and still there is an indescribable fascination and beauty about it. Now as it scratched and squealed intermittently and gradually twittered down to a zoom, zoom, zoom, a voice rose softly, and gently, insinuatingly, it entered into the music of the samisen. Only one long note had broken loose, which neither trembled nor wavered. When it had ended none could say, only that it had passed into other notes as strangely beautiful, and a girl was singing. . . . And her voice! All the notes were minors, piercing, sweet, melancholy—terribly beautiful. She was singing music unheard in any land save the Orient, and now for the first time, perhaps, appreciated by the foreigners, because of that voice—a voice meant for just such a medley of melody. And when she had ceased, the last note had not died out, did not fall, but remained raised, unfinished, giving to the Occidental ears a sense of incompleteness. Her audience leaned forward, peering into the darkness, waiting for the end. (pp. 7–9)

Rather than being repulsed, the expatriate Americans find themselves enthralled and—in the clearest sign of Yankee approval—the American theatrical manager leaps to his feet to chase after this Japanese singer, offering to make her fortune by bringing her to the United States as a vaudeville act. We will find in the next chapter that such transactions were made in reality in the first decades of the twentieth century, though Japanese sopranos were more likely engaged to perform Puccini or Tin Pan Alley songs than Japanese traditional music.

When not directly criticizing Japanese music, most American writers still tended to reveal a general disappointment. Mabel Loomis Todd—the early editor and promoter of the poetry of Emily Dickinson, active pianist and vocalist in Amherst, Massachusetts, and onetime student at the New England Conservatory of Music—traveled to Japan in 1887 and again in 1896 and attempted to transcribe some of the music she heard. Her efforts only reinforced her focus on what Japanese music lacked rather than leading her to appreciate what it possessed. When notating a geisha's song, Todd remarked that the "melodies rarely end upon the tonic, which has apparently no musical value in Japan" and, in attempting to transcribe the song of boatmen, she noted that the "voices are seldom in exact unison, and an untranscribable vocal quality makes it impossible to convey a real idea of these constantly reiterated strains."[26] Todd described a particular performance of August 1887 in some detail. Three Japanese musicians performing chamber music—the *sankyoku* trio genre—endeavored to entertain Todd and her American friends. In her journal, Todd exclaimed, "I wish I could write out the strange music they made! The singing is all in a very low key and utterly nasal. The idea of using the voice as a voice seems to be unknown here." She listened in vain for "a real chord involving the third of the scale" and concluded that the music was "without any appreciable harmonic connection, or any rhythm to speak of."[27] Multiple musical Westerners assumed that the inimical stance of Japanese music to Western notation—its resistance to being collected—was a telling sign of its musical defects.

Even the most ardent Western defenders of Japanese music frequently proved to be incapable of appreciating its subtleties. Francis Taylor Piggott, the British author of the first monograph in English devoted to Japanese music, opened his 1893 study with an extended apologia for his subject:

> If I say that Japanese music does not lack some reflex of the national grace, that it has some prettily quaint flashes of melody which strike the most inattentive listener at a tea-house festival, that it has some curious phrase-repetitions which seem to the attentive listener to indicate the possible existence of a science of construction, and that generally it is not altogether a concourse of weird sounds, it will appear to many that I have not merely stated, but have overstated, the case in its favour. . . . From our Western point of view Japanese music has everything against it, nothing in its favour.[28]

Piggott had first published an overview of Japanese music in the *Transactions of the Asiatic Society of Japan* in 1891 in which he argued that since the Japanese scale is built upon a 12-pitch division of the octave, Japanese music is not fundamentally different from Western music. Rather, he explained, the commonly perceived difference could be blamed on the misguided deviations from this scale by Japanese musicians.

> It is difficult fully to appreciate the clear tones of the Japanese flute, as the notes are seldom blown "clean." Weird quarter-tones disfigure both the beginning and the end of all sustained notes, the musicians being specially taught to acquire the art of producing them; and for some reason which much enquiry has not revealed to me, the music would be considered as shorn of its beauties if they were omitted. . . . *Hichiriki* players are even greater sinners than the flautists in the matter of those superfluous quarter tones.[29]

Clearly, Piggott never quite realized that the musical problem in this cross-cultural encounter might have been his own inability to appreciate such subtle treatments of pitch, the very feature that so enlivens Japanese traditional musics. Piggott paradoxically called upon the Japanese to create a truly national music through the process of Westernization: "it remains for the Japanese musicians of to-day, for whose skill I have the most profound respect, to yield to the influence of the ebbing and flowing of the waves of Western melody and harmony which is surely coming upon them" (p. 352).[30] The multiple manifestations of the desire for Japanese music to yield to Western influence in the late nineteenth century will be discussed below.

Given all its blatant defects, several American writers remarked that it was no wonder that Japanese music was primarily a pursuit of women and blind men. (The assumption being that the deficiencies of the music apparently echoed the deficiencies of the performers.) Japanese music was frequently perceived by nineteenth-century Americans in gendered terms. This is not terribly surprising given the fact that the majority of Americans traveling to Japan encountered Japanese music in entertainment situations featuring female performers.[31] Recall that the only musical genre alluded to in the official published report of the 1853–1854 expedition quoted at the opening of this chapter was that of the geisha. A particularly close encounter with Japanese music was reported by an officer in Perry's Expedition:

> One day the sound of a guitar attracted me, and I found an olive girl, of some fifteen or sixteen years, who, not perceiving my presence, continued her play. It was a strange tune, wild and melancholy, and often abruptly interrupted by harsh accords. After a while some women that had assembled around us made the girl aware of my presence; she threw down her instrument and began to cry, and I could not induce her to play again. The guitar was made of wood, with the exception of the upper lid. Of the three strings, two were in the octave, the middle one giving the fifth. The strings were not touched by the fingers, but with a flat piece of horn, held between the thumb and third finger of the right hand, in shape not unlike the one painters use to clean their palettes and mix their colors.[32]

Apparently unmoved by the tears of the young Japanese woman, this American clearly proceeded to enter her room and seize her *shamisen* for further study. Here, at the very onset of America's sustained communication with Japan, we witness what will prove a common conjunction in American popular culture: an American male's voyeuristic and erotic experience of Japanese music with a surprisingly detailed musical description ultimately leading to critical rejection.

Cross-Cultural Lessons and Collections

Were these negative descriptions of Japanese music primarily knee-jerk outbursts of cultural chauvinism rather than sober, considered responses? Can I, an admirer of Japanese traditional music, credit and even feel the professed pain of these writers? Some of the descriptions smack of virtuosic vitriol, more a form of entertainment than an attempt at careful explication. Even the great consistency of negative response could be explained by the fact that later writers on Japan tended to parrot or even plagiarize prior descriptions of the country. However, I have come to realize that the negative shock potential of Japanese music for nineteenth-century Americans should not be underestimated, particularly since much of this music remains so foreign to most twenty-first-century Americans. Even those late nineteenth-century Japanophiles, such as Ernest Fenollosa, Lafcadio Hearn, William Sturgis Bigelow,[33] and Edward Sylvester Morse, who were predisposed toward Japanese music and who experienced a more sustained exposure to it, found cross-cultural understanding an elusive goal. As the major American architect Ralph Adams Cram put it: "Japanese architecture is at first absolutely baffling; it is like Japanese music, so utterly foreign, so radically different in its genesis, so aloof in its moods and motives from the standards of the West, that for a long time it is a wonder merely, a curiosity, a toy perhaps or a sport of nature, not a serious product of the human mind, a priceless contribution to the history of the world."[34] Judith Becker has stated the dilemma in stark terms: "Given enough time, one can come to appreciate the arts of an alien culture (partly by superimposing one's own set of values and aesthetics upon the listening act), but one cannot be taught to hear music as someone from another culture hears it."[35] Becker's statement assumes, of course, rather clear demarcations between musical cultures and perhaps is more apt for describing the period considered in this chapter than for our own globalized musical world. Gilded Age Americans certainly did superimpose their own musical values and aesthetics upon Japanese music in a variety of fascinating ways. Listening in on how three of the most famous American *yatoi* heard Japanese music, and how divergently they responded to the experience, may prove revelatory for understanding the dynamics of cross-cultural musical encounters.

The celebrated zoologist Edward Sylvester Morse from Salem, Massachusetts, lived in Japan for extended periods from 1877 to 1883 and served as a distinguished professor in the Imperial University at Tokyo. Morse had an extraordinary mind, insatiable curiosity, and remarkable energy for learning and collecting. He proved a virtuoso at describing all things Japanese for his fellow Americans, both in his published writings and in his extensive lectures. In his monumental two-volume work *Japan Day by Day*—877 pages of text with 777 illustrations from his notebooks—Morse attempted to present Japan to his American readers in as much detail as possible, from brachiopods to ancient burial pots to the bracing employed in house construction.[36] Some of his very first observations were of Japanese sea chanties and workers' songs with their "odd, monotonous chant" (I., 4; also II., 62; 64). Morse encountered a very wide range of Japanese musical genres, including the music of *kabuki, noh, bunraku*, the *biwa, koto*, geisha song (*kouta*), *gagaku* court music, *matsuri* festival music, and the *shakuhachi*.[37] His early impressions of

Japanese music—while tending toward a far greater precision in descriptive detail—differed little from those of his compatriots. He referred to "a lazy, absentminded thrumming on the Japanese banjo with now and then a toot of a flute" (I., 30) in *kabuki* and stated early on that from "a foreigner's standpoint the nation seems to be devoid of what we call an ear for music. Their music seems to be of the rudest kind. Certainly there is an absence of harmony. . . . They have no voice, and they make the most curious squeaks and grunts when singing." However, even at this early point, Morse included a telling footnote: "Later I learned from a student that our music was not music at all to them" (I., 115).[38]

As his references to music accumulate in *Japan Day by Day*, it becomes clear that Morse was increasingly frustrated by his inability to describe and appreciate Japanese music. It is also clear that Morse made a real effort at cross-cultural understanding. On hearing *matsuri* music he wrote: "I listened in vain to detect a strain of what we regard as music and gave up in despair; I not only could not understand the music, but was equally ignorant of what it was all about" (I., 302). Likewise, in October 1877: "The native music is utterly indescribable. I listened intently for nearly two hours, much to the wonderment of my friends, and although I have a fair ear for music I managed to carry away only three consecutive notes of an air and these I still have in my head. It is one constant wail of the saddest sounds" (I., 359–360). Near the end of the first volume, and the start of his second stay in Japan in 1878, Morse appears to have arrived at a temporary accord with Japanese music: "The question constantly arose, 'Is this music in our sense of the word?' It is, but widely unlike ours. . . . It may be that their music will ultimately prove to have merits of which we get no hint at present" (I., 401–402). To a far greater extent than most Americans in Japan, this scientist stood ready to be convinced by the data.

During his third and final stay in Japan in 1882–1883, recounted in the last half of the second volume of *Japan Day by Day*, Morse's relationship with Japanese music blossomed. Demonstrating a keen understanding of Japanese musical aesthetics, Morse described hearing *shakuhachi* music in the summer of 1882: "The enjoyment for us consisted in the delicious contrasts between note after note. The notes were long and of exquisite purity. It was a revelation to us" (II., 224). The importance of the *shakuhachi* in reshaping Morse's opinions of Japanese music was echoed in the experience of the painter John La Farge.[39] La Farge traveled to Japan in 1886 with the famed American historian Henry Adams. Soon after arriving in Yokohama, La Farge and Adams "sauntered out into the Japanese quarter" and heard "fiendish music" accompanying a theatrical performance.[40] Nearly two months later they heard *shakuhachi* music and La Farge was inspired to write in a rather different prose style:

It was like a hymn to nature. The noise of the locusts had stopped for a time; and this floating wail, rising and falling in unknown and incomprehensible modulations, seemed to belong to the forest as completely as their cry. The shrill and liquid song brought back the indefinite melancholy that one has felt with the distant sound of children's voices, singing of Sundays in drowsy rhythms. But these sounds belonged to the place, to its own peculiar genius—of a lonely beauty, associated with an indefinite past, little understood; with death, and primeval nature, and final rest.[41]

The *shakuhachi* continues to play a crucial role in converting Americans to Japanese music and in fostering visions of Old Japan, as we will find in chapter 9.[42]

Later in the summer of 1882, Morse reported on the performance of both Western and Japanese traditional music at a graduation ceremony:

> The music was certainly very weird and very impressive, and with the peculiarly sweet accompaniment and curious rhythm, gave me an impression of the merit of Japanese music that I had never had before. Their music sounded distinguished as they sang it, compared with ours. Of course they did not sing the best of our music, or in the best way; nevertheless, here was a chance for some one to secure ideas in regard to the power of music in a new direction. (II., 237)

As astonishing as it is rare, in this statement a Gilded Age American suggests that he might actually prefer Japanese music to "ours." Moreover, he also imagines the role that Japanese music might play in pointing toward a "new direction" for Euro-American music, thus prefiguring musical modernists by several decades. In December he attended a concert performance of *bunraku* music and had a slight relapse: "When one hears this form of story-telling it impresses one as highly absurd; becoming accustomed to it one can somewhat understand the reason for the vocal accompaniment in expressing emotions of pain, anger, despair, etc., but it is entirely beyond description" (II., 375). But then during his final month in Japan, Morse took a remarkable step in his journey toward Japanese music. In January of 1883, he began lessons in *noh* singing—becoming the first American (to my knowledge) to study any form of Japanese musical performance. I find Morse's descriptions of his lessons moving:

> [My teacher] sang a line and I sang it after him; then he sang another; and so on through the eleven lines of the piece. After trying it twice in that way we sang together. I realized how very rich and sonorous his voice was. Then I observed that, do what I would, my notes sounded flat and monotonous while his were full of inflections and accents, though all on one note. I felt awkward and embarrassed at the absurd failure I was making and perspired freely, though it was a cold day in January. Finally, in desperation, I threw off all reserve and entered into it with all my might, resolved, at any rate, to mimic his sounds. I inflated my abdomen tensely, sang through my nose, put the tremulo [*sic*] stop on when necessary, and attracted a number of attendants who peeked through the screens to look on, in despair, no doubt, at a foreigner desecrating the honored precincts by such

infernal howls. Be that as it may, my teacher for the first time bowed approvingly at my efforts, complimented me when I got through my first lesson, and told me, probably in encouragement, that I would in a month's time be able to sing in *no* play. (II., 401–402)

In the 777 illustrations for this two-volume book Morse only once includes himself in an image and that appears in his depiction of a *noh* lesson. (See Figure 1.1.)

At this late stage in his Japanese experience, Morse declared: "It is by taking actual lessons in the tea ceremony and in singing that I may learn many things from the Japanese standpoint." And yet in the end, Morse appears to conclude that even following his endeavors at participant observation, complete cross-cultural understanding is impossible. In February he wrote that he had taken several singing lessons and "although I have a fairly quick ear, I have not been able to carry away two consecutive notes, or to recall any notes. It has been very interesting to see how different their music is from ours" (II., 406–407). Unable to "recall any notes," how could the frustrated zoologist collect and describe this music? While admitting his own difficulty in coming to terms with Japanese music, he distanced himself from the general run of foreigners:

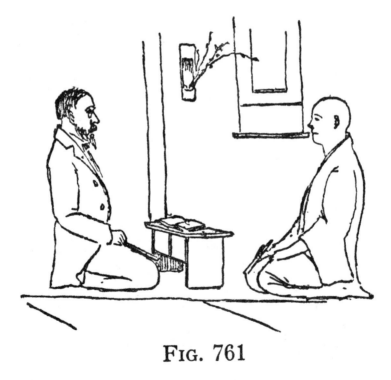

FIG. 761

Figure 1.1 Edward Sylvester Morse's depiction of his 1883 *noh* lessons. Morse, *Japan Day by Day*, vol. 2 (Boston and New York: Houghton Mifflin, 1917), 402.

The various forms or schools of Japanese music, whether vocal or instrumental, are listened to by a foreigner, first with bewilderment, and then greeted with laughter. It was a humiliating experience to attend a Japanese entertainment in which classical music was sung, music that would bring tears to the Japanese eyes, and have it greeted by the Englishmen in the audience with contemptuous laughter. You hear quaint music in the East, music that excites your interest, music that prompts your feet to beat time, but Japanese music is simply unintelligible to a foreigner. As their pictorial art was incomprehensible to us at the outset, and yet on further acquaintance and study we discovered in it transcendent merit, so it seemed to me that a study of Japanese music might reveal merits we little suspected. For that reason I studied Utai [*noh* singing] ... Professor Yatabe, a graduate of Cornell, while thoroughly approving the adoption of many features from abroad and admitting their superiority, nevertheless insisted that the Japanese music was superior to ours. (II., 407–408)[43]

This paragraph—his final statement on Japanese music—ends there, lacking the further sentence or two that could have clarified Morse's final scientific opinion. In his somewhat disjunct prose, Morse betrayed here his continued liminal position vis-à-vis Japanese music—no longer dismissive of it and yet still finding this exotic music "beyond description."[44]

*   *   *

Lafcadio Hearn, more than any other figure, instilled the image of Romantic "Old Japan" in the American popular imagination in the late nineteenth and early twentieth centuries.[45] He not only wrote prolifically on many aspects of Japanese culture, but also devoted himself to collecting and retelling traditional Japanese tales, particularly those that seemed to him most bizarre and exotic. Hearn had been a freelance writer and reporter in New Orleans when he encountered the Japanese exhibits at the 1884 World's Industrial and Cotton Centennial Exposition. He traveled to Japan in 1889 and ended up living there until his death in 1904, teaching English literature, marrying a Japanese woman, and becoming a Japanese citizen. Hearn's imaginative journey into the mysterious heart of Japanese culture knew no limits. He even wrote of becoming a Shinto god himself and of having festivals held in his honor. In this extreme exotic reverie, Hearn saw and heard the priests' daughters, the *miko*, dancing for him "with tinkling of little bells, with waving of silent fans, that I might be gladdened by the bloom of their youth, that I might delight in the charm of their grace. And there would be music of many thousand years ago,— weird music of drums and flutes,—and songs in a tongue no longer spoken; while the miko, the darlings of the gods, would poise and pose before me."[46]

Hearn was an avid student of exotic folk musics, as is evident in his letters to the music critic H. E. Krehbiel,[47] and he referred repeatedly to Japanese folk music throughout his many writings on the country. Hearn's widow recalled that he frequently sang folk songs with their children and made up his own tunes for Japanese poems, attributing "his compositions to Basho [the famous poet] by way of jest."[48] Hearn clearly sought those forms of Japanese music that he presupposed would exhibit the most primitive mystery. In an 1892 letter to Basil Hall Chamberlain, the most widely respected English-language authority of his day on "things Japanese," Hearn wrote: "I cannot like the professional music of the Japanese,—that is, vocal,— as I like the chants of the peasantry, the occasional queer bursts of quaverings and long weird plaintive tones breaking here and there into fractions of notes. Some of these seem to me very pretty, and savagely natural, like the chant of a semi, or a wild bird."[49] He once described *gagaku* music as "music which at first no Western ear can feel pleasure in, but which, when often heard, becomes comprehensible, and is found to possess a weird charm of its own."[50] In describing Japanese culture for his American audience, "weird charm" was one of Hearn's highest forms of praise. Hearn craved contact with the exotic throughout his life, whether in New Orleans, the West Indies, or Japan. He cherished the thrill of the foreign: "As first perceived, the outward strangeness of things in Japan produces (in certain minds, at least) a queer thrill impossible to describe,—a feeling of weirdness which comes to us only with the perception of the totally unfamiliar."[51] For Morse, the inability to describe and retain Japanese music in scientific detail was an intensely frustrating experience. For Hearn, the ineffability of Japanese music, its utter foreignness, was precisely its appeal. As with many other Japanophile Orientalists, "understanding" Japanese music was never Hearn's objective.[52]

Hearn repeatedly found himself "bewitched" by Japanese music and was inspired to ponder questions of universal musical expression as he appreciated this music's connections to the natural world. In 1894 he described a *bon-odori* performance as follows:

> And, at another tap of the drum, there begins a performance impossible to picture in words, something unimaginable, phantasmal,—a dance, an astonishment. . . . a strain of song, full of sweet, clear quavering, like the call of a bird, gushes from some girlish mouth. . . . Utterly impossible to recall the air, with its fantastic intervals and fractional tones;—as well attempt to fix in memory the purlings of a bird; but the indefinable charm of it lingers with me still. Melodies of Europe awaken within us feelings we can utter, sensations familiar as mother-speech, inherited from all the generations behind us. But how explain the emotion evoked by a primitive chant totally unlike anything in Western melody,—impossible even to write in those tones which are the ideographs of our music-tongue?[53]

At this point, Hearn concludes that the secret expressive power of this music, its ability to move him across the cultural divide, lies in its accord with "Nature's most ancient song."[54] Another folk performance inspired Hearn to more radical speculations along these lines. Recounting the voice of an itinerant peasant musician who appeared outside his home, Hearn wrote:

> She sang as only a peasant can sing,—with vocal rhythms learned, perhaps, from the cicadae and the wild nightingales,—and with fractions and semi-fractions and demi-semi-fractions of tones never written down in the musical language of the West. . . . long after the singer had gone that voice seemed still to stay,—making within me a sense of sweetness and of sadness so strange that I could not but try to explain to myself the secret of those magical tones.[55]

This experience led him to consider the possibilities of cross-cultural musical expression more generally. He states that just as language varies from nation to nation, so does music and thus "melodies which move us deeply have no significance to Japanese ears" (p. 45). He then wonders, however, why he had been so powerfully affected by the woman's song: "Surely that in the voice of the singer there were qualities able to make appeal to something larger than the sum of the experience of one race" (p. 45). Waxing proto-Jungian, he concludes that deeper, pan-human musical connections must exist: "Inherited memory makes familiar to even the newly-born the meaning of this tone of caress. Inherited, no doubt, likewise, our knowledge of the tones of sympathy, of grief, of pity. And so the chant of a blind woman in this city of the Far East may revive in even a Western mind emotion deeper than individual being."[56]

Hearn's Romantic experience of Japanese music, his evident delight in exotic acoustic reveries, can still inspire a certain envy in the most sober of readers of his virtuosic purple prose. His writings had a demonstrable impact on later artistic responses to Japan, including on specific musical compositions, as we shall discover in chapter 3. We can clearly hear the echo of Hearn's voice in the works of many of the American authors who followed him in praising the mysteries of Japan, as in this 1921 summary of Japanese music in a book entitled *Mysterious Japan*:

> The native Japanese music, with its crude five-tone scale, is demonstrably inferior to that of Western peoples. To the foreign ear it is unmelodious, even barbarous, and yet I must say for it that the more I heard it the more I felt in it a kind of weird appeal—an appeal not to the ear but to the imagination. Even now, when I am far away from Japan, a note or two struck on a guitar, a mandolin, or a ukulele, in imitation of the samisen, conjures up vivid pictures in my mind. . . . The sound that evokes the picture is not harmonious, but the picture itself is harmonious beyond expression.[57]

Japanese music recalled and retained the wondrous and bizarre features of the Old Japan that Hearn saw passing away before his eyes. He frequently lamented Japanese modernization and laid some of the blame on the United States: "The opening of the country was very wrong,–a crime. . . . Fairyland is already dead."[58] Yet, he could still hear Old Japan in Japanese music. Listening to a Japanese military song (a *gunka*—a genre directly shaped by the West) Hearn experienced a "flash of Japanese soul,—the old military spirit. Oh! what pains should be taken to preserve it!"[59] Cherishing the exotic signification of Japanese music—the "vivid pictures" that it represents in the Orientalist imagination rather than its audible sounds—has long been a habit of certain American Japanophiles. Rather than "recall the air" in any detail, Hearn hoped to capture and convey in his writings some of the "indefinable charm" of his exotic musical experiences.

*   *   *

In his travel diary entry of 20 July 1879 during a trip to Nikko, Ernest Fenollosa recorded his meeting with Mr. and Mrs. Ulysses S. Grant as follows: "Mrs. G. didn't come in for some time. G. was not talkative these days. Said he liked Japanese music better than our orchestra."[60] The former president was on a goodwill tour of Japan and had famously enjoyed a demonstration of *noh* theater on 8 July, allegedly urging the Japanese to preserve the art form.[61] What, in particular, Grant found appealing about *noh* and Japanese music appears to have been left unspecified. However, perhaps Grant's laconic comments served to spark Fenollosa's own interest in Japanese music and theater. Born in Salem in the year of Perry's expedition, Fenollosa appears to have been destined to travel to Japan.[62] With the personal encouragement of Edward Sylvester Morse, Fenollosa arrived in Japan in 1878 to serve as a professor of political economy and philosophy at Tokyo University. He ended up becoming the premier American authority on Japanese art—serving as the director of the Imperial Museum in Tokyo and the Curator of Oriental Art at the Boston Museum of Fine Arts—and posthumously, through his literary executor Ezra Pound, was the primary catalyst for the later Euro-American modernist interest in Japanese theater and poetry.[63]

Unlike Morse and Hearn, Fenollosa appears to have felt sufficiently equipped to study Japanese music in detail. Fenollosa's father, Manuel Fenollosa, had been an active and prominent musician in Salem and Boston, and some of Ernest's earliest memories were of his parents playing music in the home. In Japan, Fenollosa transcribed boatmen's songs for Morse and later transcribed vocal melodies from *noh* theater.[64] In his study of *noh* singing, Fenollosa literally picked up where Morse had left off—taking over Morse's lessons when the scientist departed for the United States in February 1883.[65] Fenollosa claimed to have studied *noh* for twenty years, "learning by actual practice the method of the singing and something of the acting."[66] Akiko Murakata has revealed that Fenollosa's initial attempts to study *noh* were half-hearted as he frequently skipped his vocal lessons.[67] His serious study of *noh* began during his second period in Japan in 1898. In his publication based on Fenollosa's papers, Ezra Pound quoted Fenollosa's diary entry of 20 December 1898 in which he recounts a visit to Minoru Umewaka, the restorer of *noh*:

I apologized to him for the mistake of years ago, thanked him for his frankness, his reticence to others, and his kindness in allowing me to begin again with him. . . . He asked me to sing, and I sang "Hansakaba." He praised me, said everything was exactly right and said that both he and Takeyo considered my progress wonderful; better than a Japanese could make. He said I was already advanced enough to sing in a Japanese company. . . . Morse and I are the only foreigners who have ever been taught Noh, and I am the only foreigner now practising it.[68]

Pound referred to Fenollosa's extensive notes on music, but chose not to present them in detail since he was unsure "how much or how little general interest there is in the Japanese drama and its methods of presentation."[69] Thus, an important opportunity for transmitting one prominent American's enthusiasm for Japanese music was missed.

Fenollosa took detailed notes while experiencing performances of *noh*. As Richard Taylor has observed, these marginalia reveal Fenollosa's intimate knowledge of *noh* music, including the specific styles of singing and elements of the instrumental accompaniment.[70] What is striking about Fenollosa's musical descriptions, and what sets him apart from virtually all other American commentators on Japanese music in this period, is his ability to appreciate the full range of musical expression in *noh*. In April 1899 he remarked that the "transition of sound, in solos or duets, from the 'strong voice' to the 'tone voice' is very striking, like ones from minor to major."[71] He rightly refers to the occasional "shriek" of the *noh* flute and to monotonous sections in the plays. However, he also observes when the flute plays "sweetly" and repeatedly proclaims the beauty and power of this musical tradition. Fenollosa appreciated both the "impressive" silences in this music as well as the passages of "loud and fierce" singing.[72] In reading Fenollosa's descriptive marginalia on the details of *noh* performance, I am struck by how closely they resemble my own observations made over a century later.

In a heading to a section reproducing some of Fenollosa's transcriptions of *noh* singing, Pound stated "it seems to me that many things in the singing are wholly unindicated in his script."[73] However, Fenollosa's attempts to transcribe this music are actually quite impressive, particularly when we note orthographic details omitted in Pound's published transcription of Fenollosa's original.[74] For instance, Pound repeatedly employs a normal slur mark between notes where Fenollosa employed a straight line indicating a glissando. In other spots, Fenollosa appears to indicate a repeated wavering between a main pitch and a secondary pitch but Pound, again, simply indicates a slur between pitches of equal value. Pound is careful to include nearly all of Fenollosa's zigzag lines above pitches, but fails to note that in numerous cases the line begins straight and then wavers up and down. This allowed Fenollosa to indicate the common vocal gesture of initializing a pitch before beginning to shake it in a broad vibrato. Without having heard the music himself, it is not surprising that Pound was unable to appreciate fully Fenollosa's efforts to capture the vocal subtleties in notation.

Although he is celebrated as *the* modernist pioneer in his devotion to *noh*, Fenollosa was not alone in his admiration for its music. His second wife, Mary McNeil Fenollosa, was one of the earliest and most prominent women in the creation of American literary *japonisme* and joined him in attending *noh* performances and demonstrations. In fact, she initially appears even to have participated in some of his *noh* lessons.[75] Mary was a novelist and poet from Alabama who had traveled to Japan previously with a former husband. Two of her poems attest to her general attraction to Japanese music. In "The Koto-Player," she describes a *kotoist*'s performance with subtle observation and evocative description: "O wondrous hush!—Then three slow notes, like tears,/Roll down the cheek of silence, one by one."[76] She admires both the "lowly" *shamisen* player and the "high-born" *kotoist* in her later poem "The Musicians."[77] Her diaries reveal her charged initial impressions of Japanese music:

> . . . quite late at night, I hear from the lower story the slow round notes of the old ladies' samisen, "plunk" like white pebbles, one by one into the great night-sea of silence—then I creep to my bedroom veranda, and, bending to listen, catch the rich, plaintive murmur of a man's voice—old Wakai, perhaps—singing ancient *No* songs. There is nothing exactly like this singing in the whole world. It plays on our senses and nerves, rather than on the one crass organ of the ear. It seems the low plaint of a hero-soul imprisoned in the commonplace. It has long pauses, and slow quaverings, sudden risings of the voice, like a bird bestirring itself at dawn; gradual deep fading like the death of a soul. It is more than music—it is poetry symbolized in sound. . . . It affects me differently from any other music. It is the very nerve-thread of melody.[78]

Like Hearn, and in language similar in tone to his, Mary reveals here the fundamental importance of Japanese music to her experience of Japan. Again, this exotic music is deemed valuable for what it evokes and symbolizes, rather than as performed music.

Japanese music also played important symbolic and dramatic roles in several of Mary Fenollosa's novels and poems. In both *The Breath of the Gods* (1905) and *The Dragon Painter* (1906) a major turning point in the narrative occurs through a musical performance. *The Breath of the Gods* is set in 1903, just before and during the Russo-Japanese War. Much of the story centers on the friendship of Yuki, a Japanese woman who has gone to school in the United States, and Gwendolen, the white American daughter of a diplomat who moves to Japan with her family. Late in the novel, Yuki decides to hold a sewing party to sew bandages for the war effort.[79] She invites both Japanese and foreign women and plans to entertain her guests with "music of the two worlds."[80] The narrator pokes fun at the musical chauvinism of the British character, Mrs. Wyndham, who will represent Western music by performing a few songs. Perhaps with the publications of some of the travel writers quoted earlier in this chapter in mind, the narrator states: "As may be inferred, all Japanese music was, to Mrs. Wyndham and her intimate associates, mere squeaking, caterwauling, an excruciating discord" (p. 301). Mrs. Wyndham declares that she is not thinking of the Japanese in attendance as she picks her pieces since she knows they "are incapable of appreciating any real music" (p. 302). Gwendolen pointedly answers her by stating that Yuki loves the music of Brahms. At first the Japanese women are so shocked by Mrs. Wyndham's singing that they are unable to contain their laughter. However, as her performance continues they begin to admire the music. Gwendolen then plays a Chopin fantasy, "music that even the untutored Japanese girls could feel. It held the sound of their own koto strings" (p. 303). The Japanese portion of the recital begins with the arrival of the Satsuma *biwa* player—Mrs. Wyndham making a hasty exit.[81] The narrator indulges in a breathless description of his performance and relates its impact on Gwendolen: "In the sense of Western harmony there was none, but something in the weird vibrations of long notes, the intricacies of overtone, and, above all, the unbelievable subtleties of rhythm, gave to one eager American listener, at least, her first insight into a new world of sound" (p. 308). For Gwendolen, this music demonstrated how the Japanese "are nearer . . . to nature" and are able to "summon the very essences of being." Echoing Mary's own experiences of Japanese music, the narrator states that the music "swept in [Gwendolen's] soul strained chords of un-known feeling. She felt in herself the vibrations of the trembling lute. In its cell a soul, just wakened, fumbled at a new discovered latch" (p. 309). After the *biwa* per-formance ends, Gwendolen approaches Yuki: " 'Yuki-ko,' she faltered, 'I just wanted to say that at last I understand,—I think I understand entirely' " (p. 310). Japanese music is framed here as a mysterious key to cross-cultural understanding, or at least momentarily sensing the secret exotic soul of Japanese culture.

Music plays an even more mysterious, even cosmic role in Mary Fenollosa's *The Dragon Painter*—a tale in the spirit of Hearn's fantastical Japanese stories. At the crucial, mystical moment early on in the story (and illustrated in the book's frontis-piece) the young male protagonist (the "dragon painter") encounters our heroine, Umè-ko, as she suddenly enters to sing and dance at her father's bidding: "A singing voice began, rich, passionate, and low, matching with varying intonation the mar-velous postures of fan and throat and body. At first low in sound, almost husky, it flowered to a note long held and gradually deepening in power. It gathered up shadows from the heart and turned them into light."[82] Of course, the young man immediately recognizes her as the "dragon maiden," the wife he has been searching for through multiple lifetimes, and he falls headlong into a frenzy of passion. Not all of Mary Fenollosa's evocations of Japanese music were this high-strung. In her 1899 poem "The Samisen," collected in *Out of the Nest: A Flight of Verses*, Japanese music serves as a cover for a young Japanese couple's erotic tryst.[83] In this comic vignette, a maiden tells her family that she wants to stay home to practice her "little samisen. Plink! Plunk!" while they attend a festival. This ruse allows her admirer to sneak into her home and soon "a boyish face bends o'er her samisen." This lighthearted poem on Japanese music called forth a musical setting by Albert A. Mack, published by G. Schirmer in 1903. In Mack's song, the music of the *shamisen* appears to be represented indirectly by the open fifth, "staccatissimo sempre," four sixteenths and two eighths tattoo in the piano accompaniment—the chief musical stereotype signaling East Asia in Western popular music. The vocal line representation of the *shamisen*'s "Plink! Plunk!" is set with an octave fall. An awkward rest here and there might be intended to signal the perceived odd formality of Japanese speech, while the song's minor mode contrast with the comic tale signals the exotic setting throughout. In 1902 Mack had set Fenollosa's "Miyoko San," from the same collection, in which Fenollosa celebrates the ethereal beauty of an ideal Japanese woman whom the protagonist will paint with the aid of all sorts of magical materials, such as the "soul of a dragon-fly," a "star's quick eye," and "a single note/Gone mad to float/To its own sweet death in the upper air." We will discover in the next chapter that the literary *japonisme* of Mary Fenollosa and, particularly, Hearn had an extensive impact on American song throughout the early twentieth century.

Hearn's influence on Mary Fenollosa's writings on Japan is quite evident, particularly in her descriptions of the exotic Japanese soundscape. For example, Hearn was clearly fascinated by bells in East Asia and published several Chinese and Japanese tales in which bells figure prominently.[84] He repeatedly attempted to describe the impression that these bells made on him. A priest once invited him to ring the big bell at Kamakura and Hearn described the result as "a sound deep as thunder, rich as the bass of a mighty organ,—a sound enormous, extraordinary, yet beautiful,—rolls over the hills and away. Then swiftly follows another and lesser and sweeter billowing of tone; then another; then an eddying of waves of echoes."[85] Before traveling to Japan, Hearn had translated Pierre Loti's "The Big Bell" in which Loti, in his typical sarcastic tone, relates how he paid two cents to pull the battering-ram with the help of some Japanese children and produced "a sound awful, cavernous, and prolonged into mighty orchestral vibrations, which must be heard through the whole of the sacred city."[86] Picking up directly from Hearn, Mary Fenollosa described the sound of the big Japanese bell in her fiction, attempting to approximate that sonic experience in her sentence structure:

> About half the distance up the steep the temple bell above them sounded six slow deliberate strokes. First came the sonorous impact of the swinging beam against curved metal, then the "boom," the echo,—the echoes of that echo to endless repetition, sifting in layers through the thinner air upon them, sweeping like vapor low along the hillside with a presence and reality so intense that it should have had color, or, at least, perfume; settling in a fine dew of sound on quivering ferns and grasses, permeating, it would seem, with its melodious vibration the very wood of the houses and the trunks of living trees.[87]

These mystical and generally positive descriptions of this Japanese sound are striking considering that the sound's significance would be dramatically recast in such anti-Asian films as *The Mask of Fu Manchu* (1932), in which a white character is tortured by the sound of an exotic bell, and in Frank Capra's 1945 *Know Your Enemy—Japan*. Furthermore, the ubiquitous use of a gong to signal East Asia has likewise been incessantly framed as an ominous, rather than alluring, sound in American popular culture.

Mary was not the only Fenollosa to appreciate the writings of Lafcadio Hearn. In his review of Hearn's *Glimpses of Unfamiliar Japan*, Ernest Fenollosa contrasted Hearn's "sympathy and exquisiteness of touch" with Chamberlain's "cynical, unfeeling" views expressed in his *Things Japanese*.[88] Ernest's condolence letter to Hearn's widow attests to his devotion to Hearn: "And now that he has passed to the spirit world of which he thought so often and wrote so much, it seems to us who are left behind as if the brightest star in the sky had gone out."[89] Like Hearn, Fenollosa was dismayed by the rampant modernization of Japan. He famously championed older traditions of Japanese art at a time when the Japanese appeared intent on deserting their cultural heritage. In "East and West," his 1892 poetic address to the Phi Beta Kappa Society at Harvard, he lamented: "O you West in the East like the slime of a beast,/Why must you devour that exquisite flower?/Why poison the peace of the far Japanese?/Is there no one to tell of the birthright they sell?"[90] In this poem, as in his lectures to American audiences and other writings, Fenollosa prophesied a new union between the feminine Japan and the masculine America for the greater glory of all humankind, and he envisioned this synthesis in musical metaphors.[91] Thus, Ernest Fenollosa's experience of Japan and of Japanese music seems to fall somewhere between those of Morse and Hearn. Fenollosa approached the study of Japanese culture in a more academic manner than did Hearn and yet was drawn to spiritual interpretations and imagery absent from the descriptive catalogs of Morse. Where Morse appeared content with collecting and describing genres of Japanese music for his readers, Fenollosa late in his life was eager to launch a promotional campaign for Japanese *noh* in America, along the lines of what he had achieved for Japanese painting. In a 1903 lecture on *noh* in Washington, D.C., Fenollosa exclaimed:

> If, in some obscure corner of the Hellenic mountains, there lingered still a legitimate descendant of the Art of Thespis, how we should flock to study it, as we do the miracle play of Oberammergau! But how few visitors to Japan avail themselves of an opportunity to study the living analogue of Greek drama in Japan, the *No*.[92]

Promoting Japanese art in Japan and the United States had been a relatively straightforward task for Fenollosa. At the time of his death, however, Fenollosa had published only one article on *noh* and had delivered a few lectures on the subject. Pound's idiosyncratic edition of Fenollosa's *noh* manuscripts would not appear until 1916. The initial presentation of Japanese music and theater in the United States would proceed instead along other lines.

Domestic Encounters and Exotic Masquerades

The number of nineteenth-century Americans who heard Japanese music in Japan, while perhaps surprisingly large, represented but an infinitesimal portion of the population. While a handful of American sailors may have encountered Japanese music as early as the late eighteenth century—and, as we have seen, seemingly every American globetrotter passing through Japan heard some form of traditional music—only a handful of Americans toward the end of the nineteenth century experienced a sustained encounter with Japanese music in Japan. Was Japanese music heard by a broader public in the United States itself? At a time when Americans were purchasing Japanese art and decorative objects in vast quantities, creating "Japanese corners" in their homes and "Japanese gardens" outside, incorporating Japanese design in luxury domestic architecture from Pasadena bungalows to Adirondack cabins, donning the kimono and using "Japanese soap" in their baths, reading novels set in Old Japan and breathless reports on Japan's modernization, did music play a role in their *fin-de-siècle* craze?[93]

Nineteenth-century Japanese immigration to the United States likely resulted in isolated cross-cultural musical encounters, but Japanese immigrants did not serve as a significant source of contact with Japanese music for white Americans until the early decades of the twentieth century, as will be discussed in subsequent chapters. Instead, such musical encounters took place in particular public venues and in specific limited formats. Aya Mihara has documented the reception of Japanese music in the highly popular performances by Japanese acrobatic troupes in Europe and the United States starting in the 1860s.[94] Seven or more troupes toured the country in the mid-1860s, bringing for the first time a form of Japanese theater to broad audiences in the West. Mihara reveals that the consistent intensely negative references to their *kabuki*-style music in the otherwise positive reviews of their acrobatic performances led most troupes to abandon the use of Japanese music altogether. Thus some of the earliest encounters with Japanese music in America resulted in its silencing.

However, one quite prominent musical member of the audience at a New York performance by one of these troupes underwent a striking change of heart. Clara Louise Kellogg, the first American operatic soprano to achieve fame in Europe, reported in *Scribner's Monthly* in 1877 that she had repeatedly seen and heard the Japanese perform "several years ago" in New York and had been disturbed by the "exceedingly harsh and disagreeable noise made by the Japanese orchestra."[95] At one performance, she "suddenly noticed a melody, at first indistinct, but afterward assuming definite shape as I was able to shut out the discordant accompaniment." She memorized this tune and then played it for one of the performers on the piano backstage. She described the melody as "perfect in construction, original, beautifully simple, full of sentiment, and suggestive of touching words." When she later attended performances by the troupe in London she was disappointed to discover that they had dropped their Japanese musicians. Kellogg declares that she would "like to awaken an interest" in Japanese music and predicts that there must be even more of musical value in the art music traditions of Japan. This example, and a handful of others from the nineteenth century, might suggest that Americans only needed to become familiar with Japanese music through repeated hearings in order to appreciate it. But Kellogg's conversion tale represents a rather pyrrhic musical victory for the Japanese. She was never reconciled to the torturous timbres of Japanese music, only to its tunes.

Throughout the history of US-Japan musical interaction, entrepreneurial managers from the vaudeville era to the summer performing arts festivals of our time have capitalized on Japanese exoticism by bringing Japanese performers to the United States. As early as 1866, Thomas F. Smith imported a troupe of Japanese acrobats and the California-based impresario Tom Maguire, paying Smith $10,000 "for rights to the attraction," toured this and a second troupe throughout the country in 1866–1867.[96] The actual nationality of nineteenth-century "Japanese" performers in the United States is not always clear. An 11 March 1897 program of a performance at Williams College indicates that one Soto Sunetaro (the Brooklyn-born Wellington King Tobias), a "Japanese Wonder Worker," performed "novel paper tricks," "curious Hindoo feats," and "Japanese Conjuring" in alternation with a "musical humorist" who performed in the "negro dialect." The student newspaper described Sunetaro as "an intelligent and handsome Japanese, having perfect mastery of the English language and possessing the art of magic in no small degree."[97] Sunetaro was one of several prominent American magicians in the late nineteenth century to perform in Japanese guise. For example, a female magician named Adelaide Hermann performed in Japanese costume and with an elaborate set in a successful act titled "A Night in Japan."[98] Similarly, an 1867 advertisement announced a Japanese performance in Worcester, Massachusetts, featuring Eye-EE-Nos-Kee as a conjurer and Sing-Kee-Chee as an "Eccentric Character of Japan," who promised to demonstrate "their delight in music and dancing in their old age." The performance was billed as "being an Entire Japanese Performance, the Stage will be conducted in precisely the same manner as in Japan."[99]

By far the most famous and influential actual Japanese performer in the West at the turn of the century was Sadayakko, who toured Europe and the United States with her husband's Kawakami Theater Troupe and then with her own productions.[100] Sadayakko's fame was such that even Puccini traveled to attend one of her performances as he worked on *Madama Butterfly*.[101] J. Scott Miller states that Sadayakko and Kawakami were "aggressive and shrewd promoters who took every available opportunity to satisfy their audiences' demands for a vision of Japan that conformed to orientalist expectations."[102] Furthermore, according to Ingrid Fritsch, "sounds that were strange if not disturbing to the Western ear were reduced or omitted, prompting an English reporter to remark, 'Finally, the coincidental music, which strikes so oddly on European ears, was kept within wise limits.'" In addition, "traditional Japanese music was not allowed as an interlude during scene changes. During the scene changes in London, for example, the orchestra played a potpourri of melodies from the operettas *The Mikado* (Arthur Sullivan, 1885) and *The Geisha* (Sidney Jones, 1896)."[103] Sadayakko performed throughout the United States in 1899–1900. For example, her troupe performed two plays in Boston "accompanied by weird and monotonous instrumental music and strident chanting or singing."[104] Repeatedly, Sadayakko's accommodations to Western styles of acting and drama met with great success, but elements of Japanese music in her productions were criticized and subsequently removed.

The next most likely sites for cross-cultural musical encounters in the United States were the series of late nineteenth-century world's fairs, starting with the 1876 Philadelphian Centennial Exhibition.[105] The extensive Japanese displays at the Centennial have been widely credited with igniting American *japonisme*. Interest in Japan was so intense that crowds turned out to observe the Japanese carpenters constructing the Japanese buildings and fences had to be erected to keep these pre-Exhibition spectators at bay.[106] Frank Lloyd Wright credited his trip to the Centennial Exhibition as the start of his lifelong interest in Japan and the stimulus for the influence of Japanese art and architecture on his work. Where was music in this stunning presentation and enthusiastic reception of Japanese culture? My research has uncovered no evidence of Japanese musicians performing at the Centennial Exhibition. In fact, the Bostonian music educator Luther Whiting Mason remarked on the complete absence of Japanese music.[107] Perhaps the Japanese government, so eager to showcase nearly every aspect of both its traditional culture and its modernization, feared that Japanese music would not be well received in the States. Japanese music did make an appearance of sorts. An orchestra under the direction of Theodore Thomas performed the "National Airs of all Nations" at the Opening Exercises on 10 May 1876. This piece appears to have been C. F. Blandner's "Grand International Medley, Containing the National Airs of all the Principal Nations of the World" which included an arrangement of a Japanese *gunka* (military song) in 2/4 with an Alberti bass slapped on.[108]

At the 1893 World's Columbian Exposition in Chicago, the government of Japan again created multiple buildings and large displays that included Japanese instruments and information on musical education in Japan. However, despite the fact that many "exotic" nations on the Midway presented musical performances, I have found no evidence of Japanese music being officially performed at the fair.[109] Instead, several commentators reported on the work songs sung by the Japanese carpenters as they created the Japanese pavilions: "the happy group of imported workmen are putting their materials together on the island, making hardly a sound with their work—for there are but few nails in this building—but making the park resound with their happy songs . . . wild songs something like those of our sailors."[110] The Japanese Village at the 1894 California Midwinter International Exposition included a "Royal Japanese Theatre." Rather than presenting *noh* or *kabuki*, a Japanese troupe performed balancing acts in this space.[111] A Japanese theater was also built in the amusement area at the 1904 Louisiana Purchase Exposition in St. Louis and apparently the *kabuki* play *Tsuchigumo* was performed in an English translation, but I have found no discussion of the music employed at this performance.[112] Instead, songs such as the 1905 "Cho-Cho-San: A 'Pike' Memory" (words C. L. Boye and music W. H. Hynson) celebrated Japan's presence at the fair and, in this case, capitalized on Puccini's opera. The sheet music cover featured a Japanese woman's face peeking from behind a parasol, and the lyrics referred to her "feet so teenie wee" and "accent most beguiling." An ad for this song placed by its St. Louis publisher appeared in *The Billboard* and stated: "The eyes of the world are upon Japan, and we have the song the people wish to hear. It is timely, original, characteristic and a distinct novelty." Typical of Japan's musical presence at these fairs is the following description of the 1915 Panama-Pacific International Exposition in San Francisco. This reporter relates his experiences of the Japanese pavilions and tells of being served tea by "a pretty little geisha" while

> The band—John Philip Sousa's, probably—strikes up airs from "The Mikado" in the musical concourse over by the Inside Inn. "Three Little Maids From School," it plays. You hum the airs, and look about you. . . . It is a concession—a colossal affair, with the biggest Buddha ever seen outside of Japan standing guard. . . . A band is playing American ragtime inside. And before you there stretches a long vista of Japanese buildings.[113]

Apparently at nearly every opportunity in nineteenth-century America, Japanese music was displaced by Euro-American musical representations of Japan.

One white American attendee at the 1893 Columbian Exposition was inspired by the exotic music he encountered on the Midway to pursue a career as a comparative musicologist. Albert Gale (1870–1952) was born in Michigan, had graduated from the University of Michigan, Ann Arbor, and had set out as a pharmacist. He then studied at the Chicago Conservatory in 1895, taught music at Albion College in Michigan, and later helped launch the music department at the University of Washington in Seattle in 1903.[114] His research and collections focused primarily on Native American music but included Chinese and Japanese music as well. Gale styled himself "the Ethnologist of Music" and claimed to be the only person scientifically studying the racial relationships between "primitive peoples" as expressed in music.[115] Writing on Chinese music, Gale noted that "to most people of the Occident the music of the Orient makes little or no appeal except from the standpoint of novelty. . . . this confusion of sounds, at first meaningless, begins after several hearings to reveal beneath its rough exterior many gems of exceeding worth and beauty."[116]

Gale and his wife, the vocalist and choral director Martha Brockway Gale, gave numerous lecture recitals across the country through the Chautauqua and Lyceum lecture circuits for two decades starting around 1906, including ones entitled "Music and Myth of Old Japan" and "Tone Pictures of Chinatown."[117] Gale had never traveled to Japan but instead encountered Japanese immigrant musicians in Seattle where he "took lessons on Japanese and Chinese instruments which made it easier to appreciate the native music."[118] Publicity brochures promised that their productions would include: "Elaborate Stage Setting of Handsome Japanese Draperies . . . Priceless Musical Instruments from the Buddhist and Shinto Temples . . . A Glimpse of the Queer and Quaint Customs of the 'Little Brown People,'" all of which would take "You Away From the Commonplace and Transports You to a Wonderland of Fancy—A Land of Myths and Mystics."[119] (See Figure 1.2). Their programs featured "[t]inkling myth-music" at the start followed by Mrs. Gale singing "Kimigayo" in "true Japanese fashion." Gale lectured on how Japanese music expressed the Japanese character and demonstrated on the *shakuhachi, hichiriki, koto, shamisen*, drums, and other instruments. He played "Banzai March" on the violin with piano accompaniment to demonstrate "the possibilities of the Japanese music through its development into art forms." He also performed a Japanese piece on the *shakuhachi*, in costume, and then a "developed" and harmonized version on the violin with piano accompaniment. Gale explained that "[p]iano accompaniments were added so that an audience could judge the music by the standards with which all of us have so long been familiar. Melodies need harmonic support to be generally appreciated."[120] Mrs. Gale sang and played the *koto* and Mr. Gale played "Sakura" on the *fue* (flute) with piano accompaniment. In the second half of their production this white couple presented a dramatic scene "in Japanese" illustrating the domestic life of a Japanese couple, emphasizing the duty of the Japanese wife to "think of her husband's comfort" and to "obey his every command." Thus, scholarship and gendered Orientalist representation were closely aligned in these early public introductions to Japanese music.

*　*　*

In the 1904 novel *My Japanese Prince*, two white American women in Japan decide to disguise themselves as geishas. To complete their transformation, one of them grabs a *shamisen* and hands the other a *koto*. When our heroine protests that she is unable to play the *koto*, her friend replies, "'Well, of course, you can't play it, but you can play at it! Accompany me, strike these chords, see! You know enough about general music to understand.' I have had a few lessons on this curious instrument and can do as she directs." The friend then pretends to sing a Japanese song "in the sweet plaintive manner that is common to the country and emphasizing the accompaniment on her *samisen* with some of those curious glissandos peculiar to native music."[121] This conceit of white women dressing up Japanese and transforming themselves through music—frequently in an attempt to compete with Japanese women for the admiration of white American men—is one that will reappear in American representations of Japan throughout the twentieth century and into the twenty-first. This period also witnessed an increasing American tendency to "dress up" Japanese music itself in Western features. For example, the artist Helen Hyde lived in Japan in 1899–1910 and again in 1912–1914 and published a collection of

Figure 1.2 Albert Gale's program for "Music and Myth of Old Japan." Courtesy of Redpath Chautauqua Collection, University of Iowa Libraries, Iowa City, Iowa.

Japanese children's songs with harmonizations by her sister Mable Hyde. Helen Hyde's illustrations in this oddly titled collection (*Japanese Jingles: As Set Forth by the Chinks*) featured a red-haired girl, clearly intended to represent the protagonist of many of the poems who is so often bemused by Japanese customs. In one image, the girl plays a drum and is followed by some Japanese women and in another she leads Japanese gods in song as she strums a *shamisen*.[122]

Actual Americans were also encouraged to immerse themselves in *japonisme* at special festivals and balls. As early as the 1890s, the white citizens of Salem, Massachusetts, held Japanese-themed fairs, including a *matsuri* in 1901.[123] Such opportunities to masquerade as Japanese were more commonly held as benefit events sponsored by wealthy individuals or by cultural institutions. For example, the Art Students League of the Art Institute of Chicago held a "Japanese Pageant" in 1911 for its annual Mardi Gras Festival fundraiser. A variety of musical performances were included at this two-day event attended by some 1,500 people, "most of them in Japanese costumes."[124] *The Daimio's Head: A Masque of Old Japan* by Thomas Wood Stevens and Kenneth Sawyer Goodman, with musical setting ("appropriate to the rest of the production")[125] by Harold E. Hammond, was created specifically for this event. Mrs. Michitaro Ongawa (Clara Page, the white wife of a Japanese acrobat who had settled in Chicago) performed a sacred Japanese dance at the end of the second performance and a Shinto ceremony by other dancers and "priests" was enacted. (Like the Gales, the Ongawas also offered Japanese performing arts costumed presentations on the Chautauqua circuit in the first decades of the twentieth century.) A *Chicago Tribune* article announcing the festival noted that it would feature a Japanese wedding: "It will be carried out with all possible solemnity and with the traditional ceremonies of the far east, but it is expected that the odd rites, costumes, and ornamentations will convulse the onlookers."[126]

This extravagant display of *japonisme* in Chicago was not an isolated case. For example, having spent five months in Japan in 1903 as the guest of Kakuzo Okakura, the famed soprano Emma Thursby helped to arrange a Japanese fête the following summer at Green Acre in Maine.[127] Japanese garden parties, frequently featuring musical performance, continued well into the twentieth century. As late as May 1920, Frank A. Vanderlip and his wife held such a party at their Scarborough estate, wearing Japanese clothes and featuring a play put on by Japanese students from Columbia University with selections from *Madama Butterfly* sung by Nobuko Hara, a *shakuhachi* concert, fencing, and a demonstration of judo.[128] The numerous didactic pieces published in the late nineteenth and early twentieth centuries offering white American children and women the chance to perform as Japanese in pageants and plays will be explored in the next chapter.

The most prominent Bostonian Japanophile to host such events at the turn of the century was Isabella Stewart Gardner. Gardner produced a "Japanese Festival Village" in 1905 for a charity benefit in the Music Room at her Boston mansion, Fenway Court. Inspired by Morse, she had traveled to Japan in 1883 and, with the guidance of William Sturgis Bigelow, had heard the music of *kabuki*, geishas, *matsuri*, and more.[129] On her domestic version of a Japanese Festival, Gardner wrote: "Such a thing was almost the very first sight I saw in Japan. They are delightful little things of the people, held at times of fête in some temple grounds, little shops on both sides; the temple, the Tea House and the merry little people."[130] The *Boston Globe* reported that at Gardner's festival one could experience "novel songs and dances by native Japanese."[131] By offering this Japanese charity event at her home, Gardner was attempting what so many nineteenth-century Japanophiles had likewise attempted: to bring exotic Japan closer to the American public.

Gardner famously served as a patron for European classical music in Boston and thus her general failure to comment in any detail in her correspondence and diaries on the music she heard in Japan is striking.[132] However, Gardner's explorations of Japanese culture continued long after her trip, primarily through her intense friendship with Kakuzo Okakura.[133] As author of *The Book of Tea* (1906) and consultant for Fenollosa on Japanese art, Okakura was the most influential ambassador for Japanese culture in the West in the early twentieth century and was a major force in art education in Japan. A letter from Okakura on 8 March 1905 from San Francisco indicates that he sent Gardner "assortments of things for the Fox-God festival," including lanterns and baskets to sell at her charity bazaar. Gardner eventually devoted a room in her museum home to works of Chinese and Japanese art. Okakura played the *koto*, but it is not clear whether he ever played for Gardner. In her turn, Gardner introduced Okakura to European music in her home and she took two young Japanese gentlemen placed under her care by Okakura to performances of such operas as *Carmen* and *Samson et Dalila*.[134]

Gardner's friendship with Okakura nearly resulted in what might have proved a major theatrical work of modernist *japonisme*. In 1912, Charles Martin Loeffler agreed to Gardner's request to set Okakura's poetic drama *The White Fox* as an opera. A 1913 script for this "Fairy Drama in Three Acts Written for Music" was dedicated by Okakura to "the Presence, Fenway Court"—Okakura's typical poetic address for Gardner. However, multiple letters from Okakura and Loeffler to Gardner reveal that the two artists were unable to agree on revisions to the libretto. A letter from Loeffler to Gardner on 25 January 1920 indicates that following Okakura's death, Loeffler proposed to revive his efforts on *The White Fox*. However, as with several other dramatic projects, Loeffler never completed the opera. Gardner's correspondence reveals that other composers proposed during this period to compose the opera themselves, but Gardner remained committed to Loeffler. Most intriguingly, Gardner's friend Henry Furst warned her during World War I that a Frenchman had translated the play and aimed to have an opera composed for Paris without her permission, but that the war intervened and scuttled that project. Furst urged Gardner to read the works of the modernist director Edward Gordon Craig and, in a letter of 10 December 1916, suggested that Gordon Craig should himself direct *The White Fox* in "an intimate representation, perhaps in your house, for you only and a few friends." Had Gardner agreed, *The White Fox* might well have served as an American answer to W. B. Yeats's *noh*-inspired "plays for dancers." As it was, American modernist works inspired by Japan and Japanese theatrical traditions would appear later.

"Hail Columbia!": Hearing America in *Japonisme* and in Japan

A member of Perry's Expedition described the 1854 landing in Japan as follows: "the squadron band struck up 'Hail Columbia' in a style, and with a force that made the Japanese open their ears (they may have to listen to it again), and the hills around sent each note of 'Hail Columbia' back again. 'Hail Columbia' never sounded better."[135] This particular musical statement of American force directed at the Japanese was somewhat ironic, given the rousing call of the lyrics: "Immortal patriots, rise once more,/Defend your rights, defend your shore!/Let no rude foe, with impious hand,/Invade the shrine where sacred lies/Of toil and blood, the well-earned prize." A mere quarter of a century later, General Grant's 1879 arrival in Japan was marked by a Japanese band playing "Hail Columbia."[136] A rather significant historical shift is delineated by these two prominent performances of this patriotic anthem. As an indisputably "American" musical specimen, "Hail Columbia!" never sounded better to this expeditionary American than when it trumpeted his 1854 forced entrance into the forbidden exotic land. Recalling the role of *mehter* music in the period of Ottoman imperial conquest, or the blaring broadcasts of heavy metal by US forces in twenty-first-century military operations, the tune apparently served to intimidate the Japanese. Just as the miniature locomotive and telegraph presented as gifts by the Perry Expedition were intended to display the superiority of Western culture and the potential benefits to the Japanese of opening up their country to trade, so too were the performances of Perry's military bands intended to impress the Japanese and to offer a clear alternative to their deficient music. And yet, the "American" status of these tunes was soon put into play after being adopted by the modernizing (i.e., Westernizing) exotic nation and then sent echoing back again. Had our 1854 informant been present also at the 1879 performance, would he have welcomed this particular acoustic boomerang?

From a twenty-first-century perspective, the initial American responses to Japanese music reveal a remarkably firm belief in the superiority of "our music" and an equally sure understanding of what "our music" consists of. Such conviction left little room to consider Japanese music from the perspective of Japanese aesthetics—making the cases of Edward Sylvester Morse and the Fenollosas all the more remarkable. Given that Japan in the popular imagination represented the cultural antipode, American listeners were predisposed to focus on musical difference and to question the status of Japanese music *qua* music. By describing their first impressions of Japanese music, American writers were unintentionally revealing their own musical values and how they heard their own music. In a sense, we can hear nineteenth-century musical America in American literary *japonisme*. In bashing Japanese music, Americans expressed pride in Western harmony and scales, the construction of modern musical instruments, and in the clearly defined melodic lines they heard in their music. By attacking Japanese vocal music they indirectly affirmed the "natural" singing techniques and "pleasant" timbres of *bel canto.* While complaining of immoderate expression in Japanese music and of the physical pain it inflicted upon them, these writers indicated their assumption that music's ultimate goal should be to relax the body and soothe the nerves through logical and moderate expression. (I will note in chapter 9 the nearly ubiquitous use today in the United States of the *shakuhachi* in music designed to relax the mind and to accompany massages.) The very features of Japanese music that inspired the greatest outrage—absence of tonal harmony, its timbral intensity, immoderate expression, melodic ambiguity—are those that would soon provoke listeners encountering Euro-American musical modernism.

Expressing disdain for Japanese music also enabled Americans to display confidence in American musical abilities vis-à-vis Europe. It was an American, the Bostonian Luther Whiting Mason, who was employed by the Japanese government to reform musical education along Western lines in 1880.[137] Mason had little sympathy for Japanese music and felt it impeded his work, complaining that "their ears are prevented by a wrong scale of music."[138] He assumed that his charge was to replace Japanese music with Western music, ignoring the suggestions of Shuji Isawa, the Japanese musical educator and bureaucrat assigned to work with him, that Japanese music should be retained alongside Western music in Japan. Isawa had spent three years in the United States and was central to musical Westernization efforts in Japan.[139] However, Mason displayed little interest in Isawa's desire to explore connections between Japanese and Euro-American music and to pursue musical hybridity.[140]

Mason carried out his musical missionary work for two years in Japan and proved astonishingly successful in his attempt to convert the Japanese. His work was celebrated at home in such periodicals as *Dwight's Journal of Music*: "hitherto the Japanese have known nothing of music, in our sense of the word. Their scale consists of only five tones, and their ears have actually to be attuned to the complete scale, which is the basis of all real music. He [Mason] has therefore almost to create the sense, as well as teach the music."[141] Mason was described as a conquering musical hero: "Verily, the tuneful missionary who has set out to make a musical people of the Japanese, exhibits a faith, a courage of conviction, like that which revealed a new world to Columbus! But we have no doubt his faith will be rewarded, since we believe that music is a principle divinely planted in the soul, and that it exists potentially, if not actually, in our common human nature everywhere."[142] Mason was determined to replace Japanese scales with the "true scale" and employed both the organ, his "grand assistant missionary," and science to prove his case. He asked an American physics professor in Tokyo to deliver a series of lectures on musical acoustics for his Japanese music students and this, he claimed, settled the subject concerning the "true scale."[143]

Mason was but the most prominent American musical missionary active in converting Japan to Western music. The former music and drama critic of the *Boston Courier*, Edward H. House, first arrived in Japan in 1870 and by 1901 had spent over twenty years there. House founded an ensemble that would become

Japan's first symphony orchestra and in 1900 was employed to teach Western music to the court musicians.[144] Like Mason, House was no fan of Japanese traditional music. Describing a Japanese vocal performance, House wrote in 1871: "The voice of the very gifted singer is heard warbling and vibrating in that strange involution of shake and trill which constitutes the highest form of Japanese vocalization. . . . We vow that we are enchanted—and are in the mood to enjoy anything—but we do not press her to a repetition."[145] He described the "tumult" and "acoustic anguish" he experienced in Japanese theater and stated that the Japanese actor is "needlessly hampered in a variety of ways. It is no excuse for anomalies like the perpetual jingle of orchestra and clamor of chorus, to say that others just as bad exist in other theatrical systems; and, so long as the Japanese actor has to contend against *samisen* and song-singers, he will always be at a disadvantage."[146] For such musical missionaries as House and Mason, the goal was not simply to transplant Western music in Japan but to weed out the exotic music that they encountered there.

In the 1880s, a significant number of musical performances in Japan presented European and Japanese music in direct juxtaposition. Perusing *The Japan Weekly Mail* from this period reveals that expatriate Americans sponsored numerous such performances. For example, a Professor Sauvlet directed a performance in June 1886 by the Yokohama Choral Society of Gilbert and Sullivan's *Pirates of Penzance* and then appeared in November at a benefit performance that featured music "by performers of note on the *Koto, Samisen, Kokiu*, and *Shakuhachi*; and European pieces under the direction of Professor Sauvlet, Instructor in the Institute of Music under the control of the Department of Education."[147] Clara Whitney had attended just such a cross-cultural musical display in 1879 at the Academy of Music at Ushigome. The performance started with *bugaku*, and was then followed by a Western style band "who made too much noise with the bass drum." Whitney found the *bugaku* dance "altogether irresistible to a poetical temperament. Of course the European music not being first class by any means was cast entirely in the shade, making me quite ashamed of its rattle, bang, slam, and general racket as if its merit consisted in its noisiness."[148] Most American attendees at such experimental musical demonstrations drew the opposite conclusions concerning the relative merits of Japanese and Western musics.

Some of these mixed concerts featured Japanese performers for both the Western and Japanese traditional selections. In 1888, a concert by the Nippon On-Gaku Kwai (the Musical Society of Japan) started with a Beethoven overture by the Imperial Marine Band directed by Franz Eckert, a Miss Koda played a Liszt piano solo, Eckert conducted the string band of the Shikibushoku in a work by Haydn, and the concert included Japanese music by one *shakuhachi* and two *shamisen* musicians. The reporter stated: "Although we are not competent to pass judgment upon the quality of Japanese music, a remarkable feature of its execution in this instance was that of the two samisen players who, both blind, played with perfect accord and in exact time throughout a long piece."[149] At the 1889 annual meeting of the Musical Society of Japan, the society's President Marquis Nabeshima stated that the purpose of the association was "to further the cause of music, whether Japanese or foreign." The report announced that a concert in March would feature both European and Japanese music, explaining that "what chiefly attracts notice is the practical comparison thus instituted between Japanese and European music. The two are placed upon the same stage and allowed to speak for themselves. Will both survive the ordeal, or will the one reduce the other to perpetual silence?"[150]

Despite celebrating Japanese participation in Western musical performances, many American commentators felt impelled to note a Japanese failure to reach Western musical standards. An 1889 report on the Commencement Exercises of the Tokyo Academy of Music stated that the singing had been good but that the Japanese lacked strength in singing Western music: "Why such should be the case we cannot tell, unless it be that the Japanese method of singing, as practised [sic] for the past ten or fifteen centuries, is unsuited to the development of vocal power. And indeed, from an Occidental point of view, there is no real singing in Japan. There is lilting, as when one hears a girl piping a lullaby, or a rustic quavering to his pack-horse, and there is intoning, as in the recitative of the joruri or the hayashi. But there is no genuine, open-lunged singing in Western style."[151] The ceremony included music performed by a koto trio. The director of the academy, Shuji Isawa, was reported to have "dwelt on the indisputable fact that the music of Japan today is virtually identical with the music of Greece two thousand years ago, from which the European music of the nineteenth century differs only in the extent to which it has progressed. In adopting the music of the West, therefore, Japan will not be taking anything new or foreign, but will be merely availing herself of the improvements others have grafted on a stock that is as much hers as theirs."[152]

The astonishing success of Mason, House, and others in encouraging the Japanese to adopt the music of the West was praised back at home and by Americans in Japan.[153] Edward Sylvester Morse, for example, repeatedly betrayed his astonishment at hearing "our music" being played by Japanese musicians. Remarking on a performance by the Japanese naval band, he wrote: "Had we not seen their faces we should have supposed them to be Occidentals." He was particularly impressed since by this point he had "heard nothing in Japan that we could regard as music from our standpoint, and so the performance of our music by Japanese was as startling to me as if a North American Indian should suddenly be able to produce an Inness or a Bierstadt."[154] Morse had been involved in a cross-cultural musical exchange himself. In return for a demonstration concert at the Educational Department of Japanese music, Morse, Fenollosa, Leland, and Mendenhall (four expatriate professors) formed a quartet and gave a concert for the Japanese teachers who were asked to record their impressions, which (unfortunately) I have been unable to locate.[155] Morse described Mason's work as being "little short of marvelous" (II., 209). In July 1882 he attended an exhibition by Mason's students and felt that "it was amazing to hear them sing in our way. Their voices lacked the vim and snap that are characteristic of our school-children, yet there was no doubt that the Japanese could be taught to sing in our way; whether it is desirable to engraft our musical methods on them is another question."[156] Mason had requested in a letter thanking him for attending the exhibition that Morse put in a good word for his musical missionary work.[157] Mason surely had not counted on the cultural relativism implied in Morse's final phrase. Other Americans wondered whether aspects of Western music might be grafted onto Japanese music to strengthen it. For example, Mabel Loomis Todd visited Doshisha University in 1896—an institution founded by Joseph Hardy Neesima, an 1870 graduate of Amherst College—and reported that the "girls sang for us some weird native melodies, remarkable harmonies being supplied by a foreign teacher at a small organ. Harmonizing Japanese airs is an almost untried musical field, offering many curious opportunities for original effects."[158] This particular musical field would be repeatedly tilled by numerous Japanese and American composers in the early twentieth century.

Some Americans would soon come to lament the Westernization of Japanese music and the passing of Old Japan. Encountering Japanese playing American music proved a particularly perplexing experience and Japanese forays into Euro-American musical styles and attempts at cross-cultural mixture have repeatedly been met with derision in the United States. In John Luther Long's 1895 novel *Miss Cherry-Blossom of Tokyo* the Japanese heroine complains that she studied music in the United States "a liddle. But they say I play like I speak. Ah, you know how that is! How crule that was,—to say I play like I speak!"[159] Later in the novel a young Japanese male's piano performance is described as exhibiting a "machine quality" (p. 84)—a criticism that Asian and Asian American performers of European classical music contend with to this day. Lafcadio Hearn offered an anecdote suggesting that the Japanese were just as incapable of understanding Western music as were Euro-Americans of understanding Japanese. He reported that at a restaurant specializing in Western food,

> Suddenly I observed on a table at the other end of the room something resembling a music-box, and covered with a piece of crochet-work! I went to it, and discovered the wreck of a herophone. There were plenty of perforated musical selections. . . . The herophone gurgled, moaned, roared for a moment, sobbed, roared again, and relapsed into silence. I tried a number of other selections . . . but the noises produced were in all cases about the same. . . . There was a queer melancholy in the experience, difficult to express. One must have lived in Japan to understand why the thing appeared so exiled, so pathetically out of place, so utterly misunderstood. Our harmonized Western music means simply so much noise to the average Japanese ear; and I felt quite sure that the internal condition of the herophone remained unknown to its Oriental proprietor.[160]

For American travelers of Hearn's ilk, hearing Western music in Japan could only spoil their reveries in this exotic land.

Throughout the Meiji Era, European music was introduced into the schools, traditional musicians were taught to perform on European instruments, and traditional instruments were retuned for the performance of European compositions. Thus, this initial encounter with Japan resulted in a campaign to silence Japanese music. We will find that periods of silence and retreat have been central to the history of American encounters with Japanese music. When not repelled by the perceived stridency, the "strummings and squealings," and the stasis of Japanese traditional music, Westerners have repeatedly proved unable to hear this music at all—often willfully ignoring the sounds before them in their general celebrations of Japanese performing arts. Of course, silence is fundamental to Japanese music itself, based, as it is, on the aesthetic principle of *ma*—on discovering beauty in emptiness, beauty in the most subtle of sounds. Rather than remain silent, we will find that many American musicians followed up on the initial encounters described here by creating their own representations of Japanese music. Indeed, most Americans have encountered Japanese music only through composed representations manufactured by other Americans.

2

Strains of *Japonisme* in Tin Pan Alley,
on Broadway, and in the Parlor

The period from 1890 to 1930 was particularly volatile in the history of US-Japan relations. American public opinion veered dramatically from ardent support for the "Yankees of the Far East" to serious fears of a coming war with the Asian upstarts. Throughout the Russo-Japanese War of 1904–1905 the United States was openly sympathetic to the Japanese cause. Upon hearing of Japan's stunning victory over the Russian navy, President Theodore Roosevelt admitted: "I grew so excited that I myself became almost like a Japanese."[1] However, these warm feelings were not to last. Japan quickly developed into an economic rival in the Pacific and a steady increase in Japanese immigration to California fueled racist exclusion movements on the West Coast. Reports of Japanese military aggression in China were not well received. Although Japan and the United States were allied during World War I, tensions between the two nations increased sharply by the war's end, particularly as a result of "Yellow Peril" fears stoked by the American press. Anti-Japanese sentiment led eventually to the 1924 Exclusion Act which barred Japanese immigration to the United States and further strained relations.[2]

This mercurial political context determined—and was shaped by—representations of Japan and the Japanese in American popular culture. Initially, as we have seen, *japonisme* had been primarily an elitist cultural endeavor in the United States. Collecting woodblock prints and other objets d'art, dressing up in kimonos for Japanese-style garden parties, and traveling to Japan itself offered some Gilded Age white Americans a means for signaling an elite status, just as the consumption of sushi and indulgence in Japanese-themed day spas would in the late twentieth and early twenty-first centuries. At the opening of the twentieth century, however, *japonisme* gradually became more democratized and commercialized. A middle- and lower-class interest in consuming Japan, evidenced first in the late nineteenth century by attendance at Japanese pavilions at world's fairs and at performances across the nation by Japanese jugglers and acrobatic troupes, became increasingly apparent in the early twentieth century. "Japanese things"—whatever the actual provenance of their manufacture—were highly visible in the United States. Audible representations of Japan followed as songs and piano pieces proved a major avenue for the popularization of *japonisme*.

The earliest significant American musical responses to Japan were composed in this period, with musical *japonisme* particularly evident in Tin Pan Alley and on Broadway. I have discovered some 375 pieces with Japanese subjects—including parlor songs, show tunes, and piano dances and novelty pieces—that were published between 1890 and 1930 in the United States.[3] (For detailed publication information on these pieces, see Appendix 1.) Prior to 1911, just over 30 percent of these pieces were composed for solo piano. Of the pieces in this collection published after 1911, approximately 85 percent are songs. These include a few of the most successful numbers ever published in the United States such as "The Japanese Sandman" and "Poor Butterfly" as well as more minor works by such major composers as John Philip Sousa (the 1900 "Sen-Sen March"), Rudolf Friml (the ballet *O Mitake San* of 1911 and the 1924 song "Dream Maker of Japan"), Irving Berlin ("Hurry Back to My Bamboo Shack" of 1916 and "Tokio Blues" of 1924), George Gershwin (the 1920 "Yan-kee" and the 1921 "In the Heart of a Geisha"), and Sigmund Romberg ("Lotus Flower" of 1923 and the 1927 musical *Yo-San/Cherry Blossoms*). Such songs were created at the intersection between Tin Pan Alley's general devotion to stereotyped ethnic and racial representation and the phenomenon of American *japonisme*. These songs were often included in shows that otherwise had nothing to do with Japan. Musical representations of Japan were performed in all of the popular genres of the day, including operetta, vaudeville, burlesque, musical theater, parlor song, novelty piano piece, and characteristic dances. Pieces concerning East Asia and Asian Americans comprise, of course, but one subset of the entire output of American popular music during this period. And yet the numbers are significant and, in the case of Japan, they quite clearly indicate periods in which national interest was intensely focused on things Japanese. As revealed in Figure 2.1, nearly

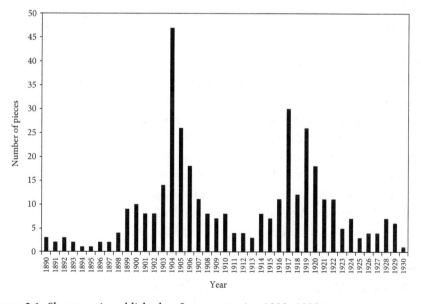

Figure 2.1 Sheet music published on Japanese topics, 1890–1930.

two-thirds of the pieces I have studied were published in less than one-third of the total years surveyed and were clustered in two specific subperiods: 1903 to 1907 and 1916 to 1922. By far the largest number of songs on Japanese topics appeared in 1904, followed by 1917 and then 1905 and 1919. Although the 1920s were particularly productive years for Tin Pan Alley generally, the number of songs decreases in this decade and in the 1930s barely a couple of Japanese-inspired songs appear to have been published each year. Before considering why this particular concentration of songs occurred, and why composers of American popular music were especially interested in Japan around 1904, I will offer more general observations on the representation of Japan and the Japanese in American popular song and musical theater during the long Tin Pan Alley era.[4]

My goal in this chapter is not only to identify the particular features that served as "Japanese" markers in the music, lyrics, cover art, and staging of these songs, but also to trace the development of American perceptions of Japan as reflected in and shaped by these works. The representation of African Americans and of specific European immigrant groups has received much scholarly attention. Comparatively less work has been undertaken on Tin Pan Alley's engagement with Asians and Asian Americans and the staging of "Asianness" in musicals and vaudeville.[5] By including discussion of such representations on the popular American stage in the late nineteenth and early twentieth centuries, I am able to explore the context in which many of these songs were first experienced. What did becoming "like a Japanese" entail for the performers of these songs? In surveying this collection of sheet music, I investigate the impact of specific works such as *The Mikado* and *Madama Butterfly* and of particular political events such as the Russo-Japanese War on American popular music and also explore the relationship between representations of the Japanese in popular song and representations of African Americans, Chinese and Chinese Americans, and Native Americans. Finally, composers of parlor and recital songs in this period frequently made gestures toward "exotic authenticity" that prefigure a century of cross-cultural appropriations, influence, and stylistic explorations in all forms of American music. These composers set the stage for American modernists who would define themselves in part in contradistinction to these earlier examples of musical *japonisme*. Many of these pieces accumulated significant mileage during this period as they were performed at home, heard in musicals and vaudeville shows, and eventually heard in recordings, radio broadcasts, and in films.[6] Repeated encounters with specific songs, the repetition of stereotypical representational techniques throughout the period, and the repetition inherent in the typical musical forms employed in these pieces, helped to reinscribe specific images of Japan in the American imagination. As Robert Lancefield has aptly put it: "Professionals and amateurs alike could sing that raciologically imagined essence into and out from their own bodies, learning to know it as both a means of temporary amusement and a key part of longer-lasting structures of belief. Those musically supported beliefs concerned, among other matters, the relationship widely imagined between orientality, whiteness, and Americanness."[7]

"On Many a Screen and Fan": Popularizing
Japonisme Musically

Americans were first invited to participate musically in *japonisme* through dance. Prior to 1890, Japan and Japanese-related terms and imagery appear in the titles and covers of a few pieces that are otherwise entirely standard dances, presumably to be danced with the normal steps. The 1872 "Japanese Galop," 1875 "Japan Waltz," and 1883 "Ichi-ban: Waltzes," for instance, betray no stylistic abnormalities that might be heard as responding to the exoticism indicated in their titles. Most striking to me is the doubly ethnic terpsichorean indications suggested in such titles as the 1898 "Japanese Picnic: Schottische"—Bohemia meeting East Asia over lunch. How did these titles function for performers and dancing participants? Was the appearance of the label "Japan/Japanese" equivalent to dedications that imply no stylistic reference to the piece itself, or did these titles suggest Japanese qualities that would be encountered beyond the cover? The title of the very earliest piece I have located, the 1815 "Japanese Air," raises the question of whether consumers were to assume that the piece was somehow "Japanese," or—given the lack of cover art and of any other exotic indications—whether the attribution was made more casually as a promise of novelty. Regardless of representational intent and reception, the mere appearance of "Japan" in the titles of such works attests to the widespread interest in the exotic nation and the presupposed possibilities for capitalizing on this craze.

When Japan and the Japanese are featured as subjects in the lyrics of songs published around 1900 the tone is often comical and involves Japanese couples, dolls, or mothers singing lullabies. In many cases, the titles and lyrics of songs from this period reflect the contemporary desire to collect Japanese bric-a-brac, particularly dolls, fans, screens, and lanterns. Given the current ubiquity of products manufactured in East Asia in American commerce, it is perhaps difficult to appreciate the novelty of encountering objects from Asia a century and more ago. The famous 1877 "Chopsticks" (originally entitled "The Celebrated Chop Waltz" by its British composer Euphemia Allen) acquired its association with the exotic East Asian dining implement only after its widespread success. In one c. 1900 publication of the piece by De Luxe Music Co. in New York, the *ukiyo-e*-inspired cover design features two geishas, with one holding a *shamisen*. In this case, a piece was co-opted for musical *japonisme* through its tangential association with a Japanese object, implying an imagined transition in performance practice from chopping the piano keys with the sides of the hands, to playing with the index fingers as though they were chopsticks, to plucking the *shamisen*.[8] A few pre-1900 examples, discussed below, offer satirical perspectives on *japonisme* and the exotic imagination itself. Japanese dolls were particularly popular collector's items in the late nineteenth and early twentieth centuries and they inspired multiple pieces.[9] In several of these a Japanese doll is involved in an ill-fated romance. For example, in the 1894 "Two Little Japanese Dolls: An Oriental Romance" the male Japanese doll commits suicide after his beloved is purchased. The sheet music cover depicts within four bamboo frames the stages of this romantic tale of kimono-clad dolls. In "The Jap Doll" of 1898 the protagonist relates that she is a homesick "slant eyed doll from Japan so far away." As though prescient of the mid-twentieth-century desirability—from a white American heterosexual male perspective—of obtaining a Japanese wife, the white female creators of this song presented a Japanese female doll who attracted no buyers in the United States. Such works contributed to the stereotypical impression that the Japanese themselves were a doll-like people.

Some early pieces of American musical *japonisme* were inspired by specific political events. For instance, Perry's efforts to "open" Japan called forth "The Japan Expedition Polka" in 1853 from a publisher in Baltimore. Presumably the composer and those who performed the piece in their parlors considered a polka suitable for celebrating America's new intercourse with Japan. In 1860 Japan sent its first diplomatic mission to the United States to ratify the Treaty of Friendship, Commerce, and Navigation that stemmed from Perry's successful expedition. The comic potential of this historic cross-cultural encounter immediately inspired several works. Joseph Jefferson, one of the foremost American comic actors of the nineteenth century, starred in *Our Japanese Embassy* in June and then again in *Tycoon; or Young America in Japan*, a burlesque that ran in June and July with music by Thomas Baker.[10] (The term "tycoon" was derived from a Japanese word employed during the negotiations following Perry's expedition and was commonly used to refer to the political ruler of Japan in the US press in the 1860s.) In a June 1860 review lamenting the general state of burlesque productions, Quelqu'un (William Winter) made reference to both of these productions and also poked fun at Bostonians who felt slighted that the Japanese would not be visiting their city. He proclaimed that a burlesque may well travesty "any particular event of the day such as the Reception of the Japanese" but that it should "grow naturally out of the subject," which he felt *Our Japanese Embassy* failed to do. He predicted that *Tycoon; or Young America in Japan* would prove a hit and, indeed, in a positive review in July proclaimed it a hilarious production, even though it had nothing to do with Japan.[11] We will find that throughout the history of the fraught US-Japan relationship specific events have called forth an outpouring of musical responses, both comic and tragic in tone.

The American press exhibited a keen interest in observing the activities of the 1860 Japanese diplomatic delegation in detail. For example, the *New York Times* reported on the visit by the Japanese to a performance at the Academy of Music and on their reactions to hearing an American musical representation of Japan:

> Oddly enough, they did not seem to be melted to tears by the "Japanese March." Either they are less sensible to nostalgia than the Swiss, or the "Japanese March" is not good Japanese. The American audience, unluckily, seemed to suppose it was and accordingly maintained a respectful silence, so that, between the guests and the hosts, the "March" became rather a Dead March, although somebody came to the wings and encored it very angrily and yet very deliberately.[12]

A more successful musical response to the visit of the Japanese delegation was the 1860 "Tommy Polka."[13] This topical piano piece celebrated and was dedicated to one specific personage involved in the burgeoning US-Japan relationship: Tateish Onogero, a seventeen-year-old accompanying the 1860 Japanese diplomatic mission and known in the American press as "Japanese Tommy." The sheet music cover features a portrait of him, in samurai dress with swords, sitting on a chair at a table on which rests a helmet. (See Figure 2.2.) The following text appears above the music: "Wives and maids by scores are flocking/Round that charming, little man,/ Known as Tommy, witty Tommy,/Yellow Tommy, from Japan." This is a surprising

Figure 2.2 "Tommy Polka," sheet music cover (Lee and Walker, 1860).

and rare suggestion in the history of American Orientalism of a white American female attraction to an Asian man.[14] Indeed, contemporary press reports indicate that he enjoyed a celebrity status among young white female citizens of New York.[15] (In his review quoted above, Quelqu'un suggested that Bostonians should actually rejoice at the absence of Boston on the Japanese diplomatic itinerary, for "the Boston-girls have not been exposed to the seductive machinations of Tommy.") Tommy's popularity was such that an African American minstrel performer took on the stage name "Japanese Tommy" and was quite successful.[16] This multilayered racial representation was not unique. Also capitalizing on the intense public interest in the Japanese delegation, the famed minstrel George Christy produced "The Japanese Treaty" in June 1860 and claimed in advertisements that some members of the delegation would attend matinee performances.[17] Robert C. Toll has stated that "minstrelsy's most exotic foreigners were the Asians" and has noted that white minstrel troupes—styling themselves "The Flying Black Japs"—also picked up on the sensation of touring Japanese acrobats between 1865 and 1867. Toll argues that "although on the surface they just sang songs and told jokes about peculiar people, minstrels actually provided their audiences with one of the only bases that many of them had for understanding America's increasing ethnic diversity."[18]

At the turn of the century, Americans were offered numerous opportunities to dress up Japanese and participate in the musical performance of *japonisme* themselves, thereby learning about the exotic other through acts of participant representation or, as in Robert Lancefield's formulation, by indulging in the "educational pleasures of racial mimesis."[19] Mari Yoshihara has noted that many of these opportunities were intended specifically for, and were in many cases created by, white American women.[20] I have identified a set of musical works intended for children and women that, in effect, functioned as forms of didactic *japonisme*. In "drills" and "action songs" such as the 1891 "Japanese Parasol," the 1904 "Little Maids of Japan," and the 1906 "The Japanese Fan," children were instructed to dress, walk, and dance in "Japanese style," while singing or moving to music exhibiting strong Orientalist stereotypes. Operettas "for ladies" or children, such as the 1899 *The Japanese Girl*, the 1904 *A Garden of Japan*, and the 1928 *O Cho San: or, the Stolen Jade*, also proved popular.

Such works allowed the exotic masquerading featured at elite benefit events sponsored by the likes of Isabella Stewart Gardner to be engaged in by a much broader public. "Ladies" performing in *The Japanese Girl* would have sung the anthem "Kimigayo" in addition to marching away "to the sound of the koto and the drum," singing a chant of lamentation on "Sayonara," and re-enacting a Japanese "coming-of-age" ceremony. This work didactically incorporated multiple Japanese words in the lyrics with translations provided in the score. In a performance of *O Cho San*—a work set at a Japanese street fair—young performers would have welcomed their parents in the audience to the land of "japanee" as they sported "Japanese" costumes and reaffirmed their parents' conceptions of these exotic, childlike, superstitious people. (For some of the parents in the audience, the operetta's title might have called to mind Cio-Cio-San of *Madama Butterfly*.) This work included a diegetic song (a song sung within the world of the story), "Fuki No Kame," that featured a particularly static melody and that required the vocalists to "all draw in breath with hissing sound." Both of these operettas relied on repeated open fifths and obsessive grace note gestures to signal the exotic. Women and children were also invited to enact *japonisme* in the numerous lullabies referencing Japan that were published in this period. Eugene Field, a major nineteenth-century author of children's poems, penned the most successful version of the "Japanese Lullaby," which appears to have been first set to music in 1890. Field's poem was then set by at least ten different composers, with one rendition published as late as 1925. Several of these settings circulated widely. I have located six more "Japanese" lullabies composed before 1925 and speculate that these, and even the famous 1920 hit "Japanese Sandman," may have been partly inspired by Field's poem. Through such songs, the American experience of musical representations of Japan can be said to have begun at the cradle.

Although my focus here is on works composed and published in the United States, numerous British songs and shows about Japan were performed in America during this period. Indeed, important features of American musical *japonisme* can be traced back to Great Britain. By far the most popular and influential of nineteenth-century Japanese-themed works was Gilbert and Sullivan's *The Mikado* of 1885. This operetta has been continuously performed throughout Europe and the United States since its premiere, with a couple thousand performances being staged in the second half of the twentieth century in the United States alone.[21] Indeed, the continued relevance of this British work to American popular culture was celebrated by the American performance artist Taylor Mac in the 2016, 24-hour extravaganza *A 24-Decade History of Popular Music*. Mac selected songs from *The Mikado* to represent the decade 1876–1886 in US history. Aiming to bypass Gilbert and Sullivan's Orientalist representations, and achieving an apotheosis of exoticism, Mac set this version of *The Mikado* on Mars, complete with glow-in-the-dark costumes and makeup, vocoder-manipulated voices, and an unforgettable rendition of "Three Little Maids" performed in a spaceship rising above the stage. In typical Orientalist fashion, Gilbert and Sullivan's original exotic Japanese setting served as a foil for a work of domestic parody aimed at contemporary British society. This is not to suggest, as some Gilbert and Sullivan commentators have claimed, that the work is not simultaneously also involved in proffering representations of the Japanese people. Throughout the operetta, the Japanese are portrayed as irrational, quaint, puppet people who take themselves far more seriously than they should. The actual Japanese were not thrilled by this representation and the British government banned the operetta for several weeks in 1907 to appease them. In a sarcastic, witty, and revealing response to the government's ban, Gilbert wrote:

It has recently been discovered that Japan is a great and glorious country whose people are brave beyond all measure, wise beyond all telling, amiable to excess, and extraordinarily considerate to each other and to strangers. This is the greatest discovery of the early years of the twentieth century. . . . The Japanese, however, attained their present condition of civilization very gradually, and at the date of my story they had peculiar tastes, ideas and fashions of their own, many of which they discarded when they found that they did not coincide with the ideas of the more enlightened countries of Europe. So if my readers are of opinion (as they very likely will be) that some of their customs, as they are re-vealed in this story, are curious, odd or ridiculous, they must bear in mind that the Japan of that time was very unlike the Japan of to-day. It is important to bear this in mind, because our Government being (in their heart of hearts) a little afraid of the Japanese, are extremely anxious not to irritate or offend them in any way lest they should come over here and give us just such a lesson as they gave the Russians a few years ago.[22]

Thus, in one fell witty swoop Gilbert suggests that he had been aiming his satire at the Japanese back in 1885, that his representations were accurate, and that the recent Westernization of Japan has cured the exotic nation of all its ills while also posing a significant new threat to the West.

In one of the earliest studies of exotic representation in opera to engage with Edward Said's concept of Orientalism, Michael Beckerman detailed the extent to which Sullivan's music had been shaped by the work's Japanese setting. In partic-ular, Beckerman traces the impact of the Japanese *gunka* "Miya sama" throughout the score.[23] The *gunka* genre consisted of Western-style march songs composed in quadruple meter with heavy accentuation, and often accompanied by prominent brass and drums. As Beckerman notes, the impact of "Miya sama" on the score occurs most prominently at the very opening in "We Are Gentlemen of Japan." As the curtain rises we find the Japanese noblemen frozen in poses "suggested by native drawings" as in Japanese art, but they are soon animated by the music. They openly profess their own exoticism: "Our attitude's queer and quaint; You're wrong if you think it ain't." Their vocal line is emphatic and pompous in its blunt rhythm and re-peated pitches, and yet their self-assertion is undercut by the odd juxtaposition of very short and very sustained notes, scurrying sixteenths in the accompaniment, and accentuated syncopated slurs in the vocal line that warp one-syllable English words into two syllables (e.g., "paint" is transformed into "pay-ain't"). Sullivan's set-ting for all winds and voices creates, perhaps, a more exotic sound than would have the typical instrumentation in Japan for these military pieces. On the other hand, Sullivan domesticated the tune somewhat, reworking it into three clear phrases of four bars each and emphasizing thirds in the melody instead of seconds. Sullivan extrapolated several features from the tune and employed them throughout the score, particularly the repeated note motif at the start which is heard in multiple pieces in *The Mikado*. Some of these stylistic features became clichés for Japanese representation in American music, as did the particular mispronunciations of English by Gilbert's gentlemen from Japan.

Gilbert and Sullivan's comic operetta was by far the most influential British model for American musical *japonisme* in this period, yet it was not the only such work. *The Geisha* by Sidney Jones also became an international hit following its 1896 premiere—indeed, it proved to be one of the most successful works in the history of British musical theater.[24] Specific character names from this operetta begin to appear in Tin Pan Alley songs around 1900 and the prevalence of the term "geisha" itself in American popular music may have initially stemmed from the success of this British work. *The Geisha* presents a twist on the standard Orientalist opera paradigm of the Western soldier and the exotic femme fatale. A British sailor in Japan becomes increasingly attracted to a Japanese geisha. After receiving warning of his roving eye, his British betrothed arrives on the scene and—prefiguring a gambit followed by American female characters in later Hollywood films (e.g., the 1962 *My Geisha*)—disguises herself as a geisha to win back his attentions. This work inspired a parody production from the famed comic duo Weber and Fields, with music by John Stromberg and book by Joseph Herbert, entitled *The Geezer* (1896) in which the two star performers dressed in Chinese fashion but maintained their stock German and Irish dialects, resulting in what Gavin Jones describes as a "multiethnic polyphony of individual sentences."[25]

The impact of *The Mikado* and *The Geisha* in American popular song and theater played out along a continuum. At one end, we might tentatively place examples that suggest a *Mikado* or *Geisha* influence based on the accumulation of stylistically similar details and shared subject matter. At the other end of the continuum we are able to place with confidence numerous songs and shows that made specific reference both in the lyrics and musical setting to *The Mikado* or *The Geisha* or both. Specific character names from *The Mikado* reappeared in numerous American popular songs. This is particularly true of the heroine Yum-Yum. For example, befitting her typically suggestive stage persona, in her performances of the 1899 song "In Japan" May Irwin declared/promised that in that exotic land, "half your life is pass'd away in yumy yumy yum." In the 1897 "Darling Little Yum-Yum" the "pitter patter girls from distant Asia" explicitly celebrate Yum-Yum and declare the primacy of *The Mikado* over *The Geisha*. The song proclaims that although in *The Geisha* they "toddled 'round and sung a lot of tum-tum," displaying the flirtatious nature of geisha, in truth "Mister Gilbert showed the way/To produce that kind of play." A similar multiple intertextual reference is evident in "Whoa San" from the 1903 *The Darling of the Gallery Gods*, a burlesque of Belasco's hit drama, coauthored with John Luther Long, *The Darling of the Gods*.[26] This song features a newlywed couple who fall into an argument when the wife—referred to as a "little yum-yum Jap"—asks to be taken to see *The Mikado* and the husband refuses. Another musical theater example from 1903, *Otoyo/Japan by Night*, set in the Tokyo of the present, exhibits clear *Mikado* influence in its plot, excepting that the male lead is now a white American.[27] Similar plot devices and musical stylistic features derived directly from *The Mikado* appear in both the 1904 *Fantana* and the 1905 *The Mayor of Tokio*, in which the lead male is again a white American. By this point spinoffs of

The Mikado had become so common that a *New York Times* reviewer of *The Mayor of Tokio* remarked: "The pink and white parasol of gay Japan never seems to lose its property of casting rose light over a couple of hours of dance, dialogue, and song."[28]

Throughout the late nineteenth and early twentieth centuries, and on the heels of *The Mikado* and *The Geisha*, a series of popular songs and stage works made direct comic reference to American *japonisme*. For example, in the 1886 "Mikado Mc. Allister" the Irish American protagonist complains of having to dress up Japanese at his wife's insistence. He laments that everyone is calling him the "red-headed, squinty-eyed mick from Japan!" and he quotes several snippets of text and tune from *The Mikado*. Thus, music plays a role in transforming this Mick into a Mikado. It is rather ironic that an operetta parodying the Japanese is claimed in such songs to have inspired an addictive desire to imitate the Japanese. These songs gain comic mileage by trading in what Gavin Jones has referred to as the fear of "dialect contagion" in late nineteenth-century America.[29] New immigrants were not only potential carriers of foreign disease and distressing customs, but of terrible tongues that grated on the ears and threatened to contaminate the sound of the nation's speech (i.e., "standard" American English). Dialect became a central feature in post–Civil War American literature, stage performance, and song and the full impact of the songs considered here clearly depended on the timbral effects of dialect exoticism in their performances. Jones convincingly claims that through the comic treatment of dialect, "threatening foreign tongues were transformed into gibberish."[30]

The influence of *The Mikado* and *The Geisha* on American musical *japonisme* was clearly extensive, but it should not be considered determinative. I noted above the several musical theater examples that were directly inspired by the 1860 Japanese diplomatic mission to the United States. One additional American work predating Gilbert and Sullivan's operetta is highly significant to this history. Although not first performed until 1886, a year after the premiere of *The Mikado*, Willard Spenser's "American-Japanese comic opera" *The Little Tycoon* was actually composed and published in 1882.[31] Perhaps inspired by the extensive Japanese displays at the 1876 Centennial Exposition in Philadelphia, it has been referred to as the first American comic opera and was performed some 500 times in Philadelphia before traveling to New York for another very successful run. The play is neither set in Japan nor does it include Japanese characters, but instead lampoons the British and those Americans similarly overly concerned with social status. A young white American male disguises himself as the Royal Highness Sham, Great Tycoon of Japan, in order to win approval to wed his sweetheart from her class-obsessed father General Knickerbocker. The father becomes increasingly overexcited as he learns of the imminent arrival of the fake Japanese tycoon and exclaims "everything Japanese all the rage. Never was there such a craze for everything that's Japan*ase*." He instructs his servants to dress up Japanese and to hang lanterns to honor their faux exotic visitor. In Japanese costume, the white American chorus also takes on Orientalist musical traits that prefigure several of the major sonic stereotypes for representing the Japanese found in later examples.[32] The suitor, in Japanese disguise, enters to the music of the "Tycoon March" and then, with friends also in Japanese disguise, sings a "Japanese" song with nonsense text. The father praises their music: "Bravo! Sublime! It has the true, classical, Wagnerian ring. [*sic*, pun] I shall have to go to a Japanese conservatory and finish." A nice bit of satire is lodged in this praise for a deliberately ridiculous American attempt at faking Japanese music. The father's delight at the prospect of his daughter marrying this Japanese aristocrat is comically framed as evidence of the excesses of American *japonisme*. Of course the possibility of miscegenation is presented only at a certain remove—not only is the actor playing the young suitor not Japanese, neither is the character being portrayed. In *The Little Tycoon* the sonic and visual signs of Japaneseness are held at arm's length.

"Sing a-high sing a-lee sing a-low": Sounding and Looking Japanese

By 1900, American composers, lyricists, and graphic artists had begun to develop a set of specific stereotypes for the representation of the Japanese in sheet music.[33] In a sense, these publications functioned as multimedia works, offering an experience akin to that of Hindustani *ragamala* paintings. Consumers of these pieces received an Orientalist representation of the Japanese through verbal, aural, and visual conduits simultaneously. Encountering a number of these songs in succession offered both a pleasurable aesthetic experience and served as a memory aid for Orientalist cultural understanding, for reinforcing the stereotypes. Given the exotic erotic subject matter of many of these songs, domestic performance in the parlor must have involved a certain frisson for white American heterosexual couples. In typical Orientalist fashion, implications of miscegenation in these songs would not have caused concern given that the romantic narratives were set in the exotic locale and almost never suggested a white female interaction with exotic males. In addition, the typical public performance of these songs within a white performer/audience context made clear that imagining oneself in an interracial romance or viewing staged presentations of such relationships could prove titillating in the absence of any actual miscegenation aspirations. The performance of such songs by Japanese, Asian American, and African American musicians put into play different racial representational dynamics, which will be considered below.

In addition to shaping the consumer's imaginative engagement with the music, the cover images and lyrics served to cue performers on how to dress and move in public performances of these songs. The cover illustrations drew upon and participated fully in American artistic *japonisme*, in terms of both their content and their design. The core set of icons consisted of: women in kimonos, fans, paper lanterns, bamboo, Mount Fuji, and cherry trees in bloom. As with many European and American *japonisme* paintings, the kimono-clad figures on these covers often appear more Caucasian than Asian in their features. Furthermore,

Tin Pan Alley's cleavage-revealing version of the kimono clearly deviates from the Japanese model. Numerous covers depict women holding Japanese instruments as though to suggest a connection between the music to be found inside and the music of Japan. Indeed, the frequency of such depictions likely created the impression in the United States that Japanese women spent most of their time making music. (Images of Japanese male musicians are comparatively rare on these covers.) Depictions of Japanese women with either a *shamisen* or *koto* had been common both in nineteenth-century European and American paintings and in postcards and other mass-produced images of Japan. In turn, depictions of Japanese women with instruments were also very common in Japanese export art and crafts and the *shamisen* was indeed central to the life and work of geishas.[34] Neither Japanese art nor Tin Pan Alley songs made clear, however, that most Japanese women were not geishas.

These sheet music covers functioned as a poor man's version of *ukiyo-e*, the Japanese wood block prints that had been prized objects in nineteenth-century French and early twentieth-century American *japonisme*. In numerous examples, representations of Japanese artworks are contained within the cover's frame, and a small number of examples imitate Japanese *ukiyo-e* prints quite closely. The distinction between the "real" and the represented occasionally becomes blurred as in the cover of the 1908 "Lotus San" (see Figure 2.3). The inserted photograph of the white female performer of this song is placed within a drawing of a standing bamboo frame as though the photographed image is itself a Japanese art object within this Japanese woman's room. (A similar arrangement is found on several other covers, as with the 1902 "The Maid from Tokio.") Occasionally, the overall layout of the covers was influenced by the shape and segmentation of Japanese painted screens and scrolls. In addition, the covers consistently exhibit a "Japanese" font, which appeared in two varieties. The first was created in imitation of Japanese brush strokes in its tapering from thick to thin in each segment of each letter (as in Figures 2.3 and 2.4). The second type employs stylized bits of bamboo which reference both the plant itself and the articulated quality of Japanese written characters. Occasionally text is printed vertically on the covers, in further imitation of Japanese script. The earliest example of these font styles that I have located in American sheet music is from 1888. This font received its most emphatic treatment in World War II anti-Japanese propaganda and continues to appear ubiquitously in commercial copy today. Indeed, much of the visual imagery and representational techniques employed on the covers of these early twentieth-century songs retains currency in American popular culture.

One particularly striking example illustrates the extent to which American women participated in the creation of musical *japonisme* and the role of cover art in framing these songs. Marie Hall-Brimacombe not only wrote the words and music for the 1918 "Little Sally-San (Of Old Japan)" and published the song through her Marion, Indiana–based company, but she also performed the song herself on tour in the Midwest and appeared on the cover in full Japanese costume, sporting a parasol

Figure 2.3 "Lotus San," sheet music cover (Jerome H. Remick, 1908).

and fan for good measure. Her name, along with the title, is printed in the typical brushstroke font, as though she and "Sally-San" are fully equivalent. (See Figure 2.4.) Hall-Brimacombe appeared again in this Japanese costume in her company's promotional brochure and on her Circuit Chautauqua programs.[35] In this song, an Irish captain journeys to Japan and instantly becomes captivated by Sally-San. He offers to do all of her domestic work—thereby suggesting that her beauty has completely unmanned him—and vows that if she fails to pick him from among her many suitors he will "steal this maiden from Japan." By wearing a faux kimono and (like Sally-San) placing blossoms in her hair, perhaps Hall-Brimacombe sought to compensate for the lack of Japanese musical signals in this piece.

Figure 2.4 "Little Sally-San (Of Old Japan)," sheet music cover (Marie Hall Brimacombe, 1918).

The lyrics of these songs often set the exotic scene in a fashion parallel to the covers.[36] We are frequently asked by a narrator to imagine ourselves in "far off old Japan" and to admire a "lovely little Jap," or "Japansy," or "Japaneesee"—the words "little" and "old" seem obligatory in these songs as does some distortion of the word "Japanese." (This conceit of an "Old Japan" runs nearly constant throughout this period, starting in 1892.) Several songs make direct reference to the erotic enticements of Japanese art objects, celebrating the materiality of *japonisme*. In "Laughing Little Almond Eyes," from the 1904 musical *Fantana*, an American male is aroused by a Japanese woman pictured on a fan and pledges that "if your tiny face of tan is like this one on the fan, Look no further I'm your man."[37] The 1901 "My Little Belle of Japan" relates a "Fan Tastic Episode" in which a geisha possessing "sweet almond eyes" and her beloved, along with some flowing pentatonic gestures, are tragicomically washed off their fan. Japanese women, repeatedly referred to as geisha, are by far the most common subjects of these songs. Unlike Tin Pan Alley's presentation of other foreign or minority women in this period, Japanese women are often praised for their beauty, although this praise tends to be qualified by such lines as: "I love her although her face is shady."[38]

The most striking aspect of the lyricists' role in these songs is the attempt to pen a form of Japlish, an imaginative and comic dialect that served to ridicule the song's Japanese subjects, just as parallel forms of dialect and pidgin English were deployed in representations of several other ethnic and racial groups in American popular song. This Japlish dialect drew upon nineteenth-century novels and short stories set in Japan by such authors as John Luther Long as well as the stereotypical dialect employed for African American representations. As was common in the Tin Pan Alley era, the verses are frequently delivered in a narrator's voice while the chorus section features an exotic ethnic voice speaking or singing a "sung song"—diegetic Japanese vocal and instrumental performance is implied in many of these songs. A good deal of the lyricists' creative energy was devoted to parodying the sound of spoken Japanese and the Japanese dialect in spoken English through the use of awkward grammar, mispronunciations, excessive rhyming, and nonsense words. Japanese terms and place names are occasionally strung together to similar effect. For instance, in *Fantana* a white valet in disguise as a Japanese minister emits the following nonsense, which is echoed by the chorus: "Nagasaki, Hi pagoda! Yokohama, Yi kimona! Semisen, riksha, satsuma, Hoi! Hoi! Hoi!" Political tension with Japan appears particularly to have inspired the use of inane rhymes and nonsense text. In "That Tango Tokio," a 1913 song that includes the line "tho' you sometimes make us mad," the chorus section reads as follows:

> Oh, oh, you Jap, little Jap, little Jap, little Japanese!
> Oh, oh, you cute little yap, little yap, little yapanese!
> How we love to see you prance, When they play that tango dance;
>   It just puts us in a trance
> Oh, pinky panky poo, pinky panky poo!

Presaging the racist lyrics of World War II propaganda songs, this song continues by referring to the "sly little . . . Japanese" and stating "You are a fly little . . . Japanese!" In the 1914 song "I Want to Go to Tokio," a "Japanee" male longs to return to his homeland and offers a translation of his cry as he sings it: "I sing a-high sing a-lee sing a-low, That means I want to go to Tokio." Exhibiting an even greater linguistic dysfunctionality, the male protagonist of "Poor Little Japanese Doll" from 1900 is said to be able to produce only "an ambiguous, discordant squawk squawk" every time he opens his mouth to speak. Ridicule of the Japanese language was occasionally enhanced in live and recorded performances of such songs. For instance, in a recording with Victor Roberts of the 1920 "So Long! Oo-Long" (Victor Records 18672-B)—a song that was recorded numerous times in the 1920s—the vocalist rattles off in a high-pitched voice a bit of spoken "Japanese" which he then translates as "Did you pay your income taxes?"[39]

In synch with the graphic and verbal attempts at Japanese representation, the composers and performers of these songs sought the most efficient means for signaling the exotic Japanese through sound. However, evidence of musical *japonisme* is less consistent in this period than are the visual and textual stereotypes. In fact, a good number of the songs appear devoid of any specific exotic musical *tinta* and instead rely on generic forms of contrast within the musical context.[40] In many cases, exotic musical signals appear only in the opening measures of the instrumental introduction—announcing, like the songs' titles, the representational target as clearly and quickly as possible before moving on and cadencing with the normal. The two most prominent musical signs for Japan are a conspicuous use of grace note ornamentation (viz., the acciaccatura) and variations of a particular rhythm—four sixteenth notes followed by two eighths, or four eighths followed by two quarter notes, most often with staccato articulation and involving some pitch repetition. The rhythm frequently appears in the introduction and in other cases is embedded conspicuously at certain spots in the song in response to a Japanese reference in the lyrics. This stereotypical rhythmic gesture is related to "Miya sama" but it also developed independently of *The Mikado* and can be traced back to examples from as early as the mid-nineteenth century. Between 1890 and 1930 seemingly every possible melodic variation of this basic rhythmic pattern appears in songs representing Japan. The gesture has appeared also in music composed in Japan itself. Edgar W. Pope locates the first occurrence of this rhythmic pattern and pentatonic melody in Japanese popular music in "Shanhai Kōshinkyoku" ("Shanghai March"), a 1931 Japanese song representing China. Pope refers to this as the "Shanghai March pattern" and notes its appearance in other Japanese pieces of intra-Asian exoticism.[41] By far the most common current musical stereotype for East Asia—heard in ringtones and in soundtracks for video games, films, television shows, and commercials—employs this rhythm, as well as pitch repetition and, frequently, parallel fourth harmonization. This contemporary "standard" version of the melodic cliché appears to have achieved its ubiquitous status only in the 1970s, following the 1974 number-one proto-disco hit "Kung Fu Fighting."[42] The motif also appeared particularly prominently and with parallel fourths in the 1980 hit song "Turning Japanese" by the Vapors. (See Example 2.1 for the contemporary standard form of this motif.) Searching for the origin of this trope proves a fool's errand.

Example 2.1 The standard musical sign for East Asia.

The earliest potential prototype I have discovered appears in the earliest piece of American music referencing Japan that I have located, the 1815 "Japanese Air." However, as with several of the later polkas and galops mentioned above, the appearance of a four-sixteenth, two-eighth-note rhythm devoid of any other exotic signals is surely merely coincidental. The representational significance of this rhythm as a Japanese marker was, however, established by 1903 and is prevalent thereafter. Example 2.2 offers a small selection of excerpts (primarily from pieces referencing Japan) providing some indication of the wide variety of applications of this gesture while focusing on those examples that most closely prefigure the post 1970s version. A few of these excerpts approximate the "standard" version of the motive quite closely. "My Little Japaneesee" (1903) includes stacked fourths and fifths and a downward gesture. "Jappy Johnny" (1907) presents the same melodic profile, includes fourths, but lacks the quadruple sixteenth-note repetition.[43] The 1920 "Yo San" lacks the parallel fourths and four repeated pitches, but might otherwise be cited as a direct model if not for the fact that the collection taken as a whole suggests a more evolutionary process, complete with randomly generated variants over the decades rather than a direct linear path of influence leading up to 1974. In numerous examples, the obsessive repetition of the rhythm suggests that it was conceived as an exotic signal, frequently appearing at the start as a head motif and in other cases shaping the vocal melodic line. Several pieces, such as the 1921 "In Old Japan," use the rhythm in a long sequential descent and others repeat the rhythm as an accompanimental tattoo. In the majority of examples, staccato eighths and sixteenths more generally comprise much of the rhythmic material, as though offering an imagined approximation of the plucked sounds emanating from the *shamisen* appearing on the covers.

Other musical devices were less frequently employed to enhance musical representations of the Japanese. Pentatonicism appears in these songs but is not nearly as omnipresent as one might expect. The topical use of the pentatonic scale is first encountered in this collection in late nineteenth-century art songs intended for recital performance. The earliest (most often, fleeting) appearances of pentatonicism in popular representations of the Japanese seem to first occur around 1900, becoming more prevalent in the mid-1910s and early 1920s. However, pentatonicism never emerges as the dominant exotic signal. Rather, in many cases the minor mode and a somewhat heightened chromaticism are more prevalent exotic markers within the musical context. In a rather unique example, Romberg established the exotic Japanese scene in his 1923 "Lotus Flower" by employing the whole-tone scale as the narrator calls upon us to listen to the voice of a *shamisen*-playing Japanese poet. Perfect fourth and fifth intervals are frequently emphasized in melodic lines as, for instance, in the Japanese protagonist's call for his lover in the 1914 "I Want to Go to Tokio" (see Example 2.3) and open fourths and fifths appear in the accompaniment as a repeated tattoo and then frequently move in parallel motion in songs from the 1910s and 1920s.[44] The 1902 "Ko Ko" features bold open fifths in the accompaniment and, in the third measure, prefigures a gesture also found in the final measures

Example 2.2 Variations of the standard musical sign for East Asia.

a. 1880, "Japanese Love Song," Cotsford Dick
b. 1881, "Japanese Tone Picture," Chas. J. Newman
c. 1888, "Lady Picking Mulberries," Edward Stillman Kelley
d. 1903, "My Little Japaneesee," Max Hoffman
e. 1904, "Yokohama Intermezzo," Ralph E. Kenny
f. 1905, "The Geisha Girl," Fred T. Ashton
g. 1907, "Jappy Johnny," Theodore Morse
h. 1910, "Chinatown, My Chinatown," Jean Schwartz
i. 1916, "When He Comes Back to Me," Dave Stamper
j. 1919, "Lantern Time in Tokio," F. Henri Klickmann
k. 1920, "Yo San," R. L. Harlow
l. 1929, "Japanese Toyland," Raymond Klages, Jesse Greer, and Harry Carroll

Example 2. Continued

g)

h) Allegro Moderato

i) Allegretto Scherzando.

j) Vamp k)

l) Moderato

Example 2.3 "I Want to Go to Tokio," Fred Fischer, 1914

grow - ing, Ho, Yo-san, Hear your man, Soon you're goin' to be___ Sit-ting on my Jap-a-(k)nee

I sing a-high sing a - lee sing a-low, That means I want to go___ to To-ki - o.___

of Puccini's *Madama Butterfly*. In addition, some of these songs employ the more typically "Middle Eastern" musical clichés such as the augmented second sonority. Awkward interval leaps and inordinate repetition of motives in the vocal melody often enhance the text's parody of the Japanese voice and dialect in these songs. For example, in the 1904 "My Little Kokomo" the vocal line of a male Japanese doll longing for a female doll residing on a higher shelf jumps an octave from high to low between all syllables of the line: "She high, Me low, Come down to me my Ko-ko-mo." Just as the actual textual content of the sheet music covers is Western while the font style vaguely suggests Japanese calligraphy, the music of these songs only remotely resembles any traditional Japanese musical style. Nevertheless, many of these songs seem to make a bid for ethnic musical "authenticity" in their use of such subtitles as "a song of old Japan" and "an odd Japanese lullaby" and a few claim to employ Japanese tunes and even to have been created by Japanese composers.

Certain typical narrative structures in these songs offered composers a clear opportunity for distinguishing the exotic. For example, the 1905 "My Lu Lu San" provides one such test case for detecting musical *japonisme*. (See Example 2.4a and 2.4b). The verses describing the "cute little maiden named Lu Lu San" (Example 2.4a), with a variation on the clichéd rhythmic gesture, contrast clearly in melodic style with the syncopated refrain of the Yankee sailor (Example 2.4b). Shifts between a neutral (i.e., white) narrator's voice and an exotic Japanese voice prompted comic timbral and enunciation changes by some performers of these songs resulting in a form of yellowvoice performance. A similar structural shift to the exotic realm is suggested in multiple songs in which a narrator takes us on a journey to "old Japan."

By far the most famous song to take Americans on an imaginative trip to Japan is Raymond Egan and Richard Whiting's 1920 hit "The Japanese Sandman." On the cover of the first printing of this song we see a Japanese woman leaning over her sleeping child on a tatami mat floor with Mt. Fuji visible outside a screen door. We seem to sink into the song in the introduction's descending chromatic line and are perhaps a bit drowsy as the narrator invites us to journey to Japan and "hide behind the cherry blossoms" in order to eavesdrop on the lullabies and sighs of this Japanese lady. The melodic line of the verses ascends and descends in waves—in the first verse these melodic waves carry us to Japan and then in the second, we float away quietly on them in order not to "wake the little people of old Japan." Clearly, we are positioned within the song as voyagers and voyeurs. In the chorus we hear the voice of the Japanese mother singing about the Sandman, and at the end of the second verse we hear the Sandman himself call "New days near for all" in a voice the narrator describes as "like an echo of the song" the mother sang in the chorus.

This mysterious and exotic figure seems rather double in nature. On the one hand, the Sandman offers something like a nocturnal laundry service, taking our worn-out day and "every sorrow" with him and leaving us with a fresh new day in exchange. We are left a "bit older" and a "bit bolder" and with new life. And yet this "old second hand man" sneaks up on children in their sleep and—as E. T.

Example 2.4a and 2.4b "My Lu Lu San," Bob Cole, 1905

A. Hoffman and Metallica demonstrated—might therefore be considered rather sinister. Would the promise of such a visit soothe a child? If not, Whiting's suave rocking minor thirds in the melody of the chorus very well might charm children as they have countless audiences of the numerous recordings and performances of this pop standard. The minor-third/augmented-second sonority as well as the modal flavor and chromatic alterations in the verses and in the concluding measures of the song suggest the typical musical stereotypes for the "Middle East," but the isolated measure of cascading fourths in the chorus might help point us further east. Japanese, or more generally East Asian, markers such as a gong stroke at the opening of the song could as well and were added in various arrangements and performances. Perhaps to compensate for the lack of specific "Japanese" musical signals in this famous tune, the 1928 Red Nichols and His Five Pennies recording of "The Japanese Sandman" prominently features an inserted bit of the "Miya sama" melody from *The Mikado*.

Ever since Nora Bayes popularized the piece in vaudeville and Paul Whiteman hit gold with his first Victor recording, "The Japanese Sandman" has had a presence in American popular culture. This song and the image of a Japanese Sandman have appeared in a wide variety of contexts since 1920. During World War II, Hirohito was portrayed as a duck singing "The Japanese Sandman" in the Warner Bros. cartoon *The Ducktators* (1942). In opposition to such anti-Japanese ridicule, the Nazi-sponsored propaganda swing band Charlie and His Orchestra released a version of the song in which the Sandman is described as "no second hand man" but as a serious threat and an Axis power deserving of respect. One Japanese American swing band active in Los Angeles in the 1930s went by the name "The Japanese Sandmen."[45] In an interesting twist on the Japanese Tommy phenomenon from a century prior, in 1957 the Cellos—an African American doowop group—recorded a song entitled "I Am the Japanese Sandman" in which the lead vocalist celebrates his prowess: "I am the Japanese Sandman/From across the sea/I got all the girls loving me." In two episodes from the 1968–1969 season of the animated TV cartoon series *The New Adventures of Superman* entitled "The Japanese Sandman," the American superhero fought against industrial sabotage and subdued the supernatural exotic Sandman in Yokohama—perhaps a Cold War allegory of the United States protecting Japan against its own subversives. Finally, the song itself was frequently employed in the HBO television series *Boardwalk Empire* in 2009–2010 to evoke the Prohibition period. These examples, and numerous others, reveal that the Japanese Sandman has been portrayed as either benevolent or malign depending on the current political relationship between the United States and Japan.

My detailed summary of the "Japanese" signs employed in these songs and in their performance is somewhat misleading, for Tin Pan Alley was not very particular in its representations of different East Asian peoples. The musical features I identified above as signals for "Japan" also appear in songs about China and the Chinese.[46] In fact, in anthologies of silent film music from the period one finds pieces entitled "Prelude to Chinese *or* Japanese drama" or simply the label "Chinese-Japanese." The 1921 song "My Cherry Blossom," which is set in "old Japan by the sea," includes a musical section headed "Chinese music box" that is intended to supplement the piano accompaniment of the chorus section as an optional four-handed duet. Blurred representation also occurred in a more graphic fashion. The visual signals on the 1922 cover of "Sing Song Man"—women in kimonos, Mount Fuji, the *shamisen*—suggest that this "sing song man" must be from Japan. (See Figure 2.5.) However, this song is set in "Far off China land" and is concerned with a Chinese musician. This transposition of visual stereotypes also occurred in staged

Figure 2.5 "Sing Song Man," sheet music cover (Jerome H. Remick, 1922). Courtesy of York University Libraries, Clara Thomas Archives & Special Collections, John Arpin fonds, JAC004859.

performances of these songs. A c. 1905 cover for Gustav Luders's "Little Japanese Baby" (originally published in 1900 as "A Japanese Baby Song") from the show *By the Sad Sea Waves* includes a photograph of two male performers, one dressed in a Chinese-style costume with a long *queue* and the other holding a *yueqin*, a moon-shaped Chinese lute. A similar confusion in ethnic representation frequently occurs in the lyrics. Songs such as the 1899 "In Japan" refer to characters with names such as "Foo Chang" and draw on stereotypical Chinese dialect style while the 1920 song

"Yo San" is set in China. Some songs concerned with China surprisingly refer to kimonos, geishas, and the "land of the rising sun" in their lyrics.

Of course, the Japanese and Chinese were not the only ethnic others blended together in Tin Pan Alley's melting pot. Remaining within the sphere of East Asian representations, *The Sho-gun* of 1904 was set in Kachoo "an imaginary and secluded island in the Sea of Japan between Japan and Corea." This popular work exhibits strong parallels to *The Mikado* and some clear Japanese references as when Moo-Zoo May refers to her *shamisen*. However, the staging also includes a Korean dance by "sing-song girls" with small drums and one program for an October 1905 production at the Metropolitan Opera House in Minneapolis suggests an attempt at achieving Korean authenticity.[47] On the other hand, the composer Gustav Luders—who also published several songs on Japanese subjects—stated in an interview that the music for *The Sho-gun* was 100 percent American since he had "never heard of a Corean school of music."[48] The Japanese, Chinese, and Koreans were, however, treated differentially in certain respects in this period. In her study of the representation of the Chinese in Tin Pan Alley songs, Judy Tsou implies that the Chinese were consistently represented negatively, whereas we have found numerous exoticized (and often eroticized) celebrations of Japan.[49] Determining the exact racial, cultural, and political position of the Japanese vis-à-vis other Asians and minority groups in the United States proved problematic throughout the Tin Pan Alley era.

"Your Tiny Face of Tan": Racial Positioning

When did the Japanese turn yellow in the white American racial imagination? In American popular song, the skin color of the Japanese remained in flux until World War II, when such phrases as "look out, you yellow Japs" stained the Japanese for good. The Japanese were commonly referred to as tan or brown skinned in the late nineteenth and early twentieth century, although the 1860 "Tommy Polka" celebrated "yellow Tommy, from Japan." References to the "brown" Japanese range from "The Little Brown Man of Japan" in 1904 to the "happy little brown-skinned man" in the 1928 song "Moon of Japan." In "My Belle of To-ki-o" (1904) an American male relates that in Japan "the cutest tanned-skin maidens wreathe and deck their raven hair" and we learn that he found his own "sun browned beauty" there. (In light of these lyrics, the placement of a studio photograph of a Japanese woman on the cover suggests that the song will function to lure other men to Japan, if only in their dreams.) An equivalent status for Japanese and African Americans is suggested in some early comic songs. Specific racist terms normally denoting black characters, such as "pickaniny" and "mammy," occasionally appear in songs describing the Japanese, and in the 1893 "The Sunny Side of Thompson Street"—a dangerous, but enticing street for white folks to visit—the Japanese are simply grouped with the "colored population."

Although their skin color would remain a shade of brown for another couple of decades in American popular song, by 1910 representational devices for the Japanese were clearly distinguished from those for African Americans. In fact, the ability to employ the same white performers to represent African Americans and then Asians in quick succession was considered a virtuosic special effect in vaudeville productions. The Hippodrome's 1909 extravaganza *A Trip to Japan*, with book by R. H. Burnside and music and lyrics by Manuel Klein, ran for 447 performances in an auditorium seating over 5,000 and offers one example of staged racial transformation.[50] Describing the production, which begins in New York City and is then transported to Japan, the *New York Times* reviewer wrote:

> It is in the first of these scenes that a clever negro song and dance is introduced, in which so many chorus girls take part that it is impossible to count them, all apparently blacked up. It was heartrending to feel that they would be compelled to get their faces clean in time to be Japanese ladies in the ensuing scene.[51]

An advertisement for Pond's Extract Company's Vanishing Cream, featuring Nanette Flack in Japanese costume, in the 4 October 1909 program for this show suggests how such a transformation might be realized.[52] While it is clear that the white female performers in *A Trip to Japan* would have had to remove their black faces before appearing as Japanese ladies, the appropriate color for Japanese-face performance is not specified. This "spectacular melodrama" included a circus performance with a troupe of performing monkeys, acrobats, and clowns. Japanese agents hire this circus in order to disguise a shipment of submarine models that they are smuggling to Japan. After some struggles and intense adventures in Tokyo, the submarine plans are recovered and, in a final scene set in the Mikado's garden, the Japanese government punishes the culprits and promises to restore the submarine models to the Americans.[53] Clearly the plot was inspired in part by the 1908 visit to Japan by the US Great White Fleet, a gesture of naval power by President Theodore Roosevelt intended to remind the little brown Japanese men of American superiority during a period of tension between the two nations.

Racial divisions are particularly significant in these songs when romance is in play. John Luther Long's 1898 short story *Madame Butterfly* famously presented an interracial relationship between a white male and a Japanese female. However, early Tin Pan Alley comic versions of this tale tended to give the American sailor a different skin color. The 1901 musical *Hoity-Toity*, a Weber and Fields production that ran for 225 performances and featured Fay Templeton as Cho-Cho San "known as 'Madame Butterscotch' and in search of a lost husband," included a song entitled "My Japanese Cherry Blossom." In a strong dialect voice, with absurdly repeated ee sounds at the end of words and the substitution of l's for r's, Cho-Cho San tells us about her American lover in the first verse. She relates that her sweetheart "singee me a songee likee 'Mel'can coon." We hear the voice of this American coon in the song's ragtime refrain in which he refers to himself as a "ragtime 'Mel'can man."

(It appears that association with the Japanese has caused this African American to lose his ability to pronounce r's.) In the 1903 song "My Japanese Baby," from *The Darling of the Gallery Gods*, we learn of the love affair between a "Hottentot man" and a Japanese woman. The song's introduction abruptly shifts from "Japanese style" to ragtime and offers a music history lesson by explaining that this is "the way that the coon 'a song 'a came 'a to Japan!" and later that this is how the "rag 'a time 'a came 'a to Japan!" Similarly, "a coloured coon who came from far Mobile" decides to stay in Japan after falling in love with a "pretty little geisha girl" in the 1902 "The Geisha and the Coon." Soon, all the geishas fell in love with him and all of the Japanese men rushed to their barbers and "frizzled up their hair, with paint each one just made himself a coon" so that the geishas would fall in love with them.[54] Multiple songs from this period associate the Japanese with ragtime for comic effect. "A little man from old Japan" cures his homesickness by listening to ragtime in the 1906 "A Ragtime Jap: A Genuine Up-to-Date Novelty." On the 1911 cover of "Oh That Oriental Rag" a dragon is depicted with the notation for "Miya sama" emerging from his mouth and that tune alternates with a ragtime style in the song.[55] *The Mikado* was itself reworked with African American musical styles as early as 1886 when a black minstrelsy troupe performed *The Black Mikado, or the Town of Kan-Ka-Kee*. More famously, Gilbert and Sullivan's operetta was refashioned as the *Swing Mikado* in 1938 and then as *The Hot Mikado* in 1939 with Bill Robinson starring in the title role.[56] In such songs and productions, African Americans engaged in yellowface performance and racial representation proved multilayered.

Racial positioning and racial transformation forms the very subject of some of these songs and theatrical works. In multiple pieces, the beautiful Japanese woman turns out in the end not to be brown, butterscotch, or yellow, but white beneath her kimono. In a sense, this allows the white American male characters to have their geisha and their white woman too, avoiding any actual miscegenation. For example, in the 1914 *Miss Cherryblossom: or A Maid of Tokyo* an "American" (i.e., white) girl is orphaned in Japan at an early age and is brought up as a Japanese maiden, never knowing her true race. When she matures, a visiting white American male falls in love with her, noting that although she speaks Japlish and dresses Japanese her "eyes . . . don't look like Japanese eyes." They are finally allowed to marry only after her true racial identity is revealed. In the 1932 operetta *Maid in Japan, or When Dreams Come True*, an American male—trying to sell suspenders in Japan but in need of an official "Made in Japan" seal—falls in love with the Lord Keeper of the Seal's (Hirohito's) only daughter. It turns out that this "Japanese" beauty is actually the daughter of a white American missionary. Hirohito—the name of the actual Japanese Emperor—relents and decides to bless their marriage. In this work, the American male also complains of gender confusion in exotic Japan as he attempts to sell suspenders in a land of no pants: "You can't tell which from what. They all wear skirts." (I should note that both of these works involved the collaboration of a husband and wife compositional team.) Such examples simultaneously suggest that race is an ambiguous concept and that the maintenance of racial difference is crucial.

Racial and gender ambiguity and comic confusion are not limited to female characters in these works. Charlotte Salisbury, the composer and lyricist of "Japanette," appears herself in Japanese costume on the cover of this intriguing 1918 song. The lyrics are delivered in the voice of a white male addressing a white female whom he met and fell in love with at an "Oriental masquerade." Apparently, she was dressed in a Japanese costume that evening and he now proclaims: "I long the day you're goin' to be/My own little Japanee." He promises that they will go to the "land of flowers, old Japan" on their honeymoon, fulfilling their dream of living out a Japanese romance. In a few examples, white males complain of "turning Japanese" themselves instead of celebrating the romantic possibilities of such a transformation. In "The Jap," an 1893 number published in Boston and performed in the United States by the famous British music hall comic Dan Leno, an American male claims he was forced into marrying a Japanese woman and that he has become a "mixed up half-and-half." In this exotic land where everything is opposite, his wife sings with a tomtom and we hear strong "Middle Eastern" Orientalist signals—a quarter-eighth-eighth tattoo in the left hand with vaguely modal melodies in the right. This hapless male's speech is infected by nonsense words ending in -ang and -ing. A prolonged sojourn in Japan has clearly eroded this American's language and, thus, his identity. As with the 1886 "Mikado Mc. Allister," the comedy in this song seems fueled both by a semi-serious fear of infection by all things Japanese and by a desire to satirize *japonisme* itself.

"Poor Butterfly" and Poor Pinkertons

The primary musical and racial strains of Tin Pan Alley *japonisme* were rather tightly interwoven in the 1928 song "Japanese Mammy," particularly in Eddie Bard's arrangement. As the narrator implores "little Japanese Mammy rock your baby to rest," his word choice and imagery invoke the coon song and lullaby predecessors and his melodic line echoes the rocking interval of "The Japanese Sandman" from 1920 and alludes to its Japanese mother's song. "Japanese Mammy" also features a clear inserted reference to the "Miya sama" tune from *The Mikado*, as well as prominent open staccato fifths, parallel fifths, and pentatonicism. The 1928 arrangement recorded by Paul Whiteman (Columbia 1701D) featured woodblocks and a conclusive gong stroke.[57] Finally, we learn that this Japanese woman sits "watching alone, waiting for a sailor man, who never, never comes home." In the two decades leading up to this number, almost any allusion to an abandoned Japanese woman—particularly one deserted by a lover from across the seas—inescapably pointed to the archetypal tale of Madame Butterfly.

Tin Pan Alley's interest in Japan did not remain constant throughout the first decades of the twentieth century, but instead was aroused by specific cultural works and political events. The success of John Luther Long's 1898 short story, David Belasco's 1900 play, and Giacomo Puccini's 1904 operatic treatment (first performed in the United States in 1906) of the "Madame Butterfly" narrative in-spired a significant response in American popular song. I have collected some 345 songs dealing with Japan published between 1900 and 1930 alone. At least eighty of these exhibit specific connections to Butterfly.[58] (These songs are marked with an asterisk in Appendix 1.) This tally does not include songs that involve white male/ Japanese female love but that lack direct reference to the "Madame Butterfly" nar-rative, nor does it include the numerous songs in which a Japanese woman yearns for her departed Japanese sailor. The earliest piece in my collection that is clearly inspired by this tale is "O Mona San: A Tokio Tragedy" from 1900 which was dedicated to Belasco. ("The Jewel of Asia" from *The Geisha* might be considered an earlier prototype, although in a comic mode, for this song topic.) The fad for "Madame Butterfly" songs eventually called forth Irving Berlin's "Hurry Back to My Bamboo Shack" in 1916 and George Gershwin's "Yan-Kee" in 1920 and "In the Heart of a Geisha" in 1921. Several songs even referred textually to Tin Pan Alley's "Madame Butterfly" corpus, thereby attesting to the prevalence of such songs. For example, a unique twist on the tale was offered in the 1917 "Mister Butterfly" where we hear of the Japanese geisha who could say no. Turning the Butterfly image back upon the American, this geisha accuses him of flitting from one flower to the next and declares that she is fully aware of Madame Butterfly's fate and has "not the least desire to play her part." These songs more typically present us with the lament of an abandoned Cho-Cho-San, or with a pining American male who longs to return to his geisha girl. However, Tin Pan Alley rang a number of changes on the basic story and in some versions the American sailor returns to live happily ever after with his Japanese lover or they decide to depart together for America. In a period of intense anti-Asian racism and fears of miscegenation, the number of songs celebrating the love between white males and Japanese women is striking. Of course, as I have noted, Tin Pan Alley's representation of interracial love abides by the regulations of Euro-American Orientalism—the white lover is always male and the affairs are most often set in "far-off Japan." These songs surely stoked the fantasy for white American heterosexual males of having an exotic woman pining for one's return, even though a significant number of these works were created by white female composers and/or lyricists, as will be discussed below.[59] Somewhat surprisingly, some female performers even performed these songs. For example, the sheet music cover for the 1900 "My Geisha of Tokio" reveals that Belle Archer sang this song in the show *A Contented Woman*.

References to the "Madame Butterfly" narrative and to Puccini's opera include indirect quotations in the lyrics, as in the 1919 "Fan Tan: Oriental Fox-Trot," which includes the line "she's waiting, while the robins mating"—Pinkerton had prom-ised to return when the robins mate again—and that year's "Won't You Come Back to Tokio" in which "little Cho-Cho San" is said to be waiting and "still for one fine day she's praying"—an allusion to Butterfly's undying belief that "Un bel dì"/"One fine day" Pinkerton would return. Numerous songs feature names derived from either "Cho-Cho-San" or "Madame Butterfly." These popular Butterflies tend to be a bit more flirtatious behind their fans than the operatic heroine, but the opera appears to have firmly established the icon of the singing geisha in American popular culture. Tin Pan Alley's Pinkerton often fantasizes that he hears Butterfly's "plaintive" and "quaint" melodies floating across the seas to him and he appears to derive comfort and even pleasure from imagining her longing. When we do hear the voice of the Butterfly character, it is often through his ears. In a number of the "Madame Butterfly" songs, such as the 1917 "My Little Sing Song Girl" and the 1923 "Japanese Lullaby," the Japanese woman is praised for her angelic vocal art and, in some cases, for her *shamisen* playing. In the 1922 "Japanese Love Moon," the Pinkerton character imagines that he hears his "own butterfly" singing and playing the *shamisen*, that she dreams of him, and that her "plaintive melodies" are floating across the seas to his ears. Similarly the American male lover in the 1915 "Won't You Be My Little Fan Tan Girl" longs to return to Japan for the "quaint little melodies from my sweet Japanese haunt me daily." Both the ideal Japanese woman and her music are perceived as equivalently small and quaint. Multiple other songs quote or paraphrase the main theme from Butterfly's famous "Un bel dì" aria, including three songs from 1917. We hear a hint of this melody in "Suki San (Where the Cherry Blossoms Fall): Japanese Novelty Song" as we are told that "she hums a lonesome lovesick tune." Robins are mentioned in "Good-bye, Cherry Blossom" and we again hear the "Un bel dì" melody in both the introduction and with the phrase "a voice she longs to hear." The Pinkerton character asks his Butterfly to "sing me once more your plaintive Oriental strain" in "Good-bye Little Yo Ho San" and sings a near quotation of Puccini's tune as he makes his farewell in the refrain.

The appearance of "Madame Butterfly" songs between 1903 and 1906 is not surprising, given the dates of Belasco's highly successful play and Puccini's opera, however the far greater concentration of similar songs in the years 1916 to 1922 is not so readily explained. Performances of Puccini's opera in New York City were no more common during this later period than in the preceding years nor were large numbers of American sailors returning from the Pacific at this time.[60] The 1915 silent film *Madame Butterfly* staring Mary Pickford might well be cited as one prominent, but not singular, stimulus. Much of the credit for this later popularity of the "Madame Butterfly" narrative in American popular song may be directly attributed to the immense success of one particular song—John L. Golden's and Raymond Hubbell's 1916 "Poor Butterfly," a title that echoes the servant Suzuki's "povera Butterfly" delivered late in Puccini's opera upon learning that Pinkerton has married a white American woman.

In this standard number the Butterfly narrative is told quite efficiently, allowing the narrator to focus on Butterfly's painful anticipation of her foreign lover's return. The opening phrase, "there's a story told," coyly refers to the long tradition of the "Madame Butterfly" narrative. The narrator then dismisses any ambiguity by referring to the protagonist as "Miss Butterfly" and sums her up as having been "a sweet little innocent child." The past tense is maintained as we learn that an

American male "taught her to love in the 'Merican way" and then "sailed away with a promise to return."

> There's a story told of a little Japanese
> sitting demurely 'neath the cherry blossom trees.
> Miss Butterfly her name
> A sweet little innocent child was she,
> till a fine young American from the sea.
> To her garden came.
> They met 'neath the cherry blossoms ev'ry day
> and he taught her how to love in the 'Merican way,
> To love with her soul! t'was easy to learn;
> Then he sailed away with a promise to return.

In the first half of the refrain, the narrator laments Butterfly's fate but then slips from the past tense of "she loved him so" to the present, inviting us to listen for "as she smiles through her tears, She murmurs low." Thus, in the second half of the refrain we hear her voice as she proclaims that the American will return to her. She concludes, however, by envisaging a future in which he has failed to return, and stating that she would "never sigh or cry" but "just mus' die."

> Poor Butterfly! 'neath the blossoms waiting
> Poor Butterfly! For she loved him so.
> The moment [*sic*] pass into hours
> The hours pass into years
> And as she smiles through her tears,
> She murmurs low,
> The moon and I know that he be faithful,
> I'm sure he come to me bye and bye.
> But if he don't come back
> Then I never sigh or cry
> I just mus' die.
> Poor Butterfly.

The narrator shifts back to the past tense in the second verse and quotes her words once again, but leaves us at the end of the verse longing with her in an endless present.

> "Won't you tell my love," she would whisper to the breeze
> Tell him I'm waiting 'neath the cherry blossom trees.
> My sailor man to see.
> The bees and the humming birds say they guess,

> Ev'ry day that passes makes one day less.
> 'Till you'll come to me.
> For once Butterfly she gives her heart away,
> She can never love again she is his for aye.
> Through all of this world, For ages to come,
> So her face just smiles, tho' her heart is growing numb.

The framing of the song implies her (impending?) demise without specifying the act or freeing her (or us) from the narrative's loop. These shifts in tense allow us, and the Butterfly character, to re-experience the tale yet again through her murmuring voice in this song.

The three-pitch chromatic climb on the syllables "poor but-ter" followed by an ascent of a minor sixth for "fly" in the refrain serves as an effective melodic hook for the entire song. The gesture is first heard at the start of the instrumental introduction, appears at the opening of the refrain with the title words as noted, and then again at the start of the second half of the refrain as Butterfly murmurs the words "the moon and I." This melodic gesture and its accompanying text were emphasized further in the numerous recorded performances that omitted the lyrics of the second or even both verses. Larry Hamberlin has suggested that the song alludes to the harmonic style of Puccini.[61] One might also hear a connection between the rhythmic profile and general melodic shape of the refrain and Puccini's "Un bel dì" aria and note the pentatonic quality in the verses. The song became a hit through early recordings by Edna Brown and by the Victor Military Band, and was also recorded with success over the decades by Red Nichols, Deanna Durbin, Al Hibbler, Fritz Kreisler, and Sarah Vaughan, among others.[62] The most bizarre recording must be the 1963 entomological mashup by The Three Suns in which "Poor Butterfly" is performed simultaneously with "The Flight of the Bumblebee." However, by far the most elaborate performance of this song occurred in its initial production.

On the sheet music cover of "Poor Butterfly" the largest font is reserved for the show title and theater of the song's premiere: *The Big Show* at the New York Hippodrome. The line "staged by R. H. Burnside" appears above the credits for both the lyricist and composer. *The Big Show* apparently ran for over 400 performances and included a section entitled "Somewhere in Japan" lasting roughly nine minutes, which involved four Japanese dancers, a mixed chorus of ninety-six performers dressed in Japanese costume, and the premiere of "Poor Butterfly" sung by Haru [Haruko] Onuki.[63] Correspondence and other production materials reveal that this high-profile example of staged *japonisme* and "Poor Butterfly" itself may have been inspired by the opportunity to feature this Japanese female performer at the Hippodrome, demonstrating once again that theater's tireless efforts to bring the exotic world before the eyes and ears of the New York public. In February 1916 Burnside received letters from a promoter suggesting specific Japanese performers for the Hippodrome's season. On 2 February the agent offered:

> SUMIKO AND HER FOUR REAL GEISHA GIRLS If you have anything like that in view, then this combination would be very interesting as she is a very good singer, and perhaps we could get ONUKI, who is a great singer at the same time and perhaps two or three big Japanese troupes, to make up a big combination.

In a 25 February follow-up, the agent focused specifically on the talents of Onuki:

> Re MISS HOROKU ONUKI, a wonderful Japanese singer, whom we brought from Chicago on purpose to get a line on her talent, I would strongly advise you to see her as she might be a wonderful acquisition for one or the other production. She has a most wonderful voice and is something entirely out of the ordinary. Of course, any night you want to go kindly let me know as only members are admitted.[64]

Her contract—$200 weekly for ten weeks with an option of two more ten-week renewals—was signed in May of that year. Onuki went on to enjoy a modest career in opera in the 1920s, appearing as Madama Butterfly with the San Carlo Opera Company in 1926. In this case, the *New York Times* stated that she "made a striking entrance in the first act, giving to the opera its exotic flavor," as though Puccini's opera lacked sufficient exotic representation without such a performer.[65] Apparently, Onuki was also called upon to satisfy the need for exotic performance at several benefit parties in the 1920s. One such Japanese-themed garden party in May 1927 in Montclair, New Jersey, included Japanese dances by Michio Ito, "a jiu jitsu exhibition by Isuke Shinmen, a group of Japanese children folk-songs by the Okajima sisters, interpretative dances by Mm. Michitaro Ongawa and several arias from 'Madame Butterfly' by Miss Haru Onuki." Refreshments at this event were served by "Japanese girls in native costume."[66] Clearly, the taste for public displays of *japonisme* did not die with Isabella Stewart Gardner.

However, the conceit of having a Japanese performer sing Madame Butterfly's lament and thus transport the audience, through her vocal timbre and appearance, to "Somewhere in Japan" in *The Big Show* was not well received and she was replaced for subsequent performances. (I have not been able to determine whether the song was divided in any way between Onuki and the chorus in their performance.) Reviews suggest that this performer and song were not deemed to be sufficiently exotic. A generally positive review in *Theatre* stated that: "In Act I we also have a Japanese dance, along with a song, with chorus, by Haru Omuki [*sic*], a Japanese singer of feminine charm, Oriental, but accomplished after a manner that is not foreign to us."[67] The reviewer for the *New York Times* complained that a greater musical effort was needed in order to fuel the exotic voyage: "It would be well . . . to find a less blatantly Occidental song for the Japanese soprano to sing and some exit for the lion tamer's entire episode."[68] One very disgruntled patron, writing from his winter home in St. Petersburg, Florida, chose to complain directly to Burnside about his staged *japonisme* in a ten-page critique of the production. He too cited a lack of sufficient "Japanese character":

"Somewhere in Japan" was not much better than the "Fifth Ave." affair. . . . The singing of the main singer lacked any special Japanese character of suggestiveness. The man who attended the sedan or palanquin, or whatever it is called, seemed to be a real Japanese so far as his actions and appearance went; but the whole scene lacks any apparent motive. It is no more than a passing scene with no especial interest, and no especially beautiful surroundings. Some incident of the Flower Festival, some feature of the Japanese home, most anything that had obvious character to it would have been far more effective.[69]

Later arrangements of this song, such as Ferde Grofé's recorded by Paul Whiteman, remedied this "defect" by adding musical Orientalisms not present in the original score. Hubbell's other Japanese-themed works, including the 1904 *Fantana* and the 1919 "Say-on-ar-a," also lack prominent exotic musical markers. Creating an exotic impact with such songs was left, to a large extent, in the hands of the performers. Indeed, the song's retelling of the "Madame Butterfly" narrative itself proved somewhat performance-dependent.

In the refrain of "Poor Butterfly" we hear her lament and her conclusion that "if he don't come back/Then I never sigh or cry/I just mus' die." Several of the recordings of this song in the 1920s and 1930s were made by male vocalists. In one of these recordings (Andy Kirk and His Clouds of Joy, Pha Terrell vocalist, Decca 1663-A, 1937) the text was changed in the refrain: "I'm sure *she* comes to me bye and bye, But if *she* don't come back . . . I just must die." This apparently insignificant alteration to the "Madame Butterfly" narrative is not a unique occurrence in American versions of the tale. In fact, many of the songs considered here emphasize the longing and suffering of the American male, as though Pinkerton was the tragic victim. In "Poppy-Time in Old Japan" (1915) an American male has dreamed of returning to Old Japan but when he finally does so his beloved has vanished. As late as 1972 in the number-one hit song "Made in Japan" by the country artist Buck Owens we hear an American male pining for the girl he left behind in Japan. (A performance of this song by Owens on the TV show *Hee Haw* featured his band in red, white, and blue striped ties with matching guitars.) In this case the Japanese girl was forced to marry someone else and the American male's own transistor radio, which was "made in Japan," painfully reminds him of his Japanese maid and his own broken heart. I should note that not all versions of the tale ended tragically for Pinkerton and Butterfly and that in some cases the story was treated satirically. In a comic twist in "My Nagasaki Girl" from 1915 the American marries "Cho San" only to have her become a nagging wife. A US Marine, whose speech has been comically impacted by his exotic romance, relates in the 1921 "My Little Rose of Tokio" that he longs to return to his Japanese girl because "she can do things that would amaze ya." In a rather convoluted version of the scenario, the American male of the 1915 "The Yellow Fan" (a "Japanese Fantasy, Humourous Romantic Recitation") explains that he had once traveled to Japan and had missed his American sweetheart until a fan depicting a Japanese lady caught his eye. He then fell for a live Japanese girl but discovered she was already married and so he returned home to the American woman. As though to affirm his rightful place in the United States, the song quotes the "Star-Spangled Banner," the "Wedding March," "Dixie Land," and "Yankee Doodle" at the end. Again, the emphasis here is on Pinkerton and his search for love and a solid masculine identity.

We should recall that Puccini's opera ends with Pinkerton's threefold anguished cry "Butterfly." It is the echo of *his* remorse and pining that we hear in many of these American popular songs. In 1921, Ricordi, Puccini's own publisher, released "Cho-Cho-San," a fox trot "on melodies by G. Puccini." This song begins with the humming chorus melody heard in the passing of the night between parts one and two of Act II. The song's refrain section employs Butterfly's famous aria "Un bel dì" and the song ends, in the arrangement used by Paul Whiteman and recorded by him in 1921 and 1926, with the final measures of the opera. Instead of Butterfly's voice and her hopes, we hear the American male's promise to return in this contrafact refrain. In fact, many of these songs are in the voice of a pining Pinkerton who relates his pain to the "Un bel dì" tune. Considering the entire "Madame Butterfly" corpus, Pinkerton appears the central musical figure. In Long's short story and Belasco's staged production, we hear Butterfly sing the songs that Pinkerton has taught her. In Puccini's opera, Pinkerton's is the first and last voice that we hear and his aria of Yankee bravado is the closest piece resembling a true sung-song or diegetic performance in the final version of the work. Rather than giving full voice to Butterfly's anguish near the opera's end, Puccini allows Pinkerton to lament his tragic mistake.

Numerous subsequent songs referred directly to "Poor Butterfly," often to comic effect. Hubbell capitalized on his own success in 1917 by giving voice to Pinkerton in "I'm Coming Back to You Poor Butterfly." Far off Broadway, Captain Frank Glick of the US Army stationed at Camp Lee, Virginia, followed suit in 1919 with "I'm Coming, Butterfly," in which Pinkerton asks to be pitied and forgiven and declares that he longs to "hold you to my bleeding heart." This number was introduced in *I'll Say So*, a musical extravaganza produced by the officers of Camp Lee. In the 1919 "Poor Little Butterfly Is a Fly Girl Now," the Japanese heroine appears in blackface on the cover in some printings and the music includes a quotation from Hubbell's hit. This Butterfly wins back her man by dancing a shimmy and an "Oriental dance."[70] The protagonist of the 1917 "If I Catch the Guy Who Wrote Poor Butterfly" complains that he cannot get Hubbell's tune out of his head. Several songs, such as the 1917 "My Yiddisha Butterfly" and the 1920 "Happy Butterfly" refer musically or textually to both "Poor Butterfly" and to Puccini's opera. Similarly, the 1917 "My Broadway Butterfly" directly references both Puccini's opera and "Poor Butterfly" and presents the most blatant attempt to rehabilitate Pinkerton through popular song. Here the American male explains his side of the story. He sings the "Un bel dì" tune as he describes his longing and then, following Puccini's Pinkerton, quotes the "Star-Spangled Banner." (See Example 2.5.) By 1927 in "Nagasaki Butterfly," the revisionary project is explicit as Pinkerton, claiming that he has been

Example 2.5 "My Broadway Butterfly," Willy White, 1917

maligned, declares to his Japanese sweetheart: "Tell the 'Europeany' guys, And the old Puccini guys, That their Madam Butterflies Don't go for me."

"The Yankees of the Far East": Representations of the Russo-Japanese War

Of the numerous variations on the theme of an American male and Japanese female romance, the version told in the 1905 "My Jap From Tokio" is particularly significant. In this song the Yank gets to marry his "sweet brown-eyed fairy" but only after first proving his valor in battle and fighting to defend her nation. In this song, the "Madame Butterfly" narrative intersected with a momentous political event in Japan's relationship to the West: the Russo-Japanese War of 1904–1905.[71] The year 1904 was by far the biggest one for the publication of Japan-related songs. This musical outpouring was not inspired primarily by Puccini's *Madama Butterfly*, as we might suppose, but by Japan's military exploits. As Charles K. Harris put it in his influential *How to Write a Popular Song* (1906): "the late war between Russia and Japan aroused interest in Japanese songs, not necessarily treating on war themes, but Japanese in subject and atmosphere."[72] Indeed, one-fifth of my entire collection of songs was published in 1904 and 1905 and a full half of those songs refer to the Russo-Japanese War. These songs reflected (and helped to shape) the strong pro-Japanese position of the United States during the conflict.[73] Enthusiasm for the Japanese is clear in the American media coverage of the war and this political interest in Japan inspired a more general interest in Japanese culture. The front page of the 17 April 1904 edition of the *New York Times* reported another stunning Japanese naval victory over the Russians. On page two of this edition one finds an article entitled "Japanese War Songs: What the Mikado's Men are Singing in These Stirring Times." This article discussed two new Japanese songs and explained that "though the tunes to European or American ears are not very musical, yet both are said to have become quite popular." Would musical appreciation follow political sympathy for the exotic nation?

Several examples attempted to bridge the cultural divide by employing Japanese tunes, or at least by claiming to do so. The "Christmas music supplement" of the 11 December 1904 *San Francisco Examiner* offered "Battle Hymn," a song allegedly composed by "the Mikado of Japan and sung by the Japanese armies on the battle fields." The introduction does indeed draw upon "Kimigayo," the unofficial Japanese national anthem that was composed by a Japanese court musician and harmonized by Franz Eckert, a German bandsman, in 1880. However, the balance of "Battle Hymn" was most likely not composed by anyone in Japan. Instead, this piece offers a striking case of putting words and music in the mouth of the other. In the second verse, the fictitious Japanese soldiers refer to themselves as "new men of Nippon, redeem'd from ancient error" and boast that they are "hermits no longer" but have learned instead to be "proud hosts of ev'ry comer." In this song, San Francisco readers would have heard the Japanese voice they preferred—a voice grateful to the American "redeemers." Similarly, the 1905 march "Japanese Heroes" is in the voice of a Japanese soldier preparing to fight Russia and includes the phrase "I suppose you have read in the papers" and makes specific references to contemporary events. Such pieces tend to avoid the stereotypical Japanese musical markers mentioned above that were emerging in this period and thus, perhaps, demonstrate solidarity with, rather than an Orientalist distance from, these "Yankees of the Far East."

Distinct from other periods, songs from the Russo-Japanese War years focus intently on Japanese male protagonists, both in the lyrics and in the cover art. Figure 2.6 presents an illustration of this new cover style. These songs

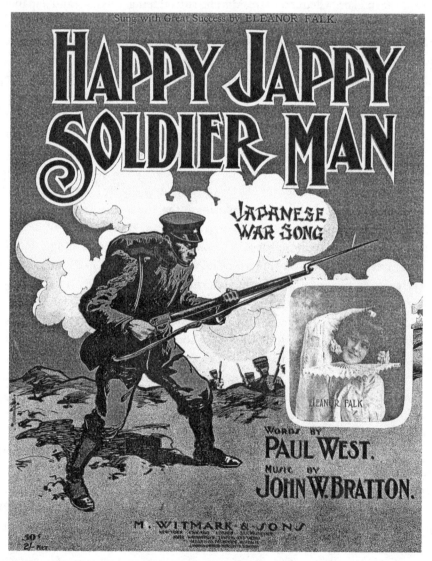

Figure 2.6 "Happy Jappy Soldier Man," sheet music cover (M. Witmark and Sons, 1904).

simultaneously praised the pluck of the Japanese while subtly aiming to keep the "little" men in their place. For example, in "The Little Brown Man of Japan" (1904) we are told: "In that land of Kimona and Fan, They'll be peaceful as long as they can, And the best friend to know, or the bitterest foe, is that little brown man of Japan." The cover of "Little Japan" depicted Japanese soldiers advancing and a bear, representing the Russians, creeping around the frame. This song claims that the Japanese were fighting for civilization and protecting the weak Chinese from the Russians. Multiple pieces were inspired by Theodore Roosevelt's role in brokering the peace treaty between Japan and Russia and by the extended stay of the Japanese delegation in Portsmouth, New Hampshire, where the negotiations took place. For example, Roosevelt was celebrated in "The Peacemaker: Characteristic March, Introducing Russian and Japanese Battle Songs" (1905), which—in a rather Ivesian fashion—employed bits of "Miya sama" battling the 1812 Overture, with the American tunes "The Star-Spangled Banner" and "Dixie" achieving the peace.

The war also offered American songwriters another prompt for portraying Japan as the land of painful romantic separations and tragic love. In several songs published in 1904 and 1905, a Japanese woman awaits the return of a Japanese soldier. "Sayonara: A Japanese Love Song"—sporting an odd singing humanoid butterfly on the cover—presents a Japanese woman singing "sayonara" to her "little fighting Jap" as he goes off to battle. In "A Tale of Tokio," a "dainty little oriental maid" waiting for her soldier "of old Japan" sings a "plaintive lay, in such a fascinating captivating way." The narrator informs us that the soldier lies dead in Russia. Not all such songs ended tragically. The narrator in Paul West and John W. Bratton's "Happy Jappy Soldier Man: Japanese War Song" asks a "little geisha" to sing, but she refuses explaining that she is in mourning for a soldier. However, in the second verse she agrees to sing because her lover has returned from war. Most musical responses to the Russo-Japanese War remained quite serious in tone, but the events of the day also inspired comic works. The 1904 show *The Japskys* included such songs as "Susie Oo: A Japanese Coon Song" and "The Way to Rush a Russian." Willard Spenser, the creator of *The Little Tycoon*, was inspired by the war to return to Japanese themes. His 1906 *Rosalie or, The Japanese Fairies* was set during the war and was subtitled "an original Japanese-Russian Romantic Opera." The odd tale involves an American (Rosalie) who becomes involved in the war and is reunited with her American man through some fairy magic. The work offers a satirical perspective on American war correspondents and the Red Cross and ends with a "Japanese Grand Army March." Outdoing Spenser in its oddity is the 1906 comic operetta *The Yellow Peril* by Alice Brandon Caldwell and Annie Laurie Nance, which these women created for the literary society in Abingdon, Virginia.[74] The work, set during the war, is subtitled "A Solution of this Most Vexing Problem"—the true "Yellow Peril" problem turns out not to be the military might of the Japanese, but the attraction experienced by American men for the irresistible Japanese women. The work opens with a dignified and serious first scene presenting Japanese soldiers and the final number, marked "very staccato," is "Hats Off to the Japs." However, the threat of Japanese feminine charms and of miscegenation drives the comedy.

The stunning military success and fears of miscegenation led many other Americans to believe that the "Yellow Peril" was no laughing matter. As noted above, Lothrop Stoddard's warnings against Japanese immigration in his widely cited 1920 book *The Rising Tide of Color against White World-Supremacy* were particularly dire. The relationship between Japan and the United States was rather erratic in the two decades leading up to Stoddard's pronouncements and the landmark 1924 exclusion of the Japanese in US immigration policy. The general enthusiasm expressed by Theodore Roosevelt for the Japanese victory over Russia quickly turned to anxiety as Japan assumed its new position as a power in the Pacific. Tensions surrounding Californian segregation efforts, which resulted in the 1907 "Gentleman's Agreement" restricting Japanese immigration, and war fears leading up to the cruise of the Great White Fleet were temporarily resolved by the very warm welcome the fleet received in Japan, including the spectacle of "hundreds of thousands of Japanese waving the Stars and Stripes and singing 'The Star-Spangled Banner'–in English."[75] However, Japan's "21 Demands" imposed on China in 1915 shocked American public opinion and Japan's attempts to achieve parity with Western nations during the peace conferences following World War I further strained relations. A period of relative calm was broken after Japan attacked Shanghai in 1932, and American opinion of the Japanese remained generally negative in the years leading up to the attack on Pearl Harbor.[76]

Several songs in my collection betray a more wary attitude in response to the growing military and economic power of the Japanese during this period, including the 1905 "When America Is Captured by the Japs" (discussed in the Introduction) and the 1913 "Tango Tokio."[77] "The Modern Japanee" (also published as "My Japanee") was rather more explicit concerning fears of a "Yellow Peril" in 1909 and alluded directly to *The Mikado*: "We figured once on fans and screens, We figure now on the Philippines, It's not the style to pat my head, The white man shakes my hand instead." This piece was composed by Gustav Luders, who had earlier contributed a lullaby and a Japanese march, in addition to *The Sho-gun*, to American musical *japonisme*. Such songs demonstrate the close coordination between political events and cultural responses in the history of the US-Japanese relationship. As US interest in Japan and in Japanese culture waned during the 1930s, American popular music became virtually silent on the subject. My collection includes only eleven pieces referring to Japanese subjects published during the decade of the 1930s. The trials of the Great Depression were not conducive to popular *japonisme*. With the bombing of Pearl Harbor in 1941, Tin Pan Alley would again turn its attention to Japan, no longer framing the Japanese as feminized others always available to the "vagabond Yankee," or as political protégés across the Pacific, but instead as an exotic subhuman enemy inspiring new strains of Orientalist representation. Many of the stereotypical devices of exotic representation developed in the songs discussed in this chapter would be redeployed during World War II. In some cases, entire songs would be repurposed for anti-Japanese propaganda efforts. In the 1914 "I Want to Go to Tokio" the white American narrator relates how a little Japanese male sings about his "little sweetheart" Yo San (a reference once again to Belasco's *Darling of the Gods*) and of how he longs to return to "old Japan." A recording of this song by Louis Prima in the 1940s (HIT: 7123) added a martial introduction and adapted the lyrics, referring to the Japs as monkeys and declaring that in response to the bombing of Pearl Harbor, "soon the Yanks will be a going, where the lanterns are a glowing." Seemingly light pieces of popular *japonisme* could rather easily be transformed into ominous musical threats.

"Founded Upon Genuine Themes": Aspirations of Exotic Authenticity

Multiple American composers chose to express their solidarity with the Japanese during the Russo-Japanese War by attempting to incorporate Japanese music into their works, or at least by claiming to have done so. This is evidenced, for example, by Ferdinand Wagner's 1904 "Nippon Banzai!: Characteristic Japanese War March," which was "Inscribed by the Composer to the Heroes of the Army and Navy of Japan." Various moments and sections in this instrumental piece are labeled "Japanese Drum," "War Song (Battle Hymn) of Japanese Warriors," "Banzai Nippon!," and "Hymn of Praise to the Japanese Deity," without clear musical evidence supporting such labels. The 1904 "Banzai: Japanese Victory March" by Chas. E. Lepaige—which was "Respectfully Inscribed to Hon. S. Uchida Consul General of Japan"—does present the words and music for "Kimigayo" on the first page. Such gestures toward a form of "exotic authenticity" can be found in pieces throughout this collection. Indeed, many examples were casually billed as "Japanese" pieces and others specifically claimed to employ a "Japanese Air," as in the first movement of the 1883 "Ichi-ban: waltzes," the earliest example of such a claim that I have located in American popular music. In rare cases, works credited to Japanese-sounding names or by actual Japanese composers such as Kosaku Yamada were published in the United States during this period.[78]

Bids for exotic authenticity are most commonly encountered in songs and larger works intended for the recital and concert hall and, often, produced by composers active in classical genres. Such pieces are more likely to present tragic narratives and to celebrate the romantic nobility of an "Old Japan" where Japanese women commit suicide for the "sake of love," as in the 1907 cantata for women's voices, *The Fate of Princess Kiyo: A Legend of Japan*. (The most famous example of such *japonisme* cantatas is the 1911 *A Tale of Old Japan* by the African English composer Samuel Coleridge-Taylor.) Numerous examples proclaim an elevated status by employing Japanese terminology and documenting exotic cultural and musical sources in introductory notes. Markings such as "quasi samisen" appear in these scores—implicitly suggesting that the composer and performer have heard *shamisen* music—and specific songs or movements are headed by notated Japanese folk tunes. For example, each of the six songs in the 1920 "Drolleries from an Oriental Doll's House" is prefaced by the notated Japanese or Chinese tune employed in that song. American art song composers of the period also frequently turned to nineteenth-century works of literary *japonisme* by such writers as Pierre Loti, Sir Edwin Arnold, Mary McNeil Fenollosa, John Luther Long, and, especially, Lafcadio Hearn for their lyrics, character names, and general perceptions of Japan.[79] Attempting to delimit Tin Pan Alley numbers, parlor songs, novelty piano pieces, and works of popular musical theater from "art" or "cultivated" examples in this period is by no means a simple task. Indeed, although many of the art songs, cantatas, and instrumental works on Japanese themes avoided the musical styles and forms employed in Tin Pan Alley and on Broadway, many of the same representational strategies and narrative topoi appear in all of these genres. However, the examples considered in this final section of the chapter appear to have been created more in the bourgeois *japonisme* spirit of the Arts and Crafts movement rather than in the vein of mass-mediated popular culture.

Straining to suggest exotic authenticity was nowhere more evident than in theatrical works that, taking their cue from such nineteenth-century Orientalist operas as Mascagni's 1898 *Iris*, occasionally employed Japanese instruments as props. For example, Belasco and Long's *Darling of the Gods*—with music by William Furst—called for the presentation of the *biwa, shamisen, koto, tsuzumi,* and *fuye* on stage.[80] Works of staged *japonisme* took a wide variety of forms. An 1897 pantomime written by Vance Thompson and presented at the new Astoria Hotel in New York by the Society of Musical Art included music composed "in the Japanese mode" by Aime Lachaume. This music was said to preserve "the fantastic rhythms, the strange tonality and exotic color of Japanese music, and, in addition, it has all M. Lachaume's modernity, grace, and French delicacy." Exotic authenticity was promised in this advance publicity: "A Japanese artist has supervised the costumes, and is lending his assistance at the rehearsal. Japanese dancing girls, with one exception the only troupe of Mousmees seen in this country, will appear."[81] The composer of the 1925 opera *Namiko-San*, Aldo Franchetti, had spent three months in Japan in 1922 accompanying the Japanese soprano Tamaki Miura who took the title role in his opera, thus lending her own mark of authenticity to this production in Chicago. The libretto was based on a book by a French American who had lived in Japan ten years and drew upon a Japanese tale for his narrative. Rather than raising issues concerning its Japanese features, *Namiko-San* apparently inspired a debate on whether the work counted as an "American" opera due to the composer's nationality.[82] Some figures acquired certification as purveyors of authentic exotic representations primarily through repeated activity in this field. John Luther Long, for example, was celebrated not only for David Belasco's stagings of *Madame Butterfly* and *The Darling of the Gods* but for other works of theatrical *japonisme*, in addition to his multiple novels and short stories set in Japan. Long expanded his *Andon* to serve as the libretto for *Hoshi-San*, an opera composed by Wassili Leps and premiered in Philadelphia in 1909. Leps had previously set *Andon* for soprano, tenor, and orchestra and it was performed by the Philadelphia Orchestra. Leps had also composed a very successful cantata for women's chorus on a text by Long in 1905 entitled *Yo-nennen: A Japanese Cicada Drama* in which a warrior dies and then returns to visit his beloved in the form of a cicada.[83]

A particularly prominent theatrical work in this period of American *japonisme* is the 1917 play *The Willow Tree* by Joseph Harry Benrimo and Harrison Rhodes.[84] The play quite clearly presupposed an interest on the part of its audience in the consumption of all things Japanese. Indeed, even as late as the 1931 publication of the work, any future director was instructed to "bear in mind that his scene should resemble a Japanese garden such as one sees in the little Table-Bowl gardens, with water and bridge, etc., which are so fashionable now."[85] Benrimo (1874–1942), most often referred to by last name only, was a central and versatile figure in Orientalist theater as a writer, actor, designer, and director. In addition to writing the landmark Chinese-inspired play *The Yellow Jacket* (with George C. Hazleton, 1912) he appeared as a Chinese character in *The First Born*, as Japanese in Belasco's *The Darling of the Gods*, and as the Native American Billy Jackrabbit in Belasco's *The Girl of Golden West*. *The Willow Tree*, based on a Japanese legend,[86] was reworked in at least five different forms including the original spoken play with incidental music, a novel (1918), a silent film (1920), and an operetta (1927), in addition to inspiring multiple individual songs during this period. Again, repetition alone tends to certify authenticity and expertise in exotic representation. A review of a 1933 revival of *The Willow Tree* celebrated Benrimo's extensive work in theatrical exoticism and reported that he had received a complimentary letter from Japanese residents in New York. The review was titled "Knows His Orient."[87]

Music played a central role in establishing the play's exotic authenticity in its 1917 and subsequent productions. Though it is not clear who composed the music, the memorandum of agreement for the original production of *The Willow Tree* stipulated that Benrimo and Rhodes would provide the producers (George M. Cohan and Sam H. Harris) with a copy of the score and the exclusive right to use the music.[88] The 1931 publication of the play only includes the rather unremarkable music for "The Song of the Street Singer," an excerpt of the "Song of the Image," and a solo flute part, all without attribution. The stage directions and promptbooks reveal that Benrimo paid close attention to details of the production's soundscape and called for the use of a *shamisen* at several points. For example, the directions for the opening of Act III state: "After the house lights have been lowed [sic] and just before the screen folds back we should hear the tolling of the deep toned bell which keep [sic] up until the screen has fully opened" and when the tolling bell stops "we hear the flute play a plaintive melody which should die away in a mournful wail."[89] The directions, perhaps inspired by the writing of Lafcadio Hearn, go on to call for buzzing insects, croaking frogs, and singing crickets. Less specific directions appear in other spots in the typescript promptbook, such as "a Japanese song is heard off stage."

Sigmund Romberg's attempts to create Japanese music in the 1927 "musical play" or operetta *Yo-San/Cherryblossoms*, which was directly based on *The Willow Tree* with book and lyrics by Harry B. Smith, received mixed reviews.[90] A reviewer of the Boston production at the Wilbur Theatre in June 1927 pointed to similarities with *Madama Butterfly* and stated that the music "is far above the commonplaces of our theatre, and you cannot but conjure up no less a name than Sir Arthur Sullivan." However, the New York critical response suggests that, by 1927, theatrical *japonisme* and *The Willow Tree* itself were considered rather old hat. Writing in the *New York Herald Tribune* (30 March 1927), Arthur Ruhl reveals that the belatedness of this work was indirectly signaled even in its opening number:

> . . . their opening chorus was a noisy song about "the new Japan, which had lost its Oriental charm," and in which the temple bells still ring "but play only jazz." Having drummed this point in, with all the strength of the large orchestra and the well developed lungs of the double-sized chorus, it was a bit hard to go back the next minute and try to pick up the sentimental tone of "The Willow Tree."

The reviewer for the *New York Times* (29 March 1927) compared Romberg's musical *japonisme* unfavorably with previous landmarks:

> Musically, "Cherry Blossoms" suffers from the effort to blend the "song hit" limitations of style to some desultory rambles in Oriental motifs. These latter are achieved by the usual handy use of dissonances, muted cornets and banging of gongs, with phrases strangely suggestive of Puccini's masterpiece and of "The Mikado." All this is rather shoddy and unnecessary in view of the experiments that have been made to give a more exotic flavor to the performance, through the use of a chorus stationed in the orchestra [in Japanese costume] and of chroniclers who record the action which separates the several acts.

Such experimental attempts to surpass the exotic authenticity of *The Willow Tree* itself also included hiring Michio Ito to choreograph the dances, decorating the lobby with Japanese lanterns, and having the ushers dress in Japanese costume.

Despite the work's mixed critical reception, Romberg's eminence ensured that multiple songs from the musical circulated widely. The play itself had already inspired several songs published between 1917 and 1922, including "My Princess of the Willow Tree" and "Japanese Willow (The Legend of the Bride)." Works such as the 1920 "Oriental Operetta" *Yo-San* might have been referring to Belasco's *The Darling of the Gods*. Following Romberg's 1927 operetta, songs featuring the name Yo-San could have been inspired by either work, given that this is the name of the Japanese woman in both works. In fact, in the collection of songs and shows considered here, the ideal Japanese woman is just as likely to be named Yo-San as she is Butterfly/Cho-Cho-San. In both cases, she seals her ideal feminine status through self-sacrifice.

The longevity of *The Willow Tree: A Japanese Fantasy in Three Acts* in its multiple manifestations can be credited to the fact that this work presented the most cherished fantasy of American *japonisme* in a particularly direct form. In this Pygmalion-esque tale based on a Japanese legend, a wooden sculpture of an ideal woman—named "The Image" in the play—comes to life and marries the man who has willed her into existence.[91] The twist in the play is that her lover is a white male named Hamilton who is slowly turning Japanese himself (through diet, dress, home decor, etc.), to the annoyance of his white male friend. Music serves as one marker of the ideal exotic woman's absolute innocence and naiveté. In Act II we hear from offstage the song of an old street singer accompanying herself on the *shamisen*. The Image mistakes the sound for the song of a bird and is corrected by Hamilton. She then attempts to sing herself, making "a few unmusical attempts to imitate the singer" and Hamilton, like John Luther Long's Pinkerton in the Madame Butterfly tale, laughs at her. The old singer enters and performs on stage before the Image interrupts, seizing the *shamisen* and announcing that she will sing a song of youth, which she proceeds to do accompanied by a flute in the pit and, apparently, her own *shamisen* playing.

Later, Hamilton is visited in Japan by his British sweetheart Mary who, upon noticing the Image, again in her form as a sculpture, declares: "I know why you bought her. She looks like me. . . . That is, I could be like her." Hamilton becomes instantly enthused and responds: "I've always thought perhaps she was what you could be like if you only would. Mary, won't you be like her?" (p. 65). Here we have the most blunt statement of the white male heterosexual fantasy of having one's ideal of an exotic submissive woman transubstantiated into the form of a white woman, thereby avoiding miscegenation and safely reasserting one's masculinity—a fantasy replayed in numerous works in multiple genres throughout the following century, as we shall see. This message was underscored in the original 1917 productions by having the same white actresses play both Mary and (in brown or yellow face) the exotic Image.[92] In the end, like any good Japanese woman in American *japonisme*, the Image sacrifices herself by instructing a servant to chop down the magical willow tree, thereby ending her life and leading Hamilton to shed his Japanese trappings, reclaim his manhood, return to England to fight in World War I, and, presumably, to wed Mary who has likely absorbed the lessons of ideal womanhood through her sojourn in Japan. I note that the Irish writer Henry De Vere Stacpoole dedicated his 1918 novelization of the play to his own wife.[93]

Though works of musical *japonisme* typically express white heterosexual male fantasies, women also contributed substantially to the composition of Orientalist parlor and recital songs in the early twentieth century. By far the most popular example is the British composer Amy Woodforde-Finden's *Four Indian Love Lyrics* of 1901, and particularly her "Kashmiri Song."[94] Woodforde-Finden also published *Five Little Japanese Songs* in 1906, which likely inspired Americans to compose similar sets of songs that could be performed in a wide variety of venues. For example, the rather prominent American composer Kathleen Lockhart Manning (1890–1951) published *Japanese Ghost Songs* in 1924, possibly referring to the works of Hearn, at least in spirit, in the cycle's title. Though not drawing on Japanese music itself, Manning encouraged the pianist to approximate the sound of Japanese walking in sandaled feet in performances of her "The Maid of Mystery." The pianist is instructed to play in "half staccato fashion—like clicking foot-steps—and extremely light touch—but marked accents." Mary Turner Salter (1856–1938) offers a less well-known but intriguing example. She was the wife of Sumner Salter, the first director of music at Williams College, and lived in Williamstown, Massachusetts, starting in 1906. (Sumner Salter participated in a minor way in musical *japonisme* himself by arranging Clayton Thomas's "Japanese Love Song," concerning an affair between a girl on a fan and a boy on a tea packet, for female chorus in 1917.) Mary published a number of Japanese-inspired works, including the 1907 "Japanese Cradle-Song" with lyrics by the female Indian poet Sarojini Naidu, and the 1911 *From Old Japan: A Cycle of Songs*, setting the poems of Alfred H. Hyatt.[95] These texts pay homage to the two major landmarks of *japonisme* by referring to "three maidens in Japan" (an allusion to *The Mikado*) and to "Little Miss Butterfly." Salter's setting of "Three Maidens of Japan"—an odd text about these "un-wooed" maidens in their garden—is rather striking in its chromaticism, starting with a tritone and featuring some pentatonicism and melismatic "ah's" before concluding with stacked fifths and fourths.

One of the most peculiar cases of American musical *japonisme* is presented by Fay Foster (1886–1960) who was, allegedly, a descendant of Pocahontas, Stephen Foster, and President James Monroe.[96] Foster composed five operas, two on Chinese subjects, in addition to one of the more successful American war songs of World War I.[97] She also published at least six rather eccentric Japanese-themed works in 1917. Infused by martial and patriotic sentiments, Foster composed both "A Nipponese Sword Song" and "The Red Heart," the latter of which employs material from a Japanese march and features a drawing on the cover of a Japanese male resembling a *kabuki* actor in appearance. Some of her songs, including "The Honorable Chop-Sticks" and "The Shadow of the Bamboo Fence," draw on the works of Lafcadio Hearn for their texts. Her "Sunset in a Japanese Garden" is a programmatic piece for piano that aims to depict the following image: "Under the Cherry blossoms the Japanese maidens dreamily dance and sing." Specific spots in the score are labeled "they dance" or "they sing" presumably to assist the performer. Finally, Foster's "The Cruel Mother-in-Law (Humorous)" defies generic labels. This mini melodrama was fashioned by adapting "fragmentary translations by Lafcadio Hearn from the original Japanese." The work begins with spoken text over tremolo octave Es before introducing an odd vocal melody and echoing responses from a female trio. Foster also includes a dance section featuring nonsense text in this "humorous" work.

Some female American composers actively pursued exotic authenticity in their works of musical *japonisme*. Perhaps most striking are the songs of Gertrude Ross, a pianist, accompanist, and composer, active in California starting in 1898. In a note to her 1917 *Art Songs of Japan (Yamata Shirabe)*, Ross explained:

> My interest in the music of the Japanese was awakened when a little Japanese woman played for me on the samisen. The weirdness of this music founded on scales so entirely different from ours, impressed me with its unusual intervals and rhythms. The unresolved melodies, without our cadence, gives a sense of something so foreign to our occidental ears, that it is indeed an awakening.[98]

Ross related that she had transcribed the tunes for these six songs during this cross-cultural encounter in Los Angeles and that she employed *koto* melodies as well. (A drawing of a Japanese woman playing a *koto* appears on the cover.) The Japanese melodies are featured prominently in the songs, supported with conventional harmony, with the balance of the pieces consisting of diatonic material. The canonical *koto* piece "Rokudan" appears in "Slumber Song of Izumo," while in other songs, such as "Fuji," the Japanese material consists simply of such gestures as a descending pentatonic *yo* scale. The "Love-Lay Indited by the Mikado Temmu" features the standard four-sixteenths, two-eighths gesture discussed above along with multiple fragments of Japanese melodies. Ross praised Japanese poetry for "merely suggesting, and not weighing down with detail and elaboration" and thanked a certain Kenzo Kubota for help with the cultural notes and translations that appear with the songs. (One of the songs is based on translations by Lafcadio Hearn.) Ross further displays her expertise by providing the Japanese melodic source material, encouraging performers to sing a couple of the songs in Japanese, and referring to the cycle as "this little group of uta [song]."[99]

Female performers and male composers frequently collaborated in this period—increasingly with the assistance of "native" informants—in an attempt to achieve exotic authenticity. The most active such performer was likely the French-Canadian mezzo-soprano Eva Gauthier (1885-1958).[100] Gauthier had a significant presence in the United States, concertizing in New York City starting in 1914 and performing a wide repertoire that included the North American premiere of Stravinsky's *Three Japanese Lyrics*, popular works by Gershwin, and Indonesian songs (often in native costume). Gauthier traveled widely throughout Asia, collecting Javanese folk songs in Indonesia and providing them to composers with the aim of performing the resulting works herself.[101] She also collected folk melodies in Japan, which the New York composer Charles Tomlinson Griffes used in such works from 1916–1918 as *Sho-jo* and *Sakura-Sakura*.[102] Griffes collaborated directly with the choreographer Michio Ito on several theatrical works and encountered the Japanese composer Kosaku Yamada in New York.[103] Japan proved the most significant source of exotic influence for Griffes but not, apparently, for Gauthier. A lengthy press release promoting her recitals explained that Gauthier was engaged in a musical quest, searching the globe for a "strange melody—her song supernal." She had searched throughout the East, aiming "to have gone where no white woman had ever been before her," including in Japan, "but that which she sought she could not find. It is somewhere in the beyond."[104]

In her vast repertoire of musical exoticism, Gauthier included songs composed by Charles Wakefield Cadman based on Native American tunes.[105] Cadman, one of the most prominent American composers in the early twentieth century, is primarily known as an "Indianist."[106] However, he also composed several works "founded upon Japanese melodies" in collaboration with the lyricist and librettist Nelle Richmond Eberhart (1871–1944), which he frequently performed in prominent venues across the country with the soprano Alice Nielsen between 1910 and 1913. Eberhart had helped to introduce Cadman to Native American music. In his bid for exotic authenticity in *japonisme*, Cadman benefited from his association with Tomijiro Asai, a Japanese immigrant and tenor active in New York. Asai is credited with translating the lyrics in *Two Little Songs from Japan*.[107] Cadman and Eberhart's 1910 song cycle *Sayōnara: A Japanese Romance* is one of the more significant works in this early period of American musical *japonisme*. Nielsen and Cadman performed the songs in such venues as Carnegie Hall in New York and Pittsburgh's Carnegie Music Hall. The New York Philharmonic Orchestra performed two of the songs from the cycle in 1911–1912 and they were featured by the Metropolitan Opera soprano Jeanne Jomelli.[108] *Sayonara* is a dramatic cycle consisting of a prelude and four songs with an "Argument" or preface that lays out the basic story of the meeting of two Japanese lovers, the blossoming of their love affair, and their inevitable tragic separation. A note in the score suggests that "for certain occasions the duet would be effective given in costume."

It is not immediately evident how each movement was "founded upon Japanese melodies," as proclaimed in the score. The Japanese *in* scale is prominent in the prelude as are planing chords in the style of Debussy and stacked fourth and fifth intervals. A rather slight suggestion of the "Miya sama" opening gesture is heard in the transition to the second song. The *in* scale appears in other movements as well and recurring themes unify the work. The penultimate song, "All My Heart Is Ashes," is the most striking and seems most closely based on a Japanese tune in its repeated descending line. Cadman clearly viewed *Sayonara* and his other Japanese-inspired works as being in the same vein as his Native American pieces. In an 18 May 1912 letter to Eberhart, Cadman referred to his *Two Little Songs from Japan* as follows:

> You see Davison just had dedicated Two Little Japanese Songs which a fellow named Tomijiro Asai and myself did a few months ago. They are similar in treatment to the Indian songs but of course more popular in style and simpler because the melodies themselves which the Jap [sic] gave me were simple.[109]

These two songs, "Harvest Song" and "Love Song," were "founded upon genuine themes" and "harmonized and idealized" by Cadman. The songs are brief and repetitive, as though to suggest that the composer has attempted to present these samples of Japanese music in the most direct manner possible while leaving out the "strummings and squealings" that so offended Americans encountering Japanese music in the raw.

In his 1900 overview of "famous American composers," Rupert Hughes predicted that Japanese music would have a significant influence on American music in the new century:

> The influence of Japanese and Chinese art upon our world of decoration has long been realized. After considering the amount of interest shown in the Celestial [i.e., Chinese] music by American composers, one is tempted to prophesy a decided influence in this line, and a considerable spread of Japanese influence in the world of music also. Japanese music has a decorative effect that is sometimes almost as captivating as in painting.[110]

Hughes's prediction appears in a chapter entitled "The Innovators" in a discussion of the work of N. Clifford Page (1866–1956), whom Hughes considered to be one of America's leading composers, but whose work, unlike that of Cadman's, is now nearly entirely unknown. Page was born in San Francisco and was a student of Edgar Stillman Kelley, a significant figure in American musical Orientalism who had studied Chinese music in San Francisco and composed *Aladdin*, a high-profile suite for orchestra influenced by Chinese music and premiered in 1894.[111] A great deal of Page's own career was devoted to musical Orientalism, in both popular and more elevated genres. His first opera included scenes set in Morocco[112] and he also published the songs "A Romance in Porcelain: A Japanese Ditty" (1892) and "The Girl with the Bamboo Legs: A Japanese Oddity" (1902).[113] Page came closest to achieving lasting fame by providing the incidental music for the 1903 theatrical version of Onoto Watanna's (Winnifred Eaton) 1901 novel *A Japanese Nightingale*, a play that competed directly with Belasco's *Madame Butterfly* and, alas for Page, lost in the court of popular opinion.[114] Hughes reports that Page had successfully achieved exotic authenticity in his incidental music for Chester Bailey Fernald's *Moonlight Blossom*, "a play based upon Japanese life" produced in London in 1898. According to Hughes, the "overture was written entirely on actual Japanese themes, including the national anthem of Japan" and Page employed "two Japanese drums, a whistle used by a Japanese shampooer, and a Japanese guitar." Prefiguring Harry Partch, Page had even adapted a "Japanese fiddle" with a violin fingerboard but had needed to substitute a mandolin for this part in the end. Page's success in creating Japanese music is particularly celebrated by Hughes: "The fidelity of the music is proved by the fact that Sir Edwin Arnold's Japanese wife recognized the various airs and was carried away by the national anthem."[115]

Extensive emulation of an exotic culture's music by an American composer might ultimately call into question what constitutes musical Americanness itself. Such questions assume a particular urgency during wartime. Some fifteen years after Hughes's celebration of this composer, Page, and his librettist Frederick

H. Martens,[116] dramatized the question of national musical identity in their *Contest of the Nations*, an "Operetta with Dances" published in Boston in 1915. An ad for the piece proclaimed its success in encouraging "Americanization" during wartime and cited a review claiming that 8,000 had attended one performance.[117] In this operetta, allegorical characters representing various nations vie for cultural supremacy through music. Spoiler alert: the work ends with the United States triumphant in the musical contest, with all the other nations having served to define America through contrast. A clear preference is expressed for the music of one particular exotic nation at the expense of another. A Chinese man attempts to make acquaintance with the ladies, but they find him strange. His later appearance is marked by the sound of gongs and the international throng asks him to keep it short. He speaks in standard pidgin and then sings "Mo Li Hua," the most famous Chinese folksong, in a "'sing-song' style, semi-falsetto." His contribution is not enthusiastically received. In contrast, Japan is represented by O-me-san, a woman who "toddles forward, bows Japanese fashion." Her song is labeled "Hime Matsu" and "Japanese koto melody" in the score and she sings in Japanese. Page calls for a "crisp touch like picking strings" in the score and employs parallel octaves and the *in* scale. Lady Utopia declares: "This gentle maid has charmed us all. We'd like to hear her song again." The operetta concludes with the appearance of Miss Columbia accompanied by "American Indian, Puritan, Continental Soldier, Quakeress, Arkansaw Traveler, Country Fiddler, Farmer Folk, Dixie Girl"—a list of American types that is conspicuous for its omission of certain ethnic and racial groups. Each of Miss Columbia's companions receives a musical turn and is formally presented. For example, the American Indian is marked by a low octave tattoo, the Puritan gets a hymn, and the Continental Soldier is heralded by "Yankee Doodle." At this culmination of the competition, "American" is defined through music, dance, costume, and lyrics as not including African or Asian Americans. (The "Dixie Girl" is not marked as "black" by costume or through any other stereotypical means.) Not surprisingly, "O Columbia! The Gem of the Ocean" features prominently. Columbia, of course, wins this musical contest of nations and all join in for a concluding "Star-Spangled Banner."

* * *

Throughout the period considered in this chapter, American composers and performers assumed "Japanese" voices in numerous comic songs, tragic cantatas, and eccentric operettas. By appropriating Japanese melodies, American composers appeared to dress up their music as Japanese, at least momentarily. This cross-cultural masquerade, playacting, or ventriloquism was most often inspired by a professed admiration for certain aspects of Japanese culture, however imaginary or exaggerated. Following President Theodore Roosevelt's lead, these musical works offered Americans the opportunity to feel "almost like a Japanese." Authenticity claims were made in the attempt to distinguish certain works within the general cacophony of musical *japonisme*. These composers, performers, and publishers appear to have operated under the assumption that creating Japanese music was entirely possible for a Euro-American and that American audiences would accept such works as exotic surrogates.

As we have seen, the possibility of "turning Japanese" was repeatedly treated comically throughout this corpus of popular song. Yet, in many of these works, we can hear traces of nervous laughter. What would become of "American" music if composers indulged too extensively in musical *japonisme*? Was it possible to experience the feeling of being "almost like a Japanese" while retaining one's white, American identity? What would it feel like to cross over all the way? One song from 1926, "If I Were Japanese," posed this very question. Appearing near the end of the period considered here, the song remains squarely within Tin Pan Alley's framework for representing Japan. The expressive marking "quaintly" appears in the score and "quaint" is heard in the lyrics to describe the exotic land of "fair Japan." The protagonist expresses a keen fascination with Japanese domestic architecture. The song ends with the speaker, and, presumably, us, musing on what it would feel like to be Japanese. The title line, "if I were Japanese," is repeated three times, first with a poco ritardando, then a più rallentando. Finally, the phrase is delivered sotto voce and quasi parlando, as though the speaker is mulling over what this would mean, imagining their way into an exotic existence. In this last statement, the vocal line is a dissonant second away from the piano and is marked "morendo" (dying), with a final, wistful third scale degree in the voice. This musical ending suggests that the possibility of becoming Japanese is enticing, unclear, and somewhat unsettling. We will discover in the next chapter that those American composers seeking a "modernist" status in the first half of the twentieth century repeatedly pursued direct encounters with Japanese music while attempting to achieve exotic authenticity and to distinguish their work from earlier strains of musical *japonisme*.

3

Japonisme and the Forging of American Musical Modernism

Late nineteenth-century Euro-American encounters with Japan not only inspired a widespread fascination for all things Japanese, they also served as a primary stimulus for the development of modernist aesthetics in many fields including painting, poetry, architecture, theater, dance, and (eventually) music. The Imagist poetry of Ezra Pound and Amy Lowell, the designs of Frank Lloyd Wright, the experimental theater of W. B. Yeats, dances by Ruth St. Denis and Martha Graham, the paintings of the Impressionists and Post-impressionists—all were fundamentally shaped by either direct or imagined contact with Japanese arts.[1] Like popular *japonisme*, modernist interest in Japanese culture closely tracked political developments. This is quite clear, for instance, in a 1915 statement by the arch modernist Japanophile Ezra Pound. In this document, Pound defended his Imagist style of poetry by pointing to the power of the image in Japanese drama: "The European thinks by 'ideas,' the Jap by 'images.'" For Pound, the exotic model provided a justification for his modernist breach with Euro-American poetic conventions. Pound suggested that such artistic cross-cultural engagements might lead to forms of cross-cultural understanding with positive political ramifications. Referring to geopolitical alignments at the time of World War I, he stated: "If we are in for a Japanese alliance we may as well use whatever means we have of trying to understand the Japanese mind. I do not imagine that we shall succeed, but the arts are the only peace-makers, and they survive any number of conquests."[2] From his vantage point in the poetic avant-garde, Pound predicted that Western audiences would eventually catch up aesthetically and embrace Japanese-influenced modernism and, perhaps, Japanese drama itself: "I do not expect to see Noh satisfactorily performed in Europe for another forty years, but I think there may sometime be an audience, even in the west, which will dispense with the sheer mechanics of plot as cheerfully as our poets now dispense with the rigid elaboration of the canzone."[3]

The widespread influence of *japonisme* on European art in the late nineteenth and early twentieth centuries eventually did receive a great deal of attention in major exhibitions and publications in the late twentieth century. However, though many art lovers are now well aware of the profound impact of Japanese prints on the work of Van Gogh, for example, far fewer are likely to think of Japanese influence on such celebrated American painters as Georgia O'Keeffe. Arthur Wesley Dow, O'Keeffe's teacher and a major figure in art pedagogy, had spent three months in Japan in 1903 and through his writings, teaching, and art served as a vital intermediary between Japanese stylistic features and the development of American painting.[4] In hindsight, it is clear that in several artistic fields, figures such as Dow served in the early twentieth century to translate Japanese aesthetics for their better-known modernist successors. The influence of *japonisme* and Japanese music on comparable figures in American musical modernism has received even less attention.

The role of *japonisme* in the formation of American artistic modernism may appear somewhat paradoxical given the fact that some Victorians initially turned toward Japan as an antidote to the ills of industrialized modern life. Edward Sylvester Morse, for example, celebrated the pre-industrial attention to detail and craftsmanship in the construction of Japanese homes. The American Arts and Crafts movement in particular was spurred by an *anti*modernist appreciation for Japanese culture. As T. J. Jackson Lears put it: "Antimodern dissenters . . . groped for alternatives in medieval, Oriental, and other 'primitive' cultures."[5] However, the aesthetics of artistic modernism did not necessarily require a celebration of the modern world. Turning toward exotic sources valued for their antiquity and as alternative models to nineteenth-century genres, aesthetics, and artistic techniques was common modernist practice across the arts. Elite American writers consistently lamented the "passing of Old Japan" and the Westernization they observed in Japanese arts—thereby betraying their fear of losing the exotic model. Yet, many of these writers called for the Westernization of Japanese music. In surveying American *japonisme* it appears that Americans were attracted to nearly all aspects of Japanese culture, save its music. However, the early negative American reaction toward Japanese music in turn marked this music as an ideal model for those twentieth-century composers eager to break away from European conventions and Gilded Age aesthetics. Representing the cultural antipode in the American imagination, Japanese models proved particularly irresistible to those engaged in the making of modernism.

Schoenberg's Nightmare Coming True

It seems a nightmare to imagine what might have become of music if Japan had succeeded in conquering America, England and finally Germany. The Japanese idea of music has no resemblance to ours. Their scales are not based on a harmonic concept, or, if so, at least it is not ours. Friends of Eastern Asiatic music claim that this monodic music is capable of such variety as to express every nuance of human feeling. This may be true, but to the Western ear it sounds—ah—different. If it is not completely impossible to add a harmonic accompaniment to melodies of this kind, it is certainly impossible to derive it logically or naturally from these scales. For this reason alone it seems they would rather destroy our music than comply with its conditions.[6]

This statement, made by Arnold Schoenberg in 1947, calls out for comment. In this essay, he chided those who rely on folk music in their compositions and banished them from the realm of "real composers." In doing so, he reveals a fascinating conception of what constitutes "our music." Schoenberg proceeds as though in the recent war a united and homogenized Anglo-Germanic culture had been threatened by an Asiatic menace, suggesting an underlying Western bond that transcended any recent political difficulties. By pointing to Japanese music as a potentially dangerous influence, Schoenberg was able to place his own music within the sanctuary of a Euro-American *Heimat*. He erroneously assumed that a singular "idea of music" exists in Japan and that it is mutually exclusive with a monolithic Western "idea of music." As a Jewish refugee in the United States, and as a composer who had repeatedly faced critical rejection, perhaps the alienated Schoenberg needed to live by such fictions.[7] It is less easy to account for the fundamental musical assumptions revealed here. Why would Schoenberg, a composer who had famously extended the "conditions" of the common practice period, take for granted the need to add harmonic accompaniments to exotic material? Ignoring, for a moment, the unstable foundations of his assertions, Schoenberg's nightmare actually suggests an ideal status for Japanese music as source material for those European and American composers aiming to reinvent "our music" and in need of an exotic model. Japanese music, either directly experienced or imagined, served in this capacity throughout much of the twentieth century for composers negotiating a wide variety of routes to the "ultra-modern," a territory that Schoenberg had himself done so much to map.

Perhaps Schoenberg intuited that Japanese music and aesthetics offered models for rival versions of musical modernism. In the first half of the twentieth century, numerous European composers responded to Japan and Japanese music in a wide range of styles, though rarely in forms that suggested direct Japanese musical influence. Some scholars have heard the impact of *japonisme* on works by French Impressionists. Robert F. Waters, for example, even suggested that some of Debussy's chords approximated *sho* clusters.[8] Jessica E. Stankis has argued that Japanese art profoundly shaped the music of Ravel.[9] In 1947 Schoenberg might even have recalled specific works (or their titles) that had embraced or signaled Japanese culture, such as Stravinsky's *Three Japanese Lyrics* and Orff's opera *Gisei—Das Opfer*, both from 1913,[10] or the 1924 *Improvisation on a Japanese Tune* by the violin virtuoso Efrem Zimbalist, or Delage's *Sept Haikai* and Holst's *Japanese Suite* (based on tunes provided by Michio Ito), both from 1925, or Shostakovich's *Six Romances on Texts by Japanese Poets* (1928–1932), or Roberto Gerhard's *7 Haiku*, composed in 1922 (rev. 1958) just before he became a student of Schoenberg's, or even the more recent 1940 *Japanese Festival Music* by Richard Strauss, featuring such section titles as "Cherry Blossom Festival" and "Attack of the Samurai," though betraying little sense of Japanese style.

Box 3.1 Chronology: Henry Eichheim (1870–1942) and Japan

1906   *Gleanings from Buddha Fields: Poem for Piano*
1912   Retired from the Boston Symphony Orchestra
1915   First trip to East Asia
1918–1920   *Oriental Sketches* (piano): *Japanese Sketch* 1918, *Japanese Nocturne* 1920
1919–1920   Second trip to East Asia
1921   *Oriental Impressions* (chamber orch.), performed at Coolidge's Berkshire Festival: *Japanese Sketch, Japanese Nocturne*, and *Entenraku* [sic]
1922   Third trip to East Asia
1922   Premiere of *Oriental Impressions* by Boston Symphony Orchestra, followed by performances by the Chicago, Cleveland, Philadelphia, London, and Los Angeles orchestras
1923   Stokowski and Philadelphia Orchestra tour *Japanese Nocturne*
1924   *The Rivals* (ballet)
1927–1928   Fourth trip to East Asia
1928   Studied Japanese music with Hisao Tanabe
1929   Stokowski records *Japanese Nocturne*
1937   Final trip to East Asia

Schoenberg's musical xenophobia, of course, represented but one branch of musical thought in midcentury America. Henry Cowell (1897–1965) was instrumental in promoting the contra-Schoenbergian position on the world's musical resources.[11] Although far less well known, Henry Eichheim (1870–1942) was also committed to exploring exotic musics and was one of the first American composers to pursue Asian music studies. Japanese music proved pivotal as these two composers set out to break with the "conditions" of Euro-American art music and to forge new forms of musical modernism.[12] Both composers also sought to distinguish their Japanese-inspired works from those of such predecessors as Cadman, Griffes, and Whithorne. (Refer to Box 3.1 and 3.2 for timelines of Eichheim's and Cowell's interactions with Japanese music.) Eichheim and Cowell were far from alone in their interest in Japan. The influence of Japan was particularly widespread in works of American composers between 1910 and 1935 and, as we shall see in chapter 8, again between 1955 and 1970, with significant reverberations in recent decades. Encounters with Japanese music have ranged from domestic perusal of transcribed melodies to long-term study of a specific genre and performance tradition within Japan. Elements of this influence appeared in a variety of forms, including: a new conception of silence in music; a wider exploration of timbre and subtle pitch bending; the use of pitch clusters; a new expressive range in vocal music;

Box 3.2 Chronology: Henry Cowell (1897–1965) and Japan

1911   *Adventures in Harmony*, section titled *Oriental*

1913   *Music for Creation Dawn*, poetic drama by Takeshi Kanno

1915   *Red Silence*, poetic Japanese drama

1924   *Snows of Fujiyama* (piano duo)

1927   Cowell performs in percussion section for Eichheim's *The Rivals* (includes Eichheim's *Entenraku*)

1932   Teaches course at the New School for Social Research, includes Japanese music with demonstrations by Soichi Ichikawa

1934   Meets Kitaro Tamada

1935   Attends Japanese festival in San Francisco, hears *sankyoku*

1936–1940   In San Quentin prison, studies *shakuhachi*

1946   *The Universal Flute* (*shakuhachi*)

1957   In Japan two months, sponsored by Rockefeller Foundation and State Department

1957   *Ongaku*, recorded by Robert Whitney and Louisville Orchestra in 1959

1959   *Characters*, including "The Mysterious Oriental"

1961   Attends Tokyo East-West Music Encounter Conference

1961   *Koto Duet; Family Rondo*

1961/1963   *Music from a Visit to a Japanese School*

1962   Concerto [no. 1] for Koto and Orchestra

1962   Concerto for Harmonica and Orchestra

1964   Stokowski, Eto, and the Philadelphia Orchestra premiere Concerto [no. 1] for Koto and Orchestra

1965   Concerto no. 2 for Koto and Orchestra

---

abandonment of bar lines and strict synchronization between parts; heterophony; and, of course, an emphasis on pentatonic melodies. Japanese music was clearly not the sole source of inspiration for these musical features but instead tended to reinforce existing compositional predilections. Motivations for encountering Japanese music varied widely as did the sites and contexts of encounter.

The critical reputations of Eichheim and Cowell and of their respective cross-cultural endeavors are quite divergent. Eichheim, when remembered at all, tends to be dismissed as a Romantic Orientalist who, in his limited body of works, deployed tunes heard during his sojourns abroad. He is occasionally acknowledged in surveys of twentieth-century American music as perhaps the first American composer to travel extensively in Asia, but his music has attracted very little scholarly discussion. Cowell, by contrast, is most often celebrated as an incredibly prolific composer and serious student of the world's music, an artist whose works and musical philosophy foreshadowed later "postcolonial" engagements with other cultures. Juxtaposing these two composers might seem a forced, or even perverse, critical gambit. But by comparing their Japanese experiences I do not seek to reverse their current positions. Rather, I hope to offer a more nuanced account of their similarities and differences and, by doing so, to demonstrate that categorical critical approaches to cross-cultural composers consistently fall short. I aim to question the standard criteria and assumptions that continue to be employed when we analyze and critique cross-cultural compositions and that shape (and often limit) our experience of such works. Experimentation and abstraction tend to be valued over quotation and imitation and extended engagement over brief encounter; labels such as "appropriation" and "influence," and "modernist" and "postmodernist" appear to be assigned with confidence. The application of these labels, of course, plays a large role in determining the repertoire that we are likely to hear. Evaluations often proceed as though some ideal form of cross-cultural interaction is available as a standard, despite the fact that every musical engagement with another culture has been delimited by both personal motivations and broader social factors as well as by current conceptions of compositional prowess. I find that justification for employing such evaluative criteria is rather shaky and that individual works, composers, performers, critics, and audiences show the nature of musical exoticism to be contradictory and multifaceted.

The influences and representations of Japan and of Japanese music in Eichheim's and Cowell's works and their concomitant actual and imagined encounters with this exotic culture can be traced in their compositions, lectures, articles, photographs, and correspondence. Their histories of engagement with Japan offer particularly rich case studies for reconsidering our common approaches to cross-cultural works. Juxtaposing the musical journeys of these two composers and proselytizers also allows us to trace the developments and recapitulations of cross-cultural influence and Orientalist attitudes in the United States throughout much of the twentieth century and prompts us to question the persistent temporal, geographic, genre, and high/low boundaries we typically employ in modernist taxonomy. Following Cowell's career, in particular, will offer one focused perspective on a time period investigated more extensively in chapters 4 through 8. Despite the clear differences between these two composers and the radical changes in the American musical landscape throughout the century, I find strands of continuity in their attempts to compose American cross-cultural and "universal" music. I will first turn to the impact of literary *japonisme* and travel on Eichheim's Japanese-inspired pieces and will consider his aesthetic and didactic motivations. I will then chronicle Cowell's encounters with Japanese music throughout his life—deliberately emphasizing his similarities with Eichheim—and will discuss his mature works in the context of Cold War cultural politics. Although my approach is clearly composer- and concert hall–centric, the histories of Eichheim and Cowell recounted in this chapter show how crucial specific audiences and performers were to the staging of cross-cultural events. They lead us, moreover, to alternative performance sites and sources and elucidate some unexpected parallels in other art forms and branches of American music.

Henry Eichheim and Japan: Gleanings
from Buddha Fields

It might seem unlikely that a "Friend of Eastern Asiatic music" obsessed with collecting those scales and melodies that so worried Schoenberg—not to mention the exotic instruments that played them—could be considered a viable protagonist for a novel and movie, and yet the titular character in Samuel Merwin's 1914 *Anthony the Absolute* is just that.[13] The fictional Anthony Eckhart is an American comparative musicologist who, while on a research trip to Japan and China, falls in love with a white American opera singer after hearing her voice on the other side of his hotel room door. He is aroused by her ability to sing microtonal scales and he records her using the same wax cylinders that store his exotic finds. Exactly like Béla Bartók in Biskra, Algeria, in 1913, Anthony is determined to collect only the most "pure" music and decides to record the singing of Japanese prostitutes (pp. 25–26), planning ultimately to send his specimens to "von Stumbostel" (i.e., Erich M. von Hornbostel) in Berlin. In his "scientific" studies he sounds very much like a member of the New York Musicological Society of the early 1930s, and in his impassioned attacks on the evils of equal temperament and his celebration of ancient Greek and Asian intonation systems he prefigures Harry Partch and Lou Harrison (pp. 9–11).[14] Anthony becomes disillusioned with Japan when he discovers that two of the prostitute's songs are in equal temperament. Declaring that Japan has been spoiled musically by the West (pp. 28–29), he decides to "push on to China, where the ancient music may still be caught in its pure form, uncorrupted and unconfused by the modern touch. For my purposes, time spent in Japan would be wasted" (pp. 35–36). In creating his fictional comparative musicologist, Merwin evidently did his homework. And yet it almost seems as though his true models appear only later in American music history. Henry Eichheim was almost an exact contemporary of the fictional Anthony, but he did not set sail for Asia until the year after Merwin's novel was published. In his pursuit and celebration of Asian melodies and instruments, Eichheim embodied a good deal of Anthony's scholarly approach. Yet, Eichheim's engagements with East Asia were also inspired by a poetic sensibility entirely absent in the character of the fictional musical scientist.

Following twenty-one years as a violinist in the Boston Symphony Orchestra, Eichheim retired in 1912 to devote himself to composition and travel. During his second trip to East Asia in 1920, Eichheim declared that Japan "has a mysterious charm, a poetry no other country seems to possess for me."[15] The "poetry" of Old Japan was a feature consistently celebrated by proponents of American *japonisme*. To *fin-de-siècle* Euro-Americans, Japan was a Baudelairean "forest of symbols" (or, better, a Barthean "empire of signs") just waiting to be interpreted by master

Japanophiles for an eager general audience back home. Eichheim, directly inspired by late nineteenth-century publications on Japan, journeyed to Japan and other East Asian nations repeatedly between 1915 and 1937 and approached these trips as a collector, amassing an impressive set of musical instruments (now housed at the University of California, Santa Barbara), taking numerous photographs of performers (which he exhibited and published back in the States), and transcribing over two thousand tunes.[16] His abilities as a cross-cultural interpreter were proclaimed repeatedly in the press: "To [Eichheim] the Orient has been less an exotic and curious panorama, a medley of strange sights and sounds, than a land rich in meaning, charged with poetry."[17] However, Eichheim's own poetic vision of Japan was formed well before he first traveled to the "land of [his] dreams" in 1915. His knowledge of Japan's mysterious meanings was acquired secondhand, gleaned from extensive readings in popular studies of Japanese culture. Eichheim was particularly entranced by the writings of the unparalleled Japanophile Lafcadio Hearn.[18]

Hearn's influence on Eichheim was profound and is but one example of the substantial impact of literary *japonisme* on musical *japonisme* in the early twentieth century. In 1920 Eichheim explained that "the aspect I like best of this beautiful country can only be described by a poet like Hearn, the power and vigor is not as sympathetic to me as the mystery—the soft lights—mist, fantastic angles, color. Contradictions abound here."[19] Indeed. Eichheim apparently realized that 1920s Japan did not perfectly reflect Hearn's visions. He could not ignore the signs of Japan's vigorous modernization, and yet he admits to seeking out and enjoying only those features of Japanese culture that he had been taught to cherish by Hearn.

Eichheim's first musical response to Japan, the 1906 *Gleanings from Buddha Fields: Poem for Piano*, takes its title from a work by Hearn published in 1897.[20] At the end of his manuscript score, Eichheim copied the following from Hearn: "Religion, indeed, is everywhere in Japan associated with landscapes, cascades, peaks, rocks, islands; with the best places from which to view the blossoming of flowers, the reflection of the Autumn moon in water, or the sparkling of fireflies on Summer nights." This notion of a pervasive spirituality in the exotic nation manifests itself in the work's seemingly unending musical flow; or, at least, that is the only perceptible connection either to Hearn's writings or to Japan and its music in this early composition. However, Eichheim's subsequent Japanese-inspired pieces suggest that Hearn not only provided the composer with a ready-made set of impressions of Japan, but also determined Eichheim's approach to Japanese music and directly shaped his compositional responses.

To glean is to gather bit by bit things left behind by others. One of Hearn's main objectives in *Gleanings from Buddha-Fields* was to celebrate the "divine art of creating the beautiful out of nothing" in Japanese culture.[21] In his multiple discussions of Japanese music, Hearn focused on ephemeral forms that he felt most others would ignore. In a chapter entitled "Out of the Street," Hearn praised the "vulgar songs" of daily life in Japan. He described their "long, queer, plaintive modulations" and how the songs were "characterized by the greatest possible simplicity, directness, and sincerity. The real art of them, in short, is their absolute artlessness. That was why I wanted them."[22] Hearn was also capable of waxing mystical on the sounds of Japan:

> In the boom of the big bell there is a quaintness of tone which wakens feelings, so strangely far away from all the nineteenth-century part of me, that the faint blind stirrings of them make me afraid,—deliciously afraid. Never do I hear that billowing peal but I become aware of a striving and a fluttering in the abyssal part of my ghost,—a sensation as of memories struggling to reach the light beyond the obscuration of a million million deaths and births.[23]

For Hearn, the ineffability of Japanese music, its utter foreignness, was precisely its appeal. I will note Eichheim's musical attempts to match Hearn's mysticism and to represent the sound of this big bell below.

Hearn repeatedly lamented his inability to capture and describe the "weird" songs of Japan. In a letter to the prominent Japanologist Basil Hall Chamberlain, Hearn wrote "Happy, happy, thrice happy the traveler who is able to write music by ear. Oh, if I could only give you musical copies of the extraordinary peasant songs I have heard,—strange, melancholy, penetrating things, that seemed to be of the earth, of the land,—the cry of the ancient soil itself, or of its ancient soul!"[24] Clearly, Hearn's appreciation of Japanese music was framed within a primitivist imagination.

Such paeans to the musical minutiae of Japan were not lost on Eichheim, a traveler particularly adept at collecting these treasures. Like Hearn's, Eichheim's ultimate goal was to present these exotic cultural artifacts to American audiences. Writing from Japan to his important patron, Elizabeth Sprague Coolidge, Eichheim is explicit: "We hope to hear some of the music that will be used at the coronation of the Japanese Emperor and as this is chiefly for small orchestra I hope to find some priceless old imperial music that I may use in a piece I hope I may write for you."[25] In addressing her as "Lady Coolidge" in this hopeful letter, Eichheim appears to be assuming the role of an imperial explorer in the age of discovery, or perhaps is serving as her art buyer, playing the part of a musical Bernard Berenson to her Isabella Stewart Gardner.

Eichheim gained a wide experience of Japanese traditional music, theater, and dance and enjoyed most all of it. In 1927 he stated:

> I like the Japanese No dramas and also koto, shakuhachi and biwa music . . . and I take interest even in the simple flute played by Japanese masseurs wandering the streets on a cold night. I wanted to incorporate those pathetic notes in Western music, and for this purpose composed a "Japanese Nocturn." . . . I should like to devote myself to the study of Oriental music, and will make a study of Japanese music next year under Mr. Hisao Tanabe.[26]

His repeated praise of *noh* is not exceptional in the context of Euro-American modernism. Numerous modernist composers, dramatists, and choreographers would have agreed with his statement that the "mixture of play and music in the 'Noh' theatre seems to me to be better than anything the white races have evolved."[27] For example, Ruth St. Denis, often referred to (along with Isadora Duncan) as a founding mother of modern dance in the United States and a near contemporary of Eichheim's, created a Japanese dance-drama featuring Japanese dialogue and performers entitled *O-Mika* in 1913 based on a tale by Hearn and with music by Robert H. Bowers.[28] In June 1927 she created a "Japanese Dance" that, based on my reading of her choreographic notes, was inspired by *noh*, which she had witnessed during a trip to Japan.[29] Finally, in 1935 St. Denis referred to creating a sketch for an "Easter pageant" based on *noh* and stated that she had "said to my students for years, if you will learn Japanese dancing every other thing you do will be better done."[30] Japanese dance proved significant to the further development of American modern dance. Martha Graham's interest in Japanese aesthetics was most obviously manifested in her long-term collaborations with Isamu Noguchi, who served as her set designer. In addition, one of her principal dancers, Yuriko, was a Japanese American who had pursued dance training in Japan and who was interned during World War II. Although modernist devotion to *noh* theater was widespread, Eichheim's general declaration that the "music of Japan, like the other arts of this strange and wonderful country, is a source of constant delight to the musician" is striking given the general Euro-American negative response to Japanese music in this period.[31]

In addition to offering a "mysterious charm," Eichheim felt that Japanese music could help direct Euro-American art music out of what he perceived to be its late-Romantic impasse. In 1923, Eichheim complained that he could no longer work with the "stiff and antiquated patterns" of European forms, and prophesied that the music of the Orient "will make our music ever more free and flexible in expression."[32] He also claimed in 1928 that "the future of European music can be enhanced and enriched by the finer sense of line and proportion and greater rhythmic scope of some of the music of the Orient."[33] More immediately, he hoped that his own study of Asian music would help to separate his music from the conservative strand of current American composition. Writing to Carl Engel, Eichheim enthused:

> Church festivals are fertile fields for strange sights and sounds, crowded streets, costumes and floats always designed from traditional subjects, and the rhythms of drums, O' My! how you would enjoy these broken China effects that make the wildest ragtime sound like the safe and respectable 4-4 so dear to the heart of Arthur Foote and sworn to by those arch anarchs Kneisel and Zach.[34]

Clearly, Eichheim was boasting in such statements of his unwillingness to "comply with [the] conditions" of Western music.

Gleanings from Buddha Fields acknowledges Hearn's influence explicitly, yet Hearn's most significant impact on Eichheim appeared later in the composer's

Oriental Sketches for piano (1918–1920). Eichheim's reputation as a composer rests in large part on this set of short pieces, each inspired by his travels to a specific East Asian nation (viz., Korea, China, Thailand, and Japan).[35] The movements of *Oriental Sketches*, including *Japanese Sketch* and *Japanese Nocturne*, were arranged by Eichheim for chamber orchestra in 1921 as *Oriental Impressions*, with the addition of *Entenraku* [sic, correct spelling is *Etenraku*] and *Nocturnal Impressions of Peking*. Finally, three of these short works, including *Japanese Nocturne*, were arranged by Eichheim for large orchestra in 1922.[36] Like Hearn, Eichheim employed in these pieces the seemingly inconsequential "vulgar songs" and mystical sounds that he had gleaned in his travels. In his prose, Hearn carefully framed the exotic legends and "glimpses of unfamiliar Japan" that he had collected, often setting the exotic scene in his introductions and suggesting profound insights on the hidden nature of Japanese life in his conclusions. Likewise, Eichheim deliberately displayed each of his cherished exotic musical objects within his works, particularly by creating transparent musical textures. Just as Hearn's prose served as a surrogate for actual travel to Japan, Eichheim attempted to evoke the sound of "being there" in these pieces.[37]

In the *Japanese Sketch* (1918), Eichheim presents four exotic finds: the "boom of the big bell" at the Chion-In Temple in Kyoto, the chant of a Buddhist priest, a *shakuhachi* tune, and a country boy's song. They are presented with the utmost clarity, with even greater melodic profile than heard in Stravinsky's treatment of Russian folk songs in *Petrushka*. Unlike Stravinsky, Eichheim almost always identified his borrowed material in his scores and program notes; his compositional motivations were clearly different. Eichheim's representation of the bell—a struck and sustained octave and open fifth with the reverberation rendered as a vaguely octatonic wash of rapid ascending runs in thirty-second notes—provides the primary connective tissue and structural definition in the piece. (See Example 3.1.) The implication of this score is that we are hearing little more than a collage of the actual sounds of Japan, one formed of juxtapositions that we might encounter if we could but travel to the exotic land ourselves. Eichheim dodged Schoenberg's dilemma by not attempting to harmonize his exotic tunes and aiming instead at a continual linear flow.[38] A performer could be forgiven for seeing something of a bel canto profile in Eichheim's decorated version of the *shakuhachi* tune. (See Example 3.2.) Here Eichheim seems to give prominence to pitches and gestures that in *shakuhachi* performance are concealed as ghostly graces to the pillar tones of the melodic line. By attempting to capture the original in terms of pitch notation he actually undermined his bid for authenticity in other dimensions. The orchestration choices in Eichheim's chamber version of this piece, commissioned by Coolidge in 1921, are not surprising: the bell is realized by the piano and harp, the priest's chant is given to the flute as is the *shakuhachi* melody, and the boy's song is presented by the oboe, which is employed only for this final tune. Perhaps this placement of the boy's song was not arbitrary, given that the final piece mentioned in Hearn's chapter on Japanese folk music is sung by a boy, the tune Hearn declares to be the best, "the soul of all the rest."[39]

Example 3.1 Eichheim, *Japanese Sketch*, measures 1–4

Example 3.2 Eichheim, *Japanese Sketch*, measures 10–16

Eichheim came closest to translating the spirit of Hearn into music and transporting his audience to Japan in his orchestral versions of *Japanese Nocturne* (1922).[40] (He is also at his most Debussian in this beautiful piece.) Here the cherished sounds of Japan heard from his bedroom window—the tunes of blind masseurs, the "shrill piping of food-vendors," the plucking of a *koto*, and the chanted prayer of an old man beating a wooden bell—float through a nonharmonic drone of tolling octaves and fifths and the lulling pulse of arpeggiated triplets befitting a nocturne. (See Example 3.3.) Each fragmented tune is presented clearly, except for the "playing of a koto" which may or may not be represented by a few gestures in the harp in the chamber orchestra version. With this piece Eichheim sought to recreate for his American audiences his nightly aural experience of Japan.

Example 3.3 Eichheim, *Japanese Nocturne*, measures 1–8

The most striking feature of this piece occurs near the end as the old man's prayer, played by the oboe, is accompanied by his constant beating of a Japanese fish-head wooden slit drum or temple block (a *mokugyo*)—the instrument specified by Eichheim.[41] Eichheim's historical significance is credited largely to his early incorporation of numerous East Asian percussion instruments in his orchestral works, many of which he made available from his own collection for performances. At the moment the fish-head drum enters, the representational system has been breached. Rather than translating the old man's drum, Eichheim purports to place the actual exotic musical object before his audience. Of course, such bids for authenticity often prove difficult to realize in performance, and Eichheim allowed for exotic substitutes in his manuscript score: "If no Fish Head drum—a small Japanese wood bell or drum used in Budahistic [*sic*] prayers—is available, kindly use a small Chinese wood block, made by Deagan in Chicago."

In assessing the products of cross-cultural influence, it may seem natural to search for evidence of integration and a "deeper engagement" with the fundamental elements of exotic artistic traditions, of "true influence" rather than "mere imitation." Rather than describing the affect and significance of direct borrowings, analysis is tooled to uncover the more pervasive impact of abstract technical features.

Example 3.3 Continued

In this endeavor critics, consciously or not, follow Bartók's maxims concerning the proper form cross-cultural influence should take, maxims formulated by Bartók as he labored to differentiate Romantic exoticism from its modernist successors.[42] The evidence for such engagement in Eichheim's works is relatively slim, which perhaps partly explains his later obscurity. Eichheim appears to have been most struck by the floating pulse and ambiguous meter of some forms of Japanese traditional music, and this interest is manifested in several of his Japanese-inspired works, not to mention in remarks such as the sarcastic reference to "safe and respectable" meters quoted above. A note pasted onto the second page of the manuscript score of *Japanese Sketch* (chamber version) that he presented to Coolidge states that "extreme legato is to be observed throughout the piece. I would like it to sound as if there were no bar lines." In the score of the original piano version of *Japanese Nocturne*, Eichheim went one step further by abandoning bar lines for the final melody and noting that "the left hand and the right hand are to be played without time relation." In his notes to the chamber version of this piece he instructs the oboist to "play the motives marked 'Solo' with all possible elasticity and freedom."[43] An even more provocative feature is the occasional occurrence of pitch clusters in these pieces. In

Example 3.3 Continued

measure 19 of *Japanese Sketch*, we hear the following isolated seven-pitch cluster lasting two beats: CC♯EF♯GG♯A♯ (an unmistakable echo of Stravinsky's *Petrushka* chord, but with an added G♯). In the *Japanese Nocturne* a five-pitch cluster is sustained for several measures near the opening (CD♯EF♯G♯, with the violins playing harmonics in the large orchestral version) and other clusters appear later in the work (such as CDEF♯A in measures 21–22). Clearly, these sonorities do not correspond with "our" harmonic concept. I tend to assume that any pitch cluster in a Japanese-inspired work is a sign of the composer's knowledge of the Japanese *sho*, a mouth organ that sustains clusters of 5–6 pitches used in *gagaku* (the ancient court orchestral music). In Eichheim's case, such knowledge is a real possibility as some of his clusters resemble *sho* chords in both pitch and interval content quite closely and since he was likely the first Euro-American composer to hear *gagaku*. (He certainly was not the last.)[44]

Gagaku lies at the opposite end of the traditional Japanese musical spectrum from Hearn's cherished "vulgar songs." The *gagaku* ensemble includes flutes (*ryuteki*) and piercing double-reed instruments (*hichiriki*) carrying the melody in heterophony, the sustained clusters of the *sho*, plucked string instruments playing brief repeated gestures, and a few percussion instruments that mark specific moments in a piece. This intense and stately music, considered the oldest surviving orchestral music in the world, prompted Eichheim to take a different approach. Rather than quote or translate snippets of this music in juxtaposition with other exotic material, he decided to present the most famous *gagaku* piece, *Etenraku*, on its own in an "adaptation for modern European instruments" complete with *sho* clusters arranged for violins. Acknowledging the Chinese origin of *gagaku*, Eichheim subtitled the piece "Chinese Elegy, A.D. 700." In a response typical of Euro-American modernists after encountering ancient material, Eichheim (and numerous other later composers) looked upon the elite *gagaku* as an ideal resource for the creation of modern music. In fact, *gagaku* itself could be claimed for the modernist flag: "Here we have music fourteen hundred years old, yet so modern that if I had been told that the composition was by a radical ultra-modern European, I would have believed it."[45]

It is instructive to compare Eichheim's 1921 *Entenraku* [*sic*] with a 1931 version for European orchestra by the Japanese conductor Hidemaro Konoye (Konoe).[46] As works of musical translation, these pieces invite investigation of their respective swerves from the original. Eichheim's version is a bare-bones reduction, suggesting that he may not yet have heard *Etenraku* or even *gagaku* himself and was basing his work on a transcription.[47] (He notes in the published score that the piece had been "translated" into European notation for him by Hisao Tanabe.) Eichheim omits the quite prominent role of the *kakko* drum and the flute introduction. He also leaves out a substantial section of the piece and clarifies the musical form, which is presented more ambiguously in *gagaku* performances. Furthermore, he makes no attempt to suggest the pitch bending and sliding tones heard in *gagaku*. In contrast, Konoye offers a richer and more complete arrangement of *Etenraku*. He provides detailed notes to the score that are aimed at pushing the instrumentalists toward *gagaku* timbres and playing techniques. However, in a note concerning his dynamic markings, Konoye frames the piece with the programmatic image of an approaching procession. This note, and the use of bar lines and quadruple meter, resulted in a transformation of *Etenraku* into the solemn and steady march of Stokowski's Philadelphia Orchestra 1934 recording.[48] The floating pulse and loose metric organization heard in *gagaku* are absent in both Eichheim's and Konoye's versions.

A nitpicking critique of this kind prompts the question of why such direct cross-cultural translations were ever attempted. In a period of ubiquitous musical recordings we are apt to forget the educational function that Eichheim's works served. Just as Eichheim's *Java* and *Bali* and Colin McPhee's 1936 *Tabu-Tabuhan* helped to introduce audiences to the music of the Indonesian gamelan, it is likely that Eichheim's *Entenraku* was the first representation of *gagaku* ever heard in the United States. Konoye's version reached a particularly large audience when it was performed at the Hollywood Bowl in 1937 with Konoye conducting and choreography by Michio Ito.[49] The question of how best to translate Japanese music into a form playable by Western musicians and consumable by Western audiences had been hotly debated in the decades prior to Eichheim's works, particularly in Germany. The specific bone of contention was whether or not Japanese melodies should be presented with harmonizations. The major German music theorist Hugo Riemann had published his own harmonizations of Japanese and Chinese melodies early in the century.[50] Georg Capellen published multiple collections of Japanese melodies and his work was central to this debate.[51] In 1905 Capellen called upon composers to harmonize Asian melodies and offered his own harmonization of a Japanese *gunka* as an example.[52] In his review of Capellen's collection of Japanese melodies, Erich M. von Hornbostel argued that harmonization defeated the goal of introducing Japanese music to the West: "The gap is unbridgeable. Compromise is a priori doomed to failure, and Capellen's arrangements confirm this view."[53] The German cellist Heinrich Werkmeister, who lived in Japan for eighteen years, encouraged direct encounters with Japanese music in a 1927 article in *The Musical Quarterly*, placing the burden of cultural compromise on the Western listener and, thus, prefiguring Cowell: "it is necessary, first of all, to 'listen one's self into' and not simply condemn or dismiss as ridiculous something which one does not understand."[54]

Throughout the history of American encounters with Japanese music, certain native informants have repeatedly served as sources and musical translators. The Japanese composer and conductor Kosaku Yamada (1886–1965) had been trained in Germany and first traveled to the United States in 1917, conducting his own works in Carnegie Hall in 1918 and collaborating with Michio Ito in New York.[55] David Pacun has shown that Yamada was expected to "sound Japanese" and his music was received by American critics, publishers, musicians, and audiences in this light.[56] Carl Fischer and G. Schirmer both published numerous songs and piano pieces by Yamada between 1919 and 1922, many of which were prominently advertised as featuring authentic Japanese melodies. Frederick H. Martens provided notes in several of these scores detailing the ways in which Yamada's settings approximated features of Japanese music. In the 1919 publication of *Three Old Japanese Art Dances* for piano, Martens explained in a prefatory note that the piece offered "authentic musical documents because their transcriber, a Japanese by birth, who has devoted much time and attention to the music of his native land, has also studied *au fond* the music of its antipodes in European institutions. He is able, therefore, to present the exotic beauty of the music of his native Nippon in a manner at once intelligible and exact." The implication is that Yamada was able to make the piano sound more "Japanese" than would a white American composer. Yamada's published scores circulated widely in the United States and appear to have provided "authentic" sources of Japanese melodies for numerous composers, silent film musicians, choreographers, and theater directors.[57]

Eichheim's own influence on later American composers and on other artists interested in non-Western cultures has been underestimated. His extensive collection of exotic instruments attracted significant attention throughout his career (see Figure 3.1), and he frequently lectured on Asian music, often in conjunction with performances of his works.[58] In addition to highlighting the didactic motivation

Figure 3.1 Henry Eichheim demonstrating a Javanese gong for Martha Graham. Orig. lost. Reproduced from Dolores M. Hsu, *The Henry Eichheim Collection of Oriental Instruments: A Western Musician Discovers a New World of Sound* (Santa Barbara, CA: University Art Museum, 1984).

behind these pieces, Eichheim's lectures shaped his audiences' aural expectations and experiences. His wife performed the piano version of *Oriental Sketches* throughout Asia and the United States. The chamber version of these pieces was first performed at Coolidge's Berkshire Festival in Pittsfield, Massachusetts, in 1921, and the full orchestral version of three of the movements was performed by multiple leading orchestras in the United States and Europe.

Reviews of these US performances indicate that Eichheim's authority on all forms of Asian music was unquestioned and his ability to transport his audiences to exotic locales through sound was repeatedly celebrated. By attending performances of Eichheim's Japanese-inspired pieces, American audiences—buttressed by his authoritative lectures and detailed program notes—were able to experience the "ultramodern" and "ancient" exotic simultaneously. Eichheim was also well received in Japan, at least by resident Westerners. As late as 1936 Frederic de Garis cited Eichheim in a Japanese publication as a major authority on Japanese music and a leading composer whose use of Japanese themes offered "a pleasant change from European music."[59] At least one Japanese audience, however, laughed at hearing Eichheim's incorporation of street vendor's tunes in his compositions. A 1919 review in the English language *Japan Advertiser* is illustrative:

It will take several hearings of Eichheim's "Oriental Sketches" to get their full aroma. The laughter of the audience at homely sounds heard every day in Tokyo streets was a tribute to faithful transcription; the applause at the end was the recognition of art, making . . . out of two street melodies not a new melody, but a star—something shiny and high up. Afterwards one remembers that the Eichheim way is not to take a workman's ditty and throw it to the wild beasts of harmony and counterpoint to be tossed and worried.[60]

The audience's laughter points directly to a fundamental contingency of modernist expression. The same musical gesture—in this case a Euro-American's quotation of exotic folk tunes—can offer one audience a transcendent and "ultra-modern" cross-cultural experience, while prompting another to laugh at the composer's amalgamation of high and low aesthetics. "Forging" can refer to faking as well as to making. The audience's laughter at Eichheim's attempt to stage modernist *japonisme* points to the exotic counterfeiting central to the crafting of American musical modernism. The modernist attempt to elevate the exotic to "something shiny and high up" occasionally backfired.

Olin Downes of the *New York Times* repeatedly paid tribute to Eichheim's "truly Oriental" pieces and contrasted his music with "pseudo-Oriental" works by others. In a review of Eichheim's *Chinese Legend*, Downes wrote: "Whether the listener comes from Oshkosh or Jersey City the music has the right feel; there is no doubt that it is a genuine artistic result of first-hand contacts."[61] (Music critics have rarely hesitated in adjudicating exotic authenticity, regardless of the extent of their own personal experience of exotic music, or lack thereof. Later critics would dismiss Eichheim for creating "pseudo-Oriental" works as they sought to celebrate the cross-cultural works of more recent composers.) Eichheim's musical impressions of the Orient were received by his audiences as an aural travelogue. In the program for the Boston Symphony Orchestra's premiere of *Oriental Impressions for Orchestra* (*Korean Sketch, Siamese Sketch, Japanese Nocturne, Chinese Sketch*) in March 1922, a concertgoer would have found an advertisement for Cook's Travel Service to the Far East immediately following the notes for Eichheim. The ad beckoned the Bostonian patrons: "The world is calling you. Beyond the horizon be strange and beautiful places." One could even "spend Springtime in Japan."[62] Perhaps Eichheim's music helped stir up some business for Cook's tours that week. It was an ad of this nature that had caught Eichheim's own attention in 1915 and provided the immediate stimulus for his first exploration of his beloved East Asia.

Other Exotic Others

In composer-centric scholarship, there is always the danger of overstating uniqueness and misattributing precedence. While Eichheim was likely the most famous composer and lecturer engaged in promoting East Asian musics in the early decades of the twentieth century, he was by no means the only such figure active in the United States. For example, we encountered the earlier costumed lecture recitals of Japanese music by Albert Gale in chapter 1. Claude Lapham (1890–1957) traveled to Japan in 1934, composed multiple major works inspired by Japanese music, and presented lecture-recitals on Japanese music in the United States throughout the 1930s and up until Pearl Harbor, resuming these in the 1950s. (Lapham's musical engagements with Japan and the Japanese American community of Los Angeles will be considered in chapter 7.) John Hazedel Levis, a British citizen, was born in Shanghai and lived there for twenty-six years before spending five years in the United States and then returning to China in 1936 where he was interned for two and a half years in a Japanese camp during World War II.[63] He was referred to in the American press as being of "Arab/Russian" or "Arabian-Hebrew" heritage and was thus considered a bit exotic himself. Levis was able to play several Chinese instruments and, like Eichheim, toured major cities in the United States in the 1930s offering lecture-demonstrations on Chinese traditional music and performing his own compositions based on this music. He presented his lecture-recitals at major institutions such as Harvard, Columbia, and Stanford universities and the Brooklyn Academy of Music; was presented by such organizations as Pro Musica in Los Angeles; and was reviewed in major newspapers. A review of a 1933 appearance by Levis at the Little Theatre in New York noted that he performed two ancient pieces, one of which "was accompanied effectively and eerily by the drum and rare bells of its own era," and also demonstrated multiple traditional instruments, sang folk songs, and performed his own piano tone-pictures "utilizing Chinese themes and harmonized with excellent taste and discretion to suggest, in so far as possible on a Western instrument, the color and feeling of the melodies themselves."[64] In 1936 he published a book on Chinese music.[65] Again, like Eichheim, Levis extolled the modern potential of ancient East Asian music: "If some of the Chinese musical masterpieces were introduced into this country now they would fascinate and intrigue beyond measure. Their very pattern of moving tones and rhythm is so entirely unlike that of Western melody that many people would judge them to be the most modern of modern music."[66]

The dynamics of exoticism appear to observe a form of Newton's third law of motion: attraction toward one exotic culture is most often counterbalanced by an equal and opposite repulsion from another. China and Japan have been consistently played off one another in this fashion in American popular culture since the mid-nineteenth century. The Chinese were particularly denigrated during the height of American *japonisme* and—conversely—were praised during World War II for their ancient wisdom and fortitude as the noble ally bearing the brunt of Japanese brutality. The success of Levis's tours in the United States may have owed a good deal to the increasing anti-Japanese sentiment and more sympathetic general view of the Chinese during the Sino-Japanese War. Eichheim was attracted to both Chinese and Japanese culture and appears, at first glance, to have enjoyed the pretense of temporarily collapsing the space between self and exotic other. In a letter to Coolidge he relates that he and his wife were staying in a mountain resort and living "in a semi-Japanese manner, so that I eat raw fish with chop sticks and do many other Japanese things" all for "the sake of 'local color.'"[67] Musically, he believed that he had strayed far from the domestic: "Can you imagine the amount and kinds of music I shall hear during this time. I am sure a plain C major triad will sound like a strange exotic thing to me when I return."[68] In 1922 he declared that he was "no longer staggered by the strange ways of the Chinese and Japanese—these two countries seem natural to me now, and I feel as much at home in Peking as in Boston and the city is far more sympathetic to me than New York, possibly because I prefer the Chinese to the Jews when taken en masse."[69] Here Eichheim not only boasts of having become acclimated to the "strange ways" of an exotic culture, but also reveals that his attraction to the peoples of East Asia was at the expense of another exotic other.

In this respect, Eichheim was not alone. Pointed—and rather odd—attempts both to associate and disassociate Asian musical influence, Jewish culture, and ultra-modern music were made throughout the mid-twentieth century. Five years prior to Schoenberg's published remarks on the unredeemable otherness of Japanese music, the Jewish American composer Lazare Saminsky made the following statement in *Modern Music* in an overview of the contemporary Californian musical scene:

> The war has fastened our eyes on the Pacific coast where the danger we were always aware of has taken a sharper outline. But the danger from the East is not that of musical infiltration—not any more, at least. We do not quite gather that the Orient is already upon us. South California, of course, is Oriental; Hollywood, eminently so. Hollywood is East minus uniformity; not a house but looks like no other, not a man but looks like no other. And it is not coincidence that the foremost Western creative minds of Oriental heritage—Schönberg, Bloch and Milhaud—have settled, after much drifting, on the Pacific shore. No coincidence, but a gravitation.[70]

Here we have proof of the special theory of Orientalist relativity—we all run the risk of being someone's exotic other. This casual association of three Jewish composers, lumped together with the exotic enemy in spite of the fact that they represented markedly different musical styles, is astonishing. However, it was not entirely a unique view. Paul Nettl made a similar argument based on more technical grounds in the same journal one year later. Nettl explained that Schoenberg's music was Oriental in its abandonment of the tension and resolution of tonal harmony and in its use of what he identified as heterophony.[71] Rather more fancifully, John Cage in 1946 compared Schoenberg's twelve-tone rows to Indian ragas.[72] Perhaps Schoenberg's 1947 attempt to quarantine Japanese music from "our music" was motivated by such writings.

Eichheim's own concerns on being taken for an exotic other may, in part, explain his casual anti-Semitism. In a letter complaining of the number of Jews on board his ship home from Europe, Eichheim wrote: "Even I cannot prove my Catholic ancestry—having worn off my foreskin in early youth, and my name sounds suspicious to my fellow travelers who seem to be returning pilgrims from a back to Zion movement."[73] He signed this letter, and several others, "Heinie." Strikingly, we find Henry Cowell expressing a similar concern in 1936 while imprisoned at San Quentin for homosexual acts: "Today I had a surprise. I was called by the secretary of Jewish activities—I dashed toward his office, wet and in boots from scrubbing, to assure him that he was making a grave error in supposing that any Irishman would ever permit himself to be taken for a Hebrew—when he came out and informed me that he had heard I played—would I play for a program he had arranged."[74] Moreover, and again like Eichheim, Cowell's own warm embrace of Asian musics and musicians was in contrast to his envy of some of his more successful Jewish colleagues. In 1931 he wrote to his parents from Berlin:

> I had a wonderful success with my lecture and playing at the Edition Adler on the 8th. All critics in Berlin, and nearly all orchestra conductors were there, and my music was very vigorously applauded. This concert, of several composers, served to offset the concert of all Jews—Copland, Gruenberg, etc. recently given here. They really do band together, and have made every effort to be taken for the only composers existing in America.[75]

From the vantage point of Cowell and other self-proclaimed "ultra-moderns," both race and musical style distinguished the different camps of American composers.

Eichheim's phobia of being mistaken as Jewish resonates with the form assumed by his cross-cultural music. Rather than absorbing specific features of an exotic musical style and system into his own compositional language, as demanded by Bartók, Eichheim primarily played the part of a musical translator. By carefully identifying his borrowed material and presenting it as directly as possible, Eichheim was keeping the exotic music somewhat at arm's length. In a lecture given in conjunction with a 1926 performance of his *Oriental Impressions* for chamber orchestra, Eichheim stated: "The music of the Orient does not at any point touch the music of the Occident. The underlying principles of these two arts evidently have no connection."[76] Here it seems almost as though Eichheim would have found common ground with Schoenberg's postwar initiative to police cultural borders.

Henry Cowell and Japan: War and Musical Diplomacy

The notion that Eichheim's "Romantic" engagement with Asian musics was of an entirely different order from Cowell's "modernist" explorations is not of recent origin. In his 1933 systematic classification of contemporary American composers, Cowell dismissed Eichheim as one "who superimposes Oriental instruments and impressions upon a conventional French style."[77] Cowell's critique of Eichheim was even more pointed in a speech he delivered at the 1961 Tokyo East-West Music Encounter Conference: "[Eichheim] was attracted by the beautiful and unfamiliar tone colours, but he never realized that the music he had heard was part of a formally organized system. 'Of course, I know oriental music is not real music,' he said to me naively. 'But still it haunts me,' he added apologetically. This was not an attitude that could develop any lasting influence from the East upon the West!"[78] Cowell's quotation of Eichheim here does not ring entirely true with Eichheim's other statements on Asian music and, in any case, is clearly intended to separate Cowell's own approach to Asian music from that of his predecessor. Cowell continues by apologizing for bringing himself "into the narrative," but states that he has "not been able to learn of any western composer who studied several eastern musical traditions from within, with eastern teachers, before I did."[79] Neither Cowell, nor his mentor Charles Seeger (who once referred to Eichheim as an "exquisite"[80]), nor most other composers who considered themselves to be "ultra-modern" in the 1930s or beyond looked upon Eichheim as a fellow traveler.[81] And yet, some specific connections between Cowell and Eichheim can be drawn, suggesting that their juxtaposition here is not capricious. Eichheim served on the "Resident Cooperating Committee" and as a conductor for the first concert of Cowell's New Music Society in 1925 and remained associated with the Society for a decade.[82] Leopold Stokowski was a champion of both Eichheim's and Cowell's Asian-inspired pieces and served a crucial role in the careers of both composers, as he did for numerous other Americans. Stokowski was a personal friend of Eichheim's, traveling with him to East Asia and visiting him in Santa Barbara.[83] Percy Grainger took the piano part at the premiere of Eichheim's *Oriental Impressions* for chamber orchestra in 1921 and twenty years later was instrumental in securing Cowell's release from prison. In 1933, Grainger had referred to "a few discerning composers, such as Henry Eichheim, Henry Cowell and Charles Seeger" who qualified in his estimation as "enlightened appraisers of the exquisite beauties found in 'exotic' music."[84] Both Eichheim and Cowell sought the guidance of the prominent Japanese musicologist Hisao Tanabe while in Japan. Most significant, Cowell's first exposure to the music of *gagaku*, and thus to a representation of *sho* clusters, likely occurred in 1927 at a performance of Eichheim's *Entenraku*.[85]

Japanese music and culture were of sustained importance to Cowell throughout much of his life. The influence of Japanese music is evident in one of his earliest works, the "Oriental" movement of *Adventures in Harmony* (1911–1912), and in one of his last, the Concerto no. 2 for Koto and Orchestra (1965).[86] At the risk of accusations of myopia, I claim that Japanese musical culture was the most persistent exotic influence on Cowell, or at least that Japan was the musical port he most consistently returned to at crucial moments in his career of living in the "whole world of music."[87] Cowell, unlike most other white American composers, famously encountered East Asian music at an early age in San Francisco, and he himself emphasized its prominence in his musical formation.[88] I find, however, that the importance and lasting influence of this early (and limited) exposure to East

Asian music was more philosophical than directly musical. Nancy Yunhwa Rao has argued that Cowell's engagement with this music was categorically different from that of other American modernists because Asian music was part of Cowell's own cultural background. She has convincingly argued that "ideologically the Orient was the privileged other in Cowell's pursuit of the new and modern, yet in practice the audible Orient had always existed as part of his native musical self."[89] However, I believe that for Cowell something close to the opposite was also true: Ideologically he viewed all the world's music as native to himself, yet in practice he heard much of East Asian music through Orientalist ears. Pertinent to this cultural stance, as I will show, is the fact that the final formation of his musical ideology and the height of his compositional interest in Asia coincided with a particularly hot period in the Cold War.[90]

While it is certainly true that Cowell encountered Japanese folk songs and *koto* music as a child, it is highly unlikely that he would have heard *gagaku*, the Japanese ceremonial music that had the strongest influence on his mature works, not least because this music was not central to the Japanese American musical experience. Cowell may have heard recordings of Japanese music, including recordings of *gagaku*, during his 1931 studies at the Berlin Phonogramm-Archiv. The archive held 132 wax cylinder recordings of Japanese music that had been recorded in Berlin and in Japan between 1901 and 1925.[91] It is clear from his letters home, however, that he devoted most of his time in Berlin to listening to recordings of musical cultures that he had not yet encountered and that he was quite busy organizing concerts of his own and other American composers' music.[92]

Cowell's earliest works on Japanese subjects reveal little working knowledge of Japanese music. Instead, they are roughly equivalent to Eichheim's *Gleanings from Buddha Fields* in that they were inspired by texts and programmatic images worthy of Lafcadio Hearn. Cowell's incidental music for the 1913 "vision drama" *Creation Dawn* written for the Carmel Forest Theatre by the poet Takeshi Kanno, the mystic *issei* (first-generation Japanese American), consisted of a compilation of earlier pieces and some new fragmentary works designed to accompany specific moments, none of it requiring Japanese musical representations.[93] In the 1915 monodrama *Red Silence*, Cowell—still a teenager—relied primarily on a naive pentatonicism and open fifth and fourth intervals to signal the exotic.[94] The work is for a solo female character, Red Silence, who is waiting for her lover to return; she receives a sign of his death, and then—as a good samurai's daughter in the Euro-American *japonisme* tradition—commits suicide on stage. In setting her song "Fresh Flowery Sprays," Cowell employed the black keys of the piano for the vocal line and mostly parallel-fourth black keys for the piano accompaniment. This form of musical exoticism did not require contact with Asian music; rather, as Michael Hicks argues concerning Cowell's invention of piano tone clusters, it is the sign of East Asia most readily at hand as one sits at the keyboard.[95] Red Silence's subsequent prayer to Kwannon resembles, at least at the start, a Belliniesque bel canto aria, and is followed by a solo flute melody that might be mistaken for an *erhuang* aria in Beijing opera. In the resplendent 1926 piano duo *The Snows of Fuji-yama*, Cowell seems to run through the various possible permutations of a five-pitch tune with chromatic scale clusters, accompanied by ringing octaves. The piece was inspired by the "old legend" that the snows of Fuji are actually the souls of maidens shed on the mountain at their approach to Nirvana. The forte "black key" clusters heard toward the end of the work, with their triumphant tintinnabulation, seem to signal the maidens' ascension.

In 1932, in preparation for teaching at the New School for Social Research, Cowell was in contact with the Japanese musician Soichi Ichikawa of the Museum of Natural History in New York.[96] But his serious and sustained study of Japanese music did not begin until two years later at age thirty-seven, when he met the *issei* musician Kitaro Tamada (see Figure 3.2). Tamada is an important but hitherto neglected figure in the history of American cross-cultural music. He met Eichheim in the early 1920s,[97] was Cowell's most crucial connection to Japan for three decades, and inspired several other American composers both directly and indirectly to study Japanese music, including John Cage, Lou Harrison, and Gerald Strang. Immigration records reveal that Tamada was born in 1894 and first arrived in the United States in 1918, landing at San Francisco. Except for a two-year return visit to

Figure 3.2 Kitaro Tamada playing the *shakuhachi* at Cowell's home in 1962. Reproduced with the permission of the Music Division, The New York Public Library for the Performing Arts, Astor, Lenox and Tilden Foundations, and the David and Sylvia Teitelbaum Fund, Inc., as successors to Henry and Sidney Cowell.

Japan, Tamada worked in agriculture (he was a graduate of the Tokyo Agricultural College and had also studied at the Massachusetts Agricultural College, Amherst), owned a flower shop in Mountain View from 1931 to 1940, and taught *shakuhachi* until his internment in Manzanar in 1942.[98] When Cowell met Tamada in 1934[99] he was immediately introduced to the Japanese American musical community and invited to numerous performances of *sankyoku* (popular chamber music for *koto, shakuhachi*, and *shamisen*) and Japanese dance.[100] Cowell, in turn, organized a New Music Society concert of "ancient traditional music of Japan" performed by Tamada and other musicians at his home on 1 April 1935. In the invitation Cowell explained his rationale for sponsoring this performance, the only concert of this nature sponsored by the Society: "Since the music, although ancient, is new to most Occidentals, the New Music Society feels it to be within its province to sponsor this presentation."[101] As did Eichheim, Cowell thus suggested an equivalence between traditional Japanese music and ultra-modern composition.

Tamada taught Cowell *shakuhachi* for a period of four years, continuing his lessons during Cowell's imprisonment; he also assisted Cowell in his studies of spoken and written Japanese.[102] Cowell received a *shakuhachi* in prison in early August 1937,[103] studied the instrument, and went on to introduce it to other American composers (see Figure 3.3). He wrote to his stepmother on 11 October: "Tamada came again,

Figure 3.3 Henry Cowell demonstrating the *shakuhachi* for Edgard Varèse, ca. 1944. Reproduced with the permission of the Music Division, The New York Public Library for the Performing Arts, Astor, Lenox and Tilden Foundations, and the David and Sylvia Teitelbaum Fund, Inc., as successors to Henry and Sidney Cowell.

and gave me some valuable pointers on how to play the shakuhachi. He seems to be reconciled to the idea that I am going to try to learn it willy-nilly, and is willing to help. He also very kindly offered to come and play for programs here, and I think it will be arranged." In April 1938 Cowell referred to Tamada as his "most regular visitor" and on 25 November 1938 he wrote to his parents:

> I don't know whether I told you that my playing on the shakuhachi has taken a turn for the better recently. As you know, it is extremely difficult to produce any tone at all, and to control the tone after it is made. I do not spend a great deal of time at it, as there are so many other things to do, but I have been playing a few minutes each evening, and recently have been getting a very musical tone, so that I might really be able to play something on it that one would like to listen to. I have a shakuhachi record here, and I tried playing along with the record, and was able to play all the main parts with it, although the very refined variations of course were far over my head. However, I am able to play all the notes which the player in the record played, as far as the range of tones employed is concerned, and I feel quite set up over it, as no one who has not tried can quite appreciate how great an accomplishment it really is![104]

In 1941 Cowell made recordings of Tamada's *shakuhachi* performance. His friendship with Tamada and devotion to the *shakuhachi* inspired later American composers in their own explorations of the world of music.

Within two years of Cowell's release from San Quentin and move to New York, Tamada himself was behind barbed wire in the Manzanar Japanese American internment camp. He would spend the next three years and eight months attempting to continue his *shakuhachi* performance and teaching while worrying about the future of Japanese culture in America.[105] The report of an official War Relocation Authority (WRA) interview with Tamada held at Manzanar on 15 January 1945 documents his musical concerns and aspirations:

> Mr. T. is well-known in Japan as a musician. He has toured the world in this way. Before evacuation he had a number of students and also did some concert work to private groups such as university groups. . . . Mr. T. hopes to continue with his musical career in the future. He would like to settle in New York as he feels Oriental culture would receive a favorable reception there. Also, he has several friends including a Caucasian friend [i.e., Cowell] who is a musical critic for the Office of War Information in New York. . . . He feels that Japanese culture will have a definite place in the United States after the war. The type of music and instrument that he plays is very classical and is not even appreciated by the majority of Japanese Americans including Issei. He said that Caucasian music scholars and university professors were those who understood the music that he had to present. . . . Therefore, in light of limited reception anticipated for his music, he is concerned as to how he will be able to support himself until the war is over.

Interviewer suggested that he might write to his friend in New York and inquire about possibilities in the music field there.

Tamada did write to Cowell numerous times during his internment. His letters were probing and poignant and reveal his determination to continue his musical career. A November 1942 letter related the situation for Japanese traditional music in the camps and the difficulties faced by Tamada as a musician.

> Well, I am allright and working as farmer and teaching my shakuhachi music in the evening. But Japanese music is not so good now even in the relocation center. Few months ago, from the W.R.A. explained as following. The W.R.A. does not intend to promote ideals and cultures of nations with which we are at war. So long as patriotic music is not played, Japanese music may be played in the Center but it will not be sponsored by the government. Paid teachers or special room or quarters cannot be provided for them. . . . I like to write that Mrs. Adams from the regional office came to Manzanar and gave specific order that administrative recognition of Japanese music must stop. I like to know how is your opinion about my music in the relocation center? Time is fly so soon, I am stay here now over seven months and all my music friends are away in the other relocation center.[106]

Japanese music eventually found a limited place in camp life and Tamada, under difficult conditions, was able to teach and perform in the evenings after working at agricultural jobs during the day.[107] In a 3 February 1943 letter, Tamada thanks Cowell for sending *koto* strings and discusses his participation in a recent performance of *sankyoku* music at Manzanar. On the back of his letter, white camp officials described their impressions of Tamada's performance at his request. The camp's project director, Ralph R. Merritt, stated:

> Because I am not a musician I am unable to comment except in a very personal way. The more I hear the Japanese instruments the more I enjoy them,— particularly the harp [*koto*]. The numbers played are beautifully executed but the mood of the first three numbers is hard for a western mind to grasp. Some time I hope to hear the symphonic music to which we are accustomed enriched by these Japanese instruments.

Mrs. Nielsen, the head of the camp's high school music department, wrote:

> The quality of tone of the shakuhachi is hauntingly lovely. The artistry of the players in blending their tones to such a fine unison is evident. All the selections successfully established a real mood and sense of the beautiful. The ensemble work for kotos and shakuhachi was very fine. The [?] selection might well have been Dibussy's [*sic*] inspiration for 'L'apres-midi d'une fanne' [*sic*]. Our artists

tonight do speak a truly international language. The last selection is especially fine music—even to my 'western ears'. Sincere thanks for a real treat.

The prospect of leaving Manzanar caused Tamada much anxiety and he remained in the camp for as long as possible. In February 1945 he wrote to Cowell:

> I rather like to stay in this center until the war is over. Most of all people are same. . . . We, musicians will be on chance to teach music long years to Japanese until they settled down some where, someplace like Los Angeles or San Francisco. Sometimes I thinking that I am very eager to hear from you about Japanese music in this country after war is over, for the culture, education and better understanding. Tell me, what is your opinion for this? When you have a time, please write to me.[108]

It is clear from references in Tamada's correspondence that Cowell did write to him, but I have been unable to locate these letters. Cowell's correspondence to both his wife and parents throughout this period is notably silent on both the war and on the Japanese American internment camps. Perhaps Cowell's role as a senior music editor in the Office of War Information and his recent imprisonment encouraged him to remain quiet on these matters. However, a most eloquent response and expression of gratitude to Tamada can be heard in the 1946 solo for *shakuhachi*, *The Universal Flute*, which Cowell dedicated to him.[109] This work is one of the earliest by a Euro-American composer for an Asian solo instrument. The piece is in an ABA′ structure, typical of *shakuhachi* solo music, and Cowell calls for a great deal of the pitch bending and sliding tones central to *shakuhachi* idioms. The emphasis on pillar tones through extended duration, grace-note worrying, and accelerated repetition of one pitch is also evident here. Joscelyn Godwin claimed that this piece represented "almost pure pastiche."[110] One could say with equal validity that the work represents an impressive creative act within an exotic tradition. It was certainly a worthy gift by Cowell to his teacher.

Although living on opposite coasts, Tamada and Cowell remained in contact until the early 1960s. Tamada introduced Cowell to Kimio Eto (the *koto* virtuoso for whom Cowell would compose his first *koto* concerto) and to Takefusa Sasamori (a musicologist who studied composition with Cowell),[111] and he helped establish contacts and made suggestions as Cowell prepared for his first trip to Japan. He also visited Cowell in New York in 1959, as Cowell related to his stepmother: "Mr. Tamada is here for a few days . . . will go to Japan soon to retire. His playing is still superb; better than anything I heard in Japan (including his teacher there.)"[112] Tamada visited Cowell again in 1962, bringing his own teacher with him to New York City to meet his most famous student. Cowell had just returned from his second and final trip to Japan. After visiting Cowell, Tamada vanishes from the historical record of American music, and yet his subtle influence can still be traced.[113]

For a composer who wished to "live in the whole world of music," Cowell spent relatively little time outside the United States. Unlike Eichheim, who traveled in East Asia five times and for extended periods, Cowell visited East Asia only twice, in 1956–1957 and in 1961. He spent approximately two months in Japan in 1957 and one month in 1961. Cowell's first trip to Japan was part of a larger tour funded by the Rockefeller Foundation and sponsored by the Department of State, US Information Agency.[114] In 1961, Cowell served as President Kennedy's representative to the Tokyo East-West Music Encounter Conference. Just as he had served as a shaper of musical propaganda during World War II, selecting music for the Office of War Information to be broadcast on US radio abroad with the aim of inspiring home-sickness in the Japanese enemy, Cowell proved an important participant in Cold War cultural diplomacy.[115] His universalism and attempts to synthesize East and West in his music, however benign in motivation, worked hand-in-hand with US Cold War efforts to form political bonds with Asian nations, particularly with Japan, as did state-sponsored radio broadcasts, lectures, and concerts of American music abroad. (This topic and the transnational Cold War dynamics of the Tokyo East-West Music Encounter will be examined in detail in chapter 8.) In the United States, popular Orientalism kept public sentiment in line with official US Cold War strategies. In 1957, the year of Cowell's most famous Japanese-inspired work, *Ongaku*, the *Reader's Digest* published an article urging American readers to, as Christina Klein puts it, "cultivate mutual understanding between the US and Japan."[116]

In May 1961, Cowell wrote a "personal credo" that elucidates the particular form of nationalism at work in his aesthetic and cultural leanings.

> In my own music I believe I coordinate . . . musical means from all parts of the world, and from all ages of musical history. Into my inner creative needs I may feel the necessity of drawing on resources from any part of the world, folk or cultivated, and from any age, simple or complex. . . . In a way, I think of this as truly American, because America more than any other country, is made up of all the peoples of the world, and less than any other great composer-producing country does it have any one specific old tradition of musical composition.[117]

With this credo, Cowell points back to the nineteenth-century ecstatic multicultural visions of Walt Whitman and forward to the allegedly postcolonial cross-over music of the late twentieth century. Cowell's argument that East Asian musics are part of American music is literally true in that East Asian immigrants brought their music to the United States.[118] Such pluralist perception is to be applauded. However, living "in the whole world of music" and subsuming all musics under an American label do involve a certain problematic egotism that resonates with US covert imperialism. Indeed, claims to universalism most often seem to imply ingestion to one's self rather than the dissolution of the self into the other. In "drawing on resources" from nations such as Japan, Cowell's explicitly stated goal was to counter international serialism with a new musical universalism—on American terms.[119]

Cowell's "transethnic" (Lou Harrison's term) works of this period repeatedly present a rather formulaic dialectic: the most obviously exotic material appears first in a piece, followed by a more recognizably Euro-American style, and ultimately an attempt is made to integrate the two.[120] His desire to achieve musical universalism also determined his understanding and reception of exotic musics. In program notes for his 1957 *Ongaku* Cowell wrote:

> The foreign music strangest to Western ears is certainly that of the Far East: China, Korea and Japan. But the strangeness seems to be largely superficial: a matter of tone color and technique rather than structure. The basic relationship between music East and West is attested, I think, by the fact that Western orchestra performers will find nothing particularly surprising in their individual instrumental parts [in *Ongaku*] . . . in spite of the unfamiliar style in which the music is couched.[121]

This statement is revealing. First, it is striking that Cowell would consider "structure" to be more fundamental than "tone color and technique" when discussing Japanese music. It is also clear that he casually considered his *Ongaku* to be equivalent to Japanese music, at least to the extent that Western musicians' reactions to it could be cited as revealing their understanding of Asian music in general. If critical commentary can be taken to reflect basic audience perceptions, Cowell's American audiences, like Eichheim's, did receive these works as examples of "Japanese" music. Cowell can be celebrated for hearing and appreciating the connections among all nations and all musics. However, he can just as readily be criticized for failing to hear and respect cultural difference.

Cowell's major Japanese-influenced works of the 1950s and 1960s include *Ongaku* (1957), the Concerto [no. 1] for Koto and Orchestra (1962), the Concerto for Harmonica (1962), and the Concerto no. 2 for Koto and Orchestra (1965). In program notes, interviews, and personal correspondence, Cowell repeatedly addressed the relationship between these pieces and Japanese music in a way that emphasized originality, creative synthesis, and the use of foreign compositional procedures (as opposed to the citation of Japanese melodies). In his program notes for *Ongaku*, Cowell stated that the piece "is not an imitation of Japanese music, but an integration of some of its usages with related aspects of Western music" and declared that "all the thematic material is my own; there are no actual Japanese themes in the work. The themes are extended by means of techniques for melodic variation that are common to both cultures. Western techniques for thematic development are not applied to the material." Similarly, Concerto no. 2 for Koto was introduced with program notes (likely written with Sidney Cowell's assistance) that claimed "all themes are original, but Japanese and Western modes and scales are used freely and often entwined. . . . The bright main melody [in the third movement] might be a Japanese fisherman's song, although the syncopation is American in style; but of course, like the rest of the Concerto, it is composed music."[122] (The reverberations of Schoenberg's and Stravinsky's criticisms of Bartók's use of folk material appear to be haunting Cowell here.)[123] In Cowell's statements, as in the majority of critical works on cross-cultural music, the implication is that borrowing is a form of cultural theft and a sign of artistic weakness and that the composition of original tunes, no matter how similar to actual exotic melodies, constitutes a form of true cross-cultural engagement, as does extrapolating exotic materials "according to a logic inherent in the basic materials themselves."[124] Cowell's insistence that he never borrowed Japanese tunes in his music is a constant refrain that seems propelled by some form of anxiety. Perhaps he sought to put as much distance as possible between himself and such early twentieth-century "Romantic Orientalists" as Henry Eichheim.

The two traditional Japanese genres shaping Cowell's mature works were *gagaku* and *sankyoku*. Cowell's long-term devotion to the solo *shakuhachi* is also evident in the melodic style of several of these pieces. The degree to which Cowell imitated *gagaku* and *sankyoku* in *Ongaku* is suggested by details in his manuscript short score.[125] He labeled the various orchestral parts with the *gagaku* instrument names and transcribed *koto* scales at the bottom of the first page of the second movement, presumably as a compositional aid. Several melodic gestures in *Ongaku*, including the flute introduction and the initial melody for trumpets (in imitation of the *ryuteki* and *hichiriki* parts), appear derived from the most famous of *gagaku* pieces, *Etenraku*. The most striking *gagaku* feature in Cowell's Japanese-influenced works of this period is his use of *sho*-style pitch clusters. During his first visit to Japan, a group of young Japanese musicians pointed out to Cowell that tone clusters appeared in *gagaku*, indirectly implying that his famous invention might have been influenced by Japanese music. They were mistaken. Cowell's piano tone clusters from the 1910s and 1920s are not similar to the clusters of the *sho* nor to those found in his *Ongaku*. His use of *sho*-inspired clusters in pieces from the late 1950s and early 1960s, however, might prompt us to associate Cowell with the dense clusters heard in contemporaneous works of "textural music," such as Penderecki's *Threnody for the Victims of Hiroshima* (1960), Ligeti's *Atmosphères* (1961), and in related works by Xenakis, who traveled to Japan in 1961 and whose 1963–1964 *Eonta* for brass and piano, for example, contains clusters approximating the interval content and timbre of those of the *sho*. Of course, composers of "textural music" themselves perhaps owed a debt to Cowell's early piano clusters.

Cowell was quite proud of *Ongaku* and of its reception in Japan, something evident in the program notes he wrote. Not only did he postulate the supreme ability of the American composer to embody the transethnic role, he even suggested that an American might be able to understand and produce exotic music more readily than the exotic other: "The degree of success with which Mr. Cowell has caught the flavor of Japanese music is illustrated by the reaction of a Japanese audience to [*Ongaku*] in 1959. It was enthusiastically received by older members of the audience. But some of the younger ones, whose musical leanings and experience are increasingly Western, were puzzled. 'Frankly, it's too Japanese for us,' said one, 'it's way over our heads.'" (The *kotoist* Kimio Eto in reference to Cowell's Concerto [no. 1] for Koto is reported to have said: "Do you know, in some ways, Cowell has written music more Oriental than I play in Japan.")[126] However, echoing the Japanese reaction to Eichheim's use of folk tunes in his compositions, some Japanese audience members were apparently disturbed by Cowell's juxtaposition of the sacred and ritualistic *gagaku* alongside the *sankyoku* genre of secular entertainment.[127] Cowell continued in this vein in his *koto* and harmonica concertos. For example, while the first movement of the Concerto [no. 1] for Koto presents Cowell's hieratic *gagaku* style (see Example 3.4), the 6/8 lullaby second movement is so entirely without traditional Japanese musical elements that Cowell was able to reorchestrate it as a new piece entitled *Carol* (see Example 3.5). Similarly, the Concerto for Harmonica opens with *sho*-inspired clusters in the winds and then in the violins. The harmonica part, surprisingly, avoids any suggestion of the *sho* and contains no chords and only two dyads in the entire piece.[128]

Cowell's works from the Cold War might at first appear far removed from the musical *japonisme* of Eichheim. However, evidence from Cowell's sketches suggests a closer correspondence to Eichheim's poetic impressions. To what extent does a composition's title shape our experience of the work and our understanding of the composer's artistic stance? Cowell's original title for the 1962 Concerto for Harmonica was *Haiku (Spirit of Japan)*, which is crossed out on his manuscript score, perhaps to steer listeners clear of poetic evocations of Old Japan in the piece and toward an appreciation of a skillful modernist abstraction of fundamental Japanese musical features.[129] (The work is beautiful and is my personal favorite among Cowell's Japanese-influenced pieces. In general, Cowell was more successful when writing with the *shakuhachi* in mind rather than the *koto*. His writing for the *koto* is frequently awkward.) Likewise, Cowell's original title for *Ongaku* was *Impressions of Court Music (Gagaku)*, and he initially subtitled the work's first movement "An American in Japan." Unlike Eichheim, however, Cowell composed impressions of a musical style rather than of an exotic soundscape. Cowell's discarded titles also call to mind such contemporaneous musical responses to Japan as Dave Brubeck's *Jazz Impressions of Japan* and the exotica albums of Martin Denny. An even stronger connection can be made between Cowell's works of the late 1950s and early 1960s and those of another contemporaneous group of composers not normally associated with the "ultra-moderns."

Cowell began composing *Ongaku* in June 1957 while in Japan and finished the piece in September in Shady, New York. Contemporaneously, Franz Waxman composed the score for the Warner Bros. film *Sayonara* between May and late August 1957 in Los Angeles. Here we should recall that Sputnik was launched in October of that year—*Sayonara*, based on James Michener's novel, was as much a product of Cold War cultural diplomacy as was *Ongaku*. Music proved central to Hollywood's parallel efforts to reshape American perceptions of the Japanese, as we shall see in chapter 6. In such films from the 1950s and early 1960s as *The Teahouse of the August Moon*, *The Barbarian and the Geisha*, *Sayonara*, *A Majority of One*, and *My Geisha*,

Example 3.4 Cowell, Concerto [No. 1] for Koto, introduction, measures 1–16

Hollywood proved determined never to miss an opportunity to display Japanese musical traditions on the screen and soundtrack. In fact, these films provided perhaps the most sustained exposure (carefully framed, of course) that Americans have ever had to Japanese traditional music.

Waxman's Main Title music for *Sayonara*, at least in its original version, runs parallel to Cowell's contemporaneous Japanese-inspired works. Like Cowell, Waxman begins and ends his short piece in a style influenced by *gagaku*, complete with very close approximations of *sho* chords. (See Example 6.1 in chapter 6.) Likewise, the middle section of Waxman's piece bears a close resemblance to *sankyoku*, as

Example 3.4 Continued

do several of the middle movements of Cowell's Japanese-influenced works.[130] The opening sonority and entire Largo introduction of Cowell's Concerto [no. 1] for Koto sound very much like the opening of Waxman's *Sayonara*. These two composers offer a natural experiment for the study of musical exoticism. Apparently, encountering exotic music firsthand in a foreign nation and remaining at home do not necessarily result in dramatically different musical responses. This comparison can be pushed further. The opening of the third movement of the Concerto for Harmonica sounds a good deal like Hollywood's typical "arrival in Japan" music from this period. This whole movement, in fact, seems so cinematic that one can almost see the lyrical pans of the quaint Japanese villages and countryside in full technicolor. (The resemblance to Max Steiner's version of the Hollywood Japanese pastoral in his score for the 1957 film *Escapade in Japan* is particularly strong.) And I am not the first to draw such a comparison. In his review of the premiere of Cowell's Concerto [no. 1] for Koto, Irving Lowens stated that he "might have been happier had there been somewhat less use of 'Oriental' tone-color—the woodblocks and the percussion sounded a bit movie-ish."[131] From the other side of the great divide, the Hollywood composer Dimitri Tiomkin proclaimed in reference to the

Example 3.4 Continued

concerto: "We have overcome our mystification of Oriental music *per se*. To many of us, professional and layman alike, Japanese music, in particular, is hauntingly lovely."[132] Tiomkin claims here that Cold War American composers approached exotic musics rationally as a source of material to be mined rather than as a Romantic inspiration à la Eichheim. The midcentury Hollywood composer and the American experimentalist no longer seem quite so far apart.

Cadenza: Critical Cross-Cultural Reflections

In a 1928 letter, Eichheim mentioned that he would be giving recitals in Tokyo and joked that he hoped "this will discourage the Japanese from learning our music and stick to their own."[133] Eichheim was not the first to lament Japan's musical modernization. As noted above, in 1903 Otto Abraham and Erich M. von Hornbostel had concluded their study of Japanese music by stating their concern that this exotic musical tradition was in danger of vanishing and that this would constitute a great loss to Western musical science and to future composers who would miss an opportunity for the "widening of musical horizons."[134] Abraham and Hornbostel

Example 3.4 Continued

were prophetic. Euro-American musicians, while turning to Japan for their own modernization projects, have been chronically concerned with the health of Japanese traditional music ever since Western influence began to take hold in Meiji Era Japan. This concern was repeatedly aired at the 1961 Tokyo East-West Music Encounter Conference by the American delegates.[135] In his speech, Cowell famously countered his fellow conferees by coming to the defense of musical hybridity.[136] Cowell's championing of hybrids has been celebrated as proof of his postmodern sensibility and as a precursor to recent sanguine views on musical globalization. However, Cowell was a more interesting and complex figure than his current historical image would suggest. First, his formal remarks at the conference did not diverge entirely from those of his compatriots and may even be heard as an echo and extension of Abraham's and Hornbostel's call for recorded collections:

It seems to me we all agree that music should all be different. We also all agree that traditions should be preserved. I want to make a plea also for preserving that sort of hybrid music coming into being. It all should be recorded just as we need so desperately to record the traditions that are still here. On the other hand, it is very interesting to me that the most urgent plea, to which I add my own, should mostly

Example 3.5 Cowell, Concerto [No. 1] for Koto, second movement opening, measures 9–16

have been made here by the Westerner. They are pleading with the East to preserve its traditions.[137]

Moreover, two weeks later Cowell scolded a group of Japanese music educators for their failure to preserve Japanese traditional music: "You really ought to know something about the traditions of Japanese music. If you will come to Columbia University, I have a class there."[138] This seems an instance of the Euro-American modernist, disturbed by the cross-cultural reverse image in the mirror, exhorting his exotic model not to change. Cowell's later engagements with Japanese musicians reveal that not all hybrids were deemed acceptable by him.

Euro-American distaste for cross-cultural works emanating from Asian nations has been evident for well over a century. Japanese forays into Euro-American musical styles and attempts at cross-cultural mixture have been met with especial derision in the United States. This is conspicuous in the American reception of the Japanese *koto* virtuoso and composer Kimio Eto in the 1950s and 1960s. Eto was most often presented as an ambassador of the exotic culture of Old Japan (see Figure 3.4). Eto's concertizing in the United States began on the West Coast where he was repeatedly featured in the *Los Angeles Times*, starting in 1954 with his Evenings on the Roof concert along with Robert Craft, who conducted two German baroque cantatas. Peter Yates, the organizer of the Evenings on the Roof, wrote to Cowell about this concert and explained that he had programmed the other "neutral" European works in order to prepare his audience for the shock of the Japanese music.[139] Active throughout the Los Angeles musical scene, Eto's playing also appeared on the soundtrack of the 1956 film *The Teahouse of the August Moon*. Media coverage of Eto tended to fetishize his blindness and was generally positive on his performances. Eto's impact in California was broad. For example, Barry Melton of the band Country Joe and the Fish has testified, albeit vaguely, to

Figure 3.4 Album cover for Kimio Eto, *Art of the Koto*, Electra EKS 7234, 1963.

Eto's wider influence: "I was a big Hamza El Din fan. Kimio Eto mixed the traditional Japanese koto with a sort of American influence. I learned from both of them, 'cause I heard both of them play a lot in Southern California when I was growing up. So I brought that with me, that sort of Japanese and Middle Eastern influence, and Indian ragaesque thing."[140] Eto recorded an album entitled *Koto and Flute* with the jazz musician Bud Shank in 1960.[141] In 1965, he received a citation from the mayor of Los Angeles for his "contributions to international music." In a sense, Eto was continuing in the footsteps of his famous teacher Michio Miyagi (1894–1956) in exploring fusions with Western music.[142] Eto's first East Coast performance occurred at a gala dinner hosted by the Japan Society in honor of Crown Prince Akihito's visit in September 1960, and the Cowells were present at this black-tie event.[143] Reviewers of Eto's multiple recitals in New York City in the early 1960s frequently complained that his style of music was not "Japanese" enough. For example, in a review of Eto's Carnegie Hall recital in October 1961, which Cowell attended, Alan Rich groused that "the 'modern' school of koto composition seems not at all interested in preserving this native quality" and that the recital was "an evening's journey through a musical No Man's Land, a series of strange and unsettling stylistic anachronisms."[144]

Cowell apparently made a similar complaint regarding Eto's cadenzas in the first performances of his Concerto [no. 1] for Koto, a work he composed specifically for Eto. The concerto received solid media coverage and was considered a major cross-cultural musical event. Following the 1964 premiere in Philadelphia, Stokowski performed the work with the Philadelphia Orchestra and Eto in New York, Baltimore, and Washington, D.C., before conducting the work with Eto and other orchestras in Tokyo and Honolulu (see Figure 3.5). Eto also performed the concerto with the Seattle Symphony. Ed Arian, a bassist who performed at the premiere and who retired from the Philadelphia Orchestra in 1967, recalls that the "audience took it very well" and that the "composition itself wasn't too ultra-modern" and was not particularly challenging for the orchestra to play. Arian also remembers that he and his fellow string players were struck by Eto's ability to move bridges while performing and by his technical skill.[145] Eto allegedly drew upon nineteenth-century European music for his cadenza which caused the audience in Philadelphia to laugh and annoyed Cowell greatly.[146] According to Sidney Cowell:

The reason this cadenza is of special interest is because the famous koto virtuoso Kimio Eto was an arrogant and stubborn man whose cadenzas he intended as evidence of his mastery of the Western idiom. They are made up almost entirely of echoes of unsuitable music, from the call of the Valkyries to Hansel and Gretel to Gounod's Ave Maria. This aroused laughter in the Philadelphia audience at the first performance, which he took as a measure of success, so that he stubbornly refused to listen to polite representation, made both separately and together by L. S. and H. C. in favor of something more suitable to the Japanese character of the work. The piece was played several times, and each time Eto bowed politely in response

Figure 3.5 Cowell, Stokowski, and Eto at the 1964 premiere of Cowell's Concerto for Koto. Reproduced with the permission of the Music Division, The New York Public Library for the Performing Arts, Astor, Lenox and Tilden Foundations, and the David and Sylvia Teitelbaum Fund, Inc., as successors to Henry and Sidney Cowell.

to L. S.'s expression of interest in the new Japanese cadenza he anticipated. But then here came Wagner again, and the rest was always the same. L. S. was irritated but in the end, I think, amused at Eto's wonderful bad taste; the composer, however, was mortified at what seemed to him a cheapening of the performance. After the piece was played in Tokyo, Columbia-Japan proposed to record the work, but Mr. Cowell would not give his permission for a recording unless Mr. Eto changed to a more suitable cadenza. This Eto refused to do, so there was no recording.[147]

Cowell's annoyance and his audience's laughter reveals an inability or unwillingness to hear and accept Eto's cadenza as a modernist (or postmodernist?) gesture. In a sense, with his cadenza and recitals Eto undermined midcentury American attempts to create cross-cultural music on American terms.

Cowell's alleged mortification over Eto's cadenza is ironic, given that Cowell himself juxtaposed a nineteenth-century Japanese musical style with the more ancient *gagaku* in this piece. The irony is compounded when we consider Cowell's 1965 Concerto no. 2 for Koto, a disappointing work that begins in Cowell's *gagaku* style complete with *sho*-influenced clusters and continues in its second and third movements with the *koto* playing variations on tunes vaguely reminiscent of "My Country, 'Tis of Thee" and "Greensleeves."[148] Finally, I should note that the *koto* style that influenced Cowell and other midcentury Euro-American composers had been shaped by Michio Miyagi, a major Japanese composer and *koto* performer who early in the century had set out to Westernize Japanese music and who had been influenced by *fin-de-siècle* French composers who, in turn, had been influenced by Asia. Both of Cowell's *koto* concerti were written for students of Miyagi's.[149] Was Cowell himself superimposing "Oriental instruments and impressions upon a conventional French style"?

The Concerto no. 2 for Koto was composed for Shinichi Yuize, a composition student of Cowell's in the mid-1950s and a member of the executive committee of the Tokyo East-West 1961 conference. Yuize had composed numerous Western-influenced pieces for *koto* before beginning his studies with Cowell. (Yuize's cadenzas for Cowell's concerto, however, make no reference to European pieces and instead draw on melodic gestures from the piece itself. Yuize premiered this work at Dartmouth College in May 1965 with Mario di Bonaventura conducting.) Exemplifying the tight interconnections in cross-cultural musical circles, Yuize performed at a private party given by Oliver Daniel celebrating Stokowski's seventy-fourth birthday.[150] Yuize went on to release numerous recordings, including of his own works, and in 1982 appeared on Jean-Pierre Rampal's album *Japanese Melodies, Vol. 3: Yamanakabushi* (CBS Records 37295). Most famously, he collaborated with Hozan Yamamoto (*shakuhachi*) and the jazz clarinetist Tony Scott on Scott's 1964 album *Music for Zen Meditation and Other Joys*. This recording has been referred to as the first World Beat album, and its suggestive "Other Joys" is indicative of the Orientalist marketing of exotic musics throughout this period.[151] In his associations with Eto and Yuize, Cowell was but one step removed from the musical worlds of midcentury jazz and popular exotica.

Conclusions and Credos: Exoticism, Modernism, and Historiography

A good deal of critical energy has been devoted in recent decades to determining which examples of cross-cultural influence in the twentieth century can be celebrated and which are to be condemned. John Corbett's dismissal of Cowell as a producer of mere "decorative Orientalism" has made careful investigation of Cowell's cross-cultural endeavors vitally important.[152] Although he salutes Cage for his "systematic experimental work," by claiming that certain composers were guilty of "cheap imitation" and of coming "perilously close" to sounding like their exotic models in their cross-cultural music, Corbett upholds the Romantic and modernist notions of autonomous creativity and unique style that Cage's revolution supposedly had overthrown. (Such criticism might well prompt us to question the "postmodern" status of Cage and the received tenet of the gulf between "modernism" and "postmodernism" more generally.) Corbett is right to suggest strands of continuity between nineteenth-century Orientalism and the works of twentieth-century

American composers, but he then too rigidly sets apart those composers who qualify for his "experimental" designation from such broader trends. David Nicholls, in contrast, has sought to separate Cowell from the "appropriative musical exoticism" of such early twentieth-century figures as Eichheim.[153] One could argue in response to Nicholls that Cowell's "engagement" with Japanese music was far more appropriative than Eichheim's in that he drew upon a greater number of Japanese musical features. (Eichheim primarily focused on melody and claimed to be simply presenting or translating his exotic collection. In addition, Cowell's involvement with East Asian music appears somewhat sporadic and selective when compared with Eichheim's devotion to these musical cultures.)[154] Framing Eichheim as a *kleinmeister* foil for appreciating Cowell's allegedly more advanced interactions with other cultures is not without its complications. As we have seen, it is not possible to keep separate the apparently neutral label "cross-cultural influence" from the politically charged terms of "Orientalist representation" and "cultural appropriation" when discussing the music of either of these composers.

In multiple ways Eichheim and Cowell differed greatly in their interactions with Japan and Japanese music. Whereas Cowell heard fundamental similarities across all cultures and claimed to identify with the other, Eichheim spoke of fundamental differences between the domestic and the exotic. Yet, I argue that in spite of their different approaches, we have little grounds for privileging one composer's form of cross-cultural music over the other. Even if I felt confident in such an endeavor, which of Cowell's own approaches to other cultures would I select to represent his position? The Cold War high modernist who in 1959, hoping to counter international serialism, called for a form of cross-cultural internationalism in which "musical materials developed in a single culture are carried beyond the customs of that culture according to a logic inherent in the basic materials themselves"[155] is the same composer who in 1959 composed "The Mysterious Oriental," an Orientalist character sketch replete with augmented seconds and reminiscent of the silent film period, one that he hoped could be used for TV or radio.[156]

A good deal of critical energy, including some of my own, has also been focused on determining which twentieth-century composers qualify as "modernists." Some of these studies have sought to push back the start date of musical modernism to include composers who are otherwise stranded between categories. (My discussion of Eichheim here might appear to be aimed in this direction, as is the work of Denise Von Glahn and Michael Broyles on Leo Ornstein or that of Charles Fisk on Rachmaninoff.)[157] Other scholars have argued for more inclusive accounts of musical modernism that would validate the music of composers from marginalized groups.[158] Given the intense political critique aimed at modernist aesthetics in recent decades, receiving the "modernist" designation might seem a rather dubious honor for a composer's current reputation.

My juxtaposition of Eichheim and Cowell for the purpose of reconsidering exoticism and modernism is not without precedent. In her comparative study of Albert Roussel's and Maurice Delage's encounters with the music of India, Jann

Pasler identifies Delage as a modernist who engaged "with the culture on its own terms" and determines in contrast that Roussel's background prepared him for a "spiritually enriching experience of India . . . resulting from a projection rather than an induction of value in its culture."[159] Pasler details four ways in which Delage's interactions with Indian music might be seen to qualify as modernist: 1. his "tone of resistance and critique" toward Western music; 2. his support for "Indians' resistance to foreign contamination" and his "respect for authenticity"; 3. his "preoccupation with the timbral richness of Indian music"; and 4. his devotion to "musical traditions of India's contemporary elite" rather than to Indian folk or popular music.[160] How do Eichheim and Cowell measure up in their interactions with Japanese music? Both composers turned toward East Asian musics as they turned away from Western musical traditions, although this is more explicit in the career of Eichheim. However, Eichheim only briefly referred to the musical Westernization afoot in Japan and, in theory, Cowell's celebration of hybridity transcends notions of cultural "authenticity." Both composers were attracted to the exotic timbres of East Asian instruments and made some attempts to incorporate and/or approximate these timbres and instruments in their scores. Finally, Cowell was more devoted to the elite music of *gagaku* while Eichheim drew upon a full range of Japanese traditional musics. In these terms, the contest between Eichheim and Cowell for "most modernist engagement with the exotic other" appears to end in a draw.

The differences between postmodern, modernist, and Romantic exoticism are often overstated, for the aesthetic aims and philosophies of each can be illustrated by examples taken from throughout the last century, frequently from within the oeuvres of individual composers.[161] As we seek to expand our understanding of where and when modernism happened and to define the set of aesthetics and techniques that should be grouped under that label, we will continue to discover unexpected traces of modernism in unexpected places. The comparative case study of Eichheim's and Cowell's engagements with Japanese music has involved a wide range of performance sites and meeting grounds for cross-cultural encounter. From the Imperial Palace in Tokyo to major urban concert halls in the United States, from Hollywood soundstages to movie theaters across the nation, and from the San Quentin penitentiary to the Manzanar internment camp—exotic encounters motivated would-be modernist musical expression across the board. The "high" and "low" and "East" and "West" interpenetrated each other throughout the twentieth century, not only in the celebrated "crossover" examples of the century's final decades.

I believe it is possible to celebrate the cross-cultural creations of Henry Cowell (and Colin McPhee, John Cage, Harry Partch, Lou Harrison, Alan Hovhaness, etc.) without ignoring the context that shaped his music, musical philosophy, and the strains of Orientalism that can be heard throughout his oeuvre. Attempting to tailor the mantle of "prophet of postmodern pluralism" to fit Cowell distorts our understanding of his long and varied career. Neither is it necessary to privilege his brand of the American cross-cultural at the expense of earlier composers such as

Eichheim or to sequester his music in the category of the "experimental" and "ultra-modern" far away from the mass-mediated music of his time. Indeed, in the following three chapters we will encounter numerous composers of film music who engaged in stylistic experimentation closely paralleling Eichheim's and Cowell's in their attempts to represent Japan. The professed goal of creating exotic authenticity was prevalent on both sides of the high/low cultural boundary.

4

Two Paradigmatic Tales, between Genres and Genders

Systems of exotic representation rely on repetition. The stereotype, as Homi K. Bhabha has put it, "vacillates between what is always 'in place,' already known, and something that must be anxiously repeated."[1] Repetition maintains and reaffirms the beliefs embedded in the stereotype and ensures that the distance of difference will not be collapsed. Repetition, of course, also points to a fundamental element of representational laziness or, perhaps, to the paramount importance of achieving once again the desired response from one's intended audience, of duplicating representational success. Finally, despite all calls to "make it new" from cultural mavens both high and low, there is clearly a certain comfort and pleasure in experiencing representational repetition.[2]

Documenting the longevity of a stereotype, or of any archetypal form of representation, is itself an important act of cultural criticism. And yet, identifying the subtle and not-so-subtle reinterpretations and refigurings of a stereotype over time, its multiple uses and disguises, can prove even more revealing. By far the most influential and long-lived narrative in the shaping of popular perceptions of Japan has been the tale of Madame Butterfly. Indeed, the self-sacrificing and subservient exotic woman abandoned by her white American husband has proved emblematic of Asian women more generally in countless American representations.[3] Likewise, tales of the deceitful and dangerous exotic male stalking white American women also exhibit an impressive track record in American popular culture. One of the most successful versions of this narrative, and one that initially focused on the Japanese male, was launched by the 1915 silent film *The Cheat*. Both tales deal with miscegenation, but from different perspectives.[4] The (brief) union of the Japanese woman and the white American male is typically presented in rosy terms, even though the tale ends badly for the exotic woman. However, the threat of a sexual union between the exotic man and the white American woman—while likely titillating for some heterosexual female audience members—is clearly presented as an abomination within the narrative frame.[5] Ultimately, the multiple versions of both *Madame Butterfly* and *The Cheat* and other similar tales seem primarily concerned with educating white American women on their proper relationship to white American men. In this chapter, I trace both of these exotic archetypes as they reappear across a range of genres and time periods, focusing on their early cinematic manifestations.[6]

In doing so, I reveal evidence of both evolution and stasis in perceptions of race and gender and raise broader issues of comparative genre analysis.[7]

Strikingly, these two representational lineages have involved multiple intersections between opera and film. In fact, these works offer an ideal case study for a comparative exploration of these two genres. Puccini's operatic treatment of the Butterfly narrative inspired numerous cinematic treatments, and DeMille's film *The Cheat* eventually inspired a French opera. How do film and opera differ in their methods of exotic representation and in their approach to manufacturing "exotic authenticity?" And to what extent does the inherent reflexivity faced by new versions of these tales undermine attempts at realism? In addressing such questions, it is important first to consider what the ultimate aims of veristic exoticism might be. Attention to details of local color is rarely, if ever, motivated solely by entertainment values. Rather, creating persuasive exoticism is more generally useful to the art of persuasion. For example, if a film can convince its audience of the authenticity of its depiction of the Japanese landscape and soundscape, then perhaps the audience is that much more likely to respond with credulity to its portrayal of Japanese women or to its position on the US-Japan political relationship. More broadly still, these works prompt us to assess the relative roles of aural and visual signification in each genre and how these expressive capabilities are redistributed when film and opera converge.

The intriguing practical and interpretive issues involved in bringing these two media together inspired discussion not only in recent film-opera studies but also during the early period of film's and opera's intersection.[8] Writing in *Opera Magazine* in 1915, E. H. Bierstadt observed: "The question of putting an operatic work upon the moving picture screen presented some obvious difficulties. As there could be no singing, the action of the whole opera must necessarily be pulled together, and quickened in such a way as to move with a natural rapidity." Bierstadt offered practical advice for realizing film-opera in the silent period: "If the facilities are at hand, the music of the opera may be played in time to the pictures. The score, of course, has to be arranged in such a way that the music and the pictures will fit perfectly, and in many instances this has been found thoroughly satisfactory." Bierstadt assumed that the primary motivation for producing film-operas was the desire to achieve a realism in representation not available within the theater, and noted that, with film, it "becomes at once possible to produce 'Carmen' in Seville or Toledo. 'Madame Butterfly' may come to us straight from the heart of Japan."[9] This assumption of film's ability to bring realism to opera and of the allegedly more "natural" dramatic pace of cinema is echoed in a 1919 article on the superiority of the screen over the stage for the presentation of opera[10] and some eighty years later in Jeongwon Joe's 1998 reference to the "clash between cinematic realism and operatic theatricality."[11] However, filmed versions of these tales reveal that cinematic exoticism proves no more realistic than does operatic representation of exotic others.[12]

Cinematic Realism, Reflexivity, and the American "Madame Butterfly" Narratives

This is a tale that has no beginning. In the opening of John Luther Long's 1898 *Madame Butterfly*, an American naval officer starts to tell the tale of the "Pink Geisha." Pinkerton cuts him short, complaining that he has heard this story of an American sailor's romance with a Japanese woman a thousand times before.[13] "Madame Butterfly" narratives have been retold in multiple genres at least since Pierre Loti's 1887 *Madame Chrysanthème* and Long's 1898 short story. The tale has appeared in the form of the fictionalized memoir, short story, staged melodrama, popular song, opera, musical, silent film, sound film, opera telecast, film-opera, pornographic novel, and concept album. (See Box 4.1.) Just as Long's Pinkerton alludes derisively to previous tellings, each successive rendition of the narrative either covertly or overtly reflects back upon earlier versions. Inescapably, versions of the tale following Puccini's 1904 opera have taken into account not only its plot, but its sonic representations of Japan as well. Butterfly's lament continues to reverberate across genres, propagating multiple intertextual echoes.

Why have "Madame Butterfly" narratives proven so compelling for so long, particularly in the United States? Is Long's damning story a persistent irritant that white American males have sought to assuage or does the Orientalist fantasy of following Pinkerton's example continue to inspire multiple reworkings? Clearly, Butterfly has been made to perform a good deal of cultural work over the past hundred years and has always been entangled in the web of race and gender perception in American popular culture. The Butterfly canon and productions of Puccini's opera have both reflected and redirected the mercurial American image of the Japanese. In fact, successive Butterfly works often reflexively worked against the established narrative tradition in order to promote an (allegedly) new position on issues of race, gender, and Pacific Rim politics. Hollywood's Butterflies have been repeatedly engaged in such endeavors. I will focus here on specific cinematic presentations of the "Madame Butterfly" tale and on their relationship to Puccini's opera. I will start, however, by considering the relationship between the visual and the musical elements in some of the earliest versions of this exotic story.

"Proto-cinematic" Butterflies?

In retrospect, Butterfly—like several of her late nineteenth-century exotic sisters—seems destined for the screen: the careful coordination of music and visual image present in the earliest versions of her tale appears almost cinematic. Such anachronistic descriptions are inspired not only by products of the nineteenth-century melodrama tradition, but also by works not intended for stage or screen. For example, Loti's *Madame Chrysanthème* is so heavily illustrated that in some sections his text functions as commentary on the pictures, in a fashion parallel to the role

Box 4.1 Selected Works Related to "Madame Butterfly"

1887   *Madame Chrysanthème*, Pierre Loti, novel

1893   *Madame Chrysanthème*, mus. André Messager, opera based on Loti

1898   *Madame Butterfly*, John Luther Long, short story

1900   *Madame Butterfly*, David Belasco (based on Long), mus. William Furst, melodrama

1901   *A Japanese Nightingale*, Onoto Watanna (Winnifred Eaton), novel

1903   *A Japanese Nightingale*, William Young (based on Eaton), mus. N. Clifford Page, melodrama

1904   *Madama Butterfly*, mus. Giacomo Puccini, opera, revised 1906

1915   *Madame Butterfly*, dir. Sidney Olcott, silent film

1916   "Poor Butterfly," w. John Golden, mus. Raymond Hubbell, popular song

1918   *His Birthright*, dir. William Worthington, silent film

1919   *Harakiri*, dir. Fritz Lang, silent film

1922   *Toll of the Sea*, dir. Chester M. Franklin, cue sheet by Ernst Luz, silent film

1932   *Madame Butterfly*, dir. Marion Gering, mus. W. Franke Harling, sound film

1934   *One Night of Love*, dir. Victor Schertzinger, mus. Schertzinger and Gus Kahn, sound film

1936   *Il sogno di Butterfly/Premiere der Butterfly*, dir. Carmine Gallone, sound film

1939   *First Love*, dir. Henry Koster, mus. Charles Previn and H. J. Salter, sound film

1950   *The Toast of New Orleans*, dir. Norman Taurog, mus. George Stoll, sound film

1952   *Japanese War Bride*, dir. King Vidor, mus. Emil Newman and Arthur Lange, sound film

1955   *Madama Butterfly*, dir. Gallone, Italian-Japanese production, film-opera

1957   *Sayonara*, dir. Joshua Logan, mus. Franz Waxman, sound film

1962   *My Geisha*, dir. Jack Cardiff, mus. Waxman, sound film

1974   *Madama Butterfly*, dir. Jean-Pierre Ponnelle, film-opera

1984   *Fans*, Malcolm McLaren, concept album

1987   *Fatal Attraction*, dir. Adrian Lyne, mus. Maurice Jarre, sound film

1988   *Butterfly*, Paul Loewen, novel

1988   *M. Butterfly*, David Henry Hwang, play

1989   *Miss Saigon*, mus. Claude-Michel Schönberg, musical

1993   *M. Butterfly*, dir. David Cronenberg, mus. Howard Shore, sound film

1993   *Household Saints*, dir. Nancy Savoca, mus. Stephen Endelman, sound film

1995   *Madama Butterfly*, dir. Frédéric Mitterrand, film-opera

1996   *Pinkerton*, Weezer, concept album

of intertitles in silent film. Loti's geisha sings compulsively throughout the novel—
"melancholy" music permeates the very atmosphere of Loti's Japan—and the French
protagonist's evolving opinion of the geisha's singing serves as our clearest gauge of
his feelings for her.[14] As we read his descriptions and view the illustrations of her
music-making we are prompted to audiate our own version of her exotic song.

More clearly "cinematic," the experience of David Belasco's 1900 staged melodrama *Madame Butterfly* resembled that of later silent film or even of the earlier
lantern slide presentations in its lighting effects and coordination of music with
image. The manuscript score of William Furst's incidental music for Belasco's play
includes detailed dynamic markings and other indications to the musicians to ensure that the music would closely underscore the dialogue, action, and stage images
throughout the work.[15] The most celebrated feature of this production was the (allegedly) fourteen-minute nonverbal section in which lighting and music realized
the passing of Butterfly's night of anticipation.[16] Furst's note for this scene offers
cues precisely coordinating the music with the changing lights. Similarly, notes
contained in the manuscript piano score indicate that, not unlike a cinematic Main
Title sequence, the prelude to Belasco's *Madame Butterfly* offered a series of drops
presenting scenes of exotic Japan accompanied by Furst's music.[17] Belasco's *The
Darling of the Gods*, a 1902 play set in Japan, also began with a series of still images
accompanied by music, and Belasco repeatedly insisted that the success of both
plays was primarily due to his innovative lighting effects and their musical accompaniment.[18] Belasco exhibited an auteur's concern with musical details: "if the play
has a musical accompaniment, I read it to the composer I have engaged, indicating
its moods and feeling. He must interpret every scene and speech as if he were
writing the score for a song."[19] Blanche Bates, the performer who premiered the
title roles in both Belasco's *Madame Butterfly* and *The Darling of the Gods*, discussed
the musical quality of Belasco's production style in 1903 and related that "no one is
like Mr. Belasco as far as regards times. Everything is timed to a 'T.' The play runs to
music."[20]

A. Nicholas Vardac has claimed that Belasco's "popularity continued into the
years of the early film because his theatrical technique was highly cinematic."[21] Of
course, the "cinematic" elements of Belasco's *Madame Butterfly* were actually indebted to the nineteenth-century melodrama tradition, and Belasco's production
style—and the tradition he represented—influenced the production of silent film.
Silent film also modeled itself on such melodramas as Belasco's *Madame Butterfly*
in its use of music. As Anne Dhu Shapiro notes: "The functions of music in melodrama were transferred very directly into music for the early silent film. Several
films were in fact made of the most popular melodramas. Theater musicians went
from stage productions to making live music for the silent film. Not surprisingly,
they brought some of their traditions and styles of music making with them."[22]
Belasco addressed the relationship between theater and cinema himself in a chapter
entitled "The Drama's Flickering Bogy—The Movies." He argued that "motion
pictures have been a parasite feeding upon the arts of the theatre" and that films

were not a direct threat to staged performance because the flickering images on the screen could only achieve a superficial realism.[23] Perhaps Belasco's confidence vis-à-vis the emerging cinema stemmed from the fact that his theater already offered stunning images and musical accompaniment, as well as the audible dialogue absent from the silent film.[24]

Like Belasco, Puccini has also inspired repeated comparisons with cinema. Peter Franklin observed that "long before the advent of the sound film, German critics had used the term 'Kino-Oper' with reference to Puccini."[25] Franklin himself has pointed to Puccini's *Tosca*, in particular, as illustrating "the proto-cinematic role of music" in opera and has imagined an ideal film version of *Tosca* in which "the actors would have spoken their lines above Puccini's music, turning the opera into the literal melodrama that veristic literature unerringly sought when it first ventured onto the stage heading, via the opera-house, for the cinema screen."[26] Any "cinematic elements" in Puccini's *Madama Butterfly*, however, are likely traceable to the inchoate "cinematic" features of Belasco's melodrama.

Puccini famously understood not a word of the dialogue when he experienced Belasco's production in London. Contrary to Belasco's oft-quoted and inaccurate demurral—"I never believed he [Puccini] did see 'Madame Butterfly' that first night. He only heard the music he was going to write"—Puccini's attention must also have been focused on the relationship between Belasco's images and Furst's music. In a 1916 article in the *New York Tribune*, H. E. Krehbiel presents "Japanese" tunes from Furst's and Puccini's scores. He offers no comparative commentary beyond the following: "If Signor Puccini had needed the suggestion that Japanese music was necessary for a Japanese play (which of course he did not) he might have received it when he saw Mr. Belasco's play in London."[27] Although my study of Furst's score has revealed no obvious signs of borrowing by Puccini, certain musical parallels are evident between the two works.[28] Both Furst and Puccini employ running sixteenth-note figures and prominent grace note ornamentation in their overtures. Both turn to a lilting 6/8 meter for Butterfly's and Suzuki's preparation for Pinkerton's expected imminent return. In Furst's score, this joyous preparation music returns near the play's end as Suzuki exits sobbing. Similarly, in Puccini's opera we hear musical allusions to the homecoming preparation as Suzuki exhorts Pinkerton to look at the scattered flowers as evidence of Butterfly's tragic faith. Finally, both Furst and Puccini underscored Butterfly's pantomimed suicide with a martial pentatonic melody. These detailed correspondences may well be coincidental, but they nevertheless point to the rampant intertextuality evident in the Butterfly corpus and caution against attempts to pin down a single Ur-version of this tale.

The first silent films of the "Madame Butterfly" narrative tended to turn back to Long's story for their plot and dialogue and to sources other than Puccini for their musical *japonisme*. This is particularly true of Sidney Olcott's 1915 *Madame Butterfly*, a vehicle for Mary Pickford. This is not to say that the opera is entirely absent from our experience of this film, nor to suggest that the absence of Puccini indicates a more general musical abdication. While it is possible that some screenings of this silent film were accompanied by excerpts from Puccini's opera, played either on a phonograph or by live musicians, it is more likely that the organist or ensemble drew upon musicals and Tin Pan Alley songs dealing with Japan and on published silent film music anthologies.[29] Nick Browne has stated that the "erasure [in the 1915 film] of Puccini's music and the singing, with their coordinated power of elevation, significantly alters the conditions of reception. It is manifestly a silent film."[30] This is a surprising assertion. Perhaps even more so than with other films of the period, the 1915 *Madame Butterfly* appears to call for musical accompaniment.[31] The film prompts the realization of diegetic musical performance (performance framed within the world of the narrative) in three sections. Butterfly sings and plays the *shamisen* twice in the film and Pinkerton and Butterfly meet at a theatrical performance that resembles low budget *kabuki*. (See Figure 4.1.) I have discovered one published cue sheet for this film, which offers a suggestion of the music likely heard at its screenings.[32] This 1916 cue sheet draws heavily on Sidney Jones's *The Geisha*, a late nineteenth-century British musical comedy that was second only to *The Mikado* in popular *japonisme*, as well as on several Tin Pan Alley songs. None of Puccini's music is called for. Similarly, Ernst Luz's compiled score for the 1922 *Toll of the Sea*—a version of the "Madame Butterfly" tale set in China—also avoids Puccini.[33] Luz explains in his preface to the score: "While the music selected must continually suggest the Chinese or Japanese character, nevertheless, care must be

Figure 4.1 Mary Pickford as the silent singing geisha. Famous Players publicity still for *Madame Butterfly* (1915). Courtesy of the Academy of Motion Picture Arts and Sciences.

taken in proper programming so that it does not become tiresome." He specifically warns that Puccini's music should not be employed to accompany the film without the publisher's permission and calls for a Chinese gong during the introduction to the pieces "By the Japanese Sea" and "Japanese Legende." Puccini clearly created the most famous soundtrack for the Madame Butterfly legend, but his influence on later manifestations of the tale was rarely straightforward.

My focus now will be on two sound films—Paramount's 1932 *Madame Butterfly* and that studio's 1962 *My Geisha*. Neither of these works are film-operas, that is, screened productions of an opera. Instead, each incorporates musical and narrative material from Puccini's opera and simultaneously comments upon it. Produced near the beginning of the sound era, the 1932 film struggles to co-opt the opera and thereby to create a fully cinematic Butterfly. *My Geisha*, created three decades later, aspires to subvert Orientalist representation by reflecting back upon Puccini's and Hollywood's Butterflies with hip sophistication. I will concentrate on the complex relationship between the music heard in these films and in Puccini's opera, and on how pre-existent versions of the Madame Butterfly narrative are reworked to promote and shape prevailing race and gender ideology. I will also consider the relationship between operatic and cinematic Orientalist representation more generally and will investigate whether, in its bid to project exotic realism in both sound and image, film succeeds in surpassing the experience of staged Orientalist opera. In addition, these films prompt a discussion of the differences between opera's ability to stage itself as opera-within-an-opera and film's potential for reflexive screenings. Both the 1932 *Madame Butterfly* and 1962 *My Geisha* point back to earlier presentations of the tale and both seek to capture the "real" Butterfly on film.

"La Ghesha canterà"?: Avoiding Opera

In most versions of the narrative Butterfly is a singing geisha. She does not sing, however, in the 1932 Paramount sound film. Similarly, Butterfly only briefly sings in Puccini's opera. After Sharpless suggests that Pinkerton will never return and that she should marry Yamadori, Puccini's Butterfly brings out her child and, imagining a return to her life as a performing geisha, cries out "E come fece già/la Ghesha canterà!" Although her momentary acting out of this possible future performance has been referred to by some as diegetic or a sung song, I do not believe the designation is warranted. Butterfly's musical style does not change to signal a diegetic performance, and the text suggests that, in her imagination, she is soliciting her audience rather than performing for it. In the original version of the opera Butterfly sang twice to her child, whereas in the final version she sings only a brief lullaby as she ascends the stairs with the boy following her night of anticipation. In Long's story Butterfly sings several songs, including a lullaby that Pinkerton had frequently sung to her: "Rog-a-by, bebby, off in Japan,/You jus' a picture off of a fan."[34] Butterfly did fulfill her role as a singing geisha in the draft versions of the

1932 film.[35] The preliminary scripts also reveal other intended vocal performances. For example, the Americans' arrival at the port was to be heralded by the "Star Spangled Banner being sung by shrill boyish voices, mostly off key." The shot of these Japanese schoolboys was described as follows: "PAN to get the effect of the bland, expressionless faces, the mechanically moving lips." In the final shooting script, only Pinkerton sings.

One might assume that in 1932 Hollywood would have been eager finally to realize Thomas Edison's dream of merging opera directly with film. Producers frequently had been interested in opera during the silent period and had used opera to raise the cultural status of the movies.[36] In addition, 1932 has been identified as the year when sound film began to embrace the use of nondiegetic music.[37] Rather than creating a film of Puccini's opera, however, the producers of the 1932 *Madame Butterfly* appear to have been somewhat opera-phobic, or perhaps assumed their audience to be so.[38] From their initial negotiations with Ricordi it is clear that they never intended to include the vocal music. In fact, Paramount attempted to disassociate the film from the opera as clearly as possible in its publicity materials. Exhibitors were instructed that the film was "NOT a picturization of the opera—the music does not play an important part in the production, furnishing only the incidental background. Say nothing about the opera or its music in your campaign . . . but bill it as a romance, for that's what it is!"[39] While music is heard throughout almost every minute of the film, the volume of the music is often quite low. By 1932 at least some Hollywood executives were concerned that a film-opera would limit rather than expand their potential audience.[40]

The 1932 *Madame Butterfly* is primarily a "film-melodrama" in which the spoken dialogue is heard over a continuous orchestral accompaniment and much of the onscreen movement appears choreographed. Rather than openly embracing Puccini, the film harnesses his music to support its own version of the tale. The credits acknowledge both Long's and Belasco's versions and production files reveal that the 1915 silent film was also consulted. However, this film goes far beyond the short story, play, opera, and silent film by considerably fleshing out the narrative. In particular, we are privy to Pinkerton and Butterfly's domestic life to a far greater extent than in the prior versions.[41] We hear sections of Puccini's music—both at their original narrative positions and transposed to new episodes—along with new Orientalist music by the Hollywood composer W. Franke Harling.[42] Some sections of the film appear to illustrate Marcia Citron's term "opera in prose"—that is, films that employ operatic music beneath dialogue that is based on the opera's literary source.[43] Alternately, certain scenes of the film do qualify as "film-opera" in that we hear Puccini's music in the same narrative spot accompanying the same dramatic action. The screening of these purely orchestral sections from the opera, and others without dialogue but supported with Harling's music, also resembles silent film. In a memo, the film's producer Ben Schulberg wrote: "We have played substantial portions of the story in pantomime with a minimum of dialogue . . . which should make for effective picturization, all the more so because of the Puccini music which we will play against these scenes."[44] (The passing of the night sequence, which employs Puccini's music and ten graceful dissolves, is particularly illustrative of this intention.)

Despite Paramount's professed opera-phobia, the soundtrack proves operatic not only in its use of Puccini's score but also in the style and form of Harling's original music. For instance, Harling employs Puccini's "curse motive" for his own dramatic purposes and creates his own leitmotifs for the American consul Sharpless and for Pinkerton.[45] A good deal of Puccini's music is heard in the film and often quite prominently. Most of the major themes are employed, save Pinkerton's aria of Yankee bravado. (The significance of this omission will be considered later.) Also absent from the soundtrack are sections of the operatic score in which Puccini conspicuously reworked Japanese folk tunes. Since Harling did not draw upon Japanese folk tunes himself, we actually hear less "Japanese" music in the film than in the opera.[46] The use of Puccini's music and the coordination between music and image in the film's Main Title sequence suggest that we are about to view a screened production of the opera. The film begins with Puccini's orchestral introduction heard in its entirety. We first see the logo for Paramount Studios as the music starts and then view a still image of Mt. Fuji. This visual rhyme thus offers a reflexive wink at the very start of the film. Puccini's fugal music works closely with the succession of still images in this title sequence. The change from one shot to the next is achieved by the opening and closing of a fan covering the entire screen. The first fan movement occurs with the second fugal entry and the third fan appears to open and close with the ascending and descending lines heard at Puccini's rehearsal no. 3.[47] The two stills of the male leads in uniform appear with the brassy music at rehearsal no. 4 in Puccini's score. As the title sequence ends, there is a brief silence before Harling's music is heard. It is only at this point that one realizes this will not be a film-opera.

Puccini's opera offers only one extended love scene between Pinkerton and Butterfly. In contrast, the 1932 film shows several shorter intimate scenes between the couple and thereby establishes the exotic woman's ideal nature. Harling drew upon Puccini's Act I love duet music for these scenes, most often leaving Puccini's vocal melodies out. He occasionally used Puccini's music in precisely parallel dramatic locations. For example, in the film, Pinkerton first encounters Butterfly at Goro's teahouse and pursues her in a moonlit garden. At the moment when it is clear that Pinkerton is entirely smitten with her, when he realizes that she is completely innocent of the ways of love and seems eager to please, Harling employed Puccini's soaring theme (rehearsal no. 128) heard in the opera just before Butterfly's plea "Vogliatemi bene, un bene piccolino, un bene da bambino" ("Love me, just a very little, as you would a baby"). In a later scene in the film, as we see Suzuki preparing the bridal chamber, we hear the music from Act I in the opera as Butterfly undresses for their nuptial night. In order to match the faster dramatic pace of the film's bridal chamber scene and to reach Puccini's musical climax at the moment of Butterfly and Pinkerton's onscreen kiss, Harling radically cut and pasted the opera's love duet material. In general, film moves at a much quicker (but not necessarily more realistic) dramatic rate and unfolds on a smaller dramatic scale than does opera. Harling skillfully negotiated these differences in creating his score.

In contrast to Long's short story and to Puccini's opera, the 1932 Pinkerton does return to confront Butterfly directly and to explain to her that he is saying farewell for good. In this scene, Harling poignantly employed excerpts from the operatic Butterfly's "Un bel dì" aria and from the Act I love duet—a dramatic decision as effective as the return of the *bacio* theme in Verdi's *Otello*. For Pinkerton's arrival, Harling chose the precise moment in Puccini's score when Butterfly describes what she will do when Pinkerton returns and then acts out what she hopes he will say. We hear the musical climax from Act II, rehearsal no. 16 as we see Butterfly embrace Pinkerton onscreen while he stands starkly unresponsive. Finally, as Butterfly formally bows and slowly reenters the house alone, closing the sliding *shoji* for the last time, we hear the music from the very end of Act I in Puccini's opera when the operatic lovers retire indoors together. Harling carefully reworked Puccini's music to powerful effect so that it appears to have been composed to underscore this very sequence.

This film reflects back upon the Madame Butterfly tradition not only in its use of Long, Belasco, and Puccini, but also in its references to Tin Pan Alley's *japonisme*. Golden and Hubbell's 1916 song "Poor Butterfly" was perhaps the most widely known version of the Madame Butterfly narrative in the United States in the early 1930s. In the film, the song is heard diegetically and inscribed with a new significance during a scene set in a New York City restaurant. As Pinkerton sits glumly, his fiancée draws his attention to a robin on a branch outside the window. At this significant moment, we hear an instrumental rendition of the chorus of "Poor Butterfly," presumably played by an unseen ensemble or phonograph in the restaurant. In the song, the text of this section is in the voice of the lamenting Japanese woman. This music might be intended to remind us and Pinkerton of Butterfly and her pining voice, of *her* suffering. However, since we see Pinkerton's dejected demeanor and hear *his* dispirited speech, the tune becomes the accompaniment to his feelings of guilt and discomfort. The sequence ends exactly with the end of the song. Such blatant reflexivity, similar to the Paramount and Mt. Fuji visual rhyme mentioned above, would seem to undermine the film's diegesis and cinema's vaunted realism.[48] By drawing attention to the Butterfly canon in this way, the film simultaneously asserts its authority to tell the tale anew and betrays its inability to escape its predecessors and to claim genuineness.

The only vocal music heard in the entire 1932 film is Pinkerton's diegetic singing of Harling's and Rainger's newly composed song, "My Flower of Japan." Thus, the film's most "operatic" sequence avoids Puccini entirely. As we have seen, a significant number of the Tin Pan Alley songs dealing with Japan in the first decades of the twentieth century were set in the voice of an American male longing to return to his Japanese lover. This song's lyrics and its appearances in the film imply its preexistence. Typical of Tin Pan Alley's *japonisme*, the lyrics reveal that the male protagonist has been inspired by Japanese art objects and has dreamed of Japanese women: "Long have I waited to hold you enfold you, My flower of Japan, You have created a dream world, my dream world, A picture off a fan." We first hear an excerpt of the tune whistled by Pinkerton in his cabin as he packs up to disembark. Oddly, he begins to whistle the song just as he picks up a photograph of his American sweetheart after agreeing to join his buddy Barton for an exotic night on the town. Perhaps this whistling offers a subtle suggestion that the white woman will eventually replace or become his "flower of Japan." Since the song and its lyrics have not yet been heard by the film's audience, any irony is lost. In retrospect, however, this whistling suggests that Pinkerton has brought Tin Pan Alley's images of Japanese women with him in his mental baggage.[49]

The entire song is sung by Pinkerton—Cary Grant drawing upon his musical theater experience—only once in the film. In the previous scene, Butterfly has learned by accident at dinner that Pinkerton will be departing for the United States the very next morning. The sequence in question begins with silence and a shot of Butterfly praying. The silence is momentary and the rest of the sequence was cut precisely to allow for a complete orchestral statement of the song immediately followed by Pinkerton's vocal rendition with orchestral accompaniment. After Pinkerton tries to comfort Butterfly, and she attempts to perform her domestic duties with a smile, she asks him to sing his song "same as always, please." Her request is delivered just as the orchestra reaches the end of the song and Pinkerton complies by joining the orchestra for the repeat. The diegetic/nondiegetic divide appears to be collapsed, or is at least boldly transgressed several times in the sequence, most obviously when Pinkerton begins to sing with the unheard(?) orchestra. During the first orchestral statement of the song, the background music crescendos with Pinkerton's movements as he helps Butterfly rise following her prayer. Not only do most of the movements of Pinkerton and Butterfly appear choreographed, the camera movement is also closely coordinated with the music. The camera pans smoothly during the longest held note in the melody and the cutting rhythm is in synch with the beginnings of musical phrases. Pinkerton's song ends and the screen fades to black as we hear Butterfly's violent sobbing. In this film, the most intensely emotional scenes are treated most like a film-opera.

In the film's final sequence we hear a full minute without music—the longest musical silence in the entire film—as we see and hear Butterfly offering a final prayer at her altar. Unlike in the opera, where she is interrupted by her child, Butterfly remains alone in the film for the final two and a half minutes as she prepares for death. This allows the film to focus more intensely on the pathetic suicide of this exotic woman. Puccini's music begins as Butterfly picks up her father's sword, a movement punctuated by Harling with a gong crash. We hear fourteen bars starting from Puccini's rehearsal no. 55. After a brief musical silence for Butterfly's final line "I love you for always," the final eleven bars of the opera mark her death as the camera pulls back and the screen then fades to black. Butterfly's singing voice remains silent to the end in this sequence. As it was displaced by Pinkerton's singing earlier in the film, the operatic Butterfly's final lines are taken here by the violins.[50] She dies at the foot of Pinkerton's chair where we had earlier witnessed her dance attendance on him like an eager puppy.

"What do your excellencies desire?": Avoiding Exotic Possibilities

In the publicity materials generated for *Madame Butterfly*, Paramount professed an ardent desire to achieve exotic veracity. Such claims—presupposing a definable and attainable "exotic realism"—have been made throughout Hollywood's history and are most often spurious. For example, the filmmakers sought to suggest exotic authenticity by crediting the Japanese dancer Michio Ito as both technical adviser and dance director.[51] However, an interoffice memo from the producer dated 28 October 1932 reveals that the decision to credit Ito was made in order to disarm expected criticism of the film's inaccurate presentation of Japanese customs. Taking for granted a general American ignorance of Japanese culture, the producer stated that by citing Ito's assistance they would "undoubtedly lead many a critic, who might otherwise think and state we are wrong, to fear to present such a conclusion." A 16 December 1932 review of the film in *Variety* reveals that, at least for one critic, their stratagem backfired: "Picture at times becomes too technical, under direction of Michio Ito, Japanese dancer. There can be little fault with the authenticity of Japanese customs, but they clutter up the picture and drag the tempo to a snail's pace." We learn from a "ready-to-publish" article included in the film's publicity package that "thirty Japanese girls" were hired for the film. Despite Hollywood's best intentions to hire the "authentic other," "it was soon found that all but two of them had been born in the United States or had been brought here while very young, and knew little of their native land. The other two were real geisha girls who married wealthy countrymen and moved to Los Angeles." This Paramount press release is entitled "East Meets West and Learns Forgotten Customs of Native Orient from Movie Mentors," and it claims that the Japanese girls "were found to have so completely succumbed to Western influence that they had to be taught the customs of their own country." Hollywood has repeatedly proved determined to teach the other exactly how to look and sound exotic for its cinematic representations of Japan.

The 1932 *Madame Butterfly* introduces several new scenes of local color not found in previous versions of the narrative. During the early stages of the production, a cameraman was sent to Japan to shoot "atmospheric" footage. Some of this on-location footage was employed in double-exposed shots—as just before Butterfly and her family are shown praying at a temple—thereby placing the film's actors "in Japan" without actually sending them there.[52] Later we witness (what is framed as) the traditional Japanese wedding ceremony of Pinkerton and Butterfly, presented in far more detail than in the opera. The most extended scene of exotic realism, and one that well illustrates the care the filmmakers took to shape this reality, occurs at Goro's teahouse. This cinematic teahouse is constructed through image and sound as a site of erotic suggestion. We hear offscreen female laughter, glimpse the faces of Japanese women in mirrors and through lattice windows, and are led to hidden rooms behind multiple sliding doors. The scene begins with a woman lighting a lantern outside. This shot then dissolves as the image of Butterfly's face fades into her handheld mirror which perfectly replaces the illuminated lantern on the screen. Harling's melody at this reflective moment is somewhat mirrored itself around the pitch B♭, which roughly splits the tune's octave ambitus. The arrival of Pinkerton and Barton sets in motion a veritable ballet of scurrying geisha, with multiple vortices in multiple planes. (The brief five-shot entrance sequence is demarcated by the length of the music, which consists primarily of a nervous ostinato figure in the low strings and a clopping woodblock.) This intricate onscreen movement, along with the multiple layers of sliding doors, suggests that the geisha house is a mysterious, enticing labyrinth that these two American males are penetrating. The camera pans to the right in the first shot to reveal a line of geisha who then rise and in two groups patter offscreen in opposite directions. In the second shot, we see Pinkerton and Barton enter from the left with a geisha who continues toward the back as two geishas advance from the right to greet them, followed by two other geishas who head off toward the back. In the fourth shot, Pinkerton and Barton abruptly redirect their path toward an offscreen room on the right. This redirection of their movement coincides with a bit of syncopated jazzy material on the soundtrack, a striking stylistic shift that (stereotypically) suggests something alluring lies just behind the next sliding *shoji*.

Harling's manuscript short score discloses some effort on his part to approximate Japanese traditional music and to participate in the film's professed representational goals.[53] However, this objective was somewhat compromised in the recording of the final soundtrack. This is apparent from early on in the film. Harling composed the music in Example 4.1 for the dock scene as the sailors arrive in Japan. The use of pizzicato strings moving in parallel fifths, fourths, and octaves and the rapid xylophone figuration hardly represent innovations in musical *japonisme*. However, a note written at the top of this score indicates that Harling planned to enhance

Example 4.1 Arrival in Japan, W. Franke Harling, *Madame Butterfly* (Paramount, 1932).

his musical exoticism: "add native percussion effects." In the final soundtrack this music is barely audible beneath the dialogue.

Following their choreographed entrance sequence discussed above, Goro welcomes the Americans to his teahouse and the following exchange ensues:

GORO: What do your excellencies desire?
PINKERTON: Music.
BARTON: And girls.
PINKERTON: And, uh, dancing.
BARTON: And girls.
PINKERTON: And, uh, um, girls.
GORO: How many?
PINKERTON: Well, one's enough for me.

Harling responded to Pinkerton's demands for exotic music and dance with his own simulated Japanese music. (See Example 4.2a.) This tune employs the Japanese *in* scale—a pentatonic scale featuring two semitones. In addition, Harling called for a "Japanese bamboo flute" and harp, mandolin, and a pizzicato violin for this melody, thus roughly approximating the timbres of the Japanese *sankyoku* ensemble. The following note appears above this music: "under the ensuing dialogue, native music steals into the scene as though blown by a soft breeze from the tea-room adjacent

Example 4.2a and 4.2b Geisha teahouse music, W. Franke Harling, *Madame Butterfly* (Paramount, 1932).

to the garden." Harling also gave the indication: "ad lib = no specific tempo or time signature." This represents his boldest gesture toward approximating Japanese traditional music which, in several of its most refined forms, projects an ambiguity in pulse and meter. However, bar lines were added in pencil on the score at some point and the poetic cue was crossed out. As the music begins, the American men are led deeper into the teahouse and we catch glimpses of geishas playing *shamisen*, although we do not hear their music. We also briefly view three dancing geishas and do hear their footstomps. These moments of dance and the general close coordination between onscreen movement and the music suggest to the viewer that Harling's musical *japonisme* is diegetic and authentic. As the American men settle into their private room and their hired geishas arrive to entertain them, Harling develops his tune by adding a countermelody in the harp and cymbalon and by calling for a *shamisen* in his score. (See Example 4.2b.)

While being entertained by his geisha, Pinkerton idly picks up her *shamisen* and admires it. However, his attention is quickly diverted by a striking image and he puts the *shamisen* aside. Butterfly is amusing herself in another room by flitting around in her new kimono, like a butterfly. The soundtrack abruptly switches from Harling's musical *japonisme* to a graceful waltz to accompany her flowing dance, which casts a shadow through several sets of sliding paper walls.[54] Although he had glanced only briefly at the pseudo-Japanese dancing of the geishas during his entrance into the teahouse, Pinkerton is now transfixed by this shadow dance projected on the *shoji* screen and immediately deserts his geisha and her *shamisen*. With a strong sense of entitlement, he opens several doors and barges into Butterfly's room. Startled by this sudden appearance of a tall American in uniform, Butterfly flutters around and then flies out into the garden, accompanied by a staccato woodwind cascade and pursued by the enchanted Pinkerton. Just as Pinkerton is aroused by the very dance style that looks least Japanese, we are intended to recognize Butterfly's singular beauty in part through the shift to a more obviously Euro-American musical style.[55]

The possibilities for enhancing musical exoticism in the 1932 *Madame Butterfly* were not fully realized. Why did this film not employ actual Japanese music for the scene set in the teahouse? Why was the *shamisen* put aside? In another Orientalist feature from 1932, Frank Capra's *The Bitter Tea of General Yen*, Harling (or the film's producers) chose to include the performance of Chinese *sizhu* music in addition to Harling's own musical *chinoiserie*. Perhaps the use of Japanese music in *Madame Butterfly* was avoided because it would have virtually excluded any original composition by Harling since he was already obliged to use so much of Puccini's score. As it turned out, even some of Harling's intended *japonisme* effects were left out in the recording of the soundtrack. Similarly, production notes reveal that the filmmakers considered casting the Japanese actress Toshia Mori in the role of Butterfly. (Mori had just played the role of the Chinese servant girl in *The Bitter Tea of General Yen*.) However, the filmmakers eventually rejected this possibility for achieving "authentic" exoticism. In the end, Sylvia Sydney played the role in yellowface. (See Figure 4.2.)

Figure 4.2 Sylvia Sydney and Cary Grant as Butterfly and Pinkerton. Paramount publicity still for *Madame Butterfly* (1932). Courtesy of the Academy of Motion Picture Arts and Sciences.

"An unpleasant hangover on the picture": Avoiding Miscegenation

The American characters in the Madame Butterfly narrative have undergone an extensive rehabilitation ever since Long. In Long's original story there is no indication that Pinkerton entertains any serious feelings for Butterfly and he disappears from the tale without displaying any remorse. His white American wife is all business and refers to Butterfly as a "pretty plaything." Pinkerton is considerably improved by the final version of Puccini's opera. Not only is he given an aria to display his caring, sentimental side toward the end, but he is also allowed the last heartfelt cry. The writers and director of the 1932 film attempted to make the American couple look as compassionate and guiltless as possible. Pinkerton is presented as Butterfly's savior. Barton and Goro both explain to him, within earshot of Butterfly, that a Japanese marriage is a casual, nonbinding act and Butterfly repeatedly thanks him for his charity. Instead of boasting of amorous conquests in multiple exotic ports, Pinkerton sings a song of praise to the exotic woman. Finally, in the 1932 film Pinkerton remains unaware of their child's existence.

The ending of the 1932 film is unique: Butterfly instructs Suzuki to take the boy to his grandfather and then commits suicide. This ending was determined not solely for dramatic reasons, but for racial ones also. Race was at issue from the early stages of the film's production. Telegrams from July 1932 reveal that the "miscegenation angle" in the Madame Butterfly narrative was considered by the censors responsible for upholding the industry's code. Colonel Jason S. Joy of the Association of Motion Picture Producers wrote on 22 July 1932 that Paramount would not have trouble securing permission to film the story since "the interpretation of miscegenation under the code has always been guided by the second dictionary definition which specifies whites and negroes only." In a long memo dated 5 October 1932, Ben Schulberg, the film's producer, explained that the script had been revised in order to make Pinkerton a more likable character than in the opera and the play. He also discussed the new ending, arguing that since the Pinkertons are presented as a nice couple in the film, it would not be fair to have the mixed-race child "hang over their lives as a constant reminder of the tragedy." Schulberg refers to the evolving American perception of the Japanese:

> at the time that BUTTERFLY was first presented as a play or an opera, there was no strong, anti-racial feeling toward the Japanese; there were not as yet even immigration laws against their wholesale entry into any country; there were in evidence no consequences of inter-racial marriages between Japanese and white people so that the tragedy of the half blood Japanese-Caucasian was not discernable or thought of. It seems to us to be an unpleasant hangover on the picture after its completion to feel that the half Japanese half American child of Butterfly's and Pinkerton's will have to go through a miserable life in America as a social misfit.[56]

With such concerns in mind, the filmmakers were determined to avoid the most telling signs of miscegenation on the screen. Although Butterfly's child is described as having curly blonde hair and purple eyes in several of the earlier versions of the tale, Trouble is played by a dark-haired Japanese-American boy in this 1932 film.

This film takes for granted the notion that Pinkerton's only real wife is the white woman and that Butterfly is tragically naive to imagine otherwise. Adelaide (Kate in other versions) is far more present in the 1932 film than in the short story, play, opera, or 1915 silent film. Her status as Mrs. Pinkerton is affirmed by a brief shot of the couple exiting a white clapboard church following their wedding, complete with the requisite Mendelssohn march heard on the soundtrack. Adelaide proves immediately forgiving upon learning of Pinkerton's affair with Butterfly and never betrays the slightest apprehension about her Japanese rival. She reassures Pinkerton: "Don't feel so badly about it dear, it isn't your fault." Just as the film assumes that raising a mixed-race child in the United States would be an inordinate punishment for Pinkerton's simple exotic fling, Adelaide's equanimity suggests that it would be absurd to fear that an American male would ever ultimately choose a

Japanese woman over the blonde-haired girl back home. White women formed the film's intended audience. A preproduction report on the script stated that the film would likely "appeal greatly to women and to men who are sentimentally inclined." While reaffirming the paramount precedence of white heterosexual marriage, the film lingers lovingly over scenes of Butterfly's and Pinkerton's domesticity. We hear Puccini's joyful "flower duet" music as we observe Butterfly's ideal feminine behavior—removing her husband's shoes, mixing his drink, preparing his pipe. The intended moral of the Madame Butterfly story has never been concerned with the behavior of American men overseas. Rather, the real cultural work of this perennial narrative has been to provide an exotic fantasy for the white American heterosexual male and a model of feminine subservience for the American woman.[57]

Filming the Filming of the Film-Opera: Framing Puccini

Paramount Pictures paid G. Ricordi & Co. $13,500 for permission to use Puccini's music in the 1932 *Madame Butterfly*. In 1962 Paramount paid $52,400—over $20,000 more than in 1932, after adjusting for inflation—for permission to employ portions of Puccini's opera, sung in Japanese and Italian, in the soundtrack of *My Geisha*.[58] In this film, an American movie star (Lucy, played by Shirley MacLaine) decides to follow her French film director husband (Paul, played by Yves Montand) in secret to Japan and then disguises herself as "Yoko" in order to counter her imagined exotic rivals. Pretending to be a Japanese geisha, she fools her husband—who is filming an "authentic Japanese" version of Puccini's opera—and is cast in the part of Butterfly herself.[59] Paul had planned to prove himself with this film and had refused to allow Lucy to be cast in the role. By the film's end, Lucy learns from a "true geisha" to sacrifice her own ambitions for those of her husband. While parodying both previous cinematic presentations of the opera and Hollywood's attempts at presenting "the real Japan," *My Geisha* nevertheless participates in the quest for exotic authenticity and benefits from Puccini's music. Japanese instruments appear in Franz Waxman's score and the film offers stunning shots of Japan in "vivid, arresting colors." *My Geisha* purports to criticize and distance itself from the Madame Butterfly narrative tradition, but actually furthers its Orientalist ideology.

The relationship between the film and the opera becomes quite complex and layered in *My Geisha* and the boundary between diegetic and nondiegetic music is often thoroughly blurred. In certain sequences we see and hear Puccini's opera as though through the "diegetic camera," while in others we witness the creation of the film-within-the-film from a nondiegetic position as we hear either Puccini's or Waxman's music. Puccini's music is heard as we observe the rehearsing and filming of the film-opera, as we see the diegetic screening of the film-opera, and to indicate to us that the diegetic screening of the film-opera is occurring offscreen. In one instance, we witness the rehearsing and filming of the wedding scene in the film-opera as we hear Waxman's own Orientalist music. In this sequence, we are likely to

assume, at first, that Waxman's music is nondiegetic—particularly if we are familiar
with the opera. This scene resembles silent film in that we see the moving lips of the
performers but hear only Waxman's music. However, when we hear and see Paul
cut the filming of this scene, the music immediately ends as though it had been the
soundtrack to the film-opera and was thus diegetic all along.

Puccini's music is first heard in *My Geisha* during a thirteen-shot montage sequence of the production of the film-opera. Immediately before the sequence
begins, Paul is seen reading a love letter from Lucy—a letter he believes she has sent
to him from home. His assistant yells "quiet on the set," but Paul is engrossed in
the letter and replies "No you can talk, go ahead." However, Puccini's music enters
nondiegetically and does silence the diegetic sound world of the "set." Again, although we occasionally see moving lips, we hear only the opera, as though we are
experiencing a silent film with a phonograph playing Puccini's music in the dark. In
this sequence we hear the love duet from Butterfly's "dolce notte" through to the end
of Act I. Although most of the shots in the montage present mundane moments of
filmmaking, in which Paul frequently mimes directorial frustration and tantrums,
Puccini's music makes clear that the sequence is concerned with the love of this
working Hollywood couple, or at least with her love for him. The lyrical camera
movement and the six gentle dissolves between shots also suggest this dramatic
interpretation.

Throughout this extended sequence, we assume that we are hearing nondiegetic
music and are seeing through a nondiegetic camera whenever the movement within
the frame appears unconnected to our music and camera. The extended third shot
in the sequence offers a graceful pan of Paul rehearsing a *bugaku* dancer—both the
dancer and the camera appear to move to Puccini's gliding melody, although the
camera angle suggests that we are nondiegetic voyeurs. Some moments in this sequence more pointedly call into question the nondiegetic status of Puccini's music
and of the camera through which we are viewing the filming of the film-opera. In
one shot, Lucy (in disguise as Yoko in the costume of Butterfly, of course) gracefully
pivots and strikes a pose in preparation for the next take in perfect synchronization
with Puccini's musical climax and cymbal crash and directly facing the diegetic(?)
camera. The camera angle and her apparently choreographed movement momentarily suggest a diegetic status for Puccini. The sequence ends with a gorgeous long
shot of Lucy/Yoko/Butterfly—it is unclear which persona MacLaine is portraying at
this point—walking along the beach, seemingly in pace with the music, as the sun
sets and Puccini's Act I music reaches its cadence.

Puccini's music achieves a more secure diegetic status in *My Geisha* during Paul's
filming of Butterfly's death scene. By this point in the film, Paul has discovered that
Yoko is actually his wife Lucy.[60] He is humiliated by this realization and has determined that Lucy loves her career more than him and that their marriage will end
with this film. Without revealing his knowledge, and in order to prepare Lucy for
her performance in Butterfly's tragic scene, he propositions Yoko/Lucy in her hotel
room the night before the final shooting. When she repulses him, he suggests that

he will easily find satisfaction elsewhere. Lucy is crushed, believing that Paul's behavior proves that he has routinely had affairs with geishas the world over—that he is simply another Pinkerton.

The next sequence presents the filming of the final scene in the film-opera. We hear Puccini's music from rehearsal no. 55 to the end. The music starts exactly with Paul's hand signal and the camera movement is far more lyrical during this diegetic sequence. We hear Butterfly's vocal lines sung in Japanese and the camera pans over the landscape, reaching MacLaine/Lucy/Yoko's face as she lip-syncs the word "sayonara." (MacLaine's acting is powerful and her lip-syncing adept, indicating that she could indeed have starred in a stunning film-opera version of *Madama Butterfly*.) Immediately after Butterfly dies, and before the music has ended, we hear Pinkerton's threefold cry "Butterfly" and the camera pans to Paul as he cuts the filming.[61] Suddenly, our confidence in the diegesis has been shaken—a diegetic camera would not have panned to film the director, the diegetic opera music would not have continued after the filming had ended.[62] We hear the final eleven bars of Puccini's opera as we follow Paul's abrupt departure from the set and see him drive off alone as the film's producer, Sam, and members of the crew stare at him in confusion and dismay. Just as the 1932 film reframed "Poor Butterfly" to express Pinkerton's pain, here Puccini's music becomes the soundtrack to Paul's tragedy after the diegetic filming has ended. Although we have just witnessed a female character commit suicide on screen, the story of *My Geisha* has become the tragedy of this man.

The "True Geisha"?: Framing Exotic Realism

In the Main Title sequence of *My Geisha* a drawing of a *shamisen* appears behind Franz Waxman's name. Although separated by thirty years, Harling's and Waxman's versions of musical *japonisme* are quite similar. Waxman's "Arrival in Tokio" music (see Example 4.3) might remind us of Harling's (compare with Example 4.1).[63] Waxman had stretched his musical resources to include Japanese instruments, timbres, and scales more significantly in his score for the 1957 Warner Bros. film *Sayonara* (which will be discussed in chapter 6). Perhaps to avoid composing in a style too dissimilar from Puccini's, Waxman's few gestures toward Japanese music are far less bold in the later *My Geisha*.

Example 4.3 Arrival in Tokyo music, Franz Waxman, *My Geisha* (Paramount, 1962).

Like the 1932 *Madame Butterfly*, *My Geisha* includes an important scene set in a teahouse. However, in this film we arrive at the teahouse with the American wife. Breaching Hollywood convention, Lucy enters the exotic/erotic setting normally restricted to male characters in order to gaze voyeuristically upon her husband as he sits surrounded by geishas.[64] As we peek with Lucy's eye through a gap in the *shoji*, we hear vocal music accompanied by *shamisen*. We briefly see one of the geishas playing the *shamisen* but never see the source of the vocal line. The diegetic status of this music is confirmed as we see and hear Paul hum along with the tune and snap his fingers while rocking in syncopation. Thus the film, however briefly, presents Japanese music in a somewhat positive light, although Paul (under the *sake*'s influence, of course) seems to hear it with ears conditioned by jazz and rock 'n' roll. This tune is a famous Japanese folk song entitled "Kyūshū Tankō Bushi" ("The Coal Miner's Song of Kyūshū"). Published sheet music for this song is found among the *My Geisha* score materials at Paramount Studios, and a printed note explains that coal miners' tunes have, since World War II, "become quite popular all over Japan, and are often sung even at banquets." Continuing a long tradition of composers in quest of "ethnographic authenticity," the filmmakers must have felt authorized in selecting this particular folk song for the diegetic background music at their cinematic geisha feast. The scene continues with music for *shamisen* and banjo composed by Yajuro Kineya and then, as Lucy enters the room in disguise, with a simple *koto* theme by Waxman which employs the Japanese *in* scale. Again, Waxman's musical *japonisme* appears to recapitulate Harling's of three decades prior.

From the very opening of the film, Paul explains that with his film-opera he hopes to "capture the real traditional Japan" by casting a "real Japanese girl" in the role of Butterfly.[65] Puccini's opera, ironically, will serve as his vehicle for authenticity. Paul's quest for exotic realism provides some of the comic energy in *My Geisha*. Paul becomes increasingly frustrated during the auditions as none of the Japanese female hopefuls come close to his ideal image of a Japanese woman. After listening to the rock 'n' roll singing of a trio of Japanese girls in modern American dress, Paul complains: "They're more western than the girls at home. I knew there was an American tendency, but they are making a fetish of it. They're not Japanese anymore. . . . That's just why I want to do this picture. I want to capture the old spirit of Japan while it still exists." Hearing American music emanating from Japanese bodies provokes this outburst.[66] Paul claims that all he wants is to "use a plain old fashion real Japanese girl who doesn't sing Rock and Roll." However, what he actually has in mind is the mythic mute Oriental woman and he acknowledges as much when he states that all he needs is the right "face." He is looking for a Japanese puppet through which he, the ventriloquist, will project Puccini's vocal music. While the fictional director, Paul, only required a body that looked Japanese, the plot of *My Geisha* demanded that Lucy Dell (and thus Shirley MacLaine) apply extensive and painful cosmetics and manipulate her voice in order to convince us that she could fool both Paul's eyes and ears.[67]

The conceit of the film-within-a-film in *My Geisha* suggests that there is a sharp division between reality and fictional depiction on the screen. By framing some sequences and settings as part of the fictional film, this film creates an aura of authenticity for the other settings. As we view the film, we are being taught not only that the fictional Lucy Dell is astonishingly skillful in her imitation of a Japanese woman, but that MacLaine is actually doing a tremendous job of cultural cross-dressing herself. Similarly, the recognizability of Puccini's music and its frequent "on-set" diegetic status in the film-opera frames it as clearly not Japanese and thus, in contrast, suggests that certain pieces of musical *japonisme* by Waxman are authentic specimens. (This "figure/ground" dynamic is, of course, at work within Puccini's score itself.) This process of implied authenticity through representational counterpoint is particularly in play as we encounter the "true geisha" in this film.

In order to carry out her deception Lucy seeks training from a geisha teacher. (In a sense, this fictional white American actress follows in the footsteps of both Blanche Bates and Geraldine Farrar, who both studied Japanese women in preparation for their portrayals of Butterfly.) The venerable teacher provides Lucy and Sam (the producer), and thus us, with a stern lecture on what constitutes a "true geisha." (The film also takes the opportunity at this point to introduce us to the tea ceremony—we see the "true geisha," framed by open *shoji*, enacting the ritual in a back room.) The geisha teacher lectures at such length that we are compelled to accept the veracity of his words and likely assume, at least momentarily, that the woman he introduces is herself a real geisha. The foolish misconceptions and obvious cultural ignorance of the two American characters further supports the authenticity of the characters presented to us as being "Japanese." The low-angle shot of the teacher and Waxman's musical *japonisme* also encourage this perception. As the Americans arrive at the geisha teacher's home, we hear repeated stacked fifth sonorities in the marimba, flutes, and strings and the plucking of harps and *koto* accented by finger cymbals. (See Example 4.4: We hear bars 1–9 as they arrive and enter into the house. The general pause of measure 9 occurs as they are introduced and enter the room. Bar 10 begins as they seat themselves on the floor and we arrive at bar 17 as the teacher asks whether they are interested in the tea ceremony. In these final eight bars the melody is taken by the viola, viola d'amore, banjo, *shamisen*, *koto*, celli, and two harps, while the accompaniment calls for *koto*, two flutes, marimba, and harp.) Waxman's music resumes with the start of the teacher's lecture, supporting him as he rises to his feet.

The "true geisha" is named Kazumi, perhaps a reflexive reference to Katsumi in the 1957 hit film *Sayonara*.[68] The geisha teacher suggests that Kazumi could serve as Lucy's personal trainer and states that "it would be an honor to see a geisha truly portrayed on the screen." However, this "true geisha" is played by Yoko Tani, an actress born in Paris who was a successful figure in European B-grade movies and sci-fi films from the 1950s to the 1970s. (Her first film appears to have been *Ali-Baba et les quarante voleurs* in 1954.) Of course, the irony is compounded since Lucy assumes the name "Yoko" in her geisha disguise. While recognizing that Yoko

Example 4.4 The "True Geisha," Franz Waxman, *My Geisha* (Paramount, 1962).

Tani was only playing the role of a geisha, the *New York Times* reviewer of *My Geisha* still credits her with adding authenticity to the picture and assumes that this was the goal of the producer: "Yoko Tani, as a perceptive geisha who teaches our heroine the trade, and Tatsuo Saito are among the native players who add authenticity to the proceedings."[69] Paramount's own press releases for the film encouraged this view of Yoko Tani's role: "Also adding to the authenticity of Miss MacLaine's portrayal was the advice of lovely Yoko Tani."[70] Ironically, the technical adviser for the 1932 *Madame Butterfly*, Michio Ito, likely knew more about geisha than did this Japanese actress in 1962. MacLaine herself has revealed that she spent two weeks

in a geisha training school in Japan "learning the intricacies of the delicate tea ceremony, the Japanese dance and how to play the stringed instrument."[71] This claim to
special knowledge of Japanese culture resonates oddly with the film's lampooning
of Hollywood's quest for exotic authenticity, particularly since the skills listed by
MacLaine are not demonstrated by her in *My Geisha*.

In *My Geisha*, we see the white American actress MacLaine playing the role of
an American actress pretending to be a geisha who plays the role of a geisha in a
film (with a French director) of an opera by an Italian based on an American play
and short story. We hear the voice of the Japanese soprano Michiko Sunahara
singing the part of Butterfly in Japanese as we see MacLaine lip-sync these lines as
an American actress lip-syncing as a geisha lip-syncing in the role of Butterfly. Sam
refers to the arrival of the opera recordings for the film-opera's soundtrack and to
their superior quality, yet we never see the source of Butterfly's voice—the Japanese
vocalist and the audio technology remain invisible. This singing voice is heard as either a voice-off or a voice-over, depending on the diegetic status of Puccini's music
in any given moment in the film. The jacket notes for the 1962 RCA soundtrack
recording of *My Geisha* state that Sunahara "instructed Miss MacLaine on the elo-
cution of the lyrics while the film was being shot in Japan."[72] Of course, Sunahara
actually did not coach MacLaine in speaking or singing Butterfly's lines in Japanese.
Rather, she taught MacLaine how to mouth the words sung by this Japanese soprano convincingly.[73] (See Figure 4.3.) A parallel, although fictional, form of cross-
cultural ventriloquism occurs in the climactic scene as Kazumi teaches Lucy the
proper lines of an obedient wife.

"No one before you, my husband, not even I": Framing the American Woman

Seemingly the most lighthearted treatment of the Madame Butterfly narrative, *My
Geisha* may actually be the most sinister. The very title of this film implies male
dominance and female submission and in the film's final scene we witness a double
fictional suicide by a woman on screen. The opening night of the film-opera takes
place in a *kabuki* theater in Tokyo. The diegetic screening of the film is indicated, at
first, only indirectly. A diegetic gong signals that the film-opera will begin and we
see the audience settle down and direct their attention to the offscreen screen. We
hear Puccini's overture as the film-opera begins but do not see the diegetic screen.
Instead, our camera cuts between shots of Paul and shots of Lucy and Sam in the
theater. The cutting rhythm is precisely synchronized with Puccini's fugal entries
and thus oddly suggests that these images constitute the diegetic film-opera. After
Lucy and Sam move backstage, Puccini's music is heard at a lower volume, and any
confusion regarding diegetic status is at least momentarily clarified. Following this
brief backstage scene, the screen dissolves back to an image of the audience and thus
suggests the passing of time. We see the diegetic screening of Butterfly's "Un bel dì"

Figure 4.3 Shirley MacLaine lip-syncing "Un bel dì" in Japanese. Paramount publicity still for *My Geisha* (1962).

aria and see and hear the audience applaud at the end of the number as though they were attending a live performance. Another dissolve serves to indicate a further passage of time and to return us to Lucy's dressing room for the climactic moment in *My Geisha*.

Lucy is changing into her disguise as Yoko with the assistance of Kazumi. Her plan is to surprise her husband and the entire audience by removing her wig during her curtain call and revealing that Lucy Dell, rather than an authentic Japanese geisha, has just been seen in the role of Butterfly. Sam remarks that this stunt and the moment of *stupore universale* it will inspire will surely earn her an Oscar. After Sam leaves, Kazumi offers Lucy a gift of an inscribed fan. Lucy thanks Kazumi and requests a translation of the fan's text. Kazumi then deliberately reads the inscription twice: "No one before you, my husband, not even I." Lucy is clearly not thrilled by Kazumi's none-too-subtle hint, but the inscription has struck a chord.[74] Throughout this sequence, we hear Butterfly's final death-scene aria from our backstage position. Lucy continues to dress as Yoko and applies one of her dark-colored contact lenses. At the moment when we, and Lucy, hear Pinkerton's cries of "Butterfly," Lucy employs the fan to contemplate her natural blue eye and then assumed brown eye in the mirror.[75] We abruptly cut to the diegetic screen and witness Butterfly's suicide. (See Figure 4.4.) This sequence involves an odd temporal disjunction, or at least a stuttered replay, since we have already heard from backstage the music that accompanies this moment in the opera and are now hearing Puccini's final bars. Perhaps this deliberate visual discontinuity was intended to suggest the symbolic suicide which occurs offscreen at this moment in *My Geisha*.

Figure 4.4 Shirley MacLaine's Japanese suicide. Paramount publicity still for *My Geisha* (1962). Courtesy of the Museum of Modern Art/Film Stills Archive.

As the audience applauds madly, Paul takes the stage. Aware of Lucy and Sam's planned surprise, Paul introduces Yoko and calls her to take a bow. Lucy surprises him and the audience by entering as herself, dressed in Western clothes. She explains to the audience that Yoko has entered a convent and will be seen in public no more. By killing off her fake geisha persona and thereby forgoing the chance to win an Oscar by claiming the credit due to her, Lucy "internalizes the 'lesson' she learned from being a Japanese woman," the lesson of the "true geisha," and of this film.[76] As though having heard Paul's pained voice in Pinkerton's sung cries, Lucy has decided to renounce her own ambition. Only by removing the kimono, the exotic disguise that allowed her to assume the role denied to her by her husband, has Lucy assumed her "proper" role as Paul's wife. In a sense, Lucy "speaks" the lines of the "true geisha" by appearing on stage in Western dress. *My Geisha* arrives at a conclusion common to Hollywood films of the late 1950s and early 1960s (and to the 1932 *Madame Butterfly*): Japanese women represent an ideal that American women can and should emulate.[77] In comparison with other Madame Butterfly settings, *My Geisha* is a much more direct presentation of the lesson to be learned from this well-worn narrative. With a bit of training, even a white American wife can succeed as a "true geisha." The comedy ends with a clear *lieto fine*: Paul gets to have his blue-eyed wife and his geisha too.[78]

"Not just an opera, but real!"

Locating a clear vantage point from which to construct a critique of *My Geisha* is quite difficult. To what extent is the representation of Japanese culture in this film a progressive parody of previous Hollywood Orientalist products? To what extent can *My Geisha* be separated from the heritage of the Madame Butterfly tradition and from its own comic plot? Gina Marchetti has argued that *My Geisha*'s "own self-consciousness tends to solidify its conservatism."[79] Looking beyond the superficial layer of parody, my detailed analysis has uncovered strains and strategies of Orientalist representation endemic to this film. Although the film pokes fun at Paul's quest for a "real Japanese girl" and the "old spirit of Japan" with arch sophistication, traces of Paul's fictional desires and of his appropriations of Puccini are evident throughout this Paramount production. The quest for exotic realism clearly inspired the film's cinematography and the film repeatedly assumes an unearned authoritative tone as it introduces us to the tea ceremony, sumo wrestling, and the art of the geisha. However, my critique of the film's agenda along gender lines is complicated by consideration of its parodistic elements. Although the fictional director, Paul, receives the public's adulation as Lucy sacrifices her success, Shirley MacLaine did receive top billing in *My Geisha*. The fact that the film's producer, Steve Parker, was MacLaine's husband at the time further confuses matters. Was *My Geisha* a vehicle for Parker or for MacLaine? Were the gender implications of the plot part of an elaborate joke shared by Parker and MacLaine, or was Parker calling out to his wife through the film? Rather than delving further into Hollywood biographies and *My Geisha*'s self-reflections, we should pull back in this conclusion to consider the reflexive potential of film and opera more broadly.[80]

Film can never escape the nondiegetic camera. As Christopher Ames has stated: "Films about Hollywood purport to take the viewer behind the scenes and behind the cameras, but by definition what appears on the screen must be taking place in front of the camera."[81] Opera, however, can more easily and more transparently construct and expose multiple proscenium arches and its own theatrical mechanisms. Opera can stage itself as an opera-within-an-opera relatively easily, where film can only pretend to accomplish this because it can never present itself from a distance. Similarly, opera can literally incorporate film on the stage, whereas a film-opera never quite replicates the live performance experience of opera, no matter how enthusiastically the audience (either actual or onscreen) may applaud. Both of the films considered here contain film-opera sections, although this merging of genres is achieved in very different ways. In the 1932 *Madame Butterfly* the film itself appears to become a film-opera in certain sequences. *My Geisha* includes actual film-opera footage, but attempts to present this material diegetically as a film-within-the-film. Considering cinematic reflexivity further, *My Geisha* appears to aim for exotic realism by emphasizing the self-referential. However, reflexivity ultimately proves corrosive for realism, as does rampant intertextuality. *Madame Butterfly* undermines its attempts to present authentic images and sounds of Japan simply by referencing the Madame Butterfly narrative itself. By 1932, the tale had been told too many times to hold claim to an audience's suspension of disbelief. *My Geisha* overtly reflects on the Butterfly tradition, whereas the 1932 film cannot avoid covertly commenting on it.

In *My Geisha* Paul states that with his film-opera of *Madama Butterfly* he seeks to create a work that will be "not just an opera, but real!" This aspiration, and the generic assumptions behind it, was also expressed by the real film director Anthony Minghella at an October 2006 press conference held in advance of his new Metropolitan Opera production of *Madama Butterfly*, which had premiered in 2005 at the English National Opera. Minghella related that he had initially faced a daunting problem in approaching this production. He explained that "film is the most literal medium in the world. . . . The verismo element of cinema is unassailable. If you are making a film about a fifteen-year old Japanese girl, you go to Japan and you meet Japanese girls." He referred to the "squabbling" that arose when non-Japanese actresses were cast in *Memoirs of a Geisha* and asked: "Can you imagine the squabble that would be going on if those criteria were brought to bear in the opera house?" He then revealed that after having been invited to stage Puccini's opera, he had asked "how many good teenage Japanese sopranos are there?" and, when told that the answer was none, had declared "then we won't do the opera." Fortunately, Minghella overcame his objections to opera's "unreality" and created a stunning production.[82]

What exactly did Paul and Minghella assume to be unreal about opera vis-à-vis film, and what could possibly satisfy their desires for and standards of authentic exotic representation? Paul is clearly a victim of the delusions of cinematic realism. The notion that film could bring a new standard of realism to opera has been expressed since the earliest days of silent cinema, and the promise of cinematic realism has always been particularly pronounced in productions involving exoticism. Where opera is faulted for its unrealistic temporal distension, film's penchant for abrupt leaps in both time and place are even further removed from lived experience.[83] Opera's alleged shortcomings in visual representation find certain compensations. Although Citron refers to the realism of cinema in other dimensions, she rightly notes that "the realism-artifice relationship is inverted when it comes to sound."[84] In Orientalist opera, music sustains the exotic impact of the otherwise static set and can direct our attention as would camera angle and movement in film—we are repeatedly taught to see through our ears.[85] Film might seem particularly well suited to presenting the "authentic" exotic through both sound and image. Film shot on location can "take us there" in a way not possible on the operatic stage. However, rather than collapsing the distance between the audience and the exotic setting, film can seem to emphasize it. A travelogue presents images and sounds of distant lands on our local movie screen—it does not literally bring the exotic other to us nor does it transport us there. Instead, we experience the exotic at a definite remove. (Opera performed "on location" before a live audience might represent an attempt to outflank film in these terms. For example, in 1923 Isabel Longdon Stine—a founder of the San Francisco opera who had spent six months in 1917 studying *kabuki* in Tokyo—hosted an informal performance of *Madama Butterfly* by the opera company in her Japanese-style garden.[86] Alternately, the tendency toward lavish Orientalist decoration in major movie palaces throughout the United States certainly heightened the audience's exotic experience during the silent and early sound periods.) As a form of live performance, opera has a (much-celebrated) presence and a literal realism not found in the movie theater. By repeatedly representing opera as somehow deficient in terms of realism, film has simultaneously staked out its claim to the real and has condescendingly offered opera its services. Rather than make further claims here for realism in the operatic experience, I will simply assert that film's strategies for exotic representation come no closer to reality in any sense of that word.

Orientalist film is often indebted to Orientalist opera, even when not directly linked by a shared narrative. It is not immediately obvious why this should be the case. Sound film would appear to have a tremendous advantage over opera for representing the acoustic exotic. Consider the *shamisen*. To include genuine Japanese *shamisen* music in either silent film or opera, one would either have to hire a performer who would need to be present at every performance in every city or one would need to make do with a recorded performance.[87] Sound film can easily splice in exotic performances. However, throughout the entire history of Hollywood *japonisme* this potential for enhancing musical exotic realism has rarely been realized.[88] In fact, opportunities for including the other and the other's music were routinely turned down. Why did the creators of the 1932 *Madame Butterfly* not choose to include footage of actual dancing geishas? Why has Hollywood repeatedly turned to composers such as Harling and Waxman—or to Puccini—for "Japanese music"? Perhaps these filmmakers feared that the presence of the "real" would prove too disruptive. Perhaps they intuited that actual Japanese traditional music and Japanese actors would undermine the representational style of exotic realism. In studying Hollywood Orientalism, it soon becomes apparent that the legendary "authentic" exotic is not really wanted even if it can be had, despite the vociferous protestations by filmmakers to the contrary. This is particularly true of music.

In Long's 1898 short story Butterfly envisions herself as a singing beggar: "Me with my samisen, standing up bifore all the people, singing funeral songs." Long's Butterfly then acts out this dreaded future by singing a Japanese song and accompanying herself on *shamisen*. In addition, she sings a song that Pinkerton had taught her in a jargon he had made "as grotesque as possible, the more to amuse him." The lyrics of this song rival the most sophomoric examples of Tin Pan Alley *japonisme*: "I call her the belle of Japan—of Japan;/Her name it is O Cho-Cho-San— Cho-Cho-San;/Such tenderness lies in her soft almond eyes,/I tell you she's just ichi ban." For over a century, Butterfly has been made to sing "bifore all the people" and to re-enact her grotesque suicide. She has sung countless exotic songs and endures in American fantasies of race and gender, for this is a tale that has no end.

A Tale of Musical Orientalism, in Four Genres
and Two Nations

Cecil B. DeMille's astonishing 1915 silent film *The Cheat* tells the story of Tori, a Japanese millionaire, who becomes a member of Long Island's "smart set" by befriending Edith, the spendthrift wife of a stockbroker, and by offering his house for the Red Cross Ball. Edith's husband, Richard Hardy, is wary of Tori from the beginning and disapproves of his wife socializing with this exotic man. Hoping to obtain money to satisfy her sartorial obsession, Edith pilfers the Red Cross funds entrusted to her and manages to lose the entire sum on the stock market. Tori takes advantage of this scandalous situation by offering to provide Edith with the necessary funds on condition that she visit him alone at his home. Edith agrees to the bargain in Tori's exotic *shoji* room. (See Figure 4.5.) However, her husband strikes it rich the very next day and assents to Edith's request for $10,000. That night, Edith goes to Tori's home to repay him with this money, but he demands payment in the manner promised, or at least implied. As they violently struggle, Tori drags her by the hair to his desk, rips her dress, and brands her shoulder with his seal. She then shoots him before fleeing. (See Figure 4.6.) Richard has followed Edith to Tori's and enters the house immediately after her escape, only to find the Japanese man suffering a gunshot wound and clutching a piece of Edith's dress. When the police arrive and confront him, Richard claims to have fired the shot himself. In jail, he forbids Edith

Figure 4.5   The Bargain, *The Cheat* (1915). Lasky publicity still. Courtesy of the Museum of Modern Art/Film Stills Archive.

Figure 4.6 The Branding, *The Cheat* (1915). Lasky publicity still. Courtesy of the Academy of Motion Picture Arts and Sciences.

to reveal the truth so that he can preserve her honor. Edith returns to Tori's home to beg the wounded man to help clear her husband. She offers him money and even herself, but Tori chillingly replies: "You cannot cheat me twice." At the trial Edith finds it impossible to remain silent and watch her husband condemned to prison. She leaps to her feet, violently bares her branded shoulder for the jury, and relates the entire sordid affair. The courtroom explodes and Tori is nearly lynched.[89]

The Source of an Exotic Lineage

This seminal film inspired an extraordinary series of works in multiple genres and in two nations spanning a quarter of a century.[90] Each successive version reworked the tale, inspiring new Orientalist musical settings. (See Table 4.1.) Following the success of the DeMille film, this story was transformed into a play entitled *I.O.U.* and produced in New York in 1918.[91] Camille Erlanger's *Forfaiture*—apparently the first opera to be based on a film—premiered at the Opéra-Comique in 1921.[92] A silent film remake was made by Paramount in 1923 and a sound version appeared from that studio in 1931.[93] A novel published in 1923 by Russell Holman was loosely "based upon the story by Hector Turnbull [coauthor of the 1915 screenplay]" and was directly connected to the 1923 film, featuring stills from that screened version.[94] Finally, in 1937 the French film *Forfaiture* reflected back upon

Table 4.1 Versions of *The Cheat*

Date	Title	Genre	Creator(s)	Production co./publisher	Villain's ethnicity (actor)	General notes
1915	*The Cheat*	silent film	dir. Cecil B. DeMille; screenplay by Hector Turnbull and Jeanie Macpherson	Lasky Feature Play Company	Japanese (Sessue Hayakawa)	no cue sheet published; major success in Paris
1918	*The Cheat* (rerelease)	silent film	edited by Frank Wards and Mary O'Conner	Lasky Feature Play Company	Burmese (Hayakawa)	no cue sheet published; minor changes to the 1915 film
1918	*I.O.U.*	stage play	Turnbull and Willard Mack	opened in Asbury Park, then Belmont Theatre in NYC	orig. Japanese then Hindu for NYC production (José Ruben)	a "musical program" was performed by a quartet; only the final act takes place in the exotic home of the villain
1920	*Forfaiture*	opera (comédie musicale)	mus. Camille Erlanger (died 1919); libretto by Paul Milliet and André de Lorde	Opéra-Comique, 1921	Japanese (Vanni-Marcoux)	villain sings with *shamisen* prop; Japanese servants sing to tune of "Kimigayo"
1923	*The Cheat*	silent film	dir. George Fitzmaurice; adapted by Ouida Bergère; published cue sheet by James C. Bradford	Paramount/Famous Players-Lasky	European con artist disguised as an Indian prince (Charles De Roche)	includes Hindu dance and musical performance; the wife is Argentinean; set in Buenos Aires, Paris, NYC, and Long Island; no print available
1923	*The Cheat*	novel	Russell Holman (based on the 1923 film and on Turnbull)	Grosset & Dunlap	Indian/Hindu prince	no musical performance in the plot; no disguised European
1931	*The Cheat*	sound film	dir. George Abbott; anonymous composer; screenplay by Harry Hervey	Paramount	white American who has traveled much in Orient (Irving Pichel)	"Japanese" musicians and servants; "Cambodian" dance by Ruth St. Denis; white guests at ball in "Oriental costumes"
1937	*Forfaiture*	sound film	dir. Marcel L'Herbier; mus. Michel Lévine	Societé du Cinéma du Panthéon, Fr.	Chinese (Hayakawa)	set in Mongolia; documentary performance footage included, opening includes footage from the 1915 film
1994	*The Cheat*	silent film score	mus. Robert Israel	video release of 1918 version	Burmese (Hayakawa)	1915 film is repeatedly cited in 1990s in studies of race and film

this tradition by casting Sessue Hayakawa, the Japanese actor who played Tori in the original film, as the villain.[95] These works display the fundamental tension in Euro-American Orientalism between a professed desire to present the "authentic" exotic other and the tendency to conflate all others in a general representation of enticing and shocking difference. Versions of the tale that emphasized an exotic setting for the charity bazaar or ball were reflecting common contemporaneous high-society Orientalist practice, as exemplified by Isabella Stewart Gardner's 1905 "Japanese Festival Village." At the same time, works such as *The Cheat* were clearly in a codeterminant relationship with rising fears of a coming "Yellow Peril." The multiple *Cheat*s could be considered in terms of their mercurial political contexts, in light of the evolving social conceptions of race and gender, and with respect to the basic differences between American and French exoticism and cinematic style in the early twentieth century. This lineage also provides a rare opportunity to compare in a precise and intertextual fashion the role of music and the realization of musical Orientalism in multiple distinct genres.

In visual terms, Tori's exotic difference in DeMille's 1915 silent classic is signaled particularly through the film's stunning lighting effects—a cinematic feature much commented upon at the time and more recently. The film emphasizes shadows, particularly on the walls and sliding doors of Tori's *shoji* room. In his opening title shot, we see Tori wearing a kimono and branding Asian art objects at his desk, his face lit by the light of the burning brazier. We do not see him again in exotic costume until his violent confrontation with Edith. The typed synopsis of this scene indicates that during their struggle, Tori was originally to have pointed to "their shadows on the *shoji*—reflected plain in the moonlight on the outside so that the husband is sure to see.... Tori pulls her to him in an embrace; laughs as he points to the shadows on the screen, showing the embrace clearly to the husband outside." (Japanese paper walls repeatedly suggested the potential for dramatic shadows to American filmmakers. Recall that in the 1932 film of *Madame Butterfly*, Pinkerton first encountered Butterfly as a dancing silhouette.) During the Red Cross ball, Tori leads Edith (and thus us) on a tour of this exotic office, pointing out such highlights of his collection as a sculpture of the Buddha and samurai's armor and offering her an exotic dress.[96] A striking, high-angle shot and a smoking incense burner enhance the exoticism and the general sense of unease. The various versions of the script and scenario called for rather sinister and blatant acting for the portrayal of Tori. However, the film owed a great deal of its success to the fact that Hayakawa ignored many of these directions and instead gave a much more subtle performance of this exotic "villain." Hayakawa's portrayal offered a villain who was both far more realistic than the various Fu Manchu types of exotic male evil and far more alluring and, thus, ultimately more threatening to the white social order. As Edith faints in Tori's office after learning of her financial loss, Tori steals an interracial kiss—an act that, along with his later branding of her bare shoulder, caused *The Cheat* to become a cinematic sensation.

What music likely accompanied this film as it was screened across the United States and then Europe? As foreshadowed in chapter 2 and noted in relation to early *Madame Butterfly* films, a music director or silent film organist in 1915 would have been faced with two basic forms of Tin Pan Alley–produced *japonisme* to draw upon for *The Cheat*—either delicate tunes in praise of Japanese women, or marches commemorating Japan's victory over Russia, and often devoid of any exotic signals. No cue sheet or score was published for the original DeMille film nor for its 1918 rerelease.[97] However, we can arrive at a close approximation of the music that would have been heard during screenings of the 1915 *Cheat* by studying cue sheets compiled for other films from this period dealing with Japan and starring Hayakawa. For example, in the 1917 Paramount feature *The Secret Game*, directed by William C. deMille [*sic*] (Cecil's brother), Hayakawa played Nara-Nara, a Japanese spy assisting the United States against the Germans during the first World War. The publicity packet for this film included a musical cue sheet credited to Louis F. Gottschalk.[98] While the cue sheet called for an exotic musical mixture, most of Nara-Nara's cues were set with examples of Tin Pan Alley's musical *japonisme*. For Hayakawa's title shot, musical directors and organists were prompted to select Tobani's "Japanese Patrol," a march employing a Japanese military song (*gunka*) from the 1904–1905 Russo-Japanese war.[99] This music called for in *The Secret Game* works equally well for Hayakawa's title shot in the 1915 *Cheat* if played *molto maestoso* as we see the villain in dramatic lighting at his desk branding art objects with his seal.[100] Further evidence for determining the music that might have been used for *The Cheat* is discovered in organists' trade magazines. Writing in *The Diapason* in October 1917, Wesley Ray Burroughs noted that "in endeavoring to portray the strains of the Japanese, we find that there is a preponderance of string effects, both pizzicato and legato. . . . While there is no organ stop at present on most of the theatrical organs that imitates the Japanese samisen and other native instruments (with the exception of two inventions by Hope-Jones, one of which is named the kinura), we suggest that as a solo player the organist lay stress on the clarinet, orchestral oboe and a combination of these with string effects."[101] Burroughs then proceeded to offer an extensive list of songs, musicals, and operas on Japanese subjects that the silent film organist should draw on, including *Madama Butterfly*, *The Mikado*, *The Geisha*, and *The Mayor of Tokio*.

DeMille's *The Cheat* inspired some unique experiments in genre transformation. *I.O.U.* was perhaps the first stage play to be based on a film. Although a string quartet apparently played several selections at the performance, it is unclear whether incidental music was heard throughout the play. The transformation of a silent film into a staged performance involved certain challenges. For example, unable to switch settings as nimbly as in film, this play was set in the Hardy's living room for the first two acts, thus reserving the villain's exotic home for the final act. The entire trial scene was cut, with the villain committing suicide instead. A note in the original program reveals an attempt to find an equivalent for cinematic transitions in order to represent the passage of time on stage: "During the action of [Act III], the curtain will be lowered one minute to denote the passing of fifteen minutes." Norman

Bel Geddes, the major theatrical and industrial designer, designed the sets and lighting and became scene designer for the Metropolitan Opera that year. Reviews of *I.O.U.* did not approve of this experiment in genre-crossing. For example, the *Evening Post* reviewer wrote: "Dialogue and plot proved entirely irreconcilable. The words were mere fillers, banal, and tiresome. . . . Decidedly, in this instance, spoken drama proved distinctly inferior to film."[102] We will find below that transforming *The Cheat* into an opera proved even more problematic.

The Metamorphoses of the Exotic Man

This lineage presents a bizarre exotic mélange, frequently within individual works and particularly in scenes involving diegetic performance. With successive versions of the tale, the ethnicity of the villain changed and the Orientalist representation intensified. Protests from Japanese American organizations and the Japanese government, a US ally in World War I, and a long-running campaign against the film by the Los Angeles Japanese American newspaper *Rafu Shimpo* resulted in a re-release of the original film in 1918 with the title cards changed to identify the villain as Burmese rather than Japanese.[103] Likewise, *I.O.U.* previewed in New Jersey with José Ruben playing a Japanese villain, but by the time the play opened in New York City the character had become Hindu.[104]

In the 1923 silent film, the villain (Prince Rao) is actually a French con artist who passes as an Indian prince. As though to compensate for the villain's whiteness, the Edith character in this film (Carmelita) is an Argentinean played by Pola Negri, a Polish actress who was rumored to have Gypsy blood. (At one point in the film our heroine dances a tango with the faux Indian prince.) Early in the film's development, in a complex twist to the original plot, the heroine was to cheat and be branded by an older Spanish gentleman (Don Carlos) to whom she was betrothed. At the moment in the courtroom scene when the heroine reveals her brand and denounces the older Spanish gentleman, there is a revealing parenthetical note in the original typed scenario: "(NOTE: I do not agree that audience would here turn on Don Carlos. Before the audience turned on Tori because he was a Jap—racial hatred; but, Don Carlos being a Spanish gentleman, I consider the following scenes out of place.)" In the end, the filmmakers reverted to the original plot structure, with the faux exotic prince as the villain. Although the threat of actual miscegenation is defused in this film, the screenplay emphasizes racial difference and Orientalism. According to the film's scenario, in a spoken title the heroine's white American boyfriend declared: "I'm not crazy about the idea of trotting about with this Hindu. He may be a prince but his color is offensive to me—*especially* when I see him near you." The film featured a "Hindu" ball with "Hindu" musicians and the scenario states that "the Prince delighted his guests by giving them a taste of real India. . . . There are soft lights and much incense, something very exotic and queer. . . . Girl dances in the middle of the floor while Hindu musicians play for her."

(See Figure 4.7.) The cue sheet, compiled by James C. Bradford, called for Latin American–themed pieces near the opening, a piece entitled "The Bayaderes" (perhaps intended to signal the "Hindu" villain), and Zamecnik's "My Cairo Love."[105] At least one New York theater attempted to enhance the exotic experience of this 1923 film even further. The Broadway Rivoli Theatre screening of *The Cheat* in August 1923 was preceded by several musical numbers including "Priere Hindoue" ("Hindu Prayer") which was performed on stage by four female dancers.[106] Racial difference was emphasized even more bluntly in Russell Holman's novel based on this film. In the novel, the Hindu prince (who is not unmasked as a European fraud, but retains his exotic status) is described as "sinister" and "possessive" throughout. Alone with Carmelita in his secret room, Rao declares: "You and I are different from the others, the Americans, you know. We are of older, warmer-blooded races. We take love where we find it" (p. 34). Later, at the moment when he went to brand her with his Bengal tiger brand, the "mask was gone. He was wholly the hate-maddened Oriental!" (p. 238). Both the 1923 film and novel, released but one year before the 1924 Exclusion Act, prove to be the most explicit in dealing with race in the lineage of *The Cheat*.

As the first sound film of the narrative, the 1931 *Cheat* exploited the possibilities for diegetic Orientalist performance. (Except for the emphatic brass and gongs of the Main Title music, all of the music in the film is diegetic.) The villain in this version is a white American named Hardy Livingstone whose "code of honor has been perverted by life in the Orient."[107] Livingstone has not only collected an impressive

Figure 4.7 A "Hindu" Performance, *The Cheat* (1923). Paramount publicity still. Courtesy of the Academy of Motion Picture Arts and Sciences.

number of Asian art objects, but has adopted a Japanese character as his crest, wears a kimono-like outfit in one scene, and understands his servants' Japanese dialogue. He has also "collected" international women in his travels—they are represented by small dolls that he keeps in a cabinet. Early in the film Livingstone declares: "The Oriental woman isn't really a slave, she's simply well trained . . . she knows her business." This film attempts to outdo previous versions of the tale in its Orientalist mise en scène and in its lessons for white female audience members. As Livingstone shows Elsa (the Edith character) his *shoji* room, she asks what lies behind the *shoji* door. Livingstone slides the door open, revealing a moonlit garden in which a male and female musician are performing. Although they are referred to as "Japanese musicians" and the female appears to be wearing a kimono, they are seen playing two Indian instruments—a *sarangi* and a *sitar*—as we hear a vague bowed string line on the soundtrack. Elsa, ever the reckless flirt in this film, remarks: "I must admit you are very clever at planning your conquests." This is not the only exotic performance to take place at Livingstone's house. The 1931 charity ball sequence is one of the most striking scenes in any version of *The Cheat*. The theme of this costume party is "Oriental" and we witness the white American guests foxtrotting while dressed up in an array of exotic costumes. (A character refers to the theme of last year's party as having been American Indian.) Elsa appears in an elaborate "Siamese" dress provided by Livingstone himself; Livingstone's Japanese servants remain in tuxedos. The evening climaxes in the performance of a "Cambodian" dance accompanied by a "Cambodian" ensemble. The dance was actually choreographed and performed by Ruth St. Denis and her company. Both the dance and the soundtrack music were influenced to some degree by Cambodian (Khmer) dance and music. The instruments on the screen include a Cambodian *ranat-ek* and the soundtrack music features a bowed string instrument, drums, a marimba, and small finger cymbals which correspond to the Cambodian *ching*.[108]

The final cinematic version of the tale both transports it far beyond its origins and returns it to its original screening. It also clearly refers to previous versions knowingly. With the 1937 French sound film *Forfaiture* the story is transplanted from Long Island to Mongolia—perhaps America had lost its exotic tinge for French audiences by this point in cinematic history. In this film, the Richard Hardy character is a French engineer leading a joint French-Mongolian team in building a bridge. More than any other version of the tale, the 1937 *Forfaiture* emphasizes the mortal dangers inherent in dealing with the exotic. The Frenchmen are shot at by snipers and the bridge itself is blown up by native terrorists before completion. The Edith character becomes obsessed with an exotic form of gambling that has been rigged against her. The villain, Lee-Lang, is clearly behind all of this Oriental treachery. This film declares its reflexivity from the start and pays homage to DeMille by literally incorporating shots from the 1915 film, reworking them, and providing them with new music by Michel Lévine. In the introductory sequence, we first see two shots of the wounded Tori. However, these shots are presented in reverse order from the original film, the third shot is taken from earlier in the 1915 scene, and the original intertitle with Edith's spoken text has been deleted. In addition, the newly composed music functions simultaneously as the Main Title music for this new film and as accompaniment to the silent original. This theme, punctuated by a gong, consists of a marcato brass line based on an anhemitonic pentatonic scale and a plodding rhythm. (See Example 4.5.) Thus, this Main Title music draws directly on the Euro-American sonic signals for the "evil Oriental," musical markers that arose in large part from Orientalist opera. Here, at the start of the 1937 film, and at the end of this cinematic lineage, we see the original mute cinematic actors inhabiting the new musical genre of Orientalist sound film.

In an ultimate act of homage to the original film, a significantly older Hayakawa was cast as the villain Lee-Lang. The exoticism of Lee-Lang's home is primarily conveyed through music. In fact, his house seems oddly permeated by music of ambiguous diegetic status. For example, during the first scene set in the villain's home we hear an ethereal melody played by celesta and vibraphone above a sustained chord in the strings. This music eventually transmutes into the Main Title theme, which is bluntly stated by the strings after we witness Lee-Lang branding an art object. Lee-Lang proves himself the master of diegetic musical performance later in the film. At one point we hear the celesta theme and assume again that it is nondiegetic or background music, only to have Lee-Lang gesture to an offscreen performer to stop playing. The camera then pans to reveal a musician holding a long-necked lute. As host of the Red Cross Ball, Lee-Lang arranges for an elaborate exotic outdoor performance. In this scene the dancing Europeans are interrupted by brash ceremonial music that, to my ear, resembles nothing so much as Steve Reich's *Different Trains*. In general, the film's Orientalist music points to a Southeast Asian influence, perhaps reflecting France's colonialist experience. In a bid to achieve a degree of "exotic authenticity" not encountered in earlier versions of the narrative, the filmmakers spliced in documentary footage of exotic musical performance. However, although we see men playing cymbals and a large drum, we hear newly composed music that, in its close coordination with the musical performance on the screen, attempts to pass as authentic. In a surprise narrative variation, we do not witness the branding scene, but stumble upon its aftermath along with the husband. However, we do see the scene later as a flashback during the trial scene—the film thus treats itself reflexively as it did the sequence from the 1915 original; in both cases we first see the villain wounded. Perhaps seeking closure for the narrative, Lee-Lang appears to be dead in this version. The 1937 *Forfaiture* was not the first

Example 4.5 Orientalist Main Title Music, Michel Lévine, *Forfaiture* (Societé du Cinéma du Panthéon, 1937).

French reworking of DeMille's film. Some French audience members might have recalled an intriguing, although short-lived 1920 opera bearing the same title.

Giving the Exotic Cinematic Male an Operatic Voice

> What the hell, Mah-jong,
> what the hell, since it's not understood,
> it will have, it will have, it will have,
> it will have, cascara, harakiri, Sessue Hayakawa,
> ha! it will always have a Chinese air.
>
> The Chinese Cup, L'enfant et les sortileges[109]

Writing in 1917, Colette, the French novelist and critic, lamented: "They tell me the thing is decided: *The Cheat* is going to be made into an opera. The news was given me by one of those 'friends of film' whose enthusiasm crushes me and whose conversation temporarily deprives me of any taste for cinema."[110] Colette reported that after hearing of the impending genre metamorphosis that *The Cheat*—a film she had celebrated in print—was fated to undergo, she decided to goad her "friend of film" by helping him determine exactly how to achieve the operalization. Her friend was most concerned with the question of who could sing the role of the Japanese villain, particularly since "really, the Japanese has nothing to say in the story." Colette offered the following advice: "I have an idea. Supposing that the Japanese, in your opera, were made evil, seductive, and . . . mute?" She then explained how she proceeded to lead her friend step by step to the only satisfactory solution: the original silent film should simply be screened in the opera house. *The Cheat* and Hayakawa were clearly very much on Colette's mind during this period for she also paid homage to the silent screen star in her 1918 libretto for Ravel's opera *L'enfant et les sortileges* (premiered in 1925). In lines for the Chinese Cup, quoted above, Colette wittily twisted the French language to simulate a faux Chinese sound and deliberately mixed Japanese and Chinese references, presumably to poke fun at fashionable Orientalism itself. Following the Cup's reference to Hayakawa, the Cup is joined by the Teapot as they sing "Ping, pong, ping, pong, ping./Ah! What the hell have you done with my Kawa?"—perhaps an oblique reference to her own critical fears concerning the operatic treatment of the silent cinematic masterpiece. Colette concluded her 1917 lament by complaining that such self-proclaimed champions of the cinema do not rest until they have "transformed [a successful film] into a bad play, an ankylosed opera, or a dislocated pantomime-ballet." However, her plea to keep the new art of the cinema quarantined from opera at all costs was clearly not respected in the twentieth century, as my discussion of Madame Butterfly's multiple screen appearances attests. In her study of opera and silent film, Michal Grover-Friedlander queries: "How would a mute operatic voice appear in film?"[111] Colette asks us to consider how a mute cinematic actor would appear in opera. DeMille's 1915 silent film and Camille Erlanger's 1920 opera *Forfaiture* allow us to consider the cinema/opera dynamic from a new angle.

Over six decades before the cinematic experiments of Philip Glass, Erlanger's *Forfaiture* was the first opera—to my knowledge—to be based on a film.[112] *Forfaiture* apparently received only three performances, but attracted significant attention. Given the intense French fascination with DeMille's film and the scandalous nature of Erlanger's 1906 *Aphrodite* and that opera's depiction of women, it is not surprising that *Forfaiture* would stir interest in certain quarters.[113] The opera is set specifically in "present-day" New York and Erlanger created *couleur locale* with a heavily syncopated theme marked "très rythmé," making this one of the earliest European works to suggest a representation of early jazz. (See Example 4.6.) In style and genre, the opera presents a mixture of *verismo*, Orientalist, and proto-*Zeitopern* elements. In addition, Erlanger's opera reveals the influence of Debussy, particularly in its harmony. The transformation from silent film to opera required the addition of dialogue—opposite the process of transforming a spoken play into an opera—and a restructuring of the plot into five episodes or acts. The opera condenses the plot and omits several scenes from the film, presumably to avoid additional set changes. For

Example 4.6 The New York Setting, Camille Erlanger, *Forfaiture* (Max Eschig, Paris, 1920).

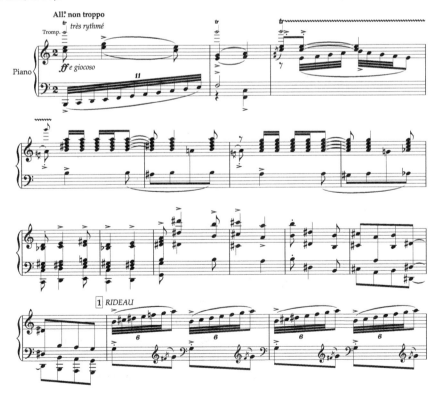

example, elements of the action from the film's first four scenes, involving multiple settings, are presented in one setting in the first episode of the opera.

In her review of DeMille's film, Colette asked: "Is it only a combination of felicitous effects that brings us to this film and keeps us there? Or is it the more profound and less clear pleasure of seeing the crude '*ciné*' groping toward perfection, the pleasure of divining what the future of the cinema must be when its makers will want that future, when its music will finally become its inevitable, irresistible collaborator, its interpreter; when the same slow waltz or the same comic-opera overture will no longer accompany, and impartially betray, a tragedy, a love duet, and an attempted murder?"[114] Colette imagined a new cinematic genre, an ideal form of sound film in which newly composed music would support the screen so closely as to appear inevitable. Although Colette's temporary "solution" for the operalization of film (simply screening the film in the opera house) is no solution at all, it does pay the most direct homage to DeMille's *Cheat*, the source of this astonishing exotic lineage.

In his review of *Forfaiture*, Émile Vuillermoz complained that situation and character are presented far less efficiently and quickly in opera than in film.[115] He claimed that film has a unique ability to present a character's personality and motivations instantly with one arresting image while opera had no such resources. However, the immediate visual impact of Tori's title shot in the 1915 *Cheat*, for example, is directly paralleled in the opera by his striking leitmotif heard as he first appears on stage—in both cases Tori remains mute during his first appearance. Although many comparative discussions have focused on the temporal differences between the experience of operatic and cinematic drama, I suggest that the oft-bemoaned sense of stasis in opera vis-à-vis film may have more to do with spatial and visual elements than with the rate of text delivery and action. The relative visual stasis in opera is felt keenly in Orientalist works, although I reassert that opera's slower rate of location change is much closer to our experience of life than is film's instant cutting between different locations. (The triumphal march in Act II of Verdi's *Aida* offers one solution to this problem. On the other hand, French Grand Opera's construction of stunning singing tableaux points to the potential pleasures of operatic stasis.)[116] In the case of *Forfaiture*, the need to compensate for relative visual stasis was particularly acute.

The composer and librettists had already experienced DeMille's kinetic presentation of the tale and knew that the astonishing cinematic images would be fresh in the minds of their audience. Their attempt to compensate for the loss of visual flexibility and the ability to cut instantly to other settings and viewing angles is most apparent in the second episode, which is set in Tori's exotic home. The stage directions describing this setting are extensive and, in their specificity and use of Japanese terms, reveal an attempt at ethnographic authenticity. The episode begins with an instrumental introduction and a raised curtain, allowing us to gaze upon the multiple rooms of the Japanese interior and the garden beyond. (The garden in the original 1915 film was also Japanese in design.) Unlike several of the cinematic versions, the entire interior of the villain's home is exotic in style. A great deal of the dialogue in this episode is devoted to visual descriptions of Japan and of Tori's home. First, we hear Tori's servants describe their homeland (prefiguring the nostalgia of Ping, Pang, and Pong in the opening of Act II in Puccini's *Turandot*) and later hear Richard Hardy, who has spent time in Japan, catalog all the images he remembers of the exotic country and that he now sees reproduced in Tori's home. The female guests simply gush in their descriptions of Tori's charming and enchanting house, drawing our visual attention to various details of the set. Finally, Tori offers Edith a tour of the *shoji* room and presents his collection of Japanese art objects for Edith, and the audience, to admire. The amount of visual description in the dialogue of this episode implies that we are unable to see the exotic setting with our own eyes. The librettists betray an anxiety that their operatic audience is blind, or has been visually spoiled by cinema, and that dialogue must serve as a surrogate camera. As I claimed above for Orientalist opera more generally, in *Forfaiture* we are repeatedly prompted to see through our ears.

In Orientalist opera, music sustains the exotic impact of the otherwise static set and can direct our attention as would camera angle and movement in film. Tori's otherness is far more pronounced in the opera than in the original film and his enhanced exoticism is directly reflected in Erlanger's musical setting, which represents a step beyond earlier examples of operatic *japonisme* by Saint-Saëns, Messager, and Mascagni.[117] Three specific musical elements repeatedly serve as acoustic signs of the exotic in Erlanger's opera: parallel fifths, melodic tritones, and the use of the Japanese national anthem, "Kimigayo." In silent film, music often functions as precise commentary as it reacts to the images and intertitles on the screen. In opera, music appears more autonomous, providing a consistent sonic atmosphere that does not necessarily respond moment by moment to stage action. Erlanger's simple use of leitmotifs does, however, resemble the function of music in silent film.

Tori's first appearance is signaled with a conspicuous leitmotif marked "un poco misterioso" in the score. (See Example 4.7a.) We hear this theme again during Tori's first lines and frequently whenever he appears on stage. In the original silent film, Tori's difference was signaled by smoke and shadows. In the opera, the exotic and sinister are signaled by a plunging melodic line accompanied by open fifths (as in Example 4.7a) and by a low-register, cyclic theme with a prominent augmented fourth and brooding parallel fifths (see Example 4.7b). The music is telling us something not otherwise apparent. Tori's musical themes also appear when other characters refer to him and later in the third episode when Edith reads his letter. Japanese music is represented explicitly in one crucial scene in the opera. After making his crude bargain with Edith, Tori sings a "Japanese song" (with stereotypical open fifths and fourths in the melody and strummed accompaniment), and mimes accompanying himself on *shamisen*—thus, performing his difference within the drama. (See Example 4.8.) In this dramatic context, Tori's exotic sung song, and thus Japanese music itself, is coded as sinister. Richard Hardy responds to

Example 4.7a and 4.7b Tori's Leitmotifs, Camille Erlanger, *Forfaiture* (Max Eschig, Paris, 1920).

this performance by declaring Tori to be a "singulier homme," one who is "curious, bizarre, strange, original, and rare!" Erlanger approximates Japanese traditional music most closely in the instrumental introduction to the second episode. (See Example 4.9.) As we gaze upon the exotic setting, we hear a heterophonic relationship between the upper and middle lines. Both lines employ the Japanese *in* scale, the upper line emphasizes augmented fourths, and the middle line features characteristic grace notes. The accompanying drone of stacked fifths enhances the exoticism but points away from any Japanese influence. (This texture suggests a possible encounter with Japanese *sankyoku* music by Erlanger.) Finally, the Japanese national anthem "Kimigayo" is used repeatedly in the score for scenes set in Tori's

Example 4.8 Tori's "Japanese" Song, Camille Erlanger, *Forfaiture* (Max Eschig, Paris, 1920).

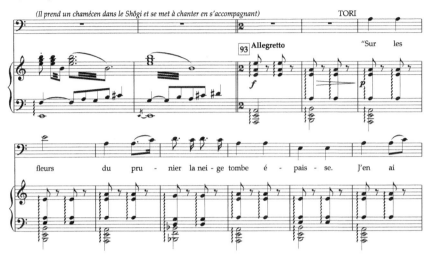

Example 4.9 Introduction to the Second Episode, Camille Erlanger, *Forfaiture* (Max Eschig, Paris, 1920).

home and for explicit references to Japan, and his Japanese servants sing a duet about their homeland to this tune.

Considered along nationalistic lines, the lineage of *The Cheat* suggests a greater French devotion to representing the exotic. Taking genre and chronological differences into account, the two French works seem to revel in their musical exoticism; American versions of the tale are more concerned with offering a lesson for their female audience members.[118] One might think that Edith is a victim, but the tale clearly brands her as a cheat who learns the hard way that her husband knows best. One might also assume that as the villain became increasingly white in successive American versions, race played a diminishing role. These changes in the villain's race attest to the fact that miscegenation between a white woman and an Asian male was seen as a threat, while the affair between a white sailor and his Japanese lover was viewed and presented as an enticing exotic fantasy. And yet we have seen that exoticism was actually enhanced in later versions of *The Cheat* and that music was repeatedly employed not only to create exotic settings, but also to define race.

Other Exotic Men

Although *The Cheat* proved to be one of the most seminal depictions of the enticing and horrifying exotic male, it was certainly not unique in the early twentieth century, nor were Japanese males the exclusive target of these representations. Franz Lehár's 1929 Viennese operetta *Das Land des Lächelns* (*The Land of Smiles*), an international success based on his 1923 *Die gelbe Jacke* (*The Yellow Jacket*), offered a more lighthearted depiction of the miscegenation of a white woman and an Asian male, but this time with a Chinese focus.[119] In the first act, the countess Lisa has fallen in love with a Chinese diplomat Prince Sou-Chong—a part written for Richard Tauber who made the number "Dein ist mein ganzes Herz" ("You are my heart's delight") his signature song. She moves with him to China only to discover that he is obligated by his new social standing to take four wives. When she protests, he forbids her to leave his home and she comes to hate him. Following the late eighteenth-century mode of *alla turca* operas, Sou-Chong proves magnanimous upon discovering her attempts to escape in Act III and allows her to leave.

During this period, cinematic depictions of exotic men along the spectrum of Orientalist allure and repulsion ranged from *The Sheik* (1921) to the nefarious Dr. Fu Manchu. In *The Sheik*, the white heroine's infatuation with the dangerous exotic man is ultimately whitewashed in the narrative when she (and we) learn near the film's end of the true European identity of Rudolph Valentino's dashing character. White female audience members enjoying the cinematic spectacle of Valentino's beauty could remind themselves of his own whiteness—something not possible in their experience of Hayakawa. Dr. Fu Manchu first appeared in print in 1912 and remained a fixture in American popular culture over four decades. As the "Yellow Peril" incarnate—complete with grotesque yellowface depictions on screen—it is unlikely that Fu Manchu inspired much in the way of sexual desire. And yet, his daring and nearly magical brilliance were certainly appealing and awe-inspiring. As the United States engaged in a series of East Asian wars throughout the mid-twentieth century, the Fu Manchu approach to depicting the Asian male predominated.

Hayakawa will repeatedly return in succeeding chapters as we trace representations of the Japanese male throughout much of the twentieth century. In fact, it could be argued that Hayakawa's multiple film and television appearances in the United States profoundly shaped the American imagination of Japanese men more generally, just as the self-sacrificing Madame Butterfly character did for the image of Japanese women. Asked late in life about *The Cheat* and his portrayal of the Japanese villain, Hayakawa insisted: "He might have been a Russian, a Frenchman, a Spaniard—the nationality didn't count. . . . The man was merely a villain, and a new twist was given the scenario by making him a Japanese."[120] However, even when the villain in versions of *The Cheat* was represented as a white American or European, it was his association with the exotic and the accompaniment of Orientalist music that marked him as evil. Hayakawa himself played characters of many nationalities— Chinese, Japanese, Indian, Mexican, Native American, Hawaiian—during his long career. The closest he got to playing a white American was as a Spanish matador and in the roles of a mixed race Chinese-American and—most significant for this discussion—as the mixed-race son of a Madame Butterfly and Pinkerton couple in *His Birthright* (1918).[121] In this film, the first released by his own production company, Hayakawa portrayed Yukio, a young man whose Japanese mother had committed suicide after having been abandoned by his father, a white American sailor. Yukio sets sail for America seeking revenge on his father for denying him "his birthright," but ends up dedicating himself to the United States after learning that his Pinkerton-father had remained in love with his mother despite being unable to return.[122] Daisuke Miyao has argued that the Americanization of Yukio in this film was constructed to emphasize the actor's own embrace of his new home during World War I. Furthermore, Miyao notes that music marks Yukio's development and signals his "racial identification" at different moments in the film. Early in the film, Yukio responds enthusiastically to the music of an African American dance orchestra, moving "his hands exactly in rhythm with the orchestra" while looking disapprovingly upon the movements of the white dancers. At the end of the film he responds positively to the music of a white US Navy band and is inspired to make a patriotic pro-American declaration.[123] In the period leading up to the 1924 Exclusion Act, Hayakawa's attempts to establish bonds between the United States and Japan through the cinema proved, of course, ultimately unsuccessful.[124] As he explained in a 1929 interview with none other than Onoto Watanna, he came to feel unwelcome himself in the United States and eventually moved to France.[125] His attempt to rewrite the Madame Butterfly narrative in order for the Japanese American child to accept and be accepted by his American fatherland also met with some stiff resistance. (Apparently, naval officers in New Orleans protested against *His Birthright* and the film was confiscated and sent to Washington.)[126] Ultimately, it was Hayakawa's stunning success in the role of Tori, the Japanese millionaire who remained unassimilable, that launched his career and it was in the role of the exotic other that Hayakawa would remain in the American imagination. In 1927, Hayakawa used the money he had made in Hollywood portraying exotic men to purchase his own Tudor mansion on Long Island.

5

An Exotic Enemy

Musical Propaganda in Wartime Hollywood

As the Japanese pilots flew to Pearl Harbor for their 7 December 1941 attack, they tuned their radios to Honolulu station KGMB and used the popular music being broadcast as a sonic beacon to their bombing sites. A second anecdote: in Studs Terkel's best-selling oral history of World War II entitled *"The Good War,"* a Japanese American woman (Yuriko Hohri) tells the story of her family's internment by the US government. She recounts the day in her Californian childhood a few months after Pearl Harbor when two FBI agents searched her house and then took her father away:

> A black car came right into the driveway. One man went into the kitchen. As I watched, he looked under the sink and he looked into the oven. Then he went into the parlor and opened the glass cases where our most treasured things were. There were several stacks of *shakuhachi* sheet music. It's a bamboo flute. My father played the *shakuhachi* and my mother played the *koto*. At least once a month on a Sunday afternoon, their friends would come over and just enjoy themselves playing music. The man took the music.[1]

During World War II, music served as a weapon—as an instrument of racist propaganda and as an agent of militant patriotism. Although FBI agents did not make a habit of confiscating Japanese sheet music, from fear that it might be a form of coded espionage, and American popular music did not normally play a direct part in battles, music was thoroughly implicated in the war.[2]

The propagandistic potential of music was taken for granted in both the United States and Japan during World War II. In both nations, national committees were established and competitions held to encourage the creation of patriotic war songs. The US Office of War Information formed a National Wartime Music Committee for this purpose, and the music industry followed suit.[3] Each US soldier was issued an "Army Song Book" containing such expected pieces as "Anchors Aweigh" and the "Marines' Hymn" as part of his standard equipment.[4] Although most musical contributions to the war effort emanated from Tin Pan Alley and Hollywood, some American art music composers also sought to serve. Aaron Copland stated in a 1942 speech to the League of Composers Board that American composers wanted to "help in the war effort" and had "offered Washington the services of the composer to write background music for war films, to arrange music for army band, to write songs or production numbers for the entertainment of troops."[5] Japan deployed music more directly by broadcasting American popular songs to US GIs in the Pacific with the intent of instilling homesickness and weakening the American will to fight.[6]

In a 1946 article entitled "Shaping Music for Total War," Henry Cowell explained his own contributions to the war effort, focusing particularly on the important role of music for US radio propaganda efforts. Capitalizing on Cowell's knowledge of the world's music, the Office of War Information employed him to select pieces to be played on US radio in various nations. Cowell stated that to "direct listeners away from radio Tokyo, our newscasters find that it is especially the *music* we offer which must be more attractive than that on Japanese programs." Directly countering similar Japanese propaganda efforts, Cowell explained that his unit selected "love songs adored by the Japanese people but forbidden by their government, which fears they will make their soldiers homesick." Cowell found that the global musical hybridity of the mid-twentieth century ("distasteful to musicologists") proved helpful for propaganda purposes: "Our popular tunes are to be found in every Oriental country played and sung on native instruments in the style of the land."[7] Indeed, the Japanese-controlled radio station in Shanghai played Stephen Foster's "Old Folks at Home/Way Down upon the Swanee River"—a song taught to Japanese schoolchildren since the late nineteenth century—following the broadcast of the Emperor's statement of defeat. The Japanese stationed there "could not repress our tears, hearing the melody. To us Foster's music sounded like a mixture of deep sorrow and warm humanity. We felt as though hatred and despair had been swept away."[8]

At home, the Japanese government attempted to ban certain forms of "enemy music," but this proved difficult since American music had become thoroughly integrated with Japanese musical life since the 1868 Meiji Restoration.[9] Of course, there was little need to ban Japanese music in the United States, *pace* the overzealous FBI agents mentioned above. Even in the internment camps, Japanese Americans primarily performed and listened to swing music.[10] In the rare instances when US propaganda took any notice of it, Japanese traditional music was presented as a sign of that culture's fanaticism and inexplicable nature, of its dangerous difference. The general ignorance of Japanese culture in the United States facilitated American propagandists' attempts to portray the Japanese as a completely foreign enemy.

The belief in Japan's irreconcilable cultural difference was confirmed by the anthropologist Ruth Benedict, perhaps the most influential interpreter of Japanese culture in the United States. Benedict began her 1946 study *The Chrysanthemum and the Sword* by stating: "The Japanese were the most alien enemy the United States had ever fought in an all-out struggle. In no other war with a major foe had it been necessary to take into account such exceedingly different habits of acting and thinking." Benedict had been hired by the Office of War Information to assist in understanding the Japanese. She interviewed Japanese Americans in internment camps and watched Japanese films in her venture to carry out fieldwork "at a distance." As indicated by the title of her first chapter, "Assignment: Japan," Benedict's cultural anthropology presents a clear case of Edward Said's Orientalist scholar in the service of her state.[11]

As John W. Dower has powerfully demonstrated, the war between the United States and Japan was as much a race war as a geopolitical conflict.[12] This is evident in statements made during the war by US servicemen and civilians, in the propaganda created in both nations, in the treatment of Japanese war dead by US soldiers, and in Japan's calls for (and US fears of) a unification of Asian races in league against the "decadent whites." In sharp contrast to American depictions of the German enemy, anti-Japanese propaganda consistently and negatively focused on the physical characteristics, social customs, and religious beliefs of the Japanese people.[13] Propaganda in the initial stages of the war tended to underestimate the Japanese as nearsighted and bucktoothed children. But long cherished images of a "queer and quaint," and ultimately harmless, feminine people remembered from *The Mikado* and *Madama Butterfly* would soon vanish. Indeed, a wartime cartoon appearing in the *New Yorker* depicted two Japanese men in swastika-design kimonos with bombs and paratroopers descending in the background declaring: "If you want to know who we are, We are gentlemen of Japan." A cartoon by Helen Hokinson appearing in the 17 January 1942 issue of the magazine featured two women heading to the opera, with one remarking to the other: "Well, there's *one* good thing about it. We won't have to feel so sorry for Madame Butterfly any more." Throughout all forms of American media, the Japanese were referred to derogatively as "Japs" and were routinely depicted as back-stabbing monkeys lurking in the jungle or as vermin in need of extermination. The phrase "sneaky little yellow rats" sums up the common racist stereotype. (The sneakiness of the Japanese had been more light-heartedly depicted before the war in Ogden Nash's 1938 poem "The Japanese.") Wartime Orientalist representation of the Japanese understandably emphasized the repulsive alien qualities rather than the potential exotic enticements of the enemy. Frequently, the question was raised whether the barbaric Japanese were even members of the same species as the rest of the world's peoples. Thus the Japanese were presented as the ultimate exotic other.

American popular songs such as "We're Gonna Have to Slap the Dirty Little Jap" kept pace with these representations in their racist and jingoistic lyrics. The favorite devices of this form of propaganda included ridiculing the accent and linguistic usage of the Japanese when speaking English, rhyming "Japs" with as many negative terms as possible, and drawing on stereotypical images. (The roots of these representational techniques are found in Tin Pan Alley songs of the late nineteenth and early twentieth centuries.) The 1941 song "Goodbye Mama (I'm Off to Yokohama)," with words and music by J. Fred Coots, offers one example: "A million fightin' sons of Uncle Sam, if you please,/Will soon have all those Japs right down on their 'Jap-a-knees'" (Chappell and Co.). The following text is from Lu Earl's 1944 "A-Bombing

We Will Go (Right Over Tokio)": "Look out, you yellow Japs/You thought that we were saps, We're gonna blast you from away up high./Now you bombed Pearl Harbor in your mean and sneaky way,/So we're gonna jar your little island night and day" (STASNY Music Corp.). Other titles include "Taps for the Japs," "We'll Nip the Nipponese," "We're Gonna Change the Map of the Jap," "We're Gonna Play Yankee Doodle in Tokyo," and "You're a Sap, Mister Jap."[14] In American popular culture, the "us" in the "US," the audience referred to as "American," and the "we" in these titles from Tin Pan Alley denoted white, Euro-American (and predominately Christian) US citizens. (Hollywood's calculated attempts to present a more ethnically diverse and harmonious America—excluding Asian Americans and with only token African American presence—will be discussed below.) Although major popular song composers such as Irving Berlin ("The Sun Will Soon Be Setting for the Land of the Rising Sun") and Hoagy Carmichael ("The Cranky Old Yank") also contributed anti-Japanese songs, none of these achieved much prominence. Instead, the most effective medium for anti-Japanese propaganda in the United States, and the site of music's most important wartime role, was the cinema.

From shortly after the entrance of the United States into the war in late 1941 to the end of the American occupation of Japan in 1952, Hollywood produced a large number of films offering negative depictions of the Japanese. The Japanese had been relatively ignored in American film in the 1930s. From 1931 to 1940, approximately twenty-five films dealt with Japan or with Japanese characters, and eight of these formed the "Mr. Moto" detective series, which actually had little to do with Japan. In contrast, approximately twenty-five anti-Japanese feature films were released in the United States in 1942 alone.[15] Hollywood's anti-Japanese propaganda films of the war period included the combat genre, in which the Japanese were often represented as a ship on the horizon, a plane in the sky, or a faceless mass of approaching infantrymen. Films set in the period leading up to Pearl Harbor included Japanese characters involved in espionage, while those set during the war frequently presented Japanese officers who delighted in torturing American prisoners.

Hollywood films served as a primary connection to the war for those on the home front and as an introduction of sorts for those heading to battle. The war was inescapable in American theaters, even on nights when the feature presentation was not war-related. Before the feature, the audience watched newsreels chronicling the war's progress and cartoon shorts urging them to buy war bonds (available for purchase in the lobby) and to conserve and contribute scrap metal for the war effort. Almost half of the American population went to the movies at least once a week during the war, and box office revenues increased sharply with each year of the conflict.[16] Following Japan's surrender, apparently no anti-Japanese films were produced for almost three years. Starting in 1949, however, the anti-communist witch hunt led by the House Un-American Activities Committee encouraged Hollywood to reaffirm its patriotism by making more celebratory World War II films. While such films appeared sporadically throughout the 1950s and onward, often serving as indirect propaganda for the Cold War or more recently as nostalgic memorials to the "Good War," 1952 represents the end of the central decade of anti-Japanese feature films. Another type of propaganda film was also created in the United States during World War II: a series of pseudo-documentary indoctrination films produced (primarily in Hollywood) as part of the official efforts of the War Department. These films were initially intended for the instruction of soldiers, but were considered so successful that several were released to public theaters in the United States and Allied nations. My research has focused on the soundtracks of some seventy films—both Hollywood features and US government documentaries—dealing with the war against Japan. (A selected filmography, listing credited composers' names, is available in Appendix 2. Film dates given in this chapter represent the year of the film's general release.)

In this chapter, I will investigate the multiple roles assumed by music in anti-Japanese feature and documentary films created in Hollywood. Never had Orientalist and racial politics been more clearly evident in music heard by so many as in these World War II American films. Despite its manifest cultural significance, this large body of music has been hitherto either ignored or quickly dismissed as too blatant and utilitarian to merit serious analysis and interpretation. These films have repeatedly been investigated by political scientists and historians of American cinema, but their music appears to have offered little to scholars devoted to establishing a canon for film composers.[17] My research has uncovered some sophisticated examples of musical propaganda that offer new perspectives on the study of musical exoticism. Before turning to an analysis of anti-Japanese representation in these films, I will briefly assess the ability of film music to function as racist propaganda. The remainder of the chapter will focus both on how the Japanese were represented through film music and how Japanese music itself was presented.

Film Music as Racist Propaganda

"Propaganda" encompasses both the act of purveying certain beliefs or attitudes to a group of people in order to shape their opinions and ultimately direct their behavior toward a desired action, as well as the cultural products and texts appropriated or created to transmit those meanings and information and to incite the desired action. In order for propaganda to function, the agent of meaning should not lead to ambiguous interpretations, at least not within the mind of an intended recipient. Without recourse to an established lexicon, film music might instill a general feeling within a particular audience, but it would be unable to direct that emotion toward a specific action and thus would not fully succeed as propaganda. Of course, music with text has the potential of conveying (as well as modifying) propaganda embedded in the text. Utilizing a melody from a song well known to the intended audience could serve to bring the text and its meanings to the minds of the audience. In the absence of text, a distinctive musical style with a traditional signification might be employed. In all such cases, the immediate cinematic and cultural context will reshape the associated meaning. The films considered here demonstrate how, through associative mechanisms, music can be made to bear certain simple meanings and can thus be wielded as an agent of propaganda. In most cases, music strengthens the propagandistic function of the film by helping to cram multiple channels of perception with the same basic message. Propaganda thrived on new forms of multimedia in the twentieth century.

In his *Theory of Film*, Siegfried Kracauer states: "The moviegoer is much in the position of a hypnotized person. Spellbound by the luminous rectangle before his eyes—which resembles the glittering object in the hand of a hypnotist—he cannot help succumbing to the suggestions that invade the blank of his mind. Film is an incomparable instrument of propaganda."[18] But while Kracauer's assessment of film's propagandistic potential is accurate, he vastly overstates the "blank slate" condition of the audience and the autonomous power of the "luminous rectangle." The perception of any film is radically determined by context—in relation both to other films and to the current social environment. The same images and sounds can suggest a strikingly different meaning to different audiences (or individual audience members) or to the same audience at different times. Within each film, meaning is constructed through the interaction of the several visual, verbal, and aural elements. Reinforcement and repetition are required to establish a film's semiotic code in each of these dimensions. Music's signification in film is fashioned by associative meanings previously established in other genres, by the various visual and verbal techniques and contents of the film, and by cultural context. Within a film, the impact of a particularly striking screen image can determine our reading of the music heard. For example, when the image seen has been coded as "evil" by various visual and verbal elements, the music heard may also assume this connotation. Of course, this associative process works equally well in the opposite direction. Music does not passively take up the meanings created by such contexts. Often it is the music that dramatically shapes the perceived meaning and thus actualizes the propaganda. Kracauer offers pertinent examples of this in his study of World War II German film:

A conspicuous role is played by the music, particularly in *Victory in the West* [a 1941 full-length Nazi documentary celebrating the German victory in France]. Accompanying the procession of pictures and statements, it not only deepens the effects produced through these media, but intervenes of its own accord, introducing new effects or changing the meaning of synchronized units. Music, and music alone, transforms an English tank into a toy. In other instances, musical themes remove the weariness from soldier faces, or make several moving tanks symbolize the advancing German army.[19]

We will find that the propagandistic potential of music within film is realized in large part through the exploitation of a system of rudimentary leitmotifs formed by *mutual implication* (Claudia Gorbman's term) between specific images and sounds.[20]

The question of what element—visual, verbal, or aural—has priority in producing meaning in film has long engrossed film scholars. Although experience reveals rather quickly that each of these elements may serve as "dominant signifier" at different moments of a film, such determinations in film criticism are too often predetermined by the field of the critic. In extreme cases, music (or sound in general) may appear to have a "blinding effect" (Kracauer's term) in relation to the screen image, or the image may prove "deafening."[21] Music can cause us to "see" something not actually present on the screen and can determine how we interpret what is projected there. Screen images can prove similarly deceptive, by causing us to assume that what we hear is an original product of what we see. Music can influence our perception of the rate of visual movement both within shots and between shots, just as a rapid succession of images may cause us to hear the music at a quicker tempo. (Examples of how each of these cinematic potentialities can be harnessed for propaganda will be encountered below.) With so many signifying variables at play in film, it may seem a wonder that any single, coherent propagandistic meaning can be produced or perceived. And yet, when its various semantic systems are aligned, film can communicate with an impact greater than that produced by other media. Throughout the period covered in this chapter, cinematic ambiguity was rigorously rooted out by an army of censors. In addition, the majority of American audience members were already quite receptive to anti-Japanese messages and were inclined to think in a stereotypical fashion about the enemy. War proved a powerful inducement for bringing cinema's signifying systems into alignment for the purposes of propaganda.

The propagandistic aim of both Hollywood and US government World War II films was to convince US soldiers and the home front of the evil of the enemy and the necessity of fighting them. With respect to Japan, this aim was pursued along Orientalist lines. The "Japanese mind" and Japanese beliefs and values were presented as being antipodal to "ours." It is easier to kill when one's target is perceived as being utterly unlike oneself. Racist propaganda was accomplished in these films through dialogue concerning Japanese villainy, through repeated use of derogatory names for the Japanese, by showing Japanese characters committing atrocities onscreen, and through the various cinematic and musical techniques that will be analyzed in this chapter. In the 1943 film *China*, for example, two Japanese soldiers arrive at a Chinese peasant family's farm and quickly kill the elderly father. The camera then offers an extreme close-up of the leering grin of one of the Japanese soldiers as he spots the attractive daughter. We are not surprised to learn in the next scene that the young Chinese woman was brutally raped by the Japanese men. After the white American hero arrives at the farm, discovers the atrocity, and then shoots the two Japanese soldiers, he states that he now has no more compunction about shooting Japs "than if they were flies on a manure heap. Matter of fact, I kind of enjoyed it." In *Guadalcanal Diary*, also from 1943, we watch in disgust as Japanese soldiers bayonet the bodies of wounded and dead American GIs on a beach.

Hollywood's musical stereotypes for the Japanese frequently accompany such depictions of Japanese brutality. Typically in these films, we learn which musical sounds signal "Japanese enemy" by repetitive narrative association with images of "Japs" or in conjunction with dialogue mentioning the Japanese. These musical stereotypes needed to be unambiguous for propaganda purposes, although the meanings themselves ("evil Japs," "friendly Chinese," etc.) were not very subtle. I argue that these musical stereotypes are analogous to verbal stereotypes. Racist slurs such as "dirty little Jap" and "yellow rats" rely far more on how they are pronounced aloud or heard within the reader's inner ear than is normally recognized. Their sound is part of their racist sting. Within the context of anti-Japanese films, Hollywood's musical stereotypes for the Japanese are equally racist. In addition, the mechanical repetition of these musical stereotypes can itself serve as a dehumanizing representational technique. (The repetitive use of patriotic tunes accompanying footage of the white heroes in these films must be assumed, in contrast, to help define these characters as ideal types.) If propaganda inspires an audience to despise an enemy and ultimately to join the war effort, then propaganda and its agents serve as successful weapons of war.[22]

The examples discussed in the following three sections will illustrate the various ways music functioned within the propaganda network of anti-Japanese films. We will encounter film scores that employ preexistent European music to represent the Japanese enemy, scores that use stereotypical Orientalist signs for Japan, and films that include actual Japanese music or music that was composed with the intent to pass as Japanese music. My analysis and interpretation will be based on two fundamental premises: first, that the music we hear in a film informs both our specific comprehension of and our more general feelings about what we see in the film (whether or not we are aware of hearing the music); and second, that what we see on the screen, as determined by the cinematic techniques that shaped the moving images, influences how we perceive and evaluate the music we hear.[23] The first assumption is one on which most film music criticism is based. The second is a less commonly explored feature of the visual-aural dynamic, and is one that offers important implications for the study of cross-cultural musical encounters in film.

Propagandistic Pastiche

When surveying this large body of film music, one major compositional technique stands out: pastiche. These soundtracks offer a radical collage of musical styles, including American military tunes, contemporary popular music, jazz, Protestant hymns, American folk songs, nineteenth- and twentieth-century European classical music, anthems and folk songs of various European and Asian nations, and several forms of Orientalist musical representation. While pastiche has been exceedingly common throughout the history of Hollywood film music, its most striking usage is found in films from the World War II period. Musical pastiche is nowhere more evident than in the propaganda films created for the US War Department, including the famous *Why We Fight* series, the *Know Your Enemy/Know Your Ally* films, and the Army-Navy Screen Magazine productions.[24] Many of these films were made under the supervision of Frank Capra, the celebrated Hollywood director who had been enlisted to serve as Commanding Officer of the 834th Signal Corps Photographic Detachment. It is immediately apparent that they are composed chiefly of clips from pre-existent footage, often taken from films made in enemy nations. Pastiche is thus their basic cinematic technique. Capra wrote that his methodology was to "let the *enemy* prove to our soldiers the enormity of his cause—and the justness of ours."[25] These films were made primarily in Hollywood with the resources and staff of Hollywood studios. Capra also turned to academic experts for help, particularly for films concerned with Japan. On 5 October 1942, Capra wrote to Professor Nathaniel Peffer of the Columbia University Department of Public Law and Government to request assistance, since he had been told that Peffer knew "more about the Far East than any man alive."[26] Staff members of the Museum of Modern Art in New York City assisted the project by studying some 109 reels of confiscated Japanese film and selecting 42, which they then sent to the Office of War Information in February 1942.[27] Finally, each film produced by Capra's unit was subject to scrupulous oversight and censorship by various branches of the Armed Forces and the federal government.

At the start of the project in 1942, Eric Knight, a member of Capra's unit, submitted a report on the value of film for propaganda, in which he wrote: "Silent film was the only true international language. . . . The birth of the talkie ruined the growing technique of the film as the one readily comprehensible international medium, and made it nationalistic in scope again."[28] By providing film with a distinct nationalistic dimension, film sound (including film music) expanded the possibilities of cinematic propaganda. While these films were in part composed of moving images created by the enemy, the enemy's original soundtrack was most often silenced. Instead, the didactic messages were transmitted primarily through the voice-over of the narrator and, I argue, the added or substituted music. Music was called on to inspire confidence in the might of the United States, to distinguish each enemy and ally on the screen, and to instill in the American soldier a devotion to fighting the Axis powers.

The soundtrack to *Prelude to War*, the first film in the *Why We Fight* series, illustrates music's propagandistic role as well as the principle of musical pastiche. Seen and heard by an estimated 9 million soldiers by 1945, *Prelude to War* was released to public theaters in the United States at the direct request of President Roosevelt and won the Academy Award for best documentary. Alfred Newman served as the film's "musical director"—aptly so designated, since (as was the norm in Hollywood) the scores of these government films were often a team project.[29] Several major Hollywood composers and arrangers contributed to the score for *Prelude to War* by composing a few measures of music, reworking and developing music composed by a colleague, or helping to rework material from the most important musical source for this film series, identified on the cue sheets as "P.D."—that is, music "in the public domain."

Pre-existent music used in *Prelude to War* included everything from Americana such as "Yankee Doodle" to the "Siegfried" leitmotif from Wagner's *Ring*. In one typical section we hear, within a mere twelve measures, the "Jap Theme" composed by Newman, two measures derived from Wagner labeled "Nibelungen March," a snippet of the Italian march "Giovinezza!," and some music labeled "Chaos" composed by David Raksin (see Figure 5.1). Throughout the film, each enemy is identified by its own distinctive theme and images, which are often presented in quick succession.[30] Newman's "Jap Theme" contains most of the musical traits that emerge as the stereotypical sonic signals for the Japanese in World War II Hollywood.[31] In the most detailed study to date of the *Why We Fight* series, Thomas Bohn argues that music is overused in *Prelude to War* (forty-eight of its fifty minutes include music) and complains that because the music follows the abrupt cutting pace of the images, the result is "sometimes chaotic."[32] But a chaotic effect is precisely what was intended in several of these documentary films. By overwhelming the audience with a collage of images and sounds, the filmmakers sought to represent the fanaticism of the enemy and to impress on American soldiers the urgency of their mission.

Although musical styles representing Germany, Italy, and Japan are juxtaposed in rapid alternation throughout *Prelude to War*, thus suggesting that these national musics are equivalently dangerous, it is far more common in US government films for actual Japanese music to be decreed ugly and beyond comprehension. A brief example from the 1945 *Know Your Enemy—Japan* will suffice to illustrate here.[33] In a sequence concerned with Japan's attempts to root out elements of American culture, we witness two shots of musical performance apparently taken from Japanese newsreels. In the first shot (lasting three seconds) we see and hear a female Japanese singer accompanied by a male jazz orchestra consisting of violins, guitar, tuba, and drum set and led by a conductor. The woman, wearing a Western evening dress and a Western hairstyle, stands casually with her weight shifted to one side. She expressively raises her right arm and glances offscreen as she sings. We view her in a medium shot from a slightly lower angle as though positioned comfortably near the stage. Then the narrator announces in voice-over: "Western music was banned. Instead, the government approved this," and we see and hear an ensemble of geisha, each with a *shamisen*. The composition of this four-second shot is striking. The women are shown sitting in a diagonal line that, from our perspective, sharply recedes into the background and appears to continue infinitely off the left edge of the screen. We are placed extremely close to the player on the right edge of the screen and are looking down this line of nine performers. As is traditional in Japanese performance, these women wear identical kimonos and the same formal hairstyle. Each woman sits utterly immobile, save for her right hand holding the plectrum and left hand moving along the neck of the instrument. The narrator provides no further commentary. Clearly, the filmmakers assumed that their

-23-

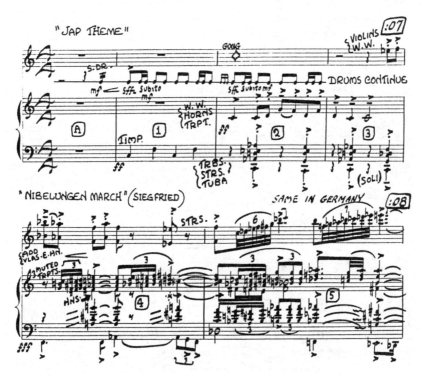

Figure 5.1 Propagandistic pastiche in *Prelude to War* (1943). Courtesy of the University of Southern California Cinema and Television Library.

Figure 5.1 Continued

audience would immediately recognize the fanaticism of a government that would ban the freedom, expressivity, and fun represented by American dance music and mandate performances of the apparently stoic and conformist music heard and seen in the second shot.

The narrator also influences audience perception of enemy music in films deploying pastiche against the Germans. The dangers of German music are specifically addressed in *Your Job in Germany*, a film shown to US soldiers following Germany's surrender in preparation for the occupation. This film warned GIs not to trust the peaceful facade that the Germans would present in their defeat. As we hear and see a German folk band and dancers in traditional costume, the narrator declares sarcastically, "Tender people, the Germans, and very sweet music indeed." And as the sounds and images of a German orchestra are presented, he states in mock awe that "when it comes to culture, they lead the whole world." But this beautiful German music is denounced in the film as being deceitful. It is accused of serving as an acoustic disguise, as a form of cultural camouflage cloaking the true German militant spirit. These US government films do presume that the significance of some forms of German music is transparent. Wagner's music is repeatedly used against the Germans—we hear leitmotifs from the *Ring* for footage of German attacks and appearances of Hitler on the screen—while the symphonies of Beethoven are consistently mined for positive representations of various sorts.[34] Beethoven's music thus evades its Germanic origin and becomes a universal good in these propaganda films.

German music and German musicians are revealed to be particularly duplicitous in the 1942 *Secret Agent of Japan*. The final script for this film was completed on 30 December 1941, making it one of the first anti-Japanese films to come out of Hollywood following Pearl Harbor.[35] At the opening, we see and hear a pianist performing in a hotel bar. This character is known as Alecsandri, a Romanian, and he repeatedly switches between a late Romantic style and syncopated jazz, transforming such works as Brahms's Hungarian Dance no. 5 in D minor. His musical performance and open smiles suggest innocence and bonhomie and he repeatedly invites the American leading man to his home for "good food, good drink, good music." But we eventually learn that Alecsandri is actually a German serving as a secret agent in league with the Japanese and using music and an Eastern European accent as a disguise, cloaking his true evil personality and dastardly intentions. (The actor portraying this secret agent was Steven Geray, a Hungarian born in what is now part of Ukraine. Thus the Eastern European accent we hear is actually authentic and true.)

Late in the film Alecsandri plays a waltz for the American hero at his home as a sample of the hospitality that he had promised. He is then suddenly revealed to be the German agent Mulhauser. As the American leaps to his feet Mulhauser strikes a cluster on the piano, which immediately brings in two Japanese thugs to defend him. Mulhauser then stages a fake torture scene in order to get the American to talk, pretending that the leading lady—a British agent and love interest of the

American—will be tortured in another room until he does so. Mulhauser begins to play an early modernist–style piano piece, seeming to cue the fake screams from his German wife in the other room with his repeated descending bass gestures, as though his musical performance is choreographing torture and is sending an audible signal or message that the "torturers" or, actually, his German wife understands and responds to with her expressionistic performed screams. The American hero apparently believes this musical communication is taking place and is not surprised but, rather, relieved when the screaming stops and does not resume at the moment Mulhauser stops playing the piano in response to his promise to reveal the location of an important coded document.

Having finally obtained the crucial paper, Mulhauser sits again at the piano to decipher the code. He looks at the sheet placed to his right to read the coded numbers that were typed in a six-by-twelve array of number strings, each set consisting of four to six numbers. Mulhauser plays clusters with his right hand as though each string of numbers somehow indicates notes and, oddly, as though hearing the resulting clusters assists him in the decoding process. (These numbers do not appear to represent scale degrees, interval content, or fingering and, thus, are apparently arbitrary.) After playing each cluster, he then glances to the left at a sheet of notated music, which appears also to have text, and he reads the coded message. (Actually, the sheet music on the left looks a good deal like a piece of manuscript paper from a Hollywood film score, complete with big bold lettering and numbers for cues in the upper right.) Mulhauser speaks the coded message: "Plan 21 has been completed." The Japanese villain then "translates" this ("That is operation for area of Hawai'i") and the German wife repeats the last word of each line Mulhauser speaks as she transcribes the message. Thus, in this film Germans working for the Japanese lie with Romantic and popular musical styles and communicate with a modernist musical style and vaguely serial numerological techniques to conceal their violent plans.[36]

Many of the Hollywood composers (such as Bronislaw Kaper, Miklós Rózsa, Max Steiner, Dimitri Tiomkin, and Franz Waxman) who created scores for anti-Japanese propaganda films were recent European immigrants to the United States. Thus, it is not surprising that in these films they drew on European classical music for both style and content. That they used European music for representations of the Japanese enemy is somewhat unexpected, however. This is most striking in the pastiche scores for *The Battle of China* and *Know Your Enemy—Japan*, in which Russian American Dimitri Tiomkin borrowed excerpts from Igor Stravinsky's *The Rite of Spring* and Modest Mussorgsky's *Pictures at an Exhibition* for sequences representing Japanese aggression. In *The Battle of China*, for example, we hear an unaltered excerpt from Stravinsky's own recording of *The Rite* as we watch newsreel footage of the Chinese attempting to flee the brutal bombardment of Shanghai.[37] Throughout the film, Mussorgsky's "gnome" motive from the "Gnomus" movement of *Pictures at an Exhibition* proves to be Tiomkin's favorite tune for the Japanese. For example, as the narrator states that the "enraged Japs saw their whole plan of conquest bogging down," we hear an arrangement of the "gnome" motive scored for marimba, xylophone, and piccolo. Tiomkin marked this passage "wery ligth and nasty" [sic] in his original short score. (This particular expressive marking was not carried through into the conductor's score.) For representations of the Chinese, Tiomkin incorporated different material from the Mussorgsky work. As we witness the epic westward flight of the Chinese from the Japanese invaders, an extremely powerful sequence in the film, Tiomkin employs the theme from the "Bydlo" or "Ox Cart" movement in *Pictures*. This theme is heard in several arrangements throughout the "migration sequence," including one for a chorus singing in Chinese.[38]

Considering that these films were scrutinized minutely for any elements that might offend America's allies, it may seem odd that Russian music was used to accompany scenes of the Japanese engaged in mass murder. But in the vast quantity of government reports and memos produced on these films, I have found no discussion focused on music. It should be noted that Tiomkin, an economical composer, also employed *The Rite* as background music for footage of China's scorched-earth defense in *The Battle of China*, and in *The Battle of Russia* to accompany a clip appropriated from the famous "Battle on the Ice" sequence in Eisenstein's *Alexander Nevsky*. Although Tiomkin's use of modern Russian music proves not to have been consistently aimed at the Japanese, his use of *The Rite* in *Know Your Enemy—Japan* is tied much more directly to this exotic enemy. For a thirty-second sequence illustrating the militaristic history of the Japanese, Tiomkin selected the first twenty measures from "The Naming and Honoring of the Chosen One" section in *The Rite*. As the narrator recounts the samurai civil wars fought in Japan for "the right to become the shogun," we are shown battle footage taken from a Japanese period film. Crosscuts between two advancing armies and closer shots of hand-to-hand fighting are followed by an animated pyramidal diagram representing Japanese society with bowing peasants placed on the bottom level, fighting samurai above, and finally one warlord ascending to the apex as shogun with the shadowy image of the emperor behind him obscured by clouds. The sequence begins visually with a close-up shot of a drum being beaten and aurally with part of Stravinsky's drum and string tattoo in the measure before rehearsal no. 104. Stravinsky's music is thus framed at the start within the diegesis of the film and is closely associated with the battling Japanese.

The Rite is further identified with the Japanese in a two-part sequence of *Know Your Enemy—Japan* focused on Japan's trade wars and militant industrialization in the 1930s. In the first part, we hear the entire "Naming and Honoring of the Chosen One" section, starting two measures prior at rehearsal no. 103, as we are told about Japan's "unfair" trade practices and piracy of American and European products. Tiomkin added a drumroll and cymbal crash to the soundtrack three measures after rehearsal no. 113 to match the visual climax of animated arrows on a map revealing the nefarious routes of Japanese exports. This section of *The Rite* perfectly matches the length of this first part of the sequence, starting with a fiery belch from a steel furnace and ending as we learn from the voice-over and images how the Japanese "even undersold us with our own American flag." The music then immediately jumps to "The Dancing Out of the Earth," the final section of part one of the ballet, which is also heard in its entirety. The first shot in this second half of the sequence is an extreme close-up of a mechanical stamp printing the phrase "Made in Japan." As the instrumental lines move to shorter note values building to the climactic ending of this part of *The Rite*, the narrator intones, "A fanatic nation turning its sweat into weapons for conquest: sweat for guns, sweat for planes, sweat for ships, sweat for war." This music and narration is heard as the screen alternates between shots of frantic workers engaged in various forms of manual labor and images of smoothly moving war machines. The sense of increasing frenzy is primarily achieved by the music, and the sequence ends with the sound of explosions that are perceived as the musical conclusion to this passage from *The Rite*. In this film, as occurred more generally in primitivist and futurist works of European modernism, Tiomkin called on a single musical style to represent the subhuman Japanese in both a barbaric past and a mechanized present. His association of *The Rite* with violence is in line with Hollywood's typical framing of modernist musical styles, equivalent to its use of jazz for sexy or seedy scenes.[39] Brandishing modern European music, however, was not the most common strategy adopted in Hollywood's musical representations of the Japanese.

Conventional Orientalist Warfare

Anti-Japanese Hollywood feature films drew on an astonishing array of musical, cinematic, and dramatic conventions. For example, in addition to presenting a negative portrayal of the enemy through stereotypical means, Hollywood developed multiple stock devices to project the image of a unified and ethnically balanced America. Within the narrative frame of these films, music was often presented as *the* cohesive force uniting Americans of different races and religions. In *Guadalcanal Diary* (1943), a priest leads a Christian church service aboard ship. We hear the crew singing "Rock of Ages" and overhear this exchange between two Marines: "Say Sammy, your voice is OK." "Why not, my father was a cantor in the synagogue."[40] In another 1943 film, *Bataan*, a group of Americans attempts to hold off the advancing Japanese deep in the jungle. Ramirez, the token Hispanic American in the group, manages to pick up an American radio station broadcasting swing music. The white Sergeant queries, "Don't tell me that's Jap jive." Ramirez answers, "No Sarge, no, that's good old America, that's USA." The myth of racial harmony among Americans was repeatedly manufactured through music in these films. The one black soldier in *Bataan*, a character who sings more often than he speaks, habitually hums "St. Louis Blues." The group's midwestern white chatterbox claims that it is his favorite song, too, thus establishing a bond of solidarity.

Music was employed in World War II propaganda films in numerous specific symbolic ways: for example, Hawaiian music in anti-Japanese films often conveyed the foolish unpreparedness of the United States before Pearl Harbor, and fragments of "Taps" inevitably informed the audience that a wounded American had died. What were some of the most common musical signs drawn on to signal the exotic enemy? The Japanese are frequently represented in these films by tunes based on a pentatonic scale, most often played by brass (or by woodwinds and strings in a lower register with brass punctuation), and often with an aggressive timbre and at a loud dynamic. These themes, which tend to be supported by perfect fourth or fifth intervals moving in parallel motion, are set in quadruple meter with plodding marchlike rhythms consisting predominantly of quarter and half notes, often marked marcato or with heavy accentuation. A gong regularly punctuates the first beat of each phrase. In dramatic situations calling for a more sudden musical statement, the enemy is signaled by either a stinger *sforzando* cluster chord of five to seven pitches or an abrupt rhythmic statement composed of an accented eighth-note chord, a second eighth-note chord normally one step lower in pitch, and then a sustained return to the first chord. The following examples will reveal the range of applications for some of these archetypal stylistic features.

Walter Scharf composed the music presented in Example 5.1 to accompany shots of the advancing Japanese during an attack in *The Fighting Seabees* (1944).[41] Confident that, given the film's context, his arranger would recognize the musical cliché—evoked here by heavy accentuation, a martial rhythm, and stacked fourth and fifth intervals—Scharf did not indicate the orchestration of this section in his pencil sketch. As expected, the material was scored for trumpets, trombones, and bass. For a cue marked "Jap sez 'Hey!'" in *Three Came Home* (1950), Hugo Friedhofer instructed his arranger to make the "'Jap' color not too heavy (only one small Jap!)."[42] A slightly different version of the same material, scored for brass instruments with heavier "Jap color," is heard in reel 3, part 1 and is labeled "The Enemy" in the full score. (See Example 5.2; note the similarity between Friedhofer's concluding iambic gestures and the final two emphatic measures in Scharf's theme.) Friedhofer composed a "Brutality" chord, consisting of the pitches F–C–Db–Gb–Bb–C, to accompany a scene of Japanese officers torturing and savagely kicking the British heroine in *Three Came Home*. Max Steiner provides the apotheosis of Hollywood's "evil Japanese" musical cliché—scored for low strings,

Example 5.1 Walter Scharf, *The Fighting Seabees* (Republic, 1944).

woodwinds, horns, and pianos—in his score for the 1951 film *Operation Pacific* (see Example 5.3).[43] This music is heard at the moment when the American submarine crew raises their periscope and realizes that they have arrived in the midst of the entire Japanese fleet. We are informed of the situation as much by the music as by the visual images.[44]

Behind the Rising Sun (1943) is unlike the usual Hollywood war film in that it is set in Japan and focuses on Japanese characters. In addition to employing the stereotypical sonic signs for Japan, Roy Webb called for the "weird" sound of a novachord (an electronic organ invented in 1939) in several spots in his score.[45] The vibrating reeds of the novachord created a thin, ethereal timbre that enhanced Webb's exotic musical setting. As we watch the sun rise over the ocean during the opening credits, we hear Webb's version of the "Japanese theme" in his Main Title music (see Example 5.4).[46] This theme is electrically charged by a sustained chord (A–B–D–E) in the novachord and strings. The film tells the "true-to-life" (i.e., entirely fictitious) tale of a Japanese father and son, both played by white American actors. When the

Example 5.2 Hugo Friedhofer, *Three Came Home* (20th Century–Fox, 1950).

Example 5.3 Max Steiner, *Operation Pacific* (Warner Bros., 1951).

Example 5.4 Roy Webb, *Behind the Rising Sun* (RKO, 1943).

son returns home in the late 1930s upon graduating from Cornell, he is dismayed to discover that Japan has become increasingly jingoistic during his absence and that his father has been swept up in the nationalistic fervor. The son is eventually drafted and the father is appointed "minister of propaganda." By the film's end, however, father and son have completely reversed their original political outlooks. The father, who has narrated the entire story retrospectively in an outlandish "Japanese" accent, comes to despair over what fanatic militarism has done to his country and his son. At the film's end, the young zealot is shot down by an American fighter over Tokyo, and the father finishes his narration by deciding to commit ritual suicide: "I die for the repudiation of the Emperor and everything he has stood for. I die for the hope that somewhere, somehow the people of Japan may one day redeem themselves before the eyes of the civilized world. But if that is to be, then the Japan that I knew must die with me and the sooner the better." (See Figure 5.2, a publicity photograph that closely matches the final two shots of the film.) Just as the Axis powers were forced into self-incrimination by Frank Capra in his films for the War Department, *Behind the Rising Sun* ends with the father praying: "Destroy us as we have destroyed others. Destroy us before it is too late." This propagandistic fantasy compels the Japanese enemy to condemn itself on the screen to the tune of the "evil Japanese" cliché and the synthetic wheeze of the novachord.

As with operatic leitmotifs, the musical signals in these films serve multiple narrative functions. They can inform the audience of the enemy's approach before the

Figure 5.2 A Hollywood wartime fantasy. RKO publicity still for *Behind the Rising Sun* (1943). Courtesy of the Museum of Modern Art/Film Stills Archive.

characters are aware; they serve to clarify the nationality of distant planes or ships visible on the screen; they often serve to reinforce negative images of the Japanese or to underscore statements about the Japanese made in printed text or spoken voice-over; and they can create a general atmosphere of danger or establish Japan as the setting. These markers are most often nondiegetic; that is, they are perceived as being part of the composed soundtrack rather than music emanating from within the world of the film. Thus, they acquire a narrational authority that shapes our perceptions of what we see, just as what we see helps determine our attitude toward what we hear. In the final extended section of the 1950 film *Sands of Iwo Jima*, we witness a fictionalized re-enactment of the American attack on Mt. Suribachi.[47] Victor Young engages the stereotypical "evil Japanese" musical signs in multiple ways in his score.[48] In Example 5.5, his theme recalls Scharf's idea in *The Fighting Seabees* (compare Example 5.1). At one point, a version of this theme is heard as a Japanese soldier suddenly appears from behind a rock with his sword raised against Sergeant Stryker, the John Wayne character. In this instance, music is not essential for identification; rather, it simply reinforces our visual perceptions. The brass gesture is heard again as we witness the death of a Japanese soldier shot by Stryker. Soon thereafter, we hear Young's Orientalist theme *before* a Japanese soldier appears onscreen and stabs an American in the back. Finally, after Stryker has been shot, a rapid-fire version of the theme reveals the identity and location of the invisible Japanese assailant as an American soldier aims his machine gun into a sniper pit.

What were the sources of these conventional musical devices for representing the Japanese? Had pentatonic brass tunes and gong strokes been clearly coded as inevitably "evil" sounds in Euro-American musical traditions before the advent of World War II? Or was the negative reception of these sounds dependent primarily on the current context in which they were heard? The roots of World War II anti-Japanese musical representations are less obvious than one might suppose. Puccini provided one model for Hollywood composers (see especially the final eleven tragic Orientalist measures of *Madama Butterfly*), but not all of the features of the cliché can be found in his music. Neither do silent film music anthologies nor Tin Pan Alley songs about Japan reveal a direct lineage. A more immediate source for comparison is Hollywood's representations of Native Americans in the 1930s. In multiple ways, the Japanese replaced Native Americans on the screen during World War II as Hollywood's favorite exotic enemy.[49] Similarities are immediately evident in the visual, aural, and narrative conventions used to represent these two "savage enemies." Japanese cries of "Banzai!" replaced the whoops and war chants of

Example 5.5 Victor Young, *Sands of Iwo Jima* (Republic, 1950).

cinematic Native Americans. Several of the composers active in anti-Japanese representation during and after World War II had composed music for "Indian" attacks in prewar films. In both Roy Webb's score for *The Last of the Mohicans* (1935) and Alfred Newman's for *Drums along the Mohawk* (1939), marcato pentatonic brass tunes signal the Native American enemy. Unlike the Japanese musical stereotype, however, these tunes move at a moderately fast tempo and are invariably supported by an eighth-note drum tattoo.[50] While some musical kinship is evident between Hollywood's "Japs" and "Injuns," the similarity is most striking in how these separate musical stereotypes were employed.

Film music, particularly in the service of propaganda, tends to be very cost-effective, imparting its meanings as clearly and quickly as possible. Immediate comprehension of symbolic allusion is a measure of the soundtrack's success. Dimitri Tiomkin addressed this point in 1951: "Much of the music that is accepted as typical of certain races, nationalities and locales, is wholly arbitrary. Audiences have been conditioned to associate certain musical styles with certain backgrounds and peoples, regardless of whether the music is authentic." With reference to Hollywood's sonic signals for Native Americans, Tiomkin asserted that such "arbitrary" musical signs were valuable not only because they served as "a telegraphic code that audiences recognize," but because "authentic" music of exotic peoples would have little impact on the audience.[51] The decision to "avoid the authentic exotic" in Hollywood music has been upheld by composers and critics alike. Roy M. Prendergast echoes Tiomkin in his survey of film music:

> A related technique is the use of musical devices that are popularly associated with foreign lands and people; for example, using the pentatonic idiom to achieve an Oriental color. The "Chinese" music written for a studio film of the 1930s and '40s is not, of course, authentic Chinese music but rather represents our popular Occidental notions of what Chinese music is like. The Western listener simply does not understand the symbols of authentic Oriental music as he does those of Western music; therefore, Oriental music would have little dramatic effect for him.[52]

Such discussions rarely raise the question of how closely a stereotypical style need resemble the actual musical tradition referred to in order to function within the associative process. While propaganda may require either the exaggeration of genuine attributes of the enemy or, alternatively, a "toning down" of exotic difference in order to appease the intended audience, rare examples (presented below) in which Japanese music *was* heard in US propaganda films will prove the communicative potential even of unfamiliar musics.

The analysis of conventional Orientalist representation in World War II Hollywood films raises another important comparative topic. A major concern of US propaganda makers was for the American people to understand that the Chinese were allies and should be carefully differentiated from the Japanese. Elements of the conventional negative musical signal for the Japanese enemy had appeared, for example, to depict the Chinese villain in the 1940 film *The Drums of Fu Manchu* (with a score by Cy Feuer and, uncredited, Paul Sawtell). However, two weeks after Pearl Harbor, *Time* magazine printed a brief guide to distinguishing Chinese from Japanese men entitled "How to Tell Your Friends from the Japs," focusing on visual clues.[53] While offering a list of contrasting characteristics, the author warned that "there is no infallible way of telling them apart, because the same racial strains are mixed in both." In Hollywood this became an important problem, since many anti-Japanese World War II films were set in China. But the industry had always assumed that "American" audiences would be unable to distinguish one Asian nationality from another on the screen and throughout the war enlisted Chinese American, Hawaiian, and Korean American actors, as well as Euro-American actors transformed by "racist cosmetics," to portray the Japanese.[54]

Confusion in identifying Asian ethnicity was taken to an extreme as a plot point in favor of the Chinese in the 1942 *China Girl*, one of the first films to be released in response to Pearl Harbor. In this film the white American leading man does not initially realize that the woman he has fallen for in Mandalay is Chinese or, at least, Eurasian, played (of course) by a white actress. They engage in an onscreen "interracial kiss" and he declares that he wants to take her back home to Akron, Ohio, prefiguring the plot of the 1957 film *Sayonara*. However, this exotic woman decides to return to China to help her people and he recklessly follows her there, flying into the heart of the war. The Japanese—whom we witnessed executing Chinese peasants early on in the film—bomb the orphanage that she and her father run and she dies in the American hero's arms, thus avoiding bringing any troublesome miscegenation back home to the United States. In numerous wartime films, the Chinese were consistently depicted as feminine and infantile victims of the barbaric Japanese in need of the strong protection and rescue of white American Air Force men.

Hollywood film directors and composers repeatedly faced with the task of distinguishing between the Chinese and Japanese through image and music drew on separate sets of conventional Orientalist signs for the exotic ally and enemy.[55] The 1942 film *Flying Tigers* is set in China and depicts the efforts of American volunteers to defend the Chinese people against Japanese air raids. During the opening section of the film, we see a poster of Chiang Kai-shek as the text of his speech thanking American volunteers rolls across the screen. This image and text are interrupted by an announcement made on a loudspeaker of a new Japanese attack. Victor Young's score uses the standard brassy signal for Japan as a stinger in the Main Title music and at the moment when the Japanese attack is announced. In contrast, as we read the text of Chiang Kai-shek's speech we hear a melody derived from the Chinese folk tune "Mo Li Hua," the same tune that Puccini had employed in *Turandot*.[56] Throughout the film, Young maintains his two Orientalist musical idioms. Example 5.6 offers a sample of his "lighter" Orientalist style from a scene involving a group of Chinese children. The pentatonic melodic material is played by high woodwinds and strings with a gentle staccato articulation. The rhythms are lilting rather than

Example 5.6 Victor Young, *Flying Tigers* (Republic, 1942).

martial, and the music is punctuated not by a crashing gong but by a delicate alternation between a small cymbal and a wood block. (However, both the exotic enemy and the exotic ally are marked by fourth and fifth intervals and parallel motion in Young's score.) For the innocent, yet nonetheless exotic, Chinese, Young has turned here to the style of Mahler's "Von der Jugend" and "Von der Schönheit" movements in *Das Lied von der Erde*.

Just as Hollywood directors frequently opted to hire white actors for prominent Asian roles, actual Japanese and Chinese music was avoided in Hollywood films in favor of the conventional tunes. In *Dragon Seed* (1944), Katharine Hepburn portrays Jade—a young Chinese woman who overcomes traditional Chinese gender norms to lead her people in fighting the Japanese (see Figure 5.3). Herbert Stothart's score, like Young's for *Fighting Tigers*, establishes the Chinese setting with delicate pentatonic Orientalism and represents the Japanese enemy with occasional brass stingers.[57] Scenes of intense emotion or intimacy, such as those between Jade

Figure 5.3 The noble Chinese in yellowface. MGM publicity still for *Dragon Seed* (1944). Courtesy of the Museum of Modern Art/Film Stills Archive.

and her husband, are underscored in the film with Hollywood's trademark lush strings. Although Chinese culture was consistently celebrated in both Hollywood feature films and US government documentaries, Chinese music fared little better than did Japanese. In *Thirty Seconds over Tokyo* (1945), we see and hear a record player playing "Chinese" music in the American ward of a Chinese Red Cross station. One of the wounded Americans declares, "I think the Chinese are a swell bunch of people, but I can't say I go for their music." The cue sheet credits Herbert Stothart with the composition of this "Chinese" music.[58] During a romantic scene between an Irish American named Nick (played by James Cagney) and a Eurasian women named Iris in *Blood on the Sun* (1945), a Chinese female servant enters with a *yueqin*, a Chinese lute, and offers to perform for them. Iris sharply tells the servant to go away, pointedly rejecting the possibility of Chinese music. Miklós Rózsa's romantic love theme scored for European strings and winds enters instead as the two lovers continue their assignation. This rejection of even sham Asian performing art forms was common in Hollywood's World War II films. A young Javanese nurse offers to perform a "beautiful Java dance" for wounded Americans in *The Story of Dr. Wassell* (1944). As she softly hums and moves in a slow, stylized fashion—only vaguely suggestive of genuine classical Javanese dance—the GIs yell, "When do you start?" She replies, "Oh, you mean like they do in the movies?" She then begins to shimmy and dance Hollywood's version of the Hawaiian hula to the delight of the men. Similarly, in *First Yank into Tokyo* (1945) a group of Japanese officers is entertained by a "Japanese" woman whose performance, accompanied by flute and drum, resembles nothing so much as a parody of Middle Eastern belly dancing.

Today we may perceive martial brass tunes, parallel fourths, gong crashes, and dissonant chords as obvious, offensive, and rather trivial musical clichés—that is, as signs of the "evil Japanese" that have lost their emotive impact and semiotic power through overuse. But in the 1940s and early 1950s, the propagandistic value of these musical markers was as potent as any other element of the films.[59] The question remains whether other stylistic features deviating from the standard cinematic musical milieu might have served equally well for Hollywood's representation of the Japanese. Might it not have been possible to avoid associative mechanisms entirely by projecting painful sounds for appearances of the enemy, or did the omnipresent sound of explosions and machine gun fire (albeit synthetic) in these soundtracks neutralize this possibility? Perhaps the use of more immediately repulsive sounds would have turned the audience against the screen and sound system, rather than against the Japanese. In addition, it is difficult to judge the degree of sonic violence that the "evil Japanese" musical signals may have induced in the ears of the original audience members.

We should certainly consider the possibility that, within the context of World War II propaganda, the original audiences heard these themes as authentically Japanese. A general presumption of authenticity on the part of the audience is crucial to the success of propagandistic representation. We will find that, in many cases, World War II American filmmakers went to great lengths to establish an aura of authenticity, however false their representations may actually have been. Their films proclaimed this "authenticity" in various ways: by interpolating documentary footage, by including actual participants in the events reenacted, by citing assistance from branches of the armed forces, and by stating at the film's start that a true story would be presented. In addition, we should ask whether the Orientalist musical signals were indeed "wholly arbitrary," as my earlier quotation of Tiomkin on this subject would imply.

Military band music was the first Euro-American musical style adopted in Japan following the country's "opening" by Commodore Perry in 1853–1854. In the Meiji period of modernization and Westernization, Western military music was embraced as part of a more general reform program. In 1869, a British bandsman was hired by the Japanese government to train a military brass and drum band to perform marches. This bandmaster composed the first unofficial Japanese anthem ("Kimigayo") in 1870, setting a classical poem about the emperor that would remain the text for future Japanese national anthems. In 1880, new music was composed for the anthem by a *gagaku* court musician, and this tune was then harmonized by a German bandsman.[60] Japanese military music retained pentatonicism as its one Japanese musical feature into the twentieth century.[61] Throughout the 1930s and the Pacific war, the Japanese government encouraged the composition and performance of *gunka:* patriotic lyrics set in a Western march style, in quadruple meter with heavy accentuation, and often accompanied by prominent brass and drums. *Gunka* are thus somewhat similar in style to the Hollywood "evil Jap" musical cliché, although they tend to emphasize dotted rhythms.[62] Consequently, Hollywood composers were to some extent using a Japanese musical style against the Japanese. Japan's propaganda films of the 1930s frequently included *gunka* in their soundtracks. A particularly relevant example is the 1939 film *Tsuchi to Heitai* (*Mud and Soldiers*).[63] As was common in Japan's war films, military life is presented in all of its drudgery, and the enemy (in this case the Chinese) is rarely represented on the screen at all. Music is scarcely present on the soundtrack. Instead, we hear the incessant sound of marching feet as the Japanese soldiers advance through one muddy field after another. A Western-style diatonic march serves as the Main Title music. We also hear diegetic singing of *gunka* by men in their barracks early on and again near the end of the film as the soldiers relax and the camera pans their earnest faces and then over the buildings they have destroyed. The use of *gunka* was banned in postwar Japanese films by the US occupation authorities.

It is worth noting here that *Japanese* filmmakers also engaged in forms of conventional Orientalist representation in World War II propaganda films. One example must suffice to support this claim. Yoshiko Yamaguchi was a major Japanese actress raised in Manchuria who played Chinese characters in Japanese wartime propaganda films intended for Chinese audiences in the occupied areas. Before embarking on her astonishing film career, Yamaguchi had studied voice with an Italian teacher in Manchuria. Following the war, she traveled to Japan and then to the United States where, as Shirley Yamaguchi, she starred in the Hollywood films

Japanese War Bride (1952) and *House of Bamboo* (1955).[64] In the 1940 Japanese film *China Nights*, Yamaguchi portrayed a Chinese woman who—even though Japanese bombs had killed her parents—falls in love with a kind and noble Japanese naval officer. Chinese opera arias and *sizhu* (chamber music for strings and winds) are heard during street scenes and thus provide Chinese local color. The Japanese hero pointedly states his admiration for the *sizhu* performance that the lovers hear while strolling, thus reinforcing their amorous cross-cultural bridge. Although genuine Chinese music is heard, the film's composer (Ryoichi Hattori) relied primarily on Hollywood styles of light pentatonicism and lush European strings to underscore scenes of intense happiness. Toward the end of the film, the Chinese heroine, backed by a Western orchestra, sings to her Japanese lover a song celebrating exquisite China entitled "China Nights" (which became hugely popular). It was taught to her, she tells him, by Toshiko—the Japanese woman who has secretly loved the officer throughout the film and has nobly suffered as the cross-cultural romance developed. Japan consistently presents a complex case for the study of twentieth-century musical exoticism.[65]

Diegesis and the Manipulation of "Authenticity"

The Japanese enemy was most often represented musically by nondiegetic Orientalist themes in both Hollywood feature films and US government documentaries. In a few significant cases, however, Japanese music was itself conscripted as a tool of anti-Japanese propaganda. In some of these films, we hear Japanese music with either the original source, a counterfeit source, or no musical source visible on the screen. In other films, we see actual Japanese performers but hear nondiegetic music that has been composed to sound "Japanese." Occasionally, we hear diegetic Japanese music and newly composed Orientalist background music simultaneously. When a musical source is visible, whether or not it is the genuine source, the viewer is likely to credit the music heard with a greater degree of authenticity. Furthermore, if the mise en scène projected on the screen is a plausible setting, then the music may be accepted as genuinely Japanese even when it is not strictly diegetic. Finally, although tight synchronization between onscreen movements and accompanying musical rhythms ("mickey-mousing") often seems artificial, it may also suggest that the music not only is part of the world of the images but is actually animating the movements seen. These observations help to open up an ambiguous space in any rigid division of film sound into source or background, diegetic or nondiegetic.[66] Michel Chion's comments on this subject are particularly apt here: "Let us note that in the cinema, causal listening is constantly manipulated by the audiovisual contract itself, especially through the phenomenon of synchresis [i.e., the immediate connection one tends to make between something heard and something seen simultaneously]. Most of the time we are dealing not with the real initial causes of the sounds, but causes that the film makes us believe in."[67] Chion also notes that "sound that rings true for the spectator and sound that *is* true are two very different things. . . . If we are watching a war film or a storm at sea, what idea did most of us actually have of sounds of war or the high seas before hearing the sounds in the films?"[68] For most American audience members during World War II and after, the same question may equally well be asked of Japanese music.

Wartime filmmakers exploited and exaggerated those aspects of Japanese culture that they felt Americans would find most shockingly foreign. Music and religious ceremony were considered especially prime targets. Traditional Japanese music *is* strikingly different from the musical styles familiar to most Americans. But actual musical life in 1930s Japan was not that different from the contemporaneous American musical scene. American vernacular musics, European classical music, and new styles derived from these traditions were widespread in Japan. In a sense, the use of traditional Japanese music, religious ceremony, and folk performance in certain US propaganda films succeeded in presenting a "Japan" that was more "Japanese" and wholly "foreign" than the actual modern nation. Negative representation of Japanese music was achieved through visual cinematic techniques, voice-over commentary on the performance, and manipulation of the audio recording technology. While Orientalist musical propaganda was certainly not peculiar to World War II, several techniques of cinematic propaganda were. In the following examples we will focus on how Japanese music was appropriated for anti-Japanese representation in films and on how this music was contextualized.

In the film *Know Your Enemy—Japan*, produced by Capra's unit in 1945, Japanese traditional music serves as a sign of the barbaric and inscrutable nature of the enemy. The film begins with a group of Japanese men pulling ropes attached to the striker of a huge bell. As a visual reverberation accompanying this sound, the Japanese written characters spelling "Nippon" zoom toward us from the bell's surface. No longer the enticing and mystical sound celebrated by the likes of Lafcadio Hearn, this Japanese bell is exotically ominous. We then witness the most negative possible contextualization for the traditional Japanese music heard on the soundtrack. As we hear "Banzai" shouts and the music of a male vocalist accompanied by a *shamisen*, we see a newspaper illustration of a sword-wielding Japanese soldier about to behead a captured American. This image dissolves to a close-up of a gleaming sword held at the appropriate angle to suggest the decapitation. As the music continues, we then witness a staged, ceremonial demonstration of sword technique by a Japanese officer. In the next extended sequence, defined in part by a change in the musical style, the film alternates between images of traditional and modern Japanese society. Brief shots of folk dance performance, religious processions, and rustic waterwheels alternate with shots of fast-moving trains, modern urban buildings, and typewriters. Virtually every shot in this sequence contains onscreen movement, and the direction of these movements changes abruptly from shot to shot. Visual disorientation is enhanced by quick-cutting rhythms and shifting camera angles. The nondiegetic music continues throughout this montage—supporting both traditional and modern images and thus exposing the fact that beneath Japan's facade of modernity lies a primitive fanaticism.

Several of the shots of traditional performance in this sequence are inserted with their original music, or with simulated sound, thus producing sonic confusion through musical layering with the continuous nondiegetic music. For example, in shot 12 of the film we see Buddhist nuns, clad in white from head to toe, march from the left-screen background to the right-screen foreground while chanting and playing *uchiwa-daiko* (fan drums). During this momentary shot, we hear not the original source sounds but a female voice singing to the accompaniment of a drum and a *shamisen*. Shot 14 offers a corresponding image from modern Japanese society. The camera dollies quickly from the left-screen background toward the right-screen foreground, along a diagonal line of female telephone operators—clad in identical white blouses and dark skirts—working a huge switchboard. At another point in this sequence, we see what appears to be a performance of the Iwate deer dance and hear the actual drums and chant of the performers. Toward the end of the sequence, a group of bare-chested men are shown heaving a *matsuri omikoshi* (large portable shrine) up and down in rhythm. The audience has been denied any interpretation from the narrator throughout the first three and a half minutes of the film. In fact, this entire opening sequence was intended to bewilder the audience and arouse an intense desire for explanation, a desire that the continuation of the film would presumably satisfy. The accumulated tension is finally released when the narrator's voice enters: "We shall never completely understand the Japanese mind." As a large group of chanting men lean from side to side with stylized leg lifts in shot 49, the narrator states, "We are dealing with a fantastic people." The entire opening section of the film concludes with a return to the initial shot of the temple bell being struck. This time, the reverberation of this Japanese religious sound causes the screen image to rip from the center, revealing in close-up a group of Japanese soldiers marching menacingly toward us. Throughout this sequence, traditional Japanese music is shown to make the job of "knowing your enemy" all the more unpleasant for an American audience.

US anti-Japanese films of the World War II and postwar periods present a remarkable case of rampant intertextuality. Throughout this collection of films, one repeatedly encounters clips and musical passages borrowed from or influenced by other films, in addition to the customary recycling by Hollywood composers of their own material for multiple soundtracks. Hollywood feature films and War Department documentaries drew on some of the same sources of footage and music, and also on each other. In a few cases we can compare multiple musical settings of the same pre-existent footage. For example, the shot of the marching Buddhist nuns in *Know Your Enemy—Japan* also appeared in *Our Job in Japan* (1946), in the television episode "Suicide for Glory" from the *Victory at Sea* series (1952), and in the 1961 US-France coproduced documentary film *Kamikaze*. The complex web of borrowing among these films prompts the question, which films served as the initial sources of enemy footage? In the case of propaganda films produced by Capra's unit, "March of Time" newsreels provided not only a model for documentary filmmaking and compilation techniques, but also a store of reusable material.[69] The image in *Know Your Enemy—Japan* of Japanese men pulling the striker of a huge bell appeared earlier in both the 1935 newsreel "Okitsu, Japan!" and in "Japan—China!"—a 1936 newsreel critical of Japan's militarism (with the requisite brassy statements) but approbatory (with lighter Orientalist tunes) concerning the "modernization" that the Japanese were bringing to China. The images in *Know Your Enemy—Japan* of Japanese telephone operators and Japan's cottage industries busy underselling American goods were taken from the "March of Time" newsreel "Tokyo—1939: Japan, Master of the Orient." Prophetic in multiple ways of US films to come, this 1939 newsreel concluded by denouncing the Japanese as "ruthless aggressors" and "lawless men of destiny."[70] In addition to other domestic and European newsreels on Japan, enemy films were also tapped as source material.[71] Confiscated Japanese period films yielded images of ferocious samurai, and films such as *Tsuchi to Heitai (Mud and Soldiers)* provided scenes of modern Japanese warriors in battle. Documentary travelogues and ethnographic films offered footage of traditional Japanese performances and religious ceremony. The same sources of Japanese ritual and martial arts footage drawn on in *Know Your Enemy—Japan* proved particularly popular for US propagandists and were mined for several other anti-Japanese films.

A masterful sequence in the 1946 War Department documentary *Our Job in Japan* presents the most striking example of the use of Japanese music and film against the Japanese. In this section, the film's didactic purpose is to reveal connections between Japan's religious beliefs and its militarism.[72] Two parallel shots—appropriated from source footage—serve as signifying bookends for this segment. Near the start, the camera zooms in on a Shinto priest who advances from the distance. This shot is suddenly "stamped" with the emblem of the "rising sun," with the text "Official State Religion" bursting onscreen at the sound of a gong. At the end of the section, one and a half minutes later, the camera similarly zooms in on a medieval Japanese warlord dressed in full armor. Following the initial shot of the Shinto priest, the narrator explains how Shinto was appropriated and perverted by the Japanese militarists in the 1930s in order to inspire jingoistic nationalism in the Japanese people. The sequence that follows is presented as evidence of the Japanese people's hysterical devotion to their cause. As the narrator declares in somber tones, "up from Japan's murky past, bring back the 'mumbo jumbo,'" Okinawan folk music, consisting of a female vocalist accompanied by a *jamisen* and a drum and echoed by a female chorus, fades in.[73] This "mumbo jumbo" music continues throughout the sequence and thus flows beneath the fragmentary clips of ritual and martial arts performance on the screen. The sequence, as defined by the duration of the folk music and (less strictly) by the extended silence of the narrator, contains thirty-nine shots carefully crafted in order to create a chaotic effect. We first see torchlit outdoor shots of a group of bare-chested men being blessed by a Shinto priest. Following this ceremonial introduction, the sequence juxtaposes a series of images, including various costumed drummers, men engaged in *kendo* stick fighting, a dragon dancer, several different flutists, dancers with drums, a sword ceremony, and religious processions. Japanese traditional music and ritual are thus framed as the primal energy sources fueling the militaristic mania.

Our aural perception of this music is profoundly shaped by the film images we see. Repeated pictures of drummers cause us to focus our attention on the music's rhythmic ostinato. In addition, the sequence exhibits careful synchronization between the sound and the film images. Several shots contain onscreen movements that are in synch with the rhythm and tempo of the music. In the fifth shot, we see (but do not hear) an *o-daiko* drummer who seems to offer a drumroll introduction for the female vocalist. In shot 11, a man gestures and thus appears to cue in the female chorus heard (but not seen) an instant later. In shot 26, we see men who appear to sway from side to side with the beat of the music. An extraordinary effort was made in this brief but powerful sequence to suggest that the projected chaos was an "authentic" presentation of Japanese culture. Even though the soundtrack music remains constant throughout this montage of conscripted clips, sounds of instruments corresponding to those seen on the screen are occasionally added in order to suggest that the music is diegetic and thus authentic. A couple of these "added sounds" seem to be the original source sounds accompanying the appropriated clips, while others clearly were simulated by the filmmakers to correspond to the momentary performances on the screen. Several of the added sounds occur at "appropriate" musical points—often, at the end of phrases sung by the female soloist. For example, in shot 10 the metallic clangs of the hammers we see striking an anvil are heard during a long note held by the soloist, and in shot 15 we hear and see a shell trumpet blown at the conclusion of a vocal phrase. On closer inspection, it is obvious that the instrumentalists we see are most often not producing the music we hear. In shot 20, the uncertain strokes of a boy learning to play the *taiko* are clearly not producing the audible drum rhythm. In shot 27, we hear the added sound of a flute as we see a flutist . . . taking a breath. On an initial viewing, however, none of this aural/visual craft(iness) would likely be evident. Each shot lasts only about two seconds, and the cutting between them is very abrupt. In contrast, shots before and after this sequence are much longer in duration, are relatively static, and are accompanied by music in a slower tempo. (This sequence must have proved far more shocking to an audience unaccustomed to the fast-moving images and abrupt cutting rhythms of rock music videos and TV commercials.) By offering a disorienting collage of images and sounds, then, the sequence presents these various performance traditions negatively. In a draft version of the script, the writers here called for a "murky MONTAGE of ancient pagan rites, growing in violence."[74] Authorial intent is simply not in question in these propaganda films.

Portions of the same Japanese performance footage were also utilized, with Orientalist music by Richard Rodgers and Robert Russell Bennett, in the hugely successful 1952 television documentary series *Victory at Sea*.[75] *Victory at Sea* was produced as a twenty-six-part series by NBC in association with the US Navy and was frequently broadcast throughout the 1950s. Episode 25, "Suicide for Glory," begins with images and music representing "the Japan that most of the world wants to know," the imaginary Japan that had inspired late nineteenth- and early twentieth-century American *japonisme*. Geishas, blossoming cherry trees, temple gardens, and tranquil pools grace the screen in long shots or slow pans, with either static content or slowly moving images. These pictures are accompanied by a soft pentatonic tune in solo flute and xylophone, which floats above a gentle oscillation between two tones played by french horns, low woodwinds, and vibraphone. The narrator interrupts this placid scene by reminding us of Japan's militarism and asserting that "spiritually" the Japanese "belong to the East." We then see some of the same shots of Japanese performances and religious ceremonies as appeared in the earlier War Department films. But the bouncy and somewhat bombastic musical setting sounds more like eighteenth- and nineteenth-century European Orientalist representations of Turkish *mehter* music than like anything Japanese.

Japanese performance footage appeared once again as late as 1961 in two brief sequences on Japanese religion in the documentary film *Kamikaze*, with a score composed by Norman Dello Joio.[76] The first employs several shots from *Know Your Enemy—Japan,* including the striking of the large bell (which punctuates this sequence six times) and the shot of men carrying a *matsuri* float. In the second, many of the same shots used in the "Shinto" sequence of *Our Job in Japan* reappear, but in a different order. This one-minute segment of twenty-two shots, as delineated musically, starts with the narrator's observation, "Japan has not one religion, but many." As in *Our Job in Japan*, the sequence is preceded and followed by a slower camera movement and musical tempo, and it leads to representations of Japan's militarism. Unlike in *Our Job in Japan*, no attempt is made to match the soundtrack to the sounds of the performances shown on the screen. Dello Joio's music starts with a nervous sixteenth-note figure in the strings, punctuated by wood block taps, and then emphasizes a staccato rhythmic motive (eighth–eighth–quarter) played quickly. This loud, brash music is quite similar in style not only to the music heard in the film's first display of Japanese ritual performance, but also to that heard in an earlier sequence in this film showing Japanese children playing in an elaborate mock battle complete with child-size tanks. By reusing this musical style for the segments presenting Japanese ritual performance, Dello Joio contributes to the film's mocking representation of Japanese culture. Rather than attempting to manufacture "the shock of diegetic authenticity" in these two sequences, then, the creators of *Kamikaze* chose to ridicule Japan's "little religions." Dello Joio's nondiegetic music provided the necessary distancing, the alienation.

Unlike the US government documentary films, which were intended to instruct American GIs on various aspects of Japanese culture, Hollywood feature films were rarely set in Japan. I have encountered only one World War II Hollywood feature film employing traditional Japanese music. In *Behind the Rising Sun* (1943), music performed on *koto* and *shakuhachi* is heard during a scene set in a geisha house.[77] The sequence preceding this scene plays an important role in shaping audience perceptions of this Japanese music. Clancy (an Irish American engineer) is attempting to brush off the matrimonial aspirations of Sarah (an American reporter) as they sit at a table in an upscale Tokyo bar. At the entrance of Taro (a young Japanese man), Clancy sees a chance to escape and tells Sarah as he leaves, "I'm sorry darling, where we're going is no place for ladies, not nice ladies anyway." At this moment a small jazz combo (consisting of violin, piano, and drum set) is heard on the soundtrack, as though to cover Clancy's escape or to underscore the fact that Sarah has been left without a dance partner while the men depart for a mysterious Japanese realm inaccessible to Euro-American women. The camera pans the barroom allowing us to see a Japanese man sitting at a piano and a dancing couple—evidence that the jazz we hear is diegetic. While the Japanese and Euro-American patrons enjoy themselves, the camera zooms in, first on Sarah's dejected face as she smokes a cigarette and then on the ashtray as she extinguishes it.

The transition from this scene to the geisha house sequence is remarkable. As the image of the ashtray dissolves, a close-up shot of a small Japanese brazier with smoking coals fades in. This transition is also achieved musically. There is a momentary musical superimposition as the jazz trio in the bar comes to the conclusion of their piece and the Japanese duet in the geisha house begins. The close-up of the smoldering coals dissolves in a slow disclosure to reveal a medium shot of a geisha making tea and a second geisha dancing next to her. The camera then pulls back and pans to the left in order to focus fully on the dancer, who waves two fans in her (not very convincing) "Japanese" dance. Although we never see the *shakuhachi* and *koto* in this sequence, the dancing and the mise en scène lead us to accept the music as diegetic. The camera then pans farther to the left to reveal that the Euro-American expatriate men and the young Japanese man, immersed in a poker game, are ignoring both the music and the dancing geisha. An American in the group hears a cat howl outside and complains that the sound annoys him. He is told by Clancy to "forget it, it's just the music." The men eventually discuss the life of geishas and the general social position of Japanese women as the music continues. The Euro-Americans address their comments to Taro in an effort to teach him the truth about Japanese women. Although Max (a German secret agent) insists that a geisha is lucky since she merely "sings a little, plays a little, and . . . is very well paid for it by the few patrons she has to work for," the men agree that the position of the average Japanese woman is very dire. Boris (a Russian secret agent) declares that their sympathy should be saved for the "wives and mothers who are the real drudges in this slave society." (Ironically, in post-occupation Hollywood films, the dutiful Japanese wife is repeatedly celebrated as the ideal woman.) In this scene, the Japanese music is regarded by the characters as either trivial and somewhat irritating noise or as a sad reminder of the lamentable condition of Japanese women.

Another significant scene set in a geisha house occurs in *The Purple Heart* (1944). This sequence offers a striking example of "counterfeit Japanese music" that, within the context of the film, will be heard as both sinister and authentic. *The Purple Heart* has been called "the most terrifying and incendiary product Hollywood ever would produce dealing with the Japanese."[78] It is based on the famous incident in which some of the Doolittle fliers—American airmen who early in the war led a daring bombing raid on Tokyo—were captured by the Japanese and then tried in a kangaroo court in Japan. The soundtrack contains a striking amount of silence, and Alfred Newman's score offers music in but a few pivotal spots. Thus, Newman's "Pentatonic Intermezzo"—music heard during a scene when the Japanese officers prosecuting the trial dine at a geisha house—is particularly conspicuous.[79] We have been taught to hate these Japanese officers after seeing the results of their techniques of torture. The music is closely tied to both the movement within shots and the movement between shots, creating a sense of cool precision and a false diegesis. The sequence begins as a geisha enters bearing a written message. Her entrance shot lasts five seconds. In the second shot we see a second geisha kneeling as the first enters the frame with the message and kneels next to her. This shot also lasts five seconds. A long shot then reveals the entire room, with three Japanese officers drinking at a table while being served by a third geisha, who kneels at the end of the shot. The camera then cuts back to the pair of geisha, and we see the second one rise with the message. The next shot closely resembles shot 2 in this sequence: the second geisha now enters the frame, kneels next to the third, and transfers the message. Finally, geisha three rises and in the next shot delivers the message to the Japanese officer at the head of the table as she kneels. He flirts briefly with her, and the remainder of the sequence is devoted to the officers' reactions to the message.

The movements of the three geisha seem carefully choreographed in a fluid, cascade-like rhythm. They are made to look identical both by their parallel movements within each shot and by the similar camera angle and length of their shots. Newman's music exhibits a similar sense of mechanical precision. The pentatonic musical lines are punctuated precisely by the gong, cymbal, triangle, and drum (see Example 5.7). The relationship between the music and the images is also precise as the cuts between shots occur on the musical downbeats. Newman's music moves in parallel fourths and establishes a succession of dyads at measures 1, 4, and 14—one dyad and set of instruments corresponding to each geisha. During the final extended shot the music incorporates two altered statements of the opening phrase of "Kimigayo," the Japanese national anthem. The clockwork music contributes to our uncanny sense that these women are less than fully human. In a different context, in a different film, this same music could be perceived as a form of light Orientalism, pleasant musical *japonisme*. (It might have served Victor Young equally well for the representation of the innocent Chinese in *Flying Tigers*.) In anti-Japanese propaganda films, however, Japanese music (either authentic or contrived) is consistently presented as a barrier to cultural understanding and is heard in a decidedly negative context.[80]

In a 9 March 1944 review of *The Purple Heart* focused on the question of the film's authenticity, Bosley Crowther suggested that even though the story presented might not be exactly accurate, "so honest and thoroughly consistent with American character is the tale of individual heroism . . . so clearly in keeping with the nature

Example 5.7   Alfred Newman, *The Purple Heart* (20th Century–Fox, 1944).

of the enemy is its grim detail, that we are safe in accepting this picture—along with the atrocity reports—as general truth."[81] This assertion prompts the question, from where did Crowther's readers learn about "American character" and "the nature of the enemy" in the first place? For wartime audience members the answer was most likely, from Hollywood films. Crowther appears to have accepted Newman's "Pentatonic Intermezzo" as actual Japanese music. In a second review of the film on 19 March 1944, Crowther stated that in *The Purple Heart*, music

> is used but in three places: The Air Force Song is faintly played when the eight American fliers are first marched into the solemn courtroom; the popular song "Memories" moods the passage wherein the men retrospect in their cells . . . and again, in a surge of muted triumph, the Air Force Song carries the men off as they march with dignity and honor out of the courtroom to their deaths. For the rest the track carries only voices and realistic sounds.[82]

Hollywood's manufactured musical "authenticity" has always been at least sub-liminally accepted by most audience members as "realistic sounds." Such acceptance is apparent even in current historical and critical writing on Hollywood's representations of the Japanese in World War II.

In his study of Japanese society during the occupation period, John W. Dower considers the role film played in shaping the views of the American occupiers:

> In wartime propaganda films, it was standard practice to convey the utterly alien nature of the enemy by introducing jarring montages of the "most exotic" Japanese behavior—such as footage depicting seasonal festivals and traditional dances, in which distinctive garments were worn and the accompanying music was inevitably atonal and offensive to Western ears. *Our Job in Japan* exploited this familiar formula.[83]

Dower's assumption that Japanese music would "inevitably" offend American ears is striking. No acknowledgment is made of the crucial role of the various other cinematic factors in shaping the reception of this music. Film music critics have also been quick on occasion to identify "authenticity" in Hollywood's musical representations of Japan and to assume an "inevitable" negative reception of this music by American audiences. In Jerry Goldsmith's Main Title music for *Tora! Tora! Tora!*—a 1970 Japanese and American coproduced epic re-enactment of the attack on Pearl Harbor—the title first appears written in Japanese characters and is accompanied by a violent, crunching electronic sound and a few plucks on a *koto*. The title then appears in roman type as violent string stabs are heard, reminiscent of Bernard Herrmann's shower scene music from *Psycho*. As the camera pans the Japanese warship (actually a US Navy vessel outfitted for the film with a Japanese flag), a theme played on *koto* and accompanied by a wood block begins. This melody is treated fugally as the European instruments enter, and is eventually transformed into a militant march. George Burt has described this Main Title music as being "distinctly Japanese in its melodic and rhythmic style."[84] The *koto* plucks are heard at various points throughout the film to signal a Japanese setting. In his discussion of *Tora! Tora! Tora!* Irwin Bazelon refers to "ominous oriental sounds" heard as the Japanese approach Pearl Harbor.[85] Hollywood films have taught these critics what to accept as "distinctly Japanese" sounds and which musical styles to perceive as "ominous."

Shaping and Reshaping Musical Perceptions

In his best-selling comic travel guide *Dave Barry Does Japan,* Barry reports that his first, intensely negative impressions of the Japanese had been formed by watching old World War II movies on television as a child in the 1950s.

> You could always tell when the Japanese were about to appear because brass instruments on the sound track would play an ominous, Oriental-sounding

musical chord. A group of GIs would be walking through the jungle, nervous but still making spunky American wisecracks, and suddenly the sound track would go:

BWAAAAAAAAAMP

And right away you knew there were Japs in the trees, ready to pounce.

Or a US Navy ship would be motoring along, and the lookout would put his binoculars to his eyes, and

BWAAAAAAAAAMP

there would be a Jap destroyer. Probably one of the major reasons why the Japanese lost the war is that the sound track kept giving their position away.[86]

What lasting effect did these propaganda films and their soundtracks have on US audiences? Did Americans consciously hear the music in anti-Japanese films, and did they assume that some of these sounds were authentically Japanese? If so, did these films create enduring negative conceptions of Japanese music and culture in the United States?

In January 1995, I visited my grandfather, a World War II veteran, while on a research trip to the Harry Partch Archive. We attempted to discuss my research while watching a news broadcast concerning the recent Kobe earthquake. As I explained how I was searching for evidence of the influence of Japanese music and theater on Partch's works, my grandfather sharply asked, "You aren't a Jap lover, are you?" He was especially shocked to learn that I enjoyed traditional Japanese music. After this visit, I began to wonder how my grandfather's views of the Japanese people and of Japanese music had been formed fifty years earlier. He had fought almost entirely in Europe and was transferred to the Philippine island of Luzon at the war's end to "clean out" the remaining Japanese soldiers. In 1943, an official study was carried out by the US Army to measure the success of several of the early *Why We Fight* films, including *Prelude to War*, in shaping soldiers' attitudes. It found that although the films had little success in generating enthusiasm for fighting, they did affect the attitudes of soldiers toward the enemy and were successful in teaching American GIs "facts" about enemy nations.[87] It is not unreasonable to assume that American perceptions of Japanese music were equally shaped by these films, however subliminally, and that the attitudes formed were negative. These films continue to be viewed on video and on television by veterans as well as younger audiences. In addition, some of the representational techniques and clichés analyzed in this chapter were drawn on for films made during the US-Japan trade wars of the 1980s and 1990s and in commemorations of the attack on Pearl Harbor.[88] For many in the United States, Hollywood films continue to define their sonic impressions of Japan.

In World War II Hollywood film, one is far more likely to encounter brash Orientalism and the sounds of explosions and machine gun fire than the traditional music of Japan. In a draft script of *Our Job in Japan*, the writers had called for a shot of a "geisha girl playing [a] Japanese instrument." The narrator was to say: "Don't get close. The piece she's playing isn't Yankee Doodle."[89] This shot and music did not appear in the final film. But in the decade following the US occupation of Japan, from 1952 to 1962, Hollywood repeatedly presented Japanese music and performing arts on the screen and introduced American male characters who ventured quite close to that musical geisha. In this later period, Japanese music was presented as a positive sign of exotic romance, cultural refinement, and exquisite peace. In fact, by 1962 in *The Horizontal Lieutenant* even my grandfather's assignment "to clean out the Japs" at the war's end served as the basis for a comic plot, complete with a subservient and gently seductive jazz-singing geisha (played by Miyoshi Umeki) and the performance of Japanese traditional music to express the gratitude of the conquered and cultured Japanese people. Hollywood's image of Japan switched from the repulsive, sword-wielding, and screaming soldier to the ideal woman who offered a massage, a cup of *sake*, and a charming song. Having been recently conquered and reformed, the exotic other could now resume its earlier role as a feminine purveyor of quaint pleasures.[90]

As we will discover in the next chapter, in these later films, Japanese music served an Orientalist narrative function as a bridge to cultural understanding between white American (male) and Japanese (female) lovers. Several of the same major Hollywood composers encountered in anti-Japanese films stretched their compositional language and orchestral resources to create scores celebrating their newfound enthusiasm for Japanese music and culture.[91] With the United States involved in new wars in the 1950s and 1960s—the Korean and the Cold—Hollywood grew determined to erase the very prejudices it had done so much to create during World War II. Music and Orientalist modes of representation were again enlisted to project propaganda in American theaters—musical propaganda that Hollywood hoped would reshape perceptions of America's new exotic ally.

6

Singing Sayonara

Musical Representations of Japan in Postwar Hollywood

We hear the shrill, piercing timbre of the engine before we spot the distant fighter jet coming in for a landing at the start of the 1957 film *Sayonara*. "Korea 1951" appears emblazoned on the screen as the jet comes into view, announcing the film's setting in a new time of war with new representational goals in Hollywood's long history of *japonisme*. The camera lingers briefly over a shot of an African American crewman on the tarmac, thus making an oblique reference early on to the filmmakers' hopes for racial inclusion. As the jet's cockpit opens, another crewman asks the pilot, Air Force ace Lloyd Gruver, how many he shot down. Lloyd raises two fingers and then remains seated, looking rather pensive. In the next scene, Lloyd learns that one of his men, Joe Kelly, intends to marry a Japanese woman and that he and Kelly both have orders to fly out to Japan. In sharp contrast with the postcard images of a Japanese garden displayed in the Main Title sequence, all we see of Korea in these opening scenes is the gray US military base. The rest of the film will unfold in the colorful land of the new exotic ally. As they begin to descend over Japan, Kelly points out the "nice scenery" below, the grounds and buildings of the "Matsubayashi" all-female theatrical troupe, and the city where the all-male *kabuki* is performed—gendered exotic musical landmarks that will prove pivotal to the interracial romantic stories depicted in the film.[1]

Near the beginning of *Sayonara*, Lloyd declares: "I haven't got anything against the Japanese anymore, I mean not really." From the end of the US occupation in 1952 through the early 1960s, Americans were encouraged to follow Lloyd and revise their views of Japan, their new Cold War ally.[2] The seven-year American occupation had ended just one year prior to the hundredth anniversary of Perry's arrival in Edo Bay and the beginning of Japan's "opening" to the world. Once again, the United States would set out to orchestrate Japan's reintegration into the global community. Though most commonly expressed in romantic Orientalist tales set in postwar Japan, revisionist efforts are evident even in postwar combat films from this period. Both *Three Came Home* (1950) and *The Bridge on the River Kwai* (1957) featured Sessue Hayakawa as a more fully human and multidimensional exotic enemy. Rather than denigrate Japanese Americans as likely spies for the enemy, Hollywood began to offer more positive depictions as well as sympathetic references to the internment experience, as in *Hell to Eternity* (1960). The 1951 film

Go For Broke! celebrated the much-decorated 442nd Regimental Combat unit of Japanese American soldiers who fought in Europe, and *Operation Bikini* (1963), featuring elements of the contemporary exotica style in its score, offered a positive depiction of a Japanese American translator who makes the ultimate sacrifice against the Japanese enemy to save his fellow soldiers. Finally, two decades after the war, the 1965 *None but the Brave*, directed by Frank Sinatra and with a score by John Williams, offered not only a reevaluation of the Japanese enemy but of the Good War itself. We hear a white American soldier declare, "I want to whip the enemy as much as you do. Not because he's Japanese, but because he is the enemy," and we see the blunt antiwar phrase "Nobody ever wins" printed on the screen at the end of the film after the Japanese are killed.

Hollywood released one of its most focused revisionist treatments of anti-Japanese racism two years prior to *Sayonara* in the 1955 film *Three Stripes in the Sun* (also released as *The Gentle Sergeant* and occasionally erroneously referred to as *The Gentle Wolfhound*, the title of the *New Yorker* article that inspired the film). This film is based on the experiences of Master Sergeant Hugh O'Reilly and his unit, the "Wolfhounds," who established an orphanage in Japan during the occupation. O'Reilly—a veteran of multiple battles against the Japanese during World War II—begins the film virulently anti-Japanese, unable to understand how his fellow soldiers in occupied Japan have made peace with the enemy. Upon arrival, he is taken to a nightclub featuring a Japanese male jazz band, but becomes disgusted by the sight of interracial dancing couples, refuses a Japanese woman's offer to dance, and leaves in a huff. The music of a noodle vendor playing the *charumera* (a double reed shawm) outside on the street proves one alien sensation too many, seeming to set him off as he initiates a fight. O'Reilly is then reprimanded by his wise commanding officer, Colonel William Shepherd, who offers one of the most explicit statements in a Hollywood film of the need for American military personnel to form positive relationships with the new Japanese ally in order to be fully prepared as the Cold War threatens to heat up. (In fact, the Korean War begins and O'Reilly is transferred there, returning to Japan after being slightly wounded in combat.) Shepherd recognizes O'Reilly's racism and reveals that he has overcome his own antagonistic feelings despite having lost his wife during the attack on Pearl Harbor.

O'Reilly gradually falls in love with a Japanese interpreter named Yuko. As a Catholic and orphan himself, his hard exterior is pierced during a visit to a destitute orphanage run by nuns and he then takes on the lead role in planning, fundraising, and building a new orphanage for these Japanese children. George Duning's score helps to trace O'Reilly's evolving perceptions of Japan and the developing romance.[3] Though we hear music highlight certain moments, as when O'Reilly sees a view of Mount Fuji from a plane, which is marked on the soundtrack with a gong and plucked harp, the first half of the film is shot in a *vérité* style accompanied by very little music at all. As the romance develops, Duning draws on both the Japanese *in* scale and on anhemitonic pentatonic melodies, composing multiple melodic fragments reminiscent of *koto* pieces. Duning repeatedly approximates the timbres and textures of Japanese music by employing alto flutes and the banjo. His musical *japonisme* comes to the fore during a long sequence in Yuko's family home as O'Reilly has dinner with Yuko's father. The most striking musical sequence, however, occurs late in the film when O'Reilly seeks out Shepherd to ask to be discharged so that he may marry Yuko and live in Japan. O'Reilly finds a contemplative Shepherd at a Shinto shrine where he likes to retreat to think. Shepherd jokes that O'Reilly should not worry, he has not converted, but he admits that he finds Shinto interesting. Throughout the first half of this sequence we hear Duning's approximation of *gagaku* music, scored for "Japanese flute and oboe," Irish harp, "harp-banjo," muffled bell, and bass drum. The banjo and harp play a gesture from *Etenraku* and the "Japanese flute and oboe" play the opening melodic gesture of this most famous *gagaku* piece. The "Japanese oboe" in this scene does not sound exactly like a *hichiriki* to my ear, unless it was played weakly at a low volume and, perhaps, by a novice. A small drum simulates the *kakko* of *gagaku* and string harmonics realize a specific *sho* cluster (minus one pitch). This music abruptly ends and the soundtrack turns to ambient street noise as Shepherd accuses O'Reilly of being too cowardly to bring a Japanese woman back to the States and bluntly denies his request. O'Reilly had been disgusted upon seeing and hearing Japanese performing and dancing to American music in the jazz club at the start, but his success in transcending racism is signaled near the end as a chorus of the Japanese orphans, accompanied by a nun on a portable organ, sings a newly composed hymn in his praise. In their final dialogue, O'Reilly proposes marriage and Yuko expresses her own fears of living in the United States and of raising mixed-race children. He reassures her that they will work through everything together, she accepts, and the film ends with text informing us that the real O'Reillys currently live at West Point. In the course of roughly ninety minutes, this film depicts the transformation of one white American soldier from feeling revolted by the Japanese to successfully proposing to marry and bring home a Japanese woman. As John W. Dower explains in his history of occupation-period Japan, "Japan—only yesterday a menacing, masculine threat—had been transformed, almost in the blink of an eye, into a compliant, feminine body on which the white victors could impose their will."[4]

Throughout the 1950s and 1960s, Japan was advertised in the United States as an ideal vacation destination, a new democratic nation that had been thoroughly tamed. One figure particularly active in encouraging this new perception of Japan in the 1950s was the novelist James Michener, author of the 1953 best-selling novel *Sayonara*.[5] Michener based his celebrations of Japan on two claims: the superior artistic sensibilities of the Japanese and the ideal model offered by "the" Japanese woman. In multiple writings, Michener praised the refined and devoted behavior of Japanese wives and attempted to explain why, during the Korean War, thousands of American soldiers were marrying the former enemy.[6] One striking indication of just how pervasive this idealized image of Japanese women became (at least in the American heterosexual male imagination) appeared in the 7 December (Pearl Harbor day) 1957 edition of the *New Yorker* in an advertisement suggesting that the mere purchase of Japanese-style silk shirts would encourage American wives to kneel as geisha and "put slippers on feet of honorable husband." In this ad a white, smiling, kneeling woman sporting such a shirt performs the promised act at the foot of her husband who is suggested only by a protruding trousered leg.[7]

During the early 1950s, Michener's Japan articles frequently appeared in such popular serials as *Reader's Digest* and *Life* magazine. Michener repeatedly presented Japanese women as a model for American women to emulate and, in contrast, his white female characters in *Sayonara* are rather disagreeable. Michener's praise for Japanese women was deemed "extravagant" by Yukio Mishima, who referred to *Sayonara* as "a reworking into a modern legend of the story of *Madama Butterfly*" and concluded that Michener must have been thinking of the geisha since "even in Japan there are wives and wives."[8] In an article entitled "Madame Butterfly in Bobby Sox," Michener explained that although the traditional Japanese woman had been the "world's loveliest gift to man," the United States had bestowed freedom and rights on Japanese women during the occupation period and thus, unlike in other Asian nations, the newly liberated Japanese woman would find no appeal in the false promises of communism.[9] Michener's discussions of Japanese women and the alluring pervasiveness of art in all aspects of life in Japan encouraged American tourism to the exotic nation. *Holiday* magazine's 1952 introduction to postwar Japan, penned by Michener, was echoed over a decade later by an entire issue devoted to the exotic nation by *Life* magazine in 1964.[10] American tourism in Japan began to increase sharply starting in 1951. The increase in tourism between 1957 and 1958—the period of *Sayonara*'s general release in movie theaters—was nearly double all previous increases, and the increase between 1958 and 1959 was even greater.[11] Clearly, many American readers and filmviewers embraced what Mishima had dismissed as Michener's "cherished myths" of Japan. Michener himself married a *nisei* in 1955. A model method actor, Marlon Brando—perhaps fully identifying with his *Sayonara* character, Major Lloyd Gruver—exhibited a preference for Asian women and stated that they made better wives than did white American women.[12]

In his novel, Michener tells the story of a love affair between a white American Air Force officer and a Japanese female performer that ends with the exotic woman renouncing her illicit love for her life in the Takarazuka musical theater. In the 1957 Warner Bros. film adaptation, the cross-cultural lovers—Lloyd Gruver and Hana-ogi (played by "Miiko Taka," a Japanese-American amateur actually named Bette Ishimoto)—decide to defy racial bias and professional regulations and are united, instead of separated, at the end.[13] (See Figure 6.1.) The film's director, Joshua Logan, related that Brando had demanded this change to the ending and had initially refused to do the film because he felt it was not serious enough and belittled the Japanese.[14] A 1987 staged musical version of *Sayonara* followed the original plot of the novel by having Hana-ogi leave Lloyd.[15] However, the director and actors clearly studied the film quite closely, imitating numerous details from the film in blocking, staging, and costumes. In fact, in their first intimate meeting in the musical when Hana-ogi tells Lloyd that she has been watching him too we hear a bit of

Figure 6.1 One of multiple interracial kisses in *Sayonara* (1957). Warner Bros. publicity still. Courtesy of the Museum of Modern Art/Film Stills Archive.

Irving Berlin's "Sayonara" melody—a song prominently featured in the film—on the flute and again on English horn and then clarinet at the end of her speech.

The film includes two other cross-cultural relationships central to the plot—one ends tragically, the other, as we will see further on, remains ambiguous. Joe Kelly marries his Japanese girl, Katsumi, played by Miyoshi Umeki, a Japanese jazz vocalist and naturalized US citizen. (The novel and musical include this interracial relationship as well.) Her impossibly sweet, subservient, and childlike depiction of Katsumi earned Umeki the Academy Award for Best Supporting Actress—one of the four Academy Awards garnered by the film and, to date, the only Oscar won by an Asian American actress.[16] (See Figure 6.2.) Their blissful love and idyllic domesticity is admired by Lloyd who, in the film, more or less moves in with the couple and goes native himself by donning a kimono, watering their bonsai, and learning to avoid hitting his head on the low door frames. (Dower claims that during the occupation period, "While the media in the United States were chuckling and enthusing over the 'Americanization' of Japan, the Japanese were quietly and skillfully Japanizing the Americans.")[17] Like Hamilton in the 1917 play *The Willow Tree*, Lloyd clearly becomes fully domesticated within this exotic setting. In the novel, Lloyd states that he had never seen a better wife than Katsumi: "she seemed to me one of the most perfect women I had ever known, for she had obviously studied her man and had worked out every item of the day's work so that the end result would be a happy husband and a peaceful home."[18] However, a racist officer—framed

Figure 6.2 Sweet Katsumi, *Sayonara* (1957). Warner Bros. publicity still.

as such in the narrative and clearly disgusted by Kelly's marriage to Katsumi and Lloyd's affair with Hana-ogi—declares the house off-limits to US military personnel and arranges to have Kelly transferred stateside, even though regulations require that he leave his pregnant Japanese wife behind. After attending a *bunraku* performance of a lovers' double-suicide play, and seeing no alternative for their own hopeless situation, Kelly and Katsumi commit suicide themselves, thus ending their cross-cultural romance and the life of their unborn child as well. Lloyd's discovery of their bodies is depicted with searing poignancy in the film, primarily through the exquisite string scoring of "Katsumi's Love theme."[19]

Lloyd's transfer to Japan had been on the orders of General Webster, the father of Lloyd's white American girlfriend, Eileen. Eileen had been brought to Japan by General Webster and his wife on the assumption that Lloyd would soon propose marriage. After their initial romantic reunion and attendance at a *kabuki* performance, Lloyd soon becomes estranged from Eileen, whose (rather mild) feminist notions have pushed him to seek out Japanese women. Thirty years after the film in the 1987 staged musical, Eileen appears to be quite conservative, with conventional ambitions to follow her steely mother as a well-established military wife. After Lloyd announces that he plans to marry a Japanese girl, Eileen runs after him and, rather awkwardly, blames herself for not stopping to think more about his desires. She sings a "you know I'll always love you" song and then exits from the narrative by saying "I'm proud of you Lloyd, sayonara." At one point in his affair with Hana-ogi in the novel, Lloyd, seeing a white woman who reminds him of Eileen, almost "cried aloud with pain to think that something had happened in

American life to drive men like . . . me away from such delectable girls" (p. 138). Michener's message to white American would-be wives seems quite clear. Equally clear in *Sayonara*, and in multiple other Hollywood films from this period, is the promise that white American males suffering a crisis of confidence can reclaim their manhood in Japan. (With this narrative trope Hollywood was recapitulating any number of nineteenth-century Orientalist operas.)[20] Gina Marchetti has argued that films set in Asia, such as *Sayonara*, reaffirmed heterosexual love and the patriarchal home, teaching white American women how to return to a passive prewar role in American society, and that in these films "the romantic hero functions as a white knight who rescues the nonwhite heroine from the excesses of her own culture while 'finding' himself through this exotic sexual liaison."[21]

Lloyd becomes intensely attracted to Hana-ogi, a female performer of male roles. He finds her alluring precisely because she dresses in masculine clothing. In Michener's novel, Lloyd attends performances of *Swing Butterfly* by the all-female Takarazuka musical theater, with Hana-ogi in the role of Pinkerton.[22] This production functions as a sendup of American males and Butterfly avoids suicide. Lloyd is bemused by the confusing juxtapositions in the show of "old Japan dances" and "jitterbugging to represent 1890 America," but is also clearly angered by "this burlesque of a great opera" and by Hana-ogi's portrayal of Lt. Pinkerton: "She was all Japanese women making fun of all American men" (p. 94). However, he finds her "more essentially feminine than any of the other girls on stage" and he falls "under the spell of Japanese art" as he watches her dance as a samurai, suspecting that the spell may have been cast by the "horribly weird sounds" (p. 94) of the music. Hana-ogi introduces Lloyd to many aspects of her exotic culture, and Lloyd becomes increasingly entranced. Echoing Lafcadio Hearn, or even Henry Eichheim, Lloyd tells of his last night with Hana-ogi and how he was lulled to sleep by "the sweetest night sound I have ever heard, the soft passage of the noodle vendor, pushing his belled cart while he played a rhythmic melody upon his flute" (p. 226). (A document entitled "General Music Notes" indicates that the noodle man's music was recorded in Japan for the film. We hear this brief tune—an unlikely lullaby for Lloyd—on the piercing *charumera* double-reed shawm late in the film after the *bunraku* performance as Kelly and Katsumi go to enter their boarded up "off-limits" house.) By the end of the novel, and at the end of their affair, Lloyd sees Hana-ogi portray Pinkerton on stage one final time and finds himself enjoying her burlesque, a performance he believes to be clearly improved by her intimate study of himself (pp. 198–199). The novel ends with Lloyd learning that Hana-ogi has left him forever, choosing to honor her obligations to the Takarazuka theater and remaining within character as a cross-dressed, exotic Pinkerton.[23]

Gender ambiguity is one of several tropes of exoticism that were repeated in numerous Hollywood films from the 1950s and 1960s set in Japan, such as *Three Stripes in the Sun* (1955), *The Teahouse of the August Moon* (1956), *Joe Butterfly* (1957), *Escapade in Japan* (1957), *The Geisha Boy* (1958), *The Barbarian and the Geisha* (1958), *Cry for Happy* (1961), *A Majority of One* (1962), and *A Girl Named*

Tamiko (1962). Many of these films were clearly influenced by *Sayonara*, either by Michener's 1953 novel or the 1957 Warner Bros. film, and certain songs from this period were as well. For example, the 1955 "Sayonara-Goodbye (Japanese Farewell)," with words and music by Marguerite Arneth and Lanny Grey, tells of a romance between a Yankee boy and a Takarazuka girl, "Tho' their eyes were diff'rent as each other's name." The 1955 "Japanese Farewell Song" by Hasegawa Yoshida, with English lyrics by Freddy Morgan, might also have been published in response to the success of Michener's novel. Hank Locklin had a hit with the 1957 rockabilly number "Geisha Girl" by Lawton Williams, which was also covered successfully by Country Johnny Mathis. This song's male protagonist has found love in Japan and asks us to "tell the home folks that I'm happy."[24] (Numerous comments on YouTube reveal that this song continues to remind aged GIs of the good times they had in Japan during the occupation period and Korean War.) Characters in these films—and, thus, audiences—were repeatedly lectured on the true nature of the geisha, on removing one's shoes upon entering a Japanese home, and on proper etiquette at the Japanese table. Much comic mileage was derived from American anxiety upon visiting coed Japanese bathhouses, returning bows of greeting, or fumbling with chopsticks. Many of these films also made reference to the Madame Butterfly narrative, as we saw most explicitly in chapter 4 with *My Geisha*. Music played a central role in the attempt in these films to reverse the racism Hollywood had stoked during World War II and to transform American public opinion of Japan once again. Japanese musical performance serves as evidence of the cultured and refined nature of the Japanese, as indication of the feminine ideal represented by Japanese women, and as a symbol of racial reconciliation. Hollywood assumed the role of public enthnomusicologist, rather didactically introducing mass audiences to numerous forms of Japanese performance. We repeatedly witness white American characters learn to enjoy Japanese music and, thus, the Japanese themselves. For instance, at a performance of *noh* in the film, Hana-ogi turns to Lloyd and asks whether he likes "this old and curious play," and he responds affirmatively.[25]

Sayonara is particularly ripe for the study of musical exoticism in American popular culture, and I will focus on this prominent film while referencing multiple others throughout this chapter. The desire to present "authentic old Japan" was repeatedly compromised by a need to satisfy Hollywood's aesthetic ideals. Sketches and correspondence reveal how this dilemma played out in the creation of the *Sayonara* soundtrack. Multiple forms of "Japanese" music are heard, creating a complex and contradictory musical portrait. Franz Waxman's score employs Berlin's song "Sayonara" and numerous Japanese folk tunes, and offers original music scored for Japanese instruments. In addition, Japanese composers provided music for sections of Hana-ogi's Takarazuka performance and the traditional musics of *noh*, *kabuki*, *bunraku*, and the *koto* are briefly heard.[26] These divergent musical sources interact and collide in the creation of a Japanese sound and in the representation of Japanese performance. Tracing the sources of the soundtrack forces us to consider what constituted Japanese music in the mid-twentieth century.[27] We will explore not only what is heard in such films, but how it is presented. In classic Orientalist fashion, Japanese performances are framed within a highly charged erotic context, revealing an intense fascination with the gender ambiguities inherent in these traditions. However, Orientalist and cultural imperialist critiques ultimately fail to capture fully the complexity of American/Japanese cultural encounters that such works as *Sayonara* reveal.

Hollywood's Singing Geishas

Consistently, it has been through exotic musical performance that the Japanese woman displays her charms and attracts the white American male in Hollywood films. In the 1931 cinematic travelogue *Around the World in Eighty Minutes with Douglas Fairbanks*, Fairbanks sends his cameraman to go "window shopping" and film a Japanese maiden at home.[28] Through the voyeuristic lens, we see both the exotic sleeping maid and the white American males peeking in on her as we hear a light pentatonic melody in the orchestral music. Watching her morning routine, Fairbanks makes suggestive jokes here and there while providing detailed commentary. We see the "charming, intelligent, gentle people" at breakfast and hear this woman of "ethereal fragility" play and sing during the *shamisen* and dance lessons that follow. The two peeping toms are discovered and their flight is accompanied by variations on "Yankee Doodle." However, this faked documentary scene ends with the exotic woman catching up to Fairbanks and asking him in English for his autograph. Unlike the tearful and shy Japanese woman encountered by the voyeuristic officer in Perry's 1853–1854 expedition, this exotic woman turns the tables on the intrusive white man. Apparently, she has been watching him as well from the other side of the world on the silver screen.

Major Gruver (and, thus, the audience) spends a significant amount of time watching and listening to singing and dancing Japanese women in *Sayonara*. Tipped off by a Marine buddy about the "lovely stuff" that passes over the bridge to the Matsubayashi grounds, Lloyd hangs out at this bridge watching the women parade by in groups distinguished only by different pastel-colored simple kimonos. Images of these women are most often accompanied on the soundtrack by Japanese folk and children's songs. We first hear a female chorus singing "To Ryan Se," but the lips of the onscreen practicing women remain closed. This is also the case for later shots of these women accompanied by "Sakura," "Tanko Bushi," "Hanayome Nigyo," and other folk songs. The songs are perceived as emanating from the parading Japanese women even though we do not see them sing nor do we see the *koto* or other instruments that occasionally accompany these songs. In fact, Lloyd and his buddy hear and react to this music before seeing the women approach. The men are enticed and decide, with a leer, to go to the theater and catch the show.

One aspect of the Matsubayashi scene that differs strikingly from the reality of Takarazuka theater is its erotic presentation. Once inside, we are treated to several shots of the American men as they ogle the performers, particularly during the climactic closing number. (See Figure 6.3.) LeRoy Prinz drew on this choreography again for the analogous female climax moment of the staged "Honey Bun" number in the 1958 movie *South Pacific*. Although Hana-ogi is an *otokoyaku* (that is, a female performer of male roles in Takarazuka theater), we see her dressed in masculine attire for only thirty seconds during the entire performance, as though to avoid any suggestion of homoerotic desire on Lloyd's part. While *otokoyaku* performers do appear occasionally in female attire during a performance, they primarily appear as males. Erotic tension is part of the Takarazuka theater experience, but this scene in *Sayonara* has almost completely reversed the erotic and gendered aspects of this musical theater tradition. Takarazuka, to contradict the impression created by this scene and reinforced in male critics' reviews of this film, is not a "girlie show" presented for the pleasure of heterosexual male audiences. The audience for Takarazuka has been predominantly female and under the age of twenty-five since at least the end of World War II.[29] Sociologists of Takarazuka performance have discovered that the *otokoyaku* performers provide a strong homoerotic experience for their devoted teenage female fans. Hollywood's assumption that all Japanese female musical performance must exist within the geisha model is nowhere more strongly evident than in *Sayonara's* presentation of the Takarazuka tradition.

Lloyd attends two Matsubayashi performances in the film. The first, extended Matsubayashi sequence includes shots of the full stage with Hana-ogi appearing with a large cast as well as a montage sequence of Hana-ogi dancing alone. The music for the full stage segments of Matsubayashi performance was composed by

Figure 6.3 The Matsubayashi grand finale in *Sayonara* (1957). Warner Bros. publicity still. Courtesy of the Museum of Modern Art/Film Stills Archive.

Japanese composers and recorded in Japan during the shooting.[30] (Songs that were recorded in Japan for *Sayonara* are referred to in the production documentation as "wild tracks.") We see the orchestra and conductor in the pit and hear an uptempo piece entitled "Sakura Sakura" (credited to Shiro Matsumoto and Suifu Kishimoto), which is melodically unrelated to the famous folk song, the title simply designating on the cue sheet this Japanese-composed show music. The solo Hana-ogi montage sequence was filmed in Los Angeles and is accompanied by newly recorded music composed or arranged by Waxman. LeRoy Prinz directed the full-stage dances and collected Japanese music during the shooting in Japan. Throughout the film's production a great deal of attention was paid to determining and securing the legal rights for the various songs used in the bridge and theater scenes. There was also much discussion concerning which songs and which recordings to use in the film and how the music might be enhanced. For example, a document entitled "General Music Notes" and dated 14 June 1957 includes the following directive: "As we see the Matsubayashi girls coming across the bridge, utilize one of the vocal tracks recorded wild and add some additional and varied instruments to this."[31]

Employment records and various inter-office memos reveal that Japanese American vocalists were hired to rehearse and record for the soundtrack.[32] In a memo dated 27 May 1957, Waxman requested that Ray Heindorf, as musical director for the film, invite as many female singers, under twenty years old, as possible to audition. Several sets of employment cards reveal that two separate choruses were auditioned and hired. These two groups were kept separate based on race. The first group consisted of about twenty Japanese American US citizens and they performed the Japanese songs on the soundtrack. The second group, based on their names, appear to have been Euro-American women and men. This second chorus is heard singing and humming in the Main Title sequence and in the film's finale version of "Sayonara." Both groups were paid the same wage rate and rehearsed and recorded separately throughout the end of August 1957.

Japanese folk songs are heard in multiple other sequences in *Sayonara* and at least once the text of a song appears to correspond closely with the action taking place. For example, we hear a jaunty double-time version of the children's song "To Ryan Se" ("Please Let Me Pass") when Lloyd asks some Japanese children for directions as he visits Kelly and Katsumi's house for the first time. The song warns, "on your way back, you'll have trouble." Late in the film we hear a nasty brass version of this tune when Lloyd is leaving their home after discovering their bodies and is attacked by a male gang of anti-American Japanese who block his way. Other performances of Japanese songs are included to reinforce the film's exotic and erotic locale. "Tanko Bushi" is heard emanating from a radio in Kelly's kitchen when Lloyd visits the second time and we see Kelly soaking in his bath and receiving a back scrub from Katsumi. Eileen's fascination with and romantic attraction to the *kabuki* performer Nakamura is further stimulated musically as they observe, from a distance, Japanese men and women singing at a nocturnal garden party. Eileen finds the scene "beautiful." Though Japanese song and instrumental music has proved pleasurable for the white characters throughout the film, near the end this music appears to mock Lloyd. After Hana-ogi has decided to end their relationship and has been transferred to Tokyo, Lloyd crosses the bridge once more and forcefully enters the Matsubayashi compound in search of her. We hear scales and fragments of the same songs that he had previously enjoyed hearing at the bridge and in the theater, but now each brief performance is abruptly curtailed as he barges into the practice rooms, only to be disappointed each time by the absence of the one vocalist he seeks.

Romantic encounters with singing Japanese women were central to numerous films in this period. Projecting back historically, Hollywood imagined that white American males have been serenaded by geishas ever since the years of first contact. The 1958 film *The Barbarian and the Geisha*, directed by John Huston with a score by Hugo Friedhofer, offers a particularly striking example of a period film that resonated with contemporary Cold War *japonisme*.[33] In this film, John Wayne—instead of flushing out "Japs" on Iwo Jima as Sergeant Stryker—portrays Townsend Harris, the first US diplomat sent to Japan in 1856. Apparently, the Japanese provided the historical Harris with, what would later be termed, a "comfort woman" named Okichi. In the film, the relationship between Okichi (played by the Japanese actress Eiko Ando) and Harris is fictionalized as the very first enactment of the romantic Madame Butterfly narrative.[34] In a twist on the standard Orientalist approach, this film frames the story from Okichi's perspective. The Main Title music of low gong and pentatonicism in treble instruments is interrupted by Okichi's voice-over as she begins to recount the tale. She relates that the arrival of the American "black ships" occurred during an *obon* ceremony as we hear the folk music of *shamisen*, drum, flute, and voices and see a long shot of a large group of Japanese dancing in a circle in an accurate rendition. The camera then zooms in to bring this particular historical geisha into focus. She declares "my name is Okichi, this is my story too," at which point the Main Title sequence resumes with a standard Hollywood love theme in the strings. Thus, the film begins by placing us in a voyeuristic position, observing their exotic folk customs, but we then gaze apprehensively from the position of the Japanese as they see the approaching American ship.

Japanese musical performance features prominently throughout *The Barbarian and the Geisha*. Harris attends a dinner which is accompanied by geisha music and dance. When Okichi first enters we see and hear a *shamisen*, two *kotos*, and a flute, all played rather unconvincingly. Okichi then sings with a distinctly European sultry vocal timbre and Harris is instantly taken by her. When she begins her period of service she brings her *shamisen* along to Harris's house. Harris is portrayed as an entirely honorable Pinkerton, who permits Okichi to live in his house only so that he may learn more about Japan. She obliges by singing "To Ryan Se" and explaining the geisha tradition. Harris, like so many other white American male characters, is entranced by his singing geisha and declares: "You know Henry, I've seen some pretty attractive dancing girls from Siam, sing-song girls from China, but I think I prefer the geisha of Japan." Harris gradually becomes accustomed to the Japanese lifestyle. Later in the film, as Harris makes his grand procession to the capital, we see a group of Japanese men dancing with swords. Documentary footage of this type of male traditional performance had been included in anti-Japanese documentary films during the war, but a smiling John Wayne joins in this Japanese folk dance himself.

Japanese folk songs typically underscore Harris's increasing attraction to Okichi. We hear a bit of "Sakura" in the violins as Harris explains to Okichi the differences between Japanese and American women. She is perplexed and says: "In Japan, different husbands." Harris, with a laugh, replies: "No, in America different wives." Okichi sings for Harris once more in the film on the night of an attempt on his life and he proclaims her music "beautiful." As a more sympathetic incarnation of Pinkerton, Harris promises to return to Japan in order to live with her forever. Okichi foils the assassination plot on Harris and then makes the painful decision to leave him for his own good. In the end, this geisha has sacrificed her happiness and is left alone, accompanied by rather schmaltzy strings. In an interview, Friedhofer revealed that music from his score for the film *Three Came Home*—a film set during the war in a Japanese prison camp—was used as a temp track in *The Barbarian and the Geisha* and that in the end he decided to reuse "some thematic material and also some sequences practically in toto" from that earlier score.[35] Indeed, there is a good deal of brassy pentatonicism accompanying the samurai men in the later film just as such music signified the cruelty of the Japanese camp guards in *Three Came Home*. Huston had originally planned to use Japanese music throughout the soundtrack, but Friedhofer argued against this since he felt *The Barbarian and the Geisha* was not really about the Japanese but was, instead, another take on the Madame Butterfly theme. Friedhofer insisted that it "should be a romantic, dramatic score, with certain ethnic overtones, but fundamentally something that wouldn't be puzzling to a European or American audience."[36] Apparently, composer and director reached a compromise given that the soundtrack alternates between Japanese traditional musical performances, Friedhofer's more typical Romantic style, and his own attempts to compose with "ethnic overtones."[37]

Though set in a period a full century prior, *The Barbarian and the Geisha* certainly resonated (however subliminally) with the US occupation of Japan and Cold War preoccupations.[38] For example, following an ineffectual Shinto purification dance accompanied by flute, drum, and chanting voices, Harris burns down an entire Japanese village to cleanse it of the cholera brought by American sailors and then defends his destructive action by declaring "we've given them money to build new houses." The Japanese eventually agree that this cleansing by fire was for their own good. Harris delivers a speech to the Shogun asking Japan to assume its responsibility as a member of the global community and to "take what the world has to offer." Throughout the film the Japanese are presented as superstitious, foolish, and stubborn, but they are amazed by American technology and eventually march in Harris's procession to the capital bearing American emblems as grateful fans of Uncle Sam. Just as Michener claimed that the United States had "liberated" Japanese women during the occupation period, Harris declares at the official reception banquet that Japanese women will benefit if Japan opens her ports to the outside world. Music speaks volumes in this scene. As Harris asserts that progress will mean "not having to kill girl babies in time of famine," the camera pans slowly to the right, and we see and hear a large ensemble of women playing *koto* and *shamisen* from behind a bamboo screen that resembles a cloister. These exotic musical women remain otherwise silent as Harris speaks on their behalf.

A rather more comic presentation of Hollywood's singing geisha is encountered in *Cry for Happy* (1961).[39] This film once again cast Miiko Taka and Miyoshi Umeki of *Sayonara* fame in a tale of American military men falling in love with Japanese women and with Japan itself. The film is set in 1952 on a US naval base in Japan and the Departments of Defense and the Navy are thanked for assistance in the production. The Main Title song performed by Umeki features Japlish lyrics recalling Tin Pan Alley–era songs, and includes the *shamisen*, banjo, *koto*, *taiko*, *tsuzumi*, and *ko-tsuzumi*, which, along with *sho*-like sustained clusters, are also heard at other points in the soundtrack. Again Miiko Taka is required to feign trouble with English and Glenn Ford (as in the 1956 *The Teahouse of the August Moon*) is led comically astray by his geishas. The film opens with a shot of US ships in the harbor, and then cuts to an indoor private geisha performance for an American admiral. We see the geisha dancing and hear, but do not see, the vocalists and *shamisen* players. The admiral, clearly pleased by the performance, turns to a Japanese minister at his side to inquire about the geisha's availability and has his misconceptions quickly corrected—a lesson repeated multiple times throughout the film. The minister's translator explains that "in the Orient, it is man who is on pedestal." The Admiral replies: "I'm for that, but don't tell my wife I said so!" The comic plot is driven by the desire of a unit of navy photographers to improve their quarters. The men end up moving into a geisha house and learn that the geisha will serve them but only up to a certain point. In one scene, we hear a *shamisen* solo (composed by Tak Shindo) and see these American navy men—including the Japanese American actor James Shigeta, playing the part of a Japanese American translator who does not actually speak Japanese—relaxing on the floor and wearing kimonos. We also see a geisha "playing" the *shamisen*, which we continue to hear after she puts the instrument down. One of the men declares: "of all the girls I've ever known—European, Latin, American—you are the most beautiful . . . there is something about you geisha." As the men relax in their hot baths and receive massages from their geishas, their leader (the Glenn Ford character) announces: "When I make Admiral, I'm going to see to it that every man in this Navy has his own personal geisha." Ford's character becomes a "Papa-san" of this geisha-house-turned-orphanage at the end, and—comically displacing the geisha's role—is seen bathing a small boy.

In *Sayonara*, Hana-ogi most clearly assumes the role of "singing geisha" in two intimate scenes with Lloyd as they dine alone at Kelly and Katsumi's home. When she first meets with Lloyd at the house, Hana-ogi remains silent for an extended period as Lloyd awkwardly attempts to engage her in conversation. Throughout this sequence—the longest and most innovative musical piece in the film at roughly seven and a half minutes—the orchestra speaks for the exotic woman. Waxman scored for *kotos*, bass flute, *shamisen*, and bass marimba, playing dissonant chords and a shimmering texture with harmonics in the string parts. The music is tentative and marks Hana-ogi as mysterious. She eventually speaks, revealing to Lloyd that she does indeed understand English and, thus, that he was not in the clear position of power that he, and we, had assumed. In fact, the extended orchestral music indicates that she has been in control throughout this scene—rather than having been silenced by Lloyd or the orchestra, she has chosen to remain silent as she studied the behavior and intentions of this American male.

Throughout the film, Irving Berlin's 1953 "Sayonara" melody is very closely associated with Hana-ogi.[40] For example, we hear a fragment of the melody accompanying a close-up shot of her on the bridge and again after the show as someone calls out "there is Hana-ogi." As Lloyd awaits Hana-ogi's arrival at Kelly's house we hear a jazzy big band version of the tune on the radio and then a lush string nondiegetic setting at the moment of her arrival. Hana-ogi finally performs as a singing geisha herself when, after dining alone with Lloyd, she sings "Sayonara" while manipulating a hand puppet. Berlin's lyrics indicate a Japanese persona in their flawed grammar: "No more we stop to see pretty cherry blossoms." In this private performance, "Sayonara" is framed as a folk song that she sings to entertain her American lover. Lloyd is tickled pink: "Well, that's the cutest thing I ever saw honey." The "General Music Notes" document reveals that Miiko Taka post-synched "Sayonara" for this scene. We see her singing, but do not see the accompanying harp and *koto*. Perhaps surprisingly, Miyoshi Umeki–though a professional singer–does not have a similar scene of vocal performance. Rather, the intensely lyrical, delicate, and poignant "Sweet Katsumi" theme in the strings marks her musically, particularly when she serves the American men on her knees, functioning as a geisha for Kelly and Lloyd. This utterly subservient behavior prompts Lloyd to declare "she's just as cute as a bug"—a rather unfortunate analogy given the racist references to the Japanese as insects during World War II. Katsumi does (very briefly) sing wordlessly to her own theme as she cheerfully works away in the kitchen preparing the meal for these men. Hollywood geishas cannot suppress their musicality or their desire to serve white American men for long.

The Attraction and Repulsion of the Exotic

In filming *Sayonara*, Joshua Logan sought to capture the "authentic Old Japan" whose passing in the process of postwar recovery and modernization was mourned by many Americans reporting on the country. Projecting exotic authenticity was a common aim in the creation of the films under consideration here. These films frequently boasted of having been shot on location in Japan and of capturing the beauty of the exotic land with the latest in color film technology. *Sayonara*, for example, was advertised as having been "filmed in Japan in the never-before-seen beauty of TECHNIRAMA and TECHNICOLOR." Scrolling text at the start of *The Barbarian and the Geisha* promises that it was "filmed in its entirety in Japan." Filming on location in search of visual authenticity had its parallel in attempts to achieve an aural authenticity in the soundtracks. Samples of traditional Japanese culture—including forms of music, theater, and ritual—were appropriated to realize these aspirations. Although film directors, producers, and composers during this period genuinely hoped to present the "real Japan," the "authentic exotic" rarely met their expectations. As is so often true of Orientalist exploits, the quest for the exotic frequently ended with a retreat and a return to a reliance on the voyager's imagination. In the end, these films often reverted to what the filmmakers knew would look and sound "Japanese" to a Euro-American audience. Thus, the mechanics of Orientalism are found to have been as predominant in 1950s Hollywood as in any *fin-de-siècle* French opera.[41]

Initially, Logan was determined to film at the exact locations mentioned in Michener's novel. In preparation for the shooting, Logan first visited the Takarazuka theater campus. However, he was immediately disappointed and felt that "the general atmosphere didn't look very photogenic, certainly not as lushly romantic as James Michener had made it seem in the novel."[42] Since the actual bridge at Takarazuka where Lloyd first sees Hana-ogi proved disappointing, Logan embarked on a quest throughout Japan to find the ideal bridge and exotic setting of his imagination. As he searched for a location to serve as the Matsubayashi grounds, he became convinced that all Japanese parks were too small and insignificant. Finally, he discovered one bridge and park that were "on a magnified scale." It was this atypical Japanese locale that ultimately matched his exotic imaginings. When it was determined that filming at this ideal location would prove too expensive, the production team sought permission to film in a private royal garden in Kyoto that also met their aesthetic demands. In order to win permission to film at this secluded site, a formal dinner was held at which Marlon Brando succeeded in charming the royal officials by making a speech in Japanese. While the outdoor scenes were primarily shot in Japan, much of the film was made back in Hollywood. The production team hired a Japanese builder to create Kelly's house on the Warner Bros. backlot entirely from materials shipped from Japan.

To further his bid for authenticity, Logan decided that performances of *noh*, *kabuki*, and *bunraku* would all make brief appearances in *Sayonara* and would serve as "symbol[s] of old Japan."[43] In addition, Logan decided to create a new role in Michener's story for a "real" *kabuki* actor. This decision was motivated by a progressive desire to show that a white woman could find herself attracted to a Japanese man. However, in the end Logan felt that no actual Japanese male actor could play the part, since no Japanese male "would look romantic to an American girl,"[44] thereby undermining his professed goals on racial representation. Logan then planned to hire a *kabuki* actor to serve as a stand in for the long shots of the dance. However, he was rebuffed by *kabuki* actors and the rumor of his demeaning request was met with scorn in Tokyo newspapers.[45] (The 1987 musical version of *Sayonara* represented *kabuki* on stage in a brief scene transition with a single female dancer accompanied by music that resembled *kabuki* music only slightly. Indeed, Japanese music and performance traditions are far less central to the musical than they were in the film.)[46] After rejecting the notion of using a Japanese actress for the part of Hana-ogi, Logan instructed his Japanese American amateur, Miiko Taka, to drop "that very strong nisei-American accent of yours" and to sound more Japanese.[47] He had hired a Japanese American since it would be easier to film with an English speaker, but then directed her to disguise her "American" sound and to feign difficulty in speaking English. The ability to sound and look "Japanese" was felt to be crucial to the film, even though actual Japanese sources were repeatedly rejected as being inadequate.

Academic scholarship has served as an oracle for would-be Orientalists throughout the history of Euro-American exoticism and Hollywood's quest for the genuine exotic in the 1950s perpetuated this tradition. The Warner Bros. Research Department was kept busy throughout the filming and post-production periods of *Sayonara*. For example, ten days after Waxman was hired to work on the film, a request was made for a book on Japanese music.[48] The Research Department provided *Japanese Music* by Katsumi Sunaga—a brief introduction published by the Japanese national railway for English-speaking tourists.[49] Logan also turned directly to scholars specializing in Japanese culture. The most prominent American scholars of Japanese literature and theater, Donald Keene and Faubion Bowers (with Charles Saito's assistance as well), were paid $200 to provide a Japanese version of Irving Berlin's lyrics for "Sayonara," which we hear sung by a Japanese male vocalist on a jukebox in the Officers' Club. A request for information on "Japanese fan language," likely for the brief shot of Hana-ogi dancing with fans in the Matsubayashi performance, was met with the suggestion that Spanish traditions could serve as a model instead. In May 1957 the Research Department sent a copy of *The Kabuki Theatre* by Earle Ernst to the actor Ricardo Montalbán so that he could prepare for a lecture at a college. Finally, as the film was nearing completion, the department was asked to find "classical Oriental sayings for SAYONARA publicity" and provided quotes from Confucius, Japanese proverbs from *We Japanese* by Frederic De Garis, and examples of *haiku*.

The ideals of authenticity and realism shaped all aspects of this film. However, "authentic" sources of expertise were not always willing to comply. During World War II and the occupation period, Hollywood films had routinely received assistance from the US armed forces in making combat related pictures. Most of these films began with printed text thanking the Department of Defense. Such a certification of authenticity was also sought in the filming of *Sayonara*. Multiple cables between Warner Bros. and the Office of Information Services, US Air Force, reveal that the Air Force was extremely displeased by aspects of *Sayonara*'s plot and ultimately refused all assistance.[50] Similarly, the Takarazuka theater company refused to participate in the making of *Sayonara*. Both the US Air Force and Takarazuka found the film's plot offensive. Logan had similar troubles in hiring professional *noh, bunraku,* and *kabuki* performers. The production team was eventually forced to rent a theater and hire freelance performers. A troupe of communist puppeteers, presumably desperate for the work, was engaged for the film's *bunraku* scene.[51]

Efforts to achieve or simulate musical "authenticity" in *Sayonara* proved particularly multifaceted. Logan employed recordings of Japanese folk songs as a temp track while filming on location and may have expected some of this music to be retained in the final soundtrack.[52] Sheets of manuscript paper found near the end of Waxman's sketches for the film include Japanese songs transcribed in Japan during the filming.[53] LeRoy Prinz worked with Kineya Jorokuaki on the choreography for the Matsubayashi scenes and this Japanese choreographer "played" Japanese melodies for him, which Prinz transcribed. (It appears that these transcriptions were made from recordings in Japan, though this is not entirely clear. One sheet includes the indication: "authentic melody played for me by Jorokuaki Kineya.") As noted above, some of the music for the Matsubayashi scenes heard in the final film was recorded in Japan. However, within three weeks of being hired, Waxman had decided to arrange and re-record the Japanese folk songs rather than employ prerecorded performances sent from Japan. Waxman also initially rejected a proposal to employ Japanese instrumentalists on the soundtrack.[54] Rather than presenting Japanese performances of Japanese folk tunes, Waxman rescored them, but then went to considerable lengths to include Japanese instruments in his arrangements and to have the songs sung by Japanese-American vocalists in Japanese.[55] Of course, the most distinctive musical features of these Japanese songs are absent. They are performed with a European-style vocal timbre and in a very strict and regular rhythm by the chorus. Presumably to enhance the exotic flavor of these songs, Waxman added punctuation on drum, small bells, triangle, and woodblock.

To what extent did Waxman pursue research on Japanese music as he worked on the *Sayonara* score? In addition to the possible influence of the book mentioned above, other sources of information are evident. A small receipt in the Warner Bros. *Sayonara* correspondence file reveals that two recordings of Japanese music were purchased on 1 July 1957 from a Los Angeles store.[56] Waxman composed mostly in July. Several recordings of *gagaku* were available at the time and one may well have served as Waxman's inspiration for the *sho* tone clusters approximated closely in the "Main Title" music. Most significant, the Japanese American arranger and bandleader Tak Shindo was hired as a technical musical adviser on the film—renting a *shamisen* and *koto* for the recording session, composing a number for the Matsubayashi scene, and scouting musicians for the Japanese instruments—activities he performed for numerous Hollywood films in this period, as will be discussed in chapter 7.

Waxman's attempts to compose in a "Japanese style" are evident throughout his score. When Hana-ogi takes Lloyd to a tea ceremony the filmmakers were careful to ensure that we hear the bubbling sound of the boiling kettle—an essential acoustic element in the experience of this Japanese ritualistic tradition and an indication of the filmmakers' authenticity aspirations and attention to detail. However, Waxman gilded the lily, or exoticized the exotic, by adding a melody played by *kotos* at this moment, even though instrumental performance is not typically part of the ceremony. Waxman and his orchestrator Leonid Raab called for a rather elaborate instrumentation for this soundtrack, including bass flute, bass marimba, crotales, mandolin, celeste, and banjo. (Waxman frequently gave detailed orchestration indications and orchestrated some cues himself.) Waxman's score for this film has been repeatedly praised by film historians, particularly for its exotic authenticity. Christopher Palmer deemed the score for *Sayonara* Waxman's "most significant contribution to the 1950s" and claimed that "the idea of using ethnic music, not merely scenically but also *dramatically*, to underscore important action and dialogue scenes, was almost unheard of in the Hollywood of the 1950s."[57] In his liner notes for the re-release of the soundtrack album, Royal S. Brown writes: "What immediately strikes the listener in Waxman's music . . . is the general lack of the gong-xylophone-open-fifth cliches that pervade so much of the pseudo-oriental music heard in film scores."[58] Brown claims that Waxman bridged East and West by incorporating "native instruments" and that he "was also able to subtly incorporate various Japanese modes into some of the thematic material."

Of course, Waxman was not alone among film composers in the 1950s and 1960s in expressing his exotic aspirations instrumentally. Alfred Newman's music for "The Moon Festival" scene in the 1955 film *Love Is a Many-Splendored Thing*, set in Hong Kong, calls for banjo, celesta, vibraphone, bass marimba, gong, temple blocks, claves, anvil, finger cymbals, triangle, and glockenspiel. Parts of this score were created by other composers, including Hugo Friedhofer's contribution titled "Chinese Ballad" for a scene starting on a busy Hong Kong street and then entering a tea shop. Bernard Mayers's orchestration of this number included mandolin, marimba, banjo, tuned temple blocks, bass drum, Chinese cymbal, alto sax, and accordion.[59] Waxman was not the first choice for *Sayonara*. Bronislaw Kaper had been offered $16,000 in March 1957 to compose the score.[60] (In the end, Waxman was signed in May for $25,000.) Kaper later scored the 1965 film *Lord Jim* and related in a 1975 interview that he traveled throughout Cambodia searching for music for this film, but found it all dull.[61] Instead, after conferring with the ethnomusicologist Mantle Hood at the University of California, Los Angeles, he used Balinese gamelan-style music and "smuggled in a little piece which had a little of the *gagaku* character, regardless of geography, and all this. After he dies, after his funeral, I used this high oboe [*hichiriki*] that they have, and the drums. It's an unbelievable effect."[62]

Although he initially rejected the use of actual Japanese music and musicians, Waxman's score reveals his devotion to the film's purported ideal of authenticity and represents a serious attempt at simulating Japanese music.[63] This is evident from the very opening moments of *Sayonara*. Waxman's Main Title music begins with a sustained pitch cluster in the woodwinds and brass. (See Example 6.1.) This "frozen chord" matches the first shot's frozen screen image of birds in flight above a pagoda rooftop. This opening tone cluster, as well as several of the other sustained

Example 6.1 Waxman, *Sayonara*, Main Title opening (Warner Bros., 1957).

chords, corresponds in both pitch and timbre almost exactly to specific clusters produced on the *sho*, the mouth organ used in *gagaku*. (In Example 6.2 I have provided transcriptions of Waxman's chords scored for horns and winds alongside corresponding *sho* clusters.) The twelve shots of the Main Title sequence function as static picture postcards of beautiful Old Japan. These shots are relatively long in duration: nine of them last between ten and fifteen seconds, while one is twenty

Example 6.1 *Continued*

seconds and two are approximately eight seconds each. The camera remains still within each shot and thus increases each shot's perceived length. The transitions between shots also serve to prolong their duration as each shot dissolves into the next. Even the printed titles subtly fade in and then out. While only the first shot is an actual still image, movement within the frame is minimal and gentle and consists of views of tranquil flowing water, strolling people, or light rain falling on a

Example 6.2 Waxman's cluster chords and sho clusters.

a. Main Title, chord held measures 1–5
b. *sho* "otsu" cluster
c. Main Title, chord at measure 11
d. *sho* "takai-ju" cluster

pond. Most of the shots are seen from a medium long distance and there is nothing striking about their camera angles. Eight of the twelve shots feature a bridge within the frame and most of the shots include water and reflections in the water. The printed titles appear in red *japonisme* font.

Waxman's first fifteen bars are closely coordinated with the images of the opening minute of the movie. A large gong stroke is heard at the moment when Marlon Brando's title card appears. Its reverberation appears to set the birds in motion and we hear an ascending spiral of thirty-second note runs in the harpsichord, *kotos*, and harps as the mass of birds circle above the rooftops. The film's title appears just as we hear a female voice sing the first of three statements of the word "sayonara." (The "sayonara" statements here and at the end of the Main Title sequence were sung by a Japanese American named Atsuko Kunimura.) While the first sixty seconds contain both clichéd signals of Japan (gong punctuation) and more innovative simulations of Japanese music (*sho*-like tone clusters and use of the *koto*), the next twenty-five measures are in a strikingly different style. This middle section of the Main Title music consists entirely of an arrangement of Irving Berlin's song "Sayonara" for orchestra and wordless chorus echoing the strings and winds. Prominent violin harmonics, sweeping harps, and the use of a novachord impart an ethereal timbre to this otherwise straightforward setting of the Berlin tune. Berlin's Tin Pan Alley–style pentatonic song contrasts sharply with Waxman's own *japonisme*. The humming chorus was performed by the Euro-American vocalists and is thus even further removed from Waxman's assumptions and attempts at a Japanese exotic sound.

Waxman reluctantly accepted the task of incorporating Berlin's song in his score. His sketches reveal that his original version of this opening music featured an extended duet for *kotos* rather than the arrangement of Berlin's "Sayonara." Waxman's original music was far more mysterious and dramatic in affect, more in synch with the opening and closing sections of the Main Title music and, thus, serving as a true prelude to the story rather than resonating with the timeless beauty depicted in the Main Title shots. (Or, perhaps, the perceived tranquil beauty of the Main Title shots emanates, in part, from Waxman's lush setting of Berlin's melody.) This original music was more rhythmic and quicker in tempo and, thus, worked in counterpoint against the slow shot rhythm, giving the film's opening a particular charge. (The final version of the Main Title music works much more closely with the filming.) This original middle section was clearly structured in five contrasting sections of varying lengths, dynamics, timbres, and textures. We hear an initial tremolo on the two *kotos*, a circular gesture outlining a tritone sonority, parallel tritones, a measure in 5/8, etc. The instrumentation is also distinctive: novachord, "Japanese woodblocks," xylophone, marimba and bass marimba, two harps, harpsichord, two *kotos, shamisen*, bass flute, and a crotalli set. This original music builds to an agitated climax, with *fp* chordal punctuation, completely in contrast with the mood of Waxman's setting of Berlin's "Sayonara" melody in the final version. Thus, the original version of the Main Title score foregrounded Waxman's attempts at creating a Japanese sound, achieved primarily through timbre and texture.

Although he had been informed when hired that Berlin's song would need to be incorporated in the soundtrack, Waxman resisted employing the theme in the Main Title music. This generated a good amount of correspondence between the composer, the director, and the producer who, ultimately, demanded the use of Berlin's song in place of the *koto* duet. Initially, Logan was quite adamant about not allowing Berlin's song—a stylistic intrusion from the past—to be heard with the opening credits. In a telegram from Hawai'i, Logan wrote:

> My one fear in using berlins song has always been that someone would put a big hollywood violin or vocal chorus under the name [*sic*] title . . . i would hate to cheapen this picture by one of those cornball arrangements of a popular song under the titles. I like the use of it over the end title and the other places i dictated to waxman stop please cable me assurance that berlins song is not being sung or played under main title except the few phrases i heard when i was there.[64]

Logan cabled Waxman explaining that he had:

> agreed to put Irving Berlin's song in the picture only after carefully explaining to Bill Goetz [the film's producer] that in doing so I did not want it used as a big theme song in the main title. I didn't mind how often it was used later as long as it fitted the mood of the picture. . . . The thought of it being used as a theme song and pumped across in typical Hollywood fashion with the usual "lush" violins or the angel-choir voices is something I cannot stand. My one horror in doing this picture was the thought that it might in any way be like LOVE IS A MANY SPLENDORED THING.[65]

Clearly, however, Hollywood was determined to have its "lush violins" at the expense of a more persuasive representation of Japanese musical sound.

This significant and late revision to the Main Title music clearly continued to nettle Waxman. Logan did his best to smooth things over, writing to the composer:

have played both titles and must say you orchestrated hours [*sic*] so beautifully that I found no lush hollywoodisms in it both titles are equally beautiful to me and if bill and steve prefer the second one I cannot in all honesty say that I disapprove i cannot tell you how much i admire you and how much i know you have done for the picture even tho i have not heard it all gratefully.[66]

This rings somewhat false given that the final Main Title music does indeed contain the entire song played by lush violins and a humming ethereal chorus. Perhaps the absence of the text made the difference for the director.[67] Logan continued to reach out to Waxman after the film's premiere, informing the composer that Brando said the song had been successfully handled "so as not to hurt the mood of the picture" and that:

> Irving Berlin just called me—exstatic about the picture and your job. He said "I wrote Waxman but I didn't say to him how I appreciated the extra work he had to do because of me. It must have been very difficult for him to have been stuck with my song. He could have written it all him self and suffered less."[68]

Finally, in an undated letter to Waxman, Logan expressed his shock that the composer had not been nominated for an Academy Award for the *Sayonara* score. At this late date Logan assuaged Waxman by putting the blame on Berlin: "Would to god we had never got involved with Irving on it—but that has a long history and it was the only decent thing to do under the circumstances."

Gender Ambiguities and Exotic Masculinities

Sayonara presented American audiences with two cross-dressed Japanese performance traditions. In addition to Hana-ogi's appearance as a performer of male roles in Takarazuka, the film introduces its audience to the *onnagata*, or male performer of female roles in *kabuki*. Several characters inform Lloyd about this cross-dressed performance tradition and he appears flummoxed or bemused each time. As noted above, Logan was determined to create a new role in the narrative for a *kabuki* actor but was concerned that an American female audience would find implausible Eileen's attraction to an actual Japanese male body. He therefore filled the role of Nakamura, a star *onnagata*, with the Mexican actor Ricardo Montalbán, who later starred on the TV series *Fantasy Island* as Mr. Roarke and as the exotic villain Khan in *Star Trek*. (Logan's aspirations for *kabuki* authenticity remain evident in the film given that "Nakamura" is the family name of an actual *kabuki* lineage.) To summarize *Sayonara*'s character and casting alignments: on *this* fantasy island, a white American male falls in love with a Japanese female performer of male roles who is played by a *nisei*, while a white American female apparently falls in love with a Japanese male performer of female roles played by a Mexican in yellowface.

In Hollywood's imagination, exotic music and theater allow for all sorts of cross-cultural fantasies to be realized.

Soon after Lloyd's arrival in Japan, Eileen's mother announces that Eileen will take him to a *kabuki* performance. Lloyd confirms with her that men play the female roles in this tradition and she replies yes, "like at Princeton," in a reference to the Princeton University Triangle Club's long tradition of male cross-dressed performance. (Joshua Logan was himself an alum of this ensemble.) Lloyd is clearly uncomfortable at the performance and, perhaps to affirm publicly his own sexuality, demonstratively kisses Eileen, drawing the attention of a few Japanese members in the audience. (See Figure 6.4.) Eileen is clearly a *kabuki* enthusiast and is rather titillated by the tradition, teasing Lloyd about the gender reversals taking place on stage. We actually hear little of the music given their dialogue in the balcony and the extended backstage shots. At one point Eileen glances off screen and the camera cuts directly backstage to a muscular Montalbán (as Nakamura) wearing only a loincloth as he applies his makeup and is assisted with dressing in his feminine costume. Thus, the film allows us to admire his masculinity before we see him impersonate a Japanese female. Nakamura then changes costumes and appears in the famous lion dance, achieving a transformation in both gender and species. Upon Nakamura's re-emergence as a ferocious lion, Lloyd exclaims: "My lord, that's my father!" (I will forego unpacking the film's rather blatant Freudian underpinning in its representations of Eileen's mother and Lloyd's absent father.) Eileen taunts: "Is he man enough now for you Lloyd?" Lloyd is impressed and asks, "Is that the same fellow?"

Figure 6.4 Representing Kabuki in *Sayonara* (1957). Warner Bros. publicity still.

Viewers might well ask Lloyd's question themselves. Montalbán's performance in the *Sayonara kabuki* scenes is quite impressive. However, just as Lloyd is confused as to the gender of this performer, it is not entirely clear whom we are watching on the *kabuki* stage at every moment. Allegedly, Montalbán used no stand-in for this scene, though in some of the medium long shots of the dancing the performer's identity seems ambiguous to me.[69] While we see Montalbán assume this role, we significantly do not hear him attempt the *onnagata* voice in this scene, a voice that Michener had described as follows:

> Then comes a shock, for they start to speak and they sound like nothing ever heard before on earth. In unbelievably cruel distortions of the human voice they throw sounds to the top of the distant balcony. At first the *kabuki* voice is appalling but soon it weaves an intense dramatic spell. It sounds like Japan centuries ago: harsh, unearthly, powerful. . . . The voice is a piercing cry that rises and falls at least two octaves and sounds like a distant siren in the wind.[70]

We do, of course, hear Montalbán's stilted attempts to sound Japanese in his speech throughout the film, particularly in his awkward, romantically charged dialogue with Eileen.

Eileen and Lloyd meet with Nakamura in his dressing room following the performance. When Nakamura inquires whether he enjoyed the performance, Lloyd quips, "I thought you could use a Marilyn Monroe," but quickly apologizes, embarrassed by his own cultural discomfort. Nakamura seeks to reassure Lloyd and to affirm his own heterosexual masculinity by saying that he is also a great admirer of Ms. Monroe. Their shared admiration for America's most famous white female body is played out in front of Eileen—perhaps suggesting that these two men are somewhat equivalent as potential heterosexual partners for her. In fact, it is evident from early on in the film that Eileen has attended *kabuki* performances and has become acquainted with Nakamura before Lloyd's arrival. She even seems slightly put off when another white American woman interrupts her conversation with Nakamura at a reception in order to request his autograph for her young daughter. When Lloyd eventually forsakes Eileen for Hana-ogi, Eileen appears to turn to Nakamura for comfort. She arrives late and alone at the second *kabuki* performance in the film and receives a message from an attendant inviting her to meet with Nakamura after the performance. From her box, she catches Nakamura's eye as he appears in male costume on the *hanamichi* and, pointing to his note, nods yes. This seems to inspire his exuberant and macho *roppo* exit that follows. Eileen and Nakamura attend a dinner party and, alone with her in a moonlit garden, Nakamura praises her beauty but then rather inscrutably states: "I am not necessarily making love to you." Though their flirtation and some erotic tension is clear, the film does not explicitly depict a romantic union between this Asian male and white female. The film opens up this possibility but ultimately avoids screening this particularly forbidden form of fictional miscegenation. Eileen appears to find her feelings for this Japanese male somewhat peculiar as well. After Lloyd announces in front of the Websters his plans to marry a Japanese woman, Eileen dramatically exits, declaring that there is only one person she wishes to talk to and "oddly enough, he's Japanese!"

Despite these ambiguities, Montalbán's portrayal of Nakamura stands out in this period in Hollywood film for not simply replicating the stereotypical presentation of Japanese men as effeminate and impotent goofs or houseboys.[71] These characters—somewhat like Puccini's marriage broker Goro in *Madama Butterfly*—are most often ridiculed within the narrative for their attempts to imitate the West and for falling awkwardly between two cultures. For example, much of the satirical energy in *Cry for Happy* is aimed at Endo, a would-be Japanese film director who creates a ridiculous Japanese Western titled *The Rice Rustlers of Yokohama Gulch* with Japanese men appearing on the diegetic screen as cowboys and Indians. This film-within-the-film employs "Home on the Range" scored for *tsuzumi, taiko, koto,* and *shamisen.* We watch as the onscreen audience howls with laughter at this ineffectual Japanese male's attempt to create Western popular culture. In a related role in the 1957 *Joe Butterfly,* Burgess Meredith appeared as a subservient middle-aged houseboy in outlandish yellowface, speaking Japlish and walking with wobbly steps. His efforts to aid his impoverished postwar community lead to a large *obon* celebration—complete with chanting, *shamisen,* and *taiko*—featuring the gag of having Japanese children attempt to sing "Chatanooga Choo Choo" with *shamisen* and *taiko* accompaniment.[72] In one of the most notorious examples of yellowface cinematic performance in Hollywood history, Mickey Rooney appeared as a bucktoothed, aesthete, Japanese artistic photographer who lives directly above Holly Golightly in the 1961 *Breakfast at Tiffany's.* We see him stumbling around his Japanese-decorated apartment without his glasses, sitting in a steamy bath, and attempting to hold a solo tea ceremony during one of Golightly's noisy parties. We hear his shouted Japlish with its rapid-fire machine gun rhythms, absurdly sustained vowels, and false-toothed distorted enunciation and timbre. Rooney achieved an extreme yellowvoiced performance to match his exaggerated racist facial cosmetics.

Marlon Brando himself appeared in yellowface and yellowvoice as Sakini, an Okinawan interpreter, in the 1956 *The Teahouse of the August Moon.* (See Figure 6.5.) The film was based on a hugely successful 1953 Broadway play that was derived from a 1951 novel, both of which served as the basis for a 1970 Broadway musical entitled *Lovely Ladies, Kind Gentleman* which had a limited run.[73] The film kicks off with a drum roll as though we will witness a *kabuki* performance and a *shamisen* plays "Sakura" for the producer and director credits. Sakini acts as our narrator, speaking in Japlish, for this postwar tale set in Okinawa in 1946. He declares that Okinawans are grateful for their history of colonization and that they are "most eager to be educated by conquerors, not easy to learn, sometimes very painful, but pain make man think." The grateful villagers present the American officer Captain Fisby (played by Glenn Ford) with a geisha as a present and she sings "Sakura" and plays the *koto* and teaches the Okinawan village women to dance, since they decide that they would all like to be geishas as well. Once the geisha has managed to get

Figure 6.5 Brando in yellowface in *The Teahouse of the August Moon* (1956). MGM publicity still.

the American military men and villagers to build a teahouse, we are treated to a big traditional-style dance and vocal number. The American men lead a chorus of "Deep in the Heart of Texas" in turn. This geisha initially makes Fisby very nervous since he assumes geisha are prostitutes and he protests "don't give me any of that Oriental hanky panky business." However, they fall in love and his self-confidence and effectiveness increases through his relationship with this exotic woman. At the end, Fisby speaks about how he has learned from these clever and charming natives "the wisdom of gracious acceptance" and finds himself unsure "who is the conquered and who's the conqueror." Sakini remains a rather subservient exotic bumpkin throughout, ending the film by addressing us directly on screen with "sayonara."

Perhaps the most ambiguous Hollywood depiction of gender and masculinity in a Japanese setting is discovered in the 1958 Jerry Lewis vehicle, *The Geisha Boy*. Lewis plays a struggling American magician who performs as the Great Wooley in a U.S.O. unit entertaining troops in Japan. His asexual and childlike behavior suggests that he is the "geisha boy" of the film's title. Wooley appears immune to the romantic interests of a white American female character (a masculinized uniformed Sergeant) who complains: "What is it you see in these girls? What is the big difference between American girls and Oriental girls?" Having lost out to a Japanese woman, she declares: "Believe me, the next man I meet I'm gonna forget that so-called American emancipated woman type of independence and treat him just the way the girls in Japan do." Wooley responds: "Good luck." Wooley is a flop as a magician but his performance cheers a Japanese orphaned boy whom he adopts. Wooley's relationship with this boy proves far more central to the film than does his relationship with the boy's aunt, Kimi. Though Kimi appears in a bikini at one point and gazes at Wooley longingly, he seems mostly unaware of this romantic opportunity until they kiss briefly late in the film.

As in most Hollywood narratives set in Japan, the white American male is given a tour of Japanese culture, experiencing all the typical cross-cultural comic confusion and mishaps, but is led by the exotic boy rather than by the Japanese woman. Wooley protests that he has "seen everything there is to see" and has no interest in visiting a geisha house—the geisha phenomenon provokes his anxiety—but the boy leads him inside nevertheless. We hear and see a geisha *kotoist* playing "Sakura" and the music sets Wooley at ease as he eats with chopsticks in rhythm. In a cute sight gag, three young Japanese girls appear as dancing geisha for the entertainment of the boy. Music proves central to Wooley's experience of the exotic nation and he even briefly imitates a pseudo-Chinese operatic voice himself to distract Japanese baseball players and sports an exaggerated *kabuki* facial expression at another point. The film and its music, composed by Walter Scharf, emit a peculiar erotic charge throughout. The Main Title sequence is scored with staccato pentatonicism in counterpoint with soaring string melody as we see a series of posing Japanese women with fans and a final one (apparently nude) with feathers. At the end of the film, Wooley's rabbit Harry gives birth during their magic act to many baby rabbits and is quickly renamed Harriet by a shocked Wooley. Though Wooley unites with Kimi and the boy as a performing family in Japan, no romantic consummation is suggested between this white American male and the Japanese beauty. Wooley does acknowledge Kimi's exotic attraction at one point, declaring: "You're beautiful. I can understand now why Marlon Brando dug this place."[74] This is one of several examples of Hollywood's reflexivity in the film. For example, Sessue Hayakawa appears as the boy's grandfather and we see him directing the building of a small bridge in his garden, wearing the same military uniform and accompanied by the same tune heard in *The Bridge on the River Kwai*, which was released the previous year. Though Wooley's relationship with Kimi remains somewhat unclear and miscegenation is avoided, this film manages to work within the typical Hollywood *japonisme* narrative of the period while making wry allusions to its stereotypical devices. As Naoko Shibusawa remarks, *The Geisha Boy* demonstrates that "[e]ven a feckless American man can become manly by going to Japan and making the right choices."[75]

A handful of films from this period attempted to go further than *Sayonara* in reversing racist representations of Japanese men and in condoning white female/ Japanese male relationships, with mixed success. This required going beyond the infantilism of romantic Japanese men found in early twentieth-century song lyrics, echoed in Burt Bacharach's 1964 "Me Japanese Boy I Love You," and framing them instead as sexually attractive potential partners.[76] These efforts coincided with a campaign to promote the Japanese American actor James Shigeta as the first Japanese matinee idol in Hollywood since Hayakawa's silent film triumphs. (Shigeta's career had been launched as a standards singer in Los Angeles and, particularly, in Japan.) However, Shigeta's characters in this period tend to offer a conflicted amalgam of the traditionalist, stern, samurai-inspired role, recalling Hayakawa's appearance in *The Cheat*, and the refined, poetic, and inscrutable Japanese artist, like *Sayonara's* Nakamura. Repeatedly, Shigeta's characters struggle with their relationship to both Japanese (or, in the case of his character in *The Flower Drum Song*, Chinese) and Western cultures and this tension is frequently symbolized musically. These exotic male characters often feel lost between two worlds.

In Samuel Fuller's 1958 *The Crimson Kimono*, with an intriguing score by Harry Sukman, Shigeta plays a Japanese American homicide detective in Los Angeles named Joe Kojaku who shares an apartment with his white partner and fellow Korean War veteran, Charlie Bancroft. Joe and Charlie investigate the murder of a stripper who had been researching Japanese culture for a new Las Vegas act she planned to call "The Crimson Kimono." As her manager describes the act to the two detectives, we hear fragments of accompanying music as though we too can imagine how this *japonisme* strip show would have looked and sounded in performance. As the manager envisions "this gorgeous geisha makes her entrance in a crimson ki- mono," we hear pentatonic gestures, a film noir–style jazz saxophone line, and some primitivist percussion. Their investigation becomes complicated as both Joe and Charlie fall for their main witness, a young white American female painter. Joe is depicted throughout the film as an artistic type—in sharp contrast to Charlie—and has decorated the apartment with Japanese porcelain figurines and his father's own paintings. He is musical—perhaps even his license plate, MUS 737, was intended to suggest as much—and the white woman is particularly attracted to him when he plays "Aka Tombo (Red Dragonfly)" on the piano for her. (Note that in this scene Joe is offering her Japanese music through a Western medium.) She approaches his piano, her prominent bust visually rhyming with a bust of Beethoven (which is par- ticularly evident in a publicity still of this scene), as Joe seems to fulfill the role of a cultured musical geisha. Knowing that Charlie is in love with this woman as well, Joe feels torn and doubts whether, as a Japanese American, he has any right to enter into a relationship with her. He wrongly believes that Charlie himself holds this racist view and their friendship is torn apart. (The film's publicity poster, however, supports Joe's fears given that the image of Shigeta kissing the white female lead is accompanied by the lurid and racially loaded text: "Yes, this is a beautiful American girl in the arms of a Japanese boy!") Marchetti makes the perceptive point that the film unrealistically has Joe claim that he had never experienced racism before this love triangle developed. The film ultimately ignores the actual racism of the late 1950s and suggests instead that racism in the narrative is but an illusion within Joe's mind.[77]

Racial tensions are paralleled by gender ambiguities in *The Crimson Kimono*. As Marchetti argues, the film's female characters "transgress gender boundaries and engage in behavior considered unacceptable within a male-defined and male-dominated society."[78] The female painter assumes the masculine position by initiating her romance with Joe. In addition, an older female artist named Mac (a rather masculine name) lives as a bohemian with her ear open to all that goes on in the seedy city. We see her smoking a cigar and drinking hard, and first encounter her playing a record of the overture to Rossini's *Barber of Seville*, singing a bit of Figaro's tune. (As an informant to these detectives, she serves as a factotum paid with a flask.) Finally, the initial murder suspect—an effeminate white male librarian and collector of Japanese art—turns out to be the lover of the real killer, a jealous and tough older white woman. The climax of the film takes place during the 1959 Nisei Week Festival in Little Tokyo. During the final chase scene we see the Nisei Week parade and hear an abrupt alternation between the *obon* style music with fake *shamisen* accompanying the dancing Japanese girls and the brass band music of the marching Nisei Boy Scouts. In the end, Joe asserts his masculinity by shooting the fleeing murderer and passionately embracing the young painter. The film ends unambiguously with the sensitive and refined, but also tough, Japanese American male winning the white American girl.

Racial tensions do not resolve as peacefully for the Japanese male, also played by James Shigeta, in *Bridge to the Sun* (1961). This film was based on the autobiography of Gwendolyn Terasaki, a white American woman who married a Japanese diplomat, Hidenari "Terry" Terasaki, in the years leading up to Pearl Harbor. (As though to prove its basis in fact, the film starts with a shot of the book itself.) Music plays a major symbolic role throughout the film. Georges Auric's Main Title music opens with a brassy dissonant assertion, only to shift abruptly to gentle variations on "O Susanna," a song we will see and hear Terry and Gwen sing together on their first date, allowing Gwen to express her Southern heritage and Terry to display his knowledge of American culture. Terry and Gwen first meet at a reception at the Japanese Embassy in DC in 1935. He leads her from the party with its (implied) diegetic cocktail jazz to a private room in order to show her the embassy's collection of Japanese *objets d'art*. This scene seems to refer directly, even in the camera movement and angles, to the parallel sequence in De Mille's *The Cheat*. Terry, like Hayakawa's Tori in the silent film, is clearly refined and highly knowledgeable and Gwen appears to be immediately attracted to him as he points out paintings and *noh* masks. They kiss less than fifteen minutes into the picture and are then married and travel to Japan. Throughout the film, Gwen clearly finds Terry sexually attractive and typically takes the lead in moving toward intimacy. The contemporary significance of the representation of interracial romance was surely heightened, as Marchetti notes, by the decision to employ c. 1960 fashions rather than costumes approximating clothing of the 1930s and 1940s.[79]

In Japan, Gwen experiences difficulties, both comic (chopsticks, coed baths, learning to bow, etc.) and more serious, in adjusting to Japanese customs. Terry suddenly begins to act like a traditional Japanese husband and expects her to play the role of a traditional Japanese wife.[80] Gwen attempts to play the part of a Japanese hostess, donning a kimono and black wig, but she rebels and in a fight with Terry indicts the Japanese treatment of women, declaring that in Tennessee "at least they treat women like human beings!" After their fight, Terry fails to find comfort at a geisha house where we see and hear a geisha singing and playing *shamisen* and another dancing, and returns home to apologize and to declare "I do not want a Japanese wife, I want you." This marks Terry's gradual alienation from his own culture, which is confirmed musically in a scene right before the attack on Pearl Harbor when the Terasakis are living once more in DC. Terry returns home from work to find Gwen and their young daughter playing on the floor of the living room with a visible record player playing "Japanese music," which seems to employ a harpsichord and celesta to approximate the *koto*. Terry rejects Auric's fake Japanese music and asks his daughter to put on something "happy" instead, proceeding to waltz around the room with Gwen to the Western music recording his daughter chooses. Following Pearl Harbor, the family is deported to Japan and the film incorporates documentary footage of war scenes, including a shot of the emperor on horseback accompanied by an excerpt of "Kimigayo" on the soundtrack, as though we have slipped back into a *Why We Fight* series film. As the war plays out, Terry works ineffectually to encourage Japan to surrender and experiences a crisis of confidence in his manhood, feeling impotent as other Japanese men have donned military uniforms. He becomes increasingly ill and weaker, and is seen walking with a cane. Knowing he will soon die, he sacrifices by sending Gwen and their daughter back to the United States for a better life, assuming the role of a male Madame Butterfly by deciding to die alone.

In a final racial twist to Hollywood's Cold War representations of exotic men and white American men in Japan, the protagonist of *A Girl Named Tamiko*, Ivan, is identified as being half Chinese and half Caucasian (Russian) and, thus, initially appears hopelessly trapped between the two positions. Ironically, Ivan is played by a white British actor (of Lithuanian Jewish heritage) and Tamiko, the ideal Japanese woman, is played by France Nuyen who was half Vietnamese and half French. Before the film begins, Ivan has had a casual relationship with a bar girl named Eiko who sweetly tells him that he is the only man she does not charge for her pleasures. However, he ultimately rejects Eiko, the one Japanese female love interest in the film actually played by a Japanese woman, Miyoshi Umeki. The plot of both the 1959 novel by Ronald Kirkbride and the 1962 film directed by John Sturges, with a score by Elmer Bernstein, is racy in every sense of that word.[81] Ivan is terribly racist against the Japanese at first, and wants to emigrate to the United States in order to "lose the Oriental part of himself." In an astonishing exchange proclaiming the utopian virtues of the United States in this racially charged Cold War period, Ivan claims that in America "you get your chance, no matter what color you are." Tamiko admits that the Japanese are racist, but that they "are learning." He quips that they had "to lose a war to learn" and she responds, "then perhaps it was a healthy experience." However, Ivan's racism is "cured" once he rejects the white American woman and falls fully in love with Tamiko.

Music proves pivotal to Ivan's conversion in racial perception. In the novel, he hears music ("a group of musicians played a weird dirge on flutes and other wind instruments, which echoed eerily through the woods") that seemed like "a scene from the Kabuki, not real at all" and sees the funeral procession out his window. This exotic sound and vision tells him, with the "chanting still ringing in his ears," to go to Tamiko and propose marriage.[82] He feels unworthy of this ideal exotic woman: "In her simplicity and oneness with nature she possessed an eternal essence that was alien to him, almost frightening. She was, like the earth upon which her temples were placed, inexplicable and inexpressible" (p. 203). In the cinematic version of this nocturnal scene, we hear a recording of a Japanese funeral chant counterpointed with Bernstein's instrumental backing of solemn string chords punctuated by conga, tam-tam, finger cymbals, and bell tree. Representations of Japanese music occur at various crucial moments in the film. In an earlier scene Ivan takes the blonde American woman to a geisha house and we see geishas dancing to the folk songs "Ume Ni Mo Haru" ("The Spring Plum") and "Sakura," which are sung and played by two geishas on *shamisen* and *koto*. (A transcription of "The Spring Plum" made by Phil Boutel is found on a single sheet in the short score materials at Paramount Studios, and the cue sheet credits a brief, ascending *koto* line heard in this scene to Walter Scharf and the soundtrack of *The Geisha Boy*.) Bernstein composed his own version of Japanese music to accompany a sequence depicting a Judai festival parade as Ivan snaps photographs. The film lingers on this exotic procession, which resembles similar exotic processions in World War II anti-Japanese documentaries. At other points in the score, Japanese music is approximated by such instrumental combinations as English horn, three alto flutes, and *shamisen* and with indications such as "banjo ala shamisen." Tamiko introduces Ivan to other cultural sites and sounds and his initial aversion to Japan is entirely overcome. Tamiko's love and devotion allows the racially ambiguous Ivan to reassert his manhood and to achieve his goal of assuming the dominant position of the white American male in Japan.

Disdaining Musical Miscegenation

The two most significant alterations in the 1957 *Sayonara* to Michener's original story (Hana-ogi ultimately agreeing to marry Lloyd and the suggestion of romance between Eileen and Nakamura) were both aimed at making clear anti-racist statements. Just before the end of the film, Lloyd confronts Hana-ogi and once more proposes marriage. She is torn and asks what their children would be, to which he replies: "They'd be half Japanese and half American. They'd be half yellow and half white. They'd be half you and half me." Thus, the film makes a strong statement endorsing miscegenation, at least in cases involving white men and Japanese women. (Lloyd's formulation appears to leave Japanese Americans out of the equation and takes for granted that the term "American" actually implies a European heritage.) Several of the filmmakers made their socially progressive aspirations for *Sayonara* quite clear. Joshua Logan had also directed Rodgers and Hammerstein's Broadway musical version of Michener's 1947 *Tales of the South Pacific* which sought to counter racism with the number "You've Got to Be Carefully Taught."[83] In an interview for the *New York Times*, Logan claimed that with *Sayonara*:

> We are trying to say that the twain have met, and we ought to do something about it. We have brought the old Japanese-American Madame Butterfly theme up to date. . . . We hope that American men and women will be more understanding of the problems of our two races after they see the picture. It will give them an illuminating view of a problem they have only heard about. . . . We also show that the Japanese are just as prejudiced against our race as we are against theirs in regard to marriage.[84]

Again, by "American men and women" and "our race" Logan had in mind white US citizens, his target audience. Franz Waxman was also committed to the film's progressive messages and suggested in a memo to the film's producer that they hold a "Sayonara Ball" in conjunction with "big organizations concerned with racial problems or other peace organizations" in New York on opening night. His plan was for the invited guests to appear in Japanese costumes "which will lend color and excitement to this opening" and he assumed that Japanese citizens and the ambassador's staff in DC would be happy to assist.[85] Of course, Waxman's plan to "lend color" and counter racism by dressing up Japanese was constrained by the norms of his time, as was noted above with Logan's casting conundrums for the *kabuki* actor.[86] As Robert Stam and Louise Spence have concluded: "In many consciously anti-colonialist films, a kind of textual uneven development makes the film politically progressive in some of its codes but regressive in others."[87]

For his part, Brando adopted a Southern accent in order to emphasize Lloyd's struggle to overcome his disdain for miscegenation. (Truth be told, his version of a Southern accent is rather odd and inconsistent. When his Marine buddy asks in an incredulous tone, "What part of the South are you from?" Lloyd responds: "from all over.") In Orientalist fashion, *Sayonara* played out in an exotic setting domestic concerns in the late 1950s about (primarily) black and white miscegenation. A few works predating *Sayonara*, of both the Romantic Madame Butterfly and combat film molds, actually dealt with issues of American racism more directly. For example, in Ted Pollack's March 1957 play *Wedding in Japan* (preliminary versions of which had been performed as early as 1949 and 1952), a racist white Southern officer becomes infuriated when he discovers that the Japanese woman he desires plans to marry an African American soldier under his command.[88] The play opens with the Japanese woman dancing to an American jazz record, with the stage directions indicating that "she is graceful but obviously learning something new." Her African American boyfriend arrives and replaces the jazz record with a recording of Japanese music, explaining that he needs to learn Japanese customs in order to please her mother. She proceeds to attempt to teach him to dance Japanese style. The Southern officer fails in his effort to transfer the African American and then frames him for attempted murder and successfully has him court-martialed. In the initial version of the script, the Japanese woman was to rush into the courtroom and proclaim his innocence before stabbing herself to death. The final version of the script replaces the suicide with a love dialogue between the two, before the African American is declared guilty. In this radically progressive play, the exotic Japanese setting serves as a backdrop for a blunt anti–Jim Crow statement.[89] However, even this work deflects domestic fears of miscegenation by focusing on a Japanese female/black male relationship rather than on one involving white and black protagonists.

As we have seen, in numerous Hollywood films from this period, music symbolizes both romantic and broader cultural forms of miscegenation. Although he failed to win a third Oscar for his efforts in *Sayonara*, Waxman's attempts to meld Japanese and Western music did receive some critical praise. Writing in the *New York Times*, Bosley Crowther found that: "On the whole, the musical score of Franz Waxman suggests the crystal tinkling music of Japan and helps the moods."[90] Waxman's cross-cultural musical fusion was deemed a selling point for the film and soundtrack, with the liner notes to the 1957 RCA soundtrack recording proclaiming: "All the music will charm and delight you as it evokes and combines images of the Eastern and Western worlds." However, not all of the music in *Sayonara* proved to delight the critics. The two Matsubayashi performance scenes received mostly negative comments and caused confusion in the press. Critics of the film were bewildered by these scenes, claiming that the performance "looks rather like Oriental week at the Music Hall."[91] In fact, the depiction of this form of exotic performance undermined the entire film for some critics. This was clearly the case for the reviewer in *Time* magazine:

> *Sayonara* (Warner) is a modern version of *Madame Butterfly* which has gained in social significance but lost its wings—Puccini's music.... Having already seen the overdressed girlie show she works in, a Western viewer may be somewhat confused by her attitude. But Brando has to pretend to take the situation seriously, and it plainly bores him.[92]

On close investigation, these scenes prove to be a complex example of cultural collision and fusion through music, one that challenges all notions of musical "authenticity" and forces us to reconsider what constituted "Japanese music" in the twentieth century.

"Matsubayashi" is a fictional term that Logan employed when the real all-female Takarazuka theater company flatly refused to participate in the making of this film. Instead, the "Shochiku Kagekidan Girls Revue" is given credit, with LeRoy Prinz as supervisor and Masaya Fujima as technical adviser for these scenes. The actual Takarazuka company was founded in 1914 as a form of all-female musical theater performance featuring both "nippon pieces" and *yōmono* (Western) pieces. From its inception, Takarazuka was intended to merge elements of Japanese traditional culture with Western musical and theatrical traditions. In an oft-quoted indicative remark, Ichizo Kobayashi, the founder of Takarazuka, expressed the genre's embrace of Western influences by proclaiming in 1923 that "if a shamisen can't be heard [in a modern theater] then use an orchestra."[93] Takarazuka has always actively absorbed features of contemporary Western performance styles. Indeed, *otokoyaku* performers in the 1950s allegedly studied Marlon Brando movies as a model of male posture and body language.[94] Betty Grable's diegetic staged performance of "Japanese Girl Like 'Merican Boy" in the 1951 film *Call Me Mister*—sung in Japlish with exotically enhanced orchestration—might be said to resemble Takarazuka production numbers. Grable first appears as a geisha in yellowface, along with numerous other fan fluttering and toddling female performers dressed in pseudo-Japanese fashion, before her quick gender and nationality change into an American male sailor for the tap dance closer to the song that she performs with three white male dancers. (Through the magic of Hollywood, it is as though the exotic Butterfly singing of her longing for an American GI is suddenly transformed into Pinkerton displaying his prowess through dance.) However, any resemblance between this staged sequence and Takarazuka is likely due to the fact that Busby Berkeley was responsible for the choreography in this film and his production style has been said to have influenced Takarazuka in the 1930s and beyond. Cross-cultural influence between Japan and the United States has repeatedly proved circular.

Critics were equally hostile during both Takarazuka's 1939 and 1959 tours of North America. New York reviewers reacted with horror. In 1939, John Martin dismissed Takarazuka in the following manner: "It is a girl show, frankly billed as such, and whether in Niponese or any other language, the aroma of honky-tonk is virtually the same the world over." He confessed that the experience made him "want to rush home and browse in Zoe Kincaid's book on Kabuki or read one or two of Arthur Waley's Noh translations to remind one's self of some of the true glories of Japan's theatre and dance arts."[95] The Japanese male performance traditions are honored here by the critic, while the female performance with its threat of musical miscegenation is rejected. Martin's verdict was no more positive twenty years later when, once again in the *New York Times*, on 17 September 1959 he referred to a performance by the Takarazuka company at the Metropolitan Opera House as "an unclassifiable hodgepodge," reporting that in the show "a Western orchestra discourses in old-fashioned Tin Pan Alley style, with hints of the later Caribbean rhythms, and a great deal of fox-trotting" and summing up the production as "a long, thin, and sterile crossing of East and West, and not the best aspects of either. Happily, we are all aware of the rich artistic and theatrical heritage of the Japanese, and will not be deceived." In Martin's view, the West is to be blamed for the abomination of Takarazuka since America had sent over the lowest elements of its culture to Japan and the Japanese repackaged them, sending them back with the Takarazuka tour to haunt American audiences.

Despite the consistently negative criticism that Takarazuka received from American reviewers, I note that the 1987 musical of *Sayonara* emphasized and expanded the presentation of this genre. Takarazuka is even celebrated within these scenes. In the Act I performance, Hana-ogi sings "Welcome to Takarazuka World!" and the lyrics of this number emphasize the gender reversals of this performance tradition. This scene also features performance by bare-legged dancers in a fairly accurate representation of the typical big finale numbers in Takarazuka. However, both Takarazuka scenes in the musical feature substantial *taiko* drumming performance by a female ensemble, a creative decision inspired, perhaps, by the contemporaneous popularity in North America of the touring Japanese *taiko* ensemble Kodo. Act II opens with a second Takarazuka performance scene that enacts the Tanabata festival and again features the *taiko* ensemble. As they conclude the Tanabata tale the ensemble sings a "sayonara" song as a closer.

What American critics found most disturbing, whether in the scenes from *Sayonara* or at performances of the actual Takarazuka company on tour, was the presumed inauthentic use of American stage music and, more generally, the exotic other's attempts to imitate the West. Whether acknowledged or not, a false equation of racial purity with musical authenticity appears to undergird much of the negative reactions to Japanese attempts to appropriate features of American popular culture. However, a glance at the cue sheet reveals that in the *Sayonara* Matsubayashi scenes, several of those musical moments sounding most Western were the work of two Japanese composers, while those sections sounding at least vaguely Japanese were composed by the German-American Waxman. Again, the actual Takarazuka theater company was founded, in part, with the aim of "catching up" to Euro-American music—a process that had been encouraged by Americans in the late nineteenth century and that was driven by the premise that modernization required cultural Westernization. By the 1950s, Takarazuka was perhaps the most popular form of music theater in Japan and was presenting revues and musicals based on Euro-American literature and opera, in combination with *kabuki* production techniques, and in a fundamentally Western musical idiom. The fragmented representation of Takarazuka performance in *Sayonara* proves no less authentically Japanese than most of the film's presentations of Japanese music and theater. I note that the more recent July 2016 performance of *Chicago* by a Takarazuka company at the Lincoln Center Festival in New York was met with critical complaints that the company had not offered a production more Japanese in style.

Cultural anxiety is often cloaked by comedy. Numerous films, songs, and television episodes from this period treated cultural cross-dressing and musical mixtures as hilarious. In "The Ricardos Go to Japan" (first broadcast on 27 November 1959), the penultimate episode of one of the most successful television series in history (*The Lucy and Desi Comedy Hour*), Lucille Ball and Desi Arnaz travel to Japan to perform in Tokyo and to scout Japanese musical talent. This episode makes comic reference to the full tradition of American musical *japonisme*—past, present, and future. Robert Cummings, appearing as a guest star, is featured singing "The

Japanese Sandman" in his bubble bath, and announces that he is "starting a picture next week" in Japan. (He would soon appear in *My Geisha* as the fictional actor who assumes the role of Pinkerton in the filming of *Madama Butterfly*.) When Lucy is asked how she knows so much about Japan, she responds "I sat through *Sayonara* twice," poking fun at that film's attempts to introduce Americans to Japanese culture. In a typical sight gag, Fred is described as the "American Sessue Hayakawa" when he appears in a kimono. Prefiguring *My Geisha*, Lucy and Ethel spy on their men at a geisha house and then disguise themselves as geisha, speaking Japlish and, in Lucy's case, gamely attempting to dance with the geishas to *shamisen* and flute in front of their deluded husbands. However, the oddest moment of musical miscegenation in the episode occurs right before these American wives enter into the geisha dinner party room. Dressed in male Japanese attire, Desi Arnaz (as Ricky Ricardo) performs his hit rhumba number "Cuban Pete," but here retitled with Japanese lyrics as "Tokyo Pete" and accompanied by three geishas on *taiko*, flute, and *shamisen*. This awkward performance is comically undermined as Robert Cummings begins to clink out a rhythm by beating his chopsticks on an empty bowl.

Just as Tin Pan Alley–era songs had joked about the (im)possibility of Japanese jazz, songs and films in the 1950s and 1960s presented Japanese attempts at rock 'n' roll for their comic potential. In Jack Burger and Jay Haskell's 1957 song "Japanese Rock and Roll/Tonkabushi Rock and Roll" (spelled "Tonkobushi" on recordings of this novelty number), a Pinkerton character has apparently tarried too long in Japan and sings accompanied by open fifths ("Yoi, yoi, yoi!") and in Japlish and pentatonicism, declaring (with a blue third): "I go back to the land of Rock and Roll." His Butterfly answers him, first in something like *sprechstimme*, insisting that the Japanese have rock 'n' roll as well and pointing to the folk song "Tonka Bushi" as an example. She then promises that there will be "no more Shina no yoru" (though she sings a bit of the "China Nights" melody at this very moment). The American male decides to stay so that "Butterfly no hab to griebe." However, the musical punch line at the heart of this clever song is that Butterfly's "Tonkabushi Rock and Roll" in the chorus is presented as yet another failed attempt by a Japanese to imitate American popular music. I noted in chapter 4 the rejection of Japanese women singing rock 'n' roll by Paul, the fictional director, in the 1962 film *My Geisha*. Similarly, in yet another 1962 film set in Japan, *A Majority of One*, the Jewish American mother's cultural unease in the foreign land (as well as her discomfort with youth culture more generally) is symbolized by her unsuccessful attempts to select a source of entertainment in her new exotic home. She turns on the television but rejects the Low-Highs playing "Oh My Darling Clementine," complaining that she can hear this back home in the States. (Her Japanese houseboy protests, declaring "oh, but we are hep cats for American music" as he plays a bit of air guitar.) She changes the channel and is met with a broadcast of a *kabuki* play, but she rejects this music of *shamisen* and voice as well. She then hears "Japanese music" on the radio (played on *shamisen* but apparently newly composed for the film) and says "Oy. Try the Armed Forces station maybe." Finally, in *Japanese War Bride* (1952) the exotic woman's inescapable foreignness in the United States is displayed as she attempts to dance to boogie woogie at a party. Emblematic of the community's rejection of her, the white women at the party laugh at her attempts, disdainfully dismissing her dancing as "the old Japanese one-step."

Though Japanese attempts to emulate American popular music have been consistently derided in American popular culture, there is one exception that proves the rule. Kyu Sakamoto's 1960 recording of "Ue wo Muite Aruko" ("I Look Up as I Walk"), by Hachidai Nakamura and Rokusuke Ei, topped the charts in the United States in 1963 and is one of the best-selling singles of all time—a unique feat for a Japanese popular song. However, the song owed its success to a fundamental cross-cultural misunderstanding of authorial intent. In the United States the song was released as "Sukiyaki," despite the fact that this Japanese beef dish has nothing to do with the lyrics. The new title was selected because it was a Japanese word that many Americans knew, though routinely mispronounced. The song was intended to express the author's frustration and dejection given the failure of Japanese student protests against the US occupation. The lyrics have been consistently understood instead as expressing the protagonist's lament for a lost love. The song has been repeatedly recorded by American artists, including in 1980 by the African American disco group A Taste of Honey. The sheet music and album cover for their smooth and slow R&B version of the song features the two female African American lead performers of the band—Janice-Marie Johnson (who was also of Native American heritage) and Hazel Payne—both dressed in kimonos and standing on a bridge in a Japanese-style garden. Their version of the song featured new lyrics in English that made the dejection after a failed romance topic explicit and that ends with a sultry whispered "sayonara." Though in English, their version of the song aimed for enhanced musical *japonisme* by including a solo part for *koto*, played by June Kuramoto (a founding member of the jazz fusion group Hiroshima) on the recording. In live performances, Payne played the *koto* part herself and Johnson danced with a fan. Both women typically appeared in kimonos when performing the song, as in their appearance on the television show Solid Gold.[96] A Taste of Honey's performances of "Sukiyaki" point to Afro-Asian musical fusions, new forms of musical miscegenation that developed in jazz and then hip-hop in the late twentieth century, as will be noted in subsequent chapters.

Reversing Cross-Cultural Perspectives

The word "sayonara" is spoken at a couple crucial moments in *Sayonara*. As Lloyd discovers the dead bodies of Kelly and Katsumi, Hana-ogi peers in through a window herself and whispers a sad "sayonara" to the dead couple and then to Lloyd, whom she plans to leave forever in order to retain her traditional performance role in Takarazuka and, perhaps, to avoid the sad fate of her friend Katsumi. At the film's end we hear the word once again, but this time spoken publicly in response to a reporter who asks the happy couple what they wish to say to the military brass and the Takarazuka directors. Lloyd ponders for a moment and then speaks for them both: "you can tell them we say sayonara." (Of course, it is not at all clear that Lloyd will follow Hana-ogi in leaving his profession behind.) Embedded within Lloyd's final line are several significant farewells—a farewell to exotic Japan now that Lloyd has regained his manhood; a displacement of exotic music as we hear the jubilant closing rendition of Berlin's "Sayonara" melody and the voices of the white chorus; and a silencing of Takarazuka as Hana-ogi leaves her career. The implication of the ending is that with the film's mission accomplished—having presented a positive depiction of the new exotic ally, an exotic feminine model for white American women to emulate, and a partial rebuke of the racism so clearly festering on the home front—the Japanese setting has served its purpose.

Contemporaneous with Hollywood's positive depictions of the seductive singing geisha, some Japanese films attempted, in striking contrast, to suggest a break with this particular past. The US Occupational authorities proved keenly interested in shaping the development of postwar Japanese cinema, initially banning period films and pressuring directors to include shots of kissing.[97] Much of the American focus on monitoring Japanese film worked in tandem with a broader attempt to reform the position of Japanese women in Japanese society. Representations of a "new Japanese woman" continued in Japanese film after the occupation ended. For example, in Mizoguchi's 1953 A Geisha a young geisha refuses to accept a patron and asserts that the new constitution should protect women's rights in Japan. The film's diegetic geisha music is so strongly associated with the parties at which the heroine must appear traditionally subservient that it takes on an oppressive tone in the film. Strikingly, at a moment of emotional climax between the young geisha and her older protector a solo violin expresses their sisterly bond, before the music shifts back to the diegetic geisha music signaling that they must return to work and to the claustrophobic realm of the geisha party. The subtle implication of this moment is that only Western-style music expresses true emotion and that it offers some promise for a better future for Japanese women.[98] Again, at the very moment when Hollywood presented the subservient Japanese geisha as a model for white American women, the US Occupational authorities were promoting the liberated American wife as a model for postwar Japanese women. These representational efforts inevitably proved problematic as American servicemen increasingly married Japanese women and attempted to negotiate their relationships either in Japan or back home. Sayonara ends with the triumphant and defiant union of Lloyd and Hana-ogi. However, despite the celebratory full orchestral and choral statement of "Sayonara" at the film's end, it is not clear what the future will hold for this cross-cultural couple.

The representation of children in popular japonisme most directly shapes an audience's understanding of a work's position on miscegenation and cross-cultural relationships. Recall that Madame Butterfly named her child Trouble and that with their love suicide, Kelly and Katsumi sacrificed the life of their unborn child.

(*Sayonara* ends before Lloyd and Hana-ogi begin their married life and thus avoids the task of representing their children.) Miscegenation was treated tragically by Pearl S. Buck in her 1952 novel *The Hidden Flower*. This story is centered on the life of a Japanese American woman whose father had moved her family to Japan in order to avoid internment. During the Korean War she falls in love with a white GI and marries him. Back in the States, she internalizes the widespread opposition to interracial children and to their marriage. Discovering that she is pregnant, she leaves her white husband and travels to Los Angeles in search of someone who will adopt her mixed-race child. Only a female doctor, who is also a Jewish concentration camp survivor, agrees to do so. After the failure of her interracial marriage and giving up her child, the Japanese American woman returns to Japan in order to marry a Japanese man. In each of these cases, the mixed-raced child constitutes a social problem, one most often resolved with a sacrifice by the exotic mother.

Hana-ogi's concerns about what life would be like for her and her children in the United States remain unexplored in *Sayonara*. However, an earlier film addressed these questions head-on. The 1952 *Japanese War Bride*, starring Shirley Yamaguchi as Tae (the Japanese bride) and directed by King Vidor, focused almost entirely on the US reception of interracial marriage between white men and Japanese women, with only the first fifteen minutes set in Japan. The requisite plucked harps, pentatonic woodwind melodies, and gong mark Tae's exotic home and are heard again as she unwraps and displays her Japanese dolls in her new American house. (Her five court musician dolls are accompanied by a faster figuration on piano that more closely resembles Indonesian gamelan music.) Tae is rejected by her husband's American friends and by her duplicitous sister-in-law who is nearly always accompanied on the soundtrack with a jazz clarinet line. Tae runs away with their baby after an anonymous letter claims she committed adultery with their Japanese American neighbor. She nearly jumps into the sea, following the Madame Butterfly character in the 1922 *Toll of the Sea*, but is stopped by her husband. The film—like the later *Sayonara*—emphasizes and ultimately condones this cross-cultural relationship by screening multiple kisses between Tae and her husband, as well as by focusing on her pregnancy and their baby. However, *Japanese War Bride* makes clear that many white Americans (particularly white women) were not ready to accept miscegenation.[99]

Hollywood films of this period frequently turned to children to make anti-racist statements. In *Escapade in Japan*, released along with *Sayonara* in 1957, the friendship and adventures of a white American boy (Tony) and a Japanese boy (Hiko) serve to project a message of racial tolerance and reconciliation.[100] Traveling to join his parents who are on the verge of divorce, Tony survives a plane crash off the coast of Japan and is rescued by Hiko and his parents. Hiko speaks English and befriends Tony. When the Japanese father calls the police, the young boys mistakenly assume Tony is in trouble and they agree to run away together. We are then given a grand tour of the Japanese countryside during their travels. The exotic setting is signaled musically in the soundtrack, credited to Max Steiner, in several anhemitonic pentatonic melodies with a banjo and cimbalom suggesting the *shamisen* and *koto* and an alto flute approximating the *shakuhachi*. When the boys witness a large-scale geisha performance at a theater, we see the geisha playing *shamisen* and drums and dancing and appear to hear actual geisha musical performance. The boys stay at a geisha house and are charmingly entertained as though they are tired Japanese businessmen after a long day at the office. When the geisha give them a bath, Tony exclaims "just like in the movies!"—a Hollywood character acclaiming Hollywood's didactic *japonisme*. Both of the boys thoroughly enjoy the geishas' musical performance and clap along. Tony's assimilation into this exotic culture and the film's general premise that children are innocent of racist perceptions are most clearly symbolized late in the film when the boys join in with the singing of other Japanese children on a school bus. In the film's final chase scene the worried parents finally catch up to the boys. Of course, it is the white American father who rescues them from a precarious rooftop perch and it is clear that the entire escapade has succeeded primarily in reuniting the white American parents.

At an early point in the adventure, Tony asks his exotic friend: "How come your eyes go up?" Hiko responds in kind: "I don't know. How come yours don't." This innocent exchange suggests an alternative perspective on Hollywood's revisionist attempts to represent the Japanese in the postwar period. Perhaps such moments hinted to white American audiences, however briefly, that the exotic other is capable of looking and listening and even speaking back across the cultural divide. As Hana-ogi reveals to Lloyd following her extended silence during their first private meeting in *Sayonara*: "You have been watching me, but I have been watching you too." Indeed, while American interest in Japanese music has been rather fickle during the past century and a half, the Japanese have more consistently employed Euro-American musics for their own purposes. Following Hana-ogi, Japan continues to sing "sayonara" to its musical past while embracing the west.

Such films as *Sayonara* betray an interest in reshaping Japan and Japanese music in conformance with Hollywood's imagination. Repeatedly, as we have seen, white filmmakers appeared determined to speak and sing for the Japanese, at first moving toward, but then turning away from actual Japanese voices and musical sounds. We will discover in the next chapter that Hollywood films and other forms of American entertainment frequently turned to Japanese American composers and musicians for assistance with musical representations of exotic Japan.

7

Representing the Authentic from Japanese American Perspectives

In the 1949 Columbia Pictures film *Tokyo Joe*, Humphrey Bogart portrays an American in postwar Japan searching for his missing wife.[1] Early in the film, he thinks he hears her singing the song she always sang, only to discover that it is a recording of her voice. Her song, "These Foolish Things," will haunt him throughout the film. At one point, he hears from his upstairs office the song performed below by a Japanese nightclub singer in unaccented English and appears momentarily entranced. However, recalling that a Japanese body is producing the music, he rejects the performance. Going downstairs to see the Japanese singer would have only deepened his disappointment. Late in the film we see and hear the Japanese vocalist again performing "These Foolish Things" as Joe (the Bogart character) rushes into the nightclub and ascends the stairs, only to discover his Japanese male friend committing ritual suicide. At the moment of discovery, we hear the singer downstairs switch to Japanese lyrics and reach the song's final cadence just as Joe pulls the sword from his friend's belly and the sequence ends. The switch in language helps to underscore the friend's (and the vocalist's) ultimate otherness.

Racial perception is most commonly considered a task for the eyes achieved at the moment anatomical difference is encountered.[2] In fact, visible racial signs can racially predetermine auditory perception. Hearing alone is often not deemed trustworthy in the (apparently) crucial process of discerning and classifying race. Consider the initial reception of Elvis Presley, Nat "King" Cole, or non-black rappers. These performers surprised and provoked some listeners who perceived a disjuncture between their racialized voices heard on the radio and their skin colors observed on TV or in live performance. Moments of racial confusion, particularly those arising from a perceived racial mismatch in sound and image, seem to produce a psychological shock as they blur the boundaries between self and other. Seeing an Asian body producing an assumed "white" or "black" sound has repeatedly provoked such confusion, disappointment, or even ridicule in mainstream American popular culture.

The *Tokyo Joe* sequence offers an apt allegory of the Japanese American social condition. To a greater degree than other minorities in the United States, Asian Americans remain stuck in limbo as "perpetual foreigners"[3] no matter how white they may sound. As Henry Yu writes: "For Asian Americans, whether you dance an exotic dance or try to waltz like everyone else, you are still exotic."[4] This perceived doubleness was strikingly illustrated by sociologist Robert Parks in 1926. Upon interviewing a Japanese American woman who sounded perfectly "white" to his ears, Parks remarked: "I was still not able to escape the impression that I was listening to an American woman in a Japanese disguise."[5] Ironically, in the nightclub sequence from *Tokyo Joe* we actually are seeing and hearing an American woman producing the music, a woman whose singing voice lacked any trace of a Japanese accent. Not the white woman whom Bogart seeks, but a Japanese American—the *nisei* (i.e., second-generation) singer Karie Shindo, who at certain points in her career appeared with Lionel Hampton and the Mills Brothers and who was the sister of Tak Shindo, himself barely visible in the background as the accordion player.[6]

Tak Shindo (1922–2002) led an extraordinary musical career while remaining primarily in the background.[7] He served as arranger, composer, and musical adviser for film, television, radio, and Las Vegas revues. (See Box 7.1 for a chronology of Shindo's career.) He released several successful albums in the exotica genre, was a dance band leader who never missed a New Year's Eve in forty years, performed in recording sessions on *koto* and on a variety of band instruments, acted in bit parts in Hollywood, served as a translator and tour guide in Japan, was a musical columnist and publisher, studied historical musicology and Asian religions—earning a master's degree with a thesis on *shakuhachi* history—and, as an associate professor, taught world music courses and directed jazz ensembles at the college level. Prefiguring the dynamics of 1980s world beat, Shindo suddenly found the mainstream spotlight shining on him in the late 1950s as the representative of Japanese musical culture in Hollywood film and television. Several of his albums from the 1950s and 1960s—combining elements of Japanese music with the big band style—received renewed attention in the 1990s as part of the exotica/cocktail/lounge revival. Shindo's career is significant for the study of Asian American history, musical exoticism and racial representation, and the history of Japanese American jazz. Although he was clearly exceptional and not representative of *nisei* musicians, his life and career were fundamentally shaped by the *nisei* experience and will serve as a framework in this chapter for considering Japanese American perspectives on exoticism.

Early in his career, Shindo frequently inspired confusion by composing and arranging jazz music. As he put it: "They were just kind of surprised by the fact that I could write jazz; they thought I was just writing some Oriental music. . . . Frankly, the thing is, whether I'm Japanese, or black, or white, doesn't make any difference. If you're born and raised here you know more about jazz than you would [anything else]."[8] Shindo's statement appears to resonate with Ingrid Monson's observation: "Since whiteness tends to be a sign of inauthenticity within the world of jazz, the appeals of white musicians to universalistic rhetoric can be perceived as power plays rather than genuine expressions of universal brotherhood."[9] Shindo's claims of racial universalism for jazz and his participation in popular primitivism and Orientalism might seem to constitute a "move toward whiteness" on his part.

Box 7.1 Chronology: Tak Shindo (1922–2002)

1922	Born in Sacramento, California, in November
1927	Family moved to Los Angeles
1941	Enrolled at Los Angeles City College
1942	Entered the Manzanar Relocation Center in March
1944	Departed Manzanar in November after enlisting in US Army
1947	Discharged from the Army, joined musicians union, formed own dance band
1949	*Tokyo Joe*, Columbia Pictures, uncredited assistant composer
1951	BA in Music, Los Angeles State College
1957	"The Japanese Drama," *CBS Radio Workshop*, composer/director
1957	*Escapade in Japan*, RKO Pictures, uncredited assistant composer
1957	*Cinerama Seven Wonders of the World*, Warner-Adventure, composer
1957	*Sayonara*, Warner Bros., music adviser and uncredited assistant composer
1957	*Stopover Tokyo*, 20th Century–Fox, uncredited assistant composer
1957	*Gunsmoke*, CBS, music supervisor for several episodes
1958	*Mganga*, Edison International, composer/director
1958	"The Kurushiki Incident," *Studio One*, CBS, composer/director
1958	"The Sakae Ito Story," *Wagon Train*, NBC, composer
1960	Rod McKuen's *The Yellow Unicorn*, Imperial Records, composer/ arranger
1960	*Brass and Bamboo*, Capitol Records, arranger/composer/director
1960	*Accent on Bamboo*, Capitol Records, arranger/composer/director
1961	*Cry for Happy*, Columbia Pictures, arranger and uncredited assistant composer
1962	*A Majority of One*, Warner Bros., uncredited assistant composer
1962	*Geisha Fantasy*, Las Vegas Desert Inn, arranger
1962	*Far East Goes Western*, Mercury Records, arranger/director
1964	*Mood in Japan*, Nippon Victor, arranger
1964	Associate Professor, California State University, Los Angeles
1966	*Sea of Spring*, Grand Prix, arranger
1966	*Midnight in San Francisco*, Nippon Victor, arranger
1968	Associate in Arts degree, Los Angeles City College
1970	Master's degree in Asian Studies, University of Southern California, Thesis: "The Shakuhachi: The Classic Myōan School"
1979	Grand Opening of Japanese Pavilion, EPCOT Disney, arranger/ director
1979	Retired from California State University–Los Angeles
1980	Okinawa Peace Memorial, arranger/director

1980	*Encounter with the Past*, Shindo's documentary film on Manzanar
1982	*Siegfried and Roy Superstar*, Las Vegas Stardust Hotel, composer
2000	Composed two marches for Go For Broke Monument anniversary celebration
2002	Died in San Dimas, California, in May

However, this option was never fully viable for Shindo, and his motivation for this particular statement was to lay claim to a musical style generally perceived as lying beyond the boundaries of "Japaneseness." The insistence on belonging fully to mainstream American culture and the desire to distance oneself from all exotic association were very common *nisei* responses to mid-century American racism.

Shindo, however, never entirely separated himself from his exotic status. As he explained: "Everyone is looking for a style. So in my case, I decided being Oriental, I had something I should draw upon and so I decided to go 'exotic sound.'" What, exactly, did he have to "draw upon?" What was that "something" that he possessed as an "Oriental"? Was it the limited knowledge of traditional Japanese music that he had acquired as a child, or was it the exotic status of "perpetual foreigner" generally attributed to Asian Americans by white Americans? Because he was seen as being Japanese rather than American, Shindo's "exotic sound" was automatically accepted as "authentic" and his knowledge of the foreign taken for granted. As the Hollywood composer David Raksin told me: "We all went to him when we didn't want to do something stupid."[10] By helping Hollywood avoid doing "something stupid" on the soundtrack, Shindo provided directors and composers a sense of security that their films were somehow achieving or at least approximating "authenticity." In attempting to define his musical identity one needs to consider whether Shindo was primarily a product or a producer of musical Orientalism and whether his exotic status ultimately proved to be a limiting or an enabling condition for his career. Was he moving musically toward or away from the categories of white, black, and yellow, or did his music point in multiple directions on the racial compass simultaneously?

A *Nisei* Musical Education

Susan Asai, Jo Anne Combs, and Minako Waseda have documented the history of Japanese American music in Los Angeles and have discussed the particular duality of the *nisei* musical experience.[11] Shindo's musical background clearly illustrates their findings. His mother sang traditional and popular Japanese songs at home and on KRKD radio, and there was a *shamisen* and a large collection of Japanese recordings in the house. His family lived in Little Tokyo next door to a Japanese classical dance studio and across the street from a movie theater. As a child, Shindo sat in on the dance lessons and was taken to the silent film theater by a neighbor who played violin in the pit. During Japanese films, Shindo heard the narration of the *benshi* accompanied by *shamisen*. During the American films he gained his first experience of Hollywood film music. Shindo attended Japanese language school where he was introduced to basic features of Japanese traditional culture. His first public musical performance took place at around age fourteen when he sang "Blue Hawaii" on stage at the Olivers' Japanese American youth club. In his teens Shindo played E♭ horn in a Boy Scouts drum and bugle corps, receiving private lessons and learning Western notation. Finally, of course, like most American teenagers he listened enthusiastically to 1930s swing.

With the internment in concentration camps of some 120,000 Japanese Americans, roughly two-thirds of whom were US citizens, the *nisei* were bluntly informed by the federal government of their perpetual foreignness. As David K. Yoo has stated: "No other second-generation group has had to face the questions of its place in America under the extraordinary conditions that the Nisei encountered."[12] The swirl of racist conspiracy theories that supported the interment decision and process is nowhere more blatantly expressed than in the 1942 film *Little Tokyo, USA*, with Emil Newman credited for musical direction. The film begins with Main Title music featuring the typical brassy pentatonic stereotype for evil Japanese and a voiceover referring to the "vast army of volunteer spies" that will be depicted in "this film document," framing the fictional movie as a documentary exposé. The entire film is aimed at denouncing Japanese Americans on the West Coast as spies for the emperor of Japan and purports to re-enact the days leading up to Pearl Harbor. Produced during the evacuation of Japanese Americans, referred to as "dangerous aliens," the film crew was sent out to film on the streets. Near the end of the film we see a sequence just over a minute long, without dialogue or voiceover, of newspaper headlines about the evacuation and the Manzanar internment camp and actual footage of Japanese Americans being evacuated. The upbeat and even jaunty music bears the primary responsibility for directing our interpretation of this sequence. A big and brassy pentatonic gesture with gong punctuation accompanies footage of "deserted Little Tokyo." The film ends with the white heroine looking directly at the camera and beseeching "be vigilant America," as we hear nondiegetic strings play "My Country, 'Tis of Thee." The film is unambiguous in placing Japanese Americans well beyond the frame of "America."

One common *nisei* reaction to internment was to attempt to assert one's identity as an American as strongly as possible, often through music. Music continued to play a central role in *nisei* identity formation, as George Yoshida showed in his study of dance band music in the camps.[13] For many interned *nisei*, performing or dancing to swing music offered a simulation of normality and was an enactment of their hopes of being accepted as Americans. In her autobiographical account of the internment, *Farewell to Manzanar*, Jeanne Wakatsuki Houston recalls her attraction as a young girl to American popular music and her rejection of Japanese traditional culture. At one point during the internment she went to an old geisha in the camp to learn *odori* (traditional dancing for the *obon* festival), but this "occult figure" and the culture she represented proved too exotic for the young *nisei* girl and she never went back.[14] A most dramatic depiction of the *nisei* rejection of Japanese culture occurs in the 1990 20th Century–Fox film *Come See the Paradise*. After her father has been arrested by the FBI and as her family prepares to leave their home for the internment camps, Lily, the eldest daughter, and her siblings energetically break all of their father's recordings of Japanese music. This is a poignant and symbolic moment. We have witnessed her father lovingly caring for this collection early in the film and will hear him sing Japanese folk songs in camp as a lament for his lost patriarchy.[15] Many *nisei* disavowed the inheritance of Japanese music, attempting to avoid yet another stigma of cultural difference.

Had it not been for his internment at Manzanar, Tak Shindo would most likely have become an electrical engineer. Shindo entered Manzanar in March 1942 as one of the first one thousand Japanese Americans who had volunteered to evacuate. He primarily worked as a supervisor of fuel oil delivery in the camp, but also had several work furloughs in agriculture and industry in Utah and Idaho during his internment period. His internment ended when he entered the US Army in November 1944.[16] While he had some musical experience, he had just begun college before Pearl Harbor and had no thoughts of pursuing music as a career. In his 10 July 1942 internment interview, Shindo did not list music under "educational specialization" and "significant activities." Music does appear under "skills and hobbies," but only in ninth place after such activities as radio, baseball, and bowling. Asai has referred to the "abnormal opportunities for music making" afforded to the *nisei* by their internment.[17] Shindo performed in one of the camp orchestras and took advantage of the camp's musical education program. Most significantly for his later career, he also took correspondence courses in orchestration.[18] Although traditional Japanese music was present in the camps, most *nisei* performed and listened to the mainstream popular music of the day. Articles in the *Manzanar Free Press* provide one source of information revealing the diverse musical life found in the internment camps. For example, articles appearing in the summer and fall of 1944 include references to a farewell concert for the instructor of the Manzanar Sankyoku Club (*sankyoku* is a form of traditional Japanese chamber music); a "Symphony under the Stars" concert series including an all-Tchaikovsky night, a night of selections from *Oklahoma!*, and an evening of Tommy Dorsey's music; enrollment opportunities for Japanese folk dancing classes; and an announcement of music classes on European instruments taught by Japanese American instructors.[19] However, unlike other *nisei* musicians, Shindo never renounced his Japanese musical heritage. At the end of his life he still owned his family's Japanese music collection of 78 rpm records, which had been placed safely in storage during the internment.

Near the end of the war, Shindo was enlisted as a translator in the Military Intelligence Service. He continued his correspondence courses and took piano lessons when off duty while "most of the guys were out raising hell." At Fort Snelling, Minnesota, Shindo served as an arranger for the Nisei Eager Beavers band.[20] George Yoshida, a member of that band, remembers Shindo arranging the 1938 Japanese hit song "China Nights." However, the band refused to play the song as it fell outside the mainstream American big band music they were devoted to and would have served as an unwanted marker of otherness.[21] Apparently, this initial attempt at exotica by Shindo was premature. Shindo had more success in composing a musical show for the camp and it was this experience that encouraged him to pursue a career in music. Initially, his internalization of mainstream racial prejudice (against both Asian and African Americans) almost forestalled his attempts at a musical career. As Shindo put it: "I always thought that the Caucasians are the best—they could write music, they're outstanding in jazz . . . that I didn't have a chance. Because during that time there was so much prejudice going on, why should they hire me when they could hire a Caucasian?"[22] The success of this show made him change his mind: "I couldn't go up and play the instrument and direct an all-Caucasian band, but I think I could write professionally and stay in back of the curtain." During his tour of duty at the Counterintelligence Corps in Baltimore, Shindo made multiple trips to New York City to hear Latin jazz, particularly as performed by Tito Puente. After his discharge, he returned to college, this time for music studies. He simultaneously took courses in jazz writing at the American Operatic Laboratory school and formed his own dance band in 1947. In addition, he worked with Latin dance bands in Los Angeles—sitting in with bands on Olvera Street, traveling with them to Mexico, and releasing an album of his Latin-style compositions and arrangements in 1949.

Shindo's racial identity was at issue from the inception of his professional career: "I joined the musicians' union [in 1947], which at that time was a very strange situation. There was no Japanese American in the union. You had the black union and the white union . . . I could have probably joined either one. . . . I joined the white one."[23] Shindo's band performed primarily for Japanese American audiences at high school and returnee club dances and in smaller combos at Chinatown restaurants. However, the band itself was racially diverse. As Shindo explained in a 9 May 1947 interview: "As long as a player can produce good music, that's all I'm interested in. My band is supposed to be Japanese-American. But besides the four Nisei on it, I have Jewish, Negro, Russian, Irish, and Mexican-American boys on it. And we have a swell time together."[24] (See Figure 7.1.)[25] This article continued by paraphrasing Shindo: "Tak says musicians speak a common language. And that the question of minority groups would be settled in a hurry, if we could all get together through music." Throughout his life, however, music proved just as likely to reinscribe racial boundaries as to transcend them. While leading his multiracial band, Shindo also pursued educational goals that would ultimately shape the rest of his career. He enrolled in graduate school at the University of Southern California in order to study composition with the famed film composer Miklós Rózsa and to pursue a master's degree in musicology and Asian studies.

Figure 7.1 Tak Shindo and his band (c. 1949), publicity still. Courtesy of Sachiko Shindo.

Extravagant *Japonisme* in the Hollywood Bowl

As a *nisei* growing up in Los Angeles in the 1930s, Shindo was likely exposed to numerous events that attempted to bridge the perceived cultural divide between "Japanese" and "American" Angelenos through music. On 24 June 1933 over 10,000 spectators witnessed some 2,000 performers in the premiere of *Sakura*, a "Japanese opera-pageant" at the Hollywood Bowl. This production was likely the most significant musical event for the Los Angeles Japanese American community in the decade before World War II.[26] Hundreds of children from all the *gakuens* (Japanese schools) in the Southland participated as did the "Izuchi dancing girls of Lil' Tokio," female *kabuki* performers, and geisha dancers.[27] The Japanese American newspaper *Rafu Shimpo* covered the production in intense detail with articles appearing almost every other day in the month leading up to the premiere. Both US and Japanese government officials proclaimed their support for this event and even President Roosevelt expressed "interest" in *Sakura*.[28] The Japanese Chamber of Commerce of Southern California had organized and sponsored the production, intending "to promote a better understanding between Japanese and other racial groups in Los Angeles and surrounding communities"—a timely intervention given the rampant anti-Japanese sentiment of the day.[29] The Chamber also took the opportunity to donate cherry trees to be planted at the Hollywood Bowl as a goodwill gesture.

In the mode of self-exoticism, the producers of *Sakura* claimed that their production would "transport a typical cherry blossom celebration direct to the bowl stage, with all the color, mystery and drama of an oriental celebration" and on a scale allegedly impossible to achieve within Japan itself.[30] An editor of the *Rafu Shimpo*, Yaemitsu Sugimachi, wrote the script, which perhaps explains that publication's incessant promotion of the production. Sugimachi apparently spent five years developing the work and (echoing the Chamber's statement) dedicated it "to a better understanding between the races, and as a gesture of appreciation for the contribution of America to the life of Japan."[31] The plot of the opera might call to mind that of Donizetti's *Lucia di Lammermoor*: A tragic heroine (Sakura, also the title of Japan's most famous folk song), is in love with a young priest (named Zen) but their love meets with her father's disapproval. The father owes money to an uncouth lender (named Oni, a term for ogres) who demands the heroine's hand in marriage as compensation when the father is unable to repay. The young priest and the moneylender later struggle violently and the priest is stabbed to death. The heroine goes mad and, in the final scene, murders the moneylender and then wanders off alone into the forest.

Sugimachi was clearly influenced by European operatic depictions of exotic Japan and intended his work as a vehicle for his wife Miyoshi Sugi Machi [*sic*], a soprano who had recently performed the title role in *Madama Butterfly* in San Francisco. Raynum K. Tsukamoto, heralded as a "well known artist and designer of Japanese architecture, whose skill has found expression in artistic productions for Mary Pickford, the Long Beach Exposition, and gardens and houses on Pasadena estates," designed the set and—in pursuit of exotic authenticity—imported props and set items from Japan.[32] The set, which extended to the back of the shell and spread to the sides and in front, featured a large statue of the Buddha, a waterfall with a viewing bridge, a small pavilion, and a *torii* gate. (See Figure 7.2.) Attending *Sakura* at the Hollywood Bowl, the general public was able to experience something of the same sensation of being transported to Old Japan that some wealthier Angelenos achieved daily in their domestic Japanese-style gardens.

Enthusiasm for *Sakura* was not limited to the Japanese American community. The mayor of Los Angeles declared 11 June "Japanese-American Day" in honor of the production and such dignitaries and white socialites as Governor James Rolph Jr., President Rufus B. von Klein Smid of the University of Southern California, Chancellor Ernest C. Moore of the University of California–Los Angeles, Mrs. Cecil B. DeMille, and Douglas Fairbanks lent their names and assistance in support. *Sakura* also inspired benefit events including a "bridge tea" by the Assistance League at a member's Japanese-style home and gardens. At this gathering, white women dressed up à la Japanese along with "ten of the most beautiful girls representing the elite of the Japanese colony in Los Angeles, who [assisted] as co-hostesses and serve[d] tea attired in the beautiful costumes of their native land." The chairwoman of the event reportedly sang in Japanese costume.[33] Such cultural cross-dressing and yellowface performances were central to the production of the opera itself, for Sugi Machi was the only nonwhite performer among the principals.

Figure 7.2 Publicity postcard of the miniature set for *Sakura* at the Hollywood Bowl (1930) by Raynum K. Tsukamoto. Courtesy of the Japanese American National Museum (Gift of Grace Warren, 99.168.11).

In the press coverage of the event, including in the *Rafu Shimpo*, the white performers and audience members were consistently referred to as "Americans" while the majority of the cast were referred to as "Japanese," rather than "Japanese Americans." (The terms "Japanese colony" and "native land" in the description quoted above of the Assistance League's tea make this explicit.) In one *Rafu Shimpo* article the hope was expressed that the opera-pageant would become an annual or biannual event, and that in the future *nisei* could take the lead roles instead of the "American" singers.[34] Given that this publication was aimed at a Japanese American readership, the Orientalist hype running throughout the articles on *Sakura* indicates that the traditional cultural elements of Old Japan showcased in the production were assumed to be nearly as foreign to Japanese Americans as to any other group of Los Angeles citizens. In a sense, the production implicitly encouraged Japanese Americans to display their inherited exotic culture in pursuit of acceptance by white Americans in the exclusion era. By casually excluding themselves from the "American" category, dressing up in their "native costumes," and presenting a work of extravagant *japonisme* in the Hollywood Bowl, these Japanese Americans simultaneously proclaimed their cultural pride and demonstrated an internalization of otherness. *Sakura* offers a telling example of an American sub-cultural group attempting to gain the attention and acceptance of the superculture by—somewhat paradoxically—drawing on a musical heritage and foreign plot and setting that they themselves considered exotic. Throughout American music history, countless individual musicians have followed this performative route. In 1933 in Los Angeles, a besieged minority community negotiated its status as Americans through a major public musical production of exoticism at the Hollywood Bowl.

Although *Sakura* has vanished from the history of American music—and even from the history of music in Los Angeles—the work was revived in Los Angeles in August 1933 in a scaled-back production, was performed four times in June of 1936 in Portland, Oregon, and was apparently scheduled for production in San Francisco.[35] A change made in advance of its second performance at the Hollywood

Bowl in July indicates resistance to the self-Orientalist representation of *Sakura* on the part of some of its performers. Following the premiere, a *nisei* girls' organization asked to introduce a "modern jazz ballet" in lieu of one of the traditional numbers in the second act. Apparently, they supported their successful petition with a claim to greater authenticity, arguing that modern musical styles were included in Cherry Blossom festivals in Japan itself.[36] This late inclusion of a popular musical style that many Japanese Americans—particularly *nisei*—would have considered more central to their own musical lives than the music of *kabuki* and the songs of the geisha is rather ironic considering that the composer commissioned to write the score for this Japanese American extravaganza was the white jazz band arranger and songwriter Claude Lapham (1890–1957).[37]

Lapham was an unlikely figure to be tapped for the composition of a work trumpeted (inaccurately), by both the composer and the press, as the world's first "Japanese opera." Born in Ft. Scott, Kansas, Lapham attended both Washington University and Juilliard. He served as an arranger for Irving Berlin and Paul Whiteman, as a silent film organist, as a music staff member for Hollywood studios, and as a conductor for Broadway revues, and was a virtuosic pianist who apparently was the first soloist to perform Gershwin's *Rhapsody in Blue* on the radio. Lapham also published some 250 works, including popular songs, collections of dance music, a book on scoring for dance orchestras, and brief language guides to Chinese, Japanese, and Russian. Prior to his work on *Sakura*, Lapham appears to have had no experience of Japanese traditional music.[38] (See Box 7.2 for a chronology of Lapham's career.)

The *Los Angeles Times* declared Lapham's score for *Sakura* to be "the first notable amalgamation of the two races in an art" and reported that in preparation for this work Lapham had "made an extensive study of Japanese music and customs in the Japanese homes in Los Angeles" during a six-month period.[39] General reviews of the premiere were quite positive, with a more mixed response to Lapham's "strange" score.[40] *Sakura* calls for a range of Japanese traditional instruments, including the *shamisen* and *tsutsumi*. Lapham employed several Japanese folk tunes that he labeled in his score, thereby suggesting that his other folk-like melodies were original. At several points instrumental lines mimic the gradual accelerando of the *kakko*'s drum rolls in *gagaku* or of the *hyōshigi* clappers of *kabuki* theater. The vocal lines remain almost entirely syllabic and tritone intervals frequently appear for dramatic expression. At several points the accompanying harmony is marked by five-pitch clusters that might have been inspired by the clusters of the *sho*. In the press coverage and in his later writings, Lapham claimed to enjoy the challenges posed by this commission. In fact, *Sakura* was only the beginning of Lapham's extensive engagement with Japan and Japanese music.

Just as Tak Shindo was prompted by his Hollywood commissions to interrupt his devotion to big band jazz and to study Japanese music in depth, Lapham became devoted to Japanese music following his work on *Sakura*. His career focus changed dramatically as he followed in Henry Eichheim's footsteps by traveling to Japan

---

Box 7.2 Chronology: Claude Lapham (1890–1957)

1929 *Americana: A Suite of Modernistic Piano Solos in the American Idiom*
1933 *Love's Victory: Opera Romantique*
1933 *Low and Behold* at the Pasadena Playhouse
1933 *Sakura*, Hollywood Bowl
1934 Traveled to China and then on to Japan
1934 Sonata Japonaise
1934 Symphonie Japonaise
1935 *Mihara Yama: Japanese Tone Poem for Grand Orchestra*
1935 Japanese Concerto in C minor for Piano and Orchestra
1936 Lecture-recital on Japanese music at International House in Chicago
1936 *Amor Verito*, opera
1934 *Songs of the Insects (Mushi No Uta)* Suite for Piano in the Japanese Idiom
1937 *Scoring for the Modern Dance Band*
1938 Concerto in A♭ for E♭ Alto Saxophone and Orchestra
1938 *Dream of a Loved One (Yume No Aijin): Japanese Melody*, solo violin with piano
1938 Claude Lapham Salon International "The World and Its Music" at Hotel Astor
1939 Directs a concert of Oriental music at the New York World's Fair
1940 "Soirée Orientale" Town Hall Club, with dancers Saki and Nishimura
1940 Japanese musicale at the Ritz-Carlton, New York
1940 *Songs of America for Little Americans*
1942 *Iphigenia in Tauris*, opera
1942 *Montezuma*, opera
1943 Musicale Intime Orientale "Bali," music and lecture, Los Angeles
1948 *Nisei Romance* operetta, International Studio Theatre in Hollywood
1948 *Japanese Self Taught*, book
1948 *Modern Course for Piano*
1950 Directs "South Pacific Idyl," music and dance of Polynesia, Matinee Musical Club, Los Angeles
1954 "Japanese Musicorama" at Carnegie Recital Hall, New York
1956 "Tokyo Matinee Revue," Los Angeles

and then becoming a proselytizer back in the United States for this exotic musical culture.[41] Four months after the premiere of *Sakura*, Lapham sailed to Shanghai to lead a Broadway-style revue. Three months later he accepted an invitation from the Columbia Record Co. to work in Japan on jazz recordings.[42] He remained in Japan for a couple of years and his compositional output accelerated markedly. During this period he composed numerous works, including a suite for piano "in the Japanese idiom" entitled *Songs of the Insects (Mushi No Uta)* (1934); the Sonate Japonaise for piano (1934), which won a gold medal from the Japanese government; the Symphonie Japonaise (1934); *Mihara Yama* (1935), a Japanese tone poem for grand orchestra, premiered by the Tokyo Symphony Orchestra; the Japanese Concerto in C Minor for Piano and Orchestra (1935), which was commissioned by the Victor Record Co. of Japan, premiered in Tokyo by the Tokyo Symphony Orchestra with Lapham as soloist, and awarded a silver medal by the Takarazuka Film Co.; the 1938 *Dream of a Loved One (Yume No Aijin): Japanese Melody* for solo violin with piano accompaniment; and the 1938 Concerto in A♭ for E♭ Alto Saxophone and Orchestra. Lapham also wrote on Japanese music and its history. In 1936 he declared that Japan was an "endless source of inspiration" for him and that "Japanese music is not easy to understand. In fact, it is subtle, complex, elusive, but withal, extremely colorful and exciting to a serious student."[43] In his works he "sought to blend the two viewpoints by producing a new type of musical idiom in which at least 75 percent of the music would be of Japanese texture, with the remainder European."[44] As late as 1941 he lamented that Oriental music "loses much of its original flavor" when transcribed for piano and orchestra and prophesied that "in time, the beauty of both the Oriental and Occidental music will be merged into a transcendental form representing a truly universal medium of expression."[45] In 1937 he recounted his own nocturnal experiences of a Japanese soundscape, but rather than echoing Eichheim's enthusiasm, Lapham lamented Japan's rapid musical modernization: "I shall never forget how, when wandering out into a Tokyo suburb one twilight and mounting a beautiful curved bridge over a tiny stream to look over the thatched roofs, my meditations and illusions were shattered with a startling suddenness by the raucous strains of 'St. Louis Blues.' "[46] Some two decades after Eichheim's trips to Japan, and two decades before Henry Cowell's (both discussed in chapter 3), we find another white American composer equally fascinated by Japanese music and repeating many of the same claims and aspirations for its potential influence.

Lapham's Japanese-inspired works range broadly in their relation to Japanese traditional music. His six-minute tone poem *Mihara Yama* is devoid of any obvious Japanese musical influence and received the following description from the composer:

> Based on the prevalent custom of young lovers to leap into this volcano, and die together, due to objections of parents. Composed during the first week of January 1935 when these double-suicides occur. Action in tone-poem depicts Mountain Theme and Lover's theme, their farewells and tragic leaps to death.[47]

(This tragic fiery custom apparently fascinated Americans living in Japan at this historical moment, given that the novelist and educator Bradford Smith published *To the Mountain* in 1936, a novel set entirely in Japan that climaxes with a double-suicide lovers' leap into an active volcano.)[48] Lapham's piece features a rather generic, dramatic style that would not seem out of place as the Main Title music for a Hollywood gangster movie. One of the work's major themes recalls a tune from the New World Symphony of Dvořák. Similarly, Lapham's *Songs of the Insects (Mushi No Uta)*—recalling Lafcadio Hearn's homage to these creatures—present six character pieces, each inspired by the movements or sound of a particular insect as described in poetic headings. Although these pieces are marked "in the Japanese Idiom," this appears only to indicate a penchant for the Japanese *in* pentatonic scale. A similar point can be made concerning the 1938 *Dream of a Loved One (Yume No Aijin)*. However, Lapham's 1934 Sonate Japonaise for piano includes a cluster that closely approximates a *sho* cluster and the score is marked at one point "a piacere quasi samisen" with a rhythm resembling the accelerando and ritardando pattern of the *hyoshigi* clappers of *kabuki*.

The most substantial of Lapham's Japanese-influenced works following *Sakura* were his Symphonie Japonaise and Concerto Japonesa (later retitled Japanese Concerto in C minor for Piano and Orchestra). In addition to featuring the Japanese elements also present in his other works discussed above, the symphony appears to call for a *shakuhachi* solo in its second movement, which would make this one of the earliest of American works to employ this instrument. At various points in the score, one finds the markings "koto style," "quasi samisen," or "ondo"—a term from the third movement referring to Japanese folk songs and dances. Lapham's piano concerto is extraordinary and extends the style and materials of his symphony.[49] In this work, Lapham includes a banjo part in *shamisen* style and calls for *tsutsumi* and *taiko* drums and a brass bowl imitating a small metal gong. The concerto lunges through stylistic shifts, recalling in turn the music of Rachmaninoff, Gershwin, and Japanese *matsuri byashi* (street religious celebrations featuring flute and percussion) as well European musical evocations of the "Gypsy." A specimen of the interlocking percussive rhythms of Lapham's *matsuri*-style intrusions can be seen in Example 7.1.

Example 7.1 Claude Lapham, Japanese Concerto in C Minor for Piano and Orchestra (1935); excerpt with piano, percussion, and banjo parts only.

Between 1937 and 1940 Lapham gave a series of lecture-recitals on Japanese music that featured his Japanese-inspired works at such venues as the Hotel Astor and the Ritz-Carlton in New York City. Typical of these events is one in July 1936 at the International House in Chicago. The *Chicago Daily Tribune* announcement referred to Lapham as a "unique latter day Loti" and "an authority on Japanese music, and a pioneer in the efforts to adapt something of its peculiar idiom to the demands of accepted western forms," thus forgetting its own native son Henry Eichheim.[50] Lapham's presentation in Chicago was to include excerpts from *Sakura*, the Japanese piano concerto, and *Mihara Yama*. Following the attack on Pearl Harbor, Lapham—not surprisingly—ceased his "Japanese musicales" and instead delivered lectures on Balinese music[51] and composed works such as *Iphigenia in Tauris* (1942), which employed Dorian and Mixolydian modes, and the opera *Montezuma* (1942). Following the war, Lapham resumed his focus on Japan and in 1948 composed the operetta *Nisei Romance*, which was performed at the International Studio Theatre in Hollywood, in a sense offering a long-delayed response to the *nisei* girls' club members who had requested the inclusion of the popular mode in *Sakura*.[52] In 1954 Lapham presented a "Japanese Musicorama" at Carnegie Recital Hall which featured several of his own Japanese-inspired works, including excerpts from *Sakura*.[53] Finally, in 1956 (a year before his death) Lapham created a "Tokyo Matinee Revue" which featured "interpretative dances and native instruments by guest Japanese artists," including the mezzo-soprano Karie Shindo, the sister of Tak Shindo.[54]

Playing the Authentic Other in Hollywood

Sakura and Lapham's career offer striking examples of the cross-cultural and high/low fusions of early and mid twentieth-century American music and of how suddenly and thoroughly a composer's career may change direction through an encounter with an exotic musical tradition. It also points to the role of white musicians, composers, and producers in shaping a minority group's self-representation. Decades after Lapham's collaborations with the Los Angeles Japanese American community on *Sakura*, Shindo—rather than another white composer—would be turned to by his community for celebratory compositions. But first, Shindo found himself repeatedly commissioned by the mainstream media for Japanese musical representations.

As explored in the previous chapter, from the end of the US occupation of Japan in 1952 through the early 1960s, Hollywood repeatedly presented America's new Cold War exotic ally on the screen. Authentic representation of Japanese culture was a persistently professed goal in the creation of these films. However, as is often true of Orientalist exploits, the actual exotic rarely lived up to Hollywood's ideal. Although devoted to Latin jazz, Shindo was repeatedly called upon to "represent the authentic" during the postwar years by serving as the "Japanese musical adviser" for such films as *Sayonara, Stopover Tokyo, Escapade in Japan, Cry for Happy*, and *A Majority of One*. Shindo had come to the attention of the studios through his earlier work on *Tokyo Joe* and, perhaps, through a brief article on Japanese music that he had published in 1952.[55] Shindo provided Japanese instruments for recording sessions, hired Japanese and Japanese American performers, arranged Japanese folk tunes, and decided what Japanese material to use and where it should appear in a film. In addition, my research reveals that some of the Orientalist music that appears to have been created by white composers such as Franz Waxman and Max Steiner was actually composed by Shindo. (This fact is not always evident from the cue sheets, but is clear in the signed pages of the manuscript scores.) Although much of Shindo's music in these films bears little resemblance to traditional Japanese styles, apparently his mere participation offered an aura of authenticity. For example, at the moment of arrival in Japan in the 1962 Warner Bros. film *A Majority of One*, we hear a dramatic shift in musical style. (See Example 7.2.) Searching through the manuscript score in the Max Steiner collection at Brigham Young University reveals that this music featuring gong, xylophone, piccolo, glockenspiel, sleigh bells, wood blocks, and *shamisen* was composed by Shindo.[56] The *shamisen* part is marked with numbers in pencil and blue ink that suggest the musician playing this part required assistance on tuning the strings and finding the pitches. This hustle-and-bustle music of offbeat accentuation and staccato eighths and sixteenths is quite similar to that composed for analogous moments in other films by white composers—cf. Franz Waxman's cue for landing in Japan in the 1962 *My Geisha* (Example 4.3 in chapter 4).

Based on a stage play of the same title, *A Majority of One* addressed the difficulties inherent in overcoming racial prejudice in a rather heavy-handed fashion. Rosalind Russell portrays Bertha Jacoby, a Jewish American widow whose son died fighting the Japanese during the war. She travels to Japan with her daughter and son-in-law who will serve as an economic adviser at the US embassy. From near the very start of the film, and again near the end, a connection is made between prejudice against African Americans and against the Japanese. In addition, the white American characters repeatedly state that it is crucial for them to learn more about Japanese

Example 7.2 Tak Shindo, "Debarkation," *A Majority of One* (Warner Bros., 1962).

culture, given that such knowledge is advantageous during this early period of trade wars between the two nations. On board their ship to Yokohoma, Mrs. Jacoby meets and befriends a Japanese businessman and widower named Mr. Asano, played in yellowface by Alec Guinness. Russell's depiction of an aging Jewish woman is nearly as awkward and overdone as Guinness's attempts to impersonate a refined Japanese man.[57] Steiner penned a mournful "Jewish" theme, most often heard on cello, for her memories. Shindo was called upon to provide much of the "Japanese" music and he frequently scored for *koto, shamisen*, alto flute, and Japanese drums. When Mrs. Jacoby hears and reacts negatively to what is framed as Japanese traditional music on the radio, we actually hear a piece by Shindo titled "Out of Tune," which is indeed out of tune in a deliberate misrepresentation of this exotic music. The most extensive musical representation of Japan occurs when Mrs. Jacoby visits Mr. Asano and is enthralled by his exotic home and customs, exclaiming, "so this is how you live. It is like a travelogue." She changes into a kimono and refers to herself ironically as "Madam Butterfly." As Asano gives her a tour of his home we hear Shindo's version of musical *japonisme*, though a jazzy clarinet line intrudes to accompany her first taste of *sake*. Mrs. Jacoby's cultural rapprochement and their budding friendship is most directly symbolized by her enjoyment of a diegetic performance of "Sakura" on two *kotos* and one *shamisen*, to which she even taps her feet. Mr. Asano declares his romantic attraction to her but they agree to remain friends for the time being. *A Majority of One* avoids depicting an interracial union between a white American woman (marked somewhat as exotic herself) and a Japanese man. At the film's end it is unclear whether their friendship will develop into romance as she explains that she is still in mourning. It is clear, however, that a decision was made to turn to Shindo at nearly every moment in the film calling for a representation of Japan and of Japanese music. Shindo's contributions to Hollywood films in the 1950s and 1960s repeatedly centered on sequences celebrating the ideal nature of Japanese women, as is evident, for example, in his arrangements for geisha scenes in *Cry for Happy*. To some extent recapitulating the position of Duke Ellington at the Cotton Club and Josephine Baker in Parisian primitivism, we discover a Japanese American Orientalist at the heart of Hollywood's musical *japonisme*.

Sayonara proved to be the crucial film in Shindo's career. As he put it, after the striking success of this film "the whole thing just lined up one after the other . . . it just rode and rode to the point I couldn't keep up with it anymore." The compositional history of the *Sayonara* soundtrack offers some lessons in the mechanics of Hollywood's musical Orientalism. The film's composer, Franz Waxman, professed a desire to achieve authentic exotic representation, as discussed in chapter 6. However, the exotic other was repeatedly rejected. For example, Waxman initially refused Shindo's proposal to employ Japanese instrumentalists on the soundtrack. In a memo, Waxman wrote:

> I would also suggest that our property department try to rent three of the Japanese harps (Lotos) [*sic*] so that we can assign three of our musicians to practice on

them between now and the recording. They are comparatively easy to play and I am sure that our people will have no trouble studying their parts. The players recommended by Tak Shindo do not read Western style notation and it would make the recording exceedingly difficult.[58]

A compromise solution for achieving timbral authenticity was reached when Waxman had his harpist insert paper between the strings and this adapted Western instrument doubled the Japanese *kotoist*. Although hired to help insure authenticity, Shindo ironically played a large role in displacing Japanese music in the film. He successfully argued that the recordings made in Japan were of poor quality and that the Japanese folk songs should be arranged for Western orchestra and chorus and rerecorded in Hollywood. Shindo ultimately devoted much of his career to Westernizing Japanese music and Japanning jazz standards.

Shindo was extraordinarily active in film, television, and radio in the late 1950s and early 1960s and was, most often, hired to represent Japan. For example, he composed and conducted the music accompanying the 1957 CBS Radio Workshop episode "The Japanese Drama." Shindo's score for this broadcast employed several *gagaku* instruments, the *gagaku* piece *Etenraku*, and the *shamisen*, and was more clearly influenced by Japanese traditional music than were his other works of this period. The announcer introducing this "free adaptation of a noh play" referred to him as "the noted Japanese composer"—a moment Shindo marked with a brassy fanfare in sharp contrast to the prevailing "Japanese" style. Early in the 1957 film *Escapade in Japan* we see a group of geisha playing *koto* and *shamisen* and then hear a white American woman declare: "It's charming. Now I can really believe that I am in the Far East." Although Shindo remained uncredited, apparently his musical contribution at such moments in the film was deemed essential for creating credible "atmosphere" on a soundtrack otherwise composed by Steiner. For the 1961 film *Cry for Happy*, Shindo was paid $273.70 by Columbia Pictures to transcribe and arrange one Japanese folk song, to arrange two other pieces composed by George Duning (the film's credited composer) for *koto* and European instruments, and to compose a solo for *shamisen*.

By far the most bizarre of Shindo's Hollywood assignments was his score for the 1958 *Wagon Train* episode "The Sakae Ito Story." In this episode of the popular television series, the samurai Sakae Ito (played by Sessue Hayakawa) is attempting to return to Japan in c. 1860 with the ashes of his recently deceased master. As he crosses the Wild West he decides to join the wagon train of Major Seth Adams (Ward Bond). Shindo employed the *shamisen* and *koto* and pentatonic melodies moving in stacked fourths and fifths, punctuated by gong and timpani strokes, to represent Ito throughout the episode and hired Kaoru Matsuda and Kazue Kudo (a famous Los Angeles–based *koto* performer and teacher who also performed on the *Sayonara* soundtrack) to perform on this soundtrack. (See Figure 7.3.) In one scene, Shindo approximates the timbres and style of *gagaku* as we watch Ito and his servant at prayer in their covered wagon. As the *Time* magazine reviewer noted, "The samisen sounded across the plains eerier than any coyote's howl."[59]

Figure 7.3 Publicity still for "The Sakae Ito Story," *Wagon Train* (NBC, 1958).

Some members of the wagon train come to imagine that this exotic man must be carrying precious jewels and they decide to rob him. Upon breaking open the urn they had stolen from Ito's wagon, they are disgusted to find it filled with nothing more than ashes, which they toss to the ground. Ito tracks the thieves down and then challenges them to fight, armed only with his samurai sword against their pistols. At this very moment, Sharp Knife the Indian (played in redface) arrives with a band of braves and forces the three white men to drop their guns. Ito's mysterious ethnicity has puzzled and fascinated the white wagon train men from the start. At the climactic moment of armed confrontation, Ito's identity is fully revealed as he is defined through a process of racial triangulation with the white and red characters. The camera cuts pointedly between shots of the "red," "yellow," and "white" faces, prompting the television viewer to make racial comparisons. Shindo's music in this sequence helps us locate the position of yellow on the spectrum between white and red. Sharp Knife is accompanied by a blunt timpani tattoo. He proceeds to study Ito's face in great detail as the samurai stands fearlessly with sword bared. Sharp Knife's timpani line alternates and then overlaps with Ito's *koto* line, which plays "Rokudan," one of the instrument's most famous pieces. Through the resultant parallel motion in racial musical counterpoint, Shindo signals a fundamental connection between these two exotic warriors. Although puzzled by Ito's facial features—particularly his eyes—Sharp Knife recognizes him as a fellow "noble savage" and announces "Not white man." He then decides to level the playing field by forcing the three white men to fight this exotic warrior with tomahawks. Ito cuts the men down offscreen.

As Major Adams arrives upon the grisly scene, he stares at Ito and asks, "What are you, savage?" Ito gestures to Sharp Knife and replies that perhaps he is "savage like him." The *gagaku* style returns as Ito prepares to commit hara-kiri in order to join his master in death and declares: "Perhaps Indian understand Ito much more than you could. I think Ito and Indian are more alike." A little more than a decade after Hiroshima, the noble Japanese warrior can now join the ranks of the Red Man as an exotic conquered figure in the white Romantic imagination.[60]

Shindo's Exotica

Leading up to Hawai'i's statehood in 1959, Americans had been increasingly introduced through films, novels, and the popular press to exotic Asian and Pacific Rim lands that had suddenly taken on strategic geopolitical importance.[61] With the launch of Sputnik in 1957, the popular imagination was also turned toward the equally exotic realm of outer space. In the 1950s and 1960s new styles of "mood music" developed that paralleled this popular interest in the beyond and that seemed aimed at calming Cold War jitters.[62] The coexistence of "exotica" and "space-age bachelor pad" music in the Cold War period recapitulated the earlier simultaneity of European primitivism and futurism. Whether employing recorded "jungle sounds" or the electronic bleeps of a flying saucer, both musical genres promised to transport listeners to alternative fantastic realms. Joseph Lanza has described exotica music as "an enchanting, teeming, intoxicating, and festering easy-listening sub-genre that vexed many an unsuspecting ear with the dark forces of 'foreignness' while staying within the bounds of propriety."[63] In the Cold War, defining the "foreign" took on a new urgency. Christina Klein has argued that the "dual identity" of Asian Americans gave them a particular value as Americans during the Cold War.[64] In certain political quarters, Asian Americans were assumed to be capable of aiding US expansionist efforts in Asia and, as a "model minority," could serve as symbols of America's pluralism to counter stinging Soviet critiques of American racism aimed at Third World audiences. In this context, being a Japanese American cultural ambassador could prove particularly advantageous both at home and abroad.

In one of the few surveys of the genre, Philip Hayward listed Tak Shindo as one of the "notable exponents [of exotica] who merit individual study."[65] Shindo's inescapable doubleness as an Asian American musician is nowhere more evident than in the packaging and reception of his exotica albums of the late 1950s and early 1960s. The album covers and jacket notes of both *Brass and Bamboo* (February 1960) and *Accent on Bamboo* (August 1960) promise an enticing bicultural music and forcefully predetermine our encounters with this music. (See Figures 7.4 and 7.5.) The cover image on both albums is divided vertically or horizontally into two utterly different racial/musical realms. In each case, the white female model is presented as sexually sophisticated and modern as she appears caressing and surrounded by phallic instruments in front of modish studio backdrops. The

Figure 7.4 Album cover for *Brass and Bamboo*, Capitol ST 1345, 1960.

Japanese women, in contrast, are presented in kimono in a natural setting or with flowers, demurely holding their instruments and representing an alternative form of sensuality. Clearly, the traditional conflation of the exotic and the erotic is at play here. The photos, line drawings, and text on the reverse side of each jacket emphasize the Japanese instruments and Shindo's expertise in Japanese music, while also mentioning his military service and native Angeleno status (actually, he was born in Sacramento).[66] These albums promise music that is both exotic and familiar. The *Brass and Bamboo* notes proclaim: "Each tune is cleverly 'oriented' to this brilliant blend of two musical cultures in a dynamic fusion of sounds and ideas. So here is Brass and Bamboo–Tak Shindo's new Japanese-American plan for musical enjoyment, as American as 'Ichiban'—as Japanese as 'it swings.'" The *Accent on Bamboo* notes reassure us that "[a]ll in all, this well-arranged meeting of East and West is a swinging thing, and oriental too—but scrutable." The emphasis placed on Shindo's exotic status was carried over into the promotional campaign for *Brass and Bamboo*. For instance, in a radio interview in March 1960 introducing this album, Shindo was made to speak in Japanese and the interviewer translated his lines: "I will be overjoyed and humbly grateful if my latest effort meets with your approval," and "The conditions here are, well . . . groovy!"[67] The success of *Brass and Bamboo*

Figure 7.5 Album cover for *Accent on Bamboo*, Capitol ST 1433, 1960.

prompted Capitol Records to request a follow up album to be completed within thirty days.[68]

Although the album covers promise an exotic sonic experience of "musical sukiyaki" and "far-out sounds of the Far East," the music consists primarily of strong but somewhat straight big band arrangements of American pop standards. Shindo's arrangement of "Poinciana," with its evocative tinkling bell tree and sweeps on the *koto*, offers a representative example. This approach to Japanese-inflected exotica is also heard on Shindo's cool and liquid arrangement of Puccini's "Un bel dì" in which Shindo adds a *koto* introduction, finger cymbals, and a hip *koto* interlude to Butterfly's aria. The three original Shindo compositions on these two albums incorporate Japanese (or at least Orientalist) elements a bit more prominently. Shindo featured gong rolls, *koto* plucking, *taiko* drums, and mallet instruments in "Brass and Bamboo." "Festival in Swingtime" on *Accent on Bamboo* begins with a festive *ondo* call and response. In general, however, the listener should be surprised, given the album's packaging, by the relative paucity of Japanese sounds. Several of the pieces begin with exotic introductions featuring the momentary color of *koto* and *shamisen*, only to switch somewhat theatrically and abruptly to a brash big band style.[69]

Rather than consistently signaling Japan, a few of the numbers reference the exotic realms of other others. We begin our journey on *Brass and Bamboo* in the imaginary Middle East with Shindo's arrangement of "Caravan," and hear a strong tom-tom tattoo in "Cherokee" at the beginning of *Accent on Bamboo*. Furthermore, both albums are actually mistitled. The Japanese instruments that we do hear—primarily *kotos* and *shamisen*—are not of the bamboo category. Ironically, the arrangements on *Brass and Bamboo* containing the most sustained exoticism were not by Shindo but, rather, by Bill Holman. In fact, when compared with his exotica compatriots such as Martin Denny and Les Baxter, Shindo's music sounds rather "white."

Japanese instruments are particularly highlighted in Denny's musical *japonisme*. For example, when Denny employed *koto* for his arrangement of "My Funny Valentine" or *shamisen* for Irving Berlin's "Sayonara," the Japanese instruments were given the melody throughout the number. Denny made arrangements of Japanese traditional songs, such as "Sakura," as well as of Tin Pan Alley *japonisme* tunes, like "Japanese Sandman," and repeatedly turned to Japan for inspiration in his exotica albums. Shindo himself performed on *koto* for Denny's 1958 *Primitiva* and Denny scored for *koto, shakuhachi*, and *shamisen* on *Hypnotique* (1959) and for *koto*—enhanced with a strong echo and doubled by marimba—in "Sake Rock" on *Quiet Village* (1959). He employed *shamisen* to humorous effect in his arrangement of "St. Louis Blues." Shindo and Denny were far from alone in creating Japanese-tinged exotica circa 1960. For example, Arthur Lyman released an arrangement of "Ottome [sic] San (Japanese Drinking Song)" in 1958 and the Hawai'i-based Paul Mark produced two albums of jazzified Japanese tunes in 1961—*East to West* and *Golden Melodies from Japan*—featuring himself on Hammond organ, with other musicians on *koto, shamisen*, and (of course) bongos, as well as the 1963 *12 1/2 Geishas Must Be Right* and the 1965 *Kokeshi Shindig*.

A striking feature of Japanese-tinged exotica from the 1950s and 1960s is its clear continuity with older forms of American musical *japonisme*. Though emblematic of the Cold War period, these examples of exotica frequently redeployed tunes from the Tin Pan Alley era and arranged specific Japanese folk songs first published in the United States in the early twentieth century by such figures as Kosaku Yamada. This spanning-of-the-decades is particularly exemplified in George Wright's 1958 album *Flight to Tokyo*, released on Hi-Fi Records, the same label of exotica stalwart Arthur Lyman. Wright's career was rooted in the silent film era (his mother was a movie organist) and he became the most famous American theater organ virtuoso of the mid-twentieth century, performing in such venues as the Paramount theaters in Oakland and New York. The photograph on the album's cover actualizes the promise of the title as we see Wright posed with a woman in kimono at the bottom of the landing stairs of a Pan Am jet with his huge, yellow-crated Wurlitzer in the background. As the liner notes explain: "George naturally is accompanied by the mighty 5 manual Wurlitzer console and by a Japanese cutie to act as his guide." The album consists primarily of arrangements of such standards as "Japanese Sandman," "Nagasaki," and "Poor Butterfly," as well as Puccini's "Un bel dì," the ubiquitous Japanese hit "China Nights," and Edgar Stillman Kelley's 1888 "Lady Picking Mulberries" based on a Chinese melody. Wright does not imitate the sound of Japanese instruments but achieves a full range of timbral exotica on the organ, all in the spirit of musical novelty. We are told that "George has invented new Oriental sounds of Tokyo with a few other startling ear ticklers thrown in just for fun" and, with a wink at the faux authenticity inherent to all exotica, we are urged to let our "imagination travel to the land of the Buddha, to the Palace Theatre of Tokyo as George Wright plays for you the following, which are as Japanese as Chop Suey is Chinese."

Avoiding such adjectives as "odd," "bizarre," and "unique" is a challenge in attempting to describe exotica albums. A late and, to my mind, particularly eccentric echo of Japanese-inspired exotica is encountered on Van Dyke Parks's 1989 concept album *Tokyo Rose*. Parks was a collaborator with Brian Wilson and the Beach Boys in the 1960s and had released several albums influenced by Caribbean musics in the 1970s. The album jacket art for *Tokyo Rose* suggests that this is exotica with a twist. On the cover we see a scantily clad Japanese woman standing poised at the prow of a whaling boat holding a large phallic harpoon ready to strike at a whale. The flip side presents the same image of the whale and the boat but replaces the woman in the prow with Van Dyke Parks dressed as a sailor barely holding on, leaning back with mouth and legs wide open in surprise. The feminine Japan has assumed the masculine position, an interpretation supported by the numerous erotic references in the lyrics and the general message of anxiety evidenced in the album. As Jon Fitzgerald and Philip Hayward put it, Van Dyke Parks expresses a "deep sense of ambiguity about Japan—a simultaneous fascination with Japanese culture and an anxiety concerning its (once) military and (current [late 1980s]) economic power."[70] This concept album loosely traces the history of the US-Japanese relationship, from the opening of Japan to the 1980s trade wars, and employs two Japanese musicians performing on the *biwa*, *koto*, and *shakuhachi*. The introductory track opens with brief *shakuhachi* sounds and then warped variations on "My Country, 'Tis of Thee/America" and concludes with a bit of "Miya sama." A good deal of goofy humor is evident throughout the album, obscuring Van Dyke Parks's position on the historical events he references. For example, "Manzanar" refers to the shame of the concentration camp experience but with a stylistic silliness that undercuts any sense of serious tribute or political statement, and "Tokyo Rose" ends with a schmaltzy bit of "Sakura." Similarly, the tone of "Trade War" seems rather tongue-in-cheek rather than admonitory, and it remains unclear whether Van Dyke Parks regrets Commodore Perry's mission himself in "Yankee Go Home." Fitzgerald and Hayward acknowledge that "there is something politically indelicate" about the album, but then claim (unconvincingly, but predictably) that it "transcends 'mere' orientalism and exotica and utilises these practices in an applied, détourned and dialogic form."[71] Though prompted by serious political concerns with a resurgent samurai Japan in the late 1980s, in *Tokyo Rose* Van Dyke Parks draws most clearly on the humor and eroticism of 1960s exotica imaginings of the land of geishas.

In the basic concept of their exotica albums, Denny, Baxter, Wright, and even Parks are understood to be musical explorers, bringing the exotic to us or leading us on a global tour. Perhaps Shindo, being exotic himself, could choose to be more economical in his use of exotic signals since *any* music he created would be deemed exotic. (Shindo attributed the success of these albums to the fact that they were "different . . . not because they were Japanese." The albums' difference may be more apparent to the eye than to the ear.) Perhaps Shindo was able to create a particular form of Japanese American exotica by "just being there."[72] Shindo's most Japanese-sounding exotica is encountered on a particularly strange 1960 melange of an album entitled *The Yellow Unicorn*, headlined by the hugely popular poet and songwriter Rod McKuen. In conversation with me, Shindo referred to the album as containing "some hippie music," and, indeed, McKuen serves as a bridge between the beatnik and hippie sensibilities. The album alternates between tracks of McKuen's rather syrupy spoken word/poetry (accompanied at first in Beatnik style by a bass and then, surprisingly, by harpsichord and other instruments), humorous ethnic (Scottish, Russian, Caribbean) songs by Julie Meredith, and four tracks by Shindo offering arrangements of Japanese folk songs and music of Michio Miyagi. Rather than offering his more typical big band brand of exotica, Shindo's arrangement of "Sakura" ("Cherry Blossoms") is much closer to the approach of Martin Denny, with the *koto* taking the lead throughout. "Summer Festival" includes some rhythmic and melodic gestures from *matsuri*, and "Autumn Rain" features harp, *koto*, and flute, in a thinly veiled reworking of Miyagi's "Sea of Spring." The inclusion of an arrangement of "Moon over the Ruined Castle," an early twentieth-century Japanese children's song, offers yet another example of the recycling of the same limited number of Japanese melodies in American *japonisme*, as this tune also appeared as "Japanese Folk Song" on Thelonious Monk's 1967 *Straight, No Chaser* and was recorded by Jean-Pierre Rampal with Shinichi Yuize on *koto* in 1981. Exactly why Shindo was invited to participate on *The Yellow Unicorn* remains unclear and I have found no evidence suggesting a racial implication in the album's title. Though he declares on one of the tracks that "sex is in, Zen is out," the inclusion of Shindo's arrangements suggests that McKuen recognized the commercial potential and longevity of evocative musical *japonisme*. Indeed, on his 1967 album *The Love Movement*, McKuen offered "The Complete Madame Butterfly," presenting the tale in less than a minute to a jazzed-up version of Puccini's "Un bel dì" melody.

Shindo between Black and White

Shindo's first and most exotic exotica album, *Mganga* (1958), avoided Japanese associations almost entirely. In preparation for this album of original compositions, Shindo spent two weeks in the Los Angeles Public Library perusing books on Africa. Once he had collected some evocative names and programmatic ideas for this "Africanized" album, he "wrote the music according to the title."[73] Shindo's acoustic Africa consists primarily of Afro-Cuban rhythms he had learned from his Latin jazz band days and recorded animal sounds and chanting. On this album's cover, we see the striking image of a black man in dramatic red and green lighting, wearing a pseudo-African mask and holding a spear, with just a bit of arm and muscular chest visible in the shadows. (See Figure 7.6.) There is no mention of Shindo's Japanese heritage in the jacket notes and no photo of him. The notes claim that "Mr. Shindo's knowledge and continuous research of primitive music has produced the extraordinary sounds found in *Mganga*" and that this album offers a "musical high fidelity safari." The album begins with the "Mombasa Love Song" which "opens with a stirring roll of native drums" and continues with a repeated percussion tattoo and mystic wordless chorus. When listening to the "Bantu Spear Dance," we are asked to imagine the dancers "brandishing spears, their gesticulations grow wilder with each successive beat" before they finally "fall to their knees, exhausted." (To some ears, the shrill timbre of the piccolo and the general rhythmic pattern might instead call to mind a Japanese *matsuri*.) Shindo referred to this album as Afro-Cuban in style and *Billboard* magazine singled out *Mganga* on 10 November 1958 as a top "specialty album," noting that "Shindo produces a colorful and exciting series of sounds with his excellent scoring for instruments and voices. Over-all feeling of

Figure 7.6 Album cover for *Mganga*, Edison International CL 5000, 1958.

the set is African." Actually, the over-all style of this album resembles music heard during the "Boar's Tooth Ceremonial" number in the contemporaneous 1958 film of the Rodgers and Hammerstein musical *South Pacific*.

Where do we locate this album on the exotica map and in what ways does this music relate to Shindo's racial and ethnic heritage? Can we hear *Mganga* as a form of Asian American music? Joseph Lam has argued that the absence of all Asian musical signs can still point to a powerful Asian American significance.[74] Where does this leave *Mganga*? Could this album represent a lateral "move toward blackness" in Deborah Wong's terms? Building upon the work of Gary Okihiro and others who have theorized connections between the African American and Asian American experience in the United States and who have argued powerfully for the political implications of this view, Wong states that "as Asian American jazz musicians and rappers move toward Blackness, their self-conscious movement away from Whiteness is unequivocal. . . . When Asian Americans explore African American performance traditions, they describe their transit as lateral."[75] Shindo's *Mganga* might be considered a lateral move toward blackness on the part of a minority musician whose ethnic group had been defined at various points in American cultural history as either black, brown, or yellow, but emphatically not white. However, the musical style of this exotica album clearly does not represent any actual African American musical tradition and therefore is not equivalent to the work of more recent Asian American rappers. Having experienced internment and other acts of racial prejudice, perhaps the option of moving towards blackness seemed less than prudent to Shindo.[76]

Wong acknowledges that Asian American performance of traditionally black styles might have "points of contact" with nineteenth-century minstrelsy. I imagine that some black musicians would point out that claims of "lateral" motion toward blackness have been made before by economically disadvantaged white jazz and rock musicians and rappers and that the option of such "lateral" moves still depends upon a certain racial hierarchy. In addition, when we consider the full spectrum of Asian American musical performance, the "choice to move away from Whiteness" appears to be the road less traveled. I argue that *Mganga* can be more readily understood to represent a move in the opposite direction, a move toward whiteness. Shindo's models for his big band arranging style were primarily on the white end of the jazz spectrum. (Shindo cited Glenn Miller, Tommy Dorsey, and Artie Shaw as the bandleaders he most admired.) By creating this Africanized album, Shindo was momentarily assuming the powerful position of a white primitivist offering a predominately white audience a "musical high fidelity safari." When I asked him to reflect on the impact of race on his career, Shindo answered that had he been white "the competition would have been greater, however I might have become more successful." In another interview, Shindo offered the following speculation on his racialized career options: "If I had a beautiful black voice. . . . And I'm on the stage along with a black person. And I'm singing the greatest blues. Other fellow is pretty good too. He's black. Chances are I'd never succeed. That black person would succeed. Only because the fact that the blues is associated with the blacks."[77] Near the end of his life, Shindo repeatedly complained that "despite all my work for years with large film orchestras for TV and commercials, many still think of me just for Oriental music."[78] Perhaps *Mganga* represented not a conscious step toward whiteness or toward blackness but toward his later self-Orientalizing, or perhaps it constituted a step beyond standard racial/musical categorization.

No matter how clearly we may hear the Orientalist and primitivist features of Shindo's music, his exotic authenticity is celebrated by fans of exotica. The Spaceagepop website—one of the most comprehensive sites devoted to exotica music—proclaims that "Tak Shindo was responsible for some of the more authentic uses of exotica instruments in exotica recordings."[79] Shindo himself had a more practical view of musical representation. On the one hand, he was scornful of colleagues who were ignorant of Asian musical traditions: "the thing about Hollywood I always say, it's a farce to think that parallel fifths or perfect fourths are Oriental, that's not true, that's far from being true, but I think someone came up with the idea that because Europeans used it during the Middle Ages . . . and because it was ancient, they thought that Japanese and Chinese would be the same way, but it isn't." On the other hand, Shindo told me that he "purposefully" used parallel fifths in his albums. Shindo clearly felt the historical burden of Orientalist musical clichés. By employing them in his music, and thus adopting "musical yellowface," he was satisfying his audience's expectations and was creating—to risk an oxymoron—"authentic exotica."[80] Shindo's music reflected and supported the Orientalist visions of Hollywood. Yet, in my discussions with him, Shindo seemed detached from the racial implications of these soundtracks and albums, as though he had worked within the mythical sanctuary of absolute music. By concocting exotic orchestrations, setting a Gregorian chant to a Japanese rhythm, and employing the same melody in both *Mganga* and in a *noh*-adaptation radio drama (minus the Afro-Cuban rhythm, of course), Shindo was also satisfying his own experimental impulses, his own desire to create an individual sound. While participating— somewhat reluctantly—in musical Orientalism, Shindo asserted his musical individuality. Shindo's exotic status both enabled and limited his musical career as he sought alternately to capitalize upon and transcend it.

Arranging Identity: Jazz and Japanese Americans

In his *New Grove* entry on "Third Stream" jazz, Gunther Schuller—who coined the label in 1957—states: "Third stream, like all musical syntheses, courts the danger of exploiting a superficial overlay of stylistic exotica on an established musical idiom, but genuine cross-fertilization has occurred in the work of musicians deeply rooted in dual traditions."[81] Clearly, Shindo's exotica goes further in this direction than mere courtship, although he was certainly "rooted in dual traditions." What, exactly, is "the danger" of "superficial" exotic musical syntheses? Did Shindo in some way inflict damage upon "Deep in the Heart of Texas" on his 1962 *Far East Goes Western* album by adding Orientalist elements in his arrangement?[82] Schuller's implication that some forms of musical synthesis are more legitimate than others and that "genuine cross-fertilization" should be held as a constant goal suggests that we should be able to judge Shindo's brand of exotica in light of other exemplars of the style. Is Shindo somehow deficient in comparison to the more exuberant exotic displays of Martin Denny? Shindo's more detailed knowledge of Japanese music did not result in a more "authentically Japanese" form of exotica, whatever that designation might entail. In Schuller's terms, both Shindo and Denny would likely be found wanting when juxtaposed with the more creative (i.e., composed and/or improvised) fusions of jazz with Japanese musical elements heard in recordings by Thelonious Monk, Dave Brubeck, and Herbie Mann (a topic to be addressed in the following chapter). And yet, if we can manage to hear more than "superficial overlay" in the arranger's art, it might be possible to place a greater value on the exotica of Denny and Shindo than has hitherto been the case. Perhaps the actual "danger" of radical stylistic synthesis for the practitioner is losing one's sense of musical individuality. Was Shindo assuming a series of borrowed exotic masks as he jazzed up Japanese folk tunes and arranged Latin jazz and Country and Western tunes in exotica style, or was such extreme multiplicity at the very core of his musical identity? Were none of these musical traditions—swing, *koto*, cowboy—exactly native to Shindo, or did he possess a peculiar form of the Midas touch, making exotic anything he arranged?

In the 1950s and 1960s, jazz and Broadway slowly began to offer *nisei* and Japanese musicians a limited route toward participation in mainstream American popular culture, a way of "blending in." One of the most successful Asian American performers during this period was the vocalist and actress Pat Suzuki, who starred as Linda Low in the 1958 Broadway production of Rodgers and Hammerstein's *Flower Drum Song*, premiering the hit "I Enjoy Being a Girl." (In this musical, of course, Suzuki, a *nisei*, was impersonating a Chinese American on stage.) Suzuki also released a highly successful album of jazz standards that year, *The Many Sides of Pat Suzuki*. Neither the liner notes nor the album art play up her Japanese American identity. The only obvious reference to her ethnicity is the inclusion of "Poor Butterfly," which she takes quite slow in an arrangement devoid of any added exotic markers. Performers from Japan, however, tended to appear in the United States during this period with clearer visual signals of exoticism and with jazz serving as their visa. In addition, they frequently collaborated with American jazz and popular musicians to facilitate their introductions to audiences in the United States. For example, the *kotoist* Kimio Eto accompanied Harry Belafonte in "Sakura" on Belafonte's 1963 album *Streets I Have Walked*. As part of his general campaign to introduce Japanese music to an American audience, Eto released *Koto and Flute: The Japanese Koto Music of Kimio Eto* in 1960. The album features the jazz saxophonist and flutist Bud Shank, but only on side one in performances on flute of three works by Michio Miyagi, including "Sea of Spring." Beyond the participation of a jazz musician, jazz is not foregrounded on the album. Instead, on side two we hear three solo pieces composed by Eto and two by other Japanese composers. Eto's pieces slip briefly into Western styles as he would again a year later in his controversial cadenza for Cowell's *koto* concerto (as discussed in chapter 3).[83]

Female Japanese jazz singers were repeatedly introduced to the US market during this period. Lionel Hampton featured the Japanese female vocalist Miyoko Hoshino on his 1965 album *East Meets West*.[84] Hoshino appears on the album cover wearing a kimono and standing back-to-back and holding hands with Hampton who wears a tux. The album consists of standard songs along with one Japanese number on each side, "Hamabe No Uta" and "Here's Happiness (Kokoni Sachiari)." The album's opening gesture is a brief variation of the stereotypical Chinese/Japanese lick (discussed in chapter 2), played here on vibraphone and brass and signaling the ethnicity of the vocalist rather than having any connection with this opening song, "What a Little Moonlight Can Do." The second track, "Hamabe No Uta (Song of the Beach)," begins with a very brief brass gesture alluding to the standard cliché and then Hoshino sings in Japanese and speaks the lyrics in English. She again alternates between Japanese and English in her performance of "Kokoni Sachiari" on side two, but there are no Orientalist musical signals in the arrangement. In an interview for *Jet* magazine, both Hampton and Hoshino referred to the "universality" of jazz, a particularly common and useful Cold War concept, and Hampton explained that he had discovered Hoshino on tour in Honolulu on a stopover after his band's own tour of the "Far East."[85] We are told in the jacket notes that we will be delighted by Hoshino's "Far Eastern breath-of-spring vocal shading"—an essentialist sound apparently too subtle for my ears.

One of the more elaborate attempts to introduce a Japanese jazz vocalist to American audiences in the spirit of promoting Cold War cross-cultural understanding unfolded on the *Dinah Shore Chevy Show* from 1959 to 1961. Shore devoted a week of programs to Asian/Pacific cultures in October 1959, culminating in the joint appearance of the Chinese movie and music star Grace Chang and the Japanese jazz vocalist Yukiji Asaoka. Asaoka had been a performer in the Takarazuka Review from 1952 to 1955 and later became a television and movie star in Japan. On the 25 October show, Shore, Chang, and Asaoka performed "Getting to Know You" from the Rodgers and Hammerstein Orientalist musical *The King and I* in an arrangement featuring a repeated gesture of staccato parallel fifths for winds and mallets. Asaoka appeared in a kimono and Chang in a cheongsam. The three vocalists kneel as they begin the song and pick up a cup of tea at the appropriate moment in the lyrics ("you are precisely my cup of tea"). Chang interjects that she would "like to show you how we sing this in Chinese," and she does so. Then Asaoka takes her turn: "Dinah, in Tokyo we sing it this way." To the delight of both exotic guests, Shore then sings a bit in Chinese and Japanese. Of course, in each case only the language of the lyrics change and the music remains Western—"getting to know" each other plays out entirely on Western terms. The three dance in perfect synch with wind chimes on their hands—enhancing their stilted, marionette-like movements—and then kowtow at the end of the number.[86] Shore repeatedly featured Japanese and Japanese American celebrities with, for example, Miyoshi Umeki of *Sayonara* and *Flower Drum Song* fame appearing four times during this period. Shirley MacLaine served as guest host on 1 February 1959 in a "Japanese variety" episode which helped launch the US career of actor and singer James Shigeta and included a Japanese female *kotoist* and the Japanese female jazz and rock and roll singer Izumi Yukimura. Shore devoted an episode to Japan on 25 December 1960 and featured Asaoka once again, along with a Japanese acrobat and jugglers performing a "Kabuki Warrior Dance" and the Yamakawa Sisters performing on *shamisen*. On this episode, Shore and Asaoka sang a song entitled "I'd Like to Know More about You," again affirming the show's goal of promoting cultural appreciation of Japan in the United States. Shore culminated the episode by joining her guests for performances of "Dance of the Kyoto Dolls" and "Sayonara." Finally, according to Tak Shindo's personal records, Asaoka also appeared on the *Dinah Shore Show* on 29 January 1961—an episode for which Shindo served as the composer and arranger as he had for the episode hosted by MacLaine.

These examples of Japanese and Japanese American jazz and Broadway performance in the United States in the 1950s and 1960s point to an assimilationist program and a universalist rhetoric for jazz. However, in some cases (e.g., Hampton with Hoshino) a potential alliance between African American and Japanese American musicians and the extensive Afro-Asian musical crossings of recent decades is suggested instead. As Tamara Roberts notes, in many Afro-Asian fusions, black music (blues, jazz, hip-hop, etc.) may appear to lose its blackness and vanish within the label "American" while Asian elements remain distinct.[87] In the 1970s and 1980s, *sansei* (third-generation) Japanese American musicians were more likely to embrace jazz to express pride in ethnic identity and to participate politically in civil rights and internment reparations movements rather than to blend in. As Susan Asai, Deborah Wong, Loren Kajikawa, Eric Hung, and other scholars have detailed, some particularly prominent Asian American musicians—most notably, the Chinese American baritone saxophonist and composer Fred Ho and the pianist and composer Jon Jang—were profoundly influenced by free jazz and the rhetoric of the Black Power movement during this later period.[88]

A range of Asian American musical approaches to political engagement is evident in popular music and jazz of the 1970s and 1980s. Hailed as the "first Asian American album," the 1973 *A Grain of Sand: Music for the Struggle by Asians in America* presented politically focused lyrics directly referencing Asian American identity in a folk revival style with no Asian musical elements beyond a Chinese flute (*dizi*) introduction in "Somos Asiaticos (We Are Asians)." This album was recorded by a trio of political activists, the *sansei* musicians Nobuko JoAnne Miyamoto and Chris Kando Iijima and the Chinese American William "Charlie" Chin.[89] The light jazz/rock fusion band Hiroshima, consisting primarily of *sansei* and other Asian American musicians, has made less overt political statements and has featured Asian musical instruments more prominently in a string of albums since the late 1970s, including those with Japanese-referenced titles such as *Hiroshima* (1979), *Odori* (1980), *Third Generation* (1983), *East* (1989), and *Obon* (2005). Some of the band's lyrics are lightly political in reference, but are delivered in a relaxed vocal style, as with "I still remember Manzanar" in "Living in America" on *East*, an album explicitly aimed at celebrating the cultural diversity of the United States. As Susan Asai notes, the *koto* playing of June Kuramoto and her use of traditional scales has been a consistent and distinctive feature of the band's sound.[90] The titles of certain pieces, such as "Kokoro" on *Hiroshima*, also signal Japan. The band's style is often referred to as "easy-listening" and combines jazz with funk and disco grooves in an extension of earlier exotica. Several tracks on various albums begin with a *koto, shakuhachi,* or *taiko* solo before the piece gets going. For example, in "Lion Dance" on *Hiroshima* we hear the sound of the *shakuhachi* in the first thirty seconds, and during the first ninety seconds of "Midtown Higashi" on *East* we hear traffic sounds with a *taiko* roll, *shakuhachi,* and *shamisen.* Other numbers feature Japanese musical elements more prominently, as in the *sho* clusters, *bon odori* choral chant style, *shamisen,* and *taiko* on the 1981 "Odori." Finally, despite the absence of clear exotic markers in their hit song "One Wish," the 1986 music video of their performance of this piece featured a Japanese female dancer in kimono dancing with fans, parasol, and flower petals.

Some of the most politically charged works combining jazz and Japanese musical elements were inspired by the reparations movement for Japanese Americans who had been interned during World War II or by a general desire to memorialize the internment experience. Loren Kajikawa and Susan Asai have offered analyses of such works as *Manzanar Voices* (1989), *Poston Sonata* (1991), and "Terminal Island Sweep" (1992) by Glenn Horiuchi that employed Japanese instruments and were inspired by internment camp history and the redress and reparations movement.[91] Eric Hung identifies a shift in works responding to the internment experience after passage of the Civil Liberties Act of 1988, which provided reparations for Japanese Americans who had been interned. Hung focuses on four major jazz compositions by Jon Jang, Glenn Horiuchi, Anthony Brown, and Soji Kashiwagi.[92] One of the most active *sansei* musicians to explore fusions between Asian traditions and jazz has been Mark Izu, a jazz bassist and performer on multiple Japanese and Chinese instruments, including the *sho* and the *sheng* mouth organs. Izu played in a *gagaku* ensemble in San Francisco led by Suenobu Togi in the mid-1970s and has incorporated Japanese instruments and musical aesthetics in numerous collaborative works of music theater with his wife Brenda Wong Aoki. His 1992 "Scattered Stars" was composed in response to his parents' interment experience, as was his score for the 1998 *Last Dance.*[93] Izu's historical interests also led him to compose a new score in 2004 featuring *koto, sheng,* and *sho,* for the 1919 Sessue Hayakawa silent film *The Dragon Painter,* which, in turn, was based on Mary Fenollosa's 1906 novel set in Old Japan.

Shindo in Japan

World War II and the subsequent Cold War ultimately inspired in the United States a renewed and more urgent interest in Asian cultures, resulting in both the scholarship of William Malm (whose book on Japanese music was first published in 1959) and the musical exotica of Martin Denny. While continuing to produce exotica, Tak Shindo became a student of the exotic himself. Shindo represented the authentic in the classroom by teaching world music courses for fifteen years at California State University, Los Angeles, focusing primarily on East Asia. He also became an important contact in the United States for Japanese musicians and served as a promoter of Japanese traditional music. In addition, Shindo founded his own music publishing company, Eurasia Music, and in 1961 published several works composed by Kimio Eto. Starting in the early 1960s, he traveled to Japan nearly fifty times and during several of these trips pursued fieldwork on Japanese traditional music. For example, in 1964 he spent two weeks filming and studying the Imperial *gagaku* orchestra and this scholarly interest eventually led him to Taiwan and Korea. What were Shindo's primary motivations in pursuing these studies? Was he enacting a "strategy of authentication," in E. Taylor Atkins's terms,[94] to bolster his exotic authority back in Hollywood? Had he devoted himself fully to musical scholarship? Or were his studies intended to support his new career in Japan? As always with Shindo, the answers are multiple.

In the 1960s, Shindo recorded several albums in Japan. His albums for Nippon Victor from this period consisted primarily of straight arrangements of American swing numbers. He explained that with some of his albums recorded in Japan he was competing against the Japanese in creating "Japanese music." The 1966 *Sea of Spring* offers an example of Shindo's "Japanese music." The album consists of beautiful arrangements for Japanese instruments and Western orchestra of works by Michio Miyagi and traditional folk tunes that Shindo had known since childhood. The *Sea of Spring* cover—a picturesque photo taken by Shindo of the Inland Sea in Japan— is strikingly different from those of his exotica album jackets. I find it remarkable that, for Shindo, adding Japanese exotic sounds to big band tunes transformed those tunes into exotica, while making orchestral arrangements of Japanese pieces and folk tunes did not alter their status as Japanese music, even after Shindo reset the traditional "Sakura" as a lilting waltz. Shindo told me that he did not continue working in his more exuberant exotica style while in Japan because Japanese musicians would not have been capable of playing it and that jazz was behind in Japan. (This, in spite of the fact that Shindo's blending of jazz and Japanese music had been prefigured by Ryoichi Hattori and others in Japan in the 1930s.)[95] When asked in 2000 to offer advice to young Japanese Americans interested in entering the entertainment business, Shindo replied that they should make their careers in Japan since in the United States "you can't hide looks" and are inevitably typecast. Atkins has explained how the enticing hybridity of *nisei* jazz musicians resulted in

Figure 7.7 Tak Shindo, June 2000, photograph by the author.

their enthusiastic acceptance in Japan in the 1930s.[96] Shindo's own bicultural status clearly proved advantageous for his multiple projects in Japan in the 1960s.

The essential duality of Tak Shindo's musical experience continued to the end of his life. When I interviewed him in June 2000 he had just composed two marches for a *nisei* veterans commemoration and was looking forward to using his computer to explore "wild polytonal" possibilities, continuing his experiments in sound. (See Figure 7.7.) He was rather bemused by my desire to study his life and career and seemed most interested in convincing me to assist him in writing a book on Japanese music history. As I prepared to leave his home, he presented me with both an autographed copy of *Sea of Spring* and several mimeographed handouts from his East Asian music course. Tak Shindo was a musician equally proud of having been named a "Giant of Jazz" by Leonard Feather in 1966 and of possessing a detailed knowledge of Japanese notational systems.[97] When asked by another interviewer to name the most important projects of his career, Shindo singled out his work on *Sayonara*, his music for the EPCOT Center's Japanese Pavilion in 1979, and conducting his own choral arrangement of a Japanese song for the dedication of the Okinawan Peace Memorial in 1980 in Japan.[98] In each of these projects, Shindo explored multiple ways of sounding Japanese as a Japanese American. In doing so, he was also exploring new ways of being a musical American.

What's in a name, or more precisely, what cultural assumptions are embedded in the pronunciation of a name? When I made my initial telephone call to Shindo, I was careful to proceed as politely as possible in order to secure his willingness to discuss his career. As he answered the telephone, I asked whether Mr. Takeshi Shindo was at home. Initially suspicious of my use of his full Japanese first name, Shindo hesitated and then replied "Yes, this is Tăk." I did not quite catch his pronunciation of his first name at that time, but after many hours of conversation with him and subsequent extended discussions with his widow and youngest daughter, one might assume that I would have eventually mastered this. However, I still catch myself referring to Tăk Shindo, avoiding the sound of the more nasal American ă. Why did I initially attempt to pronounce Shindo's first name in a "more Japanese" manner? When I arrived at his home for our interview, why did I remind myself upon ringing his doorbell to remove my shoes? As it turns out, Shindo did have a pair of slippers waiting for me just inside the door. In the last decades of his life, Shindo became more "Japanesey," to borrow Myra Shindo's (his youngest daughter's) term.[99] Myra sang with his big band for twenty-five years. However, her father would never let her sing Japanese songs "because I couldn't pronounce it properly." Like her father, Myra was always interested in Japanese music and culture and became an amateur *shamisen* player. As a *sansei* her engagement with Japanese music was inspired in part by her more general desire to explore her cultural roots. For Tak Shindo, Japanese music was simultaneously a part of his cultural inheritance and a racialized sign of his difference—a marker that he embraced but at times resented as he sought to be heard by other Americans who expected him to represent the exotic.

"Making Japanese Music Cool": The Perspective of Paul Chihara

For Paul Chihara (b. 1938), being a Japanese American with an abiding interest in Japanese culture has proven an important, but not determinative, factor in his long career. Chihara has been active for over five decades as a composer and arranger in multiple styles and genres, including Hollywood film, ballet, electronic music, Broadway musicals, television, orchestral and chamber concert music, and music for *cirque nouveau*. He has composed for over a hundred films and television series in addition to serving as composer-in-residence for the Los Angeles Chamber Orchestra and the San Francisco Ballet. Emblematic of the wide range of his commissions is the fact that in 1975 he composed both the electronic soundtrack for the sci-fi cult classic film *Death Race 2000* and a high modernist ballet inspired by the plays of Chikamatsu for the San Francisco Ballet. He has received numerous prominent grants and prizes for his compositions, including from the Naumberg Foundation, the Guggenheim Foundation, and the National Endowment for the Arts. He has also served in academic teaching and administrative positions, developing the Visual Media graduate program at the University of California, Los Angeles, and teaching film music composition at New York University.[100]

As a *nisei*, Chihara's childhood and early musical experiences resembled those of Tak Shindo. Chihara's father had emigrated to Seattle as a teenager from a farming community in southern Japan and owned a jewelry store in downtown Seattle where he also sold Polydor and Japan Victor 78 rpm records from Tokyo of Japanese popular music, including such songs as "China Nights." Chihara's father also owned a violin, which Paul later studied. Chihara heard both recorded Japanese popular music and folk songs as a young child in Seattle, but he also heard the big band music prized by his older siblings. On 7 December 1941 Chihara's father was arrested and imprisoned for being a Japanese American and the rest of the family was transported to the Minidoka internment camp in Idaho several months later. Chihara was almost four years old when he entered Minidoka and he spent the next three years there. His family brought many of their recordings of Japanese popular music with them, as well as the violin. Other families brought traditional Japanese instruments to Minidoka and Chihara remembers occasionally hearing *shakuhachi, shamisen, koto, sho*, and *fue* played in the camp.[101] He more frequently watched the older kids in Minidoka dancing to the swing music of Artie Shaw, the Dorsey Brothers, Glenn Miller, and Duke Ellington. (Decades later, Chihara would serve as a musical consultant and arranger of Ellington's music for the 1981 *Sophisticated Ladies* on Broadway.) In the camp mess hall Chihara became something of a child entertainer, standing on a table and singing popular songs on Saturdays. Finally, Chihara was given his first violin lessons by nuns who visited Minidoka.

Chihara focused on classical violin in high school after encountering the music of Dvořák at a summer music camp and "always knew" that he wanted to pursue a musical career. During the Korean War, he performed popular music on violin with his pianist sister in a touring USO troupe at military camps throughout the Pacific Northwest. As he recalls:

> I played pop violin—favorites like "Hot Canary," "Fiddle Faddle," and "Perpetual Motion." We were billed as the Young Chiharas, [. . .] Korean refugees! The young soldiers seemed to love us and the entire troupe. They were so homesick and really not looking forward to being shipped out to the Far East, especially in the first years of the War, when things were so desperate for America and the UN.

Chihara attended the University of Washington where he majored in English while continuing musical studies. He then pursued a master's in English, focusing on linguistics, at Cornell University while also studying musical composition. It was at Cornell that he met the great musical pedagogue Nadia Boulanger, who invited him to study with her in France on a scholarship. He studied composition in Paris and at Fountainbleu and won the Lili Boulanger Memorial Award, resulting in a premiere at Carnegie Hall. Chihara completed the doctorate in music at Cornell and in 1965 went to the Berlin Hochschule on a Fulbright for further composition studies. He also worked with Gunther Schuller as a composition fellow at Tanglewood.

Chihara's career was launched in Los Angeles where he became a tenured faculty member at UCLA. During his final quarter of teaching—having decided to leave academia—Chihara took a telephone call from a film studio asking him to send one of his students to compose an electronic music score for *Deathrace 2000*, featuring the young Sylvester Stallone. Chihara decided to accept the commission himself and thus launched his film career while also embarking on a position with the San Francisco Ballet. He was then hired to compose the score for Universal's 1976 television movie *Farewell to Manzanar*. Chihara has stated that he was offered that particular commission "because I'm Japanese American." It is also likely that his ethnicity proved a factor in his being hired to work on the 1978 *Bad News Bears Go to Japan*. For this film, he was instructed by the director to employ melodies from Gilbert and Sullivan's *The Mikado*. For example, we hear "Miya sama" during a baseball game as the American boys begin to crush their Japanese opponents. However, in most cases, being Japanese American has apparently had little bearing on his career in film and television. Chihara is quite proud of his Hollywood scores, noting that "going Hollywood" opened up his stylistic range and freed him "from all those academic wars." At one point in our interviews, Chihara queried: "Can you name another Asian American composer in Hollywood?" (Chihara had never met Tak Shindo, but did recognize the name.)

During his time at UCLA, Chihara became increasingly interested in Japanese traditional music and culture. At the invitation of the composer Roger Reynolds, whom he had met at Tanglewood (and whose own extensive engagements with Japanese culture will be discussed in the next chapter), Chihara spent several months each year in Tokyo in 1967–1969.[102] Working with Reynolds on his CROSSTALK performance series, Chihara also met the prominent Japanese composers Toru Takemitsu and Joji Yuasa. Chihara notes that these trips to Japan reinforced his feeling of "being Japanese" and that he was searching for his cultural roots during the late 1960s. (As Reynolds commented in an interview with me, Chihara "was very powerfully affected by Japan.") Looking back, Chihara considers himself to be part of the generation that succeeded in "making Japanese music cool," both in the United States and in Japan. He was particularly influenced by Takemitsu who offered a model for pursuing a career in film and concert music simultaneously. Chihara served as Takemitsu's translator and they spent part of the summer at Marlboro in 1971. As Chihara recalls: "Takemitsu was not the Yoda everyone thinks he is, he was more like Jabba the Hutt, we had a lot of fun . . . he's the one who said, 'you should do movies.'"

While in Japan, Chihara attended multiple performances of traditional Japanese music and theater. However, his most substantial encounter with Japanese musical traditions took place back at UCLA with his colleague Suenobu Togi. Togi, a Japanese *gagaku* musician, was an Associate Professor at UCLA for nearly three decades and introduced numerous young American composers to *gagaku* performance.[103] Chihara recorded Togi and other Japanese musicians on *biwa*, *shakuhachi*, *hichiriki*, and chanting at UCLA and then created electronically manipulated

collages of these source sounds (through ring modulators) that he employed in multiple pieces, including the score he considers "very Japanese" for *Shin-ju*, a ballet in
one act choreographed by Michael Smuin. The scenario for *Shin-ju* is based on the
lovers' suicide plays by the great *bunraku* dramatist Chikamatsu. Smuin's choreography exhibits elements inspired by *bugaku* and *kabuki* dance—particularly the angular high knee steps and deliberate placement of feet, heel first. The costumes also
suggest Japanese culture, with the father character appearing in a Shinto priest hat,
the women's costumes with long sleeves suggesting kimonos, and two stage hands
appearing in all black and manipulating two butterfly puppets on long poles. In
addition to the taped material, the score for live orchestra also suggests Japanese
influence with a close approximation of a *sho* cluster in the first measure (played by
flutes, oboe, bassoons, and horns) and pitch-bending on the oboe reminiscent of
the *hichiriki*. The ballet was also likely influenced by Balanchine's 1963 *Bugaku* with
music—marked by *sho*-style clusters—composed by Toshiro Mayuzumi. (Jerome
Robbins's 1971 *noh*-inspired *Watermill* for the New York City Ballet, with a score
featuring *shakuhachi* by Teiji Ito, was another potential source of influence.)[104] In a
clear nod to the Japanese genre, Balanchine had his male dancers in *Bugaku* move
with exaggerated angular high steps and all dancers processed ritualistically onto
the stage and appeared in black wigs with eye makeup bordering on yellowface.
Chihara reused his electronically modified tape of Japanese traditional instruments
in several other works from this period as well. After discussing Takemitsu's score
for the 1971 film *Geishiki* (*Ceremony*) with the composer, Chihara composed a series of three works himself entitled *Ceremony I, II, III* from 1971–1973. All three
pieces employ the same tone row from an unfinished piece by Anton Webern as
well as the tape of Togi's performance on *gagaku* instruments.

Gagaku instruments are also heard in the two Chihara scores most directly related
to his family's internment during the war: the 1976 score for the television movie
Farewell to Manzanar (based on Jeanne Wakatsuki and James D. Houston's 1973
memoir of the same title) and the 1996 score for *Minidoka*, a chamber music work
commissioned for the clarinetist David Shifrin and the Chamber Music Society of
Lincoln Center. In both works, Chihara juxtaposed 1940s swing with Japanese folk
songs and the sounds of traditional Japanese instruments. Music is foregrounded
in the narrative of *Farewell to Manzanar* in a performance of Japanese folk songs
and American popular music in the Japanese American family's home before Pearl
Harbor and in performance sequences in the internment camp, including of an aria
from Puccini's *Madama Butterfly* sung by a Japanese American in Italian. Chihara
establishes a clear dichotomy between "Japanese" and "American" music on the
soundtrack, drawing on "Kimigayo" as we witness the father burn his Japanese flag
and on swing music for the mother's memories of meeting her husband. Traditional
Japanese music is most consistently associated with negative moments in the
film as when we hear *shakuhachi* for the father's imprisonment, *sho* and *hichiriki*
accompanying an image of the bodies of dead Japanese American protestors in the
camp, *gagaku* as the father gets drunk, and *koto* for the son's funeral.[105]

In his moving 1996 chamber work *Minidoka*, Chihara once again used the tape of his electronic alteration of Togi's performance on Japanese instruments. This three-movement piece is scored for clarinet, viola, percussion (including wooden wind chimes, a temple prayer drum, and temple blocks), and harp. Quotations of and allusions to Japanese folk songs and "Kimigayo" and to 1930s and 1940s popular numbers such as "I'll Be Seeing You" emerge in the score at several points. Several passages for harp are marked "koto" while other moments for clarinet receive the indication "a la Artie Shaw." The *gagaku* music on tape appears at several points and in the third movement we hear Togi's taped Buddhist chanting followed by the sound of a dance band and a male jazz vocalist singing "Away Beyond the Hills of Idaho"—a song that Chihara notes was a hit while his family was interned in Idaho. Though *Minidoka* stands out in his oeuvre for most clearly expressing his personal history and musical experiences by drawing both on Japanese traditional music and swing, Chihara has increasingly referenced Japanese culture and employed Japanese folk melodies in works from the past decade.[106] For example, "Aka Tombo (Red Dragonfly)," credited to Kosaku Yamada, appears in several of his works, including in the piano duo *Ami* (2008) and the fourth movement of *Concerto Piccolo* (2011) for four violas. In multiple scores, he has employed the term "*haiku*" in piece titles and movement labels as an indication of a general aesthetic of brevity and distilled expression. In the 1997 flute duet *Haiku* one flute is called upon to approximate the sound of a *shakuhachi* through pitch bending and a "breathy attack," while the second is intended to reference American ragtime. In *Bagatelles: Twice Seven Haiku for Piano* (2014) Chihara employed Japanese folk and popular songs, including "Sakura" and "Tonko Bushi," in three of the short, imagistic movements and in the fifth, "Bon odori . . . ," two staccato chords are marked "Small Taiko drum" in the score. The ellipses in each movement title indicates that the pieces, like *haiku* poems, are suggestive of something not fully stated. Both "Sakura" and "Tonko Bushi" were also drawn upon by Chihara in the 2002 Pierrot-type ensemble piece *Amatsu Kaze (Winds of Heaven)*, composed for Joel Sachs and the New Juilliard Ensemble. Each movement sets a Japanese poem for soprano and alludes stylistically both to Japanese music and to jazz, with a flute portamento gesture and the timbre of an alto flute approximating a *shakuhachi* along with a clarinet (or optional alto saxophone) line marked "sexy (à la film noir)." Finally, Chihara's *A Matter of Honor*, a work for speaker and orchestra commemorating the internment camp experience and drawing on his musical memories of that period, received its premiere in March 2019.

Chihara's music most closely approximates the exotica of Shindo in two high-profile works: *Shōgun: The Musical* (1990) and *Yulan* (2012). James Clavell's 1975 novel *Shōgun* was first transformed into one of the most successful miniseries in television history in 1980, with an average viewing audience of 26 million for each of the five episodes. This novel and television series—filmed on location in a bid for exotic authenticity—inscribed a powerful image in the American imagination of Old Japan, a Japan of perverse eroticism and intense and violent macho samurai, just in time for the 1980s trade wars between the two nations. Maurice Jarre incorporated Japanese musicians on multiple traditional instruments (*biwa, koto, shakuhachi, shamisen*) in his soundtrack, which stands as one of the most widely heard musical representations of Japan in the history of American *japonisme*. The Broadway musical version—with Clavell directly involved as a producer, book and lyrics by John Driver, direction and choreography by Smuin, and score by Chihara—did not fare well, closing after only two months. Based on the experiences of an Englishman who arrived in Japan in 1600, the plot's political intrigue and religious conflicts confused audiences, despite the centrality of the requisite romantic tragedy that unfolds between the leading white Western male and subservient Japanese female. In the spirit of exotic authenticity, several Asian American actors were cast in major roles and Clavell was joined as producer by Haruki Kadokawa—a Japanese publisher, director, poet, and Shinto priest who led a Shinto ceremony for the cast and crew to bless the production, flying in priests from Karuizawa to join him in the ceremony. Chihara provided program notes for this ceremony for the benefit of cast and crew.

Clavell had initially wanted a Japanese composer for this musical. Chihara did not draw on Japanese melodic material and instead, as he put it, "was being Andrew Lloyd Webber" in his score. He was also drawing on long traditions of exotic representation. The show's opening choral number features a pentatonic lick, pitch bending, and a big tom tom–style primitivist pulse. Pentatonicism, bell tree, gong, and a breathy flute timbre appear prominently in several other numbers. In a comic relief number that was cut before opening night, "Yin and Yang," two villains (a Japanese and a Portuguese) gleefully plot the murder of the Protestant English hero. Music symbolizes their devious cross-cultural alliance as they call us to "hear the mandolin and the koto's twang" and then imitate Japanese and early European vocal styles with an absurdly melismatic "alleluia/oh." By far the oddest number in the musical, and one of the strangest musical artifacts in American *japonisme*, is "Pillowing," in which Japanese female characters—putting Japan's alleged perverse eroticism on full display—praise the dildo. The extremely breathy female vocalists, singing in Japlish, are accompanied by a jazzy synthesized *koto* and the song includes a mechanical, toylike pentatonic melody. To my ear and mind, Chihara's score for *Shōgun: The Musical* resonates with the sound and spirit of Van Dyke Parks's contemporaneous album *Tokyo Rose*.

Chihara's most prominent recent work of musical exoticism is *Yulan* (2012), an "acrobatic, dance and visual extravaganza" commissioned for the Dalian Acrobatic Troupe of China and recorded and conducted by the composer in Beijing. The scenario of *Yulan*, by Dennis Nahat, offers a creation story with scenes from the Big Bang, to the Flood, to the rise of photosynthesis, and culminating in the appearance of Yulan, the "Flower of Love, Peace and Harmony." The production is quite stunning—even overwhelming—and has been seen in San Jose, California, and Dalian, China, and in excerpts on YouTube. The music, eclectic even by Chihara's standards, includes a prominent solo for the Chinese *erhu* and draws (repeatedly) on the most famous Chinese folk tune "Mo Li Hua (Jasmine Flower)." Lush orchestral sections are juxtaposed with synthesized, atmospheric numbers and with sections featuring the percussion section. The rhythmic drive of EDM/techno, a touch of tango, and the timbres of Chinese operatic percussion all make appearances. Stylistic traces of nineteenth- and twentieth-century orchestral music abound (Prokofiev, Stravinsky, Copland, Puccini, etc.), with Wagnerian Rhine music for "The Flood" and a lilting Viennese style for "Mating." I even hear a brief, melted version of the concluding phrase of "Miya sama" in the "Winds of Fire" movement, but, then again, it proves difficult to pin down the many musical memories that appear to emerge in the later works of Paul Chihara.

Like Shindo, Chihara has embraced his Japanese heritage at various points in his career while negotiating exactly how to participate in American music as an "American." I was repeatedly struck in my interviews with Chihara by his references to himself and his family as "Japanese" and to me and other white Americans as "American." Looking back, he explained that "we were aware of being Japanese American from the very beginning" and that anti-Japanese attitudes persisted in the immediate postwar years. Only during and after the Korean War did he sense that sentiment had switched to a more positive view of both Japan and Japanese Americans—"Being an Asian American didn't hinder me at all in the 60s . . . it was a great blessing." Not only did Chihara feel unconstrained by being Japanese American, he also believes that his ethnicity was even invisible at certain crucial moments in his career. He recounted a day when he had been invited to meet with a studio executive and found himself cooling his heels in the waiting room, ignored by both the secretary and the executive himself. He recalls that because nobody expected to see a Japanese composer they had misread his name as "Chihuahua and were looking for a Chicano. I was there and nobody saw me." However, Chihara also told me that at various points in his career he told everyone he "was an expert on Japanese music." While Shindo found a strategic position for his career "in back of the curtain," Chihara has sought and achieved a much higher degree of visibility. Deciding when and whether to embrace Japanese music and culture, and when and under what circumstances to accept commissions to represent the exotic other, has been a persistent challenge for Japanese American musicians and the Japanese American community more generally throughout its turbulent history.

8

Beat and Square Cold War Encounters

Mr. Moto, John P. Marquand's Japanese secret agent, had appeared in multiple novels and films throughout the 1930s. This highly popular character vanished from the scene during the war, but was brought back once more in 1956 in Marquand's *Stopover: Tokyo* to assist Americans in thwarting a violent, nefarious Russian plot designed to stir up anti-American sentiment in Japan.[1] Japanese traditional music does not play a role in this Cold War novel. Instead, the dastardly Communists appropriate American jazz for propaganda purposes aimed at the Japanese.[2] A film version of this espionage thriller appeared in 1957 with a score by science fiction and horror film composer Paul Sawtell. In the film, *Stopover Tokyo*, Mr. Nobika (the Mr. Moto character) is killed off after attempting to help the dashing American agent Mark (played by Robert Wagner). Mark, as a paternalistic good American, meets Koko, Nobika's newly orphaned daughter. Koko, accompanied by Tina (Mark's white love interest) on *shamisen*, dances for Mark and, as a good little geisha, explains her exotic dance as she performs. At the end, Mark invites Koko to return with him to the United States, but this young Butterfly insists that she must remain in Japan and, so, the American hero departs accompanied by lush romantic strings. Staking a claim for exotic authenticity, the film credited "supervisor of Japanese music Tak Shindo." Throughout the film, picture postcard shots of old Japanese settings, such as a garden party scene, are accompanied by Shindo's music for *koto*, *shamisen*, and alto flute and we hear his arrangements of Japanese folk tunes. As part of the updated exotic ambience, we also hear pentatonic jazz-inflected music composed by Shindo for scenes set in the neon-lit streets of modern Tokyo.

With the end of the American occupation of Japan in 1952 and the conclusion of the Korean War in 1953, Japan emerged as a key American ally in the Cold War. More than any other period considered in this book, the Cold War requires a transnational historical approach, encompassing musical events that took place in Japan, works by both American and European composers, and their interactions with Japanese composers. The number of transnational musical exchanges that occurred between Japan and the West during this period—particularly from 1952 to 1972— is striking. Post-occupation Japan witnessed an intense influx of American popular music, along with a renewed devotion to the performance of Western classical music and jazz, and a new, niche market interest in avant-garde trends from the West. Musical life was transmuting at an astonishing rate within Japan's national borders, which were themselves in flux during the occupation and immediate post-occupation periods. A more limited, but nevertheless highly significant and consequential flow of influence may be traced from Japanese traditional music to the compositions and publications of prominent European and American musicians. Western composers, performers, and scholars transported musical products and ideas to Japan—indeed, their very presence stimulated Japanese interest in the musical styles and techniques they represented. In turn, these Westerners brought home elements of what they had heard and studied during their visits to the exotic nation. The extensive impact of Japanese traditional music (particularly the ancient court orchestral music of *gagaku*) may be heard in some of the most prominent concepts and forms of mid-century Euro-American modernist music, such as sound mass, moment form, textural music, and timbral explorations.[3]

All of this transnational musical activity was shaped and even inspired by war–the end of World War II, the strategic importance of Japan during the Korean War, and the cultural diplomacy efforts of the United States during this particularly hot period in the Cold War. Japan became a major musical destination for composers and ethnomusicologists based in the United States and Europe. For example, William P. Malm pursued his fundamental research on Japanese music in Japan from 1955 to 1957. American composers such as Henry Cowell and Alan Hovhaness made several trips to Japan and wrote multiple pieces reflecting their encounters with Japanese performing arts in the late 1950s and early 1960s. The range of musical Americans who journeyed to Japan is astonishing: jazz musicians such as Benny Goodman, Duke Ellington, Art Blakey, and Dave Brubeck; conductors such as William Strickland and Leonard Bernstein; and ensembles including the Westminster Choir College, the Symphony of the Air, and the Boston Symphony Orchestra.

Leading European figures were equally enthralled by Japan. Upon returning to Paris from Japan in 1961, Iannis Xenakis declared, "I am a Japanese."[4] His passion for Japanese traditional music was such that he "couldn't understand why young Japanese composers were writing tonal or serial music. . . . I realized that most Japanese composers didn't actually know the wonderful traditional Japanese music, they didn't understand it and were indifferent to it."[5] In 1962, his teacher Olivier Messiaen traveled to Japan himself and explained that he "tried to live like a true Japanese. I forgot about my music, and the concerts, and I began with the cuisine. . . . I went about in slippers rather than shoes."[6] Messiaen hailed *noh* as "the most powerful theatrical expression in existence" and praised *gagaku* for being "incredibly modern," composing his own version of *gagaku* music for Western instruments that very year.[7] Karlheinz Stockhausen made the first of his several trips to Japan in 1966 and went even further in his identification with this exotic culture and its music: "What I've actually experienced is that I came to Japan and discovered the Japanese in me. I immediately wanted to become that 'Japanese,' because it was new to me that I could live like that."[8] By the mid-1970s, Stockhausen had concluded that he must have lived in Japan in a previous existence and declared that his encounter with Japanese music "suddenly changed my whole way of thinking and approach to composition" and that he was "ready to integrate Japanese music into compositions of my own and to transform them."[9] In 1967, Pierre Boulez celebrated the "wonderful Gagaku," though, unlike his colleagues, felt that "there is no sense in trying to build specimens of Oriental music into contemporary music; no influence is good except when it is transcended."[10]

Numerous Western artists across a range of disciplines sought spiritual transcendence in Japan in the postwar period. Indeed, both Allen Ginsberg and Karlheinz Stockhausen reported that they had experienced their *sartoris* (epiphanies) while in Japan. Other figures approached Japanese culture with a more technical and analytical inclination. Throughout this chapter we will encounter examples of a philosophical, Zen-influenced artistic engagement with Japanese music and performing arts, as well as the work of composers who pursued high modernist technical advances befitting a Cold War emphasis on scientific inquiry and artistic progress. The body of Western music inspired by encounters with Japan in this period is vast and varied, encompassing programmatic *haiku*-inspired "impressions," technological interfacing with traditional Japanese instruments and multimedia pursuits, and, eventually, the influence of contemporary music by avant-garde Japanese colleagues. Employing the lingo of this period, we might view these approaches as offering a "Beat" or "Square" binary, though both sensibilities frequently coexisted in American Japanese-influenced music from the Cold War.

Jazz *Japonisme* Diplomacy

In 1954, Charles E. Tuttle Publishers produced a special edition of James Michener's *Sayonara* for sale only to US personnel stationed in Japan, Okinawa, and Korea. The back jacket featured a blurb by Pearl S. Buck, praising the novel as an "illuminating description of a rarely beautiful country; as a powerful portrayal of Americans and Japanese as they must live together upon Japanese soil." Buck concluded by pointing to the blunt warning she found in Michener's novel: "But deeper than all this is the authentic explanation of why, if we Americans do not change, we can never win in Asia."[11] In addition to reshaping white American perceptions of the Japanese during the Cold War, the arts were harnessed for cultural diplomacy aimed at improving perceptions of the United States abroad, particularly in such nations deemed of high strategic importance as Japan. To counter Soviet claims of American cultural inferiority, the US government sponsored numerous projects to showcase American classical musicians and composers. As Danielle Fosler-Lussier has documented, these included tours to Japan by the Westminster Choir College that aimed to deploy Christian choral music against communism and, specifically, to counter Soviet propagandistic choral music efforts.[12] Fosler-Lussier has also detailed the extensive Japanese career of the American conductor William Strickland who was frequently sent by the State Department starting in 1958 as a guest conductor and who made multiple recordings with Japanese orchestras.[13]

Similarly, the US government funded tours to Japan by American orchestras. For example, Jonathan Rosenberg has discussed the very positive reception by Japanese audiences of the 1955 Symphony of the Air tour.[14]

Countering Soviet accusations of endemic American racism—claims that were particularly easy to make as the world viewed shocking images of police brutality against peaceful civil rights demonstrators—proved an even more urgent mission. The State Department sponsored numerous tours by African American jazz musicians of Africa, the Middle East, Latin America, and East Asia throughout the Cold War.[15] Many of these musicians produced some form of musical response to their Japanese experience. The range of American jazz musicians' engagements with Japanese culture is quite wide. There is nothing specifically Japanese about the music released on Julian "Cannonball" Adderley's 1963 album *Nippon Soul* or on *Cannonball in Japan* (1966). Similarly, Horace Silver's 1962 *The Tokyo Blues* features Japanese-inspired titles and album images—including one of Silver sitting with two kimono-clad Japanese women in a garden—but no apparent Japanese musical influences. John Coltrane toured Japan in 1966 and purchased a *shakuhachi* and *koto*, though India remained his primary source of exotic musical inspiration. Thelonious Monk's arrangement of the early twentieth-century Japanese song "Moon over the Ruined Castle" was released as "Japanese Folk Song" on the album *Straight, No Chaser* in 1967. McCoy Tyner strummed a *koto* on "Valley of Life" on his 1972 album *Sahara*, featuring an image of a *koto* on the cover as well. In some cases, jazz musicians have pointed to broader aesthetic connections with Japanese culture and performing arts in their work. In the liner notes for the Miles Davis 1959 landmark album *Kind of Blue*, Bill Evans compared the group's approach to improvisation with a genre of spontaneous Japanese painting. Similarly, Cecil Taylor pointed to the influence of *kabuki* in his 1978 album *Live in the Black Forest*. Taylor went on to collaborate extensively with the *butoh*-style Japanese dancer Min Tanaka starting in the late 1980s.

Though most of these examples represent limited encounters with Japanese culture, they may be viewed as paving the way toward the more extensive Afro-Asian fusions of the 1970s through 2000s. For example, Anthony Brown's 2005 album *Rhapsodies* pays homage to and culturally reinterprets George Gershwin's *Rhapsody in Blue* with a Japanese musical inflection. Several of the six tracks include Japanese flutes and percussion. The shortest movement, "Rhapsody in Blue: Gagaku," includes the Chinese *sheng* and *yangqin* along with the *shakuhachi*, thereby connecting Gershwin, Japanese *gagaku*, and *gagaku*'s Chinese roots.[16] Furthermore, tours by American jazz musicians in the Cold War proved to have a major impact on the development of jazz in Japan. E. Taylor Atkins points to the 1961 Art Blakey and the Jazz Messengers tour as "epoch-making" and credits it with having led to the "*rainichi* [travel to Japan] rush" phenomenon of American musicians traveling to Japan and, occasionally, collaborating with Japanese jazz musicians. For example, the Jazz Messengers were joined by a Japanese big band positioned well back onstage behind Blakey's combo in their 1961 performance. Atkins notes that "from 1961 to 1964, the peak of the *rainichi* rush, some seventy-five jazz and popular music acts from America performed in Japan."[17] Two of the most prominent of these figures were Duke Ellington and Dave Brubeck, both of whom subsequently offered jazz "impressions" of Japan.

In 1963 Ellington led his orchestra on a State Department–sponsored tour of the Middle East. This was the first of his tours of duty for US cultural diplomacy, which included a trip to Japan in 1964.[18] Ellington's concerts were publicized as major cross-cultural events, as were similar tours by Dizzy Gillespie and Louis Armstrong. Ellington and Billy Strayhorn composed *The Far East Suite* (recorded in 1967) as a musical impression of the band's travels through the Middle East and Japan. "Ad Lib on Nippon" appears last on the album and is considerably longer than the other tracks. Ellington avoided being directly influenced by the music he heard in Asia, and this is particularly evident on "Ad Lib on Nippon." There is nothing specifically Japanese about this music unless we hear the pointillist piano style and, particularly, the bass as sounding *shamisen*-like in timbre in the track's opening section (at 1:14), with its sparse, slack-string pizzicato and repetition of individual pitches. However, no listener would likely make this association without the encouragement of the track's title.

Several scholars have wrestled with determining the extent to which Ellington and Strayhorn engaged in musical exoticism in this suite. Penny M. Von Eschen states that "Ellington was not engaging in a form of colonial appropriation" but that he and Strayhorn did rely on some clichés.[19] Mark Lomanno pushes back at attempts to interpret the album as a form of exoticism, but then suggests that "despite Ellington's sensitivity to appropriation and self-aware subjectivity, the lack of other cultural viewpoints in the *Far East Suite* emphasizes the mostly one-dimensional nature of this intercultural exchange and invites exoticist critiques."[20] More pointedly, Travis A. Jackson concludes that by musically evoking exotic sites from their tours without imitating specific musical features that they had heard, Ellington and Strayhorn apparently had two aims in mind:

> The first was to insulate themselves from criticisms regarding the accuracy or ethics of musical borrowing. The second, more cynically, was to avoid their having to do anything other than what they usually did, perhaps trusting that the expressive power of their existing style could sustain any associations arising from the titles, narratives, or contexts. . . . Although they might have been tourists in addition to being cultural ambassadors as they traveled the world and produced albums "documenting" their experiences, they approached their task unlike stereotypical tourists—neither with a shallow understanding nor with an exploitative aim.[21]

Whether Ellington and Strayhorn composed from a "tourist point of view," the power of their programmatic titles to evoke exotic aural associations allowed *The Far East Suite* to function in the listening experience as a form of musical tourism not dissimilar to that experienced while consuming contemporary exotica.[22]

The Dave Brubeck Quartet also toured Japan in 1964 for the State Department. Brubeck was a particularly active cultural diplomat and, along with his wife and Louis Armstrong, even created a musical entitled *The Real Ambassadors* (1961– 1962) that satirized the State Department's programs, from their insiders' point of view.[23] However, Brubeck generally welcomed these tours and the opportunity they offered for him to encounter musicians from other cultures and to "absorb" aspects of their music.[24] Brubeck appears to have embraced the role of cultural diplomat as well and viewed his music, as he put it, "as an instrument for peace, rather than a Cold War weapon."[25] Brubeck's trip to Japan inspired the 1964 album *Jazz Impressions of Japan*. In his jacket notes, Brubeck explained: "The music we have prepared tries to convey these minute but lasting impressions, somewhat in the manner of classical haiku, wherein the poet expects the reader to feel the scene himself as an experience." His notes for several of the pieces conclude with a quotation of a *haiku*.[26] Brubeck also details the musical and cultural inspirations for several of the tracks, pointing to "Koto Song" as "the most consciously Japanese of these pieces." This blues tune was apparently inspired by the "delicate music" he heard "performed by two Japanese girls in Kyoto." Brubeck states that he was fascinated by the *koto*, "which blended with voice or flute seems to suggest the ethereal quality of Japan's gardens and misty landscapes." I hear a suggestion of *koto*-like strumming gestures in the piano part, especially at the start, and pentatonicism, but nothing else indicating a Japanese influence. Brubeck had composed "Toki's Theme," the third track, before the trip for the Japanese secretary character in the CBS *Mr. Broadway* TV series. Brubeck heard Japanese pop music in Japan and was shocked, but was also convinced that his groovy tune had been apt for this contemporary character. He found that the Japanese parody themselves in their pop music "using parallel fourths and other Western ideas of how the Oriental should sound" and noted that "to hear the authentic traditional music of Japan one has to seek it out." The album also includes "Zen Is When," a song by Bud Freeman (words) and Leon Pober (music) that sounds a good deal like Martin Denny's exotica, though lacking the bird calls. In an additional note for the 2000 CD reissue of *Jazz Impressions of Japan*, Brubeck places the album within his long-standing interest in Japan. He relates that growing up in California he had always found Japanese aesthetics appealing and that the home he built in Connecticut is very Japanese in style, including the dining room furniture and the *shoji* screens in his studio. However, *Jazz Impressions of Japan* does not suggest that Brubeck had "absorbed" very much from Japanese music during his goodwill tour.

A new wave of woodwind jazz soloists embraced elements of Japanese music in the 1970s and 1980s and their music may be heard, in retrospect, as preparing the prominent role that the *shakuhachi* would play in American New Age music. These musicians tended to be white and some participated in official cultural diplomacy programs. The clarinetist Tony Scott, who had traveled to Japan in 1959, led the way with *Music for Zen Meditation and Other Joys* in 1965. However, the most prominent figure in this later group was the jazz flutist Herbie Mann. Mann had toured

Africa for the State Department in 1959 and released an album based on this experience. In 1961 he toured Brazil and became especially prominent for promoting bossa nova in his music. In step with Henry Cowell and Duke Ellington, Mann released *Impressions of the Middle East* in 1966. Like Cowell, Mann exhibited a universalist approach to global flute music, appearing on the album cover for his 1961 *The Family of Mann* with a collection of flutes from across the world.[27] Mann toured Japan multiple times and during his 1974 visit he attempted to immerse himself in the culture, eating sushi, reading Japanese poetry, and listening to Japanese music.[28] In 1976, Mann released *Gagaku and Beyond*, an album that Cary Ginell has referred to as "probably the most esoteric album Herbie recorded in his career" and as Mann's "ultimate experiment in fusion."[29]

Gagaku and Beyond was recorded in Japan in 1974 and consists of five tracks. The first three tracks offered a collaborative performance between Mann's ensemble and Minoru Muraoka and His New Dimension ensemble and feature the *shakuhachi, sho, koto, shamisen, o-daiko*, and *taiko*. Minoru Muraoka pursued jazz rock fusion as a *shakuhachi* player, composer, and arranger. His music exhibits some similarities with that of Tak Shindo, but with a funkier vibe. For example, Muraoka's 1970 album *Bamboo* mostly consists of his arrangements for *shakuhachi, shamisen*, bass, and drum set of Western pop and jazz tunes such as "The House of the Rising Sun," "And I Love Her," "Do You Know the Way to San Jose," and "Take Five." His 1973 album *So* is more in the style of psychedelic rock. In an increasingly familiar dynamic of cross-cultural exchange in this period, something like two ships passing in the night, Mann turned to Muraoka as a source of Japanese influence, but Muraoka's albums prove even less traditionally Japanese in style than Mann's own *Gagaku and Beyond*.

The first track, "Shomyo (Monk's Chant)," begins and ends with chanting by the Modern Shomyo Study Group and the sound of a prayer bell. Mann's ensemble begins to jam on top of the sound of *sho* clusters, disconnected from the *sho* and ultimately burying it in the texture. A *shamisen* solo accompanied by a drum and bass with a driving rhythm pushes Japanese music toward jazz, but Mann's flute playing remains removed from any Japanese style or techniques. "Mauve over Blues" was composed by the keyboardist Pat Rebillot and points toward a New Age style, starting off in free time with *sho* clusters and punctuations from a prayer bell. Muraoka enters with a *shakuhachi* solo but is then displaced by a synthesized keyboard and Mann's flute solo, which move the track to a gentle, meditative, and non-Japanese style melody. The *shakuhachi* takes a solo turn with the jazz melody at the halfway point and the track ends with the return of the Japanese instruments and style from the opening. Again, elements of Japanese music and instrumentation seem merely to frame Mann's jazz music. The third track, however, is built on the Japanese melody "Kurodabushi (Sake Drinking Song)" and is kicked off with a "yo" *kakegoe* call and an accelerating *taiko* pattern, followed by *shamisen* and *shakuhachi*. Mann plays the folk melody himself in a slightly more breathy timbre than his typical style. The fourth track is a straight recording by the Ono Gagaku Society of the

most well-known *gagaku* piece, *Etenraku*. The album closes and appears to culmi-
nate with Mann's "Gagaku and Beyond," a funky and somewhat exotica-sounding
track performed by the Family of Mann alone with no Japanese elements. Mann
recorded three other tunes in this session in Japan and they eventually appeared
on the 1976 album *Surprises*. "The Sound of Windwood" is a brief recording that
includes Minoru Muraoka on *shakuhachi*, along with *sho, koto, shamisen*, and *taiko*.
Despite its evocative title, "The Butterfly in a Stone Garden" is devoid of Japanese
features and remains in Mann's funky style. Finally, "Anata (I Wish You Were Here
with Me)" is a soft-rock song opening with *koto* and a Japanese flute and closing
with a Japanese vocalist, Akiko Kosaka, in the final minute of the track.

Mann and Muraoka's jazz and fusion explorations on Western flute and Japanese
shakuhachi in the 1970s served as a model for multiple musicians in both the
United States and Japan in the final decades of the twentieth century. Though I will
consider the phenomenon of American *shakuhachi* music, focusing on several
musicians and composers, in my final chapter, I will mention briefly here one of
the more prominent musicians who pursued a form of jazz fusion on *shakuhachi*
in the 1980s and 1990s. John "Kaizan" Neptune was born in California in 1951 and
studied the *shakuhachi* at the University of Hawai'i and in Kyoto in the early 1970s,
earning his master's certification in *shakuhachi* in 1977 and then making Japan
his home. He has recorded nearly two dozen albums since 1979, most frequently
with Japanese jazz musicians on tracks of light, easy-listening jazz, occasionally
emulating the funkier style of Mann and on other albums resembling a New Age
extension of mid-century exotica. His 1980 album *Bamboo* helped to launch his
career, with his *shakuhachi* playing resembling Mann's jazz flute style more than
any traditional *shakuhachi* music. On *Jazzen* (1987), Neptune is accompanied by
Japanese musicians on vibraphone, guitar, and percussion and most of the album
is in his typical light jazz style. However, the album concludes with the track "Zen
Forest" based on a traditional *shakuhachi* piece. In the late 1980s and into the 1990s,
Neptune explored a world music fusion approach to instrumentation. He included
Indian instruments alongside *koto*, Japanese drums, and his *shakuhachi* playing
on *The Circle* (1986), recorded the 1988 album *Tokyosphere* with all Japanese traditional instruments, and performed with multiple Indian musicians on traditional
instruments on *River Rhythm* (1994). On these albums Neptune pursues a musical
hybridity within the framework of American jazz, emulating Cowell's approach to
living in "the whole world of music" as an American composer.

Postwar Occupations and the 1961 Tokyo East-West Music Encounter

Recapitulating the wave of elite Americans who arrived in Japan during the late
nineteenth-century Meiji Era, numerous American intellectuals were again
invited by the Japanese, or sent by US cultural agencies, following the postwar

occupation period. These scholars participated in a broader Cold War cultural exchange intended to promote American interests in East Asia. In turn, many of these scholars encountered postwar remnants of traditional Japanese culture and returned home as proselytizing preservationists for Old Japan. For example, the American philosopher Morton White lectured in Japan multiple times between 1952 and 1979 and later he and his wife published an account of their experiences based on their travel diaries. During their initial trip, White found that his leftist-leaning Japanese students distrusted American professors. He attempted to convince these students that he had not traveled as an agent of the State Department but that his trip was funded instead by the Rockefeller Foundation.[30] (We will discover below that, unbeknown to many of these American scholars, such private foundations frequently served as conduits for government-funded initiatives aimed at Japan.) The Whites, along with other American professors and US Army personnel, were taken to performances of *kabuki, bunraku,* and *noh.* They described *noh* chanting as "level recitative, sounding something like Gregorian chants but without much range of tone" and the drummers' *kakegoe* as "a low growling exclamation and then a growl that ended in a very high hoot like that of an owl."[31] Their aural experiences of nocturnal Japan echo those of Lafcadio Hearn and Henry Eichheim from half a century prior. Describing a 1952 outdoor *noh* performance, the Whites wrote:

> All this occurred to the accompaniment of rhythmic drums and low, undulating chants and screaming flutes. Even after the performance, we heard powerful drums being played far off in the gardens and came to realize that they had been throbbing all evening. At first we had thought this was another element of the performance, but while going home that dark night through the pine avenues, we came upon a circle of light and there saw a small raised stage like a bandstand where festival dancing was still going on to the droning accompaniment of those drums.[32]

The Whites were less intrigued by musical indications of Japanese modernity and complained at several points during their 1952 visit that loud jazz kept them awake at night.[33] During a dinner at the Osaka Hotel in 1966 they heard "a robot-like young Japanese [who] strummed jazz of the nineteen-twenties and other light music on a combination piano and electric organ."[34] In 1979 they experienced *karaoke* for the first time and were surprised to learn that all of that evening's musical entertainment would be "self-entertainment." They were particularly struck by the performance of a middle-aged Japanese man who, accompanied by the house pianist and electric guitarist, crooned "a sentimental Japanese ballad [*enka*] and seemed for all the world like a professional singer as he poured his soul into his number." The patrons took turns at the microphone, singing Japanese popular songs, an American popular song in English, and old college songs. The Whites, however, refused to perform themselves.[35]

The range of American intellectuals active in Japan during the occupation and post-occupation periods was wide and included figures who proved to have a major impact on traditional Japanese performing arts both within Japan and in the United States. Earle Ernst, a theater scholar and director, studied Japanese language at Fort Snelling, Minnesota, and then served as the head of theatrical censorship in occupied Japan. His censorship work led to his devotion to *kabuki*, on which he published a major study in 1956, and to his later productions of *kabuki* in English translation and traditional performance style at the University of Hawai'i.[36] The literary and musical scholar Faubion Bowers served as General MacArthur's personal Japanese language interpreter and, like Ernst, then served as theater censor during the occupation. Bowers is widely credited as being "the man who saved *kabuki*" when American occupation officials planned to ban the form. Bowers published the influential *Japanese Theatre* in 1952.[37] Donald Keene, the most prominent American scholar of Japanese literature in the second half of the twentieth century, had studied at the US Navy Japanese Language School before serving as an intelligence officer during World War II. He visited Japan soon after the war ended and returned to study as a graduate student in Kyoto in 1953. Keene later dedicated his 1966 book on *noh* to the American composer Alan Hovhaness and his wife.[38]

This American trio of Japanese literature scholars was matched by three prominent Western scholars of Japanese music in the postwar period. The first, Eta Harich-Schneider, was a German musicologist and harpsichordist who had refused to join the Nazi party and had emigrated to Japan in 1940. After the war, she served as the director of the US Army College music department and taught Western music to imperial court musicians, as the German bandmaster Franz Eckert had done in the 1880s. She then pursued Japanese studies at Columbia University starting in 1949. Harich-Schneider published in English on Japanese music in such journals as *The Musical Quarterly* and the *Journal of the American Musicological Society* in the 1950s, offering a detailed discussion of *gagaku* in 1953, complete with transcriptions, tuning systems, and transcribed *sho* clusters.[39] The other two major English-language scholars of Japanese music in this period, William P. Malm and Robert Garfias, were both students at the University of California, Los Angeles, in the 1950s when they first traveled to Japan. These scholars served a crucial role in introducing numerous American musicians, composers, and audiences to Japanese traditional music in the next half century.

Malm's first trip to Japan as a pianist and composition PhD student in 1955–1957 was supported by a Ford Foundation Grant, a source of funding for a good deal of the cross-cultural musical exchange between the United States and Japan throughout the Cold War.[40] He published his seminal study *Japanese Music and Musical Instruments* in 1959. This book opens with a description of the varied Japanese soundscape he encountered upon arrival in 1955, a scene in which popular music and jazz from TVs and radios competed with street festival instrumental music, folk songs, and an itinerant *shakuhachi* musician playing for alms.[41] In the early 1960s, Malm directed a *nagauta* (*kabuki* music) ensemble at the University of Michigan. In 1972, reflecting on his career as a scholar of Japanese music, he noted that his interest had remained focused on "pure music studies" rather than on music's social context.[42] A focus on the performance of Japanese traditional music at UCLA, the University of Michigan, the University of Hawai'i, and Wesleyan University influenced the careers of multiple American composers, as we will discover below.

Robert Garfias played perhaps the leading role in introducing *gagaku* to Americans in the 1950s to 1980s. Garfias started graduate school at UCLA in 1956 and first went to Japan for a three-year period in 1958 on a Ford Foundation grant.[43] In 1959 he served as a translator and attaché for the United Nations–sponsored Imperial Gagaku tour of the United States and published a short introduction to *gagaku*. He started the *gagaku* ensemble at UCLA with Los Angeles musicians and then brought to the University the Japanese Imperial court musician Suenobu Togi, who led the ensemble from 1962 to 1996. The Canadian-American architect Frank Gehry was a student member of the ensemble in 1958 and has claimed, "when I designed Disney Hall, I always imagined *gagaku* sounding in it."[44] The UCLA *gagaku* ensemble also had a significant impact on American composers, such as La Monte Young and Lois Vierk.

In addition to the opportunities to encounter Japanese music and musicians at major universities during this period, other cultural institutions sponsored national tours, bringing Japanese performing arts traditions to a broader audience. The Yoshida Trio, sponsored by Pro Musica and the Japan Society, had toured the United States in 1931–1932 with *sankyoku* music, and the *kabuki*-style Azuma dance troupe toured in 1954.[45] Barbara E. Thornbury has chronicled the efforts of the New York City Japan Society, starting as early as March 1912 when "the Society built a Japanese garden and teahouse on the roof of the [Hotel] Astor," where "for over two weeks visitors could observe tea ceremonies and *nō* presentations in the garden."[46] The Japan Society formed a Performing Arts Department in 1957. In 1959 *gagaku* and *bugaku* were presented for the first time outside of Japan at City Center, and the Japan Society played a role in setting up the major 1960 Grand Kabuki tour of the United States, an event that Joshua Logan and James Michener had proved instrumental in promoting.[47]

One cardinal transnational musical event, briefly noted in chapter 3, both climaxed and further stimulated the postwar Western interest in Japanese music: the 1961 Tokyo East-West Music Encounter.[48] The Encounter opened in mid-April 1961 and consisted of a three-week festival of performances and a concurrent conference during the first week. This complex and ambitious transnational event was conceived and largely designed by an equally transnational figure—the Paris-based American citizen, Russian émigré composer, and secretary-general of the Congress for Cultural Freedom, Nicolas Nabokov. The United States was represented at the Conference by the UCLA scholars Robert Garfias and Mantle Hood and the composers Colin McPhee, Lou Harrison, Virgil Thomson, Elliott Carter, and Henry Cowell. Nabokov enlisted the French ethnomusicologist Alain Daniélou to help organize several of the sessions and concerts of Asian music.[49] The former director of the Edinburgh Festival, Ian Hunter, was charged with arranging the details of the festival concerts from his office in London. Planning meetings were held in New York and Venice, and the planning committee initially included such figures as Ravi Shankar (India), William Schuman (New York), José Maceda (Philippines), and Purbotjaraka (Indonesia). The international roster of participants itself served as a political statement during this particularly charged period in the Cold War.

Correspondence reveals that Nabokov first conceived of the Encounter in 1955, but that the Soviet invasion of Hungary in 1956 postponed one planning meeting and Japanese anti-American sentiment and protests in 1959 and 1960 delayed the event itself.[50] Igor Stravinsky's 1959 visit to Japan had been intended to coincide with the Encounter. Stravinsky apparently heard *gagaku*, enjoyed *kabuki*, was particularly attracted to the *mokugyo* (fishhead drum) and to the *joruri* vocal style in *bunraku*, and dismissed *noh* as "insanely boring," though he found Nabokov's imitations of *noh* vocal style to be highly humorous.[51] From the start, Nabokov's plans were hugely ambitious. He invited numerous composers, many of whom, in the end, proved unable to attend, including: Britten, Tippett, Boulez, Chavez, Dallapiccola, Messiaen, and Milhaud. The broader impact of the Encounter is evident in the fact that some of the composers who were not able to attend, such as Messiaen and Boulez, would soon travel to Japan themselves or at least express serious interest in Japanese music. Nabokov had also contacted George Balanchine about the possibility of including the New York City Ballet and had considered the Jerome Robbins Ballet Company. The festival ultimately included performances of *gagaku, noh, kabuki*, Indian and Thai dance, the New York Philharmonic under Leonard Bernstein, the Japan Philharmonic, the Juilliard String Quartet, Isaac Stern, Hermann Prey, and (as a token gesture) the Modern Jazz Quartet. Most of the concerts featured European and American composers, though Cowell successfully and diplomatically suggested to Bernstein that the New York Philharmonic drop his *Ongaku* in favor of a piece by Toshiro Mayuzumi. The selection of Western ensembles proved far more troublesome than did the conference participants for, as Fosler-Lussier has noted: "Nowhere was the assessment of music's quality more stringent than in Japan. . . . Japanese audiences demanded not only elite Western classical music but also impeccable performances by the most famous musicians America could offer."[52] Conspicuously absent from both the festival and conference were musicians and scholars from the Soviet Union, most Eastern Bloc nations, and China.

The talks presented at the conference reveal fundamentally different perspectives on transnationalism between the majority of the Western participants and the Japanese scholars, critics, and composers. Several of the Japanese speakers, including Shinichi Yuize (the kotoist and former composition student of Cowell's), offered straightforward histories and explanations of various genres of Japanese traditional music, as though fulfilling a didactic obligation for their Western visitors. Others made clear a desire for Japanese musicians and composers to pursue Western music at the highest levels. For example, in a talk on "Religious Music" Yoshio Nomura asserted that European music "has an international character in the same manner sciences and technology do."[53] Most of the Western speakers lamented what Robert Garfias referred to as the "degeneration of Eastern traditions" in the face of postwar globalization and importation of American popular culture in particular.[54] Colin McPhee complained about the modernization of Balinese gamelan, describing new gamelan styles in terms that, ironically, seemed to describe quite aptly his own compositions based on this music.[55] Peter Crossley-Holland from the United Kingdom complained about the negative impact of Western popular music in Japan: "East and West are thrown together and destruction proceeds at an alarming pace." He then called for a campaign of speedy preservation, the creation of a musical Noah's ark, for the musical traditions that were extant.[56] Lou Harrison railed against equal temperament and expressed dismay that it was spreading throughout Asia.[57] As noted in chapter 3, in his speech, Henry Cowell made a case for accepting and conserving rather than condemning hybrid musics. In contrast, and in his typically blunt manner, Virgil Thomson (who had been enlisted early on to help plan the conference) called upon those Japanese composers "involved with Western music" to "make that involvement complete." He brazenly declared that the situation is different for Western composers involved with exotic musics since they "are not really changing their musical language" but are "refreshing it and clarifying it . . . through contact with other idioms," concluding that the "Western music language permits that. Yours does not. Don't be afraid to lose your own."[58] Dedicated to Shinichi Yuize, Thomson's musical response to this trip consisted of his *Variations for Koto* (1961). In triple meter and marked "Rhythmically Precise," the piece is devoid of Japanese style and aesthetics and it remains unclear how Thomson's musical style had been either refreshed or clarified through this encounter.[59]

One Japanese participant pointedly responded to his Western colleagues. Appearing on a panel at the end of the conference, the music critic and professor Takeo Murata pushed back at the Western advocates of Japanese traditional music, asserting that they needed to understand "the psychology of the modern-day audience." In reference to Garfias's talk, he explained that traditional Japanese music is "more exotic than Western music" for the Japanese youth and argued that traditional music should be presented on its own terms rather than selectively adopted as "when a foreign composer shows interest in our traditional music and tries to seek some materials in it," which he found "really annoying."[60] Cowell, who had famously declared in 1955 his desire to "live in the whole world of music," felt called upon to respond to Murata and declared that composers should "have the freedom to draw on worldwide musical resources." Cowell pointed to Mantle Hood's UCLA model of teaching Americans to play "oriental instruments from all nations" and concluded "we would like to include this and to have a world wide and international field by drawing on the music which appeals to people all over the world."[61] Thus, Cowell called for a musical universalism, but one that clearly seemed founded on specifically American terms to some of his Japanese colleagues.

Nabokov's published statements offered a rationale for the Encounter that resonates with Cowell's calls for musical universalism. Nabokov placed the focus of the Encounter on "the new relations which now exist in the modern world between traditional cultures of various new countries and western musical traditions," and he stated that the Encounter "has been devised as a means of a free confrontation and of a thoughtful understanding of [the] variety of traditional cultures of Asia and of their relation to the western tradition of music as it has evolved in the last fifty odd years in the western world and indeed in the world at large." He professed a transnational ultimate goal, moving beyond national boundaries to a utopian universalism: "Our modest beginning is only the first signpost on a long road the goal of which is an universal musical culture, preserving and protecting the values it inherited from the past and developing new ones for future generation[s]."[62]

Despite Nabokov's professed idealism, the Encounter did not actually offer a meeting between equals, but was instead primarily a venue for the West to encounter the novelty of the East. The published handbook listed three pages of Japanese names as members of the Encounter's organizing committee, but this gesture, in actuality, was an attempt to apply a "Made in Japan" sticker on an event that had been almost entirely planned from a Western point of view. Recapitulating the flow that had occurred following the forced "opening of Japan" in the mid-nineteenth century, the 1961 East-West Music Encounter also involved Americans traveling to Japan bringing their expertise to diagnose and pass judgment on musical life in postwar Asia. To appreciate the situation more fully, we need to follow the money. The funding for this Encounter and for a good deal of the trips by American musicians and composers to Japan in this period came in large part from the US government, with the goal of supporting US Cold War propaganda efforts. As Frances Stonor Saunders has revealed, the CIA was engaged in a long-term covert campaign to counter the Soviet Union through intellectual and artistic endeavors run, primarily, by the Congress for Cultural Freedom, with private foundations such as the Ford, Rockefeller, and Carnegie serving as "covers" for this CIA funding.[63]

This is not to say that American composers and scholars were all consciously participating in this Cold War outreach—the degree of their political awareness and commitment existed on a continuum. For instance, Lou Harrison, in particular, appears to have been unaware of the funding for this event. He had misunderstood the financial arrangements and had booked passage on a ship which he paid for himself, not realizing that funds were at hand to pay for his flight. Taking the slow boat to Tokyo proved beneficial, however, as it allowed Harrison to compose *Concerto in Slendro* onboard.[64] Nabokov's planning meetings for the Encounter were funded by the Rockefeller Foundation's Council on Economic and Cultural Affairs. Nabokov sent applications to other private foundations for further support, occasionally indicating that he expected to receive federal support as well. For example, in his application to the Catherwood Foundation, Nabokov claimed that "the US Government, as well as Cultural Relations Offices of various

European Governments, are very much interested in this Festival and have promised to extend a helping hand to make it a success."[65] In the Information Handbook for the Encounter, private sponsors are listed, as is UNESCO. However, the US State Department is not listed even though the travel costs for the Americans were directly covered from this source.[66] Nabokov was insistent in planning memos that US governmental involvement should not be mentioned. The Ford and Rockefeller Foundations funded not only aspects of the 1961 Encounter but supported, for example, Hovhaness's 1962 trip to Japan. Cowell's first trip to Japan was part of a larger goodwill tour funded by the Rockefeller Foundation and sponsored by the Department of State, US Information Agency. In retrospect, the entire funding situation and goals for these transnational encounters appear somewhat paradoxical. Clearly, the US funding agencies hoped that American political values and culture would be carried to Japan through musical diplomacy. However, most of these American musical diplomats warned the Japanese not to embrace Western musical culture, but to preserve their own. In addition, these diplomats almost all encountered something in Japanese music that they deemed valuable and worthy of transporting back home.

In planning the Encounter, Nabokov worked with a new Japanese organization named the Society for International Cultural Exchange, and his main contact was Katsujiro Bando, the organization's secretary-general. This organization came under intense pressure from left-leaning Japanese musicians to break ties with the Congress for Cultural Freedom. Anti-American sentiment in Japan was particularly strong in 1959 and 1960. In a 6 October 1960 letter from Nabokov in Paris to his Japanese counterpart in Tokyo, Nabokov states that he is "quite incensed" to learn that [Shūkichi] Mitsukuri, a prominent composer, had referred to Nabokov as a "leader of the Cold War." Nabokov protested, "nor do I understand how our Festival could possibly be considered political anti-communist action. If Mr. Mitsukuri and his group want to make out of it a political event, that is their business but they will be certainly acting in bad faith."[67] Such correspondence reveals that Japanese members of the executive committee of the International Music Council of UNESCO were speaking up against the Encounter, which they viewed as a blatant act of US propaganda. Indeed, a "Society for Criticizing the Tokyo World Music Festival" (as the Encounter was referred to in Japanese) published a document entitled *We Criticize the Tokyo World Music Festival* on 10 April 1961 in which Nabokov's previous anti-communist propaganda work in Germany was cited as well as his public attack on Shostakovich. These Japanese critics pointed to the absence of communist countries from the Festival and Conference programs and argued that the entire event was set up from a Western rather than Japanese perspective.[68]

In his final report on the Encounter, Nabokov claimed that socialist countries had been invited to participate in this transnational encounter but had declined: "Representatives from socialist countries were invited by the Japanese sponsors to participate both in the Conference and the Festival, with the full agreement of the Congress for Cultural Freedom." He also noted that "the Japanese and Western organizers met with strong opposition to the East-West music Encounter among a section of the Japanese intelligentsia on account of the anti-American feeling which prevailed in Japan at that time."[69] Other US participants also noted the negative impact of the political climate on the Encounter. In his 28 June 1961 report on his experience of the Encounter, Garfias referred to the "unfortunate" and "misguided" attitude of the Japanese press, which he felt had intimidated Japanese musicologists from participating.[70] At least one American participant in addition to Nabokov appears to have been aware of the role of the US government in funding the Encounter. In his 31 May 1961 report on the Encounter, Elliott Carter wrote: "To me the EWME was a very stimulating and important international exchange of ideas which will always remain with me as an example of what men who are occupied with cultural affairs can accomplish with the help of intelligent government assistance."[71] There is no doubt that the Congress for Cultural Freedom aimed to promote US interests in Japan through the East-West Music Encounter. However, it is also clear that the Encounter was a special project for the composer Nabokov, who relished his role as a musical impresario as much as he did his role as an anti-communist crusader.

The Transnational Influences of Gagaku

The opening ceremony for the 1961 Tokyo East-West Music Encounter began with a performance of three *gagaku* pieces. Refined, stately, slow, and intense—*gagaku* was never intended as musical entertainment for the masses. Instead, throughout its nearly millennium-and-a-half existence this orchestral genre has served as ritualistic court and temple music and as accompaniment for the equally refined dance genre of *bugaku*. The few Americans who heard *gagaku* in the late nineteenth and early twentieth centuries were, by and large, not entranced, though, as we have seen, Lafcadio Hearn did praise its "weird charm" and Henry Eichheim celebrated this ancient music's modernity. The austerity of *gagaku* made it a particularly appealing model for an astonishing range of mid-century European and American modernist composers, just as *noh* had been embraced across genres by modernists in the first decades of the twentieth century. Though the UN-sponsored Imperial Gagaku tour brought this music to American audiences in 1959, multiple European and American composers first heard *gagaku* performed live during their trips to Japan in the late 1950s and early 1960s, including at the East-West Music Encounter. Reverberations of these encounters are audible in their subsequent works.

As early as 1936, the Japanese musicologist Hisao Tanabe heard connections between *gagaku* and modern European music: "to take the quality of harmony alone, *Gagaku* is considered to be more congenial to the people of today than the modern music of the West. This may be well proved by the fact that the recent compositions of Debussy, Fauré, Scriabine, Stravinsky, etc. have come nearer to the Japanese

Gagaku in their combination of sounds."[72] Though his list of composers is some-what surprising, and his claims for the genre's acceptance seem premature and a bit confusing, Hisao's vision for *gagaku*'s potential influence would be borne out two decades later. Pointing to musical time, rather than harmony, Ann Stimson states that for the mid-century European and American avant-garde, "Japan symbolized intensity in the present moment. The West, on the other hand, symbolized urgency for the future. . . . To have a Japanese sense of time meant to saturate the present moment with intensity and leave no trace of the duality of present vs. non-present," and she points out that "although Boulez, Stockhausen, Varèse, and Messiaen reacted differently, each discovered aesthetic principles in Japanese music which were similar to his own."[73] Ieda Bispo has noted the "superiority of tone color over other parameters, [the] freedom of form, and absence of meter" found in both mid-century European music and *gagaku*.[74] More broadly, Robert Garfias claims in a retrospective statement that, starting in the late 1950s, "really important western composers were all interested in *gagaku*, and no other kinds of Japanese music. *Gagaku* is the only one."[75] Though other forms of Japanese traditional music proved influential as well, I will focus briefly in this section on the influence of *gagaku* on the music of several major European composers before turning to Americans and, particularly, to the extensive impact of Japanese music on the career of Alan Hovhaness.

Messiaen's encounter with and musical response to *gagaku* has received sub-stantial scholarly attention. He first traveled to Japan in 1962 and composed his own musical impressions of the exotic nation in that year. *Sept Haïkaï: Esquisses Japonaises* refers in its title to a poetic form of playful linked verse and consists of an introduction and coda, musical "sketches" of four Japanese sites, and a central movement entitled "Gagaku." Cheong Wai Ling notes that the Introduction and Coda are related through retrograde and that Messiaen said that the two movements symbolized the pair of guardian sculptures found at the entrance to Buddhist temples.[76] Messiaen employed Indian rhythms and Japanese bird calls, which are labeled in the score, in several of the movements. In "Gagaku," correspondences in orchestration are made explicit as the trumpet, English horn, and two oboes stand in for the *hichiriki* and eight violins playing sul ponticello approximate the *sho*. Messiaen marked the trumpet line "noble, religious, nostalgic" and referred to the timbre of the *sho* as "sour and acid." Cheong points to Messiaen's heterophonic tex-ture, characteristic of *gagaku*,[77] and notes that the violin clusters are related to those appearing in *Chronochromie*, the work Messiaen completed just prior to his trip, suggesting that "Messiaen might have found the Japanese gagaku attractive not just because of its intrinsic beauty, but perhaps also because he hears in it vivid sugges-tion of his own music."[78] Messiaen did not aim for a direct translation of *gagaku*—leaving out the *kakko*, which he felt would have been "unbearable for the Western ear," and referring to the sonic "violence" of the *hichiriki*'s timbre as "absolutely ag-onizing for a Westerner"—but instead claimed to have "preserved the essence" and composed "in the spirit" of *gagaku*.[79]

Messiaen scholars have sought both to distance Messiaen's "Japanese sketches" from earlier programmatic works of musical *japonisme* and to suggest the piece's impact on contemporaneous and later works by other composers. Bispo concludes that "although it is not rigorously faithful to the original sources, *Sept Haïkaï* is very distant from the crude applications of Japanese music made by early twentieth century composers."[80] Paul Griffiths identifies "resemblances of motif" and "structural similarity" between Messiaen's "Gagaku" and the traditional piece *Etenraku* and hears an echo of Varèse's *Nocturnal* (1961) in Messiaen's approximation of *sho* clusters.[81] Luigi Antonio Irlandini hails "Gagaku" as marking a return to religious expression in the music of Messiaen and as emblematic of Stockhausen's "moment form."[82] Finally, Stimson finds that Messiaen was "at the root of the avant-garde's interest in time in Japanese music" and that Boulez and Stockhausen repeatedly referred to having encountered Asian music in Messiaen's classes.[83]

Several of the mid-century modernist composers who were interested in Japanese music held fairly decided views on how or whether cross-cultural musical influence might transpire. In his typically assertive and proscriptive mode, Pierre Boulez addressed these questions in a 1967 article entitled "Oriental Music: A Lost Paradise?" In a sweeping statement, Boulez claimed that the "musical systems of East and West cannot have any bearing on one another, and this will be quickly realized by experienced composers of character."[84] Complaining of colleagues who "form a too sentimental and emotional idea of Oriental music" and who "dive into it like tourists setting off to visit a landscape that is about to vanish," Boulez related that he admired Asian music for the "stage of perfection" that it had achieved but concluded that "otherwise the music is dead."[85] Boulez did not approve of other composers' engagements with Japanese music, declaring that John Cage had composed interesting music before he "became infatuated with Zen."[86] Nevertheless, Boulez celebrated traditional Japanese music and performing arts, stating, for instance, that "Noh remains the peak of Oriental art," that he "would like to study it more closely, also the relations between Noh and *Sprechgesang*, and hope one day to be able to spend a long period in Japan in order to do this." Boulez declared that a "new vocal technique should now be created based on the Noh style" and that he "would like to investigate all the Noh schools, to make a thorough study in Japan of the techniques, and to take lessons long enough to discover the secret of the Japanese, the ease with which they pass from speech to singing."[87]

Like many of his colleagues, Boulez was also particularly attracted to *gagaku*, which he first heard recordings of in 1945 or 1946 and then live in Japan in 1967, noting that "the first thing which is very impressive is the expansion of time, because the sustained pace of this music is very slow for a long time. And that's completely different from our conceptions of time."[88] Boulez adored what he considered to be the use of *sho* clusters in Stravinsky's *Symphony of Psalms* and planned to use this sound in his own works.[89] Acknowledging the influence of *gagaku* on his music, Boulez pointed to parallels between the Japanese genre and his 1975 orchestral work *Rituel*.[90] Phillip Huscher states that *Rituel* "mirrors Boulez's infatuation with gagaku in its stately, ceremonial pacing—its evocation of timeless ritual—and in the slowly unfolding brass chords that sound from center stage."[91] Ultimately, despite his pronouncements warning against fetishizing exotic music and his skeptical views of cross-cultural influence, Boulez found in Japanese music "a beauty so far removed from our own culture and so close to my own temperament."[92]

Xenakis made his first of multiple trips to Japan in 1961 to attend the East-West Music Encounter, which he found to be "an unforgettable experience, because I became acquainted with a different way of life."[93] During this first trip he attended performances of *noh, kabuki,* and *gagaku*.[94] Following this trip, Xenakis repeatedly suggested that there must have been a deep historical connection between ancient Greek theater and Japanese *noh*.[95] He even heard a resemblance in *noh* chanting to Byzantine psalmodies and hypothesized: "Noh, coming as it does from Buddhist chant, it is not improbable that this resemblance comes from a historical relation lost in the centuries of Greco-Buddhism."[96] Xenakis acknowledged the influence of *noh* on his own music theater works and, more generally, celebrated the "economy of means" as the "strength of traditional Japanese art."[97] Japanese influence is evident in several of his instrumental works as well. Given that Xenakis had been interested in East Asian music prior to his first trip to Japan, Matossian makes an analogy to *gagaku* in a discussion of the polyphonic texture of Xenakis's 1956 *Pithoprakta* and points to a similar tension between stasis and motion.[98] Xenakis created the electronic tape piece *Hibiki-Hana-Ma* ("reverberation-flower-interval") in Tokyo, employing the orchestra of the Japan Broadcasting Corporation with added *biwa*, for the 1970 World Exposition in Osaka.[99] In Xenakis's 1964 *Eonta* for piano, trumpets, and trombones, I hear distinct allusions to the *sho* in the muted brass clusters that swell from pianississimo to forte and fortississississimo. Xenakis's interest in Japan and Japanese culture was sustained through his association with contemporary Japanese musicians and composers as well as through encounters with traditional Japanese performing arts. For example, the piano solo in *Eonta* was realized by Xenakis's student Yuji Takahashi at the premiere, and Xenakis enjoyed a close friendship with the composer Toru Takemitsu.

Though Stockhausen's interest in Japan emerged a bit later than several of the other mid-century composers considered here, he attempted to make up for lost time through cultural immersion. A decade after his initial 1966 trip to Japan, Stockhausen recalled that he had attended the Omizutori ceremony (the Buddhist water drawing festival in Nara) and had not felt "like a stranger," instead he felt "like someone who is coming home. I was so much in love with Japan." Spiritually, Stockhausen claimed that for him "it all started in Japan."[100] In rather stark contrast to Boulez, encountering exotic musical traditions instilled in Stockhausen a feeling of obligation to "conserve as many musical forms and performing styles as at all possible" and a universalist belief that "every person has all of mankind within himself."[101] He viewed daily life in Japan as an art form[102] and was struck by the perception of time in Japanese performing arts, observing that the Japanese have a "far larger time scale at the bottom, which means they have much slower and longer events than we ever would admit."[103] Stockhausen's remarks on Japanese music frequently center on temporal perceptions and on ritualistic forms.[104] Stimson suggests that Stockhausen's admiration for Japanese temporal sensibility, for the perception in Japanese art of a complete focus on "nothing but the present moment," shaped the composer's approach to musical time, including his concept of "moment form."[105] Stockhausen both acknowledged details of Japanese influence and suggested more general parallels between his work and Japanese aesthetics, pointing, for example, to his large scale 1960 *Carré* as attesting to his interest in temporal perception before he had traveled to Japan.[106] He suggested a possible influence of the *sho* sonority in his explorations in vocal timbre in *Stimmung* (1968).[107] Christian Utz has identified 1966–1977 as the period of most obvious Japanese influence on Stockhausen, a period spanning from his composition of *Telemusik* to *Der Jahreslauf*.[108] The influence of Japan manifested in a variety of ways and in multiple works by Stockhausen, but it is clear that his work was most directly shaped by Buddhist ritualistic performance and by timbral and temporal aspects of *gagaku*.

Stockhausen provocatively asserted that Wagner "would have been the best gagaku composer—if gagaku had been composed—or the best No drama listener in the world."[109] Stockhausen assumed the Wagnerian mantle in his composition of the monumental, seven-evening opera cycle *Licht*. It appears that his experience of part of the Omizutori rite, which culminates a two-week long ceremony, served as an additional impetus, along with Wagner's *Ring*, for this operatic cycle. Resembling *gagaku* and *bugaku* in its ritualistic formality and pace, Stockhausen's *Inori* (1973–1974), an invocation, is scored for an eighty-nine-member orchestra, including a chromatic set of Japanese *rin* metal bowls that are used individually in Buddhist temple ceremonies. The composer calls for specific ritualistic gestures and movements by two dancers and offers lengthy notes and directions for every aspect of the performance. *Telemusik* (1966), an electronic tape composition dedicated "to the Japanese people," plays out on an even grander cultural and musical scale, employing manipulated recordings of musical sounds from a variety of cultures across the globe, thereby realizing Cowell's universal musical vision through technological means. In program notes for the premiere in Japan, and quoted in subsequent liner notes and programs, Stockhausen referred mystically to the various musical sources as "mysterious visitors" who "all wanted to participate in *Telemusik*." By far the greatest number of these eager musical sources were from recordings of Japanese traditional music.[110] The work begins and ends with silence—the final sound we hear is a modified "ee-ya" *kakegoe* call. Specific moments in the piece are marked by recordings of large bronze bells in Nara and Kyoto and by the sounds of the *mokugyo*, *rin*, and small Japanese gongs. Though Stockhausen identifies his wide range of recorded sources, many of these are submerged through electronic manipulation and layering of recordings and electronically generated sounds. Nevertheless, numerous Japanese musical traditions are audibly referenced in the work. For instance, "structure three" starts with a drum roll and the faint sound of a *gagaku* ensemble playing *Etenraku* and "structure twenty-two" features Japanese male chant layered with an Amazon female lullaby. Though Japanese references dominate in this Japanese-commissioned work, as Robin Maconie has put it, "the unambiguous message [in *Telemusik*] is of a hidden unity of world musical traditions which may be demonstrably integrated through the medium of the composer and electronic sound processes."[111]

In a similar globe-trotting spirit, Japanese music is visited in Stockhausen's *Michaels Reise um die Erde* (1978), which formed the second act of *Donnerstag aus Licht*. Various Japanese instruments—*keisu*, *rin*, Geisha bell—are heard during this cultural stop as is the influence of *gagaku*. Maconie describes Stockhausen's imitation of the "textures and sonorities" of *gagaku*, detailing parallels in orchestration between the harmonium and Hammond organ and the *sho*, the harp and pizzicato strings and the sounds of the *biwa* and *koto*, and the English horn serving as an approximation of the *hichiriki*. Maconie concludes that "the cultural allusions to Japanese music are crudely drawn, though the music itself is fascinatingly rich."[112] In 1977 Stockhausen had been commissioned by the Japanese Imperial Gagaku Ensemble. This was a landmark moment in the history of *gagaku*'s influence on European and American composers and resulted in *Der Jahreslauf*, the first part of *Licht* that Stockhausen composed and that he then reworked for Western instruments. In an interview a decade following the premiere, the *ryuteki* player Sukeyasu Shiba recalled that "although some problems may have arisen because of [Stockhausen's] lack of knowledge of the instruments, I still found it to be energetic and quite remarkable in its own way."[113]

The impact of *gagaku* is frequently cited in discussions of multiple other contemporaneous composers, though it is often more of a challenge to trace than in the music of Messiaen, Xenakis, and Stockhausen. For example, several major works by Edgard Varèse include passages that suggest the harmonic and timbral model of *gagaku*, but it proves difficult to pin down in detail this composer's encounters with Japanese music. Varèse apparently heard *gagaku* for the first time in 1958 and claimed that any similarity between *gagaku* and his *Intégrales* and *Octandre* from 1923–1925 was therefore coincidental.[114] It is possible, however, that he had heard Eichheim's version of *Etenraku* or had seen a transcription or heard a recording of *gagaku* in the 1920s. Fernand Ouellette recounts Varèse's enthusiasm for *gagaku*— "for him, it was an image of eternity"—and, pointing to the string parts in *Nocturnal* (1961), claims that *gagaku* "enabled him to conceive, with his use of the strings, another duration, and another meeting of lines in space."[115] Chou Wen-chung, who had been a student and friend of Varèse, noted in 1971 that Varèse's "music suggests a strong affinity with Asian music" and pointed to the "curious coincidence" between the opening of *Intégrales* and *gagaku*, in which the trumpet line resembles the *ryuteki* and the E♭ clarinet the *hichiriki*, piccolos and B♭ clarinet approximate the *sho*, and the trombone part recalls the *koto* and *biwa* lines of *gagaku*.[116] Similarly, Wilfrid Mellers suggests that in the 1954 *Déserts* the "dissonant heterophony, the microtonally wailing portamentos, and the immensely slow metrical organization create what is very rare—a *new sound*, yet this new sound reminds us of something immensely ancient, the imperial court music of Japanese *gagaku* that flourished in the eighth and ninth centuries."[117]

Discussion of American minimalist music rarely fails to note the impact of Indian, West African, and Indonesian musical traditions on the compositions of these composers. Japanese music, however, is only very rarely referenced though it did play a role. For example, La Monte Young's devotion to sustained sounds and glacial tempi is most often traced to his study of Indian classical music and the centrality of the *tambura*'s drone in that tradition. However, Young also encountered *gagaku* in 1957 as a student at the University of California, Los Angeles. Jeremy Grimshaw suggests that Dennis Johnson's "affinity for playing the *hichiriki*, the Japanese double-reed instrument, enhanced Young's fascination with gagaku and perhaps helps explain some of the striking similarities between gagaku textures and Young's work with sustained sounds."[118] (Johnson was a fellow composition student and friend of Young's at UCLA.) The possible impact of *gagaku* on other minimalist composers is less easy to determine. In his notes to the score of *Music for 18 Musicians* (1974–1976), Steve Reich states that "harmonic movement plays a more important role in this piece than in any other I have written."[119] Reich discusses the cycle of eleven chords heard in the opening and closing sections and the importance of a breathing pace or rhythm in the piece. The pitch content of Reich's eleven chords are only somewhat similar to the eleven clusters of the *sho*, but the swelling and overlapping of these chords does suggest the *sho*'s sonority.[120]

The East-West Music Encounter in Tokyo proved particularly important to the career of Lou Harrison who, in letters to Nabokov leading up to what would be his first trip to Asia, enthused, "the entire occasion already stimulates me almost unbearably."[121] Though Harrison found Japanese temperament and tuning disappointing and focused his studies more on the music of Korea during this trip, traces of *gagaku* are audible in some of his subsequent music. Harrison had first heard *gagaku* on a recording given to him by the *shakuhachi* musician and friend of Henry Cowell, Kitaro Tamada.[122] Following the 1961 Encounter, Harrison drew on elements of *gagaku*—the *sho* clusters and canonic form—in the odd-numbered movements of *Pacifika Rondo* (1963), combining elements of Japanese *gagaku* with Korean *aak* as Leta E. Miller and Fredric Lieberman have noted.[123] (Harrison's juxtaposition of East Asian and Latin American musical styles in *Pacifika Rondo* would be echoed in Stephen Hartke's 1988 *Pacific Rim*, which begins and ends with clear *sho*-inspired clusters and brings together East Asian and Latin American melodic, harmonic, timbral, and rhythmic influences.) Harrison again expressed his Korean preferences in a piece otherwise calling for Japanese influence in *Set for Four Haisho and Percussion* (1992). This late work had been commissioned by the Japanese National Theatre, which called on the composer to create music for this ancient and musically extinct panpipe. Harrison's piece requires tuning in a Korean rather than Japanese mode and draws on other aspects of ancient Korean music.[124] As Toshie Kakinuma has noted, "Harrison did not seem overtly concerned with Japanese traditions but turned his eyes to the Korean Confucian ritual music that was closely connected with the panpipe . . . he substituted a tangible Korean tradition for the lost Japanese tradition."[125] The third movement, however, consists of a poem Harrison wrote to be delivered in the vocal style of *noh* with percussion accompaniment.

Alan Hovhaness was by far the most prolific American composer of Japanese-influenced pieces. Though he did not attend the East-West Music Encounter in 1961, he had traveled to Japan in 1960 and would return on a Rockefeller grant to study *gagaku* in 1962–1963 at the Imperial Household music department with Masataro Togi.[126] Hovhaness had been interested in Japanese music and culture for some years prior to his first trip and studied *gagaku* performance while serving as composer-in-residence at the University of Hawai'i in 1961–1962. In his initial letter to the Rockefeller Foundation, Hovhaness declared: "I feel that I may be particularly adept in enriching Western musical techniques with principles and concepts derived from Japanese classical music."[127] Following up on his travel grant request, Hovhaness explained: "I want to study the modes of Bunraku and Noh so that I may incorporate these principles in my own music and also in my future teaching and experimentation. In connection with this study, I wish to learn to play some Japanese instruments which I wish also to incorporate later in orchestras of western instruments."[128] Hovhaness was a devoted student of *gagaku* in the early 1960s, learning to play the *hichiriki* and *sho* in particular.[129] In Hawai'i in June 1962 he wrote that he was studying six Japanese instruments and that he could already play the *sho* and *hichiriki* in public and that playing and composing for these "is a glorious experience—my wife and I play ancient Japanese gagaku music every night."[130] (See Figure 8.1.) Upon receiving the Rockefeller funding, Hovhaness attested that he and his wife "already practice the shō, ryuteki, hichiriki instruments of gagaku as well as shamisen so we will be well prepared for this wonderful study."[131] However, his application to the Rockefeller Foundation for additional funding in 1963 to travel again to Japan and to support publication of a book "of ancient Japanese scores" that he had transcribed in modern notation was denied.[132]

Throughout his career, Hovhaness repeatedly asserted in lectures, interviews, and articles that he used "principles, but not melodies" from exotic musical cultures.[133] As early as 1954, he explained that in his compositions, "[w]hile elements of style have been absorbed from Indian, Arabic, and Japanese traditions, the music is original, an addition to tradition, not an adaption—the melodies are not quoted from folk lore but are original melodies composed in traditional scales—combined cycles of rhythmic elements circle around firm centers—as the orbits of planets revolve around central suns."[134] Hovhaness was particularly interested in the triple canons and loosely organized counterpoint he heard in some older forms of *gagaku* and attributed his own compositional idea of including sections of "controlled chaos" in his scores to this exotic model.[135] He celebrated *gagaku* for prefiguring innovations in modern music, pointing to the parallels with "aleatoric music" that he found in those triple-canon textures of *gagaku*'s "Great Overtures" or *choshi*, the

Figure 8.1 Hovhaness with a *sho* and Elizabeth Whittington Hovhaness ("Naru") with a *ryuteki*. Photograph by Judy Shamoto, Spring 1962, taken in the Hovhanesses' faculty housing apartment, University of Hawai'i. Courtesy of the Armenian Cultural Foundation, Arlington, MA.

principles of Anton Webern in Japanese *netori* or "Short Preludes," and the polytonal and polyrhythmic music worthy of Charles Ives that resulted from the practice of superimposing a piece from *noh* music over *joruri* music or *nagauta* style in a *kabuki* performance.[136] He went on to lament the abandonment of this older practice in the postwar era, noting that it had "unfortunately been modified and thus destroyed to correspond with sentimental Western music of the last century" and that the different simultaneous musical forms were being transposed to the same mode to avoid clashing, even though this "old style of purely Asian music was far more modern than the diluted Western influence which brought about its destruction."[137]

Hovhaness's Japanese-influenced works are most often not as avant-garde in style as some of his commentary might lead us to suspect. I have identified some two dozen works composed in the 1950s to 1980s that indicate Japanese influence in their programmatic titles, instrumentation, and/or stylistic features. Multiple compositions were inspired by specific Japanese sites, art works, or cultural figures. The 1953 song "O Lady Moon," for soprano (or women's chorus) accompanied by clarinet and piano employs a text from Lafcadio Hearn's *A Japanese Miscellany* but otherwise exhibits no Japanese features. Hovhaness completed the first version of the *Fuji* cantata for women's chorus, flute, harp, and strings in April 1960 in Tokyo.[138] The text was taken from the eighth-century poetry collection the *Manyoshu*, and the work was dedicated to the Ueno Gakuen College. Suggestions of Japanese, specifically *gagaku*, influence are evident in the sections of uncoordinated playing (marked "very free, not together"), the general plodding rhythm, and the prominence of the flute. Hovhaness repeatedly composed for Japanese instruments during his period of *gagaku* study, including in the 1962 sonatas for Hichiriki and Sho, Ryūteki and Shō, and the *Two Sonatas for Koto*. In each case he allowed in the score for the substitution of Western instruments, calling into question how essential he felt the Japanese timbres were to these pieces.

Numerous works by Hovhaness composed during this period feature specific aspects of Japanese traditional music and resemble in certain respects works by his contemporaries. Wayne David Johnson has identified the use of *koto* scales in such piano works as *Three Haikus* (1965) and *Komachi* (1971).[139] The orchestral *Meditation on Zeami* (1963), premiered by Stokowski, includes sliding between pitches and *sho*-like violin clusters (e.g., reh. 3). Resembling Cowell's Japanese-influenced works from the early 1960s, Hovhaness's *Ode to the Temple of Sound* (1965) has an opening and closing section marked by clusters and a big pentatonic brassy theme, while the middle section of the piece is Western in style, with a folk-like rhythmic lilt and fugal texture.[140] Two Japanese-inspired orchestral works composed in 1964 stand out in Hovhaness's oeuvre. *Floating World: "Ukiyo" Ballade for Orchestra* was commissioned by Andre Kostelanetz for the New York Philharmonic and was intended, according to a note in the score, to express the "old Japanese Buddhist concept of uncertainty, change." The piece includes some typical stylistic features that Hovhaness celebrated in *gagaku*, including pitch clusters resembling those of the *sho*, "planned chaos" sections, and sliding tones. The score presents excerpts from reviews of several performances of the work, including from the Utah *Desert News* review of the premiere in the Tabernacle: "From the opening bar, *Floating World* seemed so authentically Japanese that this department half expected to see Maestro Kostelanetz conduct in a ceremonial kimono. . . . One does not paint the impression of rising mists around Mount Fuji in counterpoint but rather in shimmering whole-tone harmonies enhanced by oriental rhythms played by gongs and drums and odd-to-us imitated sounds of the Japanese guitar-like instruments."[141] This excerpt points to the generally positive and exuberantly exoticized reception of Hovhaness's musical *japonisme*. It remains unclear in what way the similarly well-received *Fantasy on Japanese Wood Prints* might represent a response to specific examples of this most famous of Japanese visual art forms. This work for xylophone soloist and orchestra features several aspects of *gagaku* style, including woodwind glissandi in the style of the *hichiriki* and *ryuteki* and sustained clusters, though it also includes a surprising stylistic shift at rehearsal no. 18 to a lilting tune in 6/8, similar to the middle movements of Cowell's Japanese-inspired concerti. Japanese influence is also abundantly clear in Hovhaness's theater works. As Tyler Kinnear has detailed, *noh* profoundly shaped Hovhaness's operas, eight of which were composed between 1959 and 1969, the height of his interest in Japanese culture.[142] Kinnear notes that Hovhaness employed harmony based on *gagaku sho* clusters and included *kakko*-style drum rolls in his *noh*-influenced stage works.[143] By combining *noh* and *gagaku* traits in his chamber operas, Hovhaness was prefiguring Benjamin Britten's Japanese-influenced Church Parables composed in the mid to late 1960s.[144]

Hovhaness was not enthusiastic about the music of many of his European and American composer colleagues. In March 1961 when asked about his favorite music, he listed music of South India and Japanese theatrical traditions, and the music of Toru Takemitsu and Toshiro Mayuzumi. He gave a nod to Lou Harrison as an American talent who was struggling, and dismissed contemporary European music entirely as being "in decay."[145] Hovhaness referred sweepingly to "Cage, Stockhausen and company" as "the new idiots."[146] Despite his antagonistic stance to other contemporary composers, Hovhaness's approach to incorporating the world of music in his compositions shared a good deal with that of Cowell, Harrison, and Messiaen. Like Messiaen, Hovhaness sought to combine detailed aspects of Indian and Japanese music. Whereas Messiaen employed Indian rhythms with *gagaku* textures and timbres, Hovhaness composed melodies based on Indian ragas in works for *gagaku* instruments, harmonies, and temporal features. Like Harrison, Hovhaness occasionally combined features of Japanese and Korean music. Hovhaness's Symphony 17 (1963) for flutes, trombones, and percussion offers an example of his syncretic approach. He referred to this piece as a "neo-gagaku" and "neo-aak" work that employed individual Indian ragas for each movement. The six flutes create a *sho* sonority but with the pitches of a raga scale and near the end they play in canon in a free rhythm. He described one section of the symphony as resembling Indonesian gamelan music and explained that he decided to score for metal percussion instruments because he had been commissioned by the American Metal Association. A similar syncretic approach to combining the world's musical traditions is evident in contemporaneous works by a wide range of American and European composers. Hovhaness also shared with Messiaen an intense desire to convey religious expression through his music and, again like Messiaen (and even Stockhausen), turned to exotic musical traditions to serve his spiritual aspirations. Much of Hovhaness's mysticism was rooted in explorations of his Armenian heritage. However, he found the music of South and East Asia equally stimulating in spiritual terms. As he wrote in 1960: "The music of India, especially South India, also ancient Japan, cannot be separated from religious thought and feeling . . . I am searching for many things which the West and modern thought have lost but which still remain in the East, although these things are hidden from all tourists."[147] Hovhaness was far from alone in the mid-twentieth century in turning to Japan in a spiritual *cum* musical quest.

Zen and the Art of Experimental Music: From the Beats to Cage and Beyond

At the turn of the twentieth century, American artistic perceptions of Japanese culture were largely shaped by the aesthetic explanations of Kakuzo Okakura and the stories and essays of Lafcadio Hearn. Fifty years later, this role was assumed by the Japanese philosopher D. T. Suzuki and several of the American Beat poets and novelists. Japanese aesthetics, as perceived through mediated encounters with Zen Buddhism, inspired experimentation in multiple forms of American art throughout the Cold War period. As Bonnie Marranca has claimed:

> Japan has been an extraordinary influence on the New York experimental arts scene, beginning at least in the 1940s with Martha Graham, and spreading in the postwar period in the "downtown" worlds of dance, music, video, performance, and theater. It would be difficult to imagine the New York arts scene without the Japanese influence, whether philosophically through Zen and its spread by Cage, or aesthetically in the highly formal theater that has influenced artists from the era of Black Mountain, Happenings, Judson, Fluxus, and the more recent decades of the 1970s and 1980s.[148]

The influence of Zen, and of Japanese traditional culture more generally, in the postwar decades was also evident in experimental art created far beyond the New York epicenter, particularly in San Francisco and elsewhere on the West Coast, and encompassed everything from a widespread *haiku* craze to the esoteric music theater of Harry Partch.[149] Here, I will briefly consider representative composers who were, to varying degrees, inspired by the writings of Suzuki and the Beats and by John Cage's engagement with Zen.

The American perception of Zen as coextensive with Japanese culture is off the mark, given that Zen is far from being the dominant form of Buddhism followed in Japan. The American fascination with Zen can be traced to the impact of a few specific prominent figures. Daisetz Teitaro Suzuki offered a version of Zen Buddhism that American artists in the 1950s found particularly useful, for, as Kay Larson has put it, Suzuki "was probably just Zen enough, at the time."[150] Suzuki served as the primary exponent of Zen in the United States and taught at Columbia University in the 1950s.[151] Jane Naomi Iwamura notes that American fashion magazines helped to introduce Suzuki as the face of Zen to a broader public, replacing the image of the Japanese male as evil soldier with his kindly and wise visage.[152] D. T. Suzuki's image in the United States would soon be joined by that of Shinichi Suzuki, music instructor of the famous "Suzuki Method." Robert Fink has referred to Shinichi Suzuki's method as the Zen of repetitive practice and documents the rise of his impact on American musical pedagogy from 1958 to the 1971 establishment of the Suzuki Association of America.[153] Both the Suzuki Method and D. T. Suzuki's Zen teachings were simultaneously embraced and derided through Orientalist stereotyping during this period. In 1958, D. T. Suzuki addressed the Western reception of his writings:

> Zen is at present evoking unexpected echoes in various fields of Western culture: music, painting, literature, semantics, religious philosophy, and

psychoanalysis. But as it is in many cases grossly misrepresented and misinterpreted, I undertake here to explain most briefly, as far as language permits, what Zen aims at and what significance it has in the modern world, hoping that Zen will be saved from being too absurdly caricatured.[154]

Zen had become hip in the late 1950s largely through such Beat works as Jack Kerouac's *The Dharma Bums*, published in the same year as Suzuki's statement of concern. Carl Jackson speculates that *The Dharma Bums* "did more to spark American interest in Zen Buddhism in the late 1950s than all the excellent Zen studies authored in the years before 1958 by the great Japanese Zen scholar, D. T. Suzuki."[155]

In *The Dharma Bums*, Kerouac portrayed the countercultural, Zen-inspired "Buddhist anarchism" of his fellow Beat writers, particularly the poets Gary Snyder and Philip Whalen, both of whom studied Zen in Japan. Kerouac's narrator describes visiting the humble Californian home of an honorary "Dharma Bum," with its woven straw mats on the floor, "low, black-lacquered, Japanese style table," and collection of Chinese and Japanese records—a hipster, male pad version of Victorian *japonisme* interior design.[156] Late in the novel, the Gary Snyder character enthuses about his upcoming trip to Japan to live in a monastery and reveals his general devotion to Japanese culture. He imagines how he will wear clothes with "huge droopy sleeves and funny pleats" in order to "feel real Oriental." Kerouac's character, the narrator, remarks that the Westernizing Japanese are currently "mad about Western business suits." Snyder's character appears unfazed by this remark but instead expresses regret that the people financing his trip to Japan are only interested in "elegant scenes of gardens and books and Japanese architecture and all that crap."[157] In short, Snyder and other Beat writers (in Kerouac's telling) viewed their Zen devotion as hip, and elite American *japonisme* aesthetics as square.

1958 saw a third crucial publication on the American mid-century reception of Zen—Alan W. Watts's article "Beat Zen, Square Zen, and Zen."[158] Watts, a philosopher and Buddhist scholar, argued that

> the Westerner who is attracted by Zen and who would understand it deeply must have one indispensable qualification: he must understand his own culture so thoroughly that he is no longer swayed by its premises unconsciously . . . Lacking this, his Zen will be either "beat" or "square," either a revolt from the culture and social order or a new form of stuffiness and respectability.[159]

For Watts, both "Beat Zen," requiring no discipline, and "square Zen," demanding stern devotion, had diverged in the United States from true Japanese Zen.[160] American composers, however, proved rather more ecumenical concerning their Zen inspirations.

In his study of music and hip culture, Phil Ford appears ambivalent on the role of Zen: "I do not argue that Zen is the key to understanding hipness, or even that it is especially important to hip culture."[161] However, he lists seven "points of contact between the Beats' hip sensibility and Zen" and notes that the writings on Japan of Fenollosa and Pound proved "particularly relevant to the Beats."[162] Ford points to a superficial connection between Japanese culture and hipster/Beat music in Fred Katz's 1957 jazz album *Zen* and to Zen's role in the work of jazz pianist and composer John Benson Brooks.[163] A more explicit attempt to associate a Beat sensibility with things Japanese appeared in Rod McKuen's "Haiku Poems" on the 1959 album *Beatsville*, an album Ford wittily deems an example of "Beatsploitation," a "commercial co-optation" of hipster culture and Zen fetishism.[164] "Haiku Poems" is a two-minute recitation in ABA′ form in which McKuen refers to writing *haiku* poems in the A sections—accompanied atmospherically by an acoustic guitar (perhaps in reference to a *koto*)—and to a violent bar brawl in the B section—accompanied, inevitably, by a driven, jazz-inflected drum set and bass line. The brief track reads now as a (presumably) unintentional parody of Kerouac in which Japanese culture and music are entirely absent beyond the hipster reference to writing *haiku*. (Kerouac, who demonstrated a long-term interest in this Japanese poetic form, had recorded his readings of his own American *haiku* interspersed with statements by jazz saxophone soloists in 1958.) As noted in chapter 7, McKuen dove further into musical *japonisme* in his collaboration with Tak Shindo on the 1960 album *The Yellow Unicorn*, a rather belated example of Ford's "Beatsploitation."

The term "*haiku*" and the poetic form retained a hip association in the United States for several decades. Countless amateur as well as professional American poets tried their hand at writing seventeen-syllable poems, most often in the three-line form of 5, 7, and 5 syllables.[165] In addition to Snyder, Kerouac, Kenneth Rexroth, and Allen Ginsberg, the impact of *haiku* has been identified in the work of American poets as divergent as Richard Wilbur and John Ashbery. During his 1961 tour of Japan with the New York Philharmonic, a tour made in conjunction with the Tokyo East-West Music Encounter, even Leonard Bernstein penned a set of *haiku* that later served as the text for Jack S. Gottlieb's 1967 song cycle *Haiku Souvenirs* for voice and piano. (The song cycle was published in 1978 with a brushstroke font for the cover text reminiscent of Tin Pan Alley *japonisme*.) Bernstein's *haiku* are effective and evocative. Gottlieb, Bernstein's assistant on that tour, employed in the first song an approximation of the *in* scale, three different types of fermata, and an accelerando trill in the voice and piano reminiscent of the *kakko* rolls in *gagaku*. In the second *haiku*, Bernstein wrote of learning to "hear the sound of silence" by listening to a waterfall at a Buddhist temple. In his setting, Gottlieb breaks the word "sound" into its four component sounds and repeats a twelve-tone row in the piano accompaniment followed by an a cappella setting for the words "of silence." In the fourth *haiku*, Bernstein imagines being able to "reverse at will," wittily transforming "To-kyo" into "Kyo-to." Predictably, Gottlieb provides melodic retrogrades for these repeated city names. He also calls for the vocalist to "exaggerate all grace-note figures, oriental style" in this song. Finally, in the fifth song Gottlieb requires that the pianist silently depress clusters in the right hand while playing melodic lines in the left, creating a resonant sonority that quite successfully sounds "in imitation of the Sho," and, thereby, extends Henry Cowell's piano cluster techniques from earlier in the century in an explicitly Japanese direction. Several of Gottlieb's piano clusters match the exact pitch content of *sho* clusters as notated in William Malm's 1959 *Japanese Music and Musical Instruments*.[166] In singing the word "haiku" in this final song, the vocalist delivers a rising glissando on each syllable and is asked to employ a "strongly aspirated H" and a "bark, in the throat," thereby approximating either the *kakegoe* calls of *noh* drummers or the vocal style of *bunraku*.

Throughout the 1960s and 1970s, numerous American composers created works with "*haiku*" appearing in their titles. These included settings of *haiku* texts and instrumental works inspired to some degree by the *haiku* aesthetic and form by such diverse composers as Vincent Persichetti, Marilyn J. Ziffrin, Mel Powell, and Dennis Riley. For example, Powell's 1961 *Haiku Settings* is pointillist in style and calls for a wide range of vocal utterance. However, rather than indicating an emulation of Japanese *ma* and the vocal styles of *noh* and *bunraku*, Powell's work seems more clearly derived from Schoenberg's *Sprechstimme* and Webern's miniaturist approach. In fact, numerous American composers appear to have been attracted to *haiku* poetry for its intensity and brevity, qualities that lined up with a post-Webern aesthetic. Numerous American composers set *haiku* and other forms of Japanese poetry during the 1960s and 1970s in styles that did not resemble Japanese music or Zen aesthetics at all, as in Robert F. Baksa's *Madrigals from the Japanese* (1966), Mary Howe's *Three Hokku* (1959, setting poems by Amy Lowell), Robert Fairfax Birch's volume of sixty-one *haiku* settings (c. 1963), and Fredric Myrow's 1965 *Songs from the Japanese*. Above, I noted Dave Brubeck's responses to specific *haiku* in *Jazz Impressions of Japan*. In his 1974 album *Haiku*, for jazz quintet and strings (recorded in 1973), the jazz trumpeter and composer Don Ellis likewise claimed to have based each track on a specific *haiku*. However, any connection to Japanese music or even, in most cases, to these poems eludes me. As with Robert M. Pirsig's 1974 philosophical and semi-autobiographical *Zen and the Art of Motorcycle Maintenance*, the appearance of the term "Zen" or "*haiku*" in a work's title was only occasionally indicative of a specifically Japanese influence in the Cold War period.

Tania León's 1973 ballet *Haiku* for the Dance Theatre of Harlem is rather more intriguing than most of the *haiku*-inspired works from this period. The ballet was conceived by León and the African American choreographer Walter Raines. In an early proposal for this project, Raines stated that "with this ballet, I hope to create a visual Haiku."[167] Raines intended each scene in the ballet to be accompanied by a Japanese woman reading a *haiku* in English translation, and stated in the proposal that it was a "vital necessity" that the reciter have a trace of a Japanese accent. Raines based his costume designs on the kimono. Photographs of the original production reveal that the ensemble wore short tunics and that a female solo dancer (Virginia Johnson) appeared in white geisha-style makeup. In an interview with me in March 2017, León explained that Raines was "very into Japanese culture in the early 1970s" and that she had read some *haiku* herself and together they decided to select seventeen *haiku* to match the seventeen syllables in the poetic form. In preparation for the piece, León "immersed" herself in Japanese culture to the extent possible in New York City by "hanging out in an area where Japanese lived," listening to lots of Japanese traditional music records, and eating sushi for the first time. In her liner notes, León explained that she had "tried to speak in a language whose expressive tension has Japanese overtones." This is most evident in her orchestration and electronic manipulations of prerecorded material. The score calls for a regular *koto* and a "prepared" *koto* with a timbre that resembles a toy guitar with plastic strings, perhaps in an attempt to emulate the *shamisen*. This newly created instrument consists of metallic strings stretched through a board and played with drumsticks. In addition, León manipulated recorded voices to approximate Japanese *shomyo* chant, though in some sections this vocal material sounds more like an imitation of overtone Tibetan chanting. The piece opens with cello and bass harmonics that resemble the sound of *sho* clusters and there is an emphasis on sparse textures and dry percussion timbres throughout. Haiku I and II are marked by a high pitched synthesized flute-like line floating above the chanting voices along with a steady low drum tattoo resembling the large *o-daiko* in *gagaku*. In Haiku IV, text referring to geishas is accompanied by a running line on the *kotos*. As in *noh*, the score features flute solos and percussion, though León's percussion section resembles Partch's *noh*-inspired *Delusion of the Fury* (1969) more than any form of Japanese music. León's five percussionists play a large battery of instruments, including temple bell and block, Chinese cymbals, wood blocks, African Harp, bongos, tam tam, stick marimba, talking drum, stones, African maracas, and *kalimbas* (*mbiras*). As a Cuban-born, New York–based composer of mixed French, Spanish, Chinese, African, and Cuban heritage, León viewed Japanese music and aesthetics as another ingredient to experiment with in her transnational musical explorations.

In nearly all of these cases, the *haiku* piece or pieces represented an isolated musical response to Japanese culture on the part of the composer, a temporary interest in Zen aesthetics, or, in some cases, nothing much beyond an evocative title. However, John Cage's works list reveals a career-spanning interest in Japanese poetic forms: *Haikus* (1950–1951, piano), *Seven Haiku* (1951–1952, piano), *Haiku* (1958, for any instruments), *Renga* (1976), *Haikai* (1984, flute and zoomoozophone), and *Haikai* (1986, gamelan). These works tend to be based on details of poetic form rather than on an imitation of Japanese music. For example, the movements of *Seven Haiku* each consist of three measures of five, seven, and five quarter notes and a good deal of *ma* (silence) surrounding the isolated tones. The two pieces entitled *Haikai* use a five-seven-five distribution for attack points. As we will see below, some of Cage's late works did respond to other more immediately identifiable aspects of Japanese music and culture.

Cage, particularly through his writings, served as the most significant catalyst for other American composers' interest in Zen and Japanese culture more broadly in the mid-twentieth century.[168] In the foreword to his most famous publication, *Silence* (1961), Cage directly addressed the impact of Zen on his work:

What I do, I do not wish blamed on Zen, though without my engagement with Zen (attendance at lectures by Alan Watts and D. T. Suzuki, reading of the literature) I doubt whether I would have done what I have done. I am told that Alan Watts has questioned the relation between my work and Zen. I mention this in order to free Zen of any responsibility for my actions. I shall continue making them, however.[169]

Two decades later, Cage commented on his own substantial impact in Japan by referring to performance tours that he had made there with David Tudor and by noting that his music "was the only music that could afford them [Japanese composers] an appreciation analogous to their appreciation of traditional Japanese music, something they couldn't find in the different modern musics. So we deserve a small part of the credit for the fact that contemporary Japanese music features elements similar, although not identical, to those of ancient Japanese music."[170] Cage's implication here—similar to comments that Henry Cowell had made during his own visits to Japan—is that his music deeply resembles ancient Japanese music and that Japanese composers had become turned on to Japanese tradition only after encountering Cage's work.

Though Cage's role in stimulating a widespread interest in Zen in American experimental arts is undisputed and has been discussed in numerous publications, detailing the impact of Japanese culture on Cage's own music has proven more problematic. Cage had been introduced to Japanese music by Henry Cowell and had attended *shakuhachi* performances by Kitaro Tamada in San Francisco and Los Angeles in the early 1930s.[171] David W. Patterson has offered the most detailed and considered studies of Cage's engagements with Asian traditions. Patterson notes that 1950–1952 was a particularly transformative period for Cage as he pivoted from an interest in Indian thought to East Asian philosophy and that it is difficult to determine the exact date of D. T. Suzuki's initial impact on the composer.[172] Cage appears to have initiated his attendance at Suzuki's lectures at Columbia University in 1952, though he had referenced Suzuki in 1950 and his interest in Japan had also been sparked through reading R. H. Blyth's *haiku* translations.[173] (His experience of sound within silence in the anechoic chamber at Harvard took place in 1951.) Patterson states that "there is little if anything in Cage's music that suggests any kind of compelling interest in the musics of Asia, and even less that might constitute direct stylistic borrowing" and concludes that "the most elemental facet of Cage's contact with Asian culture is the way in which he studied, absorbed, and sifted through a variety of texts during the 1940s and 1950s, extracting with single-minded discrimination only those malleable ideas that could be used metaphorically to illuminate the artistic themes that were always the focus of his writings or reshaped to reinforce the tenets of his own modernist agenda."[174] Similarly, James Pritchett remarks that "Cage's understanding of Zen was shaped as much by his compositional concerns as his composition was shaped by his interest in Zen."[175] When asked in 1987 about why Japan seemed of such importance to Cage, La Monte

Young answered rather more bluntly: "Opposites attract. The East has needed the technology of the West and the West needed spiritual reinforcement on a believable level. . . . John found in Zen a philosophy that really tied in with his way of making music."[176]

Cage's more general interest in Japan is evident throughout his writings and letters. In a letter from Tokyo during his 1962 performance tour with David Tudor in Japan, a trip made at the invitation of Toshi Ichiyanagi, Cage is clearly excited and delighted to be experiencing the exotic country firsthand. He notes that he will see a *kabuki* performance and that he will be able to stay at a Zen monastery in Kyoto and that finally "the stone garden I've always talked abt. + only seen on postcards will be outside my bedroom!"[177] On his return from Japan in 1963 in Honolulu, Cage noted that "what is so special—at least in my experience—to the Japanese people: a high regard for things in the world, for plants, for wood, for metal, for the things of nature."[178] Cage's appreciation of what he viewed as a particularly Japanese sensibility resonates with the writings of Lafcadio Hearn. At the end of the nineteenth century, Hearn had celebrated the natural sounds of Japan and had noted a Japanese penchant for silence at momentous moments and he quoted a Japanese acquaintance's explanation: "We Japanese think we can better express our feelings by silence."[179] Hearn wrote of the profound impact he experienced from listening to a large temple bell in Kamakura and Cage clearly enjoyed an immersive experience with this same bell some seven decades later (See Figure 8.2).[180] Though Cage certainly did not require a knowledge of the aesthetic concept of *ma* to become interested in silence, in 1958 he did point to the raked gravel "empty" space in the Zen rock gardens he encountered in Japan as being equivalent to the use of silence in American experimental music.[181] I note that a new interest in silence emerged for Kerouac as he increased his production of *haiku* and as his Buddhist readings focused more on Zen. This is evident in aphoristic statements that appear in his *Some of the Dharma*: "THE SILENCE ITSELF IS IN THE SOUND" (late December 1955) and "*SILENCE IS THE PERFECT SOUND*" (early January 1956).[182]

Cage's late works suggest a renewed engagement with Japanese culture. In 1991–1992 he composed multiple pieces for *sho*—*One9* (1991), *Two3* (1991), *Two4* (1991), and *Perugia* (1992)—for the *sho* virtuoso and contemporary music specialist Mayumi Miyata. Rob Haskins has explained how the poetic form of Japanese *renga* shaped the structure of *Two2*.[183] Cage's most substantial late musical response to Japan is found in his 1983–1985 series of works entitled *Ryoanji*, a title indicating that the composer responded in some way to the famous Zen temple rock garden in Kyoto that he had encountered with such enthusiasm in 1962. Cage was neither the first nor last composer to base a work on Japanese garden design. Such works include Takemitsu's *A Flock Descends into the Pentagonal Garden* (1977), David Kechley's *In a Dragon's Garden* (1992), and Saariaho's 1995 *Six Japanese Gardens*.[184] Cage offered an unexpectedly clear programmatic intention in his score for *Ryoanji*.[185] An oboist had asked Cage for a piece to perform in Japan and Cage turned to the image of the temple garden in Kyoto that had made such an impression on him

Figure 8.2 John Cage and David Tudor in the Tokeiji Temple Garden (Kamakura, Kanagawa Prefecture, Japan, 1962). Photograph by Matsuzaki Kunitoshi. Courtesy of the John Cage Trust.

two decades earlier. In a rather literalist approach, Cage selected fifteen stones to correspond with the fifteen rocks in the Ryoanji temple garden. The placement of these stones on a piece of paper was determined through the Chinese *I Ching*. Cage then traced the shapes of the stones to create the score, with the resulting lines indicating glissandi to be played by the soloist within given pitch ranges. The soloist is also instructed to pre-record the parts of the score that cannot be simultaneously realized in live performance and these recordings are to be played back on four speakers surrounding the audience, creating a physical sound garden. Cage allowed for variable instrumentation for the solo part and called for obbligato percussion as accompaniment, using two sounds of metal and wood played in unison, or, alternatively, the accompaniment may consist of a twenty-member ensemble with each player playing a tone in the loose fashion of the ancient Korean *aak* ensemble. As

James Pritchett notes, this accompaniment "stands for the raked sand" just as the soloist's part corresponds with the fifteen rocks of the Japanese garden, and in this work "Cage's music does not so much comment *about* this model of the garden as it *embodies* it."[186]

At the end of his life, Cage was planning to compose a "Noh-opera" inspired by a work of Marcel Duchamp.[187] This work would have placed him within a long lineage of modernist American and European composers who had engaged with this most refined and austere form of Japanese music theater. It would also have underscored his long-term interest in Japanese culture that dated at least from the early 1950s. Though Cage's own works only rarely signal a specifically Japanese influence, his appreciation of Zen aesthetics clearly inspired numerous other composers. A striking number of these composers were women. (I note, more generally, that a simple search for pieces composed since the 1950s with the term "*haiku*" in the title returns a disproportionate number of women composers.) Several women composers who were either influenced by or otherwise associated with Cage created significant feminist statements in their Japanese-related compositions. I will briefly consider four of these composers here.

For example, though Cage did not complete his projected *noh*-opera, Meredith Monk's *Atlas* was premiered in 1991, the year before Cage's death. "Ghost Stories" was Monk's initial title for this opera and she had planned to include a traditional Japanese section based on a story by Lafcadio Hearn and inspired in part by *noh*. Monk had thought that the central character would be male but then decided to focus this portrait opera more clearly on Alexandra David-Néel, the Belgian-French female explorer who traveled to Tibet in 1924. In *Atlas*, Alexandra travels symbolically across the globe and beyond, exploring all manner of exotic lands. In the course of the opera, we also travel throughout this extraordinary woman's life, as she is represented as a teenage, adult, and elderly woman by three different performers. In representing this journey, Monk's score includes music for the *sheng*, a Chinese mouth organ and ancestor of the Japanese *sho*, and employs overtone singing. Chen Shi-Zheng performed the role of Chinese traveling companion in the premiere production, occasionally employing a Chinese opera vocal timbre. China, however, is not the only exotic musical reference point on Monk's map.

Several commentators have noted traces of Japanese theater and music in the opera. As Bonnie Marranca notes, "The Japanese influence in *Atlas* is striking, not only in Monk's collaboration with Yoshio Yabara, who worked on the scenario and designed the opera's storyboards, costumes, and co-designed . . . the sets. More specifically, it defines the opera's second section, 'Night Travel,' which is performed in the style of Bunraku."[188] Monk claimed that polygenesis was in play and that any similarity with Japanese music and theater resulted from her own vocal experimentation rather than from exotic influence: "the more that I heard these different musics from the world, [the more] I realized that when you work with your own instrument, you come upon these things that exist transculturally. . . . it's a wonderful thing, because you become part of the world—what I would call the world vocal family—just by working with your own instrument in a non-Western way."[189] Monk's Alexandra projects a spirit of adventure, perseverance, wisdom, and humor through nonverbal vocal music that occasionally resembles the vocal styles of traditional Japanese music theater.

In his five *Europeras* from the late 1980s and early 1990s, Cage radically sampled and collaged the European operatic past, thereby deconstructing the genre before the ears and eyes of his audience. Cage's radical reuse of opera had been prefigured in 1965 by Pauline Oliveros in *Bye Bye Butterfly*, a pioneering work composed at the San Francisco Tape Music Center involving two-channel tape, improvisation with oscillators, amplifiers, and tape delay employing a turntable playing a recording of *Madama Butterfly*. We hear a long, sustained high pitch buzzing and glissandi and then (at 3′22″) Butterfly's entire entrance music with tape delay, which eventually becomes submerged by electronic music. Martha Mockus offers an apt description of the work: "Oliveros constructs a listening experience of tuning in to the opera 'station,' but not fully, and tuning out again to continue down the radio band."[190] Though Oliveros said that she had used this particular opera only because she happened to find the LP in the studio, and though we are hearing Puccini's music for Butterfly's entrance scene, Oliveros wrote that her piece "bids farewell not only to the music of the 19th century but also to the system of polite morality of that age and its attendant institutionalized oppression of the female sex."[191] As Mockus put it, *Bye Bye Butterfly* is "a real-time improvised performance that enacts an eerie and forceful feminist critique of the opera."[192] Cage's Zen-inflected influence was evident later in Oliveros's career as she developed her concept of and techniques for "Deep Listening" following her own study of Zen in the early 1980s.[193]

When Cage and Tudor toured Japan in 1962 at the invitation of Cage's composition student Toshi Ichiyanagi, they famously performed with his wife, the Japanese artist Yoko Ono. The dramatic impact of Cage on Japanese composers stemming from this tour came to be referred to as "Cage shock" (*Cage shokku*).[194] As an exceedingly transnational artist, Ono played a significant role in this phenomenon, bridging the Cage-inspired conceptual art scenes in New York and Japan.[195] Born and raised in Japan, Ono attended college at Sarah Lawrence near where her family had settled in New York State following World War II. As a leading member of the Fluxus group, Ono's conceptual art works frequently resembled Zen koans in their allusive and elusive instructions for artistic realization and, presumably, enlightenment.[196] (A similar *haiku* or *koan* quality is evident in contemporaneous works by La Monte Young.)[197] Ono's performance art pieces of the 1960s, such as the 1964 *Cut Piece* in which the audience was invited to employ a pair of scissors to her clothing as she sat motionless on stage, exhibited an intensity and provocative challenge similar to that experienced in postwar Japanese *butoh* dance. The seemingly simple, but precise instructions in the works of Cage, Ono, and the Fluxus group in this period find their corollary in *noh*'s "art of walking" and in the multiple precise movements leading up to and away from moments of sonic realization in much traditional Japanese musical performance, as with *taiko* drum strokes. Simple acts, performed with precision and discipline, may impart an intimation of the profound at specific moments in time.

Ono's creative work eventually turned more consistently in a musical direction, particularly through her collaborations with her third husband, John Lennon. Ono's intense, experimental vocal style has been aptly described by Tamara Levitz as resembling "a living electric guitar," a feminist musical response proving her entirely capable of holding her own in rock performances alongside male electric guitarists.[198] Shelina Brown hears "abjection and cultural resistance," a feminist performative gesture, in Ono's extreme vocalizations and suggests that Ono's phrase "shout from the heart" ("Sisters, O Sisters," 1972) refers to the Japanese concept of *kokoro*.[199] Barry Shank has gone further in connecting Ono's music with her Japanese heritage by detailing aspects of *kabuki* vocal style in Ono's performances, going so far as to refer to her performance on *Life with the Lions* (1970) as "a fine example of *kabuki* singing."[200] Given that her mother was devoted to Japanese traditional music and that Ono had been exposed to *kabuki* and other vocal traditions during her formative years in Japan, detailing elements of Japanese influence in her performances makes sense. However, it is also possible to hear her vocal style as part of a larger avant-garde transnational movement, including the contemporaneous experimental vocal music of such British composers as Peter Maxwell Davies, or, for that matter, as an extension of the Little Richard–inspired falsetto outbursts of early-Beatles Paul McCartney. John Lennon's own explorations of what we may term "screamstimme" on the 1970 *John Lennon: Plastic Ono Band* were prompted by his turn to primal scream therapy and should be heard as an intensification of rock and blues vocal styles, rather than as exhibiting any Japanese influence. However, Lennon did appear in a kimono in some photographs from this period and the album art for the 1975 *Shaved Fish* includes imagery such as the Japanese flag, a drawing of a box of "Lennon Brand" shaved fish with Japanese lettering, and brushstroke font for the album title. In 1971 Lennon referred to his "My Mummy's Dead" as resembling a *haiku* and noted that he had "got into haiku in Japan just recently. I think it's fantastic. God, it's beautiful."[201] Clearly, Lennon's association with Yoko Ono had led him to follow the same trajectory from Indian to Japanese aesthetics that the Beats and Cage had traveled some two decades earlier.[202]

The influence of Cage, Ono, and Oliveros is evident in the work of *kotoist*, experimental composer, and improviser Miya Masaoka. Masaoka, a *sansei* (third-generation) Japanese American, has interviewed and celebrated the work of Ono, Oliveros, and Meredith Monk, collaborated with Oliveros in 2004 on an album of *koto* and accordion improvisations (Deep Listening DL 36-2007), and has acknowledged her debts to the work of Cage. In summarizing her career in 2000, Masaoka writes: "I am a kotoist and a composer, simultaneously navigating the varied worlds of Gagaku (Japanese court music), jazz, improvisation, new music and electronic music."[203] Masaoka studied *gagaku* with Suenobu Togi and formed the San Francisco Gagaku Society in 1989, which she led for seven years. She has composed not only for *koto*, but also for *sho* and *hichiriki*.

Masaoka has cited her bicultural status in support of her experimental approach to the *koto* and credits Cage's prepared piano pieces as a direct model.[204] In her compositions and improvisations she has bowed and struck the *koto* with a variety of objects and has developed what she terms the "Koto Monster"—a traditional *koto* connected to a laptop, thereby creating a digital interface in live performance that dramatically extends the *koto*'s capabilities. She also performs simultaneously with the "Koto Monster" and a "laser koto," which translates her choreographed gestures into sound. She terms this approach "aural gesturalism," extending the fundamental emphasis on precise physical movement in the creation of sound found throughout Japanese musical traditions, including in traditional *koto* playing technique. Much of Masaoka's collaborative work as a *koto* improviser has been with experimentally minded jazz musicians, including with her husband, the composer and trombonist George Lewis.[205] Her dedication to African American jazz is particularly evident on her 1997 album *Monk's Japanese Folk Song*, with Reggie Workman and Andrew Cyrille, which includes covers of Thelonious Monk and improvisations on Japanese folk song. Masaoka has explored her position as a female Japanese American musician in several striking works. Her 1993 piece *How to Construct a Tar Paper Barrack* for *koto* and tape makes direct reference to her parents' experience in a Japanese American internment camp. In the spirit of Ono's *Cut Piece*, Masaoka made her Japanese American female body both subject and instrument in her *Ritual, Interspecies Collaboration with Giant Madagascar Hissing Cockroaches* (1997–1999). In this work, Masaoka appears nude on stage, lying on a table. The cockroaches crawl on her body, activating infrared sensors that trigger sampled sounds, and closeup footage of the moving cockroaches is projected on a screen. Masaoka has stated that *Ritual* is "about the Japanese American experience."[206] She has also created a piece involving bees (e.g., *Bee Project #1*, 1996) and one for plants (*Pieces with Plants*, 2002) that translates the responses of plants to their physical environment and to her movements into sound. Masaoka has collaborated with other electronic improvising musicians such as Richard Teitelbaum, an American experimental composer who has, like Masaoka, devoted much of his career to interfacing traditional Japanese instruments with electronic musical technology.

In his numerous Japanese-inspired and influenced pieces from the 1970s through 1990s, Teitelbaum blended the approaches to this exotic culture of both John Cage and Henry Cowell.[207] Teitelbaum met Cowell in the late 1950s as a student at Haverford College and was named executor of the Cowell Estate by Sidney Cowell, who had responded favorably to a piece of his for *shakuhachi*. Teitelbaum cites Cage as his most formative influence and believes that Cage's music and writings helped prepare him to appreciate Japanese traditional music. Throughout his career, Teitelbaum has been interested in creating live electroacoustic music and fostering collective improvisation. Along with Alvin Curran and Frederick Rzewski, he was a cofounder of the experimental and improvisational Musica Elettronica Viva in Rome in the mid-1960s, and he later founded World Band at Wesleyan University as a global music improvisation group in the early 1970s, creating a model that

would be followed by numerous cross-cultural "fusion" ensembles in the late twentieth and early twenty-first centuries.[208] Teitelbaum viewed his role as a facilitator
rather than as the director of World Band, aiming to bring together musicians from
Asia and North American without, as he has explained, claiming the dominant role
typically assumed by Western composers.

In a retrospective interview in 2003, Teitelbaum stated that his "connection to
Japan is huge. There are a lot of similarities between shakuhachi and electronics,
the compositional use of timbre, the microtonal bending of pitch, etc. . . . Japanese
music presented a greatly expanded world that took me outside the limitations of
piano and Western musical culture."[209] A Fulbright Fellowship first took Teitelbaum
to Japan in 1976 where he studied *gagaku* music with Masataro Togi, who had also
served as Hovhaness's teacher. Teitelbaum also studied *shakuhachi* with Katsuya
Yokoyama, who had premiered Takemitsu's *November Steps* and who would collaborate with Teitelbaum on several pieces. Teitelbaum had studied *shakuhachi*
at Wesleyan in 1970–1971 with Kodo Araki V in order to absorb its techniques
and sensibility rather than with the goal of becoming a performer himself. As he
explained to me, *shakuhachi* taught Teitelbaum "how to create music on synthesizer with sensitivity, that's why I wanted to study it." He has composed multiple
works for *shakuhachi* (including the 1998 *Reibo Universe* for *shakuhachi*, computer,
and visual projections) in addition to pieces calling for *shamisen* (*Man Made Ears*,
1987), for *noh* flute (*Intera*, 1992, with the *noh* flute player Maesho Tosha, Anthony
Braxton on Western reeds, and an interactive computer music system), for *shomyo*
male chorus (*Iro Wa Nioedo*, 1986, a piece for twenty Japanese Shingon Buddhist
monks that drew on preexistent *shomyo* chants and employed chance techniques of
the *I Ching*), for temple bell (*Kei-san*, 1975), and a piece for violin and synthesizers
inspired by *noh* theater (*Ranbyoshi*, 1976). Teitelbaum also practiced Zazen in
Japan, explaining in that 2003 interview: "There is a side of me interested in spiritual and mystical matters. I read Suzuki at an early age and became attracted to
Zen, an interest that was later reinforced by my encounters with Cage."[210]

Teitelbaum has composed for *shakuhachi* throughout much of his career. His first
piece for solo *shakuhachi*, *Hi Kaeshi Hachi Mi Fu* (composed in 1974 at Wesleyan),
is in a traditional style, recalling Cowell's *Universal Flute* but employing the chance
operation techniques of Cage on a traditional Japanese piece and reordering the
words in its title to signal his new work. Teitelbaum dedicated the 1974 *Threshold
Music* for *shakuhachi* to Cage. This piece is written in *shakuhachi* notation with
instructions for the performer to listen to the environment and play "long sustained
sounds" at the same dynamic or softer than the environment "on the threshold of
audibility" such that the performer plays "so closely with the environment that you
merge with it/play the environment until it plays you." His two most striking works
for *shakuhachi* are both programmatic in nature. The 1977 *Blends* (dedicated to and
premiered by Katsuya Yokoyama) for *shakuhachi* solo, synthesizers, and percussion
is a programmatic piece in terms of cultural geography, exhibiting an all-embracing
global vision worthy of Cowell, an approach, as we have seen, not uncommon in

works by American composers. Teitelbaum's 1995 *Kyotaku/Denshi* ("electric sha-kuhachi," employing an ancient name for the *shakuhachi* and with a pun on the Japanese word "denki/history") is a multimovement work for *shakuhachi*, sampler/synthesizer, computer, bass, and drums that was inspired by the history of the in-strument itself and is structured programmatically, moving from the instrument's "mythical origins in ancient China to its role in modern day Japan."[211]

Teitelbaum has explained that *Blends* metaphorically celebrates a recent Japanese overcoming of their traditional "xenophobic isolationism," as it aesthetically moves eastward from Japan to the American West Coast spirit of La Monte Young, to a European expressionist sensibility, to the steppes of Central Asia, and then back to Japan.[212] The piece begins with Teitelbaum's 1974 *Hi Kaeshi Hachi Mi Fu* played simultaneously on both the *shakuhachi* and the micromoog, with the traditional *shakuhachi* notation appearing right to left on the lower half of the score and the synthesizer part transcribed in the upper left, with a graphic depiction of sonic con-frontation in the middle. (See Figure 8.3.) The micromoog synthesizer matches the *shakuhachi* at first and then gradually detunes to suggest the sound of a student player attempting, but failing, to play in unison with a teacher. Teitelbaum thereby wryly recapitulates his own experience as a student of this instrument. However, by transcribing and then reproducing the *shakuhachi* piece on the synthesizer, Teitelbaum suggests that the Western composer has other means for mastering Japanese music. The ghostly imitation of the acoustic *shakuhachi* through tech-nology, with the composer performing live on the synthesizer, calls into question both acoustic reality and authorial control in this work. The polymoog synthesizer plays *sho* chords at several points, thereby displacing that instrument. The elec-tronic music eventually overcomes the acoustic *shakuhachi* sound, which later returns embedded in a dense searing electronic texture, an intense section of the piece that suggests the sound of live reportage from the scene of a violent disaster, with a Nancarrow-esque, frantic, cascading keyboard part. The percussionist re-serves the *tabla* specifically to signal that we have arrived somewhere near India and the sound of wolves howling marks the steppes of Central Asia. Though the piece's programmatic structure may appear contrived, the work makes a pow-erful sonic impression. The acoustic *shakuhachi* and the moog, perhaps serving as proxies for East and West, do not actually blend but instead slip in and out of agree-ment, leading to the central sonic confrontation in the work.

Kyotaku/Denshi more directly foregrounds the relationship between acoustic and electronic musical performance, though in a far less confrontational and aes-thetically challenging manner than in *Blends* from two decades prior. Each move-ment in *Kyotaku/Denshi* is referred to by the composer as a "scene" in the history of the instrument. The piece begins with the legend of the *shakuhachi*'s origins, when a Chinese musician attempted to imitate the sound of a bell by creating a flute (a "false bell"). In the first movement, "Kyorei (False Bell); Imperial Procession," the synthesizer assumes the part of the false *shakuhachi* by playing a sampled Japanese prayer bell along with the acoustic *shakuhachi* performer, thereby bringing into play the question of whether live performance on a synthesizer is somehow less real and original than live performance on an acoustic instrument, a question complicated by the fact that the composer consistently plays the samplers, synthesizers, and computers in the multiple performances of each of these works. Teitelbaum then depicts the historical entrance of the *shakuhachi* into the ancient *gagaku* ensemble as the sampler keyboard and the Mac Powerbook realize an imitation of *gagaku*. This programmatic conceit is quite spectral as it recreates a sonic *shakuhachi* presence within an ancient ensemble environment that the instrument has been absent from for centuries. The second "scene," "Kichiku's Dream," is inspired by the story of a dreaming monk's creation of two classic *shakuhachi* pieces. We hear the live acoustic *shakuhachi* play one of these pieces as the sampler keyboard accompanies with a distant echo of phrases of the piece and with sampled "natural sounds" and praying monks, thereby suggesting an acoustic "realism" for this programmatic work. The Edo period use of the *shakuhachi* as a clublike weapon by the *ronin* (masterless samurai) is depicted in movement three as the *shakuhachi* player performs another traditional piece with the synthesizer responding with violent sampled percussive sounds resembling the resonant crack of bamboo and including the "snaps and scrapes" of a sampled *biwa* as well. The work concludes with "Ronin's lament: The Coming of the West." In this final movement the encounter of East and West is musically realized with late nineteenth-century, Mahleresque chords and melodic gestures on the sampler meant to symbolize the arrival of Perry's black ships and with the *shakuhachi* player playing an early twentieth-century Western-influenced piece. The entrance of live drums and bass along with sustained airy synthesizer chords accompanying the *shakuhachi* solo suggests a Herbie Mann or John Kaizen Neptune vibe. We eventually hear looped samples of voices singing *enka* played by Teitelbaum on keyboard, which both symbolizes an ultimate Westernization of Japanese music and, according to the composer, recalls a particular evening he spent singing *enka* at a bar with his teacher Yokoyama. Unstated and unprogrammed in this musical journey through the long history of the *shakuhachi* is the fact that Teitelbaum's own music and the widespread twentieth-century American engagement with this Japanese instrument represents another astonishing stage in the *shakuhachi's* surprising history.

"Seemingly Remote Associations": Roger Reynolds and Japan

One of the more sustained and varied engagements with Japan and Japanese music by a prominent American composer during the Cold War is evident in the career of Roger Reynolds. Born in 1934, trained as an engineer, cofounder of the experimental ONCE Group in Ann Arbor, recipient of the Pulitzer Prize, and on the faculty of the University of California, San Diego, since 1969, Reynolds is a composer known for works involving musical spatialization, multimedia, algorithmic

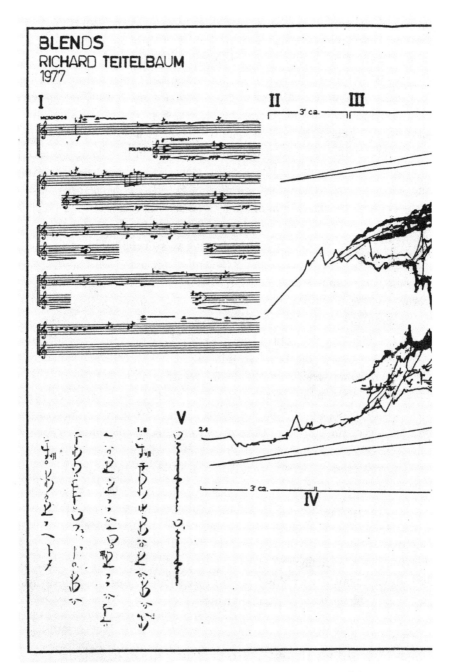

Figure 8.3 Teitelbaum's graphic score for *Blends* (1977). Courtesy of the composer.

processes, and analog and digital technology. Reynolds's influence has been particularly extensive through his work as an educator, a writer, and an organizer of music festivals.[213] It has been through these roles that Reynolds has most clearly engaged with and promoted Japanese music and composers both in the United States and in Japan.

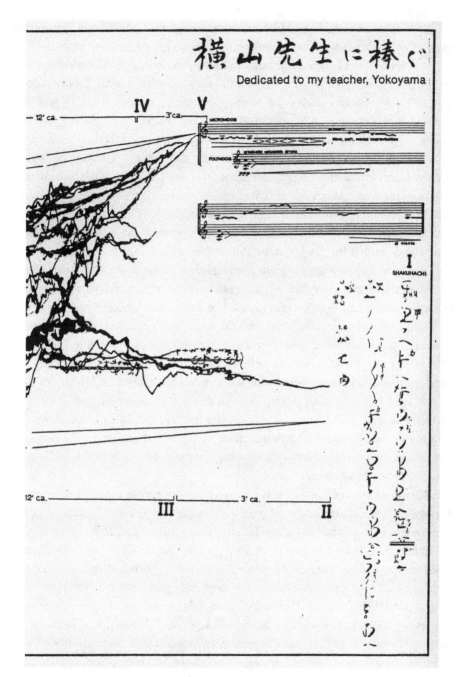

Figure 8.3 *Continued*

Reynolds lived in Japan from 1966 to 1969, returned in 1977, and traveled to Japan on multiple other occasions in the following decades. Given the paramount importance of his initial trip to Japan, it comes as a surprise to discover that he almost did not accept the invitation from the Institute of Current World Affairs (ICWA). Correspondence from March and April 1966 between Martin Bookspan (serving as "Consultant in Music") and Milton Katims (conductor of the Seattle Symphony) reveals that Reynolds was considered for the newly created position of composer-in-residence with the Seattle Symphony, funded by the Rockefeller Foundation, and that he had considered delaying his trip to Japan in order to accept. However, in the end Hovhaness was offered the position, beginning his decades-long relationship with that orchestra, and Reynolds departed for Japan.[214] Reynolds's initial residence in Japan at the height of the Cold War was sponsored by the ICWA. With his wife Karen (Hill) Reynolds, a flutist, editor, and graphic designer, he organized the highly successful CROSSTALK concerts and INTERMEDIA festival, also with two Japanese colleagues, Joji Yuasa and Kuniharu Akiyama. These programs were inaugurated in 1967 and the 1969 CROSSTALK INTERMEDIA festival drew an attendance of nearly 10,000. They were sponsored by the American Cultural Center and funded by the US Information Service specifically in an attempt to sway opinion of the young Japanese avant-garde and intellectuals in favor of the United States—a more targeted and successful endeavor than Nabokov's East-West Music Encounter of 1961.[215] Reynolds has had a remarkably extensive engagement with Japan, even though, compared with the music of his contemporaries, traces of Japanese musical influence in his works may not be particularly audible. In January 1966 Stockhausen and Reynolds both stayed at Frank Lloyd Wright's Imperial Hotel in Tokyo, meeting each morning at the hotel's newsstand, and Reynolds later encountered Teitelbaum several times in Japan in 1977. However, unlike many of the other European and American composers we have considered here, Reynolds not only studied Japanese traditional music and theater, but studied the language and collaborated substantially with contemporary Japanese composers, musicians, theater directors, and artists.

Rather than serving primarily as a proselytizer for traditional Japanese music, Reynolds played a significant role in promoting the music of such Japanese composers as Toru Takemitsu, Yuji Takahashi, Joji Yuasa, and Toshi Ichiyanagi in the United States. His very first monthly report for the ICWA, from 24 December 1966, was focused on contemporary Japanese music.[216] Reynolds has published numerous articles on Japanese composers, frequently admiring the "intensity" and "restraint" of their music.[217] He also collected, edited, and co-translated a series of articles previously published in Japanese by Takemitsu, Takahashi, and Yuasa. These appeared in successive issues of *Perspectives of New Music* in the early 1990s.[218] In addition, his decades-long relationships with major Japanese composers resulted in their travels to and residencies at the University of California, San Diego. (See Figure 8.4. In this image Reynolds is seen at his home in Del Mar, California, with composers Takemitsu and Yuasa.) Ichiyanagi, who had been heavily influenced by Cage and who was married to Yoko Ono from 1956 to 1963, returned to Japan in 1961 and composed some works that incorporated traditional instruments. Reynolds has identified Ichiyanagi as one of his initial acquaintances in Japan who served as a language teacher and who offered "an immediate entree to their artistic world." Reynolds obtained an appointment for Takemitsu as Regents Lecturer in

Figure 8.4 Reynolds, Takemitsu, and Yuasa, Del Mar, CA (1976). Photograph by
Karen Reynolds. Courtesy of the photographer, Reynolds Archive.

the late 1970s at UCSD and Joji Yuasa served on the UCSD faculty for over a decade
in the 1980s and 1990s. The pianist and composer Yuji Takahashi, a student and
then assistant of Xenakis, made several visits to San Diego in the 1970s, as did the
pianist Aki Takahashi in the 1980s. Reynolds composed both the virtuosic *Traces*
(1968) and *imAge/piano* (2007) for Yuji Takahashi.

Reynolds always felt a particular "immediacy of engagement and comprehension" with Takemitsu and said that "with him there was nothing in the way."[219]
His 1977 diary (held in his personal archive) reveals that Reynolds spent a good
deal of time with Takemitsu during this trip, attending together numerous movies,
concerts, and contemporary art exhibits in addition to performances of *bunraku*.
Takemitsu's music and approach to composition is discussed by Reynolds in multiple articles and interviews. Reynolds has remained rather wary throughout his
career concerning deliberate cross-cultural fusions and "willed" influence. In a 21
April 1977 diary entry he recorded his very negative views on the use of traditional
Japanese instruments in new pieces and quoted Takemitsu as saying to him "when
I use traditional things, I feel pain." As Reynolds had put it in 1975, "Cross-cultural
influences are hard to meld without sacrifice, although it is evident that actual
melds are imperative if the disappointments of translation are to be overcome."[220]
He went on to cite Takemitsu as being "foremost among those who have confronted
this problem" in creating "genuine radical cross-cultural compounds" such as *The
Dorian Horizon* (1966) and *November Steps* (1967), which Reynolds found to reflect
the "profound sense of spaciousness and the unfamiliar attitude toward the pacing
of events that characterize the Japanese traditions, while the language of the music

remains basically Western and thoroughly elegant in its craftsmanship."[221] Again, over a decade later, Reynolds pointed to Takemitsu's *The Dorian Horizon* as "one of the most vivid early manifestations I encountered of elements of Japanese sensibility that were then unfamiliar, striking: a taste for deliberate pacing of events and an awareness of the potential for interaction that resides in the space physically separating two entities (of *ma*, in short)." Considering the profound impact of Takemitsu's music on him, Reynolds concluded: "Aside from the sonorous elegance of Takemitsu's music, its lyrical poise, I have been most moved by his sense of spaciousness—both temporal and physical. He has the authority, the technical skill and equanimity of spirit to move his music forward at a most deliberate and undemanding pace."[222]

Throughout our interviews, Reynolds frequently mentioned Takemitsu. He recalled hearing Xenakis once tease Takemitsu for composing music that was "too pretty," too full of "perfume." As an act of homage, Reynolds deliberately took on aspects of Takemitsu's style in his 1996 *Elegy for Toru Takemitsu*, a moving and rather lyrical work in which he expressed his feelings for his departed friend. The piece lasts six and half minutes, corresponding to the Japanese composer's six and half decades of life and engaging with the "phases of his development." Reynolds "used scalar materials which appealed to Takemitsu" and scored for flute, percussion, and strings, employing a higher tessitura than in most of his own music. Some timbral exploration in the flute and percussion parts might also signal a Japanese aesthetic. The piece is more conventionally "pretty" than most of Reynolds's compositions and sounds more elegiac and even programmatic than is typical of his work, with sighing gestures and an abrupt ending.[223]

Encountering Japan in his early thirties, Reynolds found the great cultural differences to be formative, giving rise to "a dawning awareness of unfamiliar models, unexpected ways of doing things, of thinking about the world that spoke so strongly to us. Interacting with the Japanese, one was inevitably confronted with the disorientating divides between their ways and American ways. The cultural differences were more marked than in Europe."[224] The extremity of Japan's cultural difference for Reynolds was crucial: "The Japanese experience, more orthogonal to my background than Europe, was the breeding ground for a conviction that has remained with me: the dimensionality of one's mental life, the topography of one's intellectual landscape, is determined by the models that one places in it, references established largely (though perhaps not exclusively) through experience."[225] In addition to the catalytic stimulus of cultural difference, Reynolds explained to me that the relative economic weakness of Japan during the 1960s enhanced his position and experience as an American living in Tokyo. As was common for mid-century American artists and intellectuals, Reynolds's first explorations of Japanese culture were literary. He has cited his early experience of *haiku* while still a student at the University of Michigan and then his reading of R. H. Blyth's translations while in Japan as alerting him to "the merits of concentration."[226] Clearly, Reynolds was already receptive to the world of Japanese aesthetics before his arrival in Japan.

Looking back on his initial experiences in Japan in the 1960s, he finds that "all the traditional arts had a very, very strong impact on me because of their sense of reserve, and pacing." Reynolds immersed himself in Japanese culture and turned to traditional art forms as particularly revelatory cultural guides. As he later put it: "Art manifests values in their most concentrated form. It can be confidently said, for example, that careful attention to the performance of a single Japanese tea ceremony in context could reveal more of this culture than a year of studying its language."[227] He was most struck by what he perceived to be a uniquely Japanese sense of timing. In a 1982 interview Reynolds was asked whether his "non-teleological approach to articulating or structuring time" was influenced by contemporary developments in European music. The composer answered emphatically in the negative, and pointed instead to the profound impact on him "of Japanese theatre, the Noh, and more than anything else Bunraku. Also I would have to say sumo-wrestling. Same kind of thing: Extraordinary sensitivity to the capacity of one to *wait* in the proper context."[228] As we have seen, numerous American composers have similarly turned their backs on European models while turning toward Japanese traditional aesthetics over the past century.

Reynolds has referred to his interest in Japanese music at various points throughout his career. In an unpublished recorded conversation with John Cage in Toronto in 1984, Reynolds said: "One's idea about what sounds are effective is most, certainly for me, is most strongly influenced by the Orient . . . not only the presence and absence duality, where things not being there are as important as being there, but also this question of variability . . . [in the Orient] there is so much less concern with agreement."[229] (Cage immediately agreed with him fully.) Despite his primary engagement with the contemporary scene in Japan, Reynolds has said that "the most powerful impact came from the traditional things . . . the tea ceremony, and the *shakuhachi*, and the *biwa*, and *joruri*, and *bunraku*, and less *noh*, but certainly also the temples, Ryoanji."[230] His introductions to the traditional Japanese performing arts came through both Japanese colleagues and Western scholars. Takemitsu took him to *bunraku* performances several times at the National Theatre and Reynolds "was really so deeply impressed by the vocal intensity, and the whole idea of pushing against, well, both against improbability and against one's own efforts, and the idea of delivering energy which one also at the same time inhibited from being released . . . this is, I think, really essentially Japanese."[231] A diary entry from 1977 relating his experience at a *gagaku* performance indicates the role of Western scholarship on his perceptions of Japanese music: "Having just finished Garfias book on gagaku, everything was strikingly more meaningful. . . . Clearly, the sense of time becomes tied to the pace, for the passage of time, e.g. 100 minutes without interruption, is not at all a trial." Unlike Cowell, Hovhaness, Teitelbaum, and other American composers, Reynolds has not pursued performance study of any Japanese instrument. However, he found the *shakuhachi*—an instrument "capable of stunning subtlety and power"[232]—particularly appealing and later referred to the instrument's "timbric heterogeneity" and how "each note of the *shakuhachi* literature is allowed to live naturally, to reflect unashamedly the facts of its acoustic origin."[233]

Attempting to document specific instances of Japanese musical "influence" in Reynolds's oeuvre is not a straightforward task. For example, are instances of expressive silence or sonic space in such works as the 1968 *Traces* indications of Reynolds's appreciation of the Japanese aesthetic of *ma*, or should they be traced back to the pointillist works of such European composers as Anton Webern?[234] Is "cross-cultural influence" an active and conscious rather than passive or subliminal experience? Reynolds's own views on influence and engaging with an exotic culture's musical traditions have remained fairly consistent over the decades. In 1975, Reynolds noted the difficulty of cross-cultural aesthetic impact: "intercultural aesthetic impact is, of course, difficult to achieve to any degree . . . for the cultural outsider there are still almost impossible barriers to the full comprehension and responsiveness fostered by an imposed congruence of values and conditioned relationships."[235] In a 1968 report on his activities in Tokyo for the ICWA, Reynolds addressed the question of "influence" directly, explaining that he had been irritated by being asked repeatedly on a return trip to the States how Japanese music had influenced his work. He was also exasperated by the works of colleagues who employ exotic musical features "adopted in calculated fashion during an artificially brief acquaintance" and was averse to melodic borrowing and direct timbral imitations, explaining that he was able to avoid this in his own music since he was "inhibited from such practices by a musical style that does not depend on melodies or rhythms of any sort."[236] Echoing the views of Bartók, he stated in our interview: "I think a genuine influence never arises out of will, but out of experience." In the 1968 report he also pointed to specific features of Japanese music that he found appealing— the sense of space, the sound of the *sho*, timbral intensity—and felt sure "that the Japanese sense of spacing [physical and temporal] has had and will continue to have impact on my work." Reflecting on his multiple encounters with Japanese traditional performing arts during his first two years in Japan, he concluded: "Which of these diverse spectacles—at times garishly theatrical and at other times stiffly ceremonial—will eventually show results in our work, I have no idea (though I have preferences). That some will, there is no doubt."

I hear and intuit a good deal of correspondence between Japanese traditional and modern music and many of the works of Reynolds. He has repeatedly set and been inspired by Japanese literary texts, has composed for Japanese performers, and has responded to specific Japanese places and aesthetic concepts in his music. Although his awareness of Japanese music and culture before 1966 was minimal, I note that in an early vocal work from 1961 entitled *Sky* Reynolds set *haiku* poetry and that his Japanese colleagues felt that several of his pre-1966 pieces displayed a Japanese sensibility. As he relates:

When I went to Japan, the composers there told me they thought my music sounded quite Oriental. Well I'd never been to the Orient, I never had any interest in it, and I never had any experience with it. But, at that time, what they were referring to, I think, was the existence of very long background sounds and my willingness to start something and just stay with it—not to immediately go on to another point, but to start a sound and let it go on for a while. And they perceived that as being Oriental.[237]

He elaborated to me on why he thought Ichiyanagi, Mayuzumi, Yuasa, and other Japanese composers felt that his *Quick Are the Mouths of Earth* (1964–1965) and *Blind Men* (1966) sounded Japanese: "the reason is, that those pieces, in a more abstract way . . . have these passages that are not melodic and are not rhythmically driven, there is no sense of tempo . . . a suspension of drive . . . even the idea of three cellos and three flutes . . . some textures that could be related to *gagaku*." Though I am aware of the compositional and travel chronology, I too hear correspondences with specific features of Japanese music in these earlier works. For instance, the timbral effects and pitch bending called for in the flute part of *Quick Are the Mouths of Earth* (particularly at pages 12–13 of the score) suggest the spectral timbre of the *noh* flute.[238]

Before focusing on a few specific works exhibiting more extensive Japanese influence, I will provide some sense of the range of Japanese aesthetic sensibility and the differing degree of audibility of Japanese musical traits evident throughout Reynolds's career. *Threshold* was completed in Tokyo in 1967 and simultaneously suggests the textural style of Penderecki and Xenakis while hinting at the Japanese sonic world of sustained *sho* clusters and plucked *koto* or *shamisen* in the mandolin and harpsichord parts. Equally ambiguous is the possible traces of *shakuhachi* techniques in the opening solo flute section of *Transfigured Wind II* (1983). A stronger cultural and timbral correspondence—one recognized by Reynolds himself—is evident between the vocal style heard in *bunraku* and Reynolds's *VOICESPACE* series (1975–1986), and in the use of a text by Basho in *Voicespace III: Eclipse* (1979).[239] Reynolds points to the geographical reality of Japan as having influenced his *Archipelago* (1982–1983), while I note a good deal of *ma* and a focus on isolated sounds in *Autumn Island* (Islands from *Archipelago*: II) (1986). I also detect the impact of Japanese theater in several of his works, from the ritualistic *noh* sensibility of *I/O* (1970) to his 1991 electroacoustic music for Tadashi Suzuki's production of Chekhov's *The Ivanov Suite* (1991), with its digitally transformed Japanese speech.

Reynolds has referred to his 1968 multimedia work *Ping* as "definitely the most Japanese" in his oeuvre. The work is stately, even meditative, with isolated notes and a good deal of space, punctuated by events of searing timbral and dynamic intensity. The score documentation, typical of Reynolds's works, is exceedingly detailed in its specifications for both the aural and visual components of the piece. The production requires coordinated colored lighting, slides, projected text, and either a live or filmed male *butoh* dancer in a box—an alien body painted white, in reference to the first line of Samuel Beckett's *Ping*, which inspired the work: "All known all white bare white body fixed one yard legs joined like sewn." A Japanese review, in English, of the performance of *Ping* at the 1969 CROSSTALK INTERMEDIA is intriguing:

> Roger Reynolds' *Ping* is doubtless a treatise on Japanese culture as seen by a foreigner in Japan. I guess he saw in the star of the "Theater of Situations," troupe, Sekiji Maro, a model for Japanese tradition, and used him in the film. The projected titles are said to have been taken from Beckett, but when the words were shown on the screen, they read like Japanese thoughts. Also the live performance had passages which sounded like our *Gagaku* music. The work was truly suitable for this intermedia festival, but the composer's eye is as askance as the eyes of the projected women in the Ashley piece [*That Morning Thing*]. That is why his work did not appeal as strongly as it should have.[240]

The 1990 orchestral piece *Symphony[Myths]* offers a particularly pertinent and impressive example.[241] The work was dedicated to Takemitsu, commissioned by Suntory Hall, and premiered by the Tokyo Philharmonic. The first movement, entitled "Futami ga ura," was inspired by a famous rock formation off the coast of Honshu—a large "male" and a somewhat smaller "female" rock connected by thick ropes with a third smaller "spirit rock" that is often submerged in the sea. (These "married rocks" are the same formation visited by Lloyd and Hana-ogi in the film *Sayonara* and it is the one location Lloyd visits after Hana-ogi leaves him, a consequential moment in the film for the legendary amorous site inspires Lloyd to fly to Tokyo to ask her to marry him once again.) Reynolds first saw this famous formation in 1966 and in the first movement of *Symphony[Myths]* he "attempts the direct *musical manifestation* of a physical model" by employing logarithmic proportions to determine the duration of each segment in the various musical strata. Furthermore, he "attempted to represent over an interval of time the sense of vital massiveness that these rocks . . . impressed upon me" and made a "first attempt at enlarging the sense of 'the perceptual present'" by representing the massive rocks as a thirteen-layered ostinato.[242] As noted above, Cage had responded musically to the shape of the fifteen rocks of the Ryoanji temple garden in several works in the 1980s.

In Figure 8.5 we see a drawing by Reynolds of the two main rocks with the three ropes linking them. This first movement consists of three main sections. Reynolds has aptly described the outer two sections as "massive pyramids of sound, tonally static, but densely figured with inner detail." The middle section represents the ropes in the formation, as three musical lines intertwine in a counterpoint that resembles heterophony, or what William Malm termed the "sliding doors effect" prevalent in the texture of Japanese traditional music. The second sketch (see Figure 8.6) begins to document the creative process Reynolds employed to translate this visual image into musical architecture. There is nothing exceptional or indicative of Japanese music in the instrumentation, beyond a few prominent gong strokes and a marimba part that suggests the wood block sounds of a *mokugyo*, but Reynolds does call for playing techniques that create a "rapid, irregular iteration" in pitch and

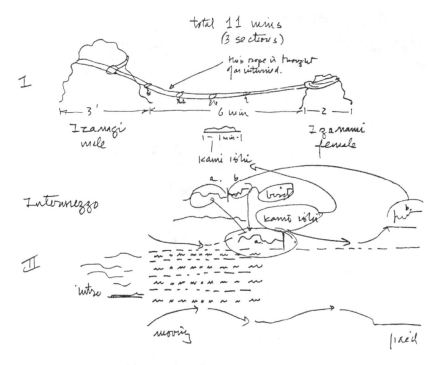

Figure 8.5 Roger Reynolds, *Symphony[Myths]* (1990), sketch 1. Courtesy of the composer.

a smooth accelerando that might, at least visually in the score, prompt a comparison with the accelerating *kakko* drum rolls in *gagaku*. The most suggestive feature of this music in terms of a potential Japanese musical influence is the use of sustained pitch clusters, which are constantly reshaped by the changing logarithmic proportions. In this opening movement we experience a sense of stasis punctuated by lines of intense activity spiraling within. The pitch clusters heard in the first and third sections of this movement consist primarily of five and six pitches, as do the clusters of the *sho*. In fact, the interval content of these clusters is quite close to a couple of the *sho* clusters and the dynamic swelling and ebbing of these clusters resembles the breathing rhythms of the *sho*, even though the register and timbre do not highlight this similarity.

Reynolds's work has been influenced not only by specific Japanese genres and instruments, by Japanese literature, and by geographical features, but also by writings on Japanese culture more generally. As was true for many American intellectuals and artists of his generation, Reynolds's perceptions of Japan were partially shaped by reading Suzuki's *Zen and Japanese Culture*. Reynolds was particularly struck by Suzuki's extended definition of the term "kokoro." Just as Henry Eichheim's approach to Japan had been shaped in the early twentieth century by the writings of the American Japanophile Lafcadio Hearn, including Hearn's 1896 book *Kokoro: Hints and Echoes of Japanese Inner Life*, Reynolds

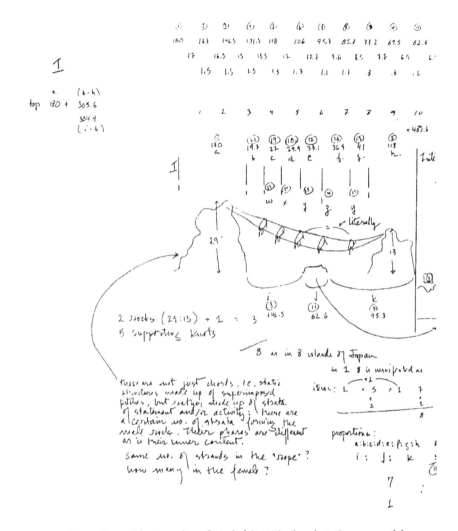

Figure 8.6　Roger Reynolds, *Symphony[Myths]* (1990), sketch 2. Courtesy of the composer.

responded to his reading of Suzuki by composing a work for solo violin directly shaped by Suzuki's discussion of this aesthetic term. A note in the score to Reynolds's 1992 *Kokoro* reveals that five of the twelve sections in the piece correspond specifically with the five aspects of *kokoro* listed by Suzuki. Reynolds calls upon the performer to "inhabit their subjective distinctions in mood" for each part in the work, creating what we might term "hints and echoes" of an inner life. Pinpointing the psychological states of *kokoro* in Reynolds's piece, despite the extensive verbal descriptions in the score, proves as elusive for me as detailing the alleged correspondences between the Indian *rasas* and the movements of Cage's *Sonatas and Interludes for Prepared Piano*. However, Reynolds's sketches for the piece include a detailed diagram (dated 25 March 1992) relating quite precisely

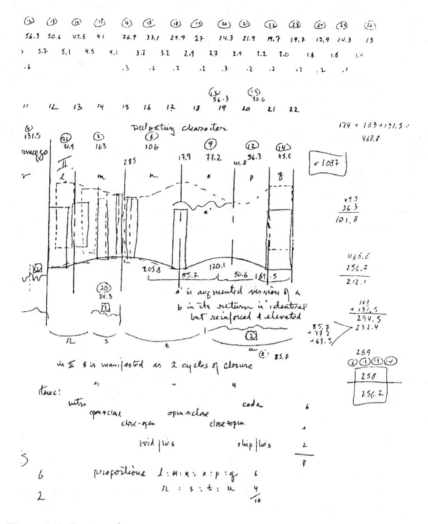

Figure 8.6 *Continued*

Suzuki's key concepts through ratios to the structure of the piece. The diagram also reveals the composer's idea that "a 'mature form' of musical manifestation could be viewed from the perspective of where it came from (nascent) and also of where it might go in a more extreme from (heightened)." A more general aesthetic correspondence between Reynolds's piece and Zen aesthetics is more readily audible. In his liner notes, Ciro G. Scotto refers to the "haiku quality" of the brief second section and Reynolds's long-term interest in Japanese approaches to time inspired a new fermata sign that suggests "stopping of the heart and—so long as the pause remains 'alive'—these may be very long." (I note that Benjamin Britten had similarly created a new "curlew" fermata sign for his *noh*-inspired Church Parables in the mid 1960s.)

A final example from 2010 illustrates the two forms of Reynolds's engagement with Japanese culture and music: the traditional and the contemporary. *not forgotten* is a set of six movements for string quartet, each in some way depicting or responding to a cherished memory of a person or place. Two of the middle movements—the order of which is not specified—are entitled "Ryoanji" and "Toru." "Ryoanji," according to the composer's note in the score, "responds to the raked sand and surrounded rocks" of the most famous Zen temple rock garden in Kyoto. As in *Symphony[Myths]*, Reynolds translated and abstracted a feature of Japanese landscape that is imbued with Japanese aesthetics into his score while also, at least to my ear, drawing on aspects of Japanese traditional music. As explained in the prefatory notes in the score, the work is "almost devoid of pitch" as it offers "a parched landscape of sounds with only the faintest touch of the lyric." The string parts feature nine distinct "noise sources," which include striking the wood of the bow on the fingerboard and knuckle knocking on the body of the instruments. This movement may well represent the most extreme exploration by this composer of timbral possibilities on acoustic instruments in response to some Japanese stimulus. Following the solo cello introduction, the score is clearly marked with section titles: "rock groups" 1–5. One might assume that a precise correspondence exists between these musical sections and the size and shape of each of the five rock groupings. Perhaps the number of measures for each musical section corresponds to the relative size of each rock grouping or perhaps there is a graphic correspondence in the score with these physical shapes. However, no such mathematical connection between the physical garden and Reynolds's musical structure is evident nor, as the composer has attested to me, was any intended. I speculate that some association exists between this work by Reynolds and Cage's 1984 *Ryoanji*, given that two of the other movements pay homage to other departed composer friends. The "Toru" movement pays homage to Takemitsu by incorporating "a central, expressive quote" from Takemitsu's *Dorian Horizon*, which "forms a core" of this movement from which the music "converges and then departs." Reynolds also includes what he referred to in his prefatory note in the score as "some startling interruptions in the form of auditory wasabi" and he labels these two loud, separate measures "wasabi" in the score.

*   *   *

In a conversation with Takemitsu published in 1996, Reynolds asserted: "It's the making of seemingly remote associations that's the most essential part of exciting art. I like art which is revelatory, and revelation often comes as a result of being shown that relationships exist which you had not at first imagined but which you immediately grasp and accept. They're plausible."[243] I have attempted in this chapter to tease out the numerous unexpected connections between Cold War politics, the popularization of Zen aesthetics, experimental American music, American ethnomusicology, and the reception of Japanese traditional and contemporary music by

European and American composers both in Japan and in the United States during the mid-twentieth century. The imperatives of musical diplomacy, funded in large part by the US federal government, shaped the work of a good deal of American composers and musicians during this period. For some, the Japanese connection proved career-defining, while others chose to release one or two albums reflecting their immediate impressions of the exotic nation. Starting in the mid-1950s, and continuing throughout the Cold War period, geopolitical agendas forged relationships between musicians and musical styles that would have been entirely unimaginable in the previous decade. The challenge, of course, in tracing such fascinating associations, in connecting the dots between musical and cultural influences, between political objectives and individual pieces, is knowing when to stop.

9

Conclusions? or, Contemporary
Representations and Reception

Amy Lowell, the early twentieth-century American imagist poet and younger sister of the astronomer and Japanophile Percival Lowell, never traveled to Japan herself nor studied the Japanese language. Yet, she produced effective English adaptations of Japanese *haiku* in addition to versions of Chinese poetry. She also published an astonishingly imaginative work of "polyphonic prose" over a century ago on the American opening of Japan—the 1918 "Guns as Keys: and the Great Gate Swings."[1] In this poetic work, Lowell employs a montage technique, cutting back and forth between the approaching American ships and the daily life of the Japanese people. As Adrienne Munich observes, "the poetic rhythms evoke the historic confrontation by alternating a muscular, often crude, tempo for the American West with a lyrical, elegant cadence for the Japanese East."[2] Relying on her brother's accounts and on travel books, Lowell described a *matsuri* celebration in Japan, attempting to capture the incessant drumming in her poetic repetition:

> Six black oxen,
> With white and red trappings,
> Draw platforms on which are musicians, dancers, actors,
> Who posture and sing,
> Dance and parade,
> Up and down the honey-gold streets,
> To the sweet playing of flutes,
> And the ever-repeating beat of heavy drums,
> To the constant banging of heavily beaten drums,
> To the insistent repeating rhythm of beautiful great drums.[3]

Lowell offers a critical view of the American mission, describing it as "commerce-raiding a nation; pulling apart the curtains of a temple and calling it trade" (p. 63). She even appears offended by the brash American music, echoing its assertiveness through alliteration while also referring derogatorily to the Japanese men:

> Braying, blasting blares from two brass bands, approaching in glittering boats over
> glittering water. One is playing the "Overture" from "William Tell," the other, "The

Last Rose of Summer," and the way the notes clash, and shock, and shatter, and dissolve, is wonderful to hear. Queer barbarian music, and the monkey-soldiers stand stock still, listening to its reverberation humming in the folded doors of the Great Gate. (pp. 83–84)

Lowell insightfully views music as a weapon deployed by the American forces at this moment of encounter, as the Americans played "Hail Columbia" upon Commodore Perry's landing: "Bands, rain your music against this golden barrier, harry the ears of the monkey-men. The doors are ajar, and the Commodore has entered" (p. 85). Writing at a time of increasing tension between the United States and Japan, Lowell concludes her historical poem on an apprehensive note: "You have blown off the locks of the East, and what is coming will come" (p. 95).[4]

This moment of encounter was also imaginatively represented in Hal Prince's production of Stephen Sondheim's and John Weidman's 1976 *Pacific Overtures*. In the final scene of Act I, Commodore Perry appears in a Stars and Stripes costume and top hat, seemingly inspired by the iconic image of Uncle Sam, and sporting the long flowing white hair wig of the *kabuki*-style lion dance, the same dance that was approximated by Ricardo Montalbán in the 1957 film *Sayonara*. (See Figure 9.1 and compare with Figure 6.4 in chapter 6.) As the stage directions note, "suddenly the lion-like figure of Commodore Perry leaps out Onstage and performs a strutting, leaping dance of triumph which is a combination of the traditional Kabuki lion dance and an American cake walk."[5] The dance music, composed for this scene by Daniel Troob, alternates abruptly between music alluding to the style of *kabuki* and music in the syncopated style of American marches and ragtime of the late nineteenth century. Choreographed by Patricia Birch and lasting just under four minutes, this dance similarly shifts abruptly between Broadway's assertive kicks and soft-shoe, and elements of *kabuki* dance such as the vigorous head nodding of the lion and allusions to dramatic *mei* poses. The dance concludes with a stylized patriotic march down the *hanamichi* bridge through the audience by Commodore Perry as he waves two small American flags in triumph. In the 1976 premiere, the nonspeaking role of Commodore Perry was played by the *issei* dancer Haruki Fujimoto, who was more accustomed to Western dance styles than to Japanese traditional performing arts. Fujimoto began his career in modern dance but became active in Broadway. Nevertheless, he was credited as the "kabuki consultant" for *Pacific Overtures*. The historical US-Japan encounter had included minstrel show performances by the Americans of cakewalk music; however, Commodore Perry, unlike Sondheim and Prince, does not appear to have witnessed performances of Japanese theater and music. *Pacific Overtures* is simultaneously a work shaped by cross-cultural encounter and a work that is about the encounter of Japanese and American culture, the subject we have been investigating.

In this concluding chapter focused on the final decades of the twentieth century and the first decades of the twenty-first, I will highlight multiple parallels with the more distant past, selecting examples that are both representative of contemporary

Figure 9.1 Haruki Fujimoto as Commodore Perry in the 1976 production of *Pacific Overtures*. Photograph by Martha Swope. Reproduced with the permission of the Billy Rose Theatre Division, The New York Public Library for the Performing Arts, Astor, Lenox and Tilden Foundations.

culture and that frequently exhibit surprisingly direct links with earlier works encountered throughout this book. These examples will make it abundantly clear that none of the techniques and forms of cross-cultural representation and influence in American musical *japonisme* have concluded. Representations of Japan in American popular culture have continued to toggle between extremes, reflecting shifting perceptions based on the dynamic economic and political relationship between Japan and the United States. The Madame Butterfly narrative has reappeared in various guises and the dichotomous representation of Japan as either submissive geisha or dangerous samurai has persisted, though frequently framed as an act of postmodernist distanciation. During this most recent period, Asian Americans have increasingly pushed back at these stereotypical binary representations, either through works of postmodern parody or by retelling historical moments from a new perspective. At the same time, the influence of traditional Japanese music and performing arts in general on composers, directors, and choreographers in America has never been more evident than in the past several decades. In addition, numerous American musicians have pursued study of traditional Japanese instruments, most especially the *shakuhachi*, but including the *koto* and even *noh* singing as well, picking up where Edward Sylvester Morse, Ernest Fenollosa, and Henry Cowell had left off. This more recent American creative engagement raises the question of whether Americans are now producing Japanese music themselves or whether, in this more intense period of musical globalization, such labels as "American" and "Japanese" have become increasingly difficult to delimit.

Pacific and Gung-ho Overtures

In his 7 July 1853 letter to the Emperor, Commodore Perry requested that the "reasonable and pacific overtures" of the United States government be accepted by Japan, threatening to bring more and larger warships should this request be refused.[6] *Pacific Overtures* dramatizes this landmark cross-cultural encounter and, more succinctly, points to its long-term ramifications. Sondheim has repeatedly explained the basic concept—a rather postmodernist conceit—that he, Weidman, and Prince shared in creating this work:

> What we actually did was to create a mythical Japanese playwright in our heads, who has come to New York, seen a couple of Broadway shows, and then goes back home and writes a musical about Commodore Perry's visit to Japan. It's this premise that helped to give us tone and style for the show.[7]

Sondheim goes further to identify himself with this "mythical Japanese playwright" when he claims to have approached the story "completely through Oriental eyes."[8] There is a certain chutzpah in the notion that one could create a musical not only in the style of another culture but as though one were from that other culture. In preparation for this extraordinary work, Sondheim passed his mythical Japanese colleague somewhere in the middle of the Pacific, for he spent two weeks in Japan, attending performances of traditional music and theater and, most crucially, purchasing a three-album set of Japanese music.[9]

Sondheim incorporated many features of Japanese traditional poetry and music in this show.[10] Stephen Banfield has detailed Sondheim's careful imitation of the form and tone of *haiku* in his lyrics.[11] Sondheim himself has professed admiration for the Japanese "less is more" Zen-inspired aesthetic and noted that in *Pacific Overtures* he "tried to infuse the lyrics with the evocative simplicity of haiku."[12] Music for *shamisen*, *shakuhachi*, and Japanese drum appears in the score and drum patterns, scale types, pitch clusters (from the *sho*), and melodic gestures can be directly traced back to their Japanese sources—and specifically to the recordings he purchased in Japan.[13] Sondheim has related how he first got into the composition of this work. Noodling at a harpsichord in Leonard Bernstein's apartment, Sondheim realized, "wow, there's a texture here, now I'm getting—it may be Hollywoodized—but I'm getting an oriental feeling here," and that this encouraged him to start work on *Pacific Overtures*. The first music that he wrote, later dropped, was for a prepared piano with thumbtacks stuck in the felt hammers.[14]

By incorporating many traits of Japanese traditional music in his score, Sondheim pays homage to this exotic music. Yet, paradoxically, within the very plot of the work Japanese music is parodied for comic effect. In one scene, the Shogun's wife sings and plays the *koto* (the actor miming *koto* performance as a harpist performs in the pit). The stage directions indicate that she performs "to no one's pleasure" and that her song is "irritating." This comic business was emphasized in the 1976 production—her wailing, nasal voice was repeatedly silenced by withering glances from the other Japanese characters.[15] Sondheim has attempted to distance *Pacific Overtures* from other Orientalist musicals, claiming that "it is *deeply* Japanese as opposed to, say, 'The King and I' or 'Madame Butterfly,' which are merely Western treatments of Eastern subjects. . . . What we're attempting to create in 'Pacific Overtures' is a genuinely Oriental musical. Most Westerners haven't seen any Japanese theater in their lives."[16] Most critics point to the undeniable uniqueness of this cross-cultural hybrid and Sondheim himself has stated, "it's certainly the most bizarre and unusual musical ever to be seen in a commercial setting."[17] The "commercial setting" phrase is an important qualifier, given the history of modernist music theater, and yet even in the popular realm Sondheim and Co.'s Japanese musical is not entirely unique. Contrary to Sondheim's claims, *Pacific Overtures* seems not only to participate in the history of musical Orientalism but, in certain dimensions, to surpass its predecessors.

Many of the classic Orientalist stereotypes appear in this work: Japanese men are represented as irrational and bloodthirsty; geisha appear as mere prostitutes while, barely twenty minutes into the musical, an honorable wife commits suicide when her husband faces being dishonored at work. The Japanese appear simultaneously as a hysterical and a highly refined poetic people. Banfield has noted the clear lyrical and musical parallels between the opening of *Pacific Overtures* and the opening of Gilbert and Sullivan's *The Mikado*, as both numbers ("If You Want to Know Who We Are" and "The Advantages of Floating in the Middle of the Sea") directly address the Western audience and offer a quick education in Japanese culture.[18] Banfield also acknowledges the possibility of Orientalist representation in *Pacific Overtures* as "the narrative is still in some respects a Western imposition in its very claim to be a drama about Western imposition."[19] Sondheim's brief trip to Japan and encounter with Japanese music mirrored the historical cross-cultural encounter dramatized in the musical and allowed him to imagine a work in the Broadway idiom as though from a Japanese vantage point. However, given that he credits an encounter with a particular screen in an exhibit of Japanese art at the Metropolitan Museum for revealing fundamental aspects of Japanese aesthetics to him, perhaps his trip to the exotic nation was not essential.[20]

Frequently in European and American musical exoticism, traits from multiple exotic sources are confounded and combined. Just as frequently, the artist in search of exotic influence travels far and wide only to end up borrowing those stylistic features that had always been close at hand. Sondheim's compositional journey in *Pacific Overtures* illustrates both of these hallmarks of musical Orientalism. In a discussion of his favorite number from the show, the powerful "Someone in a Tree," Sondheim noted a general exotic aesthetic influence on his score: "One of the qualities of Japanese music—or let's call it Oriental music—that wasn't being taken advantage of enough in the score was its relentlessness, how it goes on and on and on."[21] He then pointed to the first sixty-six bars of "Someone in a Tree" in which a basic accompanimental figure is repeated with only the slightest of changes to "sustain interest." He referred to this as "the endless stretching out of the time." The parenthetical "or let's call it Oriental music" is telling in the Sondheim quotation, for nothing in Japanese music—not even the repetitive short melodic patterns of the *noh* flute, *matsuri* music, or of *gagaku* string instruments—quite resembles this endless vamp and motoric rhythm. Rather, this style resembles the stratified texture, colotomic structure, and percussive bell-like timbre of Indonesian gamelan music. Several writers have remarked on Sondheim's temporal sensibilities in this work. Paul Attinello referred to the influence of Buddhism and claimed that Sondheim and Weidman derived a "pantemporal 'awareness' " from Zen.[22] However, Attinello also refers more aptly to "Someone in a Tree" as a "curious piece of minimalism" resembling the music of Philip Glass and Steve Reich.[23] Sondheim himself recognized and was proud to acknowledge the similarity between American minimalism and his score.[24] The additive and phase shifting techniques of Glass and Reich and the drones and cyclic feeling of much late 1960s and early 1970s minimalist music can be traced in part to the influence of Indonesian, West African, and Indian musical traditions, but not as directly to any Japanese sources.

The most celebrated feature of *Pacific Overtures* has been the elements of *kabuki* theater adopted by Prince for the original production.[25] As in *kabuki*, the show began formally with the entrance of three Japanese musicians, the sound of wooden clappers, and then a stagehand running the curtain horizontally across the stage. The stage design included a *hanamichi*, the runway in *kabuki* used for entrances and exits through the audience. Set and costume changes were achieved on stage by stagehands dressed in black from head to toe as in *kabuki*. In the 1976 premiere production, the typical *kabuki* stylized and exaggerated delivery of spoken lines was employed in several sections of the work and elements of *noh* performance style (including *kakegoe* calls and the use of a mask) were incorporated as a samurai described setting up defenses against the American landing.

Critics have also remarked particularly on the decision to employ an all-male cast, typical of traditional Japanese theater (e.g., the *onnagata* role in *kabuki*), and to cast only Asian and Asian American actors, thereby creating a historic opportunity for these performers. (In the 1976 production, the male actor playing the role of the wife, Tamate, succeeded remarkably in passing as a woman.) This casting decision required Asian Americans to appear in whiteface for the white American and European roles. Were Sondheim and Prince attempting to express political solidarity with Asian and Asian American actors by avoiding yellowface performance in this casting? Or were they motivated by a peculiar ideal of "authenticity?" Most obviously, by casting only Asian and Asian Americans, they were playing out their conceit of creating a Broadway show from the perspective of a Japanese author and were also helping to deflect criticism of their own representations of the Japanese. Sondheim credits Weidman with the decision to have the Japanese characters speak in formal English while the American and European characters speak in pidgin.[26] Given that the audience saw an Asian American (Alvin Ing) depicting the American Admiral in "Please Hello," they likely assumed, incorrectly, that the actual performer was limited to Japlish pronunciation himself. A similar issue was raised by the performance of Mako, the highly successful film, stage, and TV actor who was born in Japan but who made his career in the United States and who starred in *Pacific Overtures* as the narrator.[27] The intense distortion of Mako's natural speaking vocal timbre likely marked him as particularly exotic for the audience from the start. Just as Sondheim pushed his compositional style to incorporate Japanese musical sounds, perhaps the creative team was drawn to the exotic sounds of Asian-inflected English. Whatever their motivations, their determination to achieve an "Asian" cast was carried out to great lengths. When some of the actors were found not to look "Asian enough" under the spotlights, makeup artists were tasked with making them "look more Asian on stage."[28] The parallels here with black blackface minstrelsy are clear.

Within the historical narrative of *Pacific Overtures* two characters serve a symbolic role illustrating the tensions of Westernization in Meiji Era Japan. Manjiro (a character based on the Japanese fisherman who had lived in the United States for years before the arrival of Perry in Japan) and Kayama (a samurai who is enlisted by the Shogunate to convince the Americans to leave Japanese waters) start out as friends and end up bitter enemies, victims of cross-cultural passing. In the first act Manjiro extols the virtues of America to his traditionalist friend. By the end of the second act, he has become a samurai set on re-establishing the culture of Old Japan. Kayama, on the other hand, trades in his kimono for Western business attire and settles ever more comfortably into his role as a Westernized bureaucrat. These transformations occur before our eyes and ears. In Act I, the two friends sing a number entitled "Poems" in which they jointly write a poem while walking (Sondheim drawing on the genre of *renga* poetry here) and are accompanied in Sondheim's score by a *shamisen*. In Act II we witness their tragic cross-cultural passing in a number entitled "A Bowler Hat." (Two scenes later, Manjiro will fight Kayama in a vain attempt to defend the honor of Old Japan.) To ensure that we make the connection to the earlier Act I duet and that we note the dramatic significance of this number, Sondheim starts "A Bowler Hat" with the *shamisen* quoting the main melody of "Poems." We view a split stage, with Kayama in his Western-style study on one side and Manjiro in his traditional Japanese home on the other. Two temporal dimensions are represented here: during the song, multiple years pass for Kayama as he tells us of his work and dealings with Westerners, but for Manjiro, as for traditional Japan "floating in the middle of the sea," time stands still as he performs the same tea ceremony throughout the number. While only Kayama's voice is heard here, the instrumental interludes consist of a duet for *shamisen* (playing bits of the "Poems" melody and presumably representing Manjiro) and a piccolo (playing Kayama's main melody from this number). The *shamisen* is the only Japanese element in this song. In general, Sondheim parallels Japan's process of Westernization in his score by moving further away from Japanese musical and poetic elements as the show progresses.[29] A similar cross-cultural passing has occurred in the production history of this musical.

There have been three major productions of *Pacific Overtures*: the 1976 original, the 1984 Off-Broadway revival, and the 2000 Tokyo New National Theater production directed by Amon Miyamoto that was brought to Lincoln Center in the summer of 2002 and that (retranslated into English) was produced on Broadway in 2004. Comparing these three productions in detail, it is clear that traditional Japanese music and theater have progressively disappeared from this work. (John Doyle's recent 2017 Off-Broadway production, starring George Takei, offered a further stripped-down approach, eliminating even the Act I–ending *kabuki*-style lion dance.) This process began with the original cast recording of the show in which many of the Japanese musical features, such as the *shamisen* part in "A Bowler Hat," were simply cut. In the 1984 production, the opening entrance and music by Japanese musicians was dropped as was the use of *noh* vocal style by the samurai describing the defense preparations.[30] In general, this Off-Broadway production was simply cheaper than the 1976 original—the wife's onstage *koto* prop was smaller and no *shamisen* was used in the performance.

Amon Miyamoto's 2000 production has been repeatedly hailed for being the most "Japanese" of all *Pacific Overtures* productions and for being the first Broadway appearance by a Japanese director. The publicity for the 2002 Lincoln Center Festival performance trumpeted Miyamoto's "traditional Japanese set designs" and his synthesis of "Noh, Kabuki, Bunraku, and Rokyoku" in a production that brought "a Japanese theatrical sensibility to an American perspective on the westernization of Japan." Most critics pointed to the replacement of the original production's *kabuki* features with a new sparseness brought from *noh* theater. Edward Rothstein referred to the replacement of the *kabuki* elements with a "Noh-style minimalism."[31] For Ben Brantley, this production blew a needed "gust of authenticity" into the sails of *Pacific Overtures*.[32] Such remarks appear to have been prompted by an astute marketing ploy, for Miyamoto himself claimed a *noh* influence in his production. However, it is clear to me that Miyamoto's production gets to pass as the most "Japanese" simply because he is from Japan. Unlike Sondheim's mere passing encounter with Japanese theater, Miyamoto has been a devotee of the Broadway musical for many years. Rather than being the most Japanese of productions, I would argue that Miyamoto's is the most Broadway in style. Miyamoto need not have traveled to New York to study Broadway style since the Takarazuka theater has been fusing elements of the American musical with some features of Japanese traditional theater since the 1920s. In a sense, Sondheim and Miyamoto bypassed each other as one traveled to Japanese theater and the other to Broadway.

Pacific Overtures invites reworkings in the very structure of its final number, entitled "Next!" At the very end of the show, in the original 1976 version, we suddenly leap from the nineteenth century to the present day, skipping over a good deal of fraught US-Japanese history but thereby placing an emphasis on the contemporary ramifications of the story. (The original plan had been to survey all of this history within a puppet show framework.) The entire cast, many now in contemporary everyday costume, face the audience and belt out an aggressive, almost rock-style song tracing the Westernization of modern Japan. The negativity of "Next" seems to conclude *Pacific Overtures* with a lament on the passing of Old Japan even though Old Japan was made fun of, rather than romanticized, earlier. The number declares that modern, polluted Japan has surpassed its American master in the pursuit of capitalist imperialism. Interspersed in the song are spoken lines detailing facts of contemporary Japan's place in the world. In 1976 and 1984 such lines as "there are eight Toyota dealerships in the city of Detroit" had a particular resonance for American audience members as Japan was widely perceived as posing a serious economic threat to the United States. With each successive performance, these lines are updated. In July of 2002 a line was added referring, with a negative implication, to the post 9/11 decision by the Japanese government to allow Japanese defense forces to participate in foreign operations for the first time since World War II. In a musical that presents a critical take on American imperialist adventures and that ends with a moralistic number on the unintended consequences of such militaristic imperialism, this line resonated all too clearly with the contemporary comparisons being made between 9/11 and Pearl Harbor. I imagine that the spontaneous standing ovation (in which I participated) at the end of this particular production was not only a response to the strong performance, but was also an expression of the political sympathies of that particular New York audience.

The aggressive musical style, biting humor, and topicality of Sondheim's "Next!" prefigured a series of Hollywood films released during the trade wars of the 1980s as tensions escalated between the United States and Japan. These films typically drew on representational techniques from the World War II era, both to dramatic and comic effect in depicting Japanese economic power and uncanny technological mastery. The 1986 comedy *Gung-ho!* opens with a black screen and the intense aural shock of screaming Japanese men—who are revealed to be businessmen rather than World War II Japanese soldiers.[33] A failing plant in Pittsburgh is taken over by a Japanese auto company and most of the dramatic and comic energy of the movie arises from tensions and misunderstandings between the new Japanese management and the American workers. Though the plot resolves these cultural tensions as the Americans and Japanese eventually find common ground and cooperate, the music suggests that this resolution is ultimately on American terms. A prominent *shakuhachi* timbre accompanies the inflexibility of the Japanese boss at several points. In contrast, the Japanese and Americans dance and work together on the line to a diegetic American pop song ("Breakin' the Ice") and, in a gesture of acquiescence to Japanese corporate culture, the American workers join the Japanese in calisthenics at the close of the film, but to the accompaniment of diegetic American rock music.

The trade war period also saw the release of numerous films that depicted a more violent and austere Japanese culture, frequently employing Japanese instruments and approximations of Japanese traditional music to accompany ominous scenes. This is true of Maurice Jarre's score for the televised *Shogun* (1980) and for representations of Japanese soldiers in John Williams's score for *Empire of the Sun* (1987).[34] These representational techniques are heard quite prominently in films that specifically exploited trade war fears of a new Yellow Peril, of an inscrutable and economically dominant Japan buying up America and of what might come next. The dystopian future of Los Angeles represented in the 1982 *Blade Runner* is marked by a conspicuous Japanese cultural and commercial domination. In one of the eeriest deployments of Japanese traditional music in a Hollywood film, we hear a sample from a Nonesuch Records recording of the traditional Japanese song for voice and *biwa*, "Ogi no Mato," as we repeatedly see a floating blimp drift above the darkened city displaying a large screen advertisement featuring a geisha. (This song was also sampled in John Williams's later soundtrack for *Memoirs of a Geisha* in a scene of fiery destruction.) Similarly, Hans Zimmer's score for the 1989 *Black Rain* features a breathy synthesized *shakuhachi* sound for depictions of the evil Japanese mafia aiming to undermine New York.

By far the most controversial and complex film of this kind is the 1993 *Rising Sun*, based on a best-selling novel by Michael Crichton which warned readers about the threats of Japanese economic power. In an early scene in the film held at a lavish reception in a Japanese company's Los Angeles office tower, we witness a *taiko* performance intercut with shots of a white woman engaging in aggressive sex in a boardroom with a man whose identity is obscured, but whom we assume to be Japanese. As Deborah Wong has convincingly argued, despite the plot's eventual twists and turns, this scene frames Japanese music negatively and is offensive to *taiko* musicians. As Wong claims, Japanese music is harnessed in this scene and elsewhere to reinforce the fundamental xenophobic message of the film.[35] We typically hear *shakuhachi* and *koto* on the soundtrack for moments of great tension. Though not responsible for the music in the *taiko* scene, Toru Takemitsu composed this film's score. Timothy Koozin has attempted to defend the role of music in this film's depiction of the Japanese by noting that Takemitsu claimed to have parodied Hollywood's stereotypical use of Japanese instruments.[36] As always, the question remains whether audience members are likely to perceive this "ironic reversal of stereotypes." Koozin goes further in his discussion of the *taiko*-accompanied sex scene, weakly claiming that though "purists might lament to see the materials of traditional Japanese music used to this end," it is excusable given that unexpected musical juxtapositions occur throughout the film, though he does acknowledge that "shakuhachi sound is used elsewhere in the film to project exotic Japanese tropes of warrior-like conflict."[37]

Though many Hollywood representations of Japan in this period emphasized trade war tensions and the economic encroachment of the Japanese in the United States, others picked up where such postwar films as *Sayonara* had left off by suggesting that Japan and Japanese culture could still provide white heterosexual men with the means for reclaiming their manliness. In *The Karate Kid* (1984) a teenage Italian American boy befriends Mr. Miyagi, an Okinawan immigrant portrayed by the Japanese American actor Noriyuki "Pat" Morita, who teaches him the secrets of karate, enabling the boy to prove himself against a group of bullies and to win the girl. Miyagi's mysterious power and exotic wisdom are reinforced by his vocal timbre and speech rhythms, which resemble Yoda's from the *Star Wars* series, and by the recurring sound of the panpipe on the soundtrack. Bill Conti, the film's composer, has explained that he used "a couple of tricks" to signal Japan in the film and that he happened to have heard a performance in Pasadena by the Romanian pan flute musician Gheorghe Zamfir, whom he then invited to record on the soundtrack, presumably as a surrogate for the *shakuhachi*.[38] More explicit connections between the postwar films discussed in chapter 6 and films from the late trade war period—including a similar playing out of domestic racial and sexual concerns in exotic Japan—is evident in *Mr. Baseball* (1992). Jack Elliott, a white American baseball player down on his luck, is sent to Japan to play for a Japanese baseball team. As his plane lands we hear approximations of both *koto* and *shakuhachi* in Jerry Goldsmith's score. An African American player who has adjusted to life in Japan explains that in Japan they are both in the same situation: "like being a black guy back home, only there is less of us." A character fulfilling the role of the ever-available erotic Japanese woman introduces Jack to the pleasures of Japanese culture and additional gestures to Japanese traditional music are heard on the soundtrack. Jack succeeds in regaining his baseball skills and manhood in Japan and the film ends with a scene of him back in spring training in Florida with his newly acquired Japanese woman cheering him on in the stands. As in *Sayonara*, this lucky Pinkerton is able to have it all in the end.

Pinkerton's Lingering Lament

The "Madame Butterfly" narrative has had an astonishingly persistent presence in American popular culture, appearing in multiple musical genres in addition to the innumerable performances of Puccini's opera in the United States over the past century. Though the tale is focused on the tragic death of a Japanese woman, a great deal of creative energy has been devoted to rehabilitating Pinkerton, requiring a general swerve away from John Luther Long's original ugly American male character. Rather than a Bloomian-Freudian attempt to disown a particular artistic patriarch, whether Long or Puccini, this suggests a concerted effort spanning the century to revise a Jungian cultural archetype in the collective unconscious, as though Pinkerton presents a guilt that needs to be assuaged. The persuasive powers of music have repeatedly been enlisted in this campaign.

Puccini's own attempt to soften Pinkerton's image by giving him a remorseful exit aria in his revision of the opera has been criticized for awkwardly interrupting the dramatic arc. The recasting of Pinkerton's voice even occurs in embryonic form in the original short story. Long describes Pinkerton's first sound as a "savage snort," a noise befitting this self-centered and sardonic sailor.[39] However, before his abrupt departure from the narrative, Pinkerton's voice modulates to suggest some degree of affection, even as his patronizing tone remains audible to the end. Long's initial publication of the tale was apparently met by angry complaints from US Navy personnel who sought to defend their honor. In his preface to the 1903 edition, Long queries, with a trace of skepticism, "and where is Pinkerton? At least not in the United States navy—if the savage letters I receive from his fellows are true."[40] Long more vigorously defended the Pinkerton type in response to news that, following the official 1902 conclusion of the Philippine-American War, a Filipino woman had attempted to track down her American husband but the US War Department had declared nothing would be done to assist her. Long supported this decision, claiming that both Japanese and Filipino women were less prudish than their American sisters and that "according to Oriental ideas, no great wrong was done these Japanese girls by their sailor lovers, and no great wrong has been done the Filipino girls by their soldier boys."[41] Long thereby let his own brutish Pinkerton entirely off the hook within a mere five years after having released Butterfly into the world.

The revision of Pinkerton's character in songs from throughout the Tin Pan Alley era, traced in chapter 2, was paralleled in numerous films. The 1915 silent film treatment of the tale presents Pinkerton as a decent guy who is egged on by a friend into marrying Butterfly and who is clearly sad and guilt-ridden at the end. In *The Toast of New Orleans* (1950), a rustic with a great voice from the French Louisiana bayou is discovered and transformed into an operatic tenor who loses and then regains his virility by appearing in *Madama Butterfly* as a particularly passionate Pinkerton, thereby winning his girl. Redirecting the tale to focus on Pinkerton's emotional needs has even occurred in film versions of the opera. The entire opera is framed as a flashback in Jean-Pierre Ponnelle's 1974 film-opera, leading us to experience the tale as Pinkerton's, rather than primarily Butterfly's, tragedy—a conceptual shift that had occurred in multiple Tin Pan Alley songs earlier in the century. Pinkerton appears as a rather genial fellow in Frédéric Mitterrand's 1995 film-opera. Consistently, he sports a warm smile, remains mostly seated playing against the bombast of the text in his "Dovunque al mondo" aria, displays racial tolerance by treating his black servant (an added role) with kindness, and exhibits anguished pain and regret at the end. In other films, the Butterfly tale is referenced for its symbolic potential, though the white male, rather than the exotic woman, typically is presented as the victim. In the 1993 *Household Saints* a white man infatuated with Puccini's opera romantically pursues a Chinese American woman. He brings along a recording of *Madama Butterfly* to play for her, but is scared away after his encounter with Chinese music and ultimately commits suicide. A similar destructive infatuation with *Madama Butterfly* is central to *Fatal Attraction* (1987), in which we hear almost no nondiegetic music. Instead, fragments of Japanese classical music are heard during a book signing party at which the married white male protagonist encounters his *femme fatale*, leading to their ill-fated affair. Back at her apartment she cranks up the volume of a recording of *Madama Butterfly*, and they discuss their shared love for Puccini. Though this Pinkerton eventually attempts to abandon this white woman, who is coded as exotic through her obsessive and psychotic behavior and repeated association with *Madama Butterfly*, our sympathies lie with him for he proves to be her victim as she becomes increasingly monstrous and sets out to ruin his life.[42]

The most popular, controversial, and discussed version of the Madame Butterfly narrative has been the 1989 musical *Miss Saigon*, with music by French composer Claude-Michel Schönberg. This musical updates the Butterfly tale by setting it during the Vietnam War and climaxing with the fall of Saigon. As Ellie M. Hisama has pointedly argued: "By re-presenting the complexities of the Vietnam War as merely a 'cross-cultural' love story, *Miss Saigon* assuages the United States' guilt about the Vietnam War while also reproducing age-old Western stereotypes about Asians and about women, already familiar from Puccini's *Madama Butterfly* of 1904 and Rodgers and Hammerstein's *South Pacific* of 1949, but updating and reinforcing them for the new millennium."[43] Hisama notes that, despite the Vietnamese setting, the orchestrator "reserved the Japanese shakuhachi to signify Kim: in his words, 'the wailing of the Oriental flute comes to represent the sacrifice of the Oriental woman.'"[44] The reliance on yellowface performance in several productions of this musical inspired protest, though given its plot and general representation, others have asked why any Asian or Asian American actor would clamor to participate in this work.[45] I note that productions of *Madama Butterfly* with exactly the same casting issues do not appear to inspire such protests, suggesting that, unlike *Miss Saigon*, Puccini's opera is perceived as being a museum piece. In this musical, the Pinkerton character, Chris, appears guiltless, a victim of geopolitical history just as much as the left-behind exotic woman.[46]

The American heterosexual male fantasy of the ideal Japanese woman and nagging concerns regarding Pinkerton's portrayal have not vaporized in popular songs of the later postmodern period. In fact, one of the most arresting and perplexing musical renditions of the Madame Butterfly theme in any genre is the alternative rock band Weezer's 1996 album *Pinkerton*, which I will attempt to unpack in some detail here.[47] Weezer's *Pinkerton* is a concept album or song cycle fueled by the romantic complaints of the band's lead singer and songwriter, Rivers Cuomo. Much of the album is delivered in the apostrophe mode of address, as the male persona (more or less coextensive with Cuomo) pleads with, propositions, curses, criticizes, and apologizes to several actual and fictional women and to Cuomo's female fans at large. As one moves through the album the male persona proves something of a shape-shifter. In the first four songs, we encounter: an apologetic Don Juan who, on the verge of a breakdown, just wants true love; then a tough blue-collar stud who hopes it is not too late to patch things up with his woman; next a wimpy hay-seed who pledges to stand by his exotic and spooky girl; finally, a petulant college boy who has given up on love, turned to onanism, and whose voice resembles Elvis Costello circa 1977.

The Butterfly narrative, and particularly Puccini's opera, serve as both frame and ironic subject for this album, which overtly points to Puccini in its title and in lyrical references to Cio-Cio San, Butterfly, and robins making nests. These cultural allusions were likely not transparent for the average Weezer fan. (Case in point: the Pinkerton Detective Agency sued Weezer for what the company assumed was an unauthorized use of its name.) Some detective work proves necessary even for reading this CD's packaging. On the rim of the CD itself, one discovers (in Italian in very small font) the opening text to Pinkerton's aria "Dovunque al mondo," as though this Yankee's boast of finding pleasure in ports across the globe is the album's ultimate message. When one lifts out the disc and its cradle, the image of a hidden map is revealed. With a magnifying glass, it becomes apparent that this historic map of Korea and Japan has been altered to serve as a guide to this album, and particularly to its sexual geography. Here, Japan is labeled in Italian as the "Island of the Butterfly," while Korea—appearing phallic in shape—is the "peninsula of the dog." On Japan we find labels such as Cio-Cio San, Callas (as in Maria), bitch, Paglia (presumably as in Camille), and a misspelling in Italian of "cat." Korea is clearly meant to represent Cuomo, who refers to himself in one song as a pig and a dog. The names Pinkerton, Sharpless, Stern (as in Howard), and Don Giovanni (Pinkerton's operatic forebear) appear on the masculine western side of the map. Finally, the USS *Pinkerton* is shown sailing from Korea toward Japan. Perhaps to ensure that no listener miss the autobiographical aspects of this album, the names Rivers Cuomo and Pinkerton both have a star instead of a dot for the letter i—the letter appears in two of the other band members' names but with the standard dot. This esoteric mapping out of the album's theme spurs the listener to pursue close analytical investigation of the songs.

"Across the Sea" is the central and longest number on *Pinkerton*. This song and the album's "Madame Butterfly" concept were inspired by a fan letter Cuomo received from Japan.[48] As in the 1917 "My Broadway Butterfly," this is Pinkerton's lament and his letter back. The introduction—consisting of pentatonic melodies for piano and reedy flute and a faint sweep of the piano strings—presents the only highlighted musical Orientalism in the album. Cuomo has revealed that the text of the first verse and part of the chorus were taken directly from the Japanese fan's letter and that she receives royalties.[49] However, we only hear this Butterfly's voice through Pinkerton's mouth and from his perspective. The textual Japlish of the first line (signaled by the dropping of articles and botched verb forms) is matched by Cuomo's setting, in which over half of the syllables receive melodic dissonances, the disjunct line shifts direction seven times, and the vocal melody is rife with awkward syncopation and misplaced emphasis. (See Example 9.1.) Cuomo's voice is brought far forward in the texture and he employs clear diction and an airy, intimate, and innocent timbre. His customary ironic inflection is absent for he is clearly cherishing, rather than mocking, this Japanese female voice.[50]

In the chorus, Cuomo directly appropriates the Japanese woman's line ("Why are you so far away from me?") to express his own pain to an anhemitonic pentatonic tune. Here Pinkerton turns the table on Butterfly by blaming her for their separation. Cuomo's vocal timbre, slurred enunciation, guttural emphasis, and bent vowels signal that he is speaking in his Pinkerton voice. In the extended second verse, the musical and emotional tension is systematically increased. Now, the male persona derives pleasure from imagining the Japanese teenager fantasizing about him. He fetishizes her fragile and refined letter with a melisma and an obscene emphasis on the "sn" of "sniff" and the "k" of lick. By the end of the verse his voice climaxes with the strained timbre of a scream. This mini opera takes a Freudian turn toward self-analysis in the bridge section as we reach the heart of Pinkerton's lament. The repeated descending bass line (a trace of the conventions of the Italian operatic lament) and the clean guitar timbre frame this moment as a spiritual revelation. As he then cries out to his "momma" one might recall another mini rock opera, Queen's *Bohemian Rhapsody*. In verse three, the melodic line is emphatic as the syncopations, scansion, and dissonance have been mostly ironed out. While it remains unclear whether it is his situation or his excuses that he finds "really lame," the timbral sneer in "send," the derisive melisma on "love," and the mock dramatic shake of the voice in "all around the world" ("Dovunque al mondo," indeed) make plain that this Japanese fan's letter is not sufficient for his needs.

Cuomo composed much of this album while a student at Harvard. "El Scorcho" divulges his frustration in pursuing a particular Japanese American female student cellist. Cuomo's character is a lower-class Don Giovanni, serenading his ideal woman in a borrowed voice from "down on the street." Musical difference symbolizes the apparently insurmountable cultural distance between him and this cellist, with European classical instrumental study serving as an East Asian marker by the late twentieth century. (A similar musical symbolism is at play in "Falling for

Example 9.1 Weezer, "Across the Sea" (E.O. Smith Music, 1996), opening of verse 1.

You," when he finds himself unable to play her cello, which she has left at his level in the basement, and laments, "What could you possibly see in little ol' three-chord me?") In fact, as in many Tin Pan Alley songs and Hollywood films, it is the exotic woman's music that particularly turns him on. As though to exaggerate their difference, his musical style is stripped down—employing a simple riff rocking primarily between two chords, nasty little melismas, and an aggressive, at times lecherous, vocal timbre. Cuomo emphasizes their cultural/musical difference even further by appropriating other racial/musical signifiers for his voice. While the Japanese American is associated with European classical music and has never even heard of Green Day, Cuomo identifies himself with the seminal rap group Public Enemy and adopts, albeit subtly, musical blackface—recalling "geisha and coon" songs circa 1900. Both the bluntness of "Goddamn you" and the enriched vocabulary of "epitome" in this song's lyrics reference Public Enemy's language. As he accuses her of not speaking to him, he moves from a pentatonic line to the monotone of rap. The hip-hop feel arises from the smaller subdivisions of the beat, the short textual phrases, the explosive "p" consonants, and the propulsive rhythmic vocal line. (See Example 9.2.) Both his musical style and lyrics consistently undercut his wooing refrain, "I'm a lot like you so please hello"—a line that might recall the American Admiral's words in the show-stopping number "Please Hello" in Sondheim's *Pacific Overtures*. The attempt to downplay cultural difference has been a familiar gambit of invasive amatory Pinkertons, as well as of political strategists when exotic nations suddenly assume political importance.

Example 9.2 Weezer, "El Scorcho" (E.O. Smith Music, 1996), excerpt from verse 1.

Frustrated in his attempts in getting to know her, he invades her privacy by reading her diary in verse two:

> So I went to your room and read your diary:
> "Watching Grunge leg-drop New Jack through a press table . . ."
> And then my heart stopped:
> "Listening to Cio-Cio San fall in love all over again"

The esoteric references to wrestling and opera juxtapose one of the lower forms of pop culture with one of the highest forms of art.[51] What is his reaction to the heart stopping, stop-time revelation of this Japanese American woman's interest in Cio-Cio San? The return of the chorus delays his response, which, I assume, is then offered in the bridge as he sings "How stupid is it?" Is his anger directed at her for being trapped in this Orientalist conception of interracial love, or is he disgusted with himself for his failure of nerve to act on this perfect opportunity to play Pinkerton? A tension between fantasy and guilt, between Yankee bravado and self-abasement, runs throughout this "record of [his] heart."

Why does Cuomo so overtly identify himself with Pinkerton in this album? Is this an act of self-castigation or a boastful assertion of his prowess in defiance of the Orientalist critique? Might he be engaged in both simultaneously? In several interviews, Cuomo relates that he had been attempting to "get in touch with that masculine part of myself" and admits to being "fascinated by Asian girls."[52] Cuomo is nothing if not self-aware: "the album kind of tells the story of my struggle with my inner Pinkerton."[53] Weezer's *Pinkerton* was released in the middle of a decade that saw an intense backlash against feminism and a new defense of American masculinity. The decade began with Robert Bly's *Iron John* in 1990, a *cri de coeur* for new forms of male bonding and masculine rites of passage, and ended with a more direct riposte to feminism in Susan Faludi's 1999 *Stiffed: The Betrayal of the American Man*. "Madame Butterfly" has repeatedly provided a vehicle for male characters to discover or reassert their masculinity, particularly at points in American cultural history in which masculinity appeared in crisis. Cuomo's Pinkerton is a product of this rich Orientalist tradition.

Ellie Hisama's cogent critique of 1980s Western male Asiaphilia as expressed in popular music at first appears readily applicable to Weezer's *Pinkerton*.[54] Indeed, Cuomo eventually married one of his Japanese fans.[55] As in the examples Hisama discusses, this album fetishizes and homogenizes Asian women and celebrates what they have to offer white men, while also hinting at a self-mocking parody of the Orientalist mindset. Weezer's first album exhibited postmodern parody— even the font of the band's logo serves as a tongue-in-cheek reference to the logo of Van Halen. Cuomo has indicated that the band's first album was intended for "kind of a post-modern audience" that would listen with a sense of irony, but that *Pinkerton* "left behind some of that irony."[56] Of course, even if such works intend a postmodern irony aimed at rupturing the Orientalist cocoon, that parody is likely lost on most audience members. I argue that, rather than outright Orientalism or parody, a more complicated dynamic is at play in this album.

In a 2001 *Rolling Stone* interview, Cuomo called *Pinkerton* a "sick album, sick in a diseased sort of way."[57] He had earlier referred to Pinkerton as a "thoroughly despicable" character, said that "I can't deny that there's some of that in me," and, in attempting to describe the personal significance of the album, claimed that he found it "so hard to talk about this stuff without making myself sound like a complete asshole, which I suppose I am."[58] I do not parrot Cuomo's mea culpa in order to derail criticism of his album. Instead, I argue that Cuomo's statements and his songs reveal at least three possible disheartening aspects of the postmodern condition. First, Weezer's *Pinkerton* is not the only work in recent decades that draws on Orientalist clichés while also projecting an awareness of the negative critique of Orientalist representation. For some, Orientalism has taken on a new forbidden allure post-Said that offers an enticing space for bad-boy rebellious play—yet another opportunity to shock and thumb one's nose at the ideals of political correctness. Second, the possibility of parodying Orientalism without simultaneously indulging in Orientalist representation seems remote. From John Corigliano's *The Ghosts of Versailles* to David Bowie's "China Girl," when we laugh at our own cultural clichés of the exotic do we not still laugh at the other being represented? Finally, the tendency to conceive of oneself as encompassing multiple personalities that can be compartmentalized or played against each other, readily allows for self-absolution. This postmodern pose of honest self-analysis assumes all such characters to be available as masks to adopt and drop casually and too often constitutes a disavowal of personal responsibility.

Cuomo's postmodernist approach to representing Japanese women finds a corollary in an unexpected niche in the contemporary music scene. The avant-garde composer, producer, and improviser John Zorn has repeatedly been hailed as an exemplar of musical postmodernism for his eclecticism, incorporating aspects of free jazz, klezmer, experimental music, and hardcore rock. His compositions are marked by the techniques of collage and sampling and by jolting stylistic juxtaposition. Though his work has frequently drawn on Jewish cultural references, Japanese culture has also played an outsized role in shaping his artistic output and he has spent considerable time in Japan. Indeed, contemporary Japanese culture writ large has offered him a model of postmodernist mixing. In addition, Zorn has been active as a curator of concerts in New York devoted to the works of modern Japanese composers and typically sponsored by the Japan Society. Zorn's artistic engagements with Japan—as evidenced in his titles, album art, and musical details—have been highly controversial. This controversy stems most directly from his album artwork which has featured violent and highly sexualized displays of East Asian and particularly Japanese female bodies. As Hisama has argued, equally problematic is Zorn's cavalier attitude to accusations of misogynist and racist expression, and attempts to shield his work with the "postmodernist" label.[59] Zorn's disturbing depictions of Japanese people and culture are not limited to the visual. For example, Hisama has discussed several pieces by Zorn that exhibit a parallel representation between the visual and musical. In Zorn's *Forbidden Fruit* (1987), featuring an exuberant mashup of samples and styles, we hear a female Japanese voice speaking in Japanese.[60] Her text describes a sexual encounter and, though her language is incomprehensible to most members of Zorn's target audience, this Japanese actress's vocal timbre, speech rhythm, and subsequent wordless singing produces an eroticized impression. Similarly, her baby-talk timbre at the end of the work creates an infantilized representation of this Japanese woman. Rather than acknowledging criticisms of his depictions of East Asian women and culture, Zorn has boasted that his "dark is nasty dark."[61] Presenting as a rather forlorn postmodern Pinkerton figure, Zorn has complained of feeling alienated while living in Japan: "Japan was a culture I gave so much to, tried to immerse myself in, and I wasn't accepted."[62]

The hyper-erotized and sadomasochistic Japan encountered in the products of Zorn's artistic imagination resemble a contemporaneous literary retelling of the Madame Butterfly tale in the form of a pornographic novel—Paul Loewen's 1988 *Butterfly*, surely the most bizarre twist of Long's tale.[63] The novel is framed as though written by Pinkerton's fictional grandson who has based his account on Pinkerton's own abandoned autobiography. In this version, Kate (Pinkerton's white wife) is sadomasochistic and takes cruel revenge on Pinkerton by turning him into her slave and forcing him to wear a chastity belt. Pinkerton cherishes the memory of Butterfly: "You will continue to be a vision and an inspiration; your beauty and goodness will forever haunt me like the exquisite and melancholic strains from your *koto*."[64] Kate forces Pinkerton to return with her to Japan and to encounter Butterfly in order to humiliate the Japanese woman. Late in the novel, Pinkerton is further tortured by Kate by being made to attend a performance of the opera at its Paris premiere. The narrator laments on Pinkerton's behalf: "But the worst part was the music; for images and words he could keep at a distance and shut out at will, whereas the singing voices floated up and enveloped him like a penetrant perfume, living phantoms of the timeless sorrow or joy contained in moments long buried."[65] The "real" Pinkerton is tortured by Puccini's music and ultimately is killed by his own country, dying from exposure to the atomic fallout at Nagasaki.

The concluding number on Weezer's *Pinkerton* album, "Butterfly," suggests one final interpretive clue for reading Pinkerton's lingering laments. Both fans and reviewers have referred to this song, the only acoustic number, as the most sincere of the album's tracks. Sincerity is signaled by Cuomo's simple folk guitar accompaniment, breathy timbre, and slight vocal strain as he moves up in range. This song is Pinkerton's last letter to Butterfly. He has caught a butterfly in a jar, only to discover it withered away the next morning. This man-child laments his actions and the fact that "every time I pin down what I think I want it slips away—the ghost slips away." He ends by matter-of-factly singing, "I told you I would return when the robin makes his nest. But I ain't never comin' back," followed by a contemplative vocal pause and then a threefold "I'm sorry," echoing the threefold cry "Butterfly!" of Puccini's Pinkerton. That enigmatic pause simultaneously suggests the snide and cruel tone of a clipped goodbye and a moment of remorseful realization on his part, and thus maintains the album's ambiguity. A clearer moral is heard earlier in the song's second verse. Here, Cuomo/Pinkerton sings in a confessional mode: "I guess you're as real as me, maybe I can live with that. Maybe I need fantasy. Life of chasing butterfly." Is it too soon or too late to put Butterfly to rest, to stop chasing Orientalist fantasies in popular song? Neither Orientalism nor Pinkerton himself appears ready to give up the ghost.

Pop Geishas and Singing Samurai

Postmodern Pinkertons are not the only holdovers from Tin Pan Alley–era songs and Hollywood's musical representations of Japanese women and men. Considered broadly, American popular culture (in the form of novels, songs, films, etc.) has likely led many American consumers over the past century to assume that most women in Japan are like geishas and that many Japanese men harbor a samurai spirit. It is clear that American fascination with the geisha has not diminished. In the early twenty-first century, globe-trotting American tourists armed with mobile phones dash through the Kyoto Gion district in hope of capturing live geishas through photography.[66] At the same time, the image of the Japanese geisha has been assumed by a number of the most prominent white American female popular musicians. These recent trends were inspired in large part by the highly successful 1997 Arthur Golden novel, and subsequent 2005 film, *Memoirs of a Geisha*. In this work of historical fiction, Golden—a white American male—writes from the first-person perspective of a Japanese woman, a geisha who lives through the World War II period. In multiple ways, this novel resembles numerous late nineteenth-century works of American fiction set in Old Japan. Golden is clearly proud of his cultural research and, for instance, offers a rather didactic discussion of geisha musical performance within the frame of this fictional memoir, going so far as to inform us on details of instrument construction.[67] The novel's fictional memoirist notes that she enjoys geisha songs, finding "most of them enchanting," but she realizes that "foreigners often seem to think they sound more like cats wailing in a temple yard than music."[68] The 2005 cinematic version of this poignant tale reinforces such negative associations with Japanese traditional music at multiple key moments.

John Williams so admired Golden's novel that, for the first time in his career, he requested to compose the film score.[69] Williams appears to have welcomed the challenge of incorporating Japanese and other Asian instruments, calling for *koto, shakuhachi, shamisen*, large *taiko* drums, Chinese *erhu*, and bowed metal prayer bowls. Throughout most of the film, Japanese and other Asian instruments accompany scenes of tragedy, danger, and violence. The dark and ominous opening sequence in which the young heroine is sold by her parents to become a geisha features a prominent *shakuhachi* part. The child's subsequent attempted escape from the geisha house is set with *shakuhachi* and *taiko* drum punctuations. (With mixed exotic inspirations, Williams has said that his use of these Japanese drums signaled that the young heroine was being sacrificed "to a Mayan god somewhere.")[70] We hear a traditional Japanese male vocalist during a horrific fire and a lamenting Chinese *erhu* as the heroine stands poised on a cliff edge and tosses away a handkerchief, her one link to a man she has loved since childhood and who she now fears is lost to her forever. In contrast, Western solo string instruments provide the audience with comfort and reassurance on the soundtrack, as the heroine receives a prominent cello theme and her noble love interest is associated with a solo violin, played respectively by Yo-Yo Ma and Itzhak Perlman.

The filmmakers went to considerable lengths to create a sense of exotic authenticity. This included hiring Liza Dalby—an American scholar of geisha culture who famously trained as a geisha herself in the 1970s—to coach the actresses, offering them a one-month "geisha boot camp" in which she taught everything from *shamisen* to tea pouring. In preparation for filming, the camera crew recorded footage throughout Japan. Finding that all of the streets in Kyoto itself contained visual signals of our modern world, the production team decided to build their own Hanamachi (geisha district) back in California, importing some building materials from Japan to establish visual authenticity. As is so often the case in Hollywood's representations of Asian characters, this quest for authenticity did not extend fully to casting choices and the decision to hire three famous Chinese actresses for the main Japanese female roles proved controversial. Both the filming and the film score are stunningly beautiful, and both remain firmly within the long tradition of Hollywood's depictions of Japan.

Madonna's embrace of the geisha image at the turn of the twenty-first century was directly inspired by her admiration for a self-destructive geisha character in Golden's *Memoirs of a Geisha*, and her own use of Japanese cultural imagery likewise emphasizes violent expression.[71] This particular form of yellowface performance actually required heavy white makeup to indicate Madonna's transformation into a geisha. Madonna appears in kimono-like costumes and stylized geisha makeup in her music video for the EDM, techno-futuristic 1999 song "Nothing Really Matters." She first appears on screen in an elaborate black kimono-influenced costume, cradling a bag of water like a baby, as she sings of overcoming selfishness and becoming more self-effacing. The music video includes a few suggestions that this new maternal, rather than material, Madonna is channeling Madame Butterfly. The choreography for both Madonna and the large number of dancers is clearly inspired by the Japanese avant-garde postwar genre of *butoh*, including the genre's typical white body paint and intense facial expressions of horror. *Butoh* is certainly an effective style for suggesting Japanese ultimate exotic otherness in an American popular music video. (Madonna's jerky movements also suggest martial arts and, perhaps, even the movement style of Laurie Anderson.) Madonna's 1999 Grammy Awards staged performance of this song also adopted a Japanese theme, with a set featuring two *torii* gates and a stylized curved moon bridge.

Madonna more fully incorporated Japanese imagery in an extended section of her 2001 *Drowned World Tour*. This nearly twenty-five minute song sequence opens with silhouettes of two figures bowing on a large white screen with a central red circle—an unambiguous reference to the Japanese flag. The extravagant multi-media staged performance featured nearly nude *butoh*-style male dancers dangling suspended from the ceiling—a likely homage to the dance "Sholiba" (1979) by the seminal *butoh* company Sankai Juko. The basic narrative of this sequence carries Madonna from the role of a submissive, mincing, and apologetic geisha (who is brutally treated and nearly beheaded by a sword-wielding male samurai emitting angry, irrational shouts), to a flying fighting heroine straight from a Chinese martial arts blockbuster who eventually defeats the samurai—a dramatic arc suggesting a path to power for female victims of domestic violence. Playing out domestic concerns in exotic garb and settings has long been a core feature of Orientalism in the performing arts. Rather incongruously, a male dancer performing in what most closely resembles the Balinese *baris* solo genre also appears at several points. In this sequence, the song "Frozen" ends with a *koto* timbre motive carrying into the next song, *taiko*-style drumming marks the entrance of the samurai, and some gamelan-inflected music accompanies the solo Balinese-style dancer—otherwise, there are no Asian stylistic musical elements. After defeating the samurai, a cocky Madonna struts before the audience and then dramatically removes her black wig, revealing her signature blonde hair. She then grabs a rifle and inexplicably shoots the Balinese-style male dancer—the final revenge of the white geisha over Asian men. The stage goes dark and reworked clips from a particularly violent, even sexually violent, Japanese anime film (*Perfect Blue* 1997) are projected on the screens, accompanied by new techno-style music.

Madonna's appropriations of the geisha image has garnered some rather convoluted postmodernist apologias. For instance, after acknowledging that it is "plausible to dismiss Madonna's use of Eastern images as capitalist racism," Rahul Gairola goes to great lengths to suggest a rather surprising alternative interpretation.[72] He argues that the music video is not ethnically offensive since there is no " 'real' I" present, suggesting that the jerky camera movement "destabilizes rather than confirms any set notion of a stable ethnic identity."[73] Going quite a bit further, Gairola states that in her "Nothing Really Matters" music video,

> the natural body of Madonna is a slate upon which the impact of East Asian immigration into the USA and cultural influence is inscribed—East Asians, in this sense, have appropriated her in a dualistic (rather than one-way) shuttling of identities. Saying otherwise risks ignoring the immigration of East Asians into and the birth of diasporic identities within the USA, and thus underestimates the monumental effects of Asian culture in America.[74]

This interpretive stance strikes me as blaming the victim by suggesting that yellowface performance has somehow been thrust upon this astonishingly successful white performer by East Asian immigrants. Gairola takes a step away from this position in the end, conceding that "it may indeed be that Madonna needs to take more responsibility for the ways that her representations facilitate pan-marketing strategies that exploit other cultures while boosting her record sales."[75] Such recent and convoluted critical maneuvers are all too common as critics attempt to reconcile their assumptions of postmodernism with the clear persistence of Orientalism in our contemporary cultural life.

Given that Madonna continues well into the twenty-first century to serve as the primary model for pop success for white North American female singers, we should not be surprised to discover a number of performers following her with Japanese-themed music videos. Early in the new century, Gwen Stefani began to appear with her "Harajuku Girls"—four nearly interchangeable Japanese and Japanese American female dancers who offered a background from which Stefani more clearly stood out. These women also performed behind Stefani in multiple music videos and live performances. "Harajuku" refers to a specific district in Tokyo and to the postmodern youth street fashion associated with it. In the 2004 song and music video "Harajuku Girls," Stefani celebrated her love of this alternative fashion scene, concluding that harajuku offers "Style detached from content/A fatal attraction to cuteness." Beyond some inserted Japanese words in the lyrics and a brief synthesized *koto* line and a few notes on an end-blown flute in the introduction, the song contains no other Japanese musical signifiers. In the music video, the Harajuku girls run their hands over Stefani's body as though in sexual submission to this white woman. A similar but stronger suggestion of lesbian erotic exoticism is present in the lyrics of Avril Lavigne's 2014 "Hello Kitty," as Lavigne begs a pretty kitty to stay for a slumber party where they may "play truth or dare now/We can roll around in our underwear how/Every silly kitty should be." Celebrating the Japanese culture of cuteness (*kawaisa/kawaii*), Lavigne followed Stefani's lead from a decade earlier by inserting Japanese text in the lyrics and appearing with four identical, expressionless Japanese women who robotically dance and follow behind her in the song's music video. The song, and particularly the music video, were likely inspired by the J-Pop star Kyary Pamyu Pamyu's 2012 "Candy Candy." Lavigne adopts a squeaky high vocal timbre and some pitch bending, perhaps in emulation of the affected Japanese *kawaisa/kawaii* (cute) style female voice heard in some J-Pop.

By far the most prominent and controversial recent faux geisha performance was Katy Perry's 2013 over-the-top Orientalist staging of her powerful hit song "Unconditionally" at the televised American Music Awards (AMA). This example dramatically illustrates the power of an Orientalist production to reshape the meaning of a piece of music. (Perry's impressive vocal performance succeeds in overcoming the song's defective text setting, particularly in the case of the title word.) The lyrics suggest a simple romantic situation; however, the rather operatic official music video employs religious imagery (a Madonna and Child image, cross-shaped earrings, martyrdom by fire, heavenward glances, etc.) suggesting an unconditional love for God. This music video contains nothing remotely suggestive of Japan and resembles Madonna's "Like a Prayer" video rather than her "Nothing Really Matters." Perry's AMA performance, however, made an explicit connection between female unconditional devotion and obedience to a man through its *japonisme* staging. Dressed in an odd mashup of a Japanese kimono and Chinese fashion, Perry put the most common Orientalist stereotype on display: the submissive self-sacrificing Asian woman, a sister of Madame Butterfly and Miss Saigon.[76] (See Figure 9.2.) Musically, this performance added a *shamisen* and *shakuhachi*

Figure 9.2 Screenshots of Katy Perry performing as a geisha at the 2013 American Music Awards.

introduction in addition to *taiko* drummers and dancers carrying long-necked lutes as props.

This overwhelming performance must mark an apotheosis of Orientalist spectacle. Even the requisite claims of authenticity were proffered, as, for example, when Perry's stylist, Johnny Wujek, explained that a woman in a Pasadena kimono store "oversaw everything we were doing and made sure that it maintained all of its authenticity."[77] The number opened with Perry dancing in silhouette behind a screen, recalling Pinkerton's first encounter with Butterfly in the 1932 film *Madame Butterfly* or the opening of the Japanese sequence in Madonna's *Drowned World Tour*. Outdoing Belasco's original 1900 *Butterfly* staging or the 1933 Hollywood Bowl *Sakura*, nearly every stereotypical image of Japan appeared on stage or projected on the multiple screens, including: floating and rising lanterns, umbrellas, an ink wash painting animation, Hokusai's *The Great Wave*, a *torii* gate, Mount Fuji, and female performers dressed as geishas descending an upstage hill as though entering scene one of Puccini's *Madama Butterfly*. Furthermore, Perry was accompanied by dancers who appeared in yellowface and who, in their stylized stepping and jerky head movements called to mind minstrelsy performance. In a supreme act of self-annihilation, Perry seemed to vaporize at the end, vanishing in an eruption of steam.

This stunning (in every sense of the word) performance provoked a standing ovation from the live audience followed by an eruption of controversy throughout the blogosphere and in numerous mainstream publications, far too many to cite here. The Japanese American Citizens League issued a measured statement:

> The JACL respects the space needed by performance artists to apply their creativity. However, this space does not extend to the perpetuation of racial stereotypes that hold the potential for harm. The thoughtless costuming and dance routines by Katy Perry played carelessly with stereotypes in an attempt to create a Japanese aesthetic.[78]

Other commentators proved more pointedly critical. For example, Gil Asakawa noted how Japanese and Chinese signifiers were carelessly mixed together in the production, just as they had been for well over a century of American Orientalism.[79] Others seized the opportunity to offer lessons in cultural appropriation and racist representation.[80] On balance, the majority of commentators and posts in response to critical articles sought to defend Perry, typically arguing that she sincerely admired Japanese culture and therefore was innocent of cultural appropriation or racist representation. More sophisticated responses tended to suggest that Perry's production should be considered within the framework of postmodernism. Noting that numerous popular musicians (including David Bowie, Bono, Garth Brooks, and Madonna) have assumed a series of personas, arguments were made that Perry's geisha image was but a transparent and casually assumed mask, a form of playful postmodernist identity shifting that should not be taken too seriously. For instance, for the music video "Roar" Perry clearly copied the "jungle girl" style from 1960s Exotica album cover art and she walked like an Egyptian in "Dark Horse." These videos read as tongue-in-cheek acts of dress-up and provoked no comparable controversy as occurred following the AMA performance of "Unconditionally." As I have indicated above, it strikes me as far too convenient to inoculate contemporary works against the label "Orientalist" by declaring that the present is post the problematic past. Any assumption that we have somehow made it past the goalposts of history and now find ourselves in the end zone free to play with representational systems and stereotypes from the past without concerning ourselves with their stigma seems dubious at best. Labeling a performance "postmodernist" does not make its use of Orientalist representational techniques and stereotypes void of potential Orientalist impact.

The apparent majority response aimed to defend Perry and to hail the AMA performance as an act of homage to Japanese culture. Actually, Perry's performance paid homage (consciously or not) to the full history of Orientalist representations of Japan going back through Madonna, 1950s Hollywood films, to silent film Madame Butterflies, and to all of the Tin Pan Alley sheet music covers that depicted white female performers dressed up as Japanese. The AMA production of "Unconditionally" was a simulacrum of a simulacrum. It was not modeled so much on any specific aspects of Japanese culture and performance traditions as it was a faithful reflection and, indeed, even celebration of white European and American *japonisme*, with some rather obvious nods to Madonna's 1999 Grammy Awards performance. Less obvious are resonances between Perry's performance and two other earlier, more avant-garde productions. In her 1986 concert film *Home of the Brave*, Laurie Anderson featured a Korean *kayagum* musician in traditional Korean dress who relates a saying that he refers to as Japanese. He then accompanies Anderson's performance of her Japan-inspired 1984 song "Kokoku," which includes lyrics in Japanese. The song starts with a Western flute solo and Anderson, similar to Perry nearly two decades later, is accompanied by two African American backup singers who sing in Japanese and dance with fans, all in front of a large screen with a projected rising sun image.

Surpassing the estrangement experienced by Madonna's audience in her *butoh*-influenced presentations of Japanese culture is Björk's transformation into a Japanese woman in Matthew Barney's 2005 film *Drawing Restraint 9*, for which Björk composed some two hours of music. Japanese culture is positioned at a most bizarre limit point. In this film, Björk and Barney portray two Occidental characters. They are guests who have been brought together on a Japanese whaling ship and who are ceremonially prepared for their transformation into sea mammals, which involves carving off each other's flesh in ecstasy. These ritualistic preparations include being dressed in kimonos, bathing, and a tea ceremony, all leading to the beautified violent sacrifice of their human forms. On the impact of Japanese music in her film score, Björk has stated: "I think the oriental influence was unavoidable to some degree. When I was starting the project I tried to listen to a lot of Japanese music, but I gave up because I had so little time." She decided that listening to a lot of Japanese music would have resulted in an artistic theft, and so she decided to rely on all the Japanese music she had already heard throughout her life.[81] For the initial "Gratitude" section Björk decided to use a "music box song." (In this section we witness a Japanese woman engaged in ceremonial gift wrapping and hear a male vocalist deliver English lyrics based on an actual letter a Japanese citizen sent to General MacArthur thanking him for lifting a whale moratorium during the occupation period.) Björk's first impulse was "to use koto, and I even experimented with it, but it just sounded like restaurant music. So I used the harp instead." She did compose music for the *sho* near the opening and ending of the film, hiring the *sho* virtuoso Mayumi Miyata for the recording. However, Björk decided to use the *sho* more percussively and has explained that "Mayumi had never used her instrument in that way. It was very exciting for both of us."[82] Miyata, who had inspired and premiered several pieces by John Cage in 1991–1992, also appears onscreen performing the *sho* with strings of pearls cascading down her bare back, erotically heightening the music's outré associations in the film.

Running concurrently with the recent female pop star embrace of Japanese cultural signifiers has been a parallel American popular culture celebration of the manly virtues of the samurai. (Though representations of Asian men in Western popular culture have frequently tended toward the effeminate, we have seen that in certain periods the Asian male has been presented as either irrationally dangerous and ruthless or mysteriously powerful and skilled in ancient fighting techniques.) An extreme manifestation of this trend appeared in the 2003 film *The Last Samurai*. The soundtrack with a score by Hans Zimmer—a Hollywood favorite for films of exotic violence—introduces us to the samurai spirit in the opening sequence by accompanying shots of a meditating Japanese man with a low flute, sustained string chords, and a plucked harp, followed by a *sho* cluster and the sound of a *shakuhachi*. This noble samurai is portrayed by Ken Watanabe, the same Japanese actor who played the role of the heroine's love interest in *Memoirs of a Geisha*. We later hear a *hichiriki* during the Emperor's dialogue.[83] Tom Cruise stars in this period film as US Calvary Captain Nathan Algren, who suffers from PTSD and profound guilt after having served in battles against Native Americans at the end of the nineteenth century. He is hired to assist the Japanese government as a military adviser in its struggles against renegade samurai groups resisting Japanese modernization—a process obliquely signaled musically as we spot a piano being offloaded from a ship when Algren arrives in Japan. However, this white American is captured by the enemy and gradually comes to view the noble and traditional samurai warriors as equivalent to the Native Americans he had helped slaughter back home. His own gradual transformation and transference of allegiance is marked by *sho* clusters and the *shakuhachi*. Music thus assists in signaling that he has gone native and is turning Japanese. Algren regains his sense of honor by joining these Japanese renegades in their final hopeless battle against the pro-American forces of modernization in Japan and, as their sole survivor, emerges as "the last samurai."

CONCLUSIONS? OR, CONTEMPORARY REPRESENTATIONS & RECEPTION 399

Similar bold assumptions of the samurai image appear in numerous music videos from both 1980s British-led New Wave groups who found significant success in the United States and from African American hip-hop musicians in the early twenty-first century. This phenomenon might be traced, in part, back to the 1970s embrace of *kabuki*-style makeup and costuming by popular musicians as diverse as David Bowie and the band Kiss. (Bowie's and Brian Eno's 1977 album *Heroes* even featured Bowie playing the *koto* "like some cat from Japan" on the instrumental ambient track "Moss Garden.") The most prominent example from this period is the Vapors' 1980 hit song "Turning Japanese," with words and music by the band's lead singer David Fenton.[84] As noted in chapter 2, this song opens with the most blatant of statements of the Asian musical cliché—repeated perfect fourths that then move in parallel motion, with a rhythm of four sixteenth notes followed by four eighths and a concluding quarter note. The male protagonist's complaint that the absence of his female partner has left him "turning Japanese"—widely assumed to refer here to masturbation—echoes the fears of white male characters in such comic late nineteenth-century songs as "Mikado Mc. Allister" (1886) and "The Jap" (1893). The music video of "Turning Japanese" opens with a red Rising Sun circle that zooms away, revealing a geisha. The band performs in a room with suggestions of *shoji* walls and *tatami* mats. Abrupt cuts between Fenton and an older Japanese sword-wielding samurai, who occupies the same space in the frame visually, imply that our protagonist is turning Japanese before our eyes. Fenton then appears wielding the sword himself—rather uncertainly and comically—with the geisha giving him wry looks. Pushing his racialized performance further, in two shots Fenton uses his fingers to pull back the skin at the outer corners of his eyes. Any actual anxiety concerning the threat of "turning Japanese" and the elements of visual and musical yellowface performance are veiled by a suggestion of parodic intent in this Vapors video.

A tongue-in-cheek quality and indications of postmodern parody are prevalent in multiple examples of New Wave pop *japonisme*. For example, Wang Chung's "Let's Go" music video is, inexplicably, loaded with Japanese cultural images, including geisha, origami, sushi, and sumo wrestlers. Ultimately, the Orientalist scope of this video is widened to include Egyptian pyramids, a belly dancer and two dancing men sporting fez hats, and, finally, an African American New Orleans–style funeral parade complete with a skeleton dancing on top of a casket, capping the carpe diem message of the lyrics. (This British group's Chinese-derived name translates as "yellow bell," the first note of the Chinese classical scale.) Griffin Woodworth has pointed to the prevalence of a camp sensibility in New Wave *japonisme*.[85] This is particularly evident in the German band Alphaville's 1984 hit "Big in Japan." The song's title itself is a phrase that has been used for decades with derisive wit in reference to the phenomenon of washed-up Western bands finding success in the Japanese market.[86] Beyond a synthesized plucked string sound, the song does not engage in clear musical Orientalism. However, the male protagonist in this breakup song suggests in the English lyrics that he will find comfort and companionship in Japan instead, reclaiming his manhood in an exotic land as have so many other white male characters before him. The music video features a white female performer appearing both in Western street clothes and then in full geisha costume, suggesting a common heterosexual white male fantasy depicted in the 1962 film *My Geisha* and in numerous other examples considered throughout this book. At one point, a geisha face is projected on the face of the lead male singer himself, and this gender and sexual ambiguity is furthered when he declares, "I will wait here for my man tonight." In this song and music video the white male appears as likely to assume the role of the Japanese geisha as that of the samurai.

No such ambiguity is evident in multiple hip-hop examples from recent decades in which Japanese culture and samurai traits, and a more general celebration of Asian martial arts, affirm and celebrate masculinity and heterosexual prowess. As Deborah Elizabeth Whaley has noted, in the early twenty-first century yellowface performance has gained "enormous momentum in popular music, especially in hip-hop music and Black visual culture."[87] Whaley asks whether "the construction of the 'Oriental' in Black visual culture obstruct[s] or help[s] to facilitate solidarity and cultural crossroads between people of Asian and African descent in the United States" and concludes that:

> Black musicians' yellowface indirectly contributes to the power relations that seek to relegate Asians and Asian Americans as perpetual foreigners. Further, their bodies repeatedly act as instruments to perform typical forms of Orientalism that the dominant culture has propagated as natural and audiences view as pleasurable.[88]

One of the more flamboyant examples of such sexualized performance is encountered in the music video of R. Kelly's "Thoia Thoing" (2003). Scantily clad African American female bodies are prominently on display throughout the video. Though the lyrics contain no references to Japan, referring instead to a woman from Africa, Kelly states he is communicating from "Japan via satellite" and calls out "America get your hands up." The nonsense words in the title, apparently referring to sexual sounds, are repeated as a riff by a female vocalist who employs a somewhat robotic voice. Late in the video we see an African American woman playing an end-blown flute and this main melody, with its prominent augmented seconds, stereotypically signals the Middle East rather than East Asia. However, multiple listeners' comments on YouTube and elsewhere on the web indicate that this Japanese-themed music video leads some listeners to hear a phantom Japanese musical influence in the song. Kelly appears in a room with *shoji*-style walls and a *tatami* mat floor and wears a martial arts costume with a red circle on the back. We later see him, in front of a large screen of Hokusai's *The Great Wave*, wearing an East Asian–inspired robe along with two African American women in similar robes who serve him. Three African American women in white makeup and kimono-inspired costumes dance with fans—thus, these black women employ white facial makeup to perform in yellowface as geishas. Kelly dances next to a Japanese male twirling samurai swords and he then supervises a martial arts duel, implying that he has become a master of Japanese masculinity.

Ken McLeod has pointed to the appearance of Japanese imagery employed in hip-hop to signal a general dehumanized futuristic aesthetic and the popular trope of the black samurai.[89] As a precedent to this trend of futuristic musical *japonisme* McLeod notes Styx's 1983 "Mr. Roboto," with its use of the vocoder creating an "eerily detached mechanical or robotic quality to the vocals" and the appearance in the music video of a "Japanese racial caricature of a threatening robot."[90] "Mr. Roboto" laments the influence of technology on modern life and indicts Japan. As noted above, a dystopian association between Japanese culture and futurism was also clear in the 1982 film *Blade Runner*. In the music video for Kanye West's 2007 "Stronger," featuring a Tokyo setting and based in part on the 1988 anime film *Akira*, Japanese technology appears in a more positive light, as it transforms West into a hypermasculine cyborg samurai. The song features no Japanese musical signals, though its futuristic techno style traits likely were redefined for some listeners as being Japanese through association with the visual imagery of the music video.

A final example of connections between recent hip-hop and the image of the samurai is particularly notable for this study. In 2011, the French beatmakers and production duo Sizemen released an album entitled *A Tribute to Tak Shindo*. This album samples multiple Japanese-tinged arrangements by Shindo, including his arrangement of Puccini's "Un bel dì," as well as his 1958 primitivist African-themed album *Mganga*. The Sizemen also sample on this album recordings by the Japanese American vocalist Ethel Azama who appeared on Martin Denny's 1959 album *Exotic Dreams*, which included standards and popular Hawaiian and Japanese songs. In line with the machismo of recent hip-hop *japonisme*, several track titles on *A Tribute to Tak Shindo* reference Musashi, the famous seventeenth-century Japanese samurai swordsman. The stark black and white album cover is dominated in the foreground by a samurai sword and we see a Japanese man brandishing a sword further in the background. The figure of the noble, macho samurai of Old Japan continues to be channeled in contemporary popular culture in unexpected contexts.

Asian Americans Rewriting the Story

The persistence of the geisha and samurai tropes in American popular culture in recent decades indicates a clear continuity with the past. However, the late twentieth and early twenty-first centuries also witnessed an attempt, particularly on the part of Asian American artists, either to undermine Orientalist representation by dismantling such stereotypes through parody, or to offer commemorative works that retell major historical moments from an Asian American perspective. By far the most prominent and most discussed example of these trends has been David

Henry Hwang's 1988 Tony Award–winning play *M. Butterfly*, which was subsequently reworked as a film in 1993.[91] The play was inspired by an actual event—a 1986 Paris trial in which a white male French diplomat was convicted of engaging in espionage for the Chinese government along with his male Chinese lover, a Chinese opera performer, who the diplomat claimed to have believed was a woman throughout their two decades-long affair. In his play, Hwang merged this tale with that of Puccini's *Madama Butterfly* with the aim of exposing cultural stereotypes, particularly the persistent white heterosexual male idealization of Asian women.

In the original production of Hwang's play both Puccini's opera and Chinese opera are integral. In addition to the use of recorded excerpts from *Madama Butterfly*, music for this production was created by the Chinese American film, television, and theater composer Lucia Hwong and was based in part on Chinese operatic traditions. Hwang reveals his own views of Chinese music in his first stage directions: "percussive clatter of Chinese music" (p. 1). The play begins with the sound of gongs, cymbals, drums, an *erhu*, and a Beijing opera vocalist.[92] However, this Chinese operatic music is soon displaced by a recorded excerpt from Puccini's opera. Gallimard, the French diplomat, calls out "Butterfly, Butterfly" in his first line (p. 1), which, in the opera, is Pinkerton's concluding line, thus suggesting the cyclic nature of this tale. As Gallimard puts it in scene three, he is "always searching for a new ending, one which redeems my honor, where she returns at last to my arms" (p. 4). He then pushes the play button on his tape recorder. Puccini's overture starts and Gallimard begins to tell the audience the opera's story, which he then acts out, lip-syncing a bit and presenting a particularly nasty and crude portrayal of Pinkerton. Hwang, through Gallimard, thus deconstructs the opera before our eyes and ears, adopting Brechtian techniques of stylized and exaggerated acting and vocal delivery, which suggest that the entire play is a didactic parable. In contrast, the 1993 film treats the narrative realistically without any of the alienation and comic elements found in the play. In addition, the rather ferocious critique of the opera evident in *M. Butterfly* is largely absent in the film version, which, of course, was experienced by a much larger audience. Hwang later explained that he initially had considered Cio-Cio-San as simply representing the "stereotype of the submissive Asian woman" but that he eventually came to feel Puccini had "done something bold and progressive by making his Japanese heroine the virtuous character and rendering her American lover as the cad or villain."[93] In both the play and film, Gallimard, as an aspiring Pinkerton figure, is clearly obsessed with Puccini's opera, recalling a similar destructive obsession experienced by characters in such contemporaneous films as *Fatal Attraction* and *Household Saints*. Gallimard's white wife even seduces him by wordlessly singing a bit of Puccini's music and he is seen fetishizing the record of the opera.

Chinese opera and Puccini's opera are juxtaposed at several key points in the play. The original production included a substantial section of a Chinese opera martial arts fight scene acted out with the ensemble performing behind a scrim. Given that Act I and Act II both opened with Chinese opera music and that this music returned for the final curtain call, the entire performance appeared to be framed as a Chinese opera. The actual audience applauded this diegetic Chinese opera performance in 1988 but did not applaud the diegetic performance of *Madama Butterfly* excerpts. Chinese and Japanese musical signals were freely intermixed by Hwong in her score and interspersed with Puccini's music.[94] As Gallimard dreamed, a *shakuhachi* played the "Un bel dì" melody which was also performed during the production on *pipa* and *shakuhachi* as he related his repeated attendance at the Chinese opera. These instruments played the melody again on stage during the Act II Austrian embassy scene. In the film, Gallimard even sings a bit of "Un bel dì" to a Chinese man on the street in order (rather oddly) to ask him for directions to the Beijing opera theater—a subtle indication of his conflation of Puccini's heroine with the Chinese opera star. Similarly, in the film we see floating Japanese images during the Main Title sequence despite the fact that the story is set in China. Excerpts from *Madama Butterfly* are frequently heard at appropriate moments in the play's own narrative. For example, Act I of the play ends with the lovers in bed as we hear the end of Act I in Puccini's opera and Gallimard and Song, the Chinese male opera performer, speak Pinkerton's and Butterfly's love duet lines in Italian.

Though Gallimard claims that "very few of us would pass up the opportunity to *be* Pinkerton" (p. 42), *M. Butterfly* represents the ultimate metamorphosis of the dominant Western male into a tragic victim. Echoing numerous Tin Pan Alley Pinkertons, Gallimard claims the role of the abandoned lover, stating that he "never doubted you'd return" (p. 77). He achieves some measure of self-knowledge and concludes that "tonight, I've finally learned to tell fantasy from reality. And, knowing the difference, I choose fantasy" (p. 90). (This strikingly resonates with the lyrics of Weezer's "Butterfly" in which the Pinkerton persona concludes: "Maybe I need fantasy. Life of chasing butterfly." Such self-knowledge clearly does not deter postmodern Pinkertons.) Hwang's "poor Pinkerton" is transformed into the exotic female Butterfly before our eyes at the play's end. Gallimard has told his tale from the start in flashback as he sits alone in his Paris cell and, at the end, applies the makeup and costume of a Japanese woman. The play ends with his suicide and, as he stabs himself, we hear the music from the love duet at the end of Act I in the opera, rather than music from the opera's conclusion. Thus, the music signals that Gallimard holds on to his romantic exotic fantasy to the bitter end. Hwang reworks the Butterfly narrative as the product of the white heterosexual male's self-destructive fantasy and resultant mental illness. Though Hwang may have set out to punish Pinkerton—a form of creative revenge aimed at Orientalist narratives—Pinkerton emerges as the true victim. We feel Gallimard's pain and loss and feel nothing for his Chinese male lover who, by calling "Butterfly? Butterfly?" (p. 93) at the end of the play, has become Pinkerton himself. Hwang had set out to undermine the Orientalist Asian Butterfly fantasy but actually appears to have perpetuated the lament of Pinkerton in American popular culture.[95]

M. Butterfly dramatically depicts gender ambiguity in an exotic setting and, in so doing, recapitulates any number of Orientalist works. Initially, in both the staged play and film versions, Gallimard's encounters with the exotic East enable him to reclaim his stereotypical manhood and sexual prowess, as had been the case for Lloyd Gruver in Hollywood's *Sayonara* and for numerous other fictional white heterosexual male characters in European Orientalist operas. However, in the end Gallimard is feminized and exoticized himself, becoming the ideal self-sacrificing geisha he has fantasized about for so long. At the same time, the play furthers the stereotypical Western representation of Asian men as effeminate by having Song (Gallimard's Chinese male lover) played convincingly by an Asian American actor (B. D. Wong), who succeeded in depicting an ideal Asian woman for both Gallimard and the audience. The Asian male body is presented as androgynously enticing as Song strips nude on stage. Extending the traditional cross-dressed roles of the Chinese opera *dan* and Japanese *kabuki onnagata*, Hwang created the ultimate exotic Butterfly—the Asian male performer who surpasses any actual woman in depicting the feminine ideal on stage. As Song indicates toward the end of the play that he may have actually loved Gallimard, the white male finds it impossible to move beyond feelings of homosexual shame, a feature of the play that may well date it for twenty-first century theatergoers. Given that this fictional Chinese male delivers the most pointed critiques of Western Orientalist fantasy and of Puccini's opera, this character serves as something of a stand in for the Chinese American author himself.

M. Butterfly raises a crucial question relevant more generally to postmodern treatments of Orientalist narratives and representations—is it possible to undermine Orientalism through parody without perpetuating it? Rather than relinquish the Orientalist fantasy, Gallimard sacrifices himself by assuming the crucial role of Butterfly and, thus, provides the requisite ending. Hwang's play and the film have inspired considerable debate along these lines. James S. Moy argues that the mainstream success of this play makes it suspect in terms of its true critical potential and suggests it is an example of "stereotypical representations created by Asian Americans."[96] Moy and Karen Shimakawa both suggest that it is difficult to determine whether *M. Butterfly* was such a success because its purported critique of Orientalism was understood or because it was missed.[97] As Hwang himself noted, his attempt to deconstruct the *Madame Butterfly* narrative in *M. Butterfly* was soon answered on Broadway by the hit megamusical *Miss Saigon*, a straight retelling of the romantic Butterfly story.

Allegiance, a rather different and far less commercially successful musical, appeared on Broadway in 2015 and starred the Filipina actress Lea Salonga, who had originated the role of Kim in *Miss Saigon* when she was eighteen.[98] Rather than tackling stereotypes through postmodern irony, *Allegiance* offered a more sentimental tale commemorating the experiences of one Japanese American family interned and torn apart during World War II. The book was based loosely on the experiences of George Takei (of *Star Trek*'s Sulu fame) and his family and appeared on Broadway, with Takei in a starring role, at a time of intense anti-immigration sentiment in the United States, which included politicians and presidential candidates calling for bans on Syrian refugees and suggesting that the World War II internment of Japanese Americans might serve as a model for dealing with the perceived terrorist threats of American Muslims.[99] Takei, emerging as an outspoken liberal voice in the years leading up to the musical's premiere, has consistently emphasized the relevance of his family's story to early twenty-first-century America and the importance of "gaman," the Zen term his mother frequently used in the camp meaning "endurance with dignity," which is also the title and subject of one of the main numbers in Act I. The musical opens with a prologue set in 2001 in San Francisco before jumping back to 1941 and then to a relocation camp from 1942 to 1945, with a final return to San Francisco in 2001. Writing in the *New York Times*, Charles Isherwood complained that *Allegiance* "often feels more like a history lesson than a musical."[100]

With music and lyrics by the Chinese American Jay Kuo, *Allegiance* has been hailed as offering an Asian American perspective on Asian American history—a rare occurrence in American musical theater. After the attack on Pearl Harbor the grandfather character, played by Takei, hides his Japanese wind chimes behind an American flag, explaining: "Looks like America, sounds like Japan." Similarly, Kuo attempted to tinge this American story with elements of Japanese traditional culture, incorporating *haiku* poetic style in the lyrics and injecting "Japanese flavor" into the score.[101] Though most of the score draws on the style of 1940s big band swing music or 1980s megamusical lyricism, we hear the Japanese *shinobue* and other bamboo flutes (and Western flutes played with techniques approximating Japanese) and *koto* (or at least a synthesized version of its timbre) at several key points. The musical opens with the sound of wind and windchimes followed by a bamboo flute and *koto* sound, and several melodies employ Japanese pentatonic scales and folk song melodic material. The *Allegiance* artistic team made several gestures toward cultural authenticity—similar to those encountered in examples throughout this book. For example, the choreographer, Andrew Palermo, consulted Japanese traditional dance instructor Miyako Tachibana who had served as the dance consultant for *Memoirs of a Geisha*, in which she also appeared briefly as a geisha dance teacher. (Tachibana is the daughter of the famous Japanese American dance instructor Fujima Kansuma, who first opened a Japanese traditional dance studio in Los Angeles in 1938 and who has been active in the community's Nisei Week festival ever since.) Palermo also worked with a member of the cast, Rumi Oyama, who had some training in Japanese traditional dance, though her career has primarily involved Off-Broadway and touring musical productions.[102]

The Japanese American internment camp experience has also been commemorated in a meditative work of postmodern dance far removed from the style and sensibility of *Allegiance* and from attempts to incorporate Japanese traditional culture. June Watanabe's *5/14/45–the last dance* (2001) was labeled by Watanabe a "performance installation/1940s swing dance with audience participation." As a child, Watanabe was interned at Heart Mountain (the primary setting of *Allegiance*), and she has created a number of dances inspired by this experience, including her 1989 piece *E.O. 9066*—the title referring to the executive order that established the camps. As a teenager, Watanabe appeared as a dancer in the film versions of both the Rodgers and Hammerstein musical *The King and I* and *The Teahouse of the August Moon*. She then studied Martha Graham technique, taught dance at Mills College for over two decades, and, in the 1990s, created works influenced by Japanese *noh*. For *5/14/45–the last dance* Watanabe collaborated with George Yoshida and his J-town Big Band. Yoshida, who had performed with Tak Shindo at Fort Snelling following their internment, contributed his memories which shaped the piece and performed narration in the final section of the dance. The dance climaxes with a performance by Yoshida's band of the 1940 hit "In the Mood" as Yoshida invites the audience to join the dancers. Alvin Curran, who had been a colleague of Watanabe's at Mills College, composed the taped soundscape that runs throughout the rest of the piece which also includes a drum set solo. As Wendy Ng has explained, Curran's composition incorporates "electronically processed sounds of basketball games, Boy-Scout marching bands, and found sounds."[103]

5/14/45–the last dance was performed on a basketball court in a gym.[104] The intense slowness and minimal choreographed walking in the opening suggests Watanabe's interest in the intensity of *noh* dance. The dancers appear in 1940s period costumes and carry vintage suitcases, which are then positioned to suggest, perhaps, the borders of barracks. Projections offer historic footage of the displacement and barbed wire images and the lighting suggests the perimeter guard lights of an internment camp. The dancers' movements progress to include skipping, but this more upbeat movement is soon undercut as individuals fall to the floor and roll. Much of the opening fifteen minutes is accompanied by constant brushes in a relentless swung rhythm on the snare drum, suggesting the temporal distortion and boredom of long-term confinement. Big band chords moving up and down and drone-like sustained tones resemble other works by Curran. Approximately at the dance's halfway point, an electronic drone sound resembling an alarm appears to trigger more active dance movements—faster skipping and running—recalling the choreographic style of Lucinda Childs. A male/female pair of dancers gradually moves toward the style of 1940s social dance. The solo drum set part becomes more active and Yoshida's narration about his personal internment experience begins, accompanying the close dancing couple. Yoshida relates how he had brought his swing records by Ellington, Dorsey, and Miller with him to the camp and how he started a band there himself. The other dancers form couples joining in the slow dancing as Yoshida references the 15 May 1945 final dance in the camp's high school auditorium. The volume of "In the Mood" increases and the audience is encouraged to join in the social dance, completing the gradual transition of the work from an intense postmodern contemporary dance aesthetic to a nostalgic and inclusive commemoration.

Commissioning Cross-Cultural Influence

Japanese music and culture shaped the works of numerous European and American composers throughout the twentieth century, from Benjamin Britten to Karlheinz Stockhausen, Harry Partch to Olivier Messiaen. This widespread influence on modernist and postmodernist composers was sparked in various ways, including through encounters with Japanese music during trips to Japan, through performances by Japanese immigrant musicians in the United States, or by hearing Japanese traditional music on a recording. As we have seen, the forms in which this influence has manifested in works by such American composers as Charles Wakefield Cadman, Henry Eichheim, Claude Lapham, Henry Cowell, Alan Hovhaness, John Cage, Tak Shindo, Roger Reynolds, Richard Teitelbaum, Paul Chihara, and Miya Masaoka is astonishing, ranging from the orchestration of transcribed Japanese folk melodies, scoring for Japanese instruments, and reworking approaches to musical texture, timbre, and time, to adopting new conceptions of musical aesthetics and of the fundamental nature of the musical experience itself. In the early twenty-first century, such cross-cultural musical creation has been frequently fostered by cultural institutions with a mission to commission composers, theater directors, and choreographers—some of whom had no prior substantive contact with Japanese culture—to create works inspired by Japanese traditional performing arts.

The promotion of Japanese music and the encouragement of cross-cultural fusions has taken multiple forms in New York City in recent decades. For example, in June 1995 the Asia Society produced a concert entitled "Crossovers: Music of Asia America," which featured Japanese-inspired jazz and Asian American musicians including the Kenny Endo Taiko Ensemble and the Jon Jang Sextet. The New York–based organization Music from Japan has sponsored concerts in the United States by touring Japanese musicians since 1975, focusing particularly on works by contemporary Japanese composers, but promoting traditional music as well. The organization celebrated its thirty-fifth anniversary in 2010, producing a concert by the Japanese Reigakusha *gagaku* ensemble featuring a newly commissioned piece composed by its director Sukeyasu Shiba. Kyo-Shin-An Arts, founded in New York in 2008 by the *shakuhachi* musician and composer James "Nyoraku" Schlefer,[105] aims to integrate Japanese traditional instruments in Western classical music and has commissioned works for Japanese instruments (most commonly *shakuhachi* and *koto*) and string quartet and other chamber works from such composers as Paul Moravec, Victoria Bond, Carlos Sanchez-Gutierrez, Randall Woolf, and Donald Reid Womack. Many of these concerts have been held at the Tenri Cultural Institute in Greenwich Village.

Specific New York–based ensembles have been particularly active in performing new Japanese-influenced works. For example, the Cassatt Quartet has repeatedly collaborated with Schlefer on pieces commissioned by Kyo-Shin-An Arts and has premiered works by Japanese composers commissioned by Music from Japan, including Hitomi Kaneko's *Almost Dusk* in 2010 for *sho* and string quartet, which they performed with Mayumi Miyata. In 2014 in Hawai'i, the Cassatt Quartet performed with Schlefer and *kotoist* Yoko Reikano Kimura in three sextets for Japanese instruments with string quartet commissioned by Kyo-Shin-An Arts and written by three composers at the University of Hawai'i: Takuma Itoh, Donald Womack, and Thomas Osborne.[106] The Cassatt Quartet has also performed a sextet with the same instrumentation by Schlefer and is scheduled to join Schlefer and Kimura in the April 2019 premiere of a new work by Daron Aric Hagen for *shakuhachi, koto, shamisen*, voice, and string quartet. (Kyo-Shin-An Arts previously commissioned Hagen's 2011 *Genji Concerto* for *koto* and orchestra.) Two current members of the Cassatt Quartet (Muneko Otani and Ah Ling Neu) and one former member (Michiko Oshima) were born and raised in Japan. However, none of them had any significant encounters with Japanese instruments until later in their careers in the United States when they performed pieces by American composers for Western strings and Japanese instruments. Both Muneko Otani and Ah Ling Neu (whose parents were Chinese) enjoy playing pieces involving Japanese instruments. However, Neu notes that the experience can prove a bit frustrating as the quartet members have to "make room" for the Japanese instruments, both in the sense of holding back so as not to overbalance them, but also more literally, as the *koto* is a large instrument and placing it in the center of the ensemble requires the quartet to spread out, diminishing the intimate feeling and tight communication that the quartet is accustomed to.[107]

One especially active organization in this cross-cultural arena is the New York Japan Society, which has increasingly encouraged cross-cultural fusions with Japanese performing arts through generous commissioning programs.[108] The Japan Society, founded in 1907, has long promoted Japanese performing arts in New York, as Barbara E. Thornbury has chronicled from the end of the occupation period to the early twenty-first century based primarily on her study of press reports.[109] The Japan Society's June 2003 Spring Gala featured the Chamber Music Society of Lincoln Center in a concert that included a piece by Takemitsu and a new commissioned work by Lee Hyla, *At Suma Beach*, which was based on a *noh* play. Hyla was able to live in Japan for two months as part of the commission which was funded in part by the Asian Cultural Council. Hyla had never experienced *noh* theater before but attended multiple *noh* performances in Japan. He then composed *At Suma Beach* for Western instruments, *kotsuzumi*, and mezzo-soprano. In remarks made at the performance, Hyla referred to the commission as a "life-changing experience."

A rather more ambitious commissioning project culminated in an October 2008 concert at the Japan Society, billed as "Gagaku Revolution: New Sounds of Ancient Bamboo." In conjunction with the concert, the Japan Society hosted a *gagaku* workshop for composers, furthering the goal of interesting more contemporary US-based composers in Japanese traditional music. This concert featured both traditional *gagaku* works and premieres of commissioned pieces by Gene Coleman, Carlos Sanchez-Gutierrez, and Ken Ueno, along with a few pieces by contemporary

Japanese composers. Sanchez-Gutierrez's *Ishi no Mori (Stone Forest)* for *ryuteki* and percussion is marked by a ceremonial, even ritualistic structure. The introduction and conclusion features a gong, bass drum, and woodblock, with the percussionist initially appearing alone on stage. The *ryuteki* is then heard from offstage as the player enters. (*Noh* theater performances similarly begin with the offstage solo "Oshirabe" performed on flute.) *Tombo* by Gene Coleman was performed by the composer's Ensemble N_JP—an ensemble of Japanese and American musicians formed by Coleman in 2001 to explore the interface between Japanese and European instruments–and is scored for *sho, hichiriki, ryuteki,* bass clarinet, electric guitar, and cello. *Tombo* was accompanied by screened projections, primarily of green followed by blue color fields with basic rectangular shapes that expanded, eventually revealing images of an urban landscape.

This Japan Society 2008 concert also included Ken Ueno's *The Vague Border at the Edge of Time,* which called for all three *gagaku* wind instruments—the *sho, hichiriki,* and *ryuteki.* The style and impact of the piece is perhaps even more slow and intense than traditional *gagaku* music. Ueno, a Japanese American composer and professor at the University of California, Berkeley, has frequently composed for Japanese traditional instruments and has been inspired by aspects of Japanese language, literature, and art. He has composed a duo for accordion and *sho,* featuring Mayumi Miyata, entitled *That I may time transcend, that a universe my heart may unfold* (2008), as well as works for *koto* and voice (the 2006 *Kizu* and 2010 *Tsuki no Uta*). His 2005 concerto for *biwa, shakuhachi,* and orchestra, *Kaze-no-Oka* (2005), was dedicated to the memory of Toru Takemitsu. As in Takemitsu's *November Steps,* the Japanese instruments are kept separate from the Western orchestra. In fact, in Ueno's concerto the *biwa* and *shakuhachi* only play in the extended cadenza section. This allowed Ueno to extract the cadenza as a standalone duo, but it also appears to have been a programmatic decision. The opening section, though devoid of Japanese instruments, features string clusters and swells that resemble the *sho* and *hichiriki* parts in *gagaku* music. In his program notes, Ueno explains that the work was inspired by the architecture of a modern Japanese crematorium that was built on the site of ancient burial mounds.[110] Ueno states that the *biwa* and *shakuhachi* cadenza is "poetically related to the ancient mounds," and thus the piece conceptually moves toward the past, in memoriam, in the Japanese instrumentation of the final section. The Japan Society also commissioned a work for *tsugaru-shamisen* by Scott Johnson in 2006 and a piece by the Indian American jazz pianist and composer Vijay Iyer inspired by the *rimpa* genre of painting, performed at the Japan Society in 2012 by the Bang on a Can All-Stars. These commissions have frequently included other performing art forms. The celebrated puppeteer Basil Twist created *Dogugaeshi* (2004), incorporating a Japanese *shamisen* player as in *bunraku,* and the choreographer Jeremy Wade, inspired by *manga* and the *kawaisa/kawaii* aesthetic, created *There is no end to more* (2009) for the Japan Society. Most recently, a fall 2018 concert at the Japan Society entitled "Shamisen Evolution" featured world premieres for *shamisen,* including works by Vijay Iyer and Nathan Davis.

One proximate model for the Japan Society's recent *gagaku*-inspired commissions is found in the works of Lois Vierk. Vierk has been described as "an ethnomusicologist who turned to composing" and as the first American ever to be commissioned to write for a *gagaku* ensemble.[111] As a student at the University of California, Los Angeles, and recapitulating the experience of La Monte Young, Vierk happened to hear the *gagaku* ensemble rehearsing as she passed through the hall. She studied with Suenobu Togi for ten years at the University and eventually studied *ryuteki* in Tokyo with Sukeyasu Shiba between 1982 and 1984.[112] Vierk has related that she was particularly attracted to the massive, powerful sound of *gagaku* and to how it remained nevertheless elegant.[113] Kyle Gann has stated that "in all of Vierk's work, one can hear the expressive glissandos of *gagaku*" and that in the small ensemble piece *Timberline* "the opening pentatonic scales and small glissandos between scale notes in the viola give the piece a mildly Japanese flavor"—prominent pitch clusters reminiscent of the *sho* point even more directly to Vierk's *gagaku* interests in this beautiful work.[114] The *gagaku* ensemble Reigakusha premiered Vierk's 1996 *Silversword*, which was commissioned by the Lincoln Center Festival—another New York institution that frequently presented Japanese traditional and contemporary performing arts in the past few decades. In her notes to the score, Vierk explained: "I have not tried to write Gagaku here. The way that I blend instruments and seek new colors from the blendings is not traditional to Gagaku." She also pointed to the high energy climax "built on increasingly dense textures, more and more volume, and repetition of ever-shortening phrases, [which] has more to do with my own sensibilities as a Western composer than with anything in Gagaku."[115]

I should note that American composers have not been alone in the past few decades in their interest in Japanese traditional performing arts. Looking beyond commissions by such organizations as the Japan Society, it is clear that Japanese *noh*, in particular, has proven as influential for American postmodernists as it was earlier in the twentieth century for European and American modernist directors and playwrights. Writing on artistic interculturalism and the influence of Japanese culture, Bonnie Marranca has noted the "enormous effect on avant-garde performance, centered historically in New York," and has highlighted the work of such artists as Robert Wilson, Meredith Monk, and Julie Taymor. Marranca states that:

> These artists declare their attachment to the highly stylized, refined sensibility of traditional Japanese aesthetics in many ways: the approach to narrative; the construction of theatrical space and time; conceptual use of puppets; separation of body and voice; and, in the general development of formalistic vocabularies attuned to rhythm, composition, silence, and abstraction. Weaving its way through the visual arts, multimedia, dance, and theatre, Japanese aesthetics joined with European modernism to create the New York school of avant-garde performance in the post-war era.[116]

The glacial tempo, minimalist and abstract stage design, abrupt emphasis on specific moments, and deliberateness of gesture that mark the operatic and theatrical productions of Robert Wilson has clearly been shaped by his interest in Japanese theater and dance, including *noh, bunraku, kabuki,* and *butoh*. Wilson collaborated directly with the Japanese choreographer Suzushi Hanayagi on most of his major productions in the 1980s and 1990s, including works ranging from the *CIVIL warS* project commissioned for the 1984 Summer Olympic Games in Los Angeles (but canceled due to lack of funding) to his 1993 production of *Madama Butterfly* at the National Opera in Paris. The epic *CIVIL warS* included a "knee play" in which Commodore Perry attempts to speak with a Japanese fisherman. The music for the knee plays was composed by songwriter David Byrne of Talking Heads fame. Byrne initially consulted with *kabuki* musicians in Japan, planning to compose *kabuki*-style percussion music for these sections of *CIVIL warS*, but he eventually settled on the style of a funky R&B update of Kurt Weill's Weimar-period style. Thus, no Japanese musical traits are apparent in the depiction of Perry's arrival in Japan. However, another section of this intended day-long production was to have included *gagaku* music. Hans-Peter Bayerdörfer has identified Wilson's 1986–1987 productions of Euripides' *Alkestis* and Gluck's *Alceste* as "a culmination and highlight of his intercultural attempts with regard to East-Asian theatre."[117] These productions featured *noh*-style gestures, the *noh* theater's *hashigakari* pathway or entrance bridge, and the insertion of a comic *kyogen* play as an epilogue.[118]

Peter Sellars, the other most prominent and controversial American opera director in recent decades, has also been influenced by Japanese performing arts throughout his career. In a 1989 interview Sellars declared *noh* to be "the most profound theatre I know" and related that he attempted to stage a *noh* play every three years.[119] Sellars's interest in Japanese theater began at an early age as he apprenticed at a marionette theater in Pittsburgh and encountered *bunraku* techniques when he was thirteen. He then studied with a *kabuki* actor at Harvard, has frequently visited Japan, and points to *noh, bunraku,* and *matsuri* (festivals) as primary interests.[120] The influence of Japanese theater is more apparent in his productions of operas by such contemporary composers as Kaija Saariaho (particularly in the case of *Only the Sound Remains*, which was based on two *noh* plays translated by Ezra Pound) rather than of operas by Mozart and Handel. When asked whether he acknowledged any "rules" for the Western artist involved in cross-cultural appropriations, Sellars replied that as long as the artist has "a kind of integrity" and a "depth of feeling and range of response," such projects were unproblematic. As a white American male, he explained that "the degree of permissibility there has to do with the degree of my honesty and specificity about my own reactions." Sellars concluded that as a director, he feels cultural products are at some point "common property" to be entered into by artists such as himself, and that artists need to be able "to cut loose" in such intercultural transactions and not be regulated.[121]

Aspects of Japanese theatrical influence in works centered on Japanese topics are evident in two plays by the Chinese American director Ping Chong—*Deshima*

(1990) and *Kwaidan* (1998).[122] Chong's explorations of racial perception and East Asian history have been funded and commissioned by such major organizations and corporations as the Rockefeller Foundation, the National Endowment for the Arts, AT&T, Absolut Vodka, the Japan Foundation, and the Japan/US Friendship Commission. This is striking given the experimental approach of this director who started his career as a member of Meredith Monk's company. *Deshima* consists of a series of provocative vignettes touching on major moments of intrusive European contact with East Asia, specifically with Japan and Indonesia and focusing on the ramifications of Dutch colonialism. Chong specifies that the work's narrator role should be played by an African American, with the rest of the roles cast with Asian American performers. The work opens with the late sixteenth-century arrival of Dutch traders and then Portuguese missionaries in Japan, and then leaps from the early seventeenth-century martyrdom of Japanese Christians straight to 1941 with an American radio announcer calling out the titles of anti-Japanese World War II propaganda pop songs during a swing dance competition. Following an extended Indonesian section, *Deshima* returns to 1941 with Japanese Americans clapping and happily singing "Go Tell It on the Mountain." This moment of campy Christian joy is abruptly interrupted by a change in lighting, sudden silence, and physical stillness, marking the moment of Japanese American mandatory evacuations to the internment camps. The narrator barks orders for the evacuation through a bull-horn, bringing home the brutality of this historic disgrace. In contrast, Chong's 1998 *Kwaidan* avoids political critique and instead returns us to Lafcadio Hearn's literary celebrations of "weird" Japan from a century prior. Chong selected three "Japanese ghost stories" from Hearn's 1904 collection. Japanese music and exotic musical effects play an integral role in this work, with mystical strokes on a bell tree signaling the start and end of each story. A *shakuhachi* solo signals the presence of a corpse-eating demon in the passing of the night in the first story, which is performed with puppets. The second section features puppets and live actors, including an actor who briefly performs on *biwa* and chants, but not in a Japanese style. The sounds of the *hichiriki* and *sho* signal the presence of the noble ghosts in this tale. Finally, a recording of Ryuichi Sakamoto's song "Ride, Ride, Ride" from the 1983 film *Merry Christmas, Mr. Lawrence*, including its Brian Eno–esque synthesized atmospheric effects, assists in moving the final ghost story forward to a contemporary setting at a McDonald's.

I will conclude this section with one of the most unexpected examples I have encountered of cross-cultural immersion in Japanese performing arts by an American—the career of *noh* performer, director, and composer Richard Emmert. Following in the footsteps of Edward Sylvester Morse and Ernest Fenollosa almost exactly a century later, Emmert began studying *noh* performance in Japan in 1973—eventually mastering not only the vocal and dance performance, but the several instruments as well. He has made Japan his home ever since. Along with numerous other white American male musicians in the 1970s, as we will see below, Emmert had initially studied *shakuhachi* with Goro Yamaguchi in Japan in 1970. In the 1980s, Emmert began to compose and direct *noh* productions in English, and he launched the Noh Training Project in Tokyo in 1991 and summer programs in *noh* performance in Bloomsburg, Pennsylvania, in 1995. In 2000, he founded a Tokyo-based and American-led *noh* company, Theatre Nohgaku, dedicated to the performance of traditional and contemporary *noh* plays in English. The company toured the United States with W. B. Yeats's *noh*-inspired *At the Hawk's Well* in 2002 in a *noh* theater production. He currently serves as a professor at Musashino University and continues as the artistic director of Theatre Nohgaku. Perhaps the most unlikely Japanese-influenced example of American theater so far in this new century is Theatre Nohgaku's recent and powerful production of the English-language *noh* play *Blue Moon over Memphis* based on the life of Elvis Presley.[123]

Blue Moon over Memphis: An Elvis Presley noh was written by the American playwright Deborah Brevoort in 2006 and was composed by Emmert in 2013. Emmert directed the first production in 2017 and the work has been performed at several colleges and universities in the United States as well as in Japan. The play is set at Elvis's Graceland mansion in Memphis on the anniversary of his death and it is typical in structure to *mugen noh* ghost plays. The *waki* (secondary) character, Judy (an Elvis fan), has arrived to pay her respects and encounters the *shite* (primary) character, a mysterious man wearing a dark kimono resembling a western suit with Elvis's trademark lightning bolt and TCB ("taking care of business") emblem appearing like a royal crest on the lapels. In the second half of the play, the *shite* reappears as the ghost of Elvis, wearing a spectacular gold and white kimono—a costume clearly inspired by Elvis's typical 1977 concert attire. (See Figure 9.3.) Judy's devotion to Elvis's music has called forth his lonely spirit and Emmert employs in

Figure 9.3 John Oglevee as Elvis in *Blue Moon over Memphis*. Image c. 2018 David Surtasky; courtesy of Theatre Nohgaku.

his score the melodies of two laments of solitude famously covered by Elvis—his haunting, high lonesome early rendition of "Blue Moon" and his late style performance of "Unchained Melody." We hear Judy sing "Unchained Melody" in *noh* style and the flute plays "Blue Moon" toward the end of the play during Elvis's climactic dance expressing his eternal longing. Emmert composed the score with the eight-beat melodic phrase structure of *noh* music and devised a three-line staff notation indicating the low-middle-high relative pitches for the vocal part. The score also includes the drum patterns and drummer's *kakegoe* calls as well as labels indicating the traditional musical and dance sections of the play. *Blue Moon over Memphis* proves a moving, poignant work, which ennobles this American pop culture icon—the King of Rock 'n' Roll—through the ritualistic style of Japanese *noh*.

American Shakuhachi, Here and There

Since the early 1970s, a surprisingly large number of Americans—predominantly white and male—have traveled to Japan to study *shakuhachi* performance. Several of these performers have become certified as masters of the instrument and have returned to the United States to teach and to build performance careers.[124] This has been the most striking and unexpected phenomenon in American interactions with Japanese music in the past half century. The prevalence of *shakuhachi* players in the United States has led numerous American composers to create new works for the instrument.[125] Many of these composers have been drawn to the instrument's timbral richness and some have been motivated by its Zen associations.[126] After briefly surveying this phenomenon as it has played out both in Japan and in the United States, I will turn to the careers of two master performers/teachers in particular: Ralph Samuelson and James "Nyoraku" Schlefer. (Names appearing in quotation marks here are Japanese professional names earned through certification.) The phenomenon of American *shakuhachi* has not been limited to concert performance of traditional and newly composed pieces. By the end of the twentieth century, the timbre of the *shakuhachi*—either in acoustic or synthesized form—had become familiar enough in the United States through Hollywood soundtracks, popular song recordings, and concert music as to suggest that it might transcend its Japanese cultural associations.[127]

In 1981 Karl Signell reported on the increased presence of the *shakuhachi* in the United States since 1965, and noted that in 1977 *Rolling Stone* magazine had selected an album of traditional *shakuhachi* music (the 1969 Nonesuch recording *A Bell Ringing in the Empty Sky* performed by Goro Yamaguchi) as one of the best popular albums of the past ten years.[128] (A track from this album was included on the Voyager spacecraft's Golden Record in 1977.) As we will find, Yamaguchi proved to be the central figure in introducing Americans to the *shakuhachi* and training numerous American *shakuhachi* players. (The American Donald Berger, who had been stationed in Tokyo in 1950 with the US Army and who taught at the

American School in Japan from 1959 to 1993, was apparently the first foreigner to study with Yamaguchi in the late 1960s. Signell had himself studied with Yamaguchi at Wesleyan University in 1967–1968 and for an additional six months in Japan in 1970.) In his study of the widespread Western adoption of the *shakuhachi*, Jay Keister has claimed that "it is the persistence of this spiritual identity of the *shakuhachi* that has contributed to the internationalization of the instrument in the 20th century and its relative independence from the protective and controlling culture of the traditional Japanese music world."[129] Keister has emphasized the Americanization of the instrument, pointing out that "while the spiritual practice of classical *honkyoku* or 'blowing Zen' plays a minor role among [contemporary] players in Japan, an explicit and conscious approach to the *shakuhachi* as a Zen instrument plays a major role among players in America."[130] Keister also claims that many American *shakuhachi* musicians were attracted to the instrument for spiritual reasons and that the "anti-authoritarianism that underlies spiritual *shakuhachi* represents the beginning of the Americanization of *shakuhachi*, which, like the Americanization of Zen, consists of a transformation of ownership of tradition by valuing the personal experience of spirituality over the social structure of religion."[131]

The number of American *shakuhachi* performers and teachers is far too large to allow for a true survey here.[132] However, before turning in more depth to the careers of two such figures, I will briefly note several representative examples. Like Richard Emmert, Christopher "Yohmei" Blasdel made his home and career primarily in Japan. Blasdel traveled to Japan in 1972 as a college student and studied with Goro Yamaguchi. Throughout the 1970s Blasdel accompanied *butoh* dancers and found that even highly educated Japanese were not particularly interested in traditional Japanese music.[133] Blasdel has concertized throughout the world and he composed numerous *shakuhachi* pieces in the 1980s. He served as a co-organizer of the 1998 World Shakuhachi Festival at Colorado University in Boulder along with David "Kansuke" Wheeler, who had lived in Japan for twenty years himself—teaching and performing *shakuhachi* there as well as in the United States—and who has been teaching in a *shakuhachi* summer program at Boulder since 1999. Other American *shakuhachi* musicians have spent less time in Japan, establishing their careers from the start in the United States. For example, Ronnie "Nyogetsu Reishin" Seldin arrived in Japan soon after Blasdel in 1973 after having been in a rock band. He devoted himself to the study of *shakuhachi* and Buddhism for three years in Kyoto, eventually following the Japanese Tenrikyo religion and becoming active at the Tenri center in New York City. From 1975 to 2017 Seldin taught approximately one thousand *shakuhachi* students in the United States. Other Americans who have studied *shakuhachi* in Japan have made their careers elsewhere. The Chinese American *shakuhachi* performer Riley Lee studied in Japan starting in 1971, became the first American to achieve Grand Master status, and settled in Australia.[134] However, given his prominence in the world of *shakuhachi* performance he has also had an impact on composers in the United States. He collaborated, for instance, with the Princeton University–based composer Barbara White who hosted Lee at

Princeton in 2012 and 2016, where he inspired such student composers as Caroline Shaw to compose for the instrument. Finally, as noted in chapter 8, the most popular *shakuhachi* musicians, such as John "Kaizan" Neptune, have pursued fusions with jazz and New Age styles.[135]

Based in the New York City area, Ralph Samuelson has been a pivotal figure in American *shakuhachi* since the late 1970s. Samuelson grew up playing the saxophone and flute in jazz music.[136] In his senior year at Cornell University he took a course in Japanese art but had no early contact with Japanese music. Instead, he became intrigued by Carnatic flute music and decided to discontinue his graduate work in anthropology at Stanford University in order to study Indian music at Wesleyan. Wesleyan had brought Goro Yamaguchi along with a *kotoist* and *shamisen* player to teach at the university in 1967 for a year and, thus, by the late 1960s was offering advanced study opportunities in Indian, Indonesian, and Japanese music. However, upon arriving at Wesleyan in 1969 Samuelson discovered that the instructor of Carnatic flute was away and so he began to study *shakuhachi* instead with Kodo Araki V and then with Shudo Yamato. The major Japanese musicologist Fumio Koizumi also visited Wesleyan during this period and advised Samuelson on his *shakuhachi* master's thesis. Thus, Samuelson arrived at Wesleyan at an auspicious moment for Japanese musical studies. (Wesleyan discontinued Japanese musical performance studies in 1979.) Samuelson first traveled to Japan with his wife in 1971 where they taught English for two years while he studied primarily with Yamaguchi in addition to playing flute in the Japanese free jazz scene. After finishing PhD coursework at Wesleyan, Samuelson returned to Japan on a dissertation research fellowship and worked with multiple major *shakuhachi* players. He was then hired by the Smithsonian Institution in 1975 to select Japanese folk artists in Japan to perform in the Smithsonian's US bicentennial celebration. This work led to a significant shift in his career away from academia.

In the fall of 1976 Samuelson was hired by the J. D. Rockefeller 3rd Foundation, which became the Asian Cultural Council in 1980. This is where Samuelson would work for the next thirty-two years, serving as director starting in 1991. This position focused on fundraising and grant allocation, which allowed Samuelson to visit Japan a couple times each year and, through his funding decisions, shape American musical interaction with Japanese musicians. Samuelson practiced *shakuhachi* at night, studied with Yamaguchi during his trips to Japan, and started performing publicly in the United States in 1977 and teaching in 1980. Beate Sirota Gordon, who directed the performing arts programs at the Japan Society and Asia Society and who served for decades as a central figure in promoting Japanese music in New York, invited Samuelson to perform at the Japan Society in 1977. At this performance, several audience members approached Samuelson after the concert to ask to study with him, thus launching his extensive teaching career. In addition, a very positive review of the concert in the *Village Voice* led to further performance opportunities.[137] In 1978 he frequently performed with the Indian *bansuri* player Steve Gorn—recording Cowell's *The Universal Flute* with him as a duet—and then, starting in 1979, began to perform regularly with a *koto* player, Reiko Kamata, touring the country with her to perform at multiple Japan America societies. A highlight of Samuelson's performance career was appearing in concert in 1987 at Wesleyan with Goro Yamaguchi. A second major highlight was performing two concerts in Tokyo with Blasdel in 1995–1996 on a program of American music composed for *shakuhachi*. These concerts included Richard Teitelbaum's *Blends*, discussed in chapter 8, along with works by Elizabeth Brown and Tania Cronin and Cowell's *Universal Flute*.[138] An injury derailed Samuelson's performance career in the late 1990s, but he was able to resume some public performances starting in 2002 and has performed repeatedly in Japan since 2008 and toured with Teitelbaum and Alvin Curran in the Czech Republic and Austria in 2012 in improvisational performances.

In addition to his concertizing, Samuelson has shaped the development of *shakuhachi* in America through his teaching. His studio has consistently had between ten and fifteen students who have ranged in age from the late teens to early eighties, with most being in their thirties and forties. Over two thirds of his students have been male and most have been white Americans, though he has had some Japanese American and Japanese students and, more recently, several students from China. Most strikingly, a few of his students have gone on as composers for the instrument. Throughout his long career, Samuelson has noted a gradual evolution of the *shakuhachi*'s cultural associations. Writing in 1993, Samuelson claimed that "in the late 20th century, we can observe the *shakuhachi* being transformed from a musical instrument tied to a particular culture and time period to one which is truly part of international contemporary musical life."[139] In conversation with me in 2017, Samuelson concluded that "*shakuhachi* is now a global instrument."

An examination of the compositional and performance careers of two of Samuelson's students, Elizabeth Brown and Ned Rothenberg, provides some indication of just how disparate American *shakuhachi* music has become. Brown performs on and composes for the Western flute, *shakuhachi* (since 1984), and the theremin and has also composed a few pieces for the Harry Partch instrument collection. Since 1990, she has composed some twenty works for Japanese traditional instruments, including the *shamisen*, *koto*, *biwa*, and *sho*, often in combination with the *shakuhachi*. Her oeuvre includes *Mirage* (2008) for *shakuhachi* and string quartet, *Cloudrest* (2010) for *shakuhachi*, soprano, and gamelan, and the 2010 *Shinshoufuukei* (*An Imagined Landscape*) for Japanese traditional instrument orchestra and inspired by her experience of Japanese stroll gardens. Her work has been supported by the Asian Cultural Council and the Japan/US Friendship Commission and she has received commissions from Music from Japan, which has presented her music in concerts in the United States and Japan, including a performance of *Rubicon* (2009) by members of the Reigakusha *gagaku* orchestra. In recent years Brown has also performed *shakuhachi* on tour with Samuelson in the United States and in Japan. Rothenberg's career has been strikingly different. Following his studies with Samuelson, he studied *shakuhachi* performance for six months in

Japan with Goro Yamaguchi as well as with Katsuya Yokoyama. As a composer and performer, Rothenberg's career resembles that of his near contemporary John Zorn. Like Zorn, Rothenberg is an active improviser, performing contemporary free jazz–inspired music on saxophone and clarinets. (I note that Zorn has produced and released Rothenberg's recordings on his Tzadik label.) Rothenberg's musical interests are quite eclectic and he has toured for five years with a Tuvan vocalist. However, his pieces for *shakuhachi* most closely resemble traditional *honkyoku shakuhachi* music rather than the style of any of his other musical areas.

A major figure in the second wave of American *shakuhachi* performers, James "Nyoraku" Schlefer was a professional Western flutist before he encountered *shakuhachi*.[140] While completing his master's degree in musicology at the City University of New York, Schlefer enrolled in an Asian music course taught by Henry Burnett, who introduced him to the *shamisen* and Japanese music. In the spring of 1979 Schlefer and his fellow students were invited to the New York residence of American music critic and musicologist Edward Downes in the Dakota building, where they heard the *shakuhachi* in a *sankyoku* concert. Schlefer also noted how frequently the *shakuhachi* was referenced during a flute seminar he took with Harvey Sollberger the next summer. He then began taking *shakuhachi* lessons with Ronnie Seldin before traveling to Japan in the early 1990s where he studied with three main teachers. He returned to Japan annually in the late 1990s for approximately a month each time. Schlefer began teaching *shakuhachi* in the New York City area in 1989 and typically has had around twenty students at a time who are in their forties or fifties. He has licensed seven students himself and has taught for several years at Columbia University, an institution that has also featured *gagaku* music performance for over a decade. Schlefer founded Ensemble East to perform *sankyoku* music in the late 1990s and has frequently toured with a *kotoist* and *shamisen* player.

As noted above, Schlefer has devoted considerable energy in the past decade to commissioning new works for Japanese traditional instruments and Western ensembles, seeking, like Henry Cowell before him, "unfettered musical exploration." As he has put it, "embracing a history of differences between Japanese and Western classical music, I set out in pursuit of a tangible way in which to reconcile them."[141] Like Samuelson, he feels that the *shakuhachi* has become a "global instrument." Schlefer has composed numerous pieces for *shakuhachi* since the late 1990s. He has aimed to compose classical music in which Japanese instruments no longer seem exotic and Western instruments are not asked to conform to an "Eastern sonority that somehow suits their style," and he has called upon audiences to "imagine a musical landscape where non-Western instruments are heard alongside Western instruments without notice."[142] Much of his music for *shakuhachi* does not require the particular timbral and pitch-bending techniques that are so prominent in the Japanese traditional repertoire. He has also avoided jazz or New Age–inflected styles for the instrument. Instead, while continuing to perform traditional Japanese music in traditional styles, he has, through his compositions for the *shakuhachi*, returned to his roots in classical Western flute training. Schlefer acknowledges that Zen's emphasis on being present and focused in the moment has profoundly impacted him, but said to me that Zen has otherwise not been a focus in his life and that he is "not particularly a Nipponophile." In his compositions from the past decade, Schlefer appears to treat the *shakuhachi* less as a tool for meditation and connection to Japanese traditional culture and more as a universal flute.

Far beyond the concert hall and the teaching studio, the timbre of the *shaku-hachi* became increasingly pervasive in the American soundscape in the late twentieth century. These timbral appearances frequently occurred in unexpected contexts. For instance, the Japanese *shakuhachi* player and New Age musician Kazu Matsui became quite active in Hollywood in the 1980s and 1990s, appearing particularly on the soundtracks for films scored by James Horner. To take one example, Matsui's *shakuhachi* playing is heard signaling the bad guys in the 1998 movie *The Mask of Zorro*, a film set in nineteenth-century California and which has no Japanese associations. Matsui's *shakuhachi* playing also appeared on Joni Mitchell's 1985 "Ethiopia," a song decrying the humanitarian crisis in that country. The breathy timbre of the *shakuhachi* is associated in the song with the desolation and broader environmental degradation expressed in the lyrics. Sampled *shaku-hachi* sounds on the E-mu Emulator II were heard in the 1980s in TV ads and also appeared prominently in popular songs, as in the opening section of Peter Gabriel's 1986 "Sledgehammer," which, again, is a song without any Japanese reference. In all of these examples, the *shakuhachi* appears primarily as a timbral effect. Rather than signaling Japanese culture, the *shakuhachi* timbre came to signify either danger (in cinematic contexts in particular) or a vague spirituality, or, in some cases, nothing beyond the intriguing, ever protean and singular sound itself.

Musical *Japonisme*, Now and Then

In the late nineteenth century, Americans who encountered Japanese music either over there or here at home, were, by and large, repulsed by the exotic timbres which they frequently complained resembled the noise of insects. As we found in chapter 1, writers such as Alice Mabel Bacon in her 1891 *Japanese Girls and Women* even blamed the irritation of Japanese musical timbres specifically on the Japanese love for caged crickets. In this period of first encounter, Lafcadio Hearn stood out for his celebrations of the exotic Japanese soundscape. Unlike the majority of writers at that time, Hearn celebrated connections between ineffable Japanese music and the sounds of nature. Occasionally, bluntly negative sentiments echoing the late nineteenth-century invective have been voiced in recent years. For instance, in 1997 the English philosopher Roger Scruton opined: "For three hundred years, Japan remained cut off from Western art music, locked in its grisly imitations of the Chinese court orchestras, dutifully producing sounds as cacophonous to local ears as the croaking of jackdaws."[143] However, Hearn's hearing and celebration of connections between Japanese music and natural sounds appears to be the more predominant popular perception today.

Indeed, after several decades of interest in Zen aesthetics—or, at least, the popularized American version thereof—Japanese instrumental music found a niche by the end of the twentieth century in New Age recordings.

This substantial body of recorded music is specifically functional, designed for the purposes of relaxation, meditation, and healing, and to accompany massages. Though my fieldwork in day spas in the past several decades has, alas, been somewhat limited, it is evident that the timbre of the *shakuhachi*, in particular, is frequently heard on a daily basis in these establishments. Indeed, many massage therapy studios participate fully in a renewed embrace of *japonisme*. In Williamstown, Massachusetts, to take but one example, the two primary massage therapy establishments over the past couple of decades both reference Japanese culture in their decor—with the entrance of one framed by a bright red *torii* and the other referencing Japan directly in its business name. The sound of the *shakuhachi* in particular—whether acoustic or synthesized—is typically heard, rather interchangeably with the Native American flute, in ambient recordings played at day spas throughout the United States. As Koji Matsunobu claimed in 2011, "shakuhachi music now is grouped in the genre of New Age, spiritual, and healing music in the market of world music."[144]

In these recordings, the *shakuhachi* is most often accompanied by atmospheric synthesized sounds or by the natural sounds of birds, insects, and water. Given its intended function, the music is deliberately pulseless, floating, and sustained, with far less dramatic timbral and dynamic contrasts than in traditional *shakuhachi* music. Recent examples of such recordings include *Zen Spa: Zen Oriental Music Soundscapes Meditation, Asian Oriental Flute Shakuhachi Music for Massage, Spa, Yoga, Relax, Tai Chi, Reiki, and Sleep* (2012) from Asian Zen Relaxation Music Records; the Easy Music Record 2017 release of *Zen Shakuhachi: Secrets Garden with Japanese Traditional Flute Music for Asian Meditation, Thai Massage & Spa*; and the 2018 Stress Fighter Records *Beautiful Ambient Japanese Flute—Meditation, Yoga, Massage, Spa Music* with such track titles as "Oriental Asian Spa," "Sleeping Zen," and "Lounge Journey to Japan," and with the image of a geisha appearing on the cover. These highly specialized album titles suggest that each track was especially designed to produce specific remedies or to accompany specific forms of massage therapy, as with the 2016 "Relaxing Shakuhachi for Sensual Massage." In actuality, this music is, by design, rather consistent in style and affect.

Joseph Browning has noted a more general marketing and design trend that appears in recordings of traditional *shakuhachi* music by Japanese master musicians, recordings of American *shakuhachi* musicians, and in New Age albums featuring the instrument. The cover art and accompanying imagery for these recordings characteristically depicts natural landscapes, suggesting—as did the exotica genre in the 1950s and 1960s—that the recorded music will transport the listener to such peaceful and often exotic locales.[145] Furthermore, Browning points to multiple recordings, including those by New Age–influenced American *shakuhachi* musicians such as John "Kaizan" Neptune, that were deliberately recorded so as to allow the natural soundscape to be included. For instance, Neptune has reported that he opened windows in order to let cricket noises be picked up by the microphones as he recorded one album.[146]

This emphasis on site-specific recordings and on ambient sounds in recent recordings of Japanese music (or Japanese-inflected music) resonates with an album produced by ethnomusicologist Steven Feld in 2006: *Suikinkutsu: A Japanese Underground Water Zither* (appearing on Feld's VoxLox Documentary Sound Art). A *suikinkutsu* is a musical Japanese garden ornament, consisting of a buried ceramic bowl upon which water drips from above, thus creating highly resonant pitches that somewhat resemble the sounds of a plucked *koto*. Feld created what he referred to as a "soundscape composition" featuring the sounds of summer cicadas and the *suikinkutsu*, along with other ambient sounds, all recorded at the Enko-ji Temple in Kyoto. Like an aeolian harp, the *suikinkutsu* is a carefully crafted and positioned manmade instrument, which appears to rely on nature to play its music, or on the chance drips of a visitor washing his or her hands in preparation for a tea ceremony. Feld dedicated the piece to John Cage and, in the spirit perhaps of Erik Satie or Brian Eno, suggests in the liner notes that the recording be enjoyed "at low volume" so that the listener may experience "the ever-changing water rhythms flowing randomly into the pulsing surround of summer cicadas." Unlike New Age recordings, Feld adds no synthesized accompaniment nor any other sounds to the recording. This beautiful and meditative album is sixty minutes long, suggesting that it could continue endlessly and that Feld is simply presenting an hour of sound from a specific soundscape. Feld, however, notes that he positioned the microphones carefully and selected the time of day in order to concentrate the recording on two sound sources—the cicadas and the *suikinkutsu*—though I believe I hear distant crows as well, but not the sounds of bustling modern Kyoto. In November 2009, during a visit to Williams College, Feld presented me with a CD of this recording. I later discovered that he had inserted a Post-It note with one word written on it: "exotica?" I have been pondering the implications of his question ever since, gradually coming to the realization that the answers are to be found in the experience of each individual musical consumer.

Feld's recording of cicadas and the *suikinkutsu* encourages a reading of Japanese musical culture as being especially tied to the natural world. However, just as primitivist and futurist representation in works of early and mid-twentieth-century modernism frequently exhibited strong stylistic parallels, a similar-seeming paradox is evident in contemporary perceptions of Japanese culture. In the past several decades in the American imagination and entertainment experience, Japan and Japanese music have stood for both the ancient soul-soothing sounds of blown Zen and the ultra techno-futuristic fantasies of video games and an encroaching robotic world. (Indeed, some American parents have feared that their children have been "captured" by Japanese entertainment culture.) Japan, tied simultaneously to nature and to cutting-edge high tech, continues to inspire both desire and anxiety, thus producing the full range of experiential exoticism.

By far the most prevalent source of musical encounters with Japan has been in video game and anime film soundtracks over the past several decades. Indeed, at no prior moment have Americans consumed as much music created in Japan as through these recent media, though, of course, much of this music is rather indistinguishable from contemporary music produced in Europe or North America. Roland Kelts has noted that the early twenty-first century ravenous consumption of Japanese entertainment in the United States in the form of anime films, computer games, manga comics, Pokémon, Hello Kitty, etc., has led to what "many cultural historians are calling a third wave of Japanophilia."[147] Through some of these entertainment forms American children and their adult caregivers have encountered representations of both traditional Japanese culture and traditional Japanese music. In terms of hours of contact, the most pervasive form of this encounter since the late twentieth century has been through video games. (From this perspective, the music of such Japanese game composers as Koji Kondo, the major composer for both *Super Mario* and *The Legend of Zelda*, may well be some of the most frequently heard music of all time.) Some popular video games have featured settings in Old Japan and elements of traditional Japanese music. For instance, *shamisen*, *shakuhachi*, and *koto* are heard in the soundtrack for the 1991 game *Legend of the Mystical Ninja*.[148] More recently, the highly popular 2017 game *Legend of Zelda: Breath of the Wild* features the *shakuhachi* in the Kakariko Village sequences. The visual design for this installment of the *Zelda* series was based on styles from the Jomon period in Japanese history and the score includes *koto*, Chinese *erhu*, and Western strings and piano. Other games that have featured Japanese instrumental timbres include *Okami* (2006) and *Muramasa: The Demon Blade* (2009). The narratives of these games typically offer old Japanese legends and thus function similarly to many of the stories of Lafcadio Hearn from over a century prior.

Most recently, in June 2018 Sony announced *The Ghost of Tsushima*, a game set in the thirteenth century in which the player's avatar is a lone samurai who must fight off the Mongol invasion of Japan. Sony introduced this new game—presumably forthcoming in late 2019—at the annual E3 Conference in Los Angeles and the presentation featured a live performance on *shakuhachi* by white American musician Cornelius Boots wearing a traditional Japanese farmer costume similar to that worn by the game's avatar. Boots studied traditional *shakuhachi* performance, receiving his master license from his teacher Michael "Chikuzen" Gould, but has recorded primarily in a style he refers to as "bamboo gospel," which draws on "rock, blues, metal, Zen and pure energy."[149] He frequently plays on the bass *shakuhachi* and has performed Hendrix, Iron Maiden, and Jethro Tull pieces. *The Ghost of Tsushima* also features the *shakuhachi* in its soundtrack. As has been the case throughout the history of musical Orientalism, video game soundtracks frequently mix Japanese instruments with other exotic timbres. This is particularly the case in the game *SOCOM 4: US Navy SEALs* (2011), in which non-Western style and instrumentation represent the bad rebel insurgents and accompany violence in this war game set in Southeast Asia. As Joseph E. Jones has detailed, "beyond the sizable gamelan,

SOCOM 4 also features several Japanese instruments including McCreary's trademark taiko drums, the biwa lute, the three-stringed shamisen, and the shakuhachi, an end-blown flute. Also permeating the score are the Chinese erhu and its slightly larger cousin the zhonghu as well as the dizi, a transverse membrane flute."[150] Thus, mixed exotic musical representation is employed for highly violent, high-tech warfare.

Representations of both old traditional and techno-futuristic Japan are juxtaposed throughout *Isle of Dogs*, a 2018 stop-motion animated film written and directed by Wes Anderson that pays homage to Japanese anime. The story is set in Japan twenty years in the future at a somewhat dystopian moment when the evil mayor of the fictional Megasaki is attempting to eliminate all dogs from his city. His nephew, Atari, goes on a rescue mission to recover his own dog Spots, who was the first dog to be banished to an island of garbage. A white female foreign-exchange high school student leads a protest against the mayor and helps to expose his nefarious plans, thereby repeating a common "white savior" trope of Orientalism. The rather minimal score by Alexandre Desplat appears to draw on the style of *matsuri* music, recycling a limited amount of musical material throughout, but the soundtrack also includes a couple of pieces that had appeared in films by Akira Kurosawa. A prologue presents the backstory of the long-term animus against dogs in the mayor's family. We see a Shinto shrine decorated with numerous cat sculptures and a stern Shinto priest (reminding me of the opening of an ominous sequence in Frank Capra's *Our Job in Japan*), as we hear "mumbo jumbo" low male chanting performed by the ensemble London Voices. The repeated three-pitch rhythmic chanting (E♭ G♭ F, G♭ F, E♭ G♭ F), likely associated with East Asian religions by most viewers, actually sounds like nothing so much as the chant of the Wicked Witch's monkey army in *The Wizard of Oz* (1939). In the Main Title sequence we see three boys playing *taiko* in a school gym as we hear drumming composed by the Japanese American Kaoru Watanabe, a Brooklyn-based musician and composer who had been a member of the famous Japanese *taiko* group Kodo. The *taiko* music and other drumming is most often associated in the film with ominous plot moments, as in the deportation of Spots and particularly with the attack on Atari and his dog friends by the Municipal Task Force and its robotic dogs and high-tech weaponry. The film includes multiple typical signals of traditional Japan, including sumo wrestling, *haiku*, and cherry trees. Following the assumed death of Atari, the Megasaki Senior High Drama Club puts on a memorial performance in pseudo-*kabuki* style, to the accompaniment of the same three student *taiko* drummers along with some male chanters.

Critics of *Isle of Dogs*, such as Justin Chang in the *Los Angeles Times*, have rightly noted that the Japanese human characters are likely alienated from the target American audience by speaking only in Japanese, while the dogs, who we sympathize with, "bark" in English.[151] As a Japanese audience member, Moeko Fujii countered such criticism, writing in the *New Yorker* that she found the Japanese dialogue to be spot on and arguing that the film is largely about the failures of translation. For Fujii, the extensive Japanese dialogue and kanji printed text plays out quite differently for a Japanese-speaking audience. She also notes that the Japanese characters can actually understand English, though not dog language, but choose to speak in Japanese. This interpretation suggests that the film is a paragon of postmodernism in that the creative team intends for the artwork to signify differently for different audiences, the author makes no attempt to predetermine a singular interpretation, nor is there an attempt to meld different cultural elements into a coherent whole. Again, this postmodern ploy does not negate the fact that much of the film will be experienced as a work of exoticism for its primary target audience.[152]

The film's representations of and references to Japanese music seem rather cheeky and half-hearted. In contrast, music is a vital motivator throughout the particularly beautiful and moving 2016 stop-motion animated film *Kubo and the Two Strings*. This film is set in Old Japan and is based in its visual style on origami and woodblock print design. Kubo, the child hero, entertains villagers through his magical *shamisen* playing, which brings origami figures to life, animating them to act out his legendary tale of a noble samurai. Dario Marianelli's score features music not only for *shamisen*, but also for *koto* and *shakuhachi*. Clive Bell, an English *shakuhachi* musician who was also heard in the soundtracks for *Harry Potter and the Deathly Hallows Parts I and II*, performed the limited *shakuhachi* moments of color, the Japanese-born but UK-based Hibiki Ichikawa took the second *shamisen* part, and Melissa Holding, likewise based in the United Kingdom, performed the *koto* lines. The primary musical role in the soundtrack was taken by Kevin "Masaya" Kmetz, a white American *shamisen* musician who also performs *shamisen* in the California rock band God of Shamisen, founded in 2004. His part in Marianelli's soundtrack is primarily in the high-octane, driven style of modern *tsugaru shamisen*, made famous internationally since 2000 by the Yoshida Brothers. The end credits for *Kubo and the Two Strings* features a cover of George Harrison's "While My Guitar Gently Weeps," from the Beatles' *White Album*, with Eric Clapton's famous electric guitar solo taken by Kmetz on the *shamisen*.

Children in the United States have been particularly fascinated by the figures of the ninja and the samurai for decades: from the Teenage Mutant Ninja Turtles in the 1980s and 1990s, to numerous examples of children's literature, through episodes of such children's television shows as *The Backyardigans'* "Samurai Pie" (2006) to the Barenaked Ladies' "The Ninjas" (2008)—a short song devoid of exotic musical signs, beyond an inscrutable final synthesized gong sound, but in which we learn that: "The ninjas are deadly and silent/They're also unspeakably violent/They speak Japanese/They do whatever they please/And if you tear off their mask,/They'll be smiling." Indeed, as I dropped off my children at preschool one morning in January 2007 I noted that in answer to the teacher's "question of the day" posted on the bulletin board, "What do you want to do when you grow up?," one preschooler had replied "fight the bad ninjas." Video games have allowed children and adults to embody or fight against samurai and ninjas and to enter virtually into the world of Old Japan through ever more realistic computer-generated imagery. However, older forms of embodying *japonisme* remain popular in the early twenty-first century as well. These opportunities are typically offered at "family day" events and festivals held at art museums and other major cultural institutions across the entire country. In their efforts to introduce Americans to the exotic culture of traditional Japan, these public celebrations of *japonisme* resemble similar events discussed in chapter 1—such as the 1901 Salem, Massachusetts, *matsuri* festival, Isabella Stewart Gardner's "Japanese Festival Village" held at her Boston home in 1905, and the 1911 "Japanese Pageants" at the Art Institute of Chicago. Some of these events in recent years have been small in scale, such as the highly controversial opportunity offered to visitors at the Museum of Fine Arts, Boston, in summer 2015 to dress up in a replica robe to pose with Claude Monet's 1876 painting *La Japonaise*.[153] Similarly, Japan served as the exotic theme for the 27 September 2008 Homecoming Dance at Westminster Choir College, as students and alumni were invited on posters, sporting brushstroke font, to "come dance the night away Zen-style! Enjoy free samples of sushi and desserts." Other public Japan-themed events have played out on a much larger scale.

A simple survey of events calendars for American art museums over the past year alone reveals that days devoted to presentations of Japanese culture are nearly ubiquitous. The number of such events is even higher when we include various cultural institutions devoted specifically to Japan or to Japanese American history. In 2017 the Detroit Institute of Arts produced "Japan Cultural Days," which included performances by the Kikuno-kai Dance Troupe, an Awa Odori festival parade which encouraged audience participation, martial arts demonstrations, several traditional artists' booths (featuring doll making, paper making, pottery, etc.), tea ceremonies, anime film, and Japanese sweets.[154] Billing itself as "the largest celebration of Japanese culture in the Gulf South," the annual Japan Fest held in October 2018 at the New Orleans Museum of Art offered samples of Japanese cuisine, traditional dance groups, martial arts demonstrations, *taiko* drumming, a Zen ceremony, and a kimono dressing demonstration. The public was invited to attend in Japanese costume.[155] *Taiko* drumming is a common feature at such events, as it was at the May 2018 Children's Day celebration at the Carnegie Museum of Art in Pittsburgh[156] and, across the state of Pennsylvania, at the August 2018 Japanese Culture Family Festival at Philadelphia's Please Touch Museum.[157] In June 2018, the Coral Gables Museum in Florida invited families to "immerse themselves in Japanese culture,"[158] and in November 2018 the Portland Art Museum offered its own Japanese-themed free family day, featuring tea tasting, poetry, calligraphy, ikebana, origami, and a performance on *shinobue* flute and *shamisen*.[159] Even the National Atomic Testing Museum in Las Vegas presented a "Family Fun Day: Journey through Japan" in August that included *taiko* and Japanese dance demonstrations, with a performance by the Las Vegas Kaminari Taiko group, and opportunities to learn origami and how to write one's name in Japanese.[160]

Clearly, these types of events are inspired by educational goals. They also clearly recapitulate or, better, continue in the long tradition of public *japonisme* in the

United States. Aside from the occasional screening of anime films or *kawaisa/ka-waii* fashion-themed activities, these festivals and family days aim to create an experience of exotic Old Japan. A similar goal is evident at the permanent exhibit of Japanese culture on display at Walt Disney World's EPCOT Center. As Benjamin Pachter explains, the Japan Pavilion at EPCOT emphasizes historical authenticity and features reconstructed famous structures.[161] Pachter discusses the role of the *taiko* group Matsuriza's performances in signaling traditional Japan for visitors. Even though this Orlando-based ensemble, which has performed at the Japan Pavilion since it opened in 1983, typically plays a variety of repertoire outside the park and includes electronic instruments, the music they perform at the Japan Pavilion is fixed and traditional. Pachter also points out that *taiko* itself is not actually an ancient genre but can be dated to the 1950s. Matsuriza typically includes members of a variety of ethnicities, but Pachter found that only performers of Asian ethnicity appear in the daily performances at the Japan Pavilion.

Over the past fifteen years, I have not only taken my family to EPCOT's Japan Pavilion, but we have also attended multiple Japan-themed family days at museums and theatrical performances of *japonisme*, such as the Williamstown Theatre Festival's Free Theatre July 2006 production of *Demon Dreams*, a show about ninjas written by Tommy Smith with music by Michael McQuilken. We also attended a most extravagant Japan-themed family day in July 2008 in Williamstown—the Clark Art Institute's "Zen and the Art of Family Day." The Clark event included Sumo wrestlers from Hawai'i, the Osaka-born Japanese American storyteller Motoko Dworkin, screenings of short anime films, and workshops and demonstrations in *haiku*, origami, and ikebana. Recordings of *gagaku* and traditional *shakuhachi* were piped in near the main outdoor dining area. The event also featured live performances of *koto* music, including Michio Miyagi's "Haru no Umi" and songs such as "Sakura, Sakura," as well as performances by the Maine Thunder Spirits, a youth *taiko* group ranging in age from ten to eighteen years old and associated with a martial arts school. The group performed traditional *taiko* music, including a piece by the famed San Francisco–based *taiko* instructor Sensei Seiichi Tanaka who had worked with them. The ensemble also included performances of a lion dance, a dragon dance, and martial arts. This *taiko* group clearly incorporated some musical and spiritual influence from Native American traditions as well, including elements of the drum circle, the design of a Native American medicine wheel on one of the main drums, and a "medicine wheel" piece on their program.

A striking feature of this Clark Art Institute Japanese-themed family day was the near total absence of Japanese and Japanese American performers, artists, and attendees. The lead *kotoist* was a white woman, though the other *kotoist* was a younger Japanese American male student of hers. The *taiko* ensemble comprised white Americans and two African Americans. Nearly all the craft displays and demonstrations, including of *bonsai* and woodblock print making, were presented by white artists. Though there are clear similarities between this contemporary festival and *japonisme* events from over a century ago, several of the examples discussed in chapter 1 actually included more significant Japanese and Japanese American participation. Recent Japan-themed events, however, tend to be more democratic in granting public access. The Clark Art Institute's event was held in celebration of the completion of a building designed by the Japanese architect Tadao Ando. Had the Clark's architect been British, Spanish, Iranian, or Italian, however, it is unlikely that those national cultures would have inspired a similar culturally focused family day, despite the fact that some of those cultures have also inspired a long history of exotic representation in American popular culture. They simply would have lacked the specific exotic aesthetic element that many white Americans, in particular, of a certain class and cultural orbit find so attractive in traditional Japanese culture. I and my family will travel for the first time to Japan in spring 2019. Our experience of Japanese culture and performing arts, old and new, *in situ* will unavoidably be shaped by the countless representations we have experienced throughout our lives in the form of films, audio recordings, concerts, video games, and at such Japan-themed festivals. Our experience will also be shaped by Japanese self-presentations aimed at foreign tourists such as us.

*   *   *

In the early twenty-first century, various forms of Japanese music and representations of Japan through music, created both in the United States and in Japan itself, are prevalent throughout American culture. Numerous American musicians have devoted themselves to serious study of Japanese instruments and more American composers than ever before are composing for Japanese instruments or with aspects of Japanese aesthetics and musical techniques in mind. Encountering Japanese culture and music today does not require attendance at a world's fair or at a rare performance by a visiting musician as it did over a century ago. However, despite the obvious and numerous differences between current and past forms of American *japonisme*, many of the same representational techniques and tropes persist. Taking note of how perceptions of Japanese music are shaped through a variety of media and how musical representations shape perceptions of the Japanese in American culture remains an important task of cultural criticism. The extent to which Japan continues to impact American music is astonishing, as are the continuities in representation and reception between now and then. Despite the current public embrace of many "things Japanese," the perception of Japanese culture and music as occupying a polar opposite position lingers in the American imagination. Japan continues to serve both as a source and as a target of extreme exoticism.

Songs, Piano Pieces, Operettas, Musicals
(1815–1940)

Title; w. (Lyricist); m. (Composer); City: Publisher
An * indicates a piece related to the "Madame Butterfly" narrative.

1815
"Japanese Air"; m. J. Gildon; New York: A. Geib

1853
"The Japan Expedition Polka"; m. Ed. Loebmann; Baltimore: Miller and Beacham

1860
"Tommy Polka"; m. Chs. Grobe; Philadelphia: Lee and Walker

1861
"The Japanese Polka"; m. Gaston De Lille; Philadelphia: Lee and Walker

1872
"The Japanese Galop"; m. Alfred H. Pease; New York: Wm. A. Pond

1875
"The Japan Waltz"; m. S. H. Marsh; San Francisco: M. Gray

1880
"Japanese Love Song"; w. W. Yardly; m. Cotsford Dick; Boston and Chicago: White Smith

1881
"Japanese Tone Picture"; m. Chas. J. Newman; n.c.: W. F. Shaw

1882
The Little Tycoon: American Japanese Comic Opera; w. and m. Willard Spenser; Philadelphia

1883
"Blossom Tea: Waltz Song"; w. R. D. Milne; m. R. L. Yanke; San Francisco: M. Gray
"Ichi-ban: Waltzes"; m. Ion Arnold; San Francisco: M. Gray
"Pearls of the Orient"; m. C. Frank Horn; Boston: W. A. Evans and Bro.

1885
The Mikado; w. William S. Gilbert; m. Arthur Sullivan; UK

1886
"Japanese Dance"; m. Fred T. Baker; Boston: Oliver Ditson
"Mikado Mc. Allister"; w. and m. J. F. Mitchell; New York: Willis Woodward

1888
"Japanese March"; m. Eduard Holst; New York: T. B. Harms

1889
"Japanese Wedding"; m. S. Markstein; New York: M. Muetzler

1890
"Japanese Lullaby"; w. Eugene Field; m. Jules Jordan; Boston: Arthur P. Schmidt
"Japanese Lullaby"; w. Eugene Field; m. Reginald de Koven; New York: G. Schirmer
"Naïka: Japanese Song"; w. Paul Ferrier, trans. Nathan Haskell Dole; m. Herman Bemberg;
New York: G. Schirmer

1891

"Japanese Lullaby"; w. Eugene Field; m. William Neil; Cincinnati: John Church

"Japanese Parasol. March and Drill"; m. arranged by "Winthrop"; Cincinnati: John Church

1892

"Japanese Lullaby: Sleep, Little Pigeon"; w. Eugene Field; m. Clark Wright Evans; Baltimore: Otto Sutro

"A Romance in Porcelain: A Japanese Ditty"; w. Florence Scollard Brown; m. N. Clifford Page; New York: G. Schirmer

"She Stoops to Conquer"; w. Frederic E. Weatherly; m. Joseph L. Roeckel; Boston: Enoch and Sons

1893

"The Jap"; w. Richard Morton; m. George Le Brunn; Boston, New York, Chicago: White-Smith Music

"The Sunny Side of Thompson Street"; w. Edward Harrigan; m. Dave Braham; New York: William A. Pond

1894

"Two Little Japanese Dolls: An Oriental Romance"; w. and m. Hattie Starr; New York: M. Witmark and Sons

1895

"Japanese Lullaby"; w. Eugene Field; m. W. H. Pommer; St. Louis: Thiebes-Stierlin Music

1896

The Geisha; book Owen Hall; w. Harry Greenbank; m. Sidney Jones; UK

"Japanese Lullaby"; w. Eugene Field; m. William K. Bassford; New York: Hamilton S. Gordon

"Sweet Ping-e-Wang (The Maiden of Japan)"; w. and m. C. T. Steele; New York: Geo. Molineux

1897

"Darling Little Yum-Yum"; w. Hugh Morton; m. Gustave Kerker; New York: T. B. Harms

"Japanese Lantern Dance"; m. John W. Bratton; New York: M. Witmark and Sons

1898

"The Jap Doll"; w. Alice C. D. Riley; m. Jessie L. Gaynor; Chicago: Clayton F. Summy

"Japanese Picnic: Schottische"; m. John St. George; Boston: G. W. Setchell

"Mimosa: Japanese Serenade"; m. Waldemar Schneider; Milwaukee, WI: William Kaun

"Wilful Woman"; w. Stanislaus Stangé; m. Julian Edwards; New York: M. Witmark and Sons

1899

"In Japan"; w. Cissie Loftus and Louis Harrison; m. Cissie Loftus; Boston, New York, Chicago: White-Smith Music

The Japanese Girl: Operetta for Ladies; w. Jeanie Quinton Rosse; m. Charles Vincent; Boston: Boston Music

"Japonica"; m. Tony Stanford; New York: Leo Feist

"Mimosa, or Love in Japan"; w. Horace Leonhard; m. W. Aletter; Boston: B. F. Wood Music

1900

From Broadway to Tokio; book George Vere Hobart; w. A. Baldwin Sloane; m. Reginald De Koven; New York: G. Schirmer

"A Japanese Baby Song (Sleep, My Little Man)"; w. and m. Gustav Luders; New York: M. Witmark and Sons

"Japanese Ballet"; m. Reginald de Koven; New York: G. Schirmer

"Japanese Love Song"; w. anon.; m. Clayton Thomas; New York: Boosey

"My Geisha of Tokio"; w. and m. Billee Taylor; New York: M. Witmark and Sons

"The Nations in Review"; w. William G. Rose; m. Max Faetkenheuer; Chicago: Sol Bloom

* "O Mona San"; w. George V. Hobart; m. Alfred E. Aarons; New York: M. Witmark and Sons

"Poor Little Japanese Doll"; w. Raymond A. Browne; m. Theodore F. Morse; Chicago: Sol Bloom

"Sousa's Sen-Sen March"; m. John Philip Sousa; Rochester: T. B. Dunn

"Susie, Mah Sue"; w. F. J. Sloane; m. A. B. Sloane; New York: M. Witmark and Sons
"Sweet San Toy: A Japanese Love Song"; w. Richard Henry Buck; m. Adam Geibel; Boston, New York, Chicago: White-Smith Music Publishing

1901

Hoity-Toity; w. Edgar Smith; m. John Stromberg; New York: Marcus Witmark and Sons
"The Japanese Doll"; m. Newton E. Swift; New York: G. Schirmer
"The Jolly Japanese: Dance Characteristic"; m. Theodore F. Morse; New York: Shapiro, Bernstein, and Von Tilzer
"Kimono Waltz"; m. A. A. Ford; New York: S. Brainard's Sons
"Miss Chrysanthemum. O Kiku San. A Japanese Intermezzo"; m. William Loraine; New York: M. Witmark and Sons
* "My Japanese Cherry Blossom"; w. Edgar Smith; m. John Stromberg; New York: M. Witmark and Sons
"My Little Belle of Japan: A Fan Tastic Episode"; w. Arthur L. Robb; m. John W. Bratton; New York: M. Witmark and Sons
* "My Yokohama Lady"; w. and m. Lee Johnson; San Francisco: J. Donigan
"Sayonara"; w. Marie Louise Pool; m. Homer N. Bartlett; New York: G. Schirmer

1902

"Cradle Song"; w. Eugene Field; m. Albert A. Mack; Cincinnati: John Church
"Formosa: Japanese Flower Dance"; m. Will M. S. Brown; Wilmington, DE: Brown and Edwards Music
"The Geisha and the Coon"; w. Walter Summers; m. Edward Jakobowski; London: E. Ascherberg
"Japanesa: Characteristic"; m. Yama Sen; New York: Century Music
"A Japanese Honeymoon: Dance Characteristic"; m. Daunt Scott; Boston, New York: B. F. Wood Music
"Ko Ko: Japanese Dance"; m. Theodore F. Morse; New York: Hamilton S. Gordon
"The Maid from Tokio: A Japanese Love Song"; w. and m. Cole and Johnson; New York: Howley, Haviland and Dresser
"Miyoko San"; w. E. F. Fenollosa; m. Albert A. Mack; Cincinnati: John Church
"Yama San: An Oriental Serenade"; w. George Totten Smith; m. Emil Biermann; New York: Leo Feist

1903

The Darling of the Gallery Gods; w. John Gilroy, Arthur J. Lamb, and Matt C. Woodward; m. Ben M. Jerome; New York: Sol Bloom
* "A Flower of Old Japan"; w. Earle Remington Hines; m. Charles Moreland; New York: M. Witmark and Sons
"In a Lotus Field"; m. John W. Bratton; New York: M. Witmark and Sons
"A Japanese Serenade"; w. Grace Hibbard; m. Lyle C. True; Cincinnati: John Church
"My Japanese Baby"; w. Arthur Ambrose; m. A. Baldwin Sloane; New York, Chicago: Sol Bloom
* "My Kimona Queen"; w. Henry M. Blossom Jr.; m. George A. Spink and W. F. Peters; New York, Chicago: Howley, Haviland and Dresser
"My Lady from Japan"; w. Ren Shields; m. George Evans; New York, Chicago: Chas. K. Harris
"My Little Japaneesee"; w. and m. Max Hoffman; Chicago, San Francisco, New York: Shapiro, Bernstein
Otoyo: A Comic Opera in Two Acts; book Henry Pincus and Melvin G. Winstock; w. Robert L. Beecher; m. William Frederick Peters
"Poppyland"; m. Frederick A. Tolhurst; Cincinnati: John Church
"The Samisen"; w. Mrs. Fenollosa; m. Albert A. Mack; New York: G. Schirmer
"Solo Koko"; w. John Gilroy; m. Ben M. Jerome; New York, Chicago: Sol Bloom
"Watch Me To-Night in the Torch-Light Parade"; w. Arthur J. Lamb; m. Ben M. Jerome; New York, Chicago: Sol Bloom

"Whoa San"; w. Matt C. Woodward; m. Ben M. Jerome; New York, Chicago: Sol Bloom

"Yo-San"; w. Ernest Hanegan; m. Byrd Dougherty; New York, Chicago: Sol Bloom

1904

"Banzai: Japanese Victory March"; m. Chas. E. Lepaige; New York: Chas. E. Lepaige and Son

"Battle Hymn"; The Mikado of Japan; Christmas Music Supplement of the *San Francisco Examiner*, Sunday, 11 December 1904, and Christmas Music Supplement, *New York American and Journal*, Sunday, 4 December 1904

"Cherry Blossoms: Japanese Dance"; m. H. Engelmann; Philadelphia: Theodore Presser

Fantana; book Robert B. Smith and Sam S. Shubert; w. Robert B. Smith; m. Raymond Hubbell; New York: M. Witmark and Sons

"Farewell, My Little Yo San!"; w. A. J. Mills; m. Bennett Scott; New York: T. B. Harms

"For the Flag of Old Japan"; w. Lewis A. Browne; m. Thomas S. Allen; Boston: Walter Jacobs

A Garden of Japan: or The Rose and the Laurel; w. Frank A. Smallpeice; m. Herbert W. Wareing; Boston: Boston Music

"Happy Jappy Soldier Man: Japanese War Song"; w. Paul West; m. John W. Bratton; New York: M. Witmark and Sons

"In My Riksha of Bamboo"; w. Robert B. Smith; m. Raymond Hubbell; New York: M. Witmark and Sons

"In Tokio: Characteristic March and Two Step"; S. Nirella; Cleveland: H. N. White

"The Jap behind the Gun: March and Two Step"; m. A. E. Wade; Hoquiam, WA: Wade Music

"The Jap Rag"; m. Alma Krautwurst; New York: Carl Fischer

"Japan's Triumphal March"; m. C. M. Vandersloot; Williamsport, PA: Vandersloot Music

"Japanesa March"; m. Albert Wood; Boston: Evans Music

"The Japanese Flirt"; w. H. C. Gouldsbury; m. Theodore S. Holland; New York: Boosey

"Japanese Minstrel Song"; w. Grace Hibbard; m. F. Flaxington Harker Boston: C. W. Thompson

"Japanese Nightingale: A Spring Idyl"; m. Emile De Bar; St. Louis: Louis Retter Music

"Japanese Patrol"; m. Theodore Moses-Tobani; New York: Carl Fischer

"Japanese War March"; m. Gustav Lüders; Cincinnati: John Church

"The Jap's Farewell"; w. Herbert Earl Munroe; m. Russell A. Dickinson; Providence, RI: Westminster Music

"The Japs' Tattoo"; m. L. P. Laurendeau; New York: Carl Fischer

The Japskys; book Louis De Lange; m. Billee Taylor; New York: Continental Music

"Karama"; w. and m. Vivian Grey (Miss Mabel McKinley); New York: Leo Feist

"Kimona Girl"; m. Milton D. Blake; Fall River, MA: Anthony Brothers

* "Kokomo"; w. Jean Lenox; m. Harry O. Sutton; New York: Harry O. Sutton

"Ky-isses"; m. William Christopher O'Hare; New York: M. Witmark and Sons

"Laughing Little Almond Eyes"; w. Robert B. Smith; m. Raymond Hubbell; New York: M. Witmark and Sons

"The Little Brown Man of Japan"; w. George Totten Smith; m. William H. Penn; New York, Chicago: Sol Bloom

"Little Japan," w. and m. J. T. Rider; New York: Theatrical Music Supply

"Little Maids of Japan," w. and m. Frances C. Robinson; Philadelphia: Theodore Presser

"My Belle of To-ki-o"; w. J. Louis MacEvoy; m. E. H. Ellis; New York: Willis Woodward

"My Japanee: You Darling of the Gods"; w. Donald Smedt; m. S. Gibson Cooke; Boston: Walter Jacobs

"My Little Kokomo"; w. Sam Rice; m. Shepard Camp; New York: Howley-Dresser

"Nippon Banzai!: Characteristic Japanese War March"; m. Ferdinand Wagner; New York: no pub. listed

"Ohayo!"; m. Mary Travers; Leipzig: Bosworth

"One Little Soldier Man"; w. Edward Madden; m. Neil Moret; New York: Shapiro Remick

"Poppies. A Japanese Romance"; m. Neil Moret; Detroit and New York: Shapiro, Remick

"Pretty Kitty San: Russo-Japanese Love Song"; w. Burkhart and Hoffman; m. Leo Edwards; New York: Leo Edwards Music Pub.

"The Rising Sun of Japan: Grand Descriptive Battle Piece"; m. Jos. Wachtel; New York, Chicago: Sol Bloom

"Russian and Japanese National Songs: The Inspiring Melodies of the Contending Nations"; "Japan's Song"; Sunday, 22 May 1904 supplement to *The North American*, sec. 4

"Russo-Japanese March and Two-Step"; m. Walter A. Rice; Boston: Harmonic Music

"Sayonara: A Japanese Love Song"; w. S. Carter Schwing; m. William Christopher O'Hare; New York: M. Witmark and Sons

The Sho-Gun: A Comic Opera; w. George Ade; m. Gustav Luders; New York: M. Witmark and Sons

"A Soldier of Old Japan"; w. and m. Richard C. Dillmore; Philadelphia: Blasius and Sons

"Susie Oo: A Japanese Coon Song"; w. and m. Billee Taylor; New York: Continental Music

"Sweet Sana-oo"; w. Vernon Roy; m. W. T. Francis; Chicago: Chas. K. Harris

"A Tale of Tokio"; w. Gerald Kelley; m. James M. Fulton; music supplement, *New York American and Journal*, Sunday, 16 July 1905

"Yokohama Intermezzo"; m. Ralph E. Kenny; Minneapolis: Pillsbury-Dana

"Yo San: A Japanese Intermezzo Two-Step"; m. Al. W. Brown; Chicago: McKinley Music

"You're the Only Girl for Me"; w. Verne C. Armstrong; m. Billee Taylor; New York: Continental Music

1905

"Blood Lillies: A Japanese Two Step"; m. Arthur Pryor; New York: Carl Fischer

* "Cho-Cho-San: A 'Pike' Memory"; w. C. L. Boye; m. W. H. Hynson; St. Louis: Boye and Hynson

"Daughters of Nijo"; m. Arthur S. Shaw; Chicago: Arnett Delonais

"The Geisha Girl: A Japanese Intermezzo"; m. Fred T. Ashton; Bloomington, IL: Independent Publishing

"Hakama: A Japanese Jingle"; m. Wilfrid Beaudry; Toronto: Harry H. Sparks Music

"A Japanese Fan Dance"; m. Theo Bonheur; Boston: Vinton Music

"The Japanese Farewell"; w. and m. E. J. Haines; Chicago: Success Music

"Japanese Heroes"; w. and m. Sadie B. Kelley, arr. Eugene Kaeuffer; Chicago: Pioneer Music Pub.

"A Japanese Legend"; m. Henry Patterson Hopkins; Cincinnati: John Church

"The Japanese Maiden"; w. Alice C. D. Riley; m. Jessie L. Gaynor; Chicago: Clayton F. Summy

"The Kingdom of Flowers (Japan)"; m. J. Ringleben; New York: Carl Fischer

"Kioto: Two Step March"; m. Anna Louise Hazen; Los Angeles: Southern California Music

"Little Fighting Soldier Man"; m. Miss Lillian Coffin; music supplement, *New York American and Journal*, Sunday, 14 May 1905; New York: American Advance Music

"The Little Jap: Characteristic Two-Step"; m. Percy Wenrich; Chicago, New York: Frank K. Root

The Mayor of Tokio; book Richard Carle; m. William Frederick Peters; New York: M. Witmark and Sons

* "My Jap From Tokio"; w. Oscar F. G. Day; m. Edward Buffington; Minneapolis: Pillsbury-Dana

* "My Lu Lu San"; w. J. W. Johnson; m. Bob Cole; New York: John W. Stern

"The Peacemaker. Characteristic March. Introducing Russian and Japanese Battle Songs"; m. Harry L. Alford; Chicago, New York: Will Rossiter

"Sayonara"; m. Mary Travers; Leipzig: Bosworth

"A Soldier of Old Japan"; w. and m. Richard C. Dillmore; Philadelphia: Blasius and Sons

"A Tokio Tea Party"; arr. F. Landry Berthoud; New York: W. F. Shaw

"The Treaty of Peace, A Japanese Intermezzo"; m. Wallace A. Johnson; Stamford, CT: Homer R. S. Klock

"Tokio"; w. Richard Carle; m. William Frederick Peters; New York: M. Witmark and Sons

"When America Is Captured by the Japs"; w. Paul West; m. John W. Bratton; New York: M. Witmark and Sons

"Yokohama Charmer: A Japanese Love Song"; w. Murray Rose; m. Alfred J. Doyle; New York: Harry Von Tilzer Music Pub.

Yo-Nennen: A Japanese Cicada Drama Set to Music in the Form of a Cantata; w. John Luther
     Long; m. Wassili Leps; New York: G. Schirmer

1906
   "The Catch of Tokio"; m. H. E. Dean; Detroit, New York: Vaux Music
   "Cherry Blossoms"; w. and m. Wallace Elliott; Davenport, IA: Moody Music
   "Fan Flirtation"; m. Ralph C. Jackson; Cincinnati: John Church
   Five Little Japanese Songs; w. Charles Hanson Towne; m. Amy Woodforde-Finden; London,
     New York: Boosey
   * "The Geisha Girl from Old Japan"; w. and m. Maude McFerran Price; n.c.: Tolbert R.
     Ingram
   "Japanese Brigade: March and Two-Step"; m. S. Nirella; Cleveland: H. N. White
   "The Japanese Fan"; m. A. L. Cowley; Philadelphia: Theodore Presser
   "Japanese Grand Army March"; m. Willard Spenser; no pub. information
   "Japanese Lullaby"; w. Eugene Field; m. Jean B. Stimpson; Boston: C. W. Thompson
   "The Japanese Nightingale"; w. Harry J. Jones; m. Robert F. McGowan; Denver: Denver Pub.
   "Japania. Japanese Two-Step Characteristic"; m. H. E. Dean; Detroit, New York: Vaux Music
   "The Lantern Dance"; m. Louie Maurice; Chicago: Will Rossiter
   "My Little Japanese Rose"; w. and m. Nellie R. Pearl; New York: North American Music
   Princess Chrysanthemum: A Japanese Operetta; w. and m. C. King Proctor; New York: G.
     Schirmer
   "A Ragtime Jap"; w. Jean Lenox; m. Harry O. Sutton; New York: Jerome H. Remick
   Rosalie, or The Japanese Fairies: An Original Japanese-Russian Romantic Opera; w. and
     m. Willard Spenser; Wayne, PA: W. Spenser
   "Tokio Polka"; m. J. H. Greenhalgh; London and New York: Francis, Day and Hunter
   The Yellow Peril: Comic Operetta; w. Alice Brandon Caldwell; m. Annie Laurie Nance; New York:
     Edgar S. Werner

1907
   "Etude Japonaise"; m. Eduard Poldini; New York: G. Schirmer
   The Fate of Princess Kiyo: A Legend of Japan; Cantata for four-part Chorus of Women's voices;
     w. Edward Oxenford; m. Henry Hadley; New York: G. Schirmer
   "The Feast of the Doll"; w. Nora Archibald Smith; m. Grace Chadbourne; Cincinnati: John
     Church
   "Japanese Cradle-Song"; w. Sarojini Naidu; m. Mary Turner Salter; New York: G. Schirmer
   "A Japanese Doll's Serenade"; w. Mary Fallah; m. Helena Bingham; Chicago: Illinois Music
   "Jappy Johnny: A Japanese American Intermezzo"; m. Theodore Morse; New York: F. B.
     Haviland
   "Kuma Saka"; m. Homer N. Bartlett; New York: G. Schirmer
   "Moon Face"; m. Abe Olman; Cleveland: Sam Fox Pub.
   "Oh Japan!"; w. A. Grant; m. M. Milinowski; Cincinnati: John Church
   "Sayonara"; w. Florence Hoare; m. Joseph L. Roeckel; London and New York: Ascherberg,
     Hopwood and Crew
   "Wistaria: A Japanese Idyll"; m. Frederic Knight Logan; New York: M. Witmark and Sons

1908
   The Isle of Spice; w. and m. Louis L. Comstock
   "Japanese Revery"; m. Homer N. Bartlett; New York: G. Schirmer
   * "Lotus San"; w. Edward Madden; m. Dolly Jardon; New York: Jerome H. Remick
   "My Japanee"; w. and m. Louis L. Comstock; Chicago: Will Rossiter
   "My Tokio Queen"; w. and m. Charles Alphin; New York: Shapiro
   "A Night in Japan, Suite"; m. John J. Braham; New York: Carl Fischer
   "Petite Tonkinoise"; by V. Scotto and Christine; Chicago: McKinley Music
   "Pretty Little Japanesee Lady"; w. and m. Charles Alphin; New York: Shapiro
   Ski-Hi; w. and m. Charles Alphin; New York: Shapiro
   "Tamamura"; w. and m. Charles Alphin; New York: Shapiro

1909

"Fair Flower of Japan"; w. and m. Manuel Klein; New York: M. Witmark and Sons

"Hanako"; w. Ballard MacDonald; m. Wilh. Aletter; New York: Jos. W. Stern

The Isle of Nippon: A Japanese-American Musical Comedy; w. J. Francis Corr and Geo. W. Raynes, Jr.; m. Glen R. Crum; Chicago: Victor Kremer

"Japanese Lantern Dance"; m. Yoshitomo; Boston: Cundy-Bettoney

"Meet Me Where the Lanterns Glow"; w. and m. Manuel Klein; New York: M. Witmark and Sons

"My Japanee"; w. George Ade; m. Gustav Luders; also published as "The Modern Japanee"; New York: M. Witmark and Sons

A Trip to Japan; w. and m. Manuel Klein; New York: M. Witmark and Sons

1910

"A Cup o' Tea: Japanese Intermezzo"; m. Karl Lenox; Boston: Lenox Music

"Heart's Flower-of-Cherry"; m. Florence Newell Barbour; w. trans. Lafcadio Hearn; New York: William Maxwell Music

"Japanese Dance"; m. S. B. Pennington; Boston: B. F. Wood Music

"A Japanese Love Song"; w. Madge Dickson; m. May H. Brahe; New York: Enoch and Sons

"Japanese Reverie"; m. Homer N. Bartlett; arr. for orch. Otto Langey; New York: G. Schirmer

"My Little Jap-o-baby"; w. and m. L. Lockwood Moore; Cincinnati: John Church

"Namrah"; m. Mabel R. Kaufman; New York: Jerome H. Remick

Sayonara: A Japanese Romance for One or Two Voices; w. Nelle Richmond Eberhart; m. Charles Wakefield Cadman; Boston: White-Smith Music

"Sayonara"; m. Neil Moret; New York: Jerome H. Remick

1911

From Old Japan: A Cycle of Songs; w. Alfred H. Hyatt, m. Mary Turner Salter

Matsuris (Our Festal Days): A Cycle of Six Japanese Songs; m. Clayton Thomas; Leipzig, Boston, New York: Arthur P. Schmidt

"Oh That Oriental Rag"; w. and m. Aubrey Stauffer and Ernie Erdman; Chicago: Aubrey Stauffer

"Veil Dance" and "Butterfly Dance"; from *O Mitake San* ballet; m. Rudolf Friml; New York: G. Schirmer

1912

"My Japanesee: A Japanese Love Song"; w. Grace Delaney Goldenburg; m. William Smith Goldenburg; Cincinnati: Joseph Krolage Music

"Tokio Rag"; m. Henry Lodge; New York: M. Witmark and Sons

Two Little Songs from Japan; trans. Tomijiro Asai; m. Charles Wakefield Cadman; Boston: White-Smith Music Publishing

1913

"Japanese Love Song"; w. Clarence Stratton; m. Ernest R. Kroeger; Boston: Oliver Ditson

"Nirvana: Waltzes"; m. F. H. Losey; Williamsport, PA: Vandersloot Music

"That Tango Tokio"; w. Al Bryan; m. Jack Wells and Arthur Lange; New York and Detroit: Jerome H. Remick

1914

"Cherry Blossom"; w. and m. May Hewes Dodge and John Wilson Dodge; Cincinnati: Willis Music

* "In Cherry Blossom Time"; w. John W. Bratton; m. Eugene Salzer; New York: Shapiro, Bernstein

"I Want to Go to Tokio"; w. Joe McCarthy; m. Fred Fischer; New York: Leo Feist

"Japanese Death Song"; w. H. K. S.; m. Earl Cranston Sharp; Boston: Oliver Ditson

"Japanese Lullaby"; w. and m. Gertrude Ross; Los Angeles: R. W. Heffelfinger

"Japanese Rainsong"; w. Pierre Louis, trans. William Rice; m. Hugo Riesenfeld; Boston: Boston Music

"Kakúda"; m. Felix Arndt; New York: G. Ricordi

Miss Cherryblossom; w. and m. Mary Hewes Dodge and John Wilson Dodge; Ypsilanti, MI: John Wilson Dodge

"Underneath the Japanese Moon"; w. Gene Buck; m. W. Gus. Haenschen; New York: T. B. Harms

1915

* "Fair Maid of Tokio"; w. Walter M. Oestreicher; m. Herbert J. Braham; New York: Maurice Richmond Music
* "In Japan with Mi-Mo-San"; w. and m. Anita Owen; New York: Jerome H. Remick
* "My Nagasaki Girl"; w. Russell Rox; m. Arthur M. Kraus; New York: A. M. Kraus
* "Poppy-Time in Old Japan"; w. Ernest J. Meyers; m. Will E. Dulmage; Chicago: Forster Music Publisher
* "Won't You Be My Little Fan Tan Girl"; w. and m. P. Hans Flath; Dayton, OH: BeeBee Confection

"Yama Nan"; w. Hal Buckingham; m. C. H. Keefer; San Francisco: Hawley Publishing

* "The Yellow Fan"; w. Edith Palmer Putnam, m. Harvey Worthington Loomis; New York: Edgar S. Werner

1916

"Fuji-ko: A Japanese Intermezzo"; m. Harry Rowe Shelley; New York: G. Schirmer

* "Hurry Back to My Bamboo Shack"; w. and m. Irving Berlin; New York: Waterson, Berlin, and Snyder

"Japanese Lullaby"; w. Eugene Field; m. Grace Louise McQuesten; Boston: C. W. Thompson

* "Japanese Nodding Doll"; w. and m. Arthur A. Penn; New York: M. Witmark and Sons

"A Japanese Sunset"; m. Jessie L. Deppen; Cleveland: Sam Fox Pub.

* "Poor Butterfly"; w. John L. Golden; m. Raymond Hubbell; New York: T. B. Harms

"Poppy Time in Old Japan"; m. Will E. Dulmage; Chicago: Forster Music Pub.

* "When He Comes Back to Me (Japanese Song)"; w. Gene Buck; m. Dave Stamper; New York: T. B. Harms

"When Jap Rose Takes Her Sunday Morning Bath"; w. and m. Donald G. Robertson; Chicago: James S. Kirk

Yokohama Maid: A Japanese Comic Operetta; w. and m. Arthur A. Penn; New York: M. Witmark and Sons

1917

Art Songs of Japan: Yamata Shirabe; w. and m. Gertrude Ross; Boston: White-Smith Music Publishing

* "Cherry Blossom"; w. Gus Kahn; m. Harry Raymond; New York: Jerome H. Remick
* "Come Back to Bamboo Land (To Your Lonely Little Mi Mio San)"; w. The Loos Brothers; m. Paul Biese and F. Henri Klickmann; Chicago: Frank K. Root

"The Cruel Mother-in-Law (Humorous)"; w. and m. Fay Foster; New York: J. Fischer and Bro.

* "Good-bye, Cherry Blossom"; w. Charles Forest Wilkins; m. Edw. Allen Stickney; Chicago: Forster Music Pub.
* "Good-bye Little Yo Ho San"; w. Wm. Baltzell; m. Aubrey Stauffer; Chicago: Aubrey Stauffer
* "Hawaiian Butterfly"; w. Geo. A. Little; m. Billy Baskette and Joseph Santly; New York: Leo Feist

"The Honorable Chop-Sticks"; w. Lafcadio Hearn; m. Fay Foster; New York: J. Fischer and Brother

* "If I Catch the Guy Who Wrote Poor Butterfly"; w. William Jerome; m. Arthur N. Green; New York: William Jerome Pub.
* "I'm Coming Back to You Poor Butterfly"; w. Andrew Donnelly; m. Raymond Hubbell; New York: T. B. Harms
* "In Old Japan"; w. and m. Walter Smith; San Francisco: Sherman Clay

A Japanese Garden: Operetta; w. and m. Kenneth and Roy Webb; no pub. information

"Japanese Love Song"; w. anon.; m. Clayton Thomas, arr. Sumner Salter; New York: Boosey

"Japanese Song"; w. Laura Rountree Smith; m. Daniel Protheroe; Chicago: J. S. Fearis and Bro.

"Let's Go Back to Dreamy Lotus Land"; w. Jack Frost; m. Paul Biese and F. Henri Klickmann; Chicago: Frank K. Root

* "Midnight in Japan"; w. Fleta Jan Brown; m. Herbert Spencer; New York: Jerome H. Remick

* "Mister Butterfly"; w. Ballard MacDonald; m. Leo Edwards; New York: Shapiro, Bernstein

* "My Broadway Butterfly"; w. E. Ray Goetz; m. Willy White; New York: M. Witmark and Sons

"My Little Japanee"; w. Sue Finley Read; m. Marie Nicholson; Louisville: Fine Arts Music

* "My Little Sing Song Girl"; w. A. J. Stasny; m. Earl Burtnett; New York: A. J. Stasny Music

"My Princess of the Willow Tree"; w. Will J. Harris; m. Carey Morgan; New York: Joseph W. Stern

* "My Yiddisha Butterfly"; w. Al. Dubin; m. Joseph A. Burke; New York: M. Witmark and Sons

"My Yokohama Girl"; w. Alfred Bryan; m. Harry Tierney; New York: Jerome H. Remick

"A Nipponese Sword Song"; w. Shotaro Kimura and Charlotte M. A. Peake; m. Fay Foster; New York: J. Fischer and Brother

"The Red Heart"; w. Shotaro Kimura and Charlotte M. A. Peake; m. Fay Foster; New York: J. Fischer and Brother

"The Shadow of the Bamboo Fence"; w. Lafcadio Hearn; m. Fay Foster; New York: J. Fischer and Bro.

* "Suki San (Where the Cherry Blossoms Fall)"; w. J. Keirn Brennan; m. Walter Donaldson; New York: M. Witmark and Sons

"Sunset in a Japanese Garden"; m. Fay Foster; Boston: Olive Ditson

* "When It's Cherry Time in Tokio"; w. and m. Ivan Reid and Paul De Rose; New York: F. B. Haviland

* "When It's Moonlight in Tokio"; w. Bobby Heath; m. Chas. P. Shisler and Billy James; New York: M. Witmark and Sons

"Ysmita: Japanese Serenade"; m. H. Engelmann; New York: Church, Paxson

1918

"Chinese-Japanese"; m. Otto Langley; New York: G. Schirmer

"Garden of My Dreams"; w. Gene Buck; m. Dave Stamper; New York: T. B. Harms

"A Japanese Fantasy"; w. G. A. Woolfall; m. Robert Huntington Terry; Philadelphia: Theodore Presser

"A Japanese Love Song"; w. Colgate Baker; m. Carl Hahn; Cincinnati: John Church

* "Japanette"; w. and m. Charlotte Salisbury; Chicago: Will Rossiter

"Little Sally-San (Of Old Japan)"; w. and m. Marie Hall Brimacombe; Marion, IN: Marie Hall Brimacombe

* "My Pretty Poppy"; w. and m. Robert Levenson and Jack Mendelsohn; Boston: Jack Mendelsohn Music

" 'Neath the Lanterns' Glow"; w. Anna Fyfe; m. H. Howard Cheney; Waltham, MA: H. Howard Cheney

"Nipponese (Japanese Dramatic Themes)"; m. Joseph O'Sullivan; New York: Carl Fischer

Shadowings: Five Poems from the Japanese by Lafcadio Hearn; m. Harold Vincent Milligan; New York: G. Schirmer

* "When the Cherry Trees Are Blooming in Japan"; w. and m. Chas. K. Harris; New York: Chas. K. Harris

"Yokohama"; w. Michael Corper and Waldo C. Twitchell; m. Arthur M. Fournier; San Francisco: Sherman, Clay

1919

"Buddha"; w. Ed Rose; Lew Pollack; New York: McCarthy and Fisher

* "Cho-San: From the Land of Japan"; w. and m. Frederick Seymour and Fred W. Pike; Toledo, OH: Waldorf Music

"Chu-Chu-San: A Japanese Fox Trot"; m. Joe Samuels; Cleveland, OH: Sam Fox

* "Fan Tan"; w. Ed. Plottle; m. Patsy Raymond; Scranton, PA: Whitmore Music

"Fu-Ji"; w. Arthur Freed; m. Oliver G. Wallace; Seattle, WA: Musicland Pub.

"The Geisha Girl in Tokio"; w. and m. Kerry Mills; New York: Kerry Mills

* "I'm Coming, Butterfly"; w. and m. Captain Frank Glick, U.S.A.; Camp Lee, VA.

"Japanese Lanterns"; m. Frederick Keats; Boston: B. F. Wood Music

"Ko-Ko-San"; w. and m. Edah Delbridge and A. Robert King; New York: Shapiro, Bernstein

"Koko-San"; m. Igushi Kamoto; Boston: Boston Music

* "Lantern Time in Tokio"; w. Harold G. Frost; m. F. Henri Klickmann; Chicago: McKinley Music

* "My Nanky Panky Poo"; w. Sam M. Lewis and Joe Young; m. Walter Donaldson; New York: Waterson, Berlin, and Snyder

"My Rose of Old Japan"; w. and m. Joseph Kiefer and Billy James; New York: Waterson, Berlin, and Snyder

* "Night-Time in Old Japan"; w. and m. Maurice Solman, Bernard Eyges, and Joe Solman; Boston: Lang Music Pub.

* "Poor Little Butterfly Is a Fly Girl Now"; w. Sam M. Lewis and Joe Young; m. M. K. Jerome; New York: Waterson, Berlin, and Snyder

"Poppy Blossom"; w. Jack Yellen; m. Abe Olman; New York: Leo Feist

* "Rose of Japan"; w. and m. Moe Thompson and Norman Herbert; New York: Joe Morris Music

"Say-on-ar-a"; w. George V. Hobart and Henry Blossom; m. Raymond Hubbell; New York: T. B. Harms

* "Sya Nara (That Means Good-Bye)"; w. and m. Arthur E. Behim and Courtney Sisters; New York: Waterson, Berlin, and Snyder

* "Where the Lanterns Glow"; w. J. Stanley Royce; m. Chas. L. Johnson; Chicago: Forster Music

"Why Do They Call Mama Poor Butterfly"; w. Louis Seifert; m. W. C. Polla; Hartford, CT: C. C. Church

* "Won't You Come Back to Tokio"; w. Hal Artis; m. Will E. Dulmage; San Francisco: Daniels and Wilson Music Publishers

* "Yo-San"; w. Jean Lefavre; m. W. C. Polla; Hartford, CT: C. C. Church

* "Yokohama Love"; w. Harry D. Kerr; m. William Alexander; New York: Shapiro, Bernstein

1920

"Ching-a-Ling-a-Loo: An Odd, Japanese Lullaby and Fox Trot"; w. and m. Chiusenji Fujiyama; New York: Metropolitan Music

"Drolleries from an Oriental Doll's House"; w. and m. Bainbridge Crist; New York: Carl Fischer

* "Happy Butterfly"; w. Bobbie Tremaine; m. Joe Meyer; Detroit: Jerome H. Remick

"Idylle Japonaise"; m. Maurice Baron; New York: Belwin

* "In Cherry Blossom Time with You"; w. Blair Treynor; m. Dorothy Jardon and Joseph M. Daly; New York: T. B. Harms

"In Fair Japan"; w. John Murray Anderson and Jack Yellen; m. Milton Ager; New York: Leo Feist

"In Old Japan"; w. Alfred Bryan; m. Ed. Wynn; New York: Jerome H. Remick

"The Japanese Doll"; m. E. R. Kroeger, Philadelphia: Theo. Presser

"Japanese Lullaby"; w. Walter Hirsch; m. Erwin R. Schmidt; New York: T. B. Harms

"A Japanese Lullaby"; w. Herbert J. Brandon; m. Robert Elkin; London, New York: Elkin

"The Japanese Sandman"; w. Raymond B. Egan; m. Richard A. Whiting; New York: Jerome H. Remick

Petit Ballet Japonais; m. G. Goublier; New York: G. Schirmer

* "Rose of Tokio"; w. and m. Ralph C. Jackson; Los Angeles: R. C. Jackson

"So Long! Oo-Long"; w. and m. Bert Kalmar and Harry Ruby; New York: Waterson, Berlin, and Snyder

* "Ti-O-San"; w. and m. Lou Traveller and L. Clair Case; San Francisco: Sherman, Clay

* "Yan-Kee"; w. Irving Caesar; m. George Gershwin; New York: T. B. Harms

"Yokohama: A Japanese Intermezzo"; m. S. E. Morris; New York: Carl Fischer

"Yo San"; w. T. Dixon; m. R. L. Harlow; Boston: Atlas Pub.

Yo-San an Oriental Operetta; book and music by R. L. Harlow, lyrics L. S. Bitner, T. Dixon, and G. G. Goldie

"Yo San"; w. May Tully; m. Jean Hazard; New York: Huntzinger and Dilworth

1921

"Almond Eyes"; m. William Chas. Schoenfeld; New York: Photo Play Music

* "Cho-Cho-San"; w. Jesse Winne; m. G. Puccini, arr. by Hugo Frey; New York: G. Ricordi

* "Fo-Tu-San"; w. and m. Charles Griswold; Boston: Charles Griswold

* "Glow Little Lantern of Love"; w. and m. Fred Fisher; New York: Fred Fisher Inc.

* "In Old Japan"; w. and m. Lee Emmett Eagan; Amsterdam NY: Thomas Eagan

* "In the Heart of a Geisha (Nippo San of Japan)"; w. Fred Fisher; m. George Gershwin; New York: Fred Fisher

"Ishki Choo"; w. Edward C. McCormick; m. Chas. Bauer; Palestine, IL: Edward C. McCormick

"Isle of Tangerine"; w. Howard Johnson; m. Carlo-Sanders; New York: Leo Feist

* "The Maid of Japan"; w. Reginald V. Darow; m. John Prindle Scott; New York and Boston: G. Schirmer

* "My Cherry Blossom"; w. Harry B. Smith; m. Ted Snyder; New York: Waterson, Berlin, and Snyder

* "My Little Rose of Tokio"; w. and m. Jack Stern, Clarence J. Marks, and Norah Lee Haymond; New York: Waterson, Berlin, and Snyder

"Silversan"; m. Ernest Golden; Chicago: Forster Music Pub.

"Tea Leaves"; w. Raymond B. Egan; m. Richard A. Whiting; New York, Detroit: Jerome H. Remick

"Toki-ama"; w. Helen Commary; m. Otto Cesana; San Francisco: Adrian-Reece

"Yokohama Lullaby"; w. Grant Clarke; m. James V. Monaco; New York: Shapiro, Bernstein

1922

* "Japanese Love Moon"; w. Clancy Boykin; m. Billy Pierce; Richmond, VA: Pierce Music Pub.

"Japanese Lullaby"; w. Charlotte Lay Dewey; m. Marian Coryell; New York: G. Schirmer

"Japanese Moon"; w. Dorothy Terriss; m. Austin Huntley; New York: Leo Feist

"Japanese Sailor"; w. C. P. McDonald; m. Thomas Hughes; Williamsport, PA: Vandersloot Music Pub.

* "Japanese Willow (The Legend of the Bride)"; w. McElbert Moore; m. J. Fred Coots; New York: Harms

* "Kimono"; w. and m. Eugene West and Mary Earl; New York: Shapiro, Bernstein

* "Little Cherry Blossom"; w. Mary McMillan and Mildred W. Wallace; m. Mildred White Wallace; Columbiana, AL: Wallace-McMillan Music Pub.

* "My Chinese Butterfly"; w. G. Cullinan and T. R. Murray; m. Vincent Dattilo; New York: Ansonia Music

"A Night in Japan"; m. John J. Braham; New York: Carl Fischer

"Sakura Blossom"; w. Marion Haddock Barnes; m. Gertrude Ross; New York: J. Fischer and Brother

"Sing Song Man"; w. and m. Cliff Friend and Con Conrad; New York: Jerome H. Remick

"Tea-Cup Tinkles: A Japanese Intermezzo"; m. Frederic Knight Logan; Chicago: Forster Music Pub.

1923

"In a Tea Garden: A Japanese Romance"; m. T. Henry Lodge; New York: Richmond-Robbins

"Japanese Lullaby"; w. and m. Lloyd Kidwell; Cincinnati: Circle Music

"A Japanese Sunset"; m. Jessie L. Deppen, arr. J. S. Zamecnik; Cleveland: Sam Fox

"Lotus Flower"; w. Cyrus Wood; m. Sigmund Romberg; New York: Harms

"Sayonara"; w. Geo. J. Moriarty and Raymond B. Egan; m. Richard A. Whiting; New York and Detroit: Jerome H. Remick

1924

"Dream Maker of Japan"; w. Sam M. Lewis and Joe Young; m. Rudolf Friml; New York: Henry Waterson Inc.

"Improvisation on a Japanese Tune"; m. Efrem Zimbalist; New York: G. Schirmer

Japanese Ghost Songs; m. Kathleen Lockhart Manning; New York: Carl Fischer

"A Japanese Sunset"; w. Archie Bell; m. Jessie L. Deppen; Cleveland: Sam Fox

"La Mousmée: Geisha Dance"; m. Irénée Bergé; New York: Ross Jungnickel

"Nippon: For Japanese Scene or Action"; m. J. S. Zamecnik; Cleveland: Sam Fox Pub.

"Tokio Blues"; w. and m. Irving Berlin; New York: Irving Berlin

1925

"Japanese Lullaby"; w. Eugene Field; m. Ethel Glenn Hier; Chicago: Gilbert Music

Prelude to "Chinese or Japanese Drama"; m. Maurice Baron; New York: Belwin

* "Rose of Japan"; w. G. Marion Burton; m. William B. Kernell; New York: Leo Feist

1926

Cherry Blossom: A Romantic Operetta; w. Edward A. Paulton; m. Bernard Hamblen; New York: Leo Feist

"If I Were Japanese"; w. Blanche Elizabeth Wade; m. William Lester; Boston: Oliver Ditson

* "Sweet Maid of Tokio"; w. Jack Edwards; m. James C. Osborne and Francis J. Allen; Philadelphia: Columbia Music Pub.

Three Oriental Miniatures: "A Little, Lovely Dream"; w. Sarojini Naidu; m. Lucile Crews; New York: G. Schirmer

1927

* "Japansy"; w. Alfred Bryan; m. John Klenner; New York: Harms

* "Nagasaki Butterfly"; w. Billy Rose; m. Dave Stamper; New York: Shapiro, Bernstein

Yo-San (or Cherry Blossoms); w. Harry B. Smith; m. Sigmund Romberg; New York: Harms

1928

From Old Japan; Cantata for Women's voices; w. Alfred H. Hyatt; m. William Berwald; Boston and New York: Arthur P. Schmidt

"A Japanese Dream"; w. Dorothy Fields; m. Jimmy McHugh; New York: Mills Music

* "Japanese Mammy"; w. Gus Kahn; m. Walter Donaldson; New York: Leo Feist

"Moon of Japan"; w. William J. McKenna; m. William Haid; New York: Denton and Haskins Music Pub.

"Nagasaki"; w. Mort Dixon; m. Harry Warren; New York: Remick Music Corp.

O Cho San: or, The Stolen Jade, Japanese Operetta for Children; w. Sarah Grames Clark; m. R. R. Forman; Philadelphia: Theodore Presser

1929

"Broken Idol"; w. Raymond Egan; m. Harry D. Squires; New York: Harms

"In a Japanese Garden"; w. Marian Gillespie; m. Wilbur Chenoweth; New York: Carl Fischer

"Japanese Toyland"; w. and m. Raymond Klages, Jesse Greer, and Harry Carroll; New York: Shapiro, Bernstein

"Najimi"; w. and m. Red Hawk and Joe Macario, Jr.; Honolulu, HI: Bergstrom Music

"Pearl of Old Japan"; w. and m. Con Conrad, Sidney D. Mitchell, and Archie Gottler; New York: De Sylva, Brown, and Henderson

"Yokohama Dream Boat"; w. Phil Ponce; m. Jack Egan; New York: Phil Ponce

1930

* "My Tokio Love Girl"; w. Dave Reed; m. E. J. Goulston; Boston: Lowe-Goulston

"Sing Song Girl"; w. and m. McCarthy and Hanley; New York: Red Star Music

1931

"Hop-Li, the Rickshaw Man"; w. and m. Kathleen Lockhart Manning; New York: G. Schirmer

"In the Happy Islands"; m. Elma T. Chapman; Boston: Arthur P. Schmidt

1932

"Japanese Night Song"; w. Ellen Janson; m. Charles Bennett; Boston: Riker, Brown, and Wellington

Maid in Japan, or When Dreams Come True: An Operetta in Two Acts; w. Helen Stilwell, m. Margaret and E. J. Gatwood; Chicago: H. T. Fitzsimons

1935

"Cherry Blossom Time in Old Kioto"; w. and m. Harriet E. Barton; Boston: H. N. Homeyer

1936

"Over a Bowl of Suki Yaki"; w. and m. Richard Jerome and Walter Kent; New York: Santly Bros.–Joy

"Thru a Window in Japan"; w. Al Bryan; m. Larry Stock; New York: Marlo Music

1939

"Chopsticks"; w. and m. Jack Lawrence and Elliot Daniels; New York: Skidmore Music

"Japanese Doll Dance"; m. Alfred G. Robyn; New York: Century Music

1940

"Two Oriental Moods: On a Japanese Screen"; m. Gustav Klemm; Cincinnati: Willis Music

Selected Filmography

title; studio; director (dir.); credited composer

1915
> *The Cheat*; Lasky Feature Play; dir. Cecil B. De Mille
> *Madame Butterfly*; Famous Players; dir. Sidney Olcott

1917
> *The Call of the East*; Lasky Feature Play; dir. George Melford
> *The Door Between*; Bluebird Photoplays; dir. Rupert Julian
> *The Secret Game*; Lasky Feature Play; dir. William C. deMille

1918
> *The City of Dim Faces*; Famous Players–Lasky; dir. George Melford
> *His Birthright*; Haworth Pictures; dir. William Worthington
> *A Japanese Nightingale*; Astra Film; dir. George Fitzmaurice

1919
> *The Dragon Painter*; Haworth Pictures; dir. William Worthington
> *Harakiri*; Decla-Bioscop; dir. Fritz Lang

1920
> *The Willow Tree*; Screen Classics; dir. Henry Otto

1922
> *Toll of the Sea*; Technicolor Motion Pictures; dir. Chester M. Franklin; Ernst Luz (cue sheet)

1923
> *The Cheat*; Paramount/Famous Players-Lasky; dir. George Fitzmaurice

1930
> "Japan in Cherry Blossom Time," *James A. Fitzpatrick's Travel Talks*; MGM; dir. James A. Fitzpatrick

1931
> Around the World in Eighty Minutes with Douglas Fairbanks; Elton Corp.; dir. Victor Fleming; Alfred Newman
> *The Cheat*; Paramount; dir. George Abbott; anon.

1932
> *The Bitter Tea of General Yen*; Columbia; dir. Frank Capra; W. Franke Harling
> *Madame Butterfly*; Paramount; dir. Marion Gering; W. Franke Harling

1934
> *Marie Galante*; Fox Film; dir. Henry King; Arthur Lange
> *One Night of Love*; Columbia; dir. Victor Schertzinger; Victor Schertzinger and Gus Kahn

1935
> "Japan-China!," *March of Time*, newsreel
> "Okitsu, Japan," *March of Time*, newsreel

1936
> *Il sogno di Butterfly/Premiere der Butterfly*; Esperia Film; dir. Carmine Gallone; Luigi Ricci
> "Tokyo, Japan," *March of Time*, newsreel

1937

Forfaiture; Societé du Cinéma du Panthéon; dir. Marcel L'Herbier; Michel Lévine
"War in China," *March of Time*, newsreel

1938

Too Hot to Handle; MGM; dir. Jack Conroy; Franz Waxman

1939

First Love; Universal; dir. Henry Koster; Charles Previn, H. J. Salter, and Frank Skinner
The 400,000,000; History Today; dir. John Ferno; Hanns Eisler
"Japan, Master of the Orient," *March of Time*, newsreel
Mr. Moto's Last Warning; 20th Century–Fox; dir. Norman Foster; Samuel Kaylin
"Tokyo!," *March of Time*, newsreel
"War, Peace, and Propaganda," *March of Time*, newsreel

1940

The Drums of Fu Manchu; Republic; dir. John English; Cy Feuer

1941

Penny Serenade; Columbia; dir. George Stevens; W. Franke Harling
They Met in Bombay; MGM; dir. Clarence Brown; Herbert Stothart

1942

Across the Pacific; Warner Bros.; dir. Jo Graham; Adolph Deutsch
The Battle of Midway; US War Department; dir. John Ford; Alfred Newman
Black Dragons; Banner Productions; dir. William High; Johnny Lange and Lew Porter
China Girl; 20th Century–Fox; dir. Henry Hathaway; Hugo Friedhofer
The Ducktators; Warner Bros.; dir. Norman McCabe; Carl Starling
Flying Tigers; Republic; dir. David Miller; Victor Young
Foreign Agent; Monogram; dir. William Beaudine; Edward J. Kay
Japanese Relocation; Office of War Information; dir. Milton S. Eisenhower
Little Tokyo, USA; 20th Century–Fox; dir. Otto Brower; Emil Newman
Prisoner of Japan; Atlantis; dir. Arthur Ripley; Leon Erdody
Secret Agent of Japan; 20th Century–Fox; dir. Irving Pichel; Emil Newman
Superman: Eleventh Hour; Paramount; dir. Dan Gordon; Sammy Timberg
Superman: Japoteurs; Paramount; dir. Seymour Kneitel; Sammy Timberg
Wake Island; Paramount; dir. John Farrow; David Buttolph
You're a Sap, Mr. Jap; Paramount; dir. Dan Gordon; Winston Sharples

1943

Air Force; Warner Bros.; dir. Howard Hanks; Franz Waxman
Bataan; MGM; dir. Tay Garnett; Bronislaw Kaper
The Battle of Russia; US War Department; dir. Anatole Litvak; Dimitri Tiomkin
Behind the Rising Sun; RKO; dir. Edward Dmytryk; Roy Webb
Bombardier; RKO; dir. Lambert Hillyer; Roy Webb
China; Paramount; dir. John Farrow; Victor Young
December 7th; US War Department; dir. John Ford and Greg Toland; Alfred Newman
Guadalcanal Diary; 20th Century–Fox; dir. Lewis Seiler; David Buttolph
Gung ho!; Universal; dir. Ray Enright; Frank Skinner
Prelude to War; US War Department; dir. Frank Capra; Alfred Newman
Report from the Aleutians; US War Department; dir. John Huston; Dimitri Tiomkin
Seein' Red, White, n' Blue; Paramount; dir. Dan Gordon; Winston Sharples
So Proudly We Hail!; Paramount; dir. Mark Sandrich; Miklós Rózsa
Tokio Jokio; Warner Bros.; dir. Norman McCabe; Carl W. Stalling

1944

The Battle of China; US War Department; dir. Frank Capra; Dimitri Tiomkin
Bugs Bunny Nips the Nips; Warner Bros.; dir. Friz Freleng; Carl W. Stalling
A Challenge to Democracy; War Relocation Authority

Destination Tokyo; Warner Bros.; dir. Delmer Daves; Franz Waxman

Dragon Seed; MGM; dir. Harold S. Bucquet; Herbert Stothart

The Fighting Seabees; Republic; dir. Edward Ludwig; Walter Scharf

The Fighting Sullivans; 20th Century–Fox; dir. Lloyd Bacon; Cyril J. Mockridge

A Guy Named Joe; MGM; dir. Victor Fleming; Herbert Stothart

Marine Raiders; RKO; dir. Robert Wise; Roy Webb

The Purple Heart; 20th Century–Fox; dir. Lewis Milestone; Alfred Newman

The Story of Dr. Wassell; Paramount; dir. Cecil B. DeMille; Victor Young

Up in Arms; RKO; dir. Elliott Nugent; Ray Heindorf

A Wing and a Prayer; 20th Century–Fox; dir. Henry Hathaway; Hugo Friedhofer

1945

Appointment in Tokyo; US War Department; dir. Jack Hively; Sol Kaplan

Back to Bataan; RKO; dir. Edward Dmytryk; Roy Webb

Betrayal from the East; RKO; dir. William Berke; Roy Webb

Blood on the Sun; William Cagney Productions; dir. Frank Lloyd; Miklós Rózsa

China's Little Devils; Monogram; dir. Monta Bell; Dimitri Tiomkin

China Sky; RKO; dir. Ray Enright; Leigh Harline

The Fighting Lady; 20th Century–Fox; dir. Louis de Rochemont; David Buttolph and Alfred Newman

First Yank into Tokyo; RKO; dir. Gordon Douglas; Leigh Harline

Fury in the Pacific; US War Department; dir. combat cameramen; Lehman Engel

God Is My Copilot; Warner Bros.; dir. Robert Florey; Franz Waxman

Know Your Enemy—Japan; US War Department; dir. Frank Capra; Dimitri Tiomkin

Objective: Burma; Warner Bros.; dir. Raoul Walsh; Franz Waxman

On to Tokyo; US War Department; dir. Frank Capra

Pride of the Marines; Warner Bros.; dir. Delmer Daves; Franz Waxman

Samurai; Cavalcade; dir. Raymond Cannon; Lee Zahler

The Stilwell Road; US War Department; dir. Frank Capra

They Were Expendable; MGM; dir. John Ford; Herbert Stothart

Thirty Seconds over Tokyo; MGM; dir. Mervyn LeRoy; Herbert Stothart

To the Shores of Iwo Jima; US War Department; dir. William Lava; Alfred Newman

Two Down and One to Go; US War Department; dir. Frank Capra; Dimitri Tiomkin

War Comes to America; US War Department; dir. Frank Capra; Dimitri Tiomkin

Your Job in Germany; US War Department; dir. Frank Capra; Dimitri Tiomkin

1946

Our Job in Japan; US War Department; dir. not credited; Dimitri Tiomkin

Tokyo Rose; Pine-Thomas Productions; dir. Lew Landers; Rudy Schrager

1948

Design for Death; RKO; dir. Sid Rogell; Paul Sawtell

1949

Home of the Brave; United Artists; dir. Mark Robson; Dimitri Tiomkin

Tokyo Joe; Columbia; dir. Stuart Heisler; George Antheil

1950

Malaya; MGM; dir. Richard Thorpe; Bronislaw Kaper

Sands of Iwo Jima; Republic; dir. Allan Dwan; Victor Young

Three Came Home; 20th Century–Fox; dir. Jean Negulesco; Hugo Friedhofer

The Toast of New Orleans; MGM; dir. Norman Taurog; George Stoll

1951

Call Me Mister; 20th Century–Fox; dir. Lloyd Bacon; Alfred Newman

The Flying Leathernecks; RKO; dir. Nicholas Ray; Roy Webb

Go for Broke!; MGM; dir. Robert Pirosh; Alberto Colombo

The Halls of Montezuma; 20th Century–Fox; dir. Lewis Milestone; Sol Kaplan

Operation Pacific; Warner Bros.; dir. George Waggner; Max Steiner
Wild Blue Yonder; Republic; dir. Allan Dwan; Victor Young

1952

Above and Beyond; MGM; dir. Norman Panama; Hugo Friedhofer
Japanese War Bride; 20th Century–Fox; dir. King Vidor; Emil Newman and Arthur Lange
Victory at Sea; NBC TV; dir. M. Clay Adams; Richard Rodgers and Robert Russell Bennett

1954

Madama Butterfly; Produzione Gallone and Toho Co.; dir. Carmine Gallone; Puccini's opera

1955

Bad Day at Black Rock; MGM; dir. John Sturges; André Previn
Battle Cry; Warner Bros.; dir. Raoul Walsh; Max Steiner
House of Bamboo; 20th Century–Fox; dir. Samuel Fuller; Leigh Harline
Love Is a Many-Splendored Thing; 20th Century–Fox; dir. Henry King; Alfred Newman
Three Stripes in the Sun (Gentle Sergeant); Columbia; dir. Richard Murphy; George Duning

1956

Between Heaven and Hell; 20th Century–Fox; dir. Richard O. Fleischer; Hugo Friedhofer
The King and I; 20th Century–Fox; dir. Walter Lang; Richard Rodgers
The Teahouse of the August Moon; MGM; dir. Daniel Mann; Saul Chaplin

1957

The Bridge on the River Kwai; Columbia; dir. David Lean; Malcolm Arnold
China Gate; Globe Enterprises; dir. Samuel Fuller; Victor Young, and Max Steiner
Escapade in Japan; RKO; dir. Arthur Lubin; Max Steiner
Heaven Knows, Mr. Allison; 20th Century–Fox; dir. John Huston; Georges Auric
Joe Butterfly; Universal; dir. Jesse Hibbs; Henry Mancini
Sayonara; Warner Bros.; dir. Joshua Logan; Franz Waxman
Stopover Tokyo; 20th Century–Fox; dir. Richard L. Breene; Paul Sawtell

1958

Barbarian and the Geisha; 20th Century–Fox; dir. John Huston; Hugo Friedhofer
The Geisha Boy; Paramount; dir. Frank Tashlin; Walter Scharf
In Love and War; 20th Century–Fox; dir. Philip Dunne; Hugo Friedhofer
The Naked and the Dead; RKO; dir. Raoul Walsh; Bernard Herrmann
Run Silent, Run Deep; United Artists; dir. Robert Wise; Franz Waxman
"The Sakae Ito Story" (3 December), *Wagon Train*; NBC TV; dir. Herschel Daugherty; Tak Shindo
South Pacific; 20th Century–Fox; dir. Joshua Logan; Richard Rodgers

1959

The Crimson Kimono; Columbia; dir. Samuel Fuller; Harry Sukman
Hiroshima, mon amour; Argos Films; dir. Alain Resnais; Giovani Fusco and Georges Delerue
Never So Few; MGM; dir. John Sturges; Hugo Friedhofer

1960

Hell to Eternity; Allied; dir. Phil Karlson; Leith Stevens
The World of Suzie Wong; Paramount; dir. Richard Quine; George Duning

1961

Breakfast at Tiffany's; Paramount; dir. Blake Edwards; Henry Mancini
Bridge to the Sun; MGM; dir. Etienne Périer; Georges Auric
Cry for Happy; Columbia; dir. George Marshall; George Duning
Flower Drum Song; Fields Productions; dir. Henry Koster; Richard Rodgers
Kamikaze; Irja Films–CBS Europe; dir. Perry Wolff; Norman Dello Joio

1962

A Girl Named Tamiko; Paramount; dir. John Sturges; Elmer Bernstein

The Horizontal Lieutenant; MGM; dir. Richard Thorpe; George Stoll
A Majority of One; Warner Bros.; dir. Mervyn LeRoy; Max Steiner
My Geisha; Paramount; dir. Jack Cardiff; Franz Waxman

1963
55 Days at Peking; Samuel Bronston Productions; dir. Nicholas Ray; Dimitri Tiomkin
PT 109; Warner Bros.; dir. Leslie H. Martinson; William Lava and David Buttolph

1965
In Harm's Way; Paramount; dir. Otto Preminger; Jerry Goldsmith
Lord Jim; Columbia; dir. Richard Brooks; Bronislaw Kaper
None but the Brave; Warner Bros.; dir. Frank Sinatra; John Williams
The Return of Mr. Moto; 20th Century–Fox; dir. Ernest Morris; Douglas Gamley

1967
You Only Live Twice; United; dir. Bobby Simmons; John Barry

1968
The New Adventures of Superman "The Japanese Sandman"; Filmation Association; dir. Hal Sutherland; John Gart

1970
Tora! Tora! Tora!; 20th Century–Fox; dir. Richard O. Fleischer; Jerry Goldsmith

1974
Madama Butterfly; Unitel; dir. Jean-Pierre Ponnelle; Puccini's opera

1976
Farewell to Manzanar; Universal TV; dir. John Korty; Paul Chihara
Midway; Mirisch Corp. and Universal; dir. Jack Smight; John Williams

1978
The Bad News Bears Go to Japan; Paramount; dir. John Berry; Paul Chihara

1980
Encounter with the Past; dir. and producer Tak Shindo; Tak Shindo
Shogun; Paramount TV; dir. Jerry London; Maurice Jarre

1982
Blade Runner; Warner Bros.; dir. Ridley Scott; Vangelis

1983
Merry Christmas Mr. Lawrence; Universal; dir. Nagisa Oshima; Ryuichi Sakamoto

1984
The Karate Kid; Columbia; dir. John G. Avildsen; Bill Conti

1985
Mishima: A Life in Four Chapters; Zoetrope Studios; dir. Paul Schrader; Philip Glass

1986
An American Geisha; Interscope Communications TV; dir. Lee Philips; Miles Goodman
Gung ho!; Paramount; dir. Ron Howard; Thomas Newman
Karate Kid II; Columbia; dir. John G. Avildsen; Bill Conti

1987
Empire of the Sun; Warner Bros.; dir. Steven Spielberg; John Williams
Fatal Attraction; Paramount; dir. Adrian Lyne; Maurice Jarre

1989
Black Rain; Paramount; dir. Ridley Scott; Hans Zimmer

1990
Come See the Paradise; 20th Century–Fox; dir. Alan Parker; Randy Edelman

1991
> *Pearl Harbor: Two Hours That Changed the World*; ABC News/NHK TV Japan; dir. Roger Goodman; Skip SoRelle

1992
> *Mr. Baseball*; Universal; dir. Fred Schepisi; Jerry Goldsmith

1993
> *Household Saints*; Jones Entertainment; dir. Nancy Savoca; Stephen Endelman
> *M. Butterfly*; Geffen Pictures; dir. David Cronenberg; Howard Shore
> *Rising Sun*; 20th Century–Fox; dir. Peter Kaufman; Toru Takemitsu

1995
> *Madama Butterfly*; Erato Films; dir. Frédéric Mitterrand; Puccini's opera

1997
> *Paradise Road*; 20th Century–Fox; dir. Bruce Beresford; Ross Edwards

1999
> *Snow Falling on Cedars*; Universal; dir. Scott Hicks; James Newton Howard

2001
> *Pearl Harbor*; Touchstone; dir. Michael Bay; Hans Zimmer

2003
> *The Last Samurai*; Warner Bros.; dir. Edward Zwick; Hans Zimmer
> *Lost in Translation*; Focus Features; dir. Sofia Coppola; Kevin Shields

2005
> *Drawing Restraint 9*; Restraint LLC; dir. Matthew Barney; Björk
> *Memoirs of a Geisha*; Columbia; dir. Rob Marshall; John Williams

2006
> "Samurai Pie," *Backyardigans*; Nickelodeon; dir. Mike Shiell and Dave Palmer; Evan Lurie

2016
> *Kubo and the Two Strings*; Focus Features; dir. Travis Knight; Dario Marianelli

2018
> *Isle of Dogs*; American Empirical Pictures; dir. Wes Anderson; Alexandre Desplat

Notes

Introduction

1. The term *japonisme* was coined in 1872 by the French art critic Philippe Burty in reference to the widespread fad for Japanese prints in France and their impact on French painters. See Hazel B. Durnell, *Japanese Cultural Influences on American Poetry and Drama* (Tokyo: Hokuseido Press, 1983), 23. Alternative terms for this phenomenon have included *Japonaiserie* and Japanism. On *japonisme* in European and American visual arts see particularly: *Japonisme in Art: An International Symposium*, edited by the Society for the Study of Japonisme (Tokyo: Committee for the Year 2001, 1980); Siegfried Wichmann, *Japonisme: The Japanese Influence on Western Art since 1858* (New York: Thames & Hudson, 1981); Julia Meech and Gabriel P. Weisberg, *Japonisme Comes to America: The Japanese Impact on the Graphic Arts 1876–1925* (New York: Harry N. Abrams, 1990); Klaus Berger, *Japonisme in Western Painting from Whistler to Matisse*, translated by David Britt (Cambridge, UK: Cambridge University Press, 1992); and Lionel Lambourne, *Japonisme: Cultural Crossings between Japan and the West* (New York: Phaidon Press, 2005).

2. Michael V. Pisani covers an even longer historical period in his study *Imagining Native America in Music* (New Haven, CT: Yale University Press, 2005). Somewhat similar approaches are pursued in Gerry Farrell's *Indian Music and the West* (Oxford: Clarendon Press, 1997) and in Nalini Ghuman's *Resonances of the Raj: India in the English Musical Imagination, 1897–1947* (Oxford: Oxford University Press, 2014).

3. On this performance, see James D. McCabe, ed. *A Tour around the World by General Grant* (Philadelphia: The National Publishing Co., 1879), 731. Also see Clara A. N. Whitney, *Clara's Diary: An American Girl in Meiji Japan*, eds. M. William Steele and Tamiko Ichimata (Tokyo: Kodansha International, 1979), 260. An image depicting this performance is reproduced in Christine M. E. Guth, *Longfellow's Tattoos: Tourism, Collecting, and Japan* (Seattle: University of Washington Press, 2004), 27. I note that the Japanese boy band Da Pump enjoyed a huge summer 2018 hit with "U.S.A.," a song celebrating the relationship between the United States and Japan in a reworking of the Italian 1992 original by Joe Yellow. The success of this song and music video was directly referenced at least twice in *kabuki* performances in Tokyo in January 2019, with *kabuki* actors in full costume incorporating the "shoot" dance move featured prominently in Da Pump's performances (as well as in the game *Fortnite*).

4. On this topic, see for example Mari Yoshihara, *Musicians from a Different Shore: Asians and Asian Americans in Classical Music* (Philadelphia: Temple University Press, 2007).

5. The score for Whithorne's *Adventures of a Samurai* is held at the Free Library in Philadelphia. I am grateful to Gary Galván for helping me to secure a copy of this unpublished manuscript. The other Whithorne scores mentioned here are held in the Music Division of the Library of Congress.

6. Apparently Whithorne's original version of *Adventures of a Samurai* had been in rehearsal in Germany in 1914 when World War I broke out and the score was lost during the war. See "To Give Whithorne Suite," *Musical America* 31 (7 February 1920): 52.

7. See W. H. James, "Max Rosen, Violinist Shows Rare Virtuosity," *St. Louis Post-Dispatch* (20 March 1920): 6, and "New Whithorne Orchestral Work," *Musical Courier* 5 (February 1920): 19.

8. Arjun Appadurai, *Modernity at Large: Cultural Dimensions of Globalization* (Minneapolis: University of Minnesota Press, 1996), 31.

9. Percival Lowell, *The Soul of the Far East* (Boston and New York: Houghton, Mifflin, 1888), 2.

10. Ibid., 4.

11. Pearl S. Buck, *The People of Japan* (New York: Simon and Schuster, 1966), 9–10.

12. See Ronald Takaki, *Strangers from a Different Shore: A History of Asian Americans*, rev. ed. (Boston: Back Bay Books, 1998), 209.

13. Edwin O. Reischauer, *The United States and Japan* (Cambridge, MA: Harvard University Press, 1950), 3–4.

14. Roland Robertson, *Globalization: Social Theory and Global Culture* (London: Sage Publications, 1992), 88.

15. Albert Einstein, *The Travel Diaries of Albert Einstein: The Far East, Palestine & Spain, 1922–1923*, ed. Ze'ev Rosenkranz (Princeton, NJ: Princeton University Press, 2018), 121. Also see Ibid., 249–250 on Einstein's views of Japanese music as fundamentally different.

16. Otto Abraham and Erich M. von Hornbostel, "Studien über das Tonsystem und die Musik der Japaner" (1903), trans. Gertrud Kurath, in *Hornbostel: Opera Omnia, Vol. I*, ed. Klaus P. Wachsmann, Dieter Christensen, and Hans-Peter Reinecke (The Hague: Martinus Nijhoff, 1975), 67.

17. Oscar Wilde, "The Decay of Lying: An Observation" (1891), reprinted in *Oscar Wilde: The Dover Reader* (Mineola, NY: Dover Publications, 2015), 445.

18. Pierre Loti, *Madame Chrysanthème*, trans. Laura Ensor (Rutland, VT: Charles E. Tuttle, 1973), 43.

19. Ibid., 56.

20. Quoted in Arthur Groos, "Cio-Cio-San and Sadayakko: Japanese Music-Theater in *Madama Butterfly*," *Monumenta Nipponica* 54, no. 1 (spring 1999): 42. Here Puccini refers to Mascagni's 1898 opera *Iris*, which is likewise set in Japan, but in olden rather than contemporary times.

21. For a more extensive discussion of the term and overview of scholarly approaches to the phenomenon see my "Exoticism," in *The Oxford Handbook of Opera*, ed. Helen M. Greenwald, 795–816 (New York: Oxford University Press, 2014). For a substantive and annotated bibliography on exoticism, see my "Exoticism," *Oxford Bibliographies in Music*, ed. Bruce Gustafson (Oxford University Press, 2012; last modified 25 February 2016), DOI: 10.1093/OBO/9780199757824-0123. Ralph P. Locke has offered particularly thorough considerations of the terminology and categorizations associated with exoticism in his *Musical Exoticism: Images and Reflections* (Cambridge, UK: Cambridge University Press, 2009) 1–84, and in *Music and the Exotic from the Renaissance to Mozart* (Cambridge, UK: Cambridge University Press, 2015), 3–43. On various forms of exotic influence, also see Yayoi Uno Everett, "Intercultural Synthesis in Postwar Western Art Music: Historical Contexts, Perspectives, and Taxonomy," in *Locating East Asia in Western Art Music*, eds. Yayoi Uno Everett and Frederick Lau (Middletown, CT: Wesleyan University Press, 2004), 15–19.

22. This understanding of the cultural, political, and economic function of exoticism is most closely associated with the work of Edward Said. See in particular Edward W. Said, *Orientalism* (New York: Pantheon, 1978) and Said, *Culture and Imperialism* (New York: Knopf, 1993). Though "exoticism" and "Orientalism" are often employed interchangeably in contemporary discourse, Orientalism perhaps more pointedly denotes the critique of works involving exotic representation given the legacy of Said's argument.

23. John Cage, "The East in the West," *Modern Music* 23, no. 2 (spring 1946): 114.

24. On Japanese "self-exoticism" see Tōru Mitsui, "Domestic Exoticism: A Recent Trend in Japanese Popular Music," *Perfect Beat* 3, no. 4 (1998): 1–12; Shūhei Hosokawa, "Soy Sauce Music: Haruomi Hosono and Japanese Self-Orientalism," in *Widening the Horizon: Exoticism in Post-War Popular Music*, ed. Philip Hayward, 114–144 (Sydney: John Libbey, 1999); and

Koichi Iwabuchi, "Complicit Exoticism: Japan and Its Other," *Continuum: Journal of Media and Cultural Studies* 8, no. 2 (1994): 49–82. With specific reference to Chinese participation in Orientalism, see Arif Dirlik, "Chinese History and the Question of Orientalism," in *Genealogies of Orientalism: History, Theory, Politics*, eds. Edmund Burke III and David Prochaska, 384–413 (Lincoln: University of Nebraska Press, 2008). Also see Tony Mitchell, "Self-Orientalism, Reverse Orientalism and Pan-Asian Pop Cultural Flows in Dick Lee's *Transit Lounge*," in *Rogue Flows: Trans-Asian Cultural Traffic*, eds. Koichi Iwabuchi, Stephen Muecke, and Mandy Thomas, 95–118 (Hong Kong: Hong Kong University Press, 2004), and my "Global Exoticism and Modernity," in *The Cambridge History of World Music*, ed. Philip V. Bohlman, 606–633 (Cambridge, UK: Cambridge University Press, 2013).

25. On the dynamics of supercultural and subcultural relationships in music, see Mark Slobin, *Subcultural Sounds: Micromusics of the West* (Hanover, NH: Wesleyan University Press, 1993).

26. Charles Hiroshi Garrett, *Struggling to Define a Nation: American Music and the Twentieth Century* (Berkeley: University of California Press, 2008).

27. For a seminal example of whiteness studies, see Richard Dyer, *White* (London: Routledge, 1997).

28. Hua Hsu, "Pale Fire: Is Whiteness a Privilege or a Plight?," *The New Yorker* (25 July 2016): 66.

29. Lothrop Stoddard, *The Rising Tide of Color against White World-Supremacy* (New York: Charles Scribner's Sons, 1920).

30. Ibid., 251.

31. Ibid., 287–289.

32. See Rotem Kowner, *From White to Yellow: The Japanese in European Racial Thought, 1300–1735* (Montreal and Kingston: McGill–Queen's University Press, 2014), 28–30.

33. Arved Ashby, "Nationalist and Postnationalist Perspectives in American Musicology," in *Postnational Musical Identities: Cultural Production, Distribution, and Consumption in a Globalized Scenario*, eds. Ignacio Corona and Alejandro L. Madrid (Lanham, MD: Lexington Books, 2008), 35.

34. See William Faulkner, *Requiem for a Nun* (New York: Random House, 1951), 92. Faulkner's line ("The past is never dead. It's not even past.") was repeatedly paraphrased in speeches by Senator and then President Obama.

35. For a particularly eloquent discussion of the dangers inherent in this type of research, and the importance of the writer's own social position, see Robert Charles Lancefield, "Hearing Orientality in (White) America, 1900–1930" (PhD diss., Wesleyan University, 2004), 12–14.

36. Hidden away in this endnote, I present the text of that political rap, which I delivered in a style approximating the contemporaneous work of Run-DMC.

> My name is Tony, which rhymes with baloney, but you all know that I'm no phoney./ Vote for me, I'm the one, who'll work real hard to get the job done./You know I'm cool, you know I'm bad, I'm the baddest candidate you ever had./So Willie, Lumpy, Bonnie and Clyde you all know where you can slide./Give me your vote and give me the chance to show I can do more than just rap and dance./Vote, vote for me, Tony Sheppard is who I be, say vote, vote vote for me, Tony Sheppard is who I be.

Chapter 1

1. M. C. Perry, *Narrative of the Expedition of an American Squadron to the China Seas and Japan*, compiled by Francis L. Hawks (New York: D. Appleton and Company, 1856), 74. I have previously presented some of the material and ideas offered in this chapter in papers delivered at the Society for American Music annual meeting (2006) and at Westminster Choir College (2006). I am grateful for comments offered by panelists and audience members at these events.

2. As Michael Cooper states of these early European visitors to Japan: "On no other point were the foreigners in such complete agreement as in their dislike of Japanese music." Michael Cooper, S.J., *They Came to Japan: An Anthology of European Reports on Japan, 1543–1640* (Berkeley: University of California Press, 1965), 271. Early European writings on Japanese music proved to have a lasting impact. For example, in his armchair account of Japan, Charles MacFarlane—relying on previous accounts—had this to say of Japanese music: "Although they are passionately fond of it, the national music—like that of all Oriental nations—appears to be utterly insupportable to European ears. Perhaps, however, this condemnation is too sweeping and general. We have heard some of the music of the Japanese ladies highly commended by one who possessed a good musical ear." MacFarlane, *Japan: An Account, Geographical and Historical* (New York: George P. Putnam, 1852), 326.

3. See, for example, Christopher Benfey, *The Great Wave: Gilded Age Misfits, Japanese Eccentrics, and the Opening of Old Japan* (New York: Random House, 2003).

4. Christine M. E. Guth, *Longfellow's Tattoos: Tourism, Collecting, and Japan* (Seattle: University of Washington Press, 2004), 17. On Charles Longfellow's Japanese experience, also see Christine Wallace Laidlaw, ed., *Charles Appleton Longfellow: Twenty Months in Japan, 1871–1873* (Cambridge, MA: Friends of the Longfellow House), 1998. It is apparent from his many letters home that Charles particularly enjoyed geisha songs accompanied by *shamisen*.

5. For example, in 1799 the *Franklin* from Salem sailed for the Dutch East India Company to Japan and returned with Japanese art objects that are still held today in the Peabody Essex Museum at Salem. See *Worlds Revealed: The Dawn of Japanese and American Exchange* (Tokyo: Edo-Tokyo Museum, 1999), 32; 61.

6. This musical instrument was included in *Pacific Encounters: Yankee Whalers, Manjiro, and the Opening of Japan*, a 2004 exhibit at the New Bedford Whaling Museum in New Bedford, Massachusetts. This object was apparently brought aboard the Henry Kneeland, a New Bedford ship captained by George H. Clark, by Japanese castaways from the 1850 Tenju-maru shipwreck.

7. Ranald MacDonald, *Ranald MacDonald: The Narrative of His Early Life on the Columbia under the Hudson's Bay Company's Regime; of His Experiences in the Pacific Whale Fishery; and of His Great Adventure to Japan; with a Sketch of His Later Life on the Western Frontier 1824–1894* (Spokane, WA: Inland American Printing Company, 1923), 175.

8. Samuel Pellman Boyer, *Naval Surgeon: Revolt in Japan 1868–1869*, ed. Elinor Barnes and James A. Barnes (Bloomington: Indiana University Press, 1963), 31, 102.

9. Ibid., 116; 181–182. On the apparent nineteenth-century American preference for Japanese over Chinese music, see Krystyn R. Moon, *Yellowface: Creating the Chinese in American Popular Music and Performance, 1850s–1920s* (New Brunswick, NJ: Rutgers University Press, 2005), 13–14.

10. His further description suggests that Griffis may have heard *gagaku* music: "a grand concert of music by twenty-four bonzes in full sacerdotal costume, with wind and string instruments, in the monastery." William Elliot Griffis, *The Mikado's Empire* (New York: Harper and Brothers, Publishers, 1876), 523–524. Griffis was a minister who traveled to Japan to teach science and English and who became one of the first American Japanologists.

11. William Elliot Griffis, *In the Mikado's Service: A Story of Two Battle Summers in China* (Ganesha Publishing reprint; orig. Boston and Chicago: W. A. Wilde Co., 1901), 352–353.

12. Arthur Collins Maclay, *A Budget of Letters from Japan: Reminiscences of Work and Travel in Japan* (New York: A. C. Armstrong & Son, 1886), 87–88. I accessed this volume at the American Antiquarian Society.

13. See "Extract from the Diary of George Cleveland, Who Visited Japan in 1801," reproduced from the *Derby Papers*, Essex Institute, Salem, Massachusetts, in Arthur E. Christy, ed., *The Asian Legacy and American Life* (New York: John Day Co., 1942), 265.

14. The famed Richard Henry Dana described in his journal his encounter with Japanese music in 1860. He recounted his trip to a theater at which he heard "high sharp unnatural tones of voice" and noted that at the side of the stage sat a man "who seemed to me to act a chorus, occasionally speaking and singing. The singing, like that I have heard in the streets, is deeper toned than the Chinese, and, even with the women, a kind of unnatural barytone seems to be the fashion." Dana, *The Journal of Richard Henry Dana*, vol. 3, ed. Robert Francis Lucid (Cambridge, MA: Belknap Press of Harvard University Press, 1968), 1005. Also see Sanehide Kodama, *American Poetry and Japanese Culture* (Hamden, CT: Archon Books, 1984), 20.

15. Isabella L. Bird, *Unbeaten Tracks in Japan: Vol. II* (New York: G. P. Putnam's Sons, 1881), 215.

16. See "Japan Entering the Commercial World" (from *The Economist*), *Living Age* 42, no. 531 (22 July 1854): 189–190.

17. Alice Mabel Bacon, *Japanese Girls and Women* (London: Kegan Paul, 2001, first 1891), 34–35.

18. Ibid., 35. Lafcadio Hearn wrote in his essay "Insect-Musicians": "The national liking for caged insects does not mean a liking for mere noise; and the note of every insect in public favor must possess either some rhythmic charm, or some mimetic quality celebrated in poetry or legend. The same fact is true of the Japanese liking for the chant of frogs." Hearn, *Exotics and Retrospectives* (Boston: Little, Brown, and Co., 1905), 42.

19. Laura Alexandrine Smith, "The Music of Japan," *The Nineteenth Century* 36, no. 214 (December 1894): 901.

20. On this general subject, see Rachel Mundy, "Evolutionary Categories and Musical Style from Adler to America," *Journal of the American Musicological Society* 67, no. 3 (2014): 735–767.

21. The final criticism in this list comes from Smith, "The Music of Japan," 900–901.

22. Francis Hall, *Japan through American Eyes: The Journal of Francis Hall, Kanagawa and Yokohama, 1859–1866*, ed. and annotated by F. G. Notehelfer (Princeton, NJ: Princeton University Press, 1992), 443.

23. Frances Little, *The House of the Misty Star: A Romance of Youth and Hope and Love in Old Japan* (New York: The Century Co., 1915), 148.

24. Edward Greey, *Young Americans in Japan* (London: Ganesha Publishing, 2001), 103–104.

25. Onoto Watanna, *A Japanese Nightingale* (New York: Harper and Brothers, 1901).

26. Mabel Loomis Todd, *Corona and Coronet: Being a Narrative of the Amherst Eclipse Expedition to Japan, in Mr. James's Schooner-Yacht Coronet, to Observe the Sun's Total Obscuration 9th August 1896* (Boston and New York: Houghton, Mifflin and Co., 1898), 191 and 270. In addition to her publications, Todd gave a series of lectures on Japan to women's clubs, including four in Chicago, starting in 1890. See Sharon Nancy White, "Mable Loomis Todd: Gender, Language, and Power in Victorian America" (PhD diss, Yale University, 1982).

27. Mabel Loomis Todd Papers: Diaries and Journals, 1871–1932, Yale University Library, (1982): Reel 8, 136–139. She also noted that the flutist played an "Introductory piece to the No dancing," and she felt this piece was more discordant than the others: "The music seems more to savor of barbarity than any other one thing in Japan, to me" (141). At the end of this performance a Mr. Pemberton played the banjo for the Japanese in return and the Americans sang a song. Todd concluded that it had been "a unique entertainment altogether, and one I shall never forget" (142).

28. F. T. Piggott, *The Music and Musical Instruments of Japan* (London: B. T. Batsford, 1893), 2. Piggott continues by comparing Japanese instruments unfavorably with those of Europe. However, on page 5 he reveals that he holds a higher opinion of Japanese music than do most Westerners.

29. Piggott, "The Music of the Japanese" (paper delivered on 14 January 1891), *Transactions of the Asiatic Society of Japan*, 19 (1891): 298–299.

30. On 8 April 1891, C. G. Knott offered a rebuttal of Piggott (*Transactions of the Asiatic Society of Japan*, p. 373), claiming that Piggott had gone too far in emphasizing similarities between

Western and Japanese music and proposing that a test should be made by taking Western tunes and trying to play them on the *koto* rather than taking Japanese tunes and playing them on the piano. Knott continued: "Mr. Piggott speaks of them as 'superfluous quarter-tones'; but they are no more superfluous in Japanese music than the swell on our organ or the trill or portamento of operatic singers" (p. 383). Similar arguments had played out earlier in the *Transactions of the Asiatic Society of Japan*. On 13 June 1877 the Rev. Dr. Syle stated that the best sources for the study of original ancient music is at "the extremities of the earth," such as in Japan. Though finding Japanese scales deficient, he argued that Japanese music is closer to Western music than was often assumed. See Syle, "On Primitive Music; Especially That of Japan," *Transactions of the Asiatic Society of Japan*, 5, part 1 (1877): 170–179. A Dr. Geerts responded to Syle's paper by stating he found it surprising that, despite Japanese and Western scales being not all that different, "Japanese music does not leave a better impression on the ears and minds of foreign musicians. Japanese music cannot be said to be 'false.' . . . but it is no less a fact that it utterly fails to favourably impress the foreign ear, or to awake any noble or pleasurable emotions in the breast of the foreign listener" (p. 180). A focus on Japanese scales continued in discussions of Japanese music well into the twentieth century. Ernest W. Clement explained that to "Occidental ears Japanese music, set, as it always is, in a minor key and abounding in discords, seems unworthy of the name of music. To characterize it as merely 'strummings and squealings' because it does not conform to our ideas, is, however, an unfair aspersion. The fact is that it is based upon a scale which differs from that which we use, one of its peculiarities being the introduction of a semi-tone above the tonic." Clement, *A Handbook of Modern Japan*, 6th ed. (Chicago: A. C. McClurg and Co., 1905; orig 1903), 231.

31. The firm association in the American imagination of geishas with Japanese music resulted in some rather striking gender reversals in fictionalized representations of Japanese performance. In a 1906 novel set at the time of Perry's expedition to Japan, two Japanese characters call for geishas accompanied by three *koto* players to perform "the ancient dance," which they refer to as *noh*. The subject of the dance was "life . . . the great drama that unfolds from the cradle to the grave" and the geishas disrobe during the performance. Of course, this is a rather odd depiction of *noh* (a form of all-male performance) in more ways than one. See I. William Adams, *Shibusawa, or the Passing of Old Japan* (New York and London: G. P. Putnam's Sons, 1906), 107–109.

32. Richard Hildreth, *Japan as it Was and Is* (Boston: Phillips, Sampson and Co., 1855), 536. Volume held at the American Antiquarian Society.

33. Bigelow traveled to Japan with Morse in 1882 and remained for seven years, with a second brief trip to the country in 1902. On the significance of Japan for Bigelow, see T. J. Jackson Lears, *No Place of Grace: Antimodernism and the Transformation of American Culture 1880–1920* (New York: Pantheon Books, 1981), 228–234. Bigelow served as a tour guide to Japanese culture for several prominent Americans who traveled to Japan. The artist John La Farge reported on an evening during which Dr. Bigelow escorted him to a Japanese theatrical performance. As they removed their shoes outside the theater they "could hear during the operation long wailings, high notes, and the piercing sound of flutes and stringed instruments; the curiously sad rhythm mingled with a background of high, distinct declamation." See La Farge, *An Artist's Letters from Japan* (New York: The Century Co., 1897, 1st 1890), 18.

34. Ralph Adams Cram, *Impressions of Japanese Architecture* (Boston: Marshall Jones Co., 1930, 1st 1905), 88. Though most famous for his "collegiate Gothic" style, Cram also designed a home in Fall River, Massachusetts, that was clearly inspired by Japanese architecture. I do not know whether Cram came to appreciate Japanese music as he did its architecture.

35. Judith Becker, "Hindu-Buddhist Time in Javanese Gamelan Music," in *The Study of Time*, vol. 4, ed. J. F. Fraser, N. Lawrence, and D. Park (New York: Springer-Verlag, 1981), 161–172, quote on p. 161.

36. Edward S. Morse, *Japan Day by Day* (Boston and New York: Houghton Mifflin Co., 1917). I will cite volume and page numbers from this source in my text. (I consulted Morse's manuscripts for this work at the Salem Peabody-Essex Phillips Library, but found his hand-writing to be nearly indecipherable.) Morse also delivered lectures at the Lowell Institute in Boston during the winter of 1881–1882, which included a lecture on temples, theater, and music, and these lectures in turn inspired several prominent Bostonians to travel to Japan. Megata Tanetaro had already delivered a lecture on Japanese music at the New England Conservatory in 1877. See Ury Eppstein, *The Beginnings of Western Music in Meiji Era Japan* (Lewiston, NY: Edwin Mellen Press, 1994), 28–29. Morse also produced an astonishingly de-tailed and richly illustrated study of Japanese domestic architecture in his *Japanese Homes and Their Surroundings* in 1886 (New York: Dover Publications, 1961). On Morse's influence on Frank Lloyd Wright, see Kevin Nute, *Frank Lloyd Wright and Japan: The Role of Traditional Japanese Art and Architecture in the Work of Frank Lloyd Wright* (London: Chapman and Hall, 1993), 36–44.

37. Robert A. Rosenstone also offers an overview of Morse's impressions of Japanese music in *Mirror in the Shrine: American Encounters with Meiji Japan* (Cambridge, MA: Harvard University Press, 1988), 219–222.

38. Morse was not entirely alone among American auditors in Japan in exhibiting some un-derstanding of cultural relativism. Clara A. N. Whitney arrived in Japan in August 1875 at age fifteen and stayed nearly twenty-five years, marrying a Japanese man and encountering numerous forms of Japanese performance, including *kabuki, noh, biwa*, Shinto music, and *gagaku*. In her diary, which covers the period from 1875 to 1884, she described hearing a girl with a *koto* in 1876: "The girl played very nicely and then began to sing. Ye gods, deliver us from Japanese singing! She squalled and yelled and mumbled and sang fearfully through her nose. But I don't believe Japanese singing sounds to us as badly as ours does to them, for most of their singing is done in a nasal monotone, and sadly, while ours is all slam-bang-and-yell in the upper notes. In church I have seen Japanese trying their best to reach E flat but in spite of screwing up their foreheads, etc., they never succeed. However, this was better music than I often hear." Whitney, *Clara's Diary: An American Girl in Meiji Japan*, ed. M. William Steele and Tamiko Ichimata (Tokyo, New York, and San Francisco: Kodansha International Ltd., 1979), 93.

39. On La Farge in Japan, see James L. Yarnall, *Recreation and Idleness: The Pacific Travels of John La Farge* (New York: Vance Jordan Fine Art Inc., 1998).

40. La Farge, *An Artist's Letters from Japan*, 7. I was unable to discover substantive comments by Henry Adams on Japanese music in my perusal of his papers held at the Massachusetts Historical Society. In his numerous letters from Japan, Adams repeatedly referred to the na-tion as an insubstantial doll-house country of ridiculous women. In a letter to John Hay on 15 September 1886 from Kyoto he reported that they had attended a "Geisha ball" the night be-fore, referring to it as "an exhibition of mechanical childishness" and finding that "their voices were metallic."

41. Ibid., 191.

42. In teaching Japanese music appreciation, I always begin the first class with a *shakuhachi* ex-ample. On the popularity of the *shakuhachi* in the United States, see, for example, Jay Keister, "The Shakuhachi as Spiritual Tool: A Japanese Buddhist Instrument in the West," *Asian Music* 35, no. 2 (spring–summer 2004): 99–131.

43. Morse himself had struggled to hold back laughter during one of his early encounters with Japanese vocal style. He remarked on the singing of a vocalist he heard in a *kibigaku* perfor-mance: "Had he been suffering from an overdose of cucumbers he could not have uttered more dismal sounds; it was really ludicrous, and one found it difficult to preserve one's gravity" (I., 399).

44. Rosenstone describes Morse's evolving engagement with Japanese music in these terms: "Once he was like any foreigner, his reaction to Japanese music a mixture of bewilderment and laughter. Now he is suspended somewhere between that and a new identity, able at special moments to live in two worlds." In summarizing Morse's experience of Japanese music, Rosenstone draws the moral: "It is far easier to step beyond the boundaries of one culture than to join another." See Rosenstone, 222.

45. On Hearn's popularity see Earl Miner, *The Japanese Tradition in British and American Literature* (Princeton, NJ: Princeton University Press, 1958), 61–65; 87–96. Also see Carl Dawson, *Lafcadio Hearn and the Vision of Japan* (Baltimore: Johns Hopkins University Press, 1992).

46. Lafcadio Hearn, *Gleanings in Buddha-Fields: Studies of Hand and Soul in the Far East* (Boston and New York: Houghton, Mifflin and Co., 1897), 8.

47. See Hearn's letters to Krehbiel in Elizabeth Bisland, *The Life and Letters of Lafcadio Hearn*, vol. 1 (Boston and New York: Houghton, Mifflin and Co., 1906), 165–245.

48. Setsuko Koizumi, *Reminiscences of Lafcadio Hearn* (Boston and New York: Houghton Mifflin and Co., 1918), 60–61.

49. Lafcadio Hearn, *The Japanese Letters of Lafcadio Hearn*, ed. Elizabeth Bisland (Boston and New York: Houghton Mifflin Co., 1910), 21. Chamberlain was the author of the widely read *Things Japanese: Being Notes on Various Subjects Connected with Japan*, first published in 1890, and was an arch-despiser of Japanese music in all its forms. Fully cognizant of Chamberlain's abhorrence of Japanese music, Hearn frequently had to apologize for his more positive remarks on it in his letters. In 1890 Hearn wrote to Chamberlain: "I am now going to pray you with all my heart and soul to change that article about Japanese Music in the next edition of the book. I am, and have been for months unspeakably charmed with Japanese music,—I think it is as dainty and playfully sweet and pretty as the Japanese girls who sing it and play it; and I feel sure there is a very fine subtle art-feeling in it." See Bisland, *The Life and Letters of Lafcadio Hearn*, Vol. 2, 14–15.

50. Lafcadio Hearn, *Glimpses of Unfamiliar Japan*, vol. 2 (Boston and New York: Houghton Mifflin Co., 1894), 472.

51. Lafcadio Hearn, *Japan: An Attempt at Interpretation* (New York: MacMillan Co., 1905), 10.

52. Hearn famously professed his inability to understand Japan in the opening of his 1905 *Japan: An Attempt at Interpretation* (Ibid., 9–10): "I cannot yet claim to know much about Japan . . . after having discovered that I cannot understand the Japanese at all,—I feel better qualified to attempt this essay."

53. Lafcadio Hearn, *Glimpses of Unfamiliar Japan*, vol. 1 (Boston and New York: Houghton, Mifflin and Co., 1894), 132–138.

54. Ibid., 138.

55. Lafcadio Hearn, *Kokoro: Hints and Echoes of Japanese Inner Life* (Boston and Rutland, Vermont: Tuttle Publishing, 1972, 1st 1896), 41; 44.

56. Ibid., 46. In the Appendix to *Kokoro*, Hearn praised Japanese folk song as having "a charm indisputable even for Western ears" and concluded that the songs "represent also something essentially characteristic of the race" (p. 337).

57. Julian Street, *Mysterious Japan* (Garden City, NY: Doubleday, Page and Co. 1921), 131–132. Of course, Hearn was not alone among Westerners in the late nineteenth century in valuing Japanese music for its evocative powers. Sir Edwin Arnold, for one, wrote of hearing a *shamisen* once in the evening. He noted its lack of harmony and that there was "not much melody," but felt that certain "little chansonettes upon the *samisen*, with their light-wandering accompaniments, live a little in the memory" and that it was pleasant to sit around a *hibachi* on a cold night listening to "song after song in the strange, dreamy, suggestive intermixture of the *samisen's* sharp string, with the voices of the women, sometimes high-pitched, sometimes

sinking to a musical sigh divided into endless notes." He found that this music made him "heart easy" for "life is never very serious in Japan." Sir Edwin Arnold writing in *Scribner's Magazine* 9, no. 1 (1891): 26–27.

58. *The Japanese Letters of Lafcadio Hearn*, 249.

59. Ibid., 184. Hearn offered another paen to Japanese military music in 1895 after the Sino-Japanese War, referring to the "melancholy sweetness" of the buglers. Hearn, *Kokoro: Hints and Echoes of Japanese Inner Life*, 103–104.

60. Fenollosa's travel diary for this Nikko trip is held at the Houghton Library, Harvard University as MS Am 1759.1 (2).

61. Grant is said to have "lauded the No and urged Iwakura to preserve it." See Komiya Toyotaka, comp. and ed., trans. and adapted by Edward G. Seidensticker and Donald Keene, *Japanese Music and Drama in the Meiji Era* (Tokyo: Ōbunsha, 1956), 94. On Grant's tour of Japan, see James D. McCabe, ed. *A Tour around the World by General Grant* (Philadelphia: The National Publishing Co., 1879); and John M. Keating, *With General Grant in the East* (Philadelphia: J. B. Lippincott and Co., 1879). Keating reported on a geisha musical performance presented to the general in which each geisha "held a fan, and in time with the music and the low, monotonous chant or wail of the musicians, twisted herself into all sorts of contortions, which though making a pretty scene at first, soon became rather tiring." See Keating, 224.

62. The standard accounts of Fenollosa's work in Japan include Van Wyck Brooks, *Fenollosa and His Circle* (New York: E. P. Dutton and Co., 1962); and Lawrence W. Chisolm, *Fenollosa: The Far East and American Culture* (New Haven, CT: Yale University Press, 1963). Also see Yutaka Ito, "'Words Quite Fail': The Life and Thought of Ernest Francisco Fenollosa" (PhD diss., Rutgers, The State University of New Jersey, 2002).

63. On Fenollosa and Japanese art see, for example, Nute, 74–84. For detailed discussion of Pound's transformation of Fenollosa's *noh* papers, see Akiko Miyake, Sanehide Kodama, and Nicholas Teele, eds., *A Guide to Ezra Pound and Ernest Fenollosa's Classic Noh Theatre of Japan* (Orono: National Poetry Foundation, University of Maine, 1994). On the general topic of Japanese influence on American literary modernism, see, for example, Earl Miner, *The Japanese Tradition in British and American Literature* (Princeton, NJ: Princeton University Press, 1958), Hazel B. Durnell, *Japanese Cultural Influences on American Poetry and Drama* (Tokyo: Hokuseido Press, 1983), and Sanehide Kodama, *American Poetry and Japanese Culture* (Hamden, CT: Archon Books, 1984).

64. Fenollosa's "Notes on the Japanese Lyric Drama" was first published in *Journal of the American Oriental Society* 22 (1901): 129–137, and is reprinted in *A Guide to Ezra Pound and Ernest Fenollosa's* Classic Noh Theatre of Japan. Fenollosa stated that he started to study *noh* with Mr. Umewaka in 1880, "from whose lips I took down the Japanese text, writing over it on an improvised 'staff,' and in European notation, an approximation to the sounds of the chant" (*A Guide to Ezra Pound*, 312).

65. See Akiko Murakata, "Ernest F. Fenollosa's Studies of No: With Reference to His and Other Unpublished Manuscripts and Ezra Pound's Edition," in Murakata, ed. and trans., *The Ernest F. Fenollosa Papers: Houghton Library Harvard University*, Japanese Edition, vol. 3, Literature (Tokyo: Museum Press: 1987), 229–230.

66. See Ernest Fenollosa and Ezra Pound, *"Noh" or Accomplishment: A Study of the Classical Stage of Japan* (New York: Alfred A. Knopf, 1917), 106. Some of Fenollosa's discussion reveals understandable confusion concerning instrument names and terminology (e.g., on p. 54) while other sections of this text indicate his broader study of Japanese music (252).

67. On Fenollosa's lessons in *noh* singing, see Murakata, "Ernest F. Fenollosa's Studies," 230–231, 234–237.

68. Ezra Pound and Ernest Fenollosa, *The Classic Noh Theatre of Japan* (New York: New Directions, 1959), 27–28.

69. Ibid., 146.

70. Richard Taylor, "The Notebooks of Ernest Fenollosa: Translations from the Japanese No," *Literature East and West* 15 (1971): 537. Taylor's article includes transcriptions of Fenollosa's marginalia from several *noh* plays.

71. Quoted in Murakata, "The Ernest F. Fenollosa Manuscripts on No at the Princeton University Library" (typescript held at the Harvard-Yenching Library), 299.

72. Murakata, "The Ernest F. Fenollosa Manuscripts," 304; 312.

73. See Fenollosa and Pound, *"Noh" or Accomplishment*, 257. Pound claims here, without explanation, to have had "this play sung to me" in order to test out Fenollosa's transcriptions. The transcriptions appear on pp. 257–268.

74. Some of Fenollosa's notes on *noh* music and his musical transcriptions are held in the Ezra Pound Collection on Japanese Drama at the Princeton University Library Special Collections. The three loose sheets of Fenollosa's musical transcriptions found in folder 16 correspond only with pp. 263–268 in Fenollosa and Pound, *"Noh" or Accomplishment*.

75. See Murakata, "Ernest F. Fenollosa's Studies of No," 236–237.

76. Mary McNeil Fenollosa, *Out of the Nest: A Flight of Verses* (Boston: Little, Bown, and Co., 1899), 30.

77. Mary Fenollosa, *Blossoms from a Japanese Garden: A Book of Child-Verses* (New York: Frederick A. Stokes Co., 1913), 3.

78. Murakata, *The Ernest F. Fenollosa Papers*, 233.

79. Sidney McCall (Mary Fenollosa), *The Breath of the Gods* (Boston: Little, Brown, and Co., 1905), 301–310.

80. Ibid., 295. See below on the prevalence of this form of East-West musical encounter in late nineteenth-century concerts in Japan.

81. Hearn had begun his collection of Japanese stories published the previous year with a supernatural tale of a *biwa* player who was summoned to perform for the spirits of the departed Heiké clan. See Hearn, "The Story of Mimi-Nashi-Hoichi," in *Kwaidan* (1904).

82. Mary McNeil Fenollosa, *The Dragon Painter*, ill. Gertrude McDaniel (Boston: Little, Brown, and Co., 1906), 54. Mary Fenollosa's *The Dragon Painter* was made into a film starring Sessue Hayakawa in 1919. More recently, the Japanese American jazz bassist, *sheng* and *sho* player, and composer Mark Izu composed a score for this silent film in 2005, premiering the work in San Francisco with the Japanese *benshi* narrator Midori Sawato.

83. Fenollosa, *Out of the Nest: A Flight of Verses* (Boston: Little, Brown, and Co., 1899), 15.

84. Frank Miller's extensive collection, housed in his Riverside, California, Mission Inn, objectifies the early twentieth-century fascination with East Asian bells.

85. Hearn, *Glimpses of Unfamiliar Japan, Vol. 1* (Boston and New York: Houghton, Mifflin and Co., 1894), 66.

86. Hearn's translation appeared on 3 April 1887 in the *New Orleans Times-Democrat*. On Pierre Loti's descriptions of Japanese music see Frederick H. Martens, "Pierre Loti: A Prose Poet of Music," *Musical Quarterly* 10, no. 1 (January 1924): 51–94. The boom of big Japanese bells became a theme in *fin-de-siècle* literary responses to Japan. In 1889 Rudyard Kipling awoke one morning to a "very deep and entirely strange" sound which he feared was an earthquake but soon learned was the toll of the big bell in Kyoto. He declared that "when you have once caught the noise you will never forget it." Rudyard Kipling, *Kipling's Japan: Collected Writings*, eds. Hugh Cortazzi and George Webb (London and Atlantic Highlands, NJ: The Athlone Press, 1988), 86–87.

87. Mary McNeil Fenollosa, *The Dragon Painter* (Boston: Little, Brown, and Co., 1906), 247–248.

88. See Akiko Murakata, "'Yugiri O Kyaku San (The Guest Who Leaves with the Twilight)': The Fenollosas and Lafcadio Hearn," in *Centennial Essays on Lafcadio Hearn*, ed. Kenji Zenimoto et al. (Matsue, Japan: The Hearn Society, 1996), 191. Also see Benfey, 235.

89. Murakata, 203. Murakata's quotations from Mary Fenollosa's 1898 journal entries indicate that the Fenollosas were rather in awe of Hearn. See Ibid., 192–194; 200.

90. Ernest Francisco Fenollosa, *East and West: The Discovery of America and Other Poems* (Boston: Norwood Press, 1893, reprint 1970 Upper Saddle River, NJ: Literature House), 39.

91. Ibid., 45–48.

92. Akiko Murakata, "Ezra Pound ed. 'Fenollosa on the Noh' as it was: Lecture V. *No*. Washington, 12 March, 1903," 276. On the general modernist fascination with both ancient Greek and Japanese theater, see my *Revealing Masks: Exotic Influences and Ritualized Performance in Modernist Music Theater* (Berkeley: University of California Press, 2001).

93. The literature on turn-of-the-century American *japonisme* is vast. See, for example, Sally Mills, *Japanese Influences in American Art: 1853–1900* (Williamstown, MA: Sterling and Francine Clark Art Institute, 1981); Wendy Kaplan, *"The Art That Is Life": The Arts and Crafts Movement in America, 1875–1920* (Boston: Little, Brown and Co., 1987); William Hosley, *The Japan Idea: Art and Life in Victorian America* (Hartford, CT: Wadsworth Atheneum, 1990); Julia Meech and Gabriel P. Weisberg, *Japonisme Comes to America: The Japanese Impact on the Graphic Arts 1876–1925* (New York: Harry N. Abrams, 1990); Kendall H. Brown, *Japanese-Style Gardens of the Pacific West Coast* (New York: Rizzoli, 1999); and Marc Treib, "Mirror for the Modern: Japan, California, Architecture, Landscape," in Paolo Amalfitano and Loretta Innocenti, eds., *L'Oriente: Storia di una figura nelle arti occidentali (1700–2000)*, vol. 2 (Rome: Bulzoni Editore, 2007), 329–341.

94. Aya Mihara, "Was It Torture or Tune?: First Japanese Music in the Western Theatre," in *Popular Music: Intercultural Interpretations*, ed. Tōru Mitsui (Kanazawa, Japan: Graduate Program in Music, Kanazawa University, 1998), 134–142.

95. Clara Louise Kellogg, "Some Japanese Melodies," *Scribner's Monthly* 14, no. 4 (August 1877): 504–506.

96. See Lois Foster Rodecape, "Tom Maguire, Napoleon of the Stage," *California Historical Society Quarterly* 21, no. 2 (June 1942): 154–156.

97. "Thompson Course Entertainment," *The Williams Weekly* 11 (18 March 1897): 6–7. I thank my colleague Douglas B. Moore for bringing this to my attention.

98. See Ruth Everett, "The Best Tricks of Famous Magicians," *Cosmopolitan* 34, no. 2 (December 1902): 147.

99. This 1867 advertisement from the *Worcester Evening Gazette* is held at the American Antiquarian Society.

100. On Sadayakko, see Yoko Chiba, "Sada Yacco and Kawakami: Performers of *Japonisme*," *Modern Drama* 35, no. 1 (1992): 35–53; Lesley Downer, *Madame Sadayakko: The Geisha Who Bewitched the West* (New York: Gotham Books, 2003); and Joseph L. Anderson, *Enter a Samurai: Kawakami Otojirō and Japanese Theatre in the West* (Tucson, AZ: Wheatmark 2011).

101. Arthur Groos, "Cio-Cio-San and Sadayakko: Japanese Music-Theater in *Madama Butterfly*," *Monumenta Nipponica* 54, no. 1 (spring 1999): 41–73.

102. J. Scott Miller, "Dispossessed Melodies: Recordings of the Kawakami Theater Troupe," *Monumenta Nipponica* 53, no. 2 (summer 1998): 225.

103. Ingrid Fritsch, "Some Reflections on the Early Wax Cylinder Recordings of Japanese Music in the Berlin Phonogramm Archive (Germany)," in Musicological Society of Japan, ed., *Musicology and Globalization: Proceedings of the International Congress in Shizuoka 2002* (Tokyo: Musicological Society of Japan, 2004), 224–225.

104. See "Japanese Plays in Boston," *New York Times*, 6 December 1899, 8.

105. See Neil Harris, "All the World a Melting Pot? Japan at American Fairs, 1876–1904," in *Mutual Images: Essays in American-Japanese Relations*, ed. Akira Iriye (Cambridge, MA: Harvard University Press, 1975), 24–54.

106. For this and other information on the Centennial Fair, see the two-volume scrapbook held at the Free Library in Philadelphia. Also see Frank H. Norton, ed., *A Facsimile of Frank Leslie's Illustrated Historical Register of the Centennial Exposition, 1876* (New York: Paddington Press, 1974); and J. S. Ingram, *Centennial Exposition Described and Illustrated, Being a Concise and Graphic Description of this Grand Enterprise Commemorative of the First Centenary of American Independence* (Philadelphia: Hubbard Bros., 1876).

107. Sondra Wieland Howe, *Luther Whiting Mason: International Music Educator* (Warren, MI: Harmonie Park Press, 1997), 55.

108. See the program for the 10 May 1876 Opening Exercises, found in the scrapbook for the Centennial Fair held at the Free Library, Philadelphia.

109. I consulted collections held at the University of Chicago Libraries and at the Chicago Public Library. On the Columbian Exposition, see Rossiter Johnson, ed., *A History of the World's Columbian Exposition*, vol. 1 (New York: D. Appleton and Co., 1897). This source reported that "Ears trained to enjoy the music of the Occident were startled at the weird sounds that greeted them in the Java and Chinese theaters and from Dahomey, Soudanese, and Samoan performers. The semibarbaric minor strains of Moorish and Arabic origin, whose mournful cadences were marked by the resounding feet of dancing girls upon the stages of the Algerian, Cairene, Morrish, Persian, and Turkish theaters, remain in many memories as the typical music of the Midway" (p. 473). Also see Carolyn Schiller Johnson, "Performing Ethnicity: Performance Events in Chicago 1893–1996" (PhD diss., University of Chicago, 1998). On Japan at the fair, see *Catalogue of Objects Exhibited at the World's Columbian Exposition Chicago, USA 1893, by the Department of Education, Tokyo, Japan* (Tokyo: The Department of Education, 1893); and Kakuzo Okakura, *The Ho-o-den (Phoenix Hall): An Illustrated Description of the Buildings Erected by the Japanese Government at the World's Columbian Exposition, Jackson Park, Chicago* (Tokyo: K. Ogawa, 1893). Okakura explained that the name of this famous structure (the Ho-o-den) referred to the mythical bird whose "song resembles the sound of the *Sho* (a Chinese musical instrument), the female accompanying the male, when he sings, in notes of marvelous purity" (9–10). This source includes a photograph of the interior revealing a *koto* leaning against a wall and a *biwa* on a table (15). On the influence of the Ho-o-den pavilion on Frank Lloyd Wright, see Nute, 48–68. On the broader encounter with Asian culture at the fair, see Judith Snodgrass, *Presenting Japanese Buddhism to the West: Orientalism, Occidentalism, and the Columbian Exposition* (Chapel Hill: University of North Carolina Press, 2003).

110. See P. B. Wight, "Japanese Architecture at Chicago," *The Inland Architect and News Record* (December 1892), reproduced as Appendix D in Nute, 195.

111. See Isaiah West Taber, *The Monarch Souvenir of Sunset City and Sunset Scenes; Being Views of California Midwinter Fair and Famous Scenes in the Golden State* (San Francisco: H. S. Crocker Company, 1894), held at the San Francisco Public Library History Center.

112. On the St. Louis fair, see Clay Lancaster, *The Japanese Influence in America* (New York: Abbeville Press, 1983. orig publ 1963), 141–142. On Frances Densmore's research on Filipino music at the St. Louis World's Fair, see Krystyn R. Moon, "The Quest for Music's Origin at the St. Louis World's Fair: Frances Densmore and the Racialization of Music," *American Music* 28, no. 2 (summer 2010): 191–210.

113. See typed sheets labeled "Wilson and July 20, 1915," "Japan Artistic and Japan Beautiful at The Panama-Pacific Int. Exp.," in the Panama-Pacific International Exposition folders held at the San Francisco Public Library History Center. In 1900 John Philip Sousa published "Sousa's Sen-Sen March" (Rochester, NY: T. B. Dunn and Co.) with images of Japanese women featured on the cover. On other forms of exotic musical encounter at this exposition, see Amanda Cannata, "Articulating and Contesting Cultural Hierarchies: Guatemalan,

Mexican, and Native American Music at the Panama-Pacific International Exposition (1915)," *Journal of the Society for American Music* 8, no. 1 (2014): 76–100.

114. This biographical information is derived from several sources, but most directly from Philip J. Norvell, "A History and a Catalogue of the Albert Gale Collection of Musical Instruments" (MA thesis, University of Southern California, 1952). Norvell quotes a letter from Albert Gale to him explaining that Gale's interest in "musical instruments and the songs of foreign lands began when I visited the World's Columbian Exposition in Chicago, 1893" (5). The Gales eventually settled in California and donated their instrument collection to the University of Southern California in 1946. On Albert Gale's career and the Gales' lecture recitals, also see Louis J. Alber, "The Gale Costume Lectures: How the Music of Primitive Peoples Is Brought to Lyceum Audience," *The Lyceumite and Talent* (May 1912): 18–21. Alber claimed that "Mr. Gale has discovered the relationship of the American Indians to the Asiatics thru their music" (19).

115. See Albert Gale's brochure advertising "The Gale Costume Lectures: Music and Myth of Old Japan," held in the University of Iowa Libraries Special Collections, Redpath Chautauqua Collection. Gale may well have begun his work as a comparative musicologist somewhat earlier than the famed German scholar Erich M. von Hornbostel.

116. Albert Gale, "Chinese Music and Musical Instruments," *The Pacific Monthly* 12 (1904): 161. Gale also claimed that this music boasted "[r]hythmic effects which would put to shame our most vaunted rag-times" (168).

117. A reference to Albert Gale's lectures on Japanese music appears in a July 1907 edition of the Albion, Michigan, *Morning Star*, quoted in the 1 July 2007 edition under "Albion 100 Years Ago—July 1907," 14. Gale likely began his costumed lectures on Japanese music in 1906.

118. See Norvell, 6. For a list of the Japanese instruments Gale collected, see 114.

119. All quotations here describing this production are from Albert Gale's brochure, "The Gale Costume Lectures: Music and Myth of Old Japan," held in the University of Iowa Libraries Special Collections, Redpath Chautauqua Collection.

120. Norvell, p. 6.

121. Archibald Clavering Gunter, *My Japanese Prince* (New York: Home Publishing Co., 1904), 52–53. This novel exemplifies the generally positive views and American support of Japan during the Russo-Japanese War. A white American woman travels to Japan after having been saved by a Japanese gentleman from a car wreck back in the United States. Attending a *kabuki* play, she is attracted to the main actor because he looks like the Japanese man who had rescued her. But then "his voice smote my ear. But, oh, that was not the same. It was at times a squeaking, creaking, high falsetto, then a portentious basso, but always in that horrible, peculiar rasping monotone of a Japanese actor when he thinks he has a great opportunity. It made me squirm upon my cushions" (22). She marries her Japanese gentleman and they agree he will act as an American husband and she as an American wife. In the history of American representations of Japan, it is very rare to encounter a depiction of a Japanese male as a suitable lover for a white American woman.

122. Mable Hyde, ill. by Helen Hyde, *Japanese Jingles: As Set Forth by the Chinks* (Tokyo: Methodist Publishing House, 1907).

123. See *"A Pleasing Novelty": Bunkio Matsuki and the Japan Craze in Victorian Salem*, 23–24, 28–29. Salem's popular interest in all things Japanese was particularly evident at the turn of the century. Matsuki quite successfully sold Japanese wares through a department store in Salem starting in 1890 and *The Mikado* had been performed in that city in 1885 (90). Morse had served as Matsuki's official guardian when Matsuki arrived in Salem in 1888 and enrolled in Salem High School.

124. "Notes," *Bulletin of the Art Institute of Chicago* 4, no. 4 (April 1911): 65. My research on this event was carried out at the Art Institute of Chicago Archives. A copy of the program for

this festival is held in the Secretary Scrapbooks file at the Art Institute of Chicago Archives. The announcement for this event states, "Please come in costume, Japanese preferred." The Art Institute featured multiple Japanese-themed events and lectures in the late nineteenth and early twentieth centuries. Fenollosa had given multiple lectures on Japanese art at the Art Institute in 1890 and 1894.

125. I found this announcement in the *Chicago Tribune*, 12 February 1911, Art Institute of Chicago Ryerson Library, clippings microfilm.

126. *Chicago Tribune*, 20 February 1911, Art Institute Ryerson Library, clippings microfilm. The program lists the participants in the Japanese wedding, with Japanese names appearing for the bride and groom only. Festivities also included Japanese fencing, a tea room, and a Chinese Opium Den.

127. See Richard McCandless Gipson, *The Life of Emma Thursby, 1845–1931* (New York: New-York Historical Society, 1940), 378–379.

128. I encountered information about and an image of this event in a display case at the Japan Society in New York City.

129. Her travel scrapbooks and correspondence held at the Isabella Stewart Gardner Museum Archives indicate that she heard a good deal of musical and theatrical performances in Japan and even owned a *sho* in her collection. (Unless otherwise specified, all correspondence to and from Gardner quoted here is held in the museum archives.) On Gardner's time in Japan, see Victoria Weston, *East Meets West: Isabella Stewart Gardner and Okakura Kakuzo* (Boston: Isabella Stewart Gardner Museum, 1992).

130. Gardner to Bernard Berenson, 3 May 1905, in a folder on the Japanese Bazaar, 1905, Isabella Stewart Gardner Museum. Also see *The Letters of Bernard Berenson and Isabella Stewart Gardner, 1887–1924, with Correspondence by Mary Berenson*, ed. and annotated by Rollin Van N. Hadley (Boston: Northeastern University Press, 1987), 364.

131. See "A Bit Out of Japan," *Boston Globe*, 2 May 1905, 7. Also see "Mrs. Gardner's Real Japan: Music Room at Fenway Court Transformed for a Charity," *New York Times*, 2 May 1905, 11. Apparently, a "Japanese play" by Joseph Lindon Smith was performed at repeated intervals.

132. On Gardner's extensive interest in music see, for example, Ralph P. Locke, "Living with Music: Isabella Stewart Gardner," in Locke and Cyrilla Barr, eds. *Cultivating Music in America: Women Patrons and Activists since 1860* (Berkeley: University of California Press, 1997), 90–121.

133. On the relationship between Okakura and Gardner, see Weston, *East Meets West* and Benfey, *The Great Wave*, 95–98.

134. See letters from K. Tomita to Gardner on 4 February 1912 and 25 March 1912 thanking her for these performances. Morris Carter has suggested that Gardner only wished to attend public events with Japanese men when they were in native dress. See Morris Carter, *Isabella Stewart Gardner and Fenway Court* (Boston and New York: Houghton Mifflin Co., 1925), 89.

135. J. W. Spalding, *Japan and around the World: An Account of Three Visits to the Japanese Empire* (New York: Redfield, 1855), 156. Bayard Taylor reported that Perry's band had played "Hail Columbia" and "Yankee Doodle" as the Americans returned to their ships in 1853 after Perry's initial landing in Japan. Taylor wrote that the band played "with more spirit than ever before, and few of those present, I venture to say, ever heard our national airs with more pride and pleasure." See Bayard Taylor, *A Visit to India, China, and Japan in the Year 1853* (New York: G. P. Putnam's Sons, 1891, first pub. 1855), 432.

136. See Richie, *The Honorable Visitors*, 49.

137. On Mason's work and American efforts at reforming musical education in Japan, see Sondra Wieland Howe, "Luther Whiting Mason: Contributions to Music Education in

Nineteenth Century America and Japan" (PhD diss., University of Minnesota, 1988); *Luther Whiting Mason: International Music Educator* (Warren, MI: Harmonie Park Press, 1997); and "Women Music Educators in Japan during the Meiji Period," *Bulletin of the Council for Research in Music Education* 119 (winter 1993–1994): 101–109. On European musical influence in Meiji Japan more generally, see Eta Harich-Schneider, *A History of Japanese Music* (London: Oxford University Press, 1973), 533–549; and Ury Eppstein, *The Beginnings of Western Music in Meiji Era Japan* (Lewiston, NY: Edwin Mellen Press, 1994). Also see Elizabeth May, *The Influence of the Meiji Period on Japanese Children's Music* (Berkeley: University of California Press, 1963).

138. Mason, "Music Teaching in Japan." *Musical Courier* 1, no. 20 (18 June 1880): 281. Cited in: Howe, *Luther Whiting Mason: International Music Educator*, 90.

139. See Donald P. Berger, "Isawa Shuji and Luther Whiting Mason: Pioneers of Music Education in Japan," *Music Educators Journal* 74, no. 2 (October 1987): 31–36.

140. Isawa's desire to merge Japanese and Western music prefigured the aims of such later figures as Michio Miyagi in Japan and Henry Cowell in the United States. See Howe, *Luther Whiting Mason*, 73, 96–98.

141. See "Music in Japan," *Dwight's Journal of Music* 40 (14 August 1880), ed. John S. Dwight (Boston: Houghton, Mifflin and Co, 1880; reprinted 1967 Arno Press), 135.

142. Ibid.

143. Mason, "Music in the Schools of Japan," *The Seventh Annual Meeting of the Music Teachers' National Association, held at Providence, RI, July 4th, 5th, and 6th, 1883* (New York: American Art Journal, n.d.): 49–50. Cited in Howe, *Luther Whiting Mason*, 91.

144. On House's work in Japan, see James L. Huffman, *A Yankee in Meiji Japan: The Crusading Journalist Edward H. House* (Lanham, MD: Rowan and Littlefield Publishers, 2003).

145. Edward H. House, "A Japanese Doctor and His Works," *Atlantic Monthly* (December 1871), cited in Huffman, *A Yankee in Meiji Japan*, 69.

146. Edward H. House, *Japanese Episodes* (Boston: James R. Osgood and Co., 1881), 215; 235.

147. "'The Pirates of Penzance' at the Public Hall," *Japan Weekly Mail*, 19 June 1886, 597; and *Japan Weekly Mail* (6 November 1886): 453.

148. Whitney, *Clara's Diary*, 236.

149. See "Concert at the Rokumeikan," *Japan Weekly Mail*, 5 May 1888, 421. The concert apparently also included "Shakkyo" performed on *koto, shamisen, kokyu*, and *shakuhachi*; songs by Schubert; and the Marine Band playing a fantasia from *Carmen*.

150. *Japan Weekly Mail*, 9 February 1889, 122–123.

151. *Japan Weekly Mail*, 13 July 1889,: 29.

152. Ibid.

153. Similarly, the ability of the Chinese in the nineteenth century to learn the music of European missionaries suggested to the West that the Chinese were not incapable of achieving civilization, according to Krystyn R. Moon. See Moon, *Yellowface: Creating the Chinese in American Popular Music and Performance, 1850s–1920s* (New Brunswick, NJ: Rutgers University Press, 2005), 17. On Western perceptions of Chinese music in the nineteenth century, see Moon, 12–19.

154. Morse, vol. 1, 295–296.

155. Ibid., 402

156. Morse, vol. 2, 225.

157. Letter of 2 July 1882 from Mason to Morse, held at the Peabody-Essex Phillips Library. Mason thanked Morse for attending his exhibition and notes that anything positive Morse could say about his work would help him. Mason states: "What I claim to have done is this—I have succeeded in creating an interest in foreign music—in many ways—and that by honest means." Bigelow also attended this musical exhibition.

158. Mabel Loomis Todd, *Corona and Coronet: Being a Narrative of the Amherst Eclipse Expedition to Japan, in Mr. James's Schooner-Yacht Coronet, to Observe the Sun's Total Obscuration 9th August 1896* (Boston and New York: Houghton, Mifflin and Co., 1898), 204.

159. Long, *Miss Cherry-Blossom of Tokyo* (1895), 53. The Japanese heroine's feelings are hurt again in response to her music making: "But one evening, as she sat tinkling her koto in the little upper room of the sick man, her spirits revolted, and she broke into one of the wild unmusical songs of Old Japan. They were very good friends now, and the invalid made a whimsical protest and a wry face; with a little laugh she stopped" (260). In the end, they marry and set sail for the United States, prefiguring later Cold War–era works of cross-cultural romance. Long's own participation in works of exotic musical representation include his text for Wassili Leps's 1905 cantata for women's chorus, *Yo-Nennen: A Japanese Cicada Drama Set to Music in the Form of a Cantata.*

160. Hearn, *Gleanings*, 53–54.

Chapter 2

1. Roosevelt's remark has been widely quoted, including in Walter LaFeber, *The Clash: A History of US-Japan Relations* (New York: W. W. Norton, 1997), 82.

2. One particularly helpful study of this fraught period is Roger Daniels, *The Politics of Prejudice: The Anti-Japanese Movement in California and the Struggle for Japanese Exclusion* (Berkeley: University of California Press, 1962). Also see Charles E. Neu, *An Uncertain Friendship: Theodore Roosevelt and Japan, 1906–1909* (Cambridge, MA: Harvard University Press, 1967); and Neu, *The Troubled Encounter: The United States and Japan* (New York: John Wiley and Sons, 1975). On Roosevelt's role in Japan-US relations, also see Thomas A. Bailey, *Theodore Roosevelt and the Japanese-American Crises* (Stanford, CA: Stanford University Press, 1934); and Raymond A. Esthus, *Theodore Roosevelt and Japan* (Seattle: University of Washington Press, 1966).

3. I compiled this collection of sheet music primarily between 1998 and 2003 through extensive keyword searching in archives across the United States and have supplemented this collection since 2003 through Internet searches and by riffling through song sheet boxes at used bookstores in the Northeast. My hope is that by canvassing many different collections and types of collections throughout the country I have, to some extent, controlled for collection idiosyncracies and have somewhat minimized the randomness inherent in any such archival retrieval. Most of these pieces were found in the following collections and archives: the Duke University Collection (online); the DeVincent Collection at the Smithsonian American History Museum; the Library of Congress; the Free Library of Philadelphia; the John Hay Library at Brown University; the Lester Levy Collection at Johns Hopkins University (online); the private collection of Sandra Marrone in Cinnaminson, New Jersey; the New York Public Library for the Performing Arts; the Paul Whiteman Collection, Williams College; the American Antiquarian Society, Worcester, Massachusetts; the Harvard University Theatre Collection; the Dartmouth College Library Special Collections; the Bagaduce Music Lending Library, Blue Hill, Maine; the Balaban and Katz Collection at the Chicago Public Library; the Driscoll Collection at the Newberry Library, Chicago; the Paramount Theater Collection in Oakland, California; the San Francisco Public Library; and the University of California–Los Angeles Music Library Special Collections.

4. For more general studies covering this period in American popular song, see: Charles Hamm, *Yesterdays: Popular Song in America* (New York: W. W. Norton, 1979); Nicholas Tawa, *A Sound of Strangers: Musical Culture, Acculturation, and the Post–Civil War Ethnic American* (Metuchen, NJ: Scarecrow Press, 1982); David A. Jasen, *Tin Pan Alley: The Composers, the*

Songs, the Performers, and Their Times (New York: Donald I. Fine, 1988); Tawa, *The Way to Tin Pan Alley: American Popular Song, 1866–1910* (New York: Schirmer Books, 1990); Jon W. Finson, *The Voices That Are Gone: Themes in Nineteenth-century American Popular Song* (New York: Oxford University Press, 1994); and Hamm, *Irving Berlin: Songs from the Melting Pot: The Formative Years, 1907–1914* (New York: Oxford University Press, 1997).

5. A pioneering study of representations of Asian Americans in the Tin Pan Alley era is found in Judy Tsou, "Gendering Race: Stereotypes of Chinese Americans in Popular Sheet Music," *repercussions* 6 (fall 1997): 25–62. For a more focused study centering on one of the most prominent examples of such representation see Charles Hiroshi Garrett, "Chinatown, Whose Chinatown? Defining America's Borders with Musical Orientalism," *Journal of the American Musicological Society* 57, no. 1 (spring 2004): 119–173. Also see Garrett's *Struggling to Define a Nation: American Music and the Twentieth Century* (Berkeley: University of California Press, 2008), which includes a chapter on Tin Pan Alley representations of Hawai'i. The most comprehensive (indeed, monumental) study to date is: Robert Charles Lancefield, "Hearing Orientality in (White) America, 1900–1930" (PhD diss., Wesleyan University, 2004). Lancefield's chapter 8 is particularly relevant here. Also see Robert G. Lee, *Orientals: Asian Americans in Popular Culture* (Philadelphia: Temple University Press, 1999) and Krystyn R. Moon, *Yellowface: Creating the Chinese in American Popular Music and Performance, 1850s–1920s* (New Brunswick, NJ: Rutgers University Press, 2005).

6. My study of recorded performances of songs in my collection of sheet music was carried out primarily at the New York Public Library for the Performing Arts, at the Library of Congress, in the Paul Whiteman Collection at Williams College, and (more recently) through YouTube.

7. Lancefield, 3.

8. On the exoticizing of "Chop Sticks" also see Moon, *Yellowface*, 100, 105.

9. For an impressive resource for information on the Japanese doll and its place in European and American culture, see Judy Shoaf, "The Japanese Doll on the Western Toyshelf," http://users.clas.ufl.edu/jshoaf/jdolls/jdollwestern/index.html.

10. An advertisement for *Tycoon; or Young America in Japan* appeared in the *New York Times* on 4 July 1860. Baker is credited with composing much of the music for the 1866 *The Black Crook*, often cited as the first American musical.

11. See Quelqu'un [William Winter], "Dramatic Feuilleton," *New York Saturday Press*, 30 June 1860, 3, 26, and the same column in the 7 July and 14 July editions of this newspaper.

12. See *New York Times*, 21 June 1860, 5.

13. The Consulate General of Japan in New York sponsored a performance of this piece in 2010 to celebrate the 150th anniversary of the delegation's visit.

14. Romance between a Chinese man and a white woman is equally rare in Tin Pan Alley songs. See Tsou, "Gendering Race," 35.

15. Apparently, a scandal developed concerning Tommy's involvement with a chambermaid during his visit ("The Scandal of 'Tommy,'" *New York Times*, 22 June 1860). He allegedly received numerous love letters from American women ("Japanese Tommy's Body-Guard—Proposed Honors to the Naval Officers," *New York Times*, 29 June 1860, 2), and he corresponded with the American women he left behind after returning to Japan (see "The Japanese Embassy," *New York Times*, 20 August 1860, 1). He was reported to be missing one American sweetheart even seven years later ("Japan: Opening of New Ports—Ratification of the Treaty with the United States—Exchange of Presents," *New York Times*, 9 July 1867, 2). Tommy's notoriety resulted in P. T. Barnum's New York museum featuring a wax figure of the young Japanese man. See Christine M. E. Guth, *Longfellow's Tattoos: Tourism, Collecting, and Japan* (Seattle: University of Washington Press, 2004), 13.

16. This performer appears to have been Thomas Dilwerd, who late in life sued a restaurant in Brooklyn for refusing to serve him (see *New York Times*, 4 March 1882, 8) and who died

in 1887 and was referred to in his obituary as a colored midget and "popular songster and contortionist" (see "'Japanese' Tommy's Funeral," *New York Times*, 13 July 1887, 8). On this performer, also see Josephine Lee, *The Japan of Pure Invention: Gilbert and Sullivan's The Mikado* (Minneapolis: University of Minnesota Press, 2010), 94–97. A selection of songs that he apparently performed was published in 1871 as *Japanese Tommy's Songster: Containing a Selection of the Most Popular Melodies of the Day*. This collection includes no Japanese references in any lyrics, but instead features a couple of songs in the voice of an Irish persona. Finally, the name "Japanese Tommy" appears to have been used by at least one other performer in this period. A French boy from Lewiston, Maine, had run away with the circus and performed in New Orleans as "Japanese Tommy." See "One Japanese Tommy Returns Home," *New York Times*, 21 February 1881, 4.

17. See Robert C. Toll, *Blacking Up: The Minstrel Show in Nineteenth-century America* (New York: Oxford University Press, 1974), 171.

18. Ibid., 169–171.

19. Lancefield, 410. On Japanese-themed plays and drills for children, see chapter 6 in Lancefield. For examples of such plays designed for amateur adult performance, see Lancefield's chapter 7.

20. See Mari Yoshihara, *Embracing the East: White Women and American Orientalism* (New York: Oxford University Press, 2003), 6–8, and see chapters 1 and 3.

21. See Michael Beckerman, "The Sword on the Wall: Japanese Elements and Their Significance in *The Mikado*," *Musical Quarterly* 73 (1989): 304, note 5. Gerald Bordman and Richard Norton note that American productions of *The Mikado* had two brief runs in July and August 1860 before the D'Oyly Carte production arrived for a run of 250 performances and that a parody of the operetta, entitled *Mick-ah-do*, sprang up by November. See Gerald Bordman and Richard Norton, *American Musical Theatre: A Chronicle*, 4th ed. (New York: Oxford University Press, 2010), 91–93. John Dizikes relates that a minstrel show premiered in 1886 entitled *The Micky-Doo*. See Dizikes, *Opera in America: A Cultural History* (New Haven, CT: Yale University Press, 1993), 205. For a recent and thorough study of the relationship between *The Mikado* and the consumerism of *japonisme*, along with a critical exploration of the work's production history in the United States and Japan, see Josephine Lee, *The Japan of Pure Invention*. On controversies provoked by twenty-first century productions of this operetta in the United States, see Michael Cooper, "Reviving 'The Mikado' in a Balancing Act of Taste," *New York Times*, 26 December 2016, C1.

22. See *The Story of The Mikado Told by Sir W. S. Gilbert* (London: Daniel O'Connor, 1921), 1–2. Beckerman (317) presents a shorter segment of this statement.

23. Beckerman, 307–314. Also see Paul Seeley, "The Japanese March in *The Mikado*," *Musical Times* 126 (August 1985): 454–456. For a broader discussion of claims to exotic authenticity in *The Mikado*, see Lee, *The Japan of Pure Invention*, 29–30.

24. Sidney Jones also composed *San Toy* 1899 and *See-see* 1906 with China as the exotic locale. William A. Everett offers an interpretation of *The Geisha* in light of contemporary British political perceptions of Japan and China in "Imagining the Identities of East Asia in 1890s British Musical Theatre: The Case of Sidney Jones's *The Geisha* (1896)," in *Franjo Ksaver Kuhač (1834–1911): Musical Historiography and Identity*, ed. Vjera Katalinić and Stanislav Tuksar (Zagreb: Croatian Musicological Society, 2013), 301–310.

25. Gavin Jones, *Strange Talk: The Politics of Dialect Literature in Gilded Age America* (Berkeley: University of California Press, 1999), 173–174. A program from an October 1896 Broadway performance of *The Geezer* is held in the Dartmouth College Library, Special Collections.

26. In turn, *The Darling of the Gods* inspired multiple songs and the name of the play's heroine, Yo San, appears in numerous subsequent songs. For example, the 1903 "Yo-San" was dedicated

to Blanche Bates, the star in Belasco's production, and it claimed to present the "Story of David Belasco's Great Drama Told in Song."

27. The script indicates that scenery was created by I. Hasegawa and K. Takahashi and one cue reads: "All sorts of Japanese instruments are heard at once" (22). Henry Pincus and Melvin G. Winstock, *Otoyo: A Comic Opera in Two Acts* (1903), held at the Library of Congress.

28. See the *New York Times*, 5 December 1905. The 1906 *Princess Chrysanthemum*, a "Japanese Operetta" for amateur performance by C. King Proctor, includes multiple echoes of *The Mikado* in its plot, characters, and music, but with the addition of some rather strange fantastical elements.

29. Jones, *Strange Talk*, chapter 1.

30. Ibid., 175.

31. David Ewen, among others, repeatedly claimed in print that Spenser had followed Gilbert and Sullivan. See Ewen, *Complete Book of the American Musical Theater* (New York: Henry Holt and Co., 1958), xxiv. Bordman and Norton discuss how *The Little Tycoon* was criticized as an imitation of *The Mikado* and how Spenser showed that he had copyrighted it in 1882. See Bordman and Norton, 95–96. Spenser also wrote *Rosalie, or the Japanese Fairies* (1906), "an original Japanese-Russian Romantic Opera" set during the Russo-Japanese War.

32. In the number "Yes, We've All Seen Sham," for example, young American female characters in Japanese costume are marked musically by striking octave leaps, distinctive rhythmic patterns of eighth notes followed by four sixteenth notes, and their utterance of nonsense syllables.

33. For further discussion of the visual representation of Asians and Asian Americans in sheet music covers, see Lancefield, "Hearing Orientality," 611–636. Lancefield also curated an extensive exhibit on this subject: "Performing Images, Embodying Race: The Orientalized Body in Early 20th-Century US Performance and Visual Culture," Davison Art Center, Wesleyan University, winter 2003–2004.

34. Also see Garrett, "Chinatown, Whose Chinatown?," 138–144. For examples of early postcards depicting Japan, see Christraud M. Geary and Virginia-Lee Webb, eds., *Delivering Views: Distant Cultures in Early Postcards* (Washington, DC: Smithsonian Institution Press, 1998). On the subject of music and musical instruments in Japanese art, see the exhibition catalog *The Ear Catches the Eye: Music in Japanese Prints* (Leiden: Hotei Publishing, 2000).

35. A copy of the Marie Hall-Brimacombe Co. promotional brochure is held in the Redpath Chautauqua Collection, University of Iowa Libraries, Special Collections Department. The cover of the 1925 song "Rose of Japan" provides but one further example of the numerous images of white American women in Japanese costume that graced sheet music covers in this period and suggests how some performers of these songs appeared on stage. On this cover, the performer holds a version of the *shamisen* and wears a rather wistful facial expression.

36. On the lyrics of such songs, also see Lancefield, 637–702.

37. A copy of the program from the week of 19 June 1905 for performances of *Fantana* at the Lyric Theatre is held at the Dartmouth College Library, Special Collections. A copy of the full vocal score—with book by Robert B. Smith and Sam S. Shubert, lyrics by Robert B. Smith, and music by Raymond Hubbell, published by M. Witmark and Sons in 1904 as performed by the Jefferson De Angelis Opera Co.—is held at Brown University. In this operetta, Commodore Everett takes his daughter Fantana to Japan to save her from marriage with an Englishman. Burnside served as the director and Douglas Fairbanks appeared in the show which had nearly three hundred performances. A 15 January 1905 review in the *New York Times* (9, col. 4) stated that the "authors have taken the liberty of calling the piece a Japanese-American musical comedy, but all save the least sophisticated of us learned long ago that in this sort of thing one name is about as good as another and equally descriptive."

38. This line appears in the 1903 song "My Lady from Japan" from *The Good Old Summer Time*.

39. In a 1935 cartoon, *A Language All My Own*, Betty Boop sings in Japanese in her own peculiar vocal timbre, transforming linguistically as she changes her costume. Prefiguring numerous later Hollywood films depicting arrival by plane in Japan, she hears musical *japonisme* before spying the exotic country from above.

40. Krystyn R. Moon's suggestion that the absence of exotic musical markers in nineteenth-century songs on Chinese subjects indicates the Chinese were not represented (or conceived of) as utterly different and exotic seems unjustified to me, particularly in light of the contemporaneous pieces representing the Japanese. (See Moon, *Yellowface*, 11–12). Rather, it appears that American composers of popular music in this period created works of exotic representation often without specific musical stereotypes, just as had been the case in, for example, the Baroque period. Ralph P. Locke has argued that the absence of such musical signals does not imply an absence of exotic representation. See Locke, *Musical Exoticism: Images and Reflections* (Cambridge, UK: Cambridge University Press, 2009).

41. Edgar W. Pope, "Songs of the Empire: Continental Asia in Japanese Wartime Popular Music" (PhD diss., University of Washington, 2003), 227–228.

42. Martin Nilsson finds traces of this standard gesture in pieces referring to the Chinese in multiple examples in the late nineteenth century, with an 1847 piece suggesting an early prototype. His examples suggest that variants of the gesture were established as Chinese musical markers by 1900 and that these variants continued to evolve. Nilsson points to pre-1970s exact occurrences of the "standard" motive only in a few 1930s cartoons and in a televised lecture by Leonard Bernstein in 1957 in which Bernstein refers to it as an example of "old Chinese music." Like Nilsson, I have been surprised by the scarcity of exact statements of this motto before the later twentieth century. (I also agree with his judgement that the four sixteenth, two eighth note gesture heard at the opening of the 1860 "Tommy Polka" does not represent an example of this stereotype.) For brief discussion and numerous examples of this musical sign, see Nilsson's website http://chinoiserie.atspace.com/. I thank Ralph Locke for bringing this website to my attention. On this stereotypical rhythm also see Lancefield, 730ff.

43. The composer of this number, Theodore Morse, also wrote the 1902 "Ko Ko" as well as two other songs in the collection. A specialization in "Oriental" numbers is evident in the songlists of several other composers in this period.

44. In his study of the musical representation of Native Americans, Michael V. Pisani states that the use of parallel fourths and fifths was not common in early twentieth century music, that the first appearance occurs in Indianist works published by Arthur Farwell between 1901 and 1911, and that parallel fourths begin to appear in songs representing Asians between 1903 and 1909. See Pisani, *Imagining Native America in Music* (New Haven, CT: Yale University Press, 2005), 228–229.

45. See George Yoshida, *Reminiscing in Swingtime: Japanese Americans in American Popular Music: 1925-1960* (San Francisco: National Japanese American Historical Society, 1997), 30–31.

46. Judy Tsou has also noted the blurring between Chinese and Japanese representation in Tin Pan Alley. See Tsou, 45–48.

47. This program states: "Particular attention has been paid in the staging of the 'Sho-Gun' to the costumes which will be found typically correct of those worn in Korea. . . . All the properties were made from originals in the famous Korean collection of Marshall Field, of Chicago, and many of the costumes were brought from China, Japan and Korea." Apparently the costumes for this production were somehow simultaneously authentically Korean and imported from China and Japan. This program is held in the Dartmouth College Library, Special Collections.

48. See Bordman and Norton, 238.

49. Tsou, 31.

50. For a historical overview of this important theater, see Milton Epstein, *The New York Hippodrome: A Complete Chronology of Performances, from 1905 to 1939* (New York: Theatre Library Association, 1993).

51. This review appeared in the 5 September 1909 edition of the *New York Times*, 9, col. 5. The reviewer quipped: "How one gets to Tokio by way of New York is one of the mysteries not explained by the authors. However, Tokio, as exhibited at the Hippodrome, is a very delightful place, and the Feast of the Lanterns with which the first piece ends is one of the most beautiful stage pictures of the production."

52. This program is held in the Dartmouth College Library, Special Collections.

53. A deluxe 1909–1910 season souvenir program for the Hippodrome production of *A Trip to Japan* is held at the New York Public Library for the Performing Arts. *A Trip to Japan* appeared on a triple bill with *Inside the Earth*—"A Marvelous Scenic and Dramatic Representation of Antipodean Wonders" featuring a "Tribe of Fighting Maoris" straight from New Zealand—and with *The Ballet of Jewels*. The program promised that "no corner of the earth is so widely distant that it is not illuminated by the searchlight of the Hippodrome management." The program also includes a photograph of white female performers in Japanese costume and an advertisement—featuring a drawing of Japanese women—for Vantines "The Oriental Store" on Broadway which offered "Oriental Things" from Japan, China, Turkey, Persia, and Egypt.

54. This song prefigures later Japanese interest in African American culture, both fictional and actual. An American newsreel from the 1930s reported on a Japanese man who tried to pass as African because blacks were considered cool at that time in Japan. (See *March of Time: The Great Depression, Economy Blues 1935–1936 Part 2: "Tokyo!"*, VHS tape compilation published by Nelson Entertainment, 1988). A Japanese craze for African American culture was most clearly expressed in the 1990s and early 2000s with the teenage fashion known as *ganguro* ("black face"), which was partly inspired by Japanese interest in hip-hop.

55. For a discussion of ragtime in songs representing the Chinese, see Tsou, 38–41.

56. The various productions of "Black" *Mikados* presented in the late nineteenth century and in the first half of the twentieth century have been discussed by numerous scholars. For example, see: Stephen Vallillo, "The Battle of the Black Mikados," *Black American Literature Forum* 16 (winter 1982): 153–157; Shannon Steen, "Racing American Modernity: Black Atlantic Negotiations of Asia and the 'Swing' Mikados," in *Afro-Asian Encounters: Culture, History, Politics*, eds. Heike Raphael-Hernandez and Shannon Steen, 167–187 (New York: New York University Press, 2006); and Josephine Lee, *The Japan of Pure Invention*, chapter 4. Sam Dennison, arguing that nineteenth-century minstrel shows did not present real "black" musical elements, stated that in minstrelsy, "black influence exists in the same proportion that Japanese influence is present in Gilbert and Sullivan's *The Mikado*." See Dennison, *Scandalize My Name: Black Imagery in American Popular Music* (New York: Garland Publishing, 1982), 90.

57. This arrangement of "Japanese Mammy" is held in the Paul Whiteman Collection in the Special Collections of the Williams College Library.

58. I initially presented my research on, and collection of, Tin Pan Alley's "Madame Butterfly" songs at the 2000 meeting of the Society for American Music and, in a paper entitled "Pinkerton's Lament," at the 2003 meeting of the American Musicological Society. Several other scholars have also written on this subject and have investigated some of the same examples. In particular, see chapter 5 in Larry Hamberlin, *Tin Pan Opera: Operatic Novelty Songs in the Ragtime Era* (New York: Oxford University Press, 2011), based on his 2004 PhD dissertation. Robert C. Lancefield in his 2004 dissertation also discusses this topic and categorizes these songs in detail. See Lancefield, "Hearing Orientality," 659ff. Also see Daniel Goldmark, "Creating Desire on Tin Pan Alley," *Musical Quarterly* 90, no. 2 (2007): 197–229.

59. For a sense of the number of female composers active in this period, see the Christopher Reynolds "Women Song Composers" collection at: http://n2t.net/ark:/13030/m5br8stc.

60. For example, the Metropolitan Opera in New York City first produced *Madama Butterfly* in 1907 and continued to stage between six to eight performances each year until 1924–1925, except when they produced only four performances in 1915–1916 and five in 1916–1917 and 1924–1925. For these statistics, see William H. Seltsam, comp., *Metropolitan Opera Annals: A Chronicle of Artists and Performances* (New York: H. W. Wilson Co., 1947).

61. Hamberlin, building on Alec Wilder, discusses the music of this song in his dissertation (263–273).

62. On recordings of "Poor Butterfly" and the use of "Un bel dì" in some songs, also see Lancefield, 788–789, 794–795.

63. Other accounts of this production differ from those I present here. Bordman and Norton state that the song was written for "a then famous Japanese soprano, Tamaki Miura" to sing in the show, but that she fell through and instead a Chinese American vaudevillian introduced the song before being hastily replaced. See Gerald Bordman and Richard Norton, *American Musical Theatre: A Chronicle*, 4th ed. (New York: Oxford University Press, 2010), 366. Thomas S. Hischak refers to Haru Onuki as a Chinese American singer and notes that 2 million copies of the song were sold. See Hischak, *The American Musical Theatre Song Encyclopedia* (Westport, CT: Greenwood Press, 1995), 276. My detailed information on this production is based on materials, including correspondence and timing sheets, found in the R. H. Burnside Papers, New York Public Library Manuscripts Division, box 72.

64. See 2 February and 25 February 1916, from H. B. Marinelli Ltd, New York, to R. H. Burnside, in the Burnside Papers, New York Public Library Manuscripts Division, box 5. On Haru Onuki's career, also see Lancefield 169, 171–174.

65. See "Haru Onuki Sings 'Mme. Butterfly,'" *New York Times*, 19 September 1926, 28. A later article stated that she lived in Long Beach, California, and was also known as Marion Ohnick. See "Singer Sues Cartoonist" for "Breach of Promise," *New York Times*, 25 February 1932, 17.

66. See "Garden Party to Aid Tsuda College Fund," *New York Times*, 29 May 1927. For a report of another such benefit at which Onuki performed, see "Garden Party to Aid a College in Japan," *New York Times*, 5 July 1925, 21.

67. See *Theatre* (October 1916): 246.

68. See *New York Times*, 1 September 1916, 7, col. 3.

69. From F. Sturges Allen to Burnside, 22 December 1916, R. H. Burnside Papers, New York Public Library Manuscripts Division, box 5. Allen appears to have been an author of a thesaurus and an editor of *Webster's New International Dictionary of the English Language*.

70. Also see Hamberlin's dissertation (290–294) on this song.

71. A related song, the 1905 "Little Fighting Soldier Man," was composed and sung by Miss Lillian Coffin and published as a Sunday music supplement in the *New York American and Journal* on 14 May 1905. It was dedicated to David Belasco, and the song's *shamisen*-playing Yo-san suggests that Coffin had Belasco's *Darling of the Gods* in mind when penning the dedication.

72. Charles K. Harris, *How to Write a Popular Song* (New York: Charles K. Harris, 1906), 12.

73. On European reactions to the Russo-Japanese War and the possible impact on works of musical *japonisme* (viz., Puccini's *Madama Butterfly*) see Jann Pasler, "Political Anxieties and Musical Reception: Japonisme and the Problem of Assimilation," in *Madama Butterfly: l'orientalismo di fine secolo, l'approccio pucciniano, la ricezione*, ed. Arthur Groos and Virgilio Bernardoni (Florence: Leo S. Olschki Editore, 2008), 17–53. Also see Domingoes de. Mascarenhas, "Beyond Orientalism: The International Rise of Japan and the Revisions to *Madama Butterfly*," in *Art and Ideology in European Opera*, ed. Rachel Cowgill, David Cooper, and Clive Brown (Woodbridge, UK: Boydell Press, 2010), 281–302. Mascarenhas

suggests that Puccini's revisions to the Pinkerton character were prompted by new negative attitudes toward Japan (285). Mascarenhas also implausibly argues that Butterfly might serve in the opera as "the embodiment of a modernizing Japan stubbornly pursuing parity with the advanced nations of the world" (291–292). I maintain that though Puccini's revisions certainly rehabilitated the Pinkerton character—thereby assuaging any Western male guilt—he did not somehow move this opera "beyond Orientalism."

74. On *The Yellow Peril* also see Lancefield, 501–513.

75. See LaFeber, 90. (Apparently, in 1917 the Japanese ambassador in New York amused white Americans with his singing. See LaFeber, 115.) For an overview of US-Japan relations at this historical moment, also see Jordan Sand, "Gentlemen's Agreement, 1908: Fragments for a Pacific History," *Representations* 107 (summer 2009): 91–127. On the increase in Japanese immigration in the late nineteenth and early twentieth centuries, and the negative response by white Californians, see Ronald Takaki, *Strangers from a Different Shore: A History of Asian Americans* (Boston: Back Bay Books, 1998), 180 and 201.

76. See Eleanor Tupper and George E. McReynolds, *Japan in American Public Opinion* (New York: Macmillan Co., 1937).

77. Thomas L. Riis reports that the West Coast–based performer Billy King once transformed the Bert Williams song "Let It Alone," which had nothing to do with Japan, into an anti-Japanese number. King's lyrics turned the song into "a jingoistic parody aimed at the Japanese at the time of the Russo-Japanese War" eliciting wild enthusiasm from the audience. See Riis, *Just before Jazz: Black Musical Theater in New York, 1890–1915* (Washington, DC: Smithsonian Institution Press, 1989): 115.

78. For example, I have not been able to identify Yama Sen, the credited composer of the 1902 "Japanesa: Characteristic," which features the tune "Miya sama." The sheet music for this piece appears to present an actual *u-kiyoe* print of two Japanese women, one with a *shamisen*, on the cover.

79. In addition to examples composed by Fay Foster and Gertrude Ross discussed later in this chapter and the works of Henry Eichheim discussed in chapter 3, Lafcadio Hearn's writings were employed in such pieces as the 1910 "Heart's Flower-of-Cherry" by Florence Newell Barbour and the 1918 song cycle *Shadowings: Five Poems from the Japanese by Lafcadio Hearn* by Harold Vincent Milligan.

80. William Furst's musical representations of Japan in Hollywood film will be discussed in chapter 4. For further discussion of *The Darling of the Gods* see Lancefield, 336–371. Other staged works in this period also called for Japanese instruments. For example, Sir Edwin Arnold's 1893 *Adzuma, or the Japanese Wife* presented female characters singing and accompanying themselves on *shamisen*.

81. "The New Astoria Hotel," *New York Times*, 16 Oct 1897, 9. Also see William Saunders, "The American Opera: Has It Arrived?," *Music and Letters* 13 (1932): 147–155. Saunders points to *In Old Japan* by Tompson and Lachaume as the first opera by Americans (149).

82. For a discussion of *Namiko-San*, see Edward Ellsworth Hipsher, *American Opera and Its Composers* (Philadelphia: Theodore Presser, 1927), 173–177. The production included a version of Kelley's Chinese-themed "Lady Picking Mulberries" with newly added lyrics.

83. On Leps, see Edward Ellsworth Hipsher, *American Opera and Its Composers* (Philadelphia: Theodore Presser, 1927), 256–260. Leps was a conductor in Philadelphia, especially of opera.

84. The play was published as: J. H. Benrimo and Harrison Rhodes, *The Willow Tree: A Japanese Fantasy in Three Acts* (New York: Samuel French, 1931). The handwritten manuscript of the play and the typescript of *The Willow Tree* production notes are found in the Joseph Henry Benrimo Papers, main branch of the New York Public Library, in folders 1 and 3.

85. Benrimo and Rhodes, 88.

86. Benrimo and Rhodes based their work on two sources of the legend: F. Hadland Davis, *Myths and Legends of Japan* (London: G. G. Harrap and Co, 1912), 177–180; and R. Gordon Smith, *Ancient Tales and Folklore of Japan* (London: A. and C. Black, 1908), 12–18.

87. This review of a 1933 performance that took place in a specially constructed outdoor theater in Woodstock (the Maverick Theatre), appeared in *The Overlook*, vol. 3, 11 (14 July 1933): 1, and is found in folder 1 of the Benrimo Papers, New York Public Library.

88. This January 1917 Memorandum of Agreement is found in the Benrimo Papers, New York Public Library, folder 2. A typescript of a program (found in folder 1) for the 1933 Maverick Theatre production at Woodstock states that the music was composed by Howard Kubic, but it is not clear whether this was newly composed music for this late production.

89. See folder 3 in the Benrimo Papers. Also see the handwritten promptbooks for the New York and London productions held at the New York Public Library for the Performing Arts. Benrimo's interest in featuring exotic instruments onstage is evident in his other theatrical works as well. Folder 1 in the Benrimo papers includes a slip of paper, without date, labeled "British Museum, London: W.C.1." The names of various Chinese instruments are written on this document in both Chinese characters and in English with notes about a few of the instruments. I assume that this document was related to a production of *The Yellow Jacket*.

90. Reviews of Romberg's operetta are found in the Harvard Theatre Collection, clippings files for *Cherry Blossoms* [*Yo-San*]. On this work, see also William A. Everett, *Sigmund Romberg* (New Haven, CT: Yale University Press, 2007), 182–183, 187. A "romantic operetta" by Edward A. Paulton and Bernard Hamblen with the title *Cherry Blossom* appeared in 1926, which perhaps explains why Romberg's work was often referred to as *Yo-San* instead. However, *Yo-San*, "an Oriental Operetta in two acts" with book and music by R. L. Harlow, had already appeared in 1920.

91. The plot is strikingly similar in outline to that found in Saint-Saëns's 1872 operetta *La Princesse jaune*.

92. In the 1933 publication of the play, Benrimo noted that having the same actress perform both roles was effective but proved impractical and, in this "Description of Characters" (90), instructs future directors to cast separate actresses in the two roles. Photographs of the original production clearly reveal that the other Japanese characters appeared in brown face. The production also included a Mr. S. Hatakenaka in the minor role of the Bird Seller.

93. H. De Vere Stacpoole, *The Willow Tree: The Romance of a Japanese Garden* (London: Hodder and Stoughton, 1918).

94. See Nalini Ghuman, *Resonances of the Raj: India in the English Musical Imagination, 1897–1947* (Oxford: Oxford University Press, 2014), 168–216.

95. William Berwald set some of the same poems in his 1928 cantata for women's voices, *From Old Japan*.

96. See *The Biographical Cyclopedia of American Women*, vol. 1, Mabel W. Cameron (comp.) (New York: The Halvord Publishing Company, Inc., 1924), 182.

97. See Stanley May, "How Fay Foster Wrote 'The Americans Come!,'" *Musical America* 29, no. 7 (December 1918): 5–6.

98. On Ross and these pieces also see Lancefield, 606. In addition to art songs, Ross composed a piano trio, choruses, and a ballet. See *Who's Who in Music in California*, ed. Willey Francis Gates (Los Angeles: Colby and Pryibil, 1920), 116.

99. Ross composed other individual songs that were also inspired by her contact with Japanese music in California. She employed the expressive marking "quasi samisen" for the piano accompaniment in both her 1914 "Japanese Lullaby" and 1922 "Sakura Blossom." A note in the score of the first piece reveals that the "first two measures are a native Japanese melody as played on the Samisen."

100. See Nadia Turbide, "Biographical Study of Eva Gauthier (1885–1958) First French-Canadian Singer of the Avant-Garde" (PhD diss., University of Montreal, 1986). The Irish violinist, Maud MacCarthy, had a similar impact on composers in the United Kingdom. MacCarthy traveled to India in the early twentieth century and studied Indian classical music and the vina. She transcribed this music and offered numerous Indian music lecture-recitals in the United Kingdom that featured Indian instruments. On MacCarthy, see Ghuman, 11–52.

101. See Henry Spiller, "Tunes That Bind: Paul J. Seelig, Eva Gauthier, Charles T. Griffes, and the Javanese Other," *Journal of the Society for American Music* 3 (May 2009): 129–154.

102. See Winthrop P. Tryon, "Mme Eva Gauthier, an Internationalist of the Musical World," *Christian Science Monitor*, 31 March 1923, 14. Also see Frederick Martens, "Folk Music in the Ballet Intime," *New Music and Church Music Review* 16, no. 191 (October 1917): 762–765.

103. The manuscript scores and sketches for these works are housed in the Griffes Collection at the New York Public Library for the Performing Arts. For more on Griffes and Japanese music, see my *Revealing Masks*, 172–173. On Griffes generally, see Donna K. Anderson, *The Works of Charles T. Griffes: A Descriptive Catalogue* (Ann Arbor, MI: UMI Research Press, 1983); Edward Maisel, *Charles T. Griffes: The Life of an American Composer* (New York: Alfred A. Knopf, 1984); and Anderson, *Charles T. Griffes: A Life in Music* (Washington, DC: Smithsonian Institution Press, 1993). Midori Takeishi has suggested that Griffes actually received the Japanese melodies from Michio Ito rather than from Gauthier. See Midori Takeishi, *Japanese Elements in Michio Ito's Early Period (1915–1924): Meetings of East and West in the Collaborative Works*, ed. and rev. David Pacun (Gendaitosho: 2006), 44, 46. Ito produced a *noh* play in English with Irene Lewisohn of the Neighborhood Playhouse in 1918, (Lewisohn had studied *noh* in Japan in 1910), at the Belasco Theatre in New York in October 1920, and several more in different theaters between 1920 and 1925 (see Takeishi, 47, 66–68).

104. This press release was produced by the Wolfsohn Musical Bureau and is found in the Eva Gauthier Collection, category 11, "Press Matter for Eva Gauthier Soprano" (7–8), at the New York Public Library for the Performing Arts.

105. See Turbide, 129.

106. On Cadman and Native American music, see Michael V. Pisani, *Imagining Native America in Music* (New Haven, CT: Yale University Press, 2005), 267–277; and Beth E. Levy, *Frontier Figures: American Music and the Mythology of the American West* (Berkeley: University of California Press, 2012), chapter 3. Pisani describes Cadman as a composer who "portrayed 'Indian music' in a distinctively sympathetic way" and who maintained a "spiritual integrity" in adapting this music. See Pisani, "'I'm an Indian Too': Creating Native American Identities in Nineteenth- and Early Twentieth-Century Music," in Jonathan Bellman, ed., *The Exotic in Western Music* (Boston: Northeastern University Press, 1998), 247–248.

107. For an extensive discussion of Asai and his association with Cadman, see Lancefield, chapter 2. A copy of Asai's immigration records is held at the Japanese American National Museum Resource Center, Los Angeles.

108. For this and other detailed information on Cadman, see Harry D. Perison, *Charles Wakefield Cadman: His Life and Works* (PhD diss., Eastman School of Music, University of Rochester, 1978), 111. Perison cites an 18 May 1912 letter from Cadman to Eberhart that refers to Tomijiro Asai as the source of the Japanese melodies (109).

109. This correspondence is found in Series IV [Corr. Cadman and Nelle Eberhart], Music-AM (letters) 83-1, "Cadman, Charles Wakefield," New York Public Library for the Performing Arts.

110. Rupert Hughes, *Famous American Composers* (Boston: L. C. Page and Co., 1900), 139–140. Hughes's evidence for a significant Chinese musical influence on American composers in the late nineteenth century is rather limited.

111. Kelley also composed the highly successful song "The Lady Picking Mulberries" (1888), subtitled "A Chinese Episode," which featured the standard four sixteenth, two eighth note gesture, as illustrated in Example 2.2c. On the impact of Chinese music on Kelley see Hughes, 65–69, who notes that Kelley called for bowing techniques in imitation of the Chinese *erhu* or *huqin*. Kelley's *Aladdin* employed a couple Chinese melodies, including "Mo Li Hua," which would later appear prominently in Puccini's *Turandot*.

112. Hughes, 141.

113. I should also note here the career of the composer and organist Homer N. Bartlett (1846–1920), who became interested in Japanese music late in his career. (See William Osborne, "Bartlett, Homer N.," *Grove Music Online*.) Like several other composers considered here, Bartlett produced works of both popular and classical *japonisme*. These include the first American song that I have found to be entitled "Sayonara," published in 1901 by G. Schirmer. He also published *Kuma saka* (1907) "founded on Japanese Themes" for piano four hands and "Japanese Revery" (1908) and *Dondon-bushi* (1918) for piano. Apparently, he left unfinished a Japanese-inspired opera entitled *Hinotito*. See Edward Ellsworth Hipsher, *American Opera and Its Composers* (Philadelphia: Theodore Presser, 1927), 70.

114. I have been unable to locate this score.

115. Hughes, 142.

116. Martens was a librettist and translator who also wrote about music. He also interviewed and apparently knew Kosaku (Kôsçak) Yamada, see David Pacun, "'Thus We Cultivate Our Own World, and Thus We Share It with Others': Kôsçak Yamada's Visit to the United States in 1918–1919," *American Music* 24 (spring 2006): 80 and 91, note 55.

117. This advertisement appeared in *Music Supervisors Journal* 2, no. 3 (1916): 9. See Terese M. Volk, *Music, Education, and Multiculturalism* (New York: Oxford University Press, 1998), 42.

Chapter 3

1. The literature on Japanese influence on Euro-American modernism is vast. For a very useful resource on Japanese influence on Western literature, see David Ewick, *Japonisme, Orientalism, Modernism: A Critical Bibliography of Japan in English-Language Verse*, http://themargins.net/bibliography.html (accessed 28 September 2015). On music and theater, see my *Revealing Masks*. For detailed discussion of the influence of Japanese design and prints on Frank Lloyd Wright, see Kevin Nute, *Frank Lloyd Wright and Japan: The Role of Traditional Japanese Art and Architecture in the Work of Frank Lloyd Wright* (London: Chapman and Hall, 1993); and Julia Meech, *Frank Lloyd Wright and the Art of Japan: The Architect's Other Passion* (New York: Japan Society and Harry N. Abrams, 2001).

2. The second sentence in this statement is actually crossed out and the following appears written over it in pencil: "I may be able to throw a little light on the subject and [?] a little concorde myself." This 1915 document is titled "Affirmations VI The 'Image' and the Japanese Classical Stage' typescript and carbon typescript with corrections," and is held in the Ezra Pound Collection, Princeton University Library Special Collections, folder 7.

3. See "Miscellaneous notes on 'The Noh'," folder 9, Pound Collection, Princeton.

4. For a broad discussion of Japanese influence on American visual art in this period see Julia Meech and Gabriel P. Weisberg, *Japonisme Comes to America: The Japanese Impact on the Graphic Arts 1876–1925* (New York: Harry N. Abrams, 1990).

5. T. J. Jackson Lears, *No Place of Grace: Antimodernism and the Transformation of American Culture 1880–1920* (New York: Pantheon Books, 1981), xi.

6. Arnold Schoenberg, "Folkloristic Symphonies," *Musical America* (February 1947), reprinted in *Style and Idea*, ed. Leonard Stein (Berkeley: University of California Press, 1984), 162–163.

7. For discussions of Schoenberg's experience as an exile in California, see Alan Philip Lessem, "The Émigré Experience: Schoenberg in America," in *Constructive Dissonance: Arnold Schoenberg and the Transformations of Twentieth-Century Culture*, eds. Juliane Brand and Christopher Hailey (Berkeley: University of California Press, 1997), 58–68; Reinhold Brinkmann and Christoph Wolff, eds., *Driven into Paradise: The Musical Migration from Nazi Germany to the United States* (Berkeley: University of California Press, 1999); Peter Franklin, "Modernism, Deception, and Musical Others: Los Angeles circa 1940," in *Western Music and Its Others: Difference, Representation, and Appropriation in Music*, ed. Georgina Born and David Hesmondhalgh (Berkeley: University of California Press, 2000), 148–154; and Dorothy Lamb Crawford, "Arnold Schoenberg in Los Angeles," *Musical Quarterly* 86, no. 1 (spring 2002): 6–48.

8. See Robert F. Waters, "Emulation and Influence: *Japonisme* and Western Music in *fin de siècle* Paris," *Music Review* 55, no. 3 (August 1994): 222; 224. I do not find a similarity between *sho* clusters and Debussy's harmony myself. Waters also more generally discusses the presence of Japanese scales in works by European composers in this period.

9. Jessica E. Stankis, "Maurice Ravel's 'Color Counterpoint' through the Perspective of Japonisme," *Music Theory Online* 21, no. 1 (March 2015).

10. See Takashi Funayama, "*Three Japanese Lyrics and Japonisme*," in *Confronting Stravinsky: Man, Musician, and Modernist*, ed. Jann Pasler (Berkeley: University of California Press, 1986), 273–283. On Orff's opera, see Peter Revers, "Carl Orff und der Exotismus: Zur Ostasienrezeption in seiner frühen Oper *Gisei–Das Opfer*," in *Musikkulturgeschichte*, ed. Peter Petersen (Wiesbaden: Breitkopf and Härtel, 1990), 233–259.

11. On the relationship between Schoenberg and Cowell, including brief reference to their different views on exotic musical influence, see Sabine Feisst, "Henry Cowell und Arnold Schönberg—eine unbekannte Freundschaft," *Archiv für Musikwissenschaft* 55, no. 1 (1998): 57–71. On Cowell more generally, see Joel Sachs, *Henry Cowell: A Man Made of Music* (Oxford: Oxford University Press, 2012).

12. I delivered papers on Eichheim, Cowell, and Japan at the 2004 meetings of the Society for American Music and the American Musicological Society New England Chapter, at the Oakley Center for the Humanities and Social Sciences, Williams College (2004), at Yale University and Texas A&M University (2006), and at the Library of Congress (2010). I remain grateful for comments offered by panelists and audience members at each of these events.

13. Samuel Merwin, *Anthony the Absolute* (New York: Century Co., 1914). The story was first published serially in *McClure's Magazine* from November 1913 to March 1914. In 1917 a film based on the novel and entitled *The Door Between* was released, but no print appears to have survived, and thus we may never know how this intensely music-centered plot was dealt with in the silent film genre.

14. At the second meeting of the New York Musicological Society on 13 March 1930, Otto Kinkeldey delivered a lecture entitled "Some Japanese Polyphony." See Nancy Yunhwa Rao, "American Compositional Theory in the 1930s: Scale and Exoticism in 'The Nature of Melody' by Henry Cowell," *Musical Quarterly* 85, no. 4 (winter 2001): 598, Table 1.

15. Eichheim to Carl Engel, n.d. [summer 1920], undated folder, Carl Engel Collection, Music Division, Library of Congress (hereafter Engel Collection–LC).

16. Unfortunately, Eichheim's transcriptions were later lost. See Dolores M. Hsu, *The Henry Eichheim Collection of Oriental Instruments: A Western Musician Discovers a New World of Sound* (Santa Barbara, CA: University Art Museum, 1984), 16.

17. W.S.S., "Mr. Eichheim's Orient," *Boston Transcript*, 23 March 1922, 8.

18. In a sense, just as Eichheim's perceptions of Japan had been shaped by Hearn, Hearn's had been shaped by the writings of Pierre Loti. See Hiromi Kawashima, "Travel Sketches of Lafcadio Hearn," in Kenji Zenimoto, ed. *Centennial Essays on Lafcadio Hearn* (Matsue, Japan: The Hearn Society, 1996), 162–172.

19. Eichheim to Engel, n.d. [summer 1920].

20. Lafcadio Hearn, *Gleanings in Buddha-Fields: Studies of Hand and Soul in the Far East* (Boston and New York: Houghton, Mifflin and Co., 1897). Eichheim's poem for piano exists in two manuscript copies in the Henry Eichheim Collection, Newberry Library (hereafter Eichheim Collection–Newberry). The nine-page "second copy" is an early draft of the work. The more complete fifteen-page "first copy" represents the final version but includes a few penciled revisions. A symphonic poem based on Hearn's "The Soul of the Great Bell" is referenced in program notes at several points in Eichheim's career, but the work is apparently lost.

21. Hearn, *Gleanings in Buddha-Fields*, 60. This statement appears two pages before the passage quoted by Eichheim at the end of his manuscript score.

22. Ibid., 29, 32. He also explained that in Japanese cultural production "the cheapest material is used . . . the art sense is superbly independent of the material" (62–63).

23. Lafcadio Hearn, "Mosquitoes," in *Kwaidan: Stories and Studies of Strange Things* (Boston: Houghton, Mifflin and Co., 1904), 227–228.

24. Hearn to Basil Hall Chamberlain, 15 June 1893, published in *The Japanese Letters of Lafcadio Hearn*, ed. Elizabeth Bisland (Boston and New York: Houghton Mifflin Co., 1910), 117–118. In a letter to W. B. Mason on 10 September 1892, Hearn described the music of a *bon-odori* at Sakai and wrote, "I wish I had had a musician with me capable of writing down the notes. It would be very difficult, however, because the notes are to a great extent *fractions* of notes." Ibid., 422.

25. Eichheim to Coolidge, 15 August 1928, folder 21, box 29, Elizabeth Sprague Coolidge Collection, Music Division, Library of Congress (hereafter Coolidge Collection–LC). Cyrilla Barr has stated that Coolidge encouraged Eichheim's "interest in Asian music by helping to finance his tours to the Far East to collect material for his *Oriental Impressions*." Barr, *Elizabeth Sprague Coolidge: American Patron of Music* (New York: Schirmer Books, 1998), 340.

26. Eichheim as quoted in a short article that ran in the Osaka *Mainichi* and Tokyo *Nichi Nichi* on 15 November 1927 (Henry Eichheim Collection, University of California, Santa Barbara). Tanabe (1883–1984) was the leading Japanese musicologist in the early twentieth century. He published a book on Japanese music in English that went through multiple editions; he was also active in supporting European music in Japan. In his introduction, Tanabe notes that European music has "come very near exhausting all its resources both in form and content" and points to Japanese music as a source for the renewal of Western music: "It is my hope that a thorough study of Japanese music will contribute much to world music in its proper development of the future." Hisao Tanabe, *Japanese Music*, trans. Shigeyoshi Sakabe (Tokyo: The Society for International Cultural Relations, 1936), 5–6.

27. Henry Eichheim, "Pinwheel Music" [letter to the Dramatic Editor, dated 12 March 1927], *New York Times*, 20 March 1927, X2. In 1928 Eichheim declared that "the constant dramatic intensity of the best European stage music soon wears out the listener whereas the wailing of a single flute or the striking of a drum to italicize a high point in the No drama is more potent in its suggestion because the listener is more fresh to receive it." Eichheim quoted in an interview by Clarence Davies, *Japan Advertiser* (5 August 1928). For a discussion of Euro-American modernist interest in Japanese *noh*, and the use of "ancient" Japanese music and theater for the creation of modernist works, see my *Revealing Masks*.

28. St. Denis had seen a *kabuki* performance in Los Angeles in 1912 and had taken dancing lessons from a former geisha. See Susan Tenneriello, "*O-Mika*: Ruth St. Denis's Image of the East," *Proceedings of the Society of Dance History Scholars* 22 (1999): 279–284.

29. See folder 341, Denishawn Choreographic notes, Ruth St. Denis Collection, New York Public Library for the Performing Arts. Lily Strickland's "Dance Moods" for piano is found among the scores in this collection, in folder 396. This suite features twelve pieces each labeled with an Asian culture, including a "Japanese" movement. In her preface to the score Strickland declared: "The composer makes no apologies for the westernization of the music. To occidental ears the purely Eastern idiom is monotonous and colourless if translated too literally.... The significance of oriental music lies in its symbolism and impersonal character. The impersonal quality of the East is intensified in the dancer's art. A mood is presented rather than a definite idea. The essential characteristics of all Eastern dances are found in beauty of line, of gesture, posture and motion, and beneath all is the eternal beat of the drum." She states that her "Japanese" dance is not that of the geisha, but of Japanese ritual music instead: "The slow-motion pictures of a cinema camera might be used as a basis of development in working out postures as the spirit of the dance must be unhurried throughout."

30. See folder 268, Addresses, Essays, Lectures by Ruth St. Denis, Ibid.

31. Eichheim, "Some Aspects of Oriental Music," 3, lecture file, Eichheim Collection, University of California, Santa Barbara.

32. Hsu, *The Henry Eichheim Collection of Oriental Instruments*, 16. Also see de Garis, *Their Japan*, 81.

33. Hsu, 20.

34. Eichheim to Carl Engel, n.d. [summer 1920]. (Franz Kneisel was the concertmaster and assistant conductor of the Boston Symphony during Eichheim's years with the orchestra. Max Zach served as principal violist in the Boston Symphony and then as conductor of the Boston Pops during this period before assuming the post of principal conductor of the Saint Louis Symphony Orchestra in 1907.)

35. His late works, such as the more expansive and orchestral *Java* (1929) and *Bali* (1933), were inspired by trips to Southeast Asia. On the influence of Indonesian gamelan on Eichheim, see Richard Mueller, "Javanese Influence on Debussy's *Fantaisie* and Beyond," *19th-Century Music* 10, no. 2 (fall 1986): 177–178, 181.

36. The manuscript copy of the piano version of *Japanese Sketch* as well as the manuscript copies of the chamber versions of *Japanese Sketch* and *Japanese Nocturne* for "small orchestra" are held in the Coolidge Collection–LC. The manuscript for the large orchestra version of *Japanese Nocturne* and the earliest piano versions of these pieces are held in the Eichheim Collection–Newberry. Both piano pieces were published in Eichheim, *Oriental Impressions for Piano* (London: J. Curwen and Sons, 1928), and the full orchestral versions were published in Eichheim, *Oriental Impressions: Suite for Orchestra* (New York: G. Schirmer, Inc., 1929). For further details on the multiple versions of these works, see Hsu, *The Henry Eichheim Collection*, 79.

37. In this sense, Eichheim's music functioned similarly to the work of photographers and painters who traveled to Japan to capture images for domestic consumption. For example, Winckworth Allan Gay lived in Japan for four years starting in 1877, knew Fenollosa, painted Japanese women with *shamisens* and *kotos*, and was apparently "the earliest American painter to reside in Japan." See *Theodore Wores: An American Artist in Meiji Japan* (Pacific Asia Museum, 1993), 15–16. The American painter Theodore Wores lived in Japan from 1885 to 1887 and again in 1892 to 1894. His paintings of Japan, which avoided depicting evidence of Japanese modernization, were quite successful in the United States. See William H. Gerdts, *The World of Theodore Wores* (Stanford, CA: Iris and B. Gerald Cantor Center for Visual Arts

at Stanford University, 1999), 9. Also see the exhibition catalog *Theodore Wores: The Japanese Years* (Oakland, CA: The Oakland Museum, 1976).

38. I disagree with Mina Yang's statement that Eichheim "resorted to 'idealizing' the music of the other by recasting it to conform to European harmonic and metrical frameworks." Yang, "New Directions in California Music: Construction of a Pacific Rim Cultural Identity, 1925–1945" (PhD diss., Yale University, 2001), 191. For an overview of Californian composers' engagements with Asian music in the first half of the twentieth century, see Yang, *California Polyphony: Ethnic Voices, Musical Crossroads* (Urbana and Chicago: University of Illinois Press, 2008), chapter 2, and her "Orientalism and the Music of Asian Immigrant Communities in California, 1924–1945," *American Music* 19, no. 4 (winter 2001): 385–416.

39. Hearn, "Out of the Street," in *Gleanings in Buddha-Fields*, 41–42.

40. Leopold Stokowski, a close friend of Eichheim's, chose to tour this piece and to record it with the Philadelphia Orchestra. Stokowski wrote to Eichheim on 19 January 1929: "can you lend me soon the score and parts of your Japanese Nocturne because I want to record it with the Victor Company?" Oliver Daniel Research Collection on Leopold Stokowski, Annenberg Rare Book and Manuscript Library, University of Pennsylvania (hereafter, Daniel Collection–U. of Penn.) A compact disc issue of this recording is available on *Stokowski: Philadelphia Rarities*, Cala Records Ltd., CACD0501, 1994.

41. Hearn describes the sound of the *mokugyo* he heard at a memorial service in *Glimpses of Unfamiliar Japan, vol. 2* (Boston and New York: Houghton Mifflin and Co., 1894), 486–490.

42. See "The Influence of Folk Music on the Art Music of Today" (1920), "The Relation of Folk Song to the Development of the Art Music of Our Time" (1921), and "The Influence of Peasant Music on Modern Music" (1931), all republished in *Béla Bartók Essays*, ed. Benjamin Suchoff (London: Faber and Faber, 1976).

43. Stokowski marked the final piccolo call in his copy of the score "free. start anywhere" in red pencil. This score is held in the Leopold Stokowski Collection of Scores, Annenberg Rare Book and Manuscript Library, University of Pennsylvania (hereafter Stokowski Collection–U. of Penn.).

44. Hsu states that Eichheim heard *gagaku* during his 1922 trip (Hsu, *The Henry Eichheim Collection*, 14); he included his adaptation of the famous *gagaku* piece *Etenraku* (dedicated to the composer Charles Martin Loeffler) in the 1929 publication of *Oriental Impressions: Suite for Orchestra*. His 15 August 1928 letter to Coolidge quoted above and his following remarks to Serge Koussevitzky indicate that he heard *gagaku* in 1928: "In Tokyo I heard the Emperor's orchestra play the ancient music that was used at yesterdays coronation and found it very noble. I have written an article for a Japanese magazine about it which you shall have when it is printed." (Eichheim to Koussevitzky, 11 November 1928, Serge Koussevitzky Archive, General Correspondence, box 18, folder 15, Music Division, Library of Congress.) It is unclear whether he heard *gagaku* during his first trip in 1915 but he may well have encountered the *sho* separately at that time. Matters of precedence in cross-cultural encounters are not easy to determine. For instance, Mervyn Cooke erroneously states that "[Benjamin] Britten was the first Western composer to borrow specific musical ideas from Gagaku." Cooke, *Britten and the Far East: Asian Influences in the Music of Benjamin Britten* (Woodbridge, UK: Boydell Press, 1998), 3. We will find below that in addition to Eichheim's pieces, Henry Cowell's *Ongaku*, Concerto [no. 1] for Koto, and Concerto for Harmonica all employ features inspired by *gagaku* and predate the completion of Britten's *Curlew River*. (The influence of the *sho* is also evident in Claude Lapham's opera *Sakura*, which premiered in 1933 at the Hollywood Bowl.) Cooke refers to Britten's approximation of the *sho* as being "disconcertingly authentic." See Cooke, "Britten and the shō," 233.

45. "Some Aspects of Oriental Music," Eichheim Collection, University of California, Santa Barbara.

46. Konoye's version was published as: Hidemaro Konoye, *Etenraku* (Tokyo: Alexandre Tcherepnine, 1935). The publisher, Alexander (Alexandre) Tcherepnin, was himself a composer who lived in China and Japan during the mid-1930s and composed pieces influenced by East Asian traditional music, including an opera based on a Chinese text (*The Nymph and the Farmer*) and a ballet (*The Woman and Her Shadow*) with a *noh*-inspired libretto by Claudel that "evokes traditional Japanese music." He also encouraged Chinese and Japanese composers to draw on their own national traditions. See Ludmila Korabelnikova, *Alexander Tcherepnin: The Saga of a Russian Emigré Composer*, trans. by Anna Winestein, ed. Sue-Ellen Hershman-Tcherepnin (Bloomington and Indianapolis: Indiana University Press, 2008), 109–111.

47. On musical transcription functioning as a form of translation, see Bennett Zon, *Representing Non-Western Music in Nineteenth-Century Britain* (Rochester, NY: University of Rochester Press, 2007), 250–251, and 265–290.

48. Stokowski recorded Konoye's version, not Eichheim's. A compact disc issue of this recording is available on *Stokowski: Philadelphia Rarities*. Stokowski also recorded Konoye's arrangement of the Japanese national anthem, *Kimigayo*. The historical significance of these recordings is attested to by the following comments made by Lou Harrison in an interview with Oliver Daniel in July 1976:

> . . . one of the reasons that I feel very strongly about Stokowski's importance in American music is, of course, the attention that he gave to Henry [Cowell] too and that wonderful thing in both their old age the *Koto Concerto* in which he showed again his interest in Asian and other music. He it was in fact who first recorded that Japanese baron's orchestration of the "Etenraku" which I still have a tape made from the old '78s and Stokowski pioneered in that area too. He was one of the few conductors who would play the oriental-styled works of American composers as well as the avant-garde from Europe and all other remarkable things.

The transcript of this interview is found in folder 634, Daniel Collection–U. of Penn.

49. On this program, *Etenraku* was followed by the *Blue Danube* with choreography again by Ito. See "Japanese Music and Dance Combined in One Program," *Rafu Shimpo* (12 August 1937): 1. A review on 20 August in this Japanese American Los Angeles newspaper claimed that Konoye "proved to the satisfaction of an appreciative audience of over 20,000 that the east can masterfully interpret western music." These articles and photographs of the production are held at the Japanese American National Museum, Hirasaki National Resource Center, Los Angeles.

50. On Riemann's theories of Japanese and Chinese scales and his perspective on the debates regarding transcription and the harmonization of exotic melodies, see Alexander Rehding, *Hugo Riemann and the Birth of Modern Musical Thought* (Cambridge, UK: Cambridge University Press, 2003), 169–181; and Matthew Gelbart and Alexander Rehding, "Riemann and Melodic Analysis: Studies in Folk-Musical Tonality," in *The Oxford Handbook of Neo-Riemannian Music Theories*, ed. Edward Gollin and Alexander Rehding (Oxford: Oxford University Press, 2011), 140–164.

51. Capellen published Japanese melodies in conjunction with Isawa Shuji in multiple formats, including piano arrangements of "Kimigayo" and *gunka* and new melodies composed by Shuji or edited by him. See Capellen's *Shogaku Shoka: Japanische Volksmelodien des Isawa Shuji* (Breitkopf and Härtel, 1904). The Capellen/Shuji collections clearly were consulted by numerous composers in Europe and the United States. For example, Ottokar Wöber's 1904 *Japanische Kriegsbilder* (Japanese War Pictures) was an orchestral work based directly on melodies in Capellen's *Shogaku Shoka*, and was published by Breitkopf and Härtel with the same cover art.

52. See Georg Capellen, *Ein neuer exotischer Musikstil an Notenbeispielen nachgewiesen* (Stuttgart: Grüninger, 1905), 44–46. On Capellen's call for the creation of a form of "world

music" through the harmonization of Asian melodies, see Alexander Rehding, "Wax Cylinder Revolutions," *Musical Quarterly* 88 (2005): 144.

53. Hornbostel also noted that Isawa's newly composed melodies already betrayed Western influence. See Hornbostel's review reprinted with an English translation by Gertrud Kurath in *Hornbostel: Opera Omnia*, vol. 1, ed. Klaus P. Wachsmann, Dieter Christensen, and Hans-Peter Reinecke (The Hague: Martinus Nijhoff, 1975), 219–220.

54. Heinrich Werkmeister, trans. Frederick H. Martens, "Impressions of Japanese Music," *Musical Quarterly* 13, no. 1 (January 1927): 104. Werkmeister wrote in admiration of the *shakuhachi* (102) and unknowingly echoed the American father in *The Little Tycoon* (mentioned in chapter 2) when he claimed to hear something Wagnerian in the gradual dynamic swells of the *sho*: "I must confess that, without any exaggeration, there have been moments when I felt I was hearing actual 'Tristan music'" (101).

55. On Yamada's score for Ito's 1918 production of W. B. Yeats's *At the Hawk's Well*, see Shotaro Oshima, *W. B. Yeats and Japan* (Tokyo: Hokuseido Press, 1965), 169–172.

56. See David Pacun, "'Thus We Cultivate Our Own World, and Thus We Share It with Others': Kósçak Yamada's Visit to the United States in 1918–1919," *American Music* 24, no. 1 (spring 2006): 67–94.

57. I have found Yamada's scores in numerous collections throughout the United States. For example, two Yamada scores appear in the Louis Horst Collection at the New York Public Library for the Performing Arts, one of which has Martha Graham's signature on the inside cover. Horst served as Martha Graham's musical director from the 1920s to 1948.

58. For example, see "Play Music of Orient: Mr. and Mrs. Henry Eichheim Talk on Its Origin to Japan Society," *New York Times*, 5 December 1920, 22.

59. Frederic de Garis, *Their Japan*, 2nd ed. (Yokohama: Yoshikawa, 1936), 81. De Garis noted that "[a]s a rule, foreigners are baffled by Japanese music, though it seems to be simple," but he referred to public *gagaku* concerts in 1934 and 1935 as "great successes, and understandable by the foreigners in the audience" (80–81). In general, de Garis demonstrates a sympathetic attitude toward Japanese music but he also writes that "[u]p to the time of the introduction of western civilization (1868), Japanese songs were more like chanting than real singing, and the music was something which the western mind has never been able to associate with the science of harmonious sound" (80).

60. This review appeared in the *Japan Advertiser* on 4 December 1919 and is found in a scrapbook in the Eichheim Collection, University of California, Santa Barbara. Not all domestic audiences and reviewers of Eichheim's music were appreciative. Stokowski wrote to Eichheim on 7 April 1923: "After studying privately and then with the Orchestra your five pieces I finally personally liked most the Japanese and Chinese, and so played those two. I played them at a pair of concerts in Philadelphia, and afterwards in Baltimore, Washington, Pittsburgh, Harrisburg and New York. Their reception was mixed. About one-third of the people liked them with wild enthusiasm, and about two-thirds were furious at me for playing them" (Daniel Collection–U. of Penn.). One reviewer wrote of Stokowski's performance of these pieces at Carnegie Hall: "But music, in a sense that appeals to those ears as music, these pieces can hardly be called. They are a collection of more or less striking and beautiful timbres, new sounds, new colors, new combinations." Richard Aldrich, "The Philadelphia Orchestra," *New York Times*, 14 March 1923, 14.

61. Olin Downes, "The Boston Symphony" review of a Boston Symphony Orchestra concert at Carnegie Hall, *New York Times*, 27 November 1925, 15. Also see similar remarks by Downes made in a 25 March 1922 review of *Oriental Impressions*: "There are composers who buy an excursion ticket, hire a guide, walk through a temple and write a symphony about it. Mr. Eichheim is not of this school." Downes praised Eichheim's works as marking "a refreshing departure from the pseudo-orientalism of our composers in big cities and seem a

more fruitful approach to the Orient itself than many an approved masterpiece by a modern European" (quoted in Hsu, *Henry Eichheim Collection*, 12–13). In the interest of full disclosure, I should note that Downes signed Eichheim's guest book at his Santa Barbara home. I am grateful to Dr. Gui Clark for allowing me to tour his home, a Spanish Colonial revival house on Mesa Road designed for Eichheim by George Washington Smith.

62. A copy of this program is held in the Eichheim Collection–Newberry. Eichheim's musical tour of East Asia in his set of *Oriental Impressions* prefigures Harrison's tour of the Pacific Rim in *Pacifika Rondo* (1963).

63. Following the end of the war, he published the camp's newsletter as a book: John Levis, ed., *Camp Chit Chat* (Shanghai: Voice Pub. Co., 1946).

64. H. H., "Chinese Music Expounded," *New York Times*, 27 March 1933, 13.

65. John Hazedel Levis, *Foundations of Chinese Musical Art* (Peiping: Henri Vetch, 1936). One reviewer of this book wrote: "Who knows but that it may also open some of those 'new paths' that composers are always fondly hoping to enter upon? There's the case of Debussy. Mr. Levis, for his part, does not dispute that Debussy's music shows Eastern influence. If, then, so much was done on a mere hint or two of an Oriental system, how much may not be accomplished on full knowledge!" Winthrop P. Tryon, "A Study of Chinese Music," *Christian Science Monitor*, 10 April 1933, 12.

66. See "Chinese Music Aeons Old to Be Played in Washington," *Washington Post*, 28 November 1933, 11.

67. Eichheim to Coolidge, 15 August 1928, folder 21, box 29, Coolidge Collection–LC.

68. Eichheim to Coolidge, 30 September 1922, folder 19, box 29, Coolidge Collection–LC.

69. Ibid.

70. Lazare Saminsky, "Composers of the Pacific," *Modern Music* 20, no. 1 (November–December, 1942): 23. Beth E. Levy has noted that Saminsky, "a practicing Jew and an authority on Jewish music . . . lambasted with all manner of anti-Semitic critique" modern music by Jewish composers. See Levy, "From Orient to Occident: Aaron Copland and the Sagas of the Prairie," in *Aaron Copland and His World*, eds. Carol J. Oja and Judith Tick (Princeton, NJ: Princeton University Press, 2005), 315. Also see Klára Móricz, "Sensuous Pagans and Righteous Jews: Changing Concepts of Jewish Identity in Ernest Bloch's *Jézabel* and *Schelomo*," *Journal of the American Musicological Society* 54, no. 3 (autumn 2001): 439–491.

71. Paul Nettl, "The West Faces East," *Modern Music* 20, no. 2 (January–February 1943): 93.

72. John Cage, "The East in the West," *Modern Music* 23, no. 2 (April 1946): 111–112.

73. Eichheim to Carl Engel, n.d. [June 1925], Engel Collection–LC. This letter was written aboard the Leviathan, and Eichheim joked that the ship should be renamed the "Levi Nathan."

74. Henry Cowell to Olive and Harry Cowell, 11 July 1936, Henry Cowell Collection, New York Public Library for the Performing Arts (hereafter Cowell Collection–NYPL). (Olive was Henry's stepmother.)

75. Cowell to Olive and Harry Cowell, 11 December 1931, Cowell Collection–NYPL. Cowell expressed similar sentiments in a letter to Charles Ives written that same day: "The concert with Ruggles work amidst the jews came off—I send a review." Ibid. For a broader perspective on this topic, see Rachel Mundy, "The 'League of Jewish Composers' and American Music," *Musical Quarterly* 96, no. 1 (spring 2013): 50–99. Also see Carol J. Oja, *Making Music Modern: New York in the 1920s* (New York: Oxford University Press, 2000), 217–218.

76. Eichheim, "Some Aspects of Oriental Music," 1, Eichheim Collection, University of California, Santa Barbara.

77. Cowell, "Trends in American Music," in *American Composers on American Music: A Symposium*, ed. Cowell (Stanford, CA: Stanford University Press, 1933), 6.

78. This passage appears on p. 3 of Cowell's manuscript for his speech "Oriental Influence on Western Music" (held in the International Association for Cultural Freedom Records, Box

429, Folder 2, Special Collections Research Center, University of Chicago Library) but was not included in the shorter version published in the conference proceedings, *Music— East and West: Report on 1961 Tokyo East-West Music Encounter Conference*, ed. and publ. Executive Committee for 1961 Tokyo East-West Music Encounter (Tokyo, 1961).

79. Ibid., 4. This folder also contains a speech that Cowell was not able to read at the conference entitled "'International' Music?" in which he nobly declared: "I have never understood why anyone should feel he must belittle other kinds of music in order to have confidence in his own."

80. See Rita Mead, *Henry Cowell's New Music 1925–1936: The Society, the Music Editions, and the Recordings* (Ann Arbor, MI: UMI Research Press, 1981), 41.

81. In a letter to Cowell on 16 March 1925 (Cowell Collection–NYPL), Carl Ruggles reported on an International Composers' Guild concert: "The Eichheim thing was dull and stupid, absolutely without the slightest creative instinct. He is eliminated." Colin McPhee wrote to Cowell in 1935 concerning his intentions to compose works based on Balinese music that would offer "authentic stuff and not dished-up impressionism à la Eichheim." Quoted in Carol J. Oja, *Colin McPhee: A Composer in Two Worlds* (Washington, DC: Smithsonian Institution Press, 1990), 93. In an overview of Asian influence on Western composers, Chou Wen-chung claimed of Eichheim that "despite his sincerity and personal experience, his works are merely experimental and technically crude" (219). In contrast, Chou finds details of correspondence between *gagaku* and the music of Varèse (217) and speculates that Cowell's tone clusters may have been influenced by his childhood encounters with Asian music (220). (Chou's discussion of the similarities between *gagaku* and Varèse's 1925 *Intégrales* is convincing; his comment on the origins of Cowell's clusters is not. I have not yet determined whether Varèse heard Eichheim's *Entenraku* before composing *Intégrales*.) See Chou Wen-chung, "Asian Concepts and Twentieth-Century Western Composers," *Musical Quarterly* 57, no. 2 (April 1971): 219, 217, 220. Of course, what is considered "authentic stuff" and "ultra-modern" one day is doomed to be discarded as passé the next. In 1946 John Cage dismissed McPhee's Balinese-inspired works as "frank transcriptions" ("The East in the West," 111) and Chou was equally dismissive of McPhee in 1971 ("Asian Concepts," 222). Lou Harrison, however, in his tribute to Cowell ("Tens on Remembering Henry Cowell") was willing to draw a connection between the two composers: "Like Gottschalk and Eicheim [*sic*] and others too/He knew a new world of human music," in Peter Garland, ed., *A Lou Harrison Reader* (Santa Fe, NM: Soundings Press, 1987), 38.

82. Mead, *Henry Cowell's New Music*, 35.

83. Stokowski and Eichheim's friendship and shared enthusiasm for Asian music was even noted in the popular press, as in Janet Mabie, "Music in the East," *Christian Science Monitor*, 2 January 1935, WM3, WM15. Stokowski was something of an amateur comparative musicologist himself, traveling the world to encounter exotic musics. In his book *Music for All of Us* (New York: Simon and Schuster, 1943) he devoted one chapter to "The Musical Languages of Africa, Asia, and Remote Cultures," in which he offered general comments on musical style, instruments, scales, and rhythms. Although the book was published during the war, Stokowski still referred to the music of *noh* as "one of the highest developments of art in Asia" and remarked that the Japanese "conception of singing is totally unlike ours" (286).

84. Percy Grainger, "Is Music Universal?" *New York Times*, 2 July 1933, X4.

85. Cowell may well have heard Eichheim's *Entenraku* in one of its multiple performances and versions, including Eichheim's ballet *The Rivals*, which incorporated *Entenraku*. In his review of a performance of *The Rivals* given by the League of Composers and the Adolph Bolm Ballet, Olin Downes related that *Entenraku* was used as a prelude. (Downes, "League of Composers," *New York Times*, 28 March 1927, 26) Moreover, Downes's preview of the performance ("Eichheim and Tansman Write for Stage of Spectacle and Pantomime; Scenario of

'The Rivals,'" *New York Times*, 13 March 1927, X8) notes that Cowell along with Marion Bauer, Aaron Copland, Lazare Saminsky, and others would be playing percussion instruments off-stage for this piece. The program, too, states that the overture to *The Rivals* employs "authentic Chinese ceremonial music" [i.e., Eichheim's version of *Etenraku*] and that this music returns in a later scene where it is preceded by a cadenza played on Chinese instruments including temple bells, cymbals, and gongs from Eichheim's collection. The program also reveals that the performance included Richard Hammond's *Voyage to the East*, a setting of Amy Lowell's poem *Free Fantasia on Japanese Themes*, which involves a female character imaging herself playing a small Japanese drum and listening to the *shamisen*. (This program and the score to *The Rivals* are found in the Eichheim Collection–Newberry.)

86. See Russell Kerr, "50 Years of Cowell . . . at 65," *The Music Magazine and Musical Courier* 164, no. 4 (May 1962): 10–12. In her notes to the Smithsonian recording of Cowell's early piano works, Sidney Cowell wrote that this piece "is a simple setting of a purely Japanese tune—not a traditional one to be found among Japanese, however, but, as is usual with Cowell, a tune in authentic folk style that he composed for himself." See *Henry Cowell: Piano Music*, Smithsonian Folkways 3349, 1963; reissued on compact disc in 1993.

87. Cowell's oft-quoted 1955 statement, "I want to live in the *whole world* of music!" appears in Hugo Weisgall, "The Music of Henry Cowell," *Musical Quarterly* 45, no. 4 (October 1959): 498.

88. Cowell referred repeatedly in his career to his early exposure to East Asian music, pointing particularly to Chinese opera and to Japanese folk songs. For example, he wrote that he lived near Japanese and Chinese districts in San Francisco as a child and "sang their folk songs in their native language." He also claimed that "by the time I was nine years old, the music of these oriental people was just as natural to me as any music." See Cowell, "Music of the Orient," *Music Journal* 21 (September 1963): 25.

89. Rao, "American Compositional Theory in the 1930s," 626–627. Rao has argued that Chinese opera and particularly its use of sliding tones had a decisive influence on Cowell. See Rao, "Henry Cowell and His Chinese Music Heritage: Theory of Sliding Tone and His Orchestral Work of 1953–1965," in *Locating East Asia in Western Art Music*, eds. Yayoi Uno Everett and Frederick Lau (Middletown, CT: Wesleyan University Press, 2004), 119–145. However, it is also possible that the sliding tones of the Japanese *shakuhachi* were of equal importance to Cowell, as Rao briefly acknowledges. The *shakuhachi*'s sliding tones were of interest to other midcentury American composers. For example, on 18 October 1942 the composer Gerald Strang delivered a lecture in Beverly Hills in which he discussed the sliding tones of Chinese and Japanese music. He noted that "one especially interesting case is the appearance of glides . . . in certain old pieces for the *shakuhashi*" and he then played recordings of the *shaku-hachi* performer Kitaro Tamada that he had made himself. (Tamada's association with Cowell will be discussed in detail below.) Strang's lecture was published as "Sliding Tones in Oriental Music," *Bulletin of the American Musicological Society* 8 (October 1945): 29–30.

90. The Cold War political climate also impacted Cowell's musical outlook in other dimensions, as is clearly evident in his and Sidney's reshaping of the image of Charles Ives in the 1950s. See David C. Paul, "From American Ethnographer to Cold War Icon: Charles Ives through the Eyes of Henry and Sidney Cowell," *Journal of the American Musicological Society* 59, no. 2 (summer 2006): 399–457.

91. Selections of these recordings, including recordings of the Japanese actress Sadayakko (Yacco), a 1911 recording of *gagaku* made in Japan, and of *shakuhachi* excerpts are available on the compact disc *Walzenaufnahmen japanischer Music, 1901–1913* (Berlin: Staatliche Museen zu Berlin, 2003). See Otto Abraham and Erich M. von Hornbostel, "Studien über das Tonsystem und die Musik der Japaner" (1903), reprinted with an English translation by Gertrud Kurath in *Hornbostel: Opera Omnia*, vol. 1, ed. Klaus P. Wachsmann, Dieter

Christensen, and Hans-Peter Reinecke (The Hague: Martinus Nijhoff, 1975), 1–84. Also see Ingrid Fritsch, "Some Reflections on the Early Wax Cylinder Recordings of Japanese Music in the Berlin Phonogramm Archive (Germany)," in *Musicology and Globalization: Proceedings of the International Congress in Shizuoka 2002* (Tokyo: The Musicological Society of Japan, 2004), 224–228; and J. Scott Miller, "Dispossessed Melodies: Recordings of the Kawakami Theater Troupe," *Monumenta Nipponica* 53, no. 2 (summer 1998): 225–235.

92. In his letters to his parents from Berlin, for example, Cowell mentions listening to the music of Pygmies, Javanese and Balinese gamelan, Indian music, and the music of Malacca, New Guinea, Colombia, the Carolina Islands, middle Brazilian Indians, and Greenland Eskimos. On 21 November 1931 he wrote to Olive Cowell: "I am working on Pygmy African music, and Pangwe African music, and now on New Guinea music. I have found things which completely upset all findings of Hornbostel, and the others here, but will not tell him— YET!" He explains in this letter that East Asian music has been "much explored" and that it "would be broadening to visit the Orient just to travel, but I have too much to do to do it just for that reason; also, the war there does not look so good!" A 4 February 1937 letter from Cowell to his father reveals that Cowell's father had traveled to Japan at some prior point (Cowell Collection–NYPL). On Cowell's work in Berlin, also see Leta E. Miller, "Henry Cowell and John Cage: Intersections and Influences, 1933–1941," *Journal of the American Musicological Society* 59, no. 1 (spring 2006): 55–56.

93. Takeshi Kanno, *Creation-Dawn (A Vision Drama): Evening Talks and Meditations* (Fruitvale, CA: by the author, 1913). On Cowell's contributions to this work see Michael Hicks, *Henry Cowell: Bohemian* (Urbana and Chicago: University of Illinois Press, 2002), 49–52.

94. A typescript of the libretto of *Red Silence* by F. L. Giffin is held in the Cowell Collection– NYPL. The manuscript score for this work is held in the Henry Cowell Collection, Music Division, Library of Congress (hereafter, Cowell Collection–LC).

95. Hicks, *Henry Cowell*, 46–48. Cowell's tone clusters, appearing initially in his early piano works, call for the performer to use his or her hand or arm to play simultaneously all the pitches on the keyboard within a defined ambitus.

96. Ichikawa performed examples for Cowell's class on Japanese music at the New School in the spring of 1932. See Olive Thompson Cowell, "Henry Cowell" (typescript compiled June 1934, held in the San José State University Library), 37. On Cowell's career as a musical educator, see Edward R. Carwithen, "Henry Cowell: Composer and Educator" (PhD diss., University of Florida, 1991).

97. Tamada to Sidney Cowell, 26 January 1959, Cowell Collection–NYPL. Tamada refers to having met Eichheim at his home in Santa Barbara "about 39 years ago."

98. This, and related information below, is based on Tamada's immigration records and Manzanar internment camp records. I would like to thank Aloha South at the US National Archives for making these materials available to me. I also consulted immigration records at the Japanese American National Museum, Hirasaki National Resource Center, Los Angeles.

99. See Tamada's 14 March 1934 letter to Cowell, Cowell Collection–NYPL.

100. For example, Cowell wrote to Olive Cowell on 5 February 1935: "The Japanese festival was great! Lasted from 1.30 to 11.15 P.M. six koto players, three samesen players, three shakuhashi players" (Cowell Collection–NYPL).

101. See Mead, 316–317. Lou Harrison stated that his first live experience of Japanese chamber music was Tamada's performance at Cowell's home. See Harrison, "Learning from Henry," in David Nicholls, ed., *The Whole World of Music: A Henry Cowell Symposium* (Amsterdam: Harwood Academic Publishers, 1997), 164. (Conversely, in 1986 Sidney Cowell reminisced about how she and Henry took Tamada to hear a performance of Harrison's symphonic works in New York in the 1950s. See Garland, *A Lou Harrison Reader*, 29.) John Cage, at Cowell's urging, arranged to have Tamada perform in Hollywood on 13

April 1935 and Cowell was in attendance. See Leta E. Miller, "Henry Cowell and John Cage," 60–61. Tamada also performed in 1948 at an Evenings on the Roof concert at the invitation of Peter Yates. See Dorothy Lamb Crawford, *Evenings on and off the Roof: Pioneering Concerts in Los Angeles, 1939–1971* (Berkeley: University of California Press, 1995), 82.

102. On Cowell's imprisonment more generally see Michael Hicks, "The Imprisonment of Henry Cowell," *Journal of the American Musicological Society* 44, no. 1 (spring 1991): 92–119. Cowell's letters to his parents while in prison reveal that he was studying the Japanese language with another inmate. In a 4 August 1940 letter to Cowell, Tamada praises Cowell's Japanese writing and returns a sample of it that he has corrected (Cowell Collection–NYPL).

103. See Cowell's letter of 11 August 1937 to his stepmother and that of 21 September 1937 to Nicolas Slonimsky in the Cowell Collection–NYPL.

104. Cowell wrote to Blanche Walton on 17 July 1939: "Recently William Russell gave me a Chinese flute, and it has a lovely, woody tone. I am learning to play it rapidly. I have finally mastered the Japanese shakuhachi to some extent, so that at least my playing sounds musical on it, and I think I can say the same of the Western flute, which I now play in the band here. So I shall be able to play the three different sorts!" (Cowell Collection–NYPL).

105. On the transformative experience of internment at Manzanar and its effect on the career of the Hollywood composer and arranger Tak Shindo, see my "Representing the Authentic: Tak Shindo's 'Exotic Sound' and Japanese American History," *ECHO* 6, no. 2 (2005), http://www.echo.ucla.edu/Volume6-Issue2/sheppard/sheppard1.html, and chapter 7 below.

106. Tamada to Cowell, 8 November 1942, Cowell Collection–NYPL.

107. An announcement of Tamada's *shakuhachi* lessons appeared in the *Manzanar Free Press* 1, no. 26 (20 June 1942), 4.

108. Tamada to Cowell, 14 February 1945.

109. A recording of this work as a duet performed by Ralph Samuelson on *shakuhachi* and Steve Gorn on *bansuri* is available on *The Universal Flute: Discovery in a Single Tone* (Innova, 2016), and a performance on Western flute is available on Rachel Rudich, *Henry Cowell: The Universal Flute* (Music and Arts CD-1012, 1997).

110. Joscelyn Godwin, "The Music of Henry Cowell" (PhD diss., Cornell University, 1969), 238. Godwin also wrote: "The westerner's need for his own formal concepts can be sensed in its binary division and the up-and-down shape of each section, but the primary intention is the representation of the shakuhachi's own semi-improvised music." I should note that an "up-and-down shape" is common in traditional pieces.

111. For Sasamori's overview of such cultural exchanges see his "Impact of Far East Music on American Music," *Bulletin of the Faculty of Education, Hirosaki University* 32A (November 1974): 65–81.

112. Cowell to Olive Cowell, 16 May 1959.

113. On the continued resonance of the *shakuhachi* in American musical life, see Jay Keister, "The *Shakuhachi* as Spiritual Tool: A Japanese Buddhist Instrument in the West," *Asian Music* 35, no. 2 (2004): 99–131. Also see the several articles devoted to this topic in *Contemporary Music Review* 8, no. 2 (1994), special issue "Flute and Shakuhachi," ed. Kondō Jō and Joaquim Bernítez.

114. Amy Beal chronicles the German leg of Cowell's tour in her *New Music, New Allies: American Experimental Music in West Germany from the Zero Hour to Reunification* (Berkeley: University of California Press, 2006), 86–89.

115. On Cowell's participation in the war effort, see his "Shaping Music for Total War," *Modern Music* 22 (1945): 223–226. For his 1957 tour, Cowell had been contacted by the US Information Agency and asked to deliver lectures on contemporary American music with the explicit goal of promoting the image of the United States as a cultured

nation to counter Soviet propaganda. Cowell suggested that the USIA should send out recordings of American art music to radio stations around the world. See Edward Downes, "American Composer Encircles the Globe," *New York Times*, 25 August 1957, 119. Cowell, of course, was but one of the numerous composers and musicians who served as US cultural ambassadors during this period, as will be discussed in chapter 8. For example, both Duke Ellington and Dave Brubeck also traveled to Japan and returned home to create their own jazz impressions of this and other exotic Asian nations. On Cowell's participation in the East-West Music Encounter in Tokyo, also see Sachs, *Henry Cowell*, 468–474.

116. Christina Klein, *Cold War Orientalism: Asia in the Middlebrow Imagination, 1945–1961* (Berkeley: University of California Press, 2003), 82. In 1959 the United Nations sponsored a tour of *gagaku* in the United States and these musicians visited Cowell in New York City. In a letter to Olive on 28 June 1959, Cowell wrote: "I hope you saw the Imperial Musicians and Dancers of Japan—did I tell you we had twenty of them here in the apartment? I played a record of my Ongaku for them (it isn't out yet, but I have a master copy) it was impossible to tell, of course, how they *really* liked it—they are so polite!" *Ongaku* was recorded by Robert Whitney and the Louisville Orchestra in 1959 on LOU-595.

117. This statement was written by Cowell in Tokyo on 1 May 1961 at Oliver Daniel's request (Cowell Collection–NYPL).

118. Cowell wrote: "the music of Japan, as well as that of China and other oriental countries, is part of American music. . . . Most people who live in the middle and eastern parts of this country don't realize that Japanese and Chinese music is a part of American music" (Cowell, "Music of the Orient," 25). Rao builds on Cowell's argument in "American Compositional Theory in the 1930s," 625–626. I should note that, in general, second generation Asian Americans tended to turn away from Asian musical traditions.

119. See Cowell's statement to this effect quoted in Hugo Weisgall, "The Music of Henry Cowell," 489.

120. Cowell was explicit concerning his cross-cultural musical dialectic in which two seemingly contrary musical idioms are synthesized in the end. For example, in a letter to Stokowski on 18 June 1963 (Daniel Collection–U. of Penn.) Cowell wrote: "I was delighted to hear from your telephone call yesterday that you like the playing of Mr. Eto, and wish a copy of the score of my Concerto for Koto. . . . As you will notice, the first movement uses Japanese koto modes in the modern Japanese tradition; the second movement is Western in style but, I think, suited to the instrument. The last movement is an attempt to coordinate these approaches." Other prominent and related works from this period include Cowell's *Homage to Iran* for violin and piano, which was performed before the shah of Iran and his cabinet ministers on 3 July 1959, and *Persian Set* (1957), a chamber piece that includes music for *tar* (a double-bellied fretted lute) and a Persian drum.

121. Cowell's drafts and proofs of these program notes are held in the Cowell Collection–NYPL.

122. The typescript for these program notes is held in the Cowell Collection–NYPL. Ironically, Sidney Cowell felt that *Ongaku* was a rather clear imitation of *gagaku* music. In a 21 November 1960 letter to Virgil Thomson (held in folder 15, box 33 of the Virgil Thomson Papers at the Irving S. Gilmore Music Library, Yale University) Sidney wrote: "He always says he writes as a Westerner, responding to the contagion of. . . . [*sic*] but actually this piece sounds so much like the Gagaku (Imperial Court Music, with the *sho* which plays massed seconds) that it is almost funny." In 1961 Thomson composed his own Japanese-influenced work, the Variations for Koto (solo).

123. On the relationship between Cowell and Bartók see David C. Paul, "From American Ethnographer to Cold War Icon," 417–420.

124. Cowell, quoted in Weisgall, "The Music of Henry Cowell," 489.

125. This score is held in the Cowell Collection–LC. Godwin, in contrast, found that the first movement of *Ongaku* "is a masterpiece of synthesis: neither gagaku nor Cowell predominates, but each one gives something to the other." Writing in 1969, he tellingly suggests that *sankyoku* is "less attractive to the westerner" because it is less elevated and strange than *gagaku* and he refers to Cowell's use of *sankyoku* in the second movement as a form of "transubstantiation" and as "one of Cowell's happiest hybrids." See Godwin, "The Music of Henry Cowell," 259–261.

126. See Daniel Webster, "An Interview with Kimio Eto," *Philadelphia Inquirer*, 18 Dec 1964.

127. In her 21 November 1960 letter to Virgil Thomson (Thomson papers, Yale University Music Library) Sidney Cowell wrote:

> The second of the 2 mvts. is less admired by Japanese, apparently, because it draws on a more "modern" (end of 18th century) trio style which, while correct and classical enough, the more conventional Japanese feel is slightly irreverent in conjunction with the sacred Gagaku. At a Japan Society playing of the record here, the consensus among the Japanese was that no Japanese would dare write in this way, but for a Westerner it was fine. Japanese composers are impressed by it, and seem to learn from it, because a Westerner has shown himself impressed with, and able to use, the same values in their music that they treasure; mostly of course they have the notion that if you write for Western instruments you must use a purely Western style; and their attempts to take off from their own musical forms is just beginning to be successful.

128. Oliver Daniel erroneously reported that Cowell used the harmonica here in the style of the Japanese *sho*. See Daniel, "Henry Cowell," *Stereo Review* 33, no. 6 (December 1974): 82. Godwin ("The Music of Henry Cowell," 265) correctly notes that the harmonica part contains no chords or clusters. The concerto was composed for John Sebastian Sr., who died before he was able to premiere the work. (Sebastian's son, John Sebastian Jr., is the harmonica player and songwriter who founded The Lovin' Spoonful. I thank Richard Cohn for drawing my attention to this connection.) I am grateful to Robert Bonfiglio, who premiered the Concerto for Harmonica with Lukas Foss and the Brooklyn Philharmonic in 1986, for providing me with a recording of this piece. Cowell's pencil sketches held at the Library of Congress reveal that he was composing the Concerto [no. 1] for Koto and the Concerto for Harmonica at the same time.

129. Titles have played a particular role in leading some scholars to discount the persistence of exoticism throughout the modernist period in European and American music. For instance, Ralph P. Locke points to Debussy's gamelan-influenced *Cloches à travers les feuilles* as not engaging in exotic representation or reference, understanding the "bells" in the title to refer to French church bells. See Locke, *Musical Exoticism: Images and Reflections* (Cambridge, UK: Cambridge University Press, 2009), 228–229. However, it seems at least as likely that Debussy had the "joyful" islands of Indonesia in mind given the resonance of this title with the language he used to celebrate the bell-like Javanese gamelan music: "There were, and there still are, despite the evils of civilization, some delightful native peoples for whom music is as natural as breathing. Their conservatoire is the eternal rhythm of the sea, the wind among the leaves and the thousand sounds of nature which they understand without consulting an arbitrary treatise." Claude Debussy, "Taste," *Revue S.I.M.* (1913), quoted in Edward Lockspeiser, *Debussy: His Life and Mind: Volume I 1862–1918* (Cambridge, UK: Cambridge University Press, 1978), 115. The title *Pagodes*, for instance, likewise seems to signal exotic representational intent to me.

130. For a full discussion of the music of this film and its relationship to the film's racial and gender politics, see chapter 6 below.

131. Irving Lowens, "Stokowski a Triumph with the Philadelphia," *Evening Star* (Washington, DC), 29 December 1964. I also find a strong resemblance between the first and third

movements of Bernard Rogers's *Three Japanese Dances* (1933, rev. for wind ensemble in 1956) and the typical Hollywood depiction of Japan. Rogers was keenly interested in Japanese prints throughout his life and also composed "Fuji in Sunset Glow" (1925) and *New Japanese Dances* (1961).

132. Dimitri Tiomkin, "Whence Cometh the 'New Sound'?" *Music Journal Annual Anthology* 23 (1965): 108. Tiomkin appears to surpass Cowell's own universalism in the sentence immediately preceding this quotation: "We happily accepted Schoenberg's atonalism and the 12-tone scale, even if we fought them at first."

133. Eichheim to Carl Engel, n.d. [1928], Engel Collection–LC.

134. Abraham and Hornbostel, "Studien über das Tonsystem und die Musik der Japaner" (1903), in *Hornbostel: Opera Omnia*, 1:67. This appears to have been Hornbostel's first published article. Note that they are concerned here with preserving specimens of exotic musics for potential benefits to the West just as some conservationists now call for species preservation not based on arguments of inherent value but, rather, on potential medicinal applications for humans.

135. See, for example, Robert Garfias, "Some Effects of Changing Social Values on Japanese Music," in *Music—East and West: Report on 1961 Tokyo East-West Music Encounter Conference*, ed. and publ. Executive Committee for 1961 Tokyo East-West Music Encounter (Tokyo, 1961), 18–22. Participants from the United States also included Elliott Carter, Alfred V. Frankenstein, Lou Harrison, Mantle Hood, Colin McPhee, Nicolas Nabakov, Isaac Stern, and Virgil Thomson.

136. As Cowell wrote to his wife on 20 April 1961: "Well, the famous talk has been delivered (the long one—I was not asked to do the other) and I think I read it clearly and well . . . I have had lots of praise for it. The content of talks here is much better than in Teheran, although the orientals to a man plug for western music, while every westerner here plugs for Eastern" (Cowell Collection–NYPL). Cowell appeared on a session devoted to the "problem of interaction between the musical traditions of East and West." See *Information Handbook for 1961 Tokyo East-West Music Encounter Conference* (Tokyo 1961), a copy of which is held in the Cowell Collection–NYPL.

137. Cowell, "Oriental Influence on Western Music," in *Music—East and West*, 71. One of the more surprising statements made at the conference was by Virgil Thomson, who advised Japanese composers to divest themselves completely of the Japanese tradition. See Thomson, "The Philosophy of Style," *Music—East and West*, 145.

138. See Cowell, "Music of the Orient," 76. Cowell wrote to Sidney on 3 May 1961: "spoke 2 hours to 27 music education supervisors from all Tokyo—talked a lot of course on lack of Trad. Jap. music in schools—I *may* have sown a good seed here." Cowell had expressed a similar concern in a 27 November 1937 letter to Nicolas Slonimsky: "If you write to the Japanese, Mr. Goh, do advise him to aid in preserving their own music, as well as adding Western ideas." Taijiro Goh was the president of the Composers' League in Japan.

139. See Crawford, *Evenings on and off the Roof*, 105–106 for this 18 January 1954 letter from Yates. Also see "Foreign Music Program Set Tomorrow," *Los Angeles Times*, 17 January 1954, E5.

140. Barry Melton, quoted in Richie Unterberger, *Eight Miles High: Folk-Rock's Flight from Haight-Ashbury to Woodstock* (San Francisco: Backbeat Books, 2003), 36. Eto's son Leonard was a member of the famous world-touring Japanese percussion ensemble Kodo from 1984 to 1992, and has also collaborated with popular musicians in recent years.

141. *Koto and Flute*, World-Pacific Records 1299, 1960. This album offers straight performances of three works by Michio Miyagi, including the ubiquitous *Haru No Umi*, and three pieces by Kimio Eto for *koto* solo. World-Pacific Records also released albums by Ravi Shankar and Martin Denny.

142. Eto can be viewed as a forerunner to Ravi Shankar, who extended the exploratory and extrovert tendencies of his own *gharana* in his cross-cultural endeavors. Shankar composed his first Concerto for Sitar in 1970. See Stephen Slawek, "Ravi Shankar as Mediator between a Traditional Music and Modernity," in *Ethnomusicology and Modern Music History*, eds. Stephen Blum, Philip V. Bohlman, and Daniel M. Newman (Urbana: University of Illinois Press, 1991), 161–180.

143. A copy of the program for this gala dinner along with Cowell's invitation is found in the Cowell Collection–NYPL. Such events continue today. In May 2007 the Japan Society held its Centennial Gala Dinner, at which former President Clinton spoke and Sakata Tojuro IV performed *kabuki*.

144. Alan Rich, "Koto Introduced to Carnegie Hall," *New York Times*, 2 October 1961, 36. A more positive review also noted, with an air of disappointment, that "much of the music sounded Westernized. For all its quarter tones, the oldest classic selection had an Occidental tang." See Miles Kastendieck, Review of Kimio Eto's Carnegie Hall recital, *New York Journal-American*, 6 October 1961. Similarly, a reviewer of Eto's Philharmonic Hall performance in November 1962 with members of the New York Philharmonic found "most dignity and interest in the two selections from the classic repertoire" and was not enthusiastic about the cross-cultural pieces on the program. See Ross Parmenter, "Kimio Eto Offers Music on the Koto," *New York Times*, 5 November 1962, 35.

145. Stokowski placed the bass players directly in front of the podium for these concerts, so Mr. Arian enjoyed a good view of Eto during rehearsals and performances. I would like to thank Mr. Arian for his phone interview with me on 28 November 2007 and Paul Krzywicki, president of the Philadelphia Orchestra Retirees and Friends association, for assisting me in contacting retired members of the orchestra.

146. The Cowells were similarly bemused when Henry's simple 1961 *Music From a Visit to a Japanese School*—a march tune in the *gunka* style and thus based on a genre influenced by the West—was harmonized by a Japanese teacher and broadcast across Japan. As Sidney relates:

> H.C. was asked to write a tune for the children of a Tokyo school district directed by a friend of mine, after he had addressed the music teachers of the district (at the time of the E-W music conference.) . . . H.C.'s subject was the importance of Japanese Traditional music to Japanese and when he said that his students at Columbia knew more about this than most J. music teachers whose training was entirely European, everybody gasped with shock. His tune was J. in character but rather westernized by the unrelated harmonization a J. teacher added–showing to my amusement that HC's point was entirely missed!

This annotation by Sidney is dated 1968 and appears on the manuscript score held in the Cowell Collection–LC.

147. Sidney Cowell to Edwin E. Heilakka (curator of the Leopold Stokowski Collection at Curtis), 10 January 1987, Daniel Collection–U. of Penn. Sidney retold this story in an 18 February 1993 letter to Susan Feder of Associated Music Publishers; Cowell Collection–NYPL. A recording of a radio broadcast of the first performance of the work is held in the Cowell Collection–NYPL. In this recording Eto sticks closely to what is found in Cowell's score, without adding cadenza material. However, Sidney may well have had other early performances of the work in mind, and a source who wishes to remain anonymous has informed me that Cowell was indeed unhappy with additions made by Eto to the piece. The recording suggests that Stokowski was uncertain when Eto's cadenza would end, for the orchestra briefly enters a few bars too soon. (A full written-out cadenza for the first movement of the concerto that remains within the "Japanese" style of the movement is found in the Stokowski Collection–U. of Penn. Although this cadenza is labeled as being "by the

composer," the staff paper is Japanese and it is possible that part of this cadenza was composed instead by the *kotoist* Shinichi Yuize.) In letters to his stepmother, Cowell did not mention the cadenza but instead reported the enthusiastic response of the audience and the generally positive reviews that the work was receiving. See Cowell to Olive Cowell, 22 and 31 December 1964, Cowell Collection–NYPL.

148. There is very little suggestion of the subtleties of traditional *koto* music in the work. Instead, the concerto exhibits the Westernized features that so provoked Eto's New York critics. As Joscelyn Godwin put it: "The virtuosity in this work lies more in the conversion of an oriental instrument to western purposes than in showing off its native plumage" ("The Music of Henry Cowell," 269).

149. Michio Miyagi cofounded the New Japan Music Movement in 1920 and composed such works as the 1923 *Kairo-chō* for seven Japanese instruments in emulation of European chamber music, the 1928 *Etenraku hensōkyoku* (*Variations on Etenraku*), and several concerti for *koto* in the 1930s.

150. See Oliver Daniel, *Stokowski: A Counterpoint of View* (New York: Dodd, Mead and Co., 1982), 652.

151. Tony Scott, *Music for Zen Meditation and Other Joys*, Verve VS-8634, 1964. In his liner notes, Scott reported that "this music was totally improvised with no premeditation or rehearsal" and that he had improvised with Yuize many times, as they had met each other during Scott's first trip to Japan in 1959 when Scott was recording traditional music with Yasuko Nakashima. On some tracks Scott takes on features of *shakuhachi* performance. In his contribution to the liner notes, the philosopher Alan Watts stated: "In some ways the result is more Zen than Zen."

152. While I too respond unenthusiastically to Cowell's "Persian pieces" and find similarities between Cowell's musical exoticism and that of his contemporaries in the popular sphere, I do not share Corbett's aesthetic hierarchies, nor his confidence in decisively adjudicating and categorizing cross-cultural exploits, nor his implicit demands for artistic progress. In his sweeping criticism, Corbett also dismisses the music of Hovhaness, Harrison, and McPhee. All of this seems counter to the spirit of Corbett's brief, but thoughtful, introduction to his essay. John Corbett, "Experimental Oriental: New Music and Other Others," in *Western Music and Its Others*, 172–173. Corbett oddly suggests that Cowell's clusters might have been inspired by *koto* music (168). For another critique of Corbett's essay, see Yayoi Uno Everett, "'Mirrors' of West and 'Mirrors' of East," in *Diasporas and Interculturalism in Asian Performing Arts: Translating Traditions*, ed. Hae-Kyung Um (London and New York: Routledge Curzon, 2005), 176–177, 193, 196.

153. David Nicholls, "Reaching beyond the West: Asian Resonances in American Radicalism," *American Music* 17, no. 2 (summer 1999): 126. Nicholls has argued that the "polylingual radicals" such as Cowell and Harrison are to be clearly distinguished from earlier American Orientalists and that "the greater the degree of transethnic influence, the greater the likelihood of rejection" by the establishment. In having his cross-cultural journeys and works sponsored and performed by major institutions and ensembles, Cowell's "transethnicism" appears to have been embraced rather than rejected during his final decade. See Nicholls, "Transethnicism and the American Experimental Tradition," *Musical Quarterly* 80, no. 4 (winter 1996): 589.

154. Of course neither Eichheim nor Cowell was as devoted to Japan as was Colin McPhee to Bali. Cowell's global musical travels were not always well received even by friends who had benefited from his support. In a confessional letter concerning his initial anger in encountering a new work by Cowell based on Balinese music, McPhee expressed feelings of guilt in light of Cowell's consistent generosity. McPhee wrote to Cowell (apparently in 1948):

Actually, when I saw the score, I was so disturbed by your use of Balinese material that I could not speak. I felt it was some violation, some invasion of a territory that was my own private world. I was literally sick at night, thinking about it. At the same time, there were several reasons why I didn't speak out at the time. You had been ill; I didn't wish to destroy your pleasure in finishing a work that meant so much to you; I also thought, I must consider all this in a different, less emotional light, for I knew perfectly well that I should not have cared had Tabuh-T. been only one of many other works of my own, instead of the last. It has taken me a month, however, for me to bring all this out into the open. (McPhee to Cowell, Cowell Collection–NYPL)

155. Cowell, quoted in Weisgall, "The Music of Henry Cowell," 489.

156. The manuscript score to *Characters* is held in the Cowell Collection–LC. The other sketches in this work include "Cowboy," "The Profound One," "Deep Thinker," "The Frightened Scurrier," "The Celestial Soul," and (including his own ethnic heritage) "The Jaunty Irishman." Of course this minor piece was an aberration in Cowell's late career. Cowell's fundamental decency and admirable open-mindedness is attested to by his major public statements such as: "I do not believe that any race or people is better or worse than any other." Cowell, "Music Is My Weapon" (1954), reprinted in *Essential Cowell: Selected Writings on Music by Henry Cowell 1921–1964*, ed. Dick Higgins (Kingston, NY: McPherson and Company, 2001), 47–48. Cowell also proclaimed: "If beauty in a musical style that has had profound meaning to the people of a large part of the world for centuries had no effect upon me, I decided some years ago, the fault probably lay more in me than it did in the music." Cowell, "The Traveling Ear," *House Beautiful* 104 no. 5 (May 1962): 34.

157. See Denise Von Glahn and Michael Broyles, "Musical Modernism Before It Began: Leo Ornstein and a Case for Revisionist History," *Journal of the Society for American Music* 1, no. 1 (February 2007): 29–55. Charles Fisk, "Rachmaninoff's Modernity," paper read at the national meeting of the American Musicological Society, Washington, DC, 2005.

158. As in Catherine Parsons Smith, "'Intellectual Interest' and the Modernism(s) of the Others," paper read at the national meeting of the American Musicological Society, Washington, DC, 2005.

159. Jann Pasler, "Race, Orientalism, and Distinction in the Wake of the 'Yellow Peril,'" in *Western Music and Its Others*, 87–88.

160. Ibid., 101–102. Also see Pasler, "Reinterpreting Indian Music: Albert Roussel and Maurice Delage," in *Music-Cultures in Contact: Convergences and Collisions*, ed. Margaret J. Kartomi and Stephen Blum (Basel: Gordon and Breach, 1994), 122–157.

161. Of course, I am not the first to claim that expressions of a "postmodern" aesthetic can be identified throughout twentieth-century music. See, for example, Jonathan D. Kramer, "The Nature and Origins of Musical Postmodernism," in *Postmodern Music/Postmodern Thought*, ed. Judy Lochhead and Joseph Auner (New York: Routledge, 2002), 14–16.

Chapter 4

1. Homi K. Bhabha, *The Location of Culture* (London and New York: Routledge, 1994), 66.

2. On the presumed pleasure inherent in repeatedly experiencing musical stereotypes and their "seductive" aesthetic appeal, see Michael V. Pisani, *Imagining Native America in Music* (New Haven, CT: Yale University Press, 2005), 331.

3. The 1917 play *The String of the Samisen* by Rita Wellman offers a rather dramatic version of the self-sacrificial Japanese woman in American *japonisme*. Tama is a rich merchant's wife who takes *shamisen* lessons and has an affair with a young samurai, an enemy of her husband. Her samurai lover asks her to help him kill her husband by signaling when he is

asleep. Instead, Tama, bound by wifely duty, warns her husband to flee, sends the signal, assumes her husband's position on the sleeping mat, and is then killed by her lover.

4. I should note that the 1915 silent film of *Madama Butterfly* and *The Cheat* are considered together more briefly in Nick Browne, "The Undoing of the *Other* Woman: Madame Butterfly in the Discourse of American Orientalism," in *The Birth of Whiteness: Race and the Emergence of US Cinema*, ed. Daniel Bernardi (New Brunswick, NJ: Rutgers University Press, 1996), 227–256.

5. These narrative tensions and temptations were, of course, a staple of nineteenth-century European Orientalist opera. For example, on the paradigmatic plot device of the European male and the exotic woman, see James Parakilas, "The Soldier and the Exotic: Operatic Variations on a Theme of Racial Encounter: Part I and II," *Opera Quarterly* 10, nos, 2–3 (winter 1993–1994; spring 1994): 33–56; 43–69. For a recent overview of operatic Orientalism and its scholarship see my "Exoticism," in *The Oxford Handbook of Opera*, ed. Helen Greenwald (New York: Oxford University Press, 2014), 795–816.

6. On Orientalist representation in early American film, see the following in particular: Randall M. Miller, ed., *Ethnic Images in American Film and Television* (Philadelphia: The Balch Institute), 1978; Richard A. Oehling, "The Yellow Menace: Asian Images in American Film," in Randall M. Miller, ed., *The Kaleidoscopic Lens: How Hollywood Views Ethnic Groups* (Englewood, NJ: Jerome S. Ozer, Publisher: 1980), 182–206; Nick Browne, "Orientalism as an Ideological Form: American Film Theory in the Silent Period," *Wide Angle* 11, no. 4 (October 1989): 23–31; Kevin Brownlow, *Behind the Mask of Innocence* (New York: Knopf, 1990); Daniel Bernardi, ed., *The Birth of Whiteness: Race and the Emergence of US Cinema* (New Brunswick, NJ: Rutgers University Press, 1996); and Jun Xing, *Asian America through the Lens: History, Representations, and Identity* (Walnut Creek, CA: AltaMira Press, 1998).

7. I have previously presented some of the material and ideas on cinematic representations of the "Madame Butterfly" narrative offered here in papers delivered at the University of California, Berkeley (2001), the American Music Research Center, the University of Colorado at Boulder (2001), at the Oakley Center for the Humanities and Social Sciences, Williams College (2003), and at the University of Kentucky (2019). I am grateful for comments offered by panelists and audience members at each of these events.

8. For more recent discussion of the relationship between film and opera see such studies as: Jeremy Tambling, *Opera, Ideology, and Film* (New York: St. Martin's Press, 1987); Alexander Thomas Simpson, "Opera on Film: A Study of the History and the Aesthetic Principles and Conflicts of a Hybrid Genre" (PhD diss., University of Kentucky, 1990); Jeremy Tambling, ed., *A Night in at the Opera: Media Representations of Opera* (London: John Libbey and Co., 1994); Jeongwon Joe, "Opera on Film, Film in Opera: Postmodern Implications of the Cinematic Influence on Opera" (PhD diss., Northwestern University, 1998); Marcia Citron, *Opera on Screen* (New Haven, CT: Yale University Press, 2000); David Schroeder, *Cinema's Illusions, Opera's Allure: The Operatic Impulse in Film* (New York and London: Continuum, 2002); Jeongwon Joe and Rose Theresa, eds., *Between Opera and Cinema* (New York: Routledge, 2002); Jennifer Barnes, *Television Opera: The Fall of Opera Commissioned for Television* (Rochester, NY: Boydell Press, 2003); Paul Fryer, *The Opera Singer and the Silent Film* (Jefferson, NC, and London: McFarland & Co., 2005); and Michal Grover-Friedlander, *Vocal Apparitions: The Attraction of Cinema to Opera* (Princeton, NJ: Princeton University Press, 2005). For examples of more focused case studies, also see David Beard, "'A Face like Music': Shaping Images into Sound in *The Second Mrs. Kong*," *Cambridge Opera Journal* 18, no. 3 (2006): 273–300, and my "Tan Dun and Zhang Yimou between Film and Opera," *Journal of Musicological Research* 29, no. 1 (January–March 2010): 1–33.

9. E. H. Bierstadt, "Opera in Moving Pictures," *Opera Magazine* (October 1915): 30–32. In 1937, Ernst Toch called for the creation of original film operas—operas that would be designed

specifically for the screen—arguing that the filming of existing operas entailed the mutilation of "either screen action or the music itself." This quotation appeared in Frank S. Nugent, "The Cinema Wields the Baton," *New York Times*, 11 April 1937, sec. 11, p. 3, and is cited in Roy M. Prendergast, *Film Music: A Neglected Art*, 2nd ed. (New York: W. W. Norton, 1992), 21–22.

10. See "Are Movies Popularizing Opera?", *Theatre* 29 (May 1919): 297.

11. Joe, "Opera on Film, Film in Opera," 11. Joe's assumption of cinematic realism is also evident in her following statement: "In opera-film . . . singing becomes alien because it appears within the realistic frame of cinema." Joe draws upon Siegfried Kracauer's description of feeling "caught in a terrific clash between cinematic realism and operatic magic" while experiencing a film-opera. However, Kracauer states earlier that the "difference in unreality . . . between staged and filmed opera, is negligible." Kracauer, "Opera on the Screen," *Film Culture* 1, no. 2 (March 1955): 19–20.

12. On the degree of realism found in two famous film-operas of *Madama Butterfly*, see Helen M. Greenwald, "Issues of Authenticity in Two Films of Puccini's *Madama Butterfly*: Ponnelle (1974) and Mitterrand (1995)," in *Das Musiktheater in den audiovisuellen Medien*, eds. Peter Csobádi et al. (Anif/Salzburg: Verlag Mueller-Speiser, 2001), 295–305.

13. John Luther Long, *Madame Butterfly* (New York: The Century Co., 1903). Long's readers had also encountered an allusion to the story in his 1895 *Miss Cherry Blossom of Tokyo*. That novel opens with a character complaining that Pinkerton himself relates the story of "the Pink Geisha" far too often. This has also been noted by Arthur Groos in "*Madame Butterfly*: The Story," *Cambridge Opera Journal* 3, no. 2 (July 1991): 133.

14. Music was central to Loti's experience of Japan and to his preconceived image of this exotic land: "Even the woman's melancholy voice, still to be heard behind the paper partition, was so evidently the way they should sing, these musicians I had so often seen painted in amazing colours on rice-paper, half closing their dreamy eyes in the midst of impossibly large flowers. Long before I came to it, I had perfectly pictured this Japan to myself" (43). Towards the end of the novel, the protagonist decides to use the word "chamécen" rather than "guitar" to denote Chrysanthemum's instrument—this switch to an authentic term is framed as a sign that he now feels "almost at home" in Japan (280–282). Finally, nearly 10 percent of the novel's illustrations feature a drawing of the *shamisen*. Pierre Loti, *Madame Chrysanthème*, trans. Laura Ensor (London: George Routledge and Sons, Ltd., 1897).

André Messager's 1893 operatic setting of Loti's tale abounds in Orientalist sung songs and Chrysanthemum's exotic singing plays a major role in the drama. The hero, Pierre, is drawn to the exotic woman in Act I by her charming song—shades of *Lakmé* Act II. He is infuriated by her public musical performance in Act III and resolves to abandon her, only to be soothed once again by her "pure, silvery song" in Act IV.

15. Furst's manuscript score is contained in the David Belasco Collection of incidental music at the New York Public Library for the Performing Arts. Furst was born in 1852 and died in 1917. He composed for many of Belasco's productions and was a major figure in San Francisco theater and then on Broadway in the late nineteenth and early twentieth centuries. He composed several light operas and the score for Cecil B. DeMille's 1916 silent film *Joan the Woman*, which starred Geraldine Farrar. In addition to his Orientalist works for Belasco, Furst wrote the music for the "Chinese plays" *The First Born* (1897) by Francis Powers and *The Yellow Jacket* by George C. Hazelton and Benrimo. Walter Pritchard Eaton complained in a 4 November 1912 review of *The Yellow Jacket* that the incessant music for this production was "played on instruments approximating the Chinese, and is made up of Chinese rhythms, square-toed and monotonous. Yet this music never obtrudes, it cleverly avoids monotony, and it consistently heightens the scenes where it is employed." The review is reprinted in Eaton, *Plays and Players, Leaves from a Critic's Scrapbook* (Cincinnati: Stewart and Kidd Co., 1916), 58.

16. Belasco claimed that his "most successful effort in appealing to the imaginations of those who have sat before my stage" occurred in this scene. David Belasco, *The Theatre through Its Stage Door* (New York: Harper and Brothers, 1919), 238.

17. A notice appearing in the *New York Times* on 11 November 1906 (page SMA 2) proclaimed that the upcoming New York premiere of Puccini's opera at the Garden Theatre would offer a setting far more elaborate than that employed by Belasco in order "to carry the atmosphere of Japan with even greater fidelity and picturesqueness." The article also announced that, as in Belasco's production, a series of tableau curtains would be presented during Puccini's overture.

18. Belasco collaborated with John Luther Long in writing this play and Furst again composed the incidental music. The stage props included several Japanese musical instruments and the *shamisen* was featured in the accompanying music. On how the work presented "the real atmosphere of Japan" see David Belasco, "'Atmosphere' on the Stage," *Frank Leslie's Popular Monthly* (August 1903): 404–405. This exotic tragedy was burlesqued in 1903 as the *Darling of the Gallery Gods*. Further evidence of the success of this work is found in comments made by the supreme American Japanologist Ernest Fenollosa, who declared that he was amazed by the play's "emotional truth and power" and that *The Darling of the Gods* opened "a new era in the possibilities of elevating our Western theatre through a vital incorporation of the best elements in oriental Drama." See "Ezra Pound ed. 'Fenollosa on the Noh' as It Was: Lecture V. *No*. Washington, 12 March, 1903," in *The Ernest F. Fenollosa Papers: Houghton Library Harvard University*, ed. and trans. Akiko Murakata, Japanese Edition, Vol. 3 Literature (Tokyo: Museum Press: 1987), 275–276. The impact of the play can be traced to such later works as the 1916 *Bushido* produced by the Washington Square Players and the 1919 Provincetown Players' production (with involvement by Michio Ito) of *The String of the Samisen*.

19. Belasco, *The Theatre through Its Stage Door*, 61.

20. "'Better to 'Score' Than to Be a 'Star',' Says Miss Blanche Bates," *Morning Telegraph* (17 May 1903): part 3, p. 1.

21. A. Nicholas Vardac, *Stage to Screen: Theatrical Method from Garrick to Griffith* (New York: Benjamin Blom, 1968), 108.

22. Anne Dhu Shapiro, "Action Music in American Pantomime and Melodrama, 1730–1913," *American Music* 2, no. 4 (winter 1984): 66. For a radically revisionary view on the purported connections between early cinema and nineteenth-century staged melodrama, see Rick Altman, "The Silence of the Silents," *Musical Quarterly* 80, no. 4 (winter 1996): 648–718. Altman's argument focuses primarily on cinema history prior to 1915 and calls into question our assumptions regarding the presence of music in the experience of early film. Also see Gillian B. Anderson, "Synchronized Music: The Influence of Pantomime on Moving Pictures," *Music and the Moving Image* 8, no. 3 (fall 2015): 3–39.

23. Belasco, *The Theatre through Its Stage Door*, 205.

24. Charles Osborne notes that Belasco "specialized in stage pictures of an almost cinematic realism," and Lise-Lone Marker states that for "Belasco, as for Appia, lighting played the part of visual music, not only in the service of illusion but also of poetic vision." See Osborne, *The Complete Operas of Puccini* (New York: Atheneum, 1982), 155; and Marker, *David Belasco: Naturalism in the American Theatre* (Princeton, NJ: Princeton University Press, 1975), 86. Helen M. Greenwald has discussed the visual elements in both Belasco's and Puccini's stage designs in "Realism on the Opera Stage: Belasco, Puccini, and the California Sunset," in *Opera in Context: Essays on Historical Staging from the Late Renaissance to the Time of Puccini*, ed. Mark A. Radice (Portland, OR: Amadeus Press, 1998), 279–296, and in "Picturing Cio-Cio-San: House, Screen, and Ceremony in Puccini's *Madama Butterfly*," *Cambridge Opera Journal* 12, no. 3 (2000): 237–259.

25. Franklin refers to Artur Seidl's 1910/11 article "*Madame Butterfly* und *Tiefland*." See Peter Franklin, "Distant Sounds—Fallen Music: *Der ferne Klang* as 'Woman's Opera'?" *Cambridge Opera Journal* 3, no. 2 (July 1991): 160. A more recent German study has viewed Puccini's operas from a similar perspective: Jurgen Leukel, "Puccinis kinematographische Technik," *Neue Zeitschrift fur Musik* 143, nos. 6–7 (1982): 24–26. In addition, Annie J. Randall has referred to the "cinematic jump-cut quality of the prelude" in Puccini's *The Girl of the Golden West*. See Randall and Rosalind Gray Davis, *Puccini and the Girl: History and Reception of* The Girl of the Golden West (Chicago: University of Chicago Press, 2005), 15.

26. Peter Franklin, "Movies as Operas? (Behind the Great Divide)," in *A Night in at the Opera: Media Representations of Opera*, ed. Jeremy Tambling (London: John Libbey & Co., 1994), 83, 88. In a 1992 production of *Tosca* directed by Giuseppe Patroni Griffi, the pursuit of *verismo* took a different form from that imagined here by Franklin. In this live telecast production, each act of the opera was performed at the specific time of day and location in Rome as indicated in the work's stage directions. Jonathan White refers to this as an act of "ultraverismo." See White, "Opera, Politics, and Television: Bel canto by Satellite," in *A Night in at the Opera*, 284ff.

27. H. E. Krehbiel, "The Tragic Outcome of 'Madame Butterfly'," *New York Tribune*, 22 October 1916. See also chapter 12 in his *A Second Book of Operas: Their Histories, Their Plots, and Their Music* (New York: Macmillan, 1917), 169–189. After suggesting that Messager's *Madame Chrysanthème* failed because its presentation of Japan was too authentic, without having himself heard or seen that opera, Krehbiel praises Puccini's use of Japanese tunes: "Japanese music is arid and angular, and yet so great is Puccini's skill in combining creative imagination and reflection that he knew how to make it blossom like a rose. Pity he could not wholly overcome its rhythmical monotony. Japanese melody runs almost uninterruptedly through his instrumental score" (186–187). Early twentieth-century critics rarely hesitated to pass judgment on the use of "Japanese" music, even though they most likely had little direct experience of it. For example, a review in *The Eagle* (collected in the *Madame Butterfly* clipping file at the New York Public Library for the Performing Arts) of Belasco's *Madame Butterfly* as performed at the Montauk Theater states: "The effect is increased by the incidental use of Japanese music in the pentatonic scale like the Chinese, but without the barbaric crashing discords which make the Chinese music hideous." Here the critic casually assumes Furst's incidental music to be somehow "Japanese."

28. Betty Ewart Evans suggests that Puccini was influenced by Belasco's and Furst's decisions on where to use music in the drama and by the style of music they employed. However, she does not compare Furst's and Puccini's music in detail. See Evans, "The Nature of Belasco's Use of Music in Representative Productions" (PhD diss., University of Oregon, 1966).

29. Michal Grover-Friedlander has stated that in "films relating to opera, highlights from the opera's orchestral music were often used to accompany the image on the screen for additional effect." See Grover-Friedlander, "'The Phantom of the Opera': The Lost Voice of Opera in Silent Film," *Cambridge Opera Journal* 11, no. 2 (1999): 180. My research suggests, however, that the cue sheets for silent films relating to opera were just as likely to ignore the opera's music entirely.

30. Nick Browne, "The Undoing of the *Other* Woman," 245. Browne notes that none of the reviews of the 1915 film mention any music. He appears to accept this unremarkable fact as evidence that no music was heard during screenings of the film (236).

31. Again, see Rick Altman, "The Silence of the Silents," on the apparent absence of music in earlier cinema.

32. Wesley Ray Burroughs, "With the Movie Organist" *Diapason* (1 February 1916): 3.

33. Ernst Luz, *The Toll of the Sea: A "Luz" Music Score* (New York: Photo Play Music Co., 1923). This film starred Anna May Wong in the title role and was the first two-color Technicolor

feature. This version of the tale is particularly notable for the intensely poignant scene in which Lotus Flower (the Butterfly character) hands over her son to his new white American mother. The adaptation was made by a female writer, Frances Marion. This is available on DVD with Martin Marks performing Luz's score: *Treasures from American Film Archives*, Vol. 2 (National Film Preservation Foundation, 2000).

34. In Belasco's play Blanche Bates sang two of these songs on stage in the role of Butterfly. In Long's *Purple-Eyes*, a woman of mixed parentage sings, "Long down behine the Suwanee River" which causes the American male to laugh and join in. Long, "Purple Eyes," in *Madame Butterfly* (New York: The Century Co., 1907), 112–113.

35. The drafts of the script for this film are housed at the Academy of Motion Picture Arts and Sciences Research Center, Los Angeles (hereafter designated by AMPAS).

36. See Grover-Friedlander, "'The Phantom of the Opera.'" Also see Alexander Thomas Simpson, "Opera on Film: A Study of the History and the Aesthetic Principles and Conflicts of a Hybrid Genre"; and David Schroeder, *Cinema's Illusions, Opera's Allure: The Operatic Impulse in Film*.

37. See Claudia Gorbman, *Unheard Melodies: Narrative Film Music* (Bloomington: Indiana University Press, 1987), 42, 51.

38. A 4 May 1937 unsigned letter found in the "Production Materials" Folder 1, *Madame Butterfly* (1932), at AMPAS reveals that Paramount considered producing a "picture opera" version of the opera in 1937. The anonymous Paramount executive wrote: "The thing has been in embryo for years. Boris Morros has surveyed it from every angle and discussed it with every visiting celebrity up to and including Stravinsky." The writer explains that Paramount has not yet pursued the project because "there has always been some doubt as to the advisability of our attempting an opera on the screen." An article in the 21 July 1937 issue of *Variety* entitled "'Poor Butterfly' Gets Jap Rewrite and Modernization; Par to Produce?" offers more information on this abandoned project. This report from Tokyo reveals that the Japanese conductor Hidemaro Konoye "has completed a modern and Japanized version of Puccini's 'Madame Butterfly.'" In Konoye's version—an attempt to improve upon the 1932 film—Pinkerton is an American musician who meets Cio-Cio-San on a musical tour of Japan. Cio-Cio-San pursues a career as a vocalist and gives a recital in America with Pinkerton conducting. The couple is united at the end. Konoye reportedly proposed to rewrite Puccini's first act music himself "to impart more Japanese spirit . . . to retain the spirit in which Puccini wrote, but be more genuinely Japanese." He also suggested that all scenes offensive to the Japanese be eliminated, that a Japanese actress play the title role, and that the film be shot as much as possible in Japan.

39. Bound copies of the Paramount Press Sheets for this film (dated 30 December 1932) are held at AMPAS.

40. Executives at Columbia studios were clearly more committed opera buffs, as evidenced by the 1934 film *One Night of Love*, in which a performance of *Madama Butterfly* at the conclusion finally brings together the film's would-be lovers, an American soprano and a (hitherto) effete Italian opera coach named Monteverdi. The 1936 *Premiere der Butterfly*, also released by Columbia and directed by Carmine Gallone, went a step further by presenting a fictionalized portrait of Rosina Storchio, the soprano who first sang Butterfly, and of the premier of Puccini's opera. In this version, the soprano's lover leaves her behind in Europe to pursue his own career in America. She gives birth to their child and waits in vain for his return. She takes on the part of Butterfly, only too painfully aware of its reflection of her own life. Her former lover, mindful of what he has done and trapped in an opera box with his American wife, is made to suffer through her performance of the opera in German in the United States much as Claudius suffers through the play-within-a-play in *Hamlet*. However, she forgives him backstage, and even thanks him for causing her a terrible anguish that led to her best role and performance.

41. This version of the tale is thus the closest parallel to Loti's story of a Euro-American man's affair with a geisha. The bulk of Loti's autobiographical novel focuses on his daily impressions of life in Japan and his evolving opinions of his Japanese wife.

42. Harling's papers had been held at the Gavilan College Library in Gilroy, CA. However, the boxes containing his papers were lost before I was able to consult them.

43. Citron, 33.

44. The memo was addressed to Sam Katz and dated 5 October 1932. All correspondence cited here concerning the production of this film is collected in "Production Materials Folders," Folder 1, *Madame Butterfly* (1932), AMPAS.

45. Some critics argued that the film was a failure because its story was too operatic for the cinema, while others suggested that its cinematic realization was not operatic enough. For example, Philip K. Scheuer wrote in the *Los Angeles Times*, 27 December 1932: "[t]he picture is an opera denuded of operatics. Its story, completely lacking in contrast or counterpoint, is eminently unsuited to the cinema—besides having been robbed of any possible suspense by interminable imitations through the years."

46. This is not to imply that Puccini's own Orientalist orchestrations resemble Japanese traditional music to a significant degree. A good deal of scholarship has been devoted to detailing Puccini's borrowings of Japanese melodies and to tracing their sources. However, much of this scholarship tends to assume that pitch and melodic shape—as opposed to timbre and inflection—are of paramount importance in assessing Puccini's approximations of Japanese music. On connections between Puccini's score and Japanese (and Chinese) traditional music, see my "Puccini and the Music Boxes," *Journal of the Royal Musical Association* 140, no. 1 (spring 2015): 41–92. Also see Kunio Hara, "Puccini's Use of Japanese Melodies in *Madama Butterfly*" (MM thesis, University of Cincinnati, 2003); Michele Girardi, *Puccini: His International Art*, trans. Laura Basini (Chicago: University of Chicago Press, 2000), 195–258; Kimiyo Powils-Okano, *Puccinis "Madama Butterfly"* (Bonn: Verlag für systematische Musikwissenschaft), 1986; and, more generally, Jürgen Maehder, ed., *Esotismo e colore locale nell'opera di Puccini* (Pisa: Giardini, 1985). Ralph Locke has stated that transplanting *Madama Butterfly* from its Japanese setting would result in a different opera and that the opera has profoundly shaped his own views of Japan. See Locke, "Exoticism and Orientalism in Music: Problems for the Worldly Critic," in *Edward Said and the Work of the Critic: Speaking Truth to Power*, ed. Paul A. Bové (Durham, NC: Duke University Press, 2000), 272, 280–281.

47. These rehearsal numbers refer to the 1907 piano-vocal score published by Ricordi.

48. David Neumeyer has offered a thorough consideration of diegesis, including its relationship to realism, in a series of articles. See, in particular, Neumeyer, "Performances in Early Hollywood Sound Films: Source Music, Background Music, and the Integrated Sound Track," *Contemporary Music Review* 19, no. 1 (2000): 37–62; and "Diegetic/Nondiegetic: A Theoretical Model," *Music and the Moving Image* 2, no. 1 (spring 2009), http://mmi.press. illinois.edu/2.1/neumeyer.html. Also see Jeff Smith, "Bridging the Gap: Reconsidering the Border between Diegetic and Nondiegetic Music," *Music and the Moving Image* 2, no. 1 (spring 2009), http://mmi.press.illinois.edu/2.1/smith.html; Robynn J. Stilwell, "The Fantastical Gap between Diegetic and Nondiegetic," in *Beyond the Soundtrack: Representing Music in Cinema*, ed. Daniel Goldmark, Lawrence Kramer, and Richard Leppert (Berkeley: University of California Press, 2007), 184–202; and Ben Winters, "The Non-Diegetic Fallacy: Film, Music, and Narrative Space," *Music and Letters* 91, no. 2 (May 2010): 224–244. For an earlier discussion of this subject as it pertains to the relationship between opera and film see Robbert van der Lek, *Diegetic Music in Opera and Film: A Similarity between Two Genres of Drama Analysed in Works by Erich Wolfgang Korngold (1897-1957)* (Amsterdam: Rodopi, 1991).

49. An early draft synopsis reveals that the film was to have followed this reflexive path even further. We were to have seen a "half-caste" child at the dock and to have heard an officer

wisecrack: "Well, I know one thing . . . the Navy's been here before." We hear the entire song as an instrumental background underneath Pinkerton's and Butterfly's initial dialogue in the teahouse garden after he catches her and we first hear a line of the lyrics as Pinkerton returns home from work singing of his Japanese flower.

50. In the standard Hollywood practice of that time, the film immediately blasts forth "Un bel dì" for the end credits—erasing the tragedy and any uncomfortable feelings of guilt, and proclaiming hope, or perhaps offering a final sentimental reminder of Butterfly's anticipation.

51. For an overview of Ito's work in Hollywood, see Mary-Jean Cowell, "Michio Ito in Hollywood: Modes and Ironies of Ethnicity," *Dance Chronicle* 24, no. 3 (2001): 263–305.

52. See the Paramount Press Sheets for this film on this "atmospheric" footage.

53. Harling's score is held in the Music Department at Paramount Studios.

54. This dance does not to my eye resemble the typical movement style of Ito. Rather, it is more reminiscent of the butterfly dance of Loïe Fuller. The earlier fake geisha dancing doesn't look much like Ito's modernist choreography either.

55. Music's role in distinguishing one "Asian" face from another on screen, or in transforming our perception of a specific exotic character, is pointedly illustrated by one astonishing three-and-a-half minute sequence in the 1932 Frank Capra film *The Bitter Tea of General Yen*. In this film, a Chinese warlord has kidnapped a white American woman who clearly is both repulsed by and attracted to this exotic man. In a bizarre dream sequence without dialogue, General Yen (Nils Asther) appears in her bedroom as a grotesque Nosferatu- or Fu Manchu–like figure intent on rape and accompanied by Harling's strong pentatonic tune. The white woman is horrified. A second, masked man in Western clothes enters the room to rescue her and then removes his mask, revealing the normal face of General Yen (Asther again, but in less grotesque yellowface). Harling provides lush amorous music at this moment, the woman is thrilled by his visage, and the two engage in a passionate kiss. Harling's music helps to erase any negative connotations of this Asiatic face and forces us to accept, rather than be shocked by, this (fake) interracial kiss. As she awakens from the dream she discovers a feminized General Yen standing next to her bed, wearing a Chinese costume and holding a fan. Her ambivalence returns.

56. Clearly, the idea that a person of Asian heritage could be considered an "American" is precluded here and the "miscegenation angle" is of chief concern.

57. This argument is made powerfully by Gina Marchetti in *Romance and the "Yellow Peril": Race, Sex, and Discursive Strategies in Hollywood Fiction* (Berkeley: University of California Press, 1993). Marchetti discusses *My Geisha* in relationship to this paradigm in chapter 9 of her book. (My reading of *My Geisha*'s racial and gender politics presented below is in close agreement with Marchetti's.) Mari Yoshihara has more recently concurred that *Madame Butterfly* is a story "written and continually adapted by white men and widely enjoyed by white female audiences in America." However, Yoshihara argues that the cultural cross-dressing by white American women involved in performing this specific tale or participating in Orientalism in general "provided an effective tool for white women's empowerment and pleasure as New Women." See Yoshihara, *Embracing the East: White Women and American Orientalism* (New York: Oxford University Press, 2003), 5, 78. I confess to being unable to see how play-acting as a subservient childlike geisha on stage helped in the campaign for establishing a new conception of womanhood and female agency in America, either from the performer's or the audience's perspective. (Presumably Yoshihara's argument would need to pertain equally to those European women who performed in nineteenth-century French Orientalist operas.) Of course, as Yoshihara notes, the indulgence in Orientalism by elite white American women did place those women in a certain powerful position vis-à-vis exotic others, both within the United States and in East Asia. The idea that Japanese women offered valuable lessons for modern white American women and were superior versions of the ideal woman was stated

bluntly in 1907 by the major American collector of Asian art, Charles Lang Freer, who had first traveled to Japan in 1895. See Thomas Lawton and Linda Merrill, *Freer: A Legacy in Art* (Washington, DC: Smithsonian Institution, 1993), 20.

58. This information is found in the Franz Waxman Collection at the Syracuse University Library, Special Collections.

59. In 1955 a film similar to Paul's fictional film-opera was produced by an Italian company and directed by Carmine Gallone with Japanese actors but with Italian opera singers singing in Italian and filmed in Italy with some settings imported from Japan. See Joseph Anderson and Donald Richie, *The Japanese Film: Art and Industry* (Princeton, NJ: Princeton University Press, 1982), 247. A 7 September 1956 review of the film in the *Beverly Hills Citizen* ("Exquisite 'Butterfly'" by Hazel Flynn) opined that the "tale is particularly timely today when, due to the Occupation, there are so many 'Americans with Japanese faces.'"

60. Paul's discovery is made, ironically, through cinematic technology itself. While watching a color negative of one day's footage, Paul recognizes his blue-eyed, red-haired wife beneath her false wig and colored contact lenses. Following a moment of stunned silence, Waxman scored this crucial section with a tragic solo cello line, musically depicting Paul's devastation as he views the revealing sequence again and as we stare at the reflection of the diegetic film as it flickers across his face in the dark.

61. The male Euro-operatic accent of the tenor might spur the audience to make an association with Montand's French accent, and thus with Paul, even before the camera pans to him. Knowledge of Montand's own musical career may also have shaped early 1960s reception of his performance in this film.

62. Of course, a true filming of this scene in the film-opera would never have been achieved in one long take anyway. We are actually viewing something that more closely resembles a screening of a film-opera.

63. Waxman's score for *My Geisha* is held in the Music Department at Paramount Studios.

64. See Marchetti, 192.

65. A similar goal of exotic authenticity has periodically shaped casting decisions in productions of this opera, as noted in chapter 2 in my discussion of Haruko Onuki. On the career of Japanese soprano Tamaki Miura and her multiple appearances as Butterfly in the West, see Mari Yoshihara, *Musicians from a Different Shore: Asians and Asian Americans in Classical Music* (Philadelphia: Temple University Press, 2007), 23–33. Also see Robert Charles Lancefield, "Hearing Orientality in (White) America, 1900–1930" (PhD diss., Wesleyan University, 2004), chapter 1.

66. Although presented comically here, Paul's complaint that contemporary Japan had been corrupted by American culture and that the ideal women of Old Japan were vanishing was commonly echoed by offscreen American males in the 1950s and early 1960s. In addition, Euro-Americans often reacted negatively and derisively toward Japanese approximations of spoken English and American musical styles throughout the twentieth century. For a more recent example, see Dave Barry's rant on Japanese rock in *Dave Barry Does Japan* (New York: Random House, 1992), chapter 6.

67. On "racist cosmetology" with reference to *My Geisha*, see Eugene Franklin Wong, *On Visual Media Racism: Asians in the American Motion Pictures* (New York: Arno Press, 1978), 40, 43. As discussed above with reference to *The Bitter Tea of General Yen*, music can play a crucial role in cinematic racial coding. Soon after Lucy decides to take on the disguise of a geisha, we see a transition from a shot of Lucy on a poster to her in geisha costume at the start of the next sequence. A note dated 15 August 1961 attached to the musical sketch for this moment (collected in the *My Geisha* music production boxes at Paramount Studios) reveals that Waxman "suggested starting with harp cadenza until dissolve from poster to Lucy, made up as geisha again, then on dissolve the harp will be changed to a *koto* playing same music." In the film,

however, a jazzy clarinet lick accompanies Lucy's poster and then is imitated by the *koto* in the next shot. Perhaps Waxman decided that the harp would not contrast enough with the *koto*, or perhaps the jazz-inflected line was intended to suggest that MacLaine's sexual appeal was in no way diminished by her geisha disguise.

68. The film makes multiple references to earlier 1950s Hollywood films set in Japan. As Paul and Bob (the actor taking the part of Pinkerton in Paul's film) leave the tea house, the men joke that "sayonara" is the only Japanese word Americans know. Bob then bids farewell by saying "Marlon Brando." (Brando played the leading man in *Sayonara* in 1957.)

69. A. H. Weiler, "*My Geisha* Arrives," *New York Times*, 14 June 1962, 23.

70. See the *My Geisha* Paramount Press Book at AMPAS.

71. See the *My Geisha* page at http://www.shirleymaclaine.com/shirley/movies-mygeisha.php (accessed 17 September 2015).

72. *My Geisha*, RCA Victor, LOC-1070, 1962.

73. MacLaine does imitate the inflections of Japanese speech, at least as Japanese is heard by un-informed Anglo ears, in one particularly comic scene in the film. While attending a sumo match with Paul, Lucy (disguised as Yoko) is approached by a wrestler who attempts to strike up a conversation in Japanese. Lucy, unable to speak the language, strings together random phrases and words in an impressively rapid and fluent "Japanese voice." The wrestler, having just recently been thrown to the mat, taps his head as though to jolt his auditory system back in operation, and walks away bewildered. Spoken Japanese has frequently been presented as gibberish in Hollywood films. In the 1932 *Madame Butterfly* the baby boy's babble is denounced by Butterfly for sounding too Japanese. She requests that he speak only in his father's English.

74. Perhaps at this moment Lucy recalls a remark made to her by Paul when he still believed she was Yoko: "The Western woman is no match for the Japanese woman." In her Yoko dis-guise, Lucy had heard Paul explain that he badly wanted to do this film-opera "mostly so I could be the man, and she [Lucy] could be the woman"—a statement supported by Waxman with intensely lyrical music. On Paul's masculine crisis and Lucy's "tomboyish gestures" see Marchetti, 187–188.

75. A shot with similar implications appears in the 1932 *Madame Butterfly*, when Butterfly discovers a photograph of Adelaide in Pinkerton's luggage and holds the photo near to her own face so that we are prompted to compare her yellowface Asiatic features with the face of the white woman back home. A similar sequence occurred in the 1922 *Toll of the Sea* as the Pinkerton character's friends persuade him that he must drop his Chinese wife. The men gesture first to a white American woman and then to a Chinese woman with bad teeth. The camera focuses on each woman in turn, forcing the audience to make the comparison also and (most likely) to draw the same conclusion.

76. See Marchetti, 198–199.

77. Up to a certain point, of course. The suicide device in these Orientalist tales allows for a final alienation from the exotic woman, and thereby clears the way not only for the white female character to reassume her rightful place, but metaphorically for the white female au-dience member to fill the void left by the exotic woman's death. On the roots of this narra-tive device in nineteenth-century Orientalist opera, see James Parakilas, "The Soldier and the Exotic: Operatic Variations on a Theme of Racial Encounter, I and II."

78. By extension, some white heterosexual male audience members may also discover a certain satisfaction in the film's conclusion. As Marchetti puts it: "For male viewers, these stories pro-mote a fantasy in which a desire for the exoticism of a nonwhite beauty can be rationalized by the fact that the beauty is really Caucasian." Marchetti, 177. This twist on the Madame Butterfly tale resonates with the plot of Saint-Saëns's 1872 operetta *La Princesse jaune*. In this work, a Dutch man on drugs hallucinates while viewing a portrait of a Japanese woman. He

imagines that his Dutch girl (Lena) is the Ming (a Chinese-sounding name) of his dreams, the exotic woman in the picture. His hallucination is signaled musically by an offstage chorus singing fake Japanese words and accompanied by a celesta with a pentatonic tune and a gong. During the hallucination, we see his vision as the set changes and the performer assuming the role of Lena changes costumes in order to become the ideal exotic woman of his dreams. When he awakens he realizes that he loves only Lena.

79. Marchetti, 183.

80. Perhaps a brief plunge into Hollywood biography is in order here since MacLaine has referred to the film as being "almost autobiographical" (http://www.shirleymaclaine.com/shirley/movies.php). Steve Parker was raised in Japan and he and MacLaine were married in 1954. Envious of her success, Parker moved back to Japan and the couple maintained an "open marriage" for the next thirty years. Their joint interest in things Japanese is reflected in their daughter's middle name, Sachiko.

81. Christopher Ames, *Movies about the Movies: Hollywood Reflected* (Lexington: University Press of Kentucky, 1997), 4.

82. See my review of Anthony Minghella's production of *Madama Butterfly* at the Metropolitan Opera, *Opera Quarterly* 24, no. 1 (winter 2008): 139–147. On attempts in the 1950s to create "authentic" productions of Puccini's *Madama Butterfly* in the United States, see Barbara E. Thornbury, *America's Japan and Japan's Performing Arts: Cultural Mobility and Exchange in New York, 1952–2011* (Ann Arbor: University of Michigan Press, 2013), 126–131.

83. Grover-Friedlander suggests more generally that "sound, music, voice and speech in film do not create greater realism. . . . Rather, they accentuate the medium's uneasiness and anxiety" ("'The Phantom of the Opera': The Lost Voice of Opera in Silent Film," 183). For a rather special example of music's potential for disrupting linear time in cinema see Stan Link, "Nor the Eye Filled with Seeing: The Sound of Vision in Film," *American Music* 22, no. 1 (spring 2004): 84–86.

84. Citron, 8. Similarly, Lydia Goehr referred to film as being more realistic than opera and quoted a 1926 statement by Arnold Schoenberg to that effect. However, Goehr concluded: "But, in the end, cinematographic realism is also about style and even operatic style and, thus like opera, has everything to do with how things *appear*, especially when what this appearance reveals is how far film (or opera) contributes to reconstructing the world in its own image." She also stated that "film is much more like opera than some have claimed, especially those who have overly separated the *realism* and *naturalism* of one from the *style* or *high stylization* of the other." See Goehr, *Elective Affinities: Musical Essays on the History of Aesthetic Theory* (New York: Columbia University Press, 2008), 223, 253. Peter Kivy has also commented on the relationship between film and opera. See Kivy, "Music in the Movies: A Philosophical Inquiry," in his *Music, Language, and Cognition: And Other Essays in the Aesthetics of Music* (Oxford: Clarendon Press, 2007), 62–87.

85. Link has independently developed a theory of film sound's potential for directing our vision in the cinematic, rather than operatic, experience. See Link, "Nor the Eye Filled with Seeing."

86. Stine took the part of Kate in this production of the opera. On this and other examples of *Madama Butterfly* associated with Japanese style gardens in the United States see Kendall H. Brown, *Japanese-Style Gardens of the Pacific West Coast* (New York: Rizzoli, 1999), 11–12, 55, 60. Stine's beautiful Hakone Gardens in Saratoga, California, were inspired by the 1915 silent film and are today open to the public.

87. Mascagni composed for the *shamisen* in his 1898 opera *Iris* as did Furst for Belasco's *The Darling of the Gods*. In neither case did the presence of the Japanese instrument result in Japanese music.

88. This option was taken, however, in several World War II anti-Japanese propaganda films, including Frank Capra's *Know Your Enemy—Japan* (1945).

89. The film ends with Tori safely led away by police officers and the reunited couple strolling down the courtroom aisle as the crowd applauds. The screenplay was written by Hector Turnbull and Jeanie Macpherson. (Macpherson was both a screenwriter and actress and appeared as a Gypsy girl in DeMille's 1915 *Carmen*.) Manuscripts of the original 1915 screenplay are held in box 1241, folder 4, in the Cecil B. DeMille archives, Brigham Young University, Special Collections, Harold B. Lee Library. Several video recordings of the film, in its 1918 version, have been commercially released. For a recording featuring a particularly appropriate score by Robert Israel, see *Manslaughter; The Cheat* (New York: Kino International Corp., 2002). DeMille's film has received sustained critical attention. See particularly: Sumiko Higashi, "Ethnicity, Class, and Gender in Film: DeMille's *The Cheat*," in *Unspeakable Images: Ethnicity and the American Cinema*, ed. Lester D. Friedman, 112–139 (Urbana: University of Illinois Press, 1991); and Higashi, *Cecil B. DeMille and American Culture: The Silent Era* (Berkeley: University of California Press, 1994), 100–112. Also see: Gina Marchetti, 10–45; Robert G. Lee, *Orientals: Asian Americans in Popular Culture* (Philadelphia: Temple University Press, 1999), 120–126; and Daisuke Miyao, *Sessue Hayakawa: Silent Cinema and Transnational Stardom* (Durham, NC, and London: Duke University Press, 2007), 21–49.

90. I delivered papers on the numerous versions of *The Cheat* at meetings of both the Royal Musical Association and the American Musicological Society in 2001 and I remain grateful for comments offered by panelists and audience members at both of these events.

91. See the *I.O.U.* clippings and program file in the Billy Rose Theatre Collection, New York Public Library for the Performing Arts. This file includes a program for the 5 October 1918 performance at the Belmont Theatre in New York.

92. The piano vocal score was published by Max Eschig, Paris, in 1920.

93. All prints of the 1923 film appear to be lost, but the scenario/script for this film and for the 1931 film are held in the Academy of Motion Picture Arts and Sciences Research Center, Los Angeles. A nitrate print of the 1931 film is available at the University of California–Los Angeles, Film Archives.

94. Russell Holman, *The Cheat* (New York: Grosset and Dunlap, 1923).

95. The 1937 French film *Forfaiture* was directed by Marcel L'Herbier and was released on video in 1989 by Editions René Chateau. Hayakawa starred in numerous silent films, including those released by his own production company. DeMille's *The Cheat* proved to be Hayakawa's breakthrough work. On this star's long and fascinating career, see Sessue Hayakawa, *Zen Showed Me the Way*, ed. Croswell Bowen (Indianapolis and New York: Bobbs-Merrill, 1960); and Daisuke Miyao, *Sessue Hayakawa: Silent Cinema and Transnational Stardom* (Durham, NC, and London: Duke University Press, 2007). Also see Donald Kirihara, "The Accepted Idea Displaced: Stereotype and Sessue Hayakawa," in *The Birth of Whiteness: Race and the Emergence of US Cinema*, 81–99. Although I conclude my genealogy of *The Cheat* with the 1937 French film, it appears that Hayakawa directed his own stage version of the tale in 1944 in France (see Miyao, 286, note 25) and there could very well have been other versions that have escaped the attention of scholars. On DeMille's Orientalist depictions of East Asia, see Sumiko Higashi, "Touring the Orient with Lafcadio Hearn and Cecil B. DeMille," in *The Birth of Whiteness*, 338–348.

96. In 1957, DeMille related that following the huge success of *The Cheat*, he ordered numerous items to be shipped direct from Japan to enhance the mise en scène for a film he planned to make of David Belasco's *The Darling of the Gods*, a work DeMille referred to as "a wonderful play . . . a marvelous play, I loved it." In explaining why he never made this film DeMille claimed, "then came the fear of Japan—that anything Japanese would not go well with the American public—they were building up for trouble, which they were, way back in 1915.

Finally they persuaded me not to do it." See "PERSONAL: Autobiography files—Research," box 13, folder 1, in the DeMille archives, Brigham Young University.

97. Archival materials suggest that DeMille's 1916 *Joan the Woman* was likely his first production for which a musical score was commissioned. (S. L. Rothapfel and Hugo Riesenfeld compiled and arranged the music for DeMille's 1915 *Carmen*.) Nick Browne refers erroneously to "the score" for *The Cheat* being housed in the Kleiner collection at the University of Minnesota. Browne, "The Undoing of the *Other* Woman," in *The Birth of Whiteness*, 231. As Rick Altman has explained, cue sheets were not regularly compiled for films until the 1920s. See Altman, *Silent Film Sound* (New York: Columbia University Press, 2004), 346.

98. The list of music cues is found on page 6 in the Paramount Pictures "Press Book and Exhibitors' Aids" for the film, held at the Museum of Modern Art Film Archives. These press sheets for *The Secret Game* include an outrageous letter from Hayakawa (5) in fake Japlish ready to be sent to local newspapers. Although Gottschalk is credited with compiling the "musical synopsis" (cue sheet) for the film, on page 2 of the press book we learn that "the music which was added by Charles Bradford, director of the great orchestra of the Broadway Theatre, New York City, will go far towards adding to the effect you wish to produce."

99. The cover to the 1904 Carl Fischer publication of Theodore Moses-Tobani's "Japanese Patrol" claims to introduce "the National Air 'Fou So Ka'." I have also collected an undated arrangement of the same piece by one M. L. Lake and the tune also appears in "The Rising Sun of Japan: Grand Descriptive Battle Piece" by Jos. Wachtel, published in 1904 by Sol Bloom. The piece appeared in John Philip Sousa's compilation *National, Patriotic and Typical Airs of All Lands* (Philadelphia: H. Coleman, 1890), 152–153; and in Victor Herbert's compilation *The World's Best Music*, Vol. 8 (New York: The University Society, 1908), 632–634. This *gunka*, or military song, stylistically resembles the final eleven tragic bars of Puccini's *Madama Butterfly* and deploys the blunt rhythms, brassy instrumentation, and pentatonicism that would become ubiquitous in Hollywood's anti-Japanese propaganda films of the World War II period. "Fou-So-Ka" was presented as the "national anthem of Japan" in a 1912 ceremony at Riverside Park in New York City to celebrate the donation by Japan of cherry trees to the city. The ceremony, attended by some 5,000 people, opened with selections from *The Mikado* and featured thirteen kimono-clad kindergarten girls who came forward to plant the final cherry trees as (fittingly) "Sakura, Sakura" was performed and then the girls danced a Japanese folk dance. The entire ceremony was motivated by the desire to counter the current tense relations between Japan and the United States. See "Cherry Tree Tablet Accepted by City," *New York Times*, 29 April 1912, 10.

100. Arthur Kleiner, music director of the Museum of Modern Art film library from 1939 to 1967, composed and compiled a cue sheet for a revival screening of *The Cheat*, now held in the Kleiner collection at the University of Minnesota. Kleiner employed a Japanese melody only once in his cue sheet; the famous folk song "Sakura, Sakura" accompanies the sinister sequence in which Edith faints and Tori lifts her helpless body and steals his interracial kiss. For Hayakawa's first appearance, Kleiner composed a dissonant stinger chord, somewhat resembling a *sho* cluster, followed by a tune based on the Japanese *in* scale. The 1994 compilation score by Robert Israel, which appears on several recent releases of the film, does not play up the film's exoticism. For example, when Edith and Tori first enter the *shoji* room Israel avoids any clear change in the musical style. The style changes only after Tori slides the door closed, thus serving to emphasize their uneasy intimacy rather than the exotic room itself, and to suggest that the previous music was diegetic.

101. Remarkably, Burroughs stresses the importance of distinguishing the Japanese from the Chinese—their "hitherto barbarian neighbors"—in the music. See Wesley Ray Burroughs, "With the Movie Organist," *The Diapason* (1 October 1917): 10. However, in his 1 January 1919 column (14) devoted to Chinese-themed films, he called for selections from *Madama*

Butterfly and for the song "Poor Butterfly." In his 1 August 1916 column (6) Burroughs noted the importance of establishing the "local color" of a drama during the first reel by playing characteristic pieces of "Oriental atmosphere."

102. *Evening Post* review of 7 October 1918. A review in the *Evening Sun* on the same date declared: " 'I.O.U.' proves that a good 'movie' can be turned into a poor play."

103. A related concern clearly shaped the 1917 Hayakawa vehicle *The Secret Game*. The advance publicity claimed that the film showed America and Japan "to be the strongest of allies and friends." These press sheets refer to Japan as "America's greatest ally" and quote Hayakawa's claim that he initially rejected the part before he understood that his character was a Japanese spy in the service of the United States: "I can't afford to take another chance of making myself unpopular with my countrymen as I did with some of them when I played in *The Cheat*" (18). In revising the original 1915 film for its 1918 re-release, the filmmakers were careful to replace certain shots, as they did with the close-up of the exotic villain's signed check revealing his new name and a new date of 15 June 1918. (However, in a shot of the newspaper headlines, only the year was changed, resulting in a mistake.)

104. The play was first produced out of town in Asbury Park, New Jersey, in August 1918 and the villain's name was listed as "Baron Tori." In this initial production an actor named R. Ko Jima played a character named "Kiku" and Robert Ayerton played "Ambassador Oto."

105. The published cue sheet that I consulted is held at the Arts Library Special Collections, University of California–Los Angeles. The cover of the sheet music for the 1924 "Carmelita Song" (words by Joan Hastings, music by Nellie Simpson, G. Ricordi and Co., London) claims to have been "inspired by and used as the theme of" the 1923 Cheat. However, the cue sheet does not mention this piece.

106. "Program Week Beginning Sunday, August 26th," *Rivoli Times* 1, mp/10 (26 August 1923): no page number; found in the clipping file for this film, Billy Rose Theatre Collection, New York Public Library for the Performing Arts.

107. Paramount Press Sheet for 1931 *The Cheat*, 2. This is part of a "ready review" designed to assist the "busy movie critic." Recall that the husband in the original film was named Richard Hardy; we may presume that the villain's last name was inspired by the famous nineteenth-century explorer of sub-Saharan Africa, Dr. David Livingstone. This version suggests that association with the exotic other is dangerous for both female and male white Americans.

108. The filmmaker's attempts at exotic authenticity were trumpeted: "The music staff at Paramount's New York studio, headed by Frank Tours, [. . .] is equal to any occasion. This is proved by their ability to furnish absolutely authentic music for the Cambodian dance staged by George Abbott and Ruth St. Denis for an important scene in 'The Cheat.' Instruments peculiar to Cambodia were also obtained, at the result of much effort and expense." Harry N. Blair, "Short Shots from Eastern Studios," *The Film Daily* (15 September 1931): 6. I have not been able to locate the score or any indication who composed the music for this film. The press sheets for the film emphasized the authenticity of St. Denis's dance and boasted that in one scene artwork was featured from fifteen Oriental countries—clearly the filmmakers felt the need to lay on the Orientalism heavily to infuse some novelty into this well-worn tale.

109. The translation of this passage is by Felix Aprahamian (1981) from the CD booklet accompanying a recording of the opera conducted by Lorin Maazel with the Orchestre National de la R.T.F. (Deutsche Grammophon 423 718-2), 41.

110. Colette, edited and introduced by Alain and Odette Virmaux, *Colette at the Movies: Criticism and Screenplays* (New York: Frederick Ungar Publishing Co., 1980), 35–36. Originally published in *Excelsior*, 28 August 1917.

111. Michal Grover-Friedlander, " 'The Phantom of the Opera,'" 179.

112. Erlanger's *Forfaiture* is widely cited as having been the first opera to be based on a film, and I have uncovered no evidence to dispute this claim. Benjamin Goose is incorrect in attributing this status to the 1926 opera *Der Golem* by d'Albert. In his discussion of that opera's relationship to film, Goose suggests that cinema influenced d'Albert in his creation of music that was "subordinate to the stage action." This does not seem entirely novel in operatic history. See Goose, "The Opera of the Film? Eugen d'Albert's *Der Golem*," *Cambridge Opera Journal* 19, no. 2 (2007): 142, 159, 163. Basing new operas on preexistent films became relatively common by the start of the twenty-first century.

113. Julie McQuinn, "Unofficial Discourses of Gender and Sexuality at the Opéra-Comique during the Belle Epoque" (PhD diss., Northwestern University, 2003), 115–211.

114. Colette, 19. (This review originally appeared in *Excelsior* on 7 August 1916.)

115. Émile Vuillermoz, "*Forfaiture* de Camille Erlanger, à l'Opéra-Comique," *Revue Musicale* (March 1921): 256–258. He compared the opera to Puccini's *Tosca* and to *verismo* more generally. (The opera also prompts a comparison with Bartók's *The Miraculous Mandarin*, which premiered in 1926.) I should note that Vuillermoz was a composer and music critic who published an article on film in 1927 entitled "La Musique des Images."

116. For a related discussion, see Rose M. Theresa, "Spectacle and Enchantment: Envisioning Opera in Late Nineteenth-Century Paris" (PhD diss., University of Pennsylvania, 2000).

117. The large scale exotic performance scenes in the 1923 and 1931 films do recall the structures of French Orientalist opera. On French musical *japonisme*, see Robert F. Waters, "Emulation and Influence: *Japonisme* and Western Music in *fin de siècle* Paris," *Music Review* 55, no. 3 (August 1994): 214–226, and Jann Pasler, "Political Anxieties and Musical Reception: Japonisme and the Problem of Assimilation," in *Madama Butterfly: l'orientalismo di fine secolo, l'approccio pucciniano, la ricezione*, eds. Arthur Groos and Virgilio Bernardoni (Firenze: Leo S. Olschki Editore, 2008), 17–53. Pasler has suggested that the negative response at the premiere of Puccini's opera was shaped in part by European fears of the Japanese given the steady news of Japan's advances in the Russo-Japanese War.

118. An ad for corsets appearing on p. 5 of the program for *I.O.U.* offers but one source of evidence that the presenters and producers of several of these *Cheat* works assumed their wartime audience would be predominately female. This ad explains that women are "doing their bit" for the war effort and that "in most cases [they are] being engaged in work which has always been considered too hard for the so-called 'weaker sex.'" The implication of this ad, and the play itself, is that women should avoid conspicuous consumption and exotic enticements and instead continue to "do their bit." This program is found in the "clipping and program" file for *I.O.U.* at the Billy Rose Theatre Collection, New York Public Library for the Performing Arts.

119. The exotic subject of this operetta prompted Lehár to stretch his musical style. In particular, I note that the choral music heard in the opening of Act II is heavily Orientalized. Edward Michael Gold has stated that "with *Das Land des Lächelns*, one observes in virtually every respect an expansion of musical means." See Gold, *By Franz Lehár–The Complete Cosmopolitan* (London: Glocken Verlag Limited, 1995), 11.

120. Sessue Hayakawa, 136–137.

121. Hayakawa's Chinese-American role was in the 1918 film *The City of Dim Faces*, set in San Francisco's Chinatown. The Paramount Press Book for this film emphasized the mixed-race nature of Hayakawa's character and proclaimed that it brought "into strong contrast in his makeup, the intellect and subtlety of the Oriental and the power, strength and physical superiority of the whites" (2). This Chinese American hero is unaware that his Chinese father has imprisoned his white mother—whom he has never known and who is now demented—in an underground den. The young man himself falls in love with a white woman whom he in turn imprisons in the same den when she breaks off their engagement. Eventually, he

learns that he is half white and that the demented imprisoned older woman is his mother and then "the white blood in his veins asserts its power and remorse seizes him." He frees both women, and dies wounded at his mother's feet.

122. On this recently rediscovered film, see Daisuke Miyao, 159–165.

123. Ibid., 163–164.

124. On the rise of anti-Japanese sentiment during this period see Roger Daniels, *The Politics of Prejudice: The Anti-Japanese Movement in California and the Struggle for Japanese Exclusion* (Berkeley: University of California Press, 1962).

125. See Brownlow, 351–352.

126. See Ibid., 350.

Chapter 5

1. Studs Terkel, *"The Good War": An Oral History of World War Two* (New York: Ballantine Books, 1984), 32. This particular oral history seems to have served as a model for David Guterson's novel *Snow Falling on Cedars* (New York: Vintage Books, 1995). In the novel, two FBI agents search the Japanese American heroine's childhood home and confiscate both a stack of *shakuhachi* sheet music and the *shakuhachi* itself before arresting her father. It is interesting to note that in Japan's Edo period the *shakuhachi* served the dual role of musical instrument and clublike weapon for itinerant priests doubling as spies (perhaps Guterson's FBI agents perceived the dangerous potential of this bamboo flute). In the 1999 Universal film version of the novel, with a score by James Newton Howard, we hear synthesized *shakuhachi* sounds, although no musical instruments are visible during the FBI scene.

2. I delivered earlier versions of this chapter as lectures at Oxford University (1999) and the University of Chicago (2000) and I remain grateful for comments and suggestions offered by audience members at both of these events.

3. For information on this campaign, see Kathleen Ellen Rahtz Smith, " 'Goodbye, Mama. I'm Off to Yokohama': The Office of War Information and Tin Pan Alley in World War II" (PhD diss., Louisiana State University, 1996). Smith finds that Tin Pan Alley failed to create strong World War II songs (in the way it had for World War I) and concludes that "Americans did not need a war song to convince them to support the war" (xii). I will argue that music successfully fulfilled this role in Hollywood films. The topic is also surveyed in Rae Nichols Simmonds, "The Use of Music as a Political Tool by the United States during World War II" (PhD diss., Walden University, 1994). Also see Les Cleveland, "Singing Warriors: Popular Songs in Wartime," *Journal of Popular Culture* 28, no. 3 (1994): 155–75. Cleveland discusses both the official American attempts to create inspirational songs during World War II and the actual, often subversive songs sung by Allied troops in the field. For a broader study of American music during the war, see Annegret Fauser, *Sounds of War: Music in the United States during World War II* (New York: Oxford University Press, 2013). Fauser focuses on the activities of the Office of War Information in chapter 2. For studies of music's role in the wartime United Kingdom, see Christine L. Baade, *Victory through Harmony: The BBC and Popular Music in World War II* (Oxford: Oxford University Press, 2012); Jeffrey Richards, "Vaughan Williams and British Wartime Cinema," in *Vaughan Williams Studies*, ed. Alain Frogley (Cambridge, UK: Cambridge University Press, 1996), 139–165; David Rosen, "The Sounds of Music and War: Humphrey Jennings's and Stewart McAllister's *Listen to Britain* (1942)," in *Coll'astuzia, col giudizio: Essays in Honor of Neal Zaslaw*, ed. Cliff Eisen (Ann Arbor, MI: Steglein Publishing, 2009), 389–427; and Kate Guthrie, "Propaganda Music in Second World War Britain: John Ireland's Epic March," *Journal of the Royal Musical Association* 139, no. 1 (2014): 137–175.

4. See Richard Franko Goldman, "Music for the Army," *Modern Music* 20, no. 1 (1942): 8–12.

5. Quoted in Ben Arnold, *Music and War: A Research and Information Guide* (New York: Garland Publishing, 1993), 186. On Copland's own contribution to the war effort—a score for the Office of War Information film *The Cummington Story* (1945)—see Neil William Lerner, "The Classical Documentary Score in American Films of Persuasion: Contexts and Case Studies, 1936–1945" (PhD diss., Duke University, 1997), chapter 5. In addition to the Copland score, Lerner focuses on Virgil Thomson's scores for *The Plow That Broke the Plains* and *The River*, and provides an overview of documentary film music in his first chapter. Also see Lerner, "Aaron Copland, Norman Rockwell, and the 'Four Freedoms': The Office of War Information's Vision and Sound in *The Cummington Story* (1945)," in *Aaron Copland and His World*, ed. Carol J. Oja and Judith Tick (Princeton, NJ: Princeton University Press, 2005), 351–377.

6. These broadcasts were part of the infamous "Tokyo Rose" radio programs. See Ryō Namikawa, "Japanese Overseas Broadcasting: A Personal View," in *Film and Radio Propaganda in World War II*, ed. K. R. M. Short (Knoxville: University of Tennessee Press, 1983), 324–27; and Katherine A. Baber, "Jazz, World War II Radio Propaganda, and the Case of Tokyo Rose," in *The Soundtrack of Conflict: The Role of Music in Radio Broadcasting in Wartime and in Conflict Situations*, ed. M. J. Grant and Férdia J. Stone-Davis (Hildesheim: Georg Olms Verlag, 2013), 57–73.

7. Henry Cowell, "Shaping Music for Total War," *Modern Music* 23, no. 3 (summer 1946): 226–228.

8. See Ryō Namikawa, "Japanese Overseas Broadcasting: A Personal View," in *Film and Radio Propaganda in World War II*, ed. K. R. M. Short (Knoxville: University of Tennessee Press, 1983), 332.

9. On Japan's January 1942 ban of "jazz and sensual Western music" see Gordon Daniels, "Japanese Domestic Radio and Cinema Propaganda, 1937–1945: An Overview," in *Film and Radio Propaganda in World War II*, ed. Short, 293–318. Also see Anthony Rhodes, *Propaganda: The Art of Persuasion in World War II* (New York: Chelsea House, 1976), 249; and Ben-Ami Shillony, *Politics and Culture in Wartime Japan* (Oxford: Clarendon Press, 1981), 144. An official Japanese announcement of 8 January 1943 sought to clarify the edict: "The recent ban on jazz music . . . was never intended as an all-round rejection of Anglo-American music. The blacklisted numbers do not include sound, healthy, popular folk songs, even if some are of Anglo-American origin. They have been well assimilated with Japanese sentiments, such as 'Auld Lang Syne,' 'Home, Sweet Home,' and 'The Last Rose of Summer'" (quoted in Peter de Mendelssohn, *Japan's Political Warfare* [London: George Allen and Unwin, 1944; reprint, New York: Arno Press, 1972], 103).

10. On the performance of jazz in the camps, see George Yoshida, *Reminiscing in Swingtime: Japanese Americans in American Popular Music* (San Francisco: National Japanese American Historical Society, 1997), chapter 3. Deborah Wong has argued that the "centrality of jazz in the Japanese American internment camps or the fame of San Francisco's Forbidden City are thus easily forgotten because those jazz sounds were neither produced nor heard by the right kind of Americans" ("The Asian American Body in Performance," in *Music and the Racial Imagination*, ed. Ronald Radano and Philip V. Bohlman [Chicago: University of Chicago Press, 2000], 68). Recordings of 1940s big band standards performed by some of the same Japanese American singers and instrumentalists who had performed in the internment camps during the war are available on *Music to Remember: A Tribute to Japanese—American Musicians and Singers of the 40s*, 1997, Lisa Joe LJMP 1001-2. Discussion of music in the Japanese American internment camps will appear below in chapter 7.

11. Ruth Benedict, *The Chrysanthemum and the Sword* (reprint, Boston: Houghton Mifflin, 1989), 1.

12. See Dower's *War without Mercy: Race and Power in the Pacific War* (New York: Pantheon Books, 1986). My understanding of American perceptions of the Japanese during World War

II is indebted to this study. Although both nations were clearly guilty of racist views and racist actions, my focus here is solely on American representations of the Japanese.

13. In the case of Hollywood films, Japan's shocking foreignness appears to have provoked more frequent attempts at representation. Michael S. Shull and David Edward Wilt report that in Hollywood films between 1942 and 1945, there were 99 "topical references" to Germany and 236 to Japan (*Hollywood War Films, 1937–1945* [Jefferson, NC: McFarland, 1996], 293).

14. My study of World War II Tin Pan Alley songs was carried out primarily in the Sam DeVincent Collection at the Smithsonian's National Museum of American History Archives (no. 300, series 2: Armed Forces ca. 1810–1980; subseries 2.5: World War II, box 57, folders AA and BB), and in the Music Division of the Library of Congress with the assistance of Wayne Shirley. Also see Krystyn R. Moon, "'There's No Yellow in the Red, White, and Blue': The Creation of Anti-Japanese Music during World War II," *Pacific Historical Review* 72, no. 3 (August 2003): 333–352; Kathleen E. R. Smith, *God Bless America: Tin Pan Alley Goes to War* (Lexington: The University Press of Kentucky, 2003); John C. Hajduk, "Tin Pan Alley on the March: Popular Music, World War II, and the Quest for a Great War Song," *Popular Music and Society* 26, no. 4 (December 2003): 497–512; and John Bush Jones, *The Songs That Fought the War: Popular Music and the Home Front, 1939–1945* (Waltham, MA: Brandeis University Press, 2006), 124, 133–134.

15. These statistics are derived from Patricia King Hanson, ed., *American Film Institute Catalog of Motion Pictures Produced in the United States: Feature Films, 1941–1950* (Berkeley and Los Angeles: University of California Press, 1999). As noted above in chapter 2, Tin Pan Alley also remained relatively silent on the subject of the Japanese during the 1930s.

16. See Thomas Schatz, *Boom and Bust: The American Cinema in the 1940s* (New York: Simon and Schuster Macmillan, 1997), 27 and 153. On the pervasiveness of propaganda in American movie theaters, see James E. Combs and Sara T. Combs, *Film Propaganda and American Politics: An Analysis and Filmography* (New York: Garland Publishing, 1994). Apparently, a desire to harness Hollywood's persuasive potential in support of US military efforts persists in the twenty-first century. As the "War on Terror" commenced following the terrorist attacks of 9/11, President George W. Bush's political adviser Karl Rove met with Hollywood executives to discuss the ways in which films could support the administration's position and aims, including through the production of film shorts to be screened before features. See John King, "White House Sees Hollywood Role in War on Terrorism" (CNN.com, 8 November 8 2001).

17. Hollywood's World War II productions have inspired a large number of general studies. See particularly Lawrence H. Suid, *Guts and Glory: Great American War Movies* (Reading, MA: Addison–Wesley Publishing, 1978); Kathryn Kane, *Visions of War: Hollywood Combat Films of World War II* (Ann Arbor, MI: UMI Research Press, 1982); Bernard F. Dick, *The Star-Spangled Screen: The American World War II Film* (Lexington: University Press of Kentucky, 1985); Jeanine Basinger, *The World War II Combat Film: Anatomy of a Genre* (New York: Columbia University Press, 1986); Clayton R. Koppes and Gregory D. Black, *Hollywood Goes to War: How Politics, Profits, and Propaganda Shaped World War II Movies* (New York: Free Press, 1987); Thomas Doherty, *Projections of War: Hollywood, American Culture, and World War II* (New York: Columbia University Press, 1993); and Robert Fyne, *The Hollywood Propaganda of World War II* (Metuchen, NJ: Scarecrow Press, 1994).

18. Siegfried Kracauer, *Theory of Film: The Redemption of Physical Reality* (New York: Oxford University Press, 1960), 160.

19. Kracauer, *From Caligari to Hitler: A Psychological History of the German Film* (Princeton, NJ: Princeton University Press, 1947), 280.

20. Claudia Gorbman, *Unheard Melodies: Narrative Film Music* (Bloomington: Indiana University Press, 1987), 15.

21. Kracauer's concept of the potential "blinding effect" of film music was explored by Berthold Hoeckner in "The 'Pictorial Turn' and the 'Blinding Effect' of Music," delivered at the Sixty-fifth Annual Meeting of the American Musicological Society in Kansas City, November 1999.

22. This conclusion raises challenging issues concerning the power of music to influence behavior and the various attempts to censor music that is deemed "dangerous." If we continue to suggest, as do I in classes on American popular music, that certain musical styles were able to propagate the political values of nonviolence and equality in the 1960s, then it seems disingenuous not to admit likewise the possibility that some forms of popular music in the 1980s and 1990s might have reinforced violent behavior or misogyny in some adolescent males. In both cases, as with World War II propaganda, context is essential for the affective powers of music to be realized. A certain type of receptivity must be present in the auditor.

23. Michel Chion refers to a reciprocal "added value" relationship between sound and image: "Sound shows us the image differently than what the image shows alone, and the image likewise makes us hear sound differently than if the sound were ringing out in the dark." He concludes, however, that "for all this reciprocity the screen remains the principal support of filmic perception" (*Audio-Vision: Sound on Screen*, ed. and trans. Claudia Gorbman [New York: Columbia University Press, 1994], 21).

24. The *Why We Fight* series comprises *Prelude to War* (1943), *The Nazis Strike* (1943), *Divide and Conquer* (1943), *The Battle of Britain* (1943), *The Battle of Russia* (1943), *The Battle of China* (1944), and *War Comes to America* (1945). On music for other Office of War Information films see, for example, Alfred W. Cochran, "The Documentary Film Scores of Gail Kubik," in *Film Music: Critical Approaches* (New York: The Continuum International Publishing Group, 2001), 117–128.

25. Frank Capra, *The Name above the Title: An Autobiography* (New York: Macmillan, 1971), 331. On the making of these US War Department films, see William Thomas Murphy, "The Method of *Why We Fight*," *Journal of Popular Film* 1 (1972): 185–96; Thomas Bohn, *An Historical and Descriptive Analysis of the "Why We Fight" Series* (New York: Arno Press, 1977); Allan M. Winkler, *The Politics of Propaganda: The Office of War Information, 1942–1945* (New Haven, CT: Yale University Press, 1978); and Charles J. Maland, *Frank Capra* (Boston: Twayne Publishers, 1980).

26. In a return letter dated 12 October 1942, Peffer agreed to look over the scripts for the anti-Japanese projects. This correspondence is held in box 6, folder "1942 October," at the Frank Capra Archive, Cinema Archives, Wesleyan University.

27. See Document 63, a letter from Iris Barry (film curator at the MOMA) to Nelson A. Rockefeller, 3 February 1943, in David Culbert, ed., *Film and Propaganda in America: A Documentary History* (New York: Greenwood Press, 1990), 3:216. According to Capra (*The Name above the Title*, 338), MOMA staff members also helped to translate the Japanese films. (Siegfried Kracauer assisted MOMA's staff in studying and reviewing Nazi films. These reviews were sent directly to Capra's unit.)

28. See Document 25 in Culbert, ed., *Film and Propaganda in America*, 3:109. Walter Murch echoed this point in his foreword to Chion's *Audio-Vision* by stating that silent films "were Edenically oblivious of the divisive powers of the Word, and were thus able—when they so desired—to speak to Europe as a whole" (*Audio-Vision*, x).

29. I would like to thank David Raksin for speaking with me about the making of these films in a telephone conversation on 9 March 2000. The final short scores for *Prelude to War* are contained in the Alfred Newman Collection, Cinema and Television Library, University of Southern California. A copy of these scores is also contained in the Frank Capra Archive, Cinema Archives, Wesleyan University. Capra inscribed his copy as follows: "This great score was composed and recorded by Alfred Newman, using the Fox–20th-Century orchestra—all at n[o] cost to the War Dept. My eternal thanks to Al Newman and his musicians—."

30. In addition to the Wagner material, the Germans are represented by such marches as George Fürst's 1933 "Badenweiler Marsch." In one sequence, the narrator's claim that "the same poison made them much alike" is supported musically as we see shots of children in each Axis nation marching to the same Italian tune on the soundtrack.

31. This "Jap Theme" was reused in various arrangements in Alfred Newman's and David Buttolph's score for *The Fighting Lady* (1945). A copy of this score is held in the David Buttolph Collection, Harold B. Lee Library Special Collections, Brigham Young University.

32. Thomas Bohn, *An Historical and Descriptive Analysis of the "Why We Fight" Series* (New York: Arno Press, 1977), 178–79.

33. Dimitri Tiomkin is credited as the "musical director" of *Know Your Enemy—Japan.* The script was first drafted in June 1942 and went through several versions until April 1945. The film was released on 9 August 1945, but it is unclear how many GIs saw it before it was recalled just before the war's end. For an account of this film's production, see William J. Blakefield, "A War Within: The Making of *Know Your Enemy—Japan,*" *Sight and Sound* 52, no. 2 (1983): 128–133. I have discovered evidence suggesting that there was some attempt to have this film released to the general public. On 3 August 1945, Taylor M. Mills, chief of the Bureau of Motion Pictures, Office of War Information, wrote to Francis S. Harmon of the motion picture industry's War Activities Committee: "We have a difficult battle ahead with our enemy in the Pacific, and no matter how long or how short our war may be with the Japanese, it would be well that the American public know and understand these barbaric Japanese and how and why they got that way. I feel this film not only would be vitally important to the American home front war effort in the immediate months ahead, but also in plans for consideration for our treatment of the Japanese people in the post war world." This correspondence is found at the US National Archives II, RG 208, location 350/73/19–20/7, box 1532. A second film, derived from much of the same material used in *Know Your Enemy—Japan,* was released in 1946 and was entitled *Our Job in Japan.*

34. In the 1942 Japanese film celebrating the attack on Pearl Harbor, *Hawai Marei Oki Kaisen* (*The War at Sea from Hawaii to Malaya*), Wagner's "Ride of the Valkyries" is heard as the planes release their bombs, prefiguring *Apocalypse Now.* See Daniels, "Japanese Domestic Radio and Cinema Propaganda, 1937–1945," 311–312. On *Your Job in Germany* also see Laurie Ruth Semmes, "Frank Capra's *Job in Germany*: Evoking Cautious Suspicion through German Musical Reassurance," in *Music and Propaganda in the Short Twentieth Century,* ed. Massimiliano Sala (Lucca: Brepols, 2014), 57–67. On Hollywood's use of Wagner, including in World War II propaganda films, also see Scott D. Paulin, "The *Ring* in *Golden Earrings,*" in *Wagner and Cinema,* eds. Jeongwon Joe and Sander L. Gilman, 225–250 (Bloomington: Indiana University Press, 2010).

35. See Bernard F. Dick, *The Star-Spangled Screen: The American World War II Film* (Lexington: University of Kentucky, 1985), 102 and 104–105. Emil Newman was credited with the musical direction for this film but, as with many documentary films of this period, several composers were involved, including Alfred Newman, Hugo Friedhofer, Leigh Harline, and Cyril J. Mockridge. The cue sheet and sections of the score for *Secret Agent of Japan* are held at the University of Cincinnati archives, in the Leigh Harline Papers, box 10, folder 13.

36. For discussion of a related cinematic example, the 1931 *Dishonored,* see Carolyn Abbate, "Cipher and Performance in Sternberg's *Dishonored,*" in *Music and the Aesthetics of Modernity,* eds. Karol Berger and Anthony Newcomb, 357–392 (Cambridge, MA: Harvard University Department of Music, 2005).

37. Tiomkin's original short scores as well as the final conductor's scores and cue sheet for *The Battle of China* are held in the Dimitri Tiomkin Collection, Cinema and Television Library, University of Southern California. The Army Air Forces Orchestra performed most of the

music heard in this film. But documents in box 3, folder 1 of the Tiomkin Collection reveal that the excerpts from *The Rite of Spring* were taken from Stravinsky's own Columbia Records (M 417-4) recording with the New York Philharmonic Orchestra. This use of Stravinsky's music reached a large audience. David Culbert reports that at least 3.75 million people had seen and heard *The Battle of China* by 1 July 1945 (" 'Why We Fight': Social Engineering for a Democratic Society at War," in *Film and Radio Propaganda in World War II*, ed. Short, 184). The film was recalled and revised at one point during the war, and two different versions have been released on video.

38. Rosalynd Chang is credited with writing these Chinese lyrics. Tiomkin's arrangement of the Mussorgsky melody with this text is found in box 3, folder 2 in the Dimitri Tiomkin Collection. The cue sheet for *The Battle of China* (found in box 3, folder 1) reveals that Tiomkin also employed the following Chinese anthems and folk tunes in his score: "Call to Arms," "Little Cabbage Head," "Riding the Dragon," "Work as One," "Song of the Great Wall," "Sword Blade March," "Chinese National Anthem," and the "Chinese Air Force Song." This was not Tiomkin's first experience with Asian folk songs. He had employed Tibetan folk songs for Frank Capra's 1937 film *Lost Horizon*. These folk songs were performed by the African American Hall Johnson Choir in arrangements made by a member of the choir. See Christopher Palmer, *Dimitri Tiomkin: A Portrait* (London: T. E. Books, 1984), 78–80.

39. Stravinsky himself famously described his *Symphony in Three Movements* as a "war symphony" and revealed that its first and third movements were inspired by war documentaries: "The first movement was likewise inspired by a war film, this time a documentary of scorched-earth tactics in China. The middle part of the movement—the music for clarinet, piano, and strings, which mounts in intensity and volume until the explosion of the three chords at No. 69—was conceived as a series of instrumental conversations to accompany a cinematographic scene showing the Chinese people scratching and digging in their fields" (Stravinsky and Robert Craft, *Dialogues* [Berkeley: University of California Press, 1982], 52).

40. In *PT 109*, the 1963 fictionalized account from Warner Bros. of John F. Kennedy's World War II experience, the black "natives" who have helped rescue the stranded Kennedy and his crew sing "Rock of Ages" as they paddle their canoe back to their island home.

41. The original pencil sketches and the full score for *The Fighting Seabees* are scattered throughout the Republic Pictures Music Archives (MSS 1507), Harold B. Lee Library Special Collections, Brigham Young University. Scharf's pencil sketch for this example, entitled "Mow Me Down," is found in box 66, folder 1; the full score is in folder 2.

42. This music is found in Friedhofer's pencil sketch labeled "Reel 3-3–Reel 4-1." The original sketches and the bound conductor's score for *Three Came Home* are held in the Hugo Friedhofer Collection, Harold B. Lee Library Special Collections, Brigham Young University. In a 1974 interview with Irene Kahn Atkins, Friedhofer remarked that he had found *Three Came Home* "an inspiring picture to work on, because it was the first picture after the end of World War II in which the Japanese were not portrayed altogether as arch-villains." When asked whether he had used "any sort of ethnic music" in the film, Friedhofer replied: "I used not so much Japanese as Indonesian scales in the thing, but not done with ethnic instruments, because it was all woven into a dramatic fabric." Atkins published this interview as *Arranging and Composing Film Music: Interview with Hugo Friedhofer* (n.p.: American Film Institute, 1975), microfilm, 274–275. The interview also appears in an abridged form in Linda Danly, ed., *Hugo Friedhofer: The Best Years of His Life* (Lanham, MD: Scarecrow Press, 1999).

43. The conductor's score (no. 1630) is held in the Warner Bros. Archives, University of Southern California. Steiner's original pencil sketches for *Operation Pacific* are held in the Max Steiner Collection (MSS 1547, vol. 123), Harold B. Lee Library Special Collections, Brigham Young University. Steiner's humorous marginalia addressed to his arrangers in these sketches reveals his low estimation of this film. Referring to yet another torpedo sequence, he quips,

"I'm awfully sick of R1 Pt3—aren't you? I could vomit!!" Steiner makes numerous sarcastic remarks regarding the dialogue and aims a few at his own music. As a torpedo is fired in reel 9, part 4, Steiner writes the expressive marking "moltissimo crescendissi'moe'—a Jewish crescendo." He then instructs the arranger to reuse material from an earlier section in the film and writes, "SHIT and I know it but I don't care, don't tell Warner." For a broad overview of exoticism in Steiner's scores, see Mark Slobin, "The Steiner Superculture," in *Global Soundtracks: Worlds of Film Music*, ed. Slobin (Middletown, CT: Wesleyan University Press, 2008), 3–35.

44. The crew had watched the 1944 film *Destination Tokyo* on board their vessel before this scene and had laughed at Hollywood's portrayal of submarine warfare, thus suggesting that the submarine film *we* are viewing (*Operation Pacific*) is a more genuine document. After the Japanese fleet has been spotted, one stunned crew member declares, "I'll never make fun of another movie as long as I live."

45. The full score for *Behind the Rising Sun* is held in box RKO-M-466 in the RKO Archives, Theater Arts Library, University of California, Los Angeles.

46. The title and credits are displayed on the screen in the typical pseudo-brushstroke font that has been employed for typographical representations of Japan (and China) in the United States at least since the days of late nineteenth-century sheet music covers. Webb reused this music for the Main Title of *Betrayal from the East* (1945).

47. This classic of the Hollywood combat genre served as a blatant advertisement for the US Marine Corps as well as an ideal vehicle for its hero, John Wayne. The film incorporates actual battle footage and was made with extensive assistance from the Marines. The famous Mt. Suribachi flag raising is reenacted in the film by three of the original Marines who had been involved in this symbolic event. See Philip D. Beidler, *The Good War's Greatest Hits: World War II and American Remembering* (Athens: University of Georgia Press, 1998), 56–65.

48. The sketches, full score, and cue sheets for this film are held in the Republic Pictures Music Archives (MSS 1507), Harold B. Lee Library Special Collections, Brigham Young University. The relevant materials for this discussion are found in box 371, folder 4; box 958, folder 4; and box 974, folder 4. Throughout the film, music functions in obvious representational ways. In the first half, music remains closely allied with the Marines, to the extent that "mickey-mousing" (the synchronization of action with sound) is evident between the soundtrack and their movements. (This soundtrack must hold the world record for most statements of and variations on the Marines' Hymn, "From the Halls of Montezuma," the melody of which is Jacques Offenbach's "Hommes d'Armes" from *Geneviève de Brabant*.)

49. Comparisons were commonly made during the war between the jungle warfare against the Japanese and the nineteenth-century Indian battles fought on the American frontier. See Dower, *War without Mercy,* 152–53; and Walter LaFeber, *The Clash: US-Japanese Relations throughout History* (New York: W. W. Norton, 1997), 222.

50. On earlier musical representations of Native Americans and for a detailed analysis of the "Indian" musical cliché, see Michael V. Pisani, "'I'm an Indian Too': Creating Native American Identities in Nineteenth- and Early Twentieth-Century Music," in *The Exotic in Western Music,* ed. Jonathan Bellman (Boston: Northeastern University Press, 1998), 218–257. For more recent examples, see Claudia Gorbman, "Scoring the Indian: Music in the Liberal Western," in *Western Music and Its Others: Difference, Representation, and Appropriation in Music,* eds. Georgina Born and David Hesmondhalgh (Berkeley and Los Angeles: University of California Press, 2000), 234–253.

51. Dimitri Tiomkin, "Composing for Films" (1951), reprinted in James L. Limbacher, comp. and ed., *Film Music: From Violins to Video* (Metuchen, NJ: Scarecrow Press, 1974), 60. On the ethics of authenticity and realism in documentary soundtracks, see Leo Murray, "Authenticity and Realism in Documentary Sound," *The Soundtrack* 3, no. 2 (2010): 131–137.

52. Roy M. Prendergast, *Film Music: A Neglected Art*, 2nd ed. (New York: W. W. Norton, 1992), 214. On Hollywood's use of musical "stock characterization" and "narrative cuing," also see Claudia Gorbman, *Unheard Melodies: Narrative Film Music*, 83; and Gorbman, "Scoring the Indian," 238. Yet another rendition of this theme is offered by Irwin Bazelon: "countless scores written in an occidental, nineteenth-century symphonic style had only to add the omnipotent gong to achieve the proper 'oriental' effect. This representative timbre in conjunction with open fifths and the pentatonic scale gave adequate testimony and still does in many recent films to a Chinese locale. In the same way the song 'Sakura' (cherry blossom) is synonymous with Japan" (Bazelon, *Knowing the Score: Notes on Film Music* [New York: Van Nostrand Reinhold, 1975], 109).

53. *Time*, 22 December 1941, 33.

54. On Hollywood's use of "racist cosmetics," see Eugene Franklin Wong, *On Visual Media Racism: Asians in the American Motion Pictures* (New York: Arno Press, 1978). In the 1945 film *First Yank into Tokyo*, the use of such cosmetics is central to the narrative itself. In this film, a white American airman who had spent much of his childhood in Japan volunteers to undergo irreversible cosmetic surgery in order to sneak into Japan and rescue a captured engineer whose knowledge is vital to the building of the atomic bomb. This heroic volunteer is played by Tom Neal—a white actor who had undergone less drastic cosmetics in order to play the Japanese son in *Behind the Rising Sun*. Cosmetic surgery is also central to the plot of *Black Dragons* (1942). In this film, several Japanese agents (played by white actors in yellowface) undergo cosmetic surgery in order to pass as white businessmen and direct sabotage operations from within the United States. Such dramatic devices might suggest that racial difference runs only skin deep. However, these Hollywood films affirm the ultimate difference of the Japanese through myriad other means.

55. Maintaining the distinction between "Chinese" and "Japanese" musical signs did not remain a priority in Hollywood film music for very long, though conventional Orientalist themes have been repeatedly recycled. A striking example of juxtaposition between "positive" and "negative" Orientalist musical signals is discovered in the Main Title and "Prelude" sections of *China Gate* (1957). This film is set during the final stages of the French war in Vietnam, and it presents the Chinese as the enemy and Vietnam as the alluring exotic land. Official credit for the music was given to Victor Young (who died during the film's production) and Max Steiner, though Howard Jackson was also involved in compiling the score. Jackson employed both a "Chinese Theme" by Max Steiner and music headed with the cue "Battlefield Japs" in the Prelude—clearly drawing on material and reworking associations from the World War II period. The bound score (consisting of pencil sketches and short scores) for this film is held in the Max Steiner Collection (MSS 1547, vol. 29) at the Harold B. Lee Library Special Collections, Brigham Young University.

56. See William Ashbrook and Harold Powers, *Puccini's* Turandot: *The End of the Great Tradition* (Princeton, NJ: Princeton University Press, 1991), 95. This material is labeled "Jasmine Flower, Chinese folk song" in Young's original pencil sketch, which suggests that his source was a folk song collection rather than Puccini's opera. The original pencil sketch and full score for this film are found in the Republic Pictures Music Archives (MSS 1507), Harold B. Lee Library Special Collections, Brigham Young University. The music for the "Prelude" section is found in box 118, folder 6.

57. In his 5 August 1944 review of *Dragon Seed* in *The Nation*, film critic James Agee declared that " 'quaint' pseudo-Chinese background-music was never more insultingly out of place" (*Agee on Film*, vol. 1 [New York: McDowell, Obolensky, 1958], 110). Agee was quite critical of Hollywood's racist depictions of the exotic enemy throughout the war. In his 11 March 1944 review of *The Fighting Seabees*, for example, he complained that the "Japanese are represented, both verbally and by mannerism, as subhuman" (Ibid., 80). On Hollywood's war

films in general, however, Agee wrote in the 3 July 1943 issue of *The Nation*: "We may not yet recognize the tradition, but it is essentially, I think, not a drama but a certain kind of native ritual dance. As such its image of war is not only naive, coarse-grained, primitive; it is also honest, accomplished in terms of its aesthetic, and true" (Ibid., 45).

58. The cue sheet is found in the MGM Collection, Cinema and Television Library, University of Southern California.

59. This is not to suggest that all audience members were equally accepting of these musical representations of the enemy. In his classic analysis of Franz Waxman's score for *Objective: Burma,* the critic and orchestrator Lawrence Morton praised Waxman for avoiding "such banalities as the characterization of the enemy by what Western ears regard as Oriental music—the clichés of the pentatonic scale, temple bells, and wood blocks" ("The Music of *Objective: Burma,*" *Hollywood Quarterly* 1, no. 4 [1946]: 395). Of course, Morton was hardly a typical wartime audience member.

60. In a draft script for *Know Your Enemy—Japan,* the writers indicated that "Kimigayo" should be heard briefly at one point in the film in order to illustrate Japan's political and cultural connections to Germany. The filmmakers assumed that the music of this anthem was entirely German and, astonishingly, that "a few bars" would suffice to reveal Germany's influence on Japan. See Document M-310 in Culbert, ed., *Film and Propaganda in America,* vol. 5 (microfiche supplement), 2442. The song has been the subject of intense controversy in Japan and was designated the official national anthem only in August 1999. Although the Japanese Ministry of Education has encouraged the singing of "Kimigayo" at graduations for years, the song reminds many Japanese of the militaristic period of the 1930s and early 1940s. See Nicholas D. Kristof, "Japan Weighs Formal Status for Its Flag and Anthem," *New York Times,* 28 March 1999, sec. 1, p. 4.

61. This historic overview is indebted to William P. Malm's essay "The Modern Music of Meiji Japan," in *Tradition and Modernization in Japanese Culture,* ed. Donald H. Shively (Princeton, NJ: Princeton University Press, 1971), 257–300.

62. For English-language discussions of the stylistic development and social history of *gunka,* see Junko Oba, "From *Miyasan, Miyasan* to *Subaru:* The Transformation of Japanese War Songs from 1868 to Today" (MA thesis, Wesleyan University, 1995); Linda Fujie, "Popular Music," in *Handbook of Japanese Popular Culture,* ed. Richard Gid Powers and Hidetoshi Kato (New York: Greenwood Press, 1989), 204–205; and Oba, "To Fight the Losing War, to Remember the Lost War: The Changing Role of *Gunka,* Japanese War Songs," in *Global Goes Local: Popular Culture in Asia,* ed. Timothy J. Craig and Richard King (Honolulu: University of Hawai'i Press, 2002), 225–245.

63. Excerpts from this film served as source footage for the US War Department's anti-Japanese films. For surveys of Japan's wartime cinema, see Joseph Anderson and Donald Richie, *The Japanese Film: Art and Industry,* expanded ed. (Princeton, NJ: Princeton University Press, 1982), 126–158; Shimizu Akira, "War and Cinema in Japan," in *The Japan/America Film Wars: World War II Propaganda and Its Cultural Contexts,* ed. Abé Mark Nornes and Fukushima Yukio (Chur, Switzerland: Harwood, 1994), 7–57; and Darrell William Davis, *Picturing Japaneseness: Monumental Style, National Identity, Japanese Film* (New York: Columbia University Press, 1996).

64. On Yamaguchi's global career, see Freda Freiberg, "*China Nights* (Japan, 1940): The Sustaining Romance of Japan at War," in *World War II, Film, and History,* eds. John Whiteclay Chambers II and David Culbert (New York: Oxford University Press, 1996), 31–46. Also see Anderson and Richie, *The Japanese Film,* 152–55; and Ian Buruma, "Haunted Heroine," *Interview* (September 1989): 124–27. Yamaguchi was known as Ri Ko-ran in Japan and as Li Hsiang-lan in China. Her Chinese audiences assumed that she was actually Chinese.

65. On Japan's musical representations of China, see Edgar W. Pope, "Signifying China: Exoticism in Prewar Japanese Popular Music," in *Popular Music: Intercultural Interpretations,* ed. Tôru Mitsui (Kanazawa, Japan: Graduate Program in Music, Kanazawa University, 1998), 111–120. Pope demonstrates that Japanese modes of exotic representation were indebted to American Orientalism and particularly to Hollywood film evocations of China.

66. Such forced distinctions are evident, for instance, in Irene Kahn Atkins, *Source Music in Motion Pictures* (East Brunswick, NJ: Fairleigh Dickinson University Press, 1983). On music's ability to blur the line between the diegetic and the nondiegetic, see Gorbman, *Unheard Melodies: Narrative Film Music,* 20–26; Neumeyer, "Diegetic/Nondiegetic: A Theoretical Model," *Music and the Moving Image* 2, no. 1 (spring 2009) http://mmi.press.illinois.edu/2.1/neumeyer.html; Smith, "Bridging the Gap: Reconsidering the Border between Diegetic and Nondiegetic Music," *Music and the Moving Image* 2, no. 1 (spring 2009) http://mmi.press.illinois.edu/2.1/smith.html; and Stilwell, "The Fantastical Gap between Diegetic and Nondiegetic," in *Beyond the Soundtrack: Representing Music in Cinema*, eds. Daniel Goldmark, Lawrence Kramer, and Richard Leppert (Berkeley: University of California Press, 2007), 184–202.

67. Chion, *Audio-Vision*, 28.

68. Ibid., 107.

69. In general, "March of Time" newsreels were scored with continuous and often newly composed music. A detailed source list of the "March of Time" material used in *Know Your Enemy—Japan* is found in Document M-311 in Culbert, ed., *Film and Propaganda in America,* vol. 5 (microfiche supplement), 2466.

70. Although the producers of the "March of Time" newsreels were themselves engaged in propaganda in the years leading up to the war, one newsreel—the 1939 "War, Peace and Propaganda"—aimed to expose the extent of propaganda then current in the United States. Focusing on the national pavilions and exhibits at the 1939 New York World's Fair, the narrator states: "By definition, propaganda is any organized effort, whether good or bad, to direct public thought. And today the governments of every nation, including the United States, are making use of it." Concerning the propaganda efforts of the future exotic enemy, we learn that "Japan's exhibit is pointedly peaceful, designed to make visitors conscious of Japanese culture, rather than her warrior spirit."

71. I have discovered correspondence from October and November 1946 in the Frank Capra Archive at Wesleyan University that includes a long list of confiscated Japanese films, several of which were used in the films made by Capra. This postwar correspondence is concerned with the efforts of a Hawaiian-based Japanese film distribution company to reclaim films that had been confiscated by the US government from several Los Angeles exhibitors during the war. (See documents numbered 1858–1863 and 1866–1867.) World War II documents in the Celeste Bartos International Film Study Center of the Museum of Modern Art reveal the titles of confiscated Japanese films that the museum temporarily stored at the request of the Alien Property Custodian and apparently studied for Capra's unit before shipping them to the Library of Congress. See "Alien Property Custodian Correspondence/Lists: Japan, November–December 1943" and "Film Lists, Department of Film—Archive: Japan 1935–1968 file."

72. Religion figured as the source of Japanese fanaticism in several other US World War II films, including the B-grade *Samurai* (1945) with a score by Lee Zahler. In this film, an orphaned Japanese boy is adopted by white American parents and is raised in California. He is secretly trained as a samurai by a Japanese priest stationed in the United States and eventually spies for the Japanese government. At various points during his training, the narrator proclaims "the magnetic power of 'samurai'!" and the camera zooms in on a Buddhist sculpture as we

hear an eerie electronic cluster. At one significant moment late in the film, the villain's face is superimposed on the sculpture as we hear this exotic sound.

Louis Applebaum describes another example of innovative musical techniques employed to accompany representations of Japanese culture in propaganda films. In preparation for composing a score for a Canadian documentary on the Japanese enemy, the French Canadian composer Maurice Blackburn (allegedly) studied traditional Japanese music. For a sequence concerned with Japan's "ancient traditions," Blackburn scored music to be played by "one flute out of tune, one piano stripped of its action and played by strumming prescribed strings with a screw driver . . . and by assorted percussion instruments. The microphone was . . . moved about and waved over the instruments. . . . In addition, many incongruous noises were recorded. . . . the sound tracks were then assembled in a cutting room, some cut in to sound simultaneously and some cut in backwards so that the normal sound process was reversed. . . . the result, if not truly Japanese [indeed!], was at least interesting. . . . The musical pirouettes were executed by a composer in search of a Japanese musical sound" (Applebaum, "Documentary Music," reprinted in Limbacher, *Film Music*, 69–70; I have been unable to locate this documentary film).

73. This use of Okinawan folk music highlights certain unintended political ironies. One of the Ryukyu Islands lying in the East China Sea to the southwest of the main Japanese islands, Okinawa presents in its culture and music a unique mixture of East Asian and Southeast Asian features. Historically influenced by China and Japan in alternation, Okinawa only became part of the Japanese nation in 1879. Near the end of World War II, in one of the war's bloodiest battles, Okinawans suffered terribly as the Japanese government pursued a suicidal defense. The island was turned into a major US military base during the occupation and was not returned to Japanese control until 1972. Continued US military presence on Okinawa remains a subject of contention.

74. This draft is dated 16 June 1945 and is entitled *Your Job in Japan*. See Document M-317 in Culbert, ed., *Film and Propaganda in America,* vol. 5 (microfiche supplement), 2516.

75. Rodgers provided a set of main themes for this series which Bennett used, in addition to his own material, in composing the extensive soundtrack. For the latter's account of the "collaboration," see Bennett, *"The Broadway Sound": The Autobiography and Selected Essays of Robert Russell Bennett*, ed. George J. Ferencz (Rochester, NY: University of Rochester Press, 1999), 208–214.

76. This film also includes footage of Japanese sailors marching in place on their ship's deck as they sing a *gunka*. This is juxtaposed with scenes of American surfers and Hawaiian music intended to reveal the unpreparedness of the United States.

77. Two pencil sketches for the score of *Behind the Rising Sun* seem to indicate that Roy Webb had considered composing the "geisha music" in this scene himself. These sketches are found in box RKO-M-466 in the RKO Archives, Theater Arts Library, University of California, Los Angeles. "Geisha Tune #1" was composed for flute and *shamisen*. The folder containing "Geisha Tune #2" included a part for alto flute, likely intended to simulate the timbre of the *shakuhachi*. Although it is unclear whether these were newly composed pieces or whether they represent some form of transcription, documents pertaining to the recording of the soundtrack (see box RKO-M-392) reveal that the final "Geisha Dance" music was not composed by Webb but was acquired from an unidentified source.

78. Wong, *On Visual Media Racism*, 157.

79. This score is found in box 6 in the Alfred Newman Collection, Cinema and Television Library, University of Southern California.

80. Some of the closest simulations of Japanese music from the World War II period are found in the soundtracks of American cartoon shorts. Ironically, however, this particular medium makes it less likely that the audience accepted the music as authentic. In the Popeye cartoon

short *You're a Sap, Mr. Jap* (1942), a title taken from a Tin Pan Alley song, we hear a clever (and comic) imitation of typical *matsuri* music issuing from a Japanese bugle that serves as a call to arms against Popeye. In *Tokio Jokio* (1943), a Looney Tunes short with music by Carl W. Stalling, we hear a close approximation of a *shamisen* or *koto*, most likely realized by a banjo, which later in the film is joined by a flute in a simulated *koto/shakuhachi* duet. Other cartoon scores, of course, suggest less interest in matters of authenticity. For example, two of Paramount's *Superman* cartoons from 1942 draw on standard musical stereotypes. In "Japoteurs," with musical arrangement by Sammy Timberg, we hear a massive gong stroke and pentatonic brass for the appearance of a Japanese spy, and in "Eleventh Hour," in which Superman commits sabotage in Yokohama, plucky staccato pentatonic music represents the Japanese setting.

81. Bosley Crowther, *New York Times*, 9 March 1944, 15. Crowther stated that the film "[is a] shocking and debasing indictment of the methods which our enemies have used" and that "Americans cannot help but view this picture with a sense of burning outrage." A reviewer in *Time*, though also positive, was less inclined to accept the film's veracity: "It is also extremely effective propaganda. But sober and well-informed cinemaddicts may have some doubts about it. *The Purple Heart* is fiction, but it is fiction about some still rather foggy historical facts. As it is very persuasively played, it is likely to be accepted as truth by a great many people, not all of whom will be able to judge where fact ends and fiction begins" (review of *The Purple Heart*, *Time*, 6 March 1944, 94 and 96).

82. Bosley Crowther, Review of *The Purple Heart*, *New York Times*, 19 March 1944, sec. 2, p. 3.

83. John W. Dower, *Embracing Defeat: Japan in the Wake of World War II* (New York: W. W. Norton, 1999), 215. In his discussion of a late contrasting section in *Our Job in Japan*, sequences in which a more positive light is thrown on the new postwar situation, Dower notes that "smiling GIs were shown talking with kimono-clad women no longer gyrating in strange dances or singing in nasal voices" (p. 216).

84. George Burt, *The Art of Film Music* (Boston: Northeastern University Press, 1994), 127. Burt presents the *koto* theme on page 128.

85. Bazelon, *Knowing the Score*, 109.

86. Dave Barry, *Dave Barry Does Japan* (New York: Fawcett Columbine, 1992), 6. Barry relates that these "maniacal" cinematic Japanese soldiers were "like some species of giant suicidal shrieking, sword-waving, spittle-emitting insect." In the 1959 film *Never So Few*, authentic Japanese music does appear to "give away" the Japanese position. As an American-led ambush unit prepares to set a Japanese military camp on fire, we hear a Japanese female vocalist accompanied by *shakuhachi* and *koto*. This music seems to emanate from a radio that the Japanese soldiers (seen in a long shot) are listening to in their tent. The siren song of this traditional music distracts the Japanese soldiers, and they do not hear the American-led attack until it is far too late.

87. See Carl I. Hovland, Arthur A. Lumsdaine, and Fred D. Sheffield, *Experiments on Mass Communication* (Princeton, NJ: Princeton University Press, 1949), 64–65.

88. The 2001 film *Pearl Harbor* is particularly exploitive of the cinematic World War II tradition. The Japanese are represented in Hans Zimmer's score primarily by a martial drum tattoo with a distinct tom-tom or, perhaps, *taiko* timbre. An ominous dotted-half-note/quarter-note figure in the low strings and brass, reminiscent of a main theme from the "Mars" movement of Gustav Holst's *The Planets*, is used to build tension during sequences of the Japanese preparation for the attack. *Pearl Harbor* uses documentary and newsreel footage from the war period to provide a quick suggestion of authentic history and acknowledges assistance from all branches of the US armed forces. Beyond a simple opportunistic commemoration of the sixtieth anniversary of the attack, the film appears devoid of any propagandistic intent or meaning. Apparently aware of the film's hollowness, the filmmakers made a half-hearted

gesture toward suggesting some motivation for the production by acknowledging African American participation in the war effort. In the end, however, the female heroine's voice-over is able to offer only the following empty moral: "America suffered, but America grew stronger."

89. This draft is dated 16 June 1945 and is entitled *Your Job in Japan.* See Document M-317 in Culbert, ed., *Film and Propaganda in America,* vol. 5 (microfiche supplement), 2524. A more extended exposition on the dangers and deceptions of traditional Japanese culture exists in an 8 July 1943 draft script of *Know Your Enemy—Japan,* reprinted by Culbert as Document M-308 (5:2407). In this outline, the writers called for a sequence illustrating the "mask of the enemy," the "Japan we knew, or thought we knew, in the years of complacent sleep—idyllic, quaint, picturesque: bent bridges; stunted pine trees, Fuji; picture postcard shrines; those pretty Jap girls in kimonos floating over a sleepy lagoon in an old barge and trailing their fingers in the clear warm water." This presentation of "Romantic" Japanese culture as a form of cultural camouflage is strikingly similar to the framing of German music in *Your Job in Germany,* as discussed above. It represents one of the rare allusions made in these films to the potential exotic allure of the Japanese and to the dominance of American *japonisme* in the early twentieth century.

90. The reframing of the Japanese female body as exotically desirable rather than as exotically repulsive began even before the conclusion of the Pacific war. Carol J. Oja has discussed in detail the rather courageous casting of the Japanese American dancer Sono Osato as a beauty contest winner in the 1944–1945 original production of the Broadway musical *On the Town.* See Oja, *Bernstein Meets Broadway: Collaborative Art in a Time of War* (New York: Oxford University Press, 2014), chapter 4.

91. For example, Franz Waxman composed scores for *Air Force, Destination Tokyo* and *Objective: Burma* during the war, and some fifteen years later composed music for *Sayonara* and *My Geisha*—films celebrating Japanese culture. Similarly, Max Steiner composed scores for *Escapade in Japan* and *A Majority of One* in the late 1950s and early 1960s. These later films will be considered in the next chapter.

Chapter 6

1. My initial research work on *Sayonara* resulted in papers delivered at Princeton University in October 1997 and at the 1998 meeting of the American Musicological Society. I am particularly grateful for comments on those earlier versions of this chapter that I received from Michael Beckerman, Ellie Hisama, and the late Philip Brett.

2. The Japanese were not the only former cinematic enemy redeemed on the silver screen during this period. Claudia Gorbman has observed that Hollywood engaged in a "project of humanizing the Indian" in the 1950s and 1960s in a series of films. See Gorbman, "Scoring the Indian: Music in the Liberal Western," in, *Western Music and Its Others: Difference, Representation, and Appropriation in Music*, eds. Georgina Born and David Hesmondhalgh, 239 (Berkeley: University of California Press, 2000), 234–253. For a particularly insightful overview of US popular culture depictions of Asia during the Cold War, see Christina Klein, *Cold War Orientalism: Asia in the Middlebrow Imagination, 1945–1961* (Berkeley: University of California Press, 2003). On efforts by such serials as the *Reader's Digest* to develop sympathetic views of the Japanese see Klein, 82.

3. Duning's short score for *Three Stripes in the Sun* is held at the University of Southern California and I would like thank Ned Comstock for providing me with access to this material.

4. John W. Dower, *Embracing Defeat: Japan in the Wake of World War II* (New York: W. W. Norton, 1999), 138.

5. James A. Michener, *Sayonara* (New York: Random House, 1954). All references, unless otherwise noted, will be to this edition of the novel. On Michener's broader role in shaping American public opinion about Asia, see Klein, *Cold War Orientalism*, chapter 3.

6. For example, see James A. Michener, "Pursuit of Happiness by a GI and a Japanese: Marriage Surmounts Barriers of Language and Intolerance," *Life* 38 (21 February 1955): 124–141; "Why I Like Japan," *Reader's Digest* 69 (August 1956): 182–191; "Madame Butterfly in Bobby Sox," *Reader's Digest* 69 (October 1956): 21–27; and "Japan," *Holiday* 12, no. 2 (August 1952): 27–41, 76–78.

7. A strikingly similar image touting the benefits of modeling domestic behavior on Japanese customs appeared as a cartoon in *Harper's Weekly* a century prior on 18 December 1858. The cartoon, illustrating "Japanese manners," depicts a gentleman lounging on a couch and being attended to by six women in Victorian dress, including one kneeling at his feet with his slippers. This image is reproduced in Christine M. E. Guth, *Longfellow's Tattoos: Tourism, Collecting, and Japan* (Seattle: University of Washington Press, 2004), 20.

8. Yukio Mishima, "The Cherished Myths," in *Party of Twenty: Informal Essays from Holiday Magazine*, ed. Clifton Fadiman (New York: Simon and Schuster, 1963), 197–198.

9. Michener, "Madame Butterfly in Bobby Sox," 22, 27.

10. This special issue of *Life* devoted to Japan (11 September 1964) coincided with the Summer Olympics held in Tokyo.

11. See Table 2, "American Visitors to Japan" in Sheila K. Johnson, *The Japanese through American Eyes* (Stanford, CA: Stanford University Press, 1988), 101.

12. See Naoko Shibusawa, *America's Geisha Ally: Reimagining the Japanese Enemy* (Cambridge, MA: Harvard University Press, 2006), 48, 267. Shibusawa's general discussion of "Hollywood's Japan" during this period appears on pages 255–287.

13. Coincidentally, a photographic carte de visite from 1871–1873 of a woman named Hannaogi, dressed in an elaborate kimono and apparently positioned on stage, was collected by Charles Longfellow during his two-year visit to Japan. See Guth, *Longfellow's Tattoos*, 57.

14. See Joshua Logan, *Movie Stars, Real People, and Me* (New York: Delacorte, 1978), 86. Given Brando's yellowface performance in the earlier film *The Teahouse of the August Moon* (to be discussed below), his initial dismissal of this script is somewhat surprising.

15. This 1987 *Sayonara*, with book by William Luce, lyrics by Hy Gilbert, and music by George Fischoff, was billed as "A New Musical Adapted from the novel by James A. Michener." The musical was first produced at the New Jersey Paper Mill Playhouse in 1987, and again in 1993 in Houston and Seattle, and the script was published by Samuel French, Inc. in 1995. In the published script, but not in the 1987 production, the narrative is framed as a flashback from the moment at the end when Lloyd is dragged into General Webster's office and is about to be told he is being shipped home. A video recording of the 1987 production is available in the Theatre on Film and Tape Archive, New York Public Library for the Performing Arts. The musical was revived in New York City in 2015 by the Pan Asian Repertory Theater, directed by Tisa Chang. See Alexis Soloski, "Review: 'Sayonara' Reimagines a Story of Cross-Cultural Love," *New York Times*, 10 July 2015, C2.

16. Umeki also played Mei Li in Rodgers and Hammerstein's *Flower Drum Song* on Broadway in 1958 and in the 1961 film. On this musical in the context of Cold War exoticism, see Klein, 226–243.

17. Dower, *Embracing Defeat*, 301.

18. Michener, *Sayonara*, 165. Similarly, a white American female secretary complains earlier in the novel that Japanese women have a secret ability to "make their men feel important." Michener has this character speak against herself and against white American women: "I try to build my husband up—as a wife should. But with me it's a game. With these ugly little round-faced girls it isn't a game. It's life." (52).

19. This melody was published by M. Witmark and Sons, New York, with newly penned lyrics—referencing "temples of old" and lotus blooms—by Carl Sigman as "The Mountains beyond the Moon" in 1957.

20. See James Parakilas, "The Soldier and the Exotic: Operatic Variations on a Theme of Racial Encounter: Part I and II," *Opera Quarterly* 10, nos. 2–3 (winter 1993–1994; spring 1994): 33–56, 43–69.

21. Gina Marchetti, *Romance and the "Yellow Peril": Race, Sex, and Discursive Strategies in Hollywood Fiction* (Berkeley: University of California Press, 1993), 115 and 109; also see 135.

22. On the actual 1931, 1946, and 1953 Takarazuka productions and reworkings of *Madama Butterfly*, see Arthur Groos, "Return of the Native: Japan in *Madama Butterfly/Madama Butterfly* in Japan," *Cambridge Opera Journal* 1, no. 2 (July 1989): 181 and 193–194.

23. Presumably unbeknownst to Michener, this ending echoed the narrative of the 1919 song "Sya Nara (That Means Good-Bye)," with words and music by Arthur E. Behim and Courtney Sisters. In this song we learn that "Toy-o San was a little girl like Butterfly" and that she has decided the cultural differences between her and her American lover are unbridgeable and that she will not travel to the United States, though she pines for him to return.

24. In a late and rather odd version of these themes, an American girl at home in the United States declares in the 1967 "Tonight in Tokyo" (w. and m. by Bill Martin and Phil Coulter) that she is confident her American boy in Tokyo will behave. The lady doth protest too much, methinks.

25. We see a brief excerpt from *Hagoromo (The Robe of Feathers)* in which a celestial female is forced to dance by a fisherman in exchange for the return of her magic robe. Of course, *noh* is an all-male performance tradition, so this celestial beauty is performed by a man beneath the mask.

26. In the novel, Michener describes Lloyd's experience of the *bunraku* voice: "To hear this man was a terrifying experience for I had not known the human voice to be capable of such overpowering emotion. I would defy anyone not to be unnerved by that stupefying voice" (223).

27. I would like to thank John W. Waxman for providing me with the cue sheet for *Sayonara* and for answering many of my questions concerning his father's work on this film.

28. This film was released by the Elton Corporation in 1931 and a print is held at the Museum of Modern Art Film Archives. Sessue Hayakawa makes a very brief appearance in the film when Fairbanks lands in Japan.

29. See Zeke Berlin, "The Takarazuka Touch," *Asian Theatre Journal* 8, no. 1 (spring 1991): 39.

30. This is clear in the production documentation held at the Warner Bros. Archives, University of Southern California. For example, in an 18 March 1957 memo, Chas. Greenlaw informs Joe McLaughlin that the following songs were recorded in Japan during the shooting: "Moon over the Ruined Castle," "The Bride Doll," "The Rainy Moon," and "The Baseball Song."

31. This document was provided to me by Tak Shindo, who worked as a technical musical adviser on the film and whose career will be discussed in the following chapter.

32. A large stack of "Employment of Singer" cards from August and September 1957 are found in Folder 3 "Sayonara" 1058, in the Warner Bros. Archives, University of Southern California.

33. The "sketches and material" for Friedhofer's score are held in a folder marked "prod #A802" in the Hugo Friedhofer Collection at Brigham Young University.

34. Kosaku Yamada composed an opera on this same historical tale in 1939 entitled *Yoáke (Dawn)* or *Kurofone (The Black Ships)*, which was premiered in 1941. The libretto was written in Japanese by an American journalist named Percy Noel who had lived in Japan since 1927 and who commissioned Yamada to write the opera. The opera is primarily in a late nineteenth-century French idiom and, apart from a flute solo approximating a *shakuhachi*, is not very Japanese in style. A recording is available on Toshiba Records, JSC 1002-3.

35. See Irene Kahn Atkins, *Arranging and Composing Film Music: Interview with Hugo Friedhofer* (N.p.: American Film Institute, 1975), microfilm, 144–145.

36. Ibid., 338–339.

37. William Darby and Jack Du Bois point to what they hear as "discordant-sounding rhythms of the East" in the film and claim that Friedhofer's love theme does not dominate the sound-track. See Darby and Du Bois, *American Film Music: Major Composers, Techniques, Trends, 1915–1990* (Jefferson, NC: McFarland, 1990), 213.

38. John W. Dower has referred to the "latter-day Okichis" of the occupation period who offered themselves to the occupying US forces in order to protect the chastity of other Japanese women. See Dower, *Embracing Defeat: Japan in the Wake of World War II* (New York: W. W. Norton, 1999), 126.

39. The score for this film was composed by George Duning and is held in the George Duning Collection at the University of Southern California in Box 16.

40. Berlin's "Sayonara" enjoyed an extensive career following the success of the film. Recordings of the song were released or live performances given by Gordon MacRae in 1958, Paul Anka in 1963, Percy Faith in 1963, Douglas Gamly and His Orchestra in 1968, and the Sandler and Young duo in the early 1970s. A track labeled "Sayonara" and credited to Berlin appears on Nina Simone's 1963 live album recorded at Carnegie Hall, but the number is actually an exotica-style instrumental version of "Sakura." Other songs entitled "Sayonara," but with no musical connection to Berlin's number, were recorded by a wide range of artists including A Taste of Honey (1982), Taco (1984), and the Pogues (1990).

41. These issues were also pertinent to American operas composed contemporaneously with *Sayonara*. In an interview held the day before the 1957 premiere of his opera *Sotoba Komachi* in New York City—a work also produced later that year at the Santa Fe Opera—Martin Levy explained that he had not been influenced by Japanese music: "The music I've written for it is, admittedly, pseudo-Oriental, but Oriental to Western ears in any case." He concluded, almost apologetically, "It's a plain old Opera . . . very much like what Puccini did in a sense, I hesitate to say it." The opera's *nisei* director, Sanae Kawaguchi, concurred, stating that even though the opera was based on a famous *noh* play, she was not aiming for Japanese theatrical authenticity in their production. A recording of this 6 April 1957 interview is held at the New York Public Library for the Performing Arts Research Collections, Dance.

42. Joshua Logan, *Movie Stars, Real People, and Me* (New York: Delacorte Press, 1978), 84. My discussion in this paragraph of Logan's quest for an authentic setting is based also on his recollections appearing on pages 97–98 in this memoir. On the on-location filming of *Sayonara* also see Jeanette Roan, *Envisioning Asia: On Location, Travel, and the Cinematic Geography of US Orientalism* (Ann Arbor: University of Michigan Press, 2010), 180–191.

43. Logan, *Movie Stars*, 85.

44. Ibid., 88. Note Logan's casual usage of "American girl" to refer to white American female audience members.

45. See Truman Capote, "Profiles: The Duke in His Domain," *New Yorker* 33 (November 9 1957): 70–73. Documentation in the Warner Bros. Archives details the filmmaker's efforts to include excerpts from *kabuki* performance. A typed sheet attached to documentation concerning permissions needed for including Japanese music in the film lists two *kabuki* plays: *Oshu-Adachi-ga-Hara* and *Lion Dance* (*Kagami-zishi*). The document reveals the initial filming plans: "We would want about two minutes of the Lion Dance, and about nine minutes of Oshu-Adachi-ga-Hara. On the latter, we would want to shoot the very beginning showing the curtain opening, and then show the most important spots from the entrance of Sada-to and Mune-to, and also the ending of the play."

46. The musical does include a second, traditional wedding for Kelly and Katsumi. For this depiction of a Shinto wedding, we hear plucked strings, the timbre of a bamboo flute and bells,

and a thin musical texture as Katsumi sings "sacred vow, sacred wine" with an odd vocal quavering. In addition, *taiko* drumming is featured prominently in the Takarazuka scenes, as will be noted below.

47. Logan, *Movie Stars*, 89. A memo dated 19 November 1956 from Harry Mayer to Steve H. Trilling (and other documents dated 12 November and 11 December) reveals that the following actresses were considered for the role of Hana-ogi: Sandra Rehn, Michi Kobi, Shirley Yamaguchi, and Reiko Sato. Sandra Rehn was also considered for the role of Eileen Webster. Not surprisingly, none of the Japanese or Japanese American actresses was considered for the part of a white female character. These documents are found in Folder 2, "Sayonara (cables)," Warner Bros. Archives, University of Southern California.

48. Documentation of this and the other research requests noted in this paragraph is found in Folder 1, "8581 SAYONARA 421," Warner Bros. Archives. As a researcher myself, I am grateful that the following directive appeared in upper case on the bottom of all Warner Bros. inter-office communication paper from this period: "Verbal messages cause misunderstanding and delays (Please put them in writing)."

49. Katsumi Sunaga, *Japanese Music* (Tokyo: Maruzen Company; Board of Tourist Industry, Japanese Government Railways, 1936). This source begins with a discussion of how Japan and its music are simultaneously traditional and modern. The book includes *koto* scales that appear to have been of use to Waxman. Finally, two illustrations in this source deserve mention. The first presents an older white woman listening to two young Japanese girls playing *koto* and is captioned: "A foreign lady is delighted with the serene and meditative *koto* music." The second image is captioned: "The *samisen* playing of a little girl attracts the attention of foreigners." These images invite future foreign tourists to experience Japanese music as well.

50. This is documented in a cable dated 8 January 1957 from Brigadier General Kinney to Colonel Dowling, a copy of which was sent to Steve Trilling at Warner Bros. Kinney had demanded specific changes to the script, but these proved insufficient and he concluded that the film is "inaccurate and unfair to an extreme, and tends to be detrimental to the air force."

51. Logan, *Movie Stars*, 103.

52. See the inter-office memo dated 1 April 1957 to William Goetz from Ray Heindorf: "We have received a lot of music from Japan, and it is imperative at this time that you and Mr. Logan make a decision whether or not you will use any of this music in the picture."

53. Waxman's sketches for *Sayonara* are held in the Franz Waxman Collection at the University of Syracuse.

54. This will be discussed further in chapter 7. I note that for the RCA recording of the soundtrack, two *kotoists* were hired, Gail Laughton and Kazue Kudo, and each was paid $82.50. The contract by the American Federation of Musicians (18 October 1957) does not list any *shamisen* players, but instead lists two mandolinists. This document is held in the Warner Bros. Archives, University of Southern California.

55. Each compositional decision in the effort to enhance musical *japonisme* in the soundtrack resulted in considerable paperwork. For example, the decision to score for *shamisen* required rental requisition forms which reveal that the instrument was obtained from the MGM Studios Property Department on 26 June 1957 and that the rental fee for one week was $12.50. Document held in a folder marked "Sayonara" and 1058, Warner Bros. Archives.

56. This receipt is from the Bun-ka Do: Japanese Books and Records store in Los Angeles, dated 1 July 1957, and documents the purchase of two records of Japanese music for $2.40.

57. Christopher Palmer, *The Composer in Hollywood* (London: Marion Boyars, 1990), 114–115.

58. Liner notes for the CD recording "The Original Film Score *Sayonara*," Soundtrack Library 010 (numbered 008 on the CD itself).

59. The score materials for *Love Is a Many-Splendored Thing* are held in the Alfred Newman Collection, University of Southern California Cinema and TV Library.

60. This contractual arrangement is documented in an inter-office memo dated 14 March 1957 from Ray Heindorf to William Goetz.

61. See the interview with Bronislaw Kaper in Irene Kahn Atkins, *Scoring Hollywood Movies* (American Film Institute, microfilm, 1975), 112.

62. Quoted in Atkins, 114–115. Mantle Hood told Atkins that he felt Kaper did a "remarkably fine job" with *gagaku* (119).

63. I studied the sketches at the University of Syracuse and the full score at the Warner Bros. Archives. Leonid Raab served as the primary arranger on the film. Waxman's manuscript short score reveals that he most often specified the instrumentation in detail.

64. Telegram dated 23 September 1957, Kilauea Kauai, from Josh Logan to Steven Trilling. Document found in the *Sayonara* Correspondence files, "*Sayonara* Cables," Warner Bros. Archives.

65. This 24 September 1957 document is found in Franz Waxman Correspondence, Box 3, Franz Waxman archives at Syracuse University.

66. Telegram dated 26 September 1957, Kauai, Joshua Logan to Franz Waxman, Correspondence files, "*Sayonara* Cables," Warner Bros. Archives. A copy is also held in Franz Waxman Correspondence, Box 3, Franz Waxman archives at Syracuse University.

67. In a separate telegram dated 26 September 1957 (Correspondence files, *Sayonara* Cables, Warner Bros. Archives) Logan wrote to Steve Trilling: "Dear steve played both titles and find them both beautiful perhaps the revised one has more variety and therefore is preferable in the long run."

68. Note dated 8 November 1957 on 20th Century–Fox stationery, Beverly Hills, found in Franz Waxman Correspondence, Box 3, Franz Waxman archives at Syracuse University.

69. See Logan, *Movie Stars*, 104. Montalbán's depiction of *kabuki* performance received praise. For example, see Arthur Knight, "Dance in the Movies: Sayonara," *Dance Magazine* (December 1957): 14–15. This reviewer commented on the "persuasively genuine" performance by Montalbán but assumed that there was a double in the long shots. The reviewer also described the "weird crooning and harsh, clacking musical accompaniments" of *noh* and referred to Waxman's "lovely score—muted, sympathetic, faintly percussive."

70. In general, Michener praised *kabuki*: "The Japanese art which affects foreigners most deeply is *kabuki*, the traditional drama. *Kabuki* hit me like a thunderbolt." For these descriptions of *kabuki*, see Michener, "Japan," *Holiday* (August 1952), 34. We do hear a stentorian *kabuki* voice in the second, brief *kabuki* sequence later in the film, but this sound does not appear to be emitted by Montalbán.

71. Christina Klein points to *The King and I* from this period as a particularly prominent example of Hollywood's depiction of a Western woman holding a strong masculine position in relation to an effeminate exotic King. See Klein, *Cold War Orientalism*, 214.

72. This film includes two musical jokes passing in the opposite cross-cultural direction. The Main Title sequence, which includes a very brief statement of the typical Orientalist cliché gesture, features a series of cartoon images, one of which depicts a white GI playing a *shamisen* for two Japanese women in kimonos. At one moment in the film, the photographer in this unit, depicted throughout as a jokester, dons a samurai suit that elicits a brassy Orientalized "Yankee Doodle" statement on the soundtrack.

73. The soundtrack credits for *The Teahouse of the August Moon* read as follows: "Musical supervision by Saul Chaplin/Okinawan songs composed or arranged by Kikuko Kanai." The song "Teahouse of the August Moon" references a Madame Butterfly narrative situation and employs the *in* scale.

74. Brando's performance in *Sayonara* has received numerous subsequent references in popular culture. For instance, as Ellie Hisama notes, David Bowie refers directly to Brando's iconic role in *Sayonara* and the Orientalist fantasy it represents in his song "China Girl." See Ellie M.

Hisama, "Postcolonialism on the Make: The Music of John Mellencamp, David Bowie, and John Zorn," *Popular Music* 12, no. 2 (1993): 102.

75. Naoko Shibusawa, *America's Geisha Ally: Reimagining the Japanese Enemy* (Cambridge, MA: Harvard University Press, 2006), 286.

76. Depictions of Japanese men engaged in romantic relationships in these films tended to adopt a comic approach. For example, the affair between the Japanese American male character named Tada and a Japanese woman played by the ubiquitous Miyoshi Umeki in *The Horizontal Lieutenant* presents them as a cute rather than serious couple and the film gains considerable comic mileage from Tada's humorous Japlish, despite the fact that this character is a *nisei*.

77. See Marchetti, 156–157.

78. Ibid., 151.

79. Ibid., 170–171.

80. The impression that Gwen is trapped in an exotic land and in a subservient role to her new exotic husband echoes the plot of Franz Lehár's 1923 operetta *Die gelbe Jacke* (*The Yellow Jacket*), revised in 1929 as *Das Land des Lächelns* (*The Land of Smiles*).

81. Ronald Kirkbride, *A Girl Named Tamiko* (New York: Frederick Fell, 1959). Kirkbride dedicated the novel to "Junko who introduced me to the magic of the wind bells."

82. Ibid., 201–202.

83. On *South Pacific*, see Klein, *Cold War Orientalism*, 160–174; and Jim Lovensheimer, *South Pacific: Paradise Rewritten* (Oxford: Oxford University Press, 2010). Michener's novel *Tales of the South Pacific* ends by pointing to racism against blacks in the United States.

84. Logan's comment was quoted in Ray Falk, "'Sayonara' Now Spells 'Change,'" *New York Times*, 10 March 1957, X5.

85. This letter on Warner Bros. inter-office paper, dated 25 July 1957, from Franz Waxman to Steve Trilling, is found in the folder marked "Sayonara" and "1058" in the Warner Bros. archives.

86. Basic racial assumptions and casual equations of "white" with "American" are evident throughout the vast collection of documents associated with the production of this film. For example, in the "General Music Notes" found in Tak Shindo's papers, labels such as "American type music" appear as do such bewildering indications as "Pit orchestra plays a Japanese chord in G."

87. Robert Stam and Louise Spence, "Colonialism, Racism, and Representation," *Screen* 24, no. 2 (March/April 1983): 18.

88. The annotated script is held at the New York Public Library for the Performing Arts, Billy Rose Theatre Division.

89. Similarly, the African American veteran's flashbacks of his combat experiences with the Japanese enemy in the 1949 film *Home of the Brave* functions as a foil for his psychological paralysis induced by domestic racism.

90. Bosley Crowther, "Screen: Brando Stars in 'Sayonara,'" *New York Times*, 6 December 1957, 39. Also see Crowther's "After the Japanese: 'Sayonara' Has Some of the Qualities of Fine Films from Japan," *New York Times*, 8 December 1957: D5.

91. Robert Hatch, "Films," *The Nation* 185, no. 21 (Dec 21 1957): 484.

92. *Time* 70, no. 25 (16 December 1957): 98–99.

93. See Zeke Berlin, "Takarazuka: A History and Descriptive Analysis of the All-female Japanese Performance Company" (PhD diss., New York University, 1988), 85. On Takarazuka in *Sayonara* also see Berlin's "The Takarazuka Touch," *Asian Theatre Journal* 8, no. 1 (spring 1994): 41–42. On Takarazuka and the representation of gender, see Jennifer Robertson, "The 'Magic If': Conflicting Performances of Gender in the Takarazuka Revue of Japan," in *Gender in Performance: The Presentation of Difference in the Performing Arts*, ed. Laurence Senelick

(Hanover, NH: University Press of New England, 1992), 46–67; and her *Takarazuka: Sexual Politics and Popular Culture in Modern Japan* (Berkeley: University of California Press, 1998).

94. See Ian Buruma, *Behind the Mask: On Sexual Demons, Sacred Mothers, Transvestites, Gangsters, and Other Japanese Cultural Heroes* (New York: Meridian, 1985), 114.

95. John Martin, "Cherry Blossom Ballet," *New York Times*, 22 May 1939, 19.

96. For their performance on *Solid Gold*, see: https://www.youtube.com/watch?v=rcad9bNv670. Johnson also wore a kimono for her August 2014 performance of the song at the Greek Theater in Los Angeles. In 2001 Johnson released a CD of new songs entitled *Hiatus of the Heart* which included the bonus track "Sayonara" featuring Kuramoto once again on the *koto*.

97. See Kyoko Hirano, *Mr. Smith Goes to Tokyo: Japanese Cinema under the American Occupation, 1945–1952* (Washington, DC: Smithsonian Institution Press, 1992), 66, 154.

98. In Mizoguchi's 1936 *Sisters of the Gion* a modernist, aggressive musical style intrudes in the soundtrack at the end after the heroine declares that geisha should never have existed. On Mizoguchi's "women's liberation films" see Hirano, 165–170.

99. In the 1955 *House of Bamboo*, again starring Shirley Yamaguchi, Japanese women reject one of their own after the Japanese heroine moves in with a white man. On *Japanese War Bride*, also see Marchetti, 161–162, 166–170. On the historical phenomenon of Japanese war brides and the image of Japanese women in the United States during this period, see Caroline Chung Simpson, *An Absent Presence: Japanese Americans in Postwar American Culture, 1945–1960* (Durham, NC, and London: Duke University Press, 2001), 149–185.

100. The short score for *Escapade in Japan* is held in the Max Steiner Collection, MSS 1547, v. 56, "Conductor; Prod. 812," at Brigham Young University. I was able to view the film at the Museum of Modern Art, film archives.

Chapter 7

1. This film, with a score by George Antheil, was one of the earliest attempts by Hollywood to portray the postwar Japanese situation. The film is equally notable for bringing the Japanese silent film star Sessue Hayakawa back to the American screen in what has to be his most evil role.

2. See Sander L. Gilman, *Difference and Pathology: Stereotypes of Sexuality, Race, and Madness* (Ithaca, NY: Cornell University Press, 1985), 25.

3. See Frank H. Wu, *Yellow: Race in America Beyond Black and White* (New York: Basic Books, 2002), chapter 3.

4. Henry Yu, *Thinking Orientals: Migration, Contact, and Exoticism in Modern America* (New York: Oxford University Press, 2001), 203. Also see Ronald Takaki, *Strangers from a Different Shore: A History of Asian Americans*, rev. ed. (Boston: Back Bay Books, 1998), 214–216.

5. Yu, 67. On hearing race wrong, particularly in a judicial context, see John Baugh, "Linguistic Profiling," in *Black Linguistics: Language, Society, and Politics in Africa and the Americas*, eds. Sinfree Makoni, Geneva Smitherman, Arnetha F. Ball, and Arthur K. Spears, 155–168 (London and New York: Routledge, 2003).

6. Karie Shindo (married name Aihara) also had several bit parts in Hollywood films and TV shows. In addition, she participated in a 1960 pageant in Los Angeles that depicted (in four tableaux of music, dancing, and drama) the history of US-Japanese relations and the loyalty of the *nisei* in World War II. (The *kotoist* Kimio Eto—a famous ambassador of Japanese traditional music to the United States, introduced above in chapter 3—also participated in this performance.) See "Program to Tell Story of Japanese Culture," *Los Angeles Times*,

11 August 1960, 15. A photograph of her performing with the Harry James Orchestra appears in George Yoshida, *Reminiscing in Swingtime: Japanese Americans in American Popular Music: 1925-1960* (San Francisco: National Japanese American Historical Society, 1997), 219.

7. I delivered a paper at the 2003 meeting of the Society for Ethnomusicology that was focused on Shindo's career and I remain grateful for comments offered by panelists and audience members at that session.

8. Unless otherwise noted, all quotations from Shindo are from transcripts of my interviews with him in April and June 2000 carried out at his home in San Dimas, California, and on the telephone. I am exceedingly grateful to Sachiko Shindo for allowing me to continue my research in her husband's papers at her home in January 2004. (Unless otherwise noted, I derived the factual information presented in this chapter about Shindo's career from his home archive.) I am also grateful to Myra Shindo for meeting with me during that research visit to discuss her father's life and career.

9. Ingrid Monson, *Saying Something: Jazz Improvisation and Interaction* (Chicago: University of Chicago Press, 1996), 203.

10. Telephone interview on 9 March 2000.

11. See Susan Miyo Asai, "Transformations of Tradition: Three Generations of Japanese American Music Making," *Musical Quarterly* 79, no. 3 (autumn 1995): 429-453; Jo Anne Combs, "Japanese-American Music and Dance in Los Angeles, 1930-1942," in *Selected Reports in Ethnomusicology Volume VI: Asian Music in North America*, eds. Nazir A. Jairazbhoy and Sue Carole De Vale (Los Angeles: University of California, 1985), 121-149; Combs, "The Japanese O-Bon Festival and Bon Odori: Symbols in Flux" (MA diss., University of California-Los Angeles, 1979); and Minako Waseda, "Japanese American Musical Culture in Southern California: Its Formation and Transformation in the 20th Century" (PhD diss., University of California-Santa Barbara, 2000). Also see Mina Yang, "Orientalism and the Music of Asian Immigrant Communities in California, 1924-1945," *American Music* 19, no. 4 (winter 2001): 385-416. A striking c. 1930 photo of a girl playing a *koto* in her family's living room with a piano in the background illustrates the musical duality of the *nisei*. See Ichiro Mike Murase, *Little Tokyo: One Hundred Years in Pictures* (Los Angeles: Visual Communications/Asian American Studies Central, 1983), 69. Lon Kurashige has discussed the cultural divergence between the *issei* (first) and *nisei* generations in his *Japanese American Celebration and Conflict: A History of Ethnic Identity and Festival, 1934-1990* (Berkeley: University of California Press, 2002).

12. David K. Yoo, *Growing Up Nisei: Race, Generation, and Culture among Japanese Americans of California, 1924-49* (Urbana and Chicago: University of Illinois Press, 2000), 9.

13. George Yoshida, *Reminiscing in Swingtime: Japanese Americans in American Popular Music: 1925-1960* (San Francisco: National Japanese American Historical Society, 1997). On music in the camps, also see Marta Robertson, "Ballad for Incarcerated Americans: Second Generation Japanese American Musicking in World War II Camps," *Journal of the Society for American Music* 11, no. 3 (2017): 284-312.

14. Jeanne Wakatsuki Houston and James. D. Houston, *Farewell to Manzanar* (New York: Bantam Books, 1973), 80.

15. This film—ostensibly focused on the plight of Japanese Americans—is primarily concerned with the life of the white male hero and with his interracial love. As Laura Hyun Yi Kang puts it: "The film ends with the happy reunification of Jack, Lily, and their daughter. One reconstituted family with its white male head-of-household is celebrated, displacing the ruptures wreaked upon numerous other Japanese American families by the Internment." See Kang, *Compositional Subjects: Enfiguring Asian/American Women* (Durham, NC: Duke University Press, 2002), 86-87. Marita Sturken similarly argues that the film's more radical elements are "undercut by its privileging of the story of its white male protagonist, played

by Dennis Quaid, whose character allows white viewers to feel atoned through their iden-
tification with his apparent transcendence of racism." See Sturken, "Absent Images of
Memory: Remembering and Reenacting the Japanese Internment," in *Perilous Memories: The
Asia-Pacific War(s)*, eds. T. Fujitani, Geoffrey M. White, and Lisa Yoneyama (Durham,
NC: Duke University Press, 2001), 40.

16. My detailed information concerning Shindo's internment experience is derived primarily
from his WRA evacuee case file housed at the National Archives and Records Administration,
Washington, DC. I am grateful to Aloha South at the National Archives for providing me
with copies of these records. In 1980, Shindo made a self-produced documentary film on
the Manzanar internment camp entitled *Encounter with the Past* that includes rare footage of
camp life, including various forms of musical performance.

17. Asai, "Transformations of Tradition," 435–436. Waseda has made a parallel point: "The internment camps, thus, ironically functioned as a 'shelter,' in which Japanese Americans
could continue to practice their ethnic cultural heritage" (Waseda, "Japanese American
Musical Culture," 126). See chapter 3 in Waseda on music in the internment camps. Also see
Waseda, "Extraordinary Circumstances, Exceptional Practices: Music in Japanese American
Concentration Camps," *Journal of Asian American Studies* 8, no. 2 (June 2005): 172, 180. For
information on the organization of music in Manzanar and the regulation of Japanese tradi-
tional music performance see Harlan D. Unrau, *The Evacuation and Relocation of Persons of
Japanese Ancestry during World War II: A Historical Study of the Manzanar War Relocation
Center* (United States Department of the Interior, National Park Service, 1996), 573–574.

18. For example, he received a certificate in "Dance Band Arranging" from the University
Extension Conservatory, Chicago, on 11 September 1945.

19. The Japanese section on 13 September 1944 included an article in which the author refers to a
recent radio broadcast of opera. This correspondent states that Puccini is their favorite composer and cites *La bohème* and *Madama Butterfly* as being "complete in drama, words and
music." The author continues: "Speaking of this reminds me that ever since the outbreak of
the war the shadow of 'Madame Butterfly' seems to have vanished somewhere." Microfilmed
copies of the *Manzanar Free Press* are housed at the Japanese American National Museum
Hirasaki National Resource Center, Los Angeles.

20. For a photograph of this band with Shindo standing in the back, see Yoshida, 206.

21. Telephone interview with Yoshida in August 2003. This song was featured in the 1940
Japanese propaganda film *China Nights* starring Shirley Yamaguchi, with a score by the famous Japanese popular song composer Hattori Ryoichi. Hattori and Yamaguchi appeared
with Shindo's band in their American debut in Los Angeles c. 1950.

22. It is striking that in the 1940s Shindo placed a higher value on writing jazz music rather than
on improvisation and that he apparently considered jazz composition and arranging the domain of white musicians. Clearly, these are not the values and skills normally celebrated today
in discussions of jazz of this period.

23. Quoted from Shindo's videotaped Go For Broke Educational Foundation Hanashi Oral
History Program interview on 6 February 2000.

24. Mark Keats, "Ear to the Ground," *Sports Journal* (9 May 1947). This clipping is found in
Shindo's papers and contains no other information for citation.

25. The caption in Shindo's hand on the reverse side of this photograph reads: "Taxco Rec Session,
Recording Murray Wilson (Beach Boys) Enamorado di Ti TamBarin."

26. Although I claim pre-eminent importance for *Sakura*, it was by no means the first Japanese-
inspired opera produced in America nor was it the only grand musical event to impact the
Japanese American community of Southern California during this period. Aldo Franchetti
completed his opera *Namiko San* in 1925 in Hollywood and it was premiered in Chicago and
then taken on a national tour. The work includes parts for *tsutsumi* and *fuye* (flute) positioned

offstage and the heroine mimes a *shamisen* performance onstage in Act I as a harp realizes the part in the pit. The score for this opera is held in the Music Division of the Library of Congress. Mina Yang briefly mentions this opera in "Orientalism and the Music of Asian Immigrant Communities in California, 1924–1945," *American Music* 19, no. 4 (winter 2001): 404. An event more relevant to the Los Angeles Japanese American community was an August 1937 performance at the Hollywood Bowl led by the Japanese conductor Hidemaro Konoye and featuring the celebrated choreographer Michio Ito. The performance included Konoye's adaptation of *Etenraku* with choreography by Ito and performed by a large ensemble of dancers.

27. A 15 June 1933 article in the *Rafu Shimpo* claimed that the production would feature a chorus of 1,200, a 70-piece orchestra, and 500 children. An article the following day in the same newspaper claimed that 800 children would participate. Unfortunately, I do not know whether Tak Shindo (age eleven at the time) was involved in the production or whether he attended one of the performances. Reviews of the production did note that many Japanese American children were in attendance in the audience.

28. See "Ambassador Debuchi Sends Greetings to 'Sakura' Cast; Governor Rolph to Attend," *Rafu Shimpo* (23 June 1933): 6.

29. "Mayor Porter Proclaims 'Japanese-American' Day," *Rafu Shimpo* (4 June 1933): 3.

30. See "Students to Get Special Rate at Opera Pageant, 'Sakura,'" *Rafu Shimpo* (21 June 1933): 6, and "Cherry Blossom Fete Reproduced on Grand Scale for First Time," *Rafu Shimpo* (18 June 1933): 1.

31. See "New Japanese Opera Wins Support of Social Leaders," *Rafu Shimpo* (11 May 1933): 6.

32. "Leading Singers Selected for Bowl Opera-Pageant," *Rafu Shimpo* (21 May 1933): 1. Tsukamoto later in life had bit parts in a few Japanese-related Hollywood films such as *Operation Bikini* and *The Teahouse of the August Moon*. A model of his set for *Sakura* is held at the Japanese American National Museum, Hirasaki National Resource Center, Los Angeles.

33. See Juana Neal Levy, "Assistance League's Bridge Tea to Have Authentic Japanese Atmosphere," *Los Angeles Times*, 25 June 1933, B1.

34. "Cherry Blossom Fete Reproduced," *Rafu Shimpo*, 1.

35. "'Sakura' to Be Feature of Art Club Festival," *Los Angeles Times*, 25 August 1933, A10. For this Los Angeles revival performance it was announced that "Japanese maids in costume will serve tea during intermissions."

36. "'Sakura' to Add Contrast," *Los Angeles Times*, 2 July 1933, 9.

37. Lapham later suggested that he had intended to compose an opera "entirely Japanese in spirit" as opposed to Puccini's *Madama Butterfly* and that he approached the Japanese community with this idea and was then directed to meet with Sugimachi. I find this account implausible. See Claude Lapham, "Japan Inspires an American Composer," *The American Music Lover* 2, vol. 3 (July 1936): 71, 74. In 1937, Lapham referred to *Sakura* as "the first grand opera composed in Japanese style and with a Japanese libretto." See Lapham, "Popular Japanese Music," *Asia* 37, no. 12 (December 1937): 859. The manuscript of Lapham's piano vocal score for *Sakura* is held at the Music Division of the Library of Congress. For a brief discussion of Lapham, see Yoshida, 46–47.

38. I delivered a paper at the annual Society for American Music meeting in 2010 on Lapham's engagement with Japanese music and the Japanese American community. I am grateful for comments made by panelists and audience members at this event.

39. "Orient, Occident Join to Produce Japanese Opera," *Los Angeles Times*, 11 June 1933, A4.

40. A 26 June review in *Rafu Shimpo* ("Colorful Nipponese Opera Receives Huge Ovation from 20,000 at World Premiere") referred to "the difficult and strange music" of Lapham. On 2 July, *Rafu Shimpo* reproduced a full page of reviews from other newspapers on its front page. The *Illustrated Daily News* reviewer Eleanor Barnes praised the libretto hugely but was not positive on the music, and Gilbert Brown of the *Los Angeles Record* declared that "ancient Japan took

another plunge into the intricate shallows of western modernism Saturday night. . . . Between 10,000 and 15,000 spectators looked and listened as an international cast of principals sang Japanese words to music moderne, Nipponese and Puccinesque, and Japanese Kabuki dancers performed inscrutably against a background of gorgeously contrasted costumes and settings."

41. I am not the first to note similarities between Eichheim and Lapham. In 1955, Robert S. Schwantes wrote, "we should not overlook the work of American composers like Henry Eichheim and Claude Lapham, who have tried to capture the spirit of Japanese music in Western forms." See his *Japanese and Americans: A Century of Cultural Relations* (New York: Harper & Brothers, 1955), 242. Frederic de Garis had also mentioned Eichheim and Lapham and their interest in Japanese music in his general guide to Japan: *Their Japan* (Yokohama: Yoshikawa, 1936), 80–81.

42. See Isabel Morse Jones, "Oriental Music to Be Played," *Los Angeles Times*, 17 January 1934, 11. Also see a brief notice by her in "Words and Music," *Los Angeles Times*, 3 June 1934, A6. Lapham discussed jazz in Japan and the prospects for American jazz musicians there in "If You Must Go to Japan," *Metronome* 52, no. 10 (October 1936): 16, 29, and "Looking at Japanese Jazz," *Metronome* 52, no. 6 (June 1936): 14, 27.

43. Claude Lapham, "Japan Inspires an American Composer," *The American Music Lover* 2, no. 3 (July 1936): 71, 74.

44. Ibid., 74.

45. Claude Lapham, "Music of the Far East," *Who Is Who in Music: 1941 Edition* (Chicago and New York: Lee Stern Press, 1940), 523–524.

46. Lapham, "Popular Japanese Music," 860.

47. This note is found on the Free Library of Philadelphia, Edwin A. Fleisher Music Collection catalog form. The score is held as number 3053 in this collection and is also held at the Library of Congress. A recording was released on the Victor Red Seal Record label, 11895, with the Victor Symphony Orchestra led by Lapham.

48. Bradford Smith, *To the Mountain* (Indianapolis and New York: The Bobbs-Merrill Co., 1936). Music symbolizes the Western fascination of Shigeo, the Japanese male member of this ill-fated couple. The author reveals his own distaste for Japanese traditional music by describing the "tentativeness" of geisha singing "accompanied by the plaintive *sam-isen* whose notes always sounded out of tune" (166). Shigeo attends a performance of Beethoven's *Kreutzer Sonata*, which he loves but finds he "failed to grasp it; he had not caught all that was meant to be expressed" (184). An encounter with a recording of Wagner's *Tristan und Isolde*, however, proves transformative, prefiguring his own romantic *Liebestod* (211–212). Smith taught English at St. Paul's University and the Imperial University in Tokyo from 1931 to 1936 and published a book on Japanese Americans in 1948 (*Americans from Japan*).

49. The score to the piano concerto is held in the Fleisher Collection, Free Library of Philadelphia, and in the Music Division of the Library of Congress. Lapham recorded the work with Alfredo Cibelli conducting on the Victor Red Seal Record label, #4306.

50. See notice in the *Chicago Daily Tribune*, 19 July 1936, D3.

51. See the advertisement for the 3 June Musicale Intime Orientale "Bali" with music by Lapham and a "Musical Highlights of the Culture of Bali" travelogue by him in the *Los Angeles Times*, 30 May 1943, C6.

52. *Nisei Romance* was produced and directed by Claude Lapham at the International Studio Theatre in Hollywood. See the announcement in *Rafu Shimpo* (27 October 1948): 1.

53. See announcement in the *New York Times*, 4 May 1954, 35.

54. See the advertisement for the 20 April performance of *Tokyo Matinee Revue* in the *Los Angeles Times*, 15 April 1956, A20.

55. Tak Shindo, "Japanese Music Today," *Film Music* 12, no. 1 (September–October 1952): 21–22. This article touches on the music employed in Japanese films and introduces the *koto, shakuhachi*, and *shamisen*. Hollywood's turn to Shindo for gestures of exotic authenticity is analogous to the role of exotic dance consultant assumed by the Japanese American choreographer Michiko Iseri in the 1951 stage production and 1956 film of *The King and I*. Though she was often in conflict with the show's choreographer, Jerome Robbins, over details of authenticity, her fan dance in "Getting to Know You" resembles Japanese traditions, particularly *bon odori*, rather than Thai court dance, and the choreography for "The Small House of Uncle Thomas" number includes elements of *kabuki* as well as movement resembling the work of Martha Graham.

56. The short score for *A Majority of One* is held as MSS 1547 vol. 106 in the Max Steiner Collection, Brigham Young University. A copy of the short score along with individual parts is also held as #1885 in the Warner Bros. archive, University of Southern California.

57. Here I am in agreement with Brendan Gill's review of *A Majority of One* (*The New Yorker*, 20 January 1962), which refers to the film's "caricature of both Jewish and Japanese life" (113).

58. Inter-office memo, 27 May 1957, from Waxman to Ray Heindorf. Collected in the Warner Bros. Archives, University of Southern California, correspondence files, folder *Sayonara* no. 1058. For evidence that Waxman's proposed solution for representing Japan instrumentally has been a common one, see various composers' statements in Fred Karlin and Rayburn Wright, *On the Track: A Guide to Contemporary Film Scoring* (New York: Schirmer Books, 1990). For example, Laurence Rosenthal points to Puccini as a model composer for the representation of ethnic music (495) and Gerald Fried explains that given the difficulty in recording with authentic performers, it is easier to "let the studio guitarist adjust his banjo to make it sound like a samisen" (497). Bill Conti details how he used a synthesized panpipe to suggest the *shakuhachi* in *Karate Kid II* and a synthesizer playing with "lute" and "giant koto" patches in addition to the natural minor scale to signal "Japanese" in the film (500).

59. "Westward the Wagons," *Time* (15 December 1958): 54.

60. On Hayakawa's own portrayals of Native Americans during the silent film era, see Daisuke Miyao, *Sessue Hayakawa: Silent Cinema and Transnational Stardom* (Durham, NC, and London: Duke University Press, 2007), 76–84.

61. Hawai'i's large Japanese American population played a direct role in shaping general American postwar perceptions of Japan. GI nostalgia for occupied Japan was met by recordings of Japanese popular and folk songs recorded by *nisei* musicians in Hawai'i and released by the 49th State Hawaii Record Company. (Hawai'i became the 50th state in 1959.) In Japan, some of this music was known by the label "Occupational Forces songs." Of course, these recordings were also marketed more generally to the Japanese American audience. Some of these recordings have been reissued on the following compilation CD: *Hawaiian Nisei Songs: A Musical Cocktail of Japanese American Songs in 1950s Hawaii* (Cord International/Hana Ola Records, HOCD 3600, 2000). On Japanese American performers and self-Orientalization in these songs, see Minako Waseda, "Looking Both Ways: GI Songs and Musical Exoticism in Post–World War II Japan," *Yearbook for Traditional Music* 36 (2004): 144–164.

62. See Joseph Lanza, *Elevator Music: A Surreal History of Muzak, Easy-Listening, and Other Moodsong* (New York: Picador, 1994), 67–69.

63. Ibid., 120.

64. Christina Klein, *Cold War Orientalism: Asia in the Middlebrow Imagination, 1945–1961* (Berkeley: University of California Press, 2003), 240.

65. Philip Hayward, "Introduction: The Cocktail Shift: Aligning Musical Exotica," in Philip Hayward, ed., *Widening the Horizon: Exoticism in Post-War Popular Music* (Sydney: John Libbey and Company, 1999), 15, note 4.

66. On the similar treatment of the *sansei* actor and singer James Shigeta, see Oliver Wang, "Between the Notes: Finding Asian America in Popular Music," *American Music* 19, no. 4 (winter 2001): 445–446. In addition to his multiple roles in Hollywood film, Shigeta starred in a 1959 Los Vegas musical revue titled *Holiday in Japan* at the New Frontier Hotel, which was produced by Shirley MacLaine's husband Steve Parker and was featured and praised in *Life Magazine* (5 October 1959).

67. Transcript of a radio broadcast in March 1960 of an interview between John Annarino and Shindo; found in Shindo's papers at his home in a folder labeled "Capitol Records Contracts."

68. The slower sales of *Accent on Bamboo* resulted in Capitol not renewing Shindo's contract in March 1961. See the letter dated 6 March 1961 to Shindo from Ed Yelin in the Capitol Records Artist and Repertoire division. This letter is found in Shindo's papers at his home in a folder labeled "Capitol Records Contracts."

69. Shindo's somewhat theatrical shifts from Orientalist signs to a big band style were prefigured in numerous Tin Pan Alley *japonisme* songs in which the introduction is strikingly split between a staccato pentatonic tune moving in fourths or fifths and a syncopated ragtime lick. The late 1920s/early 1930s *nisei* blues singer Kono Takeuchi allegedly acted out such sudden identity switches on a grander scale in her performances: "Dressed in a kimono, playing a *shamisen* ... she opened her vaudeville act singing a few Japanese tunes. This was followed by an almost instantaneous change–flinging off her kimono, now appearing in a glittering evening gown, she would break into a raucous rendition of 'My Japanese Mama.'" See Yoshida, 16–17.

70. Jon Fitzgerald and Philip Hayward, "Musical Transport: Van Dyke Parks, Americana, and the Applied Orientalism of *Tokyo Rose*," in *Widening the Horizon: Exoticism in Post-War Popular Music*, ed. Hayward, 151 (Sydney: John Libbey and Company, 1999), 145–167.

71. Ibid., 163.

72. In this sense, Shindo's position within exotica can be understood as analogous to Yma Sumac's. (As a Peruvian American, Sumac traded on her "mysterious" and "ancient" Incan heritage.)

73. During my January 2004 research work at Shindo's home, I found a piece of notebook paper with translations in a folder labeled *Mganga* that appears to be the notes referred to by Shindo in my June 2000 interview with him.

74. Joseph S. C. Lam, "Embracing 'Asian American Music' as an Heuristic Device," *Journal of Asian American Studies* 2, no. 1 (February 1999): 53–54.

75. Deborah Wong, "The Asian American Body in Performance," in *Music and the Racial Imagination*, ed. Ronald Radano and Philip V. Bohlman, 88 (Chicago: University of Chicago Press, 2000). On whether Asian musicians move toward blackness in such fusion, see Oliver Wang, "These Are the Breaks: Hip-Hop and AfroAsian Cultural (Dis)Connections," in *Afro-Asian Encounters: Culture, History, Politics*, eds. Heike Raphael-Hernandez and Shannon Steen, 157 (New York: New York University Press, 2006). On the relationships between Asian Americans and African Americans, see Gary Y. Okihiro, *Margins and Mainstreams: Asians in American History and Culture* (Seattle: University of Washington Press, 1994), chapter 2; and Frank H. Wu, *Yellow: Race in America Beyond Black and White*.

76. Some rather peculiar moves toward blackness have occurred in Japan in recent decades. Japanese teenagers have been ardent fans of hip-hop since the mid 1990s and have not only adopted hip-hop fashions but have also embraced blackface (*ganguro*) in their attempt to emulate African Americans. On the general Japanese interest in African American culture, see John G. Russell, "Race and Reflexivity: The Black Other in Contemporary Japanese Mass Culture," in *Contemporary Japan and Popular Culture*, ed. John Whittier Treat, 17–40 (Honolulu: University of Hawai'i Press, 1996); and Shuhei Hosokawa, "Blacking Japanese: Experiencing Otherness from Afar," in *Popular Music Studies*, ed. David Hesmondhalgh and Keith Negus), 223–237 (London: Arnold, 2002).

77. Quoted from Shindo's videotaped Go For Broke interview on 6 February 2000.

78. Howard Lucraft, "Tak Shindo: Hollywood Film Composers," *Crescendo and Jazz Music* 37, no. 4 (August–September 2000): 25. This very brief profile contains some errors and includes an odd overview of "Oriental music." However, the particular quotation presented here corresponds closely with sentiments Shindo expressed to me in June 2000. Some jazz musicians in Japan in the middle of the twentieth century experienced a similar pressure to "Japanize" their music. For example, the American saxophonist Sonny Rollins has been quoted as telling a Japanese jazz musician in the 1960s: "Because you all are Orientals your mission is to tie Oriental music to jazz." See E. Taylor Atkins, *Blue Nippon: Authenticating Jazz in Japan* (Durham, NC: Duke University Press, 2001), 32.

79. *Space Age Pop Music*, http://www.spaceagepop.com/shindo.htm (most recently accessed on 24 May 2016).

80. For an example of a more self-conscious form of self-Orientalism, see Shuhei Hosokawa, "Soy Sauce Music: Haruomi Hosono and Japanese Self-Orientalism," in *Widening the Horizon*, 114–144. Hosono, a founder of the Yellow Magic Orchestra, helped revive Martin Denny's exotica in Japan in the mid 1970s. Hosokawa suggests that Hosono's music presents "the Japanese way of exoticising American exoticism" (116) and "the deconstruction of orientalism by mimicry" (120).

81. Gunther Schuller, "Third Stream," *Grove Music Online*, ed. L. Macy (accessed 12 August 2003). Of course, Schuller was not referring to the exotica genre and the "dual traditions" of his Third Stream were European classical music and American jazz.

82. This Mercury Records album was produced by Quincy Jones. In my interviews with Shindo he appeared somewhat reluctant to discuss this recording and claimed to me that the album's concept was entirely Jones's idea.

83. The celebrated *taiko* performer Leonard Eto has followed his father's lead in pursuing musical fusions. After performing as a leading member of the famous *taiko* ensemble Kodo from 1984 to 1992, Leonard pursued a solo career and composed for multiple Hollywood films and dance companies.

84. Hampton's band included the Japanese American trombonist Paul Higaki in 1949–1951 and the *nisei* vocalist Susumu Takao sang with his band in the late 1940s, as did Karie Shindo. See Yoshida, 209–223.

85. "Demure Vocalist Is Called 'An Oriental Billie Holiday,'" *Jet* (20 February 1964): 60–61.

86. This performance, following Grace Chang's solo number, is currently available at https://www.youtube.com/watch?v=TD5YfqddKhY.

87. Tamara Roberts, *Resounding Afro Asia: Interracial Music and the Politics of Collaboration* (Oxford: Oxford University Press, 2016), 20. In chapter 2, Roberts focuses on Yoko Noge, a Chicago-based Japanese-born female blues musician and band leader who mixes blues and Japanese instruments and folk songs.

88. On Japanese American jazz in this period, see Asai, "Cultural Politics: The African American Connection in Asian American Jazz-based Music," *Asian Music* 36, no. 1 (winter–spring 2005): 87–108; "Transformations of Traditions," 442–448; and "*Sansei* Voices in the Community: Japanese American Musicians in California," chapter 11 in *Musics of Multicultural America: A Study of Twelve Musical Communities*, eds. Kip Lornell and Anne K. Rasmussen, 257–285 (New York: Schirmer Books, 1997); Deborah Wong, *Speak It Louder: Asian Americans Making Music* (New York and London: Routledge, 2004), 39–50, 170–180, 275–197, and 306–316; Loren Kajikawa, "The Sound of Struggle: Black Revolutionary Nationalism and Asian American Jazz," in *Jazz/Not Jazz: The Music and Its Boundaries*, eds. David Ake, Charles Hiroshi Garret, and Daniel Ira Goldmark, 190–216 (Berkeley: University of California Press, 2012); Eric Hung, "Sounds of Asian American Trauma and Cultural Trauma: Jazz Reflections on the Japanese Internment,"

MUSICultures 39, no. 2 (2012): 1–29; David W. Stowe, "'Jazz That Eats Rice': Toshiko Akiyoshi's Roots Music," in *Afro-Asian Encounters: Culture, History, Politics*, eds. Heike Raphael-Hernandez and Shannon Steen, 277–294 (New York: New York University Press, 2006); and Kevin Fellezs, "Silenced but Not Silent: Asian Americans and Jazz," in *Alien Encounters: Popular Culture in Asian America*, eds. Mimi Thi Nguyen and Thuy Linh Nguyen Tu, 69–108 (Durham, NC, and London: Duke University Press, 2007).

On Fred Ho, see Roger Buckley and Tamara Roberts, eds., *Yellow Power, Yellow Soul: The Radical Art of Fred Ho* (Urbana: University of Illinois Press, 2013); Fred Ho, *Wicked Theory, Naked Practice: A Fred Ho Reader*, ed. Diane C. Fujino (Minneapolis: University of Minnesota Press, 2009); and Tamara Roberts, *Resounding Afro Asia: Interracial Music and the Politics of Collaboration* (Oxford: Oxford University Press, 2016), chapter 4. Roberts discusses Ho's music theater work *Deadly She-Wolf Assassin at Armageddon!*, which is set in feudal Japan and incorporates Japanese instruments, and argues that it circumvents Orientalism (136–141).

89. On Nobuko Miyamoto, see Susan M. Asai, "Sansei Voices in the Community," 264–272. Asai discusses Miyamoto's 1990s one-woman show, *A Grain of Sand*, and its inclusion of Japanese instruments (268).

90. Asai, "Sansei Voices in the Community," 278–281.

91. Kajikawa, "The Sound of Struggle," 206–208. Also see Asai, "Transformations of Traditions," 443–445, on Horiuchi's *Poston Sonata*.

92. Eric Hung, "Sounds of Asian American Trauma and Cultural Trauma: Jazz Reflections on the Japanese Internment," *MUSICultures* 39, no. 2 (2012): 1–29.

93. On Izu, see Asai, "Sansei Voices in the Community," 272–278; and Hung, 17.

94. Atkins, 12.

95. See Yoshida, 43–44; and Atkins, 134–139.

96. Atkins, 82.

97. Leonard Feather, "Giants of Jazz: Miscellaneous Instruments," *International Musician* (July 1966): 7, 22–23. This was the fifteenth article in Feather's series on the "giants of jazz." Shindo was certainly not the first or only *nisei* involved in jazz to receive national recognition. For instance, Pat Suzuki had been named "Best New Female Singer" of 1958 in *Downbeat*.

98. See Shindo's Go For Broke interview.

99. In 1981, Tak Shindo married his second wife, Sachiko Shindo—a Japanese woman who left Japan to join him in San Dimas. Mrs. Shindo was an accomplished *shamisen* player who performed on the recording of the piece Shindo composed for the Japanese Pavilion at EPCOT. It appears that in making this recording, Shindo encountered a problem with his Japanese musicians similar to that which Franz Waxman had feared in the *Sayonara* recording sessions. Sachiko and the other Japanese musician could not follow Tak's conducting and were therefore recorded separately and later mixed in.

100. My discussion of Chihara's life and career and all quotations from him, unless otherwise noted, are based on our extensive interviews in November 2015 and April 2016 and on numerous emails and phone conversations from January to April 2016. I would like to thank Mr. Chihara for providing me with numerous scores and audio and video recordings of his works. Also see Chihara's interview with Drew Schnurr, at the University of California, Los Angeles on 11 November 2010: https://www.youtube.com/watch?v=pGgNZyDz4jM and the recorded interview with David Starobin appearing as the final track on *Chihara Viola Concerto and Music for Viola* (Bridge 9365, 2013).

101. My research does not support Susan Asai's comment that Chihara's "musical orientation was completely American, and he was never exposed to Japanese music." See Asai, "Transformations of Traditions," 433.

102. Chihara's relationship with Reynolds was substantial and he even played percussion on a recording of Reynolds's *All Known All White*.

103. On Suenobu Togi, see Lois V. Vierk, "Studying Gagaku," in *Arcana: Musicians on Music*, ed. John Zorn, 306–310 (New York: Granary Books, 2000). Asai mentions Togi in "Sansei Voices," 263, and Wong discusses the impact of Togi and *gagaku* on Miya Masaoka's music in *Speak It Louder*, 140–157 and 278–285.

104. On *Watermill*, see Deborah Jowitt, *Jerome Robbins: His Life, His Theater, His Dance* (New York: Simon and Schuster, 2004), 397–402.

105. In "The Asian American Body in Performance" (86), Deborah Wong briefly mentions Chihara's score for *Farewell to Manzanar*, stating that he avoided Asian sounds in his scores.

106. In his orchestral piece *An Afternoon on the Perfume River* (2003) Chihara used a Vietnamese folk tune that he had heard sung by a South Vietnamese refugee who appeared as an extra on an episode of the television series *China Beach*, which Chihara scored.

Chapter 8

1. John P. Marquand, *Stopover: Tokyo* (Boston: Little, Brown, 1956). On Marquand's "Mr. Moto" series, see Richard Wires, *John P. Marquand and Mr. Moto: Spy Adventures and Detective Films* (Muncie, IN: Ball State University Press, 1990).

2. Marquand, *Stopover: Tokyo*, 20–21.

3. I have previously presented some of the material and ideas offered in this chapter in papers delivered at the American Philosophical Society (2008), the Society for American Music annual meeting (2016), and at the University of California, Los Angeles (2017). I am grateful for comments offered by panelists and audience members at each of these events.

4. See Linda M. Arsenault, "Iannis Xenakis: 'I Am a Japanese,'" in *Musicology and Globalization: Proceedings of the International Congress in Shizuoka 2002*, eds. Yoshio Tozawa, Tatsuhiko Itoh, Keiichi Kubota, and Yasuhiko Mori, 238 (Tokyo: The Musicological Society of Japan, 2004).

5. Bálint András Varga, *Conversations with Iannis Xenakis* (London: Faber and Faber, 1996), 39.

6. Peter Hill and Nigel Simeone, *Messiaen* (New Haven, CT: Yale University Press, 2005), 249.

7. Olivier Messiaen, *Olivier Messiaen: Music and Color; Conversations with Claude Samuel*, trans. E. Thomas Glasow (Portland, OR: Amadeus Press, 1994), 100. The impact of *noh* is particularly evident in Messiaen's 1983 opera *Saint François d'Assise*.

8. Jonathan Cott, *Stockhausen: Conversations with the Composer* (New York: Simon and Schuster, 1973), 32–33.

9. Ekbert Faas, "Interview with Karlheinz Stockhausen Held August 11, 1976," *Interface* 6, nos. 3–4 (1977): 198–199.

10. Pierre Boulez, "Oriental Music: A Lost Paradise?" (1967), reprinted in *Orientations: Collected Writings of Pierre Boulez*, ed. Jean-Jacques Nattiez and trans. Martin Cooper, 422 (Cambridge, MA: Harvard University Press, 1986).

11. James A. Michener, *Sayonara: A Japanese-American Love Story* (Rutland, VT, and Tokyo: Charles E. Tuttle, 1954).

12. Danielle Fosler-Lussier, *Music in America's Cold War Diplomacy* (Oakland: University of California Press, 2015), 138–142.

13. Ibid., 49–56.

14. Jonathan Rosenberg, "'To Reach . . . into the Hearts and Minds of Our Friends': The United States' Symphonic Tours and the Cold War," in *Music and International History in the Twentieth Century*, ed. Jessica C. E. Gienow-Hecht, 148–151 (New York: Berghahn, 2015).

15. On this subject, see, for example, Ingrid Monson, *Freedom Sounds: Civil Rights Call Out to Jazz and Africa* (Oxford: Oxford University Press, 2007), chapter 4; and Fosler-Lussier, *Music in America's Cold War Diplomacy*, chapter 3.

16. On Brown's *Rhapsodies* see Ryan Raul Bañagale, *Arranging Gershwin:* Rhapsody in Blue *and the Creation of an American Icon* (Oxford: Oxford University Press, 2014), 174–179.

17. E. Taylor Atkins, *Blue Nippon: Authenticating Jazz in Japan* (Durham, NC: Duke University Press, 2001), 209. Atkins lists American jazz musicians who have "successfully incorporated Japanese folk melodies and instrumentation into their music," including Tony Scott, Herbie Mann, John "Kaizan" Neptune, and John Zorn (39).

18. On Ellington's tours of cultural diplomacy, see Penny M. Von Eschen, *Satchmo Blows Up the World: Jazz Ambassadors Play the Cold War* (Cambridge, MA: Harvard University Press, 2004), 126–147. Also see Duke Ellington, "Orientations: Adventures in the Mid-East," *Music Journal* 22, no. 3 (1 March 1964): 34–36, 104.

19. Von Eschen, *Satchmo Blows Up the World*, 146–147.

20. Mark Lomanno, "Ellington's Lens as Motive Mediating: Improvising Voices in the *Far East Suite*," *Jazz Perspectives* 6, nos. 1–2 (2012): 159–161.

21. Travis A. Jackson, "Tourist Point of View? Musics of the World and Ellington's Suites," *The Musical Quarterly* 96, nos. 3–4 (1 December 2013): 532.

22. Anthony Brown's 1999 re-orchestration of *The Far East Suite* for his Asian American Orchestra included several Chinese and Persian instruments. On Brown's album, see Lomanno, "Ellington's Lens," 160–165; and William Minor, *Jazz Journeys to Japan: The Heart Within* (Ann Arbor: University of Michigan Press, 2004), 323–329. Brown has cited Robert Garfias's book on *gagaku* (*Music of a Thousand Autumns*) and the music of Takemitsu as inspirations for his re-orchestration of Ellington's suite (327–328).

23. Von Eschen, *Satchmo Blows Up the World*, 56, 79–91.

24. Ibid., 52–53.

25. Quoted in Stephen A. Crist, "Jazz as Democracy? Dave Brubeck and Cold War Politics," *Journal of Musicology* 26, no. 2 (2009): 137. This article focuses primarily on Brubeck's 1958 tour that included Turkey, India, Iran, and Iraq. Crist discusses Brubeck's 1958 album *Jazz Impressions of Eurasia* (154–156). On Brubeck's trips for the Bureau of Educational and Cultural Affairs, see Lisa E. Davenport, *Jazz Diplomacy: Promoting America in the Cold War Era* (Jackson: University Press of Mississippi, 2009), 74–77.

26. The Dave Brubeck Quartet, *Jazz Impressions of Japan* (Columbia Records 9012, 1964), liner notes. On how specific *haiku* might be understood as related to specific tracks on the album, see Ilse Storb and Klaus-G. Fischer, *Dave Brubeck, Improvisations and Compositions: The Idea of Cultural Exchange*, trans. Bert Thompson (New York: P. Lang, 1994), 97–99. Storb points to the appearance of parallel fourths and fifths and pentatonic scales in *Jazz Impressions of Japan* as an attempt to convey "Far Eastern atmosphere" (50, 87).

27. Cary Ginell refers to a "Japanese flute" played by Mann, which might be the "stone flute" featured on the album entitled *Stone Flute* recorded in 1969. Ginell states that Mann had played this instrument on "Bedouin" from *African Suite* (1959) and that he also played "Japanese flute" on "Brazilian Soft Shoe" at the 1960 Newport Jazz Festival. Cary Ginell, *The Evolution of Mann: Herbie Mann and the Flute in Jazz* (Milwaukee: Hal Leonard Books, 2014), 66.

28. Ibid., 136.

29. Ibid., 137.

30. Morton White and Lucia White, *Journeys to the Japanese 1952–1979* (Vancouver: University of British Columbia Press, 1986), 1, 27–28. Morton White's 1960 visit to Japan was partially funded by the Center for American Studies in Tokyo (56).

31. Ibid., 31.

32. Ibid., 32.

33. Ibid., 38.

34. Ibid., 108.

35. Ibid., 143

36. Earle Ernst, *The Kabuki Theatre* (New York: Grove Press, 1956). On Ernst's career, see James R. Brandon, "Earle S. Ernst," *Asian Theatre Journal* 28, no. 2 (fall 2011): 332–340.

37. Faubion Bowers, *Japanese Theatre* (1952; New York: Hill and Wang, 1959).

38. Donald Keene, *Nō: The Classical Theatre of Japan* (Tokyo: Kodansha International, 1966). Keene, Bowers, and Ernst represent only three of the most prominent American scholars of Japanese culture during this period. Numerous other figures could be mentioned here, such as Donald Richie who first visited Japan during the occupation and later became the foremost English-language proponent of Japanese film.

39. See Eta Harich-Schneider, "The Present Condition of Japanese Court Music," *Musical Quarterly* 39, no. 1 (January 1953): 49–74. Also see her *The Rhythmical Patterns in Gagaku and Bugaku* (Leiden: Brill, 1954); "Abstracts: Regional Folk Songs and Itinerant Minstrels in Japan," *Journal of the American Musicological Society* 10, no. 2 (1957), 132–133; and *A History of Japanese Music* (Oxford: Oxford University Press, 1973). The year 1957 also saw the publication of a highly detailed introduction to *noh* in the *Journal of the American Musicological Society*. See Tatsuo Minagawa, "Japanese Noh Music," *Journal of the American Musicological Society* 10, no. 3 (autumn 1957): 181–200.

40. Don R. Baker, "William Malm: Japanese Music," *Percussive Notes* 23, no. 5 (July 1985): 26–28.

41. William P. Malm, *Japanese Music and Musical Instruments* (Rutland, VT: Charles E. Tuttle, 1959), 19–21.

42. William P. Malm, "Personal Approaches to the Study of Japanese Art Music," *Asian Music* 3, no. 1 (1972): 38–39.

43. On Garfias's career see Naoko Terauchi, "Interview with Robert Garfias," *Journal of Intercultural Studies (Kobe University)* 46 (2016): 91–120. This interview was held in March 2013.

44. Ibid., 103–104.

45. Robert S. Schwantes, *Japanese and Americans: A Century of Cultural Relations* (New York: Harper & Brothers, 1955), 241–245. Also see "Trio Gives Music of Japan," *New York Times*, 20 December 1931, 27.

46. Barbara E. Thornbury, "Cultural Policy and Private Initiative: The Performing Arts at the Japan Society, New York," *The World of Music* 46, no. 2 (2004): 126. I should note here that I served as a member of the Japan Society's Performing Arts Advisory Committee from 2007 to 2010.

47. Ibid., 127. (Logan also wrote the foreword to the 1952 publication of Faubion Bowers's book *Japanese Theatre*.) Also see Barbara E. Thornbury, *America's Japan and Japan's Performing Arts: Cultural Mobility and Exchange in New York, 1952–2011* (Ann Arbor: University of Michigan Press, 2013), 32–75. See Thornbury chapter 2 on the history of the Japan Society's promotion and production of Japanese performing arts and chapter 4 on the promotion of Japanese contemporary music by Music From Japan. Thornbury discusses the negative reception of the Takarazuka company's contemporaneous New York City performance (Ibid., 54–58).

48. Very little has been written about this major musical event. Two papers were delivered on this topic at the 2010 International Forum for Young Musicologists in Yokohama: Fuyuko Fukunaka's "Anti-Communist Propaganda or Philanthropy Misfired?: The Tokyo East West Music Encounter Festival (1961) and Its 'Political' Motives"; and Harm Langenkamp's "An Unprecedented Confrontation: The 1961 Tokyo World Music Festival." Fukunaka also delivered "The Tokyo World Music Festival (1961) and the Politics of De-Politicizing the Cold War" at the 2011 University of Nottingham conference "Red Strains: Music and

Communism outside the Communist Bloc after 1945." Langenkamp also offers a brief discussion in Harm Langenkamp, "(Dis)Connecting Cultures, Creating Dreamworlds: Musical 'East-West' Diplomacy in the Cold War and the War on Terror," in *Divided Dreamworlds?: The Cultural Cold War in East and West*, eds. Peter Romijn, Giles Scott-Smith, and Joes Segal, 217–234 (Amsterdam: Amsterdam University Press, 2012). Finally, in chapter 10 of his autobiography, the German composer and musicologist Hans Heinz Stuckenschmidt refers to his 1959, 1961, and 1963 trips to Japan and discusses the East-West Music Encounter. See H. H. Stuckenschmidt, *Zum Hören geboren: Ein Leben mit der Musik unserer Zeit* (Munich: R. Piper, 1979), 283–286.

49. On Alain Daniélou's pluralistic view that multiple "great" musical traditions existed in the world, and how this shaped Nabokov's vision for the East-West Music Encounter, see Ian Wellens, *Music on the Frontline: Nicolas Nabokov's Struggle against Communism and Middlebrow Culture* (Aldershot: Ashgate, 2002), 112.

50. My detailed discussion of Nabokov's work in organizing the East-West Music Encounter is based primarily on my research in the International Association for Cultural Freedom Records, Special Collections Research Center, University of Chicago Library, hereafter cited as IACF Records. On the initial planning for and delays of the Encounter also see Vincent Giroud, *Nicolas Nabokov: A Life in Freedom and Music* (Oxford: Oxford University Press, 2015), 299, 302, 329.

51. On Stravinsky's 1959 trip to Japan, see Igor Stravinsky and Robert Craft, *Dialogues and A Diary* (Garden City, NY: Doubleday, 1963), 121–138. In discussion with Stravinsky, Craft wondered whether Schoenberg had learned about *noh* vocal style from a student in Berlin named Abé and whether that had influenced his use of *Sprechstimme* in *Pierrot lunaire* (133).

52. Fosler-Lussier, *Music in America's Cold War Diplomacy*, 27.

53. Yoshio Nomura, "Religious Music," in *Music—East and West: Report on 1961 Tokyo East-West Music Encounter Conference*, Executive Committee for 1961 Tokyo East-West Music Encounter, ed. and publ. (Tokyo, 1961), 28.

54. Robert Garfias, "Some Effects of Changing Social Values on Japanese Music," in *Music-East and West*, 18.

55. Colin McPhee, "The Music Crisis in Bali Today," in *Music-East and West*, 61. McPhee wrote: "But the danger—at least the danger from a Western point of view—lies in the complete lack of Balinese interest in preserving the music of the past. There are a few ancient ensembles that continue to preserve, from memory, their sacred melodies, but the average Balinese gamelan of today would consider it a disgrace to perform music they had learned only a few years back." He went on to lament that the modern Balinese music does not "show the formal structure or melodic beauty of the older music. Balanced f[or]m and metric breadth have given way to restless fantasias in which short excerpts from traditional melodies follow each other in purely arbitrary succession." McPhee's landmark *Tabu-Tabuhan* (1936) could well be described as a fantasy of excerpts from traditional Balinese melodies reworked for Western orchestra.

56. Peter Crossley-Holland, "Asian Music under the Impact of Western Culture," in *Music-East and West*, 52. Tran Van Khe, from South Vietnam, noted that Asian youth were turning away from Asian music in "Problems of Sino-Japanese Musical Tradition Today," in *Music-East and West*, 54.

57. Lou Harrison, "Refreshing the Auditory Perception," in *Music-East and West*, 141–142.

58. Virgil Thomson, "The Philosophy of Style," in *Music-East and West*, 145.

59. The manuscript score is held in the Virgil Thomson Collection, Yale University, MSS 29, Box 9, Folder 6.

60. Murata quoted in *Music-East and West*, 193. A similar debate had played out at the landmark 1932 Cairo Congress of Arab Music, an earlier musical meeting of East and West.

See Ali Jihad Racy, "Historical Worldviews of Early Ethnomusicologists: An East-West Encounter in Cairo, 1932," in *Ethnomusicology and Modern Music History*, eds. Stephen Blum, Philip V. Bohlman, and Daniel M. Newman, 68–91 (Urbana: University of Illinois Press, 1991), 78–79.

61. Murata, 197.

62. Nabokov's statement appears on page 2 of the Information Handbook for the 1961 Tokyo East-West Music Encounter Conference.

63. Frances Stonor Saunders, *The Cultural Cold War: The CIA and the World of Arts and Letters* (New York: The New Press, 2000), 1, 135. Saunders also discusses Nabokov's 1952 "Masterpieces of the Twentieth Century" festival held in Paris (113–128) and his "International Conference of Twentieth Century Music" held in Rome in 1954 (220–224). Saunders is skeptical of Nabokov's claims of not knowing that the funding for such events was provided by the CIA (127–128, 395–396). On CIA funding for the Congress for Cultural Freedom, also see Wellens, *Music on the Frontline*, 11. A brief discussion of these topics appears in James Wierzbicki, *Music in the Age of Anxiety: American Music in the Fifties* (Urbana: University of Illinois Press, 2016), 172–176.

64. See the undated letter (referred to in later correspondence as having been written on 19 December 1960) from Lou Harrison to Ruby d'Arschot, in the IACF Records, Box 427, Folder 6.

65. Nabokov to the Catherwood Foundation, from Paris on 26 Nov 1959, IACF Records, Box 426, Folder 7. Other letters from Nabokov requesting funding in 1958 and 1959 appear in this folder as well.

66. A 20 October 1959 letter from Nabokov to the Department of State requesting funding is held in IACF Records, Box 426, Folder 9.

67. Nabokov writing from Paris on 6 Oct 1960 to Bando in Tokyo, IACF Records, Box 427 Folder 4.

68. See materials held in IACF Records, Box 194, Folder 3. Other documents held in Boxes 193 and 194 relate to other Congress for Cultural Freedom activities in Japan in the 1950s and early 1960s. These efforts included supporting various magazines that were clearly anti-communist and supporting an event held to benefit Hungarian refugees after the Soviet invasion. Numerous CCF staff traveled to Japan during this period.

69. Nabokov's statements in his final report appear in IACF Records, Box 429, Folder 7, pp. 5, 11.

70. Garfias's report, sent on 28 June 1961 to Ruby d'Arschot, Nabokov's assistant, is held in IACF Records, Box 427, Folder 6.

71. Carter's report is held in IACF Records, Box 427, Folder 5.

72. Hisao Tanabe, *Japanese Music*, trans. Shigeyoshi Sakabe (Tokyo: The Society for International Cultural Relations, 1936), 17.

73. Ann Michelle Stimson, "Musical Time in the Avant-Garde: The Japanese Connection" (Ph.D. diss., University of California, Santa Barbara, 1996), 5–6.

74. Ieda Bispo, "Olivier Messiaen's *Sept Haïkaï*: Beyond Japonisme," in *Musicology and Globalization: Proceedings of the International Congress in Shizuoka 2002*, eds. Yoshio Tozawa, Tatsuhiko Itoh, Keiichi Kubota, and Yasuhiko Mori, 242 (Tokyo: The Musicological Society of Japan, 2004).

75. Terauchi, "Interview with Robert Garfias," 104.

76. Cheong Wai Ling, "Buddhist Temple, Shinto Shrine, and the Invisible God of *Sept Haïkaï*," in *Messiaen the Theologian*, ed. Andrew Shenton, 242, 261 (Farnham: Ashgate, 2010).

77. Ibid., 248.

78. Cheong Wai Ling, "Culture as Reference in the 'Gagaku' of Messiaen's *Sept Haïkaï* (1962)," in *Music and Its Referential Systems*, ed. Matjaž Barbo and Thomas Hochradner, 195 (Vienna: Hollitzer Wissenschaftsverlag, 2012).

79. Quoted in Ibid., 186. On this movement also see Yayoi Uno Everett, "'Mirrors' of West and 'Mirrors' of East: Elements of *Gagaku* in Post-War Art Music," in *Diasporas and Interculturalism in Asian Performing Arts: Translating Traditions*, ed. Hae-Kyung Um, 185 (London: Routledge-Curzon, 2005), and Bispo, "Olivier Messiaen's *Sept Haïkaï*," 243–244.

80. Ibid., 245.

81. Paul Griffiths, *Olivier Messiaen and the Music of Time* (Ithaca, NY: Cornell University Press, 1985), 197.

82. Luigi Antonio Irlandini, "Messiaen's 'Gagaku,'" *Perspectives of New Music* 48, no. 2 (summer 2010): 195–197, 201.

83. Stimson, "Musical Time in the Avant-Garde," 9, 38. Taking a long view, Messiaen's *Sept Haïkaï* might be understood as a model for Kaija Saariaho's *Six Japanese Gardens* (1995).

84. Pierre Boulez, "Oriental Music: A Lost Paradise?" (1967), 424.

85. Ibid., 421.

86. Ibid., 422.

87. Ibid., 423.

88. Rocco Di Pietro, *Dialogues with Boulez* (Lanham, MD: Scarecrow Press, 2001), 48–49.

89. Quoted in Yves Balmer, Thomas Lacôte, and Christopher Brent Murray, "Messiaen the Borrower: Recomposing Debussy through the Deforming Prism," *Journal of the American Musicological Society* 69, no. 3 (fall 2016): 780.

90. Di Pietro, *Dialogues with Boulez*, 50. Boulez also refers to his interest in *noh* and *bunraku* in this source (60).

91. Chicago Symphony Orchestra 2004 program notes "Comments by Phillip Huscher."

92. Quoted in Stimson, "Musical Time in the Avant-Garde," 71.

93. Varga, *Conversations with Iannis Xenakis*, 39.

94. On this experience, see Arsenault, "Iannis Xenakis: 'I Am a Japanese,'" 238.

95. Ibid., 239. Also see Iannis Xenakis, "The Riddle of Japan," *This Is Japan* 9 (1962): 68.

96. Quoted in Nouritza Matossian, *Xenakis* (New York: Taplinger, 1986), 146.

97. Ibid., 146–147. Also see Arsenault, 239.

98. Matossian, 103.

99. James Harley, *Xenakis: His Life in Music* (New York: Routledge, 2004), 67.

100. Faas, "Interview with Karlheinz Stockhausen," 199. (The Beatles expressed similar sentiments following their 1967 trip to India.) For Stockhausen's description of the Omizutori ceremony he witnessed at Nara see Cott, *Stockhausen*, 181–184.

101. Karlheinz Stockhausen, "World Music," *The World of Music* 21, no. 1 (1979): 3–4.

102. Dieter Gutknecht, "Stockhausen und Japan," in *"Lux Oriente": Begegnungen der Kulturen in der Musikforschung, Festschrift Robert Günther zum 65. Geburtstag*, eds. Klaus Wolfgang Niemöller, Uwe Pätzold, and Kyo-chul Chung, 271. Kölner Beiträge zur Musikforschung 188 (Kassel: Gustav Bosse, 1995).

103. Cott, *Stockhausen*, 30.

104. See, for example, Karlheinz Stockhausen, *Stockhausen on Music: Lectures and Interviews*, ed. Robin Maconie (London: Marion Boyars, 1989), 91, 93, and 100; 154.

105. Stimson, "Musical Time in the Avant-Garde," 72, 85–86. Stockhausen was struck by the "wide scale between the extremely fast and the extremely slow" and by the "instant change without transition" he heard in Japanese music. Quoted in Christian Utz, *Neue Musik und Interkulturalität: von John Cage bis Tan Dun*, Archiv für Musikwissenschaft 51 (Stuttgart: Franz Steiner, 2002), 148.

106. Cott, *Stockhausen*, 31.

107. Ibid., 163.

108. Utz, *Neue Musik*, 136.

109. Cott, *Stockhausen*, 129.

110. For a highly detailed discussion of Stockhausen's sources for this piece, see Utz, *Neue Musik*, 153–165.

111. Robin Maconie, *The Works of Karlheinz Stockhausen*, 2nd ed. (Oxford: Clarendon Press, 1990), 176.

112. Robin Maconie, *Other Planets: The Music of Karlheinz Stockhausen* (Lanham, MD: Scarecrow Press, 2005), 433. Maconie also points to parallels between "the changing clusters and time strokes" of *gagaku* and Stockhausen's 1971 *Trans* (Maconie, *The Works of Karlheinz Stockhausen*, 227).

113. Susumu Shōno, "The Role of Listening in *Gagaku*," *Contemporary Music Review* 1, no. 2 (1987): 23.

114. Fernand Ouellette, *Edgard Varèse*, trans. Derek Coltman (New York: Orion Press, 1968), 204–205.

115. Ibid., 205.

116. Wen-chung Chou, "Asian Concepts and Twentieth-Century Western Composers," *Musical Quarterly* 57, no. 2 (April 1971): 216–217.

117. Wilfrid Mellers, *Singing in the Wilderness: Music and Ecology in the Twentieth Century* (Urbana: University of Illinois Press, 2001), 132. Ann Stimson states that *Déserts* shares harmonies with *Etenraku* and points to parallels between timbral groups in these two works. See Stimson, "Musical Time in the Avant-Garde," 111–112, 121–122.

118. Jeremy Grimshaw, *Draw a Straight Line and Follow It: The Music and Mysticism of La Monte Young* (Oxford: Oxford University Press, 2011), 25–26.

119. Steve Reich, *Music for 18 Musicians* (New York: Boosey & Hawkes, 2000). Note by the composer.

120. Similarly, the swelling organ and bowed vibraphone sounds heard in Reich's 1985 *Sextet* also resemble the *sho* to my ear. I would like to thank my student Nathaniel Vilas for suggesting to me in 2016 the influence of *gagaku* on these works by Reich.

121. Undated letter (referred to as 22 December 1960 in subsequent Nabokov letter), from Harrison to Nabokov, IACF Records, Box 427, Folder 6. Harrison relates that he plans to study modes from Japan to Indonesia and that he is "already wide open for the musical stimulus which I expect from all this."

122. Leta E. Miller and Fredric Lieberman, *Lou Harrison: Composing a World* (Oxford: Oxford University Press, 1998), 20. Miller and Lieberman explain that a delegate to the Encounter from Korea gave Harrison a record of Korean music which he listened to in Tokyo and which inspired him to travel to Korea after the conference ended (58–59). Harrison had composed music for an experimental production of a *noh* play at Black Mountain College in 1951 (95).

123. Ibid., 155.

124. Toshie Kakinuma, "Composing for an Ancient Instrument That Has Lost Its 'Tradition': Lou Harrison's *Set for Four Haisho and Percussion*," *Perspectives of New Music* 49, no. 2 (summer 2011): 250–253.

125. Ibid., 254.

126. My discussion of Hovhaness's travels to Japan and study of Japanese music is based primarily on research I carried out at the Armenian Cultural Foundation, Arlington, Massachusetts: The Alan Hovhaness Collection. Hereafter referred to as the ACF Hovhaness Collection.

127. Hovhaness to Burton Fahs (Rockefeller Foundation), 27 December 1961, Box 1, Folder 9, ACF Hovhaness Collection. In this letter he refers to having spent several months in Japan in 1959, though most sources date this initial trip to 1960. He had been commissioned to write a cantata for Ueno Gakuen College of Music in Tokyo and he conducted his own works with the Tokyo Symphony and Japan Philharmonic.

128. Hovhaness to Boyd Compton (Rockefeller Foundation), 12 January 1962, Box 1, Folder 9, ACF Hovhaness Collection.

129. Photographs of Hovhaness playing these instruments alongside other *gagaku* musicians, including his wife Elizabeth "Naru" Whittington Hovhaness, in spring 1962 in Hawai'i are held in Box 8, Series X, Folder 238, ACF Hovhaness Collection.

130. Hovhaness to Walter Simmons, 29 June 1962, Box 2, Folder 26, ACF Hovhaness Collection.

131. Hovhaness to Rockefeller Foundation, 7 April 1962, Box 1, Folder 9, ACF Hovhaness Collection.

132. Boyd Compton (Rockefeller Foundation) to Hovhaness, 12 September 1963, Box 1, Folder 9, ACF Hovhaness Collection. Compton suggested that Hovhaness turn to Robert Garfias for advice.

133. See, for example, Recording of Hovhaness lecture at Elmira College on 14 February 1967, "Giant Melody in Nature and Art," ACF Hovhaness Collection (24:15).

134. Hovhaness to Harry Adaskin, 9 December 1954, Box 1, Folder 1, ACF Hovhaness Collection.

135. Hovhaness, Elmira College lecture, ACF Hovhaness Collection (38:00).

136. Alan Hovhaness, "Thoughts on East-West Music," in *Essays in Ethnomusicology: A Birthday Offering for Lee Hye-Ku* (Seoul: The Korean Musicological Society, 1969), 368.

137. Ibid., 369.

138. An early version of the work included parts for xylophone and woodblock. The sketches for *Fuji Cantata* are held in the Music Division of the Library of Congress. See ML96 H853 no. 29, ML96 H853 no. 30, and M1543 H74F8 copy 2 (the published score).

139. Wayne David Johnson, "A Study of the Piano Works of Alan Hovhaness" (DMA thesis, University of Cincinnati, 1987), 90.

140. On this piece also see Chung Park, "*Ode to the Temple of Sound, Floating World–Ukiyo*, and *Meditation on Zeami*: An Analysis of Three Works by Alan Hovhaness" (DMA thesis, University of Miami, 2008).

141. Quoted in the published score of Alan Hovhaness, *Floating World: "Ukiyo" Ballade for Orchestra* (Edition Peters, no. 66021).

142. Tyler Kinnear, "Alan Hovhaness and the Creation of the 'Modern Free Noh Play'" (MA thesis, University of Oregon, 2009), 1, 63–70. Also see my *Revealing Masks: Exotic Influences and Ritualized Performance in Modernist Music Theater* (Berkeley: University of California Press, 2001), 174.

143. Kinnear, "Alan Hovhaness," 24, 74–83.

144. On Britten's Church Parables, see my *Revealing Masks*, chapter 9.

145. Hovhaness to Walter Simmons, 6 March 1961, Box 2, Folder 26, ACF Hovhaness Collection. Simmons wrote to Hovhaness as an aspiring composer and fan of his music and was a teenager during the period of their correspondence cited here.

146. Hovhaness to Walter Simmons, 2 July 1965, Box 2, Folder 26, ACF Hovhaness Collection.

147. Hovhaness to Walter Simmons, 27 October 1960, Box 2, Folder 26, ACF Hovhaness Collection.

148. Bonnie Marranca, "Meredith Monk's Atlas of Sound: New Opera and the American Performance Tradition," in *Meredith Monk*, ed. Deborah Jowitt, 182 (Baltimore: Johns Hopkins University Press, 1997).

149. On the impact of Japanese culture on the works of Harry Partch, see my *Revealing Masks*, chapter 12.

150. Kay Larson, *Where the Heart Beats: John Cage, Zen Buddhism, and the Inner Life of Artists* (New York: The Penguin Press, 2012), xii.

151. See Jane Naomi Iwamura, *Virtual Orientalism: Asian Religions and American Popular Culture* (Oxford: Oxford University Press, 2011), 23–25.

152. Ibid., 25, 32–33.

153. Robert Fink, *Repeating Ourselves: American Minimal Music as Cultural Practice* (Berkeley: University of California Press, 2005), 15, 217. Fink also considers D. T. Suzuki's impact in the United States and the relationship between different forms of Zen Buddhism and the Suzuki Method of Shinichi Suzuki and American musical minimalism (227–233).

154. Daisetz T. Suzuki, "Zen in the Modern World," *Japan Quarterly* 5, no. 4 (1958): 452, quoted by Iwamura, *Virtual Orientalism*, 40–41.

155. Carl Jackson, "The Counterculture Looks East: Beat Writers and Asian Religion," *American Studies* 29, no. 1 (1988): 60.

156. Jack Kerouac, *The Dharma Bums* (New York: Penguin, 1986), 162.

157. Ibid., 203–205.

158. Alan W. Watts, "Beat Zen, Square Zen, and Zen," *Chicago Review* 12, no. 2 (1958): 3–11.

159. Ibid., 6–7.

160. Ibid., 9. On Kerouac and Watts as representing divergent forms of Zen in the United States, see Iwamura, *Virtual Orientalism*, 38–52. Iwamura notes that Watts had read Hearn *Gleanings in Buddha Fields* during his teenage years (41).

161. Phil Ford, *Dig: Sound and Music in Hip Culture* (Oxford: Oxford University Press, 2013), 33. Ford launches his study of Hipness and Beat musical culture with Zen, but not in a very committed way: "Since I have been using the koan as an extended metaphor, I may as well consider the link between hipness and Zen Buddhism" (27).

162. Ibid., 29–32.

163. Ibid., 32–33; 187–190.

164. Ibid., 34–35.

165. For a recent anthology, see Jim Kacian, Philip Rowland, and Allan Burns, eds., *Haiku in English: The First Hundred Years* (New York: W. W. Norton, 2013). The American fascination with the *haiku* form is documented in the American Haiku Archives at the California State Library, Sacramento, and is celebrated by The Haiku Society of America, which was founded in 1968.

166. Malm, *Japanese Music and Musical Instruments*, 265.

167. I thank Paul Novosel, archivist for the Dance Theatre of Harlem, for providing me with these manuscripts. As noted in chapter 7, multiple ballets on Japanese subjects were created in the United States in the early 1970s. These include Jerome Robbins's 1971 *noh*-inspired *Watermill* for the New York City Ballet with score by Teiji Ito, and Michael Smuin's 1975 *Shin-ju* for the San Francisco Ballet with score by Paul Chihara. Balanchine's 1963 *Bugaku*, score by Toshiro Mayuzumi, was a particularly prominent precursor for these works.

168. See Alexandra Munroe, "Buddhism and the Neo-Avant-Garde: Cage Zen, Beat Zen, and Zen," in *The Third Mind: American Artists Contemplate Asia, 1860–1989*, ed. Alexandra Munroe, 199–273 (New York: Solomon R. Guggenheim Foundation, 2009).

169. John Cage, *Silence: Lectures and Writings* (Middletown, CT: Wesleyan University Press, 1961), xi. As David W. Patterson notes, Cage first made this demurral in his 1958–1959 lecture "Indeterminacy," following soon after Watts's article. See David W. Patterson "Appraising the Catchwords, c. 1942–1959: John Cage's Asian-Derived Rhetoric and the Historical Reference of Black Mountain College" (PhD diss., Columbia University, 1996), 48.

170. John Cage, *For the Birds: In Conversation with Daniel Charles* (Boston: Marion Boyars, 1981), 200.

171. On Cage's attendance at performances by Tamada, see Ingrid Grete Gordon, "Drums along the Pacific: The Influence of Asian Music on the Early Percussion Ensemble Music of Henry Cowell, John Cage, and Lou Harrison" (DMA diss., University of Illinois at Urbana-Champaign, January 2000).

172. David W. Patterson, "Cage and Asia: History and Sources," in *The Cambridge Companion to John Cage*, edited by David Nicholls, 50; 53–55 (Cambridge, UK: Cambridge University Press, 2002).

173. Patterson, "Appraising the Catchwords, 141–142, 139, 135. R. H. Blyth was an English author of multiple books on Japanese literature and Zen and his translations of *haiku* were particularly influential. Blyth studied Zen with D. T. Suzuki and later served a crucial role as liaison to the Emperor during the US occupation following World War II.

174. Patterson, "Cage and Asia," 41, 58–59.

175. James Pritchett, *The Music of John Cage* (Cambridge, UK: Cambridge University Press, 1993), 74. Pritchett also points to Cage's use of the poetic line structure of *haiku* and *renga* in the 1970s (183).

176. "La Monte Young: Interview with Peter Dickinson, New York City, July 2, 1987," in *Cage Talk: Dialogues with and about John Cage*, ed. Peter Dickinson, 155 (Rochester, NY: University of Rochester Press, 2006).

177. John Cage to Walter and Evelyn Hinrichsen (10 October 1962, from Tokyo), in *The Selected Letters of John Cage*, ed. Laura Kuhn, 275–276 (Middletown, CT: Wesleyan University Press, 2016).

178. Fredric Lieberman, ed. "'Contemporary Japanese Music': A Lecture by John Cage," in *Locating East Asia in Western Art Music*, eds. Yayoi Uno Everett and Frederick Lau, 195 (Middletown, CT: Wesleyan University Press, 2004).

179. Quoted in Lafcadio Hearn, *Gleanings in Buddha-Fields: Studies of Hand and Soul in the Far East* (Boston and New York: Houghton, Mifflin and Co., 1897), 69–70.

180. On Cage's tour of Japan with David Tudor, see You Nakai, "Of Stone and Sand: John Cage and David Tudor in Japan, 1962," *POST: Notes on Modern and Contemporary Art around the Globe*, Museum of Modern Art, 21 April 2015, https://post.at.moma.org/content_items/562-of-stone-and-sand-john-cage-and-david-tudor-in-japan-1962.

181. See Barry Shank, "Productive Orientalisms: Imagining Noise and Silence across the Pacific, 1957–1967," in *Postnational Musical Identities: Cultural Production, Distribution, and Consumption in a Globalized Scenario*, eds. Ignacio Corona and Alejandro L. Madrid, 49 (Lanham, MD: Lexington Books, 2008).

182. Jack Kerouac, *Some of the Dharma* (New York: Viking, 1997), 369, 379.

183. Rob Haskins, "On John Cage's Late Music, Analysis, and the Model of Renga in *Two²*," *American Music* 27, no. 3 (fall 2009): 335–337.

184. On musical responses to the Ryoanji garden, also see Michael Fowler, "Transmediating a Japanese Garden Through Spatial Sound Design," *Leonardo Music Journal* 21 (2011): 41–49.

185. See John Cage, "Ryoanji: Solos for Oboe, Flute, Contrabass, Voice, Trombone with Percussion or Orchestral Obbligato (1983–85)," *PAJ: A Journal of Performance and Art* 31, no. 3 (September 2009): 58–64.

186. Pritchett, *The Music of John Cage*, 190–191. Michael Fowler somewhat overstates the connection between Cage's piece and the garden: "*Ryoanji* is a literal translation of the temple's dry garden into music, in which all the aspects of the space have a composed sonic equivalent." This is true only if one, following Cage's own view, assumes that the fifteen rocks at Ryoanji could be rearranged anywhere in the space of the garden. See Fowler, "Finding Cage at Ryōan-ji through a Re-Modelling of *Variations II*," *Perspectives of New Music* 47, no. 1 (winter 2009): 175. John Corbett dismisses Cage's piece as a work of "conceptual Orientalism" that "does not resemble anything specifically Japanese at all," concluding that it represents "an oblique form of Orientalism. . . . But it is still Orientalist." See John Corbett, "Experimental Oriental: New Music and Other Others," in *Western Music and Its Others: Difference, Representation, and Appropriation in Music*, eds. Georgina Born and David Hesmondhalgh, 171 (Berkeley: University of California Press, 2000).

187. This unrealized work was to have been entitled *Noh-opera, or the Complete Musical Works of Marcel Duchamp*, and was to present "a collage of both Oriental theater and Western theater." See John Cage, *Musicage: Cage Muses on Words, Art, Music*, ed. Joan Retallack, 228 (Hanover, NH: University Press of New England, 1995). Also see *The Selected Letters of John Cage*, 561–565.

188. Marranca, "Meredith Monk's Atlas of Sound," 181.

189. Leslie Lassetter, "Meredith Monk: An Interview about Her Recent Opera, *Atlas*," *Contemporary Music Review* 16 (1997): 67.

190. Martha Mockus, *Sounding Out: Pauline Oliveros and Lesbian Musicality* (New York: Routledge, 2008), 25.

191. Pauline Oliveros, program notes for *Bye Bye Butterfly* in *The Transparent Tape Music Festival Program*, sfSound, 11–12 January 2002, http://sfsound.org/tape/oliveros.html.

192. Mockus, *Sounding Out*, 24.

193. I was fortunate to participate in a Deep Listening workshop led by Oliveros at Williams College in October 1996. Sarah Weaver has argued against emphasizing sexuality and gender in discussing Oliveros's music and has pointed to elements of continuity between *Bye Bye Butterfly* and the later Deep Listening projects. See Sarah Weaver, "Roots for Deep Listening in Oliveros's *Bye Bye Butterfly*," *American Music Review* 47, no. 1 (fall 2017): 5–12, http://www.brooklyn.cuny.edu/web/academics/centers/hitchcock/publications/amr/v47-1/weaver.php#.

194. For a very brief discussion, see Tomomi Adachi, "'John Cage Shock' in the 1960s in Japan and the Question of Orientalism," in *Cage and Consequences*, eds. Julia H. Schröder and Volker Straebel, 165–167 (Berlin: Wolke, 2012). Adachi notes that Cage eventually made a total of seven trips to Japan.

195. On Ono's role, see Yayoi Uno Everett, "'Scream against the Sky': Japanese Avant-garde Music in the Sixties," in *Sound Commitments: Avant-garde Music and the Sixties*, ed. Robert Adlington, 195–197, 201–202 (Oxford: Oxford University Press, 2009).

196. On Cage's influence on Ichiyanagi and Ono and his role as mentor to the Fluxus group, see Luciana Galliano, "Toshi Ichiyanagi, Japanese Composer and 'Fluxus,'" *Perspectives of New Music* 44, no. 2 (summer 2006): 251–254.

197. See Munroe, "Buddhism and the Neo-Avant-Garde," 204.

198. Tamara Levitz, "Yoko Ono and the Unfinished Music of 'John & Yoko': Imagining Gender and Racial Equality in the Late 1960s," in *Impossible to Hold: Women and Culture in the 1960s*, eds. Avital H. Bloch and Lauri Umansky, 223 (New York: New York University Press, 2005). On Ono's gendered musical constructions also see Elizabeth Ann Lindau, "'Mother Superior': Maternity and Creativity in the Work of Yoko Ono," *Women and Music: A Journal of Gender and Culture* 20 (2016): 57–76.

199. Shelina Brown, "Scream from the Heart: Yoko Ono's Rock and Roll Revolution," in *Countercultures and Popular Music*, ed. Sheila Whiteley and Jedediah Sklower, 171, 173 (New York: Routledge, 2014). Brown rightly notes a range of influences on Ono, including *kabuki* and Second Viennese School opera (177), but oddly suggests that Ono was "instrumental in introducing John Cage to Zen philosophy" (181).

200. Barry Shank, "Abstraction and Embodiment: Yoko Ono and the Weaving of Global Musical Networks," *Journal of Popular Music Studies* 18, no. 3 (2006): 288, 290.

201. Lennon made this statement in a 1971 conversation with Tariq Ali and Robin Blackburn, quoted in *Lennon on Lennon: Conversations with John Lennon*, ed. Jeff Burger, 181–182 (Chicago: Chicago Review Press, 2016).

202. Steely Dan offered a gentle parody of the current fad for Eastern religion that was prevalent among hippies in the song "Bodhisattva," the first track on *Countdown to Ecstasy* (1973). The lyrics include the following lines:

Bodhisattva
I'm gonna sell my house in town
And I'll be there to shine in your Japan
To sparkle in your China, yes I'll be there
Bodhisattva, Bodhisattva

203. Miya Masaoka, "Notes from a Trans-Cultural Diary," in *Arcana: Musicians on Music*, ed. John Zorn, 153 (New York: Granary Books, 2000). On her *koto* studies, see 154. For a brief overview of her career and description of one performance, see Minor, *Jazz Journeys to Japan*, 268–272.

204. Miya Masaoka, "Koto No Tankyu (Koto Explorations)" *Newsletter: Institute for Studies in American Music* 25, no. 2 (spring 1996): 8–9.

205. On Masaoka's improvised collaborations with George Lewis, see Deborah Wong, *Speak It Louder: Asian Americans Making Music* (New York: Routledge, 2004), 278–285.

206. Quoted in Frank J. Oteri, "Miya Masaoka: Social and Sonic Relationships," *NewMusicBox* 1 (June 2014), https://nmbx.newmusicusa.org/miya-masaoka/. On this piece and its controversial reception, see Wong, *Speak It Louder*, chapter 7. Also see Stacey Sewell, "Making My Skin Crawl: Representations and Mediations of the Body in Miya Masaoka's *Ritual, Interspecies Collaboration with Giant Madagascar Hissing Cockroaches*," *Radical Musicology* 4 (2009), http://www.radical-musicology.org.uk/2009/Sewell.htm.

207. Unless otherwise noted, the information presented here on Teitelbaum is from interviews and email conversations I held with him in September and October 2006.

208. As a graduate student in composition at Yale, Alvin Curran composed *The Damask Drum* in 1959, a chamber opera-ballet inspired by *noh* that, however, does not exhibit Japanese musical features. Markings on the instrumental and vocal parts indicate that the work received a performance at Yale. I am grateful to Joel Curran, the composer's brother, for providing me with access to these manuscripts.

209. Randy Raine-Reusch, "Integrating Extremes: The Music of Richard Teitelbaum," *Musicworks* 85 (spring 2003): 52.

210. Ibid., 47.

211. Teitelbaum, *Blends* (New Albion Records, NA118, 2002), liner notes, 4. In several works in the 1980s and 1990s, Jon Appleton also responded to Japanese culture and music in pieces for both acoustic and live electronic instruments, such as the 1979–1980 *Nukuoro* for live synclavier, *Degitaru ongaku* (synclavier, 1983), and the 1996 *Nihon no omide (Japanese Memories)* for solo violin.

212. Ibid., 3.

213. I credit my own early interest in the American experimental tradition to a course Reynolds offered as a visiting professor at Amherst College in 1988, and I am grateful for his assistance in my current research as he devoted many hours to our interviews and has provided extensive access to his diaries, manuscripts, recordings, and scores. Much of my discussion here is based on interviews held with him at his Del Mar, California, home in June 2011 and in numerous email conversations from 2010 to 2017.

214. Correspondence dated 7 March and 19 April, 1966, Box 1, Folder 14 in the ACF Hovhaness Collection. Hovhaness accepted the position of composer-in-residence with the Seattle Symphony in July 1966 for a term that was initially planned for one year, from December 1966 to December 1967.

215. Reynolds discussed these festivals in his ICWA report #20, "Cross Talk Intermedia I" (10 May 1969): 4, 9. He noted that the US embassy was interested in the endeavor for its potential to reach young Japanese intellectuals who were typically antagonistic toward the United States. He also expressed a negative view of the current performance of contemporary music in Japan, noting that this situation is what spurred the creation of CROSSTALK

in the summer of 1967. His ICWA reports are available at: http://www.icwa.org/roger-reynolds-newsletters/. Also see Roger Reynolds, *Mind Models: New Forms of Musical Experience* (New York: Praeger Publishers, 1975), 29–31, where in a brief section headed "Borrowed Models" he mentions his experience in running CROSSTALK INTERMEDIA in Japan. Reynolds noted to me in our email correspondence that "before we left for Japan, the Director of ICWA had given us a stern lecture about rebuffing and reporting immediately any approach by the CIA, etc. (There was none.)"

216. Roger Reynolds, ICWA report #1, "From Space to Environment—I" (24 December 1966).

217. Roger Reynolds, "Current Chronicle: Japan," *Musical Quarterly* 53, no. 4 (October 1967): 563. Concerning a piece by Teizo Matsumura, Reynolds noted that the music of Varèse is evoked in addition to *gagaku*, noting that "one of the most striking qualities of gagaku music is the wide unison, the agreement not quite achieved (or not sought)" (568). Also see Reynolds, "Happenings in Japan and Elsewhere," *Arts in Society* 5, no. 1 (1968): 90–101.

218. Roger Reynolds and Tōru Takemitsu, "A Jostled Silence: Contemporary Japanese Musical Thought (Part One)," *Perspectives of New Music* 30, no. 1 (winter 1992): 22–80. Reynolds and Yuji Takahashi, "A Jostled Silence: Contemporary Japanese Musical Thought (Part Two)," *Perspectives of New Music* 30, no. 2 (summer 1992): 60–100. Reynolds and Jōji Yuasa, "A Jostled Silence: Contemporary Japanese Musical Thought (Part Three)," *Perspectives of New Music* 31, no. 2 (summer 1993): 172–228.

219. Roger Reynolds, "Ideals and Realities: A Composer in America," *American Music* 25, no. 1 (spring 2007): 14.

220. Roger Reynolds, *Mind Models*, 211.

221. Ibid.

222. Roger Reynolds, "Rarely Sudden, Never Abrupt," *Musical Times* 128, no. 1735 (September 1987): 480.

223. Reynolds also suggested to me that his own violin concerto *Aspiration* has some Takemitsu connections, especially in the use of multiple octave sonorities.

224. Reynolds, "Ideals and Realities," 13.

225. Ibid., 14.

226. Ibid., 7. Also see his discussion of various English translations of *haiku* (47n1). As a student at the University of Michigan, Reynolds served as editor of *Generation: The University Inter-Arts Magazine*. The May 1962 issue included *haiku* by Basho, Buson, and Issa in translations by Ken Akiyama and Sara Ann Handler.

227. Roger Reynolds, "A Perspective on Form and Experience," *Contemporary Music Review* 2, no. 1 (1987): 284.

228. "Interview: Reynolds/Sollberger," in *Roger Reynolds: Profile of a Composer* (New York: C. F. Peters, 1982), 25. Emphasis in the original. In a 1980 interview, Reynolds was asked whether Japan had "a greater effect on your music than the time you've spent in other countries?" and he replied: "Oh, indeed; certainly, for several reasons," pointing to *bunraku* as having had the "largest impact" on him and noting that Japanese composers felt his early works were "very Japanese." See Cole Gagne and Tracy Caras, *Soundpieces: Interviews with American Composers*, 324. Reynolds also referred to the Japanese "lack of concern about the passage of time" in ICWA report #11, "Time (in and out of Japan)," (28 March 1968): 3.

229. This is quoted from my transcription of the recorded conversation Reynolds provided to me. Cage and Reynolds referred to Zen in a 1977 published interview. See Roger Reynolds and John Cage, "John Cage and Roger Reynolds: A Conversation," *Musical Quarterly* 65, no. 4 (October 1979): 574–576; 584.

230. Reynolds made this and the following statement in an interview with me in June 2011.

231. Also see Roger Reynolds, ICWA report #15, "Bunraku," (3 March 1969): 2, in which he offers a more detailed description and celebration of the *bunraku* narrator's voice and states that "the *shamisen* is not an immediately appealing instrument in terms of timbre and apparent flexibility."

232. Roger Reynolds, ICWA report #9, "Young Composers and Mr. Watanabe" (11 October 1967): 1.

233. Roger Reynolds, *Mind Models*, 90.

234. Of this piece, Reynolds noted to me that "the presence (also graphically, in the score for *Traces*) of a braided drone, made up of three separate stereo tapes played back over 6 loudspeakers is deeply 'Japanese' in that the particular mix one experiences is individually created, an 'in-the-air' experience had by each listener and not pre-homogenized in a fixed electronic mix. The sounds are allowed to exist together as independent strands in a multichannel listening field."

235. Reynolds, *Mind Models*, 37. It is telling that the very first sentence of Part I presents a quotation from Zeami (3), the seminal figure in the history of Japanese *noh* theater.

236. Reynolds, ICWA report #14 "Influence" (25 December 1968): 1. Reynolds's views on influence relaxed somewhat in later years. For example, when asked nearly four decades later about being inspired to compose by the development of new technological tools, Reynolds responded: "There is nothing wrong with the idea that one is seduced by opportunity. You hear a fantastic shakuhachi player or a guitarist and you think, 'Maybe I should write for that.'" See David Bithell and Roger Reynolds, "Image, Engagement, Technological Resource: An Interview with Roger Reynolds," *Computer Music Journal* 31, no. 1 (spring 2007): 17.

237. Paul Robinson and Roger Reynolds, "'I'm Always Interested in New Experience': A Conversation with Paul Robinson," in *Music with Roots in the Aether: Interviews with and Essays about Seven American Composers*, by Robert Ashley (Cologne: MusikTexte, 2000), 167.

238. For this piece, the literary inspiration was Thomas Wolfe's *Look Homeward Angel* from which Reynolds derived his title, a phrase followed in Wolfe's text by a sentence addressed by a character to the ghost of his female lover: "You who were made for music, will hear music no more." Thomas Wolfe, *Look Homeward Angel* (New York: Charles Scribner's Sons, 1957), 380.

239. Roger Reynolds, "Ideals and Realities." On *VOICESPACE* and his vocal explorations, Reynolds wrote: "some of this realization doubtless arose from hearing performances in Japan of the traditional *gidayū* narration that accompanies the *Bunraku* puppet dramas. The virtuosic extremity of these ritualized narrations, especially at moments of high drama, can seem almost searing to the ear and mind. This experience confirmed for me (and then later led me to incorporate into my work) the fact that the sonic nature of uttered words could add an important dimensionality to their experience in performance" (17).

240. Shigeru Sato, "Symposium of Light and Sound," *Ongaku Shimbun* (23 February 1969). Clipping provided to me by Reynolds, held in his home archive.

241. On *Symphony[Myths]* also see Nicholas Cook, "Imagining Things: Mind into Music (and Back Again)," in *Imaginative Minds*, ed. Ilona Roth, 130–139 (Oxford: Oxford University Press, 2007).

242. Roger Reynolds, *Form and Method: Composing Music; The Rothschild Essays*, ed. Stephen McAdams, 30–31 (New York: Routledge, 2002).

243. Roger Reynolds and Toru Takemitsu, "Roger Reynolds and Toru Takemitsu: A Conversation," *Musical Quarterly* 80, no. 1 (spring 1996): 63.

Chapter 9

1. Amy Lowell, "Guns as Keys: And the Great Gate Swings," in *Can Grande's Castle* (New York: Macmillan, 1918), xiii–xv, 47–97. For her versions of Japanese poetry see Lowell, *Pictures of the Floating World* (New York: Macmillan, 1919). On Lowell's representations of Asia, see Mara Yoshihara, *Embracing the East: White Women and American Orientalism* (New York: Oxford University Press, 2003), chapter 4.

2. See Amy Lowell, *Selected Poems of Amy Lowell*, ed. Melissa Bradshaw and Adrienne Munich, 33 (New Brunswick, NJ: Rutgers University Press, 2002).

3. Lowell, "Guns as Keys," 59–60.

4. Lowell's view is clearly distinct here from the ecstatic enthusiasm of Walt Whitman who, in "A Broadway Pageant," celebrated the first visit by Japanese dignitaries to New York in 1860. On the use of music by Commodore Perry, see Peter Booth Wiley, *Yankees in the Land of the Gods: Commodore Perry and the Opening of Japan* (New York: Viking, 1990), 368–369; and Victor Fell Yellin, "Mrs. Belmont, Matthew Perry, and the 'Japanese Minstrels,'" *American Music* 14, no. 3 (fall 1996): 257–275.

5. Stephen Sondheim, John Weidman, and Hugh Wheeler, *Pacific Overtures*, rev. ed. (New York: Theatre Communications Group, 1991), 65.

6. M. C. Perry, *Narrative of the Expedition of an American Squadron to the China Seas and Japan, Performed in the Years 1852, 1853, and 1854*, ed. Francis L. Hawks (New York: D. Appleton, 1856), 300.

7. Quoted in Craig Zadan, *Sondheim & Co.*, 2nd ed. (New York: Da Capo Press, 1994), 210. Also see Leonard Fleischer, "'More Beautiful Than True' or 'Never Mind a Small Disaster': The Art of Illusion in *Pacific Overtures*," in *Stephen Sondheim: A Casebook*, ed. Joanne Lesley Gordon, 108 (New York: Garland, 1997).

8. Clive Hirschhorn, "Will Sondheim Succeed in Being Genuinely Japanese?," *New York Times*, 4 January 1976, D1, D5.

9. Sondheim noted that he went to Japan for a "two-week crash course" and saw *kabuki* troupes at City Center. Ibid., D1. I first presented some of the discussion of *Pacific Overtures* offered here at Middlebury College in 2005.

10. Raymond Knapp has offered a table of the songs "arranged according to my rough assessment of how strongly they project Japanese or Western perspectives through situation, music, and language." See Raymond Knapp, "Marking Time in *Pacific Overtures*: Reconciling East, West, and History within the Theatrical Now of a Broadway Musical," in *Musicological Identities: Essays in Honor of Susan McClary*, eds. Steven Baur, Raymond Knapp, and Jacqueline Warwick, 166 (Burlington, VT: Ashgate, 2008).

11. Stephen Banfield, *Sondheim's Broadway Musicals* (Ann Arbor: University of Michigan Press, 1993), 262–263.

12. Stephen Sondheim, *Finishing the Hat: Collected Lyrics (1954–1981) with Attendant Comments, Principles, Heresies, Grudges, Whines, and Anecdotes* (New York: Alfred A. Knopf, 2010), 304. Sondheim has proclaimed that the Japanese "are *the* minimalist culture." Mark Eden Horowitz, *Sondheim on Music: Minor Details and Major Decisions*, 2nd ed. (Lanham, MD: The Scarecrow Press, 2010), 157.

13. See Horowitz, *Sondheim on Music*, 161–163.

14. Ibid., 160. This song with prepared piano (thumb tacks and paper) was entitled "Prayer." Sondheim has related: "John Cage was not terribly useful or influential for my own work, but I did indeed use a prepared piano to imitate Oriental sounds when I played the first song I'd written for *Pacific Overtures* for my collaborators, most of whom were unfamiliar with Cage and thus much impressed with my inventiveness." Quoted in James Klosty, *John Cage Was* (Middletown, CT: Wesleyan University Press, 2014), 25.

15. My discussion of the 1976 and 1984 productions of *Pacific Overtures* is based on my study of recordings held at the New York Public Library for the Performing Arts of performances on 9 June 1976 and 27 January 1985.
16. Quoted in Hirschhorn, "Will Sondheim Succeed in Being Genuinely Japanese?," D1. Of course, as noted in chapter 6, many Americans had seen representations of Japanese theater in Hollywood films.
17. Ibid.
18. Banfield, *Sondheim's Broadway Musicals*, 251–253.
19. Ibid., 259.
20. Sondheim, *Finishing the Hat*, 304.
21. Sondheim made this statement in an interview with Frank Rich, "Anatomy of a Song: With Stephen Sondheim, John Weidman, and Members of the Cast of *Pacific Overtures*," video recording (Kent, CT: Creative Arts Television, 1976).
22. Paul Attinello, "The Universe Will Tell You What It Needs: Being, Time, Sondheim," in *Musicological Identities: Essays in Honor of Susan McClary*, eds. Steven Baur, Raymond Knapp, and Jacqueline Warwick, 77, 82–83 (Burlington, VT: Ashgate, 2008).
23. Ibid., 82.
24. Sondheim notes that Reich praised this show to him: "It's similar to his own music, because so much of it is influenced by oriental music." Quoted in Horowitz, *Sondheim on Music*, 158.
25. For detailed discussion of the numerous *kabuki* elements in the show, see Joseph M. Piro, "Kabuki Meets Broadway: Crafting the Oriental Musical *Pacific Overtures*" (Master's thesis, Queens College CUNY, 1978).
26. Sondheim, *Finishing the Hat*, 327.
27. Mako founded the East-West Players, the important Asian American theater company in Los Angeles, which produced a small-scale version of *Pacific Overtures* in 1979. See Joanne Gordon, *Art Isn't Easy: The Achievement of Stephen Sondheim* (Carbondale: Southern Illinois University Press, 1990), 204. Mako also appeared in numerous films relevant to this study, such as *Farewell to Manzanar* (1976), *Rising Sun* (1993), and *Memoirs of a Geisha* (2001).
28. "'Overtures' Opens Door for Orientals," *New York Times*, 2 March 1976, 24. Also see Wayman Wong, "Actors Remember *Pacific Overtures*," *Sondheim Review* 4, no. 4 (spring 1998): 20–23. I note that in the 2018 Williamstown Theatre Festival production of *The Closet*, a Japanese American woman who likes to quote Broadway lyrics at the office blurts out the line "four black dragons" from Act I of *Pacific Overtures*. Her African American male boss asks in an accusatory tone whether she is saying something racist about him. She quickly identifies the line as from the Sondheim musical and laments his failure to note this allusion to "the music of my people!" The layers of irony are deep at this moment in the play.
29. On this point see Brooke Joyce, "A Broadway Hybrid: Stephen Sondheim's *Pacific Overtures*," in *Musicology and Globalization: Proceedings of the International Congress in Shizuoka 2002*, eds. Yoshio Tozawa, Tatsuhiko Itoh, Keiichi Kubota, and Yasuhiko Mori, 328 (Tokyo: The Musicological Society of Japan, 2004).
30. This 1984 production claimed to "authenticate" the work primarily through dance by hiring Sachiyo Ito, "a native of Tokyo who has thirty years of experience in kabuki" and who held two workshops on "basic walks and bows." See Kevin Grubb, "Specifically *Pacific*," *Dance Magazine*, January 1985, 74.
31. Edward Rothstein, "Japanese View of an American View of Japan," *New York Times*, 1 September 2002, A3.
32. Ben Brantley, "Repatriating the Japanese Sondheim," *New York Times*, 3 December 2004, E23. (This positive comment appears in an otherwise negative review by Brantley of the 2004 version.) Brantley, and multiple other commentators on the new Japanese productions, referred to a critical question that had been posed by Walter Kerr in his negative 1976 review: "Why

tell their story *their* way, when they'd do it better?" See Walter Kerr, "'Pacific Overtures' Is neither East nor West," *New York Times*, 18 January 1976, D1, D5. Also see Gary Perlman, "*Overtures* 'Sensational' in Tokyo: Sondheim," *Sondheim Review* 7, no. 3 (winter 2001): 11; and Perlman, "*Pacific Overtures* a Triumph in Tokyo," *Sondheim Review* 7, no. 3 (winter 2001): 6–10.

33. The term "gung ho" originated as a US Marine Corps slogan coined during World War II and was based on an inaccurate interpretation of the name of a Chinese industrial group. This film was likely inspired by the New United Motor Manufacturing, Inc. (NUMMI) plant established in Fremont, California, in 1984. This was a joint venture between Toyota and General Motors.

34. A rather unique war period film, the 1983 *Merry Christmas, Mr. Lawrence*, starring David Bowie and Ryuichi Sakamoto, is driven by a homoerotic charge associated with the excessive samurai code of the Japanese captain. Set in a Japanese-run POW camp in Java, Sakamoto's score features some synthesized gamelan-style music.

35. Deborah Wong, *Speak It Louder: Asian Americans Making Music* (New York and London: Routledge, 2004), 209–216.

36. Timothy Koozin, "Parody and Ironic Juxtaposition in Toru Takemitsu's Music for the Film, *Rising Sun* (1993)," *Journal of Film Music* 3, no. 1 (2010): 66.

37. Ibid., 71.

38. "East Meets West: A Composer's Notebook," *The Karate Kid*, special ed. (Columbia Pictures 10130, 1984: Culver City, CA: Sony Pictures, 2005), DVD, timestamp 03:29.

39. John Luther Long, *Madame Butterfly* (New York: Century, 1903), 4.

40. Ibid., xiii.

41. John Luther Long, "A 'Madame Butterfly' of the Philippines," *The World*, 7 June 1903, 5.

42. Though Butterfly is only very rarely presented in any version of the tale as a true *femme fatale*, I note that in "Kabuki Girl," released by the punk rock band Descendents on *Milo Goes to College* (1982), the male persona celebrates his mysterious Japanese woman but declares, "you'll probably stab me in the back." The male protagonist asks whether the geisha girl is a "femme fatale or ingenue" in glam rocker Bryan Ferry's "Tokyo Joe" (1977), a song replete with Japlish and which, perhaps, references the 1949 film starring Humphrey Bogart.

43. Ellie M. Hisama, "The Cultural Work of *Miss Saigon*: A Postcolonial Critique," in *Popular Music: Intercultural Interpretations*, ed. Tôru Mitsui, 18 (Kanazawa, Japan: Graduate Program in Music, Kanazawa University, 1998).

44. Ibid., 21.

45. See for example, James S. Moy, *Marginal Sights: Staging the Chinese in America* (Iowa City: University of Iowa Press, 1993), 128.

46. On the "rewriting of Pinkerton as the saintly-heroic Chris," see Karen Shimakawa, *National Abjection: The Asian American Body Onstage* (Durham, NC: Duke University Press, 2002), 53.

47. I first presented my discussion of Weezer's *Pinkerton* album at the 2003 meeting of the American Musicological Society. Malcolm McLaren's album *Fans* (Charisma Records, 1984) offers a less interesting, but equally perplexing, treatment of the Butterfly story in a popular music album dripping with irony. The album samples music from Puccini's *Madama Butterfly*, *Gianni Schicchi*, *Turandot*, and Bizet's *Carmen*, all within a musical stylistic setting drawing on light rock, R+B, and a bit of disco. The album opens and closes with McLaren taking on the spoken voice of Pinkerton with a slight southern drawl. In "Madam Butterfly," Pinkerton explains that he needs to go back to Japan for Butterfly. For her part, Butterfly relates as she awaits his return: "Gotta have something to believe in/my white honky I do miss him." Passages of Butterfly's arias heard on several tracks often remain disconnected from the basic instrumental groove. In "Death of Butterfly," some peppy and funky music combined with the wordless chorus of the "passing of the night" music from the opera serves

as background as Pinkerton speaks, standing uncomfortably outside in the garden and elaborating on his final aria sentiment of regret, with his final lines accompanied by an excerpt from "Un bel dì" on synthesizer.

48. Roger Catlin, "Weezer's Worry," *The Hartford Courant* (4 December 1996), E1.

49. Ibid.

50. This is in contrast to the sarcastic Mersey Beat style ending of "Falling for You" when he wonders whether he would "rather settle down, with you," with cocky melismas on "down" and "you."

51. In the mid 1990s New Jack, an African American wrestler, was a member of the Gangstas, and Grunge was a white wrestler who was part of the duo Public Enemy. Cuomo aligns himself in this song with Public Enemy, who defeated the Gangstas on 1 July 1995.

52. For example, see Clare Kleinedler and Michael Goldberg, "Weezer Revealed: The Rivers Cuomo Interview," *Addicted to Noise*, December 1996, http://web.archive.org/web/20040927062903/wma.weezernation.com/199612atnint.html.

53. Quoted in "Pinkerton," *Weezerpedia: The Weezer Encyclopedia*, last updated 18 December 2016, https://www.weezerpedia.com/wiki/Pinkerton.

54. Ellie M. Hisama, "Postcolonialism on the Make: The Music of John Mellencamp, David Bowie, and John Zorn," *Popular Music* 12, no. 2 (1993): 91–104.

55. Abe J. Riesman, "River's End," *Harvard Crimson*, 26 April 2006, https://www.thecrimson.com/article/2006/4/26/rivers-end-in-early-1995-a/#.XBa3hG-w3nc.link.

56. Kleinedler and Goldberg, "Weezer Revealed."

57. Quoted in Chris Mundy, "Weezer's Cracked Genius: Is Rivers Cuomo the Weirdest Man in Rock, or the Coolest?," *Rolling Stone* 877 (13 September 2001): 42–44, 46.

58. Kleinedler and Goldberg, "Weezer Revealed."

59. Ellie M. Hisama, "John Zorn and the Postmodern Condition," in *Locating East Asia in Western Art Music*, eds. Yayoi Uno Everett and Frederick Lau, 72–84 (Middletown, CT: Wesleyan University Press, 2004). For an attempt to reinterpret Zorn's graphic depictions of Asian figures by drawing on postmodern critical theory see John Brackett, "From the Fantastic to the Dangerously Real: Reading John Zorn's Artwork," *ECHO: A Music-Centered Journal* 8, no. 1 (fall 2006), http://www.echo.ucla.edu/Volume8-Issue1/brackett/brackett1.html.

60. On *Forbidden Fruit*, for example, see Hisama, "Postcolonialism on the Make," 95–97. Also see Susan McClary, *Conventional Wisdom: The Content of Musical Form* (Berkeley: University of California Press, 2000) 149–152.

61. Quoted in Fred Kaplan, "Horn of Plenty: The Composer Who Knows No Boundaries," *The New Yorker*, 14 June 1999, 88.

62. Ibid.

63. Paul Loewen [Leu], *Butterfly* (New York: St. Martin's Press, 1988).

64. Ibid., 162.

65. Ibid., 243.

66. On this phenomenon, see Miki Tanikawa, "In Kyoto, a Call to Not Trample the Geisha," *New York Times*, 6 April 2009, https://www.nytimes.com/2009/04/07/world/asia/07iht-geisha.html.

67. Arthur Golden, *Memoirs of a Geisha* (New York: Vintage, 1999), 141–143.

68. Ibid., 143.

69. The information on the production details and on John Williams's approach to the score presented here is derived from interviews included in the bonus tracks of the DVD recording: "Featurettes," Disc 2, *Memoirs of a Geisha*, special ed. (Culver City, CA: Sony Pictures 11159, 2006), DVD.

70. Disc 2 Featurette "The Music of 'Memoirs,' " timestamp: 09:23.

71. Daisann McLane, "Like a Geisha," *Harper's Bazaar* 3447 (February 1999): 128.

72. Rahul Gairola, "Re-worlding the Oriental: Critical Perspectives on Madonna as Geisha," in *Madonna's Drowned Worlds: New Approaches to Her Cultural Transformations, 1983–2003*, eds. Santiago Fouz-Hernández and Freya Jarman-Ivens, 106 (Aldershot, UK: 2004).

73. Ibid., 115.

74. Ibid., 116.

75. Ibid., 118.

76. Jeff Yang also noted these connections. See Yang, "Geisha A-Go-Go: Katy Perry's AMAs Performance Stirs Debate," *Wall Street Journal*, 25 November 2013, https://blogs.wsj.com/speakeasy/2013/11/25/memories-of-a-geisha-katy-perrys-amas-performance-stirs-debate/.

77. Quoted in Natalie Finn and Baker Machado, "Katy Perry's Stylist Explains Geisha-Inspired Outfit at AMAs: We Love Japan!," *E Online*, 25 November 2013, http://www.eonline.com/news/484980/katy-perry-s-stylist-explains-geisha-inspired-outfit-at-amas-we-love-japan.

78. Japanese American Citizens League, "JACL Statement on Katy Perry AMA Performance," *Japanese American Citizens League, Est. 1929* website, 27 November 2013, https://jacl.org/jacl-statement-on-katy-perry-performance/.

79. Gil Asakawa, "Katy Perry's Faux-Japanese American Music Awards Performance Was Terrible," *Nikkei View: The Asian American Blog*, 25 November 2013, http://www.nikkeiview.com/blog/2013/11/katy-perrys-faux-japanese-american-music-awards-performance-was-terrible/.

80. See, for example, Lauren Duca, "Cultural Appropriation 101, Featuring Geisha Katy Perry and the Great Wave of Asian Influence," *Huffington Post*, last updated 26 November 2013, https://www.huffingtonpost.com/2013/11/25/cultural-appropriation-katy-perry_n_4337024.html; and Nico Lang, "Settling the Katy Perry Controversy: 'Yellowface' Is Not Beautiful," *Los Angeles Times*, 29 November 2013, https://www.latimes.com/opinion/opinion-la/la-ol-katy-perry-american-music-awards-yellowface-20131127-story.html.

81. Quoted in Árni Heimir Ingólfsson, "Drawing New Boundaries: Björk's Expanding Territory," *Nordic Sounds* 4 (December 2005): 15.

82. Ibid.

83. June Kuramoto, the *kotoist* of the band Hiroshima, is credited for her performance on the soundtrack and "Kagura-No-Netori" was performed by the *gagaku* group Tokyo Gakuso.

84. Less well known, the lyrics in the Vapors' 1980 "Letter from Hiro" are addressed to a World War II–era Japanese pen pal, and the song features a pentatonic lick for the line "when the sun was rising somewhere in the East" and ends with a Japanese melody played on a cimbalom.

85. Griffin M. Woodworth, "'Big in Japan': Orientalism, Camp, and Cultural Anxiety in Pop Music of the 1980s" (presented at the Society for American Music, Tempe, AZ, 2003).

86. This phenomenon is likewise referenced at the end of the 1984 mock documentary *This Is Spinal Tap* as we see the hugely unsuccessful fictional metal band Spinal Tap performing before a wildly enthusiastic Japanese audience at the end of the film. Part of the joke, of course, depends on the assumption that the film's intended Western white audience finds any Asian participation in popular music culture to be amusing.

87. Deborah Elizabeth Whaley, "Black Bodies/Yellow Masks: The Orientalist Aesthetic in Hip-Hop and Black Visual Culture," in *AfroAsian Encounters: Culture, History, Politics*, eds. Heike Raphael-Hernandez and Shannon Steen, 189 (New York: New York University Press, 2006). Whaley lists examples of R&B and hip-hop performers who have engaged in Asian sexualized representations in music videos (192).

88. Ibid., 190, 194–195. For other perspectives on this topic, see Vijay Prashad, *Everybody Was Kung Fu Fighting: Afro-Asian Connections and the Myth of Cultural Purity* (Boston: Beacon Press, 2001); and Ellie M. Hisama, "'We're All Asian Really': Hip-Hop's Afro-Asian Crossings," in *Critical Minded: New Approaches to Hip Hop Studies*, eds. Ellie Hisama and Evan Rapport, 1–21 (Brooklyn, NY: Institute for Studies in American Music, 2005).

89. Ken McLeod, "Afro-Samurai: Techno-Orientalism and Contemporary Hip-Hop," *Popular Music* 32, no. 2 (May 2013): 259–275. McLeod focuses in particular on examples by Kanye West, Nicki Minaj, and RZA. McLeod also points to the 2007 *Afro-Samurai* anime series.

90. Ibid., 261–262.

91. My discussion of Hwang's play is based on my viewing of a video recording of the 16 August 1988 performance at the Eugene O'Neill Theatre held at the New York Public Library for the Performing Arts and on the published script, David Henry Hwang, *M. Butterfly* (New York: New American Library, 1988). Page numbers cited in the play's text will refer to this publication.

92. I note that Hwang also wrote the libretto for Philip Glass's opera *The Sound of a Voice* (2003), a work based on a Japanese ghost play written by Hwang in 1983 which drew on Japanese folk tales, films, and *noh*. Glass's score featured the Chinese *pipa*, the North African *dumbeck*, and the Persian *tar*.

93. David Henry Hwang, "A New Musical by Rodgers and Hwang," *New York Times*, 13 October 2002, AR1, AR16.

94. Puccini had himself drawn on both Chinese and Japanese traditional melodies in his score. On this topic, see my "Puccini and the Music Boxes," *Journal of the Royal Musical Association* 140, no. 1 (spring 2015), 41–92.

95. In reference to the film version of *M. Butterfly*, Bart Testa concludes that, in opposition to Puccini's opera, "Cronenberg [the film's director] mutates a feminine ecstatic transport into the masculine affixation of Gallimard's delicious suffering—a voluptuous masochism." See Bart Testa, "Late Mutations of Cinema's Butterfly," in *A Vision of the Orient: Texts, Intertexts, and Contexts of Madame Butterfly*, eds. Jonathan Wisenthal, Sherrill Grace, Melinda Boyd, Brian McIlroy, and Vera Micznik, 101 (Toronto: University of Toronto Press, 2006).

96. Moy, *Marginal Sights*, 124–125.

97. See Ibid., 122–123; and Shimakawa, *National Abjection*, 127.

98. *Allegiance* premiered in San Diego in 2012 and opened on Broadway in November 2015, closing there on 14 February 2016.

99. See, for example, John Eligon, "Resistance to Syrian Refugees Calls to Mind Painful Past of Japanese-Americans," *New York Times*, 26 November 2015, https://www.nytimes.com/2015/11/27/us/for-japanese-americans-resistance-to-syrian-refugees-recalls-long-ago-fears.html.

100. Charles Isherwood, "Review: 'Allegiance,' a Musical History Lesson about Interned Japanese-Americans," *New York Times*, 8 November 2015, https://www.nytimes.com/2015/11/09/theater/review-allegiance-a-musical-history-lesson-about-interned-japanese-americans.html.

101. Diep Tran, "From Orientalism to Authenticity: Broadway's Yellow Fever," *American Theatre*, 27 October 2015, https://www.americantheatre.org/2015/10/27/from-orientalism-to-authenticity-broadways-yellow-fever/.

102. On Palermo's attempts to incorporate elements of traditional Japanese dance in his choreography for *Allegiance*, see Sylviane Gold, "Cultured Choreography," *Dance Magazine*, 31 January 2016, https://www.dancemagazine.com/cultured-choreography-2307008768.html.

103. Wendy Ng, "Educating Californians about Japanese American Internment," *Mills Quarterly* (winter 2001): 14.

104. A full recording of this work is available at https://archive.org/details/csfpal_000072.

105. Names appearing in quotation marks here are Japanese professional names earned through certification.

106. Donald Reid Womack, based in Hawai'i, has been particularly active in composing works for Japanese and Western instruments in the past decade, including *After*, a 2006 concerto

for *shakuhachi, koto*, and orchestra. Thomas Osborne's career to date is marked by his extended interest in composing for East Asian instruments, which, as of 2018, has resulted in four pieces for Japanese instruments composed between 2007 and 2016, twenty-three for Korean instruments, and three for Chinese instruments.

107. I would like to thank both Muneko Otani and Ah Ling Neu, who are also colleagues of mine at Williams College, for speaking with me in November 2018 about their experiences playing this work.

108. I should note that I served as a member of the Japan Society Performing Arts Advisory Committee from 2007 to 2010 and have delivered several lectures at the Japan Society on Japanese-influenced European and American works.

109. Barbara E. Thornbury, *America's Japan and Japan's Performing Arts: Cultural Mobility and Exchange in New York, 1952–2011* (Ann Arbor: University of Michigan Press, 2013), 186–198. Also see Thornbury, "Cultural Policy and Private Initiative: The Performing Arts at the Japan Society, New York," *The World of Music* 46, no. 2 (2004): 123–136.

110. For these program notes, see http://www.kenueno.com/performancenotes.html.

111. Kyle Gann, *American Music in the Twentieth Century* (New York: Schirmer Books, 1997), 363.

112. Lois V. Vierk, "Studying Gagaku," in *Arcana: Musicians on Music*, ed. John Zorn, 307–309 (New York: Granary Books, 2000).

113. Frank J. Oteri, "Lois V. Vierk: Slideways: In Conversation with Frank J. Oteri, 30 November 2007," *New Music Box*, 1 January 2008, https://nmbx.newmusicusa.org/lois-v-vierk-slideways/.

114. Gann, *American Music*, 364.

115. The notes to the score quoted here can be found at http://iresound.umbc.edu/index.php/compositions/19-vierk/196-silversword-1996. Other works by Vierk relevant to this study include *Go Guitars* (1981) for five electric guitars and *Hyaku Man No Kyu (One Million Spheres)* 1983 for eight *ryuteki*. Vierk's compositional output has been curtailed by illness since 1998. Vierk is far from alone among composers born in the 1950s and 1960s and active in the United States who have composed for Japanese instruments. Carl Stone created works based on sampling of the Tokyo soundscape while living in Japan in 1988–1989, supported by the Asian Cultural Council, and has also collaborated with Japanese traditional instrument musicians. Lowell Liebermann composed *Fantasy* for bass *koto* in 1990 and, at the end of the decade, John Luther Adams composed *Time Undisturbed* (1999) for three *shakuhachis*, three *kotos*, and *sho*. Japan has impacted the work of Chaya Czernowin, a former student of Roger Reynolds, particularly in her 1995 trio *Die Kreuzung* for *sho* (or accordion), alto saxophone, and double bass, a piece that has been recorded by the ubiquitous Mayumi Miyata on *sho*, and an improvisatory approach to new solo music for the *sho* is heard in works by Sarah Peebles on her 2014 album *Delicate Paths*. We will discover below that the *shakuhachi* has particularly attracted numerous American composers since the 1980s.

116. Bonnie Marranca, "Thinking about Interculturalism," in *Interculturalism and Performance: Writings from PAJ*, eds. Bonnie Marranca and Gautam Dasgupta, 14 (New York: PAJ Publications, 1991).

117. Hans-Peter Bayerdörfer, "*Nô* in Disguise: Robert Wilson's Adaptation of *Nô* Elements in His Productions of *Alkestis/Alceste*," in *Japanese Theatre and the International Stage*, eds. Stanca Scholz-Cionca and Samuel L. Leiter, 370 (Leiden: Brill, 2001).

118. Ibid., 375–378.

119. John J. Flynn, "Transiting from the 'Wethno-centric': An Interview with Peter Sellars," in *Interculturalism and Performance: Writings from PAJ*, eds. Bonnie Marranca and Gautam

Dasgupta, 185–186; 191 (New York: PAJ Publications, 1991). In this October 1989 interview, Sellars discussed his perceptions of *noh* and its influence on his work (189–191).

120. Ibid., 185.

121. Ibid., 188–189. On exoticism in the operas of John Adams and Peter Sellars, also see my "The Persistence of Orientalism in the Postmodern Operas of Adams and Sellars," in *Representation in Western Music*, ed. Joshua S. Walden, 267–286 (Cambridge, UK: Cambridge University Press, 2013).

122. I am grateful to Ping Chong for discussing his work with me in October 1998 and providing access to video recordings of these works. On *Deshima*, also see Shimakawa, *National Abjection*, 133–146.

123. I am grateful to Richard Emmert for providing me with a copy of the score and a video recording of this work. The 2017 performance at Williams College was funded in part by the Japan Foundation and this followed Theatre Nohgaku's 2002 production at Williams of *At the Hawk's Well*. I have been fortunate to have participated in *noh* workshops led by Emmert.

124. Of course, multiple professional Japanese *shakuhachi* musicians have immigrated to the United States and have taught the instrument to numerous American students as well. For example, the Japanese *shakuhachi* musician Masayuki Koga founded the Japanese Music Institute of America in 1981 in the San Francisco Bay area.

125. For a listing of new music composed for *shakuhachi*, see Ralph Samuelson, "Shakuhachi and the American Composer," *Contemporary Music Review* 8, no. 2 (1993): 89–93. Also see Yoshikazu Iwamoto, "The Potential of the *Shakuhachi* in Contemporary Music," *Contemporary Music Review* 8, no. 2 (1993): 5–44.

126. Tania Cronin, for instance, has cited the aspects of "changing timbre, or timbre as movement" in *shakuhachi* music as particularly appealing. See Tania Cronin, "On Writing for *Shakuhachi*: A Western Perspective," *Contemporary Music Review* 8, no. 2 (1993): 77.

127. Though I am focusing on the predominance in the United States of the *shakuhachi* among Japanese traditional instruments, I should note that *taiko* performance has also thrived, particularly as a source of pride and empowerment for Asian Americans. On the phenomenon of American *taiko*, see Deborah Wong, "Taiko and the Asian/American Body: Drums, *Rising Sun*, and the Question of Gender," *The World of Music* 42, no. 3 (2000): 67–78; Paul Jong-Chul Yoon, "'She's Really Become Japanese Now!': Taiko Drumming and Asian American Identifications," *American Music* 19, no. 4 (winter 2001): 417–438; and Yoshitaka Terada, "Shifting Identities of Taiko Music in North America," in *Transcending Boundaries: Asian Musics in North America*, ed. Yoshitaka Terada, 37–59, Senri Ethnological Reports 22 (Osaka: National Museum of Ethnology, 2001). *Koto* performance has also been pursued by American musicians, but to a lesser extent. For example, "Ayakano" Cathleen Read began studying the *koto* in Japan in 1969 and has been teaching and performing at such institutions as Tufts University and the Boston Museum of Fine Arts for decades.

128. Karl Signell, "The Mystique of the *Shakuhachi*," *Journal of the American Musical Instrument Society* 7 (1981): 90–98. On the international presence of *shakuhachi* and university instruction in *shakuhachi* performance in the United States, see Steven Casano, "From *Fuke Shuu* to Uduboo: The Transnational Flow of the *Shakuhachi* to the West," *The World of Music* 47, no. 3 (2005): 23–25. Also see Roderic Knight, "The Shakuhachi Comes to Oberlin," *Oberlin Alumni Magazine* (1984): 17–20, and in *The Annals of the International Shakuhachi Society: Volume 1*, ed. Dan E. Mayers, 17–20 (Wadhurst, Sussex: The Society, n.d. [1990]). Knight invited a Japanese *shakuhachi* performer to teach at Oberlin in 1982.

129. Jay Keister, "The *Shakuhachi* as a Spiritual Tool: A Japanese Buddhist Instrument in the West," *Asian Music* 35, no. 2 (2004): 100.

130. Ibid., 107. Keister cites the example of Michael "Chikuzen" Gould's career and his emphasis on "natural *shakuhachi*" and a Zen-inspired approach (118–120). Gould lived in Japan from 1980 to 1997 studying *shakuhachi*, eventually earning the title of Grand Master in 1994. He has since taught Zen Buddhism and *shakuhachi* at the University of Michigan and in Ohio at Oberlin College and Wittenberg University.

131. Jay Keister, "Seeking Authentic Experience: Spirituality in the Western Appropriation of Asian Music," *The World of Music* 47, no. 3 (2005): 49. Keister notes that *shakuhachi* musicians in the United States typically speak of a "conversion" moment when the timbre of the *shakuhachi* transformed their lives (42).

132. For an incomplete database of *shakuhachi* teachers and performers active in the United States, see the International Shakuhachi Society's website: "Shakuhachi Teachers," *The International Shakuhachi Society*, accessed 7 January 2019, https://www.komuso.com/top/teachers.pl#USA.

133. Christopher Yohmei Blasdel, *The Single Tone: A Personal Journey into Shakuhachi Music* (Tokyo: Printed Matter Press, 2005), 88.

134. For his own views of *shakuhachi* music see Riley Kelley Lee, "An American Looks at the Shakuhachi of Japan" (1 April 1986), *The Annals of the International Shakuhachi Society: Volume 1*, ed. Dan E. Mayers, 113–116 (Wadhurst, Sussex: The Society, n.d. [1990]).

135. Though less well-known, John Singer, who began his *shakuhachi* studies in 1975 and who performs on antique instruments, has released multiple world fusion albums.

136. My discussion of Samuelson's career is based on my extensive interview with him in October 2017 and on our email correspondence.

137. Tom Johnson, "Ralph Samuelson, Shakuhachi Master," *Village Voice*, 25 July 1977, 53.

138. Teitelbaum has not been the only American composer interested in interfacing the *shakuhachi* with electronic and digital music. For example, Gerald Bennett's 1987 *Kyōtaku* is scored for *shakuhachi* and tape and Chris Brown's 1999 "Waves" calls for *shakuhachi* and interactive computer.

139. Samuelson, "Shakuhachi and the American Composer," 83.

140. Though I have known Schlefer since the late 1990s, much of my detailed discussion of his career is based on my interview with him held in October 2014.

141. James Nyoraku Schlefer, "The Intersection of Genres," *New Music Box*, 15 February 2018, https://nmbx.newmusicusa.org/the-intersection-of-genres/.

142. James Nyoraku Schlefer, "Some Practicalities of East-West Musical Collaborations," *New Music Box*, 28 February 2018, https://nmbx.newmusicusa.org/some-practicalities-of-east-west-musical-collaborations/. The contemporary British composer Frank Denyer has also composed numerous pieces for *shakuhachi*. He found the traditional solo style to be an "obvious danger" in terms of influence since its "seductive influence ringing in the memory has the power to subvert almost any compositional idea into a pale silhouette of itself." He therefore aimed to release *shakuhachi* techniques from Japanese tradition in order to "personalise" his use of them. See Frank Denyer, "The Shakuhachi and the Contemporary Music Instrumentarium: A Personal View," *Contemporary Music Review* 8, no. 2 (1993): 47–48. Christian Utz has a made a similar claim regarding contemporary compositions for the *sho*. See Christian Utz, "Beyond Cultural Representation: Recent Works for the Asian Mouth Organs *Shō* and *Sheng* by Western Composers," *The World of Music* 47, no. 3 (2005): 113–134.

143. Roger Scruton, "The Eclipse of Listening," in *The Future of the European Past*, eds. Hilton Kramer and Roger Kimball, 54 (Chicago: Ivan R. Dee, 1997).

144. Koji Matsunobu, "Spirituality as a Universal Experience of Music: A Case Study of North Americans' Approaches to Japanese Music," *Journal of Research in Music Education* 59, no. 3 (October 2011): 276.

145. Joseph Browning, "Assembled Landscapes: The Sites and Sounds of Some Recent Shakuhachi Recordings," *Journal of Musicology* 33, no. 1 (2016): 74–76.

146. Ibid., 78–79.

147. Roland Kelts, *Japanamerica: How Japanese Pop Culture Has Invaded the US* (New York: Palgrave Macmillan, 2007), 5. Some Japanese traditional instrument musicians have attempted to tap into the general American youth culture interest in Japan in recent years. For instance, the prominent American master *kotoist* Elizabeth Falconer, who studied in Japan for a decade starting in 1979, released multiple CDs for young children in the first years of this century in which she tells Japanese tales to the accompaniment of her *koto* playing. She has also released albums of original *koto* music intended to offer soothing sonic experiences, as with the 2004 album *Chocolate Suite—Japanese Music for Chocolate Lovers.*

148. I am grateful to my former student Alec Schumacker for bringing this example to my attention in 2005.

149. See his website for iterations of this description: "Holy Flute," *Cornelius Boots: Shakuhachi*, accessed 7 January 2019, http://corneliusboots.com/albums/holy-flute/.

150. Joseph E. Jones, "The Exotic and Eclectic in Bear McCreary's Television and Video Game Scores," *Music Research Forum* 30 (2015): 12–13.

151. Justin Chang, "Wes Anderson's 'Isle of Dogs' Is Often Captivating, but Cultural Sensitivity Gets Lost in Translation," *Los Angeles Times*, 21 March 2018, https://www.latimes.com/entertainment/movies/la-et-mn-isle-of-dogs-review-20180321-story.html.

152. Moeko Fujii, "What 'Isle of Dogs' Gets Right about Japan," *The New Yorker*, 13 April 2018, https://www.newyorker.com/culture/cultural-comment/what-isle-of-dogs-gets-right-about-japan.

153. On this controversy, see Brian Boucher, "Outrage at Museum of Fine Arts Boston over Disgraceful 'Dress Up in a Kimono' Event," *Artnet*, 6 July 2015, https://news.artnet.com/art-world/outrage-boston-museum-of-fine-arts-disgraceful-kimono-event-314534.

154. See "Japan Cultural Days," *Detroit Institute of Arts*, accessed 7 January 2019, https://www.dia.org/events/japan-cultural-days.

155. See "Japan Fest 2018," *New Orleans Museum of Art*, 6 October 2018, https://noma.org/event/japan-fest-2018/.

156. See "Children's Day Celebration with Pittsburgh Taiko Drummers," *Carnegie Museum of Art*, 5 May 2018, https://cmoa.org/event/childrens-day-celebration-with-pittsburgh-taiko-drummers/.

157. See "8/11: Japanese Culture Family Festival," *Please Touch Museum*, 11 August 2018, https://www.pleasetouchmuseum.org/event/japanese-culture-family-festival-2/.

158. See "Family Day: Kon'nichiwa!," *Coral Gables Museum*, 9 June 2018, http://coralgablesmuseum.org/event/family-day-konnichiwa/.

159. See "Miller Family Free Day: Poetic Imagination in Japanese Art," *Travel Portland*, 17 November 2018, https://calendar.travelportland.com/event/miller_family_free_day_poetic_imagination_in_japanese_art#.XBFby1VKiHs.

160. See "Family Fun Day: Journey through Japan," *National Atomic Testing Museum*, 25 August 2018, https://nationalatomictestingmuseum.org/event/family-fun-day-journey-through-japan/.

161. Benjamin Pachter, "Displaying 'Japan': *Kumidaiko* and the Exhibition of Culture at Walt Disney World," *Asian Musicology* 14 (2009): 81–121.

Bibliography

Newspapers and Periodicals

Boston Globe
Chicago Daily Tribune
Christian Science Monitor
Dwight's Journal of Music
Evening Post
Evening Sun
Japan Weekly Mail
Jet
Life
Los Angeles Times
Morning Telegraph
The Nation
New York Times
New York Tribune
The New Yorker
Rafu Shimpo
Theatre
Time
Transactions of the Asiatic Society of Japan
Variety
Washington Post
Worcester Evening Gazette

Archival Sources

Academy of Motion Picture Arts and Sciences Research Center, Los Angeles.
American Antiquarian Society, Worcester, MA.
Art Institute of Chicago, Institutional Archives and Ryerson and Burnham Archives, Chicago.
Bagaduce Music Lending Library, Blue Hill, ME.
Balaban and Katz Collection, Harold Washington Library Center, Chicago Public Library.
Celeste Bartos International Film Study Center, Museum of Modern Art, New York.
David Belasco Collection of Incidental Music, Music Division, New York Public Library for the Performing Arts.
David Belasco Papers, Billy Rose Theatre Division, New York Public Library for the Performing Arts.
Joseph Henry Benrimo Papers, New York Public Library, Main Branch, Manuscripts Division.
Boston Public Library, Special Collections.
R. H. Burnside Papers, New York Public Library, Main Branch, Manuscripts Division.
David Buttolph Collection, Harold B. Lee Library Special Collections, Brigham Young University.
Frank Capra Archive, Cinema Archives, Wesleyan University.
Carnegie Library of Pittsburgh, Music Special Collections.
Chapin Library, Special Collections, Williams College.
Chicago Public Library, Harold Washington Library Center, Special Collections.

Elizabeth Sprague Coolidge Collection, Music Division, Library of Congress.
Copyright and Public Records, Library of Congress.
Henry Cowell Collection, Music Division, Library of Congress.
Henry Cowell Collection, Music Division, New York Public Library for the Performing Arts.
Dance Theatre of Harlem Archives, New York.
Oliver Daniel Research Collection on Leopold Stokowski, Annenberg Rare Book and Manuscript
    Library, University of Pennsylvania.
Dartmouth College Library Special Collections.
Cecil B. DeMille Archives, Harold B. Lee Library Special Collections, Brigham Young University.
Sam DeVincent Collection, National Museum of American History Archives, Smithsonian.
Driscoll Collection, Newberry Library, Chicago.
Duke University Libraries, Historic American Sheet Music Collection.
George Duning Collection, University of Southern California, Cinematic Arts Library.
Henry Eichheim Collection, Newberry Library, Chicago.
Henry Eichheim Collection, University of California, Santa Barbara.
Carl Engel Collection, Music Division, Library of Congress.
Ernest F. Fenollosa Papers, Houghton Library, Harvard University.
Edwin A. Fleisher Collection of Orchestral Music, Free Library of Philadelphia.
Free Library of Philadelphia Sheet Music Collection.
Hugo Friedhofer Collection, Harold B. Lee Library Special Collections, Brigham Young University.
Isabella Stewart Gardner Museum Archives, Boston.
Eva Gauthier Collection, Music Division, New York Public Library for the Performing Arts.
Charles T. Griffes Collection, Music Division, New York Public Library for the Performing Arts.
Leigh Harline Papers, University of Cincinnati, Archives and Rare Books Library.
Harvard Theatre Collection, Harvard University Library.
John Hay Library, Special Collections, Brown University.
Louis Horst Collection, Music Division, New York Public Library for the Performing Arts.
Alan Hovhaness Collection, Armenian Cultural Foundation, Arlington, MA.
International Association for Cultural Freedom Records, Special Collections Research Center,
    University of Chicago Library.
Japanese American National Museum, Hirasaki National Resource Center, Los Angeles.
Arthur Kleiner Collection of Silent Movie Music, Special Collections, University of Minnesota.
The Serge Koussevitzky Archive, General Correspondence, Music Division, Library of
    Congress.
Lester S. Levy Collection, Johns Hopkins University, Baltimore.
Sandra Marrone Sheet Music Collection (private), Cinnaminson, NJ.
Massachusetts Historical Society, Boston.
MGM Collections, Cinema and Television Library, University of Southern California.
Mission Inn Archive, Riverside, CA.
Museum of Modern Art Film Archives, New York.
Music Department Paramount Studios, Los Angeles.
Music Division, Library of Congress.
National Archives and Records Administration, Washington, DC
New Bedford Whaling Museum Research Library, New Bedford, MA.
New York Public Library for the Humanities and Social Sciences, Manuscripts Collection.
New York Public Library for the Performing Arts, Jerome Robbins Dance Division.
New York Public Library for the Performing Arts, Billy Rose Theatre Division.
New York Public Library for the Performing Arts, Music Division.
New York Public Library for the Performing Arts, Rodgers and Hammerstein Archives of
    Recorded Sound.
New York Public Library for the Performing Arts, Theatre on Film and Tape Archive.
Alfred Newman Collection, Cinema and Television Library, University of Southern California.
Office of War Information Records, US National Archives II, College Park, MD.
Panama-Pacific International Exposition Collection, San Francisco Public Library History Center.

Paramount Theater Music Library, Oakland, CA.
Phillips Library, Peabody-Essex Museum, Salem, MA.
Ezra Pound Collection on Japanese Drama, Princeton University Special Collections.
Recorded Sound Research Center, Library of Congress.
Redpath Chautauqua Collection, University of Iowa Libraries, Special Collections Department.
Republic Pictures Music Archives, Harold B. Lee Library Special Collections, Brigham Young University.
Roger Reynolds Papers, personal collection, Del Mar, CA.
RKO Archives, University of California, Los Angeles, Library Special Collections.
Ruth St. Denis Collection, New York Public Library for the Performing Arts.
Tak Shindo Papers, personal collection, San Dimas, CA.
Max Steiner Collection, Harold B. Lee Library Special Collections, Brigham Young University.
Leopold Stokowski Collection of Scores, Annenberg Rare Book and Manuscript Library, University of Pennsylvania.
Virgil Thomson Papers, Yale University Library, Irving S. Gilmore Music Library.
Dimitri Tiomkin Collection, Cinema and Television Library, University of Southern California.
University of California, Los Angeles, Arts Library Special Collections.
University of California, Los Angeles, Film and Television Archives.
University of California, Los Angeles, Music Library Special Collections.
University of Chicago, Film Studies Center.
University of Chicago, University Archives.
University of Chicago Library, Special Collections.
University of Pittsburgh Hillman Library.
Virginia Historical Society Library, Richmond, VA.
Warner Bros. Archives, University of Southern California.
Franz Waxman Collection, Syracuse University Library Special Collections.
Paul Whiteman Collection, Special Collections, Williams College.

Interviews conducted by author

Arian, Ed, via telephone, November 2007.
Chihara, Paul, at New York University, November 2015; at Williams College, April 2016.
Chong, Ping, at Williams College, October 1998.
León, Tania, at Williams College, March 2017.
Neu, Ah Ling, at Williams College, November 2018.
Otani, Muneko, at Williams College, November 2018.
Raksin, David, via telephone, March 2000.
Reynolds, Roger, at his home in Del Mar, CA, June 2011.
Samuelson, Ralph, at his home in Chappaqua, NY, October 2017.
Schlefer, James Nyoraku, at Williams College, October 2014.
Shindo, Myra, and Sachiko Shindo, at the Shindo residence in San Dimas, CA, January 2004.
Shindo, Tak, via telephone, April 2000; at his home in San Dimas, CA, June 2000.
Teitelbaum, Richard, via telephone, September 2006; at Williams College, October 2006.
Yoshida, George, via telephone, August 2003.

Published Sources

Abbate, Carolyn. "Cipher and Performance in Sternberg's *Dishonored*." In *Music and the Aesthetics of Modernity*, edited by Karol Berger and Anthony Newcomb, 357–392. Cambridge, MA: Harvard University Department of Music, 2005.
Abel, Richard. *French Film Theory and Criticism: A History/Anthology, 1907–1939*, vol. 1. Princeton, NJ: Princeton University Press, 1988.

Abraham, Otto, and Erich M. von Hornbostel. "Studien über das Tonsystem und die Musik der Japaner" (1903). Trans. by Gertrud Kurath, in *Hornbostel: Opera Omnia*, Vol. 1, edited by Klaus P. Wachsmann, Dieter Christensen, and Hans-Peter Reinecke, 1–84. The Hague: Martinus Nijhoff, 1975.

Adachi, Tomomi. "'John Cage Shock' in the 1960s in Japan and the Question of Orientalism." In *Cage & Consequences*, edited by Julia H. Schröder and Volker Straebel, 165–167. Berlin: Wolke, 2012.

Adami, Giuseppe, ed. *Letters of Giacomo Puccini*. Trans. by Ena Makin. Philadelphia: J. B. Lippincott Co., 1931. Reprint, New York: Vienna House, 1973.

Adams, I. William. *Shibusawa, or the Passing of Old Japan*. New York and London: G. P. Putnam's Sons, 1906.

Adinolfi, Francesco. *Mondo Exotica: Sounds, Visions, Obsessions of the Cocktail Generation*. Edited and translated by Karen Pinkus with Jason Vivrette. Durham, NC: Duke University Press, 2008.

Adlington, Robert, ed. *Sound Commitments: Avant-garde Music and the Sixties*. Oxford: Oxford University Press, 2009.

Adorno, Theodor, and Hanns Eisler. *Composing for the Films*. London: The Athlone Press, 1994. First published 1947.

Agee, James. *Agee on Film*. New York: McDowell, Obolensky Inc., 1958.

Akira, Shimizu. "War and Cinema in Japan." In *The Japan/America Film Wars: World War II Propaganda and Its Cultural Contexts*, edited by Abé Mark Nornes and Fukushima Yukio, 7–57. Chur, Switzerland: Harwood, 1994.

Alber, Louis J. "The Gale Costume Lectures: How the Music of Primitive Peoples Is Brought to Lyceum Audience." *The Lyceumite and Talent* (May 1912): 18–21.

Aldrich, Richard. "The Philadelphia Orchestra." *New York Times*, 14 March 1923: 14.

Al-Taee, Nasser. *Representations of the Orient in Western Music: Violence and Sensuality*. Surrey: Ashgate, 2010.

Amalfitano, Paolo, and Loretta Innocenti, eds. *L'Oriente: Storia di una figura nelle arti occidentali (1700–2000)*. 2 vols. Rome: Bulzoni Editore, 2007.

Altman, Rick. "The Silence of the Silents." *The Musical Quarterly* 80, no. 4 (winter 1996): 648–718.

Altman, Rick. *Silent Film Sound*. New York: Columbia University Press, 2004.

Ames, Christopher. *Movies about the Movies: Hollywood Reflected*. Lexington: University Press of Kentucky, 1997.

Anderson, Donna K. *The Works of Charles T. Griffes: A Descriptive Catalogue*. Ann Arbor, MI: UMI Research Press, 1983.

Anderson, Donna K. *Charles T. Griffes: A Life in Music*. Washington, DC: Smithsonian Institution Press, 1993.

Anderson, Gillian B. *Music for Silent Films, 1894–1929*. Washington, DC: Library of Congress, 1988.

Anderson, Gillian B. "Synchronized Music: The Influence of Pantomime on Moving Pictures." *Music and the Moving Image* 8, no. 3 (fall 2015): 3–39.

Anderson, Isabel. *The Spell of Japan*. Boston: The Page Company, 1914.

Anderson, Joseph L. *Enter a Samurai: Kawakami Otojirō and Japanese Theatre in the West*. Tucson, AZ: Wheatmark, 2011.

Anderson, Joseph L., and Donald Richie. *The Japanese Film: Art and Industry*. Princeton, NJ: Princeton University Press, 1982.

Ansari, Emily Abrams. "'A Serious and Delicate Mission': American Orchestras, American Composers, and Cold War Diplomacy in Europe." In *Crosscurrents: American and European Music in Interaction, 1900–2000*, edited by Felix Meyer, Carol J. Oja, Wolfgang Rathert, and Anne C. Shreffler, 287–298. Basel: Paul Sacher Stiftung, 2014.

Appadurai, Arjun. *Modernity at Large: Cultural Dimensions of Globalization*. Minneapolis: University of Minnesota Press, 1996.

Applebaum, Louis. "Documentary Music." In *Film Music: From Violins to Video*, compiled and edited by James L. Limbacher, 66–72. Metuchen, NJ: Scarecrow Press, 1974.

"Are Movies Popularizing Opera?" *Theatre Magazine* 29 (May 1919): 297.

Armor, John, and Peter Wright. *Manzanar*. Commentary by John Hersey. Photographs by Ansel Adams. New York: Times Books, 1988.

Arnold, Ben. *Music and War: A Research and Information Guide*. New York: Garland Publishing, Inc., 1993.

Arnold, Edwin. "Japonica—Second Paper—Japanese People." *Scribner's Magazine* 9, no. 1 (1891): 17–30.

Arnold, Edwin. *Japonica*. New York: Charles Scribner's Sons, 1892.

Arnold, Edwin. *Seas and Lands*. London: Longmans, Green, and Co., 1892.

Arnold, Edwin. *Adzuma, or the Japanese Wife*. London: Longmans, Green, and Co., 1893.

Arsenault, Linda M. "Iannis Xenakis: 'I Am a Japanese.'" In *Musicology and Globalization: Proceedings of the International Congress in Shizuoka 2002*, edited by Yoshio Tozawa, Tatsuhiko Itoh, Keiichi Kubota, and Yasuhiko Mori, 238–241. Tokyo: The Musicological Society of Japan, 2004.

Asai, Susan Miyo. "Transformations of Tradition: Three Generations of Japanese American Music Making." *The Musical Quarterly* 79, no. 3 (fall 1995): 429–453.

Asai, Susan Miyo. "Sansei Voices in the Community." In *Musics of Multicultural America: A Study of Twelve Musical Communities*, edited by Kip Lornell and Anne K. Rasmussen, 257–285. New York: Schirmer Books, 1997.

Asai, Susan Miyo. "Cultural Politics: The African American Connection in Asian American Jazz-based Music." *Asian Music* 36, no. 1 (2005): 87–108.

Asai, Susan Miyo. "The Cultural Politics of *Issei* Identity and Music Making in California, 1893–1941." *Journal of the Society for American Music* 10, no. 3 (2016): 304–330.

Ashbrook, William, and Harold Powers. *Puccini's* Turandot: *The End of the Great Tradition*. Princeton, NJ: Princeton University Press, 1991.

Ashby, Arved. "Nationalist and Postnationalist Perspectives in American Musicology." In *Postnational Musical Identities: Cultural Production, Distribution, and Consumption in a Globalized Scenario*, edited by Ignacio Corona and Alejandro L. Madrid, 23–43. Lanham, MD: Lexington Books, 2008.

Atkins, E. Taylor. *Blue Nippon: Authenticating Jazz in Japan*. Durham, NC: Duke University Press, 2001.

Atkins, Irene Kahn. *Arranging and Composing Film Music: Interview with Hugo Friedhofer*. N.p.: American Film Institute, 1975, microfilm.

Atkins, Irene Kahn. *Scoring Hollywood Movies: Interview with Bronislaw Kaper*. N.p.: American Film Institute, 1975, microfilm.

Atkins, Irene Kahn. *Source Music in Motion Pictures*. Rutherford, NJ: Fairleigh Dickinson University Press, 1983.

Attinello, Paul. "The Universe Will Tell You What It Needs: Being, Time, Sondheim." In *Musicological Identities: Essays in Honor of Susan McClary*, edited by Steven Baur, Raymond Knapp, and Jacqueline Warwick, 77–93. Burlington, VT: Ashgate, 2008.

Baade, Christina L. *Victory through Harmony: The BBC and Popular Music in World War II*. Oxford: Oxford University Press, 2012.

Baber, Katherine A. "Jazz, World War II Radio Propaganda, and the Case of Tokyo Rose." In *The Soundtrack of Conflict: The Role of Music in Radio Broadcasting in Wartime and in Conflict Situations*, edited by M. J. Grant and Férdia J. Stone-Davis, 57–73. Hildesheim: Georg Olms Verlag, 2013.

Bacon, Alice Mabel. *Japanese Girls and Women*. London: Kegan Paul, 2001. First published 1891.

Bailey, Thomas A. *Theodore Roosevelt and the Japanese-American Crises*. Stanford, CA: Stanford University Press, 1934.

Baker, Don R. "William Malm: Japanese Music." *Percussive Notes* 23, no. 5 (July 1985): 26–28.

Ballagh, Margaret Tate Kinnear. *Glimpses of Old Japan 1861–1866*. Tokyo: Methodist Publishing House, 1908.

Balmer, Yves, Thomas Lacôte, and Christopher Brent Murray. "Messiaen the Borrower: Recomposing Debussy through the Deforming Prism." *Journal of the American Musicological Society* 69, no. 3 (fall 2016): 699–791.

Bañagale, Ryan Raul. *Arranging Gershwin:* Rhapsody in Blue *and the Creation of an American Icon*. Oxford: Oxford University Press, 2014.

Banfield, Stephen. *Sondheim's Broadway Musicals*. Ann Arbor: University of Michigan Press, 1993.

Barnes, Jennifer. *Television Opera: The Fall of Opera Commissioned for Television*. Rochester, NY: Boydell Press, 2003.

Barr, Cyrilla. *Elizabeth Sprague Coolidge: American Patron of Music*. New York: Schirmer Books, 1998.

Barry, Dave. *Dave Barry Does Japan*. New York: Fawcett Columbine, 1992.

Barthes, Roland. *Empire of Signs*. Trans. Richard Howard. New York: Hill and Wang, 1982.

Bartók, Béla. *Béla Bartók Essays*. Edited by Benjamin Suchoff. London: Faber and Faber, 1976.

Basinger, Jeanine. *The World War II Combat Film: Anatomy of a Genre*. New York: Columbia University Press, 1986.

Baugh, John. "Linguistic Profiling." In *Black Linguistics: Language, Society, and Politics in Africa and the Americas*, edited by Sinfree Makoni, Geneva Smitherman, Arnetha F. Ball, and Arthur K. Spears, 155–168. London and New York: Routledge, 2003.

Bayerdörfer, Hans-Peter. "*Nô* in Disguise: Robert Wilson's Adaptation of *Nô* Elements in His Productions of *Alkestis/Alceste*." In *Japanese Theatre and the International Stage*, edited by Stanca Scholz-Cionca and Samuel L. Leiter, 367–383. Leiden: Brill, 2001.

Bazelon, Irwin. *Knowing the Score: Notes on Film Music*. New York: Van Nostrand Reinhold Company, 1975.

Beal, Amy. *New Music, New Allies: American Experimental Music in West Germany from the Zero Hour to Reunification*. Berkeley: University of California Press, 2006.

Beard, David. "'A Face like Music': Shaping Images into Sound in *The Second Mrs. Kong*." *Cambridge Opera Journal* 18, no. 3 (Nov. 2006): 273–300.

Becker, Heinz, ed. *Die "Couleur locale" in der Oper des 19. Jahrhunderts*. Regensburg: Gustav Bosse Verlag, 1976.

Becker, Judith. "Hindu-Buddhist Time in Javanese Gamelan Music." In *The Study of Time*, vol. 4, edited by J. F. Fraser, 161–172. New York: Springer-Verlag, 1981.

Beckerman, Michael. "The Sword on the Wall: Japanese Elements and Their Significance in *The Mikado*." *The Musical Quarterly* 73, no. 3 (1989): 303–319.

Beidler, Philip D. *The Good War's Greatest Hits: World War II and American Remembering*. Athens: University of Georgia Press, 1998.

Belasco, David. "'Atmosphere' on the Stage." *Frank Leslie's Popular Monthly* (August 1903): 404–405.

Belasco, David. *The Theatre through Its Stage Door*. New York: Harper and Brothers, 1919.

Belasco, David. *Six Plays*. Boston: Little, Brown, and Co., 1929.

Bellman, Jonathan, ed. *The Exotic in Western Music*. Boston: Northeastern University Press, 1998.

Bellman, Jonathan D. "Musical Voyages and Their Baggage: Orientalism in Music and Critical Musicology." *Musical Quarterly* 94 (2011): 417–438.

Benedict, Ruth. *The Chrysanthemum and the Sword*. Boston: Houghton Mifflin Company, 1989. First published 1946.

Benfey, Christopher. *The Great Wave: Gilded Age Misfits, Japanese Eccentrics, and the Opening of Japan*. New York: Random House, 2003.

Bennett, Robert Russell. *"The Broadway Sound": The Autobiography and Selected Essays of Robert Russell Bennett*. Edited by George J. Ferencz. Rochester, NY: University of Rochester Press, 1999.

Benrimo, J. H., and Harrison Rhodes, *The Willow Tree: A Japanese Fantasy in Three Acts*. New York: Samuel French, 1931.

Berger, Donald, comp., ed., and arr. *Folk Songs of Japanese Children*. North Clarendon: Tuttle, 1969.

Berger, Donald, comp., ed., and arr. *Folk Songs of Japan*. New York: Oak Publications, 1972.

Berger, Donald P. "Isawa Shuji and Luther Whiting Mason: Pioneers of Music Education in Japan." *Music Educators Journal* 74, no. 2 (October 1987): 31–36.

Berger, Klaus. *Japonisme in Western Painting from Whistler to Matisse*. Trans. by David Britt. Cambridge, UK: Cambridge University Press, 1992.

Berlin, Zeke. "Takarazuka: A History and Descriptive Analysis of the All-female Japanese Performance Company." PhD diss., New York University, 1988.

Berlin, Zeke. "The Takarazuka Touch." *Asian Theatre Journal* 8, no. 1 (spring 1991): 35–47.

Bernardi, Daniel. *Classic Hollywood, Classic Whiteness*. Minneapolis: University of Minnesota Press, 2001.

Bernardi, Daniel, ed. *The Birth of Whiteness: Race and the Emergence of US Cinema*. New Brunswick, NJ: Rutgers University Press, 1996.

Bernstein, Matthew, and Gaylyn Studlar, eds. *Visions of the East: Orientalism in Film*. New Brunswick, NJ: Rutgers University Press, 1997.

Bhabha, Homi K. "The Other Question—the Stereotype and Colonial Discourse." *Screen* 24, no. 6 (November–December 1983): 18–36.

Bhabha, Homi K. *The Location of Culture*. London and New York: Routledge, 1994.

Bierman, Duane. "Interpreting Alan Hovhaness's Fantasy on Japanese Wood Prints." *Percussive Notes* 40, no. 6 (December 2002): 40–53.

Bierstadt, E. H. "Opera in Moving Pictures." *Opera Magazine* (October 1915): 30–32.

The Biographical Cyclopedia of American Women, vol. 1, Mabel W. Cameron (comp.). New York: The Halvord Publishing Company, 1924.

Bird, Isabella L. *Unbeaten Tracks in Japan*, vol. 1. New York: G. P. Putnam's Sons, 1880; vol. 2, 1881.

Bisland, Elizabeth. *The Life and Letters of Lafcadio Hearn*. Vol. 2. Boston and New York: Houghton, Mifflin, 1906.

Bispo, Ieda. "Olivier Messiaen's *Sept Haïkaï*: Beyond *Japonisme*." In *Musicology and Globalization: Proceedings of the International Congress in Shizuoka 2002*, edited by Yoshio Tozawa, Tatsuhiko Itoh, Keiichi Kubota, and Yasuhiko Mori, 242–246. Tokyo: The Musicological Society of Japan, 2004.

Bithell, David, and Roger Reynolds. "Image, Engagement, Technological Resource: An Interview with Roger Reynolds." *Computer Music Journal* 31, no. 1 (spring 2007): 10–28.

Blair, Harry N. "Short Shots from Eastern Studios." *The Film Daily* (15 September 1931): 6.

Blakefield, William J. "A War Within: The Making of *Know Your Enemy—Japan*." *Sight and Sound* 52, no. 2 (spring 1983): 128–133.

Blasdel, Christopher Yohmei. *The Single Tone: A Personal Journey into Shakuhachi Music*. Tokyo: Printed Matter Press, 2005.

Bloom, Ken. *American Song*. New York: Schirmer Books, 2001.

Blyth, R. H. *Zen in English Literature and Oriental Classics*. New York: E. P. Dutton, 1960. First published 1942.

Bohlman, Philip V. "Fieldwork in the Ethnomusicological Past." In *Shadows in the Field: New Perspectives for Fieldwork in Ethnomusicology*, edited by Gregory F. Barz and Timothy J. Cooley, 139–162. New York: Oxford University Press, 1997.

Bohlman, Philip V. "World Music at the 'End of History.'" *Ethnomusicology* 46, no. 1 (winter 2002): 1–32.

Bohlman, Philip V. "Music as Representation." *Journal of Musicological Research* 24, no. 3 (2005): 205–226.

Bohn, Thomas. *An Historical and Descriptive Analysis of the "Why We Fight" Series*. New York: Arno Press, 1977.

Bomberger, E. Douglas. *"A Tidal Wave of Encouragement": American Composers' Concerts in the Gilded Age*. Westport, CT: Praeger, 2002.

Bond, Randall Ives. "'Still Dreaming of Paradise': Rodgers and Hammerstein's *Oklahoma!*, *South Pacific*, and Postwar America." PhD diss., Syracuse University, 1996.

Bordman, Gerald, and Richard Norton. *American Musical Theatre: A Chronicle*. 4th ed. New York: Oxford University Press, 2010.

Born, Georgina, and David Hesmondhalgh, eds. *Western Music and Its Others: Difference, Representation, and Appropriation in Music*. Berkeley: University of California Press, 2000.

Boulez, Pierre. "Oriental Music: A Lost Paradise?" (1967) and "Where Are We Now?" (1968). Reprinted in *Orientations: Collected Writings of Pierre Boulez*, edited by Jean-Jacques Nattiez and trans. Martin Cooper, 421–424. Cambridge, MA: Harvard University Press, 1986.

Bowers, Faubion. *Japanese Theatre*. New York: Hill and Wang, 1952.

Bowles, Paul. "Films and Theatre." *Modern Music* 20, no. 1 (November–December 1942): 57–61.

Boyd, Michael. "The Roger Reynolds Collection at the Library of Congress." *Notes* 64, no. 3 (2008): 435–457.

Boyd, Michael. "The Evolution of Form in the Music of Roger Reynolds (I)." *Tempo* 66, no. 259 (2012): 36–48.

Boyd, Michael. "The Evolution of Form in the Music of Roger Reynolds (II)." *Tempo* 66, no. 260 (2012): 34–49.

Boyer, Samuel Pellman. *Naval Surgeon: Revolt in Japan 1868–1869*. Edited by Elinor Barnes and James A. Barnes. Bloomington: Indiana University Press, 1963.

Brackett, John. "From the Fantastic to the Dangerously Real: Reading John Zorn's Artwork." *ECHO: A Music-Centered Journal* 8, no. 1 (fall 2006), http://www.echo.ucla.edu/Volume8-Issue1/brackett/brackett1.html.

Brandon, James R. "Earle S. Ernst." *Asian Theatre Journal* 28, no. 2 (fall 2011): 332–340.

Brantley, Ben. "Repatriating the Japanese Sondheim." *New York Times*, 3 December 2004, E23.

Brewster, Ben, and Lea Jacobs. *Theatre to Cinema: Stage Pictorialism and the Early Feature Film*. Oxford: Oxford University Press, 1997.

Brinkley, Captain F. *Japan: Its History, Arts, and Literature*. Boston: J. B. Millet Co., 1902.

Brinkmann, Reinhold, and Christoph Wolff, eds. *Driven into Paradise: The Musical Migration from Nazi Germany to the United States*. Berkeley: University of California Press, 1999.

Brooks, Ray. *Blowing Zen: Finding an Authentic Life*. Tiburon, CA: H. J. Kramer, 2000.

Brooks, Van Wyck. *Fenollosa and His Circle*. New York: E. P. Dutton and Co., 1962.

Brown, Julie, ed. *Western Music and Race*. Cambridge, UK: Cambridge University Press, 2007.

Brown, Kendall H. *Japanese-Style Gardens of the Pacific West Coast*. New York: Rizzoli, 1999.

Brown, Royal S. *Overtones and Undertones: Reading Film Music*. Berkeley: University of California Press, 1994.

Brown, Shelina. "Scream from the Heart: Yoko Ono's Rock and Roll Revolution." In *Countercultures and Popular Music*, edited by Sheila Whiteley and Jedediah Sklower, 171–186. New York: Routledge, 2014.

Browne, Nick. "Orientalism as an Ideological Form: American Film Theory in the Silent Period." *Wide Angle* 11, no. 4 (October 1989): 23–31.

Browne, Nick. "The Undoing of the *Other* Woman: Madame Butterfly in the Discourse of American Orientalism." In *The Birth of Whiteness: Race and the Emergence of US Cinema*, edited by Daniel Bernardi, 227–256. New Brunswick, NJ: Rutgers University Press, 1996.

Browning, Joseph. "Assembled Landscapes: The Sites and Sounds of Some Recent Shakuhachi Recordings." *Journal of Musicology* 33, no. 1 (2016): 70–91.

Brownlow, Kevin. *Behind the Mask of Innocence*. New York: Alfred A. Knopf, 1990.

Buck, Pearl S. "The People of Japan." New York: Simon and Schuster, 1966.

Buckley, Roger, and Tamara Roberts, eds. *Yellow Power, Yellow Soul: The Radical Art of Fred Ho*. Urbana: University of Illinois Press, 2013.

Buhler, James, Caryl Flinn, and David Neumeyer, eds. *Music and Cinema*. Hanover, NH: Wesleyan University Press, 2000.

Burger, Jeff, ed. *Lennon on Lennon: Conversations with John Lennon*. Chicago: Chicago Review Press, 2016.

Burke, Edmund, III, and David Prochaska, eds. *Genealogies of Orientalism: History, Theory, Politics*. Lincoln: University of Nebraska Press, 2008.

Burroughs, Wesley Ray. "With the Movie Organist." *Diapason* (1 February 1916): 3.

Buruma, Ian. *Behind the Mask: On Sexual Demons, Sacred Mothers, Transvestites, Gangsters, and Other Japanese Cultural Heroes*. New York: Meridian, 1985.

Buruma, Ian. "Haunted Heroine." *Interview* (September 1989): 124–127.

Burt, George. *The Art of Film Music*. Boston: Northeastern University Press, 1994.

Bush, Christopher. "The Ethnicity of Things in America's Lacquered Age." *Representations* 99 (2007): 74–98.

Cage, John. "The East in the West." *Modern Music* 23, no. 2 (spring 1946): 111–115.

Cage, John. *Silence: Lectures and Writings*. Middletown, CT: Wesleyan University Press, 1961.

Cage, John. *For the Birds: In Conversation with Daniel Charles*. Boston: Marion Boyars, 1981.

Cage, John. *Musicage: Cage Muses on Words, Art, Music*. Edited by Joan Retallack. Hanover, NH: University Press of New England, 1995.

Cage, John. "*Ryoanji*: Solos for Oboe, Flute, Contrabass, Voice, Trombone with Percussion or Orchestral Obbligato (1983–85)." *PAJ: A Journal of Performance and Art* 31, no. 3 (September 2009): 57–64.

Cage, John. *The Selected Letters of John Cage*. Edited by Laura Kuhn. Middletown, CT: Wesleyan University Press, 2016.

Caldwell, Helen. *Michio Ito: The Dancer and His Dances*. Berkeley: University of California Press, 1977.

Cannata, Amanda. "Articulating and Contesting Cultural Hierarchies: Guatemalan, Mexican, and Native American Music at the Panama-Pacific International Exposition (1915)." *Journal of the Society for American Music* 8, no. 1 (2014): 76–100.

Capellen, Georg. *Shogaku Shoka: Japanische Volksmelodien des Isawa Shuji*. Leipzig: Breitkopf and Härtel, 1904.

Capellen, Georg. *Ein neuer exotischer Musikstil an Notenbeispielen nachgewiesen*. Stuttgart: Grüninger, 1905.

Capote, Truman. "Profiles: The Duke in his Domain." *New Yorker* 33 (9 November 1957): 53–100.

Capra, Frank. *The Name above the Title: An Autobiography*. New York: Macmillan, 1971.

Carner, Mosco. *Puccini: A Critical Biography*. 3rd ed. London: Duckworth, 1992.

Carr, Graham. "Diplomatic Notes: American Musicians and Cold War Politics in the Near and Middle East, 1954–60." *Popular Music History* 1, no. 1 (2004): 37–63.

Carrothers, Julia D. *The Sunrise Kingdom; or, Life and Scenes in Japan, and Woman's Work for Woman There*. Philadelphia: Presbyterian Board of Publication, 1879.

Carson, Diane, Linda Dittmar, and Janice R. Welsch, eds. *Multiple Voices in Feminist Film Criticism*. Minneapolis: University of Minnesota, 1994.

Carter, Morris. *Isabella Stewart Gardner and Fenway Court*. Boston and New York: Houghton Mifflin, 1925.

Carwithen, Edward R. "Henry Cowell: Composer and Educator." PhD diss., University of Florida, 1991.

Casano, Steven. "From *Fuke Shuu* to *Uduboo*: The Transnational Flow of the *Shakuhachi* to the West." *The World of Music* 47, no. 3 (2005): 17–33.

Castro, Christi-Anne. "Voices in the Minority: Race, Gender, Sexuality, and the Asian American in Popular Music." *Journal of Popular Music Studies* 19, no. 3 (2007): 221–238.

Catalogue of Objects Exhibited at The World's Columbian Exposition, Chicago, USA, 1893. Tokyo: Department of Japan, 1893.

Catlin, Roger. "Weezer's Worry." *The Hartford Courant*, 4 December 1996, E1.

Chamberlain, Basil Hall. *Japanese Things: Being Notes on Various Subjects Connected with Japan*. Rutland: Charles E. Tuttle, 1971. Reprint of 5th rev. ed., London: John Murray, 1905.

Chambers, John Whiteclay, II, and David Culbert, eds. *World War II, Film, and History*. New York: Oxford University Press, 1996.

Champney, Elizabeth W., and Frère Champney. *Romance of Old Japan*. New York and London: G. P. Putnam's Sons, 1917.

Chan, Sucheng. *Asian Americans: An Interpretive History*. Boston: Twayne Publishers, 1991.

Chang, Justin. "Wes Anderson's 'Isle of Dogs' Is Often Captivating, but Cultural Sensitivity Gets Lost in Translation." *Los Angeles Times*, 21 March 2018, https://www.latimes.com/entertainment/movies/la-et-mn-isle-of-dogs-review-20180321-story.html.

Chiba, Yoko. "Sada Yacco and Kawakami: Performers of *Japonisme*." *Modern Drama* 35, no. 1 (1992): 35–53.

"Chinese Music Aeons Old to Be Played in Washington." *Washington Post* (28 November 1933): 11.

Chion, Michel. *Audio-Vision: Sound on Screen*. Edited and translated by Claudia Gorbman. New York: Columbia University Press, 1994.

Chisolm, Lawrence W. *Fenollosa: The Far East and American Culture*. New Haven, CT: Yale University Press, 1963.

Chou, Wen-chung. "Asian Concepts and Twentieth-century Western Composers." *The Musical Quarterly* 57, no. 2 (April 1971): 211–229.

Christy, Arthur E., ed. *The Asian Legacy and American Life*. New York: John Day Co., 1942.

Citron, Marcia J. "A Night at the Cinema: Zeffirelli's *Otello* and the Genre of Film-Opera." *Musical Quarterly* 78, no. 4 (winter 1994): 700–741.

Citron, Marcia J. *Opera on Screen*. New Haven, CT: Yale University Press, 2000.

Clayton, Martin, and Bennett Zon, eds. *Music and Orientalism in the British Empire, 1780s–1940s*. Aldershot, UK: Ashgate, 2007.

Clement, Ernest W. *A Handbook of Modern Japan*. Rev. 6th ed. Chicago: A. C. McClurg and Co., 1905. First published 1903.

Cleveland, Les. "Singing Warriors: Popular Songs in Wartime." *Journal of Popular Culture* 28, no. 3 (winter 1994): 155–175.

Clifford, James. *The Predicament of Culture: Twentieth-century Ethnography, Literature, and Art*. Cambridge, MA: Harvard University Press, 1988.

Coaldrake, Kimi. "New Age Music and Japanese Tradition: Kitaro Live in Yakushiji." *Perfect Beat* 13, no. 1 (2012): 49–68.

Cobbing, Andrew. *The Japanese Discovery of Victorian Britain: Early Travel Encounters in the Far West*. Richmond, Surrey: Japan Library, 1998.

Cochran, Alfred W. "The Documentary Film Scores of Gail Kubik." In *Film Music: Critical Approaches*, edited by Kevin J. Donnelly, 117–128. New York: The Continuum International Publishing Group, 2001.

Cohen, Brigid. "Limits of National History: Yoko Ono, Stefan Wolpe, and Dilemmas of Cosmopolitanism." *Musical Quarterly* 97, no. 2 (summer, 2014): 181–237.

Colette. *Colette at the Movies: Criticism and Screenplays*. Edited and introduced by Alain and Odette Virmaux, translated by Sarah W. R. Smith. New York: Frederick Ungar Publishing, 1980.

Colterjohn, David. "An American Musician Blows Zen: John Kaizan Neptune Stretches the Boundaries." In *The Annals of the International Shakuhachi Society: Volume 2*, edited by Dan E. Mayers, 87–90. Wadhurst, Sussex: The Society, 2005.

Combs, James E., and Sara T. Combs. *Film Propaganda and American Politics: An Analysis and Filmography*. New York: Garland Publishing, 1994.

Combs, Jo Anne. "The Japanese O-Bon Festival and Bon Odori: Symbols in Flux." MA diss., University of California–Los Angeles, 1979.

Combs, Jo Anne. "Japanese-American Music and Dance in Los Angeles, 1930–1942." In *Selected Reports in Ethnomusicology Volume VI: Asian Music in North America*, edited by Nazir A. Jairazbhoy and Sue Carole De Vale, 121–149. Los Angeles: University of California Press, 1985.

Cook, Nicholas. "Imagining Things: Mind into Music (And Back Again)." In *Imaginative Minds*, edited by Ilona Roth, 123–146. Oxford: Oxford University Press, 2007.

Cooke, Mervyn. "Britten and the Shō." *Musical Times* 129, no. 1743 (May 1988): 231–233.

Cooke, Mervyn. *Britten and the Far East: Asian Influences in the Music of Benjamin Britten*. Woodbridge, UK: Boydell Press, 1998.

Cooper, Elizabeth. *The Heart of O Sono San*. New York: F. A. Stokes, 1917.

Cooper, Michael. "Reviving 'The Mikado' in a Balancing Act of Taste." *New York Times*, 26 December 2016, C1.

Cooper, Michael, S.J., ed. *They Came to Japan: An Anthology of European Reports on Japan, 1543–1640*. Berkeley: University of California Press, 1965.

Corbett, John. "Experimental Oriental: New Music and Other Others." In *Western Music and Its Others: Difference, Representation, and Appropriation in Music*, edited by Georgina Born and David Hesmondhalgh, 163–186. Berkeley: University of California Press, 2000.

Cott, Jonathan. *Stockhausen: Conversations with the Composer*. New York: Simon and Schuster, 1973.

Cowell, Henry. *New Musical Resources*. New York: Alfred A. Knopf, 1930.

Cowell, Henry. "Trends in American Music." In *American Composers on American Music: A Symposium*, edited by Henry Cowell, 3–13. Stanford, CA: Stanford University Press, 1933.

Cowell, Henry. "Shaping Music for Total War." *Modern Music* 22, no. 4 (summer 1945): 223–226.

Cowell, Henry. "Music Is My Weapon" (1954). Reprinted in *Essential Cowell: Selected Writings on Music by Henry Cowell 1921–1964*, edited by Dick Higgins, 47–48. Kingston, NY: Documentext, 2002.

Cowell, Henry. "Oriental Influence on Western Music." In *Music—East and West: Report on 1961 Tokyo East-West Music Encounter Conference*. Edited and published by the Executive Committee for 1961 Tokyo East-West Music Encounter, 71–76. Tokyo, 1961.

Cowell, Henry. "The Traveling Ear." *House Beautiful* 104, no. 5 (May 1962): 34–36.

Cowell, Henry. "Music of the Orient." *Music Journal* (September 1963): 25–26, 74–76.

Cowell, Mary-Jean. "Michio Ito in Hollywood: Modes and Ironies of Ethnicity." *Dance Chronicle* 24, no. 3 (2001): 263–305.

Cowell, Olive Thompson. "Henry Cowell." Compiled June 1934. Typescript held in the San José State University Library, 1934.

Cram, Ralph Adams. *Impressions of Japanese Architecture*. Boston: Marshall Jones Co., 1930. First edition 1905.

Crawford, Dorothy Lamb. *Evenings on and off the Roof: Pioneering Concerts in Los Angeles, 1939–1971*. Berkeley: University of California Press, 1995.

Crawford, Dorothy Lamb. "Arnold Schoenberg in Los Angeles." *Musical Quarterly* 86, no. 1 (spring 2002): 6–48.

Crist, Stephen A. "Jazz as Democracy? Dave Brubeck and Cold War Politics." *Journal of Musicology* 26, no. 2 (2009): 133–174.

Cronin, Tania. "On Writing for *Shakuhachi*: A Western Perspective." *Contemporary Music Review* 8, no. 2 (1993): 77–81.

Crossley-Holland, Peter. "Asian Music under the Impact of Western Culture." In *Music—East and West: Report on 1961 Tokyo East-West Music Encounter Conference*. Edited and published by the Executive Committee for 1961 Tokyo East-West Music Encounter, 50–53. Tokyo, 1961.

Crowther, Bosley. Review of *The Purple Heart. New York Times*, 9 March 1944, 15.

Crowther, Bosley. Review of *The Purple Heart. New York Times*, 19 March 1944, X3.

Crowther, Bosley. "Screen: Brando Stars in 'Sayonara.'" *New York Times*, 6 December 1957, 39.

Crowther, Bosley. "After the Japanese: 'Sayonara' Has Some of the Qualities of Fine Films from Japan." *New York Times*, 8 December 1957, D5.

Culbert, David. "'Why We Fight': Social Engineering for a Democratic Society at War." In *Film and Radio Propaganda in World War II*, edited by K. R. M. Short, 173–191. Knoxville: University of Tennessee Press, 1983.

Culbert, David, ed. *Film and Propaganda in America: A Documentary History*, vols. 1–4. New York: Greenwood Press, 1990–1991.

Currid, Brian. "'Finally, I Reach to Africa': Ryuichi Sakamoto and Sounding Japan(ese)." In *Contemporary Japan and Popular Culture*, edited by John Whittier Treat, 69–102. Honolulu: University of Hawai'i Press, 1996.

Cusick, Suzanne G. "'You Are in a Place That Is out of the World . . .': Music in the Detention Camps of the 'Global War on Terror.'" *Journal of the Society for American Music* 2, no. 1 (February 2008): 1–26.

Dalby, Liza. *Geisha.* New York: Vintage, 1983.

Dana, Richard Henry. *The Journal of Richard Henry Dana,* vol. 3. Edited by Robert Francis Lucid. Cambridge, MA: Belknap Press of Harvard University Press, 1968.

Daniel, Oliver. "Henry Cowell." *Stereo Review* 6 (December 1974): 72–82.

Daniel, Oliver. *Stokowski: A Counterpoint of View.* New York: Dodd, Mead and Co., 1982.

Daniels, Gordon. "Japanese Domestic Radio and Cinema Propaganda, 1937–1945: An Overview." In *Film and Radio Propaganda in World War II,* edited by K. R. M. Short, 293–318. Knoxville: University of Tennessee Press, 1983.

Daniels, Roger. *The Politics of Prejudice: The Anti-Japanese Movement in California and the Struggle for Japanese Exclusion.* Berkeley: University of California Press, 1962.

Daniels, Roger. *Concentration Camps: North America.* rev. ed. Malabar, FL: Robert E. Krieger Publishing Co., 1989.

Danly, Linda, ed. *Hugo Friedhofer: The Best Years of His Life.* Lanham, MD: Scarecrow Press, 1999.

Darby, William, and Jack Du Bois. *American Film Music: Major Composers, Techniques, Trends, 1915–1990.* Jefferson, NC: McFarland, 1990.

Davenport, Lisa E. *Jazz Diplomacy: Promoting America in the Cold War Era.* Jackson: University Press of Mississippi, 2009.

Davies, Clarence. Interview with Henry Eichheim. *Japan Advertiser* (5 August 1928).

Davis, Darrell William. *Picturing Japaneseness: Monumental Style, National Identity, Japanese Film.* New York: Columbia University Press, 1996.

Davis, F. Hadland. *Myths and Legends of Japan.* London: G. G. Harrap, 1912.

Dawson, Carl. *Lafcadio Hearn and the Vision of Japan.* Baltimore: Johns Hopkins University Press, 1992.

De Garis, Frederic. *Their Japan.* 2nd ed. Yokohama: Yoshikawa, 1936.

De la Campa, Román, E. Ann Kaplan, and Michael Sprinker, eds. *Late Imperial Culture.* London: Verso, 1995.

De Launey, Guy. "Not So Big in Japan: Western Pop Music in the Japanese Market." *Popular Music* 14, no. 2 (May 1995): 203–225.

Debussy, Claude. "Taste." *Revue S.I.M.* (1913). Quoted in Edward Lockspeiser, *Debussy: His Life and Mind: Volume I 1862–1918.* Cambridge, UK: Cambridge University Press, 1978, 115.

Deleuze, Gilles. *Cinema 2: The Time-Image.* Translated by Hugh Tomlinson and Robert Galeta. Minneapolis: University of Minnesota Press, 1989.

Dennison, Sam. *Scandalize My Name: Black Imagery in American Popular Music.* New York: Garland Publishing, 1982.

Denyer, Frank. "The Shakuhachi and the Contemporary Music Instrumentarium: A Personal View." *Contemporary Music Review* 8, no. 2 (1993): 45–52.

Deschênes, Bruno. "The Interest of Westerners in Non-Western Music." *The World of Music* 47, no. 3 (2005): 5–53.

de Van, Gilles. "Fin de Siècle Exoticism and the Meaning of the Far Away." *Opera Quarterly* 11, no. 3 (1995): 77–94.

Di Pietro, Rocco. *Dialogues with Boulez.* Lanham, MD: Scarecrow Press, 2001.

Dick, Bernard F. *The Star-Spangled Screen: The American World War II Film.* Lexington: University of Kentucky, 1985.

Dickinson, Peter, ed. *Cage Talk: Dialogues with and about John Cage.* Rochester, NY: University of Rochester Press, 2006.

Dizikes, John. *Opera in America: A Cultural History.* New Haven, CT: Yale University Press, 1993.

Doherty, Thomas. *Projections of War: Hollywood, American Culture, and World War II.* New York: Columbia University, 1993.

Donaldson, Laura. "*The King and I* in Uncle Tom's Cabin, or On the Border of the Women's Room." *Cinema Journal* 29, no. 3 (spring 1990): 53–68.

Donnelly, K. J., William Gibbons, and Neil Lerner, eds. *Music in Video Games: Studying Play*. New York and London: Routledge, 2014.

Dower, John W. *War without Mercy: Race and Power in the Pacific War*. New York: Pantheon Books, 1986.

Dower, John W. *Embracing Defeat: Japan in the Wake of World War II*. New York: W. W. Norton, 1999.

Downer, Lesley. *Madame Sadayakko: The Geisha Who Bewitched the West*. New York: Gotham Books, 2003.

Downes, Edward. "American Composer Encircles the Globe." *New York Times*, 25 August 1957, 119.

Downes, Olin. "The Boston Symphony" [review of a Boston Symphony Orchestra concert at Carnegie Hall]. *New York Times*, 27 November 1925, 15.

Downes, Olin. "Eichheim and Tansman Write for Stage of Spectacle and Pantomime; Scenario of 'The Rivals.'" *New York Times*, 13 March 1927, X8.

Downes, Olin. "League of Composers" [review of *The Rivals*]. *New York Times*, 28 March 1927, 26.

Duca, Lauren. "Cultural Appropriation 101, Featuring Geisha Katy Perry and the Great Wave of Asian Influence." *Huffington Post*, last updated 26 November 2013, https://www.huffingtonpost.com/2013/11/25/cultural-appropriation-katy-perry_n_4337024.html.

Dulles, Foster Rhea. *Forty Years of American-Japanese Relations*. New York: D. Appleton-Century, 1937.

Durnell, Hazel B. *Japanese Cultural Influences on American Poetry and Drama*. Tokyo: Hokuseido Press, 1983.

Dyer, Richard. *White*. London and New York: Routledge, 1997.

Dyer, Richard. *The Matter of Images: Essays on representations*. 2nd ed. London and New York: Routledge, 2002.

Eaton, Walter Prichard. *Plays and Players, Leaves from a Critic's Scrapbook*. Cincinnati: Stewart and Kidd Co., 1916.

Eichheim, Henry. "'Pinwheel Music'" [letter to the Dramatic Editor]. *New York Times*, 20 March 1927, X2.

Einstein, Albert. *The Travel Diaries of Albert Einstein: The Far East, Palestine & Spain, 1922–1923*, edited by Ze'ev Rosenkranz. Princeton, NJ: Princeton University Press, 2018.

Eligon, John. "Resistance to Syrian Refugees Calls to Mind Painful Past of Japanese-Americans." *New York Times*, 26 November 2015, https://www.nytimes.com/2015/11/27/us/for-japanese-americans-resistance-to-syrian-refugees-recalls-long-ago-fears.html.

Ellington, Duke. "Orientations: Adventures in the Mid-East." *Music Journal* 22, no. 3 (1 March 1964): 34–36; 104.

Eng, David L. *Racial Castration: Managing Masculinity in Asian America*. Durham, NC: Duke University Press, 2001.

Epstein, Milton. *The New York Hippodrome: A Complete Chronology of Performances, from 1905 to 1939*. New York: Theatre Library Association, 1993.

Eppstein, Ury. *The Beginnings of Western Music in Meiji Era Japan*. Lewiston, NY: Edwin Mellen Press, 1994.

Erdmann, Hans, and Giuseppe Becce. *Allgemeines Handbuch der Film-Musik*. Berlin: Schlesinger'sche Buch- und Musikhandlung, 1927.

Ernst, Earle. *The Kabuki Theatre*. New York: Grove Press, 1956.

Esthus, Raymond A. *Theodore Roosevelt and Japan*. Seattle: University of Washington Press, 1966.

Evans, Betty Ewart. "The Nature of Belasco's Use of Music in Representative Productions." PhD diss., University of Oregon, 1966.

Everett, Ruth. "The Best Tricks of Famous Magicians," *Cosmopolitan* 34, no. 2 (December 1902): 147.

Everett, William A. "*Chu Chin Chow* and Orientalist Musical Theatre in Britain during the First World War." In *Music and Orientalism in the British Empire, 1780s–1940s: Portrayal of the East*, edited by Martin Clayton and Bennett Zon, 277–296. Aldershot, UK: Ashgate, 2007.

Everett, William A. *Sigmund Romberg*. New Haven, CT: Yale University Press, 2007.

Everett, William A. "Imagining the Identities of East Asia in 1890s British Musical Theatre: The Case of Sidney Jones's *The Geisha* (1896)." In *Franjo Ksaver Kuhač (1834–1911): Musical Historiography and Identity*, edited by Vjera Katalinić and Stanislav Tuksar, 301–310. Zagreb: Croatian Musicological Society, 2013.

Everett, William A., and Paul R. Laird, eds. *The Cambridge Companion to the Musical*. Cambridge, UK: Cambridge University Press, 2002.

Everett, Yayoi Uno. "Intercultural Synthesis in Postwar Western Art Music: Historical Contexts, Perspectives, and Taxonomy." In *Locating East Asia in Western Art Music*, edited by Yayoi Uno Everett and Frederick Lau, 1–21. Middletown, CT: Wesleyan University Press, 2004.

Everett, Yayoi Uno. "'Mirrors' of West and 'Mirrors' of East: Elements of *Gagaku* in Post-War Art Music." In *Diasporas and Interculturalism in Asian Performing Arts: Translating Traditions*, edited by Hae-Kyung Um, 176–203. London: Routledge-Curzon, 2005.

Everett, Yayoi Uno. "'Scream against the Sky': Japanese Avant-garde Music in the Sixties." In *Sound Commitments: Avant-garde Music and the Sixties*, edited by Robert Adlington, 187–208. Oxford: Oxford University Press, 2009.

Ewen, David. *Complete Book of the American Musical Theater*. New York: Henry Holt and Co., 1958.

Ewick, David. *Japonisme, Orientalism, Modernism: A Critical Bibliography of Japan in English-Language Verse*, http://themargins.net/bibliography.html (accessed 28 September 2015).

Executive Committee for 1961 Tokyo East-West Music Encounter, ed. and publ. *Music-East and West: Report on 1961 Tokyo East-West Music Encounter Conference*. Tokyo, 1961.

Faas, Ekbert. "Interview with Karlheinz Stockhausen Held August 11, 1976." *Interface* 6, nos 3–4 (1977): 187–204.

Falk, Ray. "'Sayonara' Now Spells 'Change.'" *New York Times*, 10 March 1957, X5.

Farrell, Gerry. *Indian Music and the West*. Oxford: Clarendon Press, 1997.

Fauser, Annegret. *Musical Encounters at the 1889 Paris World's Fair*. Rochester, NY: University of Rochester Press, 2005.

Fauser, Annegret. *Sounds of War: Music in the United States during World War II*. New York: Oxford University Press, 2013.

Feather, Leonard. "Giants of Jazz: Miscellaneous Instruments." *International Musician* (July 1966): 7, 22–23.

Feisst, Sabine. "Henry Cowell und Arnold Schönberg—eine unbekannte Freundschaft." *Archiv für Musikwissenschaft* 55, no. 1 (1998): 57–71.

Felcher, Michael. *The Henry Eichheim Memorial Collection of Oriental Musical Instruments*. Santa Barbara, CA: Santa Barbara Museum of Art, 1979.

Fellezs, Kevin. "Silenced but Not Silent: Asian Americans and Jazz." In *Alien Encounters: Popular Culture in Asian America*, edited by Mimi Thi Nguyen and Thuy Linh Nguyen Tu, 69–108. Durham, NC, and London: Duke University Press, 2007.

Fenollosa, Ernest Francisco. *East and West: The Discovery of America and Other Poems*. Boston: Norwood Press, 1893. Reprint Upper Saddle River, NJ: Literature House, 1970.

Fenollosa, Ernest, and Ezra Pound. *"Noh" or Accomplishment: A Study of the Classical Stage of Japan*. New York: Alfred A. Knopf, 1917.

Fenollosa, Mary McNeil. *Out of the Nest: A Flight of Verses*. Boston: Little, Brown, 1899.

Fenollosa, Mary McNeil. [Sidney McCall, pseud.]. *The Breath of the Gods*. Boston: Little, Brown, and Co., 1905.

Fenollosa, Mary McNeil. *The Dragon Painter*. Illustrated by Gertrude McDaniel. Boston: Little, Brown, 1906.

Fenollosa, Mary McNeil. *Blossoms from a Japanese Garden: A Book of Child-Verses*. New York: Frederick A. Stokes, 1913.

Ferbraché, Lewis. *Theodore Wores: Artist in Search of the Picturesque*. San Francisco: 1968.

Fink, Robert. *Repeating Ourselves: American Minimal Music as Cultural Practice*. Berkeley: University of California Press, 2005.

Finson, Jon W. *The Voices That Are Gone: Themes in Nineteenth-century American Popular Song*. New York: Oxford University Press, 1994.

Fisk, Charles. "Rachmaninoff's Modernity." Paper delivered at the national meeting of the American Musicological Society, Washington, DC, 2005.

Fitzgerald, John, and Philip Hayward. "Musical Transport: Van Dyke Parks, Americana, and the Applied Orientalism of *Tokyo Rose*." In *Widening the Horizon: Exoticism in Post-War Popular Music*, edited by Philip Hayward, 145–167. Sydney: John Libbey, 1999.

Fleischer, Leonard. "'More Beautiful Than True' or 'Never Mind a Small Disaster': The Art of Illusion in *Pacific Overtures*," in *Stephen Sondheim: A Casebook*, edited by Joanne Lesley Gordon, 107–124. New York: Garland, 1997.

Flinn, Caryl. *Strains of Utopia: Gender, Nostalgia, and Hollywood Film Music*. Princeton, NJ: Princeton University Press, 1992.

Flynn, John J. "Transiting from the 'Wethno-centric': An Interview with Peter Sellars." In *Interculturalism and Performance: Writings from PAJ*, edited by Bonnie Marranca and Gautam Dasgupta, 184–191. New York: PAJ Publications, 1991.

Fogg, William Perry. *Round the World: Letters from Japan, China, India, and Egypt*. Cleveland: 1872.

Ford, Phil. "Taboo: Time and Belief in Exotica." *Representations* 103 (2008): 107–135.

Ford, Phil. *Dig: Sound and Music in Hip Culture*. Oxford: Oxford University Press, 2013.

"Foreign Music Program Set Tomorrow." *Los Angeles Times*, 17 January 1954, E5.

Fosler-Lussier, Danielle. *Music in America's Cold War Diplomacy*. Oakland: University of California Press, 2015.

Fowler, Michael. "Finding Cage at Ryōan-ji through a Re-modelling of *Variations II*." *Perspectives of New Music* 47, no. 1 (winter 2009): 174–192.

Fowler, Michael. "Transmediating a Japanese Garden through Spatial Sound Design." *Leonardo Music Journal* 21 (2011): 41–49.

Fraisse, Paul. *The Psychology of Time*. Translated by Jennifer Leith. New York: Harper and Row, 1963.

Franklin, Peter. "Distant Sounds—Fallen Music: *Der ferne Klang* as 'Woman's Opera'?" *Cambridge Opera Journal* 3, no. 2 (July 1991): 159–172.

Franklin, Peter. "Movies as Operas? (Behind the Great Divide)." In *A Night in at the Opera: Media Representations of Opera*, edited by Jeremy Tambling, 71–112. London: John Libbey, 1994.

Franklin, Peter. "Modernism, Deception, and Musical Others: Los Angeles circa 1940." In *Western Music and Its Others: Difference, Representation, and Appropriation in Music*, edited by Georgina Born and David Hesmondhalgh, 143–162. Berkeley: University of California Press, 2000.

Fraser, Mrs. Hugh. *Letters from Japan: A Record of Modern Life in the Island Empire*. New York: Macmillan Co., 1904. First published 1899.

Freiberg, Freda. "*China Nights* (Japan, 1940): The Sustaining Romance of Japan at War." In *World War II, Film, and History*, edited by John Whiteclay Chambers II and David Culbert, 31–46. New York: Oxford University Press, 1996.

Fritsch, Ingrid. "Some Reflections on the Early Wax Cylinder Recordings of Japanese Music in the Berlin Phonogramm Archive (Germany)." In *Musicology and Globalization: Proceedings of the International Congress in Shizuoka 2002*, 224–228. Tokyo: The Musicological Society of Japan, 2004.

Fryer, Paul. *The Opera Singer and the Silent Film*. Jefferson, NC, and London: McFarland & Co., 2005.

Fujie, Linda. "Traditional Japanese Music in New York State." *New York Folklore* 14, no. 3-4 (1988): 61–70.

Fujie, Linda. "Popular Music." In *Handbook of Japanese Popular Culture*, edited by Richard Gid Powers and Hidetoshi Kato, 197–220. New York: Greenwood Press, 1989.

Fujii, Moeko. "What 'Isle of Dogs' Gets Right about Japan." *The New Yorker* (13 April 2018), https://www.newyorker.com/culture/cultural-comment/what-isle-of-dogs-gets-right-about-japan.

Fujitani, T., Geoffrey M. White, and Lisa Yoneyama. *Perilous Memories: The Asia-Pacific War(s)*. Durham, NC: Duke University Press, 2001.

Funayama, Takashi. "*Three Japanese Lyrics* and Japonisme." In *Confronting Stravinsky: Man, Musician, and Modernist*, edited by Jann Pasler, 273–283. Berkeley: University of California Press, 1986.

Fyne, Robert. *The Hollywood Propaganda of World War II*. Metuchen, NJ: Scarecrow Press, 1994.

Gabbard, Krin. *Jammin' at the Margins: Jazz and the American Cinema*. Chicago: University of Chicago Press, 1996.

Gagne, Cole, and Tracy Caras. *Soundpieces: Interviews with American Composers*. Metuchen, NJ: Scarecrow Press, 1982.

Gairola, Rahul. "Re-worlding the Oriental: Critical Perspectives on Madonna as Geisha." In *Madonna's Drowned Worlds: New Approaches to Her Cultural Transformations, 1983–2003*, edited by Santiago Fouz-Hernández and Freya Jarman-Ivens, 104–119. Aldershot, UK: 2004.

Gale, Albert. "Chinese Music and Musical Instruments." *The Pacific Monthly* 12 (1904): 161.

Galliano, Luciana. *Yōgaku: Japanese Music in the Twentieth Century*. Translated by Martin Mayes. Lanham, MD: Scarecrow Press, 2002.

Galliano, Luciana. "Toshi Ichiyanagi, Japanese Composer and 'Fluxus.'" *Perspectives of New Music* 44, no. 2 (summer 2006): 250–261.

Gann, Kyle. *American Music in the Twentieth Century*. New York: Schirmer Books, 1997.

Garcia, Roger, ed. *Out of the Shadows: Asians in American Cinema*. Milan: Olivares, 2001.

Garfias, Robert. *Gagaku: The Music and Dances of the Japanese Imperial Household*. New York: Theatre Arts Books, 1959.

Garfias, Robert. "Some Effects of Changing Social Values on Japanese Music." In *Music— East and West: Report on 1961 Tokyo East-West Music Encounter Conference*. Edited and published by the Executive Committee for 1961 Tokyo East-West Music Encounter, 18–22. Tokyo, 1961.

Garfias, Robert. *Music of a Thousand Autumns: The Tōgaku Style of Japanese Court Music*. Berkeley: University of California Press, 1975.

Garland, Peter, ed. *A Lou Harrison Reader*. Santa Fe, NM: Soundings Press, 1987.

Garrett, Charles Hiroshi. "Chinatown, Whose Chinatown? Defining America's Borders with Musical Orientalism." *Journal of the American Musicological Society* 57, no. 1 (spring 2004): 119–173.

Garrett, Charles Hiroshi. *Struggling to Define a Nation: American Music and the Twentieth Century*. Berkeley: University of California Press, 2008.

Gates, Francis Willey, ed. *Who's Who in Music in California*. Los Angeles: Colby and Pryibil, 1920.

Gautier, Judith. *Les Musiques Bizarres à l'Exposition de 1900*. Paris: Librairie Ollendorff, 1901.

Geary, Christraud M., and Virginia-Lee Webb, eds. *Delivering Views: Distant Cultures in Early Postcards*. Washington, DC: Smithsonian Institution Press, 1998.

Gelbart, Matthew, and Alexander Rehding. "Riemann and Melodic Analysis: Studies in Folk-Musical Tonality." In *The Oxford Handbook of Neo-Riemannian Music Theories*, edited by Edward Gollin and Alexander Rehding, 140–164. Oxford: Oxford University Press, 2011.

Gerbrandt, Carl. "The Solo Vocal Music of Alan Hovhaness." DMA diss., Peabody Conservatory of Music, 1974.

Gerdts, William H. *The World of Theodore Wores*. Stanford, CA: Iris and B. Gerald Cantor Center for Visual Arts at Stanford University, 1999.

Gerstle, Andrew, and Anthony Milner, eds. *Recovering the Orient: Artists, Scholars, Appropriations*. Chur, Switzerland: Harwood Academic Publishers, 1994.

Ghuman, Nalini. *Resonances of the Raj: India in the English Musical Imagination, 1897–1947*. Oxford: Oxford University Press, 2014.

Gilbert, W. S. *The Story of The Mikado Told by Sir W. S. Gilbert*. London: Daniel O'Connor, 1921.

Gilman, Sander L. *Difference and Pathology: Stereotypes of Sexuality, Race, and Madness*. Ithaca, NY: Cornell University Press, 1985.

Ginell, Cary. *The Evolution of Mann: Herbie Mann & the Flute in Jazz.* Milwaukee: Hal Leonard Books, 2014.

Gipson, Richard McCandless. *The Life of Emma Thursby: 1845–1931.* New York: New-York Historical Society, 1940.

Girardi, Michele. *Puccini: His International Art.* Translated by Laura Basini. Chicago: University of Chicago Press, 2000.

Girardi, Michele. "Un'immagine musicale del Giappone nell'opera italiana fin-de-siècle." In *L'Oriente: Storia di una figura nelle arti occidentali (1700–2000),* vol. 1, edited by Paolo Amalfitano and Loretta Innocenti, 583–593. Rome: Bulzoni Editore, 2007.

Giroud, Vincent. *Nicolas Nabokov: A Life in Freedom and Music.* Oxford: Oxford University Press, 2015.

Godwin, Joscelyn. "The Music of Henry Cowell." PhD diss., Cornell University, 1969.

Goehr, Lydia. *Elective Affinities: Musical Essays on the History of Aesthetic Theory.* New York: Columbia University Press, 2008.

Gold, Edward Michael. *By Franz Lehár—The Complete Cosmopolitan.* London: Glocken Verlag Limited, 1995.

Gold, Sylviane. "Cultured Choreography." *Dance Magazine* (31 January 2016).

Golden, Arthur. *Memoirs of a Geisha.* New York: Vintage, 1999.

Goldman, Richard Franko. "Music for the Army." *Modern Music* 20, no. 1 (November-December 1942): 8–12.

Goldmark, Daniel. *Tunes for 'Toons: Music and the Hollywood Cartoon.* Berkeley: University of California Press, 2005.

Goldmark, Daniel. "Creating Desire on Tin Pan Alley." *Musical Quarterly* 90, no. 2 (2007): 197–229.

Goose, Benjamin. "The Opera of the Film? Eugen d'Albert's *Der Golem.*" *Cambridge Opera Journal* 19, no. 2 (2007): 139–166.

Gorbman, Claudia. *Unheard Melodies: Narrative Film Music.* Bloomington: Indiana University Press, 1987.

Gorbman, Claudia. "Scoring the Indian: Music in the Liberal Western." In *Western Music and Its Others: Difference, Representation, and Appropriation in Music,* edited by Georgina Born and David Hesmondhalgh, 234–253. Berkeley: University of California Press, 2000.

Gordon, Ingrid Grete. "Drums along the Pacific: The Influence of Asian Music on the Early Percussion Ensemble Music of Henry Cowell, John Cage, and Lou Harrison." DMA diss., University of Illinois at Urbana-Champaign, January 2000.

Gordon, Joanne. *Art Isn't Easy: The Achievement of Stephen Sondheim.* Carbondale: Southern Illinois University Press, 1990.

Grainger, Percy. "Is Music Universal?" *New York Times,* 2 July 1933, X4.

Greene, Evarts Boutell. *A New-Englander in Japan: Daniel Crosby Greene.* Boston and New York: Houghton Mifflin, 1927.

Greene, Victor R. *A Singing Ambivalence: American Immigrants between Old World and New, 1830–1930.* Kent, OH: Kent State University Press, 2004.

Greenwald, Helen M. "Realism on the Opera Stage: Belasco, Puccini, and the California Sunset." In *Opera in Context: Essays on Historical Staging from the Late Renaissance to the Time of Puccini,* edited by Mark A. Radice, 279–296. Portland, OR: Amadeus Press, 1998.

Greenwald, Helen M. "Picturing Cio-Cio-San: House, Screen, and Ceremony in Puccini's *Madama Butterfly.*" *Cambridge Opera Journal* 12, no. 3 (2000): 237–259.

Greenwald, Helen M. "Issues of Authenticity in Two Films of Puccini's *Madama Butterfly*: Ponnelle (1974) and Mitterrand (1995)." In *Das Musiktheater in den audiovisuellen Medien,* edited by Peter Csobádi et al., 295–305. Anif/Salzburg: Verlag Mueller-Speiser, 2001.

Greey, Edward. *Young Americans in Japan.* Introduction by Charles B. Wordell. London: Ganesha Publishing, 2001.

Griffis, William Elliot. *The Mikado's Empire.* New York: Harper and Brothers, 1876.

Griffis, William Elliot. *In the Mikado's Service: A Story of Two Battle Summers in China.* Boston and Chicago: W. A. Wilde, 1901. Reprinted London: Ganesha Publishing, 2001.

Griffiths, Paul. *Olivier Messiaen and the Music of Time*. Ithaca, NY: Cornell University Press, 1985.

Grimshaw, Jeremy. *Draw a Straight Line and Follow It: The Music and Mysticism of La Monte Young*. Oxford: Oxford University Press, 2011.

Groos, Arthur. "Lieutenant F. B. Pinkerton: Problems in the Genesis of an Operatic Hero." *Italica* 64, no. 4 (winter 1987): 654–675.

Groos, Arthur. "Return of the Native: Japan in *Madama Butterfly*/*Madama Butterfly* in Japan." *Cambridge Opera Journal* 1, no. 2 (1989): 167–194.

Groos, Arthur. "Madame Butterfly: The Story." *Cambridge Opera Journal* 3, no. 2 (July 1991): 125–158.

Groos, Arthur. "Lieutenant F. B. Pinkerton: Problems in the Genesis and Performance of *Madama Butterfly*." In *The Puccini Companion*, edited by William Weaver and Simonetta Puccini, 169–201. New York: W. W. Norton, 1994.

Groos, Arthur. "Cio-Cio-San and Sadayakko: Japanese Music-Theater in *Madama Butterfly*." *Monumenta Nipponica* 54, no. 1 (spring 1999): 41–73.

Groos, Arthur, and Virgilio Bernardoni, eds. *Madama Butterfly: l'orientalismo di fine secolo, l'approccio pucciniano, la ricezione*. Firenze: Leo S. Olschki Editore, 2008.

Grover-Friedlander, Michal. "'The Phantom of the Opera': The Lost Voice of Opera in Silent Film." *Cambridge Opera Journal* 11, no. 2 (1999): 179–192.

Grover-Friedlander, Michal. *Vocal Apparitions: The Attraction of Cinema to Opera*. Princeton, NJ: Princeton University Press, 2005.

Grubb, Kevin. "Specifically Pacific." *Dance Magazine* (January 1985): 74.

Gunter, Archibald Clavering. *My Japanese Prince*. New York: Home Publishing Co., 1904.

Guterson, David. *Snow Falling on Cedars*. New York: Vintage Books, 1995.

Guth, Christine M. E. *Longfellow's Tattoos: Tourism, Collecting, and Japan*. Seattle: University of Washington Press, 2004.

Guthrie, Kate. "Propaganda Music in Second World War Britain: John Ireland's Epic March." *Journal of the Royal Musical Association* 139, no. 1 (2014): 137–175.

Gutknecht, Dieter. "Stockhausen und Japan." In *"Lux Oriente": Begegnungen der Kulturen in der Musikforschung, Festschrift Robert Günther zum 65. Geburtstag*, edited by Klaus Wolfgang Niemöller, Uwe Pätzold, and Kyo-chul Chung, 271–284. Kölner Beiträge zur Musikforschung 188. Kassel: Gustav Bosse, 1995.

Gwynne, Anna Nalini. "India in the English Musical Imagination, 1890–1940." PhD diss, University of California–Berkeley, 2003.

Hadley, Rollin van, ed. *The Letters of Bernard Berenson and Isabella Stewart Gardner: 1887–1924*. Boston: Northeastern University Press, 1987.

Hajduk, John C. "Tin Pan Alley on the March: Popular Music, World War II, and the Quest for a Great War Song." *Popular Music and Society* 26, no. 4 (December 2003): 497–512.

Hall, Francis. *Japan through American Eyes: The Journal of Francis Hall, Kanagawa, and Yokohama, 1859–1866*. Edited and annotated by F. G. Notehelfer. Princeton, NJ: Princeton University Press, 1992.

Hamberlin, Larry. "American Popular Songs on Operatic Topics, 1901–1921." PhD diss., Brandeis University, 2004.

Hamberlin, Larry. "Visions of Salome: The Femme Fatale in American Popular Songs before 1920." *Journal of the American Musicological Society* 59, no. 3 (fall 2006): 631–696.

Hamberlin, Larry. *Tin Pan Opera: Operatic Novelty Songs in the Ragtime Era*. New York: Oxford University Press, 2011.

Hamm, Charles. *Yesterdays: Popular Song in America*. New York: W. W. Norton, 1979.

Hamm, Charles. *Irving Berlin: Songs from the Melting Pot: The Formative Years, 1907–1914*. New York: Oxford University Press, 1997.

Hammond, Phil, ed. *Cultural Difference, Media Memories: Anglo-American Images of Japan*. London and Washington, DC: Cassell, 1997.

Han, Arar, and John Hsu, eds. *Asian American X: An Intersection of 21st Century Asian American Voices*. Ann Arbor: University of Michigan Press, 2004.

Hanson, Patricia King, and Amy Dunkleberger, eds. *American Film Institute Catalog of Motion Pictures Produced in the United States: Feature Films, 1941–1950*. Berkeley: University of California Press, 1999.

Hanson, Patricia King, and Alan Gevinson, eds. *Meet Frank Capra: A Catalog of His Work*. Palo Alto, CA: Stanford Theatre Foundation; Los Angeles: National Center for Film and Video Preservation, 1990.

Hara, Kunio. "Puccini's Use of Japanese Melodies in *Madama Butterfly*." MM thesis, University of Cincinnati, 2003.

Harich-Schneider, Eta. "The Present Condition of Japanese Court Music." *Musical Quarterly* 39, no. 1 (January 1953): 49–74.

Harich-Schneider, Eta. *The Rhythmical Patterns in Gagaku and Bugaku*. Leiden: Brill, 1954.

Harich-Schneider, Eta. "Abstracts: Regional Folk Songs and Itinerant Minstrels in Japan." *Journal of the American Musicological Society* 10, no. 2 (1957), 132–133.

Harich-Schneider, Eta. *A History of Japanese Music*. London: Oxford University Press, 1973.

Harley, James. *Xenakis: His Life in Music*. New York: Routledge, 2004.

Harris, Charles K. *How to Write a Popular Song*. New York: Charles K. Harris, 1906.

Harris, Neil. "All the World a Melting Pot? Japan at American Fairs, 1876–1904." In *Mutual Images: Essays in American-Japanese Relations*, edited by Akira Iriye, 24–54. Cambridge, MA: Harvard University Press, 1975.

Harrison, Lou. "Refreshing the Auditory Perception." In *Music—East and West: Report on 1961 Tokyo East-West Music Encounter Conference*. Edited and published by the Executive Committee for 1961 Tokyo East-West Music Encounter, 141–143. Tokyo, 1961.

Harrison, Lou. "Learning from Henry." In *The Whole World of Music: A Henry Cowell Symposium*, edited by David Nicholls, 161–168. Amsterdam: Harwood Academic Publishers, 1997.

Hartung, Philip T. "Eastward Ho!" *Commonweal* 67 (13 December 1957): 287–288.

Haskins, Rob. "On John Cage's Late Music, Analysis, and the Model of Renga in *Two²*." *American Music* 27, no. 3 (fall 2009): 327–355.

Haskins, Rob. *John Cage*. London: Reaktion Books, 2012.

Haskins, Rob. "Aspects of Zen Buddhism as an Analytical Context for John Cage's Chance Music." *Contemporary Music Review* 33, nos. 5–6 (2014): 616–629.

Hayakawa, Sessue. *Zen Showed Me the Way*. Edited by Croswell Bowen. Indianapolis and New York: Bobbs-Merrill, 1960.

Hayward, Philip. "Introduction: The Cocktail Shift: Aligning Musical Exotica." In *Widening the Horizon: Exoticism in Post-War Popular Music*, edited by Philip Hayward, 1–18. Sydney: John Libbey, 1999.

Hayward, Philip, ed. *Widening the Horizon: Exoticism in Post-War Popular Music*. Sydney: John Libbey, 1999.

Head, Matthew. "Musicology on Safari: Orientalism and the Spectre of Postcolonial Theory." *Music Analysis* 22, nos. 1–2 (2003): 211–230.

Hearn, Lafcadio. *Glimpses of Unfamiliar Japan*. 2 vols. Boston and New York: Houghton, Mifflin, 1894.

Hearn, Lafcadio. *Gleanings in Buddha-Fields: Studies of Hand and Soul in the Far East*. Boston and New York: Houghton, Mifflin, 1897.

Hearn, Lafcadio. *Japan: An Attempt at Interpretation*. New York: Macmillan, 1904.

Hearn, Lafcadio. *Kwaidan*. Boston: Houghton, Mifflin, 1904.

Hearn, Lafcadio. "Mosquitoes." In Lafcadio Hearn, *Kwaidan: Stories and Studies of Strange Things*. Boston: Houghton, Mifflin, 1904.

Hearn, Lafcadio. *Exotics and Retrospectives*. Boston: Little, Brown, 1905.

Hearn, Lafcadio. *The Japanese Letters of Lafcadio Hearn*. Edited by Elizabeth Bisland. Boston and New York: Houghton Mifflin, 1910.

Hearn, Lafcadio. *Diaries and Letters*. Translated by R. Tanabe. Tokyo: Hokuseido, 1920.

Hearn, Lafcadio. *Insect-Musicians and Other Stories and Sketches*. Compiled with notes by Jun Tanaka. Tokyo: Kairyo-Do Press, 1930.

Hearn, Lafcadio. *Kokoro: Hints and Echoes of Japanese Inner Life*. Boston and Rutland, VT: Tuttle Publishing, 1972.

Heifetz, Robin J. "East-West Synthesis in Japanese Composition: 1950–1970." *Journal of Musicology* 3, no. 4 (fall 1984): 443–455.

Heifetz, Robin J. "European Influence upon Japanese Instrumental and Vocal Media: 1946–1977." *Music Review* 47, no. 1 (February 1986): 29–43.

Henning, Joseph M. *Outposts of Civilization: Race, Religion, and the Formative Years of American-Japanese Relations*. New York: New York University Press, 2000.

Hicks, Michael. "The Imprisonment of Henry Cowell." *Journal of the American Musicological Society* 44, no. 1 (spring 1991): 92–119.

Hicks, Michael. *Henry Cowell: Bohemian*. Urbana and Chicago: University of Illinois Press, 2002.

Higashi, Sumiko. "Ethnicity, Class, and Gender in Film: DeMille's *The Cheat*." In *Unspeakable Images: Ethnicity and the American Cinema*, edited by Lester D. Friedman, 112–139. Urbana: University of Illinois Press, 1991.

Higashi, Sumiko. *Cecil B. DeMille and American Culture: The Silent Era*. Berkeley: University of California Press, 1994.

Higashi, Sumiko. "Touring the Orient with Lafcadio Hearn and Cecil B. DeMille: Highbrow versus Lowbrow in a Consumer Culture." In *Birth of Whiteness: Race and the Emergence of US Cinema*, edited by Daniel Bernardi, 329–353. New Brunswick, NJ: Rutgers University Press, 1996.

Higgins, Dick, ed. *Essential Cowell: Selected Writings on Music by Henry Cowell 1921–1964*. Kingston, NY: McPherson and Company, 2002.

Hildreth, Richard. *Japan as It Was and Is*. Boston: Phillips, Sampson and Co., 1855.

Hill, Peter, and Nigel Simeone. *Messiaen*. New Haven, CT: Yale University Press, 2005.

Hipsher, Edward Ellsworth. *American Opera and Its Composers*. Philadelphia: Theodore Presser, 1927.

Hirano, Kyoko. *Mr. Smith Goes to Tokyo: Japanese Cinema under the American Occupation, 1945–1952*. Washington, DC: Smithsonian Institution Press, 1992.

Hirschhorn, Clive. "Will Sondheim Succeed in Being Genuinely Japanese?" *New York Times*, 4 January 1976, D1, D5.

Hisama, Ellie M. "Postcolonialism on the Make: The Music of John Mellencamp, David Bowie, and John Zorn." *Popular Music* 12, no. 2 (1993): 91–104.

Hisama, Ellie M. "The Cultural Work of *Miss Saigon*: A Postcolonial Critique." In *Popular Music: Intercultural Interpretations*, edited by Tôru Mitsui, 17–25. Kanazawa, Japan: Graduate Program in Music, Kanazawa University, 1998.

Hisama, Ellie M. "John Zorn and the Postmodern Condition." In *Locating East Asia in Western Art Music*, edited by Yayoi Uno Everett and Frederick Lau, 72–84. Middletown, CT: Wesleyan University Press, 2004.

Hisama, Ellie M. "'We're All Asian Really': Hip Hop's Afro-Asian Crossings." In *Critical Minded: New Approaches to Hip-Hop Studies*, edited by Ellie M. Hisama and Evan Rapport, 1–21. Brooklyn: Institute for Studies in American Music, 2005.

Hischak, Thomas S. *The American Musical Theatre Song Encyclopedia*. Westport, CT: Greenwood Press, 1995.

Ho, Fred. *Wicked Theory, Naked Practice: A Fred Ho Reader*, edited by Diane C. Fujino. Minneapolis: University of Minnesota Press, 2009.

Holman, Russell. *The Cheat*. Based on a story by Hector Turnbull. New York: Grosset and Dunlap, 1923.

Hoobler, Dorothy, and Thomas Hoobler. *The Japanese American Family Album*. New York: Oxford University Press, 1996.

hooks, bell. *Black Looks: Race and Representation*. Boston: South End Press, 1992.

Horowitz, Mark Eden. "The Score: Tender, Funny, and Highly Dramatic." *Sondheim Review* 4, no. 4 (spring 1998): 24–26.

Horowitz, Mark Eden. *Sondheim on Music: Minor Details and Major Decisions*. 2nd ed. Lanham, MD: The Scarecrow Press, 2010.

Hosley, William. *The Japan Idea: Art and Life in Victorian America*. Hartford, CT: Wadsworth Atheneum, 1990.

Hosokawa, Shūhei. "Soy Sauce Music: Haruomi Hosono and Japanese Self-Orientalism." In *Widening the Horizon: Exoticism in Post-War Popular Music*, edited by Philip Hayward, 114–144. Sydney: John Libbey, 1999.

Hosokawa, Shūhei. "Blacking Japanese: Experiencing Otherness from Afar." In *Popular Music Studies*, edited by David Hesmondhalgh and Keith Negus, 223–237. London: Arnold, 2002.

House, Edward H. *Japanese Episodes*. Boston: James R. Osgood and Co., 1881.

Houston, Jeanne Wakatsuki, and James D. Houston. *Farewell to Manzanar*. New York: Bantam Books, 1973.

Hovhaness, Alan. "Thoughts on East-West Music." In *Essays in Ethnomusicology: A Birthday Offering for Lee Hye-Ku*, 367–370. Seoul: The Korean Musicological Society, 1969.

Hovland, Carl I., Arthur A. Lumsdaine, and Fred D. Sheffield. *Experiments on Mass Communication*. Princeton, NJ: Princeton University Press, 1949.

"How to Tell Your Friends from the Japs." *Time*, 22 December 1941, 33.

Howard, John Tasker. *Emerson Whithorne*. New York: Carl Fischer, Inc., 1929.

Howe, Sondra Wieland. "Luther Whiting Mason: Contributions to Music Education in Nineteenth-century America and Japan." PhD diss., University of Minnesota, 1988.

Howe, Sondra Wieland. "Women Music Educators in Japan during the Meiji Period." *Bulletin of the Council for Research in Music Education* 119 (winter 1993–1994): 101–109.

Howe, Sondra Wieland. *Luther Whiting Mason: International Music Educator*. Warren, MI: Harmonie Park Press, 1997.

Hsu, Dolores M. *The Henry Eichheim Collection of Oriental Instruments: A Western Musician Discovers a New World of Sound*. Santa Barbara, CA: The University Art Museum, 1984.

Hsu, Hua. "Pale Fire: Is Whiteness a Privilege or a Plight?" *The New Yorker* (25 July 2016): 63–66.

Huang, Yunte. *Transpacific Displacement: Ethnography, Translation, and Intertextual Travel in Twentieth-century American Literature*. Berkeley: University of California Press, 2002.

Hubbert, Julie. "Race, War, Music and the Problem of *One Tenth of Our Nation* (1940)." In *Music and Sound in Documentary Film*, edited by Holly Rogers, 56–73. New York: Routledge, 2015.

Huffman, James L. *A Yankee in Meiji Japan: The Crusading Journalist Edward H. House*. Lanham, MD: Rowman and Littlefield Publishers, 2003.

Hughes, David W. "Japanese 'New Folk Songs,' Old and New." *Asian Music* 22, no. 1 (fall/winter 1990/1991): 1–49.

Hughes, David W. "'Esashi Oiwake' and the Beginnings of Modern Japanese Folk Song." *The World of Music* 34, no. 1 (1992): 35–56.

Hughes, Rupert. *Famous American Composers*. Boston: L. C. Page and Co., 1900.

Hung, Eric. "Sounds of Asian American Trauma and Cultural Trauma: Jazz Reflections on the Japanese Internment." *MUSICultures* 39, no. 2 (2012): 1–29.

Huyssen, Andreas. *After the Great Divide: Modernism, Mass Culture, Postmodernism*. Bloomington and Indianapolis: Indiana University Press, 1986.

Hwang, David Henry. *M. Butterfly*. New York: New American Library, 1988.

Hwang, David Henry. "A New Musical by Rodgers and Hwang." *New York Times*, 13 October 2002, AR1, AR16.

Hyde, Mable. *Jingles from Japan: As Set Forth by the Chinks*. Illustrated by Helen Hyde. Tokyo: Methodist Publishing House, 1907.

Information Handbook for 1961 Tokyo East-West Music Encounter Conference. Tokyo, 1961.

Ingólfsson, Árni Heimir. "Drawing New Boundaries: Björk's Expanding Territory." *Nordic Sounds* 4 (December 2005): 14–17.

Ingram, J. S. *Centennial Exposition Described and Illustrated, Being a Concise and Graphic Description of This Grand Enterprise Commemorative of the First Centenary of American Independence*. Philadelphia: Hubbard Bros., 1876.

Irlandini, Luigi Antonio. "Messiaen's 'Gagaku." *Perspectives of New Music* 48, no. 2 (summer 2010): 193–207.

Isaku, Patia R. *Mountain Storm, Pine Breeze: Folk Songs in Japan*. Tucson: University of Arizona Press, 1981.

Isherwood, Charles. "Review: 'Allegiance,' a Musical History Lesson about Interned Japanese-Americans." *New York Times*, 8 November 2015, https://www.nytimes.com/2015/11/09/the-ater/review-allegiance-a-musical-history-lesson-about-interned-japanese-americans.html.

Ito, Yutaka. "'Words Quite Fail': The Life and Thought of Ernest Francisco Fenollosa." PhD diss., Rutgers, The State University of New Jersey, 2002.

Iwabuchi, Koichi. "Complicit Exoticism: Japan and Its Other." *Continuum: Australian Journal of Media and Cultural Studies* 8, no. 2 (1994): 49–82.

Iwabuchi, Koichi. *Recentering Globalization: Popular Culture and Japanese Transnationalism*. Durham, NC, and London: Duke University Press, 2002.

Iwamoto, Yoshikazu. "The Potential of the *Shakuhachi* in Contemporary Music." *Contemporary Music Review* 8, no. 2 (1993): 5–44.

Iwamura, Jane Naomi. *Virtual Orientalism: Asian Religions and American Popular Culture*. Oxford: Oxford University Press, 2011.

Jackson, Carl. "The Counterculture Looks East: Beat Writers and Asian Religion." *American Studies* 29, no. 1 (1988): 51–70.

Jackson, Travis A. "Tourist Point of View? Musics of the World and Ellington's Suites." *The Musical Quarterly* 96, nos. 3–4 (1 December 2013): 513–540.

Jairazbhoy, Nazir A., and Sue Carole De Vale, eds. *Selected Reports in Ethnomusicology. Volume VI: Asian Music in North America*. Los Angeles: University of California, 1985.

"Japan Entering the Commercial World" (from *The Economist*), *Living Age* 42, no. 531 (22 July 1854): 189–190.

"Japanese Music and Dance Combined in One Program." *Rafu Shimpo*, 12 August 1937: 1.

Japonisme in Art: An International Symposium. Edited by the Society for the Study of Japonisme. Tokyo: Committee for the Year 2001, 1980.

Jasen, David A. *Tin Pan Alley: The Composers, the Songs, the Performers, and Their Times*. New York: Donald I. Fine, 1988.

Jenkins, Jennifer R. "'Say It with Firecrackers': Defining the 'War Musical' of the 1940s." *American Music* 19, no. 3 (fall 2001): 315–339.

Joe, Jeongwon. "Opera on Film, Film in Opera: Postmodern Implications of the Cinematic Influence on Opera." PhD diss., Northwestern University, 1998.

Joe, Jeongwon, and Rose Theresa, eds., *Between Opera and Cinema*. New York: Routledge, 2002.

Johnson, Carolyn Schiller. "Performing Ethnicity: Performance Events in Chicago, 1893–1996." PhD diss., University of Chicago, 1998.

Johnson, Robert Sherlaw. *Messiaen*. Berkeley: University of California Press, 1989.

Johnson, Rossiter, ed. *A History of the World's Columbian Exposition*. New York: D. Appleton, 1897.

Johnson, Sheila K. *The Japanese through American Eyes*. Stanford, CA: Stanford University Press, 1988.

Johnson, Tom. "Ralph Samuelson, Shakuhachi Master." *Village Voice*, 25 July 1977, 53.

Johnson, Wayne David. "A Study of the Piano Works of Alan Hovhaness." DMA thesis, University of Cincinnati, 1987.

Johnston, James D., *China and Japan: Being a Narrative of the Cruise of the US Steam-Frigate Powhatan, in the Years 1857, '58, '59, and '60*. Philadelphia: Charles Desilver, 1860.

Jones, Andrew F. *Yellow Music: Media Culture and Colonial Modernity in the Chinese Jazz Age*. Durham, NC, and London: Duke University Press, 2001.

Jones, Dorothy B. *The Portrayal of China and India on the American Screen, 1896–1955*. Cambridge: Massachusetts Institute of Technology, 1955.

Jones, Gavin. *Strange Talk: The Politics of Dialect Literature in Gilded Age America*. Berkeley: University of California Press, 1999.

Jones, John Bush. *The Songs That Fought the War: Popular Music and the Home Front, 1939–1945*. Waltham, MA: Brandeis University Press, 2006.

Jones, Joseph E. "The Exotic and Eclectic in Bear McCreary's Television and Video Game Scores." *Music Research Forum* 30 (2015): 1–21.

Jones, Stanleigh. "Puccini among the Puppets: *Madame Butterfly* on the Japanese Puppet Stage." *Monumenta Nipponica* 38, no. 2 (1983): 163–174.

Jowitt, Deborah. *Jerome Robbins: His Life, His Theater, His Dance.* New York: Simon and Schuster, 2004.

Joyce, Brooke. "A Broadway Hybrid: Stephen Sondheim's *Pacific Overtures.*" In *Musicology and Globalization: Proceedings of the International Congress in Shizuoka 2002,* edited by Yoshio Tozawa, Tatsuhiko Itoh, Keiichi Kubota, and Yasuhiko Mori, 328–332. Tokyo: The Musicological Society of Japan, 2004.

Kacian, Jim, Philip Rowland, and Allan Burns, eds. *Haiku in English: The First Hundred Years.* New York: W. W. Norton, 2013.

Kajikawa, Loren. "The Sound of Struggle: Black Revolutionary Nationalism and Asian American Jazz." In *Jazz/Not Jazz: The Music and Its Boundaries,* edited by David Ake, Charles Hiroshi Garret, and Daniel Ira Goldmark, 190–218. Berkeley: University of California Press, 2012.

Kakinuma, Toshie. "Composing for an Ancient Instrument That Has Lost Its 'Tradition': Lou Harrison's *Set for Four Haisho and Percussion.*" *Perspectives of New Music* 49, no. 2 (summer 2011): 232–263.

Kane, Kathryn. *Visions of War: Hollywood Combat Films of World War II.* Ann Arbor, MI: UMI Research Press, 1982.

Kang, Laura Hyun Yi. *Compositional Subjects: Enfiguring Asian/American Women.* Durham, NC: Duke University Press, 2002.

Kanno, Takeshi. *Creation-Dawn (A Vision Drama): Evening Talks and Meditations.* Fruitvale, CA: by the author, 1913.

Kaplan, Caren. "'Getting to Know You': Travel, Gender, and the Politics of Representation in *Anna and the King of Siam* and *The King and I.*" In *Late Imperial Culture,* edited by Román de la Campa, E. Ann Kaplan, and Michael Sprinker, 33–52. London: Verso, 1995.

Kaplan, E. Ann. *Looking for the Other: Feminism, Film, and the Imperial Gaze.* New York: Routledge, 1997.

Kaplan, Fred. "Horn of Plenty: The Composer Who Knows No Boundaries." *The New Yorker* (14 June 1999): 84–90.

Kaplan, Wendy. *"The Art That Is Life": The Arts & Crafts Movement in America, 1875–1920.* Boston: Little, Brown and Co., 1987.

Karlin, Fred. *Listening to Movies: The Film Lover's Guide to Film Music.* New York: Schirmer Books, 1994.

Karlin, Fred, and Rayburn Wright. *On the Track: A Guide to Contemporary Film Scoring.* New York: Schirmer Books, 1990.

Kastendieck, Miles. Review of Kimio Eto's Carnegie Hall recital. *New York Journal-American* (6 October 1961).

Kawaguchi, Yoko. *Butterfly's Sisters: The Geisha in Western Culture.* New Haven and London: Yale University Press, 2010.

Kawashima, Hiromi. "Travel Sketches of Lafcadio Hearn." In *Centennial Essays on Lafcadio Hearn,* edited by Kenji Zenimoto, 162–172. Matsue, Japan: The Hearn Society, 1996.

Keating, John M. *With General Grant in the East.* Philadelphia: J. B. Lippincott, 1879.

Keats, Mar. "Ear to the Ground." *Sports Journal* (9 May 1947).

Keene, Donald. *Nō: The Classical Theatre of Japan.* Tokyo: Kodansha International, 1966.

Keil, Charles, and Steven Feld. *Music Grooves: Essays and Dialogues.* Chicago: University of Chicago Press, 1994.

Keister, Jay. "The *Shakuhachi* as a Spiritual Tool: A Japanese Buddhist Instrument in the West." *Asian Music* 35, no. 2 (2004): 99–131.

Keister, Jay. "Seeking Authentic Experience: Spirituality in the Western Appropriation of Asian Music." *The World of Music* 47, no. 3 (2005): 35–53.

Kellogg, Clara Louise. "Some Japanese Melodies," *Scribner's Monthly* 14, no. 4 (August 1877): 504–506.

Kelsky, Karen. *Women on the Verge: Japanese Women, Western Dreams*. Durham, NC: Duke University Press, 2001.

Kelts, Roland. *Japanamerica: How Japanese Pop Culture Has Invaded the US*. New York: Palgrave Macmillan, 2007.

Kerouac, Jack. *Dharma Bums*. New York: Penguin, 1986. First published 1958.

Kerouac, Jack. *Some of the Dharma*. New York: Viking, 1997.

Kerr, Russell. "50 Years of Cowell . . . at 65." *The Music Magazine and Musical Courier* 164, no. 4 (May 1962): 10–12.

Kerr, Walter. "'Pacific Overtures' Is neither East nor West." *New York Times*, 18 January 1976, D1, D5.

King, John. "White House Sees Hollywood Role in War on Terrorism" (CNN.com, 8 November 2001).

Kinkle, Roger D. *The Complete Encyclopedia of Popular Music and Jazz, 1900–1950*. New Rochelle, NY: Arlington House, 1974.

Kinnear, Tyler. "Alan Hovhaness and the Creation of the 'Modern Free Noh Play.'" MA thesis, University of Oregon, 2009.

Kipling, Rudyard. *Kipling's Japan: Collected Writings*. Edited by Hugh Cortazzi and George Webb. London and Atlantic Highlands, NJ: The Athlone Press, 1988.

Kirihara, Donald. "The Accepted Idea Displaced: Stereotype and Sessue Hayakawa." In *The Birth of Whiteness: Race and the Emergence of US Cinema*, edited by Daniel Bernardi, 81–99. New Brunswick, NJ: Rutgers University Press, 1996.

Kirkbride, Ronald. *A Girl Named Tamiko*. New York: Frederick Fell, 1959.

Kivy, Peter. *Music, Language, and Cognition: And Other Essays in the Aesthetics of Music*. Oxford: Clarendon Press, 2007.

Klein, Christina. *Cold War Orientalism: Asia in the Middlebrow Imagination, 1945–1961*. Berkeley: University of California Press, 2003.

Kleinedler, Clare, and Michael Goldberg. "Weezer Revealed: The Rivers Cuomo Interview." *Addicted to Noise* (December 1996).

Klosty, James. *John Cage Was*. Middletown, CT: Wesleyan University Press, 2014.

Knapp, Raymond. *The American Musical and the Formation of National Identity*. Princeton, NJ, and Oxford: Princeton University Press, 2005.

Knapp, Raymond. "Marking Time in *Pacific Overtures*: Reconciling East, West, and History within the Theatrical Now of a Broadway Musical." In *Musicological Identities: Essays in Honor of Susan McClary*, edited by Steven Baur, Raymond Knapp, and Jacqueline Warwick, 163–176. Burlington, VT: Ashgate, 2008.

Knight, Arthur. "Dance in the Movies: *Sayonara*." *Dance Magazine* (December 1957):14–15, 81.

Knight, Roderic. "The Shakuhachi Comes to Oberlin." *Oberlin Alumni Magazine* (1984): 17–20. Reprinted in Dan E. Mayers, ed., *The Annals of the International Shakuhachi Society: Volume 1*. Wadhurst, Sussex: The Society, n.d. [1990].

Knox, Thomas W. *The Boy Travellers in the Far East, Part First: Adventures of Two Youths in a Journey to Japan and China*. New York: Harper and Brothers, 1879.

Kodama, Sanehide. *American Poetry and Japanese Culture*. Hamden, CT: Archon Books, 1984.

Koizumi, Setsuko. *Reminiscences of Lafcadio Hearn*. Boston and New York: Houghton Mifflin, 1918.

Komiya, Toyotaka. *Japanese Music and Drama in the Meiji Era*. Translated and adapted by Edward G. Seidensticker and Donald Keene. Tokyo: Ōbunsha, 1956.

Koozin, Timothy. "Parody and Ironic Juxtaposition in Toru Takemitsu's Music for the Film, *Rising Sun* (1993)." *Journal of Film Music* 3, no. 1 (2010): 65–78.

Koppes, Clayton R. and Gregory D. Black. *Hollywood Goes to War: How Politics, Profits, and Propaganda Shaped World War II Movies*. New York: Free Press, 1987.

Korabelnikova, Ludmila. *Alexander Tcherepnin: The Saga of a Russian Emigré Composer*. Translated by Anna Winestein. Edited by Sue-Ellen Hershman-Tcherepnin. Bloomington and Indianapolis: Indiana University Press, 2008.

Kowner, Rotem. *From White to Yellow: The Japanese in European Racial Thought, 1300–1735.* Montreal and Kingston: McGill–Queen's University Press, 2014.

Kracauer, Siegfried. *From Caligari to Hitler: A Psychological History of the German Film.* Princeton, NJ: Princeton University Press, 1947.

Kracauer, Siegfried. "Opera on the Screen." *Film Culture* 1, no. 2 (1955): 19–21.

Kracauer, Siegfried. *Theory of Film: The Redemption of Physical Reality.* New York: Oxford University Press, 1960.

Kramer, Jonathan D. "The Nature and Origins of Musical Postmodernism." In *Postmodern Music/Postmodern Thought*, edited by Judy Lochhead and Joseph Auner, 13–26. New York: Routledge, 2002.

Krehbiel, Henry Edward. "The Tragic Outcome of 'Madame Butterfly.'" *New York Tribune*, 22 October 1916, C5.

Krehbiel, Henry Edward. *A Second Book of Operas: Their Histories, Their Plots, and Their Music.* New York: Macmillan, 1917.

Kristof, Nicholas D. "Japan Weighs Formal Status for Its Flag and Anthem." *New York Times*, 28 March 1999, sec. 1, p. 4.

Kurashige, Lon. *Japanese American Celebration and Conflict: A History of Ethnic Identity and Festival, 1934–1990.* Berkeley: University of California Press, 2002.

Kyrova, Magda, ed. *The Ear Catches the Eye: Music in Japanese Prints.* Leiden: Hotei Publishing, 2000.

La Farge, John. *An Artist's Letters from Japan.* New York: The Century Co., 1897. First published 1890.

Ladd, George Trumbull. *Rare Days in Japan.* New York: Dodd, Mead, 1910.

LaFeber, Walter. *The Clash: US-Japanese Relations throughout History.* New York: W. W. Norton, 1998.

Laidlaw, Christine Wallace, ed. *Charles Appleton Longfellow: Twenty Months in Japan, 1871–1873.* Cambridge, MA: Friends of the Longfellow House, 1998.

Lam, Joseph S. C. "Embracing 'Asian American Music' as an Heuristic Device." *Journal of Asian American Studies* 2, no. 1 (1999): 29–60.

Lambourne, Lionel. *Japonisme: Cultural Crossings between Japan and the West.* New York: Phaidon Press, 2005.

Lancaster, Clay. *The Japanese Influence in America.* New York: Abbeville Press, 1983.

Lancefield, Robert Charles. "Hearing Orientality in (White) America, 1900–1930." PhD diss., Wesleyan University, 2005.

Lang, Nico. "Settling the Katy Perry Controversy: 'Yellowface' Is Not Beautiful," *Los Angeles Times*, 29 November 2013, https://www.latimes.com/opinion/opinion-la/la-ol-katy-perry-american-music-awards-yellowface-20131127-story.html.

Langenkamp, Harm. "(Dis)Connecting Cultures, Creating Dreamworlds: Musical 'East-West' Diplomacy in the Cold War and the War on Terror." In *Divided Dreamworlds?: The Cultural Cold War in East and West*, edited by Peter Romijn, Giles Scott-Smith, and Joes Segal, 217–234. Amsterdam: Amsterdam University Press, 2012.

Lanman, Charles, ed. *The Japanese in America.* New York: New York University Publishing, 1872.

Lanza, Joseph. *Elevator Music: A Surreal History of Muzak, Easy-Listening, and Other Moodsong.* New York: St. Martin's Press, 1994.

Lapham, Claude. "Looking at Japanese Jazz." *Metronome* 52, no. 6 (June 1936): 14; 27.

Lapham, Claude. "Japan Inspires an American Composer." *The American Music Lover* 2, no. 3 (July 1936): 71, 74.

Lapham, Claude. "If You Must Go to Japan." *Metronome* 52, no. 10 (October 1936): 16, 29.

Lapham, Claude. "Popular Japanese Music." *Asia* 37, no. 12 (December 1937): 859.

Lapham, Claude. "Music of the Far East." In *Who Is Who in Music: 1941 Edition*, 523–524. Chicago: Lee Stern Press, 1940.

Larson, Kay. *Where the Heart Beats: John Cage, Zen Buddhism, and the Inner Life of Artists.* New York: The Penguin Press, 2012.

Lassetter, Leslie. "Meredith Monk: An Interview about Her Recent Opera, *Atlas*." *Contemporary Music Review* 16 (1997): 59–67.

Lawton, Thomas, and Linda Merrill. *Freer: A Legacy in Art*. Washington, DC: Smithsonian Institution, 1993.

Lears, T. J. Jackson. *No Place of Grace: Antimodernism and the Transformation of American Culture 1880–1920*. New York: Pantheon Books, 1981.

Lee, Esther Kim. *A History of Asian American Theatre*. Cambridge, UK: Cambridge University Press, 2006.

Lee, Josephine. *The Japan of Pure Invention: Gilbert and Sullivan's* The Mikado. Minneapolis: University of Minnesota Press, 2010.

Lee, Josephine, Imogene L. Lim, and Yuko Matsukawa, eds. *Re/collecting Early Asian America: Essays in Cultural History*. Philadelphia: Temple University Press, 2002.

Lee, Riley Kelley. "An American Looks at the Shakuhachi of Japan" (1 April 1986), 113–116. In Dan E. Mayers, ed., *The Annals of the International Shakuhachi Society: Volume 1*. Wadhurst, Sussex: The Society, 1993.

Lee, Robert G. *Orientals: Asian Americans in Popular Culture*. Philadelphia: Temple University Press, 1999.

Lerner, Neil. "Aaron Copland, Norman Rockwell, and the 'Four Freedoms': The Office of War Information's Vision and Sound in *The Cummington Story* (1945)." In *Aaron Copland and His World*, edited by Carol J. Oja and Judith Tick, 351–377. Princeton, NJ: Princeton University Press, 2005.

Lerner, Neil. "Reading Wagner in *Bugs Bunny Nips the Nips* (1944)." In *Wagner and Cinema*, edited by Jeongwon Joe and Sander Gilman, 210–224. Bloomington: Indiana University Press, 2010.

Lerner, Neil William. "The Classical Documentary Score in American Films of Persuasion: Contexts and Case Studies, 1936–1945." PhD diss., Duke University, 1997.

Lessem, Alan Philip. "The Émigré Experience: Schoenberg in America." In *Constructive Dissonance: Arnold Schoenberg and the Transformations of Twentieth-century Culture*, edited by Juliane Brand and Christopher Hailey, 58–68. Berkeley: University of California Press, 1997.

Leukel, Jurgen. "Puccinis kinematographische Technik." *Neue Zeitschrift fur Musik* 143, nos. 6–7 (1982): 24–26.

Levis, John, ed. *Camp Chit Chat*. Shanghai: Voice Pub. Co., 1946.

Levis, John Hazedel. *Foundations of Chinese Musical Art*. Peiping: Henri Vetch, 1936.

Levitz, Tamara. "Yoko Ono and the Unfinished Music of 'John & Yoko': Imagining Gender and Racial Equality in the Late 1960s." In *Impossible to Hold: Women and Culture in the 1960s*, edited by Avital H. Bloch and Lauri Umansky, 217–239. New York: New York University Press, 2005.

Levy, Beth E. "From Orient to Occident: Aaron Copland and the Sagas of the Prairie." In *Aaron Copland and His World*, edited by Carol J. Oja and Judith Tick, 307–349. Princeton, NJ: Princeton University Press, 2005.

Levy, Beth E. *Frontier Figures: American Music and the Mythology of the American West*. Berkeley: University of California Press, 2012.

Lieberman, Fredric, ed. "'Contemporary Japanese Music': A Lecture by John Cage." In *Locating East Asia in Western Art Music*, edited by Yayoi Uno Everett and Frederick Lau, 193–198. Middletown, CT: Wesleyan University Press, 2004.

Lichtenwanger, William. *The Music of Henry Cowell: A Descriptive Catalog*. New York: Institute for Studies in American Music, 1986.

Limbacher, James L. *Film Music: From Violins to Video*. Metuchen, NJ: Scarecrow Press, 1974.

Lindau, Elizabeth Ann. "'Mother Superior': Maternity and Creativity in the Work of Yoko Ono." *Women and Music: A Journal of Gender and Culture* 20 (2016): 57–76.

Ling, Cheong Wai. "Buddhist Temple, Shinto Shrine, and the Invisible God of *Sept Haïkaï*." In *Messiaen the Theologian*, edited by Andrew Shenton, 241–261. Farnham: Ashgate, 2010.

Ling, Cheong Wai. "Culture as Reference in the 'Gagaku' of Messiaen's Sept Haïkaï (1962)." In *Music and Its Referential Systems*, edited by Matjaž Barbo and Thomas Hochradner, 177–200. Vienna: Hollitzer Wissenschaftsverlag, 2012.

Link, Stan. "Nor the Eye Filled with Seeing: The Sound of Vision in Film." *American Music* 22, no. 1 (spring 2004): 76–90.

Lipsitz, George. *Dangerous Crossroads: Popular Music, Postmodernism, and the Poetics of Place.* London: Verso, 1994.

Little, Frances. *The House of the Misty Star: A Romance of Youth and Hope and Love in Old Japan.* New York: The Century Co., 1915.

Littlewood, Ian. *The Idea of Japan: Western Images, Western Myths.* Chicago: Ivan R. Dee, 1996.

Locke, Ralph P. "Constructing the Oriental 'Other': Saint-Saëns's *Samson et Dalila*." *Cambridge Opera Journal* 3, no. 3 (1991): 261–302.

Locke, Ralph P. "Living with Music: Isabella Stewart Gardner." In *Cultivating Music in America: Women Patrons and Activists since 1860,* edited by Locke and Cyrilla Barr, 90–121. Berkeley: University of California Press, 1997.

Locke, Ralph P. "Exoticism and Orientalism in Music: Problems for the Worldly Critic." In *Edward Said and the Work of the Critic: Speaking Truth to Power,* edited by Paul A. Bové, 257–281. Durham, NC: Duke University Press, 2000.

Locke, Ralph P. *Musical Exoticism: Images and Reflections.* Cambridge, UK: Cambridge University Press, 2009.

Locke, Ralph P. *Music and the Exotic from the Renaissance to Mozart.* Cambridge, UK: Cambridge University Press, 2015.

Locke, Ralph P., and Cyrilla Barr, eds. *Cultivating Music in America: Women Patrons and Activists since 1860.* Berkeley: University of California Press, 1997.

Loewen, Paul. *Butterfly.* New York: St. Martin's Press, 1988.

Logan, Joshua. "A Loud 'Banzai' for Brando of 'Sayonara.'" *New York Times,* 1 December 1957, 165.

Logan, Joshua. *Josh: My up and down, in and out Life.* London: W. H. Allen, 1977.

Logan, Joshua. *Movie Stars, Real People, and Me.* New York: Delacorte, 1978.

Lomanno, Mark. "Ellington's Lens as Motive Mediating: Improvising Voices in the *Far East Suite*." *Jazz Perspectives* 6, nos. 1–2 (2012): 151–177.

Long, John Luther. *Miss Cherry-Blossom of Tokyo.* Philadelphia: J. B. Lippincott, 1895.

Long, John Luther. *Madame Butterfly.* New York: The Century Co., 1903.

Long, John Luther. "A 'Madame Butterfly' of the Philippines." *The World,* 7 June 1903, 1, 5.

Lornell, Kip, and Anne K. Rasmussen, eds. *Musics of Multicultural America: A Study of Twelve Musical Communities.* New York: Schirmer Books, 1997.

Loti, Pierre. *Madame Chrysanthème.* Translated by Laura Ensor. Rutland, VT: Charles E. Tuttle, 1973.

Lovensheimer, Jim. *South Pacific: Paradise Rewritten.* Oxford: Oxford University Press, 2010.

Lowe, Lisa. *Immigrant Acts: On Asian American Cultural Politics.* Durham, NC, and London: Duke University Press, 1996.

Lowell, Amy. *Can Grande's Castle.* New York: Macmillan, 1918.

Lowell, Amy. *Pictures of the Floating World.* New York: Macmillan, 1919.

Lowell, Amy. *Selected Poems of Amy Lowell.* Edited by Melissa Bradshaw and Adrienne Munich. New Brunswick, NJ: Rutgers University Press, 2002.

Lowell, Percival. *The Soul of the Far East.* Boston and New York: Houghton, Mifflin, 1888.

Lowell, Percival. *Occult Japan, or the Way of the Gods.* Boston and New York: Houghton, Mifflin, 1894.

Lowens, Irving. "Stokowski a Triumph with the Philadelphia." *Evening Star* (Washington, DC), 29 December 1964.

Lucraft, Howard. "Tak Shindo: Hollywood Film Composers." *Crescendo and Jazz Music* 37, no. 4 (August–September 2000): 25.

Lyne, Sandra. "Fictions of Alien Identities: Cultural Cross-Dressing in Nineteenth- and Early Twentieth-Century Opera." In *Music and History: Bridging the Disciplines,* edited by Jeffrey H. Jackson and Stanley C. Pelkey, 143–162. Jackson: University of Mississippi Press, 2005.

Ma, Sheng-Mei. *The Deathly Embrace: Orientalism and Asian American Identity.* Minneapolis: University of Minnesota Press, 2000.

Mabie, Janet. "Music in the East." *Christian Science Monitor,* 2 January 1935, WM3, WM15.

MacDonald, Ranald. *Ranald MacDonald: The Narrative of His Early Life on the Columbia under the Hudson's Bay Company's Regime; of His Experiences in the Pacific Whale Fishery; and of His Great Adventure to Japan; with a Sketch of His Later Life on the Western Frontier 1824–1894.* Spokane, WA: Inland American Printing Company, 1923.

MacFarlane, Charles, *Japan: An Account, Geographical and Historical.* New York: George P. Putnam, 1852.

Maclay, Arthur Collins. *A Budget of Letters from Japan: Reminiscences of Work and Travel in Japan.* New York: A. C. Armstrong & Son, 1886.

Macomber, Ben. *The Jewel City: Its Planning and Achievement; Its Architecture, Sculpture, Symbolism, and Music; Its Gardens, Palaces, and Exhibits.* San Francisco: John H. Williams, 1915.

Maconie, Robin. *The Works of Karlheinz Stockhausen.* 2nd ed. Oxford: Clarendon Press, 1990.

Maconie, Robin. *Other Planets: The Music of Karlheinz Stockhausen.* Lanham, MD: Scarecrow Press, 2005.

Maehder, Jürgen, ed. *Esotismo e colore locale nell'opera di Puccini.* Pisa: Giardini Editori e Stampatori, 1985.

Mahling, Christoph-Hellmut. "The 'Japanese Image' in Opera, Operetta, and Instrumental Music at the End of the 19th and during the 20th Century." In *Tradition and Its Future in Music,* edited by Yosihiko Tokumaru et al., 369–378. Tokyo: Mita Press, 1991.

Maisel, Edward. *Charles T. Griffes: The Life of an American Composer.* New York: Alfred A. Knopf, 1984.

Maland, Charles J. *Frank Capra.* Boston: Twayne Publishers, 1980.

Malm, William P. *Japanese Music and Musical Instruments.* Rutland, VT: Charles E. Tuttle, 1959.

Malm, William P. "The Modern Music of Meiji Japan." In *Tradition and Modernization in Japanese Culture,* edited by Donald H. Shively, 257–300. Princeton, NJ: Princeton University Press, 1971.

Malm, William P. "Personal Approaches to the Study of Japanese Art Music." *Asian Music* 3, no. 1 (1972): 35–39.

Malm, William P. "Layers of Modern Music and Japan." *Asian Music* 4, no. 2 (1973): 3–6.

Malm, William P. "Overseas Japanese Music and Marginal Survival." In *Tradition and Its Future in Music,* edited by Yosihiko Tokumaru et al., 417–419. Tokyo: Mita Press, 1991.

Malm, William P. "Yamada Shôtarô: Japan's First Shamisen Professor." *Asian Music* 30, no. 1 (fall/winter 1998/1999): 35–76.

Manion, Martha L. *Writings about Henry Cowell: An Annotated Bibliography.* Brooklyn: Institute for Studies in American Music, 1982.

Manjiro, John. *Drifting toward the Southeast: The Story of Five Japanese Castaways.* Translated by Junya Nagakuni and Junji Kitadai. New Bedford, MA: Spinner Publications, 2003.

Manvell, Roger, and John Huntley. *The Technique of Film Music.* London: Focal Press, 1957.

March of Time: The Great Depression, Economy Blues 1935–1936. Part 2: "Tokyo!" VHS tape compilation. Nelson Entertainment, 1988.

Marchetti, Gina. *Romance and the "Yellow Peril": Race, Sex, and Discursive Strategies in Hollywood Fiction.* Berkeley: University of California Press, 1993.

Marker, Lise-Lone. *David Belasco: Naturalism in the American Theatre.* Princeton, NJ: Princeton University Press, 1975.

Marks, Martin. "Film Music: The Material, Literature, and Present State of Research." *Notes* 36, no. 2 (December 1979): 282–225.

Marks, Martin Miller. *Music and the Silent Film: Contexts and Case Studies, 1895–1924.* New York: Oxford University Press, 1997.

Marquand, John P. *Stopover: Tokyo.* Boston: Little, Brown, 1956.

Marranca, Bonnie. "Meredith Monk's Atlas of Sound: New Opera and the American Performance Tradition." In *Meredith Monk,* edited by Deborah Jowitt, 175–183. Baltimore: Johns Hopkins University Press, 1997.

Marranca, Bonnie, and Gautam Dasgupta. *Interculturalism and Performance: Writings from PAJ.* New York: PAJ Publications, 1991.

Martens, Frederick. "Folk Music in the Ballet Intime." *New Music and Church Music Review* 16, no. 191 (October 1917): 762–765.

Martens, Frederick H. "Pierre Loti: A Prose Poet of Music." *Musical Quarterly* 10, no. 1 (January 1924): 51–94.

Martin, John. "Dance: Japanese Girls." *New York Times*, 17 September 1959, 49.

Masaoka, Miya. "Koto No Tankyu (Koto Explorations)." *Institute for Studies in American Music Newsletter* 25, no. 2 (spring 1996): 8–9.

Masaoka, Miya. "Notes from a Trans-Cultural Diary." In *Arcana: Musicians on Music*, edited by John Zorn, 153–166. New York: Granary Books, 2000.

Masavisut, Nitaya, George Simson, and Larry E. Smith, eds. *Gender and Culture in Literature and Film East and West: Issues of Perception and Interpretation*. Honolulu: University of Hawai'i, 1994.

Mascarenhas, Domingos de. "Beyond Orientalism: The International Rise of Japan and the Revisions to *Madama Butterfly*." In *Art and Ideology in European Opera*, edited by Rachel Cowgill, David Cooper, and Clive Brown, 281–302. Woodbridge, UK: Boydell Press, 2010.

Mason, William M., and John A. McKinstry. *The Japanese of Los Angeles: 1869–1920*. Los Angeles: Los Angeles County Museum of Natural History, 1969.

Matossian, Nouritza. *Xenakis*. New York: Taplinger, 1986.

Matsunobu, Koji. "Spirituality as a Universal Experience of Music: A Case Study of North Americans' Approaches to Japanese Music." *Journal of Research in Music Education* 59, no. 3 (October 2011): 273–289.

May, Elizabeth. "Encounters with Japanese Music in Los Angeles." *Western Folklore* 17, no. 3 (1958): 192–195.

May, Elizabeth. *The Influence of the Meiji Period on Japanese Children's Music*. Berkeley: University of California Press, 1963.

May, Stanley. "How Fay Foster Wrote 'The Americans Come!'" *Musical America* 29, no. 7 (December 1918): 5–6.

Mayers, Dan E., ed. *The Annals of the International Shakuhachi Society: Volume 1*. Wadhurst, Sussex: The Society, 1993.

Mayers, Dan E., ed. *The Annals of the International Shakuhachi Society: Volume 2*. Wadhurst, Sussex: The Society, 2005.

McCabe, James D. *A Tour around the World by General Grant. Being a Narrative of the Incidents and Events of His Journey*. Cincinnati: Jones Brothers, 1879.

McCarten, John. "Variation on the Puccini Caper." *New Yorker* 33 (14 December 1957): 89–90.

McClary, Susan. *Conventional Wisdom: The Content of Musical Form*. Berkeley: University of California Press, 2000.

McClary, Susan. "Mounting Butterflies." In *A Vision of the Orient: Texts, Intertexts, and Contexts of Madame Butterfly*, edited by Jonathan Wisenthal, Sherrill Grace, Melinda Boyd, Brian McIlroy, and Vera Micznik, 21–35. Toronto: University of Toronto Press, 2006.

McConachie, Bruce A. "The 'Oriental' Musicals of Rodgers and Hammerstein and the US War in Southeast Asia." *Theatre Journal* 46, no. 3 (1994): 385–398.

McLane, Daisann. "Like a Geisha." *Harper's Bazaar* 3447 (February 1999): 126–135.

McLeod, Ken. "Afro-Samurai: Techno-Orientalism and Contemporary Hip Hop." *Popular Music* 32, no. 2 (May 2013): 259–275.

McPhee, Colin. "The Music Crisis in Bali Today." In *Music—East and West: Report on 1961 Tokyo East-West Music Encounter Conference*, edited and published by the Executive Committee for 1961 Tokyo East-West Music Encounter, 60–63. Tokyo, 1961.

McQuinn, Julie. "Unofficial Discourses of Gender and Sexuality at the Opéra-Comique during the Belle Epoque." PhD diss., Northwestern University, 2003.

Mead, Rita. *Henry Cowell's New Music 1925–1936: The Society, the Music Editions, and the Recordings*. Ann Arbor, MI: UMI Research Press, 1981.

Meech, Julia. *Frank Lloyd Wright and the Art of Japan: The Architect's Other Passion*. New York: Japan Society and Harry N. Abrams, 2001.

Meech, Julia, and Gabriel P. Weisberg. *Japonisme Comes to America: The Japanese Impact on the Graphic Arts 1876–1925*. New York: Harry N. Abrams, 1990.

Mellers, Wilfrid. *Singing in the Wilderness: Music and Ecology in the Twentieth Century*. Urbana: University of Illinois Press, 2001.

Mendelssohn, Peter de. *Japan's Political Warfare*. New York: Arno Press, 1972. First published London: George Allen and Unwin Ltd., 1944.

Merwin, Samuel. *Anthony the Absolute*. New York: The Century Co., 1914.

Messiaen, Olivier. *Music and Color; Conversations with Claude Samuel*. Translated by E. Thomas Glasow. Portland, OR: Amadeus Press, 1994.

Michener, James A. *Tales of the South Pacific*. New York: Macmillan, 1947.

Michener, James A. "Japan." *Holiday* 12, no. 2 (August 1952): 27–41.

Michener, James A. *Sayonara*. New York: Random House, 1954.

Michener, James A. "Pursuit of Happiness by a GI and a Japanese: Marriage Surmounts Barriers of Language and Intolerance." *Life* 38 (21 February 1955): 124–141.

Michener, James A. "Why I Like Japan." *Reader's Digest* 69 (August 1956): 182–186.

Michener, James A. "Madame Butterfly in Bobby Sox." *Reader's Digest* 69 (October 1956): 21–27.

Micznik, Vera. "Cio-Cio-San the Geisha." In *A Vision of the Orient: Texts, Intertexts, and Contexts of Madame Butterfly*, edited by Jonathan Wisenthal, Sherrill Grace, Melinda Boyd, Brian McIlroy, and Vera Micznik, 36–58. Toronto: University of Toronto Press, 2006.

Midway Types: A Book of Illustrated Lessons about the People of the Midway Plaisance, World's Fair, 1893. Chicago: American Engraving Co., 1894.

Mihara, Aya. "Was It Torture or Tune?: First Japanese Music in the Western Theatre." In *Popular Music: Intercultural Interpretations*, edited by Toru Mitsui, 134–142. Kanazawa: Kanazawa University, 1998.

Miller, J. Scott. "Dispossessed Melodies: Recordings of the Kawakami Theater Troupe." *Monumenta Nipponica* 53, no. 2 (summer 1998): 225–235.

Miller, Leta E. "Henry Cowell and John Cage: Intersections and Influences, 1933–1941." *Journal of the American Musicological Society* 59, no. 1 (spring 2006): 47–111.

Miller, Leta E., and Fredric Lieberman. *Lou Harrison: Composing a World*. Oxford: Oxford University Press, 1998.

Miller, Randall M., ed. *Ethnic Images in American Film and Television*. Philadelphia: The Balch Institute, 1978.

Miller, Randall M., ed. *The Kaleidoscopic Lens: How Hollywood Views Ethnic Groups*. Englewood, NJ: Jerome S. Ozer, 1980.

Mills, Sally. *Japanese Influences in American Art: 1853–1900*. Williamstown, MA: Sterling and Francine Clark Art Institute, 1981.

Minagawa, Tatsuo. "Japanese *Noh* Music." *Journal of the American Musicological Society* 10, no. 3 (autumn 1957): 181–200.

Minear, Richard H. "Review: Orientalism and the Study of Japan." *Journal of Asian Studies* 39, no. 3 (May 1980): 507–517.

Miner, Earl. *The Japanese Tradition in British and American Literature*. Princeton, NJ: Princeton University Press, 1958.

Minor, William. *Jazz Journeys to Japan: The Heart Within*. Ann Arbor: University of Michigan Press, 2004.

Mishima, Yukio. "The Cherished Myths." In *Party of Twenty: Informal Essays from Holiday Magazine*, edited by Clifton Fadiman, 196–208. New York: Simon and Schuster, 1963.

Mitchell, Tony. "Self-Orientalism, Reverse Orientalism, and Pan-Asian Pop Cultural Flows in Dick Lee's *Transit Lounge*." In *Rogue Flows: Trans-Asian Cultural Traffic*, edited by Koichi Iwabuchi, Stephen Muecke, and Mandy Thomas, 95–118. Hong Kong: Hong Kong University Press, 2004.

Mitsui, Tôru. "Domestic Exoticism: A Recent Trend in Japanese Popular Music." *Perfect Beat* 3, no. 4 (1998): 1–12.

Mitsui, Tôru, ed. *Popular Music: Intercultural Interpretations*. Kanazawa, Japan: Graduate Program in Music, Kanazawa University, 1998.

Miyake, Akiko, Sanehide Kodama, and Nicholas Teele, eds. *A Guide to Ezra Pound and Ernest Fenollosa's* Classic Noh Theatre of Japan. Orono: National Poetry Foundation, University of Maine, 1994.

Miyao, Daisuke. *Sessue Hayakawa: Silent Cinema and Transnational Stardom*. Durham, NC, and London: Duke University Press, 2007.

Mockus, Martha. *Sounding Out: Pauline Oliveros and Lesbian Musicality*. New York: Routledge, 2008.

Moon, Krystyn R. "'There's No Yellow in the Red, White, and Blue': The Creation of Anti-Japanese Music during World War II." *Pacific Historical Review* 72, no. 3 (August 2003): 333–352.

Moon, Krystyn R. *Yellowface: Creating the Chinese in American Popular Music and Performance, 1850s–1920s*. New Brunswick, NJ: Rutgers University Press, 2005.

Moon, Krystyn R. "The Quest for Music's Origin at the St. Louis World's Fair: Frances Densmore and the Racialization of Music." *American Music* 28, no. 2 (summer 2010): 191–210.

Monson, Ingrid. *Saying Something: Jazz Improvisation and Interaction*. Chicago: University of Chicago Press, 1996.

Monson, Ingrid. *Freedom Sounds: Civil Rights Call Out to Jazz and Africa*. Oxford: Oxford University Press, 2007.

Mori, Setsuko. "A Historical Survey of Music Periodicals in Japan: 1881–1920." *Fontes Artis Musicae* 36, no. 1 (January–March 1989): 44–50.

Móricz, Klára. "Sensuous Pagans and Righteous Jews: Changing Concepts of Jewish Identity in Ernest Bloch's *Jézabel* and *Schelomo*." *Journal of the American Musicological Society* 54, no. 3 (autumn 2001): 439–491.

Morris, Robert D. "Aspects of Confluence between Western Art Music and Ethnomusicology." In *Concert Music, Rock, and Jazz since 1945: Essays and Analytical Studies*, edited by Elizabeth West Marvin and Richard Hermann, 53–64. Rochester, NY: University of Rochester Press, 1995.

Morse, Edward S. *Japan Day by Day*. 2 vols. Boston and New York: Houghton Mifflin, 1917.

Morse, Edward Sylvester. *Japanese Homes and Their Surroundings*. New York: Dover Publications, 1961. First published 1886.

Morton, Lawrence. "The Music of *Objective: Burma*." *Hollywood Quarterly* 1, no. 4 (July 1946): 378–395.

Most, Andrea. "'You've Got to Be Carefully Taught': The Politics of Race in Rodgers and Hammerstein's *South Pacific*." *Theatre Journal* 52, no. 3 (2000): 307–337.

Moy, James S. *Marginal Sights: Staging the Chinese in America*. Iowa City: University of Iowa Press, 1993.

Mueller, Richard E. "Javanese Influence on Debussy's *Fantaisie* and Beyond." *19th-Century Music* 10, no. 2 (fall 1986): 157–186.

Mueller, Richard E. *Beauty and Innovation in la machine chinoise*. Hillsdale, NY: Pendragon Press, 2018.

Mullen, Bill V. *Afro-Orientalism*. Minneapolis: University of Minnesota Press, 2004.

Mundy, Chris. "Weezer's Cracked Genius: Is Rivers Cuomo the Weirdest Man in Rock, or the Coolest?" *Rolling Stone* 877 (13 September 2001): 42–44, 46.

Mundy, Rachel. "The 'League of Jewish Composers' and American Music." *Musical Quarterly* 96, no. 1 (spring 2013): 50–99.

Mundy, Rachel. "Evolutionary Categories and Musical Style from Adler to America." *Journal of the American Musicological Society* 67, no. 3 (2014): 735–767.

Munroe, Alexandra. "Buddhism and the Neo-Avant-Garde: Cage Zen, Beat Zen, and Zen." In *The Third Mind: American Artists Contemplate Asia, 1860–1989*, edited by Alexandra Munroe, 199–273. New York: Solomon R. Guggenheim Foundation, 2009.

Munroe, Alexandra, ed. *The Third Mind: American Artists Contemplate Asia, 1860–1989*. New York: Solomon R. Guggenheim Foundation, 2009.

Murakata, Akiko. "Selected Letters of Dr. William Sturgis Bigelow." PhD diss., George Washington University, 1971.

Murakata, Akiko, ed. and trans. *The Ernest F. Fenollosa Papers: The Houghton Library Harvard University*. Japanese Edition, Vol. III Literature. Tokyo: Museum Press: 1987.

Murase, Ichiro Mike. *Little Tokyo: One Hundred Years in Pictures*. Los Angeles: Visual Communications/Asian American Studies Central, 1983.

Murphy, William Thomas. "The Method of *Why We Fight*." *Journal of Popular Film* 1, no. 3 (1972):185–196.

Murray, Leo. "Authenticity and Realism in Documentary Sound." *The Soundtrack* 3, no. 2 (2010): 131–137.

"Music in Japan" (from the Albany *Evening Journal*). *New York Times* (21 July 1873): 2.

"Music in Japan." *Dwight's Journal of Music* 40, no. 1026 (14 Aug 1880): 135. Reprinted New York: Arno Press, 1967.

Musicological Society of Japan, ed. *Musicology and Globalization: Proceedings of the International Congress in Shizuoka 2002*. Tokyo: Musicological Society of Japan, 2004.

Naficy, Hamid, and Teshome H. Gabriel, eds. *Otherness and the Media: The Ethnography of the Imagined and the Imaged*. Chur, Switzerland: Harwood Academic Publishers, 1993.

Nakai, You. "Of Stone and Sand: John Cage and David Tudor in Japan, 1962." *POST: Notes on Modern & Contemporary Art Around the Globe*. Museum of Modern Art, 21 April 2015, https://post.at.moma.org/content_items/562-of-stone-and-sand-john-cage-and-david-tudor-in-japan-1962.

Namikawa, Ryō. "Japanese Overseas Broadcasting: A Personal View." In *Film and Radio Propaganda in World War II*, edited by K. R. M. Short, 319–333. Knoxville: University of Tennessee Press, 1983.

Nelson, Emmanuel S., ed. *Asian American Novelists: A Bio-Bibliographical Critical Sourcebook*. Westport, CT: Greenwood Press, 2000.

Nettl, Paul. "The West Faces East." *Modern Music* 20, no. 2 (January–February 1943): 90–94.

Neu, Charles E. *An Uncertain Friendship: Theodore Roosevelt and Japan, 1906–1909*. Cambridge, MA: Harvard University Press, 1967.

Neu, Charles E. *The Troubled Encounter: The United States and Japan*. New York: John Wiley and Sons, 1975.

Neumeyer, David. "Performances in Early Hollywood Sound Films: Source Music, Background Music, and the Integrated Sound Track." *Contemporary Music Review* 19, no. 1 (2000): 37–62.

Neumeyer, David. "Diegetic/Nondiegetic: A Theoretical Model." *Music and the Moving Image* 2, no. 1 (spring 2009).

Ng, Wendy. "Educating Californians about Japanese American Internment." *Mills Quarterly* (winter 2001): 13–16.

Ng, Wendy. *Japanese American Internment during World War II: A History and Reference Guide*. Westport, CT: Greenwood Press, 2002.

Nicholls, David. "Transethnicism and the American Experimental Tradition." *Musical Quarterly* 80, no. 4 (winter 1996): 569–594.

Nicholls, David. "Reaching beyond the West: Asian Resonances in American Radicalism." *American Music* 17, no. 2 (summer 1999): 125–128.

Nicholls, David, ed. *The Whole World of Music: A Henry Cowell Symposium*. Amsterdam: Harwood Academic Publishers, 1997.

Nitobé, Inazo. *The Japanese Nation: Its Land, Its People, Its Life*. New York: G. P. Putnam's Sons, 1912.

"No Music in the East" (from the *London Truth*). *New York Times*, 30 March 1896, 4.

Noël, Percy. *When Japan Fights*. Kanda, Japan: The Hokuseido Press, 1937.

Nomura, Yoshio. "Religious Music." Executive Committee for 1961 Tokyo East-West Music Encounter, ed. and publ. *Music—East and West: Report on 1961 Tokyo East-West Music Encounter Conference*. Tokyo, 1961.

Norman, Henry. *The Real Japan: Studies of Contemporary Japanese Manners, Morals, Administration, and Politics*. New York: Charles Scribner's Sons, 1892.

Nornes, Abé Mark, and Fukushima Yukio, eds. *The Japan/America Film Wars: World War II Propaganda and Its Cultural Contexts*. Chur, Switzerland: Harwood, 1994.

Norton, Frank H., ed. *A Facsimile of Frank Leslie's Illustrated Historical Register of the Centennial Exposition, 1876*. New York: Paddington Press, 1974.

Norton, Richard C. *Chronology of American Musical Theater*. Oxford: Oxford University Press, 2002.

Norvell, Philip J. "A History and a Catalogue of the Albert Gale Collection of Musical Instruments." MA thesis, University of Southern California, 1952.

Nute, Kevin. *Frank Lloyd Wright and Japan: The Role of Traditional Japanese Art and Architecture in the Work of Frank Lloyd Wright*. London: Chapman and Hall, 1993.

Oba, Junko. "From *Miyasan, Miyasan* to *Subaru*: The Transformation of Japanese War Songs from 1868 to Today." MA thesis, Wesleyan University, 1995.

Oba, Junko. "To Fight the Losing War, to Remember the Lost War: The Changing Role of *Gunka*, Japanese War Songs." In *Global Goes Local: Popular Culture in Asia*, edited by Timothy J. Craig and Richard King, 225–225. Honolulu: University of Hawai'i Press, 2002.

O'Brien, David J., and Stephen S. Fugita. *The Japanese American Experience*. Bloomington and Indianapolis: Indiana University Press, 1991.

Oehling, Richard A. "The Yellow Menace: Asian Images in American Film." In *The Kaleidoscopic Lens: How Hollywood Views Ethnic Groups*, edited by Randall M. Miller, 182–206. Englewood, NJ: Jerome S. Ozer, Publisher, 1980.

Oja, Carol J. *Colin McPhee: Composer in Two Worlds*. Washington, DC: Smithsonian Institution Press, 1990.

Oja, Carol J. *Making Music Modern: New York in the 1920s*. New York: Oxford University Press: 2000.

Oja, Carol J. *Bernstein Meets Broadway: Collaborative Art in a Time of War*. New York: Oxford University Press, 2014.

Oja, Carol J., and H. Wiley Hitchcock. "Henry Cowell at 100." In *Henry Cowell's Musical Worlds: A Program Book for the Henry Cowell Centennial Festival*, edited by Carol J. Oja and Ray Allen, 5–6. Brooklyn: Institute for Studies in American Music, 1997.

Okakura, Kakuzo. *The Ho-o-den: An Illustrated Description of the Buildings Erected by the Japanese Government at the World's Columbian Exposition, Jackson Park, Chicago*. Tokyo: K. Ogawa, 1893.

Okakura, Kakuzo. *The Book of Tea*. New York: Fox, Duffield, 1906.

Okihiro, Gary Y. *Margins and Mainstreams: Asians in American History and Culture*. Seattle: University of Washington Press, 1994.

Ortolani, Benito. *The Japanese Theatre: From Shamanistic Ritual to Contemporary Pluralism*. Rev. ed. Princeton, NJ: Princeton University Press, 1995.

Osborne, Charles. *The Complete Operas of Puccini*. New York: Da Capo, 1981.

Oshima, Shotaro. *W. B. Yeats and Japan*. Tokyo: Hokuseido Press, 1965.

Ota, Yuzo. *Basil Hall Chamberlain: Portrait of a Japanologist*. Richmond, Surrey: Japan Library, 1998.

Oteri, Frank J. "Lois V. Vierk: Slideways: In Conversation with Frank J. Oteri, 30 November 2007." *New Music Box*, 1 January 2008, https://nmbx.newmusicusa.org/lois-v-vierk-slideways/.

Oteri, Frank J. "Miya Masaoka: Social and Sonic Relationships." *NewMusicBox*, 1 June 2014, https://nmbx.newmusicusa.org/miya-masaoka/.

Ouellette, Fernand. *Edgard Varèse*. Translated by Derek Coltman. New York: Orion Press, 1968.

Pachter, Benjamin. "Displaying 'Japan': *Kumidaiko* and the Exhibition of Culture at Walt Disney World." *Asian Musicology* 14 (2009): 81–121.

Pacun, David. "'Thus We Cultivate Our Own World, and Thus We Share It with Others': Kósçak Yamada's Visit to the United States in 1918–1919." *American Music* 24, no. 1 (spring 2006): 67–94.

Palmer, Christopher. *Dimitri Tiomkin: A Portrait*. London: T. E. Books, 1984.

Palmer, Christopher. *The Composer in Hollywood*. London: Marion Boyars, 1990.

Parakilas, James. "The Soldier and the Exotic: Operatic Variations on a Theme of Racial Encounter: Part I and II," *Opera Quarterly* 10, nos. 2–3 (winter 1993–1994; spring 1994): 33–56; 43–69.

Parish, James Robert. *The Great Combat Pictures: Twentieth-Century Warfare on the Screen.* Metuchen, NJ: Scarecrow Press, 1990.

Park, Chung. "*Ode to the Temple of Sound, Floating World–Ukiyo,* and *Meditation on Zeami*: An Analysis of Three Works by Alan Hovhaness." DMA thesis, University of Miami, 2008.

Parmenter, Ross. "Kimio Eto Offers Music on the Koto." *New York Times,* 5 November 1962, 35.

Pasler, Jann. "Reinterpreting Indian Music: Albert Roussel and Maurice Delage." In *Music-Cultures in Contact: Convergences and Collisions,* edited by Margaret J. Kartomi and Stephen Blum, 122–157. Basel: Gordon and Breach, 1994.

Pasler, Jann. "Race, Orientalism, and Distinction in the Wake of the 'Yellow Peril.'" In *Western Music and Its Others,* edited by Georgina Born and David Hesmondhalgh, 86–118. Berkeley: University of California Press, 2000.

Pasler, Jann. "Political Anxieties and Musical Reception: Japonisme and the Problem of Assimilation." In *Madama Butterfly: l'orientalismo di fine secolo, l'approccio pucciniano, la ricezione,* edited by Arthur Groos and Virgilio Bernardoni, 17–53. Florence: Leo S. Olschki Editore, 2008.

Patterson, David W. "Appraising the Catchwords, c. 1942–1959: John Cage's Asian-Derived Rhetoric and the Historical Reference of Black Mountain College." PhD diss., Columbia University, 1996.

Patterson, David W. "Cage and Asia: History and Sources." In *The Cambridge Companion to John Cage,* edited by David Nicholls, 41–59. Cambridge, UK: Cambridge University Press, 2002.

Paul, David C. "From American Ethnographer to Cold War Icon: Charles Ives through the Eyes of Henry and Sidney Cowell." *Journal of the American Musicological Society* 59, no. 2 (summer 2006): 399–357.

Paulin, Scott D. "The *Ring* in *Golden Earrings.*" In *Wagner and Cinema,* edited by Jeongwon Joe and Sander L. Gilman, 225–250. Bloomington: Indiana University Press, 2010.

Perison, Harry D. "Charles Wakefield Cadman: His Life and Works." PhD diss., Eastman School of Music, University of Rochester, 1978.

Perlman, Gary. "*Pacific Overtures* a Triumph in Tokyo." *Sondheim Review* 7, no. 3 (winter 2001): 6–10.

Perlman, Gary. "*Overtures* 'Sensational' in Tokyo: Sondheim." *Sondheim Review* 7, no. 3 (winter 2001): 11.

Perris, Arnold. *Music as Propaganda: Art to Persuade, Art to Control.* Westport, CT: Greenwood Press, 1985.

Perry, M. C. *Narrative of the Expedition of an American Squadron to the China Seas and Japan, Performed in the Years 1852, 1853, and 1854.* Edited by Francis L. Hawks. New York: D. Appleton, 1856.

Pieslak, Jonathan. *Sound Targets: American Soldiers and Music in the Iraq War.* Bloomington and Indianapolis: Indiana University Press, 2009.

Piggott, Francis Taylor. "The Music of the Japanese" (read 14 January 1891), *Transactions of the Asiatic Society of Japan* 19 (1891): 298–299.

Piggott, Francis Taylor. *The Music and Musical Instruments of Japan.* London: B. T. Batsford, 1893.

Piro, Joseph M. "Kabuki Meets Broadway: Crafting the Oriental Musical Pacific Overtures." Master's thesis, Queens College, CUNY, 1978.

Pisani, Michael V. "'I'm an Indian Too': Creating Native American Identities in Nineteenth- and Early Twentieth-Century Music." In *The Exotic in Western Music,* edited by Jonathan Bellman, 218–257. Boston: Northeastern University Press, 1998.

Pisani, Michael V. *Imagining Native America in Music.* New Haven, CT: Yale University Press, 2005.

Pitken, Walter B., *Must We Fight Japan?* New York: The Century Co., 1921.

"Play Music of Orient: Mr. and Mrs. Henry Eichheim Talk on Its Origin to Japan Society." *New York Times,* 5 December 1920, 22.

"*A Pleasing Novelty*": *Bunkio Matsuki and the Japan Craze in Victorian Salem.* Salem, MA: Peabody & Essex Museum, 1993.

Pope, Edgar W. "Signifying China: The Exotic in Pre-war Japanese Popular Music." In *Popular Music: Intercultural Interpretations*, edited by Tôru Mitsui, 111–120. Kanazawa, Japan: Graduate Program in Music, Kanazawa University, 1998.

Pope, Edgar W. "Songs of the Empire: Continental Asia in Japanese Wartime Popular Music." PhD diss., University of Washington, 2003.

Pound, Ezra, and Ernest Fenollosa. *Certain Noble Plays of Japan*. Churchtown: Cuala Press, 1916.

Pound, Ezra, and Ernest Fenollosa. *The Classic Noh Theatre of Japan*. New York: Alfred A. Knopf, 1959.

Powils-Okano, Kimiyo. *Puccini's "Madama Butterfly."* Bonn: Verlag für systematische Musikwissenschaft, 1986.

Prashad, Vijay. *Everybody Was Kung Fu Fighting: Afro-Asian Connections and the Myth of Cultural Purity*. Boston: Beacon Press, 2001.

Prendergast, Roy M. *Film Music: A Neglected Art*. 2nd ed. New York: W. W. Norton, 1992.

Pritchett, James. *The Music of John Cage*. Cambridge, UK: Cambridge University Press, 1993.

"Program to Tell Story of Japanese Culture." *Los Angeles Times*, 11 August 1960, 15.

Quigly, Isabel. "Through Eastern Windows." *Spectator* 200 (14 February 1958).

Racy, Ali Jihad. "Historical Worldviews of Early Ethnomusicologists: An East-West Encounter in Cairo, 1932." In *Ethnomusicology and Modern Music History*, edited by Stephen Blum, Philip V. Bohlman, and Daniel M. Newman, 68–91. Urbana: University of Illinois Press, 1991.

Radano, Ronald, and Philip V. Bohlman, eds. *Music and the Racial Imagination*. Chicago: University of Chicago Press, 2000.

Raine-Reusch, Randy. "Integrating Extremes: The Music of Richard Teitelbaum." *Musicworks* 85 (spring 2003): 40–53.

Randall, Annie J., and Rosalind Gray Davis. *Puccini and the Girl: History and Reception of* The Girl of the Golden West. Chicago: University of Chicago Press, 2005.

Rao, Nancy Yunhwa. "Racial Essences and Historical Invisibility: Chinese Opera in New York, 1930." *Cambridge Opera Journal* 12, no. 2 (2000): 135–162.

Rao, Nancy Yunhwa. "American Compositional Theory in the 1930s: Scale and Exoticism in 'The Nature of Melody' by Henry Cowell." *Musical Quarterly* 85, no. 4 (winter 2001): 595–640.

Rao, Nancy Yunhwa. "Songs of the Exclusion Era: New York Chinatown's Opera Theaters in the 1920s." *American Music* 20, no. 4 (winter 2002): 399–444.

Rao, Nancy Yunhwa. "Henry Cowell and His Chinese Music Heritage: Theory of Sliding Tone and His Orchestral Work of 1953–1965." In *Locating East Asia in Western Art Music*, edited by Yayoi Uno Everett and Frederick Lau, 119–145. Middletown, CT: Wesleyan University Press, 2004.

Rapée, Erno. *Motion Picture Moods for Pianists and Organists*. New York: Arno Press, 1970. Originally published New York: Schirmer, 1924.

Rapée, Erno. *Encyclopedia of Music for Pictures*. New York: Arno Press, 1970. Originally published New York: Belwin, 1925.

Raphael-Hernandez, Heike, and Shannon Steen, eds. *Afro-Asian Encounters: Culture, History, Politics*. New York: New York University Press, 2006.

Rehding, Alexander. *Hugo Riemann and the Birth of Modern Musical Thought*. Cambridge, UK: Cambridge University Press, 2003.

Rehding, Alexander. "Wax Cylinder Revolutions." *Musical Quarterly* 88 (2005): 144.

Reischauer, Edwin O. *The United States and Japan*. Cambridge, MA: Harvard University Press, 1950.

Revers, Peter. "Carl Orff und der Exotismus: Zur Ostasienrezeption in seiner frühen Oper *Gisei-Das Opfer.*" In *Musikkulturgeschichte*, edited by Peter Petersen, 233–259. Wiesbaden: Breitkopf and Härtel, 1990.

Review of *The Purple Heart. Time*, 6 March 1944, 94 and 96.

Review of Sayonara. *Time* 70, no. 25 (16 December 1957).

Review of Sayonara. *The Nation* 185 (21 December 1957): 484.

Revill, David. *The Roaring Silence: John Cage, a Life*. New York: Arcade Pub., 1992.

Reynolds, Roger. "Current Chronicle: Japan." *Musical Quarterly* 53, no. 4 (October 1967): 563–580.

Reynolds, Roger. "Happenings in Japan and Elsewhere." *Arts in Society* 5, no. 1 (1968): 90–101.

Reynolds, Roger. *Mind Models: New Forms of Musical Experience*. New York: Praeger Publishers, 1975.

Reynolds, Roger. "Rarely Sudden, Never Abrupt." *Musical Times* 128, no. 1735 (September 1987): 480–483.

Reynolds, Roger. "A Perspective on Form and Experience." *Contemporary Music Review* 2, no. 1 (1987): 277–308.

Reynolds, Roger. "The Indifference of the Broiler to the Broiled." In *Samuel Beckett and Music*, edited by Mary Bryden, 195–211. Oxford: Clarendon Press, 1998.

Reynolds, Roger. *Form and Method: Composing Music; The Rothschild Essays*. Edited by Stephen McAdams. New York and London: Routledge, 2002.

Reynolds, Roger. "Ideals and Realities: A Composer in America." *American Music* 25, no. 1 (spring 2007): 4–49.

Reynolds, Roger, and John Cage. "John Cage and Roger Reynolds: A Conversation." *Musical Quarterly* 65, no. 4 (October 1979): 573–594.

Reynolds, Roger, and Harvey Sollberger. "Interview: Reynolds/Sollberger." In *Roger Reynolds: Profile of a Composer*. New York: C. F. Peters Corporation, 1982.

Reynolds, Roger, and Yuji Takahashi. "A Jostled Silence: Contemporary Japanese Musical Thought (Part Two)." *Perspectives of New Music* 30, no. 2 (summer 1992): 60–100.

Reynolds, Roger, and Tōru Takemitsu. "A Jostled Silence (Part One)." *Perspectives of New Music* 30, no. 1 (winter 1992): 22–80.

Reynolds, Roger, and Toru Takemitsu. "Roger Reynolds and Toru Takemitsu: A Conversation." *Musical Quarterly* 80, no. 1 (spring 1996): 61–76.

Reynolds, Roger, and Jōji Yuasa. "A Jostled Silence: Contemporary Japanese Musical Thought (Part Three)." *Perspectives of New Music* 31, no. 2 (summer 1993): 172–228.

Rhodes, Anthony. *Propaganda: The Art of Persuasion in World War II*. New York: Chelsea House, 1976.

Rich, Alan. "Koto Introduced to Carnegie Hall." *New York Times*, 2 October 1961, 36.

Richards, Jeffrey. "Vaughan Williams and British Wartime Cinema." In *Vaughan Williams Studies*, edited by Alain Frogley, 139–165. Cambridge, UK: Cambridge University Press, 1996.

Richie, Donald. *The Honorable Visitors*. Rutland, VT: Charles E. Tuttle, 1994.

Riddle, Ronald. *Flying Dragons, Flowing Streams: Music in the Life of San Francisco's Chinese*. Westport, CT: Greenwood, 1983.

Riesman, Abe J. "River's End." *Harvard Crimson*, 26 April 2006, https://www.thecrimson.com/article/2006/4/26/rivers-end-in-early-1995-a/#.XBa3hG-w3nc.link.

Riis, Thomas L. *Just before Jazz: Black Musical Theater in New York, 1890–1915*. Washington, DC: Smithsonian Institution Press, 1989.

Roan, Jeanette. *Envisioning Asia: On Location, Travel, and the Cinematic Geography of US Orientalism*. Ann Arbor: University of Michigan Press, 2010.

Roberts, Tamara. *Resounding Afro Asia: Interracial Music and the Politics of Collaboration*. Oxford: Oxford University Press, 2016.

Robertson, Jennifer. "The 'Magic If': Conflicting Performances of Gender in the Takarazuka Revue of Japan." In *Gender in Performance: The Presentation of Difference in the Performing Arts*, edited by Laurence Senelick, 46–67. Hanover, NH: University Press of New England, 1992.

Robertson, Jennifer. *Takarazuka: Sexual Politics and Popular Culture in Modern Japan*. Berkeley: University of California Press, 1998.

Robertson, Marta. "Ballad for Incarcerated Americans: Second-Generation Japanese American Musicking in World War II Camps." *Journal of the Society for American Music* 11, no. 3 (2017): 284–312.

Robinson, Paul, and Roger Reynolds. "'I'm Always Interested in New Experience': A Conversation with Paul Robinson." In *Robert Ashley, Music with Roots in the Aether: Interviews with and Essays about Seven American Composers*, 153–178. Cologne: MusikTexte, 2000.

Rodecape, Lois Foster. "Tom Maguire, Napoleon of the Stage." *California Historical Society Quarterly* 21, no. 2 (June 1942): 141–182.

Rogin, Michael. *Blackface, White Noise: Jewish Immigrants in the Hollywood Melting Pot.* Berkeley: University of California Press, 1996.

"Romance in the Orient." *Newsweek* 50, no. 96 (9 December 1957): 96.

Rosen, David. "The Sounds of Music and War: Humphrey Jennings's and Stewart McAllister's *Listen to Britain* (1942)." In *Coll'astuzia, col guidizio: Essays in Honor of Neal Zaslaw,* edited by Cliff Eisen, 389–427. Ann Arbor, MI: Steglein Publishing, 2009.

Rosenberg, Jonathan. "'To Reach . . . into the Hearts and Minds of Our Friends': The United States' Symphonic Tours and the Cold War." In *Music and International History in the Twentieth Century,* edited by Jessica C. E. Gienow-Hecht, 140–165. New York: Berghahn, 2015.

Rosenstone, Robert A. *Mirror in the Shrine: American Encounters with Meiji Japan.* Cambridge, MA: Harvard University Press, 1988.

Rosner, Arnold. "An Analytical Survey of the Music of Alan Hovhaness." PhD diss., State University of New York at Buffalo, 1972.

Rothstein, Edward. "Japanese View of an American View of Japan." *New York Times,* 1 September 2002, A3.

Russell, John G. "Race and Reflexivity: The Black Other in Contemporary Japanese Mass Culture." In *Contemporary Japan and Popular Culture,* edited by John Whittier Treat, 17–40. Honolulu: University of Hawai'i Press, 1996.

Sachs, Joel. *Henry Cowell: A Man Made of Music.* Oxford: Oxford University Press, 2012.

Said, Edward W. *Orientalism.* New York: Pantheon, 1978.

Said, Edward W. *Culture and Imperialism.* New York: Knopf, 1993.

Saminsky, Lazare. "Composers of the Pacific." *Modern Music* 20, no. 1 (November-December 1942): 23–26.

Samson, Jim. "Propaganda." In *Aesthetics of Music: Musicological Perspectives,* edited by Stephen Downes, 259–275. New York: Routledge, 2014.

Samuelson, Ralph. "Shakuhachi and the American Composer." *Contemporary Music Review* 8, no. 2 (1993): 83–93.

Sand, Jordan. "Gentlemen's Agreement, 1908: Fragments for a Pacific History." *Representations* 107 (summer 2009): 91–127.

Sasamori, Takefusa. "Impact of Far East Music on American Music." *Bulletin of the Faculty of Education, Hirosaki University* 32A (November 1974): 65–81.

Sato, Shigeru. "Symposium of Light and Sound." *Ongaku Shimbun* (23 Feb 1969).

Sato, Tadao. *Currents in Japanese Cinema.* Translated by Gregory Barrett. New York: Kodansha International, 1982.

Saunders, Frances Stonor. *The Cultural Cold War: The CIA and the World of Arts and Letters.* New York: The New Press, 2000.

Saunders, William. "The American Opera: Has It Arrived?" *Music and Letters* 13 (1932): 147–155.

Saylor, Bruce. *The Writings of Henry Cowell: A Descriptive Bibliography.* Brooklyn: Institute for Studies in American Music, 1977.

Schaller, Michael. *Altered States: The United States and Japan since the Occupation.* Oxford: Oxford University Press, 1997.

Schatt, Peter W. *Exotik in der Musik des 20. Jahrhunderts.* Munich: Musikverlag Emil Katzbichler, 1986.

Schatz, Thomas. *Boom and Bust: The American Cinema in the 1940s.* New York: Scribner, 1997.

Schlefer, James Nyoraku. "The Intersection of Genres." *NewMusicBox* (15 February 2018), https://nmbx.newmusicusa.org/the-intersection-of-genres/.

Schlefer, James Nyoraku. "Some Practicalities of East-West Musical Collaborations." *NewMusicBox* (28 February 2018), https://nmbx.newmusicusa.org/some-practicalities-of-east-west-musical-collaborations/.

Schoenberg, Arnold. "Folkloristic Symphonies." *Musical America* (February 1947). Reprinted in *Style and Idea,* edited by Leonard Stein, 161–166. Berkeley: University of California Press, 1984.

Scholz-Cionca, Stanca, and Samuel L. Leiter, eds. *Japanese Theatre and the International Stage*. Leiden: Brill, 2001.

Schroeder, David. *Cinema's Illusions, Opera's Allure: The Operatic Impulse in Film*. New York and London: Continuum, 2002.

Schueller, Malini Johar. *US Orientalisms: Race, Nation, and Gender in Literature, 1790–1890*. Ann Arbor: University of Michigan Press, 1998.

Schuller, Gunther. "Third Stream," *Grove Music Online*, ed. L. Macy (accessed 12 August 2003).

Schwantes, Robert S. *Japanese and Americans: A Century of Cultural Relations*. New York: Harper & Brothers, 1955.

Scott, Derek B. "Orientalism and Musical Style." *Musical Quarterly* 82, no. 2 (summer 1998): 309–335.

Scruton, Roger. "The Eclipse of Listening." In *The Future of the European Past*, edited by Hilton Kramer and Roger Kimball, 51–68. Chicago: Ivan R. Dee, 1997.

Seeley, Paul. "The Japanese March in *The Mikado*." *Musical Times* 126, no. 1710 (August 1985): 454–456.

Seltsam, William H., comp. *Metropolitan Opera Annals: A Chronicle of Artists and Performances*. New York: H. W. Wilson Co., 1947.

Semmes, Laurie Ruth. "Frank Capra's *Job in Germany*: Evoking Cautious Suspicion through German Musical Reassurance." In *Music and Propaganda in the Short Twentieth Century*, edited by Massimiliano Sala, 57–67. Lucca: Brepols, 2014.

Senelick, Laurence, ed. *Gender in Performance: The Presentation of Difference in the Performing Arts*. Hanover, NH: University Press of New England, 1992.

Sewell, Stacey. "Making My Skin Crawl: Representations and Mediations of the Body in Miya Masaoka's *Ritual, Interspecies Collaboration with Giant Madagascar Hissing Cockroaches*." *Radical Musicology* 4 (2009), http://www.radical-musicology.org.uk/2009/Sewell.htm.

Shand-Tucci, Douglass. *The Art of Scandal: The Life and Times of Isabella Stewart Gardner*. New York: HarperCollins, 1997.

Shank, Barry. "Abstraction and Embodiment: Yoko Ono and the Weaving of Global Musical Networks." *Journal of Popular Music Studies* 18, no. 3 (2006): 282–300.

Shank, Barry. "Productive Orientalisms: Imagining Noise and Silence Across the Pacific, 1957–1967." In *Postnational Musical Identities: Cultural Production, Distribution, and Consumption in a Globalized Scenario*, edited by Ignacio Corona and Alejandro L. Madrid, 45–61. Lanham, MD: Lexington Books, 2008.

Shapiro, Anne Dhu. "Action Music in American Pantomime and Melodrama, 1730–1913." *American Music* 2, no. 4 (winter 1984): 49–72.

Sharff, Stefan. *The Elements of Cinema: Toward a Theory of Cinesthetic Impact*. New York: Columbia University Press, 1982.

Sheppard, W. Anthony. *Revealing Masks: Exotic Influences and Ritualized Performance in Modernist Music Theater*. Berkeley: University of California Press, 2001.

Sheppard, W. Anthony. "Representing the Authentic: Tak Shindo's 'Exotic Sound' and Japanese American History." *ECHO: A Music-Centered Journal* 6, no. 2 (2005), http://www.echo.ucla.edu/Volume6-issue2/sheppard/sheppard3.html.

Sheppard, W. Anthony. "Review of Anthony Minghella's Production of *Madama Butterfly* at the Metropolitan Opera." *Opera Quarterly* 24, no. 1 (winter 2008): 139–147.

Sheppard, W. Anthony. "Tan Dun and Zhang Yimou between Film and Opera." *Journal of Musicological Research* 29, no. 1 (January–March 2010): 1–33.

Sheppard, W. Anthony. "The Persistence of Orientalism in the Postmodern Operas of Adams and Sellars." In *Representation in Western Music*, edited by Joshua S. Walden, 267–286. Cambridge, UK: Cambridge University Press, 2013.

Sheppard, W. Anthony. "Exoticism." In *The Oxford Handbook of Opera*, edited by Helen M. Greenwald, 795–816. New York: Oxford University Press, 2014.

Sheppard, W. Anthony. "Puccini and the Music Boxes." *Journal of the Royal Musical Association* 140, no. 1 (spring 2015): 41–92.

Sheppard, W. Anthony. "Exoticism." *Oxford Bibliographies in Music*, edited by Bruce Gustafson (Oxford University Press, 2012; last modified 25 February 2016).

Shibusawa, Naoko. *America's Geisha Ally: Reimagining the Japanese Enemy*. Cambridge, MA: Harvard University Press, 2006.

Shillony, Ben-Ami. *Politics and Culture in Wartime Japan*. Oxford: Clarendon Press, 1981.

Shimakawa, Karen. *National Abjection: The Asian American Body Onstage*. Durham, NC: Duke University Press, 2002.

Shindo, Tak. "Japanese Music Today." *Film Music* 12, no. 1 (September–October 1952): 21–22.

Shively, Donald H., ed. *Tradition and Modernization in Japanese Culture*. Princeton, NJ: Princeton University Press, 1971.

Shōno, Susumu. "The Role of Listening in Gagaku." *Contemporary Music Review* 1, no. 2 (1987): 19–43.

Short, K. R. M., ed. *Film and Radio Propaganda in World War II*. Knoxville: University of Tennessee Press, 1983.

Shull, Michael S., and David Edward Wilt. *Hollywood War Films, 1937–1945*. Jefferson, NC: McFarland, 1996.

Siddons, James. "Favorite Japanese Sounds." In *Dika Newlin: Friend and Mentor, a Birthday Anthology*, edited by Theordore Albrecht, 88–95. Denton: Jagdhorn Verlag, 1973.

Signell, Karl. "The Mystique of the *Shakuhachi*." *Journal of the American Musical Instrument Society* 7 (1981): 90–98.

Silverman, Kaja. *The Acoustic Mirror: The Female Voice in Psychoanalysis and Cinema*. Bloomington and Indianapolis: Indiana University Press, 1988.

Simmonds, Rae Nichols. "The Use of Music as a Political Tool by the United States during World War II." PhD diss., Walden University, 1994.

Simpson, Alexander Thomas. "Opera on Film: A Study of the History and the Aesthetic Principles and Conflicts of a Hybrid Genre." PhD diss., University of Kentucky, 1990.

Simpson, Caroline Chung. *An Absent Presence: Japanese Americans in Postwar American Culture, 1945–1960*. Durham, NC, and London: Duke University Press, 2001.

The Slanted Screen: Asian Men in Film and Television. Dir. Jeff Adachi. San Francisco: AAMM Productions, 2006.

Slawek, Stephen. "Ravi Shankar as Mediator between a Traditional Music and Modernity." In *Ethnomusicology and Modern Music History*, edited by Stephen Blum, Philip V. Bohlman, and Daniel M. Newman, 161–180. Urbana: University of Illinois Press, 1991.

Slaying the Dragon. Produced and directed by Deborah Gee. VHS tape. San Francisco, CA: Cross Current Media: 1988.

Slobin, Mark. *Tenement Songs: The Popular Music of the Jewish Immigrants*. Urbana: University of Illinois Press, 1982.

Slobin, Mark. *Subcultural Sounds: Micromusics of the West*. Hanover, NH: Wesleyan University Press, 1993.

Slobin, Mark. "The Steiner Superculture." In *Global Soundtracks: Worlds of Film Music*, edited by Mark Slobin, 3–35. Middletown, CT: Wesleyan University Press, 2008.

Smith, Bradford. *To The Mountain*. Indianapolis and New York: The Bobbs-Merrill Co., 1936.

Smith, Catherine Parsons. "'Intellectual Interest' and the Modernism(s) of the Others." Paper delivered at the national meeting of the American Musicological Society, Washington, DC, 2005.

Smith, Jeff. "Bridging the Gap: Reconsidering the Border between Diegetic and Nondiegetic Music." *Music and the Moving Image* 2, no. 1 (spring 2009).

Smith, Kathleen E. R. *God Bless America: Tin Pan Alley Goes to War*. Lexington: The University Press of Kentucky, 2003.

Smith, Kathleen Ellen Rahtz. "'Goodbye, Mama. I'm Off to Yokohama': The Office of War Information and Tin Pan Alley in World War II." PhD diss., Louisiana State University, 1996.

Smith, Laura Alexandrine. "The Music of Japan." *The Nineteenth Century* 36, no. 214 (December 1894): 900–918.

Smith, R. Gordon. *Ancient Tales and Folklore of Japan*. London: A. and C. Black, 1908.

Snarrenberg, Robert. "Zen and the Way of Soundscroll." *Perspectives of New Music* 30, no. 1 (winter 1992): 222–237.

Snodgrass, Judith. *Presenting Japanese Buddhism to the West: Orientalism, Occidentalism, and the Columbian Exposition*. Chapel Hill, NC: University of North Carolina Press, 2003.

Snyder, Allegra Fuller. "Filmed in 'Holly-Vision': Hollywood Images of World Dance." In *Looking Out: Perspectives on Dance and Criticism in a Multicultural World*, edited by David Gere, 72–93. New York: Schirmer, 1995.

Sondheim, Stephen. *Finishing the Hat: Collected Lyrics (1954–1981) with Attendant Comments, Principles, Heresies, Grudges, Whines, and Anecdotes*. New York: Alfred A. Knopf, 2010.

Sondheim, Stephen, John Weidman, and Hugh Wheeler. *Pacific Overtures*. Rev. ed. New York: Theatre Communications Group, 1991.

Spalding, J. W. *Japan and around the World: An Account of Three Visits to the Japanese Empire*. New York: Redfield, 1855.

Spiller, Henry. "Tunes That Bind: Paul J. Seelig, Eva Gauthier, Charles T. Griffes, and the Javanese Other." *Journal of the Society for American Music* 3, no. 2 (May 2009): 129–154.

Stacpoole, H. De Vere. *The Willow Tree: The Romance of a Japanese Garden*. London: Hodder and Stoughton, 1918.

Stam, Robert and Louise Spence. "Colonialism, Racism and Representation." *Screen* 24, no. 2 (March/April 1983): 2–20.

Stanbrook, Alan. "The Sight of Music." *Sight & Sound* 56, no. 2 (spring 1987): 132–135.

Stankis, Jessica E. "Maurice Ravel's 'Color Counterpoint' through the Perspective of Japonisme." *Music Theory Online* 21, no. 1 (March 2015).

Starrs, Roy. *Modernism and Japanese Culture*. New York: Palgrave Macmillan, 2011.

Statler, Oliver. *Japanese Inn*. New York: Random House, 1961.

Steen, Shannon. "Racing American Modernity: Black Atlantic Negotiations of Asia and the 'Swing' Mikados." In *AfroAsian Encounters: Culture, History, Politics*, edited by Heike Raphael-Hernandez and Shannon Steen, 167–187. New York: New York University Press, 2006.

Stevens, Thomas Wood, and Kenneth Sawyer Goodman. *The Daimio's Head: A Masque of Old Japan*. Chicago: The Stage Guild, 1915.

Stilwell, Robynn J. "The Fantastical Gap between Diegetic and Nondiegetic." In *Beyond the Soundtrack: Representing Music in Cinema*, edited by Daniel Goldmark, Lawrence Kramer, and Richard Leppert, 184–202. Berkeley: University of California Press, 2007.

Stimson, Ann Michelle. "Musical Time in the Avant-Garde: The Japanese Connection." PhD diss., University of California, Santa Barbara, 1996.

Stockhausen, Karlheinz. "World Music." *The World of Music* 21, no. 1 (1979): 3–15.

Stockhausen, Karlheinz. "Eine Teezeremonie Hören." *Neue Zeitschrift für Musik* 147, no. 6 (1986): 19–21.

Stockhausen, Karlheinz. *Stockhausen on Music: Lectures and Interviews*. Edited by Robin Maconie. London: Marion Boyars, 1989.

Stoddard, Lothrop. *The Rising Tide of Color against White World-Supremacy*. New York: Charles Scribner's Sons, 1920.

Stokes, Martin, ed. *Ethnicity, Identity, and Music: The Musical Construction of Place*. Oxford: Berg, 1994.

Stokowski, Leopold. *Music for All of Us*. New York: Simon and Schuster, 1943.

Stone, Rebecca. "Cinematic Salomes: An Investigation of Dance and Orientalism in Hollywood Films." *UCLA Journal of Dance Ethnology* 15 (1991): 33–42.

Storb, Ilse, and Klaus-G. Fischer. *Dave Brubeck, Improvisations and Compositions: The Idea of Cultural Exchange*. Translated by Bert Thompson. New York: P. Lang, 1994.

Stowe, David W. "'Jazz That Eats Rice': Toshiko Akiyoshi's Roots Music." In *Afro-Asian Encounters: Culture, History, Politics*, edited by Heike Raphael-Hernandez and Shannon Steen, 277–294. New York: New York University Press, 2006.

Strang, Gerald. "Sliding Tones in Oriental Music." *Bulletin of the American Musicological Society* 8 (October 1945): 29–30.

Stravinsky, Igor, and Robert Craft. *Dialogues and A Diary*. Garden City, NY: Doubleday, 1963.

Stravinsky, Igor, and Robert Craft. *Dialogues*. Berkeley: University of California Press, 1982.

Street, Julian. *Mysterious Japan*. Garden City, NY: Doubleday, Page, 1921.

Stubblebine, Donald J., *Broadway Sheet Music: A Comprehensive Listing of Published Music from Broadway and Other Stage Shows, 1918–1993*. Jefferson, NC: McFarland & Co., 1996.

Stubblebine, Donald J. *Early Broadway Sheet Music: A Comprehensive Listing of Published Music from Broadway and Other Stage Shows, 1843–1918*. Jefferson, NC: McFarland & Co., 2002.

Stuckenschmidt, H. H. *Zum Hören geboren: Ein Leben mit der Musik unserer Zeit*. Munich: R. Piper, 1979.

Sturken, Marita. "Absent Images of Memory: Remembering and Reenacting the Japanese Internment." In *Perilous Memories: The Asia-Pacific War(s)*, edited by T. Fujitani, Geoffrey M. White, and Lisa Yoneyama, 33–39. Durham, NC: Duke University Press, 2001.

Suid, Lawrence H. *Guts and Glory: Great American War Movies*. Reading, MA: Addison-Wesley Publishing Co., 1978.

Sunaga, Katsumi. *Japanese Music*. Tokyo: Maruzen Co., Board of Tourist Industry, Japanese Government Railways, 1936.

Suzuki, Daisetz T. "Zen in the Modern World." *Japan Quarterly* 5, no. 4 (1958).

Suzuki, Daisetz T. *Zen and Japanese Culture*. New York: Pantheon Books, 1959.

Taber, Isaiah West. *The Monarch Souvenir of Sunset City and Sunset Scenes; Being Views of California Midwinter Fair and Famous Scenes in the Golden State*. San Francisco: H. S. Crocker Company, 1894.

Tachiki, Amy, Eddie Wong, and Franklin Odo, with Buck Wong, eds. *Roots: An Asian American Reader*. Los Angeles: Regents of the University of California, 1971.

"Tak Shindo." Hanashi Oral History Program, Go for Broke Educational Foundation, video. Gardena, CA: 2000.

"Tak Shindo." *Space Age Pop Music*. http://www.spaceagepop.com/shindo.htm (most recently accessed on 24 May 2016).

Takahashi, Jere. *Nisei/Sansei: Shifting Japanese American Identities and Politics*. Philadelphia: Temple University Press, 1997.

Takaki, Ronald. *Strangers from a Different Shore: A History of Asian Americans*. rev. ed. Boston: Back Bay Books, 1998.

Takeishi, Midori. *Japanese Elements in Michio Ito's Early Period (1915–1924): Meetings of East and West in the Collaborative Works*. Edited and revised by David Pacun. Tokyo: Gendai Tosho: 2006.

Tambling, Jeremy. *Opera, Ideology, and Film*. New York: St. Martin's Press, 1987.

Tambling, Jeremy, ed. *A Night in at the Opera: Media Representations of Opera*. London: John Libbey, 1994.

Tan, Margaret Leng. "'Taking a Nap, I Pound the Rice': Eastern Influences on John Cage." In *John Cage at Seventy-Five*, edited by Richard Fleming and William Duckworth, 34–56. Lewisburg, PA: Bucknell University Press, 1989.

Tanabe, Hisao. *Japanese Music*. Translated by Shigeyoshi Sakabe. Tokyo: The Society for International Cultural Relations, 1936.

Tanikawa, Miki. "In Kyoto, a Call to Not Trample the Geisha." *New York Times*, 6 April 2009, https://www.nytimes.com/2009/04/07/world/asia/07iht-geisha.html.

Taruskin, Richard. *The Danger of Music and Other Anti-Utopian Essays*. Berkeley and Los Angeles: University of California Press, 2009.

Tawa, Nicholas. *A Sound of Strangers: Musical Culture, Acculturation, and the Post–Civil War Ethnic American*. Metuchen, NJ: Scarecrow Press, 1982.

Tawa, Nicholas. *The Way to Tin Pan Alley: American Popular Song, 1866–1910*. New York: Schirmer Books, 1990.

Taylor, Anna Marjorie, comp. *The Language of World War II*. New York: H. W. Wilson, 1944.

Taylor, Bayard. *Japan, in Our Day*. New York: Charles Scribner's Sons, 1872.

Taylor, Bayard. *A Visit to India, China, and Japan in the Year 1853*. New York: G. P. Putnam, 1891. First published 1855.

Taylor, Richard. "The Notebooks of Ernest Fenollosa: Translations from the Japanese No." *Literature East and West* 15, no. 4 (December 1972): 533–576.

Taylor, Timothy D. *Beyond Exoticism: Western Music and the World*. Durham, NC, and London: Duke University Press, 2007.

Tenneriello, Susan. "*O-Mika*: Ruth St. Denis's Image of the East." *Proceedings of the Society of Dance History Scholars* 22 (1999): 279–284.

Terada, Yoshitaka. "Shifting Identities of *Taiko* Music in North America." In *Transcending Boundaries: Asian Musics in North America*, edited by Yoshitaka Terada, 37–59. Senri Ethnological Reports 22. Osaka: National Museum of Ethnology, 2001.

Terauchi, Naoko. "Interview with Robert Garfias." *Journal of Intercultural Studies* (Kobe University) 46 (2016): 91–120.

Terkel, Studs. *"The Good War": An Oral History of World War Two*. New York: Ballantine Books, 1984.

Testa, Bart. "Late Mutations of Cinema's Butterfly." In *A Vision of the Orient: Texts, Intertexts, and Contexts of Madame Butterfly*, edited by Jonathan Wisenthal, Sherrill Grace, Melinda Boyd, Brian McIlroy, and Vera Micznik, 91–122. Toronto: University of Toronto Press, 2006.

Tharp, Louise Hall. *Mrs. Jack: A Biography of Isabella Stewart Gardner*. Boston: Little, Brown and Co., 1965.

Theodore Wores: The Japanese Years. Oakland, CA: The Oakland Museum, 1976.

Theodore Wores: An American Artist in Meiji Japan. Pasadena, CA: Pacific Asia Museum, 1993.

Theresa, Rose M. "Spectacle and Enchantment: Envisioning Opera in Late Nineteenth-Century Paris." PhD diss., University of Pennsylvania, 2000.

Thomas, Tony. *Music for the Movies*. South Brunswick, NJ: A. S. Barnes and Company, 1973.

Thomas, Tony, ed. *Film Score: The View from the Podium*. Introduction by Tony Thomas. South Brunswick, NJ, and New York: A. S. Barnes and Company, 1979.

"Thompson Course Entertainment." *The Williams Weekly* 11 (18 March 1897): 6–7.

Thomson, Virgil. "The Philosophy of Style." In *Music—East and West: Report on 1961 Tokyo East-West Music Encounter Conference*, edited and published by the Executive Committee for 1961 Tokyo East-West Music Encounter, 144–146. Tokyo, 1961.

Thornbury, Barbara E. "Cultural Policy and Private Initiative: The Performing Arts at The Japan Society, New York." *The World of Music* 46, no. 2 (2004): 123–136.

Thornbury, Barbara E. *America's Japan and Japan's Performing Arts: Cultural Mobility and Exchange in New York, 1952–2011*. Ann Arbor: University of Michigan Press, 2013.

Tiomkin, Dimitri. "Writing Symphonically for the Screen." *Music Journal* 17, no. 1 (January 1959): 26, 106.

Tiomkin, Dimitri. *Please Don't Hate Me*. Garden City, NY: Doubleday, 1959.

Tiomkin, Dimitri. "The Music of Hollywood." *Music Journal* 20, no. 8 (November-December 1962): 7, 87.

Tiomkin, Dimitri. "Whence Cometh the 'New Sound'?" *Music Journal Annual Anthology* 23 (1965): 45, 108–109.

Tiomkin, Dimitri. "Composing for Films" 1951. In *Film Music: From Violins to Video*, edited by James L. Limbacher, 55–61. Metuchen, NJ: Scarecrow Press, 1974.

Todd, Mabel Loomis. *Corona and Coronet: Being a Narrative of the Amherst Eclipse Expedition to Japan, in Mr. James's Schooner-Yacht Coronet, to Observe the Sun's Total Obscuration 9th August 1896*. Boston and New York: Houghton, Mifflin, 1898.

Todd, Mabel Loomis. *Mabel Loomis Todd Papers: Diaries and Journals, 1871–1932*. Microfilms, 9 reels. New Haven, CT: Yale University Library, 1982.

Tokita, Alison. "Japanese Influence on Contemporary Australian Composers." In *Tradition and Its Future in Music*, edited by Yosihiko Tokumaru et al., 465–473. Tokyo: Mita Press, 1991.

Tokumaru, Yosihiko. "The Impact of American Popular Music on Japan." In *International Musicological Society: Report of the Twelfth Congress, Berkeley, 1977*, edited by Daniel Heartz and Bonnie C. Wade, 580–582. Kassel, Germany: Bärenreiter, 1981.

Tokumaru, Yosihiko, et al., eds. *Tradition and Its Future in Music*. Tokyo: Mita Press, 1991.

Toll, Robert C. *Blacking Up: The Minstrel Show in Nineteenth-Century America*. New York: Oxford University Press, 1974.

Toop, David. "Into the Hot—Exotica and World Music Fusions." In *Rhythms of the World*, edited by Francis Hanly and Tim May, 118–126, London: BBC Books, 1989.

Toop, David. *Exotica: Fabricated Soundscapes in a Real World*. London: Serpent's Tail, 1999.

Tran, Diep. "From Orientalism to Authenticity: Broadway's Yellow Fever." *American Theatre* (27 October 2015), https://www.americantheatre.org/2015/10/27/from-orientalism-to-authenticity-broadways-yellow-fever/.

Treib, Marc, "Mirror for the Modern: Japan, California, Architecture, Landscape." In *L'Oriente: Storia di una figura nelle arti occidentali (1700–2000)*, edited by Paolo Amalfitano and Loretta Innocenti, vol. 2, 329–341. Rome: Bulzoni Editore, 2007.

Trudeau, Lawrence J., ed. *Asian American Literature: Reviews and Criticism of Works by American Writers of Asian Descent*. Detroit: Gale, 1999.

Tsou, Judy. "Gendering Race: Stereotypes of Chinese Americans in Popular Sheet Music." *repercussions* 6, no. 2 (fall 1997): 25–62.

Tupper, Eleanor, and George E. McReynolds. *Japan in American Public Opinion*. New York: Macmillan Co., 1937.

Turbide, Nadia. "Biographical Study of Eva Gauthier (1885–1958): First French-Canadian Singer of the Avant-Garde." PhD diss., University of Montreal, 1986.

Unrau, Harlan D. *The Evacuation and Relocation of Persons of Japanese Ancestry During World War II: A Historical Study of the Manzanar War Relocation Center*. Denver: United States Department of the Interior, National Park Service, 1996.

Unterberger, Richie. *Eight Miles High: Folk-Rock's Flight from Haight-Ashbury to Woodstock*. San Francisco: Backbeat Books, 2003.

Utz, Christian. *Neue Musik und Interkulturalität: von John Cage bis Tan Dun*. Archiv für Musikwissenschaft 51. Stuttgart: Franz Steiner, 2002.

Utz, Christian. "Beyond Cultural Representation: Recent Works for the Asian Mouth Organs *Shō* and *Sheng* by Western Composers." *The World of Music* 47, no. 3 (2005): 113–134.

Utz, Christian. "Transnationale Verflechtungen in der Musik der 1950er und 1960er Jahre: Henry Cowell, Toshirō Mayuzumi, und Luciano Berio im Kontext des 'Cutural Cold War.'" Archiv für Musikwissenschaft 75, no. 2 (2018): 135–162.

Vallillo, Stephen. "Battle of the Black Mikados." *Black American Literature Forum* 16, no. 4 (winter 1982): 153–157.

van der Lek, Robbert. *Diegetic Music in Opera and Film: A Similarity between Two Genres of Drama Analysed in Works by Erich Wolfgang Korngold (1897–1957)*. Amsterdam: Rodopi, 1991.

Van Khe, Tran. "Problems of Sino-Japanese Musical Tradition Today." In *Music—East and West: Report on 1961 Tokyo East-West Music Encounter Conference*, edited and published by the Executive Committee for 1961 Tokyo East-West Music Encounter. Tokyo, 1961.

van Rij, Jan. *Madame Butterfly: Japonisme, Puccini, and the Search for the Real Cho-Cho-San*. Berkeley: Stone Bridge Press, 2001.

Vardac, A. Nicholas. *Stage to Screen: Theatrical Method from Garrick to Griffith*. New York: Benjamin Blom, 1968.

Varga, Bálint András. *Conversations with Iannis Xenakis*. London: Faber and Faber, 1996.

Varisco, Daniel Martin. *Reading Orientalism: Said and the Unsaid*. Seattle and London: University of Washington Press, 2007.

Vierk, Lois V. "Studying Gagaku." In *Arcana: Musicians on Music*, edited by John Zorn, 306–310. New York: Granary Books, 2000.

Volk, Terese M. *Music, Education, and Multiculturalism*. New York: Oxford University Press, 1998.

Von Eschen, Penny M. *Satchmo Blows Up the World: Jazz Ambassadors Play the Cold War*. Cambridge, MA: Harvard University Press, 2004.

Von Eschen, Penny M. "Jazz Ambassadors Play the Cold War: Crosscurrents of Jazz in the Twentieth Century." In *Crosscurrents: American and European Music in Interaction, 1900–2000*, edited by Felix Meyer, Carol J. Oja, Wolfgang Rathert, and Anne C. Shreffler, 299–308. Basel: Paul Sacher Stiftung, 2014.

Von Glahn, Denise, and Michael Broyles. "Musical Modernism before It Began: Leo Ornstein and a Case for Revisionist History." *Journal of the Society for American Music* 1, no. 1 (February 2007): 29–55.

Vuillermoz, Émile. "*Forfaiture* de Camille Erlanger, à l'Opéra-Comique." *Revue Musicale* (March 1921): 256–258.

Wade, Bonnie C. *Composing Japanese Musical Modernity*. Chicago: University of Chicago Press, 2014.

Wang, Grace. *Soundtracks of Asian America: Navigating Race through Musical Performance*. Durham, NC, and London: Duke University Press, 2015.

Wang, Oliver. "Between the Notes: Finding Asian America in Popular Music." *American Music* 19, no. 4 (winter 2001): 439–465.

Wang, Oliver. "These Are the Breaks: Hip-Hop and Cultural (Dis)Connections." In *AfroAsian Encounters: Culture, History, Politics*, edited by Heike Raphael-Hernandez and Shannon Steen, 146–164. New York: New York University Press, 2006.

Warak, Melissa. "Zen and the Art of La Monte Young." In *Music and Modernism, c. 1849–1950*, edited by Charlotte De Mille, 256–276. Newcastle upon Tyne, England: Cambridge Scholars, 2008.

Waseda, Minako. "Japanese American Musical Culture in Southern California: Its Formation and Transformation in the 20th Century." PhD diss., University of California, Santa Barbara, 2000.

Waseda, Minako. "Looking Both Ways: GI Songs and Musical Exoticism in Post–World War II Japan." *Yearbook for Traditional Music* 36 (2004): 144–164.

Waseda, Minako. "Extraordinary Circumstances, Exceptional Practices: Music in Japanese American Concentration Camps." *Journal of Asian American Studies* 8, no. 2 (2005): 171–209.

Watanna, Onoto. *A Japanese Nightingale*. New York: Harper and Brothers, 1901.

Waters, Robert F. "Emulation and Influence: *Japonisme* and Western Music in *fin de siècle* Paris." *Music Review* 55, no. 3 (August 1994): 214–226.

Watkins, Glenn. "Beyond Exoticism?" In *On Bunker's Hill: Essays in Honor of J. Bunker Clark*, edited by William A. Everett and Paul R. Laird, 299–308. Sterling Heights, MI: Harmonie Park Press, 2007.

Watts, Alan W. "Beat Zen, Square Zen, and Zen." *Chicago Review* 12, no. 2 (1958): 3–11.

Watts, Talbot. *Japan and the Japanese: From the Most Authentic and Reliable Sources*. New York: J. P. Neagle, 1852.

Waxman, Franz. "Progress in Development of Film Music Scores." *Music Journal* 3, no. 5 (September–October 1945): 9, 66–67.

Weaver, Sarah. "Roots for Deep Listening in Oliveros's *Bye Bye Butterfly*." *American Music Review* 47, no. 1 (fall 2017): 5–12, http://www.brooklyn.cuny.edu/web/academics/centers/hitchcock/publications/amr/v47-1/weaver.php#.

Webster, Daniel. "An Interview with Kimio Eto." *Philadelphia Inquirer*, 18 Dec 1964.

Weisgall, Hugo. "The Music of Henry Cowell." *Musical Quarterly* 45, no. 4 (October 1959): 484–507.

Wellens, Ian. *Music on the Frontline: Nicolas Nabokov's Struggle against Communism and Middlebrow Culture*. Aldershot: Ashgate, 2002.

Wellman, Rita. "The String of the Samisen, a Play" (1917). In *The Provincetown Plays*, edited and selected by George Cram Cook and Frank Shay, 207–239. Cincinnati: Stewart Kidd Company, 1921.

Wellman, William A., Jr. "Runnin' into Marlon." *Film Comment* 27, no. 4 (July 1991): 34–36.

Werkmeister, Heinrich. "Impressions of Japanese Music." Translated by Frederick H. Martens. *Musical Quarterly* 13, no. 1 (January 1927): 100–107.

Weston, Victoria. *East Meets West: Isabella Stewart Gardner and Okakura Kakuzo*. Boston: Trustees of the Isabella Stewart Gardner Museum, 1992.

Whaley, Deborah Elizabeth. "Black Bodies/Yellow Masks: The Orientalist Aesthetic in Hip-Hop and Black Visual Culture." In *AfroAsian Encounters: Culture, History, Politics*, edited by Heike Raphael-Hernandez and Shannon Steen, 188–203. New York: New York University Press, 2006.

White, Jonathan. "Opera, Politics, and Television: Bel canto by Satellite." In *A Night in at the Opera*, edited by Jeremy Tambling, 267–298. London: Libbey, 1994.

White, Morton, and Lucia White, *Journeys to the Japanese 1952–1979*. Vancouver: University of British Columbia Press, 1986.

White, Sharon Nancy. "Mable Loomis Todd: Gender, Language, and Power in Victorian America." PhD diss, Yale University, 1982.

Whitebart, William. "Madame Bountiful." *New Statesman* 55, no. 1405 (15 February 1958): 198–199.

Whitney, Clara A. N. *Clara's Diary: An American Girl in Meiji Japan*. Edited by M. William Steele and Tamiko Ichimata. Tokyo: Kodansha International, 1979.

Wichmann, Siegfried. *Japonisme: The Japanese Influence on Western Art since 1858*. New York: Thames & Hudson, 1981.

Wierzbicki, James. *Music in the Age of Anxiety: American Music in the Fifties*. Urbana: University of Illinois Press, 2016.

Wilde, Oscar. *Oscar Wilde: The Dover Reader*. Mineola, NY: Dover Publications, 2015.

Wiley, Peter Booth. *Yankees in the Land of the Gods: Commodore Perry and the Opening of Japan*. New York: Viking, 1990.

William, H. A. Williams. *'Twas Only an Irishman's Dream: The Image of Ireland and the Irish in American Popular Song Lyrics, 1800–1920*. Urbana and Chicago: University of Illinois Press, 1996.

Williams, Harold S. *Shades of the Past, or Indiscreet Tales of Japan*. Rutland, VT: Charles E. Tuttle, 1959.

Winkler, Allan. *The Politics of Propaganda: the Office of War Information, 1942–1945*. New Haven, CT: Yale University Press, 1978.

Winters, Ben. "The Non-Diegetic Fallacy: Film, Music, and Narrative Space." *Music and Letters* 91, no. 2 (May 2010): 224–244.

Wires, Richard. *John P. Marquand and Mr. Moto: Spy Adventures and Detective Films*. Muncie, IN: Ball State University Press, 1990.

Wisenthal, Jonathan, Sherrill Grace, Melinda Boyd, Brian McIlroy, and Vera Micznik, eds. *A Vision of the Orient: Texts, Intertexts, and Contexts of Madame Butterfly*. Toronto: University of Toronto Press, 2006.

Wong, Deborah. "The Asian American Body in Performance." In *Music and the Racial Imagination*, edited by Ronald Radano and Philip V. Bohlman, 57–94. Chicago: University of Chicago Press, 2000.

Wong, Deborah. "*Taiko* and the Asian/American Body: Drums, *Rising Sun*, and the Question of Gender." *The World of Music* 42, no. 3 (2000): 67–78.

Wong, Deborah. "Finding an Asian American Audience: The Problem of Listening." *American Music* 19, no. 4 (winter 2001): 365–384.

Wong, Deborah. *Speak It Louder: Asian Americans Making Music*. New York: Routledge, 2004.

Wong, Eugene Franklin. *On Visual Media Racism: Asians in the American Motion Pictures*. New York: Arno Press, 1978.

Wong, Wayman. "Actors Remember Pacific Overtures." *Sondheim Review* 4, no. 4 (spring 1998): 20–23.

Wordell, Charles B. *Japan's Image in America: Popular Writings about Japan, 1800–1941*. Kyoto: Yamaguchi Publishing House, 1998.

Wordell, Charles B. *Japan in American Fiction, 1880–1905*. London: Ganesha Publishing, 2001.

Worlds Revealed: The Dawn of Japanese and American Exchange. Tokyo: Edo-Tokyo Museum, 1999.

Wright, H. Stephen, and Stephen M. Fry, eds. *Film Music Collections in the United States: A Guide*. Hollywood, CA: Society for the Preservation of Film Music, 1996.

W.S.S. "Mr. Eichheim's Orient." *Boston Transcript*, 23 March 1922, 8.

Wu, Frank H. *Yellow: Race in America beyond Black and White*. New York: Basic Books, 2002.

Xenakis, Iannis. "The Riddle of Japan." *This Is Japan* 9 (1962): 66–69.

Xing, Jun. *Asian America through the Lens: History, Representations, and Identity*. Walnut Creek, CA: AltaMira Press, 1998.

Yang, Jeff. "Geisha A-Go-Go: Katy Perry's AMAs Performance Stirs Debate." *Wall Street Journal*, 25 November 2013, https://blogs.wsj.com/speakeasy/2013/11/25/memories-of-a-geisha-katy-perrys-amas-performance-stirs-debate/.

Yang, Mina. "New Directions in California Music: Construction of a Pacific Rim Cultural Identity, 1925–1945." PhD diss., Yale University, 2001.

Yang, Mina. "Orientalism and the Music of Asian Immigrant Communities in California, 1924–1945." *American Music* 19, no. 4 (winter 2001): 385–416.

Yang, Mina. "East Meets West in the Concert Hall: Asians and Classical Music in the Century of Imperialism, Post-Colonialism, and Multiculturalism." *Asian Music* 38, no. 1 (winter 2007): 1–30.

Yang, Mina. *California Polyphony: Ethnic Voices, Musical Crossroads*. Urbana and Chicago: University of Illinois Press, 2008.

Yarnell, James L. *Recreation and Idleness: The Pacific Travels of John La Farge*. New York: Vance Jordan Fine Art Inc., 1998.

Yellin, Victor Fell. "Mrs. Belmont, Matthew Perry, and the 'Japanese Minstrels.'" *American Music* 14, no. 3 (fall 1996): 257–275.

Yokoyama, Toshio. *Japan in the Victorian Mind: A Study of Stereotyped Images of a Nation 1850–80*. Houndmills: Macmillan, 1987.

Yoo, David K. *Growing Up Nisei: Race, Generation, and Culture among Japanese Americans of California, 1924–49*. Urbana and Chicago: University of Illinois Press, 2000.

Yoon, Paul Jong-Chul. "'She's Really Become Japanese Now!': Taiko Drumming and Asian American Identifications." *American Music* 19, no. 4 (winter 2001): 417–438.

Yoshida, George. *Reminiscing in Swingtime: Japanese in American Popular Music: 1925–1960*. San Francisco: National Japanese American Historical Society, 1997.

Yoshihara, Mari. *Embracing the East: White Women and American Orientalism*. New York: Oxford University Press, 2003.

Yoshihara, Mari. "The Flight of the Japanese Butterfly: Orientalism, Nationalism, and Performances of Japanese Womanhood." *American Quarterly* 56, no. 4 (2004): 975–1001.

Yoshihara, Mari. *Musicians from a Different Shore: Asians and Asian Americans in Classical Music*. Philadelphia: Temple University Press, 2007.

Yu, Henry. *Thinking Orientals: Migration, Contact, and Exoticism in Modern America*. New York: Oxford University Press, 2001.

Zadan, Craig. *Sondheim & Co.* 2nd ed. New York: Da Capo Press, 1994.

Zamecnik, J. S. *Sam Fox Moving Picture Music*. Cleveland: Sam Fox Publishing Co., 1913.

Zenimoto, Kenji. *Centennial Essays on Lafcadio Hearn*. Matsue, Japan: The Hearn Society, 1996.

Zheng, Su. *Claiming Diaspora: Music, Transnationalism, and Cultural Politics in Asian/Chinese America*. Oxford: Oxford University Press, 2010.

Zimmermann, Walter. *Desert Plants: Conversations with 23 American Musicians*. Vancouver: A.R.C. Publications, 1976.

Zon, Bennett. *Representing Non-Western Music in Nineteenth-century Britain*. Rochester, NY: University of Rochester Press, 2007.

Selected Discography

Adderley, Julian "Cannonball." *Nippon Soul*. Riverside: RLP-9477, 1963.

Adderley, Julian "Cannonball." *Cannonball in Japan*. Capitol: CP-8096, 1966.

Alda, Frances. "Poor Butterfly." Victor: 64653, 1917.

Anka, Paul. "Sayonara" on *Our Man around the World*. RCA Victor: LSP-2614, 1963.

Bayes, Nora. "The Japanese Sandman." Columbia: A2997, 1920.

Beautiful Ambient Japanese Flute—Meditation, Yoga, Massage, Spa Music. Stress Fighter Records: 2018.

Belafonte, Harry. *Streets I Have Walked*. RCA: LSP 2695, 1963.

Brown, Anthony, Asian American Orchestra. *Far East Suite*. Asian Improv Records: AIR0053, 1999.

Brown, Anthony. *Rhapsodies*. Water Baby Records: WBR1010, 2005.

Brown, Edna. "Poor Butterfly." Victor: 18211, 1917.

Brubeck, Dave, Quartet. *Jazz Impressions of Japan*. Columbia Records: 9012, 1964.

The Cellos. "Rang Tang Ding Dong (I Am the Japanese Sandman)." Apollo Records: 510–545, 1957.

Club Nisei Orchestra and Singers. *Sayonara Farewell Tokyo: Souvenir Songs of Japan*. 49th State Hawaii Record Co.: 3450, c. 1950.

Cowell, Henry. *Ongaku*. Louisville Orchestra: LOU-595, 1959.

Cowell, Henry. *Henry Cowell: Piano Music*. Smithsonian Folkways: 3349, 1963.

Denny, Martin. *Exotica*. Liberty: LST 3034, 1957.

Denny, Martin. *Forbidden Island*. Liberty: LST 7001, 1958.

Denny, Martin. *Primitiva*. Liberty: LST 7023, 1958.

Denny, Martin. *Exotic Dreams*. Liberty: LRP 3104, 1959.

Denny, Martin. *Hypnotique*. Liberty: LST 7102, 1959.

Denny, Martin. *Quiet Village*. Liberty: LST 7122, 1959.

Denny, Martin. *Sayonara*. Sunset: SUS-5169, 1967.

Durbin, Deanna, with Victor Young and His Orchestra. "Poor Butterfly." Decca: 18297, 1942.

Ellington, Duke. *The Far East Suite*. RCA-Victor: LPM/LSP-3782, 1967.

Ellis, Don. *Haiku*. MPS Records: MC25341, 1973.

Eps, Van, Quartet. "So Long Oo-Long." Victor: 18681A, 1920.

Eto, Kimio. *Art of the Koto*. Electra: EKS 7234, 1963.

Eto, Kimio, and Bud Shank. *Koto and Flute*. World-Pacific Records: 1299, 1960.

Falconer, Elizabeth, and Brian Falconer. *Chocolate Suite—Japanese Music for Chocolate Lovers*. Koto World: 2004.

Feld, Steven. 2006: *Suikinkutsu: A Japanese Underground Water Zither*. VoxLox Documentary Sound Art: 106, 2006.

Goodman, Benny, and Orchestra. "The Japanese Sandman." Bluebird: B10459A, 1939.

Hampton, Lionel. *East Meets West*. Glad Hamp: GHLP 1007, 1965.

Hawaiian Nisei Songs: A Musical Cocktail of Japanese American Songs in 1950s. Hawai'i, Cord International/Hana Ola: HOCD 36000, 2000.

Henderson, Fletcher, and His Orchestra, featuring Henry "Red" Allen. "Nagasaki." Decca: 18253B, 1934.

Hibber, Al. "Poor Butterfly." Chess: 1569, 1953.

Hines, Earl, and Orchestra. "The Japanese Sandman." Decca: 654B, 1934.

Hiroshima. *Hiroshima*. Arista: AB4252, 1979.

Hiroshima. *Odori*. Arista: AL9541, 1980.

Hiroshima. *Third Generation*. Epic: FE38708, 1983.

Hiroshima. *East*. Epic: E45022, 1989

Hiroshima. *Obon*. Heads Up International: HUCD 3098, 2005.

Hughes, Spike, and His Dance Orchestra. "Poor Butterfly." Decca: F1815, 1930.

Iijima, Chris Kando, Nobuko JoAnne Miyamoto, and William "Charlie" Chin. *A Grain of Sand: Music for the Struggle by Asians in America*. Paredon Records: P1020, 1973.

Kirk, Andy, and His Clouds of Joy, Pha Terrell vocalist. "Poor Butterfly." Decca: 1663-A, 1937.

Kreisler, Fritz. "Poor Butterfly." Victor: 64655, 1917.

Lapham, Claude. *Mihara Yama*. Victor Red Seal: 11895, 1935.

Lapham, Claude. *Japanese Piano Concerto*. Victor Red Seal: 4306, 1935.

Liberace. "Sayonara" on *Piano Memories*. AVI Records: AVL-1001, 1972.

MacRae, Gordon. "Sayonara." Capitol Records: F 3816, 1957.

Mann, Herbie. *Gagaku and Beyond*. Atlantic: SR9014, 1976.

Mann, Herbie. *Surprises*. Atlantic: SD1682, 1976.

Mark, Paul. *East to West*. Imperial: 9120, 1961.

Mark, Paul. *Golden Melodies from Japan*. Imperial: 12075, 1961.

Mark, Paul. *12 1/2 Geishas Must Be Right*. Sounds of Hawaii: SHS 5010, 1963.

Mark, Paul. *Kokeshi Shindig*. Sounds of Hawaii: SH-5019, 1965.

Masaoka, Miya. *Monk's Japanese Folk Song*. Dizim Records: 4104, 1997.

Masaoka, Miya, and Pauline Oliveros. *Accordion Koto*. Deep Listening: DL 36-2007, 2007.

McKuen, Rod. "Haiku Poems" on *Beatsville*. HiFi Records: R419, 1959.

McKuen, Rod. *Yellow Unicorn*. Imperial: LP12036, 1960.

McKuen, Rod. *The Love Movement*. Capitol Records: ST2838, 1967.

McLaren, Malcolm. *Fans*. Charisma Records: MMDL2, 1984.

Monk, Thelonious. *Straight, No Chaser*. Columbia: CS9451, 1967.

Music to Remember: A Tribute to Japanese-American Musicians and Singers of the 40s. Lisa Joe: LJMP 1001–2, 1997.

Nichols, Red, and His Five Pennies. "Japanese Sandman." Brunswick: 3819, 1928.

Nichols, Red, and His Five Pennies. "Poor Butterfly." Brunswick: 20062, 1928.

Noble, Ray, and Orchestra. "The Japanese Sandman." Victor: 24577B, 1934.

Oliveros, Pauline. "Bye Bye Butterfly," *New Music for Electronic and Recorded Media*. 1750 Arch Records: S-1765, 1977.

Neptune, John Kaizan. *Bamboo*. Far East: ETJ-85008, 1980.

Neptune, John Kaizan. *The Circle*. Denon: YF-7113-ND, 1985.

Neptune, John Kaizan. *Jazzen*. Denon: YF-7131-ND, 1987.

Neptune, John Kaizan. *Tokyosphere*: JVC: JD-3316, 1988.

Neptune, John Kaizan. *River Rhythm*. Kosei: CS00066, 1994.

Parks, Van Dyke. *Tokyo Rose*. Warner Bros.: 1-25968, 1989.

Peebles, Sarah. *Delicate Paths*. Unsounds: 42U, 2014.

Prima, Louis. "I Want to Go to Tokio." HIT: 7123, 1944.

Quintette of the Hot Club of France. "Nagasaki." Victor: 25558B, 1936.

Rampal, Jean-Pierre. *Japanese Melodies, Vol. III: Yamanakabushi*. CBS Records: 37295, 1982.

Reisman, Leo, and Orchestra. "Poor Butterfly." Victor: 27435-A, 1941.

Roberts, Victor. "So Long! Oo-Long." Victor Records: 18672-B, 1920.

Rothenberg, Ned. *Ryu Nashi/No School*. Tzadik: 7267, 2010.

Rudich, Rachel. *Henry Cowell: The Universal Flute*. Music and Arts: CD-1012, 1997.

Samuelson, Ralph. *Offerings*. Music of the World: MOW 153, 1998.

Samuelson, Ralph. *The Universal Flute: Discovery in a Single Tone*. Innova: 942, 2016.

Schlefer, James Nyoraku. *Flare Up*. NRCD: 102, 2002.

Scott, Tony. *Music for Zen Meditation and Other Joys*. Verve VS-8634, 1965.

Shindo, Tak. *Mganga*. Edison International CL 5000, 1958.

Shindo, Tak. *Brass and Bamboo*. Capitol ST 1345, 1960.

Shindo, Tak. *Accent on Bamboo*. Capitol ST 1433, 1960.

Shindo, Tak. *Sea of Spring*. Grand Prix GPM1, 1966.

Shindo, Tak. *Far East Goes Western*. Mercury PPS 2031, 1962.

Silver, Horace. *The Tokyo Blues*. Blue Note: 84110, 1962.

Sizemen. *A Tribute to Tak Shindo*. Palace: 2011.

Stokowski: Philadelphia Rarities. Cala Records Ltd.: CACD0501, 1994.

Suzuki, Pat. *The Many Sides of Pat Suzuki*. Vik: LX-1127, 1958.

Taco. "Sayonara" on *Let's Face the Music*. RCA Victor: CPL1-4920, 1984.

Taste of Honey. "Sayonara" on *Ladies of the Eighties*. Capitol Records: 1A 006-86606, 1982.

Teitelbaum, Richard. *Blends*. New Albion Records: NA118, 2002.

The Three Suns. "Poor Butterfly." RCA Victor: LSP-2617, 1962.

Tyner, McCoy. *Sahara*. Milestone Records: MSP 9039, 1972.

Vallée, Rudy, and His Connecticut Yankees. "Nagasaki." Bluebird: B7358B, 1933.

Vaughan, Sarah. "Poor Butterfly." Mercury: 71085X45, 1957.

Victor Military Band. "Poor Butterfly." Victor: 35605, 1917.

Victor Military Band. "I Want to Go to Tokio." Victor: 17764B, 1919.

Walzenaufnahmen japanischer Music, 1901–1913. Berlin: Staatliche Museen zu Berlin, 2003.

Waxman, Franz. *Sayonara*. RCA Victor: LOC-1041, 1957.

Waxman, Franz. *The Original Film Score: Sayonara*. Soundtrack Library: 010/008, n.d.

Waxman, Franz. *My Geisha*. RCA: LOC-1070, 1962.

Weezer. *Pinkerton*. DGC: DGCD-25007, 1996.

Whiteman, Paul, and His Ambassador Orchestra. "The Japanese Sandman." Victor: 18690, 1920.

Whiteman, Paul, and Orchestra. "Ti-O-San." Victor: 18818B, 1921.

Whiteman, Paul. "Cho-Cho-San." Victor: 18777, 1921.

Whiteman, Paul. "Japanese Mammy." Columbia: 1701D, 1928.

Whiteman, Paul. "Poor Butterfly." Victor: 24078, 1928.

Wilder, Alec, Octet. "The Japanese Sandman." Brunswick: 8410, 1939.

Wright, George. *Flight to Tokyo*. Hi-Fi Records: SR 717, 1958.

Yamada, Kosaku. *Kurofone (The Black Ships)*. Toshiba Records: JSC 1002-3, 1987.

Yamaguchi, Goro. *A Bell Ringing in the Empty Sky*. Nonesuch: H-72025, 1969.

Zen Shakuhachi: Secrets Garden with Japanese Traditional Flute Music for Asian Meditation, Thai Massage, & Spa. Easy Music Record: 2017.

Zen Spa: Zen Oriental Music Soundscapes Meditation, Asian Oriental Flute Shakuhachi Music for Massage, Spa, Yoga, Relax, Tai Chi, Reiki, and Sleep. Asian Zen Relaxation Music Records: 2012.

Zorn, John. *Spillane; Two Lane Highway; Forbidden Fruit*. Elektra/Nonesuch: 79172-2, 1987.

Index

Ongawa, Michitaro, 46, 86
Ono, Yoko, 352–53, 544n199
Onogero, Tateish ("Japanese Tommy"),
    59–60, 465n15
Onuki, Haru [Haruko], 85–87,
    470n63, 470n65
"opening of Japan." *See* Perry Expedition
opera and film compared, 151, 157–62, 177–
    79, 189–95, 492–93n9, 493n11, 495n29,
    501n84, 505n112
Operation Pacific (film), 213–14,
    511–12n43, 512n44
Orientalism, 450n22, 492n6, 498–99n57,
    505n117
Osato, Sono, 518n90
Osborne, Charles, 494n24
Osborne, Thomas, 553–54n106
Otani, Muneko, 407–8
Ouellette, Fernand, 337–38
Our Japanese Embassy, 58
Our Job in Japan (film), 225–26, 227,
    232–33, 517n83
Owens, Buck, 87–88

Pachter, Benjamin, 425–26
Pacific Overtures (musical), 373, 375–80,
    548n10, 548n12, 548n14, 549n25, 549n30
Pacun, David, 121
Page, N. Clifford
    Contest of the Nations, 102–3
    A Japanese Nightingale, 102
    Moonlight Blossom, 102
Palermo, Andrew, 405
Palmer, Christopher, 251–52
Panama-Pacific International Exposition in
    San Francisco (1915), 42–43
Parakilas, James, 492n5, 500n77
Pardon Me, Is This Planet Taken
    (musical), 15
Parker, Steve, 177, 501n80, 531n66
Parks, Robert, 276–77
Parks, Van Dyke
    Tokyo Rose, 299
Pasler, Jann, 147–48, 470–71n73, 505n117
Patterson, David W., 348–49, 542n169
Pearl Harbor (film), 517–18n88
Peebles, Sarah, 554n115
pentatonicism, 5–6, 10–11, 71–74, 81, 128–29,
    221–22, 246, 503n99
Perry Expedition, 18, 22, 26, 48, 58, 372–73,
    375, 462n135
Perry, Commodore Matthew Calbraith. *See*
    Perry Expedition
Perry, Katy, 394–97

Philadelphian Centennial Exhibition
    (1876), 42
Philippine-American War, 383
Pickford, Mary, 155–57, 284
Piggott, Francis Taylor, 25–26, 453n28,
    453–54n30
Pinkerton (character), representations
    of, 87–90
Pisani, Michael V., 449n2, 468n44, 473n106,
    491n2, 512n50
Pollack, Ted
    Wedding in Japan, 267–68
Polo, Marco, 12–13
Ponnelle, Jean-Pierre, 383–84
"Poor Butterfly" (John L. Golden and
    Raymond Hubbell) 83–88, 160, 298–99,
    304–5, 503–4n101
    songs influenced by 88–90
Pope, Edgar W., 70, 515n65
postmodernism, 6, 109–10, 140–41, 146–47,
    148–49, 373–75, 388–90, 393–94, 396–
    97, 399–400, 404, 423–24, 491n161
Pound, Ezra, 34–35, 105, 344–45,
    458n73, 474n2
Powell, Mel
    Haiku Settings, 346
Prelude to War (film), 205–9, 510n30
Premiere der Butterfly (film), 496n40
Prendergast, Roy M., 217
primitivism, 43, 113, 211–12, 277–79, 292,
    295, 302–3, 401
Prince, Hal, 373, 377
Prinz, LeRoy, 242–44, 251, 268–69
Pritchett, James, 348–51, 543n175
Proctor, C. King
    Princess Chrysanthemum, 467n28
propaganda, 197–98, 199–200, 201–12, 213,
    217–18, 221–22, 223, 229, 330, 331, 485–
    86n115, 508n16, 509n22, 515n70
PT 109, 511n40
Puccini, Giacomo
    and film, 155, 495n25
    Madama Butterfly, 9–10, 41–43, 46, 60–
        61, 71–74, 81–90, 155–62, 166, 167–70,
        172, 174–75, 178, 284, 352, 383–84,
        385, 388, 390, 396, 401–4, 470n60,
        470–71n73, 494n17, 494–95n25,
        495n27, 495n28, 496n38, 496n40,
        497n46, 501n82, 503n99, 505n117,
        527n19, 550–51n47, 553n94. *See also*
        "Un bel di"
    Tosca, 495n26
    Turandot, 191–92, 388, 474n111
Purple Heart, The (film), 228–30, 517n81